AF690950

The Moral Rights of Authors and Artists

The Moral Rights of Authors and Artists

From the Birth of Copyright to the Age of Artificial Intelligence

Second Edition

MIRA T. SUNDARA RAJAN

OXFORD
UNIVERSITY PRESS

OXFORD
UNIVERSITY PRESS

Great Clarendon Street, Oxford, OX2 6DP,
United Kingdom

Oxford University Press is a department of the University of Oxford.
It furthers the University's objective of excellence in research, scholarship,
and education by publishing worldwide. Oxford is a registered trade mark of
Oxford University Press in the UK and in certain other countries

© Mira T. Sundara Rajan 2025

The moral rights of the author have been asserted

First Edition published in 2011
Second Edition published in 2025

All rights reserved. No part of this publication may be reproduced, stored in a retrieval system, transmitted, used for text and data mining, or used for training artificial intelligence, in any form or by any means, without the prior permission in writing of Oxford University Press, or as expressly permitted by law, by licence or under terms agreed with the appropriate reprographics rights organization. Enquiries concerning reproduction outside the scope of the above should be sent to the Rights Department, Oxford University Press, at the address above.

You must not circulate this work in any other form
and you must impose this same condition on any acquirer

Public sector information reproduced under Open Government Licence v3.0
(https://www.nationalarchives.gov.uk/doc/open-government-licence)

Published in the United States of America by Oxford University Press
198 Madison Avenue, New York, NY 10016, United States of America

British Library Cataloguing in Publication Data
Data available

Library of Congress Control Number: 2024951634

ISBN 978-0-19-879185-0

DOI: 10.1093/law/9780198791850.001.0001

The manufacturer's authorised representative in the EU for product safety is Oxford University Press España S.A. of El Parque Empresarial San Fernando de Henares, Avenida de Castilla, 2 – 28830 Madrid (www.oup.es/en or product.safety@oup.com). OUP España S.A. also acts as importer into Spain of products made by the manufacturer.

This book is dedicated to Professor Colin Tapper:
Guru sakshat para brahma.

Contents

Foreword	xvii
Foreword to the First Edition	xix
Preface and Acknowledgments	xxi
Prologue	xxv
1. A Unitary View of Copyright Law	1
A. Introduction	2
B. Moral Rights: The Doctrine	4
C. The Controversy	8
1. Doctrine vs. Law	9
2. The Origins of Moral Rights	12
3. Aesthetic Reality	13
D. The Rights Protected	15
1. Attribution	17
2. Integrity and Reputation	20
a. Destruction of a Work	27
3. Disclosure and Withdrawal	30
4. A Right to Remuneration? The Example of the Resale Right (*droit de suite*)	32
E. Legal Implications of the Doctrine	32
1. Independence of Moral and Economic Rights	32
2. Inalienability, Waiver, and Inequality of Bargaining Power	33
3. Perpetual Protection	34
F. Relationship between the Economic and Moral Aspects of Copyright	36
G. The Common-Law Treatment of Moral Rights	38
H. Moral Rights and Human Rights: The Ruling of the Court of Justice of the European Union (CJEU) in *Deckmyn* (2014)	40
I. Moral Rights and Free Speech: A Dual-Edged Sword?	44
J. Moral Rights in the Technological Environment	46
K. Fame: The Currency of the Digital Era?	50
L. A Study in Contrasts: The Enforcement of Moral Rights	52
M. Moral Rights Jurisprudence: Occurrences and Outcomes	54
N. Conclusion: Scope and Structure of This Book	57
2. Moral Rights: History of an Idea	61
A. Origins of the Doctrine	62
B. Moral Rights at Home: France	66
1. "A Grace Founded in Justice": Moral Rights and Revolutionary Ideals	67

2. The Modern Doctrine: A Controversial Model Law 76
 a. The Pre-Eminence of Moral Rights 76
 b. *Les droits moraux*: The Rights Defined 77
  i. Disclosure: Article L121-2 78
  ii. Withdrawal: Article L121-4 79
  iii. Integrity vs. Reputation: "Subjective" and "Objective" Requirements of Proof 80
  iv. Criticism 82
 c. *Le dualisme*: Practical Effects 82
  i. Inalienability and the Prohibition of Waivers 83
  ii. Permanent Protection 84
 d. Technological Features 89
  i. Audiovisual Works 89
  ii. Computer Programs 90
  iii. Moral Rights in Employment 91
  iv. Press Publication Right 92
  v. Defenses to a Moral Rights Claim: Parody and Pastiche 93
 e. Conclusions 95
C. Germany and Monist Moral Rights: Romance of a Theory 97
 1. The Birth of Monism 98
 2. Monism in Practice 100
 3. The Modern Moral Rights: Germany and Austria 106
 4. Moral Rights and the Basic Law 109
 5. Conclusion 110
D. The United Kingdom: Second Thoughts 111
 1. Early History and the Statute of Anne, 1709–10 115
  a. Early Recognition of a Moral Copyright: *Millar v. Taylor* (1769) 117
  b. Protecting Free Speech: Moral Rights Revisited in *Donaldson v. Beckett* (1774) 122
 2. Modern Approach: "Shy Beauty" 123
  a. Moral Rights in the Copyright, Designs and Patents Act 1988 126
   i. Attribution 126
   ii. Integrity: The Right to Object to Derogatory Treatment 127
   iii. A Moral Right of Privacy? 132
  b. Exceptions: Limits on Moral Rights in Employment and Technology 134
  c. Parody and Moral Rights: Is There an Exception under the CDPA? 135
  d. Inalienability and Waiver 135
  e. Conceptual Confusion 137
 3. Brexit and Moral Rights: A Sobering Future? 139
 4. Conclusions: The Birth of the Common-Law Approach 140
E. Conclusion: Un-Romantic Authorship 142

3. Moral Rights in the International Copyright Regime: Article 6*bis* of the Berne Convention and Beyond 149
A. Introduction 150

B. Emergence of an Archetype: Moral Rights in Article 6*bis* of the Berne Convention 153
1. The Age of Authorship: The Original Text of 1928 153
a. Literary Language 155
b. Legal Language 156
c. Objective vs. Subjective Proof 157
2. The 1948 Amendments: Moral Rights in a Commercial Age 158
3. Revisiting the Compromise: The Stockholm Conference of 1967 159
4. The Technological Era: Moral Rights and the Unknown 161
C. Moral Rights in the Berne Convention beyond Article 6*bis* 164
1. Explicit Recognition: Attribution for Journalists in Article 10.3 164
2. Indirect Protection: Convention Rights and the "Legitimate Interests of the Author" 164
a. Moral Rights Abroad: Article 5.1 and Rights "Specially Granted by the Convention" 165
b. The Three-Step Test: Article 9.2 166
c. *Droit de suite* (Artist's Resale Right): A Hybrid Right in Article 14*ter* 168
D. Moral Rights in Other International Copyright Agreements 169
1. Russian Dolls: The Berne Convention and the TRIPs Agreements 169
a. Relation to the Berne Convention: TRIPs Article 9.1 170
b. Post-TRIPs Expansion of Moral Rights in the International Community 171
2. Moral Rights in the Digital Age: The WIPO Internet Treaties and Beijing 172
a. The WCT: A Digital Right of Disclosure 173
b. The WPPT: Dissemination Is the New Creation 176
i. Background: The Intersection of Moral and Economic Rights in Sound Recordings 177
ii. Moral Rights in the WPPT 179
c. The Beijing Treaty: Always Read the Footnotes 182
3. The European Union: An Elephant in the Room 185
a. Harmonization and Moral Rights in the EU: Policy Initiatives? 187
b. Moral Rights in the Directives: Indirect Approaches 188
c. CJEU Jurisprudence and Moral Rights 190
d. Moral Rights and the Digital Single Market (DSM) Directive 191
E. In Principle: Moral Rights and International Trade 196
1. Minimum Standards 197
2. National Treatment 198
a. Practical Implications 199
b. Choice of Law 200
c. Most-Favored Nation 204
F. Private Rights, Public Forum: Copyright and Moral Rights in Public International Law 204
G. Conclusion 205

4. A Theory in Flux: The Evolution in Progress of Moral Rights 209
A. Introduction 211
B. Spread of the Doctrine: Moral Rights and the Common Law 213
1. Canada: A Country in Transition 216
a. A Common-Law Pioneer 217
b. Innovation and Convention: Attribution, Integrity, and Association 222
c. Moral Rights after the Death of the Author 223
d. Opportunities and Limitations: The Visual Arts 223
e. Inalienability and the Canadian Penchant to Waive 226
f. Performers' Moral Rights: An Opportunity Missed 227
g. A Drought in the Courts 230
h. Theoretical Confusion and Its Practical Effects: Monism vs. Dualism 230
i. Conclusions 235
2. The United States: American Exceptionalism 236
a. Moral Rights and the Berne Convention: Chronic Dissatisfaction 237
i. From *Shostakovich* to *Dastar*: The Moral Rights Landscape in the United States 240
ii. Better to Be Foreign: National Treatment as a Way Out? 246
b. The Word on the Street: Works of "Recognized Stature" and the *5Pointz* Case 249
c. Beyond Private Law: The Preservation of Cultural Heritage 251
i. Art Preservation: The California Art Preservation Act, the DNA of the Visual Artists' Rights Act 1990 251
ii. Film Preservation: Indirect Moral Rights 253
iii. Music Modernization: Attribution by the Back Door 253
iv. Landmarks: Public Art, Public Action 254
d. Conclusions 254
3. Australia and a Moral Right in Indigenous Culture 256
4. New Zealand: Personhood for Rivers and Mountains—A New Form of Moral Rights? 262
C. Growth of the Doctrine: Moral Rights in Developing Countries 265
1. India and Other British Colonies: Common Law, or Not? 269
2. Moral Rights and the Protection of Culture: Indian Copyright Law 271
a. The Evolution of Moral Rights in the Indian Copyright Act 271
i. The 1957 Act: The Birth of Authors' "Special Rights" 271
ii. The 1994 Act: Back to Berne 273
iii. The Copyright Amendments of 2012: Perpetual Protection Restored 275
iv. Scope of the Attribution Right 276
b. Performers, Producers, and Bollywood: Moral Rights in Film 278
c. Authors' and Artists' Resale Right 279
d. Independence from Economic Rights 279
e. Remedies 280
f. Judicial Chivalry: The Practical Dynamics of India's Moral Rights 280

g. *Amar Nath Sehgal*: Duties of the Government 282
i. Interim Ruling: 1992 283
ii. Final Ruling: 2005 285
3. Conclusion 287
D. Moral Rights and "Honor" in a Technological Society: Japan 288
E. Moral Rights and Creative Freedom: Post-Socialist Countries 293
1. Historical Context: Socialism, Russia, and Post-Socialist Countries 298
2. Moral Rights in Transition: The 1991 USSR Fundamentals of Civil Legislation 302
a. Publication and Use 302
b. Authorship and Name 303
c. Integrity as Inviolability 303
d. Inalienability and Inheritance 304
e. Duration 304
f. Performers 304
3. International Influence: The Russian Copyright Act of 1993 305
a. Dualism 306
b. Duration of Protection: Perpetual Moral Rights and the Question of Inheritance 307
c. Moral Rights in the Public Domain: *Domaine public payant* 308
d. Reputation vs. Integrity 309
e. Performers' Moral Rights 310
f. *Droit de suite* for the Visual Arts 311
g. Disclosure in the Post-Socialist Context 311
4. Programmers' Moral Rights: The Law on Computer Programs and Databases and the Recognition of Scientists 312
5. Return to the Future: The 2008 Civil Code Provisions on Copyright 313
a. Moral Rights in the Civil Code: General Provisions 316
b. General Principles 317
c. Copyright 319
i. Moral Rights Defined 319
ii. Special Features 321
iii. Moral Rights vs. Exclusive Rights 322
iv. Moral Rights and Technology 322
v. Fair Use and Parody 323
vi. Visual Art 323
d. Neighboring Rights 324
e. Patents 324
6. Improvements to Moral Rights in Russia until the War in Ukraine 324
7. A New Moral Right in Russian Law: The Renewal of Copyright Terms for Rehabilitated Authors 326
8. Conclusion 328
F. Conclusion: The Modern Doctrine 330

5. The Machine as Author: Moral Rights and Artificial Intelligence 333
A. Authenticity: The Keyword of Our Era 334
B. Authorship: The Human Heart of Copyright Law 336
C. Are Machines Authors? Approaches and Prospects under Copyright Law 340
1. Copyright in "Computer-Generated" Works: The UK Model 341
2. The Authors of Authors? Moral Rights for AI Creators 343
3. Copyright Registration: An Initial Test of Machine Authorship? 347
D. The Machine as Infringer 348
1. AI Artists: In-Stability 349
2. AI Writers: Settlements and Lawsuits 354
a. The Hollywood Writers' Strike 354
b. *NYT v. OpenAI* and Its Sister Lawsuits 356
3. The Machine as Performer: "Performance Cloning" and the Hollywood Actors' Strike 358
E. The Machine as Enforcer: Moral Rights 366
F. Are Machines Creative? Existentialism Redux 368
G. Attribution and Integrity: Keys to Our Future 369
1. Authors' Moral Rights of Attribution and Integrity 370
2. Beyond Authorship: Attribution and Integrity as Stand-Alone Principles 372
H. The EU AI Act: The Role of Moral Rights in a Risk-Based Approach 375
I. Recommendations 378
J. Conclusion: Being Human in the Age of AI 380

6. More Than Musicians: Music Copyright, Moral Rights, and Music in the Technological Environment 385
A. Introduction 386
B. State of the Art: Music Streaming, the Culmination of a Revolution in Sharing Music 387
C. Beginnings: The Creative Potential of Digital Music Discovered by Classical Musicians 390
D. *Blurred Lines* and *Stairway to Heaven*: The Limits of Music Copyright vs. Moral Rights 396
E. The Impact of New Musical Technologies: Moral Rights in Creation, Production, and Dissemination 402
1. Creation or Production? Technologies for the Creation of Musical Works 402
a. Sampling 402
b. Mixing 408
c. Production 413
2. Communication 418
a. File-Sharing: Moral Rights and Illegality 419
b. Downloading: Moral Rights as Corporate Obligation 421
c. Streaming: The Future of Moral Rights? 425

F. Musical Transformations: From Mobile Ringtones to the Streaming Era 432
1. Moral Rights and Excerpts 433
a. Integrity of a Ringtone: Germany Leads the Way 433
i. Excerpts 433
ii. Modifications 434
2. Licensing: An Implicit Waiver of Moral Rights? 435
G. Musical Performers: The New Authors 438
1. Authors and Artists: Two Solitudes 438
a. Attribution of Performances 440
b. Protecting the Performer's "Honor" as an Element of the Integrity Right 442
c. Performance in a New Context 443
2. Performers and Their Public: Future Symbiosis? 444
3. Layers of Rights: The Performer Finds a Place 446
4. Recognizing the Performer: An Issue of Equity 447
5. Recording and Broadcasting 451
H. Recommendations 453
I. Conclusion: The Public Interest in Music 455

7. Authors and *Auteurs*: Copyright and Moral Rights in Film 457
A. Introduction 457
B. Commerce Meets Creation: Authorship of a Film 460
C. The Film as a Derivative Work: An Argument against Moral Rights? 474
D. Practical Challenges: Film Litigation in India and France 477
1. India: Moral Rights in a Culture of Adaptation 482
a. Producer vs. Author: *Mannu Bhandari* 482
i. Moral Rights and Film Contracts 486
ii. "Certain Modifications" 487
iii. Remedies 489
iv. Cultural Heritage 489
b. Digital Re-creation: *Anand Patwardhan* 492
2. Colorization: Producers vs. Directors in France 494
E. Film as a Technological Work 499
1. Editing, Creative Allusion, and Reuse: From Fan Films to Family Movies 500
2. The Communication of Films Online 508
3. Fame beyond the Grave: Reviving Deceased Actors through Artificial Intelligence 510
F. Recommendations 511
G. Conclusion 514

8. The Master Hand: Moral Rights in the Visual Arts 515
A. Special Rights and Privileges: Moral Rights for Artists 516
B. *Sanctum Sanctorum*: Originality and the Special Status of Art 516

C. Moral Rights for Visual Artists Alone: The Approach in the Visual Artists Rights Act 1990 (VARA) 518
1. The Dis-United States: The Genesis of VARA in State Legislation for the Protection of Art 520
2. The Workplace: Employees Are Not Artists 520
3. Attribution: Remedying Integrity Violations 521
4. The Integrity Right: Intentional Harm 523
5. The Prohibition of Destruction: Cultural Heritage Bows before Property 525
6. *5Pointz*: Threading the Eye of the Needle 527
7. The VARA Time Machine 529
8. Waiving Moral Rights 531
D. Integrity without Reputation: Canada's Approach to Art 532
E. Context and Conservation: Alteration of the Work? 533
F. Context and Meaning: "Framed by the Sky" 534
G. Author's Right Meets the Public Interest: "General Cultural Interests," "National Treasure," and "Recognized Stature" 539
H. Creative Destruction: Should Artists Be Allowed to Destroy Their Own Work? 543
I. Perpetual Moral Rights: A Bridge between Intellectual and Cultural Property 544
1. Artworks: Property or Heritage? 547
2. Moral Rights and the Life-Cycle of an Artwork 549
a. Phase 1: Intellectual Property 549
b. Phase 2: *Post Mortem Auctoris* 549
c. Phase 3: Cultural Property and Moral Rights 552
d. The Public Domain: Shiva Nataraja's Rights of "Attribution" and "Integrity" 556
i. Legal Issues Assessed by the Courts 560
ii. A Moral Rights Perspective 563
J. Architectural Works: Balancing Public Needs with Artistic Prerogative 565
K. Moral Rights and Virtual Galleries 569
1. Digital Images: New Technology to Reach Old Masters 569
2. Building Virtual Galleries 572
3. Artistic Innovation: From Collages to Parodies 573
L. Copy or Original? 3D Printed Artworks 575
M. A Critique of Originality: Bill Reid and Haida Art 579
N. A Further Critique: Yumbulul and the Legal Paradox of Living Traditions 582
O. Recommendations and Conclusion 584

9. Friends or Enemies?: Moral Rights and Open Access 587
A. Open Access: An Alternative to Copyright 588
B. The Cult of Copyleft 589
C. Creative Commons: A Licensing System Based on Moral Rights 592
1. Copyright Infringement and Creative Commons: License or Contract? 593
2. The Basic License: Attribution Affirmed 595
3. Integrity in the Basic License 596
4. Derivative Works: Integrity or Attribution? 596
5. Reputation: The Heart of Open Access 598
6. The Dark Side of Open Access: Art as a Profession in Decline 599
D. Open Access: A Practical Need for Moral Rights 602
E. Collective Creation: Wikipedia 609
F. Freedom to Create: The Price and Promise of Copyleft Movements 615
G. Recommendations 617
H. Conclusion 619

10. Conclusion: Moral Rights in the Age of Artificial Intelligence 621

Index 627

Foreword

Moral rights are a paradoxical area of copyright law. The core moral rights recognized in international law are the right of attribution—the right of an author of a work to be credited as such—and the right to integrity—the author's right not to have their work distorted, mutilated, or subjected to other modification prejudicial to the author's honour or reputation. To most non-lawyers, these rights have an obvious intuitive appeal. Moreover, empirical research has shown that most creative people value these rights even more highly than the economic rights conferred by copyright. Many authors are content to receive little or no financial reward from their works provided that they are properly credited and the integrity of the works is respected. One might expect, therefore, that moral rights would be central to copyright law; but they are not. Even now, nearly a century after moral rights were first introduced into the Berne Convention by the Rome revision of 1928, moral rights are marginalized. The common-law systems have granted moral rights reluctantly, hedged them around with restrictions such as requirements for assertion and made it too easy for authors to be pressured into waiving them. Even in countries such as France, where protection for moral rights appears strong, authors are deterred from enforcing their rights and infringements are widespread. The rise of digital culture, which should make proper attribution easier, has in practice had the opposite effect. Worse, it has enabled works to be distorted or mutilated at the click of a mouse. Moreover, the challenges of enforcement in the online environment have conferred a degree of impunity on infringers.

This leads to another paradox. No doubt because of the reluctance of authors to bring proceedings to enforce their rights due to the costs and stress involved, and the difficulties they face if they do, there is little litigation, and even fewer decided cases, concerning moral rights, particularly in common-law countries. Nor has the extension of moral rights to performers, particularly since the signature and coming into force of the WIPO Performances and Phonograms Treaty in 1996, resulted in many claims by performers. Despite this absence of case law, moral rights have benefited from the sustained attention of some distinguished scholars who have done much to elucidate this important, yet somewhat mysterious, subject. One such scholar is Mira Sundara Rajan, who made an important contribution to the field with the first edition of this book, then entitled *Moral Rights: Principles, Practice and New Technology*, when it was published in 2011. Although there have been few changes in the substantive law, apart from the signature and coming into force of the Beijing Treaty on Audiovisual Performances, and few decided cases since then, the context has changed significantly. Two obvious examples of this are the rise of streaming as the predominant mode of consumption of sound recordings and audiovisual works and the advent of generative artificial intelligence. These developments have not lessened the importance of moral rights, but rather the reverse. It is therefore welcome that Professor Sundara Rajan has produced a second edition of this book. This is not a mere updating of the previous edition, but to some extent a new text which has been recast in the light of contemporary conditions. Thus, Chapters 5 and 10 now confront the issue of artificial intelligence. As Professor Sundara Rajan writes, a proper attention to moral rights in this context can “reaffirm[] the value of human creativity at its most vulnerable”. Throughout the book Professor Sundara Rajan brings to bear not only an unusually broad legal perspective, but also a wealth of cultural references (often with fascinating details in footnotes) which help to illuminate the topics discussed. As such, the new edition makes a further valuable contribution to this field.

Richard Arnold
Royal Courts of Justice, London
March 2024

Foreword to the First Edition

At first sight, in the British context, moral rights seem to form a rather small and insignificant part of copyright law. First recognized explicitly in statute only just over twenty years ago, it is still possible to find, even amongst those not raised in the traditions of Austinian positivism, the notion that a merely moral right cannot possibly be a legal one. While the assertion of an author's attribution right is standard in books published in the United Kingdom, judicial decisions have not encouraged a wide view of integrity rights, suspicions of which also remain high in the cultural sector. When our attention turns to the international scene, we seem to find confirmation of the general unimportance of moral rights. While it is true that performers outside the audiovisual sector (i.e. outside the film and broadcasting industries) have gained moral rights under the WIPO Performances and Phonograms Treaty of 1996, the TRIPs Agreement of 1994 carefully excluded moral rights from its ambit and the European Union's harmonization of the copyright laws of its member states has deliberately not extended to this subject either.

Mira Sundara Rajan's study successfully combats such blinkered perspectives. Using the widest of comparative lenses, she perceives and documents an expansion of moral rights doctrine around the world. Particularly significant in her analysis is the deployment of moral rights in developing and post-socialist economies of, respectively, India and Russia. The latter is a jurisdiction of which Dr Sundara Rajan's previously published work has given her a deep knowledge and understanding. She further argues that moral rights are crucial in the digital environment, where they contribute to the authentication of both origin and quality in a world where works can be speedily and endlessly transmitted and retransmitted, readily modified and reshaped, and integrated, in whole or in part, in other works. Moral rights also contribute to the protection of cultural heritage: in India, a country and a culture for which Dr Sundara Rajan also has a special affinity, they have provided a remedy against what the courts took to be unjustified destruction of an artistic work in the care of the government.

Dr Sundara Rajan further challenges the common belief that moral rights are a uniquely Civil Law construct, somehow alien to and incompatible with common-law approaches to copyright. Most striking is her demonstration that what we would now call moral right ideas are prominent in the arguments of Lord Mansfield for the existence of a common-law right antecedent to the rights provided by the Statute of Anne, and which also survived the demise of the statutory term of protection. Perhaps a Scottish lawyer may be allowed to suggest, in the light of the 1773 decision in *Hinton v. Donaldson* and subsequent Scottish case law, that a crucial element in the development of "common law copyright" after *Donaldson v. Beckett* in 1774 was the position of the unpublished work and recognition of the author's right to decide when, if at all, it might be disclosed to the public. The link between this and the author's personality rather than any property rights was long maintained in Scotland before dissolving in the great case of *Caird v. Sime* in 1885–87. Today, as the concept of personality rights to identity, reputation, and dignity gains footholds in common-law thinking (helped along by the impetus provided by human rights), it may become possible to see moral rights more as part of that picture than as something necessarily to be linked to, and contrasted with, the economic rights conferred by copyright. Dr Sundara Rajan's contribution should help substantially with that process of conceptual development.

A final target of this book is the "Death of the Author" school in literary and copyright criticism. Dr Sundara Rajan shows clearly how deep and widespread (across very different cultures) is the idea of an intimate connection between author and work justifying a privileged position for that person, if not necessarily one having to be reflected in economic advantage. With digitization enabling so many would-be authors to lay their wares before any audience that it may be able to command, the case for legal reinforcement for rights of attribution and integrity is not necessarily undermined by the parallel increase in possibilities for collaboration with others and the reworking and reuse of existing material. Nor are moral rights inconsistent with ideas of open-access licensing. What may still remain to be fully tested is how far the law may go in allowing moral rights to be given up or waived in relation to all comers. The British rule allowing waivers is, as Dr Sundara Rajan demonstrates, not a unique departure from moral right norms.

Anglophone studies of moral rights have, for too long, proceeded on the basis of difference and consequential difficulties. It is more than time to accept that the rights form an important part of the modern law rather than being an isolated beachhead of no particular significance. Mira Sundara Rajan makes this case with style and formidable breadth of learning in both law and general culture, and her work deserves, and will reward, a widespread readership.

Hector MacQueen
Edinburgh, July 2010

Preface and Acknowledgments

In many ways, this book is a lesson in how *not* to prepare a new edition of a book. The fault lies mainly in the stars: the combination of a rapidly changing publishing sector and personal circumstances led to the extension of the original timeline for the second edition by approximately a decade.

During this time, to say the least, many interesting things have happened, both in the world of books and in the world at large. I could write a separate book about my own experiences over the past decade (and it would deal only tangentially with intellectual property law)!

But I would like to draw readers' attention to a development that has had an immense impact on this book. In 2013, I left Canada, where I held the Canada Research Chair in Intellectual Property Law and was a tenured professor at UBC Law School, to move back to the United Kingdom, where I was appointed Professor of Intellectual Property Law at Glasgow University. I became head of a new masters program, the LL.M. in "Intellectual Property and the Digital Economy." I had the opportunity to develop a new course based on my *Moral Rights* book, which had been published in 2011, called International and Comparative Moral Rights.

The course was an experiment. It closely followed the structure of my book: the first part examined legislation and cases on copyright and moral rights from various jurisdictions, while the second part explored practical developments in music, film, the fine arts, and technology. These areas were treated as case studies from which students could learn in a more experiential context.

Moral rights proved to be unexpectedly popular. From the time when the course was first offered in 2013/14, as the LL.M. program grew substantially in subsequent years, large numbers of students enrolled in it. The student body was very diverse, with students from across Europe, North America, Asia, Africa, and the United Kingdom. The students also came from a variety of educational and professional backgrounds.

Teaching a group of students like this was in itself a joy. What I did not expect, however, was the passion that so many of them brought to their studies—and, in particular, to their engagement with moral rights. They had the opportunity to write papers and theses. In doing so, they developed highly original research projects, touching on an astonishing range of contemporary issues, and sometimes unearthing the unexpected. As they learned from me, I also learned from them. I amassed a treasure trove of new ideas on moral rights that was shaped by their interests, and I gained new insights from my efforts to explore and answer their questions.

My students also provided something less quantifiable but equally important: inspiration and hope. In a very real sense, this work is intended for them.

Incorporating the knowledge and new perspectives that I had acquired over the years into the new edition of *Moral Rights* was a profound challenge. It became more daunting every year. As each new academic year progressed, new material, new ideas, and new approaches continued to accumulate. In the Tamil language, my parents' mother tongue, there is a wonderful word, *malaippu*, which transforms the noun for "mountain" into a verb. It describes exactly how I felt: "mountained". This is why, in the end, the new edition is much more than an updated version of the old book. As readers who are familiar with the first edition will notice, not only has the content of the book been updated in this new edition, but the book has also been more or less completely rewritten, reorganized, and rethought. I could not do less—and there is still more that could be done.

I was finally compelled to finish the work by the stunning rise to prominence of artificial intelligence (AI).

This, too, requires a brief explanation. The past decade has been a time of intense technological change—but also, of growing disillusionment with technology. The first decade of the millennium, when the first edition of *Moral Rights* was written, was a time of great technological optimism. In retrospect, it was also, perhaps, a period of naiveté. A decade later, we have seen the dark side of technology. Social media exerts a cruel pressure on its users to conform. Online communities act as judge and jury, and they have new and powerful means at their disposal to enforce their "judgments". Trust in the integrity of information is crumbling and, along with it, democracy. The answer to the ancient question "What is truth?" is rapidly receding from our grasp, perhaps forever.

In this environment, AI—a technology with immense potential—has become a force to be reckoned with. Its ultimate testing ground—the one most eagerly embraced by tech innovators—has emerged as the traditional territory of human creativity. AI-based text generators and image generators learn from the work of human creators and create "new" things. These AI creations further confuse the environment for information, knowledge, and culture in which we move. They also offer alternatives to human creation in countless sectors, including the arts. The creators of AI claim that AI is "creative." Is it? And will it one day "replace" human creators? … Does any of this matter?

This book argues that it does. It contends, simply, that human creativity is essential for us all, as human beings. Machine creativity cannot replace it. This premise lies at the heart of moral rights. Moral rights are based on the principle that human creativity is uniquely valuable. This area of the law therefore has an important contribution to make to the debates surrounding AI, and ultimately, to the development of AI technology itself.

As lawyers, many of us have a tendency to be very cautious about making broad general statements. Overall, this is understandable, even commendable. In the intellectual property field, we recognize that our knowledge is specialized. But there is also a significant negative aspect to this reticence, which is that the public remains widely misinformed about the purposes and functioning of intellectual property laws. This works to everyone's detriment.

The rise of AI shows, as never before, how the "specialized" field of intellectual property rights can intersect powerfully with important social concerns. It appears that the world may increasingly benefit from our knowledge and, more generally, that it is in need of the primary skill in which lawyers are trained: the art of critical reasoning. I will not use the term "objective," because I do not believe that law or any field of human knowledge can be purely objective. But our reasoning as lawyers can aspire to be unbiased and disinterested—oriented towards what we believe to be in the public interest. This is the approach that I have tried to take in the book.

More than ever, this book is, and has always been, a work of advocacy for authors and artists—as noted by Sir Richard Arnold in his Foreword. This is true of all my work because it has emerged from my experience as part of a family that has been dedicated to culture and creativity over many generations. The first people for whom I advocated were my own great-grandparents and grandparents, now followed by my parents. As a result, I have seen the struggles of artists directly, and, for me, there is nothing abstract about them. In the technological environment, as Richard Arnold notes, such advocacy on behalf of authors and artists is greatly needed. I hope that this book will encourage further efforts to support them, and I believe that the public will ultimately benefit from their flourishing.

I owe an immeasurable debt to Richard Arnold, who so graciously agreed to provide a Foreword for this book. He did so in spite of the extraordinary demands of his role as a Lord Justice of Appeal, and his interest in this work over many years provided strong motivation for continuing with it. (In typical style, he reviewed the lengthy draft manuscript in its entirety when preparing his Foreword!)

I was also greatly encouraged by Professor Hector MacQueen to complete the new edition, and I could not have done so without his support. (He has also read and commented on parts of the draft—notably including the historical sections in Chapter 2.) I first met Hector at my D.Phil. viva voce at Magdalen College, Oxford; since then, his contributions to my intellectual and professional development have been unstinting. It is with great pride that I include his Foreword to the first edition here.

Much of the foundational work for the new edition was done at Stanford Law School, where I was a visiting scholar in 2016/17 at the kind invitation of Professor Paul Goldstein. Paul's welcoming presence, and his unfailing generosity in sharing his knowledge, contributed to an idyllic time for me in Stanford.

Thanks are also due to Charlotte Kershaw, the enthusiastic law editor who, with the helpful production editor Karen Moore, has seen this edition through to completion at Oxford University Press (OUP) over the past year. Imogen Hill, my previous editor at OUP, also reviewed the manuscript and provided a steady stream of encouragement throughout the very difficult period from 2019 to 2022. Matt Gallaway, now of Cambridge University Press, who first commissioned this work for OUP and has continued to be an important presence; his valuable contributions are permanently integrated into this work.

The study of Norwegian law was made possible by Beatrice Ignacius and Martine Valland, both LL.M. graduates of Glasgow, who made me aware of the situation surrounding Oslo's Picasso–Nesjar murals in 2020 and shared their keen interest in exploring moral rights as a possible solution. Beatrice provided invaluable research assistance on Norwegian law. I am also grateful to Ida Gjessing, of Gjessing Reimers law firm in Oslo, who introduced me to Gro Nesjar and Espen Viksjø, the heirs of artist Carl Nesjar and architect Erlen Viksjø.

My most sincere thanks are due to Manasa Chinni, my research assistant and former student in the J.D. program at UC Davis Law School, where I was a Visiting Professor of Intellectual Property Law from 2020 to 2024. Quite simply, Manasa's help with the final preparation of the footnotes made it possible to publish this book. Her help was provided with grace and selflessness. It has been a privilege to teach her and to have her support.

Viswanath Prasanna, who led the production of the first edition of this book, has provided essential help with proof-checking and indexing of the new edition. I think of him as the book's guardian angel!

Every effort has been made to eliminate errors, but any that remain are the sole responsibility of myself and the editorial team at OUP.

Finally, this new edition continues to be dedicated to Professor Colin Tapper, whose seminal work on law and technology has inspired my work and the work of many others. He will always remain my ideal of a teacher, intellectual, and person. I hope that my efforts to improve this work since the first edition was published will now make it somewhat more worthy of him.

Mira T. Sundara Rajan
Berkeley, California
November 29, 2024

Prologue

Once upon a time, in a faraway country, lived a poet.

One evening, the poet went out for a walk. As he passed the local blacksmith's shop, he heard the sound of singing. He suddenly stopped and stood, as if riveted to the spot.

The blacksmith was singing a song that the poet recognized. In fact, it was the poet's own song—but not as he had written it. Strange words took the place of the words he had written. The rhythm was distorted.

After listening for a few moments, the poet entered the shop. Inside, the blacksmith had kept good order: the tools and implements of his trade were neatly organized on the shelves. The poet promptly began to move around the shop, removing items from their place, rearranging things at random.

The blacksmith jumped up and approached the poet. "Crazy man! What do you think you are doing?" he cried. "These tools are my property—my livelihood."

The poet replied, "I am doing to your property what you were doing to mine. I am the poet who wrote the song you were singing. Poetry is, to me, what your property is to you—it is my livelihood."

This story was written by Indian national poet, C. Subramania Bharati, who lived from 1882 to 1921 in South India, and whose writings gave birth to the Tamil Renaissance of the early twentieth century.

1
A Unitary View of Copyright Law

[C]opyright as a whole . . . serves to protect [the] intellectual and moral as well as economic interests of authors. This could . . . be called [a] . . . unitary or synthetic concept of copyright.

—*Adolf Dietz*[1]

A. Introduction 2
B. Moral Rights: The Doctrine 4
C. The Controversy 8
1. Doctrine vs. Law 9
2. The Origins of Moral Rights 12
3. Aesthetic Reality 13
D. The Rights Protected 15
1. Attribution 17
2. Integrity and Reputation 20
a. Destruction of a Work 27
3. Disclosure and Withdrawal 30
4. A Right to Remuneration? The Example of the Resale Right (*droit de suite*) 32
E. Legal Implications of the Doctrine 32
1. Independence of Moral and Economic Rights 32
2. Inalienability, Waiver, and Inequality of Bargaining Power 33
3. Perpetual Protection 34
F. Relationship between the Economic and Moral Aspects of Copyright 36
G. The Common-Law Treatment of Moral Rights 38
H. Moral Rights and Human Rights: The Ruling of the Court of Justice of the European Union (CJEU) in *Deckmyn* (2014) 40
I. Moral Rights and Free Speech: A Dual-Edged Sword? 44
J. Moral Rights in the Technological Environment 46
K. Fame: The Currency of the Digital Era? 50
L. A Study in Contrasts: The Enforcement of Moral Rights 52
M. Moral Rights Jurisprudence: Occurrences and Outcomes 54
N. Conclusion: Scope and Structure of This Book 57

[1] Adolf Dietz, *Legal Principles of Moral Rights (Civil Law) General Report*, *in* The Moral Right of the Author 54, paras. 16–17 (1993). *See* Chapter 2, *infra* note 152 and accompanying text. All websites cited in this chapter were last visited on October 22, 2024.

A. Introduction

Since the turn of the millennium, copyright law has become both prominent and controversial. It occupies a significant place in the public discourse surrounding creativity and free expression. The rise of the Internet and the spread of new technologies for the creation, copying, and dissemination of works have tested the viability and justice of established copyright norms. But, during this time, the so-called "moral rights" of authors have also been quietly growing in importance.

Moral rights are generally considered to originate in the European theory of authors' rights.[2] European copyright laws identify two distinct categories of interests based on authorship: economic rights and personal rights.[3] The latter have come to be known as "moral rights" and are broadly considered to be "non-economic" in nature.[4] Moral rights were incorporated into the Berne Convention for the Protection of Literary and Artistic Works in 1928. They are now universally protected in copyright laws worldwide.[5] These rights are actually known by a range of terms in the different copyright laws of the world—personal rights, personality

[2] This background is explored in Chapter 2 *infra*. The difference in terminology between civil and common-law systems is worth noting. In European legal systems, copyright law is referred to as the "author's right," e.g., the French *droit d'auteur*, Italian *dirritto d'autore*, Spanish *derecho de autor*, or German *Urheberrecht* ("creator's right"). These systems fulfil all the functions of modern copyright law in commonlaw legal systems and are equivalent to copyright, but they also have a different theoretical orientation which affects the rationale behind copyright rules, if not (always) the practice of copyright law. This area was the subject of an early study by ALAIN STROWEL, DROIT D'AUTEUR ET COPYRIGHT: DIVERGENCES ET CONVERGENCES—ÉTUDE DE DROIT COMPARÉ (1993), https://bib.kuleuven.be/rbib/collectie/archieven/boeken/strowel-droitauteurcopyright-1993.pdf.

[3] However, conceptions and practices involving attribution and integrity interests, which are now protected through moral rights, are also well known in non-European cultures. For example, ancient Indian poets often include a verse in their poems which specifically identifies the poet by name. These artistic practices are not usually viewed as precursors of modern moral rights, though this is what they appear to be. Rather, the tradition of narrating copyright's history begins with the adoption of the British Statute of Anne in 1709–10, which is generally accepted as the first instrument of "modern copyright law." Evaluating the construction of copyright history and moral rights history through this lens is a research project in its own right. See the discussion in Chapter 3, *infra* notes 343–45 and accompanying text.

[4] This terminology is particularly favored in countries of common-law heritage. In civil law countries, the distinction between economic and non-economic rights is more fluid: see, e.g., the discussion of the *droit de destination* in the Canadian case *Théberge v. Galerie d'Art du Petit Champlain Inc.* [2002] 2 S.C.R. 336, 2002 SCC 34, citing French law that shows how something akin to a moral right can be classified as an economic right under French law. *See* Chapter 2, *infra* notes 87–90 and accompanying text. I discuss the *Théberge* case in detail, including this element, in Mira T. Sundara Rajan, *Moral Rights and Economic Rights: Overlapping Protection of Authors under Copyright Law, in* OVERLAPPING INTELLECTUAL PROPERTY RIGHTS 303 (Neil Wilkof, Shamnad Basheer & Irene Calboli eds., 2d ed., 2023).

[5] In the United States, however, moral rights are limited to the field of artistic creation in the fine arts—an issue that is extensively discussed in this book. *See* Visual Artists Rights Act of 1990 (VARA): Visual Artist Rights Act, 17 U.S.C. § 106A (1990), https://www.copyright.gov/title17/92chap1.html#106a. Although VARA was adopted two years after the United States joined the Berne Convention, it was a response to concerns about U.S. implementation of the moral rights in Berne's Article 6*bis*: *see* Jane C. Ginsburg, *Copyright in the 101st Congress: Commentary on the Visual Artists Rights Act and the Architectural Works Copyright Protection Act of 1990*, 14 COLUMBIA-VLA J. OF L. & THE ARTS 477, 478-79 (1990), https://repository.uchastings.edu/hastings_law_journal/vol27/iss5/3

rights,[6] and simply "special" rights[7]—but moral rights is the expression most often used, and it is accordingly the one favored in this book. It is a literal translation of the original French *droit moral*.[8]

Moral rights, alongside the economic rights of authors, are an integral part of modern copyright law.[9] The core ideas embodied by moral rights—attribution of authorship, authorial agency, the value of reputation, and the preservation of the integrity of works—also resonate beyond the law, with parallel concepts informing aesthetic theory, artistic practice, cultural history, and human rights. In the technological era, these domains are riddled with new questions and vulnerabilities. The rise of artificial intelligence makes it urgent to attend to the status of our cultural environment.

In this context, this book argues that moral rights, which have long been seen as secondary to the economic rights in copyright works, should be treated as a cornerstone of intellectual property regulation. But moral rights have a further role to play. They can help to assert the value of human creativity, personhood, and culture in an extremely challenging environment. Our world is increasingly dominated by corporations and machines, and human agency is under threat and undervalued. The potential of moral rights to respond to these developments lies in the history of these rights, in how they are currently understood, in the possibilities for their further evolution—and in their significant potential to influence legal and cultural developments beyond the rarified domain of copyright theory.

With these considerations in mind, the purpose of this book is to provide a clear and, as far as possible, accurate assessment of the moral rights of authors worldwide. It considers the place of moral rights in the international copyright system and among its various member jurisdictions. In the interests of both comprehensiveness and equity, the discussion examines moral rights in jurisdictions that have traditionally been less prominent in the international copyright arena. In these countries, moral rights have often received novel and useful interpretations, and this book argues that they carry the doctrine forward in important new directions. They will help to ensure the continued relevance and longevity of moral rights.

This book is fundamentally preoccupied with the fascinating implications of the ever-changing world of technology for creative authorship. Digital technology

[6] The Germanic term is *Personlichkeitsrecht*.

[7] Copyright Act, 1957, No. 14, §57 (India), http://copyright.gov.in/Documents/CopyrightRules1957.pdf.

[8] French legal commentators have noted the apparent shift, after codification in the French statute in 1956 of what had previously been judge-made law, from *droit moral* to *droits moraux*—broad doctrine to specific rights. This issue is discussed further in Chapter 2, *infra* notes 68–69 and accompanying text.

[9] For example, the earliest references to moral rights in modern copyright doctrine occur in the English case, *Millar v. Taylor* (1769) 4 Burr. 2303, 98 ER 201—though earlier references can be found in Europe and elsewhere. In Ireland, for example, copyright as a whole was recognized in a famous judgment, "To every cow its calf, to every book its copy": *see, e.g.*, Frank McNally, *An Irishman's Diary: As Copyright Lawyers Will Know, Today Marks an Important Anniversary in Their Trade*, IRISH TIMES (Apr. 10, 2010), https://www.irishtimes.com/opinion/an-irishman-s-diary-1.650520.

has redefined our cultural landscape, bringing immense challenges to the existing copyright paradigm from which copyright laws everywhere are derived. This study argues that moral rights have a uniquely valuable role to play in the technological environment. Indeed, neglected as they often are, moral rights may, nevertheless, have the potential to redefine and shape our understanding of the entirety of copyright law. But this can only be accomplished if the importance of the rights, and of the interests that they represent, are duly recognized by the legal community worldwide.

This book argues that the greater influence of moral rights in copyright law and policy would be a useful and positive development. As such, moral rights should be welcomed and, indeed, actively explored by the international copyright community. An approach to copyright that is more closely attuned to moral rights would lead to nothing less than a timely and humane reassessment of the character and purpose of copyright law. This transformation is long overdue.

B. Moral Rights: The Doctrine

Moral rights are based on a simple idea. The author of a work develops a special bond with his or her creation. Moral rights aim to offer appropriate legal protections to this "special" relationship. In doing so, they seek to preserve it from harm in the interests of both authors and society. But what, exactly, is the nature of that relationship, and why should we protect it?

The moral right of the author is considered to be a personal right: it originates in the person, or personality, of the author. The work is considered to be an expression of the author's personality.[10] Commentators describe this relationship in a number of ways. Words such as "intellectual," "personal," and "spiritual" appear; one venerable scholar of copyright refers to the theory that a work is the "spiritual child" of the author.[11] The terminology, with its impractical overtones, is not

[10] Desbois emphasizes this aspect of moral rights in France, pointing out that moral rights are "situated among personality rights" ("les attributs du droit moral se situent parmi les droits de la personnalité"): *see* Henri Desbois, Le Droit d'auteur en France 470 (para. 381) (3d ed., 1978). Copyright, as a whole, edges towards this realization, since it protects only "original" works of authorship; the common-law countries have moved towards higher levels of "originality," surpassing the earlier notion of protecting the *labor* of creators through copyright law, e.g., in the landmark U.S. case of *Feist Publications, Inc. v. Rural Tel. Serv. Co.*, 499 U.S. 340 (1991), https://supreme.justia.com/cases/federal/us/499/340.

[11] *See* Stig Strömholm, *Droit Moral: The International and Comparative Scene from a Scandinavian Viewpoint*, 14(1) Int'l Rev. Indus. Prop. & Copyright L. 217, 228 (1983) (calling the author the "spiritual father" of the work and cites the Swedish Royal Commission on Copyright Law for the term "spiritual children"). *See also* Sam Ricketson, The Berne Convention for the Protection of Literary and Artistic Works: 1886–1986 para. 8.93 (1987) (pointing out that "[t]he adjective 'moral' has no precise English equivalent, although 'spiritual,' 'non-economic' and 'personal' convey something of the intended meaning").

universally approved. Yet, it serves to describe something that may not be less real because of its incorporeal quality.

Regardless of what happens to the economic rights in the work, the author's moral rights persist. Even after a work of art is sold and the author has parted with the economic rights, he or she retains the moral rights. Moreover, the relationship between author and work is permanent in the sense that an author is, and always will be, the author of his or her own work. This raises the possibility—some might say specter—of perpetual protection for moral rights, which is discussed in more detail below.

National approaches to the relationship between economic rights and moral rights are quite diverse. In some jurisdictions, such as those of Europe and Asia, moral rights are said to be hierarchically related to economic rights, occupying a place above them. In others, notably those of common-law heritage, they are considered almost an afterthought to copyright. Here, they have been tagged onto systems of protection for economic rights in a spirit of hesitation and doubt, reflected in significant legislative limitations and restrictions, and often further restricted in case law.

This explanation should be tempered by the observation that the exercise of many apparently "non-economic" interests can have major economic implications.[12] For example, if the author is allowed to withdraw the work from publication, the publisher of the work will face the costs of recalling and modifying, or perhaps destroying, copies of the work.[13] Indeed, the economic power of moral rights is undoubtedly among the primary reasons why they are often treated with reluctance, and even suspicion, in the common-law countries.[14]

The key concept underlying moral rights is that of harm—"moral" harm, in the wider sense of non-physical harm that can occur through the abuse of the author–work relationship. Moral rights are based on the idea that an author is personally implicated in the work. In view of the "special relationship" between an author

[12] At some level, the separation of artists' interests into "economic" and "non-economic" aspects is artificial—and is arguably becoming more so due to technological developments. Writing as early as 1976, Merryman actually notes that "[t]here is a persistent minority doctrinal position that treats the artist's moral right as an additional property right, rather than a right of personality. However the dominant view is to the contrary": *see* John Henry Merryman, *The Refrigerator of Bernard Buffet*, 27 Hastings L.J. 1023, 1025 (n.5) (1976), https://repository.uchastings.edu/hastings_law_journal/vol27/iss5/3 (citing Waline, *Le Droit moral de l'artiste sur son oeuvre et le droit public* [1936] D.P.III.57).

[13] For these reasons, in countries where the right of withdrawal is recognized, there is often a corresponding obligation on the author to indemnify the publisher for losses: *see, e.g.*, Loi 92-597 du 1 juillet 1992 relative au Code de la propriété intellectuelle (partie législative) [Law 92-597 of July 1, 1992, relating to the Intellectual Property Code (Legislative part)], Journal officiel de la République française [J.O.] [Official Gazette of France], Feb. 8, 1994 (Code de la propriété intellectuelle), arts. L121–244 (Fr.), https://www.legifrance.gouv.fr/codes/texte_lc/LEGITEXT000006069414. French moral rights are discussed in detail in Chapter 4 *infra*.

[14] Notably, the resistance of the Hollywood movie industry to moral rights has been based, to a significant degree, on concerns about the economic impact of those rights on movie production: *see, e.g.*, Stephen Fraser, *Berne, CFTA, NAFTA and GATT: The Implications of Copyright Droit Moral and Cultural Exemptions in International Trade Law*, 18 Hastings Comm. and Ent. L.J. 287 (1996).

and his or her creation, the author's interest in the work is not limited to financial gain. Rather, an author may have strong interests in the work that are still difficult to quantify—in how it is used, displayed, or treated, for example. Authors may feel that they have suffered significant harm arising out of damage to these interests.[15] To deal with this harm, the remedy of choice for a moral rights violation is usually injunctive in nature. Financial compensation to authors for moral rights violations is a relatively rare outcome, but this is not to say that it is unjustifiable. Financial awards may make sense as part of a broader attempt to compensate the author for his or her losses, including damage to reputation, which can lead to professional losses in the future—or, indeed, as a punitive measure to deter others from damaging or destroying valuable works in the future. This simple but powerful concept is what is known as moral rights doctrine.

Moral rights are said to offer legal recognition to an author's personal interests in his or her own work—to the special relationship between author and work. However, it is essential to note that the author's "personal" interest in the work also has broad social implications. This is why there are limits on intellectual property protection at all.

For example, moral rights protect individual rights: society is composed of individuals, and if we take the individual as a basic unit of the social organism, protecting individual rights is essential for social stability. Protecting the rights of some individuals is also likely to involve balancing those rights against the rights and interests of other individuals and social organisms. This is an inherent policy challenge of recognizing rights, freedoms, and obligations.

There is also at least one other social interest involved in moral rights which has immediate relevance for our purpose: the status of the public domain. The vast majority of creative works ultimately find their way into the public domain. Authors are not only aware of this possibility, but many authors also embrace it—as did Victor Hugo.[16]In the case of Indian National Poet, C. Subramania Bharati, the poet died too suddenly to give much thought to this issue, but his wife intended to "bequeath" the works to the public upon her own death.[17] Indeed, the only

[15] In a controversial and thought-provoking incident, Kim Novak objected to the use of music from the classic Alfred Hitchcock film, *Vertigo*, in which she starred, by director Michel Hazanavicius in his 2011 film, *The Artist*, with the words, "I want to report a rape." See the discussion in Mira T. Sundara Rajan, *Homage or Humiliation? Moral Rights, Vertigo, and the Artist*, 1709 Blog (May 22, 2012), http://the1709blog.blogspot.com/2012/05/homage-or-humiliation-moral-rights.html.

[16] *See* Chapter 9, *infra* note 1 (Hugo is said to have proclaimed, "The writer as a writer has but one heir—the public domain.").

[17] She wanted to publish the works first. Bharati himself said that his work should be as readily available to the public "as a matchbox"; his linguistic innovations are a stronger testament to his generosity towards the public than anything else could be, since they made poetry accessible to the "common man." This history is reviewed in Mira T. Sundara Rajan, *Moral Rights in the Public Domain: Copyright Matters in the Works of Indian National Poet C. Subramania Bharati*, 2001 Singapore J. Legal Stud. 161. But Chellamma, his wife, was prevented from doing so by various impediments, including the disadvantages that she suffered as a widow without social status in 1920s South India. The government of Tamil Nadu ultimately "purchased" the copyright from the family and gave it to the people of India. The amount paid for it was insignificant, but the government also gave small sums of money to Chellamma

exception to this principle of public inheritance is in relation to works of visual art, which, unlike other forms of creation, can be meaningfully possessed as property, as well as intellectual property.[18]

Accordingly, and especially in relation to works of cultural importance, there are strong overlapping interests between creators and the public. Protecting the "integrity" of a work—a basic moral right that is universally recognized in the copyright laws of the world—benefits society as a whole, because it ultimately ensures the preservation of culturally valuable works that *belong to the public* or are held, in some sense, on its behalf (in museums, for example). The morality of the private ownership of important artworks that have been acquired on the international art market will not be discussed here, except to point out one interesting development: the prospect that cultural artefacts returned from Western countries to Africa might become the private property of Nigeria's *oba* has caused consternation in the West.[19] The moral right of integrity, though it is an individual right of authorship, ultimately protects the integrity of cultural heritage.[20]

The right of integrity has an obvious connection with culture: its objective is to protect cultural heritage, whether material or intangible, from damage. When the right of integrity extends to works in the public domain, it can become a means of protecting cultural heritage throughout the lifetime of a work. The effectiveness of that protection depends, in part, on who is entitled to invoke it. The right of attribution, which is also a universally recognized moral right,[21] also benefits society at large—in this case, by preserving historical truth regarding identity and authenticity. Although the author may often be the best person to watch over his or her own work, the implications of both moral rights clearly extend beyond a "personal" benefit to the author and involve a benefit to the public at large.

This book suggests that, where contemporary moral rights are concerned, any search for doctrinal purity should probably be abandoned. Indeed, the bewildering array of interests involved in moral rights parallels the situation of

(who no longer owned it by then), and to Bharati's two daughters. This history is reviewed in Sundara Rajan, *supra*.

[18] For many, though, this is an uncomfortable reality. The issue is explored in a film by Nathaniel Kahn, *The Price of Everything* (2018), https://kinolorberedu.com/film/the-price-of-everything-dvd-1.

[19] As noted by Alex Marshall, *Who Owns the Benin Bronzes? The Answer Just Got More Complicated*, New York Times (June 4, 2023), https://www.nytimes.com/2023/06/04/arts/design/benin-bronzes-nigeria-ownership.html: "The oba wants the bronzes displayed in museums in Nigeria and around the world, a representative of the royal family said, but the passing of the treasures into private hands spread anxiety among some museums that are negotiating returns of looted items to Nigeria."

[20] Mira T. Sundara Rajan, *The Public Interest Case for American Moral Rights: A Response to the Symposium "Authors, Attribution, and Integrity: Examining Moral Rights in the United States"*, 8 Geo. Mason J. Int'l Com. L. 314, 318 (2017).

[21] But the United States is the only commonly known exception: *see, e.g.*, Jane C. Ginsburg, *The Most Moral of Rights: The Right to be Recognized as the Author of One's Work* (Columbia Public Law Research Paper No. 14-517, 2016), https://papers.ssrn.com/sol3/papers.cfm?abstract_id=2806316.

copyright law as a whole—elegantly summarized by historian Carla Hesse as an "impure and unstable synthesis"[22] of potentially competing policy interests underlying copyright law. The nature of copyright subject matter is inherently complex, and it is now made more complex by the advent of digital technology and the protection of technological works through copyright law. The lack of conceptual clarity underlying modern copyright law and practice is hardly surprising. The search for purity should be replaced by an emphasis on transparency: the objectives of the law should be clear, and policy should be meaningfully expressed in the law.[23]

But this work does not advocate for the expansion of moral rights in ways that would debase the spirit and purpose of the doctrine. For example, the extension of moral rights to corporations should generally be rejected, notwithstanding its recognition in Japan, Korea, and even India,[24] because the fundamental purpose of the doctrine is to protect human rights. The same principle applies to works created by artificial intelligence, though this fascinating issue deserves much fuller consideration—and receives it in Chapter 5 of this book. Above all, moral rights should be viewed comprehensively. They represent vital social interests; they are vested in authors, at least for a period of time, because authors are personally linked to their work and depend on it for sustenance. Authors are often in the best position to champion its protection; and the public, like authors, ultimately stands to benefit from moral rights protection. The characterization of moral rights as "personal" rights is both correct and useful, but it provides only a partial picture of the rights.

C. The Controversy

For all its apparent simplicity, the idea of an author's moral right leads to an amazing array of practical consequences. The implications are cultural, economic, and philosophical, as well as legal. However straightforward they may appear at first glance, moral rights are intensely controversial—which suggests the power, dangers, and opportunities that they involve.

The controversy surrounding moral rights can be distilled into three major issues.

[22] Carla Hesse, *Enlightenment Epistemology and the Law of Authorship in Revolutionary France, 1777–1793*, 30 Representations 109, 130 (1990).

[23] This is a theme that Bill Patry has discussed extensively: see, e.g., his interview at Google (Feb. 21, 2012), https://www.youtube.com/watch?v=tGkvjVl3uSg.

[24] *See* Chapter 4, *infra* notes 295 and 319–24 and accompanying text.

1. Doctrine vs. Law

First, lawyers often fail to distinguish between the doctrine of moral rights and the law. While this could also be interpreted as a positive feature of moral rights, implying flexibility and responsiveness, it is clearly impractical in the present era of copyright law. Over the past three decades, a major shift has occurred. Common-law countries, which have historically not recognized a doctrine of moral rights, have now implemented moral rights in their laws. Crucially, this has resulted from their adherence to international conventions. In particular, the Berne Convention for the Protection of Literary and Artistic Works,[25] the primary instrument of international copyright law, has been an extraordinarily important influence in this regard. Since the Berne Convention sets out minimum criteria for the recognition of moral rights, these criteria, and the language supplied by Berne to clarify their interpretation, serve as a template for the recogition of moral rights in common-law countries, reducing the uncertainty associated with the adoption of a "new" doctrine. The internationalization of moral rights has therefore implied their codification as well.

In this context, for the sake of clarity and feasibility, it has become useful to separate doctrine and law. Of course, the two have a common origin; but drawing a distinction between them emphasizes the contrast between the earlier, informal doctrine, which emerged out of the case-specific pronouncements of judges in the eighteenth and nineteenth centuries, and the later crystallization of that doctrine into a lattice of legal rules.

This very issue is discussed by a U.S. judge encountering the doctrine of moral rights in 1948:

> Conceivably, under the doctrine of Moral Right the court could in a proper case, prevent the use of a composition or work, in the public domain, in such a manner as would be violative of the author's rights. *The application of the doctrine presents much difficulty however.* With reference to that which is in the public domain there arises a conflict between the moral right and the well-established rights of others to use such works. So, too, there arises the question of the norm by which the use of such work is to be tested to determine whether or not the author's moral right as an author has been violated. Is the standard to be good taste, artistic worth, political beliefs, moral concepts or what is it to be? In the present state of our law the very existence of the right is not clear, the relative position of the rights

[25] International Convention for the Protection of Literary and Artistic Works, adopted at Berne on Sept. 9, 1886, completed at Paris on May 4, 1896, revised at Berlin on Nov. 13, 1908, completed at Berne on Mar. 20, 1914, revised at Rome on June 2, 1928, at Brussels on June 26, 1948, at Stockholm on July 14, 1967, and at Paris on July 24, 1971, and amended on Sept. 28, 1979, S. Treaty Doc. No. 99-27 (1986), https://www.wipo.int/treaties/en/ip/berne.

> thereunder with reference to the rights of others is not defined nor has the nature of the proper remedy been determined.[26]

It is interesting to note that the doctrine initially grew out of judge-made law: it was a theory of authorship, largely developed by German observers of French court decisions in the early-to-mid-nineteenth century.[27] Its development was arguably part of the larger process by which the "natural rights of man and the citizen," which emerged in Revolutionary France, were integrated into society, inaugurating a new era, not only in France, but also in the history of continental Europe and the world.[28] The law, in the current sense, emerged later in the history of moral rights: it became the expression of the doctrine as codified in the precise language of national copyright statutes.[29]

[26] *Shostakovich et al. v. Twentieth-Century Fox Film Corp.*, 196 Misc. 67, 80 N.Y.S.2d 575, 579 (1948) (U.S.), https://www.casemine.com/judgement/us/5914a149add7b04934686cf6 (emphasis added).

[27] This history is authoritatively described by the great Swedish legal scholar, Stig Strömholm, in a classic work: Stig Strömholm, Le droit moral de l'auteur en droit allemand, français et scandinave avec un aperçu de l'evolution internationale: Étude de droit comparé (1967).

[28] For an illuminating discussion of French copyright and its development during the Revolutionary period, see Gregory S. Brown, Literary Sociability and Literary Property in France: Beaumarchais, the Société des Auteurs Dramatique, and the Comédie Française, 1775–1793 116–42 (2006). A seminal article by Martha Woodmansee explores the origins of moral rights in Western European Romanticism: Martha Woodmansee, *The Genius and the Copyright: Economic and Legal Conditions of the Emergence of the "Author"*, 17 Eighteenth-Century Stud. 425 (1984). But this approach should be treated with caution—as William F. Patry remarks:

> Another, more recent trope is the idea of copyright arising out of a Romantic view of authorship. The scholarship on this is highly selective, and is limited to a few authors in a few countries. It ignores vast amounts of contrary evidence, and in any event suffers fatally from historical determinism: copyright developed as it did allegedly because authors, legislatures, and society evolved to the point of finally recognizing that no work is as much a man's or woman's as the fruits of his or her own mind. A variant on this, much beloved by some law professors, is a Lockean view of property, in which copyright came to be analogically with its real property cousin. At least one academic career was made on this theory, a theory which UK scholars have effectively debunked on many grounds, not the least of which is that when it came to intellectual property, Locke was not a Lockean.

See William F. Patry, *Why UK Scholars Eat Our Lunch*, The Patry Copyright Blog (Nov. 14, 2006), http://williampatry.blogspot.com/2006/11/why-uk-scholars-eat-our-lunch.html. In many ways, the birth of the human rights concept can be situated in the French Revolution. The Revolutionists' motto, "Liberté, égalité, fraternité," resonated as far away in space and time as twentieth-century South India, where a pioneer of the Freedom Movement took it as the motto of his nationalist, anti-British magazine. *See generally* S. Vijaya Bharati, C. Subramania Bharati (1974).

[29] To some extent, national copyright norms originate with the language of international treaties. These treaties are not necessarily "law" in the usual sense: in the case of the Berne Convention, *supra* note 25, its terms represent minimum standards, not law per se, and must be enacted in national legislation in order to become law. In this sense, the Berne system is similar to other forms of supranational law-making, from the Directives of the European Union to the *osnovy* of the former Soviet Union. A possible exception to this rule would be apparent in relation to countries whose implementation of international treaties is "automatic" and does not need to be separately implemented in national law. The Russian Federation is an example of such a country: *see Itar-Tass Russian News Agency v. Russian Kurier, Inc.*, 153 F.3d 82 (2d Cir. 1998) (U.S.). This difference means that a Russian plaintiff could invoke the Berne Convention provisions directly in court, but an American or Canadian plaintiff could not in the courts of his or her own country. This difference could create some ambiguity about the cross-border experience of copyright: for example, an American plaintiff in Russia could rely on the Berne Convention directly but could not do so in the United States. This point is significant in relation

In the sophisticated example of codification ultimately offered by France, which adopted moral rights in its copyright law at the relatively late date of 1957, the doctrine loses some of its breadth and generality, but it is translated into well-defined principles of great pragmatism. The shift is elegantly described by French professor Pierre Sirinelli and his coauthors in terms of a movement from *droit moral*—the term "moral right" in singular form, which served to describe the theory emerging from judicial decision-making—to *droits moraux*, the plural "moral rights," in the *Code de la propriété intellectuelle*.[30]

The intuitive, or common-sense, aspect borne by the doctrine leads to special difficulties, and in this sense, it is perhaps fair to say that the intuitive appeal of the idea is as much a shortcoming as a strength. To say that moral rights are intuitive is to link them with theories of natural law. But the relationship between natural law and legal instruments is complex, particularly in the common-law tradition. The claims of natural law exceed written laws. Principles of natural law are often reflected in legal instruments, but they do not depend on legal language for their existence.[31] Law may reflect natural rights, but natural law exists before, beyond, and after the law. It is a result of "nature," whereas formal law—human law—is artificial in the true sense of the word: a construction.[32] The difficulty of defining natural

to moral rights, since an American could thereby enjoy moral rights in Russia through Art. 6*bis* of the Berne Convention, without deriving a similar benefit from Berne in his or her own country.

[30] French Code de la propriété intellectuelle, *supra* note 13.

[31] John Locke is perhaps the philosopher most closely associated with reliance on theories of natural rights in the intellectual property field. See the commentaries by William W. Fisher III, *The Growth of Intellectual Property: A History of the Ownership of Ideas in the United States*, German version available as WILLIAM W. FISHER III, *Geistiges Eigentum—ein ausufernder Rechtsbereich: Die Geschichte des Ideenschutzes in den Vereinigten Staaten*, *in* EIGENTUM IM INTERNATIONALEN VERGLEICH 265 (1999), http://cyber.law.harvard.edu/people/tfisher/iphistory.pdf; ADAM D. MOORE, *Toward a Lockean Theory of Intellectual Property*, *in* INTELLECTUAL PROPERTY: MORAL, LEGAL, AND INTERNATIONAL DILEMMAS 81 (1997). For Locke's original arguments, see JOHN LOCKE, TWO TREATISES OF GOVERNMENT, BOOK II, Chapter V, "*Property*" (1689), https://press-pubs.uchicago.edu/founders/documents/v1ch16s3.html. In particular, Locke notes how property develops out of the mixture of human labor with the environment:

> Though the earth, and all inferior creatures, be common to all men, yet every man has a *property* in his own *person*: this no body has any right to but himself. The *labour* of his body, and the *work* of his hands, we may say, are properly his. Whatsoever then he removes out of the state that nature hath provided, and left it in, he hath mixed his *labour* with, and joined to it something that is his own, and thereby makes it his *property*. It being by him removed from the common state nature hath placed it in, it hath by this *labour* something annexed to it, that excludes the common right of other men: for this *labour* being the unquestionable property of the labourer, no man but he can have a right to what that is once joined to, at least where there is enough, and as good, left in common for others.

Id. at § 27.

[32] *See Artificial*, *in* OXFORD ETYMOLOGICAL DICTIONARY (C.T. Onions ed., with the assistance of G.W.S. Friedrichsen & R.W. Burchfield, 1966) (emphasizing the sense of "workmanship"). The online Etymological Dictionary says:

> Late 14c., "made by man" (opposite of *natural*), from O.Fr. *artificial*, from L. *artificialis* "of or belonging to art," from *artificium* (see *artifice*). Another early use was in the phrase *artificial day* "part of the day from sunrise to sunset" (late 14c.). *Artificial insemination* dates from 1897.

law, articulating its principles, and describing its relationship with *laws* is one of the fundamental dynamics animating twentieth-century legal theory. The issue was famously debated by Hart and Dworkin in the post-Second World War era, which confronted the inadequacy of laws when faced with the atrocities of authoritarian governments—committed, first of all, against their own people.[33]

But further changes are afoot. Does the concept of strongly codified moral rights make sense when confronted with rapidly evolving digital technology, when technological change, the needs of authors and artists, and social needs have all become so difficult to anticipate? The digital revolution may lead to a situation where the separation of doctrine and law becomes increasingly impractical and is gradually blurred through the pronouncements of case law. This would represent a cyclical return to the past, as law and doctrine converge again into a single, more fluid reality. A new, *digital* moral rights doctrine, defined by broad principles applied on a case-by-case basis, might ultimately emerge.

However, any such trend would raise questions about the impact of moral rights on freedom of expression at a time when copyright is increasingly seen as an obstacle to free speech. In particular, creative freedom—the freedom to use technology to create new work—is said to be vulnerable. For the moment, the analytical distinction between doctrine and law is a defining characteristic of the moral rights landscape, and perhaps—by imposing practical restrictions on the scope of moral rights—it offers one of the best arguments for strong implementation of the rights.

2. The Origins of Moral Rights

A second reason for the controversy over moral rights relates closely to their complex and various origins. The story of moral rights can be told in many different ways.[34] In particular, the history of moral rights in the common-law context has been insufficiently explored. This leads to a commonly held belief that moral rights are a "foreign" import, incompatible with English law and with the common-law traditions in the United States and throughout the world, that are derived from English law.

Artificial intelligence "the science and engineering of making intelligent machines" was coined in 1956.

See http://www.etymonline.com/index.php?term=artificial.

[33] *See* H.L.A. Hart, The Concept of Law (Peter Cane, Tony Honoŕe & Jane Stapleton eds., 1994) (1961). Dworkin's reply was initially expressed in R. Dworkin, Taking Rights Seriously (1977).

[34] See, e.g., the comments of a distinguished historian of India, Romila Thapar, discussing perspectives on history in a post-colonial context: Romila Thapar, *Introduction*, in A History of India, Vol. 1 xvii (1966) and Romila Thapar, *Perceptions of the Past*, *in* A History of India, Vol. 1 1 (1966). In the copyright context, see Roberta Rosenthal Kwall, *Copyright and the Moral Right: Is an American Marriage Possible?*, 38(1) Vand. L. Rev. 1 (1985).

But a deeper examination of the past shows that the history of moral rights in the United Kingdom is far from straightforward. Did the early jurisprudence view moral rights as inimical to British law? Why were moral rights suppressed in the development of British copyright? Have they remained latent within it? As one commentator observes, the doctrine of moral rights is

> still relatively new.... [M]oral rights were long known in the European continental legal systems but were accepted in the common-law countries only recently and grudgingly with the adoption of the Berne Convention. To many, moral rights are in inherent tension with common-law concepts of property ownership. As a result, the doctrine has often been misunderstood and adopted in minimalist form in those countries with more developed legal systems, particularly for copyright protection.[35]

One thing, at least, is certain: at the point in copyright's history where we have now arrived, it is important to build a more comprehensive understanding of the origins of moral rights. A better understanding of their history in the international legal community is needed, as well as a wider understanding of their presence in diverse legal systems. This will lead to a clearer conception of their future potential.

3. Aesthetic Reality

Finally, moral rights are something more than a strictly legal idea; they represent an aesthetic reality. Moral rights transcend the law. Swedish scholar, Stig Strömholm, emphasizes the quality of the rights as "writers' rights":

> The development leading to droit moral as we know it today was anything but silent. It took place to an intensive verbal accompaniment, since what was involved were attitudes, interests and disputes concerning people whose business was words, a genus irritabile which could be relied on to make sure that nobody got hanged in silence. The prehistory and history of droit moral reflect, above all, the different conceptions successively prevailing in the Western world as to the true nature of literary and artistic creativity. The development of evaluations of that activity is a subject of considerable interest for the general history of ideas, reaching far beyond the normal limits of legal history.[36]

[35] Anonymous peer review, Oxford University Press, New York, in personal communication from Matt Gallaway to the author (Aug. 21, 2008).

[36] Strömholm, *supra* note 27, at 221.

Moral rights rest on the foundation of a special relationship between author and work, a creative reality that has little to do with the law *per se*. In this sense, it must be acknowledged that the presence of moral rights in formal law could be considered something of an anomaly. In ancient Indian law, for example, the moral rights idea developed as a branch of aesthetic theory, while law codes remained silent on the issue of authors' rights.[37] Indeed, concepts of fame and integrity were widely accepted in the ancient world, but the idea of payment for an author's work seems to have been quite radical. In some cultures, including those of Western Europe as well as India, the connotations of money were frankly negative. Payment was considered fundamentally incompatible with creative work.[38] Money was associated with the rise of the print industry in Western Europe, and the onset of an era when the professionalization of the arts gradually replaced the older systems of patronage, whether royal, religious, or both, by which they had previously survived.[39]

Appropriately enough, this brief look at history leads to a fundamentally important question today. If copyright has now been largely superseded by the mandates of technology, what will serve to replace it as a means of economic support for the arts? For better or for worse, copyright has fulfilled this function since the latter part of the eighteenth century, by which time it had effectively replaced systems of official patronage of the arts. If copyright in its current form ultimately becomes obsolete, an outcome that seems increasingly possible in the light of technological developments such as Google Books and the expansion of fair use exceptions to copyright rules, the ubiquity of "open source" approaches to works such as Creative Commons, and the obvious inability of the law to keep pace, how will culture be financed?

As a consequence of their association with aesthetic theories, moral rights suffer from many of the same kinds of preconceived notions that afflict the arts themselves. In much the same way that characters in fiction can be confused with the

[37] The example is India, and the same could be said of copyright as a whole. The notion of "literary theft" is recognized by a famous writer on aesthetic theory, Anandavardhana. See T.S. Krishnamurti, *Copyright—Another View*, 15(3) BULL. COPYRIGHT SOC'Y OF THE U.S.A. 217, 218 (1968) for a description of Anandavardhana's approach. For a discussion of Anandavardhana's role in the development of aesthetic philosophy in India, see SNEH PANDIT, AN APPROACH TO THE INDIAN THEORY OF ART AND AESTHETICS 10–11 (1977). Pandit identifies his main contribution as the recognition of the special and distinct quality of aesthetic experience. Anandavardhana's famous *Dhvanyaloka* has been translated by D.H.H. INGALLS, J.M. MASSON & M.V. PATWARDHAN, THE DHVANYĀLOKA OF ĀNANDAVARDHANA (1990).

[38] *See* Woodmansee, *supra* note 28. In the society of ancient India, Brahmins were the keepers of knowledge and the teachers charged with its dissemination. Members of other social castes were responsible for bestowing wealth, and even life's necessities, on Brahmins for this service. But this was done out of their own obligation to respect social codes of conduct and the principle of *dharma*, which can be very roughly translated as "duty." It was not a payment for services rendered, per se. The culture persists today. *See generally* Prabha Sridevan, *Intellectual Property in the Ancient Indian Texts*, *in* DIVERSITY IN INTELLECTUAL PROPERTY: IDENTITIES, INTERESTS, AND INTERSECTIONS 232 (Irene Calboli & Srividhya Ragavan eds., 2015).

[39] Woodmansee, *supra* note 28.

writer who created them, the qualities of the artist have come to be associated with the artist's moral rights.[40] Like society's vision of artists, moral rights, too, are infused with stereotypes. They are seen as otherworldly in nature, esoteric, and utterly removed from the crass realities of money—a fatal idea that has made misery of the lives of countless artists! Moral rights obviously represent interests beyond commercial gain—their very purpose is to recognize those interests but, as noted earlier, there can be no doubt that the exercise of moral rights, just like the failure to protect them, can have far-reaching economic consequences. The cost of exercising an author's moral rights may be extraordinary for the entity that pays it; but the failure to protect moral rights can also destroy an artist, both personally but professionally. In particular, damage to reputation can end an artist's career. An artist's livelihood depends on his or her reputation. The economic reality underlying moral rights helps to explain the hostility that they can arouse; it is also one of the reasons why authors and artists might feel that the rights are important to them.[41]

D. The Rights Protected

As noted earlier, moral rights first developed as a practical doctrine, with French judges examining and responding to the complaints brought before them by authors in the early part of the nineteenth century. France is often considered the home of moral rights doctrine, but the rights were not actually codified in French law until 1957.[42] This history is all the more striking in view of the fact that France, like other continental jurisdictions, is a civil law country with a strong focus on legislation as the primary source of law. Moral rights are often spoken of as esoteric rights reflecting rather obscure esthetic or philosophical principles. Yet, an examination of their pedigree shows that, at their core, they developed as legal actions designed to address practical problems raised in the courts.[43]

[40] Ernest Hemingway seemed to live this dream—or nightmare! He is perhaps the most well-known victim, or beneficiary, of this confusion, as much of the reading public identifies him directly with the glamor of characters and situations in his fiction. The assumption that all writing is biographical is not true, unless in the subtle sense that a writer must use whatever raw materials he or she has, most of which are drawn from experience of one kind or another. For an interesting analysis of Hemingway's case, see Jackson J. Benson, *Ernest Hemingway: The Life as Fiction and the Fiction as Life*, 61(3) AM. LITERATURE 345, 348 (1989) (this approach, among other things, leads to what Benson calls "the biographical fallacy").

[41] Economic considerations are undoubtedly at the heart of Hollywood's objections to moral rights. For a detailed discussion of this issue, see Chapter 7, *infra*. See also the insightful discussion by Fraser, *supra* note 14.

[42] French Code de la propriété intellectuelle, *supra* note 13.

[43] The relatively little-known English encounter with moral rights—emerging, well before French jurisprudence, in the mid-eighteenth century—further supports this view: *see* Chapter 2, *infra* notes 228–305.

Given this background, it is apparent that the doctrine has always had the potential to encompass a great variety of possible rights within its scope. Indeed, in each country where moral rights are protected, different rights may be recognized. In countries where moral rights are well developed, a number of sophisticated rights have emerged—a right to withdraw your work from circulation if your ideas, or your assessment of the quality of the work, has changed; a right to protest malicious criticism of your work; and an artist's right of continued access to a work of visual art, in certain circumstances, even after it is sold.[44] The nuances of judicial interpretation may further reflect the unique qualities of a given culture, giving rise to distinctive bodies of jurisprudence in different jurisdictions.

Notwithstanding this situation, two basic moral rights are universally recognized. These are, first, an author's right to have his or her own work attributed to him or her by name, usually called the right of "paternity;"[45] and, secondly, the author's right to protect the work from harm, known as the right of "integrity."[46] The terminology of paternity is now outdated and this work prefers to refer to the right of "attribution." But it should be noted that attribution and paternity—symbolic or metaphorical parenthood with all its implications—are far from identical concepts.[47]

The universal acceptance of attribution and integrity can be traced to the Berne Convention of 1886, the founding agreement of international copyright law.[48] Following a major revision conference in 1928, the Berne Convention has included protection for the moral rights of attribution and integrity in its Article 6*bis*.[49] The United States and Russia were the last major powers to accede to this

[44] *See* Strömholm, *supra* note 11, at 238–40 (*droit d'accès*). Strömholm points out that the main purpose of the right is usually considered to be the maintenance of the author's right to make reproductions of his work and that it can also serve the purpose of allowing the author access to the work in order to gather evidence for use in disputes. In the German law of 1965, the right was not classified as either moral or economic but belonged in a special category of other rights of the author.

[45] It should be noted that recognition of the right of paternity or attribution in the United States is extremely circumscribed: it is available to artists only under VARA, *supra* note 5, and, even within that statute, the exercise of the right is subject to important limitations. Nevertheless, the right of attribution, in some form, is present in VARA. For the Bill, see https://www.congress.gov/bill/101st-congress/house-bill/2690.

[46] Once again, as noted above, the United States recognizes this right only in VARA: *see* https://www.congress.gov/bill/101st-congress/house-bill/2690.

[47] I am indebted to Professor Valérie-Laure Benabou for pointing this out at the Glasgow Moral Rights conference: *see* https://professormira.com/glasgow-conference-2.

[48] *Supra* note 25.

[49] The Convention dates from 1886; the moral rights were implemented in 1928 at the revision conference held in Rome. Currently, the Convention sets out these moral rights in Article 6*bis*. The implementation of the Agreement on Trade-Related Aspects of Intellectual Property Rights (TRIPS Agreement) at the World Trade Organization in 1994 did not really supplant Berne, as virtually all of the substantive provisions on copyright in TRIPS are drawn from the Berne Convention: *see* Agreement on Trade-Related Aspects of Intellectual Property Rights, opened for signature Apr. 15, 1994, entered into force Jan. 1, 1995, Annex 1C to Marrakesh Agreement Establishing the World Trade Organization, 1869 U.N.T.S. 299, 33 I.L.M. 1197 (1994), https://www.wto.org/english/docs_e/legal_e/27-trips_01_e.html. In fact, Art. 9.1 of the TRIPS Agreement requires its members to join the Berne Convention and "comply with" Berne's substantive articles (with the exception of Article 6*bis*). In contrast, the TRIPS provisions on computer programs and databases make specific provision for their recognition

Convention—in 1989 and 1995, respectively[50]—and virtually every country in the world is now required to protect moral rights to the minimum standard defined by Berne. Crucially, the treatment of moral rights in Berne represents a compromise approach, reflecting international discussions and attempts to arrive at an acceptable formula for protection across different legal traditions, and a special attempt to respond to the reservations of common-law countries. This may explain broad international acceptance of the Berne approach. But controversies also remain.[51]

1. Attribution

The foundational principle of all moral rights protection is the right of attribution. This right provides that the creator of a work is entitled to be acknowledged as the author of his or her own work. As noted above, the theory on which the right of *paternity* is based is the understanding of the work as the author's "spiritual child." The right of *attribution* is treated as functionally equivalent to the paternity right, and it seeks to maintain the special link between author and work. Nevertheless, the concept has even broader resonance for society: it has a particular role to play in the preservation of truth. In the digital environment, attribution has rapidly emerged as a deeply significant concept. In many ways, attribution resonates with the imperatives of technology and, as will be repeatedly illustrated by examples in the following chapters, it reflects the underlying architecture of technological creation. To what extent these manifestations of the principle of attribution can be considered equivalent or complementary to the moral rights of the author is an interesting and important question.

At first glance, the moral right of attribution of authorship might seem relatively unlikely to attract controversy. Nevertheless, the recognition of attribution has proven to be surprisingly complex. In the United States, decades of lobbying have not yet led to the adoption of a general right of attribution under U.S. copyright law.[52] Limited recognition of attribution for the creators of works of visual art is provided for by the Visual Artist Rights Act 1990,[53] but this clearly falls short of the general requirement set out in the Berne Convention. In the United Kingdom,

as "literary works"; Berne implies this without stating it explicitly. *See* Chapter 3, *infra* (on international copyright agreements).

[50] *See* Berne Notification No. 121 (Nov. 21, 1988) for U.S. accession, https://www.wipo.int/treaties/en/notifications/berne/treaty_berne_121.html; Berne Notification No. 162 (Dec. 13, 1994) for Russian accession, https://www.wipo.int/treaties/en/notifications/berne/treaty_berne_162.html.

[51] A list of the 181 contracting parties is available at https://www.wipo.int/wipolex/en/treaties/ShowResults?search_what=C&treaty_id=15.

[52] *See* Ginsburg, *supra* note 21. *See also* Mira T. Sundara Rajan, *"A Bird Doesn't Sing Because It Has an Answer": A Famous Quote and the Stamp of (In)Authenticity*, The IPKat (May 3, 2015), https://ipkitten.blogspot.com/2015/05/a-bird-doesnt-sing-because-it-has.html.

[53] VARA, *supra* note 5.

attribution depends upon the author's assertion of his or her authorship at the time of first publication of the work, effectively imposing a "formal" requirement on the enjoyment of the right and, thereby, contravening the provisions of the Berne Convention.[54]

On the other hand, private agreements, such as the guild agreements of Hollywood, attach great importance to attribution, particularly in the United States. But this has led to a curious backlash, with some commentators complaining of excessive and onerous requirements. These complaints, particularly in the digital context, seem questionable. In fact, the ideal of attribution has been known since the earliest times, and it has arguably found expression in a variety of forms—not only by publishing an author's name alongside his or her work, but also in the use of pseudonyms, in choosing to remain anonymous, by means of literary and artistic references, and through original devices such as the cameos of director Alfred Hitchcock that appear reliably in his films. These examples show that there are many ways to honor the principle of attribution. In the digital environment, technology offers new means of acknowledging authorship. The variety of possible measures is only limited by the imagination.

A further controversy relating to the attribution right arises out of an interesting point of legal interpretation: does the attribution right allow an author to make a claim for the false attribution of someone else's work to him or her?[55] This is the problem of forgery. Technically, the offense does not involve the failure to indicate the author's *name*, and it is widely accepted that the attribution right may not prevent it. However, the false attribution of one's own work to someone else as the author—the failure to indicate the true author's name—would fall within the scope of the attribution right, and it is explicitly recognized as a right against false attribution in some national copyright laws.[56] Plagiarism is accommodated, but forgery is rejected.

This point illustrates the ill-advised complexity that legalistic interpretation can bring to attribution. From a policy perspective, this right seems to demand a firm grounding in ordinary, intuitive meaning. Ideally, moral rights, controversial as they are, should seek to maintain a more or less scrupulous and transparent connection to well-defined objectives of policy. On this reasoning, the proper scope of the attribution right should be determined by our interest in maintaining the

[54] Berne Convention, *supra* note 25, at art. 2(1).

[55] See the comments in J.M. Pontier, J.C. Ricci & J. Bourdon, Droit de la culture para. 345 (2d ed., 1996). Pontier, Ricci, and Bourdon refer to the "positive" and "negative" aspects of the attribution right. The "negative" aspect is "the impossibility of attributing a work to a person who is not the author." Interestingly, not all legal commentators agree with this interpretation of attribution—at least, as the right is drafted in Article 6*bis* of the Berne Convention, *supra* note 25. *See, e.g.*, Silke von Lewinski, International Copyright Law and Policy para. 5.99 (2008). Von Lewinski suggests that a violation of the attribution right occurs where the author's name is *not* used, but this approach to the interpretation of moral rights is controversial (as further discussed in this chapter).

[56] *See, e.g.*, *Copyright Act 1968* (Cth) s 195AC (Austl.), https://www.legislation.gov.au/Details/C2019C00042. (For interest, see also s 195AH on attribution of an altered film.)

integrity of the relationship between a work and the name of its author. The purpose of doing so would be to avoid two well-known evils that can affect authors negatively in their professional lives—plagiarism and forgery, both of which are also detrimental to the broader public interest in truth. Once we recognize that the goal of attribution is, fundamentally, to maintain this connection, it becomes clear that separating an author's name from his or her work will be, at least *prima facie*, a violation of the attribution right. This will be the case, regardless of how the separation occurs—whether it involves the attribution of the author's work to someone else, or the attribution of someone else's work to the author. The legal nicety of arguing that the attribution right arises when we credit the author's work to someone else's name, but not when we attribute his or her name to another person's work, would fall short of a full realization of this policy.[57] From a practical point of view, the attribution right seems naturally to extend to forgery as well. In this context, it could offer an important legal means of addressing a vexing social problem.

The attribution right is generally considered to include an author's right to choose to remain anonymous or to be attributed by a pseudonym.[58] It is a broad right of the author to determine the terms on which he or she will be identified and, accordingly, known to the public. This aspect of attribution offers an interesting point of legal interpretation, because Article 6*bis* of the Berne Convention makes no reference to either anonymity or pseudonymity. Rather, the extension of Berne to include these realities of authorship must be implied with reference to other provisions in the Convention. Notably, the Convention makes explicit references to anonymity and pseudonymity in two other articles: Article 7 on term of protection, and Article 15 on the right to enforce protected rights. Given these detailed provisions on determining the duration of protection for pseudonymous works, and for enforcing copyright in those works, support for the right to publish anonymously, or to use a pseudonym, would appear to be unequivocally protected by Berne.[59]

[57] In the French context, the right is protected, but there is some discussion of whether the right against false attribution is a general personal right or specifically a part of copyright: see the discussion in William Strauss, Study No. 4: The Moral Right of the Author 116 (1959), https://www.copyright.gov/history/studies/study4.pdf (citing the work of Michaélidès & Desbois, *infra* note 5). This point is relevant to the discussion in this book about the general social and legal relevance of the idea of attribution, made timely by technology.

[58] *See* Georges Michaélidès-Nouraos, Le Droit moral de l'auteur: Étude de droit français, de droit comparé et de droit international 12 (para. 120) (1935). The French names for this right include *droit à la paternité (de l'oeuvre)*, or *droit de paternité sur l'oeuvre*; *droit d'attribution*, and *droit au nom*. The French Code de la propriété intellectuelle, *supra* note 13, at art. L121-1 provides that the author enjoys the right to respect for his or her name, his or her quality as author, and his or her work: "L'auteur jouit du droit au respect de son nom, de sa qualité et de son oeuvre."

[59] See detailed discussion in Richard Arnold & Mira T. Sundara Rajan, *Is There a Legal Right to Pseudonymity?*, 30 Journal of Media Law 189 (2017), https://www.tandfonline.com/doi/abs/10.1080/17577632.2017.1347082. *See also* Mira T. Sundara Rajan, *Elena Ferrante's Right to a Pseudonym*, The Atlantic (Nov. 15, 2016), https://www.theatlantic.com/entertainment/archive/2016/11/elena-ferrantes-right-to-a-pseudonym/507530.

This issue is an important one for a number of reasons. The choice of a name, or indeed, the refusal of one, points to the important issue of an author's right to privacy. For a person who chooses to publish a creative work, the need for privacy may serve fundamental professional or personal needs. This situation acquires heightened poignancy in the online environment. Indeed, the practice of publication under a pseudonym has been adopted by the number of high-profile cultural figures in recent years. For example, the author J.K. Rowling chose to write under a pseudonym when she published a work of detective fiction, a departure from the Harry Potter novels for which she had become so famous. In retrospect, it is fascinating to consider the reception of the book when its author was the unknown Galbraith, a contrast to the notoriety it later acquired as a Rowling vehicle.[60] Another kind of author, Elena Ferrante, spoke of her decision to write under a pseudonym as an essential part of her creative undertaking. When her "real" identity was extensively unmasked by an Italian journalist, many of her readers reacted with outrage, arguing that this was a violation of her prerogatives as an author.[61] In another interesting case of creative pseudonymity, speculation about the identity of the graffiti artist, Banksy, led to a police-style investigation of his identity using various technological means.[62] Banksy has never publicly confirmed his identity, and his persistent concealment of it, many observers would argue, contributes a crucial element of mystery and surprise to his work—it is an integral part of the aesthetic experience.

2. Integrity and Reputation

The author's moral right of integrity receives an interesting and distinctive treatment in the Berne Convention. Article 6*bis* seeks to prevent any mistreatment of the work—any "distortion, mutilation or other modification of, or other derogatory action in relation to" the work—that "would be" prejudicial to the author's "honor or reputation." The text of Article 6*bis* actually identifies at least two distinct interests: the integrity of the work, and the author's reputation or honor. Drawing upon the idea of a special relationship between the author and his or her work, this section identifies the locus of the harm that can occur: it lies in the author's reputation or honor, the latter being a more nebulous concept in the modern era. In effect, the Berne provision creates a bridge between two interests—the integrity of the work and the reputation of the author—by requiring proof of damage to the

[60] *See, e.g.*, Mira T. Sundara Rajan, The Cuckoo's Calling: *Has J.K. Rowling Created Her Most Interesting Character Yet?*, 1709 BLOG (July 19, 2013), http://the1709blog.blogspot.com/2013/07/the-cuckoos-calling-has-jk-rowling.html.

[61] Sundara Rajan, *Elena Ferrante*, *supra* note 58.

[62] *See, e.g.*, Henri Neuendorf, *Mystery Solved? Scientists Reveal Banksy's Identity*, ARTNET NEWS (Mar. 4, 2016), https://news.artnet.com/art-world/banksy-identity-revealed-scientists-441185.

author. This formula has been widely adopted by most countries implementing the Berne Convention. It is clearly a compromise formula, which may well explain the willingness of different countries to adopt it and experiment with it. But it is not the only possible model—and, indeed, there is no compelling reason of either theory or practice why the right of integrity must be linked to the author's reputation. In contrast, France considers any damage to the work complained of by the author to be a *prima facie* violation of the integrity right—a model that has also been followed by other countries. Germany uses a different terminology, that of harm to the author's "legitimate interests," but the German approach resembles Berne more closely than the French approach.[63]

It is important to realize that the Berne formula has certain limitations from the point of view of cultural heritage: the integrity right will only be relevant where the author can show that damage to the work has also affected him or her personally. In this sense, the compromise view of the integrity right falls short of protecting the public interest in the integrity of cultural heritage; but commentators will be quick to point out that the public interest in freedom of speech, in contrast, may be favored by a more limited integrity right. In particular, limitations on the scope of the integrity right will more readily allow the use of works without fear of the author's reaction. But the integrity right is also limited by other mechanisms supporting free speech—such as the parody exception in French, though not English,[64] law—so the necessity for this trade-off is unclear.

But another approach also exists: in many jurisdictions that limit the integrity right, outright protection for the integrity of works of visual art is still provided, with no need to show damage to the author's reputation where these are concerned. This special treatment no doubt reflects the unique nature of artworks: in general, there is only one true "original," and damage that it suffers is, in this sense, irrevocable. In contrast, damage to a literary work or a film could be (largely) corrected by withdrawing and destroying infringing copies and issuing proper copies of the work to the public.

Artworks raise another concern. Where the integrity of artworks is under threat, litigation presents a very poor solution. Once a work of art has been damaged, corrective action can be sought through the courts, but a true resolution of the harm may never be achievable. It would depend upon the facts of a given case.

[63] Urheberrechtsgesetz (UrhG) vom 9 Sept. 1965 [Act on Copyright and Related Rights of Sept. 9, 1965], berücksichtigt die Änderung(en) des Gesetzes durch Artikel 25 des Gesetzes vom 23. Juni 2021 (BGBl. I S. 1858) [as amended by article 25 of the Act of June 23, 2021 (Federal Law Gazette I, p. 1858)], art. 14 (Ger.), https://www.gesetze-im-internet.de/englisch_urhg/englisch_urhg.html (translation provided by Ute Reusch).

[64] The 2014 amendments to the Copyright, Designs and Patents Act 1988 (CDPA), c. 48 (UK), to introduce an exception for parody make no reference to moral rights, leaving open the possibility that a parody, though recognized as a copyright exception, may still violate the author's moral right of integrity: *see* CDPA, § 30A, https://www.legislation.gov.uk/ukpga/1988/48/section/30A.

Accordingly, there is, and must be, more to moral rights than having recourse to litigation. A truly effective moral rights regime should have a deterrent effect. It should ideally act to *prevent* damage to the work, rather than attempting to compensate the author or, indeed, punish the wrongdoer, after the fact. Punishment only makes sense to the extent that it could have a deterrent effect on future attacks. The damage to a work may be irreparable. Ideally, moral rights should be part of a broader process of preventing this eventuality from occurring. Moral harm to the author should be *impeded or prevented* by the possibility of legal sanctions, providing an environment of greater safety for creative work. The primary goal of moral rights is to preserve the integrity of the cultural sphere; the preservation of economic value is incidental to this objective. The norms of culture are different from those of economics.

The legal approach to moral rights also attempts to forestall moral harm in another sense: it grants privileges aimed at preserving the sanctity of the relationship between artist and work. For example, an artist who creates a work of visual art is sometimes granted a right of access to his or her work even after it has been sold. The right may have the practical objective of allowing an artist to have access to his work for the purpose of making reproductions. In the case of the German provision, the prerogatives of the artist are balanced against "the owner's legitimate interests"—presumably, the owner's privacy, or other practical concerns like distance.[65]

How have courts chosen to interpret the requirement of proof of damage to the author's reputation or honor? This latter concept remains largely untested in case law,[66] but a recent Australian case has at least examined the issue for the first time without actually ruling on it. Because of the rarity of the analysis of honor, and the interesting perspective offered by the judge, a brief consideration of the case is included here.

[65] *See* German UrhG, *supra* note 63, at art. 25 (translation provided by Ute Reusch):

Access to copies of works

(1) The author may require that the owner of the original or of a copy of his or her work make the original or copy thereof available to him or her insofar as this is necessary for the production of copies or adaptations of the work and does not conflict with the owner's legitimate interests.

(2) The owner is not obliged to surrender the original or the copy to the author.

Article 17.1 of the Law of the Russian Federation No. 5351-1 of July 9, 1993 on Copyright and Neighboring Rights, as amended, was a similar provision ("The author may require ..."). It is still available at https://www.wto.org/english/thewto_e/acc_e/rus_e/wtaccrus48_leg_94.pdf, though the 1993 Russian law has since been overruled by Part IV of the Grazhdanskiĭ Kodeks Rossiĭskoĭ Federatsii [Russian Civil Code] (GK RF), completed in 2006 and in effect since January 1, 2008. The Civil Code, updated to 2021, is available only in Russian, at https://www.wipo.int/wipolex/en/legislation/details/20306.

[66] *See also* Elizabeth Adeney, *The Moral Right of Integrity: The Past and Future of "Honour"*, 22 Intell. Prop. Q. 111 (2005).

In 2020, *Boomerang Investments v. Padgett*[67] raised the issue of whether the use of the music that was played by Air France for customers who were on hold violated the moral rights of the composers of that music. Rita Matulionyte describes the reasons why the case was ultimately heard in Australia, but this also proved to be the plaintiff's downfall: the court found that a moral rights action under Australian law was barred by the Australian Copyright Act. As noted by Matulionyte, this finding in itself was controversial:

> Economic rights, like moral rights, are subject to the territoriality principle, even if this territoriality principle is not explicitly stated in the Act....The explicit restatement of the territorial scope of moral rights under s 195AX thus does not add any new limitation if compared with economic rights. It is therefore unclear why the court adopted such a restrictive view towards moral rights, while adopting a broader approach in relation to the economic rights of authors.[68]

Nevertheless, the judge continued to analyze the moral rights issue involved, and delivered his interpretation of what should have happened if it could have been decided under Australian law. In an extremely interesting turn of analysis, the court determined that Air France's treatment of the musical work amounted to a violation not of the composers' reputation but, specifically, of their honor. The judge commented,

> This involves a conclusion that "honour or reputation" in s 195AJ involves two distinct concepts and it is not a composite expression. No question of reputation arises in this case but it would appear to me to be something which can be objectively determined. It does not necessarily precisely correspond with the concept of reputation in defamation law. For example, an artist may well have a reputation for being a dangerous person which could be damaged by depicting their work in a wholesome light.
>
> Honour, on the other hand, as a matter of ordinary language connotes in this context a personally held set of high-minded principles ("she was a woman of

[67] *Boomerang Investments Pty Ltd v. Padgett* (Liability) [2020] FCA 535 (Austl.), https://jade.io/article/726856. But note that the judge states, "it is not an infringement of an author's moral right in respect of a work to do something outside Australia": id. at para. 395. Section 195AX of the Copyright Act 1968, *supra* note 56, is cited, which states, "It is not an infringement of an author's moral right in respect of a work to do, or omit to do, something outside Australia." As noted id. at para. 396, there was also no claim under s 195AU of the Act:

> An author's moral right in respect of a work is infringed by a person who imports an article into Australia for the purpose of dealing with the article if the importer knew, or ought reasonably to have known, that, if the article had been made in Australia, it would have been an infringing article.

[68] Rita Matulionyte, *"Love Is in the Air" Case: A Missed Opportunity to Enforce Moral Rights in Australia*, KLUWER COPYRIGHT BLOG (Aug. 6, 2020), https://copyrightblog.kluweriplaw.com/2020/08/06/love-is-in-the-air-case-a-missed-opportunity-to-enforce-moral-rights-in-australia.

> honour"). Inherently this is subjective but it is circumscribed by an objective standard. Just because a person believes themselves to have a sense of honour does not mean that they do. For example, a person who believes it is honourable to betray their friends for money is not, despite their belief, an honourable person. The test for honour is therefore both subjective and objective.[69]

Perhaps for the first time in case law, the judge defines the principle of honor, calling it a "personally held set of high-minded principles," distinct from reputation, and arguing that it is a subjective sense held by an individual that must still be aligned with a more "objective" social sense of what honor means.[70]

In fact, the term "honor" is so indeterminate that it is practically ignored by the copyright community.[71] Plaintiffs typically focus on the more concrete notion of reputation. Ireland has even eliminated the concept from its provisions on moral rights, adopted in the year 2000.[72] The Irish solution is probably the most honest approach to the model provision in Article 6*bis* of the Berne Convention, but it is not necessarily the best. Perhaps in the year 2000, eliminating honor made sense. Since then, however, a new use for honor may have emerged. There may be something worth exploring in the concept of honor in the technological environment, where people and their work can suffer so many, and such varied, affronts through online publication and social media. By adding breadth, the notion of honor, as distinct from reputation, may help to protect individuals from online harm. But including the word "honor" in provisions on moral rights without any intention of "honoring" it would seem to be the worst of all possible worlds: using a word that is devoid of legal content, and from which, no effective legal claim can arise, in an already subtle area of law. It seems ill advised to deal with moral rights in this way since they are already said to involve an important element of "subjectivity," where vagueness can only increase the already considerable difficulty of bringing a successful claim.

In countries where the Berne standard is adopted, a burden of proof is clearly imposed upon the author, and it is quite a demanding one: the author must show that the treatment "would" be prejudicial to his or her honor or reputation. In the common-law countries, at least, this amounts to the application of an "objective"

[69] *Boomerang*, *supra* note 65, at paras. 400–04.

[70] Id.

[71] This point is brought up by Tania Chen-Davies in an article on honor, but she completely misrepresents my own view. *See* Tania Chen-Davies, *Honour in UK Copyright Law Is Not "A Trim Reckoning": Its Impact on the Integrity Right and the Destruction of Works of Art*, 36(2) Oxford J. Legal Stud. 272, n.9 (2016). My work has argued in favor of considering the destruction of artworks as a violation of the moral right of integrity—a point I have been making in publications since 2001. My perspective provided the basis on which the Indian courts accepted this interpretation of integrity under §57 of the Indian Copyright Act: *see Amar Nath Sehgal v. Union of India* (2005) 30 PTC 253 (Del H.C.) (India) (*passim*). However, Chen-Davies mistakenly suggests that I hold the *opposite* view.

[72] Copyright and Related Rights Act 2000 (Act No. 28/2000), s. 109 (Ir.), https://www.irishstatutebook.ie/eli/2000/act/28/section/109/enacted/en/html#sec109.

standard. In practice, this means that the author's opinion alone will not suffice; other measures, independent of the author, must be taken into account. Some of the factors that have received consideration are the expert opinions of members of the artistic community, and, somewhat ironically, evidence showing that economic harm to the author results from the mistreatment of the work. The latter form of evidence can possibly make a claim to being "objective", but the former seems doubtful. It substitutes one opinion for another. It is only "objective" in the sense that the opinion of a third party is offered, rather than that of the author. But the author's perspective may have strengths as well as weaknesses. Any claim to objectivity on these terms falls short of the more broadly accepted, traditional test of the "reasonable person" under the law. Would it be useful to ask whether a reasonable person would find a certain treatment of a work to be damaging to an author's reputation? But this approach, too, could be problematic. Indeed, apart from very obvious situations of damage, assessing the mistreatment of an artwork could be a very complex issue.[73] This problem arises from the nature of the works themselves. The work might be novel, visionary, unprecedented—in these cases, how is appropriate treatment going to be judged, and who should be responsible for making that judgment? Is a reasonable person or a third party better placed to do so than the author? Is "reasonableness" relevant, in any meaningful sense, to creativity at all?

Henri Desbois notes the potential for hypocrisy inherent in such claims of "objectivity," commenting that article 6*bis* of the Berne Convention

> bears the traces of a transactional spirit, which is very far from the ideal professed by the French law of 1957 ... [N]o modification [under Berne] can be criticized unless it affects the honor or reputation of the author. Who, then, shall have the authority to determine the gravity of the offense? ...it will therefore be up to courts to decide. But, according to what criterion will they make their judgement? Judges, it is said, will call upon the teachings, the suggestions, of their personal culture, the impulses of their taste, their aspirations towards an ideal: the answer, far from calming worry, reveals contradictory and confusing perspectives.[74]

[73] For example, is it "mistreatment" to remove a public artwork from its context as part of a building and display it somewhere else—even if the work is physically unharmed? See, e.g., the discussion of the Picasso-Nesjar murals in Oslo in Chapter 8, *infra* notes 86–88 and accompanying text (especially the comment of Jean-Louis Andral, director of the original Musée Picasso, established with the artist present, in Antibes).

[74] Desbois, *supra* note 10, at 539 (para. 450):

> [L]'article 6 *bis* porte les traces d'un esprit de transaction, qui est fort éloigné de l'idéal professé par la loi française de 1957 ... aucune modification n'encourt la critique, si elle ne porte pas atteinte à l'honneur ou à la reputation de l'auteur. Qui donc aura qualité pour apprécier la gravité de l'offense? ... il appartient donc aux tribunaux de se prononcer. Mais, selon quel critère, porteront-ils leur jugement? Les magistrats feront appel, répondra-t-on, aux ensignements, aux suggestions, de leur culture personnelle, aux impulsions de leur goût, aux

It will be difficult to answer these questions with general statements of principle that could then be applied to moral rights cases as a matter of legal rule. Rather, these questions serve to illustrate the minefield that must be navigated where creative works are concerned. "Perfect" legal solutions may simply be unattainable. Moral rights doctrine places the artist in a position to act, and it may be that, given the complexity of the circumstances, he or she is simply in a better position to take any required action than anyone else.

In contrast, the French approach is to allow the author to complain of any mistreatment of the work as a *prima facie* violation of the moral right of integrity. Traditionally, there is therefore no way to defend against an integrity claim under French law if the author personally brings that claim, or if the author's personal objections are offered as evidence in the case. As Henri Desbois comments,

> An individualist conception animates the law in its entirety, and particularly, fundamental provisions of a general kind, such as Article 1, which specifies that an author enjoys a right in [his] intangible property, exclusive and opposable against the world, *from the sole fact of its creation*.... An explanation like this would have immediate repercussions for the structure and function of the integrity right: if the economics of authors' rights were arranged for the collective interest, from the perspective of society, not every alteration would be condemned, because more than one attempt at improvement, to which the author claims to be opposed, has, for an impartial judge, a beneficial effect and improves the quality of the work.
>
> The formula of Article 1 cuts these errors short: it is enough that the author has impressed the stamp of his personality on the work, that, in other words, he has created it, for him to be entitled to protection. His work demands to be respected as it is, such as he has wanted it to be, because, through the creative act, it is the personality of the creator which receives help and protection.[75]

> aspirations de leur idéal: la réponse, loin d'apaiser l'inquiétude, dévoile des perspectives de contradiction et de confusion.

[75] Desbois, *supra* note 10, at 538–39 (para. 449) (emphasis original):

> la conception individualiste anime la loi tout entière et singulièrement les dispositions fondamentales, d'ordre général, telles que l'article 1er qui précise que l'auteur jouit d'un droit de propriété incorporelle, exclusif et opposable à tous, *du seul fait de sa création*. ... Une telle explication exercerait une répercussion immédiate sur la structure et la fonction du droit au respect: si l'économie des droits d'auteur était aménagéé dans l'intérêt de la collectivité, dans une perspective sociale, toute altération ne serait pas condamnable, car plus d'une retouche, à laquelle l'auteur prétend s'opposer, a pour un esprit impartial un effet bienfaisant et améliore la qualité de l'oeuvre.
>
> La formule de l'article 1er coupe court à ces errements: il suffit que l'auteur ait imprimé le cachet de sa personnalité à l'oeuvre, *qu'en d'autres termes il l'ait crée*, pour que protection lui soit due. Son oeuvre appelle le respect telle qu'elle est, telle qu'il a voulu qu'elle soit, car, à travers la création, c'est la personnalité du créateur qui reçoit aide et protection.

This principle is clearly illustrated by the celebrated case of *Huston*, ironically arising in France out of a complaint by a U.S. director, John Huston, on the broadcast of a colorized version of his work in that country.[76] It is one of the most famous moral rights cases ever decided. Huston's asserted that, as the film's director, he had chosen to make the film in black and white for artistic reasons. This was sufficient for the court to prevent the broadcast of colorized versions of his work in France. Indeed, the facts of this case, and Huston's explicit objections to colorization, made the claim impossible to defend under French law. Colorization was complained of by the director himself as a potential violation of the integrity of the film that he had directed; and the work had been colorized.

This approach has more recently been challenged by the ruling of the French Supreme Court in *Hugo*, where the publication of a sequel to Hugo's monumental *Les Misérables* was allowed, in spite of Hugo's explicit remark that there could be "no sequel" to his novel.[77] How was the author's own opinion circumvented in this case? The French court ruled that the moral rights of an author from so long ago should not stifle the creativity of those alive today. "Balance" needed to be achieved. Considering Desbois's commentary,[78] the *Hugo* ruling seems like nothing less than a radical revision of the French interpretive tradition surrounding moral rights—and, indeed, it is not surprising that some commentators have asked whether moral rights are truly protected in France "in perpetuity" after this judgment.[79]

a. Destruction of a Work

A work might also be destroyed. This brings to the fore one of the most puzzling aspects of the artist's moral right of integrity as it is currently understood by the

[76] *Huston v. La Cinq*, Cour de cassation [Cass.] [supreme court for judicial matters] 1e civ., May 28, 1991, Bull. civ. I, No. 172 (Fr.), https://www.legifrance.gouv.fr/juri/id/JURITEXT000007026649.

[77] *Pierre Hugo v. Editions Plon*, Cour d'appel [CA] [regional court of appeal] Paris, 1e ch., Mar. 31, 2004, 202 RIDA (Oct. 2004), *reversed* Cour de cassation [Cass.] [supreme court for judicial matters] 1e civ., Jan. 30, 2007, Bull. civ. I, No. 125 (Fr.), https://www.legifrance.gouv.fr/juri/id/JURITEXT000017627153.

[78] But it should be noted that Desbois also comments on the importance of interpreting moral rights as appropriate for each particular set of circumstances, emphasizing that "[t]he characteristics of moral rights cannot have the same energy in all circumstances .... It is up to the judges, while respecting the spirit of the law, to strike the right balance." ("Les attributs du droit moral ne peuvent avoir la même énergie en toutes circonstances ... Il appartient aux juges, en respectant l'esprit de la loi, de dégager le point d'équilibre.") *See* Desbois, *supra* note 10, at 470 (para. 382). He contrasts the "relativity" of underlying concepts—inalienability in particular—with their linguistic embodiment, which may appear "in a form that is categorical, absolute." From this point of view, *Hugo*, *supra* note 77, can be seen as following in a tradition of "balance"—at least between the theory and practice of the law—that is well accepted in the French approach to authors' rights.

[79] See Elizabeth Adeney, The Moral Rights of Authors and Performers: An International and Comparative Analysis (Oxford University Press, New York, 2006) at 60, para. 2.53 (notes omitted): she explains perpetual protection as originating in the idea that "the author ... [has] externalized part of his personality in the work. The right would therefore exist as long as the work existed." But she also notes the reservations of Vilbois, who "commented in 1928 that the existence of the public domain (where works could be freely exploited) meant the negation of any effective moral right after the economic rights had expired."

international community. Does the integrity right prevent the destruction of an artwork? It might seem obvious to some readers that this question should be answered with a resounding "Yes!" However, a tradition of commentary suggests that the moral right of integrity will *not* prevent the destruction of a work.[80] The reason for this has to do with the legal "bridge" between mistreatment of the work and the author's reputation that is constructed through the language of the Berne Convention. If the work has been destroyed, so the argument goes, an author's reputation can no longer be harmed as it would have been by displaying a damaged version of the work to the public.

The main problem with this argument is its casual dismissal of the absence of the work. First, whether or not the absence of the work is considered to violate the author's moral right of integrity, it is clearly an affront to the integrity of cultural heritage. This interpretation of the moral right of integrity imposes limits on the usefulness of the right as a tool of public policy for the protection of cultural heritage. Secondly, the disappearance of the work may also not be a benign occurrence for the author's reputation. Rather, its disappearance needs to be seen in a proper context. Eliminating any single work from an author's larger body of work—from an artist's *catalogue raisonnée,* for example—may, in itself, lead to harm to the author's reputation. This point was argued before the Delhi High Court in a case involving the destruction of a famous sculpture.[81] Counsel made the argument, drawn from my earlier analysis, that "destruction of a work can prejudice an author's reputation by reducing the volume or quality of his creative corpus."[82]

There is also the finer point that the goal of moral rights is to protect the relationship between author and work—and, specifically, to prevent harm to the author

[80] The arguments are given a helpful overview by Irini Stamatoudi, *Moral Rights of Authors in England: The Missing Emphasis on the Role of Creators*, 8(4) INTELL. PROP. Q. 478, 482–83 (1997). Surprisingly, there is even a French precedent to the effect that unauthorized modification of a work will damage its integrity, but destruction will not: *see* id. at 483. *See also L'affaire des fresques de Juvisy*, Tribunal civile [TC] [ordinary court of civil jurisdiction] Versailles, 1932, D. 487; Cour d'appel [CA] [regional court of appeal] Paris, 1934, D. 385 (Fr.). Interestingly, Stamatoudi notes id. at 483 (notes omitted), citing the scholarship of Adolf Dietz, that:

> [T]he opinion which seems to be gaining ground today is that which considers destruction the ultimate form of distortion. As Dietz points out, "[destruction] depriv[es] the author of the authentic means of proof for his artistic and professional skills and self conscience." In other words, the destruction of a work may diminish the professional image and standing of the author by eliminating one of his creations. Especially in cases where the reputation of an author depends on a limited number of creations, the destruction of even one of them, may substantially affect his status.

For more recent support for the proposition that destruction does not violate an artist's integrity, see von Lewinski, *supra* note 55.

[81] *Amar Nath Sehgal, supra* note 69.

[82] Id. (situation arose where the sculpture in question was irrevocably damaged by mishandling). *See* Mira T. Sundara Rajan, *Moral Rights and the Protection of Cultural Heritage:* Amar Nath Sehgal v. Union of India, 10(1) INT'L J. OF CULTURAL PROP. 79, 83 (2001) (the note informs the decision of the Delhi High Court, providing much of the key language in the case, and it is also quoted at para. 41 of the final judgment).

caused *through* harm to the work. Would the destruction of the work really be an act with no significant likelihood that the author might suffer injury as a result? To accept this proposition would be to question the entire basis of moral rights theory. On the contrary, interpretation of the law should acknowledge what is implicit in the theory, that an author might suffer an immense personal loss if his or her work were destroyed. If moral rights are to be true to the doctrine, they should recognize this artistic reality.

The direct testimony of authors on this issue supports this view: destruction of their work is often perceived by them as the ultimate form of harm.[83] As the muralist Kent Twitchell stated, about the whitewashing of his celebrated mural of pop artist Ed Ruscha in Los Angeles,[84]

> You learn to restrain your emotions when you're working on the streets ... But it created a real vacuum, an unnecessary sucking of aesthetic wind right out of my soul.[85]

But what about the case where an author seeks to destroy his or her own work? History offers many examples of dissatisfied and unhappy authors, including some of the most distinguished artists in history—for example, Franz Kafka and Johannes Brahms. Kafka is an extreme example, since he directed that all of his surviving works should be destroyed upon his death. But Brahms took matters into his own hands and destroyed some of his own works—works that he thought of as imperfect—shortly before his death. If destruction, overall, is prevented by the moral right of integrity, does the right also prevent authors from destroying their own work?

The profound conflict provoked by this scenario pits authors squarely against the public interest in the preservation of works. Of course, the public is, no doubt, primarily interested in the preservation of works of quality. But who is to be the judge? Is the author the best judge of the quality of the work, and if not, who can

[83] For example, Ernest Hemingway talks about the tremendous blow that he suffered, as a young writer, when a suitcase containing his original manuscripts disappeared from a train station; he believed he would never write again. *See* Ernest Hemingway, A Moveable Feast (1964).

[84] *See* Ed Fuentes, *Whitewashed Portrait Mural of Ed Ruscha Will Be Reborn, Older and Wiser*, Hyperallergic (Apr. 18, 2016), https://hyperallergic.com/291393/whitewashed-portrait-mural-of-ed-ruscha-will-be-reborn-older-and-wiser (sensitive discussion of the incident by Ed Fuentes). *See also* Hemingway, *supra* note 76 (Hemingway's discussion of his own reaction to the accidental loss of his manuscripts); Ernest Hemingway, The Garden of Eden (1986) (the theme of the destruction of works in manuscript form is powerfully revisited in this posthumously published novel).

[85] *See* Deborah Vankin, *Mural Artist Kent Twitchell Is Extra Busy at His Canvas: L.A.'s Streets*, Los Angeles Times (July 2, 2015), http://www.latimes.com/entertainment/arts/la-ca-cm-kent-twitchell-la-murals-20150705-story.html (he is now repainting the mural: "'It's a great feeling when something destroyed can be returned,' Twitchell said.") *See also* Heidi Kulicke, *Nine Years after Being Destroyed, Twitchell's "Ed Ruscha Monument" Mural to Return*, Los Angeles Downtown News (June 11, 2015), http://www.ladowntownnews.com/news/nine-years-after-being-destroyed-twitchell-s-ed-ruscha-monument/article_c1e69a5c-0fd3-11e5-ae8f-0b8fed567176.html.

convincingly step up to this role? The psychological strangeness of authorship is also laid bare—why would an author want to destroy something that he or she has created if, indeed, the relationship between author and work is so valuable? But the issue does arise in practice. Given the state of the law today, the correct legal response would probably be that the moral right of integrity cannot prevent the destruction of a work by its author. The relationship between author and work is a special one, but it is still up to the author to decide whether or not he or she wants to preserve that relationship—at least, within the accepted logic of moral rights doctrine. If society wants to prevent the destruction of artworks, a separate provision would be in order. This might involve modifying the moral right of integrity to acknowledge, explicitly, the public interest in the preservation of artworks—an approach has been taken by California, though these provisions deal with destruction of an artist's work by someone other than the artist:

> The Legislature hereby finds and declares that the physical alteration or destruction of fine art, which is an expression of the artist's personality, is detrimental to the artist's reputation, and artists therefore have an interest in protecting their works of fine art against any alteration or destruction; and that there is also a public interest in preserving the integrity of cultural and artistic creations.[86]

This powerful and direct language brings the notion of the public interest into the conception of the moral right of integrity in a new way.[87] In this, too, California is a pioneer. But the provision does not provide a rule; it only provides a rationale for including the public interest in assessing the impact of the destruction of a work of art. California stands behind the artist, but this provision also implies that the wishes of a self-destructive artist cannot be absolute.

3. Disclosure and Withdrawal

Apart from the moral rights of attribution and integrity made explicit in Berne, it is generally accepted that the Berne Convention includes another moral right within its scope: the right of disclosure or first publication of the work, known in

[86] Cal. Civ. Code § 987 (West 1979) (U.S.), known as the California Art Preservation Act of 1979 (CAPA), https://leginfo.legislature.ca.gov/faces/codes_displaySection.xhtml?lawCode=CIV&sectionNum=987 and https://www.sfartscommission.org/our-role-impact/about-commission/policies-guidelines/california-art-preservation-act. *See* Brian McDonough, *The California Art Preservation Act: Statutory Protection of Art Work against Intentional Alteration or Destruction*, 49 Cin. L. Rev. 486, 486 (1980) (noting that CAPA represented the first enactment of moral rights in the United States). See Chapter 9, *infra*, for the further case that the text of VARA ultimately reflects the influence of CAPA as its true legislative antecedent.

[87] *See* Copyright Act, R.S.C. 1985, c. C-42, s. 28.2(2)–(3) (Can.); VARA, *supra* note 5.

French law as the right of *divulgation*. On the nature of this right, Claude Colombet comments,

> It is the right of divulgation which, chronologically, precedes the other [moral rights], for, by its exercise, the work, removed from its author, enters into the economic circuit, and becomes an economic good on the basis of which the other attributes of the author's right, whether moral or economic, can be exercised.[88]

While the Berne Convention does not make explicit mention of such a *moral* right, it does provide for the protection of the right of first publication—an *economic* right that is the foundation of the entire edifice of copyright law. But it is interesting to note that the right of first publication is implicitly double-edged: it protects not only the author's right to publish the work, but also, his or her *choice* of whether or not to publish it.[89] On a similar note, it can be observed that, even in common-law traditions, the right of an author over his or her unpublished work has historically been a very powerful right. In the United Kingdom, the previously perpetual copyright in unpublished works terminate, by statutory means, in the year 2039.[90]

Sometimes seen as the inverse of the right of first publication, the right to withdraw a work from publication is widely recognized in civil law jurisdictions. For example, French law includes explicit protection for a right to withdraw one's work from circulation for personal reasons.[91] This right is sometimes put forward as an example of the excesses of moral rights protection, but in practice, the right of withdrawal is extremely circumscribed. Notably, any economic cost to the publisher of the work must generally be borne by the author who decides to withdraw it from the public.

[88] "C'est le droit de divulgation qui, chronologiquement, précède les autres, car c'est à partir de son exercice que l'oeuvre, arrachée à son auteur, entre dans le circuit économique, devient un bien patriomonial sur lequel pourront s'exercer les autres attributs, tant moraux que pécuniaires, du droit d'auteur": C. COLOMBET, GRANDS PRINCIPES DU DROIT D'AUTEUR ET DES DROITS VOISINS DANS LE MONDE: APPROCHE DE DROIT COMPARÉ 42 (2d ed., 1992) (author's own translation).

[89] *See* Strömholm, *supra* note 27, at 218–19. Drawing on the examples of French and German law, in contrast to Scandinavian countries, Strömholm points out that "a number of technical problems have been found to result from the existence side by side of an 'economic' right of disposal, which in principle can be transferred and made the object of contracts, and a 'moral' right of publication, which in principle is non-assignable." While his point is well taken, there is also a certain precision in the French and German view. Once the work has been published, it is true that the right to "divulge" it has been exercised—but that right, nevertheless, continues to exist and is vested in the author. Perhaps the practical need for it is limited, but recognizing it helps to clarify the law.

[90] *See* INTELLECTUAL PROPERTY OFFICE, REDUCING THE DURATION OF COPYRIGHT IN CERTAIN UNPUBLISHED WORKS AND GOVERNMENT RESPONSE TO THE CONSULTATION ON REDUCING THE DURATION OF COPYRIGHT IN CERTAIN UNPUBLISHED WORKS (2014), https://www.gov.uk/government/consultations/reducing-the-duration-of-copyright-in-certain-unpublished-works.

[91] *See* French Code de la propriété intellectuelle, *supra* note 13, at art. L121-4.

4. A Right to Remuneration? The Example of the Resale Right (*droit de suite*)

A final consideration in the roster of recognized moral rights is the artist's resale right, also known as the *droit de suite*. This right is protected by Article 14*ter* of the Berne Convention, and it provides that an artist is entitled to a percentage of the proceeds from sales of the work after the artist's initial sale of it—when he or she no longer possesses it, and it is exchanged between third parties. It is a point of interest that the right applies to the manuscripts of writers and composers as well. The defining characteristic of the resale right is that it persists after the author no longer owns the work. The resale right entitles an artist anew to payment after the first sale, and it does so in spite of the fact that the artist is no longer the owner of the work.

It is undoubtedly this aspect of the resale right that leads to its classification as a moral right—its powerful assertion of a right that transcends property ownership. However, the purpose of this right is to secure a royalty for the author. As such, the practical impact of the right is purely economic. It is therefore more appropriate to consider the resale right, not a moral right, per se, but a hybrid right with both moral and economic dimensions. But the example of the resale right, like the right of disclosure, shows how difficult it can be to separate the economic and moral dimensions of copyright.

E. Legal Implications of the Doctrine

The distinctive nature of the doctrine underlying moral rights leads to precise legal consequences. Those consequences are startling and, in some ways, terrifying—but they are often softened and mediated by the courts on practical grounds. Jurisprudence on moral rights has proven to be increasingly concerned with the problem of achieving a fair balance between the interests of authors and those who exploit or use their works.

1. Independence of Moral and Economic Rights

Copyright is largely, though not entirely, an economic mechanism. Copyright makes it possible to treat the work as a commodity. Through copyright, the value of a work can also be largely, though not entirely, expressed in terms of its monetary valuation. Moral rights are different: they arise out of the act of creation and seek to maintain fundamental principles alongside, or even in spite of, the commodification of the work.

In practice, this translates into a crucial distinction between moral and economic rights. Moral rights continue to be held by the author whether or not he or she retains ownership of the work. The author may sell his or her work, and thereby, part with all of his or her rights to exploit it. Nevertheless, the author retains the moral rights in the work.[92] Moral rights are said to exist "independently" of the status of economic rights in a work.

2. Inalienability, Waiver, and Inequality of Bargaining Power

Moral rights cannot be dealt with by contract—they cannot be assigned to someone else, for example, as part of the assignment of ownership or economic rights in the work. The doctrine of moral rights implies that an author cannot alienate his or her moral rights, whether by transfer, sale, or an attempt to relinquish them altogether. Interestingly, at least one French commentator sees this aspect of the doctrine as "patronizing" —a demeaning treatment of the author by the state.[93] Nevertheless, it is a logical consequence of the doctrine. The inherent quality of the relationship between the author and his or her work is not altered by the external circumstances of mere ownership or possession of the work.[94]

The power of moral rights can create a sense of unease. It leads to the question of whether mechanisms exist to limit the possibility of negative effects on industry or, indeed, culture. One approach is to allow the author to waive his or her moral rights, in whole or in part, by contractual agreement.

In an ideal world, where pure freedom of contract might reign, waivers might present a perfect solution to the problem of moral rights protection inhibiting the exploitation of a work. But the world as we know it is a place of great inequality. The bargaining power of parties to a contract is rarely equal, and contracts are shaped by the dynamics of relationships that are far from balanced.[95] In no area governed by contracts would this be more apparent than in relation to authors, where, in the vast majority of cases, bargaining inequality between author and publisher is extreme. When it comes to moral rights in publication contracts, it should therefore come as no surprise that waivers generate discomfort on both a conceptual and a practical level.

[92] Of course, in countries where it is possible for authors to waive their moral rights, moral rights could be excluded by contractual agreement between the artist and the buyer of the work. But continental European jurisdictions generally restrict or prohibit waivers. For a detailed discussion, see Chapter 2, *infra*.

[93] *See* Pierre Recht, Le Droit d'Auteur, une nouvelle forme de propriété: Histoire et théorie 278 (1969).

[94] Indeed, the term "*droits innés*," or *angeborene Rechte*, was used by German theorists of the nineteenth century to discuss moral rights. *See* Strömholm, *supra* note 27, at 242–43.

[95] John D. McCamus, *Duress, Undue Influence and Unconscionability*, *in* The Law of Contracts 403 (2005).

Practically speaking, countries like Canada and the United Kingdom have seen the development of standard-form contracts in which complete waivers of moral rights are required before any publication activity will be undertaken. In this situation, the author is in a position of great bargaining inequality. He or she is practically required to surrender his or her moral rights in order to realize the publication of his or her work. But standard-form waivers may effectively nullify moral rights, making a mockery of statutory protections for them.

At the doctrinal level, allowing moral rights to be waived would generate a degree of theoretical inconsistency. The general implication of moral rights doctrine is that the relationship between an author and his or her own creation is permanent and unbreakable, at least as long as the work continues to exist. Moral rights must therefore be inalienable by definition. However, the severity of this doctrinal conclusion may be softened by allowing authors to waive their moral rights in limited circumstances. This approach is adopted by Germany and Austria, where waivers are sometimes permitted.[96] However, Germany, as well as the Netherlands, has taken strong measures to support greater equality of bargaining power between authors and publishers, including the introduction of a special law to improve the conditions of authors.[97]

3. Perpetual Protection

Mark Twain felt that copyright protection should be perpetual, though he was willing to settle for protection that would allow him to leave a legacy for his children. In a 1906 speech to U.S. lawmakers, he stated,

> I am interested particularly and especially in the part of the bill which concerns my trade. I like that extension of copyright life to the author's life and fifty years afterward. I think that would satisfy any reasonable author, because it would take care of his children. Let the grand-children take care of themselves. That would take care of my daughters, and after that I am not particular. I shall then have long been out of this struggle, independent of it, indifferent to it.[98]

[96] *See* Gerald Dworkin, *The Moral Right of the Author: Moral Rights and the Common Law Countries*, 19 Colum.-VLA J.L. & Arts 229, 244–66 (1995) (the issue of waivers and their significance for moral rights receives a detailed treatment). *See also* Michel M. Walter, *Dualistic Aspects in Monistic Systems of Moral Rights*, 14(4) JIPLP 318 (2019), https://doi.org/10.1093/jiplp/jpz012.

[97] Jens Schovsbo, *Integrating Consumer Rights into Copyright Law: From a European Perspective*, 31(4) J. Consumer Pol'y 393 (2008). *See also* Chapter 2, *infra* notes 154–67.

[98] Steve Courtney, *Mark Twain's Copyright Fight*, USPTO Inventors Eye (Fall 2017), https://www.uspto.gov/learning-and-resources/newsletter/inventors-eye/mark-twains-copyright-fight.

The possibility of permanent copyright protection is prevented by the U.S. Constitution.[99] This argument is occasionally offered, though incorrectly, as a general argument against the protection of moral rights in the United States.

Perpetual protection of moral rights reflects the extent to which local laws implement moral rights theory, and the ways in which they understand the relationship between economic and moral rights within their copyright systems. How far does the independence of moral from economic rights extend? How co-dependent are the rights? Some countries extend the principle of the independence to its greatest reach, while others seek to limit it.

The French tradition is an example of extreme independence. Known as "dualism," French legal theory draws a clear distinction between an author's moral rights and his or her economic rights. Not only are an author's moral rights immune to his or her dealings with the economic rights in a work, but they are also protected without any limitation in time. Under dualist theory, an author's moral rights last forever.[100] The author's relationship with his or her work, as its creator, remains permanently intact.[101] However, as noted above, the French ruling in the *Hugo* case suggests a softening of this principle in the context of the perpetual protection of moral rights. In particular, as discussed above, if a significant time has elapsed since the death of the author, the interests of those who are alive today may override the opinion of the author. The *Cour de cassation* commented,

> In deciding thus, on insufficient crowns derived from the type and quality of the work or from its completed character, and without having examined the contested works ignore stating whether these would have altered the work of Victor Hugo or caused confusion about their authorship, the court of appeal ... did not characterize moral rights in this way and reached its decision in disregard of freedom of creation.[102]

[99] *See* U.S. Const., art. I, § 8, cl. 8,https://www.law.cornell.edu/constitution/articlei#section8 known as the Patent and Copyright Clause: "[The Congress shall have power] To promote the progress of science and useful arts, by securing for limited times to authors and inventors the exclusive right to their respective writings and discoveries." Annotated versions are also available at https://www.law.cornell.edu/wex/intellectual_property_clause and https://constitution.congress.gov/browse/article-1/section-8/clause-8.

[100] But consider the example of Canada, which distinguishes between economic and moral rights while creating a regime of *lesser* protection for moral rights. *See Théberge, supra* note 4. *See also* Chapter 4, *infra* (discussion of Canadian moral rights).

[101] A recent case was brought by a great-great-grandson of Victor Hugo against the publishers of a sequel to *Les Misérables* in 2001—125 years after the author's 1885 death: *Hugo, supra* note 77.

[102] Id.:

> Qu'en statuant ainsi, par des motifs inopérants tirés du genre et du mérite de l'oeuvre ou de son caractère achevé, et sans avoir examiné les oeuvres litigieuses ni constaté que celles-ci auraient altéré l'oeuvre de Victor Hugo ou qu'une confusion serait née sur leur paternité, la cour d'appel, qui n'a pas ainsi caractérisé l'atteinte au droit moral et s'est déterminée en méconnaissance de la liberté de création, a violé les textes susvisés.

Does this signify the death of perpetual moral rights in practice? An interesting contrast is presented by a recent case in Italy, which found that a picture of Michelangelo's famous statue of David in a magazine advertisement violated, not the moral rights of the author, but Italian cultural heritage laws. Professor Roberto Caso objects to the idea that the Italian state has the authority to decide who can and cannot make use of cultural heritage that has entered the public domain, and he rightly criticizes "the creation of a new form of pseudo-intellectual property (in this case, a pseudo-copyright) that would attribute to the Italian State the power to exclusively control the commercial use of cultural heritage images."[103]

In contrast, the German treatment of moral rights is known as "monism." In German jurisprudence, the author's right is perceived as a sui generis right; the author's economic and moral rights share a common origin in the author's right. The basic idea of independence is maintained in the sense that the moral rights are treated independently of the economic rights. Moral rights will still subsist in a work even after the economic rights have been sold. However, German moral rights last only for the duration of the economic rights in a work.

Despite this important difference, both schools of thought share one fundamental principle: moral rights are protected for a significant time after the author's death. Although the rights are personal to the author, he or she leaves behind a memory and a reputation that continue to command respect. Indeed, it is largely in the context of protection after the author's death that moral rights are transformed into an instrument of cultural policy. After the author's death, moral interests do not cease to be important. Rather, they become different in nature: the public continues to have an interest in maintaining the quality and integrity of its own cultural heritage.[104]

Where duration is concerned, the approach of continental countries presents a striking contrast to the common-law world. In common-law systems, the protection of moral rights is often entrusted to tort law, with the implication that the protection of personal interests ceases with the death of the author.

F. Relationship between the Economic and Moral Aspects of Copyright

Notwithstanding the rather monolithic terminology of "copyright," copyright law is properly understood as an umbrella concept; it covers a great variety of

[103] Roberto Caso, *Michelangelo's David and Cultural Heritage Images. The Italian Pseudo-Intellectual Property and the End of Public Domain*, Kluwer Copyright Blog (June 15, 2023), https://copyrightblog.kluweriplaw.com/2023/06/15/michelangelos-david-and-cultural-heritage-images-the-italian-pseudo-intellectual-property-and-the-end-of-public-domain.

[104] The importance of moral rights from the point of view of protecting a public interest in culture is considered in Sundara Rajan, *supra* note 75, at 89–91.

rights accruing either to the author of the work or, in certain circumstances, to its owner. Alongside authors' economic rights, moral rights complete the "bundle of rights" enjoyed by authors under copyright law. All of the rights included under the rubric of copyright can be grouped into one or the other of the two categories, economic or "moral." Taken together, they comprehensively define the scope of copyright law.

From an international and comparative law perspective, this point reflects a basic understanding of how copyright works. By default—outside the United States—copyright includes both the economic and moral dimensions of authorship. Accordingly, when copyright is extended to new kinds of works—as in the case of software, for example, which is treated as a new kind of "literary work" under international copyright law[105]—the author of the new work is automatically entitled to both economic and moral rights. The only way to change this conclusion is to legislate one's way out of it.

Importantly, these two categories of right are not mutually exclusive: a single author's right may have both economic and non-economic dimensions, like the right of first publication or the moral right of disclosure (*divulgation*) discussed above. The right to publish one's work is the fundamental economic prerogative protected by copyright, while the right of disclosure is also an author's *moral* right to determine whether or not his or her work should be published, and if so, how.[106] This reality is elegantly described by renowned German copyright scholar, Adolf Dietz, who comments,

> [C]opyright as a whole ... serves to protect [the] intellectual and moral as well as economic interests of authors. This could also be called [a] ... unitary or synthetic concept of copyright.[107]

This aspect of copyright theory also has some important practical consequences—particularly in relation to the common-law countries, whose shared position on moral rights is briefly outlined below. Notably, it seems clear that many actions for infringement of copyright may have a moral rights dimension; and, in some

[105] Per TRIPS Agreement, *supra* note 49, at Art. 10.1; this was previously implied through extension by analogy under the Berne Convention, *supra* note 25, at Art. 2(1).

[106] *See, e.g.*, the French Code de la propriété intellectuelle, *supra* note 13. The *droit de divulgation*, or right of disclosure, is often said to be implicit in the Berne Convention. According to Ginsburg and Ricketson, this is not through Art. 6*bis* but through other provisions of Berne—which, additionally, leads to the interesting implication that at least some moral rights may not be exempt from enforcement through the TRIPS Agreement and the World Trade Organization (WTO) system for intellectual property rights. *See* SAM RICKETSON & JANE GINSBURG, INTERNATIONAL COPYRIGHT AND NEIGHBOURING RIGHTS paras. 10.53–56 (3d ed., 2022).

[107] Dietz, *supra* note 1; Chapter 2, *infra* note 152 and accompanying text.

cases, a claim might be brought as either an infringement of economic rights or a violation of moral rights. Accordingly, in the United States, where moral rights are not generally recognized, a claim for the unauthorized creation of a derivative work, which is made by modifying an existing work without its owner's consent, has been a substitute for the moral right of integrity.[108] But in Canada, a bare majority of the Supreme Court has decided that the problem involving moral rights must be claimed under moral rights provisions of the Canadian Copyright Act; a moral rights cannot be claimed "in the guise of" an economic right.[109] The reason for this finding was the higher level of proof associated with moral rights within the terms of the Act—a requirement that damage to the work must be shown to cause damage to the reputation or honor of the author. In contrast, the commission of *any* infringing act is considered a *prima facie* violation of economic rights under Canadian law.

G. The Common-Law Treatment of Moral Rights

Given the breadth of the doctrine, which potentially includes a vast array of different interests, it is hardly surprising that legal interpretations of moral rights vary greatly across different legal cultures. The treatment of moral rights in different legal families helps to classify different approaches to the rights, to understand how the doctrine has evolved since its inception, and to explain its current status in the international copyright system.

A great divide is widely considered to separate the civil law countries of continental Europe, where the modern doctrine originated, from common-law jurisdictions.

European countries have traditionally favored strong protection for moral rights, and many of them have recognized a wide range of different rights beyond attribution and integrity.[110] The approach to interpretation of these rights can be strongly individualistic. Notably, moral rights in France historically focused on the individual prerogatives of the author, with little overt attempt to weigh the interests of the public against the author's prerogatives. But, in recent times, even the French approach has shifted. Recent case law, which has advocated an approach to "balancing" authorial prerogatives against the rights of the public, at least where perpetual protection is involved, represents an important new direction in the

[108] *Gilliam v. American Broadcasting Companies, Inc.*, 538 F.2d 14 (2d Cir. 1976) (U.S.).

[109] *Théberge*, *supra* note 4, at para. 74.

[110] Many of these rights are catalogued by Strowel and colleagues in their 2004 study for the European Union: *see* Marjut Salokannel & Alain Strowel, with Estelle Derclaye, Study Contract Concerning Moral Rights in the Context of the Exploration of Works through Digital Technology: Final Report (Study contract no. ETD/99/B5-3000/E, 2000), https://www.academia.edu/1363052/Study_contract_concerning_moral_rights_in_the_context_of_the_exploitation_of_works_through_digital_technology.

interpretation of French moral rights[111] This could well be considered an example of common-law culture affecting a civil law approach to moral rights. It is a kind of cross-pollination that will be unavoidable in the increasingly intertwined international copyright community, and it reflects the reality that broader international acceptance of moral rights has expanded the limits of the traditional doctrine in sometimes unexpected ways.

Common-law countries, where copyright is said to be rooted in a strong commercial tradition, have historically preferred to restrict the recognition of moral rights. In these jurisdictions, moral rights have often been protected through common-law actions, such as tort, which have been claimed as equivalents to moral rights. However, these protections are more limited in scope than those available through copyright law. Personal torts typically terminate upon the death of the person injured, and the level of protection is far inferior to the normal copyright span of lifetime of the author and seventy years after his or her death.[112]

In contrast, developing countries—even those with a common-law heritage—and the post-socialist countries of Central and Eastern Europe have routinely provided rigorous legislative protection for moral rights.[113] These countries routinely extend comprehensive moral rights to authors, and their jurisprudence offers novel theories that further extend the scope of these rights. In these jurisdictions, still not widely studied by Western scholars, moral rights are said to represent a means of prioritizing culture, creativity, and individual rights in circumstances where they desperately need support.[114] The juxtaposition of European legal structures against the broader background of cultural and legal traditions has pushed moral rights into new territory and influenced law for large numbers of people.

One of the interesting questions to emerge from these divisions is whether moral rights should, in fact, be protected primarily through copyright law. Common-law countries have long argued for the use of alternative mechanisms, such as torts, to protect authors' moral interest. The United States has been in the forefront of these discussions, but the use of these alternative mechanisms has gradually been foreclosed by jurisprudence. Notably, the *Dastar* case of 2003 effectively eliminated the possibility of using the Lanham Act, the consumer protection statutes, to protect attribution. This trend is particularly interesting in light of the fact that

[111] Recent case law, which has advocated an approach to "balancing" authorial prerogatives against the rights of the public, at least where perpetual protection is implicated, represents an important new direction in the interpretation of French moral rights. *See Hugo*, *supra* note 77, and discussion *infra*.

[112] *See* Berne Convention, *supra* note 25, at Art. 7(1).

[113] *See, e.g.*, MIRA T. SUNDARA RAJAN, COPYRIGHT AND CREATIVE FREEDOM: A STUDY OF POST-SOCIALIST LAW REFORM (2006).

[114] This perspective found elegant and convincing expression in the writings of French scholar Claude Masouyé: *see, e.g.*, Claude Masouyé, *Décolonisation, indépendance et droit d'auteur*, 36 RIDA 85 (1962). Masouyé's biography (accompanied by that of his wife!) is available at https://www.wipo.int/edocs/pubdocs/en/copyright/120/wipo_pub_120_1986_04.pdf.

other countries appear to be moving towards a more fluid conception of moral rights, with other areas of law offering overlapping protection to the attribution interest.[115]

More broadly, moral rights are also protected through completely distinct legal mechanisms that have no immediate relation to intellectual property laws—international human rights instruments, for example.[116]The significance of these protections for authors' moral interests, decades after their adoption, remains completely unclear. There appears to have been no relevant jurisprudence. The closest approach to judicial consideration of these issues is perhaps to be found in the Indian case of *Amar Nath Sehgal v. Union of India* from 2005: based on my own scholarship, the Delhi High Court relied upon public international law conventions protecting cultural property to uphold an artist's moral right of integrity in his damaged sculpture.[117]

H. Moral Rights and Human Rights: The Ruling of the Court of Justice of the European Union (CJEU) in *Deckmyn* (2014)

If a single force can be identified as being at the origin of the Statute of Anne, it would be a demand for freedom of speech that was put forward in a highly restrictive political environment. The history of that period has been examined in depth by Lyman Ray Patterson and others, and writers, including John Milton[118] and other notable authors, played a crucial role in lobbying the government for a loosening of restrictions on speech. Ultimately, it was the act of vesting copyright in authors that brought an end to state censorship, which the British sovereign had largely exercised through the grant of exclusive printing privileges to the Stationers' Company.[119]

Among the different threads of social policy woven into copyright law, human rights must therefore be recognized as a foundational element.[120] This is reflected at the international level, where copyright finds recognition in instruments of international human rights law, including the Universal Declaration of Human Rights.[121] Article 27 of that instrument specifically protects the "material and moral interests" of authorship, supporting this conception of copyright policy.

[115] *See Hugo*, *supra* note 77.

[116] As are economic rights: see the discussion in Chapter 3, *infra* notes 189–95 and accompanying text.

[117] Sundara Rajan, *supra* note 75.

[118] *See, e.g.*, John Milton, Areopagitica (AMS Press 1971) (1644). See also the discussion of Locke's influence in Sundara Rajan, *supra* note 112, at n.33 and accompanying text.

[119] Discussed in more depth in Chapter 2, *infra*.

[120] See, again, Hesse's comment about an "impure . . . synthesis" of conceptual bases underlying copyright: Hesse, *supra* note 22.

[121] G.A. Res. 217 (III) A, Universal Declaration of Human Rights (Dec. 10, 1948).

More concretely, the intersection of moral rights and human rights was explored by the CJEU in the *Deckmyn* case. *Deckmyn* involved the parody of a Belgian cartoon that appeared on the cover of a magazine. The drawing had been altered to show a politician making handouts to people who appeared to be immigrants from outside Europe, including Muslims ("people wearing veils and people of colour").[122] The creators of the original court cartoon protested the parody on the grounds that it was offensive, and they did not wish their work to be identified with a discriminatory message.

The CJEU explored three questions: whether a unified concept of parody existed under European Union (EU) law; if such a concept existed, whether it was an accepted "exception or limitation" to copyright; and whether the author of the original work could object to the work even if was accepted as a parody and an exception to copyright.

In assessing this case, the CJEU applied a standard approach to balancing the rights of the parties involved, stating: "[the decision] must strike a fair balance between, on the one hand, the interests and rights of [copyright-holders][123] and, on the other, the freedom of expression of the user of a protected work who is relying on the exception for parody."[124]

In doing so, it relied upon a fascinating opinion by the Attorney General. In it, he explained, not only what the Court had been asked to determine, but also, what it had *not* been asked about—moral rights and the three-step test:

> In the first place, the Court has not been asked about the scope of the concept of "moral right" in so far as it is an aspect of intellectual property expressly excluded from the scope of the Directive. Recital 19 in the preamble to Directive 2001/29 states unequivocally that ... moral rights remain outside the scope of this Directive. On that basis, the decision as to whether or not there has been an infringement of moral rights is left entirely to the assessment of the national court.
>
> Nor, in the second place, has the referring court asked the Court about the possible scope in the present case of the "threefold condition" (also known as the "three-stage test"), provided for in general terms in Article 5(5) of the Directive, according to which the parody exception is to be applied "in certain special cases which do not conflict with a normal exploitation of the work or other

[122] Case C-201/13, *Deckmyn v. Vandersteen*, ECLI:EU:C:2014:2132, ¶ 9 (Sept. 3, 2014), https://eur-lex.europa.eu/legal-content/EN/TXT/?uri=CELEX%3A62013CJ0201.

[123] See "persons referred to in Articles 2 and 3 of that directive" (meaning Directive 2001/29, and namely rightholders): id. at paras. 27–28: Directive 2001/29/EC of the European Parliament and of the Council of 22 May 2001 on the harmonization of certain aspects of copyright and related rights in the information society, 2001 O.J. (L 167) 10, https://eur-lex.europa.eu/legal-content/EN/TXT/?uri=celex%3A32001L0029. *See also* Directive (EU) 2019/790 of the European Parliament and of the Council of 17 April 2019 on copyright and related rights in the Digital Single Market and amending Directives 96/9/EC and 2001/29/EC, 2019 O.J. (L 130) 92, https://eur-lex.europa.eu/eli/dir/2019/790/oj.

[124] *Deckmyn*, *supra* note 122, at para. 27.

> subject-matter and do not unreasonably prejudice the legitimate interests of the rightholder." The determination of whether or not each of those conditions is satisfied in the present case is a matter which, again, will fall to the national court.[125]

Accordingly, the case was not examined through the lens of moral rights, nor was the EU provision on exceptions and limitations invoked. But the CJEU concluded, "holders of rights ..., such as Vandersteen and Others, have, in principle, a legitimate interest in ensuring that the work protected by copyright is not associated with such a [discriminatory] message."[126]

What, exactly, was that legitimate interest? The court provided only that authors and other right-holders have a "legitimate interest" in ensuring that their work is not associated with a message that violates European human rights law. Accordingly, the court stated that "[i]n order to determine whether, in a particular case, the application of the exception for parody within the meaning of Article 5(3)(k) of Directive 2001/29 preserves that fair balance, all the circumstances of the case must be taken into account." In this case, "[the] drawing conveys a discriminatory message which has the effect of associating the protected work with such a message"—a salient fact in the light of Article 21(1) of the Charter of Fundamental Rights of the European Union and related instruments of EU human rights law, which establish the "principle of non-discrimination based on race, colour and ethnic origin."[127]

But the language of "legitimate interest" evokes the three-step test. If the court fully intended to sidestep it, why did it choose to use this phrase? The fact that it appears here suggests that there is something about the interest involved that overrides what would otherwise be exceptions to copyright protection, whether or not the theory of law on which this occurs is based on the three-step test. Again, that overpowering force is, in *Deckmyn*, human rights—and, in particular, the human rights norms set out in EU human rights legislation.

But Eleonora Rosati of the IPKat blog asks, "what [could] the Court ... possibly mean by 'legitimate interest' if not moral rights"? Moral rights and human rights can be overlapping interests, as in the apparent overlap between the authors' moral right of integrity and anti-discrimination law in *Deckmyn*[128] (and human rights arising out of authorship are one of the theoretical strands underlying the development of moral rights, as discussed in Chapter 2). But an author's moral right in his or her creation may also be incompatible with social commitments to human

[125] Id. at paras. 28–29.
[126] Id. at para. 31.
[127] Id. at para. 30.
[128] It should be noted, however, that violations of the moral right of integrity traditionally require some modification of the work itself; association itself was not enough.

rights; the example of Samuel Beckett, who wanted to prevent an all-female presentation of his play, *Waiting for Godot,* comes to mind.[129]

And pursuing *Deckmyn* into moral rights territory may lead to further problems. *Whose* legitimate interest is at stake? Rosati notes that

> moral rights are personal rights of authors, at least in *droit d'auteur traditions.* When the copyright owner is not the author how can he [or] she enforce his [or] her moral rights now that the Court has acknowledged that right holders have such "*legitimate interest*"? Plus, does this legitimate interest of right holders subsist together with authors' moral rights or rather[,] replace them?

In answer to these questions, it may well be that the court has opened the door to a broader understanding of the integrity principle in relation to *works*—as a right not only of the author, but also, of the copyright *owner*"—at least where such serious social issues as discrimination arise. But such a right would not be an author's moral right of integrity.[130] It would be something else, a new legal creation derived from, or related to, that right.

At the same time, there is no need to read the *Deckmyn* judgment as superseding the authors' rights with owners' rights. Indeed, such an interpretation would be likely to lead to intense confusion in the member countries of the EU, all of which protect authors' moral right of integrity as an inalienable right in their legislation. Rather, if the CJEU is purporting to recognize or create a right that can be simultaneously enjoyed by both authors and owners, that right presumably subsists in addition to the moral right of integrity of the author.

What, if anything, does this decision ultimately imply for moral rights in the EU? In effect, by invoking human rights language, the CJEU decision provides a human rights-based rationale for a decision that could also have been framed in terms of moral rights. The plaintiffs could have argued, simply, that the association of their work with a discriminatory message violated the integrity of their work and damaged their reputation.

However, doing so might also have been risky. Authors' rights do not have the same legal force as human rights instruments, and it would be easier for defendants to offer a counterweight to claims brought by authors under moral rights legislation. Copyright is generally considered to represent the balancing of interest between the right-holder and the public. Human rights instruments, however, allow us to bring public interest considerations to the fore. In *Deckmyn*, it was not just the authors who objected to the treatment of the work; the work was treated in such a way that basic social norms were violated.

[129] The Dutch court rejected the author's complaint: see the discussion of this incident in Chapter 6, *infra* notes 183–86.

[130] *See supra* note 24 and accompanying text.

A further consideration arises. At the time that *Deckmyn* was decided, the CJEU was operating in the context of EU law built on a compromise between European and British approaches. The exclusion of moral rights from the harmonization project was a deliberate compromise at the level of European policy. Since the United Kingdom is no longer a member of the EU, this restriction is no longer necessary. In these circumstances, could European policymakers revisit the issue of harmonizing moral rights across the region? If so, *Deckmyn* could provide some direction on how moral rights harmonization might move forward.

I. Moral Rights and Free Speech: A Dual-Edged Sword?

The conflict between copyright law and free speech is often noted, but copyright is also an agent of free speech. It is true that copyright is a monopoly right granted to authors, but this aspect of copyright should not be overemphasized. After all, copyright is also severely limited in scope: it is granted only to the author of a work, it applies only to works created by the author, and it is in force only for a limited duration.

In common-law countries, particularly the United States, criticism of moral rights often focuses on freedom of speech. By allowing authors to restrict the uses that can be made of their works, it is argued, the freedom of speech of the public is unduly restrained. Accordingly, the ability of the "users" of works to make use of them in future creation is inhibited. This situation is generally detrimental to creativity and to culture—a classic illustration of the "chilling effects" problem that is threatened by copyright as a whole. This perspective on copyright was most recently expressed in relation to the United States Supreme Court case of *Warhol* v. *Goldsmith*.[131] Here, the Court ultimately found that Warhol's use of Goldsmith's original photograph of Prince to make silkscreen prints should have been licensed, particularly in the light of the Warhol Foundation's success in collecting a licensing fee for the use of the unauthorized image made by Warhol from Goldsmith's photograph. While this case was being decided, a number of commentators argued that a decision in favor of Goldsmith would inhibit the creativity of artists who use preexisting materials. However, Goldsmith, too, is an artist, and, at least until the case, far less of a celebrity than Warhol; and objections to her claims for a licensing fee left open the question of how an artist like her could make earnings out of her work if the right of a subsequent creator to use it without licensing arrangements were to be prioritized.

Copyright is, by definition, a restriction on "free" speech—that is to say, it limits what can be done with published works. It does so for reasons of public policy. The

[131] *Warhol v. Goldsmith*, No. 21-869 (U.S.S.C. May 19, 2023), https://www.supremecourt.gov/opinions/22pdf/21-869_87ad.pdf.

purpose of copyright restrictions is to allow owners to benefit economically from works that they own—and, though the state of modern copyright law makes this a far more complex assertion than it should be, to allow authors to earn a living from their works by selling exclusive rights to exploit them. For better or for worse, copyright is currently the chief mechanism by which a "professional" class of artists exists in modern society. No viable alternative has yet emerged.

In this sense, moral rights, like copyright as a whole, are also restrictive of free speech. But the purpose of the restriction is somewhat different from copyright as a whole—to prevent personal harm to the author, including damage to his or her reputation. Nevertheless, reputation is clearly both a moral and an economic interest. An author's ability to earn money depends largely, perhaps increasingly, on his or her reputation—demonstrating, once again, the indivisibility of the copyright concept as a whole.[132]

The moral rights perspective helps to remind us that we are dealing with a certain kind of speech—works of authorship, and, paradigmatically, creative works that emerge out of a particular author's efforts and represent that author's personality.[133] The claim that the ability to "use" works is fundamental to free speech must be approached with caution because, where creative works are concerned, there is another person involved in this equation: the author. The author, too, has a right to freedom of speech.

It is also a matter of historical fact that authors have often been in the front line of advocacy for free speech. Authors have stood against oppression in many forms, including colonialism, totalitarian government, and human rights violations. As a class, they have faced the worst possible consequences of censorship. Even "non-political" authors have found that the free flow of the imagination inevitably antagonizes authorities at some point, since individual freedom itself—and freedom of thought in particular—is the ultimate threat, perhaps more than the content of any given work.[134]

These objections to moral rights often characterize the rights as arbitrary and unpredictable—above all, as resting on the caprice of the author. With moral rights, an author can sue anyone, as the argument goes, "just because he disliked you."[135] But the legal framework for the protection of moral rights is not arbitrary.

[132] Dietz, *supra* note 1.

[133] As Justice Oliver Wendell Holmes noted in *Bleistein v. Donaldson Lithographing Co.*, 188 U.S. 239, 188 (1903), https://supreme.justia.com/cases/federal/us/188/239: "Personality always contains something unique. It expresses its singularity even in handwriting, and a very modest grade of art has in it something irreducible which is one man's alone. That something he may copyright unless there is a restriction in the words of the act."

[134] Sundara Rajan, Elena Ferrante, *supra* note 58.

[135] For example, an examination of moral rights by Creative Commons takes the following form:

> ***Moral Rights Proposal #2: Take a more proactive stance in support of moral rights.***
>
> **Pros**: strengthens the license and make it more appealing to creators; address concerns that the current version of CC (v3) has no real provisions for letting Licensor enforce his or her moral rights or author's rights.

The theory is translated into specific legal language through legislation that defines the scope and exercise of moral rights. Balance is a widely accepted principle of moral rights interpretation—even in the French courts, which interpret legislation that is strongly favorable to authors.

Freedom of speech is often a question of achieving a satisfactory, sometimes precarious, but workable and apparently fair balance. In the case of moral rights, as in relation to copyright overall, there is an obvious need for balance between the needs of the public and the prerogatives of authorship. Copyright law has historically recognized this reality overall: no author wants to write for an audience of no one. However, moral rights represent more sensitive social issues: the protection of authorial personality, creative intent, and cultural interests. These are also fragile interests, since they are not usually backed by great economic or political power. In the light of authors' overall weakness as a constituency, mirrored by the fragility of the public interest itself in creativity and culture, it is important to remember that moral rights are not just a challenge to free speech; they represent another dimension of a truly comprehensive right of freedom of speech. They protect the free speech of authors. As such, they are fundamental to the public interest, to culture, and to democracy.

J. Moral Rights in the Technological Environment

In the technological environment, moral rights have acquired a new relevance. Contrary to the neglectful approach that has often characterized the study of moral rights in the past, this area of the law should now be infused with a new degree of urgency.

The digital environment for moral rights can be evaluated in the light of three considerations. First, copyright has taken its place ahead of any other area of intellectual property rights as the primary form of legal regulation governing technology. Notably, software and databases, two major types of new creation, enjoy copyright protection as "literary works." Through them, copyright now has implications for broad areas of innovation, including artificial intelligence technologies and text and data mining, that are proving to be important in the digital context.

The logic of extending copyright to these new forms of intellectual creation follows a long tradition of bringing diverse kinds of intellectual work into the ambit of copyright law. Copyright began as a right in literary property; it was later extended to the protection of musical works, whose graphical notation in Western culture

Cons: This creates an internal contradiction where the licensor gives anyone the permission to redistribute his work, but then has the possibility to arbitrarily prevent someone from doing so, just because he disliked that someone.

See https://wiki.creativecommons.org/wiki/4.0/Moral_rights.

made them analogous to literary property, and artistic works.[136] Copyright law has generally proven to be a flexible and adaptable instrument of social policy, able to accommodate many of these new aspects of knowledge.

However, the extension of copyright concepts to technological works may stretch the literary analogy beyond its reasonable limits. As noted above, in jurisdictions where moral rights are recognized, they are automatically included within the bundle of rights enjoyed by creative authors under copyright rules. Accordingly, the policy question of whether the creators of new technologies should enjoy moral rights is important, but it remains largely unresolved. The subsistence of moral rights in the products and processes of new technology is an issue that has received little attention. Nevertheless, the presence of moral rights would clearly have implications for technology, with the potential for significant impact upon its growth and development.

A second series of concerns arises out of the new creative possibilities generated by technology. Technology offers novel ways of creating traditional artworks; it also introduces the possibility of new kinds of creation, artistic or otherwise, such as multimedia and computer-generated works.[137] In a sense, the composite work is the archetypal creative product of the Digital Age. From a legal point of view, it potentially leads to layers of conflicting rights and interests. There is also the possibility that new technologies and artistic creation will overlap—for example, where a computer program, itself protected by copyright law as a literary work, is also designed to generate a work of art or a musical composition. As is illustrated by the difficulty of developing intellectual property (IP) policy for artificial intelligence, these issues are not easy to accommodate within copyright or other intellectual property laws. Without clear legal and policy guidance, conflicts over rights and interests could proliferate, or prove to be intractable, and technological development could proceed in an environment of inadequate, and possibly harmful, development.

Finally, it should be noted that new technologies have made it possible for members of the public to intervene in creative works in a new way, making seamless and imperceptible changes.[138] A new chapter has begun for sampling, appropriation art, fan fiction and film, and other types of creation based on the creative reuse of existing works. Talk of "users' rights" has become relatively commonplace in copyright scholarship. Moral rights may help to mediate the new relationship between

[136] Copyright Act 1842, 5 & 6 Vict. c. 45 (Eng.).

[137] *See, e.g.*, Majenta, *Make Music and Art Using Machine Learning*, https://magenta.tensorflow.org.

[138] This possibility was foreseen more than three decades ago by Canadian pianist Glenn Gould. His insights are all the more striking because they emerge from the traditionally conservative world of classical music: *see, e.g.*, Geoffrey Payzant, Glenn Gould: Music and Mind (Key Porter Books 1984) (1978). Gould's ideas are discussed from a legal perspective in Mira T. Sundara Rajan, *The "New Listener" and the Virtual Performer: The Need for a New Approach to Performers' Rights*, *in* In the Public Interest: The Future of Canadian Copyright Law 309 (Michael Geist ed., 2005).

creators and their public, particularly where copyright as a whole has failed to establish effective compromises.[139]

The new role of the public deserves examination. Through technology, does the "audience" for a creative work now have the opportunity to become a more active participant in the creative process?[140] Writing in the 1960s, Canadian pianist Glenn Gould referred to a "new listener" who could intervene in music through new technologies, thereby achieving a new level of creative engagement with it. But active involvement in an aesthetic experience arguably requires something more than physical manipulation of the work. Creativity involves processes as much as products. As Gould himself observed, "The purpose of art is the lifelong construction of a state of wonder and serenity."[141]

The idea of the audience as participant in the creative experience is perhaps less familiar to Western "high" culture than to the cultures of the East.[142] The Sanskrit term *rasa*, a "keyword" of Indian aesthetic philosophy describes the essence of art

[139] For example, recent cases on music copyright infringement in the United States have led to unclear and frustrating rules, and rulings on music copyright seem increasingly arbitrary. If principles of attribution and integrity were applied to resolving these disputes, the outcomes might be quite different, and the larger effect might be to buttress the integrity of U.S. copyright law overall.

[140] This is sometimes spoken of, in copyright law, in terms of "user rights": *see, e.g.*, David Vaver, *Copyright and the Internet: From Owner Rights and User Duties to User Rights and Owner Duties*, 57 Case W. Rsrv. L. Rev. 731 (2007). The concept features in the Supreme Court of Canada case of *Society of Composers, Authors and Music Publishers of Canada v. Entertainment Software Association*, 2022 SCC 30. Writing for the majority, Justice Rowe states, id. at [5]:

> I cannot agree with the Board's interpretation of s. 2.4(1.1). The *Copyright Act* does not exist solely for the benefit of authors. Its overarching purpose is to balance authors' and users' rights by securing just rewards for authors while facilitating public access to works. When this balance is achieved, society is enriched. Authors are encouraged to produce more works, and users gain access to works which they can use to inspire their own original artistic and intellectual creations.

With even the dissenting judges agreeing to this basic principle, it is still worth questioning whether the basis of a "reasonable balance" between authors and users has actually been achieved in the technological environment. What about the tremendous losses to *authors*, as distinguished from right holders, in the course of technological evolution? It is this trend that has reached new heights with artificial intelligence. See discussion in Chapter 5, *infra*. The disadvantages flowing to authorship have been clearly recognized in the European Union's latest round of copyright discussions, culminating in the new Directive on the Digital Single Market: *see infra* note 122. *See also* European Parliament, *Questions and Answers on Issues about the Digital Copyright Directive* (Mar. 27, 2019), https://www.europarl.europa.eu/news/en/press-room/20190111IPR23225/questions-and-answers-on-issues-about-the-digital-copyright-directive. Notably, the Parliament states:

> The proposed "Directive on copyright in the Digital Single Market" seeks to ensure that creatives (for example musicians or actors), and news publishers and journalists benefit from the online world and the internet as they do from the offline world. Currently, due to outdated copyright rules, online platforms and news aggregators are reaping all the rewards while artists, news publishers and journalists see their work circulate freely, at best receiving very little remuneration for it. This makes it very difficult for artists and media professionals to earn a decent living.

[141] Payzant, *supra* note 131, at 64.

[142] See, e.g., the detailed study of Indian art and aesthetics in Pandit, *supra* note 37. The intersection of traditional culture with digital technology is explored by James Tunney, *E.U., I.P., Indigenous People and the Digital Age: Intersecting Circles?*, 20(9) Eur. Intell. Prop. Rev. 335, 335 (1998).

as that which arises out of the shared experience of artist and audience.[143] The idea is explained by Bharata, the fabled author of the Sanskrit treatise on classical performance known as the *Natya Shastra*:

> Born in the heart of the poet, [aesthetic experience] flowers as it were in the actor and bears fruit in the spectator. All three in the serene contemplation of the work, form in reality a single knowing object fused together.[144]

By enabling a rapprochement between author and audience through new possibilities of engagement with the work, digital technology seems to offer the possibility of a new relationship between them.[145] But interaction through technology is no guarantee of human closeness. Whether or not technology will lead to real human connection depends on the terms of the underlying relationship between human beings. At a minimum, an author's participation in any relationship mediated by technology should be voluntary rather than coerced. Freedom is the necessary foundation of any meaningful relationship between human individuals, whether or not it is mediated through technology.

These considerations point to the profound transformation of copyright law—concepts, interpretation, practice, and experience—through technology. But transcending these conceptual considerations, profound as they are, is overwhelming social concern, intense and widespread anxiety about an ancient and universal human preoccupation: truth. The online environment has shown itself to be a space that lends itself to manipulation and abuse—a trend that has been accelerated by poor political leadership in Western democracies and elsewhere. False information abounds. The power to manipulate creative works, language, images, and data clearly has a dark side. The spread of false information threatens, not only the integrity of knowledge, but also the integrity of the technologies that rely upon the use of that information. Foremost among these is artificial intelligence. As noted by the participants in a conference on moral rights that I held in Glasgow in 2017, with the participation of the United States Copyright Office,

> If the integrity of human knowledge and information is affected, algorithms with decision-making power will make erroneous connections and decisions. There is, accordingly, a powerful policy interest in safeguarding the integrity of knowledge for this reason.[146]

[143] For a succinct explanation of the concept, see C. SUBRAMANIA BHARATI, *Rasa: The Key-Word of Indian Culture*, *in* THE COMING AGE: C. SUBRAMANIA BHARATI'S COLLECTED ENGLISH WRITINGS 87 (Mira T. Sundara Rajan ed., 2021).

[144] Bharata's identity is disputed; but the text itself lays the foundation for Indian classical dance, drama, and music as it has developed over the past 2,000-odd years: *see* Pandit, *supra* note 37.

[145] *See supra* note 131.

[146] For further information on this event and research resources, see Mira T. Sundara Rajan, *Moral Rights and New Technologies, Conference program (March 31–April 1, 2017)*, https://professormira.com/glasgow-conference-2. I am indebted to Florian De Rouck (LL.M. Glasgow, 2014) for his

K. Fame: The Currency of the Digital Era?

Moral rights are fundamentally concerned with artistic reputation. In some countries, a moral right to one's reputation is recognized. Others follow the formula of the Berne Convention and make reputation an essential component of the right of integrity. In these jurisdictions, modifying the work will not be enough to invoke the integrity right. Rather, the author must also be able to show that the modification has damaged his or her reputation.[147]

Reputation, also known as fame, is the essence of artistic existence. Without it, an artist cannot expect to sell work; without it, there is no measure of recognition. Even an artist who disdains celebrity is, in some sense, dependent upon it for his or her survival.[148] An artist cannot live without fame.[149]

In many ways, fame has always been an unhappy master. The work of truly great thinkers tends to be ahead of its time, and fame does not arrive in time to improve their lives. Vincent van Gogh is a tragic example: the painter struggled physically and psychologically and sold only one painting, to his beloved brother Theo, during his lifetime. Now, van Gogh's paintings routinely set records on the art market for the most expensive works of art ever sold.[150] Other examples can be found in the lives of no lesser geniuses than William Shakespeare and J.S. Bach—artists whose work was valued by their contemporaries but which, after their deaths, fell into extended periods of neglect before their true stature was ultimately realized.[151] In the case of Shakespeare, his very identity is still in question. In such

remarkable insights in this area. His work has subsequently been published as part of the Glasgow conference symposium edited by Mira T. Sundara Rajan, with Sarah Harris of Oxford University Press: Florian De Rouck, *Moral Rights and AI Environments: The Unique Bond between Intelligent Agents and Their Creations*, 14(4) JIPLP 299 (2019).

147 Berne Convention, *supra* note 25, Art. 6*bis* provides that the alteration must be "prejudicial to his honour or reputation," leaving questions open about the extent and nature of the proof required.

148 An interesting example is J.D. Salinger: the writer apparently spent his youth obsessed with achieving fame only to discover, when he did become famous, his intense distaste for celebrity. *See* Charles McGrath, *J.D. Salinger, Literary Recluse, Dies at 91*, New York Times (Jan. 28, 2010), http://www.nytimes.com/2010/01/29/books/29salinger.html—a fascinating article.

149 The ideal was well known in the poetry of the Sangam age in South Indian literature, some 2,000 years ago. *See* K. A. Nilakanta Sastri (the late), R. C. Champakalakshmi, & P. M. Rajan Gurukkal, Illustrated History of South India, adapted from K. A. Nilakanta Sastri, A History of South India (2009) (1955).

150 Van Gogh's "Sunflowers," "Irises," and his "Portrait of Dr Gachet" have all set records for their sale prices. *See On This Day*, BBC News (Nov. 11, 1987), http://news.bbc.co.uk/onthisday/hi/dates/stories/november/11/newsid_2539000/2539613.stm. In 1990, the "Portrait of Dr Gachet" was purchased by a Japanese businessman, Ryoei Saito, for U.S.$82.5 million. He claimed that he wanted to have the painting cremated with him—either to avoid inheritance taxes imposed on his heirs or out of love for the work! Currently, the record for the most expensive painting sold at auction is held by Leonardo da Vinci's "Salvator Mundi". *See* Scott Reyburn, "Five years since the $450m Salvator Mundi sale: a first-hand account of the nonsensical auction," The Art Newspaper (Nov. 15, 2022), https://www.theartnewspaper.com/2022/11/15/five-years-since-the-450m-salvator-mundi-sale-a-first-hand-account-of-the-nonsensical-auction for a superb discussion of the circumstances surrounding the sale and the ultimate fate of this painting.

151 The Romantics were responsible for rediscovering both Bach and Shakespeare.

cases, fame only serves to preserve an artist's name or, perhaps, vindicates his or her descendants.[152] It is of no direct benefit to the artist.

Fame, of even the most ordinary variety, takes time to develop. What is its place in the digital world?

A characteristic quality of digital space is its curious relation to time. Digital technology involves the speeding up of everything—perhaps quite natural, since digital communication is defined by the movement of photons, particles of light that move faster than anything else in the universe. But there is also another dimension to digital time, which can perhaps be best expressed as an inverse relationship between the volume of information available and the attention span of any given individual. In the digital environment, information is produced and consumed at tremendous speed. Journalists used to speak of "yesterday's news," but the old news of the digital era could be news that is hours or minutes old. Rare, indeed, are the personalities that can command more than a few minutes or hours of fame on the digital stage.

At the same time, the range of digital technology is such that reputation, such as it is, can be communicated across a much larger population than ever before. If fame in the digital context is limited in terms of its depth, it covers a vast surface area during its brief existence. It can generate both publicity and wealth on a scale not previously known, as illustrated by numerous examples of artists and personalities who have made a sensation on Internet platforms such as YouTube, the near-ubiquitous video-streaming site.[153]

Though the nature of fame may have changed, it has not, by any means, become outmoded. On the contrary: fame has acquired a renewed importance in the digital context. Copyright rules have become difficult to enforce; since copyright has long served as the primary means of securing money from creative work in a modern society, it has now become essential to find new ways of earning wealth that can compensate for the fragility of copyright. In many popular genres, artists are increasingly bypassing the traditional formulae for public recognition—in music, recording with a label, releasing singles and albums—in favor of offering their work directly to the public. The intervention of a middleman is no longer necessary. YouTube, again, has proven to be revolutionary. Aspiring musicians post their videos online and strive to be noticed. In the Digital Age, fame, in its new incarnation, translates into new kinds of earnings (advertising revenues,

[152] The fame of Boris Pasternak, Russian poet and novelist, comes to mind. Awarded the Nobel Prize in 1958, Pasternak was vilified by the Soviet government and by the Soviet community of writers—a situation that may have precipitated his death. *See* Peter Flinn, *The Plot Thickens: A New Book Promises an Intriguing Twist to the Epic Tale of "Doctor Zhivago"*, WASHINGTON POST (Jan. 27, 2007), http://www.washingtonpost.com/wp-dyn/content/article/2007/01/26/AR2007012601758.html. Pasternak's son finally accepted the Nobel Prize on his father's behalf in 1989.

[153] Singing sensation Susan Boyle is a case in point. *See* Sarah Lyall, *Unlikely Singer Is YouTube Sensation*, NEW YORK TIMES (Apr. 17, 2009), http://www.nytimes.com/2009/04/18/arts/television/18boyle.html.

dates for live performances, media attention), and these have largely displaced older sources, including copyright royalties. No doubt, reaching out to the world through technology also satisfies a more fundamental human urge for connection that has never really gone away. Fame still matters; it matters as never before, and the protection of reputation is therefore a key requirement of modern cultural policy. To the extent that they are concerned with reputation, moral rights are not merely necessary; they have actually acquired a new importance and, in this sense, may ultimately supersede the economic aspects of copyright law in terms of their importance for culture. Technology changes, but human nature remains the same.

L. A Study in Contrasts: The Enforcement of Moral Rights

The immense difficulties of enforcing copyright in the digital environment have launched copyright law into an existential crisis that has continued, largely unabated, since the early 2000s. In contrast to copyright, however, the situation surrounding the enforcement of moral rights is different and far more ambiguous.

It is true that moral rights are increasingly subject to the possibility of an infringement because of the ease of intervention in digitized works. At the same time, an interesting interplay between moral rights and technology means that the very factors that facilitate moral rights infringement may also help to support the enforcement of the rights. This presents a marked contrast to copyright overall, where, as noted above, the possibilities for copyright infringement have surged with no real positives for enforcement. On the other hand, the relationship of moral rights with technology has shown itself to be curious symbiotic.

The example of Joyce Hatto offers a fascinating illustration of this principle. Hatto was a reclusive concert pianist who had stopped performing but suddenly began to issue new recordings. These recordings were warmly welcomed by the classical music community, which hailed the brilliant reappearance of a long-forgotten artist. But technology brought this story to an unexpected climax. When a listener put one of Hatto's CDs into his computer, Gracenote, the database on which iTunes relies to identify music, matched the tracks apparently recorded by Hatto with pre-existing recordings made by other pianists. Joyce Hatto's celebrated "new" recordings were forgeries.[154] Clearly, the availability of information and knowledge can help to protect moral rights of attribution and integrity—although, once again, the underlying information must be reliable for this function to be effective.

There is another sense in which technology may reinforce moral rights. This has to do with the underlying architecture of new technologies, which, in many

[154] *See, e.g.*, Mark Singer, *Fantasia for Piano*, New Yorker (Sept. 17, 2007), http://www.newyorker.com/magazine/2007/09/17/fantasia-for-piano.

ways, *inherently* favors the principles of attribution and integrity. For example, when exchanging music files (an issue discussed in more detail in Chapter 6 of this book), users of those files will be fundamentally concerned with their quality and are likely to make due note of the source of the file as an indication of quality—integrity and attribution interests at play. The recognition of these interests facilitates the operation of technological imperatives.

In an attempt to prevent copyright infringement, a variety of technological protection measures (TPMs), also known as "anti-circumvention" measures, have been developed.[155] These include encryption technology, which "locks" the work to prevent someone from gaining unauthorized access to it; watermarking, which allows copying of the work to be traced, though not prevented; and digital rights management, which identifies the origin of a work. From a moral rights perspective, encryption and watermarking are credible approaches to the integrity right; as for attribution, it is supported by digital rights management. Digital rights management also lends indirect support to the integrity principle by offering a way to assess the authenticity of the source. Attempts to circumvent these safeguards have become criminal offenses in some countries, including the United States.[156] However, the caveat that applies to security technologies is that technology never stands still. Every attempt to restrict access to a work through technological measures has its own, technological antidote. Technological protection measures, however sophisticated, seem doomed to obsolescence.[157]

Circumvention also involves a psychological dimension. For some users, circumventing copy protection is a technological challenge to be met; for others, it is a form of political activism against unfair restrictions on media. The fact that there is little attempt to provide policy justifications for the criminalization of circumvention can lead to anger. In the process—ironically—talent and human potential are wasted. Condemning circumvention makes a certain type of innovative activity illegal, but there may not be anything inherently nefarious about it. Context is everything. A code-breaker during the Second World War was a hero; in the Digital Age, he or she is, apparently, a criminal.

In the digital context, the enforcement of many rights is fraught with difficulties, and moral rights cannot qualify as a complete exception. However, the fact that rights are difficult to enforce does not necessarily mean that they should be

[155] This awkward term refers to technological measures that are implemented to discourage interference with copyright works: they are against ("anti") the "circumvention" of copyright rules.

[156] Digital Millennium Copyright Act, Pub. L. No. 105-304, 112 Stat. 2860 (1998), amending Title 17 of the U.S. Code.

[157] Id. at § 1201(a)(1–2) for relevant U.S. provisions. The American approach to circumvention technologies is discussed by David Balaban, *The Battle of the Music Industry: The Distribution of Audio and Video Works via the Internet, Music and More*, 12 FORDHAM INTELL. PROP. MEDIA & ENT. L.J. 235, 259–65 (2001). The relevance of anti-circumvention technology to the moral right of integrity is considered briefly by Thomas P. Heide, *The Moral Right of Integrity and the Global Information Infrastructure: Time for a New Approach?*, 2 U.C. DAVIS J. INT'L L. & POL'Y 211, 263–66 (1996).

dispensed with. Moral rights involve fundamental social issues; there is every likelihood that moral interests will be important for the future of culture. The difficulty of enforcement should not be a reason to forego what is, essentially, a form of protection for human rights in the digital context.

But problems of enforcement need to be addressed. In the case of moral rights, coercion alone will not be adequate to enforce them. Where copyright or moral rights are concerned, enforcement depends, to some degree, on persuasion. As J.A.L. Sterling observed, writing at the dawn of the digital era,

> At the end of the day, copyright will only survive because the public wants it, and knows it wants it, and knows its value. The challenge to the copyright lawyer is therefore not only to forge solutions to the philosophical and legal problems [confronting copyright] ... but to contribute to public education in every possible way.[158]

There can be no doubt that the enforcement of moral rights depends on educating the public. But the enforcement of moral rights is also supported by strong underlying forces—the mutual compatibility of technological and human imperatives when it comes to questions of authenticity. This should be recognized and reinforced. Moreover, the overlap between moral rights and technology also makes attribution and integrity potentially helpful in the enforcement of copyright overall. But this is all the more reason why public support for moral rights should be sought.

M. Moral Rights Jurisprudence: Occurrences and Outcomes

As noted earlier, the doctrine of moral rights initially emerged from French case law, and was only later codified.[159] As Strömholm, Lucas, and other scholars have pointed out, the theorizing of moral rights was largely carried out by German jurists, with the principles finding their way formally into French legislation only at the relatively late date of 1957.[160]

If European countries have had their share of moral rights litigation—Lucas points out, for example, the "wealth of case law concerning the right of integrity in France"[161]—common-law countries have seen relatively few cases on moral rights

[158] J.A.L. Sterling, *Philosophical and Legal Challenges in the Context of Copyright and Digital Technology*, 31(5) INT'L REV. INDUS. PROP. & COPYRIGHT L. 508, 525 (2000).

[159] *See, e.g.*, André Lucas, *Moral Right in France: Towards a Pragmatic Approach?*, Presentation to the British Library and Artistic Copyright Association, para. 1.0 (2010?), (copy on file with the author; BLACA's website is https://www.blaca.org/).

[160] Id.

[161] Id.

as compared to copyright disputes based on economic rights. This is obviously due, in the first instance, to the relatively late adoption of moral rights in many common-law jurisdictions. But this relative scarcity of case law is also offered as an argument that moral rights are relatively unimportant in these jurisdictions. However, this is a seriously misinformed view.

A number of factors explain the relative paucity of moral rights case law, and these considerations also suggest that moral rights litigation will always be relatively rare. Moral rights are personally reserved to authors and artists.[162] Except for the wealthiest and most successful among them—those who may also be least likely to experience moral rights violations, or to have reason to fear their consequences—cost presents a serious and often insurmountable obstacle to bringing suit.[163] Moreover, authors and artists may also be intimidated by the prospect of engaging with the legal system to sue an adversary[164]—a problem that has been observed in practice by some artists' advocates and which would benefit from further study. These factors impede litigation by artists and make legal solutions seem both intimidating and practically out of reach.[165] This is the most obvious explanation for why moral rights cases are not litigated more frequently.

More generally, though, lawyers may be prone to forgetting that litigation should be considered a last-resort solution to conflicts. As noted earlier, the presence of

[162] *See supra* note 24.

[163] This was even the case in the high-profile dispute involving murals by Picasso and Carl Nesjar in Oslo. The descendants of Nesjar and of Viksjø, the architect who designed the building where the murals were installed, were unable to sue the government because of the potential cost of the suit. Under Norwegian law, if a preliminary injunction were initially to be granted to the plaintiffs, but a *permanent* injunction was ultimately refused (i.e., the case was unsuccessful on the merits), the plaintiffs would be responsible for the financial losses borne by the government. This was a risk that they could not afford to take. *See* Mira T. Sundara Rajan, *The Moral Rights of the Artists in Oslo's Y-Block: Can a Case against the Demolition Be Made under Copyright Law?*, 15(10) JIPLP 838 (2020). *See also* Mira T. Sundara Rajan, *Growing up with Picasso: An Interview with Gro Nesjar, Art Historian and Daughter of Carl Nesjar, Picasso's Greatest Collaborator*, WOMAN OF CULTURE PODCAST (Dec. 29, 2023), https://womanofculturepodcast.com/growing-up-with-picasso-an-interview-with-gro-nesjar-art-historian-and-daughter-of-carl-nesjar-picassos-greatest-collaborator.

[164] For example, in conversation at the Richmond Arts Center on June 7, 2023, Roberto Martinez raised this problem in relation to an ongoing dispute between a group of local artists and the oil corporation Chevron about the removal and destruction of an artwork primarily located on Richmond city property by Chevron. *See* Michael Cabanatuan, *Chevron Admits It Took Down Public Art Project that Criticized the Oil Giant* (June 7, 2023), https://www.sfchronicle.com/eastbay/article/chevron-admits-took-public-art-project-18140972.php.

[165] For example, the Writers' Union of Canada has pointed out that the average annual earnings for a writer in in Canada are around CA$13,000:

> The Writers' Union believes these results represent a cultural emergency for Canada. For 81% of respondents, income from writing would not allow them to live above the poverty line, and the average writer's income ($12,879) is a full $36,000 below the national average. This [is] despite the fact that writers have invested in post-graduate education in large numbers.

See Writers' Union of Canada, *Canadian Workers Working Harder While Earning Less* (2015), https://writersunion.ca/news/canadian-writers-working-harder-while-earning-less. The press release announces the release of a 2015 report and cites a U.S. equivalent, The Authors' Guild, *Panel Explores Drop in Authors' Earnings* (May 6, 2015) https://authorsguild.org/news/ag-panel-explores-drop-in-authors-earnings.

moral rights in copyright statutes *should inhibit* litigation—not because of the inaccessibility of legal remedies, but because legal recognition of the rights should encourage respect for them. Moral rights should simultaneously reflect and create an environment of greater respect for artists.[166]

This appears have happened in the United Kingdom, for example: more than twenty years after the enactment of moral rights in the CDPA, the rights have increasingly found their way into mainstream copyright discourse in that country. Discussions of moral rights have become normalized in this environment, though empirical studies are needed to evaluate the impact of the legislative scheme on the practices of copyright-industry players. If moral rights legislation supports the establishment of a more positive environment for artists, then the owners and "users" of artworks should be seen to exercise a greater degree of care in their treatment of works, and conflicts involving moral interests might lend themselves more readily to negotiated solutions and settlements. These issues deserve to be studied.

In the case of moral rights disputes, what might negotiated solutions entail? The ideal remedy for a moral rights complaint is generally considered to be injunction: the cessation of the activity complained of, such as publication without proper attribution or circulation of a flawed product. Damages may also be awarded, though this is less frequent. Damages arguably have a rightful place in any moral rights regime in two senses: first, as a deterrent to future moral rights violations, and secondly, as a means of recognizing the *economic* cost to the author or artist of the reputational damage that can be caused by, for example, damaging or destroying a work. A good example of a case where the destruction of an artwork led to a large settlement is that of Kent Twitchell, a Los Angeles artist whose well-known mural of another artist, Ed Ruscha, was painted over and thereby destroyed.[167] The case was settled for $1,100,000, and Twitchell has since recreated his work.[168] Since then, the case of the 5Pointz graffiti center in New York led to a settlement of $6.75 million that included damages for destroying forty-five works.[169]

Indeed, in the online environment, even relatively minor interventions in a work can lead to major reputational damage because of the breadth of online dissemination. For example, images of an artwork such as a sculpture that bears an

[166] *See supra* notes 63–64.

[167] *See, e.g.*, Deborah Vankin, *Kent Twitchell to Revive Famed "Ed Ruscha Monument" Mural Downtown*, Los Angeles Times (June 12, 2015), https://www.latimes.com/entertainment/arts/culture/la-et-cm-kent-twitchell-mural-ed-ruscha-monument-20150610-story.html.

[168] Id.

[169] *Castillo v. G&M Realty L.P.*, Nos. 18-498-cv (L), 18-538-cv (CON), 2020 U.S. App. LEXIS 5228 (2d Cir. Feb. 20, 2020), https://www.mintz.com/sites/default/files/media/documents/2020-03-25/18-498_amd_opn.pdf. *See, e.g.*, Eileen Kinsella, *A Stunning Legal Decision Just Upheld a $6.75 Million Victory for the Street Artists Whose Works Were Destroyed at the 5Pointz Graffiti Mecca* (Feb. 20, 2020), https://news.artnet.com/art-world/5pointz-ruling-upheld-1782396. *See also* Steve Schindler & Katie Wilson-Milne, *Moral Rights in Street Art: The 5Pointz Story—Revisited*, The Art Law Podcast (Mar. 2, 2020), https://artlawpodcast.com/2020/03/02/moral-rights-in-street-art-the-5pointz-story-revisited/.

error in the artist's name may circulate online for a time before the error is noticed and it is removed. The period might be brief—days, or perhaps only hours. However, that brief dissemination still has the power to do practical harm, due to the speed at which information spreads, and to the further possibility that the faulty image will continue to be held by internet users, or circulated by them, even after it has been withdrawn at the source. In this situation, the author or artist may suffer both economic and moral harm, and an injunction can only provide partial relief. Damages make sense.

The question of how to deal with financial compensation for real or potential violations of moral rights after the author's death is more troubling. For example, in France, where moral rights last in perpetuity, it is common for the rights in architectural works to be dealt with by financial compensation to the right-holder—the architect's family, for instance—in exchange for the right to modify the work.[170] In the absence of indications from the artist—in posthumous writings, perhaps, or another source—it is left to the heirs or estate administrators to infer the desires of the artist. If the process becomes a cynical one—or even if the author's heirs are driven by simple financial need—transactions like this effectively amount to an alienation *post-morten auctoris* of the artist's moral rights. This is not how moral rights are supposed to function, but it is also difficult to think of alternatives in these circumstances. "Between the idea/And the reality/ ... Falls the shadow."[171]

N. Conclusion: Scope and Structure of This Book

This book is essentially divided into two parts. The first considers the origins of modern moral rights in nineteenth-century Europe and explores their subsequent development across different parts of the world, throughout the twentieth century and until the present time. The narration of moral rights history in Chapter 2 includes traces the development of the doctrine in French and German law, as is traditional, but it also goes on to examine the history of moral rights in English law. This chapter seeks to demonstrate that, contrary to the common wisdom, the notion of moral rights is neither alien to English law nor incompatible with it. Instead, the idea of moral surfaced in the English courts, as it later arose in France. However, it was suppressed in the course of a broader struggle between legislators and the powerful Stationers' Company, whose members fought to avoid relinquishing their printing privileges as censorship by the British Crown came to an end.

170 Interview with Ludovic Julié (July 2017).

171 From "The Hollow Men," T.S. Eliot's poem, published in 1925 and now widely available online: *see, e.g.*, https://allpoetry.com/the-hollow-men.

Chapter 2 also includes a too-brief discussion of the significant antecedents to modern moral rights, and to copyright law as a whole, in the world beyond Europe.[172] This is a separate area of research that waits to be developed in its own right; but no discussion of the history of moral rights can truly be complete without reference to non-European traditions.

Chapter 3 examines the form in which moral rights became part of the international copyright system as it emerged in the late nineteenth century. The adoption of a provision on moral rights in the Berne Convention was a significant milestone. Berne elevated moral rights to the status of an internationally accepted doctrine and a core element of international copyright protection. Moreover, Article 6*bis* also served as a template provision for countries that wished to participate in the international copyright system and needed to adopt moral rights in their copyright legislation as part of the internationalization process. Interestingly, this group includes the United Kingdom, which adopted moral rights for the first time in the CDPA.[173]

Chapter 4 then broadens the discussion to examine the treatment of moral rights in jurisdictions where they have been adopted more recently, and in which, the idea of moral rights has undergone significant further evolution. The objective of the discussion is to arrive at an understanding of moral rights that is current and dynamic, rather than primarily historical. Since the doctrine was first recognized in European law, it has taken flight and become a worldwide phenomenon, inspired by its European roots, yet surpassing them. The doctrine has acquired many layers of new meaning since its European beginnings.

Moral rights are explored as they are found in selected countries drawn from the world's major legal systems, including civil law and common-law regimes, developing countries, and post-socialist states. However, though examples are given from diverse countries, the coverage of moral rights cannot be truly comprehensive across all groups within a book of this size. The group of developing countries is the most difficult to examine, as it is tremendously heterogeneous. The world's poorest countries, ironically among the richest in terms of culture, deserve a special treatment in their own right. So, too, do countries affected by war, such as Iraq, Afghanistan, Syria, and Ukraine.

The book examines the treatment of all the moral rights traditionally recognized in European law, and it also deals with "new" aspects of the doctrine, including the recognition of new rights as well as novel approaches to interpretation, which often, though not exclusively, arise in non-traditional jurisdictions.[174] Proposals

[172] Researching the history of copyright concepts in non-Western cultures is a rich area of historical, legal, and cultural scholarship that waits to be discovered. My initial work on Indian tradition in this area is cited in the discussion in Chapter 2, *infra*.

[173] CDPA, *supra* note 62.

[174] For example, the balancing exercise undertaken by the French court in the 2007 case of *Pierre Hugo*, *supra* note 77, represents a new approach to moral rights jurisprudence in the most traditional moral rights jurisdiction of all: *see infra* note 100. The case is discussed (in French) in *Le droit moral*

for Indigenous cultural rights, the relationship between moral rights and cultural heritage laws (as opposed to copyright), and the reinstatement of copyright terms for persecuted authors in post-socialist countries are among the most fascinating examples of an evolving theory.

The second part of the book is an exploration of moral rights in relation to various creative fields, with a particular view towards examining their transformation through technology. These chapters undertake a more focused discussion of how moral rights relate to the particular subject matter involved, and they also make policy recommendations on issues that remain controversial or unresolved. There is necessarily a degree of overlap between the earlier and later chapters of the book, but it is to be hoped that the discussion of moral rights from different perspectives helps to clarify and enrich readers' understanding of the doctrine by examining it from both theoretical and practical perspectives.

Choices have been made about the areas to be explored. Chapters deal with music and film, relatively more conventional categories of copyright works that have, nevertheless, been profoundly transformed by technology; computer programs, a relatively new type of copyright subject matter, and one in which moral rights remain controversial; and artificial intelligence, whose relationship with copyright remains unsettled and uneasy.

A chapter examines moral rights in the context of the visual arts, which receive preferential treatment in moral rights provisions everywhere. They are the only area of copyright subject matter in the United States where moral rights are recognized.[175] Indeed, in the U.S. context, a fascinating paradox emerges. A narrower approach to moral rights—limited to the visual arts and arguably derived from state-level statutes protecting cultural heritage, notably the California Art Preservation Act of 1985[176]—yields powerful practical results, including the largest ever monetary award in the history of moral rights litigation, made, in the *5Pointz* case, to penalize the destruction of artworks.[177]

A separate chapter examines open source and the Creative Commons movement, which effectively amounts to a moral rights system via licensing for U.S. authors that has now spread around the world.[178] Many more areas could have been

et la liberté de création: Où situer le point d'équilibre?, HAAS AVOCATS (May 14, 2008), https://www.haas-avocats.com/actualite-juridique/le-droit-moral-et-la-liberte-de-creation-ou-situer-le-point-dequilibre and Xavier Skowron-Galvez, *Un (Mauvais) Coup Porté au Droit Moral de l'Auteur—L'Affair "Les Misérables"*, VILLAGE DE LA JUSTICE (May 18, 2007), https://www.village-justice.com/articles/mauvais-porte-droit-moral-auteur,5433.html.

[175] *See* VARA, *supra* note 5, and https://www.law.cornell.edu/uscode/text/17/106A.

[176] *See* CAPA, *supra* note 86.

[177] *See Castillo*, *supra* note 169.

[178] Mira T. Sundara Rajan, *Creative Commons: America's Moral Rights?*, 21 FORDHAM INTELL. PROP. MEDIA & ENT. L.J. 905 (2010–11). The licenses, and details of the organization's mission, are available at https://creativecommons.org/.

explored but had to be left out for the sake of reasonableness, as both the original book and this new edition expanded significantly beyond my plans.

By the conclusion of this book, readers should have gained a deeper understanding of the moral rights principle—where it comes from, how and why it developed, the rights that are protected, how the doctrine of moral rights is interpreted and applied in many of the world's major jurisdictions, and how the interpretation of the rights has evolved since their inception. The complexity of the challenges presented by new technological developments, and how they affect moral rights as distinct from copyright law overall, will be raised for the reader's consideration. It is hoped that readers will also gain a greater appreciation of the profound challenges and struggles faced by many, if not most, authors and artists working in the technological environment.

Above all, this book implicitly makes the case that moral rights are an essential instrument in support of human creativity and should be recognized as such. In many ways, they may ultimately prove to be the most relevant and durable aspect of copyright law. Moral rights support history and truth in the technological context, where human knowledge has been reduced to its most immaterial and ephemeral manifestations and is more vulnerable than ever before. Moral rights represent the human side of copyright law. They can help us to see, faintly, behind the dazzling brilliance of technology, the human face of the author.

2

Moral Rights

History of an Idea

[I]n English society as an author I was not of much account, but ... in France, where an author just because he is an author has prestige, I was.
—W. Somerset Maugham, The Razor's Edge[1]

A. **Origins of the Doctrine** 62
B. **Moral Rights at Home: France** 66
 1. "A Grace Founded in Justice": Moral Rights and Revolutionary Ideals 67
 2. The Modern Doctrine: A Controversial Model Law 76
  a. The Pre-Eminence of Moral Rights 76
  b. *Les droits moraux:* The Rights Defined 77
   i. Disclosure: Article L121-2 78
   ii. Withdrawal: Article L121-4 79
   iii. Integrity vs. Reputation: "Subjective" and "Objective" Requirements of Proof 80
   iv. Criticism 82
  c. *Le dualisme:* Practical Effects 82
   i. Inalienability and the Prohibition of Waivers 83
   ii. Permanent Protection 84
  d. Technological Features 89
   i. Audiovisual Works 89
   ii. Computer Programs 90
   iii. Moral Rights in Employment 91
   iv. Press Publication Right 92
   v. Defenses to a Moral Rights Claim: Parody and Pastiche 93
  e. Conclusions 95
C. **Germany and Monist Moral Rights: Romance of a Theory** 97
 1. The Birth of Monism 98
 2. Monism in Practice 100
 3. The Modern Moral Rights: Germany and Austria 106
 4. Moral Rights and the Basic Law 109
 5. Conclusion 110
D. **The United Kingdom: Second Thoughts** 111
 1. Early History and the Statute of Anne, 1709–10 115
  a. Early Recognition of a Moral Copyright: *Millar v. Taylor* (1769) 117
  b. Protecting Free Speech: Moral Rights Revisited in *Donaldson v. Beckett* (1774) 122
 2. Modern Approach: "Shy Beauty" 123
  a. Moral Rights in the Copyright, Designs and Patents Act 1988 126
   i. Attribution 126
   ii. Integrity: The Right to Object to Derogatory Treatment 127
   iii. A Moral Right of Privacy? 132
  b. Exceptions: Limits on Moral Rights in Employment and Technology 134
  c. Parody and Moral Rights: Is There an Exception under the CDPA? 135

[1] W. SOMERSET MAUGHAM, THE RAZOR'S EDGE 9 (2003) (1943). All websites cited in this chapter were last visited on August 6, 2023.

d. Inalienability and Waiver 135
e. Conceptual Confusion 137
3. Brexit and Moral Rights: A Sobering Future? 139
4. Conclusions: The Birth of the Common-Law Approach 140
E. Conclusion: Un-Romantic Authorship 142

A. Origins of the Doctrine

It is generally accepted that moral rights originated in continental Europe. The development of the doctrine saw it divide into two major streams, emanating from France and Germany. Stig Strömholm, an eminent and path-breaking scholar of comparative copyright law, calls moral rights a product of

> the strange interaction which takes place between, on the one hand, French practical solutions—with a weak or non-existent theoretical basis—and, on the other hand, German theorizing, which develops, for a long time, with no or hardly any support in legislation and case law.[2]

What is perhaps less well known, and more interesting, is the fact that the idea of an author's moral right received early recognition in English law. Within the space of five years and two historic decisions in the mid-eighteenth century, the concept was raised by the courts and then rejected.[3] The practical and political concerns of a particular historical moment eliminated moral rights from English copyright law. Contrary to the popular belief among English lawyers, there is nothing inherently hostile about the English attitude towards moral rights—except that, when the rights eventually found their way back into English law, it was as a French import that was viewed with concern about cultural and legal incompatibility.

France and Germany—the German-speaking principalities of the nineteenth century, and Prussia in particular[4]—are usually considered the heartland of the doctrine. Nevertheless, there can be no doubt that the idea of moral rights had spread throughout Western and Eastern Europe in the course of the nineteenth century, if not before. Italy's copyright law is generally based on personality rights, and French copyright scholar Georges Michaélidès-Nouaros, in his classic study of moral rights, observes even that, "Roman law recognized and developed respect

[2] Stig Strömholm, *Droit Moral—The International and Comparative Scene from a Scandinavian Viewpoint*, 14(1) INT'L REV. INDUS. PROP. & COPYRIGHT L. 217, 225 (1983).

[3] *Millar v. Taylor* (1769) 4 Burr. 2303, 98 ER 201 (Eng.); *Donaldson v. Beckett* [also *Becket*] (1774) 2 Brown's Parl. Cases (2d ed.) 129, 1 Eng. Rep. 837; 4 Burr. 2408, 98 Eng. Rep. 257 (Eng.).

[4] Prussian Law of 1794, cited in Carla Hesse, *Enlightenment Epistemology and the Law of Authorship in Revolutionary France, 1777–1793*, 30 REPRESENTATIONS 109, 110 (1990). *See also* Martha Woodmansee, *The Genius and the Copyright: Economic and Legal Conditions of the Emergence of the "Author"*, 17 EIGHTEENTH-CENTURY STUD. 425 (1984).

for the personality of the individual [author] in all its expansiveness."[5] Hungarian copyright scholar Péter Mezei identifies what he calls "the Hungarian precursor of the moral rights concept, which became clearer in Western European copyright systems during the nineteenth century," emerging in the 1838 work of Ferencz (Schedel) Toldy.[6] Copyright in Russia was based on early recognition of the author as a legal personality, first described in a statute of 1828, and moral rights were explicitly included in the landmark revision of copyright law that occurred in 1911.[7] Elena Muravina does not hesitate to identify moral rights as "the fundamental principle of Russian copyright protection."[8]

Notwithstanding their importance in European law, it should be recognized that moral rights also have a significant place in the histories of the world's legal systems beyond Europe. This is an essential part of the richness of the doctrine. Moral rights make an appearance in the Indian aesthetic theory of Anandavardhana, going as far back as the ninth century, in a far different social and economic context than that of nineteenth-century Europe.[9] Sneh Pandit notes, in a formula that has

[5] *See* Georges Michaélidès-Nouaros, Le droit moral de l'auteur: Étude de droit français, de droit comparé et de droit international para. 3 (1935): "Le Droit romain a reconnu et développé le respect de la personnalité de l'individu dans toute son ampleur." He continues: "La protection de la personnalité a eu lieu par l'extension de l'injuria. Les Pandectes lui consacrent un titre spécial–Dig. 47.10: De injuriis et de famosis libellis; il en est de même des Institutes de Justinien." The quotation is also valuable in indicating the common origin of moral rights and torts such as "injurious falsehood," slander, or libel, which effectively serve to protect moral rights in the United States and, to some extent, in other common-law jurisdictions. In her comprehensive exploration of international moral rights history, Elizabeth Adeney quotes the interesting comment of an Italian lawyer—"Roman law knew nothing of that law that is called copyright. But it fully recognized the droit moral": Elizabeth Adeney, The Moral Rights of Authors and Performers: An International and Comparative Analysis—New Edition para. 1.01 (2006), citing the statement from Bureau Internationale pour la Protection des Oeuvres Littéraires et Artistiques, Actes de la conference reunie a Rome 316, May 7–June 2, 1928 (1929). The 1928 Rome revision conference of the Berne Convention for the Protection of Literary and Artistic Works was a moment of unsurpassed significance in the history of moral rights: it introduced the text of moral rights provisions into the world's first and most important international treaty on copyright law. *See* Strömholm, *supra* note 2, at 221: Strömholm seems right to point out the absurdity of trying to find an ancient antecedent to moral rights.

[6] Péter Mezei, *The Development of Hungarian Copyright Law until the Creation of the First Copyright Act (1793–1884)*, *in* Cambridge Handbook of Intellectual Property in Central and Eastern Europe 37, 41 (Mira T. Sundara Rajan ed., 2019).

[7] *See* Mira T. Sundara Rajan, Copyright and Creative Freedom: A Study of Post-Socialist Law Reform 82–85 (2006). *See also* art. 2 of the Copyright Law of March 20, 1911, Polnoe Sobranie Zakonov Rossiiskoi Imperii (Sob III) [Third Complete Collection of Laws of the Russian Empire] 1914, Vol. XXXI, Item 34, 935, art. 2 (Russ.) (Russian Copyright Act 1911). By an interesting irony, the earlier law was entitled Устав о цензуре [Statute on censorship] (Apr. 22, 1828): see Vladimir Gsovski, Soviet Civil Law: Private Rights and Their Background under the Soviet Regime 606 (H.E. Yntema, ed., 1948), who comments that

> [Copyright] was conceived [in the provisions of 1828] as the exclusive right of the author or translator to publication and sale of his work during his lifetime.... This principle of copyright as the right of the author (droit d'auteur, Urheberrecht) was maintained by the imperial laws and taken over by the [S]oviet legislation when protection of copyright was restored under the Soviet regime.

[8] *See* Elena Muravina, *Copyright Transactions in Russia, Part II, "Post-Glasnost Days"*, 18 New Matter 25, 26 (1993).

[9] *See* Mira T. Sundara Rajan, *Moral Rights in Developing Countries: The Example of India—Part I*, 8(5) J. Intell. Prop. Rights 357, 360–64 (nn.15–31 and accompanying text) (2003); https://nopr.nis

fascinating implications for moral rights, "Abhinavagupta's singular contribution lies in freeing *the artistic consciousness* from all natural and practical relationships and in investing it with *meaning and positive value*, the meaning and value lying not in any end outside but wholly within the work itself."[10]

Strömholm affirms that moral rights principles were familiar to the ancients, whereas the Middle Ages were a time of stagnation.[11] Art flourished, but in a context dominated by religion, and authorial anonymity was accepted and even prized.[12] Even at this time, though, artists appear to have been aware of their own individuality, even if social norms did not recognize it.[13] Research reveals significant traces of this kaleidoscopic past to the outside observer, but the details are shrouded by time and distance.

cpr.res.in/bitstream/123456789/4907/1/JIPR%208%285%29%20357-374.pdf [*Moral Rights*, Part I]. *See also* Mira T. Sundara Rajan, *Moral Rights in Developing Countries: The Example of India—Part II*, 8(6) J. Intell. Prop. Rights 449 (2003), http://docs.manupatra.in/newsline/articles/Upload/C5BBF35E-1446-4453-814D-8FFF9885389C.pdf. In a work that is "beautiful" in its own right, scholar Sneh Pandit traces the development of Indian aesthetics from the time of the Upanishads, noting Bharata's articulation of the idea of *rasa*, whose "colossal attempt to codify the principles of poetry and drama" was a watershed moment. Bharata's text remains, as Sneh Pandit notes, the primary source of Indian aesthetic theory to the present day. *See* Sneh Pandit, An Approach to the Indian Theory of Art and Aesthetics 7-8 and generally 4–12 (1977).

[10] Pandit, *supra* note 9, at 11.

[11] Stig Strömholm, Le Droit moral de l'auteur en droit allemand, français et scandinave avec un aperçu de l'evolution internationale: Étude de droit comparé, vol. 1 (1967).

[12] *See* Pandit, *supra* note 9, at 134, for echoes of a similar attitude in Indian culture of a certain epoch; he quotes from a pioneering writer on Indian art and aesthetics, Ananda Coomaraswamy to explain how, in the "total traditional approach ... [t]he artist as maker, is a personality much greater than that of any conceivable individual; the names of even the greatest artists are unknown." The positions described here are not necessarily consistent with one another; they extend across extended periods of civilization and reflect artistic and social evolution over centuries (and even millennia). Treating this subject in proper depth is beyond the scope of the present study, but the comments here may help the reader to gain a foretaste of the richness and complexity of Indian aesthetic thought, including perspectives on authorship.

[13] *See, e.g.*, Jed Perl, *"Anonymous No More": Review of "Pen and Parchment: Drawing in the Middle Ages," The Metropolitan Museum of Art, through August 23, 2009*, The New Republic (July 27, 2023), https://newrepublic.com/article/60883/anonymous-no-more. Perl comments:

> The place of individual expression in art has long been a controversial subject. Many scholars are convinced that before the fifteenth or sixteenth century, artists did not see their work as grounded in some personal impulse or sensibility. And it is true that only beginning in the Renaissance was the art of drawing written about in an extended way and were drawings, those immediate records of the artist's hand, seriously collected. [Curator and author Melanie] Holcomb must be aware that she is challenging a good deal of received opinion when she argues for the importance of drawing as a distinctive creative act in pre-Renaissance Europe. She is a scholar who is as scrupulous as she is audacious, as careful as she is bold. She makes good on her promise, as she explains in the altogether admirable catalogue, "to make visible the work of the medieval draftsman, to sort out its myriad forms and uses, and to highlight where and when drawing was especially resonant as an aesthetic choice." "Aesthetic choice" is a very daring idea to ascribe to the anonymous artists of the tenth or eleventh centuries, but Holcomb goes right ahead and does it.

The doctrine seems to fascinate lawyers and a mystique has grown up around it. But the twin propositions, "it has always existed" and "we discovered it first" only serve to obscure moral rights further. As Strömholm observes,

> Those legal scholars who have written about *droit moral* have ... consciously or unconsciously [been] dominated by the ancient juristic notion that law ... improves with age: *prior tempore, potior jure.*[14]

What seems clear is that moral rights emerged informally. This should urge us towards a more practical and realistic appreciation of the doctrine today. In fact, a similar observation could be made about copyright law as a whole. As Thomas Paris observes,

> The origin of copyright is uncertain, because it is diluted. In the first place, the system was not conceived as a law fulfilling a precise objective. On the contrary, it was forged out of timely decisions made in response to particular problems. Accordingly, it emerged locally. Moreover, it did not appear immediately in its current form but acquired its different components bit by bit.[15]

The tradition of modern copyright scholarship does not seek to look beyond and before the British Statute of Anne of 1709–10, which is considered to embody the landmark moment when modern copyright law first came into existence. The study of pre-colonial or pre-modern analogues of copyright in non-Western countries remains underdeveloped.

Nevertheless, this background is one of the keys to understanding the subsequent development of moral rights in modern times, and to explaining why the doctrine has been successfully absorbed into legal cultures and traditions that are profoundly different from those where it is said to "originate." Informed by this awareness, an assessment of the "modern" doctrine of moral rights suggests that it has moved away from its European origins in interesting ways, but that these movements have also helped some countries to gain a window onto pre-colonial or pre-modern concepts of culture, authorship, creativity, and morality. Moral rights promise to evolve yet further under the pressure of technological trends, including the development of generative artificial intelligence, 3D printing, and other innovations.

[14] Strömholm, *supra* note 2, at 221.

[15] *See* Thomas Paris, Le droit d'auteur: L'idéologie et le système 105 (2002):

> L'origine du droit d' auteur est flue, car diluée. D' une part, le système n'a pas été conçu comme une loi répondant à un but précis. Au contraire, il s' est forgé à partir de décisions ponctuelles prises en réponse à des problèmes singuliers. Il a donc émergé localement. D' autre part, il n'est pas apparu dès l'origine sous sa forme actuelle mais a acquis ses différentes composantes petit à petit.

From an analytical perspective, the special place claimed by France and Germany in the evolution of moral rights is important. While both traditions prioritize the moral rights concept, the two countries also represent two somewhat distinct approaches. In particular, each situates moral rights differently in relation to the broader copyright framework protecting authors' rights, including economic rights. The "dualist" system of France theorizes that moral rights and economic rights are two distinct types of authors' rights, leading to different practical consequences. In contrast, German "monism" suggests that the two categories of rights are like two sides of a single coin, the links between an author's economic and moral interests being inseparable in theory and practice. But the choice of monist or dualist approaches to moral rights has legal and practical implications far beyond the courtliness of a Franco-Prussian exchange. These two ways of thinking about the relationship between moral and economic rights have shaped the evolution of moral rights in countries around the world that have taken French and German law as models—from Canada to India, Korea to Japan[16]—choosing to emulate, alter, or reject key tenets, and developing their own regimes to varying degrees of coherence and persuasiveness.

B. Moral Rights at Home: France

Moral rights are a French notion. The idea that they originated in French law is widely accepted by legal historians, with the existence of a legal principle of attribution being affirmed in a French court of law as early as 1813.[17]

There are many reasons why French tradition is important to moral rights, the antiquity of the law being but one. First, modern French law contains one of the most comprehensive sets of provisions on moral rights in the world. At the same time, the French text is also simple and direct—an elegant solution to the

[16] *See, e.g.*, Copyright Act, R.S.C. 1985, c. C-42, ss. 14 and 28 (Can.), https://laws-lois.justice.gc.ca/eng/acts/C-42/page-5.html#h-102964; Copyright Act, 1957, s. 57 (India), http://copyright.gov.in/Documents/CopyrightRules1957.pdf; Jeojakgwonbeop [Copyright Act], amended by Act No. 9625, Apr. 22, 2009, Section 3 (arts. 11–15) (S. Kor.), https://www.law.go.kr/engLsSc.do?menuId=1&subMenuId=21&tabMenuId=117&query=%EC%A0%80%EC%9E%91%EA%B6%8C%EB%B2%95#; Chosakukenhou [Copyright Act], Law No. 52 of 2021, Section 3 (2) (arts. 18–20) (Japan), https://www.japaneselawtranslation.go.jp/en/laws/view/4207. Canada and India have both been influenced by French law through the Berne Convention, but there are also direct influences in Canada (obviously) and in India (less obviously, but the French controlled significant colonies in India, including Pondicherry). Japan's copyright law is modeled on German law, and Korean law is influenced by Japanese law.

[17] Citing the legal treatise of Pardessus and a landmark French decision, Strömholm, *supra* note 2, at 217, argues:

> If we want to fix a definite date for the earliest manifestations of the legal view which rejects the most far-reaching consequences of the doctrine of intellectual property and recognizes that despite any transfer of his economic rights the author retains a moral right to his work, the year 1814 would probably be the strongest candidate.

challenges of legislating on moral rights. In this sense, they can be considered model provisions, worthy of study and critique by every jurisdiction in the world interested in the moral rights concept.

Secondly, the moral rights doctrine found its way into English law via France. As a result, throughout the common-law world, moral rights are generally considered a "foreign" legal import.[18] Overall, the characterization is not a positive one. The translation of France's *droit moral* into the English "moral right" is not fortuitous. English law distinguishes between morality and law.[19] In French, at a purely linguistic level, the sense of a *droit moral* is different, invoking a certain type or quality of rights. *Droit moral* protects rights of a personal or intellectual nature.[20] The French word *moral* is linked with character and integrity. *Droit moral* conveys the sense of interests beyond the commercial. But it is questionable whether the English translation fully, or even adequately, captures the meaning of the French original.

1. "A Grace Founded in Justice": Moral Rights and Revolutionary Ideals

Authors' rights in France can be traced to a series of pre-Revolutionary Book Trade Regulations. Introduced in 1777, they put forward the concept of an author's right in his or her works for the first time.[21] The regulations sought to break the publishing monopoly consolidated by the Paris Publishers' and Printers' Guild, which not only covered the printing of individual texts but also extended to "whole areas of knowledge."[22] By recognizing the author, historian Carla Hesse concludes that

[18] *See, e.g.*, Gerald Dworkin, *The Moral Right of the Author: Moral Rights and the Common Law Countries*, 19 COLUM.-VLA J.L. & ARTS 229, 237–38 (1995): common-law countries have always had their own culture around moral rights—a culture of hesitation and reluctance.

[19] This point is illustrated by the great legal theory debate of the twentieth century between H.L.A. Hart and Ronald Dworkin: H.L.A. HART, THE CONCEPT OF LAW (Peter Cane, Tony Honoŕe & Jane Stapleton, eds., 1994) (1961). Dworkin's reply was initially expressed in R. DWORKIN, TAKING RIGHTS SERIOUSLY (1977).

[20] *See* Loi 92-597 du 1 juillet 1992 relative au Code de la propriété intellectuelle (partie législative) [Law 92-597 of July 1, 1992, relating to the Intellectual Property Code (Legislative part)], JOURNAL OFFICIEL DE LA RÉPUBLIQUE FRANÇAISE [J.O.] [OFFICIAL GAZETTE OF FRANCE], Feb. 8, 1994 (Code de la propriété intellectuelle), art. L111-1 (emphasis added) (Fr.), https://www.legifrance.gouv.fr/codes/texte_lc/LEGITEXT000006069414:

> L'auteur d'une oeuvre de l'esprit jouit sur cette oeuvre, du seul fait de sa création, d'un droit de propriété incorporelle exclusif et opposable à tous. Ce droit comporte des attributs d'ordre *intellectuel et moral* ainsi que des attributs d'ordre patrimonial, qui sont déterminés par les livres Ier et III du présent code.

The use of both terms, "intellectual and moral," is noteworthy.

[21] The six royal decrees on the book trade were issued on August 30, 1777: *see infra* note 37. Hesse, *supra* note 4, at 111 (notes omitted), observes: "The first legal recognition of the author in France can be dated quite precisely to the six royal decrees on the book trade of August 30, 1777. Prior to this date there was no formal legal recognition of the author or his relation to his text."

[22] Id. at 112.

the French administration hoped to "encourag[e] ... and empower [...] both the individual author and the public at large at the expense of ... corporate monopoly."[23]

But, in contrast to the Statute of Anne, the goal of legislators was not to liberate publishing from sovereign control. On the contrary, the author would now become directly accountable to the state. As Hesse points out,

> The creation of the author by the absolutist state was the product of a political initiative within the royal administration rather than a result of commercial protest, and it had the explicit purpose of consolidating state control over the form, content, and means of disseminating knowledge by removing the publisher as intermediary between the state and the author. Now the author would be directly accountable to the Crown and its laws for the publication of knowledge.[24]

This was possible because, in contrast to the position taken in the British Statute of Anne sixty-seven years before, the recognition of the author did not involve the recognition of literary *property*. Instead, just the opposite was true: the Regulations explicitly rejected the idea of a property right held by authors (or anyone else) in literature. This was not because the idea of literary property was unknown: it had actually been advanced previously by the Paris printers' monopoly, culminating in a 1726 legal brief that was written by Louis d'Héricourt for the Publishers' Guild.[25] Having acquired extensive printing privileges from the King, the printers "ironically," as Hesse observes, sought to protect those privileges from encroachment by competing printers by developing an irrefutable justification for their rights.[26] As described by Carla Hesse, this justification took the form of an argument in favor of the recognition of authors' literary property in their work, which was then rightfully acquired by the printers through publishing contracts.[27] The Paris publishers had thereby set the terms on which authors' rights were to be discussed.

The property justification for authors' rights was explicitly rejected by the King, who continued to assert that "royal law[w]as an emanation of the kings' grace alone."[28] However, the King does call it "a grace founded in Justice."[29]

Hesse identifies two potentially competing purposes behind the French administration's actions: the "enlightened" goal of "empowering both the individual author and the public at large" by "breaking up the Parisian monopoly on the nation's cultural inheritance," and the imposition of "direct ... accountab[ility]" on authors.[30] The latter point is sobering. Censoring publication through a

[23] Id. at 113.
[24] *See* id. at 114.
[25] Id. at 112.
[26] Id. at 112.
[27] Id. at 112–13.
[28] Id. at 113.
[29] Quoted id. at 113.
[30] Id. at 113, 114.

printers' monopoly might be efficient, but the advantages of making authors personally responsible to the state are equally clear. With the Revolution brewing, this shift of focus does not seem surprising. It is rare, if not impossible, for individual authors to have power enough to confront the state. In our age, even "celebrity" authors such as Russian Soviet writers Boris Pasternak and Alexander Solzhenitsyn could not succeed in publishing their works over state objections. The threat of violence holds sway over individuals as it cannot work against groups.

But these developments in France led to an interest in exploring the nature of the author's right, mobilizing enlightenment thinkers against each other. The question of authors' "property" rights in their work now became the battleground of the Enlightenment philosophers, with Diderot arguing that ideas were the property of an author's mind and Condorcet claiming that ideas were inherent in nature and could not be held as property.[31]

What does this history tell us about moral rights—the "non-property" interests of authors? Let us remember that the Paris printers were the first to create a debate around authorial "property." Once the concept of an author's rights had been recognized, it would seem that the door was theoretically open for the recognition of authors' rights on any theoretically viable basis, including the personality of the author. Indeed, Diderot's justifications for literary property can themselves be seen as personality-based justifications, since ideas are said to originate in the mind of the author and become his or her property thereby.[32] This rationale is distinct from Locke's theory of a labor-based property right for authors. Indeed, Diderot's focus on ideas seems akin to a "natural rights" theory of authorship—a valid and proven basis for the moral rights that were to emerge in the writings of German jurists on the other side of the French Revolution. The deeper history of authors' rights in France seems to highlight the indivisibility of the author's economic and personal interests more than anything else.

Why was property, rather than personality, the initial goal? This probably has little to do with copyright per se. In European social history, property emerged as a primordial factor behind the development of individual rights. In other social contexts, though, property is not necessarily linked to the recognition of individual rights in this way. For example, India was a country with well-established laws before British colonization. Indian aesthetic theory was highly developed and sophisticated, and the notion of individual authorship appears to have been well recognized from ancient times.[33] However, the accumulation of property in Indian society was, at least formally, separated from the acquisition of knowledge. The

[31] Discussed id. at 114–17 ("The Enlightenment Engages").

[32] The *philosophes* were aware of women's rights but also ambivalent: *see, e.g.*, Stanford Encyclopedia of Philosophy, *Notes to The History of Feminism: Marie-Jean-Antoine-Nicolas de Caritat, Marquis de Condorcet* (2022), https://plato.stanford.edu/entries/histfem-condorcet/notes.html.

[33] *See* Sundara Rajan, *Moral Rights*, Part I, *supra* note 9. *See also* T.S. Krishnamurti, *Copyright—Another View*, 15(3) Bull. Copyright Soc'y of the U.S.A. 217, 218 (1968).

latter was considered a higher and more valuable goal.[34] In this context, writers and poets maintained a high degree of freedom and independence, and they prized fame and reputation above all. Poets claimed attribution,[35] but attribution also acquired a symbolic character when it was applied to literature whose authors had faded into the mists of time.[36] All of this led to an intellectually and artistically thriving society, where artists were well recognized through non-property doctrines that resemble modern moral rights in their emphasis on the individual contributions of poets. The history of these systems remains to be studied in proper depth —a problem first noted by Upendra Baxi in 1986.[37] For now, it presents an interesting and valuable counterpoint to the emergence of property interests and its literary accompaniment, copyright.

Returning to pre-Revolutionary France, the last of the 1777 Regulations codifies a right of first publication—the essence of the author's right. Article V of the Decree states,

> Every author who obtains the privilege of his work in his own name shall have the right to sell it on his own premises, without being allowed, for any reason, to sell or to negotiate the sale of other books; and shall retain this privilege, for himself and his heirs, in perpetuity, provided that he does not cede it to any bookseller; in which case, the term of the privilege shall, by the sole reason of its transfer, be reduced to the lifetime of the author.[38]

[34] This point is also made by former Justice Prabha Sridevan. *See generally* Prabha Sridevan, *Intellectual Property in the Ancient Indian Texts*, *in* DIVERSITY IN INTELLECTUAL PROPERTY: IDENTITIES, INTERESTS, AND INTERSECTIONS 232 (Irene Calboli & Srividhya Ragavan eds., 2015).

[35] *See* Sundara Rajan, *Moral Rights*, Part I, *supra* note 9.

[36] For example, the legend is that Vyasa—the poet who composed the Sanskrit epic Mahabharata, one of the foundational texts of Indian civilization—dictated the poem to Lord Ganesh, the elephant-headed god, who had to break off one of his own tusks to use as a writing instrument to inscribe the poet's rapid dictation. Ganesh also had to understand every verse fully as he wrote it down. The story has innumerable sources, but a quick overview is offered by New World Encyclopedia, *Legend of Lord Ganesha and Veda Vyasa*, https://www.newworldencyclopedia.org/entry/Mahabharata.

[37] Upendra Baxi, *Copyright Law and Justice in India*, 28(4) JILI 497 (1986). *But see* Sundara Rajan, *Moral Rights*, Part I, *supra* note 9, and, more recently, Sridevan, *supra* note 33.

[38] Quoted in *Frédéric Rideau, Commentary on Linguet's opinion on the Decree of 30 August 1777 regarding privileges (Bibliothèque nationale de France: Mss Fr. 22073 No. 146)*, *in* PRIMARY SOURCES ON COPYRIGHT (1450–1900) (Lionel Bently & Martin Kretschmer, eds.), https://www.copyrighthistory.org/cam/tools/request/showRecord.php?id=commentary_f_1777b. As quoted in the article:

> Tout auteur qui obtiendra en son nom le privilège de son ouvrage, aura le droit de le vendre chez lui, sans qu'il puisse, sous aucun prétexte, vendre ou négocier d'autres livres; et jouira de son privilége, pour lui et ses hoirs, à perpétuité, pourvu qu'il ne le rétrocède à aucun libraire; au quel cas, la durée du privilége sera, par le seul fait de la cession, réduite à celle de la vie de l'auteur.

General commentary is provided—though it is less detailed than Hesse's discussion—by FRÉDÉRIC RIDEAU, *Commentary on: French Decree of 30 August 1777, on the duration of privileges (1777) in* PRIMARY SOURCES ON COPYRIGHT (1450–1900) (Lionel Bently & Martin Kretschmer, eds.), https://www.copyrighthistory.org/cam/tools/request/showRecord.php?id=commentary_f_1777a.

Can this be considered a kind of proto-recognition of moral rights through the disclosure principle? The moral right of disclosure later came to be known in French copyright law as the *droit de divulgation*, and it is the *droit moral* counterpart to the author's economic right to publish his or her own work.[39] The concept of disclosure serves to recognize that the author has a right to determine the circumstances in which his or her unpublished work will first appear before the public.[40] The Regulation allows an author to enjoy a permanent right, or "*privilége*," to sell his own work "*chez lui*," on his own premises. As is characteristic of moral rights, this right is permanent— it continues to exist "*à perpétuité*"—"but the decision to cede this privilege to a bookseller will remove its perpetual character and make it a right that lasts only for the lifetime of the author.

By way of a modern comparison, British copyright law long recognized an author's perpetual and inviolable right in his or her own unpublished work. In practice, however, this meant that unpublished works could easily fall into the unpublishable and endangered category of "orphan" works. If an author or an author's heirs failed to publish a work, the author's right might continue to persist in the absence of any identifiable person who could legally "authorize" first publication. This threat to cultural preservation—which affected documents of historical value like the letters written by soldiers during the First World War[41]—was explicitly used by the British government when it examined the broader problem of orphan works in 2014, through a blanket provision bringing an end to the copyright term in such works in the year 2039.[42]

Le Chapelier's law of 1791 represented the first attempt to consolidate the Revolutionary cultural transition by establishing the notion of an author's right to his own literary property.[43] The law of 1791 specifically sought to resolve the

[39] Now codified in the French Code de la propriété intellectuelle, *supra* note 20, at art. L121-2. It is also considered to be implicit in the Berne Convention, though it is not articulated in Art. 6*bis*: *see* Sam Ricketson & Jane Ginsburg, International Copyright and Neighbouring Rights paras. 10.53–56 (3d ed., 2022).

[40] *See* Claude Colombet, Grands principes du droit d'auteur et des droits voisins dans le monde: Approche de droit comparé 39–40 (2d ed., 1992). He notes the distinction between *divulgation* and *publication* clarified in Spanish law; in the digital environment, the two concepts tend to merge and are generally treated in this work under the single term, "disclosure." Colombet also emphasizes the role of "secrecy"—potentially "trade secrets"—in the United States.

[41] *See, e.g.*, Adam Sherwin, *Millions of Unseen "Orphan" Artworks to Be Put on Show*, The Independent (Oct. 29, 2014), https://www.independent.co.uk/arts-entertainment/art/news/millions-of-orphan-artworks-and-historic-documents-to-be-seen-under-new-copyright-laws-9824266.html.

[42] *See* Intellectual Property Office, *Copyright Notice: Duration of Copyright (Term)* (Jan. 15, 2021), https://www.gov.uk/government/publications/copyright-notice-duration-of-copyright-term/copyright-notice-duration-of-copyright-term. A useful review of the debates surrounding this measure is also provided by Jonathan Ball (UK) & Ben Mellett, *The 2039 Rule: UK Keeps Millions of Very Old Unpublished Works under Copyright Protection for Another 24 Years*, Brand Protection Blog (Mar. 2, 2015), https://www.thebrandprotectionblog.com/the-2039-rule-uk-keeps-millions-of-very-old-unpublished-works-under-copyright-protection-for-another-24-years.

[43] See, e.g., the brief, but useful, abstract at Frédéric Rideau, *Report of Le Chapelier on Dramatic Author's property (with the Decree Adopted by the National Assembly)*, *in* Primary Sources on

decades-long debate over the exclusive use of dramatic texts by the *Comédie française,* France's national theatre, which held a monopoly on the production of classic French plays.[44] Recognition of an individual right of authorship in Le Chapelier's law was a means to this end. As Jane Ginsburg points out,

> In the 1791 decree, the author's concerns do not occupy center stage. The report on the 1791 decree arose in a dispute between dramatists and the Comedie Française—the latter once the beneficiary of the exclusive right to produce theatrical works, the former once effectively indentured to the only approved theater. The decree's main goal was to proclaim the right of all citizens to open their own theaters and to produce plays, as the decree's first article states. Authors' rights are an adjunct to this freedom.[45]

But the principle of an individual right of authorship that emerged here was subsequently extended to other areas of intellectual and creative work. As such, Le Chapelier's law provided the basic model for the regulation of publishing in the post-Revolutionary era. The law was generalized in a new statute, the Decree on the Property Rights of Authors of July 19, 1793.[46] The 1793 legislation created a general right of literary property, to be exercised by authors in all genres as an exclusive right over their work, for a limited time: the lifetime of the author and ten years after his death.[47]

Ironically, the new laws, while introducing the concept of literary property, actually reduced the practical extent of authors' rights. As Gregory S. Brown points out,

Copyright (1450–1900) (Lionel Bently & Martin Kretschmer, eds.), http://www.copyrighthistory.org/.

44 *See* Jane C. Ginsburg, *A Tale of Two Copyrights*, 64(5) Tulane L. Rev. 991, 1005–09 (1990), https://scholarship.law.columbia.edu/faculty_scholarship/620/.

45 Id. at 1006 (notes omitted).

46 Décret du 19 juillet 1793 relatif aux droits de propriété des auteurs d'écrits en tout genre, compositeurs de musique, peintres et dessinateurs [Decree of July 19, 1793 relating to the property rights of authors of writings of all kinds, composers of music, painters and designers] (L. 15, 139; B. 32, 147, Rapp. Lakanal), Duv. & Boc. 35, (Fr.). *See* Gregory S. Brown, *From Liberty to Patriotism: Conclusion Copyright, Community and Enlightenment, in* Literary Sociability and Literary Property in France: Beaumarchais, the Société des Auteurs Dramatique, and the Comédie Française, 1775–1793 116, 138 (2006).

47 But see Hesse, *supra* note 4, at 128, who mentions that the ten-year-term *post-mortem auctoris* is for the benefit of both heirs and publishers, suggesting that the author, in keeping with pre-Revolutionary practice, would normally assign his work to a publisher in perpetuity. She goes on to comment that, with the new law, "the cultural capital of the Old Regime was definitively remanded from the private hands of heirs and publishers into the public domain," because the classic authors had all been dead for more than ten years. It is worth noting that the term of protection in the Statute of Anne was fourteen years, renewable for fourteen more, with no protection after the author's death: Statute of Anne, 8 Anne. c. 19 (1710), §§II and XI (Eng.), https://avalon.law.yale.edu/18th_century/anne_1710.asp (exclusivity in books in print was protected for a transitional period of twenty-one years: id. §II).

> The limited dimension of the authors' victory has been little appreciated due to La Harpe's and Le Chapelier's broad rhetorical framing of the authors' objectives as the "liberty" of "all men of letters" and the abolition of "exclusive privilege" on behalf of "the public." These claims, politically effective in 1790–91, have confused the issue for historians, many of whom have not recognized that the law did not grant the primary concern of authors ... These writers had not sought droits d'auteur in the sense of "human rights" but instead wanted to redefine their own literary sociability as the pursuit of the public good.[48]

The point is an important one, because it shows how the authors' perceptions of their own interests were, in a sense, co-opted by the rhetoric of the French Revolution. Authors initially saw the complementarity of their rights with the public good: authors usually write to be read.[49] But Brown's analysis would also benefit from a consideration of its immediate context. The law of 1791 followed upon a period of regulatory chaos, and, measured against this, the extent of the rights it conferred upon authors, as well as the relative novelty of those rights, was significant. The post-Revolutionary scheme for authors offered less formal protection than the pre-Revolutionary Book Decrees, but the rights that were offered worked on a new conceptual footing: an individual right of authorship, based in property, over which the threat of accountability to the Crown did not cast a shadow.

The post-Revolutionary history of moral rights in France is noteworthy in two ways. First, the doctrine emerged informally, through judges' pronouncements, and continued to develop in the same way for decades. The first mention of authors' rights per se in French legislation occurs at the relatively late date, vis-à-vis English law, of 1777.[50] By this time, the English courts had already considered and rejected the concept of moral rights, and they did so by analyzing and testing the provisions of the Statute of Anne of 1710.[51]

The complexity underlying French concepts of authorship in the Revolutionary environment is striking. Carla Hesse discusses the opposing ideological forces that shaped the authorship and the law that was to contain it. In doing so, she arrives at a key insight: there is a fundamental tension at the heart of copyright between the natural rights rationale for authors' rights and corresponding copyright notions

48 Ironically, the adoption of the new law actually signified a scaling back of authors' rights, in the practical sense of a reduced term of protection, and the consequent loss of benefits to the authors' heirs. *See* Brown, *supra* note 45, at 138–39, and, in particular, his discussion at 138 of Carla Hesse's analysis of the 1777 book trade regulations.

49 See my comments on the complementarity of these two fundamental justifications of copyright policy in Mira T. Sundara Rajan, *Moral Rights in the Public Domain: Copyright Matters in the Works of Indian National Poet C. Subramania Bharati*, Singapore J. Legal Stud. 161 (2001), https://law.nus.edu.sg/sjls/wp-content/uploads/sites/14/2021/07/1719-2001-sjls-jul-161.pdf.

50 *See* Hesse, *supra* note 4, at 111–14.

51 *See* the *Millar* and *Donaldson* cases, *supra* note 3.

of property, ownership, and public interest—what she calls "an epistemologically impure and unstable legal synthesis."[52] From the very beginning, the French view of copyright was driven by competing policy rationales, a fact that is now clearly apparent in all modern copyright systems.[53] In particular, according to Hesse, the concept of authors' rights that emerged in eighteenth-century France "combined an instrumentalist notion of the public good" with a theory of authorship based upon "natural rights."[54] Reconciling these two interests—balancing the public interest against the prerogatives of authors—remains a critical challenge. The modern version of this tension is a public, ongoing debate between copyright owners and those who claim to speak in the public interest, but the language adopted by right-holders is, crucially, the language of authorship.[55]

Brown comments that the dynamics surrounding French Revolutionary copyright have colored our appreciation of the public domain by distorting the authors' vision of their own relationship to the public:

> In the longer term, this rhetoric has led to a misunderstanding of public domain as it was conceived in 1790. Intended as a claim made by authors about their own position as advocates for a shared cultural heritage, public domain became instead a value-neutral category to which commercial intermediaries—in this case, theater managers—would lay claim and thereby situate themselves as arbiters between the authors and the public.[56]

[52] Hesse, *supra* note 4, at 130, points out that:

> Contrary to Foucault's Diderotist interpretation, the revolutionary legislation actually reflected not one but both sides of the Enlightenment debate, effecting an epistemologically impure and unstable legal synthesis that combined an instrumentalist notion of the public good with a theory of authorship based upon natural rights. Precisely because of this legal instability, the regime by which the public exchange of ideas was regulated would be challenged and renegotiated repeatedly over the course of the revolutionary period. The legal history of French authorship thus suggests that Foucault's essay requires a historical revision: the central mechanism of the modern regime of knowledge, as it emerged from the epistemology of the French Enlightenment, was unstable from its very beginnings.

[53] See the discussion of English copyright history, *infra* notes 206–38 and 306–10, and accompanying text: the same was clearly true of English copyright law.

[54] Hesse's reference to "natural rights" is also noteworthy:

> The proposed law appeared incoherent and arbitrary: on the one hand it recognized a property right, and on the other, by defining it as noninheritable, it also advanced an instrumentalist notion of the public good that flew in the face of natural rights theory and explicitly undermined the actual power of individuals to exercise their constitutionally guaranteed right. It was an attempt at a compromise between the two epistemological stances, between individual and collective claims on ideas.

Hesse, *supra* note 4, at 121.

[55] See the discussion of *Millar v. Taylor* and *Donaldson v. Beckett*, *supra* note 3. The strategy of using "authorship" to promote the prerogatives of ownership is as old as the 1700s.

[56] Brown, *supra* note 45, at 139.

In other words, the Revolutionaries, like ourselves, cared about public access to knowledge as well as the recognition of authors. The simultaneous recognition of both principles made the law conceptually unstable, but it was an inevitable result of practical concerns about knowledge and its place in society. In early French law, the priority was to liberate literature from corporate control. The French sovereign wished to break the powerful monopoly of the Parisian printers. An analogous conflict had been played out in England, nearly a century earlier, but with different stakes—state censorship versus a free press—and different outcomes. The French solution was to exalt authorship—Hesse comments that "[t]he author was conceived as a little mirror of the king."[57] But the English chose to exalt law, and, in particular, to affirm the integrity, and impregnability, of the Statute of Anne.

But these solutions were never definitive. Society is constantly evolving. At best, one stream of copyright theory or policy can dominate others for a time. Copyright inherently involves diverse interests; it is an area of law that is deeply intertwined with social phenomena, which are constantly evolving. While Hesse draws attention to the dark side of this reality—"impur[ity]" and "[in]stab[ility]"—there is also a brighter side, which is copyright's adaptability. Copyright, despite the monolithic term, is a hodge-podge of diverse, interconnected concepts. Its heterogeneity gives it the potential to adapt to different social circumstances and needs and is the secret of its longevity.

In modern legal systems, the first codification of practices marks a seminal point of recognition, transforming what is customary into more formalized legal interests. In the case of French authors' rights, the moment of initial codification was one of powerful coincidence. Authors' rights were defined as the French Revolution ignited, and the concept of individual rights of authorship was part of a larger movement in which the idea of human rights was first articulated in the Western world, embodied in the epoch-making "Declaration of the Rights of Man."[58] Moral rights were not identified as such in the Revolutionary document, but the recognition of individual authorship laid the foundation for moral rights to emerge. The recognition of a right to disclose one's unpublished work is framed in terms that resemble moral rights.

The timing is also crucial from another point of view: although the French courts pioneered the recognition of moral rights, the country was a relative latecomer to formal codification of them. Moral rights were not brought into French legislation until 1957. They are now subject to detailed elucidation in the current *Code de la proprieté intellectuelle.*[59]

[57] Hesse, *supra* note 4, at 113–14.

[58] Declaration of the Rights of Man and of the Citizen, adopted Aug. 26 or 27, 1789 by the National Constituent Assembly (Fr.), https://www.elysee.fr/en/french-presidency/the-declaration-of-the-rights-of-man-and-of-the-citizen.

[59] Code de la propriété intellectuelle, *supra* note 20. The French Code was adopted in 1992 and replaced the previous copyright law of 1957.

2. The Modern Doctrine: A Controversial Model Law

The French provisions on moral rights are framed with elegance and simplicity. A formal preface provides a clear description of the rights.[60] They protect the author's "name, quality of authorship, and work."[61] The rights are inalienable.[62] They are also permanent, and may be inherited or assigned to a third party by an author's will.[63] The clarity and comprehensiveness of French moral rights language almost certainly reflects prior judicial elaboration of the relevant principles, whose character was practical and informal, and on whose foundation the legislation is built.[64]

Each right is balanced by definite limits on its exercise. These are described alongside the statement of the right itself, in each paragraph of the law. While these structural features easily make the French Code a model of legislative clarity and precision, the substance of the rights, judged by international norms, is controversial. In some respects, French law includes provisions that are unusually expansive, and in others, its terms imply practical limits on the acquisition and use of copyright works. The provisions seem to fit well with French priorities. Would a moral rights framework of such breadth be appropriate for other countries? The following analysis will attempt to shed light on the applicability of a French model of moral rights in the international copyright community at large.

a. The Pre-Eminence of Moral Rights

In the French Code, moral rights precede the economic rights of the author,[65] a structural choice that infuses them with a sense of priority. Indeed, current commentators note the "pre-eminence" of moral rights. This leads, among other things, to implications for the interpretation of artists' contracts, which must be read in conformity with the provisions.[66]

[60] Id. at art. L121-1. It is worth noting that copyright, as a whole, is approached in the same way. *See, e.g.*, id. at art. L111-1:

> L'auteur d'une oeuvre de l'esprit jouit sur cette oeuvre, du seul fait de sa création, d'un droit de propriété incorporelle exclusif et opposable à tous.
>
> Ce droit comporte des attributs d'ordre intellectuel et moral ainsi que des attributs d'ordre patrimonial, qui sont déterminés par les livres Ier et III du présent code.

[61] Id. at art. L121-1.

[62] Id.

[63] Id.

[64] Id. at Ch. 1 ("Droits moraux") (arts. L121-1–L121-9).

[65] The economic rights are known as *droits patrimoniaux* in French law: id. at Titre 2, Ch. II ("Droits patrimoniaux") (arts. L122-1–L122-12).

[66] Code de la propriété intellectuelle commenté, vol. II, Droits des Auteurs, Commentaire 92 (Pierre Sirinelli, Sylviane Durrande, Antoine Latreille & Jeanne Daleau eds., 2009). In common-law jurisdictions, too, contracts can, of course, be modified according to doctrines of fairness and equity, such as the unconscionability of contract terms or the unfair duress under which an agreement is formed. However, in the French scheme, the possibility of reading the terms of contracts into conformity with moral rights provisions is built into the Code.

But the pre-eminence of moral rights is not universally agreed upon by French authors. In his 1969 study, Pierre Recht takes issue with this view, arguing that the importance of moral rights in French law is greatly exaggerated by commentators.[67] Indeed, Recht argues that moral rights are "unreal." Instead, authors' rights include both economic and moral interests that are inseparable.[68] Recht comments,

> [M]y research seeks to show that the property right of the author, in particular, includes monetary and moral prerogatives that are indissolubly united and cannot be separated. The so-called moral right is an unreal creation, which, for a century, we have attempted in vain to define in a manner that is petty and perfectly superfluous.... The truth is that copyright should be considered a new kind of unitary property right made up of multiple prerogatives, monetary and moral, different from property in the usual sense, which, during the first half of the nineteenth century, was called upon to resolve every problem.[69]

b. *Les droits moraux:* The Rights Defined

Notwithstanding these differences of opinion about the place of moral rights within the French copyright hierarchy, there can be little doubt that the French law represents the most comprehensive and developed set of provisions on moral rights in the world.[70] When moral rights were first recognized by French judges, they referred to the author's *droit moral*, reflecting the unity of the underlying doctrine that then manifested itself in the different moral rights. The legislation, however, converts the term into its plural form, *droits moraux*. As Pierre Sirinelli and his colleagues comment,

> Before codification, it was a matter, in the law, of the "moral right." Since then, the legislation deals with "moral rights." This passage into the plural causes us to lose sight of the fundamental unity of the moral right and the importance of common

[67] Pierre Recht, Le Droit d'auteur, une nouvelle forme de propriété: Histoire et théorie 274–75 (1969).

[68] More recently, this terrain has been revisited by Vivant and Bruguière. See their very interesting commentary in Michel Vivant & Jean-Michel Bruiguière, Le Droit d'Auteur 464–66 (paras. 24–28) (2009) (where they conclude that moral rights can be considered a fundamental right, "like that of property").

[69] Recht, *supra* note 67, at 274–75:

> [M]on étude tend à montrer que le droit de propriété de l'auteur, notamment, comporte des prérogatives pécuniaires et morales indissolublement unies et qu'on ne peut séparer. Le droit dit moral est une création irréelle, que depuis un siècle on a essayé vainement de définir d'une façon congrue et parfaitement superflue.... La vérité c'est qu'il faudrait concevoir le droit d'auteur comme une forme nouvelle de propriéte unitaire comprenant des prérogatives multiples, pécuniaires et morales, différente de la propriété ordinaire à laquelle on a vainement, pendant la première moitié du XIXè siècle, demandé de résoudre tous les problèmes.

Interestingly, Recht cites Canadian commentator Fox, who succinctly expresses his critique of moral rights in the Berne Convention as "vague, poorly drafted, sententiously expressed and without practical use": id. at 273.

[70] A conviction also noted by Sirinelli et al., *supra* note 65, at 92.

rules, but it can be explained by little differences in the regime which can arise according to the specific rights. Thus, the *post mortem* treatment of these is quite different.[71]

The Code protects five moral rights: attribution,[72] integrity,[73] disclosure or first publication,[74] withdrawal,[75] and a right against abusive criticism.[76] With the exception of the right of disclosure, none of these rights is absolute; each must be weighed against the defense offered by the alleged offender. The French law has also framed specific exceptions to moral rights, including the special cases of parody and pastiche, elaborated below.

i. Disclosure: Article L121-2

The French Code specifically entitles the author to determine the circumstances in which his work is first published. Article L121-2 creates an exclusive right to decide on publication, and to negotiate the circumstances in which publication will occur. The right is as near to absolute as any right could be, but its impact is slightly softened by the subsequent Article L121-3, which makes provision for a court to intervene in the case of a deceased author whose heirs or descendants engage in "notorious abuse" of the divulgation right.[77] The exception applies only to the case of an author who is deceased. Where the author remains alive, the author alone is entitled to control disclosure of the work. No measure of reasonableness can be applied to an author's own decision to refrain from publication.[78] The right of disclosure outlasts the author's copyright.[79]

[71] Id. at 92–93:

> Avant la codification, il était question, dans la loi, du "droit moral." Depuis cette dernière, la législation traite des "droits moraux." Ce passage au pluriel fait perdre de vue l'unité de fondement du droit moral et l'importance des règles communes mais s'explique par les petites différences de régime qui peuvent se rencontrer suivant les prérogatives. Ainsi, le sort post mortem de ces dernières est assez différent.

[72] *Attribution, paternité.* Paternity, of course, is no longer favored, though the connotation of parenting is lost with the shift to attribution: Michel Walter & Valérie-Laure Benabou, *European Community Law*, Presentation to the Conference on the moral rights of authors, sponsored by the Economic and Social Research Council (ESRC), and with the participation of the United States Copyright Office (Mar. 31–Apr. 1, 2017), https://professormira.com/glasgow-conference-2.

[73] *Droit au respect de l' oeuvre.* The French terminology, "the right of respect for the work," emphasizes the cultural aspect of the right, focusing on the work rather than the author. See discussion of the French integrity right *infra* notes 84–89 and accompanying text; see also, more generally, *infra* notes 92–118 and accompanying text.

[74] *Divulgation.*

[75] *Droit de repentir ou retrait.*

[76] *See* French Code de la propriété intellectuelle, *supra* note 20, at art. L121-3 ("*abus notoire*"). This can also occur in the case of conflict amongst the representatives, in the absence of the right holder, or in the case of unclaimed works.

[77] Id.

[78] Presumably, evidence of the author's own objections to the publication of a given work would be enough to allow the heirs to continue to refuse publication. Historical circumstance could see the author's will being overridden, but this would violate the integrity of the author's individual prerogative to disclose, or withhold, his or her own work.

[79] Protected, in conformity with the EU norm, for seventy years after the author's death: French Code de la propriété intellectuelle, *supra* note 20, at art. L123-1.

ii. Withdrawal: Article L121-4

The right of withdrawal allows an author to remove a work from circulation that has already been published; it is also known as a right of recall. In a sense, it can be seen as a counterpart to the right of disclosure, but the French Code gives it its own article. An author's reasons for withdrawing a work may be diverse. Under French law, a change of mind or belief is sufficient reason to withdraw a work, as the idea of "repentance" is built into the French terminology (*droit de repentir ou de retrait*)[80] for the right. New circumstances after the publication of a work, or any other factor that leads to what Georges Michaélidès-Nouaros refers to as "profound discord between the new state of the author's mind and his work," are valid reasons to exercise the right.[81]

The objective of this right is to remove a work from circulation, but this goal generally cannot be achieved without significant costs to the publisher. Accordingly, Article L121-4 balances this right against a requirement that the author must indemnify in advance the assignee who expects to suffer a commercial loss as a result of his decision.[82] Should the author eventually decide to publish the work again, the original publisher will have the first right of refusal on the work and will be entitled to publish it on the very terms of the original agreement.[83] The clause provides safeguards against the possibility of an author using the right of withdrawal to escape from the terms of a publication contract which might later seem undesirable—or, indeed, to alter those terms through the exercise of the right by seeking to republish the work on new terms with a new publisher.

The right of withdrawal was codified only in 1992, but a consideration of French treatises such as Michaélidès-Nouaros's 1935 work shows it to be an established part of French moral rights tradition. The right was famously tested in the 1897 case of *Eden v. Whistler*.[84] Whistler had painted a portrait of Lady Eden, which he agreed to paint for a payment that was considerably less than what he had originally wanted for the work. Lord Eden, her husband, commissioned the work. He saw the finished painting in Whistler's studio and was satisfied with it. He gave the

[80] Id. at art. L121-4.

[81] Michaélidès-Nouaros, *supra* note 5, at para. 163 ("un désaccord profond entre le nouvel état d'esprit de l'auteur et son oeuvre").

[82] *See* French Code de la propriété intellectuelle, *supra* note 20, at art. L121-4 ("indemniser préalablement le cessionnaire du préjudice que ce repentir ou ce retrait peut lui causer").

[83] Id. at art. L121-4: the work must be offered to the original assignee "par priorité" and "aux conditions originairement déterminées."

[84] Whistler wrote about the conflict himself. *See* J.M. Whistler, Eden Versus Whistler: The Baronet and The Butterfly—A Valentine with a Verdict (Leopold Classic Library 2017) (1899). The incident is reviewed in detail by Elena Cooper, *Whistler's Portrait and Copyright in Artistic Works*, Institute of Art & Law (July 15, 2021), https://ial.uk.com/whistlers-portrait-and-copyright-in-artistic-works.

painter a check for the amount that (he thought) they had agreed upon. Whistler accepted the check, but he did not deliver the painting to Lord Eden, who was travelling at the time. Instead, he exhibited it at a salon in Lord Eden's absence. When Lord Eden returned, he demanded delivery of the painting, but Whistler refused and returned the money instead.

In November of 1894, Lord Eden initiated legal proceedings. Whistler then painted over Lady Eden's face with another woman's face and made some other, minor changes to the work. Lord Eden argued that the painting had been complete when he first saw it, in February of that year, but Whistler argued that he was entitled to retain it and to continue to work on it as long as, and presumably in whatever manner, he chose. His lawyer stated, "[Y]ou cannot oblige an artist, to give up an unfinished work and allow the incomplete creations of his heart and brain to circulate the world," and this argument persuaded the court.[85] Whistler was entitled to keep the painting, but he owed Lord Eden the return of the payment, as well as damages. These principles remain intact in current French law surrounding the artist's right of withdrawal.

iii. Integrity vs. Reputation: "Subjective" and "Objective" Requirements of Proof

French law frames the right of integrity in broad and direct terms: Article L121-1 tells us that the author has a right to "respect for his or her work." In contrast to the Berne Convention, there is no requirement that an author needs to show damage to his or her reputation or honor.[86] In this sense, the French right of integrity is framed in the strongest possible terms. The author need only show a modification of the work to which the author objects. The author's personal objection is sufficient grounds for a legal action. By implication, any modification of the work to which the author objects is to be considered a *prima facie* violation of the right of integrity.

This position would be labeled "subjective" in common-law countries because the author's own opinion is considered an inadequate basis on which to make a finding of an integrity violation. Common-law countries claim to be more "objective" by requiring "proof of damage" to the author's reputation (or "honor," following the language of the Berne Convention).[87] That "proof" often takes the form of expert opinions, which are said to be more "objective" than the opinion of

[85] Quoted in Cooper, *supra* note 82; original source Whistler, *supra* note 82.

[86] See in-depth discussion of the Berne provision in Art. 6*bis*, Chapter 3 *infra*.

[87] The term is legally vague and has been eliminated by Ireland: *see* Copyright and Related Rights Act 2000 (Act No. 28/2000), s. 109(1) (Ir.), https://www.irishstatutebook.ie/eli/2000/act/28/section/109/enacted/en/html#sec109 (also discussed in Chapter 4, *infra* notes 316–19 and accompanying text). Adeney explores this theme in Elizabeth Adeney, *The Moral Right of Integrity: The Past and Future of "Honour"*, 22 INTELL. PROP. Q. 111 (2005).

the author, though this claim is debatable and should not be taken at face value.[88] Alternatively, more "objective" measures of damage to reputation might include evidence about lost sales—but a measurement like this is economic in nature and highlights the reality that reputation is as much, or more, an economic issue than a "moral" issue.

Since the discussion of moral rights in common-law countries often focuses on who bears the burden of proof, and how that burden must be discharged in conflicts involving moral rights,[89] it is worth noting that such discussions are largely irrelevant in the French context. In theory, under French law, it could be said that the person who has made the modification bears the burden of showing that it does not violate the integrity of the work. In practice, though, if it is the author who is personally bringing the suit, this notional burden of proof could never be discharged. The author's opinion would be sufficient to show a moral rights violation. Only in cases where the person bringing the suit is *not* the author—where a descendant of the author or some other person acting on the author's behalf is bringing the claim—might the court be in a position to make a factual (but speculative) determination about whether or not the author would have objected to the treatment involved. On facts like these, it might be theoretically possible for a defendant to prevail against a suit for the violation of the moral right of integrity.

Indeed, a new trend in moral rights interpretation was suggested by the *Hugo* case of 2007,[90] where a defendant prevailed in spite of direct evidence of the author's words being presented in court—though the author himself, Victor Hugo, was long deceased.[91] The reasoning in *Hugo* has implications for the exercise of

[88] For example, experts are usually paid by either of the parties in common-law lawsuits and are therefore not "objective" in this sense: *see, e.g.*, *Castillo v. G&M Realty L.P.*, Nos. 18-498-cv (L), 18-538-cv (CON), 2020 U.S. App. LEXIS 5228 (2d Cir. Feb. 20, 2020), https://www.mintz.com/sites/default/files/media/documents/2020-03-25/18-498_amd_opn.pdf (the *5Pointz* case), discussed in Chapter 4, *infra* note 164 and accompanying text, and in Chapter 8, *infra* notes 53–57 and accompanying text.

[89] For example, this was a crucial factor in the Canadian Supreme Court case of *Théberge v. Galerie d'Art du Petit Champlain Inc.* [2002] 2 S.C.R. 336, 2002 SCC 34, leading to confusion surrounding the framing of copyright claims under Canadian law. In the years since that decision, delivered by a split Supreme Court, this issue has not received further clarification in Canada. The decision is discussed in detail in Mira T. Sundara Rajan, *Moral Rights and Economic Rights: Overlapping Protection of Authors under Copyright Law, in* OVERLAPPING INTELLECTUAL PROPERTY RIGHTS 303 (Neil Wilkof, Shamnad Basheer & Irene Calboli eds., 2d ed., 2023).

[90] *Pierre Hugo v. Editions Plon*, Cour d'appel [CA] [regional court of appeal] Paris, 1e ch., Mar. 31, 2004, 202 RIDA (Oct. 2004), *reversed* Cour de cassation [Cass.] [supreme court for judicial matters] 1e civ., Jan. 30, 2007, Bull. civ. I, No. 125 (Fr.), https://www.legifrance.gouv.fr/juri/id/JURITEXT000017627153.

[91] See Xavier Skworon-Galvez, *Un (mauvais) coup porté au droit moral de l'auteur—L'affaire "Les Misérables"*, Village de la Justice (May 18, 2011), http://www.village-justice.com/articles/mauvais-porte-droit-moral-auteur, 5433.html; Hugo's description of his own work was cited, and accepted as evidence of his opposition to a sequel in this case. The court states:

> "[S]i ce dernier [Victor Hugo] ne s'était jamais formalisé et encore moins opposé aux adaptations scéniques de ses livres, voire à l'adoption par d'autres auteurs de tel ou tel de ses personnages, il était en revanche établi que l'écrivain n'aurait pas accepté qu'un tiers auteur puisse donner une suite aux Misérables." ["[I]f the latter had never taken offense or even opposed theatrical adaptations of his books, even to the adoption of one or another of his

moral rights after the author's death in France, and this is discussed in more detail below.[92]

iv. Criticism

A right to protect one's work from abusive criticism is recognized in French law, but it is subject to strict limitations. The criticism must be unfair, excessive, or "vexatious"—and if critics can show that they are truly engaged in the creation of a parody or pastiche of the original work, they will, in the absence of harm to the author, be exempt from liability.[93] To this tradition, the European judgment in *Deckmyn* adds another layer by making explicit a new anti-discrimination principle: treatments of the work that imply a discriminatory intent on the part of the original author cannot be justified on the ground that they are parodies.[94] This is discussed in further detail below.[95]

c. *Le dualisme:* Practical Effects

The French Code is based on the theory of an unbreakable relationship between author and work. In French law, this ideal translates into a theory that is known as dualism, meaning that economic and moral rights are treated as two distinct and independent types of rights.[96] In practice, dualism means that legal limitations on economic rights need not apply to moral rights. Accordingly, Article L121-1 specifies that moral rights, in contrast to economic rights, are inalienable, and are protected in perpetuity.[97]

> characters by other authors, on the other hand, it was established that the writer would not have accepted that a third author could create a sequel to Les Misérables"].

Id.

[92] *See infra* notes 92–118 and accompanying text.

[93] Parody and pastiche are defined elsewhere in the Code and offer important defenses in an integrity dispute. *See* French Code de la propriété intellectuelle, *supra* note 20, at art. L122-5(4). Somewhat awkwardly, the provisions appear in the section of the Code dealing with economic rights (*droits patrimoniaux*), but the language provides clearly that the author cannot object to these reuses of his work once it is disclosed—"Lorsque l'oeuvre a été divulguée, l'auteur ne peut interdire [Once the work has been disclosed, the author cannot prohibit]"—presumably for neither economic nor moral reasons. "Lois du genre" appears to refer to harm to the author, not just intent to harm. Harm that occurs is sufficient, in other words, with or without the intent to harm. For an excellent explanation of the status of parody in French law, with a comparison to common-law systems, see Caroline Rawski, *La Parodie: Etude comparée en Droit d'Auteur et Copyright*, LES BLOGS PÉDAGOGIQUES (June 4, 2007), http://blogs.u-paris10.fr/content/la-parodie-etude-compar%C3%A9e-en-droit-d%E2%80%99auteur-et-copyright-par-caroline-rawski.

[94] Case C-201/13, *Deckmyn v. Vandersteen*, ECLI:EU:C:2014:2132 (Sept. 3, 2014), https://eur-lex.europa.eu/legal-content/EN/TXT/?uri=CELEX%3A62013CJ0201. The Court of Justice of the European Union provided a human rights justification rather than discussing moral rights: see the discussion of *Deckmyn* in Chapter 1, *supra* notes 115–28 and accompanying text.

[95] *See infra* notes 136–45 and accompanying text.

[96] The contrast with German monism, which sees the two as varieties of the same right, is discussed *infra* notes 150–55 and accompanying text.

[97] According to the U.S. Constitution, the idea of rights "prescribed for limited times" seems to be the very essence of copyright protection—an issue that defined the debate on extending copyright term

i. Inalienability and the Prohibition of Waivers

In French law, inalienability translates into a general prohibition on waiving moral rights. Waivers are explicitly forbidden: moral rights are "perpétuel, inaliénable et imprescriptible."[98] An author cannot make a contract to divest himself or herself completely of moral rights, even if he or she should want to do so. This approach is not universally approved in French scholarship. For example, Pierre Recht finds it patronizing, and he argues that authors should not be deprived of the opportunity to choose whether or not to retain their moral rights.[99]

But limiting an author's choices when it comes to moral rights may be necessary in tough bargaining environments where authors have little bargaining power. The purpose of the legislation is not to protect authors from themselves; rather, it is to protect authors' rights in an unequal, or even hostile, bargaining environment. After all, depending on the context, the right to waive one's rights may be barely a hair's breadth removed from the expectation that one will do so.

As Michel Walter comments,

> Given the inferior bargaining position of authors, this is a significant feature of monistic as well as dualistic concepts of civil law moral rights and a major difference compared with the legal tradition of common-law countries, where most commonly the transfer or waiver of moral rights is admitted and valid.[100]

In practice, making comprehensive waivers unavailable means that French copyright industries must work with authors' moral rights as a fact of doing business in France. Copyright contracts cannot be used to "contract out" of moral rights, thereby softening the French legislative regime—a typical occurrence when it comes to moral rights in common-law jurisdictions.[101] In Canada, for example, "blanket waivers" may be sought in publishing contracts.[102]

in the *Eldred* case. It does not necessarily follow that the U.S. constitutional framework is incompatible with moral rights, but the recognition of those rights in the United States would clearly require an approach different from the French: *Eldred v. Ashcroft*, 239 F.3d 372 (2001), *aff'd*, 537 U.S. 186 (2003).

[98] *See* French Code de la propriété intellectuelle, *supra* note 20, at art. L121-1.

[99] Recht, *supra* note 66.

[100] Michel M. Walter, *Dualistic Aspects in Monistic Systems of Moral Rights*, 14(4) JIPLP 318, 326 (2019), https://doi.org/10.1093/jiplp/jpz012 (note omitted).

[101] Canada is perhaps the most extreme example, as it is standard to waive moral rights in that country. Accordingly, Canadian law, despite its statutory provisions on moral rights, arguably fails to provide a legal environment conducive to their practical enforcement. Based on Canada's weak record of case law involving moral rights, Vaver argues that Canadian "exceptional[ism]" in relation to common-law moral rights is "folklore." *See* David Vaver, *Moral Rights Yesterday, Today and Tomorrow*, 7(3) INT'L J. TECH & L. 270, 275–76 (1999). Vaver discusses the 1989 UK provisions on moral rights and comments that the "widespread use of written waivers" is a serious obstacle to moral rights where great inequality of bargaining power between authors and publishers is the norm: id. at 274–75.

[102] See also, in the UK context, Society of Authors, *Before You Sign: Moral Rights*, SOCIETY OF AUTHORS BLOG (Feb. 11, 2019), https://societyofauthors.org/News/Blogs/Before-you-Sign/February-2019-(1)/Before-You-Sign-Moral-Rights.

But France has its own peculiarities when it comes to moral rights. For example, the practice of "ghostwriting," where an author writes a text to be published under someone else's name—the biography of a celebrity, for example—is common in France.[103] How can ghostwriting be reconciled with the unwaivability of the author's moral right of attribution?

To get around this problem, a trick of legal sleight-of-hand helps. The ghostwriter does not actually waive his or her moral right of attribution; rather, he or she asserts a different aspect of the moral right of attribution, the right to remain anonymous or to write under a pseudonym, both of which are protected under French law.[104] Michel Vivant and Jean-Michel Bruguière prefer to interpret French jurisprudence as allowing the right of attribution to be temporarily "suspended," implying the theoretical possibility that the author can choose to come forward and claim it at any time.[105] At the same time, the agreement for "ghostwriting" must be entered into in good faith. Any subsequent attempt by the ghostwriter to claim attribution should not have been premeditated as the contract was under negotiation. These points of legal argumentation are extraordinarily subtle, and they have given rise to what Vivant and Bruguière call a "*jurisprudence tourmentée*."[106] It may be best to admit, like Vivant and Bruguière, that the practice of ghostwriting simply amounts to "usages contra legem."[107]

ii. Permanent Protection

The ultimate outcome of French dualism is perpetual protection for moral rights. Economic rights are limited in time, but moral rights last forever. Michel Walter identifies this feature as a key distinction between dualist and monist copyright systems, though not at essential one:

[103] Also noted as a possibility in the German and Austrian context by Michel Walter, *supra* note 96, at 324 (with further citations in note 104).

[104] *See, e.g.*, Maria Mercedes Frabboni, *France*, *in* Moral Rights 374, para. 12-009 (Gillian Davies & Kevin Garnett eds., 2012) (including a brief but interesting consideration of judgments in the notes). But it is worth noting that the French Code de la propriété intellectuelle, *supra* note 20, does not mention this issue in the moral rights provisions; rather, it recognizes a right to anonymity or pseudonymity in art. L113-6, which states, "The authors of pseudonymous or anonymous works enjoy the rights over their works provided for in article L111-1" ("Les auteurs des oeuvres pseudonymes et anonymes jouissent sur celles-ci des droits reconnus par l'article L. 111-1"). Article L111-1 is the foundational provision on authors' rights in the Code, stating, "The author's right includes intellectual and moral attributes, as well as economic attributes, which are determined by books I and II of the present Code" ("Ce droit [d'auteur] comporte des attributs d'ordre intellectuel et moral ainsi que des attributs d'ordre patrimonial, qui sont déterminés par les livres Ier et III du présent code"). *See* Mira T. Sundara Rajan, *Elena Ferrante's Right to a Pseudonym*, The Atlantic (Nov. 15, 2016), https://www.theatlantic.com/entertainment/archive/2016/11/elena-ferrantes-right-to-a-pseudonym/507530.Canadian law offers explicit protection to these aspects of attribution. *See* Canadian Copyright Act, 1985, *supra* note 16, at s. 14.1(1).

[105] Vivant & Bruiguière, *supra* note 68, at paras. 464–66. They also cite A. and H.J. Lucas, who point out that it is difficult to distinguish between the abdication of the right and the assertion of anonymity: id. at para. 465.

[106] Id. at para. 465.

[107] Id. at para. 465.

> The most important difference [between the two systems] is the fact that under dualistic systems the term of protection of moral rights may outlive the duration of economic rights and even be granted in perpetuity. However, such everlasting moral rights must not necessarily be granted in dualistic systems either. The strict differentiation between moral rights and economic rights only allows legislators to establish such systems of everlasting moral rights, which on the other hand is not a mandatory feature of dualistic concepts.[108]

Accordingly, in France, even after a work has fallen into the public domain, it can never be exempt from moral rights. In contrast to the United States, the public domain in France is not a realm that is free from more or less "all" restrictions. Of course, a key practical issue then becomes who will exercise the author's moral rights after his death. The French Code provides that the rights can be exercised by the author's heirs or by a third party whom the author has designated in his or her will.[109]

The *Hugo* case, brought 122 years after the author's death, illustrates this norm.[110] However, the French Supreme Court's ruling has raised questions about the effectiveness *in practice* of perpetual moral rights.

The claim was brought by a great-great-grandson of Victor Hugo regarding a sequel to Hugo's masterpiece, *Les Misérables*, that had been written by writer François Cérésa.[111] Cérésa's novel imagines the subsequent life of the Hugo's characters after the close of the novel, including (spoiler alert) Inspector Javert, who dies at the end of Hugo's novel. As noted above, Hugo himself had stated that there could be no sequel to the novel.[112] In spite of this strong evidence of the author's own opinion, the Court found that the sequel did not violate the author's moral right of integrity.

In doing so, the Court engaged in a "balancing" exercise—a typical approach to copyright adjudication in common-law countries like the United States, but novel in the context of French moral rights. Perhaps not surprisingly, the case was sharply criticized by some French commentators, who argued that the ruling

[108] Walter, *supra* note 96, at 325.

[109] *See* French Code de la propriété intellectuelle, *supra* note 20, at art. L121-1.

[110] *Pierre Hugo*, *supra* note 90.

[111] Id. When a case is appealed to the Cour de cassation, the appeal may be rejected, accepted with the Court sending the case back to a lower court for re-examination, or accepted with the Court itself deciding on final measures in the litigation.

[112] Id. The full statement of the Court on this issue is as follows (emphasis added):

> The case demonstrates that if the latter never formally admitted and, even less, opposed, dramatic adaptations of his books, leave alone the adoption by other authors of certain of his characters, *it was on the other hand established that the writer would not have accepted that another writer could create a sequel to Les Misérables,* that accordingly, it mattered little that the characters, resuscitated for some and revived for others, remain in the books under examination which are wrongfully presented as an adaptation of the first work because Plon claimed, beyond the judicial terrain, that they were the continuation, faithful or not, of those brought into the world for literary eternity by Victor Hugo, that to prohibit every sequel to *Les Misérables*

effectively nullified perpetual protection of moral rights.[113] The Court in *Hugo* certainly moved away from the traditionally "subjective" approach that would prioritizes an author's own view of the treatment of the work—in this case, represented both by evidence of Hugo's own opinion and, further, the representations of his descendant.[114] The movement towards "objective" proof of damage to an author's reputation mirrors standards that are favored in common-law countries when it comes to reputation-based claims.[115]

But the French court also introduced a number of useful caveats. If the new works can somehow be shown to involve actual alterations of the original, or if

could not constitute, as it was wrongly asserted, an attack on the principle of creative freedom because, in this case, this work, a veritable monument of world literature, was not, in the first place, a simple novel, in the sense that it is also a philosophical and political undertaking, as Victor Hugo explained, and moreover, it follows that no sequel could be made for a work like *Les Misérables* without violating Victor Hugo's moral right.

[L]'arrêt énonce que si ce dernier ne s'était jamais formalisé et encore moins opposé aux adaptations scéniques de ses livres, voire à l'adoption par d'autres auteurs de tel ou tel de ses personnages, *il était en revanche établi que l'écrivain n'aurait pas accepté qu'un tiers auteur puisse donner une suite aux Misérables*, que dès lors peu importait que les personnages, ressuscité pour l'un d'entre eux et ranimés pour les autres, soient demeurés dans les livres présentés à tort comme une adaptation de l'oeuvre première puisque la société Plon revendiquait, hors du terrain judiciaire, en être la continuation, fidèle ou non, à ceux mis au monde pour l'éternité littéraire par Victor Hugo, qu'interdire toute suite aux Misérables ne pouvait constituer, ainsi qu'il était soutenu à tort, une atteinte au principe de la libre création puisque, en l'espèce, cette oeuvre, véritable monument de la littérature mondiale, d'une part, n'était pas un simple roman en ce qu'elle procédait d'une démarche philosophique et politique, ainsi que l'avait explicité Victor Hugo et, d'autre part, était achevée, qu'il s'ensuivait qu'aucune suite ne pouvait être donnée à une oeuvre telle que "Les Misérables" sans porter atteinte au droit moral de Victor Hugo.

[113] See, e.g., Skowron-Galvez, *supra* note 91, who comments, in an interesting article:

Thus, in the name of freedom of creativity, the moral right should bow down before every sequel to a work that is (as desired by its author) finished. Provided that, of course, the second work respects the "spirit" of the first: we have seen with what rigor the Court of Paris has compelled respect for the spirit of *Les Misérables*. Moreover—let us repeat—it is not clear why the moral right must be considered the enemy of free speech, since the undertaking of inserting oneself in the wake of the author in order to take advantage of a story and characters created successfully by him, and thereby snatching a profit from this success oneself, is not the first example of what comes to mind when we speak of creation. How much longer until economic parasitism is legitimized in the name of liberty, commerce, and industry?

[Ainsi, au nom de la liberté de création, le droit moral devrait s'incliner devant toute suite d'une œuvre se voulant (car voulue par son auteur) finie. Sous réserve, bien entendu, du respect par l'œuvre seconde de "l'esprit" de l'œuvre première: on a vu avec quelle sévérité la Cour de Paris s'est employée à faire respecter l'esprit des Misérables. Outre que–répétons-le—on ne voit pas pourquoi le droit moral devrait être considéré comme l'ennemi de la liberté de création, la démarche qui consiste à s'insérer dans le sillage d'un auteur pour s'emparer d'une histoire et des personnages créés par lui avec succès, et ainsi venir tirer profit de bribes de ce succès pour soi-même n'est pas la première illustration qui vient à l'esprit lorsque l'on parle de création. A quand la légitimation du parasitisme économique au nom de la liberté du commerce et de l'industrie?]

[114] Henri Desbois, Le droit d'auteur en France 538–39 (para. 449) (3d ed., 1978).

[115] *See, e.g.*, the Canadian case of *Snow v. The Eaton Centre Ltd* (1982), 70 C.P.R. (2d) 105: expert evidence was considered to offer "objective" proof of damage to the author's reputation. The principle has been applied in *Prise de Parole Inc. v. Guérin éditeur Ltée* [1996] F.C.J. No. 1427 (Can.).

they would lead to confusion about authorship, a violation of moral rights can still be found.[116] However, these criteria are demanding. The court clearly affirmed its intention to support "freedom of creativity" in preference to authorial control.[117]

Moreover, as a claim on the integrity right, the facts were awkward. In theory, an adaptation can violate the moral rights of the original work which it adapts, but the standards that apply to assessing any potential violation of the integrity right by an adaptation are especially stringent. The balancing of rights is involved. For example, in a case about an animated film of Antoine de St-Exupéry's *Le Petit Prince,* the court noted that

> the conclusion of an adaptation contract did not lead to any renunciation of the right to respect for the work, but the cinematic adaptation of a literary work implied that a certain liberty would be accorded to the maker of the adaptation; that having determined overall that the adapted work respected the spirit of the pre-existing work and that, while including a personal contribution of the adapter, required by transposition to the screen, it faithfully reproduced the plot and the character of the main character, the Court of Appeal, which responded to the conclusions before it, legally justified its decision on this point;[118]

It is also worth noting that a violation of integrity usually arises out of some direct treatment of the work, or of an image of it that is widely communicated. For example, a recent case involving the use of a painting as a cover for a musical album led to some confusion in the courts, but the traditional view, that

[116] The Cour de cassation criticized the earlier ruling, arguing that, "without having examined the works that were litigated, nor stated that these would have altered the work of Victor Hugo or that they would have given rise to confusion about the paternity of those works, the court of appeal ... did not thus establish a violation of moral rights and made its judgment in ignorance of freedom of creation" ("sans avoir examiné les oeuvres litigieuses ni constaté que celles-ci auraient altéré l'oeuvre de Victor Hugo ou qu'une confusion serait née de leur paternité, la cour d'appel ... n'a pas ainsi caractérisé l'atteinte au droit moral et s'est déterminée en méconnaissance de la liberté de creation"): *Pierre Hugo, supra* note 90. (The 2007 case resulted in damages of one euro to the plaintiff.) The trajectory of the case is usefully summarized by Hervé Hugueny, *Pierre Hugo ne retournera pas en cassation contre la suite des "Misérables"*, Livres Hebdo (Apr. 15, 2015), https://www.livreshebdo.fr/article/pierre-hugo-ne-retourn era-pas-en-cassation-contre-la-suite-des-miserables.

[117] Id.

[118] In the original French:

> [L]a cour d'appel a justement énoncé que la conclusion d'un contrat d'adaptation n'emportait aucune renonciation au droit au respect de l'oeuvre, mais que l'adaptation au cinéma d'une oeuvre littéraire impliquait qu'une certaine liberté soit reconnue à l'adaptateur; qu'ayant souverainement retenu que l'oeuvre adaptée respectait l'esprit de l'oeuvre préexistante et que, bien que comportant un apport personnel de l'adaptateur, exigé par la transposition à l'écran, elle reproduisait fidèlement l'intrigue et le caractère du personnage principal, la cour d'appel, qui a répondu aux conclusions dont elle était saisie, a ainsi légalement justifié sa décision sur ce point.

Cour de cassation [Cass.] [supreme court for judicial matters] 1e civ., June 12, 2001, Bull. civ. I, No. 171 (Fr.), https://www.legifrance.gouv.fr/juri/id/JURITEXT000007043124.

direct alteration of the original work (or, in this case, of its published image) is required, prevailed:

> In 2016, the Paris first instance court held that the use of the painting by the defendants caused harm to the integrity of the painting. The court of appeal disagreed because the artwork on the album cover was reproduced in its entirety, with the painter's signature, without any elements being added or deleted, and could not be regarded as having an advertising purpose.[119]

No direct treatment of the work at all was at issue in this case, but a violation of the integrity right may still occur through a change of context.[120] For example, in some countries, the conditions in which an artistic work is displayed can violate the author's moral rights.[121] The *Cour de cassation* itself has found that including a song in a compilation with music from other groups who have shadowy political associations would be a violation of the composer's right of reputation.[122] But the facts of the *Hugo* case were not seen as falling into the category of a work placed in an improper context. The *Cour de cassation* saw the making of a sequel as analogous to making an "adaptation," a right that would become freely available to all once the term of copyright expires and the work falls into the public

[119] European Union Intellectual Property Office, Recent European Case-Law on the Infringement and Enforcement of Intellectual Property Rights 104 (Jan. 2024), https://euipo.europa.eu/tunnel-web/secure/webdav/guest/document_library/observatory/documents/reports/New_Case_Law_en.pdf. See also the original decision: Cour de cassation [Cass.] [supreme court for judicial matters] 1e civ., Oct. 10, 2018, ECLI:FR:CCASS:2018:C100941, https://www.legifrance.gouv.fr/juri/id/JURITEXT000037510697.

[120] *See Shostakovich et al. v. Twentieth-Century Fox Film Corp.*, 196 Misc. 67, 80 N.Y.S.2d 575, 579 (1948) (U.S.), https://casetext.com/case/shostakovich-v-twentieth-century-fox-film. The judge notes: "There is no charge of distortion of the compositions nor any claim that they have not been faithfully reproduced. Conceivably, under the doctrine of moral right the court could in a proper case, prevent the use of a composition or work, in the public domain, in such a manner as would be violative of the author's rights. The application of the doctrine presents much difficulty however."

[121] This topic is generally discussed in Chapter 8, *infra*. It is worth noting here that s. 195AK(b) of the Australian Copyright Act 1968 provides that "an exhibition in public of the work that is prejudicial to the author's honour or reputation because of the manner or place in which the exhibition occurs" will amount to a derogatory treatment of the artist's work, which is prohibited by the Act: *see Copyright Act 1968* (Cth) (Austl.), https://www.legislation.gov.au/Details/C2019C00042. In contrast, the possibility is now explicitly excluded by an Explanatory Note to s. 57 of the Indian Copyright Act 1957, as amended in 1994, *supra* note 16—most likely a response to the interim ruling in the *Amar Nath Sehgal* case: *Amar Nath Seghal v. Union of India and ors*, May 29, 1992, Delhi High Court (Jaspal Singh, J.), https://indiankanoon.org/doc/624173/. *See* Indian Copyright Act, 1957, *supra* note 16; Copyright (Amendment) Act 1994 (India), https://copyright.gov.in/Documents/Notification/Copyright_Amendment_1994.pdf.

[122] *See also M. jean X ... dit Jean Y ... c société Universal Music SA, venant aux droits de la société anonyme Polygram et autres*, Cour de cassation [Cass.] [supreme court for judicial matters] 2e civ., Feb. 8, 2006, Bull. civ. II, No. 44 (Fr.), *revised*, Arrêt No. 773 en rectification d'erreur matérielle [Appeal No. 773 for rectification of material error], Feb. 21, 2006, http://www.courdecassation.fr/jurisprudence_2/chambre_sociale_576/arret_no_962.html. This principle is also well established in German law. *See* Stefan Michel, *You Can't Always Get What You Want? A Comparative Analysis of the Legal Means to Oppose the Use of Campaign Music*, 18 J. Marshall Rev. Intell. Prop. L. 169 (2018).

domain—as an instance of the economic right of adaptation rather than a moral right of modification.

But the use of works in the public domain to generate a new work that enjoys a new term of copyright protection could also threaten the public interest. For example, if a theatre director now wanted to stage a play imagining the future life of Hugo's characters, could a scenario arise where the person might need the permission of François Cérésa? What about the case of a person using the characters who were the subject of the sequel in a video game?

The French ruling lends clear legal support to "fan" creativity, if the sequel in this case can be characterized as such. In this sense, it represents a certain approach to updating cultural norms and encourages French people to engage with technology. The decision was arguably in tune with the times: the "aughts" were a period of enthusiasm for technology and remix culture. Does the attempt look more naïve in the era that we have since entered—where the abuse of information through technology has become a widespread problem?

d. Technological Features

French law makes special provision for moral rights in the context of film, adopted in 1992,[123] and, in 1994 amendments, for computer programs as well.[124]

i. Audiovisual Works

The French treatment of moral rights in films is worth close examination. Historically, objections to moral rights in film have been a major impediment to greater acceptance for moral rights internationally.[125] But France has arguably created a successful and efficient regime for recognizing the moral rights of those involved in the making of a film.[126]

French law recognizes film as a collaborative work. It is a product of the creative efforts of the director, a number of "coauthors," and the producer. The author of the screenplay, adaptation, or dialogue, and the composer of original music for

[123] *See* French Code de la propriété intellectuelle, *supra* note 20, at arts. L121-5 and L121-6.

[124] Id. at art. L121-7. India, with France, was in the vanguard of countries considering moral rights in computer programs, although it chose to address the issue indirectly: *see* Indian Copyright Act, 1957, *supra* note 16, §§57 and 52(1)(aa). Interestingly, in its law of 1985, France adopted an initially restrictive stance towards moral rights in programs, which it maintained in the 1992 codification—but its position was subsequently changed in a 1994 codification amendment. This history can be traced on the website of Légifrance: *see* French Code de la propriété intellectuelle, *supra* note 20.

[125] See, e.g., the illuminating discussion Stephen Fraser, *Berne, CFTA, NAFTA and GATT: The Implications of Copyright Droit Moral and Cultural Exemptions in International Trade Law*, 18 HASTINGS COMM. AND ENT. L.J. 287 (1996). It is noteworthy that the World Intellectual Property Organization (WIPO) Performance and Phonograms Treaty, which introduces moral rights for performers, nevertheless excludes moral rights in performances recorded in audiovisual works: World Intellectual Property Organization (WIPO) Performances and Phonograms Treaty, adopted Dec. 20, 1996, S. Treaty Doc. No. 105-17, 36 I.L.M. 76 (1997) (WPPT), https://www.wipo.int/wipolex/en/treaties/textdetails/12743.

[126] *See* French Code de la propriété intellectuelle, *supra* note 20, at art. L121-5, introduced in 1992.

the film, are considered to be coauthors of a film.[127] It confronts the problem of choice and potential conflict that is involved in the final production of a feature film—which takes, cuts, images, and performances to use, and how—and specifies that the final product must be agreed upon by the director, coauthors, and producer. This final product constitutes the audiovisual work for the purposes of copyright law.

Any subsequent modification of the final work requires the consent of all parties, and any conversion of the work to a new format must be "preceded by consultation with the director." The language of Article L121-5 does not go so far as to say that the agreement of the director is required, but the article should probably be interpreted to mean that only unreasonable objections by the director may be overruled. All moral rights apply only to the final work.[128]

This last point provides an important clue about potential conflicts over moral rights between coauthors and how they should be resolved. Prior to the establishment of the final version of a film, any coauthor should be able to signal objections to the use of his or her contribution by refusing to consent to the final film. Unless and until moral rights conflicts are resolved, the final version of a film cannot be settled, as the agreement of *all* coauthors *and* the producer is required. Once the final version is established, however, a coauthor can no longer object to the manner in which his or her contribution is used in the overall context of the film. What each coauthor can do is to object to the use of the film as a whole, or of his component contribution, by a third party. The section provides a neat, though indirect, solution to the potential problem of internal conflict among the makers of a film.

Should any one of the contributors be unable or unwilling to complete his or her part in the project, that contributor will nevertheless be required to allow the others to use the work that was completed before the rupture. Article L121-6 concludes with the remark—"He will have, for this contribution, the status of authorship, and will enjoy the rights that flow therefrom." This should probably be interpreted to mean two things. First, based on his or her limited contribution, the contributor is considered an author. Secondly, however, the contributor's right as an author can only be exercised in relation to the use of the final work. He or she has no right to intervene in the overall realization of the work, which has since fallen to other hands than his or her own.

ii. Computer Programs

In relation to computer programs, the French Code specifies that dealings with a computer program by the right holder will lead to a violation of the author's right

[127] *See* id. at art. L113-7.

[128] The French Code de la propriété intellectuelle, *supra* note 20, at art. L113-7, states, "Les droits propres des auteurs, tels qu'ils sont définis à l'article L121-1, ne peuvent être exercés par eux que sur l'oeuvre audiovisuelle achevée."

of integrity only if they are prejudicial to his or her honor or reputation. From the French perspective, this represents a scaling back of the general moral right of integrity under French law. By international standards, however, the French Code grants to computer programmers a moral right of integrity that conforms exactly to the requirements of the Berne Convention.[129]

This approach is extremely interesting. Not only does France recognize a right of integrity in programs, but it also frames the right in accordance with the international standard of protection that is generally supposed to be made available for intellectual creation across all areas of copyright subject matter, in all Berne member states. But the French moral right of integrity in computer programs is restrictive by French standards. The traditional French approach, which presumes that any intervention in a work to which the author objects is a prima facie violation of the right of integrity, is apparently too broad for the software context. Nevertheless, the French legislature has not refrained from applying the Berne standard to software.

The right of withdrawal is completely discarded, and, given the characteristics of software, this seems a highly practical approach. Software changes rapidly; it is subject to updates, modifications for new operating systems, and countless other changes and improvements through time. Much of this occurs in an employment context. A desire to withdraw software after its release could prove to be a logistical nightmare. Leaving the option open could paralyze companies and programmers who want to issue improved versions of programs.

iii. Moral Rights in Employment

Provisions added to France's moral rights code in 2006 and 2009 made changes in two areas. Importantly, the first of these dealt with moral rights in the employment context. The employee's rights of disclosure, integrity, and withdrawal are all affected by Article L121-7-1, introduced in 2006.[130] First, according to this

[129] *See* Chapter 4, *infra* note 394 and accompanying text.

[130] The French Code de la propriété intellectuelle, *supra* note 20, at art. L121-7-1 states:

> Le droit de divulgation reconnu à l'agent mentionné au troisième alinéa de l'article L. 111-1, qui a créé une oeuvre de l'esprit dans l'exercice de ses fonctions ou d'après les instructions reçues, s'exerce dans le respect des règles auxquelles il est soumis en sa qualité d'agent et de celles qui régissent l'organisation, le fonctionnement et l'activité de la personne publique qui l'emploie.
>
> L'agent ne peut:
>
> 1°S'opposer à la modification de l'oeuvre décidée dans l'intérêt du service par l'autorité investie du pouvoir hiérarchique, lorsque cette modification ne porte pas atteinte à son honneur ou à sa réputation;
>
> 2°Exercer son droit de repentir et de retrait, sauf accord de l'autorité investie du pouvoir hiérarchique.

Article L111-1 deals with employment and (presumably) analogous situations: *see* https://www.legifrance.gouv.fr/codes/article_lc/LEGIARTI000042814694. A useful overview of the French copyright situation surrounding employment is provided by Olivia Bernardeau-Paupe, *Q&A: copyright ownership and transfer in France*, LEXOLOGY (May 25, 2022), https://www.lexology.com/library/detail.aspx?g=11ff7a76-9378-4fd1-88ec-0930d08407da.

article, disclosure must be exercised in conformity with the "rules to which the employee is subject in his or her capacity as agent, and those which govern the organization, the functioning, and the activity of the public person who is employing him or her." Secondly, the employee still enjoys a right of integrity, but it is only valid with respect to modifications of work that will damage the employee's reputation or honor. Finally, the employee can only exercise the right of withdrawal with the agreement of his or her employer. These changes greatly limit the scope of the employee's moral rights, although it is important to note that the employee's reputation and honor are still protected as in the minimum standard for the moral right of integrity set out in Article 6*bis* of Berne. The change moves towards regulating the workplace as common-law countries do, with employers gaining more control over their employees. Still, the moral rights retained by the employee are significant and reflect Berne standards. More generally, the provision facilitates the smoother operation of a more unified corporate environment, in which the identity of the employee is submerged in that of the controlling entity – as is, once again, usually favored in common-law countries.[131] In the U.S. context, for example, the limited moral rights in s. 106A of the Copyright Act cannot arise in the employment context at all.[132]

iv. Press Publication Right

A 2009 change involved the use of works in compilations and specifically allowed journalists to retain their right to republish their works as long as the new forms of publication do not compete with the original press publication. The new rules entered into effect on June 14, 2009. They replaced earlier provisions on the re-publication of an article in a magazine or periodical which also stipulated that the new publication must not compete with the original news publication.[133]

The change reflects a valuable new definition, in Article L132-35 of the French Code, of "titre de presse," which can be translated as "press publication." The definition extends the traditional understanding of news publications to the online environment and includes online communication of works. It invokes a principle of neutrality towards the appearance of the publication in new formats.[134] The French Code identifies editorial control as the key criterion for determining

[131] *See, e.g.*, Canadian Copyright Act, 1985, *supra* note 16, at s. 13(3).

[132] Moral rights in the United States are already limited to visual arts, and moral rights cannot arise under the U.S. Visual Artists Rights Act of 1990 (VARA), if the work of visual art is created in an employment context: Visual Artist Rights Act, 17 U.S.C. § 106A (1990), https://www.copyright.gov/title17/92chap1.html#106a. *See* U.S. Copyright Act, § 101 definitions ("work of visual art"): 17 U.S.C. § 101, https://www.copyright.gov/title17/92chap1.html#101.

[133] *See* French Code de la propriété intellectuelle, *supra* note 20, at art. L121-8.

[134] Media neutrality: *see, e.g.*, *Robertson v. Thomson Corp.* [2006] 2 S.C.R. 363, 2006 SCC 43 (Can.).

whether a work is, in effect, the transformation of the old work into a new medium or a new work in its own right. This determination will decide the issue of whether or not a work has been "re-published" and, therefore, whether or not the author's permission is once again required for publication.[135]

v. Defenses to a Moral Rights Claim: Parody and Pastiche

While it is not included in the chapter on moral rights, the parody defense in French copyright law is relevant to the treatment of moral rights in the *Code*. Inhibiting the creation of parodies, a vibrant and potentially important form of creative expression in its own right,[136] is clearly among the dangers associated with strong protection of the moral right of integrity. To commentators from common-law countries, this represents a significant concern about the scope of the French moral right of integrity.[137]

However, the objection is addressed with ease by French law, which provides comprehensively for the art of parody. A parody defense to moral rights infringement is included in a list of public interest exceptions to authors' rights under French law, as a separate defense in its own right.[138] Crucially, proving a parody defense in France depends on being able to show that the work in question is a true work of parody. Intention is important. French law identifies two possible rationales for a parody: humorous intent and critical intent. The parody must be created in good faith. If the parodist intends to harm the author of the parodied work, or to cause harm by revealing facts about the author's personal life, the defense cannot be invoked. Moreover, as many commentators observe, a parody that causes harm

[135] *See* id. In the *Tasini* case, the U.S. Supreme Court found that the use of freelance work in the online publication of newspapers did qualify as a new publication and therefore required permission from the original authors: *see New York Times Co. v. Tasini*, 533 U.S. 483 (2001).

[136] It is worth noting that a parody may also stem from admiration. See the discussion of parody in the UK context *infra* note 287 and accompanying text.

[137] In a recent Belgian case, the creation of a parody could not exempt its creator from a finding that the moral rights of the original author had been violated. *See* Joris Ghent, *Parody Exception Again Denied in Belgium: NV Code v. BV Mercis/Dick Bruna, Hof van Beroep (Court of Appeal) of Antwerp, May 2, 2006*, 1(11) Oxford J. Intell. Prop. L. Prac. 694 (2006). Ghent notes that the decision "confirms the tendency in Belgian jurisprudence to be very cautious in its application of the parody exception to copyright infringement"—and, presumably, to moral rights, as well. For example, a U.S. perspective is provided by Geri J. Yonover, *The Precarious Balance: Moral Rights, Parody, and Fair Use*, 14 Cardozo Arts & Ent. L.J. 79 (1996). The analysis suffers from some misapprehensions about non-U.S. legal systems—for example, European jurisdictions do not have U.S.-style "fair-use" principles, but they approach the issue of fair uses, or fair dealing, in other ways. Notable among these is the citation defense.

[138] *See* French Code de la propriété intellectuelle, *supra* note 20, at art. L122-5(4). In contrast to Germany and Japan, there is no need to consider parody as a special form of the citation defense. Civil law countries often rely on "citation" of the work in much the same way that common-law countries invoke "fair use" (United States) or "fair dealing" (the United Kingdom and Canada), allowing for certain activities, treatments, and uses of a work to be exempt from copyright restrictions. Quoting or "citing" a work for the purpose of research would be a classic example of fair use in both systems. In the French Code, a citation defense is listed separately, in art. L122-5(3)(a).

to the original work will generally not be allowed.[139] In an interesting parallel with trademark law, the risk of confusion with the works of the original author must also be avoided—much as trademark censures the creation of confusion in the mind of the consumer about the origin of goods.[140]

The parody may legitimately qualify as a copyright work in its own right. In this case, the author of a work of parody in France will be entitled to enjoy, to the full extent, his or her own moral rights, as well as the economic rights. This point was recently reaffirmed in a Decision of the French Court of Appeal about a parody of the Mona Lisa made by a creator of appropriation art, known as *La Joconde Playmobil*.[141] Parts of the work were subsequently reproduced on panels offered for sale by the defendant, and pictures of the panels were also posted on the defendant's social media account. The defendant argued that the panels were themselves parodies of the original Mona Lisa, but the Court did not accept this position. Instead, it pointed out that the parody had been reproduced wholesale in the Playbill, and that "the defendant did not create a new original work reproducing features of a prior work: on the contrary, he took over the prior work largely unaltered. The few minor modifications added on one side were not deemed creative." Accordingly, the Court affirmed that the original appropriation artist, who created a parody of the Mona Lisa, was entitled to the full enjoyment of his moral and economic rights under the French copyright law. According to the Court, as a recent commentary notes, "this parodic version of Mona Lisa reflected the personal touch of its author and enjoyed copyright protection."[142]

The copyright in the parody is not subject to any special limitations—except, of course, that the intent of the parodist should not be to harm the author of the original work on which the parody is based.

The French approach to parody should also be considered in the light of the *Deckmyn* case (2014). Parody is a recognized exception to copyright protection

[139] See the useful and efficient overview of parody in French copyright law in Alexandra Giannopolou & Teresa Nobre, *Best Case Scenarios for Copyright: Parody Exception in France*, Communia (June 24, 2015), https://www.communia-association.org/wp-content/uploads/2016/06/report-2-parody.pdf (moral rights are discussed in Part 2.6, entitled "Other Conditions"). They also note that, "the exempted use is balanced to the personality rights of the author. The goal is to develop a balance between the right to laugh and personality rights of the author chosen as the target, taking into account the French tradition of satire." The general emphasis is on harm to the work rather than to the author per se.

[140] The similarities between moral rights and trademark have often been noted. Vaver refers to this as the protection of "truth-in-marketing": *see* Vaver, *supra* note 97, at 276; he notes that "attributions function like trade marks." Of course, a number of common-law countries rely upon tort to protect authors' moral interests, including the United States and the United Kingdom: *see* id. at 271 (remarking on the presence of "*misattribution*" in the United Kingdom's Copyright Act of 1956 and describes it as "passing-off, writ large").

[141] The Mona Lisa is known as *La Joconde* in French, derived from *La Gioconda*, the painting's Italian name. The term means "She who is jovial," and it is considered to represent a pun on the name of the presumed model for the portrait, Lisa del Giocondo.

[142] The case is summarized in European Intellectual Property Office, *supra* note 115; the original French decision is Cour d'appel [CA] [regional court of appeal] Paris, 2e ch., Sept. 30, 2022, No. 20/18194, https://www.dalloz.fr/documentation/Document?id=CA_PARIS_2022-09-30_2018194#_.

throughout the European Union; it is articulated in Article 5(3)(K) of the Directive on copyright in the information society (2001).[143] As the Court of Justice of the European Union (CJEU) clarified in *Deckmyn*, parody is therefore what is known as an "autonomous" concept under European Union (EU) law that must receive "uniform interpretation throughout the member states."[144] It found that the parody exception must be applied in such a way as to "strike a fair balance" between the "legitimate interests" of the authors of works[145] and those who wish to make use of them for the purpose of parody. On the facts of the case, the creators of the original cartoon from which the parody was derived had "a legitimate interest in ensuring that the work protected by copyright is not associated with such a message."

Is the French parody exception harmonized with the CJEU approach in *Deckmyn*? The idea of legitimate interests is certainly implied by the French approach. As noted above, these specifically include the original author's right to be protected from a malicious parody—one that intends to "harm" the author or to violate the author's privacy. These could potentially qualify as "legitimate interests" of the author within the relevant terms of the EU Directive, though no further guidance is available.

For now, in keeping with *Deckmyn*, French law does not condone parodies that cause harm to the author. It refuses to accord the status of parody to creations that are based on "illegal elements," which would presumably include inciting racial hatred under European, and French, laws.[146] Such products are not allowed as exceptions to either copyright or moral rights under the French Code.

e. Conclusions

France offers the world a comprehensive and sophisticated framework for the protection of moral rights. The extent of protection for French moral rights is beyond what they enjoy in any other jurisdiction.

The right of attribution is treated comprehensively under French law. It is considered to include rights to remain anonymous or to publish under pseudonym. It protects against false attribution. It is arguably flexible enough to accommodate the phenomenon of ghostwriting, controversial as this is.

143 Directive 2001/29/EC of the European Parliament and of the Council of 22 May 2001 on the harmonization of certain aspects of copyright and related rights in the information society, 2001 O.J. (L 167) 10, https://eur-lex.europa.eu/legal-content/EN/TXT/?uri=celex%3A32001L0029.

144 C-201/13, *Deckmyn v. Vandersteen*, ECLI:EU:C:2014:2132, ¶ 14 (Sept. 3, 2014), https://eur-lex.europa.eu/legal-content/EN/TXT/?uri=CELEX%3A62013CJ0201.

145 Id. ¶ 36:

> set out in Articles 2 and 3 of that directive, which are provided for under Article 5 thereof, seek to achieve a "fair balance" between, in particular, the rights and interests of authors on the one hand, and the rights of users of protected subject-matter on the other (see, to that effect, judgments in Padawan, EU:C:2010:620, paragraph 43, and Painer, C-145/10, EU:C:2011:798, paragraph 132).

146 This position has been affirmed at the European level by the *Deckmyn* case, *supra* note 42. *See also supra* note 94.

Integrity is a cornerstone of the French system. In general, an author may object to any changes to his or her work. Beyond certain special cases, and in contrast to Article *6bis* of the Berne Convention, the moral right of integrity does not depend on showing proof of damage to the author's reputation or honor. The special cases are thoughtfully arrived at, and they include employment and rights in computer software.[147] It is important to recognize that moral rights in these two areas, though they may be limited by French standards, still arise in both of these contexts under French law, and that they offer a level of protection that is still in conformity with the minimum set out in Article *6bis* of the Berne Convention. It is noteworthy that French law offers protection in contexts where moral rights are not recognized in other countries, particularly common-law jurisdictions, and that French legislators have not yielded to the reflex, tempting but mistaken, to exclude moral rights in technological works . The attempt to organize and coordinate the moral rights of multiple authors of a film under French law is also impressive and suggests a starting point, at least, for the treatment of moral rights in collective works—an archetype of creativit in the technological environment.

But France is also not unique in any of these respects. Other countries have recognized a broad right of integrity independent of reputation. For example, India codified a pure right of integrity in 1957, the same year the French *Code de la propriété intellectuelle* came into existence.[148] Some jurisdictions actually distinguish between a moral right of integrity and a moral right of "reputation." Protection of reputation is arguably a more accurate characterization of the "integrity" right in Article *6bis* of the Berne Convention: in the absence of damage to the author's reputation or honor, and no matter the treatment of the work in question, no offense can be said to have occurred under Berne.

The French approach to moral rights in the digital context establishes three points of principle. First, moral rights may have to be flexible in order to adapt to technology. Second, a single moral rights regime may need to include different types and levels of protection for different types of works. Third, and most important, the moral rights doctrine is capable of evolving to meet these needs. The doctrine originated in the early 1800s, but it still remains relevant— essential, French law suggests–in the technological context.

[147] The concept of honor is discussed in Adeney, *supra* note 87. See also the discussion in Chapter 4, *infra* notes 317–21 and accompanying text.

[148] In 1994, India modified the integrity right to conform to the Berne model: *see* Copyright Amendment Act 1994 (India), *supra* note 121. As noted above, this was probably a kneejerk reaction to the interim judgment in the *Sehgal* case, which held, in no uncertain terms, that the Indian government should be held responsible for violating the integrity of a work of art in its possession. This unique judgment castigated the government for its insensitivity as well as its carelessness. In any event, the court that issued the final ruling in *Sehgal* found a workaround to the amendments—through the legal approach proposed in my article on the case: Mira T. Sundara Rajan, *Moral Rights and the Protection of Cultural Heritage:* Amar Nath Sehgal v. Union of India, 10(1) INT'L J. OF CULTURAL PROP. 79, 83 (2001)). *See Amar Nath Sehgal v. Union of India*, 2005 (30) PTC 253 (Del H.C.) (India).

C. Germany and Monist Moral Rights: Romance of a Theory

Like France, Germany and the German-speaking countries place moral at the heart of their copyright laws.[149] The following discussion traces the origins of German legal theory in this area, explores how those origins are reflected in the development of the law, and considers how German legal principles are both complementary and contrasting to French law.

Like French law, German tradition must also be recognized as a source of moral rights, but the idea of moral rights emerged very differently than in France. As Strömholm points out, French courts were already developing moral rights in practice from early in the nineteenth century, but German scholars became interested in the theoretical justifications behind these developments.[150] The modern doctrine represents a synthesis of German theory and French "practical solutions." Strömholm concludes,

> Certain writers have considered the theories of the nineteenth century from this historical perspective without, however, analyzing them in detail. Hoffmann goes so far as to affirm that the moral right as it is found in the Berne Convention (art. 6 bis) is a creation of [German legal theorists] Dambach, Klostermann and Kohler, imported into France by [French legal commentator] Morillot.[151]

To these observations should be added the influence of British common law in arriving at a compromise model of moral rights in Berne. What, then, has German legal theory contributed to the evolution of moral rights?

149 Urheberrechtsgesetz (UrhG) vom 9 Sept. 1965 [Act on Copyright and Related Rights of Sept. 9, 1965], berücksichtigt die Änderung(en) des Gesetzes durch Artikel 25 des Gesetzes vom 23. Juni 2021 (BGBl. I S. 1858) [as amended by article 25 of the Act of June 23, 2021 (Federal Law Gazette I, p. 1858)], art. 14 (Ger.), https://www.gesetze-im-internet.de/englisch_urhg/englisch_urhg.html (translation provided by Ute Reusch).

150 Strömholm, *supra* note 11, at 239.

151 Id:

> Quelques auteurs ont considéré les théories du XIXe siècle de ce point de vue historique sans toutefois les analyser en détail. HOFFMANN va jusqu'a affirmer que le droit moral (*Urheberp ersönlichkeitsrecht*) tel qu'il se trouve dans la Convention de Berne (art. 6 bis) est une création de DAMBACH, de KLOSTERMANN et de KOHLER, importée en France par MORILLOT.

Strömholm goes on to comment:

> However, this judgment relates to the theory of moral rights as opposed to the solutions of [expressed by] positive law, because Hoffmann comments elsewhere that it is only in 1928 that the *Reichsgericht* finally adopted the moral right.
>
> Toutefois, il faut que ce jugement se rapporte à la théorie du droit moral par opposition aux solutions du droit positif, car HOFFMANN déclare ailleurs que ce n'est qu'en 1928 que le *Reichsgericht* a enfin adopté le droit moral.

For an interesting overview of the work of André Morillot, see PRIMARY SOURCES ON COPYRIGHT (1450–1900) (Lionel Bently & Martin Kretschmer, eds.), http://www.copyrighthistory.org/cgi-bin/kleioc/0010/exec/ausgabe/%22f_1878%22.

1. The Birth of Monism

In his classic 1967 study of moral rights, Strömholm showcases the sheer exuberance of German theorizing on moral rights. He makes a convincing case that this area held the interest of German jurists from the early years of the nineteenth century. As outlined by him, the range and rigor of German theories is impressive. It seems that almost every imaginable approach to moral rights was explored by these jurists. They discussed moral rights as authors' personal rights, as personality rights, as "innate rights" of authorship, a variety of natural rights[152]—and even the raised the possibility of rejecting moral rights as a legal concept altogether.[153]

Some German theorists favored the French approach; others diverged from it, developing their own conception of the relationship between moral and economic rights. German theorizing in the nineteenth and early twentieth centuries eventually led to a distinctive school of thought on moral rights, defined by its approach to this relationship and known as "monism."

German monism developed its understanding of moral rights through a deeper exploration of their origins. Where the French saw the moral and economic rights of authors as two categories of rights with different and distinct bases, first called "dualism" by the French writer Morillot,[154] German theorists saw moral interests and economic interests as two aspects of a single right.[155] The right was simply an author's right. This theory came to be known as "monism." It reflects the unity of *all* the interests of the author, whether they are economic or personal in nature.[156]

The distinction between French dualism and German monism presents an imperfect contrast—shades of grey, rather than black and white. As the distinguished German legal scholar Adolf Dietz observes, German and French law share the approach of dividing authors' rights into two large groups consisting of economic and moral interests. He asks,

> Why does this apparently dual structure of copyright lead in one case to a dualistic and in the other case to a monistic interpretation of copyright? The answer to

[152] *Droits innés* or *angeborene Rechte*. *See* Strömholm, *supra* note 11, at 242–43.

[153] Strömholm discusses the concept of innate rights. *See* id.

[154] Id. at 226, noting: "What is strange is that Morillot, in his eagerness to acquaint his fellow countrymen with German ideas, he failed altogether to investigate the—by that time abundant—French case law which could be cited in support of his ideas."

[155] Morillot's writing was largely based on the work of German theorists of his time. *See* id. at 239, and Strömholm, *supra* note 2, at 226–27. In fact, Strömholm notes the curious process whereby the work of German theorists was exported to France via Morillot and found its way back into Germany theory from Morillot, *unrecognized* by German theorists of the later generation.

[156] Strömholm traces monism to the earlier theories of Harum, Dambach, and Stobbe: *see* Strömholm, *supra* note 11, at 205–07.

> this delicate question is that the apparently dual structure of the content of copyright is only half of the truth.
>
> ... [I]t is copyright as a whole which serves to protect intellectual and moral as well as economic interests of authors. This could also be called [a] ... unitary or synthetic concept of copyright.[157]

For Dietz, it seems that the difference between monism and dualism is a subtle one. Dualism is based on the idea that moral rights are "chronologically and systematically primordial."[158] Accordingly, the key to dualism is not so much the distinction between economic and moral rights as the establishment of a hierarchy between them. In a dualist system, moral rights are pre-eminent; their status is superior to that of economic rights.

But in monist systems, the equality between the author's economic and moral rights does not translate into an inferior status for moral rights—which is what those of us from common-law backgrounds might anticipate. Instead, the sensibility of moral rights infuses the copyright law as a whole. This reflects the true origin of monism, as Dietz points out, in a fundamental theory of "authors' rights," regardless of any subcategory into which those rights might subsequently fall. Michel Walter additionally points out that monist copyright systems reflect an underlying appreciation of the inequality of bargaining power that authors face, no doubt arising out of the fundamental principle of authorship underlying these systems, and that the copyright law in these countries is shaped by this awareness. Accordingly, in keeping with the monist theory at its core, German and Austrian copyright law do not allow the outright transfer of copyright as a whole.[159] Instead, as discussed below, these systems function by means of a licensing approach. According to Walter, while this approach allows practical transactions involving copyright works to be pursued in monist countries, it is still qualitatively different from the transfer, or even assignment, of copyright under common-law systems:

> However, such sole and exclusive licences are of a different legal quality in comparison with copyright assignment or transfer of copyright under common-law legislations, which even may turn out in an initial ownership of copyright by employers or commissioners, eg in case of works made for hire.[160]

[157] Adolf Dietz, *Legal Principles of Moral Rights (Civil Law) General Report*, *in* The Moral Right of the Author 54, paras. 16 and 17 (1993).

[158] Id.

[159] UrhG, *supra* note 147, at art. 29 provides that the only way in which copyright can be transferred is by inheritance.

[160] Walter, *supra* note 96, at 323.

2. Monism in Practice

Why was monism the ultimate outcome of such diverse German theorizing? The intellectual power and influence of the theorists who championed this perspective, leading to their enduring recognition in German legal history, was clearly a factor.[161] Strömholm identifies the key to monism as a focus on the work, the "object" of protection in both economic and personal terms. As understood by these theorists, echoing Hegel, the work includes two intrinsic elements: the work in its realized form and the will of the author, which is ultimately responsible for making it available to the public.[162] As Strömholm comments,

> Until the author decides to publish it, the work would not be, according to Allfeld, the object of a patrimonial right; it is the will of the author that brings it into the world of commerce. On this basis, Allfeld establishes his own definition: the author's right, he says, "has its roots in the personality of the author and its foundation in the fact of intellectual creation; it is the exclusive right to decide if, when, in what form and to what end the results of his creativity should be communicated to a third party." As a result of the duality of interests involved, the author's right is neither patrimonial nor personal; it is a law of its own kind, valid against a third party, impossible to forfeit, but alienable at the author's will and transmissible upon his death.[163]

As suggested by this paragraph, the primordial author's right is therefore the right of disclosure or *divulgation*, which could as well be called by its economic rights terminology, the right of first publication.

Monism has two practical consequences that are interesting and help to distinguish German moral rights from the French approach. The first concerns the inalienability of rights, and the second relates to the duration of protection for moral rights. While monist systems accept the principle that moral rights are inalienable, they differ from French law in initially ceding to authors the *right to decide* whether

[161] The names of Kohler, Gierke, and—writing at the turn of the twentieth century—Allfeld find prominence in Strömholm's study: *see* Strömholm, *supra* note 11, at 330; Strömholm, *supra* note 2, at 225–27. Allfeld, in particular, is an important theorist of monism.

[162] On Hegel, see the useful entry in Stanford Encyclopedia of Philosophy, *Georg Wilhelm Friedrich Hegel* (2020), http://plato.stanford.edu/entries/hegel.

[163] Strömholm, *supra* note 11, at 330. Strömholm further states that:

> Tant qu[e l'auteur] . . . n'aurait pas décidé de la publier, l'oeuvre ne serait pas, d'après ALLFELD, l' *objet* d'un droit patriomonial; c'est la volonté de l'auteur qui la fait entrer dans la sphère des biens. Sur ces bases, ALLFELD établit sa propre définition: le droit d'auteur, dit-il, "a ses racines dans la personnalité de l'auteur et son fondement dans le fait de la création intellectuelle; c'est le droit exclusif de décider si, quand, sous quelle forme et dans quel but le résultat de cette création doit être communiqué aux tiers." Il résulte de la dualité des intérêts engagés que le droit d'auteur n'est ni patrimonial ni personnel: c'est un droit particulier, opposable aux tiers, insaissable mais aliénable à la volonté de l'auteur et transmissible à cause de mort.

or not to waive their rights. Subject to the caveats below, there is no *general prohibition* on the waiver of moral rights in German or Austrian law.

However, after a detailed comparison of the treatment surrounding the allowability of waivers of moral rights in Germany and Austria with France, Michel Walter concludes that the differences between dualist and monist approaches to waivers, though real, are subtle. He points out that they primarily arise from different approaches to reasoning, what he calls their "dogmatic guise":

> As has been outlined, however, these principles are well established in monistic systems as well, although in a different dogmatic guise. In any case, both systems must admit exceptions and attenuations of these principles.[164]

The availability of waivers, though limited, leaves open the practical question of how to balance the weakness of bargaining power that is likely to characterize the author-publisher relationship. This issue is addressed through a combination of legislative measures designed to protect the author from unfair treatment. These include the rules governing copyright and moral rights, including waiver, as well as, in German law, broader legislative protection for authors.[165]

Perhaps most importantly, certain aspects of the authors' moral rights cannot be waived at all. These are the rights that are considered to constitute the "core" of moral rights protection. As Michel Walter notes, comparing French and German systems with the common law,

> What is most important, in my view, is that both concepts of moral rights to a certain extent allow contractual agreements with regard to the performance or non-performance of moral rights or a waiver thereof. However, as far as the core of moral rights is concerned, no transfer nor waiver is admitted. Given the inferior bargaining position of authors, this is a significant feature of monistic as well as dualistic concepts of civil law moral rights and a major difference compared with the legal tradition of common law countries, where most commonly the transfer or waiver of moral rights is admitted and valid.[166]

Rights comprising this core include the author's moral right of attribution, which Austrian law explicitly provides cannot be waived.[167] The attribution right presumably cannot be waived under the doctrine in Germany either.[168] The author

[164] Walter, *supra* note 96, at 325.
[165] See discussion *infra* notes 177–82, on the German law on authors' bargaining power.
[166] Walter, *supra* note 96, at 325–26 (notes omitted).
[167] Id. at 324, which notes: "This latter aspect of moral right of the author is a fundamental one and may not be waived as all, as is explicitly set out in section 19 paragraph 2 of the Austrian Copyright Act, according to which a waiver of this right to claim authorship is (null and) void."
[168] Id. (note omitted): "Whereas the German Copyright Act does not explicitly state this principle in the text, in doctrine the right to claim authorship also is regarded to belong to the substantial nucleus and core of moral right, which may not be waived at all."

also has the right to choose the form in which he or she wishes to be attributed, including anonymity or pseudonymity.[169]

In what initially seems like a contrast, the moral right of integrity can be waived; the author can, for example, authorize someone to make alterations to the work, which is, of course, an implicit waiver of the moral right of integrity, or at least some part of it. But here, too, there is a limit. The "core" of the integrity right cannot be waived. Accordingly, the author's right to object to the *mutilation* of his or her work remains even where a licensee is granted the right to make modifications. Walter explains this interesting point as follows:

> Pursuant to section 39 paragraph 1 of the German Copyright Act the right to object [to] alterations is granted on the condition that the author did not agree upon otherwise. However, here again, the very core of this moral right's prerogative may not be waived completely. According to the German doctrine, the author in any case, may oppose ... mutilating alterations.[170]

And the Austrian law, he says, is "even more" precise:

> Also with this regard the Austrian Act is even more accurate: according to section 21 paragraph 3 of the Act the author may consent to specific modifications, mutilations included. However, if the author has consented to alterations in such a way that such modifications are not specified in detail, notwithstanding such general consent, he or she still may object to mutilations and other alterations, which seriously violate his or her intellectual interests in the work.[171]

A fascinating counterpart to these restrictions on the ability to waive moral rights, enacted for the benefit of the author, is the recognition of the opposite situation: waiver can make a positive contribution to the enforcement of authors' moral rights, and, in this situation, in keeping with the overall sensibility of monist copyright laws, it is therefore allowed. For example, collective societies may thereby be empowered take action on behalf of the author, particularly where it is difficult for the author to pursue a claim in court. Since this difficulty is one of the chief obstacles to the recognition and enforcement of moral rights in court systems generally, the flexibility of German and Austrian law in this respect is noteworthy. As Michel Walter comments,

> An unconditional prohibition of a transfer of moral rights can [also] be disadvantageous for the author's interests, given that the claiming and defending of moral

[169] Id.
[170] Id. at 325.
[171] Id.

> interests by the author himself (in court) may turn out to be difficult to manage, in particular in foreign jurisdictions. This is why the Austrian Supreme Court held that a transfer of moral rights to third a person is admitted and enforceable on the condition that such transfer is carried out on a fiduciary basis and in the sole interest of the author.[172]

Indeed, the empowerment of collective rights organizations to assert moral rights is clearly not a principle to be taken lightly, since these organizations are often large and powerful entities with the potential to be influenced by their own self-interest. It is therefore not surprising that the principle recognized by the Austrian Supreme Court involves the very high standards represented by fiduciary principles and the ultimate animating rationale of the "sole interest" of the author. These would seem to be absolutely necessary restrictions on the allowability of waiver in the circumstances.

The author retains a right to revoke his or her work for reasons of changed conviction, which cannot be taken from him or her by contractual or other means.[173] Interestingly, this right is not categorized as a moral right under the German law, though it is an expression of the author' s moral right of withdrawal. In addition, no agreement committing an author to the exploitation of future works can be valid for more than five years, and the author also cannot extend these rights of exploitation over yet-to-be-created works by the indirect means of waiving the right to terminate such an agreement.[174] This right also appears as a kind of moral right in form and function. The provision on future works involves the prerogatives of disclosure. It is perhaps a recognition of an "innate right" to one's own future freedom, something like a right to be protected from forced labor. Its explicit recognition in the German law seems to fit well with the general emphasis on fairness to authors as the essence of the German copyright system. As noted above, German law also provides that the person granted an exploitation right may not make alterations to the author's work unless they have been specifically agreed upon, a detail of the integrity right.[175]

Given that copyright as a whole cannot be alienated,[176] licensing is key to the practical functioning of the monist copyright system. At the same, time, as noted by Michel Walter, German and Austrian copyright law both impose specific

[172] Id. at 323. He goes on to discuss the examples of moral rights exercised by collecting societies for the benefit of the author—a situation upheld by the Austrian courts, and upheld as part of the doctrine in both Germany and France.

[173] UrhG, *supra* note 147, at art. 42: "The right of revocation may not be waived in advance. Its exercise may not be precluded."

[174] Id. at art. 40. Article 41 also includes a "right of revocation for non-exercise," which can be invoked where the publisher's insufficient exploitation of a work "causes serious injury to the author."

[175] Id.

[176] *See, e.g.*, id. at ch. IV on the *Right to Use a Work*. Copyright as a whole "shall not be transferable": id. at art. 23(3).

limitations on the content of copyright licenses, thereby ensuring the integrity of the system of protection for authors' rights:

> With regard to the fact that copyright as such cannot be transferred to third parties, a specific dogmatic construction is necessary. Instead of a transfer of economic rights the author may grant [so-called] exclusive licences (Werknutzungsrechte).... Such exclusive licences convey genuine and absolute legal positions on the licensee.[177]

Inequality of bargaining power affecting authors has been discussed in the context of EU copyright harmonization and the digital single market initiative adopted in 2017.[178] But Germany had already adopted a law on the inequality of bargaining power in authors' contracts in 2002, the "Law to Strengthen the Contractual Position of Authors and Performing Artists."[179] As Jens Schovsbo points out,

> A ... most interesting development ... has taken place in Germany, where special legislation in the context of copyright law to strengthen the legal position of (individual) authors (and performing artists) was introduced in 2002. Interestingly, from the e-consumer's point of view, the background for this legislation was also ... changing market condition[s] and [the] increased risks of misuse of market power in the contractual relationship as a consequence of ... new technologies and changing market conditions (fewer and stronger publishers and other producers). The German law aims in part to make sure that producers would not use their bargaining power to secure for themselves all the fruits of the copyright expansion.[180]

[177] Walter, *supra* note 96, at 332 (notes omitted).

[178] *See, e.g.*, European Commission, *Questions and Answers: Commission Adopts Guidelines on Collective Agreements of Self-Employed People* (Sept. 29, 2022), https://ec.europa.eu/commission/presscorner/detail/en/qanda_22_5805; European Parliament, *Questions and Answers on Issues about the Digital Copyright Directive* (Mar. 27, 2019), https://www.europarl.europa.eu/news/en/press-room/20190111IPR23225/questions-and-answers-on-issues-about-the-digital-copyright-directive. The European Writers' Council weighs in here: European Writers' Council, *Directive 2019/790 on Copyright in the Digital Single Market: Authors' Group Recommendations on the Transportation of Articles 18 to 23* (June 30, 2020), https://europeanwriterscouncil.eu/ag-recommendations-18-23. This summary by law firm Lewis Silkin is also useful: Lewis Silkin, *Fair Remuneration for Authors and Performers in the Digital Content Directive: Are You Aware of Your New Obligations?* (Apr. 21, 2022), https://www.lewissilkin.com/en/insights/fair-remuneration-for-authors-and-performers-in-the-digital-content-directive. The Directive is available at https://eur-lex.europa.eu/eli/dir/2019/790/oj.

[179] Gesetz vom 22 März 2002 zur Stärkung der vertraglichen Stellung von Urhebern und ausübenden Künstlern [Law of Mar. 22, 2002 to Strengthen the Contractual Position of Authors and Performing Artists], BGBl. I S. 1155, amending the UrhG, *supra* note 147, as amended, https://www.wipo.int/wipolex/en/legislation/details/1048. (The original German is available at https://dejure.org/BGBl/2002/BGBl._I_S._1155.)

[180] Jens Schovsbo, *Integrating Consumer Rights into Copyright Law: From a European Perspective*, 31(4) J. Consumer Pol'y 393, 403 (2008) (note omitted).

Schovsbo observes that there is a new identity of interests between authors and their public in the digital environment. He comments,

> In many ways the individual author of books, music etc. would seem to be in a position similar to that of the consumer. The present fixation in copyright on the investment interests of corporations is bad news to consumers and individual authors alike and an initiative like the German one certainly suggests a more active role … [for] copyright law to regulate the distribution of the copyright reward and to intervene in a contractual relationship to protect the weaker party.[181]

For Schovsbo, the digital context involves new vulnerabilities. As technology corporations gain unprecedented power—through their influence on copyright law reform among other means—authors, as well as the public, are subject to a new level of exploitation.[182] But the relationship between authors and their public may have the potential for greater closeness in the technological environment. In effect, digital technology has led to possibilities for the "democratization" of this relationship.[183] But its success does not depend only on authors' ability to "enforce" their rights. Rather, in the digital context, authors and their public are involved in a symbiotic relationship, and it should be recognized as such on both sides.[184] Enjoying the benefits of this symbiosis requires mutual effort. Proximity does not necessarily translate into closeness.

A second consequence of monism involves the duration of moral rights. The French dualist system allows the duration of moral rights to differ from the term of economic rights. Under French dualism, there is a longer term of protection for moral rights: as discussed earlier, they are protected in perpetuity.[185] In contrast, German monism accords an equal term of protection to moral rights and economic rights, which is a limited term of protection under German law.[186]

[181] Id. at 403–04 (emphasis added, note omitted).

[182] This is a quick summary of the dynamics behind the adoption of the U.S. Digital Millennium Copyright Act, Pub. L. No. 105-304, 112 Stat. 2860 (1998) (DCMA), amending Title 17 of the U.S. Code. A summary of the DMCA is provided by the U.S. Copyright Office, http://www.copyright.gov/legislation/dmca.pdf.

[183] See, e.g., the comments in Mira T. Sundara Rajan, *Moral Rights in the Digital Age: New Possibilities for the Democratization of Culture*, 16(2) Int'l Rev. L. Computers & Tech. 187 (2002).

[184] Indeed, the successful enforcement of copyright is likely to depend on much more than the improvement of police and customs powers. This approach is cosmetic: practical powers of enforcement are only the tip of the iceberg; deeper problems involving the credibility of law, the absence of democratic infrastructure in societies where piracy is common, and a growing public distaste for copyright reform in many countries are other relevant factors. See, e.g., the discussion of the situation in post-socialist countries in Sundara Rajan, *supra* note 7, especially 47–71 (ch. III, *Copyright Law in Transition*). An updated version of this chapter is also available in Mira T. Sundara Rajan, *Introduction*, *in* Intellectual Property: Eastern Europe and the CIS 1 (Mira T. Sundara Rajan ed., 2008).

[185] The perpetual duration of French moral rights was recently affirmed by the *Pierre Hugo* case, *supra* note 88, although the case was not decided in favor of the writer's heirs.

[186] Article 64 of the German Copyright Law, *supra* note 144, provides that economic copyright lasts for the lifetime of the author and seventy years after his or her death. By the dualist theory, moral rights endure for the same period under German law.

According to monist theory, granting a separate duration for moral rights would break the fundamental unity of the author's right.[187] However, dualism does not necessarily require perpetual protection. All that dualist theory really accomplishes is to open up the possibility of choice on the important question of duration. Dietz observes that "there is no necessary correlation of dualism and perpetuity" and points out the great diversity of moral rights duration in countries that would categorize themselves as dualist.[188] Perpetual protection of moral rights in France is the result of dualist theory combined with the primacy of moral rights in the French copyright hierarchy.

3. The Modern Moral Rights: Germany and Austria

German copyright law protects three moral rights: disclosure, authorship, and integrity. As noted earlier, German law treats the right of revocation or withdrawal separately in its copyright law. It also includes two quasi-moral rights: a right of access to one's work after sale, also discussed briefly above, and an artist's resale right.[189]

The right of disclosure is broadly protected by the German provision. Interestingly, it includes communication of both the work and any attempt to "publicly communicate or describe the content of… [the] work."[190] The right of attribution is broad and includes the right to be recognized as the author of one's work on the terms that one chooses, or to claim anonymity.[191] The integrity right is called a right against "Distortion of the Work." However, it is neither an unlimited right,

[187] But Dietz observes that:

> If the German and, perhaps, also the Swiss example demonstrate that monistic or unitary interpretation of copyright shows a natural tendency to stop moral right protection together with copyright as a whole, there exists no necessary correlation. Duration of moral rights longer than the period of protection of the economic rights is rather a question of culture and policy.

Dietz, *supra* note 155, at para. 37.

[188] Dietz's list includes Belgium, Denmark, Italy, Netherlands, Spain, and Sweden: id. at para. 32. Canada should also be considered a dualist country, but one with lower levels of protection for moral rights, overall, than economic rights and not only in relation to the question of duration. See the comments of the majority of the Supreme Court in *Théberge*, *supra* note 89, although the Supreme Court makes the ambiguous suggestion that Canada's copyright law is monist in the subsequent case of *Desputeaux v. Éditions Chouette (1987) Inc.* [2003] 1 S.C.R. 178, 2003 SCC 17, para. 57 (Can.) ("The Canadian legislation therefore recognizes the overlap between economic rights and moral rights in the definition of copyright").

[189] The artist's resale right, or *droit de suite*, is now harmonized at the European level. *See* Directive 2001/84/EC of the European Parliament and of the Council of 27 September 200, on the resale right for the benefit of the author of an original work of art, 2001 O.J. (L 272) 32, https://eur-lex.europa.eu/legal-content/EN/TXT/?uri=celex%3A32001L0084.

[190] *See* German Copyright Law, *supra* note 147, at art. 12.

[191] Id. at art. 13, on "Recognition of Authorship," provides: "The author shall have the right of recognition of his authorship of the work. He may decide whether the work is to bear an author's designation and what designation is to be used."

as in France, nor a right that conforms to the Berne formula. Instead, the copyright law opts for a prohibition against a "distortion or any other mutilation which would jeopardize [the author's] ... legitimate intellectual or personal interests."[192] The German law does not deal with reputation. Instead, it focuses on the author's "interests," and it considers these in both their professional and personal dimensions.[193] This arguably makes the law broader in scope then the Berne Convention, since showing damage to one's "interests" is something more general than having to prove damage to one's reputation.

A comparison with modern Austrian provisions is instructive.[194] The closeness of German and Austrian law reflects their shared theoretical heritage, but the Austrian law is a more ambiguous expression of monist theory. Austrian law maintains the non-transferability of copyright, but it does not explicitly recognize the right of disclosure as a moral right. Instead, the author has an exclusive right to exploit the work.[195] However, a notion of disclosure is embedded in Article 14(3) of the Austrian law, which states a special rule in relation to "work[s] of literature or cinematography." The communication of the work to the public, or of its contents, "shall be reserved to the author, for as long as neither the work nor its substance has been published with his consent." As in the German law, the emphasis on content rather than form alone is noteworthy, and presents a contrast to the common-law emphasis on protection of expression rather than ideas.[196] This provision is well adapted to the digital context, where transformations of a work can result in significant changes to the form while the content remains essentially unchanged. Indeed,

[192] Id. at art. 14, on "Distortion of the Work," provides: "The author shall have the right to prohibit any distortion or any other mutilation of his work which would jeopardize his legitimate intellectual or personal interests in the work."

[193] The inclusion of "personal" interests here seems reminiscent of the Berne emphasis on an author's "honor." *See* Art. 6*bis* of the Berne Convention: International Convention for the Protection of Literary and Artistic Works, adopted at Berne on Sept. 9, 1886, completed at Paris on May 4, 1896, revised at Berlin on Nov. 13, 1908, completed at Berne on Mar. 20, 1914, revised at Rome on June 2, 1928, at Brussels on June 26, 1948, at Stockholm on July 14, 1967, and at Paris on July 24, 1971, and amended on Sept. 28, 1979, S. Treaty Doc. No. 99-27 (1986), https://www.wipo.int/treaties/en/ip/berne; also available in a useful format at the Legal Information Institute, Cornell University Law School, https://www.law.cornell.edu/treaties/berne.

[194] Federal Law BGBI No. 111 of 1936 on Copyright in Works of Literature and Art and on Neighboring Rights (Copyright Law), amended up to Federal Law published in the Federal Law Gazette I No. 244/2021 (BGBI.I No. 244/2021) (and as previously amended by BGBI 1949/206, 1953/106, 1963/175, 1972/492, 1980/321, 1982/295, 1988/601, 1989/612, 1993/93, 1996/151 and by 1998/25) (Austria), https://www.wipo.int/wipolex/en/legislation/details/21739.

[195] *See* id. at Pt. 1 ("Exploitation rights"), §§ 14–18.

[196] The fixation requirement is another term expressing the same idea—that the form in which ideas are recorded can be protected by copyright law but not the information contained therein. *See, e.g.*, Art. 9.1 of the Agreement on Trade-Related Aspects of Intellectual Property Rights (TRIPS Agreement), opened for signature Apr. 15, 1994, entered into force Jan. 1, 1995, Annex 1C to Marrakesh Agreement Establishing the World Trade Organization, 1869 U.N.T.S. 299, 33 I.L.M. 1197 (1994), https://www.wto.org/english/docs_e/legal_e/27-trips_01_e.htm; Copyright Act, 17 U.S.C. § 102(b) (U.S.). Canadian law is noteworthy in that it does not have a fixation requirement. This feature could have led to a potentially useful degree of flexibility when dealing with both traditional culture and new technology, but Canada's courts have read it into Canadian legislation. *See* David Vaver, Copyright Law (2000).

in the technological context, the economic and moral aspects of the work seem to converge in the fundamental principle of disclosure, although the Austrian act does not identify it as such.

The attribution right is comprehensive, allowing an author to protest any situation where his or her name is not associated with the work.[197] This is accomplished by splitting the right into two provisions, on the "Protection of Authorship" and the "Designation of Author," with the first empowering the author to object to any situation of misattribution or failure to attribute him or her appropriately.[198] As noted earlier, this right cannot be waived. The combined effect of these provisions is to circumvent any doubts about whether an author can object to the association of his or her name with another person's work—the problem of forgery.[199] In Michel Walter's opinion, "the right of non-attribution may be regarded as embraced by the author's right to authorship in a wider sense, as well, since it is the author's creative work as a whole that is concerned."[200]

The Austrian law defines the integrity right as a right for the "Protection of Works." It does not allow any alteration to the work without the author's consent. Interestingly, even if the author's consent is given, he or she may still sue in the case of "distortions, mutilations or other alterations of the work which seriously violate his moral interests in the work." Once again, the broad language of "interests" is used, and there is no mention of damage to reputation. The provision effectively places limits on the contractual agreement between author and publisher.

Finally, the Austrian law has been less willing to recognize hybrid rights than its German counterpart. It instituted an artist's resale right in 2005, in order to bring Austrian law into conformity with the EU Directive on the *droit de suite*. Austrian reluctance to recognize the resale principle may have to do with the importance of the art market for Vienna; a similar concern about London led to British reluctance to implement a resale right.[201] The Austrian law does include a provision

[197] Austrian Copyright Law, *supra* note 189:

Protection of Authorship

19.—(1) Where the authorship of a work is contested or the work is attributed to a person other than its creator, the latter shall be entitled to claim authorship. After his death, the right to safeguard the authorship of the creator of the work shall, in such cases, be held by the persons upon whom the copyright devolves.

(2) Waiver of this right shall be without effect.

[198] Id. §§ 19 and 20. Section 20 is on the "Designation of Author":

20.—(1). The author shall determine whether and in what manner the work is to bear a designation of author.

(2) An adaptation may not bear a designation of author in a manner that would make the adaptation appear to be an original work.

(3) Copies of works of art may not bear a designation of author that would make the copies appear to be originals.

[199] *See, e.g.*, Silke von Lewinski, International Copyright Law and Policy para. 5.99 (2008).

[200] Walter, *supra* note 96, at 324.

[201] The British fear was that London would cease to be competitive in relation to New York, which does not recognize an artist's resale right. *See* Nobuko Kawashima, *The Droit de Suite Controversy*

on the "Obligations of Owners of Works," which provides for the artist to have a limited right of access to his or her own work even after it is sold. But the law also states that there is no obligation on an owner to "preserve" the work, effectively releasing the owner from the specter of an integrity claim for inadequate preservation.[202] Presumably, Austrian law also does not prohibit outright destruction of a work, at least by its owner.[203]

4. Moral Rights and the Basic Law

But German copyright law has one further distinguishing feature. It is rooted in the German Constitution, the Basic Law, which includes two provisions relevant to copyright. First, German federal government is empowered to legislate on copyright by Article 73.9; unlike the U.S. constitutional provision on copyright, however, the German clause is silent on policy.[204] The second provision is more interesting. It falls under freedom of expression and provides that "Art and scholarship, research, and teaching shall be free."[205]

The German framework for moral rights should be interpreted in this context. Moral rights are part of the legal realization of artistic and intellectual freedom, a

Revisited: Context, Effects and the Price of Art, 3 INTELL. PROP. Q. 223, 227 (2006). In the United States, California is unique in attempting to institute such a right. *See, e.g.*, Eileen Kinsella, *Ending a Seven-Year Dispute, a U.S. Court Rules That Artists Aren't Entitled to Royalties for Artworks Resold at Auction*, Artnet (July 9, 2018), https://news.artnet.com/art-world/us-appeals-court-strikes-royalties-law-1314857. For a general consideration of some of the moral rights issues involved in art forgery, see also Mira T. Sundara Rajan, *Moral Rights and Forgery*, *in* ORIGINAL UND FÄLSCHUNG: IM SPANNUNGSFELD VON PERSÖNLICHKEITSSCHUTZ, URHEBER-, MARKEN-UND WETTBEWERBSRECHT 71 (G. Reichelt ed., 2007). For some statistics on the importance of Vienna's art market to the Austrian economy, see http://departure.at/jart/prj3/departure_website/main.jart?rel=en&reserve-mode=active&content-id=1160330080281&presse_id=1243582751563.

[202] A similar provision was added to the Indian Copyright Law in 1994. *See* Indian Copyright Act, 1957, *supra* note 16, §57; Indian Copyright (Amendment) Act 1994, *supra* note 121. The immediate objective may have been to protect the government, as a significant owner of important Indian works, from liability for improper preservation: *see* the *Sehgal* case, *supra* note 143.

[203] Austrian Copyright Law, *supra* note 189:

> 3. OBLIGATIONS OF OWNERS OF WORKS
> 22. On request, the owner of a work shall be required to afford the author access to the work where necessary for the reproduction of the work: in such case, the author shall show due consideration for the interests of the owner. The owner shall not be required to surrender the work to the author for such purpose: neither shall he have an obligation towards the author to ensure the preservation of the work.

[204] The German provision finds a parallel in the Canadian Constitution, which contains a purely functional clause on "copyrights." *See* the British North America Act 1867, 30 & 31 Vict., c. 3, § 91(23) (UK), http://laws.justice.gc.ca/en/const/3.html#anchorbo-ga:s_91.

[205] Grundgesetz (GG) [German Basic Law] (May 23, 1949), art. 5(3), http://www.iuscomp.org/gla/statutes/GG.htm. The German original may be seen on the website of the German Parliament at http://www.bundestag.de/dokumente/rechtsgrundlagen/grundgesetz/index.html.

constitutional imperative.[206] The constitutional context in Germany reflects the progress of human rights in the post-Second World War period, and it represents a human rights rationale underlying German copyright regulation.

By way of comparison, the U.S. constitutional framework provides a policy statement in the intellectual property clause, supporting the provision of incentives to authors while also prioritizing the public interest in knowledge that is acquired by access to copyright works.[207] The principle of balance is inherent in this provision.[208] It is interesting that this most individualistic of nations may, in some ways, have the most collectivist copyright system in the world.

5. Conclusion

Historically, the approach to moral rights in German law has been characterized by an appealing theoretical rigor. The modern law of Germany has maintained remarkable consistency with the past in its approach to moral rights. Based on the fundamental principle of disclosure, the original and ultimate prerogative of the author, Germany offers a comprehensive and logically satisfying approach to moral rights. German law provides both a complement and a contrast to French law.

Finally, it is worth noting that emphasis on disclosure as the foundation of copyright law has become especially important in the technological context. When works are so easily copied, altered, and disseminated, few aspects of authors' or owners' rights can be as important as the right of disclosure. Will a time come when little else of copyright remains?

As Hector MacQueen comments,

[206] *See* id. See also the interesting comments on the Compendium (Cultural Policies and Trends in Europe) website, http://www.culturalpolicies.net/web/germany.php?aid=531:

> **Germany**
> 5.3 Sector specific legislation
> 5.3.1 Visual and applied arts
> As is the case in other artistic fields, visual and applied art activities are covered under the *Freedom of Art Guarantee* of the Federal Constitution (*Article 5.III GG*). This provision guarantees everyone the right to freely work in the artistic domain and to strive for recognition of his/her work by the public, that is: the guarantee includes not only the "sphere of the creative work," but also the "sphere of impact" of that work via its publication and distribution.

It is also worth noting that this constitutional provision could be interpreted to impose limits on copyright protection, particularly where the freedom of expression of members of the public might be threatened by the inaccessibility of published materials.

[207] *See* U.S. Const., art. I, § 8, cl. 7: "The Congress shall have power … to promote the progress of science and useful arts, by securing for limited times to authors and inventors the exclusive right to their respective writings and discoveries." *See* http://topics.law.cornell.edu/constitution/articlei#section1.

[208] *See* Ginsburg, *supra* note 43, at 991. Both Ginsburg and Carla Hesse argue that the opposition of individualistic French law and public-oriented U.S. law is generally overstated—at least, prior to the development of "personalist doctrines, such as moral rights" in the nineteenth century: id. at 995. Hesse's work shows that the concept of author as public servant is important to the development of French copyright law: *see* Hesse, *supra* note 4, at 110 and n.6.

> Copying is unavoidable in the digital world ...; so perhaps, at least in this context (which may increasingly be the only context that really matters), copyright as a right to prevent copying should be abandoned. Privacy and confidentiality rights may serve better to protect the work which the author does not intend for publication of any kind, while moral rights of attribution and integrity can be the bulwark of other authorial interests, offset by appropriately framed exceptions for education, research, news reporting, public libraries and parody.[209]

D. The United Kingdom: Second Thoughts

In relation to moral rights, as in many other respects, the contrast between the United Kingdom and the countries of continental Europe is striking.[210] European countries place moral rights at the heart of their copyright systems. The United Kingdom, however, has long been a hostile environment for moral rights. Moral rights are, it is said, incompatible with the common law.

This position is a curious one. The history of moral rights in the French and German traditions shows that the character of moral rights in those countries is essentially informal and dependent on case determinations. Moral rights evolved in this way in spite of the fact that these European legal cultures are built on legal codification.

German theorizing about moral rights occurred while French courts were already engaged in a practical exploration of the idea. In France, codification of the law did not take place until the late date of 1957, nearly a century-and-a-half after moral rights were already well established in French legal practice. English law and moral rights may be incompatible, but, as this history shows, any such incompatibility cannot have much to do with the common law. On the contrary, the flexibility and pragmatism of the common-law mirror the processes by which moral rights originally emerged in European countries. If anything, the common law would seem to be well adapted to the recognition of moral rights for authors.

And indeed, a closer look at UK copyright history shows that the accepted narrative is incomplete and misleading. In fact, the courts in England developed an early appreciation of authors' moral rights. Remarkably, their recognition of moral rights significantly preceded the emergence of moral rights in early nineteenth-century France.[211] English judges recognized moral rights in the landmark 1769

[209] Hector L. MacQueen, *The Google Book Settlement*, 40(3) INT'L REV. INTELL. PROP. COMPETITION L. 247, 249 (2009). The moral right of disclosure is also a means of protecting the work from publication against the author's will.

[210] This section refers to the United Kingdom to capture the reach of copyright law throughout England, Scotland, and Wales. As described, the struggle to define the scope of copyright law in the wake of the Statute of Anne had an interesting intra-British dimension, pitting the enterprise of Scottish booksellers against the entrenched interests of London monopolists.

[211] See Desbois's comments on the venerable laws of the 1790s in France: Desbois, *supra* note 110.

case of *Millar v. Taylor*.[212] However, they rejected the idea soon afterwards, in the subsequent judgment of *Donaldson v. Beckett* in 1775, which overruled the earlier case.[213]

A consideration of how and why the moral rights concept was purged from English law is illuminating in two ways. First, it helps to deflate the myth that English law somehow fails to comprehend the moral rights of authors. Secondly, it shows that the British attitude to moral rights was largely a product of historical accident rather than any particular policy goal or underlying antipathy towards authors' non-pecuniary concerns.

The common-law "problem" of moral rights was a product of two factors. First, moral rights were not recognized in English copyright statutes. Reflecting the preoccupations of the era, the Statute of Anne focused exclusively on authors' property rights in their work. Subsequently, through the series of eighteenth-century cases known as the "Battle of the Booksellers," copyright in the UK became a confirmed creature of statute, with the judges clearly stating that copyright was limited to what was granted in the Statute of Anne and overruling any common-law claims related to copyright.[214] The absence of moral rights from the statutory scheme and for copyright law—notwithstanding the claims of the Gregory Committee in 1952 about the effectiveness of common-law actions for the indirect protection of moral

[212] *Millar*, *supra* note 3.

[213] *Donaldson*, *supra* note 3. While a proper discussion of the distinctions between English and Scottish law at this key historical juncture requires further research, I am indebted to Hector MacQueen for pointing out that the Scottish court in *Hinton v. Donaldson*, 1773, 5 Brn 508 appeared to recognize an author's right of divulgation, though not under that label: Hector MacQueen, private correspondence with the author (Aug. 2023). Scottish law already recognized a personality right, extending to "rights of certain family members in the integrity of family life," which made it possible to prolong such rights after the death of the person affected: *see* Hector L. MacQueen, *Ae Fond Kiss: A Private Matter?*, *in* JUDGE AND JURIST: ESSAYS IN MEMORY OF LORD RODGER OF EARLSFERRY 473, para. 10 (Edinburgh School of Law Research Paper No. 2014/14, A. Burrows, D. Johnston & R. Zimmermann eds., 2013), https://ssrn.com/abstract=2430698. The 1804 case of *Cadell and Davies v. Stewart* raised the issue of whether Robert Burns' letters to a certain Clarinda could be published after his death (though the married Clarinda was alive and vulnerable to scandal). MacQueen observes id. at [9]:

> The stroke of legal genius which enabled the defeat of Stewart's enterprise was to bring in the Burns family as co-petitioners alongside Cadell and Davies ... Bringing the Burns family into the Clarinda case made possible an argument based on their interest in preventing damage to Burns' character and reputation. The argument built on the still developing law of what we would now call personality rights, the protection of body, reputation and dignity (corpus, fama and dignitas) against the crime and delict of iniuria. The concept of iniuria included the unauthorised disclosure of another's secrets.... Damages, increasingly referred to as "solatium", might be recovered for the hurt to feelings caused by the wrong or "injury", while it was also possible to claim for any patrimonial loss that had been caused.

The Burns and Clarinda letters are the subject of a two-part discussion in Mira T. Sundara Rajan, *Robert Burns and Clarinda: A Poet's Passion before the Courts of Law—with Hector MacQueen*, WOMAN OF CULTURE PODCAST (May 25 and June 7, 2024), https://podcasts.apple.com/us/podcast/woman-of-culture/id1723723726.

[214] See the detailed discussion *infra* notes 228–40 and accompanying text.

right[215]—led to a practical lack of legal force. The root incompatibility, therefore, is not between moral rights and the common law; rather, it is the absence of moral rights from the statute that has created an issue in English and Scottish law.

Secondly, legal parochialism has subsequently played a role. The modern view of moral rights sees them as an import from French, or possibly European, law. As discussed above, even the terminology has been adopted from France. Moral rights ultimately came into the UK copyright framework through implementation of the Berne Convention, which adopted a compromise formula for the international protection of moral rights in 1928.[216] In this context, British concerns about moral rights were also justified—because of the complexities involved in legal translation or "transplantation," which continue to be presented by the challenge of effective transposition of the Berne Convention into national laws.[217] There is no way around it: the problem of translating *droit moral* into the UK context requires the translation of legal and cultural principles from one jurisdiction to the other.

From a legal point of view, this is frustrating. How can we account for cultural sensibilities while remaining true to time-tested legal theories? How can we build a meaningful approach to moral rights in any "new" jurisdiction? What is normal in France may not be feasible in the UK; what is right for one society may be irrelevant to the other. But, again, this is the value of re-examining British legal history: it allows us to discover a British concept of moral rights distinct from its European counterparts and from the compromise later achieved in the Berne Convention.

Re-examining the concept of harmonization may also help to resolve the problem of legal transplantation—in this case, by the indirect route of transposing international norms into national law. Harmonization has come to mean many things in the international regulation of copyright, and it is often misrepresented as a call for identical law in different countries. Given the different soil and climate of copyright systems around the world, such crude legal transplantation is bound to fail. The prevalence of copyright piracy in so many countries is evidence of that failure. Faced with the global reality of post-colonialism, a word that captures much of the tension underlying international intellectual property regulation, our legal imagination has often fallen short.

215 See comments *infra* notes 241–45 and accompanying text.

216 The United Kingdom was an original signatory of the Berne Convention, which came into effect on December 5, 1887: Ricketson & Ginsburg, *supra* note 39, at para. 2.52. Moral rights were adopted into Berne in 1928, and Ricketson describes the circumstances in which England and other common-law jurisdictions acquiesced: *see* SAM RICKETSON, THE BERNE CONVENTION FOR THE PROTECTION OF LITERARY AND ARTISTIC WORKS: 1886–1986 paras. 3.28 and 3.60 (1987).

217 Ugo Mattei and other comparative scholars use the appropriate terminology of "legal transplants" to discuss this issue: *see* Ugo Mattei, *Three Patterns of Law: Taxonomy and Change in the World's Legal Systems*, 45 AM. J. COMP. L. 5 (1997).

But it is helpful to remember that the concept of harmonization comes from music:

> Harmonization finds its natural context, not in law, but in music. In the legal analogy, it seems to have gained currency as meaning a process of revision that makes laws broadly similar to one another. In music, however, this is not what it means. The very notion of harmony depends on difference. Two identical notes cannot "harmonize" with one another—the essence of harmony has been brilliantly described as a juxtaposition of the disparate.[218] Harmony means that two different notes enjoy a relationship of compatibility within the terms of a defined musical language.[219] What is more, harmony arises when individual notes are colored by the larger context defined by sequences of different notes. If the legal analogy is to be well-drawn, legal "harmonization" should embrace some concept of a mutually complementary relationship, a level of consensus in the international sphere, however slowly it may be achieved. Harmonized laws will work in concert with other laws, in the context of a wider legal environment. Indeed, introducing "an identically phrased rule" into two different legal contexts may actually lead to legal differences, rather than [achieving] the desired effect of sameness.[220]

[218] See the historical discussion of harmony in Carl Dahlhaus, *Harmony, Part 1, Historical Definitions, in* New Grove Dictionary of Music and Musicians (Stanley Sadie & John Tyrrell eds., 2d ed., 2001). Dahlhaus goes on to comment that "harmony considered as a structural principle is just as much an intrinsic part of ancient and medieval music as it is of the tonal system of modern times. The two-note consonance constituted the foundation of the old tonal system, the three-note consonance that of the new": id. *See* Sundara Rajan, *supra* note 7, at 10–11 and nn.13–14:

> To satisfy musicians, it may be worth noting that the closest thing to two identical notes making "harmony" is an octave—the sounding of a note with the tone that, in scientific terms, is exactly twice the frequency of the original note. The listener would hear this as "the same note" sounded above or below the original note. In his entry on the octave in the New Grove Dictionary of Music, William Drabkin clarifies its nature: "To Western and most non-Western musicians, two notes an octave apart are in a sense alike, being different only in their relative registers and often seeming to blend into one another. This acoustical phenomenon has made the division of the frequency spectrum into octaves fundamental to both the understanding and the notation of music. The ancient Greeks, who recognized this phenomenon, called the octave *harmonia*, later *diapasōn*; Ptolemy, writing in the 2nd century, distinguished the octave from the other perfect intervals, calling it *homophōnia* (the 5th and 4th were called *symphōnia*)."

[219] The use of the term "musical language" is applied here in the sense of a musical genre—e.g., the different "musical languages" of jazz or classical music. Technically, however, genres often share the same musical language: on the one hand, classic jazz makes use of the same musical language, based on harmony, as Western classical music; on the other hand, Indian classical music is based on a "modal" language, which does not use the concept of harmony as it is usually understood in Western music. Modal music was the dominant form of medieval Europe, and it was largely replaced by harmonic systems based on the relative pitch of notes by the mid-seventeenth century: J.S. Bach's "Well-Tempered Clavier" was a response to this transformation. Modal music might be familiar to modern listeners in the West through experimental works such as Eric Satie's "Gnossiennes" of "Gymnopédies," or modal jazz such as Miles Davis's "Milestones."

[220] Sundara Rajan, *supra* note 7, at 10–11. The point was emphasized in a statement by Professor Colin Tapper (in personal communication with the author, 2006).

1. Early History and the Statute of Anne, 1709–10

The Statute of Anne was the first British law to recognize an author's right in his own work.[221] Prior to this statute, printing was regulated by a "privilege" granted directly to a select group of printers by the sovereign, known as the Stationers' Company. The Stationers enjoyed the exclusive right to print works throughout the British realm. Membership of the Company was tightly restricted. This system of printing privileges enabled the sovereign to control publication. The result was censorship.[222]

This system was broken by the Statute of Anne. The means by which censorship was brought to an end was the recognition of individual rights of authorship, and this was the culmination of a decades-long struggle for freedom of the press in England.[223]

The recognition of authors was also a breakthrough in concepts, and this achievement should not be understated. It was made possible by influential thinkers and writers. John Locke's labor theory of property was easily applied to literary creation, and John Milton's arguments for freedom of the press reflected his understanding of the relationship between a work and the personality of its creator.[224] Indeed, paragraphs of Milton's famous pamphlet on free speech, *Areopagitica*, read like an exposition of moral rights philosophy:

> For books are not absolutely dead things, but do contain a potency of life in them to be as active as that soul whose progeny they are; nay, they do preserve as in a vial the purest efficacy and extraction of that living intellect that bred them.[225]

The Statute represented a political breakthrough in another sense: it broke the economic monopoly enjoyed by the stationers and, in particular, by the formidable printers' oligopoly known as the Conger, which had come to dominate eighteenth-century printing.[226] Prior to the Statute, the stationers acquired the right to print a

[221] Statute of Anne, *supra* note 46, at §19. A facsimile copy of the book can be seen online at http://www.copyrighthistory.com/anne.html.

[222] Indeed, historian Michael Wood characterizes the earlier history of England under the Tudors as a "police state": *see* MayaVision International, *In Search of Shakespeare* (June 2003), https://www.mayavisionint.com/project/in-search-of-shakespeare.

[223] *See* Lyman Ray Patterson, *Free Speech, Copyright and Fair Use*, 40(1) Vand. L. Rev. 1 (1987). The same process was mirrored in France, where the breaking of the Paris printers' monopoly supported the genesis of an authors' right into which the French Revolution would ultimately blow the breath of life.

[224] Milton's *Areopagitica* is a manifesto of the movement for a free press. *See* John Milton, Areopagitica (AMS Press 1971) (1644) with a commentary by Sir Richard C. Jebb and with supplementary material. The text is available online at http://www.stlawrenceinstitute.org/vol14mit.html.

[225] Id.

[226] *See* Lyman Ray Patterson, Copyright in Historical Perspective 151 (1968): "In 1710, copyright was the right of a publisher to the exclusive publication of a work, and functioned to prevent literary piracy; by 1774, copyright had come to be the right of an author, and still functioned to protect the exclusive right of publication." Patterson draws attention to the power of the Statute of Anne, which effectively established the notion of an *author's* copyright over this period. It is worth noting that

work from its author, and continued to exercise it without practical limitations in time. Moreover, as Lyman Ray Patterson points out, an entire industry had grown up around the printing of classics, whose authors were deceased, and where the question of the author's consent was irrelevant.[227] The stationers recognized each others' prerogatives, and the printing right of each was, in effect, the exercise of a "copyright" that fellow members of the oligopoly would respect.

The Statute of Anne shattered this system. Under the terms of the new law, the right to print was no longer a right of the stationers: it was a right of the author, to be assigned to the printer for a fourteen-year period, after which time, it would return to the author.[228] At the same time, the stationers themselves could no longer benefit from the exclusive right to print. Instead, printing was thrown open to the world at large, and the stationers had to compete in an open market to acquire that right. Finally, the stationers would no longer have exclusive rights—de facto privileges—in classic works. On this last issue, the Statute relented slightly: it did include a transitional provision for the continued protection of stationers' printing rights in classic works for twenty-one years. But under this "grandfather" clause, too, privileges would expire. After twenty-one years, the works would fall into the public domain and could then be printed by anyone.

How could the stationers and their collaborators allow the passing of their lucrative monopoly without a struggle? The issue came to a head in two now famous cases: *Millar v. Taylor*, decided in 1769, and *Donaldson v. Beckett*, which settled the issue finally in 1774.[229] Both cases involved rights to print a celebrated long poem by James Thomson, "The Seasons." The struggle arose between the booksellers of London, who wanted to hold on to their monopoly, and Scottish booksellers, represented by Alexander Donaldson of Edinburgh, who began to print inexpensive editions of classic works, arguing that the expiry of the grandfather clause in the Statute of Anne laid these works open to the public in 1731. In their struggle to hold on to power, the stationers did something that was to be precedent-setting on a grand scale: in a strategy that is weirdly familiar in our own age, the booksellers donned the mask of the author to argue for the promotion of their own interests.[230]

the thinkers who lobbied for the right over the preceding half-century, such as Milton and Locke, also offered a conceptual basis for the grant of the right. It was a reflection of an individual's property right in his own labor.

[227] *See* id. at 151–52. *See also* LAWRENCE LESSIG, *Founders*, *in* FREE CULTURE: HOW BIG MEDIA USES TECHNOLOGY AND THE LAW TO LOCK DOWN CULTURE AND CONTROL CREATIVITY 69 (2004).

[228] Statute of Anne, *supra* note 47.

[229] *Millar* and *Donaldson*, *supra* note 3. *Hinton v. Donaldson*, *supra* note 13, also had a significant effect on the later *Donaldson v. Beckett*: Hector MacQueen, in private correspondence with the author (Aug. 2023).

[230] In this regard, Patterson, *supra* note 221, at 8 (notes omitted) observes:

> [C]opyright did not come into existence until the printing press facilitated the reproduction and widespread distribution of books. To protect the right to exclusive distribution, publishers created copyright. From this protection the author who created the work gained at best a

The rejection of their suit by the English courts dealt a death blow to the formidable monopoly that they had enjoyed.

In this clash, however, there was an unexpected casualty: moral rights. As the *Miller* and *Donaldson* cases were decided, the possibility of legal recognition for the natural, non-commercial, or moral interests of authors was raised, and then definitively eliminated from English law. The concept of a moral right for British authors was not to be revisited for more than 200 years.[231]

a. Early Recognition of a Moral Copyright: *Millar v. Taylor* (1769)

When the stationers first went to court to vindicate their monopoly, they framed their arguments with care, using the very language of the Statute of Anne for a new purpose. The Statute of Anne had recognized an author's copyright for the first time, but in doing so, the stationers argued, the Statute did not enlarge authors' rights at all. Rather, the statutory copyright was one that restricted a pre-existing right at common law. The Statute of Anne limited authors' exclusive right to print their works to fourteen years, with the possibility of a renewal for fourteen more. However, their pre-existing common law right in their works was valid in perpetuity, the stationers argued.

What was the basis for the stationers' argument? As Patterson points out, the stationers' familiarity with copyright was of long standing. The copyright, or right of printing, enjoyed by the stationers was one that they had enjoyed, at least in theory, as a perpetual right. From the stationers' perspective, perpetual protection was the natural way of looking at copyright.[232]

But the introduction of the author into this equation brought a new dimension to the right. The stationers thought that copyright should be perpetual because it had always been so. But the recognition of a perpetual copyright for *authors* had to be based on some public-policy rationale that fit with the Statute of Anne. This rationale found voice as the idea of a natural right of authorship, and it was easily derived from the humanistic arguments of Milton, Locke, and their contemporaries,

> reward secondary to that of the publisher. Copyright, therefore, originally functioned to encourage not creation, but distribution. In this regard, copyright's function is essentially the same today.

[231] Moral rights provisions were finally adopted in the United Kingdom as ch. IV of the Copyright, Designs and Patents Act 1988, c. 48 (CDPA), https://www.legislation.gov.uk/ukpga/1988/48/part/I/chapter/IV. Performers' moral rights are covered in ch. 3 of Part II of the Act ("Rights in performances"), https://www.legislation.gov.uk/ukpga/1988/48/part/II/chapter/3.

[232] On the stationers' practices, Lyman Ray Patterson, *supra* note 217, at 27 (emphasis added) comments:

> The second compromise—giving the assignee all the rights of the author—played an even more important and ultimately determinative role in creating the confusion in copyright law. This provision enabled publishers to use authors as foils in their quest for recognition of a perpetual common-law copyright. *This perpetual common-law copyright, ostensibly for the benefit of authors, could be assigned to the publisher and, therefore, would effectively supersede the statutory copyright.*

dealing with not only authorship but also property. This approach was accepted by the court in *Millar v. Taylor*, and Lord Mansfield affirmed the continued existence of authors' natural rights at common law, in perpetuity, notwithstanding the intervention of the Statute of Anne.

But the author's right at common law described by Lord Mansfield was also mysterious. What common-law principle was its source? As Mark Rose points out, Lord Mansfield relied on "the author's prepublication right" as the origin of common-law rights. Lord Mansfield cites two precedents in support of the idea that the copyright in a book is something different from the possession of the book itself—that copyright is something more than a right in physical property.[233] But, as Rose points out, none of these cases conclusively establishes the nature of an author's common-law copyright, "nor [can it be found] in immemorial custom because the introduction of printing was itself within living memory."[234] Ronan Deazley suggests that common-law copyright never really existed, but that Lord Mansfield advocated for one:

> The decision, handed down by Lord Mansfield's court, represents no less than a triumph of creative historical revisionism and legal advocacy. Notwithstanding the reality of the Statute of Anne … the history of the first four decades of lawful book publishing in Britain had been carefully re-crafted. The London monopolists had picked a number of disparate legal-historical threads, bound them together within a compelling ontological framework, and created a new, altogether different, coherent form. The perpetual common-law right had literally been written, talked and argued into existence.[235]

If Lord Mansfield was engaged in a creative legal enterprise, it can be summarized as follows: he wanted to redefine the law of copyright while relying upon the pedigree supplied by recent copyright judgments. He acknowledges his own comments as the product of long experience. But the recognition of a common law copyright would have meant a re-establishment of the booksellers' monopoly—the effective re-establishment of censorship in a new form, not as the prerogative of the crown, but exercised, in fact, by the Stationers' Company for its own material gain. This position sounds depressingly familiar in our own times. But this is not to say that Lord Mansfield intended to support the printers. As Rose observes, "So far

[233] *See* Mark Rose, Authors and Owners: The Invention of Copyright 79 (1993). The cases are *Pope v. Curll* (1741) 2 Atk. 342, 26 Eng. Rep 608 (Ch.) (Eng.) (involving the rights to print letters written by Pope but in physical possession of the person to whom they were addressed) and *Duke of Queensberry v. Shebbeare* (1758) 2 Eden 329, 28 Eng. Rep. 924 (Ch.) (Eng.).

[234] *See* Rose, *supra* note 227, at 79–80.

[235] Ronan Deazley, On the Origin of the Right to Copy: Charting the Movement of Copyright Law in 18th-century Britain 178–79 (2004).

as [Lord Mansfield] ... was concerned, evidently, the justness of the fundamental principle rendered all other considerations secondary."[236]

From a moral rights perspective, Mansfield's comments on the actual substance of the common-law copyright are striking. His view of authors' rights, as distinct from copyright, is comprehensive: the author's right originates in principles of "just[ice]." Failure to offer adequate legal protection to the author will lead to ill effects:

> [The author] is no more master of the use of his own name. He has no control over the correctness of his own work. He can not prevent additions. He can not retract errors. He can not amend; or cancel a faulty edition. Any one may print, pirate, and perpetuate the imperfections, to the disgrace and against the will of the author; may propagate sentiments under his name, which he disapproves, repents and is ashamed of. He can exercise no discretion as to the manner in which, or the persons by whom his work shall be published.[237]

There could be no clearer statement of moral rights. Mansfield recognizes every fundamental moral right later described by French and German writers: attribution ("use of his own name"), integrity ("correctness," "additions," "errors"), and even a right of withdrawal (the implication that "perpetuation" of the work in circumstances where the author "repents" or feels "ashamed" should not be allowed). The principle of disclosure occupies a central position in Mansfield's understanding of the author's rights and prerogatives: he defines it as the author's "discretion as to the manner in which, or the persons by whom his work shall be published."

Lyman Ray Patterson points out the presence of moral rights in Mansfield's approach, and he goes on to a key observation: the *Millar* case inextricably links the idea of an author's moral right, in English law, with the notion of a common-law copyright. The Statute of Anne did not delineate a comprehensive right for authors. Rather, it sought to protect the *property* rights of both authors—an innovation—and publishers. Its protection of publishers was a transitional measure to accommodate and phase out the existing rights of booksellers, but it also laid the groundwork for the publishing regime of the future based on property rights to the exclusion of more or less all else. The Statute intersected with natural rights theory only in its recognition of authorship—in the specific sense that property rights in literary creation went to their creators in the first instance, reflecting the labor and, *per* Milton, the originality of authors. This natural right of authors to own their own creations was not developed any further in the language of the Statute of Anne. As Patterson concludes,

236 Rose, *supra* note 227, at 84.
237 This passage is quoted id. at 80.

> Mansfield skillfully conflated the rights of the author and bookseller and invested copyright with the author's moral rights. The end result was to foreclose the future development of the author's rights in his work independent of copyright because copyright pre-empted the field. If a copyright encompassed all the rights in the work, the author's rights would become inextricably bound with the publisher's rights in accordance with the publisher's claims. Ironically, this development was detrimental, not beneficial, to the author. It eliminated the opportunity for courts to distinguish between the work and the copyright of the work. By embracing this conflation of rights, common-law jurisdictions forfeited the development of the doctrine of moral rights by default.[238]

Patterson points to the "conflation" of the author's interests with the copyright in the work. This subsequently made it difficult – impossible, according to Patterson – to recognize any non-proprietary rights arising out of authorship.The concept that the stationers might only be entitled to hold proprietary rights while the authors retained other rights in the work—rights arising from authorship as described by Lord Mansfield—could not be conceptualized within this framework.

Nothing in the Statute of Anne suggests a moral right. But it can be said that the Statute established an author's personal right to control the initial publication of his or her own work—implicit recognition of the principle of disclosure. Disclosure is the right to decide upon the publication of one's own, unpublished manuscripts, and William Patry asserts that

> [t]he United States' earliest statutes and case law were imported from England, where, under the common law, an author's right to prevent the unauthorized publication of his or her manuscript appears to have been recognized on the principle of natural justice, the manuscript being the product of intellectual labor and considered as much the author's own property as the physical substance on which it was written. Sir William Blackstone, English jurist and writer on law, associated such protection with the law of occupancy, which involves personal labor and results in "property," something peculiarly one's own (as implied by the Latin root "proprius").[239]

The existence of this right in unpublished manuscripts is well established. By the technological era, it had become a practical problem that the UK legislature chose to deal with by enacting the 2039 rule, whereby all unpublished manuscripts over a certain age could be lawfully published in the United Kingdom after that date. But Patry's assertion that, under English law, "an author's right to prevent the

[238] *See* Patterson, *supra* note 217, at 30–31 (emphasis added, notes omitted).

[239] William F. Patry, *Copyright Law and Practice* 3 (1994), http://digital-law-online.info/patry/patry2.html.

unauthorized publication of his or her manuscript appears to have been recognized on the principle of natural justice" is open to discussion, not because the principle is in doubt, but because it is not clear whether such a common-law copyright ever existed under English law.[240] However, the right of disclosure can be said to be a feature of statutory copyright in England, expressed in the Statute of Anne, which "vest[ed] the Copies of Printed Books in the Authors or Purchasers of such Copies." As far as "Purchasers" or publishers are concerned, the right was a transitional right; the new system aimed to give *authors* a right to control the publication of their own, unpublished manuscripts. The policy rationales behind this right are clearly set out in the preface to the Statute, which states,

> Whereas Printers, Booksellers, and other Persons, have of late frequently taken the Liberty of Printing, Reprinting, and Publishing, or causing to be Printed, Reprinted, and Published Books, and other Writings, without the *Consent of the Authors or Proprietors* of such Books and Writings, to their very great *Detriment*, and too often to the *Ruin of them and their Families*: For Preventing therefore such Practices for the future, and for the *Encouragement of Learned Men to Compose and Write useful Books.*[241]

The Statute articulates three policy rationales: authorial consent, the financial need of authors and printers, and of and their families, and the desire to provide an incentive to "encourage ... Learned Men" to "Write useful Books."

Moral rights could only originate in the common law. But any expanded conception of the common-law rights of authors would have involved publishers, too. Patterson points out that "once an author conveyed his copy, all the rights that [Lord] Mansfield concluded were 'just' and 'fit' for the author passed to the bookseller,"[242] but it is not just this: publishers alone were the repositories of the right to print prior to the Statute of Anne.[243] *Two* conclusions must therefore be drawn: that publishers would be the ultimate beneficiaries through the acquisition of manuscripts, and that any common-law right held by the *author, prior to the Statute of Anne,* could not have included a right to publish the work.

This was a reflection of the historical circumstances of the time. Although the Statute of Anne established an author's copyright for the first time, it was also a transitional statute that brought an end to the previous copyright regime, of which the stationers were the primary beneficiaries. The Statute marked the boundary between censorship—of which, the printers' monopoly was an artefact—and the era of a free press. As such, the Statute had to address the rights of both authors and

240 This issue is generally discussed by Patterson, *supra* note 217, but see especially the commentary at 31–32.

241 Statute of Anne, *supra* note 46, §I (emphasis added).

242 Patterson, *supra* note 221, at 29.

243 A point also noted by Patterson, *supra* note 20.

publishers, whose position in the new regime and relationship to one another it redefined.[244]

After the *Millar v. Taylor* case, how can moral rights be said to be alien to English law? They were not. On the contrary, the *Millar* case shows that an English judge recognized the moral rights aspect of an author's copyright more than half a century before it became a matter of serious interest for the French. As Patterson notes, "Mansfield's discussion of the author's rights remains a good statement of the author's moral rights."[245] But the judgement led to a situation where there was no available legal means of recognizing authors' non-proprietary rights.

Practical concerns about the implications of a common-law copyright led to the elimination of the moral rights concept from British law. This was accomplished in the subsequent case of *Donaldson v. Beckett.* The proposed common-law copyright presented dangers to freedom of the press. But there was nothing inherently incompatible about the moral rights concept with British law. On the contrary, Lord Mansfield showed that the common law could accommodate moral rights convincingly, and with ease.

b. Protecting Free Speech: Moral Rights Revisited in *Donaldson v. Beckett* (1774)

In *Donaldson*, the court considered how the recognition of a common-law copyright would affect publishing. The Statute's purpose was to break the printing monopoly of the booksellers, and, by doing so, bring an end to state censorship of the written word. If a common-law copyright beyond the Statute was recognized, could this purpose be accomplished?

Clearly not. Invoking rights beyond the Statute would have allowed publishers to do two things. First, they could continue to enjoy monopoly rights in works that they were already printing. Through perpetual exclusive printing rights, the literary heritage of England would become the property of the booksellers. Secondly, the booksellers could lay claim to exclusive printing rights in new works beyond fourteen years (renewable once), the period stipulated by the Statute. At the same time, the supposed foundation of copyright in the will of the author would be relegated to irrelevance.

These concerns led to a definitive ruling in the *Donaldson* case, which overturned the principle established in *Millar.* No common-law copyright existed

[244] Patterson himself blurs the distinction between common-law copyright and moral rights: *see* Patterson, *supra* note 221, at 26. He states, "Finally, by limiting the rights of the copyright owner to rights that were economic in nature, it gave the user freedom to use the work for the purpose of learning." But this effect was achieved by limiting the rights of the copyright holder to the Statute. Lord Mansfield's recognition of the moral rights as part of a "common-law copyright" was not the reason behind the rejection of the common-law copyright; rather, the reason was to prevent the re-establishment of the booksellers' control over printing—a fact that Patterson has already pointed out in his detailed historical study.

[245] Id. at n.92.

beyond the Statute of Anne: to recognize one would be to thwart the very objectives of that Statute and to destroy the possibility of a free press in its infancy.[246] In the process of affirming statutory copyright, however, another idea became a casualty of the conflict, whether real or imaginary, between common-law and statutory copyright: moral rights.

No statutory basis for moral rights existed. Lord Mansfield's brilliant exposition of moral rights theory associated it with its only possible legal source, the common law. The common-law copyright expounded by Lord Mansfield reflected elements of natural law, which was at the root of the moral rights concept in France and Germany. In Great Britain, however, the problem of the booksellers meant that any rights beyond the Statute of Anne were presented under the rubric of the common-law copyright. All such rights were abolished wholesale when common-law copyright was deemed to have been superseded by the Statute. This approach was a product of hatred for censorship, whether governmental or corporate in nature. It subsequently impeded the enlargement of British copyright law to include those elements of natural law that might have warranted consideration if the booksellers had not lobbied so hard for their own interests.

2. Modern Approach: "Shy Beauty"

The formal enactment of moral rights in British copyright law finally occurred at the relatively late date of 1988.[247] International copyright relations provided the catalyst for reform. Great Britain had been a signatory to the Berne Convention since 1887; moral rights were brought in to Berne, as noted earlier, at the Rome revision conference of 1928.[248] But the United Kingdom did not amend its legislation to include moral rights, and a 1952 review of British law by the Gregory Committee found, instead, that British law met its obligations under the Berne Convention without the need for any amendments.[249] How? Ironically, adequate protection for moral rights was deemed to arise through common-law remedies, particularly the

[246] See Rose, *supra* note 227, for a description of what happened. *See also* David Saunders, Authorship and Copyright (1992).

[247] *See* CDPA, *supra* note 231, at Pt. IV (and later ch. 3 of Pt. II, "Rights in Performances"), https://www.legislation.gov.uk/ukpga/1988/48/contents.

[248] Berne Convention, *supra* note 193, at Art. 6*bis*. *See* International Convention for the Protection of Literary and Artistic Works , adopted at Berne on Sept. 9, 1886, completed at Paris on May 4, 1896, revised at Berlin on Nov. 13, 1908, completed at Berne on Mar. 20, 1914, revised at Rome on June 2, 1928 (Rome Act, 1928), https://www.keionline.org/wp-content/uploads/1928_Rome_revisions_Berne.pdf (available in French at https://www.wipo.int/wipolex/en/treaties/textdetails/12803).

[249] *See* H.S. Gregory, Report of the Copyright Committee paras. 219–226 (Cmd 8662, 1952) (Gregory Committee Report). For a detailed discussion, see Gerald Dworkin, *The Moral Right of the Author: Moral Rights and the Common Law Countries*, 19 Colum.-VLA J.L. & Arts 229, 237–38 (1995). *See also* Irini Stamatoudi, *Moral Rights of Authors in England: The Missing Emphasis on the Role of Creators*, 8(4) Intell. Prop. Q. 478, 479 (1997).

torts of defamation, passing off, and injurious falsehood. Common-law copyright, it seems, was found to be alive and well after all, even if it was not called by that name, when it stepped in to protect the moral rights of authors.

However, a subsequent review of the very same British law, in 1986, reached the opposite conclusion, and found that British law was not, in fact, in conformity with international requirements after all when it came to moral rights.[250] The Whitford Commission assessed Britain's moral rights protection as incompatible with British obligations under the Berne Convention, and therefore deficient.[251]

But between 1928 and 1986, the level of protection for moral rights in the Berne Convention was actually reduced. When international copyright law entered a crisis during the 1960s, the language of Article 6*bis* was scaled back. Among other changes, the 1967 Stockholm text of moral rights expressly accommodated the legal systems of common-law countries. It stated that, if a given country had not yet enacted moral rights at the time of its accession to Berne, the protection of "some" moral rights in that country could cease with the death of the author.[252] The purpose of this provision was to accommodate moral rights protection through tort law: personal torts cannot be protected after a person's lifetime.[253]

The 1988 revision project reflected growing momentum behind the internationalization of intellectual property rights.[254] The Agreement on Trade-Related Aspects of Intellectual Property Rights (TRIPs Agreement) of the World Trade Organization was at hand, signaling the start of a new era in international intellectual property regulation.[255] The growing importance of copyright harmonization in the European Union was a related factor influencing British reform. At this crucial juncture, as part of comprehensive intellectual property law reform efforts, Britain decided to modernize its approach to moral rights. However, this initiative proved to be stubbornly difficult to implement in practice. The end result, as William Cornish notes, was "a highly pragmatic outcome," in which, as in the United States, "the pressures of interest played a noteworthy part."[256]

[250] Department of Trade and Industry, Intellectual Property and Innovation (Cmnd 9712, 1986) (Whitford Commission Report).

[251] *See* Stamatoudi, *supra* note 240, at 488.

[252] Berne Convention, *supra* note 193, at Art. 6*bis*, setting out protection for the moral rights of attribution and integrity, was agreed upon at the Rome revision conference of 1928. A proposal to extend moral rights to prevent outright destruction of a work was put forward in the 1948 Brussels conference; the text of the Article remained unchanged, and the conference expressed its clear intention to encourage member countries to "introduce, in their domestic legislation, some dispositions prohibiting the destruction of literary and artistic works." *See* Ricketson, *supra* note 210, at para. 8.109 (citing a "*voeu*" adopted at the conclusion of the conference).

[253] But the provision did not justify tort as the exclusive means of protecting moral rights—"some," not all. By way of comparison, the United States was more cautious about the Berne provisions, but this reflects a justifiable concern about the extent of protection required by the Berne Convention.

[254] David Nimmer, *Conventional Copyright: A Morality Play*, 3 Ent. L. Rev. 94, 95–97 (1992) discusses this issue in detail.

[255] Although moral rights were not a priority in the new system, they were still part of it. See the discussion in Chapter 3 *infra* notes 71–82 and accompanying text.

[256] *See* W.R. Cornish, *Moral Rights under the 1988 Act*, 11(12) Eur. Intell. Prop. Rev. 449, 449 (1989) (where he refers to their "shy beauty").

The British provisions on moral rights, adopted in 1988, are highly complex, difficult to decipher and to understand. British copyright law is known for its "compressed drafting style," but the moral rights are drafted with an emphasis on linguistic detail that can be both exasperating and inefficient.[257] The rights are laboriously explained. Exceptions are listed in comprehensive provisions of their own—although, as discussed in the following sections, the legislation remains silent on the important question of whether a parody can still violate the moral right of integrity of the author of the work that has been parodied.[258] For all its claimed attention to detail, the act can boast neither clarity nor precision in its treatment of moral rights. A lawyer trying to understand these rights is rather like a physicist puzzled by the location of an electron: the more precise the scientist tries to be, the more indeterminate the result. The shape of Britain's moral rights legislation suggests hesitation about the policies that it is supposed to implement, and uncertainty about how those policies would best be served.

A crucial question remains: did the scheme in the 1988 Act accomplish the desired goal of making Britain compliant with the Berne Convention? Given the impetus behind reform, it is perhaps surprising to note that, in at least one respect, the provisions remain deficient. Under the UK Copyright Designs & Patents Act 1988, authors can only enjoy their moral right of attribution if the right has been asserted.[259] This unusual section apparently aims to provide adequate notice that any attribution claims will be linked to the person making the assertion. As such, they respond to the common concern that the rights might somehow lend themselves to abuse—in this case, in the form of unexpected obligations confronting property owners. Cornish observes,

> The right to be identified (unlike the right against derogatory treatment) requires as a pre-condition that it be asserted by the person entitled. This is a form of warning which is necessary, at least in the Government's view, if authors and directors are not to take undue advantage of the right.[260]

Yet, Article 5 of Berne provides that, "The enjoyment and the exercise of [authors'] ... rights shall not be subject to any formality." Under the Berne Convention, it has been accepted from the beginning that authors enjoy their rights by virtue of the act of creation—of authorship. When the Berne Convention was amended to include moral rights, this principle extended to the new moral rights just as it had

257 *Confetti Records v. Warner Music UK Ltd* [2003] EWHC 1274 (Ch) (UK).

258 *See* CDPA, *supra* note 231, §§ 79 (exceptions to the attribution right) and 81 (exceptions to the integrity right).

259 *See* id. §§ 77(1) and 78. This has led to the practical result that most books first published in the United Kingdom bear the legend "The author asserts the right to be recognized as the author of the work" on the inside cover, or copyright page, of the book.

260 *See* Cornish, *supra* note 254, at 449–50. The assertion can be made at any time, but a delay may affect claims for an injunction or damages.

previously applied to the other rights in the Convention. The requirement that attribution must be asserted under British law clearly violates this most fundamental principle of all. Full Berne compliance has therefore not yet been attained by the United Kingdom.

a. Moral Rights in the Copyright, Designs and Patents Act 1988

At first glance, the provisions in the Copyright, Designs and Patents Act 1988 (CDPA)[261] appear to create four distinct moral rights: a right to be identified as the author of a work, a right to object to the derogatory treatment of a work, a right to be protected from association with someone else's work, and a right of privacy in relation to photographs and film.

But this is primarily an impression created by the complex legislative framework. In reality, the Act protects the two moral rights explicitly provided for in the Berne Convention: attribution and integrity.

i. Attribution

The first of the moral rights protected in the CDPA is the author's right to be identified as the author of his or her own work—or, in the case of a film, as its director—and it corresponds to the right of attribution in Article 6*bis* of Berne (with the caveat noted above, regarding the need for attribution to be asserted). A specific right against false attribution, in section 84, is another aspect of the UK attribution right, though this right is oddly formulated as a right of "a person" to object to the wrongful use of his or her name, through the attribution of a work to him or her which that person did not create. As Elizabeth Adeney points out, this is not a moral right against false attribution of authorship in the sense in which it is usually recognized in other jurisdictions, where an author can complain about the use of someone else's name to make it appear that he or she is the author of the work.[262] It seems more akin to the tortious conception of "passing off" than to the author's moral right against false attribution.[263]

The author's right to complain about false attribution of authorship to his or her own work is traditionally protected in France as well—although it is noteworthy that false attribution is not explicit in Article 6*bis* and can only be implied into Berne.[264] In effect, section 84 looks like a codified version of the common law tort of passing off.[265] In recollection of tort principles, the right of false attribution also expires earlier than other moral rights, only twenty years after the author's death.[266]

261 CDPA, *supra* note 231.

262 Elizabeth Adeney, *Australia's Experience of Moral Rights*, 14(4) JIPLP 312, 315 (2019), https://doi.org/10.1093/jiplp/jpz001.

263 *See, e.g.*, https://www.merriam-webster.com/legal/reverse%20passing%20off.

264 Stamatoudi, *supra* note 240, at 490–91. Ricketson, *supra* note 210, at para. 8.105 argues that the language of Berne effectively excludes this possibility.

265 See the English case of *Moore v. News of the World Ltd* [1972] 1 QB 441 (QB), per Lord Denning on false attribution.

266 CDPA, *supra* note 231, § 86(2).

The attribution right is noteworthy in another respect: it situates the United Kingdom as one of a number of jurisdictions that specifically grant authors a right, not only to be attributed, but also, to write under a pseudonym.[267] While the UK legislation does not explicitly protect anonymity, it does provide that the author may specify "some other particular form of identification," and, at a stretch, non-identification (anonymity) could arguably be considered a "particular form of identification."[268]

These provisions suggest a wide latitude for authors to define their own identity, and it has valuable implications for building and maintaining authorial reputations, particularly in the online environment. Both anonymity and pseudonymity also emphasize an author's right of privacy as an individual. Ironically, though— as discussed below— the actual "moral right of privacy" in the CDPA only applies to "certain films and photographs," which are taken for domestic purposes, and no broader logic of respect for authorial privacy is developed or elucidated in the Act.[269]

With limited jurisprudential guidance, it is also unclear whether these provisions can protect authors from investigative attempts such as those faced by the artist known as Banksy and the writer known by the pseudonym Elena Ferrante,[270] which seek to uncover their identities against their will. In both of these cases, the public seems to side with the artists, in favor of shielding their identities through their chosen pseudonyms, while the investigators of their identities have faced strong public criticism.[271]

ii. Integrity: The Right to Object to Derogatory Treatment

The second right protected under British law is the moral right of integrity. In the CDPA, it is known as a "right to object to derogatory treatment" of a work.[272] With typical punctiliousness, the Act defines "derogatory treatment" by offering a detailed definition of each word. Section 80(2)(a) states that "[t]reatment … means any addition to, deletion from or alteration to or adaptation of the work," other than translations or transcriptions of the work.[273] The subsequent sub-section, section 80(2)(b) turns its attention to the meaning of "derogatory." It provides that "the treatment of a work is derogatory if it amounts to distortion or mutilation of

[267] Id. § 77(8) on pseudonymity or other form of identification.

[268] Id.

[269] This idea, with a particular focus on the privacy aspects of pseudonymity, is discussed in Richard Arnold & Mira T. Sundara Rajan, *Do Authors and Performers Have a Legal Right to Pseudonymity?*, 9(2) Journal of Media Law 189 (2017), https://doi.org/10.1080/17577632.2017.1347082.

[270] *See, e.g.*, Sundara Rajan, *supra* note 102.

[271] Id.

[272] CDPA, *supra* note 231, § 80.

[273] Id. § 80(2)(a). Curiously, this section also references any "arrangement … of a musical work involving no more than a change of key or register." From a musical point of view, this seems like an odd statement, since any arrangement of a work that involved only a change of key or register would, by definition, be a transcription.

the work or is otherwise prejudicial to the honour or reputation of the author or director."

This language, though familiar from Berne, is used in a way that departs significantly from the Convention. The CDPA covers "distortion" and "mutilation," incorporating these key words from Berne into the overarching idea of "derogatory" treatment, no doubt derived from "derogatory action" in Berne. Accordingly, the formulation of the British right is narrower than its Berne counterpart: it only covers "addition, deletion, alteration or adaptation" of the work. In other words, the work must be directly subject to such "treatment"; objections based on context or association will be difficult to accommodate within the language of this section.[274] This is in keeping with a restriction on the integrity right that is sometimes recognized, a limitation on its applicability to changes of context. However, it should be noted that the language of Berne transcends this approach.[275] Under the CDPA, the "treatment" is only objectionable if it amounts to a "distortion" or "mutilation" of the work, or is "otherwise prejudicial to the author's honor or reputation." The Act avoids the broad brushstroke of "modification" employed by Berne; in British law, all of the chosen terms, derived from Berne, have strong negative connotations. A change, alone, cannot suffice to invoke this provision. By excluding "modification," which is present in Berne, the interpretive possibilities of a treatment of the work are limited, and the scope of the integrity right is narrower.

Looking at this section, an interesting question arises about the relationship between the words "distortion," "mutilation," and "otherwise prejudicial." The presence of "otherwise prejudicial" expands the possibilities beyond "distortion" or "mutilation"—but how far? If we read this phrase *ejusdem generis*, the presence of the two earlier and more specific terms must color the interpretation of the final phrase, and it must be taken to refer only to something inherently negative.[276] It seems doubtful that "otherwise prejudicial" could fully replace "modification," or that it was ever intended to do so.

While the British regime for moral rights is confusing in many respects, one point is clear: the drafters of these provisions *intended* to implement Article 6*bis* of the Berne Convention in UK law. To be more precise, given the history of British ambivalence towards moral rights, it is clear that the legislative approach to Berne

[274] They might be shown to be "additions," or perhaps even "deletions" if some features of the original context for display were considered an essential part of the work, but these arguments are not straightforward.

[275] For example, Makeen comments: "This dual protection forms the basis of Article 6bis of the Berne Convention, which requires national laws to protect authors against any 'distortion, mutilation or other modification' of their works and also against 'any derogatory action in relation to the said work.'" *See* Makeen F. Makeen, *Evaluation of moral rights protection in Egypt*, 14(4) JIPLP 278, 280 (2019). See also the detailed discussion in Ricketson & Ginsburg, *supra* note 38, at paras. 10.31–35, esp. para. 10.33.

[276] The principle is that of *ejusdem generis*, where the words in a list are said to be interpreted according to the preceding words.

implementation was to *do the minimum* required by the Convention.[277] This is unobjectionable: Berne is intended as a regime for the protection of minimum standards among the member countries.

Notably, the British drafters maintained a key limitation set out in Article 6*bis*: the author must show proof of damage to his or her honour or reputation before a violation of the integrity right is allowed. Section 80(2)(b) clearly states that "the treatment of a work is derogatory if it amounts to distortion or mutilation of the work or is *otherwise prejudicial to the honour or reputation of the author or director*" (italics added).

It is therefore fascinating to discover that this crucial limitation has been challenged in two British cases—and overturned in one. Was this finding due to boundless creativity, limited awareness of historical record, or to the simple desire to interpret the actual words of the statute as a pure and self-contained statement of the law? The first case to examine the British moral right of integrity was *Confetti Records*,[278] a case about music copyright and sampling that interpreted the right in the context of hip-hop music and pop-culture values.[279] The case "led to the faintly surreal experience of three gentlemen in horsehair wigs examining the meaning of such phrases as 'mish mish man' and 'shizzle my nizzle,'" with the judges searching, largely in vain, to find the meaning of improvised phrases recited by a rapper in the course of a studio recording. The case suffered from several awkward points on the facts—the writer of an original song complaining about associations with gangster violence in a re-recorded cover of his song, even while the original recording had featured performers dressed in gangster-inspired outfits. These elements impeded the recognition of moral rights and, moreover, led to a lost opportunity to examine some interesting questions about the role of authors' moral rights in preventing abuses of free speech or socially destructive acts.

But the court also had the opportunity to make its point about the interpretation of the integrity right, in the process, referencing the process of Berne implementation in the United Kingdom. Given the placement of the clause "prejudicial to the honour or reputation of the author," the plaintiffs had argued that any "distortion or mutilation" of a work would qualify as a violation of the right of integrity under the new British provisions. The court, however, concluded that the "compressed drafting style" of the Act meant that the clause should apply to each word in this section and found, in conformity with the historical background to the adoption

[277] *See* Cornish, *supra* note 254, at 449. It is interesting to note the parallel experience in India, where, in 1994, amendments to the Act that *reduced* the scope of protection for moral rights were said to be implemented to favor India's conformity with the Berne Convention: Copyright Amendment Act 1994, *supra* note 121; comments made in private correspondence with Jagdish Sagar. *See also* Gudibanda R. Raghavender, *The Origin and Development of a Moral Rights Regime in India*, 14(4) JIPLP SYMPOSIUM ON MORAL RIGHTS 305 (Mira T. Sundara Rajan & Sarah Harris, eds., 2019), https://doi.org/10.1093/jiplp/jpz006.

[278] *See supra* note 248 and accompanying text.

[279] The music involved was specifically a subgenre known as "UK Garage."

of this provision, that a contrary interpretation would have expanded the scope of British moral rights far beyond the intention of the drafters.

But the issue was revisited again, nine years later, in *Delves-Broughton v. House of Harlot*.[280] The case was heard by the Patents County Court, which has since been subsumed into the Intellectual Property Enterprise Court, now part of the Chancery Division of the High Court.[281] These comments on the court's status are worth making, because of the incredibly contentious nature of the judgment. The case involved a photograph of a model in erotic clothing, rented from the defendant company, and artfully taken against a natural backdrop. The photograph was subsequently used on the defendant company's website in an altered form, and with the background removed. As Recorder Douglas Campbell, the judge in this case, commented,

> It seems to me that considerable time and effort went into the composition or creation of the original photograph, and it was important to the photographer that the forest background appeared in the particular photograph for artistic reasons. I am satisfied that the changes which have been made do amount to distortion of the work.

Crucially, he went on to comment on the very issue of legislative interpretation raised in *Confetti Records*, noting,

> I would not say that it was mutilation and I would not say that it was prejudicial to the honour or reputation of the author or director, but I am satisfied that it amounts to distortion of the photograph in question and that the treatment of the work is therefore derogatory.

There is only one way that this statement could be accurate: if the clause defining derogatory treatment were read, as the plaintiffs in *Confetti Records* had previously argued that it should be, by separating out the words used to define "derogatory" in the legislation and attaching the clause "prejudicial to the honour or reputation of the author" *only* to the final words of the definition. In other words, if the work is subject to distortion or mutilation, there is no need to show prejudice to the author's reputation; the need for proof of prejudice only arises if treatment *other than* "distortion" or "mutilation" is at issue. In this case, it is up to the court to determine whether the treatment of the word qualifies as distortion or mutilation and, presumably, it would resort to the usual dictionary definitions of these words in the absence of further statutory clarification.

[280] [2012] EWPCC 29 (UK).

[281] *See* https://www.gov.uk/courts-tribunals/intellectual-property-enterprise-court.

As noted earlier, such an interpretation would directly contradict the avowed purpose of the 1988 provisions—to bring UK law into conformity with the Berne Convention. When the United Kingdom undertook to do so, given its previous experience in this regard, there can be no doubt that the legislature intended to implement the *minimum requirements* set out in Berne. UK legislators never meant to surpass Berne.

The interesting question that now arises is a difficult one: to what extent should the intentions of the drafters of these provisions be considered in the ongoing interpretation of the provisions? When considering the interpretation of the provision as a matter of interpretation of the clause alone, the approach supported in *Delves-Broughton* is a credible one. Indeed, from this perspective, it seems difficult to choose one interpretation over the other, since both make sense. The fact that the argument arose in two separate cases, in an area where litigation remains relatively rare, further supports the validity of this view. The court in *Confetti* resolved it with reference to the drafters' intent—and also, with a general comment on the "compressed drafting style" of the UK legislature. But considerations of intent, and even style, in this context are both external to the provision itself. Taken as a self-contained statement of the law, if such a thing could exist, either interpretation seems equally tenable.

Accordingly, two opposing views of this provision, from two courts of similar stature, now exist. On an informed view, based on the history and context of the provision, the interpretation in *Delves-Broughton* is clearly incorrect. But, as a reading of the statute, it is credible; moreover, it has dramatically moved the law forward. Should this change be accepted? And how will future courts view it? The judgment creates a conundrum for the future claimant, though the wise and conservative course would still be to abide by the parameters so reasonably defined by the court in the *Confetti* case.

The provisions defining the integrity right are noteworthy for their distinctive application to each category of protected work, a feature that is more broadly characteristic of the approach to copyright subject matter in the UK Copyright, Designs and Patents Act 1988. Among other points of interest, the Act offers special provisions for film, where the director is entitled to claim attribution rights as the film's author,[282] and extends moral rights explicitly to the soundtrack.[283] In relation to

282 CDPA, *supra* note 231, § 9(2)(ab) identifies the producer and the principal director as the "authors" of a film, but §§ 77 and 80 on moral rights specifically identify the "director" and the "director of a copyright film" as, respectively, the beneficiary of the attribution right in films and the holder of the integrity right in a film that qualifies as a copyright work under UK law. On this last point, it should be noted that only films that satisfy the originality requirement under UK law—found in *Norowzian v. Arks Ltd (No. 2)* [2000] EMLR 67 (UK), for example, to be reflected in the narrative element of the short film in question—will benefit from copyright and, accordingly, moral rights protection.

283 This issue has been prominent in the Indian context; the relevant §17 of the Indian Copyright Act, 1957, *supra* note 16, was amended in 2012, but the requirements of royalty payments to musicians whose music is used in films have yet to be realized in practice. This has proven to be a highly charged issue because of the immense value of popular film music in India. See the generally helpful analysis by Gaurav Bhalla of Ahlawat & Associates, *Know Your Rights under the Indian Copyright Laws*,

architecture, the Act allows an architect's name to be removed from his or her work if it is displayed in conditions that he or she finds unsuitable—a curious remedy to integrity violations that reflects the public character of a work of architecture, but arguably relegates the integrity of that work, at least as the author might see it, to a place of secondary importance.[284]

The tension between the architect's rights and the practical needs of the public is invariably a theme of moral rights disputes involving architectural works. But courts have been surprisingly willing to recognize the architect's prerogatives, as well. For example, courts may require the owners of important original structures to maintain positive relationships with their architects, so that any subsequent modifications can be carried out by the original architect, with a view to maintaining the integrity of the design. This approach makes eminent sense: unless the original work is fundamentally unsatisfactory, why involve a new architect to replace the original designer of the work when modifications are needed?[285] If cost is a factor, the moral right can be modified in practice – as, for example, French law requires that the author pay the publisher for any costs incurred as a result of a decision to withdraw a work from circulation. An architect could be required to design any changes subsequently deemed "necessary" for the public good, as in the case of the Zubizuri bridge which needed pedestrian accommodations for safety, at a reasonable cost.[286]

iii. A Moral Right of Privacy?

An interesting addition to the list of moral rights in the British legislation is the right of privacy in relation to photographs and film created in a domestic context,

Lexology (Sept. 28, 2021), https://www.lexology.com/library/detail.aspx?g=3039effd-4a69-47fa-ba9b-e353abf16aa0—but note that some details could be clarified: it is s. 18, not s. 14, that provides for an unwaivable right to royalties for literary or musical works used in film (as implied elsewhere in the piece). *See also* Music Business Worldwide, India's Music Publishing Business Held Back By Lack Of Copyright Compliance, Legal Uncertainty (Report) (Jan. 24, 2024), https://www.musicbusinessworldwide.com/indias-music-publishing-business-held-back-by-lack-of-copyright-compliance-legal-uncertainty-report/.

[284] *See* CDPA, *supra* note 231, § 80(5):

> Subsection (4) does not apply to a work of architecture in the form of a building; but where the author of such a work is identified on the building and it is the subject of derogatory treatment he has the right to require the identification to be removed.

Another feature of the right of architecture that is interesting is the inherent challenge to the idea-expression dichotomy under copyright law: the architect, who designs the work but does not usually participate in its construction, is nevertheless said to hold copyright in the final structure.

[285] These were approximately the facts concerning Santiago Calatrava's celebrated Bilbao bridge, Zubizuri: see the discussion in Chapter 8, *infra* notes 173–86 and accompanying text. For an interesting overview of the controversy, see Barceló Experiences, *The Zubizuri, an iconic yet controversial bridge* (2024), https://www.barcelo.com/guia-turismo/en/spain/bilbao/things-to-do/zubizuri/. The controversy has become part of the attraction.

[286] Id. The French right of withdrawal is set out in the French Code de la propriété intellectuelle, *supra* note 20, at art. L121-4. See the discussion *supra* notes 79–84 and accompanying text.

which prohibits the public release of private images without the subject's consent.[287] The purpose of this right would seem to be the protection of the subject of a photograph from invasion of privacy or, indeed, as in the parallel Canadian case of *Gould Estate v. Stoddart*,[288] from unwanted commercial exploitation of the subject—who, in that case, subsequently became extraordinarily famous—by the owner of the photographs. In the *Gould* case, the owner of the photographs was the photographer, Jock Carroll, who subsequently entered into contract with Stoddart publishers for the book. But the Canadian court sided with the photographer, arguing that the fact that Gould was a public figure cancelled out any right of privacy in the images.[289] In the UK Act, perhaps reflecting a greater sensitivity to media exploitation of celebrities after the tragedy of Princess Diana's death in the late 1990s,[290] the privacy right effectively subordinates the ownership interests of the owner of the photograph to the privacy of his or her subject. But the formula adopted in the provision is oblique: the right is actually granted to the person who *commissioned* the photograph and not directly to the subject of the image. This would seem to prioritize ownership rather than privacy. It may be that the adoption of this provision reflects a subtle attempt to balance ownership against ownership, as the relationship between commissioner and photographer seems something akin to an employment context—even where, as in the Gould case, the photographer was formally employed by someone else. The availability of the right to protect the subject's privacy will therefore depend on the initiative of the person commissioning the image.

This right cannot be considered a moral right in the classic sense.[291] Instead, it deals with a situation where the interests of someone other than the author—the photographer in this case—will, in fact, supersede the author's right. In at least some circumstances, the person commissioning the photograph may well be the owner of the photograph, and, therefore, the holder of the copyright in it; but, by definition, a moral right depends on authorship, not ownership. It would perhaps be more accurate to call this right of privacy an exception to the author's right of disclosure or communication to the public, which attempts to balance the subject's personal privacy—or, as it may be, the privacy of the person commissioning the photo—against the moral right of the author.

287 *See* CDPA, *supra* note 231, § 85: "private and domestic purposes."

288 *Gould Estate v. Stoddart Publishing Co.*, 1996 CanLII 8209 (Can. Ont. S.C.), https://www.canlii.org/en/on/onsc/doc/1996/1996canlii8209/1996canlii8209.html.

289 The photographs of Gould had been taken in the 1950s for a journal article on his playing, but they were never published. When the photographer, Jock Carroll, assembled the photographs into a book on the pianist, the Gould estate sued, arguing (under tort law) that his privacy had been violated. Here, the subject of the photos and the person who commissioned them are different; provisions like those in the UK Act would therefore not succeed in protecting the privacy of the subject.

290 She died in a car crash in Paris, while she and her companion Dodi Fayed were being pursued by paparazzi.

291 Stamatoudi, *supra* note 240, at 491 argues that "the privacy right does not confer any additional right upon the author of copyright. In this respect it is not a genuine moral right."

b. Exceptions: Limits on Moral Rights in Employment and Technology

The British provisions on moral rights are subject to a number of practical requirements that largely function as limitations restricting their scope. The striking requirement that the attribution right must be asserted has already been noted. In addition, the attribution and integrity rights are both subject to a series of elaborate and comprehensive exceptions. Given these limitations, the question of what happens to moral rights in the technological context is a central concern.

Exceptions to the rights of attribution[292] and integrity[293] extend to several categories of works. Perhaps most importantly, neither moral right can be claimed by employees in relation to works created in the course of their employment. This is in keeping with the general common-law treatment of the copyright of employees. However, this approach to employees' moral rights also shows a fundamental ambivalence towards the idea that the relationship between author and work is personal and should be prioritized.

Moral rights are also excluded from computer programs, computer-generated works, news publications, and "collective works of reference"—all important types of new works, or works with new connotations, in a digital society.[294] Exceptions to the integrity right also include a particularly wide exception for modifications made by BBC broadcasting authorities. The provision responds to the scenario illustrated by the *Frisby* case, where the author of a play brought a case against the BBC to protest the deletion of a crucial line in the broadcast of his work.[295] The exception is noteworthy for its contribution to maintaining the sanctity of the BBC as British broadcasting authority.

The British treatment of moral rights in the technological environment is the very antithesis of the French approach. While the French have attempted to extend existing moral rights to technological creation, the British have preferred to exclude moral rights from technological works altogether. This approach is probably motivated by concerns about the implications of moral rights for rapidly growing, unpredictable, and socially important technologies; but it is a legislative shortcoming that should probably be reconsidered at some point. The pressure exerted by artificial intelligence, in particular, demands a response, and moral rights are a key policy instrument that neither the British legislature nor any other can afford to ignore.[296]

[292] Listed in CDPA, *supra* note 231, § 79.

[293] Listed id. § 81.

[294] Id. §§ 79(2)(a) and (c) and 79(3)–(6); id. § 79(2)(b) also provides an exception for typefaces; id. § 79(7) also mentions Crown copyright.

[295] *Frisby v. BBC* [1967] Ch 932 (Ch) (Eng.).

[296] This issue is discussed in detail in Chapter 5 *infra* on moral rights and artificial intelligence.

c. Parody and Moral Rights: Is There an Exception under the CDPA?

In 2014, UK legislators undertook the long-awaited step of enacting a parody exception in the copyright law. However, the formulation of the parody right in section 30A of the CDPA does not mention moral rights.[297] Can a parody violate the author's moral right of integrity under UK law, or is it an exception to the moral right of the author? As noted above, exceptions to moral rights are treated in great detail in the Act, so it is quite ironic that this question is not explicitly answered by the CDPA.

In contrast, French law, as discussed earlier, provides that a parody that harms the author goes too far. But the CDPA's silence implies that parodies must *not* be exempt from the exercise of the moral right of integrity by the author of the parodied work. In other words, if a parody causes harm to the original author's reputation, it will not be permissible under UK law. Rather, such a parody would be considered to violate the author's moral right of integrity. If this is indeed the desired approach, the point is important enough that it should be made explicit in the statute, and not left to the courts or the public to infer.

Since parodies are often equated with "mash-ups"—digital combinations of works created through technology—the introduction of the exception was interpreted by many as legalizing mash-ups.[298] But not all mash-ups are parodies. Even for those that are, as is made clear in the European context by the ruling in *Deckmyn*, they will have to remain within the bounds of socially acceptable conduct. Under UK law, by implication at least, this means that the mash-up in question should not amount to a form of "derogatory treatment" of the work under section 80 of the CDPA, which would violate the original author's moral right of integrity. Under section 80, as noted earlier, treatment that is "prejudicial to the honour or reputation of the author or director" may violate the author's or director's moral rights—an approach that seems particularly relevant to parodies. Under the CDPA, moral rights limit mash-ups, just as they impose limits on the scope of parodies overall.

d. Inalienability and Waiver

The theoretical foundation of moral rights lies in the idea of a personal right of the author. Since moral rights are vested in the personality of the author, they are

[297] Section 30A was added by The Copyright and Rights in Performances (Quotation and Parody) Regulations 2014, SI 2014/2356, arts. 1 and 5(1). It states in full:

> **30A Caricature, parody or pastiche**
>
> (1) Fair dealing with a work for the purposes of caricature, parody or pastiche does not infringe copyright in the work.
>
> (2) To the extent that a term of a contract purports to prevent or restrict the doing of any act which, by virtue of this section, would not infringe copyright, that term is unenforceable.

[298] *See, e.g.*, Glyn Moody, *New UK Copyright Exception Allows Mashups—But Only If Judges Think They Are Funny*, TECHDIRT (Oct. 1, 2014), https://www.techdirt.com/articles/20140930/05415728669/new-uk-copyright-exception-allows-mashups-only-if-judges-think-they-are-funny.shtml.

inalienable by definition. In the interest of consistency, it would be awkward to allow or to compel authors to use moral rights, a personal privilege, as a bargaining tool in negotiating professional matters.

However, it is not necessary for moral rights to be fully subject to alienation for this conflict to arise: it is also implicated in the narrower problem of waivers. Here, too, the issue is one of unequal bargaining power. When authors and publishers meet, the publisher typically enjoys vastly superior market clout. If the law allows moral rights to be waived, publishers may be in a position to take advantage of their greater bargaining strength by introducing standard-form waivers into authors' contracts. In these circumstances, the formal possibility of waiving moral rights may seriously limit the practical significance of these rights.[299] The theory of moral rights does not require waiver to be completely banned, but, in consonance with the concept, the availability of the right must be subject to careful consideration in the interest of the author. With this proviso in mind, waivers are allowed to an extent, even in a traditionally strong moral rights jurisdiction such as Germany;[300] but, as noted, the author can invoke a waiver only in specific and well-defined circumstances.[301]

In principle, moral rights in the United Kingdom are inalienable. They cannot be assigned, only inherited after the death of the author.[302] However, waivers are allowed, and, in contrast to the German model, the British provisions on waivers are especially broad.[303] The British Act allows any or all moral rights to be waived, and it also allows waivers of moral rights in relation to future works yet to be created—a provision that incites especially strong criticism from William Cornish.[304] Section 87 leaves open the possibility of standard waivers of moral rights in contracts between authors and publishers, and this probably explains why the provision "has induced a sense of relief in many entrepreneurs who deal with authors and directors."[305]

It is true that waivers will be subject to contract doctrines such as unconscionability and duress, which have developed to remedy situations of unequal bargaining power between the contracting parties. Whether they will be

[299] This is the practical situation in Canada, as well as in the United Kingdom. See the comments in David Vaver, *Authors' Moral Rights in Canada*, 14 INT'L REV. INDUS. PROP. & COPYRIGHT L. 329, 349–52 (1983).

[300] See the discussion in Walter, *supra* notes 96 and 163–70 and accompanying text.

[301] Id. It should perhaps be noted, though, that France, while disallowing waivers in theory, does allow industry practice to dominate. See, e.g., the discussion *infra* notes 101–05 and accompanying text on ghostwriting in France. As noted, French jurists have found creative ways of explaining these conventions while, in this writer's opinion, effectively conceding the admissibility of waivers in practice.

[302] CDPA, *supra* note 231, §§ 94 and 95: authors' moral rights are not assignable, but—with the exception of the right of false attribution in § 84—they are inheritable upon the death of the author.

[303] Id. § 87.

[304] Cornish, *supra* note 254, at 452.

[305] Id. at 451.

applied in disputes over moral rights in copyright contracts remains to be seen. To invoke them would require outright judicial activism based on an independent sense of justice and social priorities. Little legislative basis exists for a larger reading of moral rights beyond the text of copyright codes.

e. Conceptual Confusion

In terms of theory, British legislation appears to be divided on moral rights. In dealing with the issue of duration, it follows the monist, German model. The duration of moral rights is generally equivalent to the term of copyright, although the right against false attribution has a shortened duration.[306] In spite of the appearance of this monist characteristic, however, the Act distinguishes strongly between economic and moral rights—what Cornish most appropriately called "an extreme form of dualism." It is noteworthy that this approach is also reflected in Canadian jurisprudence.

British dualism emerges in two ways.

First, the provisions on remedies seem to establish a hierarchy between economic rights, or copyright proper, and moral rights. A violation of economic rights is considered an "infringement" of copyright, whereas a violation of moral rights is simply a breach of statutory duty. The possibility of an injunctive remedy for a violation of the integrity right is recognized in section 103, but there are no specific provisions regarding damages.[307]

This approach leads to an interesting question. To what extent are damages available for moral rights violations under UK law? In civil law countries, violations of moral rights typically lead to injunctive relief. But in common-law countries, copyright infringement usually results in damages. If they choose to limit or exclude damages for moral rights infringements, common-law countries may effectively be signaling a *reduced* status for moral rights in this jurisdictional context. This may occur because of sequestering moral rights from economic rights, limiting possible remedies, and introducing unfamiliar solutions in an essentially conservative legal environment.

More generally, common-law countries confront the challenge of finding an appropriately nuanced way of responding to moral rights violations in a context where economic damages have usually been the ultimate recourse of the courts and reward of litigants. This tension is illustrated by the comments of the court justifying the denial of a preliminary injunction – leading to the immediate

[306] CDPA, *supra* note 231, § 86. Personal torts expire with the lifetime of the person affected.

[307] CDPA, *supra* note 231, § 03, entitled "Remedies for infringement of moral rights." *See generally* Cornish, *supra* note 254.

destruction of an important site for street art in New York city – in the celebrated 5*Pointz* litigation. Judge Block states:

> Although the works have now been destroyed—and the Court wished it had the power to preserve them—plaintiffs would be hard-pressed to contend that no amount of money would compensate them for their paintings; and VARA—which makes no distinction between temporary and permanent works of visual art—provides that significant monetary damages may be awarded for their wrongful destruction… In any event, paintings generally are meant to be sold. Their value is invariably reflected in the money they command in the marketplace. Here, the works were painted for free, but surely the plaintiffs would gladly have accepted money from the defendants to acquire their works, albeit on a wall rather than on a canvas. [308]

Secondly, it is also evident that the 1988 Act is not fully informed by an understanding of the character of moral rights as rights of *authorship*. The 1988 provisions originally drew a distinction among authors, film directors, and the commissioners of works, all of whom enjoyed moral rights independently of the acquisition of copyright; revisions in 1997 corrected the curious duality in relation to film by belatedly recognizing directors as authors. As Cornish notes, "There is no scheme of thought here that an author enjoys both moral and economic rights, all of them equal in status."[309]

In any event, the underlying purpose of moral rights, at least as they are traditionally understood, is to protect the relationship between the author and the work. Whoever may actually assert the rights, their purpose undoubtedly resides within this special relationship—a principle that may be weakened, or even lost, when other interests, such as those of the subject in a photograph, also find expression through moral rights. The concern about privacy may be worthwhile, but that does not necessarily mean that it should be classified as a moral right of the author. Such an expansion of the doctrine of moral rights is confusing, and the logic behind the extension is not clear. In this area of the law, which faces a number of challenges to its legitimacy, confusion would be best avoided.[310] In this respect, at least, the terminology of the UK Act is misleading.

[308] *Cohen v. G & M Realty L.P.*, 988 F. Supp. 2d 212 (E.D.N.Y. 2013) (U.S.), https://casetext.com/case/cohen-v-gm-realty-lp/ (the written opinion explaining the decision to deny a preliminary injunction of Nov. 12, 2013; this decision was issued on Nov. 20, 2013) (citations omitted). *See* Chapter 8, *infra*, esp. notes 54–56 and accompanying text.

[309] Cornish, *supra* note 238, at 449.

[310] But it is also true that confusion may be generated whenever moral rights are extended or applied in new ways that stretch the theory or practice of the doctrine. This may be all the more reason to maintain a basic degree of integrity in the recognition of a theory of protection geared towards the relationship between author and work. This may be the only legitimate basis on which to protect moral rights in the future and to protect the integrity of the doctrine itself. It is such a powerful doctrine, particularly where waiver and termination are concerned, that abuse would have strongly negative consequences.

3. Brexit and Moral Rights: A Sobering Future?

The *Delves-Broughton* case offers an intriguing illustration of how British law might move towards a more comprehensive acceptance of moral rights. The example is especially interesting because it reflects the possible impact of judicial independence on moral rights, while showing how judicial interpretation can move the law in a dramatically different direction even *in the absence of* legislative amendment. An even stronger example is set by judges in another jurisdiction, India, where judicial interpretation has led to a new theory of moral rights—linking them directly to the international protection of cultural heritage—that should be of interest to the world.[311]

What led the British court to this result? While a definitive answer to this question may be unreachable, it is worth noting that the court showed no evidence of being overtly influenced by EU or European law. If the case reflects the influence of European law on British intellectual property decision making, this occurred at a much deeper level. There was no compulsion upon the court in *Delves-Broughton* to recognize an expanded moral right—no pressure derived from CJEU judgments, European case law, or, of course, EU copyright legislation (which, so far, has explicitly ignored moral rights).

Britain's exit from the EU was highly significant for intellectual property law in the UK. The implications for moral rights, whether in the UK or the EU, are as yet unknown. It would be easy to say that British withdrawal from the EU has paved the way for future limitations on moral rights in the UK. But the main impetus for their 1988 enactment came from Berne, not Europe. The rights now seem deeply integrated into the consciousness of not only the British creative communities but also, as illustrated by *Delves-Broughton*, the country's legal community. Only the obvious can be stated: Brexit has eliminated the need for British law to emulate a harmonized moral right across Europe, if and when such a right were ever to be realized.[312]

However, the UK will continue with its stated commitments in the light of the Berne Convention; and, depending on how creative British judges become, an expansion of the rights seems within the realm of reality. Continued recognition of moral rights also harmonizes the British creative sector with Europe and with the world at large (excepting the United States)—an advantage that the United Kingdom may want to embrace. As in other countries, the greatest influence on

[311] The specific theory is new, but the link between moral rights and cultural heritage has long been recognized. The *Sehgal* case is reviewed in detail in Chapter 4, *infra* notes 242–99 and accompanying text.

[312] This issue, too, is far from clear. Europeans offer the United Kingdom as an excuse to refrain from moral rights harmonization; experience suggests, however, that the European Union *sans* the United Kingdom might still be careful about the extension of moral rights across EU territory. Indeed, the Digital Single Market strategy, which is currently Europe's framework for copyright reform, seems, if anything, antithetical to moral rights.

their evolution may now be the perceived interactions between AI and moral rights, and the drive to maintain international competitiveness in this area,

4. Conclusions: The Birth of the Common-Law Approach

It is clear that moral rights in Britain have not kept pace with technological developments. The legislation of 1988 generally excludes the possibility of moral rights in new technological settings. Film is a notable exception, with the British law now identifying the director as the "author" of a film and endowing him or her with moral rights.[313] More generally, the provisions lack the conceptual and legal clarity needed to deal with technological pressures on authorship. This is a troubling reality, because moral rights are highly relevant to technological developments in key areas such as artificial intelligence, data protection, and privacy. As such, they should be actively explored by policymakers.

The complexity and restrictiveness of British law seem almost intentional, reflecting, as Cornish has noted, the ambivalence surrounding moral rights at the time of their adoption. A lack of commitment and direction is apparent. Moreover, in many respects, the protection of moral rights in the CDPA falls short of internationally accepted practice as embodied in the Berne Convention. In this respect, it would appear that the revision process failed to meet the immediate objective of raising the standards in UK copyright law to the level of Berne. Instead, in at least some respects, the provisions codify the informal protections under British law from before 1988.[314]

Why is this significant? Common-law countries have often claimed that informal protections through the mechanism of the common law may address moral rights effectively, and an effort to accommodate this position is also reflected in the amendments to Article 6*bis* of the Berne Convention. The Stockholm text of 1967 affirms:

> The rights granted to the author ... shall, after his death, be maintained, at least until the expiry of the economic rights.... However, those countries whose legislation, at the moment of their ratification of or accession to this Act, does not provide for the protection after the death of the author of all the rights set out in the

[313] *See, e.g.*, CDPA, *supra* note 231, §§ 77 on the right of attribution and 80 on integrity.

[314] As Stamatoudi, *supra* note 240, at 498, reports, case law on moral rights in the United Kingdom since 1988 has been very limited; prior to *Emma Delves-Broughton v House of Harlot* [2012] EWPCC 29, it appears that the only successful claim has been made in the unreported decision of *Morrison Leahy Music Ltd v. Lightbond Ltd* (1991), [1993] EMLR 144 (Ch. Div), under the right to object to derogatory treatment provided for under CDPA, *supra* note 231, § 80.

> preceding paragraph may provide that some of these rights may, after his death, cease to be maintained.[315]

The United States has made the strongest claims in this regard, historically relying almost entirely on tort, including codified torts in the Lanham Act, for the protection of moral rights.[316] Looking at moral rights through the lens of harmonization, there is nothing inherently objectionable about this approach. It is not surprising that different types of legal approaches might be appropriate in different legal systems. Indeed, the ability to implement moral rights through the legal mechanisms relied upon in different legal systems could be considered a legitimate test of their adaptability to different environments.

The comments made by American lawyer William Strauss in 1959 are striking in this regard:

> Without using the label "moral right," or designations of the components of the moral right, the courts in the United States arrive at much the same results as do European courts. Substantially the same personal rights are upheld, although often under different principles. . . . [C]ommon law principles, if correctly applied, afford an adequate basis for protection of such rights. In our view, the contention that the author's rights of personality are not sufficiently protected in the United States, and the belief that there is an irreconcilable breach between European and American concepts of protection of authors' personal rights, seem to be dispelled by close scrutiny of the court decisions here and abroad. While a few American courts may be thought to have been remiss in protecting authors' personal rights (especially in finding implied waivers in ambiguous contracts), such decisions are exceptional and may be considered erroneous under common-law principles. Given the same facts, the large majority of courts in America and abroad employ the same reasonable and suitable standards for the protection of authors' personal rights. This similarity of protection has been obscured by the differences of approach and terminology. There is a considerable body of precedent in the American decisions to afford to our courts ample foundations in the common law for the protection of the personal rights of authors to the same extent that such protection is given abroad under the doctrine of moral right.[317]

[315] Berne Convention for the Protection of Literary and Artistic Works, Sept. 9, 1886, as revised at Stockholm on July 14, 1967, 828 U.N.T.S. 221 (Stockholm Act, 1967), https://www.wipo.int/treaties/en/ip/berne.

[316] Trademark Act of 1946 (Lanham Act), Pub. L. No. 79-489, 60 Stat. 427 (1946), codified as amended at 15 U.S.C. §§ 1051–1129 (2000). This approach was ultimately rejected in *Dastar Corp. v. Twentieth Century-Fox Film Corp.*, 539 U.S. 23 (2003), https://supreme.justia.com/cases/federal/us/539/23. See the discussion in Chapter 3, *infra* notes 131–45 and accompanying text.

[317] William Strauss, Study No. 4: The Moral Right of the Author 141–42 (1959), https://copyright.gov/history/studies/study4.pdf. Strauss was attorney-advisor to the Copyright Office: *see* https://copyright.gov/history/studies/study3.pdf.

These conclusions could have served equally well as reason for rejecting or for proposing moral rights implementation under U.S. copyright law. However, the legal landscape in the United States has changed considerably since 1959. The debates surrounding Berne membership (1989), the adoption of VARA (1990), and significant case law on moral rights issues, including the restrictive decision in *Dastar,* have all had an impact. In the intervening years, authorship itself has been transformed by technology.

The fact that the theoretical foundations of moral rights lie in authorship has acquired a new importance in the technological context. As has already been discussed in some detail, the Berne Convention establishes a basic standard for moral rights that is derived from authorship. The nuances in the language of the Berne Convention reflect this cultural basis. Torts protect individuals from harm, and may be relevant to moral rights (as is also noted by Desbois).[318] However, moral rights protect *authors* in relation to their *authorial activities.* Torts are relevant because authors are also human beings, engaged in human activities such as work, but they may not be specifically or durably adapted to the specific needs and circumstances of authorship. Accordingly, conformity with Berne today is not primarily a technical matter; Berne reflects the needs of authorship.

E. Conclusion: Un-Romantic Authorship

The moral rights of authors have been recognized for at least as long as their economic rights. They are usually associated with copyright in the countries of continental Europe. In France and Germany, a theory and practice of moral rights was well established by the end of the nineteenth century. In contrast, UK copyright law, and by extension the laws of other common-law countries, have treated moral rights as a foreign legal import, giving them limited recognition and support.

But a re-examination of the history of English copyright law suggests that this narrative should be revisited. In fact, moral rights were not unknown in English law. On the contrary, they were recognized nearly a century before French judges began to deliver their rulings on moral rights. Moral rights received a clear exposition by Lord Mansfield in the 1769 case of *Millar v. Taylor*. Their subsequent rejection occurred under the tremendous social pressure generated by the booksellers' monopoly, which threatened to replace official censorship with a regime of press control through the private sector. That monopoly had to be destroyed; the era of censorship had to be brought to a close. The legal mechanism by which this was accomplished was the Statute of Anne, which, as the judges decided in the 1775 case of *Donaldson v. Beckett*, provided a comprehensive statement of copyright rules in

[318] Desbois, *supra* note 113, at 116.

the realm, with no possibility of any reliance upon a pre-existing "common law" copyright of any kind. In this process, moral rights, which were articulated by Lord Mansfield as part of a broader theory of common-law copyright in the earlier case of *Millar v. Taylor*, were abandoned.[319]

The manner in which moral rights developed in European countries is remarkable. The concept of authors' literary property, or copyright, was the first recognition of copyright, as in England, and it, too, was a creature of statute. But moral rights—as was also the case in England—were first recognized by judges. Accordingly, moral rights initially developed as an informal and flexible doctrine. They were, in effect, a sort of common law within civilian legal systems based on legislation, and, from this position, they ultimately grew into equality with—perhaps supremacy over—the economic rights of authors in the continental systems.[320] While rulings on moral rights were developing in France, German writers were exploring the conceptual implications of moral rights from almost every conceivable angle.[321] The theories of moral rights that emerged proved to be extraordinarily rich, linking the rights with human personality, culture, creativity, and human rights.

But the study of British copyright history proves to be exceptionally valuable in this regard. The historical study of copyright has greatly emphasized the importance of the Romantic ideal of authorship in the development of modern copyright law, and moral rights are considered to be the culmination of this view. This influential scholarship, spearheaded by historian Martha Woodmansee and legal scholar Peter Jaszi, among others, has been immensely influential.[322] One of its direct consequences has been to discredit what is said to be copyright's excessive emphasis on individual authorship by seeking to dismantle the underlying conception of individual genius, whose importance in human history and culture is effectively denied. Instead, a "collective, corporate, and collaborative" model of

[319] *Millar, supra* note 3. But see the Scottish case of *Cadell, supra* note 213, with its commentary on personal rights.

[320] Dietz notes the "hierarchy" between the two, with moral rights reigning over economic rights in the German system: *see* Dietz, *supra* note 155.

[321] To reduce these theories to "emotivist," as aesthetic philosopher K.E. Gover has recently done, does a great injustice to this tradition while applying an exceptionally pejorative term to the doctrine. After all, in our society, what could be less objectively valuable than "emotive" interests? Indeed, Gover has achieved something by finding a term that is even more unhelpful than "moral rights" itself, as is commented in Chapter 1 *supra*, to discuss the doctrine. Other cultures may see things differently.

[322] Woodmansee, *supra* note 4. See also, e.g., Peter Jaszi, *On the Author Effect: Contemporary Copyright and Collective Creativity*, 10 CARDOZO A. & ENT. L.J. 293, 302 (1992), who notes: "That Romantic 'authorship' is alive and well in late twentieth-century American legal culture has consequences for the law's engagement with (or failure to engage) the realities of contemporary polyvocal writing practice-which increasingly is collective, corporate, and collaborative." But this paradigm has also been disapproved. For example, prominent U.S. scholar Mark Lemley, in a 1997 book review, questions its relevance (though he does not discuss moral rights): *see* Mark A. Lemley, *Romantic Authorship and the Rhetoric of Property*, 75 TEXAS L. REV. 873 (1997), https://ssrn.com/abstract=44418.

authorship is preferred.[323] On this view, authors draw upon pre-existing materials to the extent that their original contributions to culture, if any, are quite minimal.

But a look at copyright's British history challenges these assumptions. After all, copyright, in the sense of literary property acquired by an individual author by means of the author's work, emerged as early as the late 1600s and was codified, after a long period of debate and struggle, in 1710. It is a stretch to say that Romanticism was on the horizon; indeed, the codification of law often reflects a previous generation or more of lobbying, because it is often the final manifestation of a broader process of social change (and it can subsequently become the first step in a new process of transformation, which is what happened when the Statute of Anne was adopted). In Britain, literary property was recognized first (in other words, the livelihood of authors), but it should be remembered that the recognition of literary property was hardly an end in its own right. It was specifically a device towards the accomplishment of two ends: the end of the censorship system operated by the Stationers Company, and the decision to accord authors a livelihood in the rising era of a free press. The latter was concerned about social justice and the unfair exploitation of authors, and it makes sense that this change occurred at a time when powerful institutions such as church and state were no longer the initiators and keepers of knowledge. In Britain, the idea of the moral right emerged well after the emergence of literary property, in 1769. This was closer to the era of Romanticism but, again, it seems an exaggeration to suggest that Romantic currents were well developed enough at this point for a Romantic conception of individual genius to shape the thinking of the English courts. Instead, it seems that, once the material prerogatives of authors were established, refinements in the understanding of authorship led to the recognition of moral interests. The recognition of authors' rights in Europe, considering the development of copyright and moral rights in France and Germany, followed more or less the same path, with property rights emerging in pre-Revolutionary France, and moral rights coming after the Revolution. Indeed, it is also arguable that a broader conception of authorship was also inherent in the Statute of Anne, though it was not articulated there beyond the principle of first publication or disclosure, because the recognition of those needs, to a greater or lesser extent in practice, is fundamentally implied by the recognition of authorship itself. This goes back to Dietz's notion of the unitary quality of copyright, emanating from an underlying principle of an author's right, which is at the origin of both economic and moral rights for authors. Once again, we should not forget that it was Britain, among modern European nations, which first recognized an *author's* right, though this was called a copyright in deference to the stationers' pre-existing rights in the "copies" of books, in respect of which the Statute implemented transitional measures in order to phase them out.

[323] Jaszi, *supra* note 328.

As time went on, the concept of moral rights, like the economic rights, evolved under the pressure of historical currents, technological change, and so on. In other words, Romanticism shaped and sculpted moral rights in the Romantic era, but this does not mean that the idea of the moral right of the author originated in Romanticism or that it is ultimately an expression of Romantic idealization of the author—which is deeply unfashionable today. Rather, moral rights are part of the recognition of authorship, which was a process that was perhaps truly born, in Europe, with the Renaissance, and continued to evolve over the centuries.

It must also be said that this is only Europe's history. Our relative ignorance of the history of creativity in other parts of the world does not mean that authorship was irrelevant or undeveloped, although the modern study of it certainly is.[324] For example, in the case of India, there is a profoundly different history of the relationship between religion and knowledge, as compared to Europe, which deserves to be studied if we wish to arrive at a deeper understanding of authors' rights. The *bhakti* movement emphasized the importance of individual autonomy, stressing mystical insight and individual morality unmediated by any religious authorities. Poets and philosophers regularly condemned social institutions, with their quasi-religious overtones, such as caste and gender oppression, going as far back as Vyasa, the mythic yet named author of the Sanskrit epic, *Mahabharata*.[325] From ancient times, poets maintained the practice of attribution *written into their verses*: a verse that specifically identifies the poet, by name, as the author of that particular work.

In nineteenth-century France and Germany, when the new perfume of Romanticism suffused the air of the times, it made itself felt even in the dry doctrines of the law. While the idea of moral rights existed in the European systems of law before Romanticism, Romanticism became a new lens through which moral rights have, ever since, been viewed. Strömholm speaks of "the cult of genius and originality characteristic of pre-Romanticism and the 'Sturm-und-Drang' period [which] resulted in the final discrediting of the hitherto prevailing conception of creation." For the Romantics, creation was no longer divinely inspired, or, at least, divine inspiration required a worthy human vessel to contain it.[326] The human

[324] At least in English and European languages, but part of the legacy of colonialism is that modern scholarship in these countries is often carried out in European languages and that the study of pre-colonial phenomena may not either spread outside its original languages or be enriched by modern conceptions of scholarship. Colonialism often wiped out pre-existing methodologies of knowledge generation and conservation without replacing them with anything viable: *see, e.g.*, Mira T. Sundara Rajan, *Introduction*, *in* THE COMING AGE: COLLECTED ENGLISH WRITINGS OF C. SUBRAMANIA BHARATI 1 (Mira T. Sundara Rajan ed., 2021).

[325] For example, on the authorship of Mahabharata, see New World Encyclopedia, *Mahabharata: Authorship*, https://www.newworldencyclopedia.org/entry/Mahabharata#Authorship.

[326] "Indwelling" is the poem from which this phrase is derived. The poet describes the personality in which there is no room for the divine spirit to enter—"replete with very thou." It seems that the poem, by T.E. Brown, is often misattributed to Sir Thomas Browne; it can be found in LOUISE COLLIER WILLCOX, A MANUAL OF MYSTIC VERSE: BEING A CHOICE OF MEDITATIVE AND MYSTIC POEMS 232 (1917).

author became recognized as the source of the work, a "genius" who inherently possessed, to the highest degree, that most valuable of all qualities: creativity. If this was the Romantic perspective, what will now happen to moral rights in the age of the machine?

From a social perspective, at least, human creativity is in decline. In comparison to previous ages, it is not economically valuable, except in rare cases or in technical fields. Society at large appears to be more interested in the question of whether machines are creative, and it is fascinated by the question of whether the creativity of machines can supplant human creativity. From an economic point of view, this question is immensely significant: if machine creativity could be generated and controlled by those who own the machines, they could accrue great wealth, and the need to pay or acknowledge human authors could be avoided. Something similar has happened on a much smaller scale with the ability to use musical recordings in place of live performers, for example, in musical theater.[327] The potential for artificial intelligence (AI) to heighten social inequality seems clear. In such a scenario, would human authors become obsolete? In a deeper sense, the answer must be no—at least, not as long as human beings continue to be human[328]—but it is certainly possible that human authors could become socially unnecessary. E.M. Forster wrote about just such a society in a visionary short story from 1909, "The Machine Stops." But we are now just at the point where "the machine starts."

The moral right of our age faces new challenges: the deconstruction of authorship, the dethroning of individual genius, the general discrediting of individual creativity and (not coincidentally) individual autonomy, and the dizzyingly rapid rise of machines. As befits the digital context, with its endless possibilities for layering and overlapping information, knowledge, and works, authorship in our times has also acquired multiple layers and shades of meaning.

The post-moderns believed that Romanticism had died, but, to paraphrase—"Le Romantisme est mort. Vive le romantisme!" Romanticism lives on in our society, albeit in an altered form.[329] The "cult" of Romanticism now lies embalmed deep within our collective psyche. Poststructuralism argues that authorship is a mere social function, that the author is no more than a glorified public servant, and that talk of personal or spiritual interests is senseless.[330] Yet, even in such a hostile environment, the social fascination with authorship remains—and, for many,

[327] *See, e.g.*, Peter Marks, *On Broadway, Taking the Musicians out of the Music*, WASHINGTON POST (Mar. 10, 2003), https://www.washingtonpost.com/archive/lifestyle/2003/03/10/on-broadway-taking-the-musicians-out-of-the-music/118d7be5-594f-4212-8726-e0fcecefd70f.

[328] The essential quality of art is the subject of ELLEN DISSANAYAKE, HOMO AESTHETICUS: WHERE ART COMES FROM AND WHY (1992).

[329] The attitude of mingled fascination, contempt, and respect for the arts seems like nothing but the hero worship of the nineteenth century in a new guise. Ellen Dissanayake, id., comments on the continued associations of grandeur that cling to the arts.

[330] See Foucault's brilliant essay, *What Is an Author?*, where the philosopher argues that "authorship" is a social construct that embodies a certain perspective on creativity and its role in society: MICHEL FOUCAULT, *What Is an Author?*, *in* THE FOUCAULT READER 101 (Paul Rabinow ed., 1984).

a deep sense of unease about authorship's potential demise not in the halls of academia but in the workplaces of Silicon Valley.

The essential characteristic of digital technology, particularly when it is linked to large-scale social phenomena such as social media networks, is its need for information. As humans consume food, technology consumes information. It regurgitates it, often in a garbled form, as "content." Generative AI is the ultimate expression of this phenomenon, since its "generative" ability is built on its consumption of vast amounts of pre-existing material, much of it created by authors, on which it models its "thought" processes.[331]

In the nascent technological age that is before us now, "content" that originates with a human author may go through virtually infinite transformations as it is re-used in, through, and by generative technologies. The technological processes that transform the products of human creativity are promoted not only because of our social fascination with technology but also because they generate powerful, unprecedented opportunities for wealth creation among those who control these new technologies. As initial developments have been quick to show, some significant portion of this wealth will be generated at the expense of human creators.

A profound psychological and social transformation is underway. Human creation is increasingly insecure and undervalued in this environment. The press surrounding AI is obsessed with the question of whether AI will "replace" humans in various fields of work, including literature, the fine arts, and music. Humans have always developed technologies to promote human development, and it is not clear that AI is fundamentally different from previous technologies. As chess grandmaster Garry Kasparov has said,

> Machine's triumph is man's triumph . . .
>
> Soon machines will be taxi drivers and doctors, but will they be intelligent? . . .
>
> What really matters is how humans feel about working and living with these machines. . . .

[331] Indeed, it appears that visual artists have brought a lawsuit against a group of companies creating generative artificial intelligence technology for the creation of artistic images, many of which are created by prompts using the artist's name. *See* Benj Edwards, *Artists File Claim-Action Lawsuit against AI Image Generation Companies*, ArsTechnica (Jan. 16, 2023), https://arstechnica.com/information-technology/2023/01/artists-file-class-action-lawsuit-against-ai-image-generator-companies; Kyle Chayka, *Is A.I. Art Stealing from Artists?*, The New Yorker (Feb. 10, 2023), https://www.newyorker.com/culture/infinite-scroll/is-ai-art-stealing-from-artists; Ella Feldman, *Are A.I. Image Generators Violating Copyright Laws?*, Smithsonian Magazine (Jan. 24, 2023), https://www.smithsonianmag.com/smart-news/are-ai-image-generators-stealing-from-artists-180981488. In the absence of new rules about licensing, copyright law has not been able to address this problem so far, but the moral rights of attribution and integrity are clearly relevant. *See, e.g.*, Soleil Ho, *No, Teaching AI to Copy an Artist's Style Isn't "Democratization." It's Theft*, San Francisco Chronicle (Apr. 5, 2023), https://www.sfchronicle.com/opinion/article/stability ai-art-karla-ortiz-17854282.php; Ahmed Elgammal, *The Folly of Making Art with Text-to-Image Generative AI*, The Conversation (June 23, 2023), https://theconversation.com/the-folly-of-making-art-with-text-to-image-generative-ai-207480.

> Machines have instructions, we have purpose . . . Machines have objectivity, we have passion. . . .
>
> We should not worry about what machines can do today, we should worry about what they cannot do.
>
> If we fail, it is because we grew complacent and limited our ambitions.[332]

So far, Kasparov's words seem to have fallen largely on deaf ears. Our society does not seem ready to approach AI as a new tool to be used by humans, nor does it herald the development of AI *primarily* as a triumph of human ingenuity and a testament to the power of human creativity. Instead, AI has burst onto the world stage as a threat—a threat to human creativity, to human material and social well-being, and even, as many experts are suggesting, to human existence itself.[333]

Copyright law has done little to impede the exploitation of humans by AI. This is one more reason why current copyright laws are in need of reform. However, the doctrine of moral rights already contains many key elements of what is required to balance the progress of technology with human needs. The concepts of attribution of authorship and the integrity of human creation, as well as disclosure, offer a brilliant road map for the basic regulation of AI.

The possibilities of moral rights for AI regulation are explored in detail in Chapter 5 of this book. For now, it is sufficient to point out that human authorship still exists. Notwithstanding its seductive power, the fact remains that technology is but a reflection of human creativity. Judging from individual struggles to continue creating, even in the absence of social support, it seems clear that technology simply cannot replace the human drive to create. Why would we want it to? Archeological evidence supports the view that creative activities date from our earliest existence and, in many ways, our creativity defines who and what we are as a species.[334] Given the growing pressure to sacrifice our creative impulses to some greater technological imperative, the ultimate fate of the author—the human creative individual—has become one of the most troubling questions of our time.

[332] Quoted in Jane Wakefield, *Ted 2017: I Won First Match with Deep Blue, Says Kasparov*, BBC News (Apr. 25, 2017), https://www.bbc.com/news/technology-39701222.

[333] *See, e.g.*, Chris Vallance, *Artificial Intelligence Could Lead to Extinction, Experts Warn*, BBC News (May 30, 2023), https://www.bbc.com/news/uk-65746524.

[334] This theme is explored in a fascinating book by Ellen Dissanayake, *supra* note 314.

3

Moral Rights in the International Copyright Regime

Article 6*bis* of the Berne Convention and Beyond

The perfect is the enemy of the good.
—Voltaire[1]

A. **Introduction** 150
B. **Emergence of an Archetype: Moral Rights in Article *6bis* of the Berne Convention** 153
1. The Age of Authorship: The Original Text of 1928 153
a. Literary Language 155
b. Legal Language 156
c. Objective vs. Subjective Proof 157
2. The 1948 Amendments: Moral Rights in a Commercial Age 158
3. Revisiting the Compromise: The Stockholm Conference of 1967 159
4. The Technological Era: Moral Rights and the Unknown 161
C. **Moral Rights in the Berne Convention beyond Article *6bis*** 164
1. Explicit Recognition: Attribution for Journalists in Article 10.3 164
2. Indirect Protection: Convention Rights and the "Legitimate Interests of the Author" 164
a. Moral Rights Abroad: Article 5.1 and Rights "Specially Granted by the Convention" 165
b. The Three-Step Test: Article 9.2 166
c. *Droit de suite* (Artist's Resale Right): A Hybrid Right in Article 14*ter* 168
D. **Moral Rights in Other International Copyright Agreements** 169
1. Russian Dolls: The Berne Convention and the TRIPs Agreements 169
a. Relation to the Berne Convention: TRIPs Article 9.1 170
b. Post-TRIPs Expansion of Moral Rights in the International Community 171

[1] This aphorism seems impossibly appropriate to the story of moral rights, which is why I have made use of it even though it is (ironically) difficult to attribute. It has a number of possible sources, the most literary of which is Voltaire, who quotes a closely aligned Italian proverb in his 1772 poem, "La Bégueule", which offers excellent advice to perfectionists (and he is also said to mention it in his *Dictionnaire philosophique*)—"The best is the enemy of the good":

> "Dans ses écrits un sage Italien Dit que le mieux est l'ennemi du bien; Non qu'on ne puisse augmenter en prudence, En bonté d'âme, en talents, en science; Cherchons le mieux sur ces chapitres-là; Partout ailleurs évitons la chimère. Dans son état heureux qui peut se plaire, Vivre à sa place, et garder ce qu'il a!"

2. Moral Rights in the Digital Age: The WIPO Internet Treaties and Beijing 172
   a. The WCT: A Digital Right of Disclosure 173
   b. The WPPT: Dissemination Is the New Creation 176
      i. Background: The Intersection of Moral and Economic Rights in Sound Recordings 177
      ii. Moral Rights in the WPPT 179
   c. The Beijing Treaty: Always Read the Footnotes 182
3. The European Union: An Elephant in the Room 185
   a. Harmonization and Moral Rights in the EU: Policy Initiatives? 187
   b. Moral Rights in the Directives: Indirect Approaches 188
   c. CJEU Jurisprudence and Moral Rights 190
   d. Moral Rights and the Digital Single Market (DSM) Directive 191

E. In Principle: Moral Rights and International Trade 196
1. Minimum Standards 197
2. National Treatment 198
   a. Practical Implications 199
   b. Choice of Law 200
   c. Most-Favored Nation 204

F. Private Rights, Public Forum: Copyright and Moral Rights in Public International Law 204

G. Conclusion 205

A. Introduction

In 1928, at a revision conference in Rome, moral rights were incorporated into the Berne Convention for the Protection of Literary and Artistic Works.[2] The Berne Convention was first adopted in 1886, and it was the first ever international agreement on copyright. Victor Hugo and other writers played a key role in the development of the Convention, which allowed nationals of all member countries to benefit from shared and mutually comprehensible rules on the import and export of cultural products, notably books. All member countries agreed to recognize each other's copyright laws. The year 1928 was a further watershed moment in copyright history, when moral rights first became part of the Berne framework and were thereby transformed from an informal European doctrine into an integral part of international copyright law. Article 6*bis* was subsequently amended to

[2] *See* Art. 6*bis* of the International Convention for the Protection of Literary and Artistic Works, adopted at Berne on Sept. 9, 1886, completed at Paris on May 4, 1896, revised at Berlin on Nov. 13, 1908, completed at Berne on Mar. 20, 1914, revised at Rome on June 2, 1928 (Rome Act, 1928), https://www.keionline.org/wp-content/uploads/1928_Rome_revisions_Berne.pdf (available in French at https://www.wipo.int/wipolex/en/treaties/textdetails/12803). For the current version of the Berne Convention, see International Convention for the Protection of Literary and Artistic Works, adopted at Berne on Sept. 9, 1886, completed at Paris on May 4, 1896, revised at Berlin on Nov. 13, 1908, completed at Berne on Mar. 20, 1914, revised at Rome on June 2, 1928, at Brussels on June 26, 1948, at Stockholm on July 14, 1967, and at Paris on July 24, 1971, and amended on Sept. 28, 1979, S. Treaty Doc. No. 99-27 (1986), https://www.wipo.int/treaties/en/ip/berne. All websites cited in this chapter were last visited on Oct. 25, 2024.

reflect further accommodations for common-law systems, allowing the protection of at least some moral rights through the law of tort.[3]

The larger story of Berne is one of compromise. It is a tale of what has been, and remains, workable in the highly imperfect world of copyright as it currently exists. Accordingly, the new Article 6*bis* of the Berne Convention represented a compromise provision arrived at by discussions between European countries and Great Britain. At that time, Britain also controlled a large number of international jurisdictions as its colonies. As the world eventually moved towards decolonization, Article 6*bis* became a model provision for all countries wishing to implement moral rights in their copyright laws. In this respect, Article 6*bis* has been amazingly influential, and through it, moral rights have arguably come to be more widely accepted around the world than any other aspect of copyright law. The general characteristics of the Berne system have allowed Article 6*bis* to function as guidance rather than coercion, and the model has proven malleable enough to accommodate an extraordinary range of national, cultural, and developmental priorities.

For most countries of the world, moral rights have therefore become synonymous with Article 6*bis* of the Berne Convention. Article 6*bis* offers a practical template for moral rights protection in Berne member countries, and it is also something more: a powerful symbol of the idea of moral rights and the coalescence of international unity around it.

The latter point is significant because Berne operates at the nexus between intellectual property (IP) and trade. The purpose of Berne is to enable the movement of works across borders, to the greatest extent possible without penalizing authors and owners of copyright. Accordingly, it functions as a system of minimum standards, which must be adopted by all member countries, while allowing them to exceed those standards if they so choose.[4] The result of minimum standards is a process of harmonization, rather than standardization, where the diverse laws of member states can work together at a practical level without necessarily becoming the same. Over time, the Berne compromise has further come to mean that member countries may invoke alternate forms of legal protection for moral rights beyond copyright legislation and its interpretation, and, where relevant, to implement the limitations flowing from those alternate legal frameworks to the interpretation of moral rights—particularly in the case of countries that are relatively new to the idea of moral rights, such as those from the common-law tradition.[5]

[3] *See* Sam Ricketson & Jane Ginsburg, International Copyright and Neighboring Rights: The Berne Convention and Beyond para. 10.12 (3d ed., 2022).

[4] *See* Berne Convention, *supra* note 1, at Art. 19 ("Protection greater than resulting from Convention").

[5] In most such countries, this has meant reduced levels of protection, e.g., as tort law is invoked, limiting protection to the lifetime of the person injured. However, it could potentially operate within expanded legal frameworks with broader opportunities for protection. For example, in India, a country of common-law heritage, the public international law framework for the protection of cultural property and the principle of comity of nations have been invoked to enlarge moral rights for Indian artists and, by likely analogy, authors. See the case of *Amar Nath Sehgal v. Union of India* 2005 (30) PTC 253, where

In practice, this system has largely done what might have been expected: it has succeeded in establishing an international baseline for moral rights protection while leading to inconsistencies in terms of the kinds and levels of protection available in different jurisdictions around the world.

The Berne Union has also failed in one major respect. One of Berne's original purposes was to facilitate the mutual recognition of copyright in Europe and the United States, thereby bringing an end to the widespread piracy of British works in the United States. But the United States did not join the Berne Convention for more than 100 years, finally becoming a member in 1989. Moral rights were one of two major obstacles to U.S. membership in Berne, and, today, U.S. implementation of moral rights remains entirely limited to the area of the fine arts.[6] A recent study process at the United States Copyright Office concluded that attempts to generalize moral rights across all areas of subject matter, as is the case in all other Berne member countries, would be too dramatic a shift in the United States.[7] It therefore seems unlikely that this remaining gap in Berne acceptance, at least as far as moral rights are concerned, will be closed at any time in the foreseeable future. As the Copyright Office notes,

> The Copyright Office takes very seriously the importance of attribution and integrity interests to authors. This factor was, along with the other guiding principles outlined in this section, preeminent in our considerations as we drafted this Report. While the Office recognizes that our decision not to recommend adoption of a new statutory moral right at this time may disappoint some authors, *the Office is not yet prepared to recommend a course that would represent such a significant change to U.S. law and industry practices.*[8]

The powerful archetype of international moral rights protection represented by Article 6*bis* should still not obscure the rich history of moral rights before Berne, or

the Delhi High Court found the Indian government negligent of a sculptor's moral rights in work it had commissioned. That court derives much of its language from Mira T. Sundara Rajan, *Moral Rights and the Protection of Cultural Heritage:* Amar Nath Sehgal v. Union of India, 10(1) INT'L J. CULTURAL PROP. 79, 88 (para. 41) (2001).

[6] Visual Artists Rights Act of 1990, Pub. L. No. 101-650, 104 Stat. 5128, now U.S. Copyright Act, 17 U.S.C. § 106A (VARA), https://www.copyright.gov/title17/92chap1.html#106a; *see also* the Bill at https://www.congress.gov/bill/101st-congress/house-bill/2690. The complete U.S. Copyright Act is available as Title 17 of the U.S. Code, https://www.copyright.gov/title17/.

[7] U.S. COPYRIGHT OFFICE, AUTHORS, ATTRIBUTION, AND INTEGRITY: EXAMINING MORAL RIGHTS IN THE UNITED STATES 35–36 (2019), https://www.copyright.gov/policy/moralrights/full-report.pdf.

[8] Id. (emphasis added). The report goes on to comment,

> The Office believes that the existing patchwork, supplemented by the recommended changes to various federal laws outlined below, should address many of the concerns expressed by authors during the course of this study, and believes that further study of whether those targeted changes fully address the primary concerns of artists would be warranted before adoption of a blanket broad new moral rights provision.

their continued resonance beyond it. Article 6*bis* reflects a compromise standard that has made it possible for diverse jurisdictions to find much-needed commonalities. At the same time, the pattern of moral rights evolution throughout the Berne era suggests that this very compromise may lead to new possibilities for the development of the doctrine in the technological environment, creating an opportunity to explore moral rights beyond their traditional limitations.

This chapter provides an overview of the international copyright regime and discusses the place of moral rights in each of the major legal instruments that constitute this framework. It also considers the place of moral rights in complementary copyright systems at the regional level, particularly the powerful European Union system, which exerts a profound influence on the development of international copyright norms and practices while representing the heartland of authors' moral rights. Finally, it concludes with a broader perspective on moral rights in international law, considering the presence of these rights in instruments of public international law beyond the international copyright regime.

B. Emergence of an Archetype: Moral Rights in Article 6*bis* of the Berne Convention

What is the template for moral rights offered by Article 6*bis* of Berne, and how has this template evolved over time? The moral rights of authors adopted in 1928, during the Rome revision conference of the Berne Convention, included basic statements of the rights of attribution and integrity.[9] Article 6*bis* has been amended only twice since then—in 1948, at the Brussels revision conference of the Berne Convention, and again, at the landmark Stockholm conference of 1967.[10] The amendments did not expand the provisions; changes made at both stages clarified and reduced the scope of protection for moral rights. Interestingly, at least some of these amendments sought to clarify limitations of the rights that may well have been taken for granted by previous generations of negotiators as being implicit within the system.

1. The Age of Authorship: The Original Text of 1928

The 1928 provisions on moral rights in the Berne Convention stated as follows:

9 The drafting history of Rome Act, 1928, *supra* note 1, at Art. 6*bis* receives a detailed treatment, including discussion of the negotiating process and the positions of the various national groups, in ELIZABETH ADENEY, *The Rome Revision Conference of the Berne Convention*, *in* THE MORAL RIGHTS OF AUTHORS AND PERFORMERS: AN INTERNATIONAL AND COMPARATIVE ANALYSIS 103 (2006).

10 Again, Adeney discusses these processes in some detail: id. at 129–59 (esp. paras. 7.13–7.56).

> Independently of the author's copyright, and even after transfer of the said copyright, the author shall have the right to claim authorship of the work, as well as the right to object to any distortion, mutilation or other modification of the said work which would be prejudicial to his honour or reputation.[11]

From the range of possible moral rights known in France and Germany, the 1928 provision established the protection of attribution and integrity, which were universally recognized among continental European countries.[12] In relation to integrity, the right dealt with damage to the work that was harmful to the author's reputation, or "honor."[13] In some jurisdictions, the Berne formulation of the right of integrity, reflecting the limits of Berne language, is known simply as a right of reputation.[14]

The presence of moral rights in the Berne Convention represented a significant achievement. A compromise had been reached between the civil law countries of continental Europe and the United Kingdom and its colonial possessions on an issue of fundamental difference. However, the compromise did not imply a consensus. Rather, the addition of moral rights to Berne signified the inclusion of civil law principles within the Convention which the common law countries were willing to accept. In the civilian tradition, as discussed in the previous chapter, moral rights are considered an essential part of the author's copyright, and indeed, some of the classic commentaries on French copyright law go so far as to suggest the primacy of moral rights in copyright law as a whole.[15] Beliefs are powerful, and

[11] *See* Rome Act, 1928, *supra* note 1, at Art. 6*bis*(1). Article 6*bis*(2) deals with the practical exercise of the rights, and in 1928 it provided, "The determination of the conditions under which these rights shall be exercised is reserved for the national legislation of the countries of the Union. The means of redress for safeguarding these rights shall be regulated by the legislation of the country where protection is claimed."

[12] Adeney mentions the right "to decide if the work should appear" (*divulgation*), which is arguably implied in Art. 6*bis*. *See* Adeney, *supra* note 8, at para. 6.30.

[13] The legal meaning of "honor" was, and remains, obscure. This issue is discussed by Elizabeth Adeney, *The Moral Right of Integrity: The Past and Future of "Honour,"* 2 Intell. Prop. Q. 111 (2005), although her interpretation is not entirely satisfying. See the discussion in Chapter 4, *infra* notes 320–22 and accompanying text.

[14] This was formerly the case in Russia, under art. 15 of the Law of the Russian Federation No. 5351-1 of July 9, 1993 on Copyright and Neighboring Rights, as amended, https://www.wto.org/english/thewto_e/acc_e/rus_e/wtaccrus48_leg_94.pdf, though it has since been overruled by Part IV of the Russian Civil Code, completed in 2006 and in effect since Jan. 1, 2008. The Civil Code, updated to 2021, is available only in Russian at https://www.wipo.int/wipolex/en/legislation/details/20306. This provision is discussed in Mira T. Sundara Rajan, Copyright and Creative Freedom: A Study of Post-Socialist Law Reform 173–79 (2006). The situation has changed under the Russian Civil Code, ch. IV, which came into effect on Jan. 1, 2008 and in which, following a well-established legislative tradition under the Soviet regime, the right of integrity is restored to a right of "inviolability." A pure right of reputation perhaps fails to consider the implications of honor, but legislators may also view reputation as encompassing honor.

[15] *See, e.g.*, Henri Desbois, Le Droit d'auteur en France vii, 469–71 (paras. 380–83) (3d ed., 1978). Not all the French commentators agree; at least one writer, Pierre Recht, argues that the position of moral rights in French law is both overstated and undesirable, representing a paternalistic approach to authors by the state. *See* Pierre Recht, Le Droit d'auteur, une nouvelle forme de propriété: Histoire et théorie (1969).

the conviction that moral rights are a foreign import in common law countries has long impeded their recognition in the United Kingdom as well as the United States and most other common law countries.

Given these circumstances, how did moral rights find their way into international copyright regulation at all? Two factors were largely responsible: first, the power of authors in the late nineteenth century, who lobbied for the establishment of an international copyright framework when the book trade had become important; and secondly, the specific legal bases on which common law countries accepted the protection of moral rights, which may have made their adoption more limited than it seemed.

a. Literary Language

Copyright in the nineteenth and twenty-first centuries looks remarkably similar in the sense that both periods are evidently moments of upheaval in the law. In one key respect, however, the current dynamics of copyright are very different. In the nineteenth century, with Victor Hugo in the lead, authors played a pivotal role in establishing international copyright rules. Over the following century, the status of authors and artists fell to one of near-invisibility as far as copyright law was concerned, But this attitude towards authors may now be changing. The European Union's Digital Single Market Directive, adopted in 2021 emphaszes authors' right to remuneration, and it also recognizes the underlying problem of inequality of bargaining power routinely faced by authors .[16]The upheavals brought about by artificial intelligence are also likely to raise public awareness of the plight of authors as never before, as the technology, perhaps ironically, serves to highlight the shared interests of authors and the public.

If the twenty-first century comes to be known as the Age of Artificial Intelligence, the nineteenth century probably deserves to be known as the Century of the Book. The spread of literature during this period was without precedent in the Western world, and it was based on the development of a mass publishing industry as one of the by-products of the Industrial Revolution.[17] This made authors a powerful and prestigious group.

With the rise of international trade and travel, the unhappiness of many authors with the protection of their rights outside their countries of origin was a key factor in the development of international copyright.[18] High-profile examples of wronged writers included Charles Dickens, who was profoundly unhappy about

[16] Directive (EU) 2019/790 of the European Parliament and of the Council of 17 April 2019 on copyright and related rights in the Digital Single Market and amending Directives 96/9/EC and 2001/29/EC, 2019 O.J. (L 130) 92 (DSM Directive), https://eur-lex.europa.eu/eli/dir/2019/790/oj.

[17] See the comments in Martha Woodmansee, *The Genius and the Copyright: Economic and Legal Conditions of the Emergence of the "Author,"* 17 Eighteenth-Century Stud. 425, 425 (1984).

[18] Noted by Sam Ricketson, The Berne Convention for the Protection of Literary and Artistic Works: 1886–1986 (1987).

the unauthorized printing of his works in the United States. Dickens attempted to draw attention to the issue of literary piracy by undertaking a tour of the United States in 1842, but his efforts bore little fruit, and he remained embittered about the situation until his death.[19] In another twist, Russian authors were keen to encourage the printing of their works in European countries, believing that the popularity and prestige of Russian authors had attained historic heights in Western Europe.[20] In 1878, the *Association Littéraire et Artistique Internationale* (ALAI) was founded in France with the goal of promoting authors' rights. It had no less a luminary than Victor Hugo at its head.[21]

These authors certainly recognized the idea of moral rights and were familiar with its significance as a legal concept in French and continental law. The idea needed time to gain momentum. The presence of moral rights in the 1928 document was clearly a product of their efforts.

b. Legal Language

The communiqués surrounding the 1928 discussions show that the common law countries may have been partly persuaded to accept moral rights because they believed that they were not agreeing to anything new. Instead, the rights were apparently perceived by the UK and Australian delegations to the Rome conference as a codification of rights that were already enjoyed by their authors—presumably, through the common law of tort and statutory provisions outside copyright law. Overall, it was to the advantage of common law countries to accept moral rights in the Berne Convention because of Berne's reliance on the principle of national treatment. Authors from the common law countries would enjoy moral rights abroad, while the common law countries were only constrained to apply the minimum standards in Berne within their own borders.[22]

Elizabeth Adeney refers to the Canadian delegation's silence on the issue. She attributes it to the unwillingness of Canada to stir up controversy, which would certainly be characteristic; but her suggestion that Canada had an affinity for moral

[19] Charles Dickens was a notable victim. See the interesting review of his situation in Philip V. Allingham, *Dickens's 1867–68 Reading Tour: Re-Opening the Copyright Question*, The Victorian Web (Aug. 10, 2013), http://www.victorianweb.org/authors/dickens/pva/pva76.html; Frederick Kaplan, Dickens: A Biography 91 (1988), notes Dickens's support for the improvement of copyright protection in the United Kingdom and abroad.

[20] Ricketson and Ginsburg note the growing interest in Berne membership over the early years of the twentieth century in Russia: Ricketson & Ginsburg, *supra* note 2, at para. 3.09.

[21] See the website of the ALAI, https://www.alai.org/renseignements/historique.html, which notes, "Créée à Paris en 1878, à l'initiative de la SOCIETE DES GENS DE LETTRES et sous la présidence d'honneur de Victor Hugo, l'ALAI se donna pour premier objectif de susciter la création d'une convention internationale pour la protection de la propriété littéraire et artistique" ("Established in Paris in 1878, … the ALAI's main objective was the creation of an international agreement aimed at protecting literary and artistic copyright").

[22] The clarifications that occurred at Rome are worth noting. *See* Adeney, *supra* note 9, at para. 7.15. I am indebted to Colin Tapper for pointing this out (in personal communication with the author, June 4, 2010).

rights or special knowledge of the doctrine because of Canada's French heritage seems questionable. David Vaver refers to such claims as "folklore."[23]

A more cynical truth may be in evidence. Canada's moral rights measures, though enacted at the early date of 1931, included extensive, indeed comprehensive, provisions on waivers. The adoption of waivers as a feature of standard-form copyright contracts in Canada would render it practically impossible for the great majority of Canadian authors and artists, wielding limited bargaining power, to exercise their moral rights in practice. Canadian jurisprudence can only boast one unequivocal victory for moral rights in its history: the well-known, colorful, and very brief judgment on Michael Snow's sculpture of Canada geese.[24] The most recent comments of the Supreme Court of Canada on moral rights suggest that, in fact, Canadian courts will be extraordinarily cautious in recognizing and applying moral rights principles.[25] Rather than expanding appreciation of moral rights to Canada's English-law community, the French influence seems to have produced a schism among judges from the two traditions at Canada's Supreme Court.[26]

c. Objective vs. Subjective Proof

In one particular respect, the text of Article 6*bis* implemented a highly specific vision of moral rights. This key provision involved the author's right to object to treatment of the work that would be "prejudicial to his honour or reputation." The language introduced an idea that has since become fundamental to the understanding of moral rights worldwide, but especially in the common law countries. It imposes a requirement on the author to satisfy a burden of proof. But what, exactly, amounts to "proof of damage to honor or reputation"? The phrase has come to mean that the author must be able to bring someone else to court to corroborate his or her claims. In case law, this has taken the form of offering expert evidence to the court.

[23] *See* David Vaver, *Moral Rights Yesterday, Today and Tomorrow*, 7(3) INT'L J. TECH. & L. 270, 275–76 (1997).

[24] *Snow v. The Eaton Centre Ltd*, 70 C.P.R. (2d) 105 (1982) (Can.), available on the law firm website https://zvulony.ca/2012/decisions/snow-v-eaton-centre-ltd-et-al. See the old Copyright Act, R.S.C. 1970, c. C-30, s. 12(7) (Can.). Vaver, *supra* note 22, at 275–76 provides a survey of Canadian case law on moral rights to 1999. Since then, two Canadian Supreme Court decisions have dealt with moral rights, both of which arose from unusual contexts. The first, *Théberge v. Galerie d'Art du Petit Champlain Inc.* [2002] 2 S.C.R. 336, 2002 SCC 34 (Can.), involved a claim for copyright infringement, which, the Court said, should have been framed as a moral rights claim. The second, *Desputeaux v. Éditions Chouette (1987) Inc.* [2003] 1 S.C.R. 178, 2003 SCC 17, para. 57 (Can.), commented on the place of moral rights in an arbitration problem.

[25] *See Théberge* and *Desputeaux*, id. Interestingly, the Court in *Théberge* split precisely along linguistic lines, with the anglophone judges agreeing in their restrictive interpretation of moral rights and securing a victory of one. The law is open to change in Canada, but a pro-moral rights bench would have to contend with a badly drafted law and nearly a century of industry practice working to weaken the rights. The case is analyzed in detail in Mira T. Sundara Rajan, *Moral Rights and Economic Rights: Overlapping Protection of Authors under Copyright Law*, in OVERLAPPING INTELLECTUAL PROPERTY RIGHTS 303 (Neil Wilkof, Shamnad Basheer & Irene Calboli eds., 2d ed., 2023).

[26] *Théberge*, *supra* note 23.

In theory, it is also possible that other types of evidence could be offered by the author as the required proof—a demonstration of reduced sales due to the alteration, for example—but case law so far has not borne this out. The spirit of evidence like this, which focuses on economics, also seems like a poor fit with moral rights—although its relevance here only serves to highlight, once again, the close and ultimately indissoluble link between the author's economic and moral interests.

For the time being, this need for "objective" proof seems to be satisfied by expert evidence, and the key distinction is therefore that between the author's own opinion and the opinions of others. But it should also be noted that there is something deeply dissatisfying about this approach. It is doubtful whether experts who are employed by the parties in common legal systems are well placed to offer objective assessments; their testimony has a partisan purpose. The relative objectivity of a third party may also be unhelpful in the sense that the author may be able to perceive harm and act upon it in a way that may include a third party. Such "objectivity" might end up being detrimental to the public interest in the preservation of cultural heritage. Nevertheless, the Berne formula signifies an attempt at objectivity, and it is in these terms that the laws of common law countries are generally distinguished from those of civil law countries, such as France, which are said to take a "subjective" approach to the author's moral rights by accepting an author's complaint as *prima facie* evidence of a violation.[27]

2. The 1948 Amendments: Moral Rights in a Commercial Age

The 1948 text of the moral rights provisions, concluded at Brussels, saw an attempt to clarify the relationship between moral rights and the legislation of common law countries. In particular, the duration of moral rights is specified as follows:

> In so far as the legislation of the countries of the Union permits, the rights granted to the author in accordance with the preceding paragraph shall, after his death, be maintained, at least until the expiry of the copyright, and shall be exercisable by the persons or institutions authorized by this legislation.....[28]

[27] *See, e.g.*, *Huston v. La Cinq*, Cour de cassation [Cass.] [supreme court for judicial matters] 1e civ., May 28, 1991, Bull. civ. I, No. 172 (Fr.)., https://www.legifrance.gouv.fr/juri/id/JURITEXT000007026649.

[28] Excerpt from International Convention for the Protection of Literary and Artistic Works, adopted at Berne on Sept. 9, 1886, completed at Paris on May 4, 1896, revised at Berlin on Nov. 13, 1908, completed at Berne on Mar. 20, 1914, revised at Rome on June 2, 1928, at Brussels on June 26, 1948 (Brussels Act, 1948), Art. 6*bis*(2). The new subsections (2) and (3) read:

> (2) In so far as the legislation of the countries of the Union permits, the rights granted to the author in accordance with the preceding paragraph shall, after his death, be maintained, at least until the expiry of the copyright, and shall be exercisable by the persons or institutions authorized by the said legislation. The determination of the conditions under which the rights

In a sense, the new formulation improved upon the old by establishing a definite minimum duration for the protection of moral rights. Under the Brussels Act, the rights had to be protected until the expiration of copyright. But the reach of the Article was severely limited by the proviso that this minimum duration of protection would only apply "[i]n so far as the legislation of the countries of the Union permits." The new provision was not so much an improvement in protection as a paring down, whittling, or shaping of the loose and open-ended language of 1928 in Article 6*bis*(2) of the Berne Convention. The change occurred in an environment where copyright was increasingly seen as an economic matter, and the cultural sensitivities engendered by a nineteenth-century world view were becoming obsolete. As Ezra Pound observed, "They will come no more,/The old men with beautiful manners."[29] The world of 1948 had new priorities. As Elizabeth Adeney points out, "[T]he UK Delegation stated that this country would prefer that the Convention not contain any provision for moral rights, given that the Convention was, in the delegation's view, an economic agreement."[30]

3. Revisiting the Compromise: The Stockholm Conference of 1967

In 1967, at a revision conference rife with conflict and overshadowed by the fear that developing countries would abandon the international copyright system altogether and trigger its collapse,[31] the common law understanding of moral rights was codified into the Berne Convention in the following words:

> The rights granted to the author in accordance with the preceding paragraph shall, after his death, be maintained at least until the expiry of the economic rights, and shall be exercisable by the persons or institutions authorized by the legislation of the country where protection is claimed. However, those countries whose legislation, at the moment of their ratification of or accession to this Act, does not provide for the protection after the death of the author of all the rights

mentioned in this paragraph shall be exercised shall be governed by the legislation of the countries of the Union.

(3) The means of redress for safeguarding the rights granted by this Article shall be governed by the legislation of the country where protection is claimed.

[29] Ezra Pound, *Moeurs Contemporaines*, in Quia Pauper Amavi 14 (1919). The passing of the era, for Pound, was marked by the onset of the First World War.

[30] Adeney, *supra* note 9, at para. 7.14, citing Union internationale pour la Protection des Oeuvres littéraires et artistiques, Documents de la conférence de Bruxelles 5–26 juin 1948 194–95 (para. 7.14) (1951).

[31] Ricketson, *supra* note 17, at para. 3.64, provides a quick overview of the situation. For a detailed discussion of the evolving role of developing countries in the Berne Union, see id. at ch. 11, on developing countries.

> set out in the preceding paragraph may provide that some of these rights may, after his death, cease to be maintained.[32]

Against this historical backdrop, the new clause enacted in Article 6*bis*(2) of the Convention, incomprehensible to the uninitiated, makes perfect sense. The objective was to limit moral rights in the common law countries, which did not previously protect moral rights in their copyright laws, to the lifetime of the author. In other words, moral rights were transformed into a personal tort which, like all other personal torts and in contrast to all other aspects of copyright law, could not be exercised after the author's death. It is also worth noting that the Berne provision entered into force at a time when the principle of protecting authors' rights after the time of death was well established in international copyright law.

As drafted, however, the accommodation was imperfect. Article 6*bis* states that "some" of these rights may cease to be protected after the author's death—not "all." It seems that the drafters of the provision were not quite able to relinquish the idea of maintaining moral rights after an author's death, although it is stated as subtly as possible. Ricketson points out that

> [T]his formulation now imposes a specific obligation on these countries to protect "some [one]" of these rights after the author's death, and this is a significant advance on the position under the Rome and Brussels Acts.[33]

Perhaps, after all, the United States had the wisest approach. Its commitment to a registration-based system of copyright protection and its concerns about moral rights were behind the U.S. decision to abstain from Berne membership until the

[32] Berne Convention for the Protection of Literary and Artistic Works, Sept. 9, 1886, as revised at Stockholm on July 14, 1967, 828 U.N.T.S. 221 (Stockholm Act, 1967), https://www.wipo.int/treaties/en/ip/berne.

[33] Ricketson, *supra* note 17, at para. 8.114. Ricketson's interesting discussion seems to emphasize the idea that Berne signatories which did not offer protection for moral rights after the author's death were effectively undertaking an additional obligation under this section. He notes,

> There is an apparent gap in the formulation of this clause, as it might be taken to imply that a country which did not provide for the *post mortem auctoris* protection of either of the moral rights referred to in para (1) is now obliged to protect both rights *post mortem auctoris* if it accedes to or ratifies the Paris Act. This is on the basis that the precondition that "all [both] the rights set out in the preceding paragraph" are not protected *post mortem auctoris* means that nonetheless "some [one]" of them must be protected in this period. This would be a problem for countries such as Australia which, prior to 1967, did not accord *post mortem auctoris* protection to either of the rights set out in para (1). However, the records of the Stockholm Conference indicate that this would be too restrictive an interpretation, as Australia was a co-sponsor of the amendment which embodies the present wording, and it seems clear from the discussion in Main Committee I that its purpose was to accommodate the position of those countries which did not at that time provide *post mortem auctoris* protection for any moral rights. On the other hand, this formulation now imposes a specific obligation on these countries to protect "some [one]" of these rights after the author's death, and this is a significant advance on the position under the Rome and Brussels Acts. [Square brackets in the original]

late date of 1989.[34] By an interesting irony, the two former Cold War enemies, the United States and the Soviet Union, were actually two of the last major powers to accede to the Berne Convention.[35] They did so within six years of each other, in 1989 and 1995.[36] In this respect, at least, the ghost of Dickens can, at last, rest in peace.

4. The Technological Era: Moral Rights and the Unknown

What are the implications of the Berne Convention for moral rights in the technological context? The Berne Convention has been saved from technological obsolescence by its *modus operandi*: the agreement represents a codification of the classic copyright logic of expansion by analogy, allowing it to extend copyright protection to new kinds of intellectual creation with relative ease. The method has proven its worth. It has allowed modern copyright law to embrace new types of human creativity, from music, whether written down or performed,[37] to visual arts and photography,[38] to film.[39] This process of expansion have been remarkably effective in bringing new creativity within the scope of copyright law.

[34] *See* David Nimmer, *Conventional Copyright: A Morality Play*, 3(3) ENT. L. REV. 94 (1992) (discussing the paradox of U.S. accession to Berne). Interestingly, Ricketson, *supra* note 33, suggests that concerns about U.S. "alienation" had compelled the British delegation to resist the expansion of moral rights as early as 1948. One suspects that the U.S. position offered convenient support for a view that the British already held.

[35] China joined the Berne Convention in 1992. *See* Berne Notification No. 140, dated July 15, 1992, entry into force Oct. 15, 1992, https://www.wipo.int/treaties/en/notifications/berne/treaty_berne_140.html.

[36] United States—Berne Notification No. 121, dated Nov. 17, 1988, entry into force Mar. 1, 1989, https://www.wipo.int/treaties/en/notifications/berne/treaty_berne_121.html; Russian Federation—Berne Notification No. 162, dated Dec. 13, 1994, entry into force Mar. 13, 1995, https://www.wipo.int/treaties/en/notifications/berne/treaty_berne_162.html.

[37] In both Canada (in 1993) and India (in 1994), the definition of music was altered to include its unwritten form. *See* Government of Canada, *History of Copyright in Canada* (n.d.), https://www.canada.ca/en/canadian-heritage/services/history-copyright-canada.html; Copyright (Amendment Act) 1994 (India), https://copyright.gov.in/Documents/Notification/Copyright_Amendment_1994.pdf.

[38] In England, the extension of literary copyright to the fine arts was accomplished in 1862 with the Fine Art Copyright Act 1862, 25 & 26 Vict., c. 68. See *Ronan Deazley, Commentary on Fine Arts Copyright Act 1862, in* PRIMARY SOURCES ON COPYRIGHT (1450–1900) (Lionel Bently & Martin Kretschmer, eds., 2023), https://www.copyrighthistory.org/cam/tools/request/showRecord.php?id=commentary_uk_1862, the abstract to which notes that the Act "was ... innovative ... in providing artists with a new form of 'moral rights' protection."

[39] The history of film protection in the common-law tradition is interesting. *See* PASCAL KAMINA, FILM COPYRIGHT IN THE EUROPEAN UNION 19 and 29 (paras. 15 and 22) (2002). Kamina describes how, under the landmark Copyright Act 1911, 1 & 2 Geo. 5, c. 46, British law protected film indirectly, by analogy—as a series of photographs or as a dramatic work. When the Copyright Act 1956, 4 & 5 Eliz. 2, c. 74, recognized film as a new category of copyright work, it did so in a new way, removing the requirement of originality. Kamina notes,

> According to section 13(10) of the Act, the author of the "cinematograph film" was "the person by whom the arrangements necessary for the making of the film were under taken," i.e., the producer. The Gregory Committee Report shows that the rationale behind this new subject-matter was both to avoid multiple claims for authorship in what are, in essence, composite

Computer software provides an example of how Berne relates to new technologies. Although the technology was new, it was easily accommodated by copyright law under the Berne Convention as being analogous to "written" works. Of course, this shared attribute was superficial, but it was obvious. Indeed, Colin Tapper observes that "the whole terminology of programming is literary; it is perhaps even more surprising that 'instructions' or 'commands' are 'read.'" He notes "the metaphoric use of 'libraries,' 'files,' 'documents,' 'words,' and 'characters.'"[40] The controversy surrounding copyrighted computer programs was, appropriately enough, primarily a policy question about the advisability of doing so. Was copyright in computer programs good policy? Who benefited, and how would the public interest be affected?[41]

A number of features of copyright law within the Berne framework also encouraged the software industry to look to copyright as their right of choice. The deliberate informality with which the Berne copyright system operated was a factor encouraging the extension of copyright to computer programs. The enjoyment of copyright did not depend on the satisfaction of any administrative formalities, such as registration, and as such, the creators, or owners, of computer programs could expect to enjoy a swift and easy form of control over their works.[42] Similarly, the extensive duration of protection—lifetime of the author plus fifty years after his or her death or fifty years from publication for a corporate work—was attractive.[43] The same points can, of course, apply to the copyright protection of databases.[44]

The one difficulty arises in relation to moral rights. This was not an issue that was likely to attract attention in the United States, the home of information technology. However, the Berne system fundamentally reflects a civil law picture of copyright. Under Berne, copyright is a right that includes, by definition, both

works, while complying formally with the provisions of the Berne Convention, and to avoid the problems of the determination of originality. [Footnotes omitted]

[40] In personal communication with the author (June 4, 2010).

[41] *See generally* Jane Ginsburg's analysis of copyright protection of programs and possible alternatives in Jane C. Ginsburg, *Four Reasons and a Paradox: The Manifest Superiority of Copyright over Sui Generis Protection of Computer Software*, 94 COLUM. L. REV. 2559 (1994).

[42] *See* Berne Convention, *supra* note 1, at Art. 5(2) ("The enjoyment and the exercise of these rights shall not be subject to any formality").

[43] Id. at Art. 7. ("The term of protection granted by this Convention shall be the life of the author and fifty years after his death"). Note that Art. 7 is subject to the rule of the shorter term.

[44] The case of databases is complicated by the problem of trying to decide whether the database represents an "original" contribution on the part of the creator or his or her labor only. The approach in the EU Databases Directive is to offer protection to investment in the creation of databases through a *sui generis* right: Directive 96/9/EC of the European Parliament and of the Council of 11 March 1996 on the legal protection of databases, 1996 O.J. (L 77) 20, https://eur-lex.europa.eu/legal-content/EN/TXT/?uri=celex%3A31996L0009. The right has been controversial. As Estelle Derclaye comments, "It has been said that the database sui generis right is 'one of the least balanced and most potentially anti-competitive intellectual property rights ever created'": ESTELLE DERCLAYE, THE LEGAL PROTECTION OF DATABASES: A COMPARATIVE ANALYSIS 43–50 (2008), citing J.H. Reichman & Pamela Samuelson, *Intellectual Property Rights in Data?*, 50 VANDERBILT LAW REVIEW 49 (1997). A detailed analysis of the right follows.

economic and moral components. The divergences of civil law theories, reflected in the different practices of continental European countries, generally have to do with how these concepts relate to each other. Some jurisdictions think of copyright as a single right with economic and moral dimensions, while others see it as two, fundamentally distinct kinds of rights. But, in the absence of explicit exclusion, the moral dimension is always present.[45]

In particular, the Berne Convention makes little provision for treating different classes of copyright works differently. As long as works fall within the same overall category, they are expected to be treated alike. An artistic work, whether it is a painting by Van Gogh or the simple drawing of a "a hand carrying a pencil and in the act of finishing a cross enclosed in a square,"[46] is entitled to the same kind and level of protection. Different categories of works may elicit different rights—for example, poems, songs, and photographs may each enjoy differential protection. But here, too, there are limits: no category of copyright work is simply exempt from moral rights. This lack of discrimination has often been regarded as one of copyright's strengths. The law has been successful in extending protection to works without venturing too far into the terrain, where angels fear to tread, of attempting to define artistic quality.[47]

The Berne Convention, like the civil law traditions on which it is partly based, therefore implies the following. If copyright is to be extended by analogy to new types of technological creation, those works will be treated as other works in the same class are treated. A computer program will be treated as any other literary

[45] It is interesting to consider the relationship between moral rights and, more generally, the notion of moral damage or moral harm—well established in the civil law countries but firmly rejected in the English common-law tradition. For an illuminating comparison of the two positions, with special insight into the unique position of German law, see P.R. Handford, *Moral Damage in Germany*, 27(4) INT'L COMP. L.Q. 849 (1978). Handford points out the development of the notion of *Persönlichkeit* (personality), in German law, which is also the basis of German moral rights, and draws attention to the work of legal theorist von Gierke, who "believed that the individual ought to be able to complain of any unauthorised interference not merely with his person, his property or his reputation, but also with the social, intellectual and economic activities, opportunities and amenities, which combine to form the sum total of his existence" (footnote omitted). Interestingly, in a case involving the posthumous publication of letters written by Nietzsche to a friend, the German courts were unwilling to recognize the doctrine of personality rights, arguing that it was not (yet) part of German law: *see* id. at 856. Handford cites the *Nietzsche* case as (1908) 69 R.G.Z. 401 (Ger.) and also refers to (1912) 79 R.G.Z. 397; (1926) 113 R.G.Z. 413 (Ger.).

[46] See the landmark case of *Kenrick v. Lawrence* [1890] 25 Q.B.D. 99 (Eng.). The purpose of the drawing was to show illiterate voters how to vote.

[47] *See Hensher (George) Ltd v. Restawile Upholstery (Lancs.) Ltd* [1974] F.S.R. 173 (HL) (UK). In multiple opinions, the Lords had various ideas of what would constitute "artistic" creativity. The case considered the question of whether a prototype of furniture would qualify as a work of "artistic craftsmanship" within the meaning of UK copyright law. Nevertheless, there are limits on the inclusiveness of the "sweat of the brow" principle. See, e.g., *Exxon Corp. v. Exxon Insurance Consultants International Ltd* [1982] Ch. 119 (UK), where the court found that copyright will not usually subsist in a single word—even an invented one—and used the example of Lewis Carroll's fantastic poem, "Jabberwocky," to anchor its argument. The trial judge—approved by the Court of Appeal—commented: "Such a word would, however, I think, have to have qualities or characteristics in itself, if such a thing is possible, which would justify its recognition as an original literary work rather than merely as an invented word."

work. Accordingly, if literary works in general enjoy moral rights, moral rights are also assumed to arise in software—literary works that happen to be technological in nature. But moral rights in software, under international copyright rules, have never really been a topic of discussion.

C. Moral Rights in the Berne Convention beyond Article 6*bis*

Article 6*bis* is not the only article dealing explicitly with moral rights in the Berne Convention—and certain provisions in Berne also have indirect implications for the rights.

1. Explicit Recognition: Attribution for Journalists in Article 10.3

Article 10 of the Berne Convention provides exclusively for a right of attribution to the authors of "newspaper articles and periodicals in the form of press summaries" where these works are used for "teaching." Article 10.3 provides that "mention shall be made of the source, and of the name of the author if it appears thereon."

The right is framed narrowly in the sense that it imposes no obligation on the teacher to discover, or confirm, the identity of the author. But there is also a fairly onerous requirement of attribution, as both "source" and, potentially, the name of the author should receive mention. This requirement finds an echo in the following Article 10*bis*, dealing with the communication of news articles, which states that, even where "the reproduction, broadcasting or such communication" of these kinds of works "is not expressly reserved," "the source must always be clearly indicated"; and that "the legal consequences of a breach of this obligation shall be determined by the legislation of the country where protection is claimed." Of course, requiring an indication of source is not, in itself, a moral right *of the author*. It is, however, a kind of attribution right. As such, its significance should be duly noted. Such a right may substitute, or supplement, the attribution of authorship in situations where authorship is unknown, as in the case of orphan works, or in other circumstances where there is a need to identify works, as in various technological scenarios.

2. Indirect Protection: Convention Rights and the "Legitimate Interests of the Author"

The Berne Convention makes use of at least two, largely indeterminate expressions that may be relevant to authors' moral rights. These are the reference to "rights specially granted by the Convention," as noted in Article 5.1, and the protection of authors' "legitimate interests" in Article 9.2. This latter provision mirrors similar language under the European copyright directives, borrowed from Berne and also subject to interpretation by the European Court of Justice (ECJ). The relevant case, discussed previously, is *Deckmyn*.[48]

a. Moral Rights Abroad: Article 5.1 and Rights "Specially Granted by the Convention"

Article 5 of Berne is the very heart of the Convention, specifying which rights are guaranteed to the author both within and beyond his or her country of origin. While the Article clearly sets out the principle of national treatment, stating that a national of any Berne member country will be given the same rights as the nationals of the country where relief for copyright infringement is sought, it also provides for additional rights. Those rights are rights which are "specially granted by the Convention."

This phrase has not received much clarification at the hands of international copyright experts. On its face, it appears to be language that could potentially apply to authors' moral rights. In particular, is it possible that this phrase might make up for any *lacunae* in national laws with respect to Berne requirements—any failures to provide Berne equivalents in national law, since the minimum standards in Berne should command enactment in all member countries? So, for example, would a Canadian author suing in the United States be able to expect his or her moral rights to be protected under Article 6*bis* of Berne by a U.S. court, as rights "specially granted" by the agreement?[49]

It is also telling that the phrase concerns the situation of non-nationals claiming rights in a given Berne member country. To take the example given a step further, if a Canadian author could expect those rights to be protected, could a U.S. author claim them under Berne in his or her own country? It seems quite clear that the answer to this question would be "No." These "specially granted" rights only apply "in countries of the Union other than the country of origin."

To finish the example, it is worth noting that a U.S. author would clearly be able to assert moral rights in Canada under Canadian law. There would be no need to call upon Berne in these circumstances: the Canadian Copyright Act includes protections for moral rights.

And in the Canadian example, moral rights, at least superficially, conform to Berne. Suppose, though, that the same issue were to arise in the United Kingdom,

[48] Case C-201/13, *Deckmyn v. Vandersteen*, ECLI:EU:C:2014:2132, ¶ 14 (Sept. 3, 2014), https://eur-lex.europa.eu/legal-content/EN/TXT/?uri=CELEX%3A62013CJ0201, discussed in Chapter 1, *supra* notes 117–28 and accompanying text.

[49] See, e.g., the objections raised in the pre-Berne case of *Shostakovich v. Twentieth-Century Fox* 196 Misc. 67, 80 N.Y.S.2d 575 (1948) (U.S.). If the objections raised there can be said to be effectively answered by Berne, a case can be made that this is, indeed, the position in U.S. law, based on U.S. precedent.

where moral rights in the Copyright, Designs and Patents Act of 1988 (CDPA) diverge, in certain key respects, from the provisions in Article 6*bis* of Berne. As noted earlier, the CDPA requires that the moral right of attribution be "asserted" when the work is first published, before it can be recognized under UK law.[50] Yet, Berne provides that the rights protected must be made available "without formalities." Could a foreign claimant in the United Kingdom insist that his or her attribution right must be protected, *whether or not it is asserted as the UK Act requires*, because it is a right "specially granted" by the Berne Convention?

A test case on this issue has not arisen in the United Kingdom. These legal implications remain purely conjectural. However, courts do seem to have a penchant for creative interpretation of moral rights (also in the United Kingdom[51]), and it would be unwise to say that arguments such as these can "never" succeed.

b. The Three-Step Test: Article 9.2

The important question of limitations or exceptions to copyright has particular implications for moral rights. While the international community has increasingly turned towards the creation of exceptions to copyright as a way of limiting excessive restrictions on public freedom caused by overly strong copyright protections,[52] they are necessarily subject to stringent limitations of their own. Just as copyright cannot be granted without the satisfaction of important tests, such as originality, once granted, it also cannot be restrained without serious and substantial cause. In particular, the formula of the "three-step test," set out in Article 9.2 of Berne, and reappearing in all major instruments of international copyright law from the TRIPs Agreement[53] to the EU InfoSoc Directive,[54] identifies the three conditions that a limitation or exception to copyright must meet in order to establish its validity.[55]

[50] Copyright, Designs and Patents Act 1988 (CDPA), c. 48, § 79, https://www.legislation.gov.uk/ukpga/1988/48/section/79. See the discussion in Chapter 2, *supra* notes 250–51 and accompanying text.

[51] In the UK case of *Delves-Broughton v. House of Harlot* [2012] EWPCC 29, the court supported the proposition that the language of the CDPA, *supra* note 50, provides for the prohibition of any alteration of a work, whether or not it causes harm to the author's reputation—thereby exceeding the minimum requirements of Berne Convention, *supra* note 1, at Art. 6*bis*. This clever legal point will make little sense to those familiar with the drafting history of the provision, but it is undeniably a fascinating (revisionist?) approach to statutory construction.

[52] *See* Ricketson & Ginsburg, *supra* note 2, at paras. 13.03*ff*.

[53] *See* Art. 13 of the Agreement on Trade-Related Aspects of Intellectual Property Rights (TRIPS Agreement), opened for signature Apr. 15, 1994, entered into force Jan. 1, 1995, Annex 1C to Marrakesh Agreement Establishing the World Trade Organization, 1869 U.N.T.S. 299, 33 I.L.M. 1197 (1994), https://www.wto.org/english/docs_e/legal_e/trips_e.htm#art13.

[54] *See* Art. 5.5 of the Directive 2001/29/EC of the European Parliament and of the Council of 22 May 2001 on the harmonization of certain aspects of copyright and related rights in the information society, 2001 O.J. (L 167) 10 (InfoSoc Directive), https://eur-lex.europa.eu/legal-content/EN/TXT/?uri=celex%3A32001L0029.

[55] In full, id. at Art. 9.2 sets out the three steps as follows: "It shall be a matter for legislation in the countries of the Union to permit the reproduction of such works in *certain special cases*, provided that *such reproduction does not conflict with a normal exploitation of the work* and does not *unreasonably prejudice the legitimate interests of the author*" (emphasis added).

Crucially, step three of the test states that the proposed limitation must not "unreasonably prejudice" the "legitimate interests" of the author.[56] But what, exactly, are these legitimate interests? The phrase finds little clarification in international copyright law.[57] To make matters more confusing, limitations and exceptions are sometimes framed without reference to moral rights at all—leaving open, for example, questions about whether the UK parody exception, adopted in October of 2014, exempts the makers of parodies from allegations that they have violated an author's moral right of integrity.[58] If moral rights were among the author's "legitimate interests," exceptions to copyright could not be allowed to deprive authors of their moral rights.[59] In other words, even if copyright could be set aside for reasons of public policy, the proposed use of the work must not violate the moral rights of the author.

The decision of the Court of Justice of the European Union (CJEU) in *Deckmyn*, discussed in detail in Chapter 1, found that a parody, which would otherwise have been allowed as an exception to copyright, would not be allowed because it was discriminatory in nature and created a noxious impression of the original artists' work:[60] "In those circumstances, holders of [copy]right . . ., have, in principle, a legitimate interest in ensuring that the work protected by copyright is not associated with such a [discriminatory] message."[61]

56 Id.

57 See the detailed discussion in Ricketson & Ginsburg, *supra* note 2, at ch. 13, esp. paras. 13.01–13.29. At para. 13.29, they comment,

> Moral rights considerations more generally: As noted in 13.23, "the legitimate interests of the author" in the third step of article 9(2) necessarily embraces the author's non-pecuniary or moral rights interests, meaning that any freedom to make reproductions pursuant to that article can hardly absolve the user from observing those moral rights of the author that are protected under article 6bis(1), namely the rights of attribution and respect.

58 In comparison, French law provides explicitly for a parody exception in Loi 92-597 du 1 juillet 1992 relative au Code de la propriété intellectuelle (partie législative) [Law 92-597 of July 1, 1992, relating to the Intellectual Property Code (Legislative part)], JOURNAL OFFICIEL DE LA RÉPUBLIQUE FRANÇAISE [J.O.] [OFFICIAL GAZETTE OF FRANCE], Feb. 8, 1994 (Code de la propriété intellectuelle), art. L122-5(4), https://www.legifrance.gouv.fr/codes/article_lc/LEGIARTI000042814694, but moral rights remain with the author even in relation to parodies. *See* SABINE JACQUES, *Parody and Moral Rights*, *in* THE PARODY EXCEPTION IN COPYRIGHT LAW 167 (2019).

59 Accordingly, the silence of the UK legislature on the question of whether the parody exception exempts the creator of the parody from the obligation to respect the moral rights of the author of the original work leads to the conclusion that it does not. From all perspectives, it would have been better if the legislature had clarified this issue explicitly in the text of the exception.

60 See discussion in *Deckmyn*, *supra* note 47, at ch. 1, ¶ 29, which states,

> Nor, in the second place, has the referring court asked the Court about the possible scope in the present case of the "threefold condition" (also known as the "three-stage test"), provided for in general terms in Article 5(5) of the Directive, according to which the parody exception is to be applied "in certain special cases which do not conflict with a normal exploitation of the work or other subject-matter and do not unreasonably prejudice the legitimate interests of the rightholder." The determination of whether or not each of those conditions is satisfied in the present case is a matter which, again, will fall to the national court.

61 Id.

c. *Droit de suite* (Artist's Resale Right): A Hybrid Right in Article 14*ter*

The Berne Convention provides a basis for protecting the artist's resale right, also known as the *droit de suite,* in Article 14*ter*. As framed in this article, several features of the right are interesting. Although the right is widely known as the "artist's" resale right, the right applies both to works of art and the original manuscripts of both writers and composers. This aspect of the right is curiously anachronistic in the digital context, where many writers and composers make use of computers to "compose" their "manuscripts." Indeed, what is a "manuscript," and, perhaps barring the extreme minority of writers and musicians, does such a thing still exist? Even historical musical scores are now widely available in digital formats, with musicians exploring the conveniences of digital versions over scores in print.[62]

Article 14*ter* provides that the right is both inalienable and arising in "any sale of the work subsequent to the first transfer by the author of the work." However, it also specifies that the right can "only" be "claimed in the country of the Union ... if legislation in the country to which the author belongs permits, and to the extent permitted by the country where this protection is claimed." In other words, there can clearly be no entitlement to a resale royalty derived directly from Berne.

The European Union (EU) adopted a directive on resale rights in 2001,[63] which has since been enacted in the member states.[64] The term of protection, in keeping with other aspects of copyright and moral rights in most jurisdictions, is the lifetime of the author and seventy years after his or her death. Britain adopted such a right while it was an EU member and retains it now.[65] No such right is protected in the United States.[66]

[62] *See, e.g.*, Corinna da Fonseca-Wollheim, *When Classical Musicians Go Digital*, New York Times (June 9, 2016), https://www.nytimes.com/2016/06/12/arts/music/when-classical-musicians-go-digital.html.

[63] Directive 2001/84/EC of the European Parliament and of the Council of 27 September 2001 on the resale right for the benefit of the author of an original work of art, 2001 O.J. (L 272) 32, https://eur-lex.europa.eu/legal-content/EN/TXT/PDF/?uri=CELEX:32001L0084&qid=1715153938961 (and https://www.wipo.int/wipolex/en/legislation/details/5937). On continued UK recognition for the right post-Brexit, see Wedlake Bell, *Artist's Resale Right Regulations Survive Bonfire of EU Law*, Lexology (July 3, 2023), https://www.lexology.com/library/detail.aspx?g=8dec36cb-f089-4feb-b091-2e6a781d8a16.

[64] Ireland offers an interesting example of implementation: in the case of a deceased author, the right extends to family members for the duration of copyright. *See* O'Flynn Exham, *Artist Resale Rights Directive—Time for a Comprehensive Overhaul?* (July 8, 2022), https://www.ofx.ie/artist-resale-rights-directive-time-for-a-comprehensive-overhaul.

[65] *See* Bell, *supra* note 63.

[66] Cal. Civ. Code § 986 (West 1976) (U.S.), known as the Resale Royalty Act of 1976, https://casetext.com/statute/california-codes/california-civil-code/division-2-property/part-3-personal-or-movable-property/title-2-particular-kinds-of-personal-property/chapter-3-products-of-the-mind/section-986-right-to-collect-royalty-payment. The pre-emption of the Act is reported by Amanda Svachula, *California Tried to Give Artists a Cut. But the Judges Said No*, New York Times (July 11, 2018), https://www.nytimes.com/2018/07/11/arts/design/art-royalties-ruling-california-circuit-court.html.

D. Moral Rights in Other International Copyright Agreements

A series of international agreements on copyright has been adopted since the late 1990s. There is nothing in these agreements that supersedes Article 6*bis*, but the international understanding of moral rights has been expanded in these agreements, both directly and indirectly.

In terms of direct expansion, two new treaties have introduced moral rights for performers into the international copyright framework.[67] This represents a fundamental shift in how the international community sees performers. Performers were once considered to *disseminate* the original works of others, but, under these new agreements, they are treated as *creators* of works in their own right.

In terms of indirect or implicit acknowledgement of moral rights, the TRIPs Agreement includes them without promising to enforce them. Subsequently, the WIPO Copyright Treaty (WCT),[68] which was adopted with the specific goal of updating copyright for the technological environment, arguably treats copyright from a unitary perspective that does not observe a hard distinction between the economic and moral dimensions of authorial prerogatives. Has a new form of monism emerged at the international level?[69]

1. Russian Dolls: The Berne Convention and the TRIPs Agreements

In 1994, the Agreement on Trade-Related Aspects of Intellectual Property Rights (TRIPs) was adopted as one of the foundational agreements of the World Trade Organization (WTO).[70] However, the primary achievement of TRIPs in the area of copyright law was to create a trade-based mechanism for the resolution

[67] *See* Art. 5 of the World Intellectual Property Organization (WIPO) Performances and Phonograms Treaty, Dec. 20, 1996, S. Treaty Doc. No. 105-17, 36 I.L.M. 76 (1997) (WPPT), https://www.wipo.int/wipolex/en/treaties/textdetails/12743 (general information available at https://www.wipo.int/treaties/en/ip/wppt); WIPO Beijing Treaty on Audiovisual Performances, June 24, 2012 (Beijing Treaty), https://www.wipo.int/edocs/pubdocs/en/wipo_pub_228.pdf (general information available at https://www.wipo.int/treaties/en/ip/beijing); WIPO Copyright Treaty, Dec. 20, 1996, S. Treaty Doc. No. 105-17 (1997); 2186 U.N.T.S. 121; 36 I.L.M. 65 (1997) (WCT), https://www.wipo.int/wipolex/en/treaties/textdetails/12740 (general information available at https://www.wipo.int/treaties/en/ip/wct). The WPPT and the WCT are known collectively as the Internet Treaties. Although they were both adopted in 1996, their entry into force was made conditional on a certain minimum number of signatories. In the case of the WCT and the WPPT, this requirement was met in March and May 2002, respectively. See the summary and discussion of the Treaties in Jorg Reinbothe & Silke von Lewinski, *The WIPO Treaties 1996: Ready to Come into Force*, 24(4) EIPR 199 (2002).

[68] WCT, *supra* note 67.

[69] If so, this is due to technology and the undeniable practical importance of "moral" rights and interests in the technological context.

[70] TRIPS Agreement, *supra* note 53.

of copyright disputes between countries. The dispute-settlement process allows member countries to impose trade sanctions for the inadequate implementation and enforcement of intellectual property rights.

But TRIPs has not superseded Berne as the primary source of international copyright norms. Instead, the agreements work together symbiotically. The structure of the international copyright agreement under TRIPs can be visualized as a set of Russian matryoshka dolls.

a. Relation to the Berne Convention: TRIPs Article 9.1

The genius of the TRIPs Agreement is that it develops hardly any new rules in the area of copyright.[71] Instead, it deals with copyright largely by requiring member states to adhere to the substantive provisions of the Berne Convention, thereby ensuring that the TRIPs copyright framework benefits from more than a century of experience with international copyright acquired under Berne. Article 6*bis* on moral rights is formally included in this framework.[72] However, the TRIPs Agreement also specifies that moral rights are excluded from the dispute-settlement and enforcement mechanisms at the WTO.[73] Unique among all aspects of copyright law, the enforcement of moral rights remains excluded from the TRIPs regime.

Article 9.1 of the TRIPs Agreement provides the key. It is the first article on copyright in the Agreement, and it is entitled, "Relation to the Berne Convention." It begins:

> 9.1. Members shall comply with Articles 1 through 21 of the Berne Convention (1971) and the Appendix thereto.

With respect to Article 6*bis*, however, the new Agreement adopted a special formula. Article 9.1 goes on to state,

> However, Members shall not have rights or obligations under this Agreement in respect of the rights conferred under Article 6bis of that Convention or of the rights derived therefrom.

The meaning of this phrase is simple: since member countries do not enjoy moral rights under the TRIPs Agreement, per se, but only under the Berne Convention, dispute-settlement measures at the WTO, which are normally available for

[71] The only exceptions are copyright in computer programs and in "original" databases: *see* id. at Art. 10.

[72] Id. at Art. 9.1. The first part of this Article states that member countries "shall comply with Articles 1 through 21 of the Berne Convention (1971) and the Appendix thereto."

[73] This amounts to a crucial omission. Dreyfuss and Lowenfeld identify the linking of dispute settlement with intellectual property as one of the two most important achievements of the WTO: Rochelle Cooper Dreyfuss & Andreas F. Lowenfeld, *Two Achievements of the Uruguay Round: Putting TRIPs and Dispute Settlement Together*, 37 VA. J. INT'L L. 275 (1997).

copyright disputes under TRIPs, will not be available for moral rights. In other words, in an international copyright system that is now based on the "enforcement" international copyright norms, moral rights are not enforceable.[74]

Accordingly, no country can complain of inadequate recognition of moral rights at the WTO; and, of course, no penalty can be assigned. For example, French film directors could not petition the French government to sue the U.S. government on the grounds that the moral rights of French directors are not adequately protected in the United States.[75]

b. Post-TRIPs Expansion of Moral Rights in the International Community

The treatment of moral rights in TRIPs has proven to have both advantages and disadvantages. On the one hand, the decision to exclude moral rights from the normal operation of the WTO system makes sense: these are non-commercial rights. Apart from their shared roots in the prerogatives of authorship, moral rights are not directly related to the economic aspects of copyright law.[76] The exclusion may present some advantages to policymakers who want to focus on moral rights as an instrument of *national* cultural policy, and who hope to have some freedom from international obligations when doing so.

On the other hand, however, the exclusion of moral rights from TRIPs also indicated that they were not a priority at the international level. With the advent of TRIPs, there was a danger that moral rights would lose the international acceptance they had gained under Berne. As other areas of copyright law were prioritized in the technological environment, moral rights might be left behind.

But this has not been the effect of TRIPs. Instead, the period surrounding the adoption of TRIPs proved to be an extraordinarily interesting and active time for moral rights—nowhere more so than in the common law countries. By the end of the 1990s, all the common law countries had enacted moral rights legislation. Each one has done so in its own way, accepting the rights to varying degrees. The restrictive provisions of the UK law of 1988,[77] developed in response to the Whitford Commission's reassessment of the state of UK copyright law in anticipation of

74 In theory, though, a moral rights dispute under the Berne Convention could certainly be referred to the International Court of Justice. In the history of the Berne Convention, however, this has never happened.

75 For example, this could not be a solution to the type of conflict encountered in the *Huston* case on colorization: *Huston*, *supra* note 26. The final judgment is *Turner Entertainment v. Huston Heirs*, Cour d'appel [CA] [regional court of appeal] Versailles, chs Réunies, Dec. 19, 1994, 164 RIDA 389 (1995), *on remand from* Cour de cassation [Cass.] [supreme court for judicial matters] 1e civ., May 28, 1991, 149 RIDA 197 (1991) (Fr.).

76 This is not to suggest that moral rights do not have economic implications—quite the contrary. The potential economic costs of moral rights, such as withdrawing or reprinting works, may be highly significant. For an analysis of moral rights from an economic perspective, see the pioneering work by Hansmann and Santilli: Henry Hansmann & Marina Santilli, *Authors' and Artists' Moral Rights: A Comparative Legal and Economic Analysis*, 26 J. Legal Stud. 95 (1997). See, e.g., the interesting comments on the economic and "mixed" implications of the right of integrity: id. at 104–108.

77 CDPA, *supra* note 50.

TRIPs, present an interesting contrast to the more comprehensive Australian law of 2001.[78] The United States has enacted only one statute for moral rights, the Visual Artists Rights Act of 1990, and it continues to consider the issue of Berne implementation.[79] Canada is, once again, the relatively quiet country: it has had moral rights legislation since 1931 and therefore did not face the problem of potential non-compliance with Berne. But Canada's moral rights provisions were amended in 1988, and the changes accomplished two things. They confirmed that Canada's integrity right was closely based on the Berne model and, controversially, they also expanded the right to waive moral rights into a comprehensive provision.[80]

Among the developing countries of common law heritage, India undertook a major reform of its moral rights in 1994. Its revisions were controversial. India scaled back extensive provisions on moral rights dating from the 1957 Indian Copyright Act, the first copyright law enacted by independent India in the post-colonial period. The reformers of 1994 offered the rationale that the language of Indian law should conform more closely to Berne.[81] However the changes occurred at a time when the Indian government was being sued for a major moral rights violation by a high-profile artist, and the reforms reflect concerns raised by the case.[82]

By excluding moral rights, TRIPs has had an unanticipated effect: the progress of internationalization of a different kind. TRIPs has inadvertently helped to promote moral rights internationally by bringing a higher profile to the Berne Convention. Ironically—despite their absence from the international trade arena, or because of it?—the concept of moral rights is now one of the most widely accepted and up-to-date aspects of copyright law in the world.

2. Moral Rights in the Digital Age: The WIPO Internet Treaties and Beijing

A pair of new treaties, the WIPO Internet Treaties, were adopted by the World Intellectual Property Organization (WIPO) of the United Nations in 1996, entering into force in 2002.[83] This was the first ever attempt at explicitly updating copyright

[78] *See Copyright Act 1968* (Cth) (Austl.), http://www5.austlii.edu.au/au/legis/cth/consol_act/ca1968133. The Australian moral rights legislation was the *Copyright Amendment (Moral Rights) Act 2000* (Cth), https://www.legislation.gov.au/C2004A00752/latest/text.

[79] *See* VARA, *supra* note 5.

[80] Vaver, *supra* note 22.

[81] Jagdish Sagar (in personal communication with the author, Feb. 2009). *See* Copyright (Amendment) Act 1994 (India), https://copyright.gov.in/Documents/Notification/Copyright_Amendment_1994.pdf.

[82] *Sehgal*, *supra* note 5.

[83] WIPO is a specialist agency of UNESCO, founded in 1967, replacing the Bureaux internationaux réunis pour la protection de la propriété intellectuelle (BIRPI)—which was founded in 1893 and had previously administered international intellectual property treaties—in 1970, and joining the United Nations in 1974. A brief (and selective) history of WIPO is available at https://www/wipo.int/

for the technological environment in the international arena. Notwithstanding TRIPs, this innovation belongs to WIPO and not to the WTO. By the time of its adoption, the TRIPs Agreement was already becoming obsolete—a reflection of the gargantuan scope of the WTO system, which was beginning to collapse under its own weight. Given its place within the WTO, TRIPs was a slow-moving entity, and the fact that each of its provisions was won by hard negotiation meant that amendment would be a slow and laborious process. The contrast between the TRIPs Agreement and the needs of the quicksilver world of technology could not be greater.

The WIPO Internet Treaties were drafted to address this concern. There are two treaties, of unequal weight: the groundbreaking WIPO Copyright Treaty, or WCT, and the more specialized WIPO Performances and Phonograms Treaty, the WPPT.[84] The Treaties were the product of a landmark exercise in treaty-making. Concise and to the point, they focus directly on digital issues. The second of the two treaties, the WPPT, established a moral right for performers—a major landmark in the international protection of moral rights.[85]

The adoption of the WIPO Internet Treaties has since been followed by a further treaty on the rights of performers in film and other audiovisual media, the Beijing Treaty on Audiovisual Performances of 2012.[86] This Treaty responds to a long-standing critique of major right-holders in the film industry, particularly Hollywood, who have consistently rejected moral rights protection for performers in film including, of course, actors. However, its success in doing so is questionable, as discussed in more detail below.

a. The WCT: A Digital Right of Disclosure

The single major innovation in the WCT was its creation of a right of "making available." It brought every Internet transaction involving a copyright work within the ambit of copyright restrictions. It confirmed that Internet privacy is an illusion: once we accept the WCT concept of infringement, there is no inviolable privacy of Internet use.[87] Data on Internet use must be collected to furnish the necessary evidence of copyright infringement. This issue has been uneasily avoided

about-wipo/fr/history.html (or in English, https://www.wipo.int/about-wipo/en/history.html). *See* WPPT, *supra* note 67; WCT, *supra* note 67.

84 WPPT, *supra* note 67; WCT, *supra* note 67.
85 WPPT, *supra* note 67; WCT, *supra* note 67.
86 Beijing Treaty, *supra* note 67.
87 The potential conflict between individual privacy and a need for data on Internet usage to secure evidence in copyright infringement cases has become a theme of discussions about the liability of Internet service providers for illegal file sharing. For example, see *BMG Canada Inc. v. John Doe*, 2005 F.C.A. 193 [2005] 4 R.C.F. 81 (Can.); Case C-275/06, *Productores de Música de España (Promusicae) v. Telefónica de España SAU (Telefónica)*, ECLI:EU:C:2008:54 (Jan. 28, 2008), https://eur-lex.europa.eu/legal-content/EN/TXT/?uri=CELEX%3A62006CJ0275.

by Canadian courts in the *BMG v. John Doe* litigation, and the CJEU confronted it in the *Promusicae* case. As Fanny Coudert and Evi Werkers succinctly conclude,

> The ECJ decided ... it cannot be derived from European legislation that Member States are obliged to install a duty to provide personal data in the context of a civil procedure to ensure the effective protection of copyright. It did not however provide guidelines on how the balance should be made. In sum, the "hot potato" was passed on to the Member States.[88]

The WCT does not deal directly with moral rights.[89] The Treaty makes no explicit reference whatsoever to moral rights. However, there is still a subtext of possibilities for moral rights which should not be missed. This might also provide a basis for the future expansion of the rights in the international arena.

The language of the WCT is different from that of other copyright conventions. It focuses on authorship rather than ownership, a key distinction when it comes to moral rights.

The Preamble of the WCT points out that it is largely a response to "the profound impact of the development and convergence of information and communication technologies on the creation and use of literary and artistic works." It introduces the new "right of communication to the public," which was not present in any other international copyright instrument—a pure innovation. Article 8 specifies that

> authors of literary and artistic works shall enjoy the exclusive right of authorizing any communication to the public of their works, by wire or wireless means, including the making available to the public of their works in such a way that members of the public may access these works from a place and at a time individually chosen by them.[90]

[88] Fanny Coudert & Evi Werkers, *In the Aftermath of the Promusicae Case: How to Strike the Balance?*, 18(1) Int'l J. L. Info. Tech. 50, 51 (2010). The European Court of Justice (ECJ) is the branch of the CJEU specifically responsible for adjudicating cases from national courts and appeals; in the IP community, ECJ and CJEU are often used interchangeably. See, e.g., the excellent explanation by Damian Chalmers: Damian Chalmers, *Explainer: The Court of Justice— UK in a Changing Europe* (May 18, 2016), https://ukandeu.ac.uk/explainers/the-court-of-justice/OSCOLA.

[89] An earlier version of this analysis of the WCT was presented at the Seventeenth British and Irish Law Education and Technology Association (BILETA) Annual Conference in 2002: Mira T. Sundara Rajan, *Moral Rights and Copyright Harmonisation: Prospects for an "International Moral Right?,"* Presentation to the 17th BILETA Annual Conference (Apr. 5–6, 2002), https://www.bileta.org.uk/wp-content/uploads/Moral-Rights-and-Copyright-Harmonisation-Prospects-for-an-International-Moral-Right.pdf.

[90] *See* WCT, *supra* note 67:

> Article 8 Right of Communication to the Public without prejudice to the provisions of Articles 11(1)(ii), 11*bis*(1)(i) and (ii), 11*ter*(1)(ii), 14(1)(ii) and 14*bis*(1) of the Berne Convention, authors of literary and artistic works shall enjoy the exclusive right of authorizing any communication to the public of their works, by wire or wireless means, including the making available to

The right of communication to the public is a fundamental economic right. Its French name is the right of "*représentation*."[91]As Sam Ricketson observes, it originally emerged in relation to copyright works that are disseminated to the public through non-material representation, such as dramatic or musical performances.[92] It is closely aligned with performers' rights.[93]

With the growth of digital reproduction technologies and technologies of instantaneous dissemination, the scope of the communication right has become much broader. It is no longer performance alone that presents a challenge; works of all kinds are affected—even traditional works of visual art, through images and, increasingly, copies.[94] The right of communication to the public is another form of the moral right of disclosure. The idea that an author should be able to control the circumstances in which his or her work first appears before the public is the shared foundation of moral and economic rights. For example, confiscating an unpublished work from its author and publishing it would clearly be a violation of both sets of rights, and it is recognized as such in most jurisdictions.[95] Although the right of divulgation was not explicitly stated in Article 6*bis* of the Berne Convention, it is generally accepted that the right is protected by Berne.[96]

As Claude Colombet observes,

the public of their works in such a way that members of the public may access these works from a place and at a time individually chosen by them.

[91] JEAN-MARIE PONTIER, JEAN-CLAUDE RICCI& JACQUES BOURDON, DROIT DE LA CULTURE, para. 347 (2d ed., 1996). It is also discussed in the Canadian case of *Théberge, supra* note 23, but the Canadian Supreme Court treats it as a moral right.

[92] Ricketson, *supra* note 17, at para. 8.63.

[93] Neighboring rights are known by this term because their scope is less ambitious than an author's copyright. They have been a form of protection for performers, whose status is generally inferior to that of authors, but they also extend to other types of broadcasting and dissemination activities. As a group, they are considered "secondary," or "neighboring," to copyright.

[94] Notably, 3D printing has been a major development in relation to copying art and artefacts. See, e.g., in relation to the Elgin Marbles or Rodin bronzes: Simon Jenkins, *The Answer to the Parthenon Marbles Dispute: George Osborne and a 3D Printer*, THE GUARDIAN (June 16, 2022), https://www.theguardian.com/commentisfree/2022/jun/16/parthenon-marbles-george-osborne-british-museum-greece; Anna Sansom, *Musée Rodin Could Be Forced to Release 3D Scans of Bronze Sculptures—Including The Thinker—to the Public*, ART NEWSPAPER (Mar. 5, 2021), https://www.theartnewspaper.com/2021/03/05/musee-rodin-could-be-forced-to-release-3d-scans-of-bronze-sculpturesincluding-the-thinker-to-the-public. See also, for a fun commentary, Gabe Lipkowitz, *3D Printing the Next Rodin*, THE STANFORD DAILY (Apr. 8, 2021), https:/stanforddaily.com/2021/04/08/3d-printing-the-next-rodin.

[95] On the other hand, it is common practice in developing countries to allow translations to be made on the basis of a compulsory license issued by the government. In a sense, this could amount to a trespass on an author's right of disclosure—e.g., the practice, observed in India, of translating an English-language work (whether written in English or translated into it) by a writer whose primary language is one of the Indian national languages, into that writer's first language. This example arose in relation to the publication of S. VIJAYA BHARATI, C. SUBRAMANIA BHARATI (1974)—a biography, written in English by a Tamil writer, which was subsequently translated into Tamil and published by the Government of India without the author's permission.

[96] *But see* Adeney, *supra* note 8, at para. 6.34 (showing that the idea of a right of disclosure was deliberately excluded from Berne).

> It is the right of divulgation which, chronologically, precedes the other [moral rights], as it is through the exercise [of this right that] the work, removed from its author, enters into the economic circuit, and becomes an economic good on the basis of which the other attributes of the author's right, both moral and economic, can be exercised.[97]

Why is this important in the context of the WCT? The WCT, an international instrument focused on technologically updating copyright law, introduced one major innovation for that purpose: the new, or at least repurposed, right of communication to the public granted to the author of a work. This right could only have been based on an underlying conception of first publication, or disclosure, as the key act of the technological environment: the one authorial prerogative that it is necessary to control, which, as Colombet says "precedes" all others and cannot be renegotiated in the technological context. Disclosure is the principal act that allows an author to be rewarded economically; in the digital environment, it may one day become the primary, or only, act that generates reliable returns. This is a scary future, but that does not mean we should avoid thinking about it. It is therefore doubly necessary to protect this prerogative, both as a right to *act* and as a right to *choose*. Looking ahead technologically, it would seem that this right in the WCT should be interpreted as encompassing both the economic right of first publication, or "*representation*" in French law, and the moral right of the author to choose whether or not, when, and how to disclose the work.

b. The WPPT: Dissemination Is the New Creation

The WPPT presents a different scenario, rather surprising at first glance. Negotiated and finalized alongside the WCT, any assertion of U.S. influence on that agreement must equally apply to the WPPT.[98] But the WPPT presents us with a remarkable development. It establishes moral rights of attribution and integrity for performers, just as the Berne Convention articulates them for authors in the text of Article 6*bis*.[99]

[97] Claude Colombet, Grands principes du droit d'auteur et des droits voisins dans le monde: Approche de droit comparé 42 (2d ed., 1992):

> C'est le droit de divulgation qui, chronologiquement, précède les autres, car c'est à partir de son exercice que l'oeuvre, arrachée à son auteur, entre dans le circuit économique, devient un bien patrimonial sur lequel pourront s'exercer les autres attributs, tant moraux que pécuniaires, du droit d'auteur.

[98] Id.

[99] In fact, the provisions are generally an incorporation, *mutatis mutandis*, of the language of Art. 6*bis* of the Berne Convention into the new treaty. One substantive exception to this is the omission of the idea of "honor" from the protection of the integrity of performances: a concept that is indeterminate enough in the Berne context has been eliminated from the WPPT, but this should still be recognized as a potential scaling down of the integrity right for performers as compared to the author's moral right of integrity in the Berne provision. More strikingly, the incorporation of Berne provisions of the duration of moral rights into the WPPT has led to some inconsistencies; in particular, limiting the duration of some rights to the lifetime of the performer only, while extending others beyond it, makes little sense

The WPPT scheme for moral rights is innovative and important for a number of reasons.[100] First and foremost, at a time when conceptual discussion of copyright is rare—and of moral rights, even rarer—a performer's moral right represents a fundamental innovation in the theory of the law. WPPT represents the first international progress on moral rights since they were added to the Berne Convention in 1928. A moral right for performers has never existed before in international law. Indeed, the WPPT was the first attempt at international rule-making on performers' rights since the Rome Convention of 1961, and this was one of the reasons why the initiative was thought to be important by member countries and welcomed by them.[101] It is also striking that the majority of national delegations were strongly supportive of moral rights for performers.[102]

i. Background: The Intersection of Moral and Economic Rights in Sound Recordings

On what basis did this initiative succeed in gaining the support of the United States? The United States was deeply concerned about sound recordings in the technological environment, which subsequent experience shows to have been prescient. The U.S. delegation commented on "the inadequacy of the level of protection of rights of producers of phonograms, and noted the synergy, in the area of sound recordings, among the rights of producers, performers and composers."

This background led to a willingness to accept a broad and diverse package of rights related to sound recordings, including strong rights for performers on sound recordings. But it should be noted that sound recordings present a very different landscape from film. Indeed, in certain key respects, sound recordings amount to

in countries that do not recognize performers' economic rights beyond the lifetime of the performer. The issue is discussed in detail in Jorg Reinbothe & Silke von Lewinski, The WIPO Treaties on Copyright: A Commentary on the WCT, the WPPT, and the BTAP paras. 8.5.39–8.5.43 (2d ed., 2015).

[100] For a discussion of moral rights in the WPPT, *supra* note 66, see Mira T. Sundara Rajan, *Center Stage: Moral Rights in the WPPT*, 57 Case W. Reserve L. Rev. 767 (2010).

[101] The Rome Convention—the first international agreement dealing with performers' rights—makes no mention of performers' moral interest: International Convention for the Protection of Performers, Producers of Phonograms and Broadcasting Organizations, Oct. 26, 1961, 496 U.N.T.S. 43 (Rome Convention), https://www.wipo.int/treaties/en/ip/rome/.

[102] See, notably, the summaries of comments from individual country delegations in Committee of Experts on a Possible Instrument on the Protection of the Rights of Performers and Producers of Phonograms, First Session (Geneva, June 28–July 2, 1993), *Normative Activities in the Field of Copyright*, 29(9) Copyright: Monthly Review of the World Intellectual Property Organization (WIPO) (Sept. 1993), https://www.wipo.int/edocs/pubdocs/en/copyright/120/wipo_pub_120_1993_09.pdf (WIPO Report). The objections to moral rights are strikingly few and restrained, notably, from countries such as the United Kingdom (id. at para. 31), Australia (id. at para. 36), and Ireland (id. at para. 37), though not the United States (id. at para. 21). Also striking is the European Union's remark that the economic rights of performers should initially be prioritized, presumably over moral rights (id. at para. 18): "First, the work of the Committee should initially focus on the contents of economic rights of performers and producers of phonograms." See also the comments in Reinbothe & von Lewinski, *supra* note 98, at paras. 8.2, 8.5, 8.6, 8.9, and 8.10.

a different kind of product. Notably, the moral rights of performers usually present little threat to the prerogatives of producers of sound recordings. For example, musical performers and producers work together to determine which versions of a recording ultimately constitute the final product. The relationship between production and performance is well circumscribed in all areas of the recorded music industry compared to film, and this reflects the nature of the product above all. In this environment, performers' moral rights can be secured at little cost to producers. At the same time, an additional layer of rights can help to improve the protection of recordings from piracy, and moral rights of attribution could also serve to buttress existing anti-piracy efforts by creating additional ways of reinforcing the legitimate source of sound recordings by both performers (moral rights of attribution, integrity, and disclosure) and producers (digital rights management and other anti-circumvention technologies).[103]

Interestingly, the perspective of the U.S. recorded music industry placed some distance between the United States and other common law countries in discussions around moral rights for performers[104]—notably Britain, which engaged in a more dogmatic consideration of the rights, arguing that they "did not seem ripe for inclusion in the new instrument."[105] Reinbothe and Lewinski also note that the eventual acceptance of performers' moral rights by the United Kingdom depended on the treaty principle of "application in time," which would limit the application of moral rights to performances created after the entry into force of the WPPT—a provision that was also supported by the United States.[106] However, strong U.S. and international support for performers' moral rights meant that additional measures, such as those explicitly allowing the rights to be waived—usually a source of comfort for common law countries—were not included in this provision. Reinbothe and von Lewinski note that "[t]he compromise solution was not to deal with this topic in the text of the provision."[107] The same approach is taken in the Berne Convention. It leaves open the possibility that moral rights for

[103] The means by which a producer can identify a pirated copy through, e.g., the degradation of sound quality were discussed and demonstrated by Martha de Francisco in her presentation at the Glasgow conference in April 2017: *see* Mira T. Sundara Rajan, *Moral Rights and New Technologies*, Program of the Conference on the moral rights of authors, sponsored by the Economic and Social Research Council (ESRC), and with the participation of the U.S. Copyright Office (Mar. 31–Apr. 1, 2017), https://professormira.com/glasgow-conference-2. Some reflections on the presentation were subsequently published in Martha de Francisco, *Meeting the Challenge of Producing Classical Music for Global Audiences in the Digital Era*, 14(4) JIPLP SYMPOSIUM ON MORAL RIGHTS 327 (Feb. 2019) (Mira T. Sundara Rajan & Sarah Harris, eds.), https://doi.org/10.1093/jiplp/jpz009.

[104] *But see* Reinbothe & von Lewinski, *supra* note 99, at para. 8.58 and n.227 (identifying "the U.S., UK, New Zealand, Thailand, Singapore, Australia, and Israel" as countries with "some hesitation," "or even in part opposed [to] this provision"—specifically referring to the version of the moral rights provision in Basic Proposal II 1996).

[105] *See* WIPO Report, *supra* note 102, at para. 31: "[T]he draft TRIPS text should be used as a basis. It stated that some subjects did not seem ripe for inclusion in the new instrument, including the right of adaptation, moral rights for performers, and private copying."

[106] Reinbothe & Lewinski, *supra* note 99, at para. 8.5.9.

[107] Id.

performers could be waived in their entirety—and, indeed, Canada allows comprehensive waivers of the moral rights of performers under its copyright legislation, just as it has previously done for the moral rights of authors.[108]

The focus of the WPPT is on sound recordings, and performers' moral rights are limited to this context. Within it, the moral rights in the WPPT are quite broad, extending both to live performance and to recorded, or "fixed," performances. Moral rights for performers in films remained excluded.[109] The eventual adoption of a separate treaty on audiovisual performances in 2012, the Beijing Treaty, addressed this gap, without, however, resolving the underlying tension between the moral rights of audiovisual performers, notably actors, and the prerogatives of producers (and, potentially, directors, if their moral rights were ever to be recognized in the United States).

ii. Moral Rights in the WPPT

The moral rights of performers are set out in Article 5 of the WPPT. The rights created by the Article are based on those established in Article 6*bis* of the Berne Convention, and, as noted earlier, they have largely been incorporated *mutatis mutandis* from that Convention; but they are not identical, and the differences, though small, are significant.

Like Berne, the WPPT establishes the two, fundamental moral rights of attribution and of integrity. Article 5(1) of the WPPT reads as follows:

> Independently of a performer's economic rights, and even after the transfer of those rights, the performer shall, as regards his live aural performances or performances fixed in phonograms, have the right to claim to be identified as the performer of his performances, except where omission is dictated by the manner of the use of the performance, and to object to any distortion, mutilation or other modification of his performances that would be prejudicial to his reputation.

There are four differences between Berne and the WPPT. First, the attribution right allows a performer "to *claim to be identified* as the performer," in contrast to the Berne right "to claim authorship." As Elizabeth Adeney notes, this difference

[108] *See* Copyright Act, R.S.C. 1985, c. C-42, s. 17.1(2) (Can.), https://laws-lois.justice.gc.ca/eng/acts/C-42/page-5.html#h-102964.

[109] This has been a key issue for the Hollywood film industry. See Pamela Samuleson, *The U.S. Digital Agenda at WIPO*, 37 Va. J. Int'l L. 369, 371–72 (nn.15 and 16) (1997), who comments,

> Although the U.S. and European delegations were allied on almost all other intellectual property issues at the diplomatic conference, they were bitterly divided on a proposal to universalize European norms about rights of performers of audiovisual works which the U.S. motion picture industry regarded as an anathema. After the Europeans finally agreed to put off to another day the debate over international rights for audiovisual performers, the New Instrument could be finalized. The final treaty provides a much improved framework for protecting the rights of producers and performers of sound recordings.

was discussed by the United Kingdom in a Patent Office Consultation Paper of 1999, which concluded that this right was "a right to claim to be identified rather than ... an unconditional or absolute right of identification," leading her to question the likelihood of a performer being able to assert attribution successfully.[110] The right to make a claim is a right to sue after the fact; this is something different from the right to be "identified" as the performer of one's own performance.

The second change is that attribution may be omitted "where omission is dictated by the manner of the use of the performance." This is apparently an attempt to adapt Berne to the performance context. But it also raises the question of what exactly is meant by "manner of use," and how frequently this might result in the omission of attribution, particularly online. For example, is streaming a "manner of use" that allows attribution to be dispensed with?

Thirdly, the integrity right for performers is more restrictive than Berne. "[D]istortion, mutilation or other modification" of the performance is retained from Berne, but the additional element of "other derogatory action in relation to, the ... work" is eliminated in the WPPT. A performance must be "modified" before the integrity right can be invoked, which is not explicitly the case in relation to authors' works under Berne.[111]

Finally, the WPPT eliminates "honor" from the performer's moral right. Mihály Ficsor, who was at WIPO during these discussions, notes that there was concern about performers "oppos[ing] parodies citing possible prejudice to their honour."[112] In her commentary, Adeney notes,

> This indicates that the delegates did not see the two words "honour" and "reputation" as co-extensive, but that they saw "honour" as indicating something more in the nature of subjective self-esteem or dignity, a fact that is significant for the interpretation of article 6bis of the Berne Convention and related legislation."[113]

The second part of Article 5 maintains some flexibilities in relation to the statutory enactment of moral rights. Here, too, the formula follows the compromise established by Berne. The idea that common law protection, especially through tort, may offer an adequate substitute for statutory provisions reflects from Article 6*bis*(2) of the Berne Convention.

[110] Adeney, *supra* note 8, at para. 7.74. She also notes that the United Kingdom has a requirement of assertion for the performer's attribution right. In this, as in the provisions overall, the United Kingdom was following the model of its author's right of attribution rather than being emboldened by the change of language in the WPPT, but the change is arguably more compatible with the UK model than with Berne.

[111] See discussion in Chapter 2, *infra* note 275.

[112] Adeney, *supra* note 9, at para. 7.72, citing MIHÁLY FICSOR, THE LAW OF COPYRIGHT AND THE INTERNET: THE 1996 WIPO TREATIES, THEIR INTERPRETATION AND IMPLEMENTATION 617–18 (2002).

[113] Adeney, *supra* note 8, at para. 7.73.

As in the case of Berne, however, the WPPT also suggests that some protection beyond tort law—some kind of statutory enactment, however minimal—is required. The key distinction lies in the statement, copied from Berne, that "some, but not all of these rights ... may cease to be protected."

The moral rights in the WPPT inaugurate a new status for performers. Copyright law has traditionally understood performers to be engaged in dissemination, rather than creating works of art in their own right. Accordingly, the status of performers has always been distinctly inferior to that of "true" authors. This situation is reflected in historically lower levels of protection for performers' rights, usually known as mere "neighboring" rights to copyright, and delayed recognition for them at the international level.[114]

By recognizing that performers may be personally implicated in their work much as authors are, the WPPT moves copyright into a new era. Like authors, performers, too, may be vulnerable to harm resulting from the failure to acknowledge them as the creators of their own performances, or from alteration of their work. While performers were traditionally considered mere mouthpieces for composers, the role of the performer has grown dramatically over time, and the change is long overdue. But the transition is not complete: the approach to performers' moral rights in the WPPT reveals that they are more limited than those of authors under Berne. As such, they perpetuate, in a more subtle form, the traditionally unequal status of performers.

As Adeney notes, the digital challenge to performances was among the most important factors behind the WPPT provision on performers' moral rights. A single country, Ghana, also asserted what should have been a subject of greater awareness, the importance of performers' rights for the protection of traditional culture.[115]

How will moral rights for performers be enforced in the technological environment? In particular, the development of databases of music can help to reinforce the correct attribution of musical performances. The role of recording quality in helping to identify pirated versions of a performance, a factor supporting the moral right of integrity in performances, has also been highlighted in the work of Martha de Francisco, a renowned classical sound engineer.[116] According to de Francisco, a pirated sound recording can be identified by a sound engineer who can identify changes in the audio environment of the recording.[117]

[114] "Neighboring rights" are the terminology by which performers' rights, among other rights that are related to copyright, are known internationally. The United States takes a different approach by recognizing a sound recording copyright: *see* U.S. Copyright Act, *supra* note 6, §§ 101 (definition of "sound recordings"), 106, and 114a. Practical explanation of registering sound recordings from the U.S. Copyright Office is also available at https://www.copyright.gov/eco/gram-sr/author.html.

[115] Adeney, *supra* note 8, at para. 7.65. She specifically mentions Sweden and Denmark as drawing attention to the digital issues.

[116] For example, including pianist Alfred Brendel and the Philadelphia Orchestra. *See* de Francisco, *supra* note 102.

[117] A recording may seek to recreate the environment of a silent and stately concert hall or, alternately, a lively jazz club; it may hope to evoke a historical period, as in the common case of film soundtracks for movies like *The Sting* or *Hannah and Her Sisters*—e.g., the piano playing of the main characters' elderly

c. The Beijing Treaty: Always Read the Footnotes

With the adoption of the Beijing Treaty on Audiovisual Performances, WIPO closed a loophole on performers' moral rights left open by the WPPT.[118] Article 5 of the Beijing Treaty, as the earlier Article 5 provision in the WPPT did for musical performers,[119] creates moral rights for audiovisual performers. But it does so through a complex and ambiguous formula. How effective is the provision in practice?

At first glance, the text of Article 5 looks like a variation on a familiar theme. The moral rights for audiovisual performers in Beijing are derived from Article 5 of the WPPT and, through it, Article 6*bis* of the Berne Convention. As in both earlier versions, the Beijing agreement identifies two basic moral rights of attribution and integrity for audiovisual performers. Attribution is generally allowed, although the performer may forfeit his or her right to be identified "where omission is dictated by the manner of the use of the performance." The new treaty also keeps the theory behind moral rights more or less intact. Moral rights for audiovisual performers continue to be "independent" of economic rights and must be protected "at least until the expiry of the economic rights."

The Beijing provision on duration also follows the models of WPPT and Berne. It includes the usual caveat that, in those jurisdictions which will be introducing protection for performers' moral rights after the death of the performer as a result of the new treaty, "some" but not "all" of these rights may cease to be protected at the time of the performer's death. As in the case of the WPPT, by restating the Berne provisions on duration of protection in the audiovisual context, Beijing creates potential inconsistencies between existing provisions on the duration of protection for performances and the transplanted Berne rules about protection after the death of the performer.

In contrast to the WPPT, however, audiovisual performers faced a formidable challenge: arguing against their own industry. This is particularly reflected in the treatment of the moral right of integrity in Beijing. Unlike music production, film production is relatively much more expensive and involves a large number of participants. It is hardly surprising that the industry is so strongly hierarchical. Directors ultimately decide how—if at all—a performance will be used in a final work, and producers have the ultimate word. In Hollywood, this industry has long

parents, slightly out of tune, old-fashioned, and nostalgic. *See* Adam Gopnik for a discussion of this issue in relation to a legendary recording by the Bill Evans Trio, *Sunday at the Village Vanguard*: Adam Gopnik, *That Sunday*, New Yorker (Aug. 13, 2001), https://www.newyorker.com/magazine/2001/08/13/that-sunday-2.

[118] An earlier version of this discussion of the Beijing Treaty first appeared on the 1709 Blog: Mira T. Sundara Rajan, *The Devil Is in the Footnotes: Moral Rights and the Beijing Treaty*, The 1709 Blog (July 20, 2012), http://the1709blog.blogspot.com/2012/07/the-devil-is-in-footnotes-moral-rights.html.

[119] In particular, for "aural" performances, in the language of the Treaty. *See* WPPT, *supra* note 67, at Art. 5.

had a profound aversion to the idea of moral rights, and the agency of performers has always been tightly controlled.[120] The conflict over the colorization of films in the late 1980s is a case in point.[121]

The adoption of moral rights for performers in Beijing could have been a major step forward for actors. In the end, the accompanying limitations eviscerate the integrity right. It is subject to what may be the most extensive list of qualifications and limitations ever applied to a moral rights provision in international law. In particular, the recognition of the performer's moral right of integrity is extensively circumscribed by the terms of the "Agreed Statement" set out in the footnote to Article 5.

According to the text of Article 5, the right of integrity must be interpreted in the light of "the nature of audiovisual fixations" and, a key factor in the subsequent explanations, "their production and distribution." The provision starts out innocuously enough, providing that changes made "in the normal course of exploitation of the performance" will not violate the integrity right.

A similar principle was articulated by the German Supreme Court in a 2008 case involving the use of music for mobile ringtones. The court found that the mere conversion of music to ringtones would not amount to a violation of the creator's moral rights.[122] The principle that the German court established is important in relation to the technological transformation of works. Converting music to ringtones "necessar[ily]" involves changes, including the need to create excerpts and, possibly, technical interventions to change the sound quality. The very nature of a ringtone ensures that the music will be arbitrarily interrupted by the user when he or she answers a call, creating random excerpts which, in another light, could be seen as a violation of the musicians' moral right of integrity.[123]

But the Beijing Treaty goes on to list detailed examples of what will be considered "the normal course of exploitation"—"such as editing, compression, dubbing, or formatting"—and to exempt the treatment of the work "in existing or new media or formats," as well as any dealings with the performance "that are made in the course of a use authorized by the performer" from becoming possible violations of the integrity right.

This seems like an incredibly comprehensive list of exclusions from the moral right of integrity. Is there any way of manipulating a performance for use in the

[120] The Hollywood studio system was infamous for limiting the activities of performers. *See, e.g.*, Khalid Elhassan, *Hollywood Studios Used to Own Their Actors and Actresses*, History Collection (Jan. 3, 2022), https://historycollection.com/hollywood-studios-used-to-own-their-actors-and-actresses.

[121] See, e.g., the famous case about the colorization of John Huston's film *The Asphalt Jungle*, brought in France about the moral rights of the director: *Huston*, *supra* note 26. The *Huston* case has helped to illustrate the idea of moral rights protection to many Americans.

[122] *Klingeltöne* [*Ringtones*] case, Bundesgerichtshof [BGH] [Federal Court of Justice] Dec. 18, 2008, I ZR 23/06 (Ger.), https://openjur.de/u/73874.html.

[123] It is under this rationale that, in France, a film that is broadcast on television cannot be interrupted for commercials; instead, they are shown in a single block at the end of the film.

audiovisual context that would *not* be covered by the four words “editing, compression, dubbing, or formatting”? Just in case there might be, the four activities noted here are presented as a non-exhaustive list, and any treatment of the work that could be read *ejusdem generis* would fall within the definition of “normal ... exploitation.”

The Agreed Statement in the footnote then makes a further statement regarding the moral right of integrity: that it is “concerned only with changes that are objectively prejudicial to the performer’s reputation in a substantial way.” The idea of “objective” proof of damage to the creator’s reputation is familiar from jurisprudence interpreting the Berne Convention in common law countries, including Canada,[124] the United Kingdom,[125] and the United States.[126] In these common law jurisdictions, it is considered to stand for the proposition that someone other than the artist must vouch for the damaging quality of the treatment of the work, usually an expert.[127] But, according to this jurisprudence, the idea of prejudice to reputation is inherently objective; “proof” of damage to reputation always depends on some factor beyond the author’s simple claim. This is usually the testimony of someone other than the author. What is meant by the language “objectively prejudicial”? Presumably, it simply reinforces the existing practice, but the emphasis on “objectivity” could also be taken to mean something additional. What that would be is not clear.

How do we assess whether reputation has been damaged “in a substantial way”? These words have no established meaning under international copyright law in relation to an author’s reputation. Is it some concept that is supposed to be analogous to copying a “substantial part” of a copyright work, as is required for the infringement of economic rights to occur? But this is pure speculation. The provision seeks to draw a distinction between trivial and non-trivial damage to reputation, but it provides no guidance on how to make that distinction or whose opinion will count. Looking at the Agreed Statement, the only thing that seems clear is that the performer’s own opinion of what has happened, and his or her personal sense of injury, will be the last factors to be taken into consideration.

As described by Elizabeth Adeney, the text of this footnote was originally proposed by the WIPO Working Group on audiovisual performances as a possible protocol to the WPPT, or an eventual new treaty. On December 19, 2000, it was published in a report by the Working Group as explanatory text for the proposed Article 5 on audiovisual performers’ moral rights.[128]

[124] *Snow*, *supra* note 23.

[125] *Tidy v. Trustees of the Natural History Museum* (1995) 39 IPR 501 (UK).

[126] *Castillo v. G&M Realty L.P.*, Nos. 18-498-cv (L), 18-538-cv (CON), 2020 U.S. App. LEXIS 5228 (2d Cir., Feb. 20, 2020) (U.S.), https://www.mintz.com/sites/default/files/media/documents/2020-03-25/18-498_amd_opn.pdf. Renée Vara was the expert whose opinion was preferred in that case. See the useful commentary in Erin Pamucku, *5Pointz Litigation SCOTUS-Bound?*, Hughes, Hubbard & Reid (June 30, 2020), https://www.hhrartlaw.com/2020/06/5pointz-litigation-scotus-bound.

[127] Id.

[128] Adeney, *supra* note 8, at paras. 7.79–7.84.

In itself, the idea of modifying moral rights to reflect the characteristics of a particular medium makes sense. It need not be philosophically troublesome. Various examples may be found in copyright laws, where the scope of moral rights is modified according to the type of work concerned. The moral rights of computer programmers are limited in France.[129] Special provisions often relate to works of visual art, such as the idea that conditions of display could violate the artist's moral rights, a principle that is recognized in Australia[130] but explicitly rejected in India.[131]

But the treatment of moral rights in the Beijing Treaty takes this idea to a new level. The moral rights for audiovisual performers are severely limited. Where the right of integrity is concerned, given the range of limitations imposed by the explanatory footnote, it is questionable whether performers in audiovisual works could ever expect to assert their moral rights at all. In the final analysis, the Beijing Treaty makes a nod to moral rights without taking many real steps to endorse them. Hollywood must have breathed a sigh of relief when the treaty was finalized, as it will not have to do much to honor the moral rights obligations undertaken under its terms. Even the formal implementation of the Beijing provisions on moral rights into U.S. law, if this were ever to happen, would probably have little impact on copyright practices in the U.S. film industry.[132]

3. The European Union: An Elephant in the Room

European copyright harmonization, a regional endeavor, has had an outsize influence on the international evolution of copyright norms. One of the largest populations in the world inhabiting a zone with open borders,[133] the EU has taken on a remarkable role of international leadership when it comes to copyright, pressing for higher standards of copyright protection and more effective enforcement to fight copyright piracy. The EU pioneered the extension of copyright term to life of the author plus seventy years, an initially controversial standard that has spread throughout much of the world.[134]

[129] *See* French Code de la propriété intellectuelle, *supra* note 58, at art. L121-7(1).

[130] Copyright Act 1968, *supra* note 77, at s 195AK(b) (Austl.).

[131] Explanatory Notes to the Copyright Act, 1957, s. 57 (India), http://copyright.gov.in/Documents/CopyrightRules1957.pdf.

[132] As Reinbothe & von Lewinski, *supra* note 99, usefully summarize the matter, the idea was essentially to allow Hollywood film production companies to continue with their normal practices under Beijing—or, as they put it, to ensure that "any modifications consistent with customary practice would not violate moral rights" (id. at para. 9.5.6). They also point out that Latin American countries took positions similar to the U.S. view, if not as extreme; given the largely continental European legal heritage in these countries, they ascribe this situation to the "interests of film producers, notably those from the United States" (id. at para. 9.5.6).

[133] See, e.g., the interesting summaries at European Union, *Facts and Figures on Life in the European Union* (n.d.), https://europa.eu/european-union/about-eu/figures/living_en.

[134] In its 1993 Copyright Term Directive, the European Union extended copyright term within its territory to lifetime of the author plus seventy years: Council Directive 93/98/EEC of 29 October 1993 harmonizing the term of protection of copyright and certain related rights, 1993 O.J. (L 290) 9, https://

At one point in time, this philosophy was no doubt a product of European faith in copyright as a positive complement to technological innovation, strengthened by the long tradition of copyright internationalization born in Europe and represented by Berne. If Europe took the lead in copyright modernization, then it might have a fighting chance at becoming a haven for innovation as well. In recent years, the mood has grown significantly more somber, with Europe taking aim at the activities of tech giants, particularly Google and Facebook, for what is widely viewed as the unfair exploitation of European cyberspace. The EU's lines of attack have extended from copyright to other issues generated by the dissemination of information in the technological environment, including the treatment of personal data and privacy. Europe has now become the world leader in the area of data privacy regulation through the General Data Protection Regulation (GDPR)—an unprecedented attempt at protecting European internet users by subjecting even offshore acts involving European individuals and their data to scrutiny.[135] It is, once again, in the forefront of technology regulation, though the attitude, now, is one of restraining large tech companies from profiteering. And, of course, the pattern established by the GDPR has been followed by the pioneering initiative of the EU in relation to artificial intelligence, the AI Act.[136]

In theory at least, EU copyright harmonization has always involved a greater potential for developing a transnational standard of protection for moral rights than any other international copyright forum. The dominant members of the EU,

eur-lex.europa.eu/legal-content/EN/ALL/?uri=CELEX%3A31993L0098 (since repealed and replaced by Directive 2006/116/EC of the European Parliament and of the Council of 12 December 2006 on the term of protection of copyright and certain related rights, 2006 O.J. (L 372) 12, https://eur-lex.europa.eu/LexUriServ/LexUriServ.do?uri=OJ:L:2006:372:0012:0018:EN:PDF). This led other countries to follow suit with copyright term extensions beyond the term of fifty years after the author's death (also known as *post mortem auctoris*, or *pma*) on what was sometimes a controversial measure. For example, the Sonny Bono Term Extension Act of 1998, Pub. L. No. 105-298, § 505, 112 Stat. 2877 (1998) (U.S.), https://www.congress.gov/bill/105th-congress/senate-bill/505, was challenged before the U.S. Supreme Court, which argued that the measure violated U.S. constitutional provisions that require copyright to be protected "for limited times" only. The Supreme Court responded that seventy years after the author's death, if a long time, was still "limited" and would qualify as such under the terms of the Constitution: *see Eldred v. Ashcroft*, 537 U.S. 186 (2003), https://supreme.justia.com/cases/federal/us/537/186. An interesting comparison is offered by India, which also extended its copyright term in 1992—not because of European influence but to extend protection for the estate of one of its important poets, Nobel laureate Rabindranath Tagore (1861–1941). *See infra* note 170.

[135] *See* Regulation (EU) 2016/679 of the European Parliament and of the Council of 27 April 2016 on the protection of natural persons with regard to the processing of personal data and on the free movement of such data, and repealing Directive 95/46/EC, 2016 O.J. (L 119) 1, Art. 3, https://eur-lex.europa.eu/eli/reg/2016/679/oj (general information available at https://gdpr-info.eu).

[136] European Parliament Legislative Resolution of 13 March 2024 on the proposal for a regulation of the European Parliament and of the Council on laying down harmonised rules on Artificial Intelligence (Artificial Intelligence Act) and amending certain Union Legislative Acts (Jan. 21, 2024), COM(2021)0206 – C9-0146/2021 – 2021/0106(COD)), https://www.europarl.europa.eu/doceo/document/TA-9-2024-0138_EN.pdf. The final version is available at the Future of Life Institute, *The EU Artificial Intelligence Act: Up-to-date developments and analyses of the EU AI Act* (2024), https://artificialintelligenceact.eu/.

France and Germany, constitute the heartland of moral rights doctrine, and all EU jurisdictions, without exception, have strong protection for moral rights in their copyright laws. At the WTO, U.S. objections led to the effective exclusion of moral rights from TRIPs. In Europe, however, the United Kingdom, Europe's only common law jurisdiction, effectively adapted to a changing copyright landscape, at least in principle, when it adopted its first legislative protections for moral rights in 1988. While the treatment of moral rights in the CDPA leaves much to be desired, their presence in British copyright law was still an important step forward, and one that reflected, at least indirectly, the European influence on British copyright law.[137]

In spite of these theoretical advantages, it should be made clear that the EU has made no steps towards harmonizing moral rights in its copyright framework. But moral rights, as noted above, are a deeply ingrained part of the copyright fabric of the member states, and the EU has had to confront this reality through indirect means—oblique references in the copyright directives, and indirect commentary at the CJEU. This continues to be the case in the latest round of copyright reforms, the Digital Single Market initiative culminating in a new copyright directive in mid-2019. However, the new directive reveals the extent to which the EU's relative silence on moral rights has become awkward. Apart from the concerns about authors' status in the Digital Single Market (DSM), it also raises questions about the effectiveness of the European copyright framework.

a. Harmonization and Moral Rights in the EU: Policy Initiatives?

As far back as 1995, in a Green Paper on Copyright and Related Rights in the Information Society, the European Commission made a number of statements about the need to include moral rights in the process of copyright harmonization.[138] It observed, in words that seem prescient now,

> With the arrival of the information society the question of moral rights is becoming more urgent than it was. Digital technology is making it easier to modify works. The Commission believes there is a need for an examination of the

[137] CDPA, *supra* note 50, at ch. IV on moral rights. It is worth emphasizing a possible European influence over the international one, because British membership in the Berne Convention did not compel the adoption of moral rights for six decades. Indeed, the Gregory Commission, which first studied the issue in 1952, argued that British law gave sufficient recognition to moral rights without the need for any changes—a view that was altered only when the Whitford Committee reviewed what was essentially the same law less favorably in 1977, leading to the adoption of the new provisions.

[138] Commission of the European Communities, Green Paper on Copyright and Related Rights in the Information Society (July 19, 1995), COM (95) 382 final, VII (EU Green Paper). See also the interesting and more comprehensive work by Marjut Salokannel & Alain Strowel, with Estelle Derclaye, Study Contract Concerning Moral Rights in the Context of the Exploration of Works through Digital Technology: Final Report, Study Contract No. ETD/99/B5-3000/E (Apr. 28, 2000), https://www.academia.edu/1363052/Study_contract_concerning_moral_rights_in_the_context_of_the_exploitation_of_works_through_digital_technology.

question whether the present lack of harmonization will continue to be acceptable in the new digital environment.[139]

In 2000, a second study on moral rights in the EU was completed.[140] This study concluded that there was no need to pursue the goal of moral rights harmonization in the EU, as harmonization was only desired by two countries, Italy and Greece, which enjoyed higher levels of moral rights protection than the others.[141] In contrast to the earlier paper, the general tone of the study was quite complacent about the impact of technology on copyright law and the growing relevance of moral rights in this environment.

Since the appearance of this study, it appears that there has been no further exploration of moral rights and EU copyright harmonization. This is in spite of the expansion of the European Union to include the post-socialist jurisdictions of Central and Eastern Europe, many of whom had distinguished histories surrounding moral rights in their countries.[142] These countries bring many new needs and perspectives to the European copyright arena, many of which remain underrepresented in EU policy discussions.[143] However, the most influential voice may have been that of the United Kingdom, which maintained its historic opposition to moral rights throughout the period of its membership in the EU.

b. Moral Rights in the Directives: Indirect Approaches

Lack of policy commitment in recent years is reflected in the state of European moral rights. Since the EU has not made significant progress on policy development, which is severely out of date, progress on harmonization cannot be expected. To date, none of the eight harmonization directives has dealt with moral rights in the technological environment. For example, the Computer Programs Directive addresses only the economic rights in computer programs.[144] The Term Directive states that it "shall be without prejudice to the provisions of the Member States regulating moral rights"[145]—presumably, in order to accommodate

[139] EU Green Paper, *supra* note 135, at 67.

[140] *See* Salokannel & Strowel, *supra* note 135, at 242.

[141] Id.

[142] *See, e.g.*, Péter Munkácsi, *Moral Rights and the Cultural Aspects of Hungarian Copyright Law: 1945–2000*, in Cambridge Handbook of Intellectual Property in Central and Eastern Europe 51 (Mira T. Sundara Rajan ed., 2019).

[143] Munkácsi seeks to bring some of these perspectives to the attention of the European and international copyright policy communities: id.

[144] Directive 2009/24/EC of the European Parliament and of the Council of 23 April 2009 on the legal protection of computer programs, 2009 O.J. (L 111) 16, https://eur-lex.europa.eu/legal-content/EN/ALL/?uri=CELEX%3A32009L0024, repealing and replacing original version Council Directive 91/250/EEC of 14 May 1991 on the legal protection of computer programs, 1991 O.J. (L 122) 42, https://eur-lex.europa.eu/legal-content/EN/ALL/?uri=celex%3A31991L0250.

[145] Directive 2006/116/EC of the European Parliament and of the Council of 12 December 2006 on the term of protection of copyright and certain related rights, 2006 O.J. (L 372) 12, https://eur-lex.europa.eu/LexUriServ/LexUriServ.do?uri=OJ:L:2006:372:0012:0018:EN:PDF, repealing and replacing Council Directive 93/98/EEC of 29 October 1993 harmonizing the term of protection of copyright

jurisdictions where moral rights enjoy perpetual protection. A similar approach is taken in the Database Directive, which specifies that "the moral rights of the natural person who created the database belong to the author and should be exercised according to the legislation of the Member States and the provisions of the Berne Convention ...; ... such moral rights remain outside the scope of this Directive."[146] This statement confirms only that moral rights need not be excluded from national regulation on technological creations such as databases.

The 2001 Directive on Copyright in the Information Society, the most ambitious harmonization initiative before the Digital Single Market initiative,[147] could have provided an ideal opportunity to address the issue of harmonizing moral rights. The Directive dealt comprehensively with copyright, and it sought to harmonize the reproduction right—what Michael Hart aptly calls the "very core of copyright law"[148] —as well as the rights of distribution and communication to the public. However, moral rights appear only in Recital 19 of the Directive, which provides as follows, in a formula that closely resembles Article 9.1 of the TRIPs Agreement:

> The moral rights of right holders should be exercised according to the legislation of the Member States and the provisions of the Berne Convention for the Protection of Literary and Artistic Works, of the WIPO Copyright Treaty and of the WIPO Performances and Phonograms Treaty. Such moral rights remain outside the scope of this Directive.[149]

This Directive is generally based on the WIPO Copyright Treaty.[150] As such, it emphasizes the changing quality of authors' rights in the technological environment, especially in relation to the issue of *représentation* or communication to the public. Article 3 of the Directive sets out details of the right, including, in broader language than the WIPO Copyright Treaty, an "exclusive right to authorize or prohibit any communication to the public ... including the making available to the public of their works in such a way that members of the public access them from a place and at a time individually chosen by them" (emphasis added). In Article 3.2, the right is explicitly extended to performers in the case of a fixation of their performances, and to phonogram producers in their phonograms.

and certain related rights, 1993 O.J. (L 290) 9, https://eur-lex.europa.eu/legal-content/EN/ALL/?uri=CELEX%3A31993L0098.

[146] Directive 96/9/EC of the European Parliament and of the Council of 11 March 1996 on the legal protection of databases, 1996 O.J. (L 77) 20, https://eur-lex.europa.eu/legal-content/EN/TXT/PDF/?uri=CELEX:01996L0009-20190606&from=DA.

[147] InfoSoc Directive, *supra* note 54.

[148] Michael Hart, *The Proposed Directive for Copyright in the Information Society: Nice Rights, Shame about the Exceptions*, 20(5) Eur. Intell. Prop. Rev. 169, 169 (1998).

[149] InfoSoc Directive, *supra* note 54.

[150] WCT, *supra* note 67.

As in the case of the WIPO Copyright Treaty, it seems difficult to divide this updated right of communication into neat economic and moral compartments. Indeed, the explicit right of the author to *prohibit* communication of the work to the public seems, if anything, to emphasize the comprehensive character of this right, bringing it closer to a shared manifestation of the right of first publication and the moral right of disclosure, which respects the author's choice to publish or not to publish.

c. CJEU Jurisprudence and Moral Rights

An additional factor that makes the EU a good candidate for the development of an international moral rights standard is the availability of adjudication at a high standard. At the WTO, moral rights are excluded from the adjudicative capacity of the Dispute Settlement Body, which is, in any event, an administrative body. In the EU, however, the CJEU is a strong judicial force to be reckoned with where the intra-European movement of intellectual property is concerned. The ECJ has established a highly respected "acquis" of European copyright law[151]—seminal principles on the interpretation and enforcement of copyright in the EU. Notable among early ECJ judgments are the *Phil Collins* decision of 1993, which established that copyright within the EU must apply on a non-discriminatory basis to the nationals of all EU member states,[152] and the *Magill* case of 1995, which recognized the need to "protect the moral rights in the work" as a part of the "essential function" of copyright law.[153] Digging deeper into the history of ECJ decisions, the seminal *GEMA* case of 1981 found that the presence of moral rights in copyright law did not require the differential treatment of copyright subject matter within the EU.[154] As Catherine Seville observes,

> The ECJ acknowledged that copyright comprised moral rights, but held that this was no reason to make a distinction between copyright and other industrial and commercial property rights with regard to economic rights, which were the subject of the case. It therefore confirms that copyright, like other intellectual

[151] *Acquis* meaning principles "acquired" through the court's adjudication.

[152] *See* Joined Cases C-92/92 and C-326/92, *Phil Collins v. Imtrat Handelsgesellschaft mbH*; *Patricia Im-und Export Verwaltungsgesellschaft mbH and another v. EMI Electrola GmbH*, ECLI:EU:C:1993:847 (Oct. 20, 1993), https://eur-lex.europa.eu/legal-content/EN/TXT/?uri=CELEX%3A61992CJ0092. This case receives an excellent analysis, alongside other ECJ decisions on copyright, in CATHERINE SEVILLE, EU INTELLECTUAL PROPERTY LAW AND POLICY 324–25 (2009).

[153] *See* Joined cases C-241/91 P and C-242/91 P, *Radio Telefis Eirann (RTE) and Independent Television Publications Ltd (ITP) v. Commission*, ECLI:EU:C:1995:98 (Apr. 6, 1995), https://curia.europa.eu/juris/liste.jsf?num=C-241/91%2520P. The case receives a detailed and helpful commentary in Irini Stamatoudi, *The Hidden Agenda in Magill and Its Impact on New Technologies*, 1(1) J. WORLD INTELL. PROP. 153 (1998).

[154] Joined Cases 55/80 and 57/80, *Musik-Vertrieb membran GmbH and K-tel International v. GEMA—Gesellschaft für musikalische Aufführungs- und mechanische Vervielfältigungsrechte*, ECLI:EU:C:1981:10 (Jan. 20, 1981), ¶ 12, https://eur-lex.europa.eu/legal-content/EN/TXT/?uri=CELEX%3A61980CJ0055.

property rights, could not be used to entrench the isolation of national markets or restricting parallel imports.[155]

These cases show the effectiveness of the CJEU in promoting the implementation of harmonized copyright practices across its member states. However, in the absence of legislative guidance, there are limits to what the Court can do in terms of favoring a unified conception of moral rights throughout the territory of the EU. The *Deckmyn* case of 2014[156] provides a tantalizing illustration of what the ECJ might do if it could treat moral rights as a legal concept harmonized across the Union. The caricaturing of a cartoon to make racist depictions could have been framed as a violation of the artists' moral right of integrity. Instead, these potential violations of moral rights had to be presented in ambiguous legal language, as "unreasonably prejudic[ing]" the "legitimate interests" of "right holders." If it had been brought, the claim would also have advanced the specific idea of an association between a work and discriminatory views as a basis for a moral rights violation. Given the fundamental importance of non-discrimination as a principle of human rights underlying the architecture of the EU, this could have been a worthwhile precedent.[157] But the Court never mentions moral rights in its decision.

This is in keeping with the tacit agreement among member states that harmonization of moral rights will not be addressed, in keeping with British sensitivities. Will the British withdrawal from the EU encourage a reconsideration of moral rights harmonization among the remaining member states? No other country in the EU region, including any of the "new" member states of Central and Eastern Europe, would have reason to oppose the idea in principle. However, finding workable commonalities on the details of issues such as duration and waivers could still be a task to reckon with.

d. Moral Rights and the Digital Single Market (DSM) Directive

When the Digital Single Market (DSM) initiative for copyright modernization was proposed in 2017, the strategy identified three "pillars" of reform: "access," "environment," and "economy and society." Culture was conspicuously absent from this list. In the copyright directive that came out of this process and that was adopted in 2019, however, the language of culture and creativity is prominent in the text. In spite of this apparent shift, the directive makes no attempt to harmonize the treatment of moral rights, a prominent area of copyright law that is, in a sense, *exclusively* concerned with culture—at least, in so far as it is not *directly* concerned with commerce. Rather, the culture-related priorities of the Directive[158] seem to

155 Seville, *supra* note 149, at 324–25.
156 *See Deckmyn*, *supra* note 47; Chapter 1, *supra* notes 115–28 and accompanying text.
157 In contrast to *Confetti Records v. Warner Music UK Ltd* [2003] EWHC 1274 (Ch) (UK), where the claims of the composer were contradicted by pre-existing associations between his composition and drugs and violence in the original recording.
158 DSM Directive, *supra* note 16.

fall into two main areas: improving the position of creators and right-owners with respect to technology companies, particularly with respect to fair remuneration for the online uses of works; and facilitating the uses of works by cultural institutions, particularly for the purposes of cultural preservation. From the perspective of copyright policy, it is crucial to realize that the Directive primarily aims to achieve both goals through maneuvering the exceptions and limitations to copyright protection—specifically, by harmonizing at least some of these.

A few examples should help to illustrate the Directive's approach. First, in keeping with its recent efforts to control the activities of large technology companies and create more accountability in their online activities, the new Directive creates an obligation on online platforms to ensure that content which is posted on their sites does not infringe copyright. One of the key aims of this provision was to improve revenue streams for both authors and owners in the online environment and, in particular, to prevent the enrichment of online platforms at the expense of "content creators"—including, of course, the individuals "formerly known" as authors and artists,[159] but encompassing the full range of creators, such as small and medium-sized enterprises in, for example, the arts, animation, design, and software creation, as well. The examples are limitless.

Secondly, the Directive simultaneously aims to facilitate what it calls "extended collective licensing,"[160] a scheme that allows for collective licensing bodies to collect royalties on behalf of an author or right holder until they are advised otherwise by that person—an "opt-out" scheme. The observation that such a scheme goes directly against the traditional copyright practice of requiring authorization first is, no doubt, an old fashioned observation—requiring the explicit consent of authors (or owners) to the use of a work may amount to an antiquated paradigm of copyright, particularly in the post-Google Books era.[161]

[159] Of course, they continue to be known as authors and artists as well, but the term "content creator" has arguably become ubiquitous. See, e.g., a short article by Matthew Cook, *On Content: Are You a Content Creator or Are You a Writer?*, Innovative Marketing Resources (n.d.), https://www.imrcorp.com/innovative-marketing-blog/bid/67581/On-Content-Are-You-a-Content-Creator-or-Are-You-a-Writer.

[160] *See, e.g.*, DSM Directive, *supra* note 16, at Art. 12 on "Collective licensing with an extended effect." The term itself became well known around the time of the Google Books settlement: *see infra* note 158.

[161] The Google Books settlement originally generated much controversy because of its "opt-out" scheme, which would have allowed Google to publish parts of authors' works online, in its Google Books database, until and unless the rights-holders withdrew the works. Although the settlement was disallowed by the courts, Google's initiative was ultimately successful on a much broader ground—that it amounted to fair use under the terms of U.S. copyright law. Regardless, when Google built its opt-out approach, it arguably opened Pandora's box in the sense that it permanently raised questions about the necessity or feasibility of the traditional "opt-in" approach to copyright in the technological environment. For some reflections on the ultimate fate of the Google Books repository, see the brief commentary by Tim Wu, *Whatever Happened to Google Books?*, New Yorker (Sept. 12, 2015), https://www.newyorker.com/business/currency/what-ever-happened-to-google-books. A detailed and thought-provoking review of the story is provided by James Somers, *Torching the Modern-Day Library of Alexandria*, The Atlantic (Apr. 20, 2017), https://www.theatlantic.com/technology/archive/2017/04/the-tragedy-of-google-books/523320.

The silence on moral rights in relation to Article 12, on the possibility of extended collective licensing, is striking. The Article provides for automatic representation of authors who may not have consented explicitly to representation by the collective rights management agency in question. The CJEU has considered the need for consent in the context of economic rights, in the context of the 2015 case of *Soulier and Doke*,[162] but there is also a moral rights dimension. Would authors be able to object to uses made of a work to which they had not explicitly consented? For example, could they still object to "necessary modifications" of the work in the light of technology, on the grounds that those modifications violated their moral rights of integrity?[163]

The new Directive also includes extensive provisions intended to help cultural institutions, broadly defined by the text, to undertake the preservation of works in their collections,[164] including exceptions and limitations to copyright protection that will allow these kinds of organizations to make reproductions of the works even if it would otherwise be necessary to seek often elusive copyright permissions.

Throughout these provisions, no attempt is made to address moral rights directly—though the moral rights do receive two mentions in the Directive, both in the "recitals" rather than the substantive articles, that belie their relative unimportance to the culturally beneficial scheme that the Directive purports to create for authors.

First, in relation to educational uses of works, Recital 23 provides that member countries "may" continue to require that moral rights be respected within the member states, notwithstanding the creation of a new exception to copyright rules to facilitate the uses of works in cross-border educational activities, such as teaching.[165] This could be read as implying a broader approach to copyright exceptions and limitations in the Directive, as a whole: moral rights will be tolerated

[162] See the analysis in Lucie Guibaut & Simone Schroff, *Extended Collective Licensing for the Use of Out-of-Commerce Works in Europe: A Matter of Legitimacy Vis-à-Vis Rights Holders*, 49 IIC 916 (2018), https://doi.org/10.1007/s40319-018-0748-5; see also the comments in Johann Axhamm, *The New Copyright Directive: Collective Licensing as a Way to Strike a Fair Balance between Creator and User Interests in Copyright Legislation (Article 12)*, Kluwer Copyright Blog (June 25, 2019), http://copyrightblog.kluweriplaw.com/2019/06/25/the-new-copyright-directive-collective-licensing-as-a-way-to-strike-a-fair-balance-between-creator-and-user-interests-in-copyright-legislation-article-12.

[163] See, e.g., the discussion of *Klingeltöne*, *supra* note 122, in Chapter 6, *infra* notes 140–47 and accompanying text.

[164] *See, e.g.*, DSM Directive, *supra* note 16, at Art. 6 on "Preservation of cultural heritage." *But see* id. at Arts. 8 on "Use of out-of-commerce works and other subject matter by cultural heritage institutions" and 9 on "Cross-border uses."

[165] Id. at Recital 23 states,

> While it is essential to harmonise the scope of the new mandatory exception or limitation in relation to digital uses and cross-border teaching activities, the arrangements for implementation can vary from one Member State to another, to the extent that they do not hamper the effective application of the exception or limitation or cross-border uses. Member States should, for example, remain free to require that the use of works or other subject matter respect the moral rights of authors and performers. This should allow Member States to build on the existing arrangements concluded at national level.

at the national level as long as they do not impede the cross-border movement of copyright works that the Directive aims to enable. But this creates a burden of uncertainty for users. For educational users, for example, it raises the possibility that, despite the existence of a harmonized European exception in the Directive that allows for the educational use of works across all EU member countries, the user might still face responsibility under the copyright law of the country of use because of a moral rights provision in that country. If the country in question recognized perpetual moral rights, such as France, even the use of works in the public domain would involve continuing legal obligations. To say that this is not a significant point, in practice, suggests either that the law in those countries is somehow not enforceable—an argument that would seem to bring into question the very operation of the principle of the rule of law in this area—or that no practical question involving these issues could ever arise, something that may not be as easy to predict as we might think. This would be a bad precedent in every sense.

The problem that arises in relation to educational works could, indeed, arise in relation to any "fair dealings," or free or fair uses of works covered by the exceptions and limitations to copyright protection. It would be far simpler for users if the question of moral rights requirements in relation to copyright exceptions could be resolved at the European level, providing which rights are to be recognized, for how long, and which standards of proof are to be applied.

Secondly, and in a similar vein, recital 37 of the directive refers to moral rights in the case of the copyright exception granted to cultural institutions for the purpose of cultural preservation. The baroque formula in this article is not easy to decipher, but it suggests that the treatment of any works for cultural preservation purposes, with particular reference to unpublished works, may, once again, be subject to moral rights requirements at the *national* level:

> Considering the variety of works and other subject matter in the collections of cultural heritage institutions, it is important that the licensing mechanisms and the exception or limitation provided for by this Directive are available and can be used in practice for different types of works and other subject matter, including photographs, software, phonograms, audiovisual works and unique works of art, including where they have never been commercially available. Never-in-commerce works can include posters, leaflets, trench journals or amateur audiovisual works, but also unpublished works or other subject matter, without prejudice to other applicable legal constraints, such as national rules on moral rights.[166]

This creates uncertainties just like those noted above, and begs the question: why could the DSM strategy not include a look at moral rights and, in

[166] Id. at Recital 37.

particular, examine the broadly important question, for both policy and practice, of whether moral rights provisions should be able to limit the application of copyright exceptions and limitations to use a work freely across the EU? One can only assume that the question was politically uncomfortable: at a time when the importance of copyright exceptions was widely emphasized, the last thing policymakers might want to do would be to draw attention to a potentially inalienable right that might continue to apply, regardless of the qualification of a given use of a work as an exception or limitation, fair or free. This was much the approach taken by UK legislators in their 2014 approach to an exception to copyright for works of parody and similar types of works identified by the UK Act as "caricature" or "pastiche."[167] The exception says nothing about whether or not moral rights would continue to apply in the case of parodies and similar works. It must therefore be assumed that they would, leading to the implication that a work that is a parody under UK copyright law might still be found to infringe the moral right of integrity held by the original author—or, indeed, the author's attribution right (though the fact scenario in which the latter consequence would play out is less clear).

Article 22 of the Directive creates a new and interesting right: it allows authors and performers to revoke copyright transfers or licenses to use their work "where there is a lack of exploitation" of the work. The right is a curious one, emerging out of one of the stated objectives of the Directive, that of improving equality of bargaining power between authors and those who commercially exploit their works. But, what kind of right is it? It is a right with economic implications, but it is not an economic right in the usual sense of that term under copyright law—a right to do something, in a positive sense, with the work. Instead, it is a right to intervene when a party authorized to deal with the work refuses to do so. The right aims fundamentally at creating a new area of authorial agency, that of monitoring and ensuring the exploitation of his or her work. As such, it seems to have more in common with the personal quality of a moral right than the commercial nature of an economic right. It could even be considered a form of exercise of the author's moral right of disclosure, since it effectively seeks to ensure that the author's intent to disclose the work to the public is carried out by the publisher, or other appropriate organization to whom that act is entrusted. Has the Directive thereby recognized the author's moral right of disclosure, or one part of it, without identifying it explicitly; or has it created a new moral right in the text of Article 22?[168]

In the DSM Directive, European policymakers invoke culture without, however, taking steps to affirm the cultural importance of authors' moral rights of

[167] CDPA, *supra* note 50, § 30A, http://www.legislation.gov.uk/ukpga/1988/48/section/30A.

[168] The right might also be classified as a joint economic-moral right—a hybrid, somewhat—because the *droit de suite* is arguably a hybrid right, comprising elements of both the author's economic and moral interests. In this case, those elements would be the dual moral and economic concepts of disclosure—the author's right to decide on the circumstances in which the work will be published—and first publication—the author's right to enjoy the economic benefit of doing so.

attribution and integrity. For authors, it is worth noting that the question of recognizing moral rights is arguably as much one of economics as culture, since the ability of authors to earn money has always been based on reputation and is, in today's digital environment, more dependent on reputation than ever in the past. But moral rights, like so many issues affecting authors, are also significant for culture as a whole—if, that is, we, as a society, continue to care about who said what, and why.

This last question deserves to be both asked and answered. During the COVID-19 pandemic of early 2020, words of comfort were circulated online in the form of a beautiful poem by an author named Kathleen (or "Kitty") O'Meara. But they are two different people: Kathleen, a nineteenth-century Irish writer, and Kitty, a retired Irish-American schoolteacher who posted the poem on her Facebook page in March of 2020.[169] Users noticed the dual attribution, but at least one commented that the words, rather than author of the poem were what mattered. At the same time, an Italian journalist claimed to be the author of the original, Italian-language poem, leading Kitty O'Meara to comment: "I believe the same spirit is moving through artists and we're interpreting this suffering, and fear, and anxiety in ways that are bound to echo feelings and ideas being expressed in other ways."[170] At the very least, the case illustrates the difficulty of tracing the origins of works which spread "virally" online. Authorship may matter to some more than to others. But the degradation of the online space for truth is real. This problem is just starting to capture public attention to the extent that it should. Moral rights will eventually have an important role to play in stemming the tide of human thought that is misrepresented, taken out of context, or otherwise falsified or abused. But we will, no doubt, have to await a cultural "pandemic" before that happens.

E. In Principle: Moral Rights and International Trade

An examination of this global framework highlights the unusual character of the international copyright system. It is not "law" in the domestic sense of the term, because, notwithstanding WIPO's rule-making authority, it is not governed by a law-making body in the democratic sense, it represents no specific jurisdiction, and it has recourse to no enforcement powers beyond the economic mechanisms related to trade at the WTO. At the same time, international intellectual property law can be distinguished from other areas of true public international law by its focus on highly specific rules, its emphasis on individual and right-holder action, and in the

[169] *See, e.g.*, Elena Nicolaou, *Kitty O'Meara, Author of "And the People Stayed Home," Opens Up about Writing That Viral Poem*, Oprah Daily (Mar. 19, 2020), https://www.oprahmag.com/entertainment/a31747557/and-the-people-stayed-home-poem-kitty-omeara-interview.

[170] Id.

combination of economic and non-economic, public and private elements necessarily encompassed by copyright regulation. In fact, international copyright law functions very much as a *hybrid* system, driven by rules and practices specific to its role which that incorporate elements of the public and private interest—and, indeed, often seek to accomplish public-interest goals through the management of private rights. The practical manifestation of these hybrid features can be summarized in terms of three basic principles: the establishment of minimum copyright standards as well as the international trade norms of national treatment, and, since the adoption of the TRIPs Agreement, most-favored-nation treatment.

1. Minimum Standards

The international copyright framework provided by the Berne Convention sets out the basic norms that must be respected by member countries of the Berne Union. But these norms are not comprehensive. Rather, the Berne Convention specifies the minimum standards of protection that must be observed. Any member country of Berne can choose to exceed these minimum standards by implementing a higher level of protection in its domestic copyright law.

A simple example lies in the question of copyright term. The Berne Convention establishes a minimum duration of copyright protection for the lifetime of the author and fifty years after his death.[171] However, nothing in the Berne Convention precludes a country from increasing the term of copyright protection; and, indeed, Article 19, entitled "Protection Greater than Resulting from Convention," states,

> The provisions of this Convention shall not preclude the making of a claim to the benefit of any greater protection which may be granted by legislation in a country of the Union.

Many countries now exceed this minimum term of protection. The EU has set a new benchmark for copyright term, life of the author plus seventy years after his death; India has a term of life plus sixty years, specially extended in 1992 to accommodate copyright in the works of Indian Nobel laureate in literature, Rabindranath Tagore.[172] Article 7.6 of the Berne Convention also makes specific provision for this general rule, stating that, "The countries of the Union may grant a term of

[171] *See* Berne Convention, *supra* note 2, at Art. 7.

[172] The Copyright (Amendment) Bill 1992, No. 35-C of 1992 (India) (no longer available online). For a full explanation of the story behind the change, see THE COPYRIGHT ACT, 1957 (14 OF 1957) ALONG WITH THE COPYRIGHT RULES, 1958 & INTERNATIONAL COPYRIGHT ORDER, 1999, BARE ACT WITH SHORT COMMENTS, AMENDMENT ACT 13 OF 1992, STATEMENT OF OBJECTS AND REASONS 4 (Krishan Arora ed., 2006). It is ironic that copyright term was extended by ten years to prolong the copyright in Rabindranath Tagore's works "in view of their national importance"—the same rationale given for the early termination of Subramania Bharati's copyright in 1949.

protection in excess of those provided by the preceding paragraphs." The provision is not strictly necessary; it reinforces the general rule that countries can exceed Berne requirements, as noted above.[173] But duration of copyright is a slightly unusual issue. The Berne Convention also makes an exception to the principle of upward harmonization by legislating a "rule of the shorter term." This special rule allows the duration of copyright to be generally limited to the term of protection in the country of origin of the work.[174]

This system of minimum standards leads to certain practical consequences. Notably, it is clearly not a legal regime that promotes the standardization of copyright norms around the world. On the contrary, there is considerable scope for variation in the copyright practices specific to different countries. What Berne does provide is an assurance that no country will fail to guarantee the minimum levels of protection offered by the Convention. Accordingly, the protection enjoyed by authors will vary, in practice, depending on the country where an infringement of copyright is asserted and protection is claimed.

2. National Treatment

National treatment is a cornerstone of the Berne copyright system. Codified in Article 5.1 of the Berne Convention, national treatment simply means that an author who is a national of any Berne member country can expect to be treated on a par with the nationals of the country where copyright protection is claimed.[175] For example, a Canadian author claiming infringement of his or her copyright in the

[173] See Ricketson, *supra* note 17, for a discussion of why this was done.

[174] The provision is beautifully explained by Paul Edward Geller, *Zombie and Once-Dead Works: Copyright Retroactivity after the E.C. Term Directive*, 18(2) ENT. & SPORTS LAW. 7, 7–9 (2000). Geller points out that the non-discrimination principle established by the 1993 *Phil Collins* decision at the ECJ signifies that EU member states can no longer apply the Berne rule of the shorter term and comply with EU requirements. *See Phil Collins*, *supra* note 149. See also Ricketson, *supra* note 17, at para. 3.13 on the adoption of the minimum term of protection as life plus fifty years in the Brussels Act, 1948, *supra* note 28.

Article 7(8) of the Berne Convention, *supra* note 1, states, "In any case, the term shall be governed by the legislation of the country where protection is claimed; however, unless the legislation of that country otherwise provides, the term shall not exceed the term fixed in the country of origin of the work." *See also* id. at Art. 7(7):

> Those countries of the Union bound by the Rome Act of this Convention which grant, in their national legislation in force at the time of signature of the present Act, shorter terms of protection than those provided for in the preceding paragraphs shall have the right to maintain such terms when ratifying or acceding to the present Act.

Taken together, these two subsections limit the duration of protection to the term in the country of origin.

[175] Id. at Art. 5(1), states,

> Authors shall enjoy, in respect of works for which they are protected under this Convention, in countries of the Union other than the country of origin, the rights which their respective laws do now or may hereafter grant to their nationals, as well as the rights specially granted by this Convention.

United States will be treated in exactly the same way as any U.S. national where his or her copyright status is concerned.

In practice, the law of the country where infringement is claimed is usually applied to copyright cases. This represents a pragmatic approach to litigation, as it is likely to be the best way to ensure that the defendant can be brought to justice. This principle is also articulated in Article 5.2 of the Berne Convention, which states,

> The enjoyment and the exercise of these rights shall not be subject to any formality; such enjoyment and such exercise shall be independent of the existence of protection in the country of origin of the work. Consequently, apart from the provisions of this Convention, the extent of protection, as well as the means of redress afforded to the author to protect his rights, shall be governed exclusively by the laws of the country where protection is claimed.[176]

a. Practical Implications

It now becomes apparent that the combination of national treatment with the practice of minimum standards can create certain anomalies in practice. Let us take the exaggerated case of moral rights for an example.

With the exception of visual arts, U.S. law only provides for protection of moral rights through common law actions or, potentially, economic rights, which, it argues, is in conformity with Article 6*bis* of the Berne Convention. A U.S. author who wants to claim the protection of his or her moral right of integrity under Article 6*bis* of the Berne Convention can, of course, make a claim under U.S. law like any other U.S. author—on the grounds that the modification of the work is sufficient to create an unauthorized adaptation, for example.[177] However, if the alleged infringement were to occur in France, a U.S. author could claim the protection of his or her integrity right in a French court, where he or she would expect to be treated on par with any French national. By relying on moral rights provisions in French legislation, a U.S. author could expect his or her right of integrity to be upheld by the French court. This interpretation of French law is not only based on French tradition surrounding copyright, but it is also supported by Article 19 of the Berne Convention, which states that "the provisions of this Convention shall not preclude the making of a claim to the benefit of any greater protection which may be granted by legislation in a country of the Union.."[178] Yet, this is more than he or she could expect in the United States. This situation arose in the case of Huston, where the broadcasting of colorized versions of films by the famed U.S. director,

[176] Id. at Art. 23 (emphasis added).

[177] See the well-known U.S. case of *Gilliam v. American Broadcasting Companies*, 538 F.2d 14 (2d Cir. 1976) about the modification of television skits by famed British comedy troupe Monty Python.

[178] See brief discussion in Jane Ginsburg & Edouard Treppoz, International Copyright Law: U.S. and E.U. Perspectives: Text and Cases para 4.1.1 (2015), citing Ricketson & Ginsburg, *supra* note 2.

John Huston, on French television was found to violate the moral rights of the director.[179] In the United States, however, the existing framework for moral rights was inadequate to protect film directors from colorization.[180]

The contrast between France and the United States is extreme; but similar situations can arise in relation to many aspects of moral rights. For example, Canada offers protection for the moral rights of attribution and integrity, but it does not protect an author's right to withdraw his or her work from circulation. French law does; and if a Canadian author were to ask a French court to withdraw his or her work from circulation in France, he or she would be legally entitled to have his or her claim upheld. Once again, the situation is anomalous in the sense that an author would enjoy more rights in a foreign country than in his or her own home country.

Of course, this kind of situation would be routinely experienced by "stateless" people. For example, members of certain Indigenous communities are not granted citizenship by the states controlling the territory where they live.[181] The Berne Convention clearly provides that recognition of copyright depends not on one's country of origin, but on the law of the country where protection is claimed. In these circumstances, the fact that a work has been published, or communicated to the public, in another country should be sufficient to meet the requirements for the subsistence of copyright under the Berne Convention.[182] The Berne Convention also imposes a requirement that non-nationals be treated as nationals within the country of origin of the work.[183]

b. Choice of Law

Where multiple countries are involved in the publication and dissemination of a work, the Berne Convention rules have historically avoided conflicts over choice of law. The rule seems simple: the law of the country where protection is claimed must be applied. Article 5.2 states that "the extent of protection, as well as the means of

[179] *Turner Entertainment*, *supra* note 74.

[180] For a powerful comment on the colorization issue from a film director's perspective, see the short article by Woody Allen, *The Colorization of Films Insults Artists and Society*, New York Times (June 28, 1987), https://www.nytimes.com/1987/06/28/opinion/the-colorization-of-films-insults-artists-and-society.html.

[181] For a summary of the concerns involved, see Human Rights Watch, *Nationality and Statelessness* (n.d.), http://www.hrw.org/campaigns/race/nationality.htm.

[182] *See* Berne Convention, *supra* note 1, at Art. 5(2):

> The enjoyment and the exercise of these rights shall not be subject to any formality; *such enjoyment and such exercise shall be independent of the existence of protection in the country of origin of the work.* Consequently, apart from the provisions of this Convention, the extent of protection, as well as the means of redress afforded to the author to protect his rights, shall be governed exclusively by the laws of the country where protection is claimed [emphasis added].

[183] Id. at Art. 5(3), which states, "(3) Protection in the country of origin is governed by domestic law. *However, when the author is not a national of the country of origin of the work for which he is protected under this Convention, he shall enjoy in that country the same rights as national authors*" (emphasis added).

redress afforded to the author to protect his rights, shall be governed exclusively by the laws of the country where protection is claimed." Once again, this is a practical rule. It avoids at least two potential problems: the highly practical issue of bringing a defendant to justice in his or her own home jurisdiction, as well as the more legalistic concern, though one with strong practical repercussions, that the judges of a given jurisdiction should not be asked to locate, interpret, and apply the laws of a foreign country when deciding the outcome of a copyright case.

But this well-established approach to international copyright problems was questioned in a landmark U.S. judgment—*Itar-Tass v. Russian Kurier*, decided in 1998 by the U.S. Court of Appeals for the Second Circuit.[184] In this case, a number of articles and accompanying graphics were lifted from publications in Russia, to be republished in the Kurier, a Russian-language newspaper circulating in New York. The question of standing to sue was crucial: the case was brought by a press agency, a journalists' union, and the publishers of the original newspapers. Rather than apply the U.S. rule to decide who was entitled to sue, which would simply have involved the assignment of copyright to the employer of the journalists whose articles were reprinted, the Appeals Court felt that it had to take a more nuanced approach to this problem. Accordingly, the Court explored the question of whether the Russian copyright law should be applied to the problem of establishing ownership of copyright.

What was the Court's motivation? A number of possible reasons come to mind—fairness, perhaps a desire to bring greater subtlety to the application of the law in an increasingly global environment for copyright transactions. The Court took a very sensible approach to the awkward issue of interpreting foreign laws: it called upon the opinions of experts. In the *Kurier* litigation, truly elite experts were pitted against one another. Plaintiffs and defendants each called upon leading U.S. scholars of Russian intellectual property laws, Michael Newcity and Peter B. Maggs, to clarify the meaning of the relevant provisions of the Russian Copyright Act for the understanding of the Court.[185]

[184] *Itar-Tass Russian News Agency v. Russian Kurier, Inc.*, 153 F.3d 82 (2d Cir. 1998) (U.S.).

[185] The defendants also called Svetlana Rozina, a drafter of the Russian Copyright Act, while the plaintiffs also called Professor Vratislav Pechota. The dispute centered on whether newspaper publishers had rights in individual articles published in the newspapers—the key to determining whether they would have standing to sue for the republication of those articles in the United States. Russian law of the time maintained that individual journalists retained their copyright in particular articles, while the newspaper enjoyed the rights in the publication of the compilation as a whole. In arguing for the plaintiff, the Court summarized in its judgment:

> The plaintiffs' expert witness at trial was Michael Newcity, coordinator for the Center for Slavic, Eurasian and East European Studies at Duke University and an adjunct member of the faculty at the Duke University Law School. He opined that Article 11(2) gave the newspapers rights to redress copying not only of the publication "as a whole," but also of individual articles. He acknowledged that the reporters retained copyrights in the articles that they authored, but stated that Article 11(2) created a regime of parallel exclusive rights in both the newspaper publisher and the reporter. He rejected the contention that exclusive rights could not exist in two parties, pointing out that co-authors share exclusive rights to their joint work.

A second question then becomes interesting: in taking this approach, was the Court acting in conformity with the rules of the Berne Convention on choice of law? In fact, there are two reasons to think that the Court's approach was in harmony with Berne. First, Article 5.2 is the only section of the Berne Convention dealing with general concerns about choice of law.[186] This article does provide that the law of the state where protection is claimed should apply, but it specifies that it will apply to two issues: "the extent of protection, as well as the means of redress afforded to the author to protect his rights." These cases describe the application of copyright, and remedies for infringement; they do not, however, address the question of subsistence of copyright. To say that the law of the place of infringement applies to the subsistence of copyright, as well, is to extrapolate from what is actually in these words—to apply an extension of the principle to this additional question. One further possible interpretation should be noted: the application of U.S. law principles to decide that Russian law can govern the subsistence of copyright could arguably qualify as an application of the rules of U.S. law to this particular copyright problem.

The situation is further complicated by what has happened on choice of law issues in post-Kurier copyright litigation. In the United States, the *Bridgeman Art Library* case adopted the *Kurier* approach.[187] However, in at least one influential instance, international jurisprudence has taken a perhaps unexpected turn. In 2013, the French *Cour de cassation* considered the case of a U.S. photographer working in Paris for ABC News Intercontinental, a U.S. television news network, from 1993 to 2004.[188] When the photographer was fired for redundancy, he sued

> Newcity offered two considerations in support of his position. First, he cited the predecessor of Article 11(2), Article 485 of the Russian Civil Code of 1964. That provision was similar to Article 11(2), with one change that became the subject of major disagreement among the expert witnesses. Article 485 had given compilers, including newspaper publishers, the right to exploit their works "as a whole." The 1993 revision deleted "as a whole" from the first paragraph of the predecessor of Article 11(2), where it had modified the scope of the compiler's right, and moved the phrase to the second paragraph of revised Article 11(2), where it modifies the reserved right of the authors of articles within a compilation to exploit their works "independently of the publication as a whole." Though Newcity opined that even under Article 485, reprinting of "one or two or three, at most," articles from a newspaper would have constituted infringement of the copyright "as a whole," he rested his reading of Article 11(2) significantly on the fact that the 1993 revision dropped the phrase "as a whole" from the paragraph that specified the publisher's right. This deletion, he contended, eliminated whatever ambiguity might have existed in the first paragraph of Article 485.

[186] It should be noted that the Berne Convention, *supra* note 1, at Art. 14*bis*(2)(a) deals with the specific case of the subsistence of copyright in films, providing that: "Ownership of copyright in a cinematographic work shall be a matter for legislation in the country where protection is claimed." See the discussion of this view, as developed by Paul Torremans, in Phillip Johnson, *Which Law Applies? A Reply to Professor Torremans*, 1(1) J. Intell. Prop. L. Prac. 71, 72 (2005).

[187] *Bridgeman Art Library v. Corel Corp.*, 36 F. Supp. 2d 191 (S.D.N.Y. 1999) (U.S.).

[188] Cour de cassation [Cass.] [supreme court for judicial matters] 1e civ., Apr. 10, 2013, ECLI:FR:CCASS:2013:C100347 (Fr.), https://www.legifrance.gouv.fr/affichJuriJudi.do?oldAction=

his employer, claiming infringement of copyright because his employer had made use of reports and documentaries created during his employment without his authorization. In this case, as in *Kurier*, the application of rules on the subsistence of copyright varies considerably between the United States and France because of the U.S. work-for-hire provisions that would clearly apply to the situation of the photographer: The news network would thereby become the rightful owner of copyright in the work created by the photographer. However, French law recognizes no automatic transfer of copyright from employee to employer. Given the individualistic orientation of French copyright law,[189] it can be said that France has had a long tradition of generosity in applying the principles of French copyright to foreign claimants. Notably, this approach has played out with poignancy in moral rights cases, because of France's extensive recognition of moral rights: in the *Huston* case, a U.S. film director was able to expect recognition for his moral right of integrity in France even though he could lay claim to no such right under U.S. law.[190]

In the 2013 ruling, the French court explicitly addressed the important question of how the terms of Article 5.2 of the Berne Convention should be interpreted. In its view,

> the law of the country where protection is sought governs all questions relating to the exercise and enjoyment of copyright, notably including the question of who is the right holder; that in deciding that the question of who is the right holder evades the Berne Convention to find a basis in the rules of the French law on conflicts, the judges of the lower court violated Article 5.2 of the Berne Convention, together with article 3 of the Civil Code.

This conclusion, of course, is the exact opposite of the approach favored by U.S. courts.

rechJuriJudi&idTexte=JURITEXT000027303750&fastReqId=752968854&fastPos=1. A French law firm offers a brief summary of the case: Beau de Loménie, *The Cour de cassation and the Application of the Berne Convention to the Author of a Work Created Abroad* (May 30, 2013), https://www.bdl-ip.com/en/2013-05-the-cour-de-cassation-and-the-application-of-the-berne-convention-to-the-author-of-a-work-created-abroad. Interestingly, the firm considers the case to be a direct descendant of the 1991 case *Huston*, *supra* note 26, noting,

> ... the very protective position that French Courts adopt towards authors. In fact, such a position is in line with the now old decision of the same Cour de Cassation, this time relating to the moral rights of the author, in the judgment of May 28, 1991, relating to the film by John Huston, Asphalt Jungle, whose colorization was opposed by John Huston's heirs. The Court, in that decision, discounted U.S. law, otherwise applicable, to the benefit of French law, on the grounds that the rules relating to moral rights are rules of public order and therefore it is imperative that they should apply.

[189] *See* Jane C. Ginsburg, *A Tale of Two Copyrights*, 64(5) TULANE L. REV. 991, 1005–1009 (1990).

[190] The case of *Huston v. La Cinq*, *supra* note 26, was ultimately brought in France by Huston's daughter, actor Anjelica Huston, as her father had by then passed away.

c. Most-Favored Nation

Finally, the TRIPs Agreement adds the international trade rule of "most-favored-nation" treatment to the basic principles of copyright protection established by the Berne Convention. The rule means that, generally speaking, any trade privilege granted to one country must be granted to all member countries of the multilateral trading system. The practice could have been in conflict with provisions of the Berne Convention that allow member countries to enter into bilateral copyright agreements in order to improve upon the baseline standards established by the Convention. However, the point is clarified by Article 4 of the TRIPs Agreement, which sets out exceptions to the most-favored-nation rule, including agreements authorized by the Berne Convention to provide that "the treatment accorded be a function not of national treatment but of the treatment accorded in another country."[191] The TRIPs rule therefore does not help to curb bilateralism in the international copyright community.

F. Private Rights, Public Forum: Copyright and Moral Rights in Public International Law

A discussion of the international protection of moral rights would not be complete without due consideration of the fact that the Berne Convention, an international agreement dealing with copyright law, is also part of a broader system of agreements dealing with public international law. As always, when dealing with copyright, private and public interests are enmeshed. This confusion of intermingled interests is also reflected in the overlapping structures of private and public law that deal with copyright at the international level. This interconnectedness has, if anything, been further reinforced by the TRIPs Agreement, which brought intellectual property into the ambit of a newly expanded sphere of private international law, international trade law at the WTO, but did so through the wholesale integration of norms from *public* international law, the Berne Convention, into the new agreement.

In fact, copyright as a whole is present in public international law. Protection for the property interests of authors is also a feature of these provisions. They lie primarily in international human rights conventions, including the Universal Declaration of Human Rights[192] and the International Covenant on Economic

[191] The exception in full reads "granted in accordance with the provisions of the Berne Convention (1971) or the Rome Convention authorizing that the treatment accorded be a function not of national treatment but of the treatment accorded in another country": TRIPS Agreement, *supra* note 52, at Art. 4.

[192] *See* G.A. Res. 217 (III) A, Universal Declaration of Human Rights (Dec. 10, 1948), Art. 27, https://www.un.org/en/about-us/universal-declaration-of-human-rights. These provisions are also discussed in my earlier work, *Copyright and Creative Freedom*: Sundara Rajan, *supra* note 13.

and Social Rights.[193] There are other international agreements where moral rights, at least, might have been included, but where they do not appear: international conventions on cultural property, such as the UNESCO Convention,[194] and the Convention on Biodiversity.[195]

The significance of copyright in international human rights instruments is unclear and, as far as this author is aware, has never been clarified as a matter of interpreting *moral rights*. The closest that any court may have come to doing so is the Delhi High Court, which, in the seminal moral rights case of *Amar Nath Sehgal v. Union of India*,[196] chose to interpret the moral rights of authors in India against the background of India's membership in international conventions on cultural property in order to protect a sculpture by a living artist.[197] But this case did not consider moral rights as a part of the international body of law dealing with human rights, where moral rights are directly referenced.

It is beyond the scope of this study to give fuller consideration to this issue.[198] Suffice it to say that, upon reflection, there is nothing unexpected about finding moral rights in international human rights law. The connection between authors' rights and human rights is deeply significant. The human rights framework captures something essential about moral rights that is absent from commercial and private law contexts. Human rights remind us that there is something fundamental about creativity and culture. As the world grows increasingly technological, this reminder should be welcomed and the connections between these two worlds explored.

G. Conclusion

Moral rights are well established in international copyright law. International copyright agreements have included some form of protection for moral rights since 1928, when Article 6*bis* was first incorporated into the Berne Convention.

But the international copyright regime now confronts a fundamental question: what role should moral rights play in the technological environment?

193 International Covenant on Economic, Social and Cultural Rights, Dec. 16, 1966, 993 U.N.T.S. 3; S. Exec. Doc. D, 95-2 (1978); S. Treaty Doc. No. 95-19; 6 I.L.M. 360 (1967), Art. 15, https://www.ohchr.org/en/instruments-mechanisms/instruments/international-covenant-economic-social-and-cultural-rights.

194 United Nations Educational, Scientific and Cultural Organization (UNESCO) Convention on the Means of Prohibiting and Preventing the Illicit Import, Export, and Transfer of Ownership of Cultural Property, Nov. 14, 1970, 823 U.N.T.S. 231, https://en.unesco.org/about-us/legal-affairs/convention-means-prohibiting-and-preventing-illicit-import-export-and.

195 United Nations Convention on Biological Diversity, May 22, 1992, 1760 U.N.T.S. 79, https://www.cbd.int/convention/text.

196 Sehgal, *supra* note 4.

197 The approach was originally suggested by me in a study of the sculptor's case. *See* Sundara Rajan, *supra* note 4.

198 See the more detailed discussion in Sundara Rajan, *supra* note 13.

The response has been ambivalent, if not incoherent. The TRIPs Agreement excludes moral rights, and yet, the adoption of TRIPs has still coincided with powerful new commitments to moral rights protection undertaken by the member countries. Moral rights have been adopted in a number of jurisdictions and updated in others. A historic number of common law countries has legislated on moral rights.

Secondly, the WIPO Internet Treaties and the Beijing Treaty have expanded moral rights by extending the doctrine to performers. In particular, the WPPT establishes a new moral right for performers in the musical context. Beijing attempts to extend that right to performers in the film context, but the effort falls short. The moral rights in Beijing seem "performative," granting actors rights in Article 5 while simultaneously removing any effectiveness that the rights might have in an odious footnote.

In addition to the new treatment of performers' moral rights, the WCT, which does not include moral rights explicitly, creates a framework for understanding copyright in the technological context that has implications for moral rights and for the understanding of technological copyright as a whole. The WCT effectively fuses moral and economic rights in what was then a new right of "communication to the public," which seems to unite the economic concept of first publication with the moral concept of disclosure. This right is now considered a foundational right in digital copyright law.

The trend of ignoring moral rights, while remaining covertly aware of them, seems characteristic of European copyright harmonization efforts. Notably, the major Directive on copyright that emerged from the DSM reform process of copyright law makes oblique references to moral rights, recognizing their continued operation in national legal environments without, however, attempting to clarify the status of moral rights across the territory of the EU as a whole.[199] This seems like a serious mistake. The Directive tackles a number of key copyright issues in the digital environment, including the harmonization of permitted uses of copyright materials across the region, known as "limitations" and "exceptions" to copyright law. So, for example, if moral rights continue to be enforceable where exceptions to copyright otherwise apply, does this mean that a fair or free use of a copyright work in the EU could still be subject to restrictions because of moral rights? If so, would the nature of the restriction applied to the exception depend on moral rights in the jurisdiction where the claim is made? Would the nature and extent of these limits depend only and entirely on domestic law within that jurisdiction even if there were a transnational dimension to the treatment of the work that forms the basis of the author's objection – such as a parody originating in an EU jurisdiction different from the country of origin of the original work? The failure to address

[199] DSM Directive, *supra* note 16, at Recitals 23 and 37, as discussed *supra* notes 162–67 and accompanying text

moral rights will only serve to limit clarity about the use of works across the region, bringing doubt to what might otherwise have been smooth and even seamless uses of copyright works across the borders of EU states. Harmonized provisions on moral rights across the EU states, notably in relation to copyright exceptions and limitations, could help to create a more practical, refined, and technologically up-to-date framework for the operation of fair and free uses across the EU.

The international framework for moral rights, including their absence from EU copyright reform, leaves a significant gap in international copyright harmonization efforts.

The open-ended approach of Berne to the protection of new technological works allows it to bring them under the copyright umbrella, but the Convention does not help to clarify the details of protection in the technological context. Nor does it answer broader questions about the nature, scope, purpose, and desirability of moral rights in relation to technological creation or address the implications of digital formats and online dissemination for moral rights.

These ambiguities are intensified rather than relieved by TRIPs. TRIPs affirms that technological creation—notably software, but also databases—will not be treated differently from "traditional" copyright works. TRIPs represents continuity rather than change: it is committed to foundational copyright concepts, such as authorship, originality, and fixation, although marketplace realities, public attitudes, and approaches to judicial interpretation in the member countries actually suggest that these concepts may prove to be outmoded, or in need of serious re-imagining, in the technological environment.[200]

If copyright as a whole is to adapt more effectively to technological pressures, the international community needs to address moral rights. At least three fundamental questions could be explored. First, is greater harmonization of moral rights desirable in the technological environment? Secondly, if so, which model, or models, of moral rights should guide those harmonization efforts? Finally, what specific initiatives and/or reforms would be involved at the international level if harmonization of moral rights were pursued?[201] Given the current diversity of moral rights in different countries, even across the EU, it is also worth bearing in mind that harmonization means effectiveness without necessarily achieving standardization.[202]

[200] *See* TRIPS Agreement, *supra* note 52, at Art. 9.2.

[201] It is also worth noting that these might include provisions for how different national and international schemes might (continue to) interact in this area.

[202] Even copyright term remains different in the member countries of Berne, without falling below the Berne requirement of fifty years after the lifetime of the author: compare, e.g., Canada, until 2023, and India with the European Union or the United States. Canada extended copyright term to life of the author plus seventy years as of Dec. 30, 2022, in its Budget Implementation Act, R.S.C. 2022, c. C-19, https://www.parl.ca/legisinfo/en/bill/44-1/c-19. This leads to the rule of the shorter term among Berne member countries: a shorter term of protection in the country of origin of a work will prevail internationally. This is provided for in the Berne Convention, *supra* note 1, at Art. 7(8). *See* Ricketson & Ginsburg, *supra* note 2, at n.191 to ch. 6.

The basic tools for the establishment of an "international moral right" are already available in existing international fora. What is missing is political will. In the world of copyright lobbying and diplomacy, moral rights have long been sidelined by economic rights. However, the loss of a "unitary" vision of copyright law has deprived the law of some of the most powerful ideas and mechanisms supporting its legitimacy and enforceability.

By itself, an international legislative framework will never be enough to harmonize moral rights. Harmonization requires something more—the ability to implement norms, in both their legal and cultural dimensions, across jurisdictions. Here, too, the solutions will need to address long-term problems: deeply ingrained legal biases and, perhaps, deep-seated cultural prejudices. Experience shows that identical laws are not likely to work well in different jurisdictions because their weak connection with the culture of the new country will emphasize their most unattractive qualities. This approach to "harmonization" amounts to a subtle form of coercion; it leads to poor adaptation to the new environment and a chronic inability to respond to its unique needs. In developing countries, the paradoxically outmoded character of reformed laws imported from the West may amount to a new form of legal colonialism.[203]

In terms of its adaptation to new technology, the moral rights concept, like copyright itself, has much further to travel. However, these early steps are, in a sense, "giant" ones. They show that moral rights are not only relevant to the technological environment, but that they may also prove to be pivotal in defining the future shape of copyright law. In a post-digital world, there is every chance that copyright as we now know it will become an increasingly outmoded concept. But the moral right, and all that it represents, could be more important than ever before.[204]

[203] In relation to the example of post-socialist countries, see the comments in Sundara Rajan, *supra* note 13, at 53–59.

[204] In this regard, Hector MacQueen's comments on what was then the proposed Google Book Settlement continue to have a visionary quality: Hector MacQueen, *The Google Book Settlement*, 3 INT'L REV. INDUS. PROP. & COPYRIGHT L. 247, 249 (2009).

4
A Theory in Flux
The Evolution in Progress of Moral Rights

Les lois politiques et civiles de chaque nation ... doivent être tellement propres au peuple pour lequel elles sont faites, que c'est un grand hasard si celles d'une nation peuvent convenir à une autre.

—*Montesquieu*[1]

There is today what Mr. Justice Holmes might have called a far reaching free trade in legal ideas.

—Otto Kahn-Freund[2]

A. **Introduction** 211
B. **Spread of the Doctrine: Moral Rights and the Common Law** 213
1. Canada: A Country in Transition 216
a. A Common-Law Pioneer 217
b. Innovation and Convention: Attribution, Integrity, and Association 222
c. Moral Rights after the Death of the Author 223
d. Opportunities and Limitations: The Visual Arts 223
e. Inalienability and the Canadian Penchant to Waive 226
f. Performers' Moral Rights: An Opportunity Missed 227
g. A Drought in the Courts 230
h. Theoretical Confusion and Its Practical Effects: Monism vs. Dualism 230
i. Conclusions 235
2. The United States: American Exceptionalism 236
a. Moral Rights and the Berne Convention: Chronic Dissatisfaction 237
i. From *Shostakovich* to *Dastar*: The Moral Rights Landscape in the United States 240
ii. Better to Be Foreign: National Treatment as a Way Out? 246

[1] "The political and civil laws of each nation ... must be so fitting for the people for whom they were made that it is only by a great chance that those of one country can be suitable for another": MONTESQUIEU, DE L'ESPRIT DES LOIS, BOOK I ch. 3, 32 ("*Des lois positives*") (1758). An electronic version of the 1758 text is made available by the University of Québec à Chicoutimi, Les classiques des scences sociales, as MONTESQUIEU, DE L'ESPRIT DES LOIS (Laurent Versini, ed., 1995) (1758), http://classiques.uqac.ca/classiques/montesquieu/de_esprit_des_lois/partie_1/de_esprit_des_lois_1.html; an English translation by Phillip Stewart is also available at Centre nationale de la recherche (CNRS), *Montesquieu, Unité Mixte de Recherche 5317, CNRS—1.3 On individual laws* (n.d.), http://montesquieu.ens-lyon.fr/spip.php?article2587. All websites cited in this chapter were last visited on Oct. 26, 2024.

[2] *See* Otto Kahn-Freund, *Uses and Misuses of Comparative Law*, 37(1) MOD. L. REV. 1, 10 (1974), https://www.jstor.org/stable/1094713 (referring to the dissent of Justice Oliver Wendell Holmes in *Abrams v. United States*, 250 U.S. 616, 630 (1919) (U.S.)).

b. The Word on the Street: Works of "Recognized Stature" and the *5Pointz* Case 249
c. Beyond Private Law: The Preservation of Cultural Heritage 251
i. Art Preservation: The California Art Preservation Act, the DNA of the Visual Artists' Rights Act 1990 251
ii. Film Preservation: Indirect Moral Rights 253
iii. Music Modernization: Attribution by the Back Door 253
iv. Landmarks: Public Art, Public Action 254
d. Conclusions 254
3. Australia and a Moral Right in Indigenous Culture 256
4. New Zealand: Personhood for Rivers and Mountains—A New Form of Moral Rights? 262

C. Growth of the Doctrine: Moral Rights in Developing Countries 265
1. India and Other British Colonies: Common Law, or Not? 269
2. Moral Rights and the Protection of Culture: Indian Copyright Law 271
a. The Evolution of Moral Rights in the Indian Copyright Act 271
i. The 1957 Act: The Birth of Authors' "Special Rights" 271
ii. The 1994 Act: Back to Berne 273
iii. The Copyright Amendments of 2012: Perpetual Protection Restored 275
iv. Scope of the Attribution Right 276
b. Performers, Producers, and Bollywood: Moral Rights in Film 278
c. Authors' and Artists' Resale Right 279
d. Independence from Economic Rights 279
e. Remedies 280
f. Judicial Chivalry: The Practical Dynamics of India's Moral Rights 280
g. *Amar Nath Sehgal*: Duties of the Government 282
i. Interim Ruling: 1992 283
ii. Final Ruling: 2005 285
3. Conclusion 287

D. Moral Rights and "Honor" in a Technological Society: Japan 288

E. Moral Rights and Creative Freedom: Post-Socialist Countries 293
1. Historical Context: Socialism, Russia, and Post-Socialist Countries 298
2. Moral Rights in Transition: The 1991 USSR Fundamentals of Civil Legislation 302
a. Publication and Use 302
b. Authorship and Name 303
c. Integrity as Inviolability 303
d. Inalienability and Inheritance 304
e. Duration 304
f. Performers 304
3. International Influence: The Russian Copyright Act of 1993 305
a. Dualism 306
b. Duration of Protection: Perpetual Moral Rights and the Question of Inheritance 307
c. Moral Rights in the Public Domain: *Domaine public payant* 308
d. Reputation vs. Integrity 309
e. Performers' Moral Rights 310
f. *Droit de suite* for the Visual Arts 311
g. Disclosure in the Post-Socialist Context 311
4. Programmers' Moral Rights: The Law on Computer Programs and Databases and the Recognition of Scientists 312
5. Return to the Future: The 2008 Civil Code Provisions on Copyright 313
a. Moral Rights in the Civil Code: General Provisions 316
b. General Principles 317
c. Copyright 319
i. Moral Rights Defined 319
ii. Special Features 321
iii. Moral Rights vs. Exclusive Rights 322
iv. Moral Rights and Technology 322
v. Fair Use and Parody 323
vi. Visual Art 323
d. Neighboring Rights 324
e. Patents 324
6. Improvements to Moral Rights in Russia until the War in Ukraine 324
7. A New Moral Right in Russian Law: The Renewal of Copyright Terms for Rehabilitated Authors 326
8. Conclusion 328

F. Conclusion: The Modern Doctrine 330

A. Introduction

A glance at the world's copyright systems reveals a surprising fact: moral rights are among the most widely accepted aspects of copyright law today. Countries from Mali to Bulgaria, Armenia to Tunisia, all include provisions on moral rights in their copyright laws.[3] Societies at all levels of development, and representing diverse cultures, recognize the moral right of the author.

In many cases, moral rights in new jurisdictions also take a refreshingly new approach to the law. Moral rights are not limited to the scope of protection under French or German law. Instead, international approaches expand the theory and practice of moral rights. Moral rights metamorphose into cultural rights, communal rights, national rights. Neither the rhetoric of Romanticism nor the weight of Western European tradition has limited the imagination for moral rights beyond Europe's borders.

New jurisdictions for moral rights have effectively been created by three historical movements: colonialism, decolonization, and the end of Soviet Communism. Each of these movements has brought its own color to the treatment of moral rights in the countries concerned.

The colonial era saw the preferences and prejudices of European powers exported to their colonies. To different degrees, the United States, Canada, Australia, New Zealand, and Ireland all absorbed and perpetuated the anti-moral rights bias born in England. And the common law of moral rights was also subject to new pressures in these environments. Sometimes, further restrictions were established. In Canada, extreme caution has led to a muddying of the doctrine, while in the United States, tension over moral rights has even led to arguments for a differential regime that would treat foreigners *more* favorably than U.S. citizens on U.S. soil—a perversion of the sacrosanct principle of national treatment.[4] At the same time,

[3] *See, e.g.*, arts. 15–17 ("Author's Non-Economic Rights") and 75 (performing artist's "Non-Economic Rights") of Bulgaria's Copyright and Neighbouring Rights Act, 1993, https://wipolex-res.wipo.int/edocs/lexdocs/laws/en/bg/bg027en.pdf; arts. 12 ("Moral Non-Economic Rights of the Author"), 26 (duration), and 44 ("Moral Non-Economic Rights of the Performer") of the Law of the Republic of Armenia on Copyright and Related Rights, 2006, https://old.aipa.am/en/CopyrightLaw.

[4] National treatment has been a cornerstone of international copyright relations from the beginning: the Berne Convention codifies it in Art. 5; and the Agreement on Trade-Related Aspects of Intellectual Property Rights (TRIPS Agreement) also does so in Art. 3. *See* International Convention for the Protection of Literary and Artistic Works, adopted at Berne on Sept. 9, 1886, completed at Paris on May 4, 1896, revised at Berlin on Nov. 13, 1908, completed at Berne on Mar. 20, 1914, revised at Rome on June 2, 1928, at Brussels on June 26, 1948, at Stockholm on July 14, 1967, and at Paris on July 24, 1971, and amended on Sept. 28, 1979, S. Treaty Doc. No. 99-27 (1986), https://www.wipo.int/treaties/en/ip/berne (also available in a useful format at the Legal Information Institute, Cornell University Law School, https://www.law.cornell.edu/treaties/berne); Agreement on Trade-Related Aspects of Intellectual Property Rights, opened for signature Apr. 15, 1994, entered into force Jan. 1, 1995, Annex 1C to Marrakesh Agreement Establishing the World Trade Organization, 1869 U.N.T.S. 299, 33 I.L.M. 1197 (1994), https://www.wto.org/english/docs_e/legal_e/27-trips_01_e.htm. On the U.S. twist, parallel arguments were made, ironically, when in 1976 the Soviet Union contemplated joining the Universal Copyright Convention, Sept. 6, 1952, as revised at Paris, July 24, 1971, entered into force July 10, 1974, 943 U.N.T.S. 178 (UCC), https://www.wipo.int/wipolex/en/treaties/details/

the cultural diversity of the colonies has led to the recognition of different needs and new opportunities to test moral rights doctrine. Among the most interesting of these, Australia has explored the possibility of legislating a moral right for Aboriginal culture.[5] While an initial proposal made in 2004 was not successful, it seems likely that this area will be revisited in the light of current developments on both equity and the environment.[6] New Zealand has seen the development of a surprising new legal doctrine that recognizes the unique relationship between Indigenous peoples, the environment, and their cultural and intellectual "property" by assigning legal personhood to features of the natural environment including rivers[7] and mountains.[8] This approach has been taken in other countries, including Canada and, for a time, India, which have also assigned legal personhood to rivers, though India has since withdrawn this status from the Ganges. [9]

205. *See* Mira T. Sundara Rajan, Copyright and Creative Freedom: A Study of Post-Socialist Law Reform 102–107 (2006); *see also* Michael A. Newcity, Copyright Law in the Soviet Union 152–57 (1978).

[5] Australia's proposal for an "Indigenous communal moral right" is discussed in detail, *infra* notes 193–208 and accompanying text. In Canada, Indigenous peoples have become interested in asserting intellectual property rights to protect their traditional knowledge in the form of copyright and trademark. This issue has been recognized as a priority in Canadian copyright reform, little progress has been made as yet. For an overview of concerns, *see* Mira T. Sundara Rajan, *Intellectual Property and Aboriginal Peoples: Conflict or Compromise?* (Jan. 1, 2008), https://papers.ssrn.com/sol3/papers.cfm?abstract_id=1809606.

[6] Indeed, the proposal was to be reintroduced, but that has not yet happened. Australia has felt the environmental crisis more strongly than most countries—notably, during the fires of 2020. Aboriginal traditions of environmental stewardship provide one more, powerful reason to explore the relevance of moral rights for Aboriginal culture in Australia. *See, e.g., Australia Bushfires May Have Caused Global Climate Phenomenon La Niña*, Mongabay Haze Beat (May 11, 2023), https://news.mongabay.com/2023/05/australia-bushfires-may-have-caused-global-climate-phenomenon-la-nina-study.

[7] *See, e.g.*, Kate Evans, *The New Zealand River That Became a Legal Person*, BBC News (Mar.20, 2020), https://www.bbc.com/travel/article/20200319-the-new-zealand-river-that-became-a-legal-person. On the revocation of the Ganges' status, see Riverine Rights—The Currents and Consequences of Legal Innovations on The Rights of Rivers, *India: The Ganges and Yamuna Rivers* (n.d.)[reviewing Indian case law from 2017], https://uni.oslomet.no/riverrights/india/. The case of the Ganges receives a more detailed exploration in Sudipta Sen, *Of Holy Rivers and Human Rights: Protecting the Ganges by Law* (Apr. 25, 2019), https://yalebooks.yale.edu/2019/04/25/of-holy-rivers-and-human-rights-protecting-the-ganges-by-law. Examples in Australia and India, as well as New Zealand, are discussed in Erin L. O'Donnell & Julia Talbot-Jones, *Creating Legal Rights for Rivers: Lessons from Australia, New Zealand, and India*, 23(1) JSTOR (2018), https://www.jstor.org/stable/26799037. For a thought-provoking commentary with a focus on Bangladesh, see Naveeda Khan, *Legal Personhood of Rivers and the Failure of Imagination* (Mar. 4, 2023), https://dukeupress.wordpress.com/2023/03/22/legal-personhood-of-rivers-and-the-failure-of-imagination-a-world-water-day-guest-post-by-naveeda-khan/. This issue is discussed in more detail later in the chapter: *see infra* notes 209–12 and accompanying text.

[8] *See, e.g.*, Eleanor Ainge Roy, *New Zealand Gives Mount Taranaki Same Legal Rights as a Person*, The Guardian (Dec. 22, 2017), https://www.theguardian.com/world/2017/dec/22/new-zealand-gives-mount-taranaki-same-legal-rights-as-a-person (accompanied by a striking photograph of the mountain by David Frampton of the Associated Press).

[9] India is discussed further in the following sections; on Canada, see Elizabeth Benner, *This Pristine Canadian River Has Legal Personhood, A New Approach to Conserving Nature*, CBC (Feb. 1, 2024), https://www.cbc.ca/documentaries/the-nature-of-things/this-pristine-canadian-river-has-legal-personhood-a-new-approach-to-conserving-nature-1.7100728.

If a single factor can be held responsible for the expansion of moral rights in the post-Second World War era, it is probably decolonization. The end of the colonial era brought legislative independence to a majority of the world's population and encouraged new directions in cultural policy. The mood was one of optimism and urgency—the goal, to rebuild self-esteem and to restore prestige to downtrodden cultures.[10] For these countries, moral rights were linked to the issue of cultural preservation—indeed, cultural survival in the post-colonial era. The moral right of the author was one instrument in a larger cause, and as such, it was subject to much experimentation and manipulation with the underlying objectives in mind.

Finally, the fall of the Berlin Wall reopened the gates of communication between Western and Eastern Europe after a half-century of hostility. For many ex-socialist jurisdictions, moral rights signified a return to pre-Soviet culture as well as law. By an interesting paradox, Russia counts itself among these examples. Its approach to authors' rights offers useful ways of thinking about the relationship between authorship and the rehabilitation of culture after a devastating experience of self-abuse.

Taken together, these developments suggest that the theory and practice of moral rights have reached new dimensions in the twenty-first century. A consideration of moral rights in the international community at large not only shows how they have evolved in response to social change throughout the twentieth century. It also proves the flexibility and malleability of the doctrine, features that point to its continued relevance in the technological environment.

B. Spread of the Doctrine: Moral Rights and the Common Law

British legal history reveals that common-law judges were well aware of moral rights. The doctrine was brilliantly articulated by Lord Mansfield in the path-breaking case of *Millar v. Taylor*.[11] However, moral rights were subsequently rejected by the courts due to concerns about the recognition of a possible "common law" copyright, the context in which moral rights were raised, and the possibility that recognizing such a right might overpower Britain's nascent framework for freedom of speech.[12]

When moral rights found their way into the common law at last, it was through membership in international copyright conventions. In particular, as the previous chapters have already described in detail,[13] Article 6*bis* of the Berne Convention for

10 *See generally* Claude Masouyé, *Décolonisation, indépendance et droit d'auteur*, 36 RIDA 85 (1962).

11 *Millar v. Taylor* (1769) 4 Burr. 2303, 98 Eng. Rep. 201 (Eng.).

12 This is issue is discussed in detail in Chapter 2, *supra* notes 206, 215–36 and accompanying text.

13 Especially Chapter 3, *supra*, on the International Copyright Framework.

the Protection of Literary and Artistic Works introduced moral rights for the first time in a new Article 6*bis*.[14] This provision was initiated by continental European countries, and moral rights therefore registered in the common-law consciousness as a foreign import.[15] Nevertheless, as a member of the Berne Union,[16] Britain would be required to implement the new provisions in its copyright law.

The bundle of moral rights provided for in the Berne Convention was approached in different ways by the different common-law countries. For the United Kingdom, conformity with Berne was assumed; for the United States, moral rights were one more reason to remain aloof from Berne, whose requirement of "automatic" copyright protection upon the creation of a work was incompatible with the registration-based approach to copyright that it favored.[17] Of all the common-law jurisdictions, only Canada enacted moral rights in its copyright law as a result of Berne membership, for diverse reasons and with mixed results.[18]

Negotiations for the World Trade Organization (WTO), established in 1995, led all of the common-law countries to revisit their approaches to moral rights. The WTO included an Agreement on Trade-Related Aspects of Intellectual Property Rights (TRIPs) as one of its founding agreements.[19] TRIPs dealt with moral rights in an oblique formula, making acceptance of the moral rights in Article 6*bis* a requirement for WTO member countries, while providing that those moral rights

[14] Berne Convention, *supra* note 4. *See also* Art. 6*bis* of the International Convention for the Protection of Literary and Artistic Works, adopted at Berne on Sept. 9, 1886, completed at Paris on May 4, 1896, revised at Berlin on Nov. 13, 1908, completed at Berne on Mar. 20, 1914, revised at Rome on June 2, 1928 (Rome Act, 1928), https://www.keionline.org/wp-content/uploads/1928_Rome_revisions_Berne.pdf (available in French at https://www.wipo.int/wipolex/en/treaties/textdetails/12803).

[15] Ricketson summarizes the discussions surrounding the adoption of Art. 6*bis* at the Rome revision conference of 1928 in SAM RICKETSON, THE BERNE CONVENTION FOR THE PROTECTION OF LITERARY AND ARTISTIC WORKS: 1886–1986 paras. 8.92–8.101 (1987); *see also* id. at paras. 3.28 and 3.31. Adeney also reviews this process in ELIZABETH ADENEY, THE MORAL RIGHTS OF AUTHORS AND PERFORMERS: AN INTERNATIONAL AND COMPARATIVE ANALYSIS para. 103–28 (2006).

[16] The Berne Union refers to the group of member countries of the Berne Convention, *supra* note 4.

[17] In fact, the automatic enjoyment of copyright upon creation of the work was not part of the Berne Convention until the Berlin revision conference of 1908: International Convention for the Protection of Literary and Artistic Works, adopted at Berne on Sept. 9, 1886, completed at Paris on May 4, 1896, revised at Berlin on Nov. 13, 1908 (Berlin Act, 1908). As Ricketson and Ginsburg note,

> The principle of absence of formalities was to be found in the stipulation that the enjoyment and exercise of rights under the Convention were not to be subject to any formality. This was the logical conclusion of a long process of development in which the need for compliance with formalities, both at a national and international level, had been steadily reduced. Even though there were still a number of Union countries, such as the UK, which required formalities such as registration and deposit, they were prepared to accept this change.

See SAM RICKETSON & JANE GINSBURG, INTERNATIONAL COPYRIGHT AND NEIGHBOURING RIGHTS para. 3.12 (footnote omitted) (3d ed., 2022). The original Berne Convention and amendments up to and including the Brussels revision of 1948, are available at https://www.wipo.int/edocs/pubdocs/en/wipo_pub_berne_birpi.

[18] See the brief comments in David Vaver, *Moral Rights Yesterday, Today and Tomorrow*, 7(3) INT'L J. TECH. & L. 270, 275–76 (1999).

[19] TRIPs Agreement, *supra* note 4.

could not be enforced through the newly established trade-dispute settlement mechanism at the WTO.[20]

Why were moral rights not simply excluded from TRIPs? The reason probably has to do with the political background to the WTO. The United States was the single most important motivating force behind the TRIPs system.[21] Although the U.S. copyright system did not recognize moral rights, the United States clearly needed to demonstrate solidarity with Berne principles as part of its larger agenda to establish leadership in the international copyright arena. Credibility demanded it.

Ultimately, the U.S. interest in moral rights since its acceptance of the Berne Convention in 1989, however ambivalent, has had ripple effects throughout the international community. Despite the fact that the TRIPs Agreement provides only partial endorsement for the protection of moral rights as envisioned by Berne, moral rights have been considered with a new seriousness by common-law countries.[22] Britain examined its moral rights scheme and found it deficient, leading to the adoption of moral rights provisions for the first time in 1988.[23] New Zealand has had moral rights since 1994, in a version of the rights that adheres closely to the British model.[24] Australia introduced moral rights protection for the first time in 2001, in complex provisions that are very detailed, but also confusing and extremely limited in practice.[25] In Canada, which made legislative provision for moral rights shortly after the original adoption of Article 6*bis* of the Berne Convention, the Supreme Court has made one controversial ruling interpreting moral rights; law reform initiatives have extended the rights to performers.[26]

[20] *See* TRIPs Agreement, *supra* note 4, at Art. 9.1. Dreyfuss and Lowenfeld discuss the extraordinary significance of uniting intellectual property rights with trade-based enforcement measures at the WTO: Rochelle Cooper Dreyfuss & Andreas F. Lowenfeld, *Two Achievements of the Uruguay Round: Putting TRIPs and Dispute Settlement Together*, 37 Va. J. Int'l L. 275 (1997).

[21] *See generally*)Intellectual Property Rights: Global Consensus, Global Conflict? (R. Michael Gadbaw & Timothy J. Richards eds., 1988).

[22] Unlike other aspects of copyright law, moral rights cannot be enforced through the dispute settlement system of the WTO, and they are therefore not subject to the exercise of trade-based penalties against countries that do not provide adequate recognition or enforcement of the rights.

[23] *See* Report of the Copyright Committee (Cmd 8662, 1952) (Gregory Committee Report).

[24] Copyright Act 1994, ss 94–110 (N.Z.); id. at ss 170A–170I deals with performers' moral rights. As in the United Kingdom, in New Zealand the right of attribution must be asserted by an author (id. at s 96) or performer (id. at s 170C) to be claimed.

[25] *See Copyright Act 1968* (Cth) (Austl.), https://www.legislation.gov.au/Details/C2019C00042; *Copyright Amendment (Moral Rights) Act 2000* (Cth) (Austl.), https://www.legislation.gov.au/Details/C2004A00752.

[26] *See* Copyright Act, R.S.C. 1985, c. C-42, ss. 14.1 (moral rights of authors) and 14.2 (on term of protection for authors), and 17.1 (on performers' moral rights) and 17.2 (on term of protection for performers) (Can.), https://laws-lois.justice.gc.ca/eng/acts/C-42/index.html?wbdisable=false. Section 28.1 establishes a presumption of infringement in the case of "any act or omission that is contrary to any of the moral rights … in the absence of the author's or performer's consent." Section 28.2 protects the integrity right of both authors and performers, and specifies the circumstances in which the moral right of integrity will be infringed. It is worth noting that s. 17.1(1) models the rights for performers on the restrictive scheme for authors' moral rights, while adding the further requirement that performers' claims must be "reasonable in the circumstances." *See also* Mira T. Sundara Rajan, *The "New Listener" and the Virtual Performer: The Need for a New Approach to Performers' Rights*, *in* In the

However, the Canadian scheme can be criticized on a number of grounds, both practical and theoretical. It is a half-hearted framework that is difficult to understand and (therefore) to use.

In the process of reconsidering moral rights, common-law countries have developed both new restrictions and new practices. Importantly, there is significant variation in their approaches to moral rights. With the progress of years, despite their common heritage, it will become increasingly difficult to identify a unified common-law treatment of moral rights. The starting points are different. At one extreme, Australia's 2001 implementation of moral rights represents a relatively straightforward, monist approach to the rights that is similar to that of Germany except that it includes several exceptions for "reasonable" actions.[27] At one extreme, Australia's 2001 implementation of moral rights represents a straightforward, monist approach to the rights that is very similar to that of Germany. At the other extreme, the United States has only enacted one provision on moral rights per se, the Visual Artists Rights Act of 1990, and its recognition of moral rights is exceptionally limited.[28] The common-law countries now represent distinctive variations on the theme of moral rights that will clearly influence the global operation of the doctrine in the digital context.

1. Canada: A Country in Transition

Canada, legally and otherwise, is a more or less happy combination of French and English traditions. However, the now relatively smooth surface of French–English relations should not obscure the fact that Canadian legal practice is built on the shifting sands of an alliance between two contrasting cultural traditions.[29] In

Public Interest: The Future of Canadian Copyright Law 309 (Michael Geist ed., 2005), https://www.michaelgeist.ca/wp-content/uploads/2021/08/Two_08_Rajan.pdf (pre-dating the adoption of the provisions on performers' moral rights).

[27] As Rita Matulionyte notes, "To my knowledge, a broad 'reasonable use' defense is quite a unique feature of Australian copyright law": Rita Matulionyte, *The (Forgotten) Moral Rights in the Age of AI*, Kluwer Copyright Blog (Feb. 7, 2022), https://copyrightblog.kluweriplaw.com/2022/02/07/the-forgotten-moral-rights-in-the-age-of-ai/. The reasonableness exceptions affect both the rights of attribution and integrity; see, notably, *Copyright Act 1968*, *supra* note 25, at ss 195, 195AA, 195AB, and 195AR (authors' attribution rights), as well as ss 195ABC, 195ABD, 195ABE, and 195AXD (performers' attribution rights); and ss 195AS (authors' integrity right) and 195AXE (performers' integrity right), as well as s 195AT (relating to the destruction of "moveable artistic works," and, generally, to works installed as "affixed to or form[. . .] part of" buildings).

[28] *See* Visual Artist Rights Act (VARA), 17 U.S.C. § 106 (1990), https://www.copyright.gov/title17/92chap1.html#106.

[29] French–English relations in Canada have a turbulent history. Throughout the 1960s, French Canadians saw themselves as a "*peuple colonisé*," who had more in common with developing nations than with the English Canadians with whom they shared a country. The specter of separatism has long hung over political relations between the "two solitudes," as Hugh MacLennan famously called them: Hugh MacLennan, Two Solitudes (2009) (1945). The violent October Crisis of 1970 was informed by this perspective: *see* Louis Fournier, Histoire d'un movement clandestin (1998).

relation to no area of law could the contrast, and potential conflict, be more evident than in relation to moral rights.

It is tempting to think that Canadian law must be more accepting of moral rights because of its shared French and English roots. However, the treatment of moral rights in Canada makes it clear that this is not the case. Indeed, the most recent jurisprudence in this area, the *Théberge* case[30] of 2002, showed the Canadian Supreme Court split between francophone and anglophone judges, who differed on moral rights and, not surprisingly, in their understanding of copyright law as a whole. The francophone judges saw a unity in the Canadian conception of copyright that links Canada not only to the interpretation of moral rights as they are understood in continental European legal systems but also, to the wider, more holistic conception of copyright as an author's right in European law.[31]

Canadian moral rights jurisprudence reveals a shifting history. Early case law evinced a willingness, on the part of English-Canadian judges, to explore French legal tradition. However, as illustrated by the *Théberge* case, deep divisions between French- and English-Canadian jurists ultimately emerged. *Théberge* is a confusing and divisive precedent, but it is the only recent guidance at this level that is available to the Canadian legal community. What does *Théberge* suggest about the future of moral rights in Canada?

a. A Common-Law Pioneer

Canada holds the distinction of being the first common-law country to adopt provisions on moral rights into its copyright law. It did so in 1931, only three years after moral rights were first adopted in the Berne Convention.[32] It is equally significant that moral rights became a part of Canadian law a mere decade after the country's first independent copyright law came into effect, the Canadian Copyright Act of 1921.[33]

But the idea of moral rights in Canadian law goes back further than this. Rights resembling moral rights enjoyed formal recognition even before the

[30] *Théberge v. Galerie d'Art du Petit Champlain Inc.* [2002] 2 S.C.R. 336, 2002 SCC 34 (Can.), https://scc-csc.lexum.com/scc-csc/scc-csc/en/item/1973/index.do.

[31] Indeed, their approach is reminiscent of German monism, albeit with a French accent—reminiscent of the historical moment identified by Strömholm (i.e. Morillot articulating French legal theory based on the interpretation of French cases by German theorists!).

[32] Vaver, *supra* note 18, at 275.

[33] The Copyright Act, S.C. 1921, ch. 24 (Can.). Prior to 1921, copyright in Canada was governed by the British Imperial Copyright Act of 1842, which applied to all British dominions. The Canadian government did try to enact a Canadian copyright law at various points, but the idea received serious consideration only after a British reform led to a new UK and imperial Copyright Act in 1911. The Canadian Copyright Act of 1921 was, in part, a reaction to taxes imposed on U.S. books by British legislation; Canadian legislation enacted for this purpose also created a tax on U.S. imports, but it was far less than the tax collected by the British. The reason for taxation of U.S. products was the flourishing U.S. practice of reprinting copyright-protected works from other jurisdictions—an industry norm that was limited only by bilateral conventions on copyright initiated by the United States, since the United States was not a party to the Berne Convention of 1886.

legislative amendments of 1931, but they were not in the Copyright Act. Instead, the Canadian Criminal Code provisions of 1915 included recognition for attribution and integrity.[34] Still earlier, a doctrine of moral rights had been recognized by the Supreme Court of Canada. In the 1911 case of *Morang v. Le Sueuer,* the author of an unorthodox biography of an important politician for a "Makers of Canada" series published by Morang faced the confiscation of his manuscript by the publishers, who were unhappy with the unflattering light in which he painted his subject.[35] The Court held, 2–1, that the manuscript should be returned to the author. Chief Justice Fitzpatrick commented, "[a]fter the author has parted with his pecuniary interest in the manuscript, he retains a species of personal or moral right in the product of his brain."[36] Moreover, in reaching its decision, the court deliberately turned to French legal authorities, citing "the absence of English authorities on the subject" in contrast to "the French books which treat at great length of such contracts as we are now considering."[37]

Which moral rights, exactly, were violated in the *Morang* case? The Court appears to recognize a general "moral right" not to be dispossessed of one's own work, and it is an interesting question whether this could be interpreted as implicit in the right of disclosure. But the Court also makes reference to the author's hoped-for gain from publication, pointing out that "the chief consideration which moved him to write the manuscript... is *the benefit to his literary reputation* resulting from publication."[38] It is interesting that the court focuses on the author's reputational gain as his primary motivation. Reputation is one of the core elements constituting the modern right of integrity, but, occasionally, it may also be recognized as a moral right in its stead.[39] The facts in *Morang* raise the question of whether the

[34] David Vaver, Copyright Law 159 (2000). Vaver is right to note this landmark: although the provisions were not in the Copyright Act, codification in the Criminal Code shows that these rights had already achieved significant acceptance. In the common-law context, formal recognition in criminal legislation certainly represents something beyond the informal recognition of a tort. Given the current emphasis on criminalizing copyright infringement, it is interesting to note that the idea is not a new one; indeed, other laws of the world have called infringement a criminal offense for even longer. See, e.g., the discussion of the Russian Imperial Copyright Law of 1911, *infra* note 370, in Sundara Rajan, Copyright and Creative Freedom, *supra* note 4, ch. IV ("Copyright and Tyranny"), at 82–85.

[35] *Morang & Co. v. LeSueur*, 45 S.C.R. 95, 98 (1911) (Can.), https://decisions.scc-csc.ca/scc-csc/scc-csc/en/item/2951/index.do.

[36] Id.

[37] Id.

[38] Id. (emphasis added).

[39] For example, arts. 15, 27, and 28 of the Law of the Russian Federation No. 5351-1 of July 9, 1993 on Copyright and Neighboring Rights, as amended, took this approach. This 1993 Law is still available at https://www.wto.org/english/thewto_e/acc_e/rus_e/wtaccrus48_leg_94.pdf, though it has since been overruled by Part IV of the Grazhdanskiĭ Kodeks Rossiĭskoĭ Federatsii [Russian Civil Code] (GK RF), completed in 2006 and in effect since January 1, 2008, available in both Russian and English at https://www.wipo.int/wipolex/en/legislation/details/22547 (in the English version, Pt. IV begins at 379). It should also be noted that reputation was broadly protected under post-Soviet Russian law for its citizens, and this should be seen in the context of a society where attacks on reputation were part of the traditional arsenal of the state's weapons against its own citizens. I have suspended further updates and analysis of Russian law for now (*see also infra* note 339).

failure to publish would qualify as an affront to the author's moral right of integrity by effectively depriving him or her of the right to *establish* or *further develop* a reputation. In the latter context, at least, a violation of the integrity right, or of its narrower manifestation as a right of reputation, seems possible.

Against this background, what were Canada's reasons for enacting moral rights so early? The answer seems simple enough: Canada had signed the Berne Convention and, being a good international citizen, immediately set about enacting provisions to implement its international obligations.[40] The Canadian government was probably influenced by policy considerations, as well—the intensity with which cultural issues are felt in this closest of all neighbors to the United States, as well as its growing commitment to the international human rights framework.[41] Given the *Morang* case, there was clearly a jurisprudential basis for the adoption of statutory moral rights, as well—doctrinal recognition by the Supreme Court, no less.

The language of the Canadian provision adopted in 1931 exactly mirrored the terms of Article 6*bis* of the Berne Convention.[42] However, the formalistic adaptation of the Berne provision into Canadian law led to an awkward and ambiguous result. Which aspects of attribution were protected?[43] Did the right of integrity require a showing of proof of damage to reputation or not?[44] David Vaver points out

[40] The contrast with the present should be duly noted. Canada has been a signatory to the WIPO Internet Treaties since 1997 (the Treaties were themselves finalized only in 1996), but it did not implement them in its domestic law until 2012. During that period, the failure to do so strained United States–Canada relations. Canada is not entirely at fault; the attempts of successive governments to reform Canadian copyright law have met with intense public controversy, and copyright reform has been affected by broader political uncertainty since 2004. For a consideration of the response to the proposed Bill C-60, An Act to amend the Copyright Act, 2005, cl. 29, see Geist, *supra* note 25. On July 20, 2009, the Canadian government, led by the Conservatives, initiated a public consultation process on copyright reform, with a view to introducing new legislation. The proposed Bill C-32 was tabled by the government on June 2, 2010; the Bill expired when Parliament was dissolved, in March 2011, and was revived on September 29, 2011, as Bill C-11. This Bill was adopted into law in 2012 as the Copyright Modernization Act, S.C. 2012, c. 20, https://laws-lois.justice.gc.ca/eng/AnnualStatutes/2012_20/FullText.html.

[41] The instrumental role of Canadian lawyer and professor John Peters Humphrey in preparing the initial draft of the Universal Declaration of Human Rights should be noted: G.A. Res. 217 (III) A, Universal Declaration of Human Rights (Dec. 10, 1948), https://www.un.org/en/about-us/universal-declaration-of-human-rights. At the same time, Canada's domestic approach to human rights—notably, those of Indigenous peoples—continues to fall short of these ideals, in spite of its commitment to achieving them.

[42] *See* David Vaver, *Authors' Moral Rights in Canada*, 14 INT'L REV. INDUS. PROP. & COPYRIGHT L. 329, 341 (1983).

[43] See Vaver's discussion of the aspects of the attribution, or "paternity," right: id. at 352–55.

[44] As subtle a change as the removal of a comma from the Berne Convention phrase in the UK legislation leads to doubt on this fundamental issue. The Canadian section, quoted id. at 341, states that the author may "restrain" "any distortion, mutilation or other modification of the said work that would be prejudicial to his honour or reputation." Prior to the amendments in 1994, the Indian Copyright Act, 1957 provided for moral rights in much the same language as the Canadian Act, but it divided the integrity right in its s. 57 into two parts: the first part provided that "any distortion, mutilation or other modification of the said work" would violate moral rights, *and* "any other action in relation to the said work which would be prejudicial to his honour or reputation" would also do so.

> the folly of transporting virtually verbatim a provision from an international Convention into a domestic statute, without elaborating the provision in the manner intended by the Convention and without adapting it to the existing structure of domestic laws.[45]

In comparison, a subtle ambiguity in the language of the integrity right in the 1988 British provisions—so subtle, that some would say there is no ambiguity at all[46]—has led to judicial questioning of whether or not the British right of integrity depends upon proof of damage to the author's reputation. The issue has received judicial interpretation on two occasions so far. Since the Patents County Court, in 2012, disagreed with the earlier ruling of the High Court, in 2003, the door has, in some sense, been left open enough for further breezes to blow it ajar.[47]

Subsequent amendment of the Canadian law waited a half-century and more. Reform in 1988 brought some clarification to the moral rights of authors, and the Canadian government took the additional step of codifying a right of publicity which protects authors from the commercial association of their works with products in advertising.[48] However, the greater precision of the 1988 provisions on moral rights was achieved at a cost. It is true that ambiguities in the earlier enactment were resolved, but the solutions invariably took the form of explicit restrictions on the exercise of moral rights.

Two noteworthy examples of these new limits occur in relation to the integrity right, and on the question of waivers. As noted above, the drafting of the integrity right in the 1931 amendments created some ambiguity about the need to show proof of damage to the author's reputation. When Canadian copyright law was reviewed by Claude Brunet and A.A. Keyes in 1977, they recommended that proof of

See Mira T. Sundara Rajan, *Moral Rights and the Protection of Cultural Heritage:* Amar Nath Sehgal v. Union of India, 10(1) Int'l J. Cultural Prop. 79, 83–84 (2001), and, for the current provision, Copyright Act, 1957, s. 57 (India), http://copyright.gov.in/Documents/CopyrightRules1957.pdf. The history of the Indian Act is also reviewed by Gudibanda R. Raghavender, *The Origin and Development of a Moral Rights Regime in India*, 14(4) JIPLP 305 (2019), https://doi.org/10.1093/jiplp/jpz006. Vaver's criticism of the integrity right focuses on the question of whether personal reputation, as well as professional reputation, is involved, and he concludes that both are legitimately included within the integrity right: Vaver, *supra* note 42, at 355–60. The critique could apply equally to the Berne Convention itself, which has also enshrined the term "honor," of uncertain legal connotations, in modern copyright law. Vaver also draws attention to the use of the term "restrain," clearly intended to evoke the court's power to grant an injunction: id.

[45] Id. at 330.

[46] *See Confetti Records v. Warner Music UK Ltd* [2003] EWHC 1274 (Ch) (UK).

[47] Id. The case involved Garage music, a sub-genre of hip-hop in the United Kingdom: *Delves-Broughton v. House of Harlot* [2012] EWPCC 29 (UK).

[48] Canadian Copyright Act, *supra* note 25, at s. 28.2(1)(b). Vaver, *supra* note 42, at 331–40, mentions this protection of the conditions in which a work receives public exposure as part of the common law of moral rights in Canada. Accordingly, codification in this case represents a further degree of formalization for a pre-existing right, rather than the creation of a new right in Canadian copyright law. For a useful overview of the changes in 1988, see Jonathan Herman, *Moral Rights and Canadian Copyright Reform: The Impact on Motion Picture Creators*, 20 RDUS 407 (1990).

damage to reputation should not be required under the new Canadian law.[49] The provision was, indeed, clarified, but the new version actually went against their recommendation and, instead, added an explicit requirement of proof of damage to reputation. The right was transformed from, potentially, a pure right of integrity into a limited right of reputation.[50]

In relation to the question of whether moral rights could be waived in Canadian law, the changes of 1988 made waivers fully and comprehensively available to authors.[51] Interestingly, the practical consequence of this approach was to transform waivers into a standard feature of Canadian copyright contracts.[52] The example is an important one: it illustrates one of the ways in which the influence of the law is felt far beyond the confines of the courtroom. The language of the law can fundamentally shape the terms on which industries deal with copyright works. Litigation is only the final and most extreme manifestation by which to measure the effectiveness of legal measures for the protection of moral rights.

As for the level of general clarity, an area where improvement was needed, the drafting of specific provisions was clarified, but a larger problem remained.[53] The issue concerns the structure of the Act. Canadian moral rights are contained in two different parts of the Copyright Act, and it is difficult to piece together the complete jigsaw puzzle of the scheme. The rights are expressed in sections 14 and 28 of the

[49] Andrew A. Keyes & Claude Brunet, Le droit d'auteur au Canada: Propositions pour la révision de la loi (1977), https://publications.gc.ca/site/eng/9.902362/publication.html. At that time, the Ministry of Consumer and Corporate Affairs had an Intellectual Property Bureau. Responsibility for copyright law in Canada is now shared by two ministries, Heritage Canada and Industry Canada. Each ministry also has its own policy arm: Heritage Canada, the Copyright Policy Branch; and Industry Canada, the Intellectual Property Policy Directorate. *See, e.g.*, Government of Canada, *Canadian Intellectual Property Office* (n.d.), https://www.ic.gc.ca/eic/site/cipointernet-internetopic.nsf/eng/wr00904.html. Splitting the development of copyright policy between two ministries with otherwise different portfolios has led to chronic bureaucratic failures and probably constitutes a structural obstacle to effective copyright reform in Canada.

[50] Keyes & Brunet, *supra* note 49, made two types of recommendations on moral rights: the first was a general call for clarification, while the second involved specific proposals for the treatment of moral rights in amended Canadian legislation. For a quick overview of the proposals, see R.J. Roberts, *Copyright in Canada: Proposals for a Revision of the Law: Review by R. J. Roberts*, 4(2) Canadian Public Policy 264 (1978), https://doi.org/10.2307/3549361. The tone of the review is somewhat overwrought. The proposals made by Keyes and Brunet reflect common practices in civil law countries—including damages and an accounting of profits among the remedies available for a moral rights infringement, for example. The damages awarded in a moral rights case are highly discretionary and could be symbolic. For example, the 2007 French case involving Victor Hugo's work resulted in damages of one euro to the plaintiff: *Pierre Hugo v. Editions Plon*, Cour d'appel [CA] [regional court of appeal] Paris, 1e ch., Mar. 31, 2004, 202 RIDA (Oct. 2004), *reversed* Cour de cassation [Cass.] [supreme court for judicial matters] 1e civ., Jan. 30, 2007, Bull. civ. I, No. 125 (Fr.), https://www.legifrance.gouv.fr/juri/id/JURITEXT000017627153. Roberts, *supra*, is also mistaken when he says that the report would allow authors to "force the copyright owner to withdraw from publication the author's work." In fact, the French model underlying this proposal recognizes that withdrawal could entail serious economic consequences for the copyright holder, and the right is accordingly subject to strict limitations.

[51] *See* Canadian Copyright Act, *supra* note 25, at s. 14(4).

[52] At one time, the Writers' Union of Canada advised Canadian authors to refuse to sign publishing contracts that include waivers of moral rights, but this is no longer the case. See the general discussion of waivers and contracts in Canada in Adeney, *supra* note 14, at paras. 12.108–12.123 and 12.150.

[53] Keyes & Brunet, *supra* note 47.

Act, and they are separated from each other by a variety of unrelated provisions. The rationale for doing so appears to be that section 14 defines the rights, while section 28 defines infringement. The placement of the infringement offense in section 28 may reflect the fact that other parts of the Act dealing with the infringement of copyright may be found in the same area of the Act. But these explanations are not fully satisfactory. The provisions in section 28 also serve to define the integrity right and to clarify the definitions of other moral rights which are introduced in the earlier set. In order to make sense, the two sections need to be read together.

In 2012, the Copyright Modernization Act, Canada's implementing legislation for the World Intellectual Property Organization (WIPO) Internet Treaties,[54] introduced moral rights for performers. The Canadian Act reflects the major limitation of the WIPO Performances and Phonograms Treaty, extending protection only to "a performer of a live aural performance or a performance fixed in a sound recording," thereby excluding performances on film. The language of performers' moral rights in section 17.1 (1) mirrors that of authors' moral rights in the Canadian Act, and the opportunity that copyright reform might have offered—to consider, rationalize, and improve the approach to moral rights in the legislation—slipped by unremarked.

b. Innovation and Convention: Attribution, Integrity, and Association

Section 14 of the Copyright Act defines two rights: attribution and integrity. The attribution right is comprehensive and also innovative. It not only affirms the author's right to be "associated with the work ... by name" but also protects the author's right to maintain a pseudonym and to protect any chosen anonymity. However, attribution is greatly constrained by the provision that, in relation to any use of the work, attribution may only be required "where reasonable in the circumstances." The clause is not clarified elsewhere in the act, nor has it been subject to interpretation in the courts.

With regard to integrity, this section only tells us that "The author of a work has, subject to section 28.2, the right to the integrity of the work." For the substance of the integrity right, it is necessary to refer to the latter provision directly.[55] The definition of integrity in section 28.2 exactly parallels Article 6*bis* of the Berne Convention. It states that infringement of the integrity right will occur when the work is "distorted, mutilated or otherwise modified" in such a way as to "prejudice ... the honour or reputation of the author."[56]

[54] *See* Copyright Modernization Act (Can.), *supra* note 38.

[55] It is worth noting that the electronic version of the Act does not correct this inconvenience; there is not even a hyperlink to connect directly between ss 14.1 and 17.1 and 28.2 (or any of the other sections relevant to performers in s. 17.1 (1).

[56] *See* Canadian Copyright Act, *supra* note 25, at s. 28.2(1)(a). The intrinsic vagueness of this expression can be traced to its origins in the Berne Convention, which does not clarify the nature or standard of the proof required. See the interesting comments in Silke von Lewinski, International Copyright Law and Policy para. 5.104 (footnotes omitted) (2008):

But this provision has a second part. It affirms that the author's right of integrity will be infringed if his or her work is "used in association with a product, service, cause or institution" in such a way as to "prejudice the honour or reputation of the author." This right could be considered an aspect of the integrity right, or a third Canadian moral right, known as a right of association. Given the presence of the right of association within a provision defining integrity, the first view seems more accurate. In the Canadian context, the unauthorized use of a work for commercial or endorsement purposes is not only a violation of the author's copyright. Additionally, if the author can show that the association has caused damage to his or her reputation, it may also violate the author's moral right of integrity.

c. Moral Rights after the Death of the Author

After an author's death, [57] the Canadian Copyright Act provides that an author's moral rights may be "specifically bequeathed" to a chosen individual. The framework of the Act establishes a scheme where such a bequest will override other rights of inheritance,[58] which can only be invoked where no specific heir for moral rights has been designated.

d. Opportunities and Limitations: The Visual Arts

It is striking to note that, in one specific case, Canadian law does not require proof of damage to an author's honor or reputation. This will arise where the author is an artist—the creator of a work of visual art, such as painting, sculpture, or engraving. Any "distortion, mutilation or other modification" is "deemed" to be prejudicial to the author's reputation; rather than eliminate the need for proof of damage to reputation, the Canadian Act tells us to infer it. In practice, this means that, in the case of a work of visual art, any modification is, *prima facie*, an infringement of the artist's right of integrity.[59]

It is not entirely clear whether an actual prejudice must be established or whether the threat of a prejudice would be sufficient. There are better reasons for the second option—in particular the wording 'would be prejudicial'. It is also established today that the potential prejudice refers both to any modification and to any derogatory action.

[57] Or *post mortem auctoris* (*pma*)—a (short) form commonly used by international copyright lawyers to discuss the duration of copyright. It may represent an additional layer of mystery to the uninitiated. But see the elegant explanation of the advantages presented in the law by Latin, an "intensely economical" language, in Merike Ristikivi, *Latin: The Common Legal Language of Europe?*, 10 JURIDICA INTERNATIONAL 199, 202 (2005), https://www.juridicainternational.eu/public/pdf/ji_2005_1_199.pdf.

[58] *See* Canadian Copyright Act, *supra* note 25, at s. 17.2(2)(a); as subparagraphs (b) and (c) show, bequest by choice, to a moral rights heir, will receive priority.

[59] But note that, under Canadian law, "modification" will have to be read *ejusdem generis*, in the context of a phrase beginning with "distortion ... [and] mutilation," and it is conceivable that an artist might have to show that the modification is inherently damaging or likely to cause damage to the work. *See* Canadian Copyright Act, *supra* note 25, at s. 28.2 (2).

This provision accomplishes the important result of shifting the burden of proof from artist to audience, owner, or user. The formula by which this is done is not as straightforward as it could be. The right of integrity could have been left open-ended, with no mention of reputation. This would allow the artist to act on any modification of the work that he or she found objectionable—as in many civil law jurisdictions.[60] Regardless, the moral right of integrity is much stronger for visual artists than for others. The special status of visual artists is reminiscent of the U.S. situation, where the Visual Artists Rights Act of 1990 enacted moral rights for this class of artists alone.[61] Why the distinction? It may be justified by the unique nature of an artwork. In contrast to other art forms, there is one—and only one—original work of visual art. In this sense, visual art is quite unlike a book, music, or any other type of copyright work. Damage to an original artwork can never be set right.

But the Canadian law then goes on to impose two unexpected limits on artists' moral rights.[62] The first of these involves the conditions of display: controversially, the circumstances in which an artwork is exhibited will not give rise to a moral rights claim,[63] but this position is one that many artists and curators might find objectionable, particularly in relation to certain types of site specific works. The murals created by Pablo Picasso and Carl Nesjar in Oslo, and subsequently dismounted by the Norwegian government to address damage caused in a terrorist attack, offer a poignant illustration: Jean-Louis Andral, curator of the Picasso museum in Antibes, points out that changing the location of such a work effectively destroys it *as an artwork*, even though it may be physically preserved.[64] This idea is echoed by Gro Nesjar, Carl Nesjar's daughter and an art historian, who emphasizes the public good that the artists wished to serve by the placement of the artworks at the site where they were.[65]

Secondly, the issue of conservation is addressed. The Act provides that "steps taken in good faith to restore or preserve the work" will also be exempted from

[60] *See, e.g.*, Loi 92-597 du 1 juillet 1992 relative au Code de la propriété intellectuelle (partie législative) [Law 92-597 of July 1, 1992, relating to the Intellectual Property Code (Legislative part)], JOURNAL OFFICIEL DE LA RÉPUBLIQUE FRANÇAISE [J.O.] [OFFICIAL GAZETTE OF FRANCE], Feb. 8, 1994 (Code de la propriété intellectuelle), art. L121-1 (Fr.), https://www.legifrance.gouv.fr/codes/texte_lc/LEGITEXT000006069414.

[61] VARA, *supra* note 26.

[62] *See* Canadian Copyright Act, *supra* note 25, at s. 28.2(3).

[63] The "Explanation" to the Indian Copyright Act, *supra* note 42, s. 57 states,

> *Explanation.*—Failure to display a work or to display it to the satisfaction of the author Shall not be deemed to be an infringement of the rights conferred by this section.

[64] For the text of the letter, see Save Oslo's Y-block with mural by Picasso, FACEBOOK (May 31, 2020), https://m.facebook.com/243059203235939/photos/a.601125957429260/610685876473268/?type=3&hx0026;source=57&hx0026;__tn__=EH-R (also in private conversation, June 2020).

[65] *See* Mira T. Sundara Rajan, *Growing up with Picasso: An Interview with Gro Nesjar, Art Historian and Daughter of Carl Nesjar, Picasso's Greatest Collaborator*, WOMAN OF CULTURE PODCAST (Dec. 29, 2023), https://womanofculturepodcast.com/growing-up-with-picasso-an-interview-with-gro-nesjar-art-historian-and-daughter-of-carl-nesjar-picassos-greatest-collaborator.

any infringement claim. This provision clearly aims to avoid discouraging potentially valuable conservation efforts by limiting liability for conservation work that has gone awry. The rationale for exempting the conditions of display from liability seems more arbitrary—a way of limiting the liability of galleries, companies, and perhaps government, for the mistreatment of artworks in their possession.[66]

A further limit is involved in the inability of these provisions to address the copying of artworks—a major shortcoming in the digital environment that is shared by most other treatments of the artist's moral rights. On the face of it, neither section 28.2(1) nor (2) of the Canadian Copyright Act extends to harm caused by the treatment of *copies* of a work. To extend the scope of the Act to harm caused by copying, courts would need to interpret "distorted, mutilated or otherwise modified" to include the act of copying. Such an interpretation is possible under the international understanding of the moral right of integrity, since the language of the Berne Convention may since capture harmful actions beyond direct alterations of the work.[67] It is also worth noting that Canada would be better placed than most other countries to introduce such an innovation because it explicitly prohibits "use [...] in association with a product, service, cause or institution" as a violation of the integrity right.[68] In any case, the relevance of alterations to *copies* of a work would seem to lie primarily in the impact of those changes on the author's honor or reputation. Since this is one the means by which mistreatment of the work may lead to harm to the author's honor or reputation, it may be reasonable to

[66] A similar approach is taken in Indian law; most probably, the goal at that time was to protect the Indian government from liability for damage to artworks that it own. In the context of a developing country, the fear is understandable: the government is a major sponsor and owner of works. However, the importance of the government's cultural role should not fail to attract an obligation to treat the works involved with adequate (or at least "reasonable") care. See the comments of the Delhi High Court in the landmark case of *Sehgal*, *supra* note 56.

[67] This issue is discussed in detail by Ginsburg & Ricketson, *supra* note 17, at paras. 10.33–10.35; the specific question of whether alterations of copies of works could be considered a moral rights violation is dealt with id. at para. 10.35. A traditional approach might reject this view, on the grounds that the original work remains intact and available for "further accurate reproductions or communication of the work," the key issue identified by Ginsburg & Ricketson; but a broader reading is also possible. Much depends on how we interpret the words "in relation to the said work," and in this regard, the history provided by Ginsburg & Ricketson id. at para 10.33 (note omitted) is especially useful:

> As for the word "action", this refers to something other than an actual change or interference with the work itself: the latter are covered by the composite expression "distortion, mutilation or other modification". What is in question here, therefore, is an action "in relation to" the work. It will be recalled that these words were added at the Brussels Revision Conference, where they replaced a proposal in the programme to add the words "utilisations of the work having prejudicial effects". The latter were thought to be too wide, but they did at least have the virtue of being explicit: what was intended to be covered were uses of the work that were prejudicial to the author.

Makeen suggests that this language "offers protection against the use of the work in offensive contexts, i.e. the spirit of the work": Makeen F. Makeen, *Evaluation of Moral Rights Protection in Egypt*, 14(4) JIPLP 278, 280–81 (2019), https://doi.org/10.1093/jiplp/jpz005.

[68] Ginsburg & Ricketson, *supra* note 17. The history of the Berne provision in language seeking to prevent undesirable uses is now reflected in those Canadian provisions: *see* Canadian Copyright Act, *supra* note 25, at s. 28.2(1)(b).

infer that the mistreatment of copies of a work can lead to moral rights violations if they affect the author in this way. After all, as noted by Ginsburg and Ricketson, negotiators intended to address such a situation, albeit in narrow terms, in Article *6bis* of the Berne Convention.[69]

In a case like *Théberge*, which was not brought as a moral rights claim, a further criticism of the decision of the Supreme Court majority is that it is difficult to see *how* the making of copies of the work would have been actionable as a moral rights violation under this section. Would the language of "otherwise modified" really have been sufficient for this case to succeed? This seems unlikely.

e. Inalienability and the Canadian Penchant to Waive

If the framing of moral rights by Canadian legislators seems generally more favorable than the UK approach, the caveat to the success of the endeavor is the treatment of waivers in the Canadian Copyright Act. Canadian law follows the British approach of allowing extensive waivers, but it appears to go even further than British law allows. Indeed, under Canadian law, the only meaningful restrictions on the scope of waivers would appear to be those found in the common-law principles governing the interpretation of contracts. Short of a finding of unconscionable dealings, or waiver under duress, nothing compels an author to retain his or her moral rights or restores them to him or her once they are waived.

In addition to these general concerns, Canadian law specifically includes a most controversial provision on waivers. Article 14.1(4) provides,

> Where a waiver of any moral right is made in favour of an owner or a licensee of copyright, it may be invoked by any person authorized by the owner or licensee to use the work, unless there is an indication to the contrary in the waiver.

In other words, should an author waive moral rights when selling or offering to license the copyright to a publisher, he or she cannot then claim a violation of moral rights by anyone who is subsequently authorized by the *publisher* to use the work. An example helps to understand the implications of this provision. The author of a book signs a contract with a publisher, waiving his moral rights. The publisher authorizes another publisher to produce a chapter of the book as an article in a volume of essays. The author may object to the division of his work into separately published fragments. However, he cannot object to the republication by a third party as a violation of his moral right of integrity. The practical utility of the provision is clear: it allows the publisher to exploit his own rights without any inhibition because of the possible consequences of moral rights. In effect, the provision is a kind of negative assignment—an alienation in fact, if not in name. The author

[69] Ginsburg & Ricketson, *supra* note 17.

agrees to forego his moral rights, but the publisher effectively conveys that protection to any person who acquires the authority to use the work. At the same time, Canadian law specifies that authors cannot assign their moral rights; they can only be inherited upon the author's death.[70] In this sense, moral rights are formally "inalienable"; but can they truly be considered inalienable when they can be waived in favor of a third party with whom the author has no contract?

f. Performers' Moral Rights: An Opportunity Missed

The copyright amendments of 2012 provide for a performer's right of attribution, which, like the author's attribution right, explicitly includes rights to anonymity and to the use of a pseudonym.[71] However, like the corresponding provision on authorial attribution, the Act, once again, imposes a special limitation on attribution, providing that "the right to be associated with the performance as its performer by name" can only be claimed if it is "reasonable in the circumstances." As the authorial provision departs from Article 6*bis* of Berne, the new provision varies from Article 5 of the WIPO Performers and Phonograms Treaty (WPPT), which only allows attribution to be set aside "where omission is dictated by the manner of the use of the performance." The criterion of "reasonable[ness]" seems a much broader one than the specific exception envisioned by the WPPT. It opens up the possibility that various factual circumstances might justify a failure to attribute. From the performer's point of view, this is an important weakness in the scheme.

Performers also enjoy a right of integrity, which has been incorporated into the Canadian Copyright Act by simply inserting the relevant words—"performer," "performer's," and "performer's performance"—into the existing provisions on the integrity right. Accordingly, like the author's moral right of integrity, performers, too, must show prejudice to honor or reputation. Like authors, performers, too, are protected from the use of their performances in commercial "association[s]."

Unsurprisingly, performers' moral rights, like authors' moral rights under the Act, also allow for the comprehensive availability of waivers,[72] and the particularly controversial provision that allows third party licensees to claim the benefit of any moral rights waivers granted in favour of an owner or licensee of the copyright now operates in relation to performers' moral rights as well as authors' rights.[73] In this regard, the 2012 copyright reform represents a true missed opportunity. The Canadian government should have seized the chance to examine the Canadian scheme on waivers with a view to ensuring that these provisions support good policies, particularly in the digital environment.

70 *See* Canadian Copyright Act, *supra* note 25, at ss. 14.1(2) and 14.2(2).
71 The title of this section is that of my article in Geist, *supra* note 25.
72 *See* Canadian Copyright Act, *supra* note 25, at s. 17.1(2).
73 Id. at s. 17.1(4).

Finally, the Act provides much-needed clarification on the duration of a performer's moral rights. It establishes an equivalent term of protection for performers' economic and moral rights,[74] and, like the provisions on authors' moral rights,[75] it sets out the terms for the inheritability of performers' moral rights.[76] While there is little to surprise in the rules on inheritance, which generally treat performers' moral rights as any other form of property belonging to an individual, there is one noteworthy point: performers' moral rights may be "specifically bequeathed" to a chosen individual, and such a bequest will override other rights of inheritance.[77]

The creation of performers' moral rights should be viewed as generally positive, in two senses. First, Canada has joined the ranks of countries that are signatories of the WIPO Internet Treaties, and have chosen to enact performers' moral rights as part of their implementation of the international accords. Notably, both the United Kingdom and Australia, sister common-law jurisdictions, have created moral rights for performers in their copyright laws. Australian implementation, like the Australian framework for moral rights overall, is a model of legislative reform.[78] The UK position, like its general approach to moral rights, is ambiguous, and has been criticized by commentators.[79] Nevertheless, the simple fact of adopting moral rights for performers means that each country, within its respective limits, has signaled its commitment to the international community—to the belief that obligations assumed in the international arena are to be taken seriously by member states. To whatever extent possible, their position helps to enrich international discussions and support better compromises on international copyright issues. Canada has done the right thing by respecting the letter of the law where international copyright matters are concerned.

Secondly, the implementation of moral rights for performers on the same terms governing the protection of authors' moral rights under the Canadian Copyright Act is both a strength and, as discussed earlier, a weakness. Recognizing performers' moral rights emphasizes the equality of performers with authors under Canadian law. The approach confirms that Canada will be at least as serious about performers' moral rights as it is about the moral rights of authors.

But this last point undoubtedly leads to what must be a serious and fundamental critique of the proposed reforms. The implementation of the WIPO Internet Treaties in Canadian law offered a valuable opportunity to reconsider Canadian copyright practice—to examine Canada's approaches to copyright problems and,

[74] Id. at s. 17.2(1).

[75] Id. at s. 14.2(2).

[76] Id. at s. 17.2(2).

[77] Id. at s. 17.2(2)(a); as subparagraphs (b) and (c) show, bequest by choice, to a moral rights heir, will receive priority.

[78] *See Copyright Amendment (Moral Rights) Act 2000* (Austl.), *supra* note 24.

[79] *See, e.g.*, Ilanah Simon Fhima, *The Introduction of Moral Rights for Performer, Part 1* [2006] EIPR 552; Ilanah Simon Fhima, *The Introduction of Moral Rights for Performer, Part 2* [2006] EIPR 600.

perhaps, improve the sophistication of the solutions generated by Canadian law. Unfortunately, where moral rights are concerned, this opportunity appears to have been wasted. Instead, performers' moral rights in Canada are a copy of authors' moral rights; and the flaws and dissatisfactions generated by the treatment of authors are now perpetuated in the new legislative scheme for performers.

Ironically, this problem must have arisen quite naturally. A similar approach was followed by the WPPT in its presentation of performers' moral rights: they closely resemble the moral rights of authors framed in Article 6*bis* of the Berne Convention. No doubt, Canadian drafters took their lead from the practices at WIPO itself. However, the significance of following the Berne approach is rather different—its provisions on authors' moral rights represented a series of compromises established over five decades, and it could be argued that the WPPT had little scope to move beyond the norms established by Berne. On the other hand, the Canadian treatment of moral rights may render them largely unprotected in practice. Persistent difficulties are likely to plague performers' moral interests, much as they have afflicted authors' moral rights over the past eighty years. One of those difficulties remains the relative paucity of case law to clarify the practice of moral rights, which is undoubtedly due, in at least some measure, to the difficulty of suing under these provisions. The Canadian government has missed an opportunity to take a global approach to copyright reform and make moral rights more useful in practice—particularly in the technological context.

When will the opportunity arise again? Perhaps not in the foreseeable future. Nevertheless, two points are worth noting. Subsequent to the implementation of the WIPO Internet Treaties, the Beijing Treaty on Audiovisual Performances has been brought into being but not yet entered into force. Canada is currently not a signatory, but, with the United Kingdom and the United States both having joined Beijing, Canada will almost certainly pursue membership as it gains in popularity. Beijing introduces moral rights for audiovisual performers, but the provisions are limited by an incredibly comprehensive series of exceptions, outlined in the footnote to Article 5. How powerful will Beijing be, and what will it demand of Canada, in terms of law reform, if the country joins? Would this be a likely occasion to consider Canada's moral rights scheme as a whole?

And, finally, will Canada ironically take its cue from the United States? The U.S. Copyright Office recently initiated a study process on moral rights, although that process has not led to any immediate changes of significance.[80] U.S. law lags behind that of Canada; but will an interest in reform in the United States encourage Canada to look at its own law with fresh eyes?

[80] U.S. Copyright Office, Authors, Attribution, and Integrity: Examining Moral Rights in the United States, A Report of the Register of Copyrights (April 2019), https://www.copyright.gov/policy/moralrights/full-report.pdf.

g. A Drought in the Courts

Although litigation is but one measure of the effectiveness of moral rights, the paucity of cases on moral rights in Canada is remarkable. In the entire history of Canada's moral rights provisions to 1988, only one successful case was ever brought.[81] It was the well-known case of Michael Snow, the artist whose sculpture of Canada geese decorating Toronto's Eaton Centre found itself adorned, one fine winter day, with festive ribbons for the Christmas season.[82] Snow argued that this was a violation of his integrity right. A sympathetic court ruled in his favor, issuing an injunction for the immediate removal of the ribbons. The case also established the principle of reliance on expert evidence as a way of proving the requisite damage to reputation in Canada:

> The plaintiff is adamant in his belief that his naturalistic composition has been made to look ridiculous by the addition of ribbons and suggests it is not unlike dangling earrings from the Venus de Milo. While the matter is not undisputed, the plaintiff's opinion is shared by a number of other well respected artists and people knowledgeable in his field.[83]

h. Theoretical Confusion and Its Practical Effects: Monism vs. Dualism

The Canadian Copyright Act defines the duration of authors' moral rights as the minimum required by Berne: it protects them for the same duration as the economic rights enjoyed by the author. Under Canadian law, this duration continues to be the lifetime of the author and fifty years after his or her death—the Berne minimum, which stands in contrast to the norm of life plus seventy years in the European Union and the United States.[84] In this sense, the practice of the Act is

[81] *Snow v. The Eaton Centre Ltd* (1982), 70 C.P.R. (2d) 105 (Can.). *See also* s. 12(7) of the old Canadian Copyright Act (pre-1988). Writing in 1999, David Vaver remarked,

> But decisions speak louder than statutes. No Canadian case on the moral rights provision was reported for nearly half a century, and since then moral rights claims have been upheld only six times. But, on closer analysis, these apparently favourable decisions are more equivocal. Three cases were interlocutory; and, more importantly, of the three that went to trial, two resulted in no damages for the plaintiff because of a failure to prove any decline in honour or reputation as a result of the infringement. Modest damages—less than £1,000—were awarded in the third case for infringement of a photographer's attribution right. Somewhat perversely, claimants have fared better relying on the common or civil law to vindicate moral rights interests.

Vaver, *supra* note 18 (note omitted).

[82] *Snow*, *supra* note 81.

[83] Id. at para. 6 (emphasis added).

[84] *See* Council Directive 93/98/EEC of 29 October 1993 harmonizing the term of protection of copyright and certain related rights, 1993 O.J. (L 290) 9 (Term Directive), https://eur-lex.europa.eu/legal-content/EN/ALL/?uri=CELEX%3A31993L0098; Copyright Act, 17 U.S.C. § 302(a) (U.S.), https://www.copyright.gov/title17/92chap3.html (Ch. 3 deals with copyright duration overall). *See also* the helpful flyer, U.S. Copyright Office, *Duration of Copyright* (Circular No. 15A, 2024), https://www.copyright.gov/circs/circ15a.pdf. The variability of term across Berne countries is still an interesting issue. For example, Indian copyright term is an unusual life plus sixty years, extended to cover Rabindranath Tagore's works in 1992: see the discussion *infra* note 291.

in keeping with the "monist" theory, whereby economic and moral rights are protected for the same duration. The monist theory is additionally in evidence in the Canadian Act, because no formal distinction is made between an infringement of copyright and an infringement of moral rights.[85] In a country whose law is said to be of French origin, it is noteworthy that German theory is favored over the French model.

In Canada, however, the relationship between economic and moral rights is problematic in a much deeper sense. If moral rights and economic rights are seen as two branches of the same tree, the logical possibility of a potential overlap between the two arises. In other words, depending on the facts, an infringement claim could be made on both economic and moral grounds. In a truly monist system, the same facts could give rise to both moral and economic claims. On this theory, it should matter little to Canadian courts whether a claim is framed in terms of economic rights or moral rights. It may matter to the plaintiff, because the nature of the remedies available in the two cases may be different. Moral rights can lead to the practical solutions offered by injunctive relief, while, with, economic rights, the focus is arguably on damages. And, again, in a single case, on a single set of facts, a plaintiff may be entitled to both.

For the French-speaking judges of the Supreme Court, distinguishing between moral and economic claims has not been a major preoccupation. They seem prepared to move seamlessly between the economic and moral dimensions of author's rights. For the English speakers, however, the distinction has demanded clarification. The judges appear to be concerned that a monist approach implies a degree of equality between moral and economic claims that they are unwilling to recognize. In their view, it is not supported by the Act. As a result, in the recent ruling of *Théberge*, a majority of the Canadian Supreme Court affirmed that Canadian law is based on a dualist approach, where moral and economic rights are distinct. In particular, under Canadian law, the hierarchy between the two places economic rights above moral rights. Accordingly, facts that appear to contain the potential for a successful claim on both economic and moral grounds may nevertheless fail to generate a viable claim for the infringement of moral rights. A claim that would succeed as an economic rights claim, if approached as a moral rights issue, may fail.

The reason for this duality, as affirmed by the Supreme Court, is that the nature and standard of proof required for a moral rights infringement in Canada is higher than that required for an infringement of economic rights. The Court takes its cue from the legislation. The key phrase is to be found in "damage to honour or reputation," which appears in section 28.2 of the Copyright Act, as a prerequisite for moral rights claims in relation to all works except for the visual arts. No such evidence of an effect on reputation is required to show a violation of economic

[85] But note that infringement of copyright and of moral rights are dealt with in two separate sections of the Canadian Copyright Act, *supra* note 25, at ss. 27 and 28.1.

rights. On the contrary, any unauthorized action is, by definition, a violation of the author's economic copyright, as specified by section 27(1) of the Act.[86]

A consideration of the facts of *Théberge* illustrates this point and shows how precariously balanced is the majority's reasoning. The case involved paintings by a Canadian painter, Claude Théberge, who authorized a company to make posters and art cards of his work for sale to the public. Unexpectedly, an art gallery purchased the cards and decided to make a further reproduction—this time, as a canvas-backed copy of the original image. The technique used was to lift the ink from the postcard and superimpose it onto the canvas. The card was left blank, and the ink was transferred to the canvas.

Was this a reproduction of the work? The case turned on this detail.

The majority of the Court found that no reproduction of Théberge's work had occurred. Rather, there was merely a transfer of ink from one medium to another. There was no increase in the overall number of copies of the work. The element of multiplication, required to constitute a reproduction, was missing.[87] This statement is somewhat reminiscent of the notion of media neutrality in a digital environment articulated by the Canadian Supreme Court in the 2006 case of *Robertson* v. *Thomson Corp.*,[88] affirming that the conversion of a piece of writing from print to data—newspaper to CD-Rom—would not qualify as a reproduction of the work.

No unauthorized reproduction under section 3(1) had occurred, but, according to the majority, something else was at stake: a potential violation of the artist's moral rights and, in particular, an infringement of the artist's right of integrity under section 28(1) of the Act. The artist himself had alerted the Court to this fact. In his testimony, Théberge affirmed that the canvas-backed reproductions could be confused with his original works, leading to what he considered "a dilution of my work."[89] Owners of Théberge originals might misunderstand the artist's intentions.[90]

However, Justice Binnie, writing for the majority, points out that there is an additional onus of proof that must be satisfied in relation to a moral right.[91] In the case of economic rights, any unauthorized reproduction is a *prima facie* violation of copyright, and this is clearly indicated by the language of the Act.[92] But this is not the case in relation to moral rights. The Act explicitly requires that prejudice to reputation be shown, and Théberge had evidently failed to satisfy this additional

[86] Canadian Copyright Act, *supra* note 25, at s. 27(1): "It is an infringement of copyright for any person to do, without the consent of the owner of the copyright, anything that by this Act only the owner of the copyright has the right to do." Section 3 of the Act lists the acts prohibited by copyright law.

[87] *Théberge*, *supra* note 30, at paras. 42–50.

[88] On the other hand, the republication of a work in an online newspaper, subject to a new format and regular updates, would: *Robertson v. Thomson Corp.* [2006] 2 S.C.R. 363, 2006 SCC 43 (Can.).

[89] *Théberge*, *supra* note 30, at para. 20.

[90] Id. at paras. 17–21 (esp. the statements of M. Théberge himself, reproduced at para. 20).

[91] Id. at para. 17.

[92] *See* Canadian Copyright Act, *supra* note 25, at ss. 27(1) and 3(1).

requirement of proof. Instead, the artist was asserting a moral right in the guise of an economic right. The right, said Justice Binnie, was a *droit de destination*—a right to control the use of the work, one of the moral rights recognized in civilian jurisdictions.[93] A clear distinction is drawn between economic and moral rights, with different standards of proof coming into play in relation to each. This is a dualist theory of copyright—although, in the Canadian context, the application of the term "dualist" is jarring. French dualism implies a higher status for moral rights in copyright's hierarchy. Dualism should lead to protection for moral rights that exceeds the scope of economic rights.[94] In Canada, however, it is just the reverse. Dualism means that moral rights are limited in scope.

The dissent in *Théberge* is instructive. Writing for the minority—all of the Francophone judges of the Court—Justice Gonthier argues that the majority approach is not well founded. Justice Gonthier claims that "[t]he disposition of this case is determined solely by the aspects that derive from the English concept of copyright" and goes on to affirm that "[t]he concepts of moral rights ... are inapplicable to the facts of this case."

According to the dissent, the actions leading to this complaint are in clear violation of the author's copyright. Justice Gonthier emphasizes the shifting meaning of "reproduction" in a digital environment:

> [I]t is clear that multiplication of the number of copies of a work is not an essential element of the act of "reproduc[ing it] ... in any material form whatever." It does not matter that the process which produces a new materialization eliminates another; all that matters is that a new act of fixation occurs. Therefore, what we

[93] Interestingly, it may be more accurate to characterize the "*droit de destination*" as an economic right. In French law, the *droit de destination* is recognized as an aspect of the right of reproduction, and it allows an author to exercise some control over the treatment of a work in circulation by a third party who is neither author nor *exploitant*. The reference to a moral rights aspect seems unusual; it could be considered a follow-on to the right of disclosure by allowing an author some control over the fate of a published work. *See* Pascal Kamina, Film Copyright in the European Union para. 1.97 (2002) (defining the right as "an expression of the right of the author to limit uses of copies of his work (droit de destination)"). Kamina does not mention the moral aspect of the *droit de destination*, but he makes an interesting comment in relation to Belgian law, reformed to include specific aspects of *destination* within its provisions on economic rights: he says that "the theory could still be valid to justify a control over the resale of copies of copyright works or other acts of distribution not covered by the rental and lending rights." This could be interpreted as the (continued) existence of moral aspects of *destination* under Belgian law. Other sources also emphasize the economic nature of the right: *see, e.g.*, Séverine Dussollier, *Le droit de destination :une espèce vouée à la disparition*, Institut de Recherche en Propriété intellectuelle (n.d.), https://www.irpi.fr/revuepi/article.asp?ART_N_ID=251. Another useful overview appears in *Projet de loi relatif au droit d'auteur et aux droits voisins dans la société de l'information, Rapports législatifs* Rapport n° 308 (2005-2006), déposé le 12 avril 2006, https://www.senat.fr/rap/l05-308/l05-3087.html. See also the early work of Professor Pollaud-Dulian: Frédéric Pollaud-Dulian, Le droit de destination: Le sort des exemplaires en droit d'auteur (1989), enthusiastically reviewed at the time by Claude Colombet, *F. Pollaud-Dulian, Le droit de destination. Le sort des exemplaires en droit d'auteur*, 42(3) RIDC 1055 (1990), https://www.persee.fr/doc/ridc_0035-3337_1990_num_42_3_2079.

[94] See the discussion on French dualism in Chapter 2, *infra* notes 93–118 and accompanying text.

> must *count* in order to determine whether a work has been reproduced is not the total number of copies of the work in existence after the rematerialization, *but the number of materializations that occurred over time.*[95]

Nevertheless, the reasoning of the minority does not fail to uphold the distinction between economic and moral rights in the Copyright Act. As Justice Gonthier observes,

> While the intended purposes of those rights overlap in some respects, they are nonetheless completely different legal instruments in terms of both their definition and their scope.[96]

In an interesting afterword to the case, the 2003 *Desputeaux* decision supports the monist idea in Canadian law. The case involved arbitration proceedings and the interesting question of whether copyright lies sufficiently within the ambit of personal rights to fall outside the jurisdiction of arbitrators. The Supreme Court states,

> Parliament has indeed declared that moral rights may not be assigned, but it permits the holders of those rights to waive the exercise of them. The Canadian legislation therefore recognizes the overlap between economic rights and moral rights in the definition of copyright.[97]

Ironically, while the approach seems closely aligned to Justice Gonthier's remarks in *Théberge*, this very paragraph concludes with a reference to Justice Binnie's comments. The different theory on which *Théberge* is based passes unremarked. As Justice Binnie affirms in *Théberge*,

> The [Copyright] Act provides the respondent with both economic and "moral" rights to his work. The distinction between the two types of rights and their respective statutory remedies is crucial.[98]

[95] *Théberge, supra* note 30, at para. 149 (emphasis added).

[96] Id. at para. 117.

[97] *Desputeaux v. Éditions Chouette (1987) Inc.* [2003] 1 S.C.R. 178, 2003 SCC 17, para. 57 (Can.), https://decisions.scc-csc.ca/scc-csc/scc-csc/fr/item/2048/index.do. The Court goes on to say,

> Parliament has indeed declared that moral rights may not be assigned, but it permits the holders of those rights to waive the exercise of them. The Canadian legislation therefore recognizes the overlap between economic rights and moral rights in the definition of copyright. This Court has in fact stressed the importance placed on the economic aspects of copyright in Canada: the Copyright Act deals with copyright primarily as a system designed to organize the economic management of intellectual property, and regards copyright primarily as a mechanism for protecting and transmitting the economic values associated with this type of property and with the use of it. (See *Galerie d'art du Petit Champlain inc. c. Théberge*, 2002 SCC 34 (S.C.C.), at paras. 11–12, per Binnie J.)

[98] *Théberge, supra* note 30, at para. 11.

i. Conclusions

By introducing moral rights into the common-law tradition, Canadian law has played a pioneering role in the spread of the doctrine. Its shared French and English traditions may help to account for the receptiveness of Canadian law to the concept, but the extent of French influence on Canadian copyright law remains doubtful.

Indeed, the relative surge of interest in moral rights, with two cases reaching the Supreme Court in recent years, raises the troubling prospect of a divide between English and French judges. There is confusion about Canada's moral rights framework, and the flexibility of the Francophone bench is mirrored by the strictness of the Anglophones. The status of a precedent such as *Théberge* is uncertain, and the perspective of a more united Court is to be welcomed.

The key to this dilemma may lie in Canada's commitment to human rights. In the context of a deeply entrenched culture of human rights, moral rights have the potential to appeal to Canadian judges. It also seems likely that the public will be willing to accept them as a way of supporting the human rights of Canada's authors and artists. Human rights can ultimately help to define both the potential and the limits of moral rights. In this light, Canada is best understood as a hybrid system, with elements of French and American culture superimposed upon an English base, and animated by a prevailing rhetoric of human rights.[99]

With these considerations in mind, Canadian copyright reform should make the rationalization of Canada's moral rights regime a priority of its larger agenda on the digital society. Canada's scheme as a whole needs re-examination. The criterion of "reasonableness" should be removed from the attribution right. The allowability of partial waivers of moral rights makes sense in the Canadian context, but the provision that authors may waive moral rights in their entirety should be removed from Article 14.1(2). Similarly, the controversial measures that allow a third party to claim the benefit of waiver arrangements between the author and his or her publisher, expressed in Article 14.1(4), should be eliminated. Above all, the introduction of performers' moral rights should not be allowed to mirror the weaknesses of the existing regime for authors. The time for a serious legal commitment to moral rights in Canada has arrived.

[99] For example, Industry Minister Tony Clement remarked that copyright "has an important role to play in our aspirations for an innovative economy": *see Conservatives Seek Support on Copyright*, THE CANADIAN PRESS (May 31, 2010), https://www.cbc.ca/news/conservatives-seek-support-on-copyright-1.889498. As the article notes, the federal government held a series of public sessions across Canada to consult experts and stakeholders on copyright reform. Attendance was, of course, by invitation only.

2. The United States: American Exceptionalism

It is sobering to reflect that the world's most technologically advanced country, with the most *avant-garde* copyright law in the world—the Digital Millennium Copyright Act of 1998 predated the rival Copyright Directive of the European Union by three years[100]—does not protect moral rights in its copyright law. This is not to say that the United States does not recognize the moral interests of authors. On the contrary, the *Shostakovich* case dates from 1948 and suggests that the interests giving rise to moral rights are quite well known in U.S. law.[101] But, as compared to other jurisdictions, the idea of moral rights in the United States is underdeveloped. Even among the common-law countries, the United States is an outlier: the remainder have all enacted moral rights in their copyright laws.[102] In the United States, the Visual Artists Rights Act of 1990 remains the only federal legislation on moral rights.[103]

The possible reasons behind the U.S. position are interesting, and two considerations seem compelling.[104] The first of these lies in a constitutional framework supporting U.S. copyright law. In contrast to other jurisdictions, where copyright might be seen as part of a framework for individual rights or human rights, U.S. copyright law is an engine of the free market—a monopoly that is tolerated only in so far as it "promote[s] the progress of science and useful arts."[105] From an international perspective, a constitutional framework might hold the key to understanding certain aspects of the law as human-rights-based law; but this is clearly not the U.S. approach to the constitutional framework for copyright in the United States. Rather, the limits of copyright have been set by the Constitution; and the acceptance of new measures, such as an extended duration for copyright, has depended on the approval of the U.S. Supreme Court. In the *Eldred* case,[106] a new

[100] Directive 2001/29/EC of the European Parliament and of the Council of 22 May 2001 on the harmonization of certain aspects of copyright and related rights in the information society, 2001 O.J. (L 167) 10 (InfoSoc Directive), https://eur-lex.europa.eu/legal-content/EN/TXT/?uri=celex%3A32001L0029.

[101] *Shostakovich v. Twentieth Century-Fox Film Corp.*, 80 N.Y.S.2d 575 (N.Y. Sup. Ct. 1948), *aff'd*, 87 N.Y.S.2d 430 (N.Y. App. Div. 1949) (U.S.).

[102] All of the developed common-law countries have done so: Canada, the United Kingdom, New Zealand, and Australia. India represents moral rights in a developing country that is also a common-law state. However, the United States is not alone on the question of conformity with the Berne Convention; it also remains questionable whether other common-law countries meet the Berne standard. From the perspective of Berne conformity, legislative reform in this area has met with mixed reviews in the United Kingdom, whose legislation is reflected in the New Zealand provisions. Canada's moral rights legislation dates from 1931, but various practical considerations, including the general and widespread availability of waiver in copyright contracts, throws doubt upon their practical importance. Australia's provisions on moral rights are well drafted and comprehensive, and in this sense Australia is perhaps a model for how to enact moral rights in a common-law system.

[103] VARA, *supra* note 26.

[104] I am indebted to Professor Rochelle Dreyfuss of New York University Law School for drawing attention to these points.

[105] *See* U.S. Const. art. 1, § 1, cl. 8, http://www.law.cornell.edu/constitution.

[106] *Eldred v. Ashcroft*, 239 F.3d 372 (2001), *aff'd*, 537 U.S. 186 (2003) (U.S.).

copyright term found support; but the constitutional tension remains, and it could certainly be seen as relevant to moral rights. In the U.S. discourse surrounding moral rights, they seem to be understood as an extension of copyright principles, and not as a form of recognition for underlying principles of individual or human rights.

A second consideration is cultural. The United States is the home of the digital revolution; it is the heartland of "remix" culture. The passion for engaging with digital information is an integral part of the U.S. cultural scene. Restricting the right to remix does not fit well with the *zeitgeist*. And the understanding of moral rights in U.S. discourse seems to focus on their role in restricting the ability to use works. On the other hand, the role of moral rights in maintaining attribution seems to fit quite well with the public ethos of self-made reputations and the creative commons, but this aspect of moral rights is not well publicized in the United States.

In lieu of copyright law, the United States relies on a combination of consumer protection statutes, common-law torts, and trademark legislation—the Lanham Act[107]—to protect the personal interests of its authors.[108] However, the progressive development of U.S. copyright law since it joined the Berne Convention in 1989 has tended to close off these alternative forms of recognition for moral rights, while the introduction of moral rights legislation becomes politically ever more untenable. In view of these trends, where does the future of U.S. moral rights lie? And, in particular, can the United States really afford to ignore the implications of moral rights for new technology?

a. Moral Rights and the Berne Convention: Chronic Dissatisfaction

When the United States joined the Berne Convention for the Protection of Literary and Artistic Works in 1988, the event was one of immense magnitude for the world of copyright.[109] For the first time, it signified full-fledged U.S. membership in the international copyright community. Structural features had made it difficult for the United States to join Berne and, hoping to find a viable alternative to its isolation, it joined the Universal Copyright Convention (UCC) in 1976. [110] Limited

[107] See the U.S. Trademark Act of 1946 (Lanham Act), Pub. L. No. 79-489, 60 Stat. 427 (1946), codified as amended at 15 U.S.C. §§ 1051–1129 (2000), esp. § 1125 on false designations of origin, https://uscode.house.gov/view.xhtml?path=/prelim@title15/chapter22&edition=prelim.

[108] Of course, the changes made to the U.S. Copyright Act by VARA, *supra* note 26, protect the moral rights of visual artists.

[109] The United States officially became a member of the Berne Convention on November 17, 1988: *see* Berne Notification No. 121 (Nov. 21, 1988), https://www.wipo.int/treaties/en/notifications/berne/treaty_berne_121.htm.

[110] UCC, *supra* note 4. *See* André Kérever, *The Universal Copyright Convention*, The UNESCO Courier (Apr. 20, 2023), https://en.unesco.org/courier/news-views-online/universal-copyright-convention. The genesis of the Convention is discussed in Edward W. Ploman & L. Clark Hamilton, Copyright: Intellectual Property in the Information Age 57–60 (1980). Ploman and Hamilton also comment that the "abolition of all formalities for the establishment of copyright was one of the reasons why many countries, particularly in the Western hemisphere, felt unable to accede to the Berne Convention": id. at 59. Both the United States and the Soviet Union, from 1974, have acceded to this

international acceptance of the UCC made it nothing better than a temporary solution. Indeed, by the 1980s, membership in Berne was perceived as an essential step towards defining a leadership role for the United States in the international copyright arena. Above all, Berne membership was a legal prerequisite to the TRIPs Agreement at the WTO,[111] the leading new copyright agreement of its age. Negotiated by the United States and its trading partners, TRIPs exploited the knowledge of copyright acquired in more than a century of the Berne Convention by requiring member countries of the WTO to adhere to its provisions.[112]

At the time of U.S. accession to Berne, there were at least two glaring inconsistencies between the U.S. copyright system and Berne practices. The two represent related issues. In the first place, the United States had a registration-based system of copyright. The origins of this system lie in the U.S. Constitution, which defines copyright in primarily utilitarian terms—its purpose is to "promote the progress of science and useful arts," and the "limited monopoly" granted to authors and inventors was justified for this reason alone.[113] In contrast, the Berne Convention approaches copyright as a matter of natural rights. It requires automatic protection for authors' works: copyright arises out of the act of creation, and it must be recognized "without formalities."[114] In keeping with this natural rights approach, the Berne Convention also requires that member countries must protect the moral rights of authors. Taken together, these two features of the Berne system could not be reconciled with U.S. copyright tradition.

U.S. accession to the Berne Convention necessarily entailed copyright reform. As far as registration is concerned, the United States has gracefully moved from a registration-based system to one where copyright is now recognized automatically.[115] However, implementation of a commitment to moral rights in U.S. copyright law has proven to be more complicated.

In fact, there are at least three possible routes to achieving this goal: comprehensive legal reform, specialized law reform, and case precedent. The first, and most straightforward, solution would be general reform of the U.S. Copyright Act to include moral rights protection. From a purely legal perspective, this might be the simplest alternative; from a political perspective, however, it has proven to be untenable. Instead, a second approach has been feasible: limited legislative reform

treaty. See the discussion of Soviet accession to the UCC in Sundara Rajan, Copyright and Creative Freedom, *supra* note 4, at 102–107.

111 TRIPs Agreement, *supra* note 4.

112 Dreyfuss & Lowenfeld, *supra* note 19, at 277, assess the combination of trade penalties with intellectual property rights as one of the two most significant achievement of the WTO.

113 *See* U.S. Const. art. 1, § 1, cl. 8, *supra* note 101.

114 *See* Berne Convention, *supra* note 4, at Art. 5(2).

115 But it should be noted that the combination of automatic protection with U.S. mechanisms for the automatic transfer of copyright from individuals to corporations translates into a significant new standard of corporate power in the U.S. copyright law.

leading to the adoption of specialized provisions on moral rights, the Visual Artists Rights Act of 1990, which protects moral rights in works of visual art only.[116]

Is the scheme sufficient? It depends on how we assess it. In the Berne Convention, the treatment of moral rights can be summed up in three statements. First, the interests to be protected are attribution and, to the extent that an author's reputation may be harmed, integrity. Secondly, the rights are to be protected automatically and without the need for any formalities. Rather, they arise directly out of the act of creating a work—a principle that is violated by the UK requirement that an author must assert the right of attribution to enjoy it.[117] It should be noted that the same holds true for copyright as a whole. Indeed, the fundamental right to release one's work to the public has both an economic aspect—the right to authorize first publication of one's work—and a moral dimension—the right of disclosure. Thirdly, at least "some," if not all, moral rights must be protected after the death of the author.[118] The provisions of the Visual Artists Rights Act limit the duration of protection to the lifetime of the author, and, in this sense, they closely resemble personal tort protections, which expire with the death of the affected person.[119]

A key feature of the U.S. regime for moral rights is its complexity. Here, the contrast with the French approach is at its most striking: the French *Code de la propriété intellectuelle* lists and describes the moral rights of the author in a single set of provisions,[120] while U.S. law requires us to search in many places, including in the nebulous sphere of the common law. In order to understand the U.S. scheme, it is necessary to determine how the different aspects of the U.S. legal system relate to one another. Is there any overlap between the different parts of the legal framework? Or does the diversity of legal sources for moral rights in the United States imply that the regime is based on mutually exclusive principles?

The reliance on common-law precedent, in particular, can be problematic. Given the relative novelty of the moral rights concept in U.S. law, U.S. courts seem to have some difficulty in deciding how moral rights can merge with U.S. copyright doctrines. Their uncertainty leads to vagaries of interpretation that look like errors. Indeed, in the wake of the U.S. Supreme Court ruling in the *Dastar* case of 2003, U.S. case precedents on moral rights seem to be becoming more problematic

[116] VARA, *supra* note 26.

[117] Copyright, Designs and Patents Act 1988 (CDPA), c. 48, § 78 (UK), https://www.legislation.gov.uk/ukpga/1988/48/contents.

[118] See the difficult provision in Berne Convention, *supra* note 4, at Art. 6*bis*(2).

[119] But note that VARA seems to continue to recognize a perpetual copyright at U.S. common law in unpublished works. *See* VARA, *supra* note 26, § 106A(2):

> Duration of Rights— ... (2) With respect to works of visual art created before the effective date set forth in section 610(a) of the *Visual Artists Rights Act* of 1990, but title to which has not, as of such effective date, been transferred from the author, the rights conferred by subsection (a) shall be coextensive with, and shall expire at the same time as, the rights conferred by section 106.

[120] In France, moral rights are comprehensively covered in the Code de la propriété intellectuelle, *supra* note 60, at arts. L121-1–L121-9.

with time rather than helping to clarify the harmonization of U.S. copyright practices with the Berne Convention.[121]

Following the ruling of the U.S. Supreme Court in the 2003 case of *Dastar*, the approach appears to be one of strict separation among the different parts of the U.S. legal system dealing with moral rights. The protections of VARA, the Lanham Act, and other torts are parallel lines that run alongside one another and will never meet. Moreover, there appears to be no overlap among the different legal regimes—not because statute prohibits it, but because judicial interpretation chooses to limit the availability of protection in this way. Eligibility for protection under one part of the U.S. legal regime implies limitations on the availability of protections under every other part. In itself, the approach is sound; it promotes a coherent and efficient approach to the law. However, in a situation where precedents on moral rights are not reconciled by an overarching doctrine, the rule eliminates possibilities for recognizing moral rights in U.S. law without allowing any alternative means for their protection.

i. From Shostakovich *to* Dastar: *The Moral Rights Landscape in the United States*

The two cases of *Shostakovich* and *Dastar* represent benchmarks in U.S. copyright protection.[122] *Shostakovich* was the first recognition of the moral rights principle in U.S. law; it saw an open-ended exploration of the idea of moral rights. The *Dastar* case, decided after U.S. membership in the Berne Convention, effectively restricts the scope of moral rights within very narrow limits.

(a) *Shostakovich*: The Integrity of the Public Domain The concept of moral rights has been known in the United States since at least 1948, when the landmark case of *Shostakovich* was decided by a New York court.[123] This classic case in moral rights jurisprudence revolves around the use of music by a number of prominent composers from the Soviet Union in an anti-Soviet film. The film, called *The Iron Curtain*, explored the activities of Soviet spies in Canada.

The facts make for uneasy reading. The case was brought in the United States by the Soviet government, acting "on behalf of" the composers, and not by the composers themselves.[124] As its reason for doing so, the Soviet government offered the argument that the works in question were in the public domain and therefore

[121] *Dastar Corp. v. Twentieth Century-Fox Film Corp.*, 539 U.S. 23 (2003), https://supreme.justia.com/cases/federal/us/539/23.

[122] *Shostakovich, supra* note 97; *Dastar, supra* note 117.

[123] *Shostakovich, supra* note 97.

[124] Referring to the French litigation about this film, William Strauss notes that the plaintiff, French music company Société le Chant du monde, was acting as "assignee" of the composers: William Strauss, *The Moral Right of the Author*, 4(4) Am. J. Comp. L. 506, 534–35 and n.56 (1955). In fact, the French company sold these works under agreement with Soviet record labels, which were, presumably, government-controlled.

depended on the government to intervene for their protection. All of the four composers—Prokofiev, Khachaturian, and Miaskovsky, as well as Shostakovich—were still alive at the time. Soviet copyright protection at that date had just moved from a historic low of twenty-five years from the first publication of the work, touched in legislation of 1925, to re-establishing the principle of copyright protection for the lifetime of the author and fifteen years after his or her death, in 1928.[125] The moral right of integrity enjoyed strong protection in sections 18 and 11 of the Soviet legislation of 1928.[126] Soviet law of this period was in constant transition; but, assuming that the 1928 Act applied to these works, Soviet copyright in the works had not expired.[127] Rather, there was no legal basis for recognizing Soviet copyright in the United States, and, for this reason, the New York court eventually ruled that the works in question were effectively in the public domain in the United States. In fact, in the very year 1948, Shostakovich was denounced in the infamous Zhdanov Decree; his visit to the United States a year later at Stalin's command, as part of a Soviet delegation to the United States, placed him in a most awkward position.[128]

The Soviet government wanted to suppress the film on the grounds that the moral rights of the composers had been violated by the association of their music with political views that were incompatible with their opinions. The case was brought both as a defamation suit and as a claim for the moral right of integrity. Ruling that defamation could not apply to works in the public domain, the U.S. judge was willing to explore the idea that moral rights might be a viable option under U.S. law.

His judgment does not dismiss the idea out of hand. Instead, the judge's reasoning suggests that, in certain cases, a violation of moral rights could be found under U.S. law. The two instances that he identifies are important. In the first case, direct mistreatment of the work could lead to a violation of the right of integrity in the United States.[129] The second point is more controversial: a moral right of integrity could be recognized for the purpose of protecting works in the public domain, bringing to the right of integrity the character of an instrument for protecting valuable cultural heritage from harm.[130]

The obstacles involved in acknowledging these rights are, in his view, too substantial to overcome. In particular, three practical problems arise: the standard of

[125] *See* Sundara Rajan, Copyright and Creative Freedom, *supra* note 4, at 94–97.

[126] Id. at 97.

[127] Id. at 94–97.

[128] *See* Laurel E. Fay, Shostakovich: A Life 171–73 (2000). The decree condemned the works of a number of leading Soviet composers; they were rehabilitated in 1958, after Stalin's death and in the loosening of restrictions on intellectual life known as "the Thaw."

[129] There is an interesting parallel with *Frisby v. BBC* [1967] Ch. 932 (UK), decided on the interpretation of a contractual term. Moral rights were not then part of British copyright legislation, but then neither was the United Kingdom a signatory to the Berne Convention.

[130] This argument was made by the Delhi High Court in the *Sehgal* case, *supra* note 56.

proof to be applied to an integrity claim, the effective balancing of the moral right against other rights and interests, and the nature of the remedies that would be appropriate to a moral rights violation. On the question of standards, he is eloquent—"Is the standard to be good taste, artistic worth, political beliefs, moral concepts or what is it to be?"[131] If such a right were to be recognized in U.S. law, he concludes that it would be so vague as to cause troublesome uncertainties, especially in relation to acceptable evidence and correct standards of proof. As an interesting afterword, the same case brought in France, in 1953, won.[132]

(b) *Dastar*: Limits on Alternate Legal Mechanisms for Moral Rights U.S. membership in the Berne Convention created a new opportunity for the recognition of moral rights in U.S. case law. While the provisions of Berne cannot be used directly in U.S. copyright claims, the principle that domestic law should be interpreted in ways that harmonize with international obligations is well established in U.S. law.[133]

The applicability of this principle to moral rights was tested in the *Dastar* case of 2003. In *Dastar*, a television program about the Second World War used clips from a previous program, but the creators of the original program were not credited. The plaintiffs argued that section 43(a) of the Lanham Act should apply to this dispute.[134] On the face of it, the Lanham Act provision has nothing to do with moral rights: it deals with false advertising. Nevertheless, an analogy can clearly be drawn between a "false designation of origin," as identified by the Lanham Act, and the moral right of attribution.[135] Indeed, a well-known earlier case saw this kind of argument put forward with some success. A severely edited version of television skits by the famed British comedy troupe, Monty Python, was aired in the United States and found to violate the comedians' rights.[136] The Lanham Act protected artists from potential damage to their reputations, at the very least, because of the potential economic consequences of reputational harm. As the Court in *Gilliam* noted,

> American copyright law, as presently written, does not recognize moral rights or provide a cause of action for their violation, since the law seeks to vindicate the economic, rather than the personal, rights of authors. Nevertheless, the economic incentive for artistic and intellectual creation that serves as the foundation

[131] *Shostakovich*, *supra* note 97, at 578.

[132] *Société Le Chant du Monde v. Société Fox Europe and Société Fox Américaine Twentieth Century*, Cour d'appel [CA] [regional court of appeal] Paris, 1e ch., Jan. 13, 1953, D. Jur. 16, 80 (Fr.).

[133] This rule is known as the "Charming Betsy" principle: *see* Graeme W. Austin, *The Berne Convention as a Canon of Construction: Moral Rights after* Dastar, 61 N.Y.U. Ann. Survey of Am. L. 111, 111 (2005).

[134] *See* the Lanham Act, *supra* note 103, § 43(a).

[135] *See* Vaver, *supra* note 18, at 276 (emphasizing "truth-in-marketing" as one acceptable basis for moral rights protection).

[136] *Gilliam v. American Broadcasting Companies*, 538 F.2d 14 (2d Cir. 1976) (U.S.), https://casetext.com/case/gilliam-v-american-broadcasting-companies-inc.

> for American copyright law ... cannot be reconciled with the inability of artists to obtain relief for mutilation or misrepresentation of their work to the public on which the artists are financially dependent. Thus courts have long granted relief for misrepresentation of an artist's work by relying on theories outside the statutory law of copyright, such as contract law .... Although such decisions are clothed in terms of proprietary right in one's creation, they also properly vindicate the author's personal right to prevent the presentation of his work to the public in a distorted form.[137]

However, the *Gilliam* case also succeeded through another device—the notion that the editing of the program was so extreme as to create a "derivative work." Under the usual copyright rules, the making of a derivative work must be authorized by the owner of the copyright in the work. A derivative work prepared against the owner's will simply violates the original copyright. Under U.S. law, the rules surrounding derivative works can successfully accommodate a moral right within the traditional parameters of copyright infringement.

The reasoning is reminiscent of a well-known British case, *Frisby v. BBC*.[138] This case, about the author's moral right of integrity, arose out of a dispute over the deletion of a single line from a radio play broadcast by the BBC.[139] It turned on the interpretation of a license agreement between Frisby and the BBC. The agreement was only partly contained in their contract. Importantly, the contract functioned within the larger context of a "guild agreement" between the Screenwriters' Guild—of which, Frisby was a member—and the BBC, governing the alteration of scripts. Because of these background rules, the license to use the work granted by Frisby to the BBC had to be construed narrowly, limiting the changes that the BBC could make. In *Frisby*, the court decided that the removal of a single line amounted to a significant, "structural alteration" of the work, in contravention of the guild agreement. Accordingly, the court was able to impose limits on what the BBC could do with the work under the terms of the contract.[140] Significantly, the court accepted Frisby's own sense of the gravity of the deletion, a precedent that is interesting in the sense that it favored the author's subjective view of harm to his work—an unusual approach within the British common-law tradition.

As in the *Shostakovich* case, the facts in *Dastar* are unappealing. Indeed, *Dastar* is a case that seems to exemplify the well-known cliché that "hard cases make bad law." *Dastar* involved the re-release of a television program. The original program was based on a memoir of the Second World War, written by then General Dwight

137 Id. at 24 (citations omitted).

138 *Frisby*, *supra* note 125.

139 The line was: "My friend, Silv, said it was safe standing up."

140 *See Robin Ray v. Classic FM Plc* [1998] FSR 622, 641–44 (English HC, Ch. Div.). The scope of a license is generally thought to be much more limited than the rights enjoyed through a transfer of copyright.

D. Eisenhower and entitled *Crusade in Europe*. The program aired in 1949, and the copyright was registered by 20th-Century Fox. The copyright was not renewed by Fox, however, and in 1977, the program entered the public domain. In 1995, Dastar released a video series, entitled "Campaign in Europe," which copied substantially from the earlier program. But, in its marketing for the new program, Dastar mentioned neither Fox nor Eisenhower's original work.

In this scenario, the theory of moral rights tells us that there are two potential claims. The first would involve attribution to the makers of the original program; but, in this case, the original human creators of the program would have standing to sue, not the corporate owners of copyright. In the event, the corporation responsible for commissioning the original program sued; neither the company responsible for its creation nor the human authors behind it were involved. In addition, the attribution rights of the author of the original book could have been raised, but these were not part of the litigation.

At first instance, the claim succeeded on the grounds that the program was re-released under a "false designation of origin." The ruling was made under section 43(a) of the Lanham Act, and, as Graeme W. Austin notes in his insightful commentary, led to an award of damages for "double Dastar's profits, a decision that the U.S. Court of Appeals for the Ninth Circuit affirmed in an unpublished opinion."[141] This decision was subsequently overturned by a unanimous Supreme Court.[142]

The case failed before the U.S. Supreme Court on two grounds. First, the Court was troubled by the prospect of a multiplicity of authors who could potentially claim to be responsible for the true "origins" of the work, making the facts a poor fit with the Lanham Act provisions. From the perspective of moral rights theory, too, the Court's instinctive discomfort with the uncertainty of the work's origin makes sense: it is almost always the human creator behind the work who sues.[143] Secondly, the fact that the work in question had fallen into the public domain presented a difficult obstacle to the recognition of attribution rights. Under U.S. copyright law, the public domain is supposed to be entirely free of access. In contrast to the judgment in *Shostakovich*, the Supreme Court ruminated that recognizing the right of attribution in these circumstances could invalidate the U.S. concept of public domain.[144]

The Court's intuitions on both of these issues seem well founded. Under moral rights theories, the plaintiffs in this case had no right to claim attribution.[145] Similarly, the recognition of moral rights in the public domain implies perpetual

[141] Austin, *supra* note 129, at 118.

[142] The lower court's decision was overturned by a vote of 8–0, "Justice Breyer recused." *See* id. at 119.

[143] The one notable exception might be where moral rights are granted to corporations. See the discussion of Japanese and Korean laws, *infra* notes 318–23 and accompanying text.

[144] *See Dastar*, *supra* note 117, at 37, where Justice Scalia comments that "To hold otherwise would be akin to finding that §43(a) created a species of perpetual patent and copyright, which Congress may not do."

[145] But note the status of corporations under Japanese and Korean law mentioned *supra* note 141.

protection for those rights. The prospect was one that received favorable consideration in *Shostakovich*, and it is certainly possible to imagine a legal regime that would provide moral rights for works in the public domain without establishing their protection for living authors. For example, the tort protections offered to living authors might be sufficient to protect name and reputation. Nevertheless, the idea of recognizing moral rights exclusively in public domain works seems unnatural—at least in the sense that it appears never to have been tried. Even to fulfill a special policy goal, perpetual recognition for moral rights in the public domain seems like a huge step forward for a country that has yet to recognize moral rights in the works of living authors.

Subsequent interpretation of the *Dastar* case may have extended the application of the ruling beyond what the Supreme Court intended. The facts of *Dastar* turned on the issue of public domain; yet, the ruling has been enlarged to apply to works still within the term of copyright protection in the United States. The distinction between works within copyright and works in the public domain is important everywhere, but this boundary seems to be marked with special clarity in the United States. It is therefore questionable to claim that *Dastar* establishes a principle for both.[146]

The case is also presumed to stand for an idea that is controversial in a different sense. It identifies the difficulty of locating a proper "origin" for a work as a practical problem. But subsequent interpretation seems to see this difficulty as insurmountable.[147] On this view, *Dastar* would invalidate all claims for moral rights protection under the Lanham Act provisions on false designations of origin. Accordingly, there could be no recourse to the Lanham Act to vindicate a claim for the moral right of attribution.

This conclusion is disturbing and brings the analysis full circle. The United States does not have moral rights provisions in its Copyright Act. Within the terms of the Berne Convention, it may not need them: Berne requires that moral rights be protected, but it does not specify the manner of doing so. Rather, the Convention recognizes the diversity of the world's legal systems. It embraces the flexibility of different jurisdictions to enact the rights as each sees fit. But enact moral rights they must. If the United States does not have moral rights in its copyright provisions, where can we find them? The *Dastar* case appears to close off two possible sources of law for U.S. moral rights: the Lanham Act provisions on false designations of origin and, more generally—at least temporarily—case precedents. What else remains?

[146] See Austin's insightful comments on this issue: Austin, *supra* note 129, at 103–105.
[147] See the comments id. at 108–109, 110–14.

ii. Better to Be Foreign: National Treatment as a Way Out?

In the wake of *Dastar*, proposals for implementing the Berne Convention in the United States should be reconsidered. The ruling considerably weakens claims that U.S. law is in conformity with the requirements of the Berne Convention for the protection of moral rights. By introducing further restrictions on the ability of plaintiffs to rely on alternate legal mechanisms for the protection of their moral rights, it stirs the smoldering uncertainties surrounding the issue. By limiting the availability of the Lanham Act, in particular, the case ends what could have been an interesting alternative, expressed through commercial law principles, to the cultural model of moral rights found in civil law jurisdictions.

Indeed, with respect to moral rights, the United States could find itself in an anomalous position. National treatment requires that nationals of all member countries of the Berne Convention be treated in a non-discriminatory manner. At the same time, however, the Berne Convention also sets out minimum standards of copyright protection that are supposed to be recognized in all of the member countries. In a landmark 1998 ruling from the U.S. Court of Appeals for the Second Circuit, *Itar-TASS Russian News Agency v. Russian Kurier*, these principles unite in a powerful way.[148]

Russian Kurier explored the meaning of national treatment under the Berne Convention. In this fascinating case, a U.S. court found itself applying Russian law in order to determine whether, and on what basis, plaintiffs from Russia would have a right to claim ownership of the copyright in their works in the territory of the United States.[149] The question was important, because, without standing, the plaintiffs in this case—publishers, the Itar-TASS press agency, and the Russian Union of Journalists—would not be entitled to put forward a claim for infringement of copyright on behalf of the authors of news articles which they had published. The court relied on the principle, drawn from the rules governing conflicts of laws, that the law of the country which has the closest connection to the works should be applied.[150] The resolution of the case showed that U.S. courts will have recourse to foreign law if they feel they need it in order to determine questions of copyright ownership. In this case, fairness may have demanded it; a sense of international obligation because of Berne membership could very well amount to another valid reason to defer to foreign law. Following *Russian Kurier*, where issues of copyright ownership are concerned, a French plaintiff claiming a violation of his or her moral rights on U.S. soil could ask the court to apply French rules; a U.S. plaintiff would have no such recourse.

[148] *Itar-Tass Russian News Agency v. Russian Kurier, Inc.*, 153 F.3d 82 (2d Cir. 1998) (U.S.), https://casetext.com/case/itar-tass-russian-news-v-russian-kurier.

[149] The court was assisted in this daunting undertaking by expert evidence from distinguished U.S. experts on Russian law, including Professors Peter B. Maggs and Michael Newcity.

[150] "[T]he law of the country with the closest relationship to the work will apply to settle the ownership dispute": *Russian Kurier*, *supra* note 144, at 91.

The Court also notes that the distinction between ownership and infringement issues might not always be perfectly clear. It comments,

> The division of issues, for conflicts purposes, between ownership and infringement issues will not always be as easily made as the above discussion implies. If the issue is the relatively straightforward one of which of two contending parties owns a copyright, the issue is unquestionably an ownership issue, and the law of the country with the closest relationship to the work will apply to settle the ownership dispute. But in some cases, including the pending one, the issue is not simply who owns the copyright but also what is the nature of the ownership interest. Yet as a court considers the nature of an ownership interest, there is some risk that it will too readily shift the inquiry over to the issue of whether an alleged copy has infringed the asserted copyright. Whether a copy infringes depends in part on the scope of the interest of the copyright owner. Nevertheless, though the issues are related, the nature of a copyright interest is an issue distinct from the issue of whether the copyright has been infringed . . . The pending case is one that requires consideration not simply of who owns an interest, but, as to the newspapers, the nature of the interest that is owned.[151]

Could the United States be moving towards a moral rights regime that recognizes the moral rights of foreign authors, but not of Americans?[152] This would be a perversion of the concept of national treatment.[153] National treatment is meant not only to protect foreign authors from discrimination throughout the territories of the Berne Convention but also to ensure minimum standards of copyright protection among its members. Granting additional protections to foreign authors cannot be a satisfactory solution to this U.S. problem.[154]

Ironically, this very issue was considered, albeit indirectly, in *Fahmy v. Jay-Z*.[155] In this case, the Ninth Circuit considered whether the use of music by an Egyptian

[151] Id. at 91–92 (citation omitted).

[152] The opposite problem—that Americans may have more rights outside their own country than within it—has already been illustrated in relation to the moral rights of film directors. *See Turner Entertainment v. Huston Heirs*, Cour d'appel [CA] [regional court of appeal] Versailles, chs Réunies, Dec. 19, 1994, 164 RIDA 389 (1995), *on remand from* Cour de cassation [Cass.] [supreme court for judicial matters] 1e civ., May 28, 1991, 149 RIDA 197 (1991) (Fr.).

[153] Makeen F. Makeen makes a similar point in his discussion of Egyptian law:

> The concept of national treatment requires every member of the Berne Union to protect authors of the other member states in the same way it protects its own authors. 33 Accordingly, it dictates that the assimilation of foreign authors must be unconditional. 34 Thus, by subjecting the application of the right of integrity to two different tests, one to cover national authors and another to cover foreign authors, Egyptian law might be in breach of its international obligations under the Berne Convention.

See Makeen, *supra* note 64, at 282.

[154] Austin draws attention to this "solution" to the problem, but, for the reasons discussed herein, it would be a highly unsatisfactory one: Austin, *supra* note 129, at 135–36.

[155] *Fahmy v. Jay-Z*, No. 16-55213 (9th Cir. 2018) (U.S.).

composer by Jay-Z was harmful to the composer's moral right of integrity under Egyptian law. The plaintiff's family wanted to "to stop defendants' extensive, continuing, unauthorised, and (yes) vulgar and unfortunate distortion of plaintiff's work in America." The court made it clear that the claim could not succeed, in view of the unavailability of moral rights under U.S. law to all plaintiffs, whether foreign or American, simply stating,

> [S]ince our federal law does not accord protection of moral rights to American [music] copyright holders ... neither does it recognise Fahmy's claim to moral rights. That Fahmy retains moral rights in Egypt does him no good here.[156]

The composer's claims under Egyptian moral rights legislation were strong, due to the French model of moral rights on which the Egyptian moral right of integrity is based. In fact, the integrity right under Egyptian law is a French-style right, also known as "subjective," which depends only on the author's objections for a finding that the author's moral right of integrity has been violated.[157] But the court emphasized that, in any event, Fahmy could only qualify for injunctive relief under Egyptian law. If he sought to withdraw his work from circulation, the payment of compensation to the publisher would be required. The Court summarizes Article 144 of the Egyptian Copyright Law as follows:

> Where serious reasons arise, the author alone shall have the right to request the court of first instance to prevent putting the work in circulation, withdraw the work from circulation or allow making substantive modification to the work, notwithstanding his disposal of the economic exploitation rights. In such a case, the author shall, within a delay fixed by the court, pay in advance a fair compensation to the person authorised to exercise the economic rights of exploitation, failing which the court decision shall have no effect.[158]

This case affirmed a U.S. tradition of limiting the ability of foreign authors to seek moral rights protection in U.S. courts. It also presents an interesting contrast, and perhaps complement, to the ruling of the Second Circuit in the *Russian Kurier* case, which raised the possibility of applying foreign law from the plaintiffs' jurisdiction in a U.S. court.[159] The result in *Fahmy* seems to emphasize the idea that this flexibility is limited and, above all, that such accommodations will never extend to moral rights.

[156] Id. at 151.

[157] *See* Law No. 354 of 1954 (Law on the Protection of Copyright), June 24, 1954, art. 143(1) (Egypt), reproduced in Makeen, *supra* note 64, at 281.

[158] *Fahmy*, *supra* note 151, at 17.

[159] *Russian Kurier*, *supra* note 144.

b. The Word on the Street: Works of "Recognized Stature" and the *5Pointz* Case

But the story of U.S. moral rights does not end here. The specialized provisions for the moral rights of visual artists enacted in VARA must be given their due. In fact, the only legislation enacted by the United States to implement Article 6*bis* of the Berne Convention is both restrictive and expansive. It flirts with the idea of limiting the scope of moral rights below the Berne standard in relation to artists, as well—but it simultaneously surpasses the Berne standard within its "two inches of ivory."[160]

This paradoxical situation arises when we consider the moral rights of artists protected by VARA. Artists' rights of attribution and integrity are formally protected, and the right of attribution includes protection against false attribution. However, the formulation of the integrity right is incredibly narrow. VARA offers a remedy to artists who have objected to the treatment of their work by allowing them to remove their names from these mutilated versions of their works. This scheme overall is further eviscerated by the provision that employees do not have moral rights under VARA. This accompanies the general work-for-hire rule under U.S. law, which provides that the copyright in a work created by an employee "within the scope of his or her employment" is initially owned, not by the employee, but by the employer.[161] In fact, the question of whether an artwork was created in the course of employment has come up in two cases—*Carter v. Helmsley-Spear*,[162] the first major precedent on VARA, and *Community for Creative Nonviolence v. Reid*, a 1989 ruling from the Supreme Court that still remains the seminal precedent on work for hire.[163]

VARA again performs a paradoxical maneuver by introducing the concept of "intentional" damage. VARA prevents only intentional or possibly "grossly negligent" acts; however, where "intentional" damage occurs, it also appears that there is no requirement of proof of damage to the author's reputation and that harm

160 Paraphrasing Jane Austen on her writing: *see* Zoe Louca-Richards, *Two Inches of Ivory: A New(ish) Jane Austin Acquisition*, English and Drama Blog (July 28, 2020), https://blogs.bl.uk/english-and-drama/2020/07/two-inches-of-ivory-a-newish-jane-austen-acquisition.html.

161 *See* U.S. Copyright Act, *supra* note 80, § 101.

162 In *Carter*, in spite of the work-for-hire doctrine, the court of first instance created a new and controversial "two-tiered showing" relating to "recognized stature" under VARA. *See Carter v. Helmsley-Spear, Inc.*, 861 F. Supp. 303 (S.D.N.Y. 1994) (U.S.), https://law.justia.com/cases/federal/district-courts/FSupp/861/303/2261919:

> Thus, for a work of visual art to be protected under this Section, a plaintiff must make a two-tiered showing: (1) that the visual art in question has "stature," *i.e.* is viewed as meritorious, and (2) that this stature is 'recognized' by art experts, other members of the artistic community, or by some cross-section of society. In making this showing, plaintiffs generally, but not inevitably, will need to call expert witnesses to testify before the trier of fact. [note omitted]

The appeal is *Carter v. Helmsley-Spear, Inc.*, 71 F.3d 77 (1995) (U.S.), https://casetext.com/case/carter-v-helmsley-spear-inc.

163 *Community for Creative Non-Violence v. Reid*, 490 U.S. 730 (1989) (U.S.), https://supreme.justia.com/cases/federal/us/490/730.

to the work is sufficient for a violation. Of course, this goes beyond the Berne standard for the integrity right, but this conclusion seems inescapable in view of the language of the section.[164]

VARA also provides that destroying an artwork in certain circumstances will be a violation of the artist's moral right of integrity.[165] In doing so, it surpasses the standard interpretation of Article 6*bis* of the Berne Convention, which is generally not considered to prohibit the destruction of artworks, albeit in vary narrow circumstances. While the logic behind this tradition is questionable,[166] the negotiating history surrounding Article 6*bis* makes it clear that this is the case.[167]

Under this provision of VARA, a case involving a major center for graffiti artworks in New York, *5Pointz*, succeeded in bringing an extraordinary award of damages, in the amount of 6.75 million dollars, to a group of artists whose work was painted over in the middle of the night by the owner of the property on which it appeared.[168] The developer's pernicious attitude was strongly disapproved by the court. Based on the evidence presented in the case, including the testimony of art expert Renée Vara for the plaintiffs, the court concluded that graffiti art could be work of "recognized stature" under the terms of the statute, thereby protecting them from "intentional or grossly negligent" destruction. The case was therefore both a landmark ruling on VARA and a dramatic step forward for the recognition of unconventional artworks by the law.

By a suitable irony, the most restrictive moral rights regime in the world thereby yielded the largest ever *economic* award for a moral rights violation. This is a significant achievement for what a New York Times reporter has called "an obscure federal law."[169]

But it should be borne in mind that this case was still, in an important sense, a failure. The plaintiffs wanted to prevent the destruction of their work. Under U.S. law, however, this proved to be impossible. Why? When the plaintiffs initially sought a preliminary injunction, the court chose not to grant it on the grounds that harm caused by the destruction of the work was something that could ultimately be

[164] *See* VARA, *supra* note 26, § 106A(a)(3)(A). This point is discussed in more detail in Chapter 9, *infra*.

[165] Discussed in detail in Chapter 9, *infra*.

[166] *See generally* Sundara Rajan, Moral Rights and the Protection of Cultural Heritage, supra note 44.

[167] *See* Adeney, The Moral Rights of Authors and Performers, *supra* note 14, at chs. 6 and 7.

[168] *Castillo v. G&M Realty L.P.*, Nos. 18-498-cv (L), 18-538-cv (CON), 2020 U.S. App. LEXIS 5228 (2d Cir. Feb. 20, 2020), https://www.mintz.com/sites/default/files/media/documents/2020-03-25/18-498_amd_opn.pdf.

[169] Jenna Russell, *In Vermont, a School and Artist Fight over Murals of Slavery*, New York Times (June 20, 2023), https://www.nytimes.com/2023/02/21/us/vermont-law-art-slavery.html. The term also appears in an earlier newsletter from law firm Holland & Knight, *Rights of Artist Impact Landlord and Tenant*, First Quarter (1999), https://www.hklaw.com/en/insights/publications/1999/03/rights-of-artist-impact-landlord-and-tenant.

compensated by money.[170] At some level, does this position not represent a fundamental misunderstanding of the moral rights idea?

c. Beyond Private Law: The Preservation of Cultural Heritage

Although the recognition of moral rights is limited in the U.S. Copyright Act, there is a wide variety of legislative measures in the United States for the protection of culture, and ideas similar to moral rights are implicit in these alternate legal frameworks. A comprehensive discussion of these legal measures is beyond the scope of this book, but three relevant examples include state-level art preservation statutes, the national film registry, and the protection of specific sites and landmarks.

i. Art Preservation: The California Art Preservation Act, the DNA of the Visual Artists' Rights Act 1990

Among state-level art preservation statutes, the California Art Preservation Act (CAPA) was the first, dating from 1979, and it was subsequently expanded in the Cultural and Artistic Creations Preservation Act (CACPA) of 1982.[171] CAPA includes explicit and expansive provisions on moral rights, though these have now been largely pre-empted by VARA.[172] Indeed, a case can be made that CAPA was the template legislation for VARA—and for the broader project of Berne Convention implementation overall. In a sense, rather than introducing novel legislation for the implementation of moral rights, it was the previous experience of the states, and of California in particular, that informed this process.[173] Through

[170] The *5Pointz* case, *supra* note 168, is discussed in detail in Chapter 8, *infra*, esp. at notes 54–56 and accompanying text. *See also* Chapter 2, *supra* note 307 and accompanying text.

[171] *See* Cal. Civ. Code § 987 (West. 1979); Cal. Civ. Code § 989 (West Supp. 2000) (U.S.). VARA is available at the Bill stage at https://www.congress.gov/bill/101st-congress/house-bill/269; *see also* VARA, *supra* note 26. State-level statutes on moral rights are studied in detail in an excellent article by Edward J. Damich, *State Moral Rights Statutes: An Analysis and Critique*, 13 Colum.-VLA J.L. & Arts 291 (1988). Damich analyzes statutes in New York, Connecticut, Massachusetts, Rhode Island, Louisiana, among others—which gives a suggestion of the extent to which moral rights statutes had been adopted by the states at the time of U.S. accession to the Berne Convention. *See also* Cambra E. Stern, *The Visual Artists Rights Act and the Problem of Post-Mortem Authors' Rights*, 51 UCLA L. Rev. 849 (2004).

[172] Although VARA has pre-empted the California Act, it still offers a number of surprisingly potent benefits to California artists. As Christine Steiner notes,

> Predating VARA, California enacted the California Art Preservation Act in 1979 (CAPA). The CAPA is pre-empted to the extent that it overlaps with the VARA, but it provides the following: additional rights of attribution and integrity; civil penalties and injunctive relief for violations of such rights; specifies procedures for removal of works of public art to avoid destruction; and a right to public or private not-for-profit organisations to remove a work of fine art in order to preserve it from destruction. The law also permits attorneys' fees and is therefore a potent remedy for aggrieved artists in California.

See Christine Steiner, *Art Law in California*, Lexology (Mar. 13, 2019), https://www.lexology.com/library/detail.aspx?g=780f4cf3-bb56-4b95-905a-bb60d4e4909b. The text of CAPA is available widely: *see, e.g.*, https://www.cityofventura.ca.gov/DocumentCenter/View/6037/California-Art-Preservation-Act-Ref-PDF?bidId=. *See also* Damich, *supra* note 166, esp. at 329–38.

[173] This issue is also discussed in Chapter 8, *infra* notes 13–16 and accompanying text.

VARA, the objectives of art preservation were largely kept intact and elevated to the federal level. This implicitly avoided the situation of untested international or foreign norms being adopted in the United States.

Keeping this history in mind, the language of CAPA communicates a profound understanding of moral rights based on the twin principles of recognition for the special relationship between an artist and his or her work, and the public interest in the preservation of culture. CAPA states,

> The Legislature hereby finds and declares that the physical alteration or destruction of fine art, which is an expression of the artist's personality, is detrimental to the artist' s reputation, and artists therefore have an interest in protecting their works of fine art against any alteration or destruction; and that there is also a public interest in preserving the integrity of cultural and artistic creations.[174]

By this explicit recognition of the public interest, California legislation goes above and beyond Article 6*bis* of the Berne Convention, and it also enlarges the scope of moral rights beyond its formulation in the laws of France and Germany. This is not to say that French and German law do not recognize the public interest inherent in moral rights, which is, indeed, one of the accepted underlying rationales for moral rights—only that they do not state it expressly in their legislation. In fact, as Strömholm notes, German theorizing of the nineteenth century did recognize the public interest rationale,[175] and French courts have more recently explored it, although in the more limited context of balancing the author's rights against those of the public in the *Hugo* case.[176] California explicitly recognizes the complementarity of the two principles in its distinctive legislative language.[177] As such, the California law on moral rights is extremely impressive. CAPA transcends Article 6*bis* of the Berne Convention and should completely discredit any notion that moral rights are somehow uniquely unsuited to the United States. CAPA shows that this is not the case; the failure to adopt moral rights is, above all, a political issue.

[174] CAPA, *supra* note 171, § 987(1). For a proposal to amend the Act in 2020, see An Act to Amend Sections 987 and 989 of the Civil Code, relating to Fine Art, Cal. Assembly Bill No. 2902, Feb. 21, 2020, https://leginfo.legislature.ca.gov/faces/billNavClient.xhtml?bill_id=201920200AB2902.

[175] *See* Stig Strömholm, Le Droit moral de l'auteur en droit allemand, français et scandinave avec un aperçu de l'evolution internationale: Étude de droit comparé 239 (1967). *See also* Chapter 2, *infra* notes 144–55, 156–58, and accompanying text.

[176] *Pierre Hugo*, *supra* note 50.

[177] See also the general discussion of this theme in Mira T. Sundara Rajan, *Moral Rights in the Public Domain: Copyright Matters in the Works of Indian National Poet C. Subramania Bharati*, Singapore J. Legal Stud. 161 (2001).

ii. Film Preservation: Indirect Moral Rights

The National Film Preservation Act, originally enacted in 1988,[178] provides a means of identifying films that are "culturally, historically, or aesthetically significant", and in relation to these works, the Act prohibits the distribution or exhibition to the public of any version of the film that has been "materially altered" or colorized. In 2023, a similar registry and preservation system was established for recordings.[179]

iii. Music Modernization: Attribution by the Back Door

The recently enacted Music Modernization Act (MMA) responds to an urgent need in the music community to protect compensation for musicians in the environment of music streaming. This Act unfolded against the background of the failure to introduce significant changes on moral rights by the copyright office in 2016 and 2017—a situation that developed in spite of the concerted efforts of musicians rights organizations and influential musicians to secure the implementation of moral rights. Jane Ginsburg, who has published authoritative commentary on moral rights in the United States over a number of decades, has argued strongly for the adoption, at the very least, of a general moral right of attribution in U.S. copyright law, reflecting the mood of the artists in the music industry. It is therefore ironic that the bedrock principle of the MMA is attribution. But attribution in the MMA is attribution writ large: not only does the MMA provide for a individual artists to be identified but it also provides for right-holders to be identified. In fact, the more information that can be provided regarding attribution, the better for the MMA's purpose, which is to facilitate the identification of right holders for the purpose of royalty payments. The Act simply underscores the importance of moral rights in the digital environment. As Hafsa Tout points out,

> the tension between American copyright law's protections for non-visual works and the international legal frameworks recognizing broad moral rights, to which

[178] National Film Preservation Act, Pub. L. No. 100-446, § 11(a)(5), 102 Stat. 1774 (1988) (NFPA), http://www.gpo.gov/fdsys/pkg/STATUTE-102/pdf/STATUTE-102-Pg1774.pdf. The Act has subsequently been renewed a number of times, and its provisions have expanded to include new administrative procedures. The current iteration is now in force until 2026. *See* Library of Congress, *National Film Preservation Board: Mission* (n.d.), https://www.loc.gov/programs/national-film-preservation-board/about-this-program/mission; Library of Congress, *National Film Preservation Board: Legislation Impacting Film Preservation* (n.d.), https://www.loc.gov/programs/national-film-preservation-board/resources/legislation-impacting-film-preservation. The Act is discussed in more detail in Chapter 7, *infra* note 194 and accompanying text.

[179] *See* Library of Congress, *About This Program* (n.d.), https://www.loc.gov/programs/national-recording-preservation-board/about-this-program. The program also includes a large collection of essays about the recordings preserved: *see* Library of Congress, *Index of Recording Essays* (n.d.), https://www.loc.gov/programs/national-recording-preservation-board/recording-registry/index-of-essays.

the United States is a member, seems greater and more demanding of a solution in the context of music copyright than ever before.[180]

The Copyright Office describes the framework as follows:

> The legislation establishes a "mechanical licensing collective" ("MLC") to administer the blanket license, and a "digital licensee coordinator" ("DLC") to coordinate the activities of the licensees and designate a representative to serve as a non-voting member on the board of the MLC. The MLC will receive notices and reports from digital music providers, collect and distribute royalties, and identify musical works and their owners for payment. The MLC will establish and maintain a publicly accessible database containing information relating to musical works (and shares of such works) and, to the extent known, the identity and location of the copyright owners of such works and the sound recordings in which the musical works are embodied. In cases where the MLC is not able to match musical works to copyright owners, the MLC is authorized to distribute the unclaimed royalties to copyright owners identified in the MLC records, based on the relative market shares of such copyright owners as reflected in reports of usage provided by digital music providers for the periods in question.[181]

iv. Landmarks: Public Art, Public Action

For example, in 2014, the New York Landmarks Conservancy intervened to prevent the destruction of a work by Picasso, Le Tricorne, in the lobby of The Four Seasons hotel when the hotel owner decided that a change of décor was needed. Thanks to its intervention, the work was safely moved to the New York Historical Society, where it is currently displayed.[182] The president of the Conservancy, Peg Breen, noted that, as the Conservancy notes, "the controversy surrounding the Curtain's move from the Four Seasons made the piece one of Picasso's best-known works in New York. 'It was always meant to be seen by New Yorkers', she added, 'and now even more people will have the opportunity to enjoy it.'"[183]

d. Conclusions

It seems clear that the United States has fallen short of its stated goal of implementing provisions that will bring it into conformity with moral rights requirements in the

[180] *See* Hafsa Tout, *Copyright beyond Borders: Moral Rights & the Implications of Fahmy v. Jay-Z*, MTTLR (April 2022), https://mttlr.org/2022/04/copyright-beyond-borders-moral-rights-the-implications-of-fahmy-v-jay-z.

[181] U.S. Copyright Office, *Musical Works Modernization Act* (n.d.) https://www.copyright.gov/music-modernization/115.

[182] *See* New York Landmarks Conservancy, *Picasso Curtain Moves into New Home at Historical Society* (May 17, 2015), https://nylandmarks.org/news/picasso-curtain-moves-into-new-home-at-historical-society.

[183] Id.

Berne Convention. In order to satisfy the requirements of Berne, the United States still needs one of two things: law reform to enact moral rights provisions beyond the sphere of the visual arts, or open-ended principles of interpretation to guide existing law. A combination of both would be ideal. However, the latest study process exploring moral rights at the U.S. Copyright Office has made little headway, and the reluctance to initiate legislative change suggests that this possibility is probably on hold for the foreseeable future.[184] Similarly, the unwillingness of courts to expand the interpretation of existing laws—and indeed, their apparent tendency to restrict what is there—throws the United States back to the initial difficulty of managing a legislative deficiency in this area. But it is worth noting that the fault may not only lie with the Supreme Court decision in *Dastar*; it may also be a product of the subsequent misinterpretation of the *Dastar* case beyond the reasonable limits that seem built into its unattractive facts. Arguably, the subsequent interpretation of *Dastar* in commentary has served to maximize the potential restrictiveness of the case. This probably reflects the general environment for moral rights in the United States rather than any necessity created by the case itself.

As in the case with other common-law countries, the U.S. moral rights deficit is a product of both received legal wisdom and politics. In the digital context, however, the absence of adequate protection for moral rights signifies something entirely new—a careless approach to the protection of knowledge, culture, and information in an environment of rapid technological change where they are most vulnerable. When it comes to moral rights in the technological environment, conformity with international law will probably be the least of the United States' problems. The real issue is to maintain the integrity of intangible heritage. It is a formidable problem, and, unlike doctrinal questions, attempting to argue our way out of it will accomplish nothing beyond delaying the inevitable.

Indeed, in response to these very issues, the United States has enacted diverse pieces of legislation and created various regimes protecting interests that closely resemble authors' and artists' moral rights of attribution and integrity without actually claiming to be such. Crucially, these initiatives have occurred in the sectors that are most under pressure due to technological change: music and film. At the same time, there is also a deep-seated awareness of the importance of artworks and material cultural heritage, not only from an authorship perspective but also, and equally, in recognition of the public interest in the preservation of cultural heritage. Indeed, in this regard, California language exceeds the provisions of the Berne Convention and, in a sense, the traditions of copyright scholarship as well, by openly acknowledging the link between artists, the creators of culture, and the public, to whom cultural works are ultimately bequeathed. Indeed, the only

184 Full details of the study process, including the final report of the U.S. Copyright Office and other documents, can be found in U.S. Copyright Office, *Authors, Attribution, and Integrity: Examining Moral Rights in the United States* (Apr. 23, 2019), https://www.copyright.gov/policy/moralrights.

real exception to this rule is artwork that is privately owned by collectors, but private transactions in the art world seem to create general unease for most of those involved—sometimes even for collectors.[185]

Bringing moral rights into U.S. law by way of these "back-door" approaches seems like a practical way of accomplishing what needs to be done without appearing to disrupt the legal and political status quo. Do the provisions go far enough? Do they manage to protect what needs to be protected, especially in the technological environment? And what is to be done about the enduring problem of deficient Berne implementation in a country that claims to lead the world on copyright issues?

3. Australia and a Moral Right in Indigenous Culture

Moral rights were enacted in the Australian Copyright Act at the late date of 2000.[186] With their implementation, the United States at last became the only common-law country in the world with no general recognition for moral rights in its copyright law. Australia's implementation of moral rights is a meticulous but very limited implementation of the doctrine. With the creation of a general requirement of "reasonableness" affecting the practical exercise of both attribution and integrity rights, a unique feature of Australian law, significant limits were imposed on the extent of the rights. On a more positive note, Australian law provides for the moral rights of performers as well as authors, making Australia the first common-law country to implement the moral rights provisions of the WPPT.[187]

The Australian treatment of moral rights resolves certain long-standing issues about the substance of these rights. Attribution encompasses false attribution, and –in contrast to the UK provision on false attribution, which resembles the tort of passing off [188]—the Australian protection against false attribution is clearly a moral right of the author. As Elizabeth Adeney points out, two aspects of false attribution are prohibited under Australian law: the attribution of an author's work to another person by name and the continued attribution of the author's name to an altered version of the work that is not approved by the author.[189] In the case of film,

[185] Nathaniel Kahn's film, *The Price of Everything*, explores this issue in depth: Nathaniel Kahn, *The Price of Everything* (2018), https://kinolorberedu.com/film/the-price-of-everything-dvd-1.

[186] *Copyright Amendment (Moral Rights) Act 2000* (Austl.), *supra* note 24. The moral rights provisions entered into force as of December 21, 2000.

[187] The United Kingdom implemented moral rights for performers in 2006: *see* The Performances (Moral Rights, etc.) Regulations 2006, SI 2006/18 (UK), https://www.legislation.gov.uk/uksi/2006/18/contents.

[188] This is discussed in Chapter 2, *supra* notes 253–58 and accompanying text.

[189] *Copyright Amendment (Moral Rights) Act 2000* (Austl.), *supra* note 24, at s 195AD(a)(ii) states, "to imply falsely that the work is an adaptation of a work of the person." *See* Elizabeth Adeney, *Australia's Experience of Moral Rights*, 14(4) JIPLP 312, 315 (2019), https://doi.org/10.1093/jiplp/jpz001.

attribution rights are protected in relation to the director, producer, and screenwriter.[190] The Australian law defines the right of integrity as a "right of integrity of authorship."[191] It rejects any "derogatory treatment" of the work, and derogatory treatment is considered to be any treatment of the work that causes, in the Berne formula, damage to an author's honor or reputation.[192] The Australian scheme specifically identifies the destruction of an artwork as a violation of the right of integrity.[193] So, too, is the display of an artwork in unpropitious circumstances.[194] The duration of moral rights in Australia is equivalent to the duration of copyright, but film remains a notable exception: moral rights subsist only until the death of the director.[195] It is also striking that Australian legislators decided against the possibility of waiver: the Copyright Act provides that moral rights cannot be assigned. The only exception to this rule allows coauthors to make arrangements to exercise their moral rights jointly.[196] Australia may be the only country in the world that addresses the problem of conflicting moral rights among those involved in the making of a film in this way.[197] After the author's death, an heir or a legal executor may exercise moral rights on his or her behalf.[198]

In 2003, soon after the enactment of these provisions, the Australian government introduced a bill for the recognition of moral rights in Indigenous culture.[199] The right was called an "Indigenous communal moral right," and its purpose was to maintain the attribution and integrity of works of Aboriginal culture. In the world of intellectual property regulation, Australia has been a pioneer in confronting Indigenous cultural issues – as a result of the initiative of Aboriginal communities and activists. Its test cases on copyright and Indigenous culture have yielded important insights on the relationship of Indigenous cultures and intellectual property, even where the findings may have been disappointing for Indigenous cultural interests.[200] It is therefore no surprise that Australian legislators have made an

[190] *Copyright Amendment (Moral Rights) Act 2000* (Austl.), *supra* note 24, at s 195AF.

[191] Id. at s 195AI.

[192] Id. at s 195AJ.

[193] Id. at s 195AK(a). Section 195AT provides for safeguards where the destruction of a work will not be considered a violation of the right of integrity, including situations in which the author cannot be located or the author has been given an opportunity to remove the work. Attempts made in good faith to restore the work will also not lead to a violation of the right of integrity. Canada has a similar provision in its law. *See* Canadian Copyright Act, *supra* note 25, at s. 28.2(3)(b).

[194] *Copyright Amendment (Moral Rights) Act 2000* (Austl.), *supra* note 24, at s 195AK(b).

[195] Id. at s 195AM.

[196] Id. at s 195AN on the "Exercise of Moral Rights."

[197] Id. at s 195AN(4).

[198] Id. at s 195AN(4).

[199] *Copyright Amendment (Indigenous Communal Moral Rights) Bill 2003* (Cth) (Austl.). *See* Jane Anderson, *The Politics of Indigenous Knowledge: Australia's Proposed Communal Moral Rights Bill*, 27(3) U. New S. Wales L.J. 585 (2004).

[200] *See, e.g.*, *Yumbulul v. Reserve Bank of Australia*, 21 I.P.R. 481 (1991) (Austl.), https://case.edu/affil/sce/Yumbulul.pdf.

attempt at recognizing Indigenous interests through the device of moral rights, nor that they have pre-empted both Canada and the United States in doing so.[201]

However, as introduced, the 2003 Bill raised serious concerns about the Australian legal perspective on Indigenous culture. As Jane Anderson points out,

> [T]he power of the title *Copyright Amendment (Indigenous Communal Moral Rights) Bill* is that unless one actually reads the draft Bill (and there are only a few that have been distributed) it would superficially appear to break new ground in the field of Indigenous rights to cultural knowledge.[202]

Ultimately, the Bill did not become law. But the provisions are still worth reviewing: they remain the only proposal to adopt moral rights for Indigenous communities in a Western country, and they reveal the extent of the difficulties involved in recognizing Indigenous moral rights,. They are both legal and political in nature. Given that the idea progressed so deep into the Australian copyright reform process, it also seems likely that the Australian government will revisit this important cultural issue.[203] Indeed, it appeared that the rights might receive consideration in the 2006 round of Australian copyright amendments, but rumors of a new proposal evaporated.[204]

Apart from its content, the process surrounding the introduction of the 2003 Bill was one that generated controversy in its own right. As Anderson notes, the Bill was not made available to the Australian public, and only a small number of copies were circulated to interested groups.[205] Among these groups, which included the Arts Law Centre of Australia, the Australian Copyright Council, and the Aboriginal Board of Study of New South Wales, the Bill generated strong criticism.

Two fundamental problems are apparent in the Bill. First, the posture adopted by the Bill was one of extreme caution in relation to the recognition of Indigenous rights. The Bill was more concerned with clarifying boundaries for the users of Aboriginal artworks than protecting the works from misuse. This focus led to

[201] India is another country where recognition of Indigenous, or "tribal," contributions to traditional culture is important. The issue is neglected in India, and the position of "tribals" remains one of general disadvantage.

[202] Jane Anderson, *Indigenous Communal Moral Rights: The Utility of an Ineffective Law: Who Benefits from the Bill*, 5(30) INDIGENOUS LAW BULL. 8 (2004).

[203] In fact, the idea of introducing an Indigenous moral right resurfaced in 2006: *see* PARLIAMENT OF AUSTRALIA STANDING COMMITTEE ON ENVIRONMENT, COMMUNICATIONS, *Information Technology and the Arts, Indigenous Cultural and Intellectual Property Rights, in* INDIGENOUS ART: SECURING THE FUTURE 145 (2007), https://www.aph.gov.au/Parliamentary_Business/Committees/Senate/Environment_and_Communications/Completed_inquiries/2004-07/indigenousarts/report/c11. However, it does not appear to have been revisited since. See the comments by Molly Torsen, *Inside Views: Indigenous Communal Moral Rights*, INTELLECTUAL PROPERTY WATCH (Dec. 4, 2006), http://www.ip-watch.org/weblog/2006/12/04/inside-views-indigenous-communal-moral-rights.

[204] *See* Samantha Joseph & Erin Mackay, *Moral Rights and Indigenous Communities*, ART + LAW (2006), https://www.artslaw.com.au/article/moral-rights-and-indigenous-communities.

[205] A copy of the Bill was also, apparently, made available to one individual.

a second, and still more disturbing, problem. The Bill was based on a distorted picture of Aboriginal culture, observed through the lens of a Western copyright framework. It required Aboriginal cultural relations to be structured according to copyright norms.

The Indigenous moral right could only be invoked in cases where the Aboriginal artist and his or her community had entered into an agreement prior to any transactions involving the work. This Agreement would need to clarify the mutual responsibilities of creator and community in relation to the work; but, as Jane Anderson points out,

> The presumption here is that at the time of executing a work the individual artist will first attend to ... legal affairs and formally consider the question of communal moral rights management, presumably in anticipation of commercial potential in the reproduction of the work.[206]

At first glance, this requirement may seem like a crude response to the landmark Australian case of *Yumbulul*. Mr. Yumbulul was an Aboriginal artist, skilled in the art of making a sacred object known as a "Morning Star Pole." Yumbulul eventually entered into an agreement with the Australian government to allow an image of his pole to be featured on an Australian banknote. However, Mr. Yumbulul's community was unhappy with the dissemination of this sacred knowledge, and asked him to withdraw from the agreement.[207] In the eventual lawsuit, Yumbulul tried, unsuccessfully, to withdraw his permission from the Australian government for the use of his artwork on the banknote.[208] The case failed, for the simple reason that there was nothing wrong with the contract between Yumbulul and the government. In its finding, a highly sympathetic Australian Federal Court, though unable to understand that the Aboriginal group *did not want* this image circulating on a banknote, expressed its distress about being unable to find a copyright solution for the conflict:

[206] *See* Anderson, *The Politics of Indigenous Knowledge*, *supra* note 193, at 598.

[207] *See Yumbulul*, *supra* note 194, at para. 12:

> There was evidence that Mr. Yumbulul came under considerable criticism from within the Aboriginal community for permitting the reproduction of the pole by the bank. It may well be that when he executed the agreement he did not fully appreciate the implications of what he was doing in terms of his own cultural obligations. Certainly, it appears to be the case that neither Mr. Wallis, nor anyone else at the agency, felt a need to explore these ramifications with him. Mr. Wallis saw that as a matter which was Mr. Yumbulul's responsibility. It may be that greater care could have been taken in this case. And it may also be that Australia's copyright law does not provide adequate recognition of Aboriginal community claims to regulate the reproduction and use of works which are essentially communal in origin. But to say this is not to say that there has been established in the case any cause of action.

[208] Id. The Court found that a valid copyright agreement existed between Mr. Yumbulul and the government, and it did not have the authority to intervene on the grounds of community objections by Yumbulul's clan.

> [T]he question of statutory recognition of Aboriginal communal interests in the reproduction of sacred objects is a matter for consideration by law reformers and legislators. For what it is worth, I would add that it would be most unfortunate if Mr. Yumbulul were to be the subject of continued criticism within the Aboriginal community for allowing the reproduction of the Morning Star Pole design on the commemorative banknote. The reproduction was, and should be seen, as a mark of the high respect that has all too slowly developed in Australian society for the beauty and richness of Aboriginal culture.[209]

From a purely Western law point of view, a possible solution to these kinds of conflicts would be a formal agreement between artist and community. But this approach would be utterly artificial in the context of Aboriginal art. It presumes to impose the framework of Western contractual relations on relationships that have been defined by cultural rules, probably since time immemorial. It also identifies the physical creator of the work as its author, exactly in keeping with the Western copyright approach to creativity, without a consideration of the community's contribution to the work. Why, for example, could the Bill not introduce joint or communal authorship as an alternate model of authorship for the purposes of this right? Anderson is right to emphasize the impracticality of the rule.[210]

The requirement of a pre-existing contract was one of a number of prerequisites to moral rights in the proposed Bill. The Bill also specified that a copyright work should exist—clear enough in relation to artworks, but potentially too restrictive to accommodate traditional knowledge in the form of stories or other oral traditions.[211] The work had to show a link with Aboriginal traditions. This requirement generated little controversy, although the possibility of a disagreement between an individual artist and his or her community about the "traditional" nature of the work seems significant in the modern context. The third requirement had to do with agreement between artist and community, as noted

[209] Id. at para. 20.

[210] *See, e.g., Robertson, supra* note 84. Indeed, the fluidity of relationships is not unique to Indigenous cultures: many relationships involving the transfer of knowledge in Western society also take place without written contracts, leading to disputes about their scope.

[211] The need for a copyright work to exist could imply a protection against misappropriation—e.g., a rule that copyright in any work that can be shown to be derived from Indigenous traditions must be shared with the culture from which it is drawn.

above. Fourth, the Aboriginal community's association with the work needed to be acknowledged.

Finally, as Anderson points out,

> [I]nterested parties in the work need to have consented to the rights arising, and this consent must be provided through written notice. There is no clarification in the legislation of who constitutes an "interest holder."

As in the case of the agreement, this requirement, too, is problematic. Does it mean that any contributor to the work, including members of the community at large, must consent to the moral right before it can be asserted? The position is in contrast with the general Australian approach to moral rights, which recognizes them automatically upon the creation of a work, and rejects the possibility of waiving or assigning them. In contrast, the effect of this provision is that the proposed Indigenous moral right would need to be asserted before it could exist. To make matters still more confusing, these requirements apparently need to be met "before the first dealing with the work, otherwise no rights arise."[212]

The idea of providing moral rights protection for Australian Aboriginal culture is an exciting prospect. Because of their inalienable, perpetual, and personal nature, the links between moral rights and traditional culture are readily apparent.[213] However, the form in which the Australian government attempted to express this moral right was disappointing. In practical terms, it is difficult to see how the preconditions for its exercise could ever have been met. From a conceptual point of view, the right offered little insight or enlightenment.

To be truly effective, an Indigenous moral right would have to accomplish many things. At a minimum, it would need to accommodate the reality of shared authorship between an individual and his or her community. The joint authorship option is one; communities could also be asked to designate a claimant as and when an infringement suit is filed. The moral right should be available without formal requirements of assertion or registration, just as it is available to individual authors under Australian law. Moral rights in Aboriginal culture should not be restricted to copyright works. Traditional cultures are known for oral works and other diverse forms of knowledge, all of which could potentially be protected by moral rights. And a moral right for Indigenous culture would have to operate outside time limits, which are fundamentally incompatible with traditional heritage.

[212] Anderson, *The Politics of Indigenous Knowledge*, *supra* note 193, at 598.

[213] The relationship between moral rights and Indigenous culture is explored in Sundara Rajan, *Intellectual Property and Aboriginal Peoples*, *supra* note 5.

These considerations are only the beginning. They show how truly innovative a moral right in Indigenous cultural heritage would have to be. Meeting these challenges may not be impossible, but the development of a viable moral right for Indigenous cultures will require considerable legal ingenuity—and a commitment to learning from past failures.

At a fundamental level, the purposes behind the Indigenous communal moral right should be clearly articulated. The protection of Aboriginal cultural heritage is the goal, but protection from what? Misappropriation by those who use traditional culture to create copyright works? The public release of sacred or restricted knowledge? And what about the separate goal of seeking recognition and prestige for Aboriginal culture itself?[214] All of these purposes could be fulfilled through moral rights. But the Australian attempt, sadly, reflects the desire to give nominal recognition to Aboriginal culture without the political will to translate that recognition into practical power. Above all, the proposed Australian right failed to treat Aboriginal ways of knowing and seeing their own culture on a par with the copyright framework. Any attempt at justice must first be able to acknowledge the right of Aboriginal people to define their own cultural practices, a crucial element in cultural self-determination.

4. New Zealand: Personhood for Rivers and Mountains—A New Form of Moral Rights?

The recognition of legal personhood for features of the natural environment, including rivers and mountains, has happened first in New Zealand—a common-law country. The legal innovation recalls the approach of the English court in the case of *Bumper Development Corporation Ltd v. Commissioner of Police for the Metropolis*, where personhood was recognized in the statue of a deity that had been removed from India in contravention of export controls, which a group of plaintiffs, including the Indian government, sought to have returned to the country.[215]

What is the legal theory on which this innovation is based? In the case of the Waitangui River, the first such natural feature to be recognized under New Zealand law, the recognition of the river reflected the underlying relationship between the river and the Maori people. Any harm to the river would therefore be equivalent to harm to the Maori people as well. As Kate Evans, writing for the BBC, reports,

[214] For a useful and interesting summary of "[t]he major concerns for Indigenous people," see Terri Janke, Our Culture, Our Future: Report on Australian Indigenous Cultural and Intellectual Property ch. 3, 19–42 (1998). The report was prepared by Janke as principal consultant for Michael Frankel & Company, Solicitors, for the Australian Institute of Aboriginal and Torres Strait Islander Studies and the Aboriginal and Torres Strait Islander Commission.

[215] *Bumper Development Corporation Ltd v. Commissioner of Police for the Metropolis and others* [1991] 1 W.L.R. 1362 (UKCA). The case is discussed in detail in Chapter 8, *infra* notes 140–72 and accompanying text.

> In Maori culture, *tupuna*, or "ancestors", live on in the natural world and it is the community's duty to protect both the landscape they inherited and those who came before them. Humans and water are especially believed to be intertwined—a traditional saying is, "I am the river, the river is me." Having the river recognised as a legal person means harming it is the same as harming the tribe. If there is any kind of abuse or threat to its waters, such as pollution or unauthorised activities, the river can sue. It also means it can own property, enter contracts and be sued itself.[216]

For anyone who is familiar with moral rights, this theory sounds familiar. It is reminiscent of the understanding of the relationship between author and work under the moral rights doctrine, which characterizes that relationship as essentially "spiritual" or familial. Of course, the explicit context of moral rights seems different at first glance, since the author creates the work but natural features exist independently of humans. Upon closer examination, though, the significance of this distinction, already of questionable importance, becomes more restricted. Laws in different countries prioritize authors or works, depending on the circumstances, creating different hierarchies between them according to policy needs and priorities. As has been discussed extensively, it is not always necessary to show damage to the author's reputation to establish a violation of the moral right of integrity. In the same vein, while natural features were created by non-human forces, their current state is closely linked to human activity. Indeed, this is why many features have been chosen for protection: because they are in need of intervention to safeguard their natural qualities.

As harm to the work may cause harm to the author, harm to an element of nature amounts to harm to the people with whom it is associated. This also highlights the essential concern of moral rights as the harm resulting from the mistreatment of what appears to be, at first glance, an inanimate object. In the case of moral rights, it is the work; in the case of the environmental right, it is the river, mountain, or other feature of nature. However, harm to humans can result from the mistreatment of those non-human entities. In the case of the environmental element, this harm may even result in direct physical harm by allowing environmental pollution that ultimately harms human health. It may also cause psychological harm, such as the mental distress in Inuit communities caused by global warming and the melting of sea ice. Under moral rights, harm to the work can cause psychological distress to the author. In the case of works whose authors are deceased, harm to works in the public domain—including, for present purposes, works displayed to the public in museums, if not "owned" by the public—can cause human distress, both locally and globally.[217]

216 *See* Evans, *supra* note 7.

217 Attempts to harm works like the Mona Lisa are a case in point; a more ironic example is presented by environmental activists who harm works of art to draw attention to environmental causes.

Indeed, such environmental rights should also be understood as cultural rights. The mistreatment of the environment is born of a deeper attitude, characteristic of industrial civilization and pervasive due to its spread through colonialism. It is an exploitative attitude towards the natural world—a sense of entitlement towards nature, as well as insensitivity to the consequences of abusing the environment. In contrast, Maori culture has a different attitude towards the environment and the exploitation of nature, reflected in the phrase noted above—"I am the river." The Australian courts have confronted Aboriginal attitudes towards their culture and have found themselves unable to accommodate, or even understand, those attitudes fully through Western legal language. Ideas of stewardship and fiduciary duty have filled the gap. However, Aboriginal and Maori people themselves talk about their relationship with nature in terms of identity, selfhood, gratitude, unity, and spirituality, especially in the sense of connection with one's ancestors. It is difficult to find words to describe this relationship, perhaps especially so in a Western language.[218] but the idea of moral rights, which involves the recognition of something that is similarly resistant to expression, though it is described as spiritual or personal, is an example of a Western legal doctrine that recognizes something ineffable in culture. The difficulty of the copyright system, like much else in the modern world, is often the difficulty of quantifying what is involved beyond property interests, whether we are talking about moral rights, freedom of expression, or the public interest writ large. Moral rights provide us with an opportunity to do so within the copyright system; Indigenous cultural rights in natural features of the environment represent a similar attempt. Would it be helpful to consider these rights community "moral rights" relevant to the traditional communities involved?

Finally, any discussion of this issue should not fail to mention that the benefit to be derived from such protection, should it prove to be effective in practice, will be felt by communities beyond the local Indigenous communities, beyond those who are directly or perhaps even measurably affected—and for generations who are not yet alive. The world as a whole has much to learn from Aboriginal cultures, and much to gain from this knowledge. Recognizing these rights is therefore not merely the provision of a benefit sought by Aboriginal peoples; it is a recognition accorded to our common humanity and to our common "mother," the Earth.

As the discussion here seeks to show, doing so is reprehensible in more ways than one, since such acts perpetuate psychological violence and insensitivity, which are part of the problem of environmental degradation.

[218] Similarly, in his novel *Far from the Madding Crowd*, Thomas Hardy writes, "It is difficult for a woman to define her feelings in a language chiefly made by men to express theirs." Hardy's words, published in 1874, have lately been popularized by a 2015 film of the book.

C. Growth of the Doctrine: Moral Rights in Developing Countries

In developing countries, moral rights present an enigma. These countries hold a general attitude of suspicion towards intellectual property laws. Where moral rights are concerned, however, their approach is entirely different. Moral rights are warmly embraced in the developing world, and they enjoy widespread and wholehearted recognition in an astonishing range of countries.

Why does copyright law bring out Jekyll-and-Hyde personalities in the developing world? The reasons are deeply rooted in the history of international copyright relations, long defined by a fundamental schism between developed and developing countries. Developing countries favor access to knowledge over authors' rights—at least, where the works of foreign authors are concerned. No doubt, developing countries face a special need for knowledge from the outside world. To some extent, however, their dependence on external sources of education also reflects the persistence of a colonial mentality. From the onset of the colonial period, foreign works were perceived as essential for development. Valuable knowledge was thought to come from outside the country, and not from within one's own society.

Over the past two decades, this perception has slowly shifted with the empowerment of developing countries through technology. A notable example is India, which has long been a champion of developing countries' interests in the international copyright arena and is now also a world leader in the software industry. As a result, India is no longer just a receiving country when it comes to copyright works; it is also a producing country, with a strong interest in promoting its software industry.[219] Moreover, India experiences conflict over copyright priorities in a new way—not only as a distinction between domestic and international priorities, but also as a conflict between internal priorities. The goals of its software industry and the needs of its roughly 700 million people who fall under global standards of poverty must both be accommodated.[220]

It would be suitably ironic if the growth of technology in developing countries, largely a product of knowledge acquired externally, proved to be a necessary prerequisite to the exploration of Indigenous knowledge that has developed in these cultures. In fact, this is exactly what has happened. As many developing countries

[219] The issue of whether or not a strong copyright system promotes the software industry is highly contentious. It is comprehensively discussed by Jane Ginsburg, *Four Reasons and a Paradox: The Manifest Superiority of Copyright over Sui Generis Protection of Computer Software*, 94 COLUM. L. REV. 2559 (1994), https://scholarship.law.columbia.edu/faculty_scholarship/61.

[220] See the heart-wrenching article by Moni Basu, *Seeing the New India through the Eyes of an Invisible Woman*, CNN (2015), https://www.cnn.com/interactive/2017/10/world/i-on-india-income-gap/.

enjoy a new sense of self-worth through technological success, they are encouraged to turn towards their own traditions. At the international level, the new prominence of developing jurisdictions has brought publicity to discussions of traditional knowledge, which fundamentally question accepted ways of defining and valuing knowledge in the West.[221]

Finally, it should be noted that the copyright concerns of developing countries reflect structural features of the international copyright regime. This has led to tenacious built-in biases. The status of developing countries in the international copyright system is a peculiar one. As former colonies ruled by European "Great Powers," many of these countries found their way into the international copyright regime via the membership of their governing countries in the Berne Union. When independence was won, they elected to stay, hoping that a system made by their unwanted rulers could somehow manage to accommodate their needs.

The period of decolonization that followed proved to be a rude awakening. Developing countries felt that they were in need of information and knowledge from the developed world, but ever-increasing regulatory restrictions, and the costs of obtaining materials from abroad, interfered. Policies such as the compulsory licensing of works for translation went against Western copyright norms.[222] By the 1960s, conflict between developed and developing countries had escalated to the point where the viability of the international copyright system was at stake. The result was the 1967 Stockholm revision of the Berne Convention, which modernized the Convention in a number of ways.[223] The Stockholm document included a new protocol with special provisions for developing countries, but, as Sam Ricketson notes, "These generous provisions in favor of developing countries ... were destined never to come into force."[224] The Protocol regarding Developing Countries was revisited at the Paris meeting of 1971, and, in the course of a "salvage operation," a new and "less rigorous regime" was established.[225]

But developing countries saw moral rights in a different light. While they fought against copyright standards that they perceived as inappropriate or excessive, they

[221] The problem of valuing traditional knowledge is closely related to the issue of how to value Indigenous cultures, noted in relation to *Yumbulul*, *supra* note 194. Both issues involve alternative frameworks of knowledge that, in many respects, differ fundamentally from the copyright/intellectual property system: *see* Sundara Rajan, *Intellectual Property and Aboriginal Peoples*, *supra* note 5.

[222] But it is worth noting that the United States was the country with the world's first provisions on compulsory licensing, in the Copyright Act of 1909. The license was "to allow for the use of nondramatic musical works," and it was initially established in response to an unprecedented new technology: piano rolls. *See* Subcommittee on Courts, the Internet and Intellectual Property of the House Committee on the Judiciary, *Statement of Marybeth Peters, Register of Copyrights*, 108th Cong. 2d Sess. (Mar. 11, 2004), https://www.copyright.gov/docs/regstat031104.pdf. Peters also comments that the "stringent requirements for use of the compulsory license did not foster wide use of the license."

[223] *See* Ricketson, *supra* note 14, at paras. 3.49–3.67.

[224] Id. at para. 3.64.

[225] Id. at para. 3.67. See also id. at ch. 11 for a detailed treatment of the place of developing countries in the Berne system, including the events of the Stockholm and Paris conferences.

had few reservations about moral rights. Countries as widely divergent as India,[226] Brazil,[227] Tunisia,[228] and Mali[229] were eager to embrace moral rights.

When moral rights migrated to the developing world, it was not just the law of developing countries that was affected; moral rights, too, were transformed. In the "exotic" landscape of the developing world, moral rights inhabited not only a new geographical space but also a new cultural environment. Their ties with European culture were loosened, and they were set free from familiar models of creativity.

Developing countries do not stop at the recognition of moral rights as embodied in the Berne Convention, or even as envisioned by French or German legal theorists. They approach the implementation of moral rights in original, expansive, and creative ways. The treatment of moral rights by legislators and judges in developing countries has led to new directions in the evolution of the doctrine. Apart from large developing countries like India or Brazil, the protection of moral rights even in less-developed countries is impressive, at times exceeding standard levels of protection in Continental jurisdictions.

When post-colonial countries first adopted independent copyright laws, they were in a special situation. Their approach to the law was characterized by urgency and passion. They were poor countries, yes, but they also held extraordinary cultural riches—cultural property, folk arts and folklore, traditional medicine, ancient laws, and ancient languages—and they had an intense desire to recover their dignity and self-esteem. More than half a century after Indian independence, it is not easy to understand the mindset of the Freedom Fighters. They, and the first generation of Indian political leaders after them, approached the world with

226 *See* Indian Copyright Act, *supra* note 42, s. 57.

227 *See* Lei No. 9.610 de 19 de fevereiro de 1998 (Lei de Direitos Autorais e dos Direitos Conexos, alterada pela Medida Provisória No. 907, de 26 de novembro de 2019) [Law No. 9.610 of Feb. 19, 1998 (Law on Copyright and Neighboring Rights, as amended up to Provisional Measure No. 907 of Nov. 26, 2019)] (Braz.), https://www.wipo.int/wipolex/en/legislation/details/20999 (Brazilian Copyright Act). A number of features make these provisions interesting; the state is under an obligation to check the attribution and integrity works in the public domain; in relation to film, directors are clearly designated as the sole moral rights holder; and architects have a special right to repudiate authorship if a building design is modified against their will. The law states clearly that these rights are "inalienable and irrevocable." *See* J. Carlos Fernández-Molina & Eduardo Peis, *The Moral Rights of Authors in the Age of Digital Information*, 52(2) J. Am. Soc'y Information Sci. & Tech. 109, 112 (2001), https://eric.ed.gov/?id=EJ618542f.

228 Tunisia's 1966 Copyright Act included protection for folklore as a type of work eligible for copyright protection. For an analysis, see Ploman & Hamilton, *supra* note 106, at 130, who comment that "[t]he purpose of these restrictions is to regulate teams which frequently tour Africa to record performances by local musicians and artists and secure exclusive world rights in the exploitation of the records for minuscule sums." They also note that, in the absence of international recognition for these rights, their effectiveness would be limited.

229 See Loi No. 08-024 du 23 juillet 2008 fixant le régime de la propriété littéraire et artistique en République du Mali [Law No. 08-024 of July 23, 2008, establishing literary and artistic property rights in the Republic of Mali], art. 16, https://www.wipo.int/wipolex/en/text/197931, which calls moral rights "attributes of copyright which are perpetual, inalienable, and unassignable." (The difficulty of translating "droit d'auteur" should also be duly noted; I have used "copyright" in this context.) See the interesting perspective on piracy in Mali by Alex Duval Smith, *Mali's Radio Stations to Fall Silent in Protest over Tape Piracy*, The Independent (Feb, 5, 2000), http://www.independent.co.uk/arts-entertainment/music/news/malis-radiostations-tofall-silent-in-protest-over-tape-piracy-726275.html.

passionate idealism.[230] Any and every instrument that could improve the situation of the country should be deployed. In such an environment, under such pressures, moral rights could metamorphose into something quite new.

And indeed, moral rights in developing countries were transformed. Developing countries chose to implement extensive protections for moral rights in their laws, favoring such measures as perpetual protection, broad principles of attribution, the recognition of integrity without any need to prove damage to reputation, and moral rights in folklore.[231] In doing so, they drew upon two kinds of resources.

The first was the political idealism of decolonization. The second was the availability of traditions of law that preceded colonization. For example, the aesthetic theories of ancient India supported the protection of "ideas" as well as works, which could lead to an approach to copyright protection that is more comprehensive than Western norms.[232] More importantly, it is an approach that appears interesting again in the technological context. The significance of "fixation," the requirement that a work must be recorded in a tangible medium before it becomes eligible for copyright protection, may eventually prove to be fundamentally outdated in an environment that is defined by the digital exchange of information.[233]

It is an enduring irony that the pejorative phrase "palm-tree justice" signifies arbitrary decision making in the Global South.[234] No doubt, in parts of the world where palm trees grow, humanity has had its share of arbitrary rulership and lawlessness. However, the so-called developing world also has its share of credible and legitimate legal traditions of its own. These traditions might take the form of custom, but customary law should also be given its due as a genuine manifestation

[230] See generally Louis Fischer's classic biography: LOUIS FISCHER, GANDHI: HIS LIFE AND MESSAGE FOR THE WORLD (1954).

[231] *See, e.g.*, Ploman & Hamilton, *supra* note 106, at 130 (on Tunisia); Brazilian Copyright Act, *supra* note 220.

[232] *See* T.S. Krishnamurti, *Copyright—Another View*, 15(3) BULL. COPYRIGHT SOC'Y USA 217, 218 (1968). *See* Chapter 2, *supra* note 32 and accompanying text.

[233] The protection of performers' moral rights in the WIPO Performances and Phonograms Treaty (WPPT) includes live performances: *see* World Intellectual Property Organization (WIPO) Performances and Phonograms Treaty, adopted Dec. 20, 1996, S. Treaty Doc. No. 105-17, 36 I.L.M. 76 (1997) (WPPT), https://www.wipo.int/wipolex/en/treaties/textdetails/12743. The provisions of the Treaty are limited to "live aural" performances and apparently do not extend to visual elements, audiovisual works, or audiovisual recordings.

[234] Ironically, the phrase has been used to characterize the approach of one of the most brilliant of British judges, Lord Denning: *see* Wilfrid J. Waluchow, *Hart, Legal Rules and Palm Tree Justice*, 4(1) LAW & PHIL. 41 (1985). It is not clear whether the term might be used to condemn the colonial administration of justice, also conducted, after all, "under palm trees." The term appears to have originated with Bucknill LJ in the 1950 English case of *Newgrosh v. Newgrosh* (unreported):

> Section 17 of the Married Women's Property Act 1882 (UK) gives the judge a wide power to do what he thinks under the circumstances is fair and just. I do not think it entitles him to make an order which is contrary to any well-established principle of law, but, subject to that, I should have thought that disputes between husband and wife as to who owns property which at one time, at any rate, they have been using in common are disputes which may very well be dealt with by the principle which has been described here as "palm tree justice." I understand that to be justice which makes orders which appear to be fair and just in the special circumstances of the case.

of the law.[235] Some countries, like India, also have venerable traditions of written law that predate colonial times.

Writing about the South Pacific, Sue Farran notes the difficulty of understanding and judging law in post-colonial countries:

> When Pacific Island countries gained independence in the latter part of the 20th century some colonial laws were abolished, others were retained as interim measures pending their replacement by national laws. The place of custom and customary law was reassessed and in some cases strengthened as part of the assertion of independence and national identity, a process which has continued. In some cases, foreign laws have been introduced or have served as a model for national laws. Elsewhere colonial or imperial laws remain unaltered. In addition[,] participation in the family of nations by Pacific Island countries has seen the introduction of international law into domestic law. Today it would be difficult to claim that the law of Pacific Island states neatly fitted into any one of the major legal families of the world.[236]

1. India and Other British Colonies: Common Law, or Not?

India is a striking example of a post-colonial legal system. It illustrates the case of a common-law jurisdiction that acquired its common-law heritage through colonization, flirted with European civil law concepts during the British period, and ultimately drew upon the twin forces of decolonization and the revival of Indigenous legal ideas to expand the availability of moral rights for its authors and artists. Moreover, the Indian example also shows the transformation of the moral rights concept itself to reflect the culture, needs, and priorities of a decolonizing society. Defining India's pre-colonial legal tradition is a problem of awesome complexity. Prior to British rule, Indian law included ancient law codes, precedent, and custom as sources of law. The Sanskrit law codes, notably the *Laws of Manu,* included socially restrictive and controversial, even offensive content;[237] social customs

[235] See the interesting discussion of the interplay between British law and Indian law, including its customary aspects, in Marc Galanter, *The Displacement of Traditional Law in Modern India*, 24(4) J. Soc. Issues 65 (1968).

[236] Sue Farran, *Palm Tree Justice? The Role of Comparative Law in the South Pacific*, 58 Int'l & Comp. L.Q. 181, 182 (footnotes omitted) (2009). The article is an extremely useful exploration of how comparative law works in the context of law reform and legal modernization.

[237] *Manu-smrti*: according to the generally conservative code, "the usages of good men" are still law. The ancient law code of Manu is now among the most famous examples of codified Sanskrit law, though it is questionable whether it deserves this status. What is clear is that the modern status of Manu's code was acquired through the work of Sir William Jones, a gifted linguist, poet, and judge who translated it into English. This history is widely discussed, but much "decolonization" work remains to be done in this area. *See, e.g.*, the political and social perspective offered by Subashini Ali, *The Laws of Manu and What They Would Mean for Citizens of the Hindu Rashtra*, The Wire (Nov. 10, 2020), https://thewire.in/rights/manusmriti-hindu-rashtra-rss. For a quick and current overview of the background,

ranged from flexible and progressive to rigid and repressive.[238] A complete discussion of how British colonial law interacted with this framework is beyond the scope of this book. However, it should be noted that British law was a common-law façade that was superimposed upon an ancient and therefore many-layered palimpsest of traditional law and culture.

The presence of continental European legal traditions outside the common law should also be mentioned, although it is difficult to say how influential they were on the development of modern Indian copyright law.[239] India's exposure to European civil law occurred in the course of expeditions to India run by the Portuguese, who set up a colony at Goa, and the establishment of a major French territory in Pondicherry. While the legal traditions of these civilian jurisdictions had little direct impact on India's national legal framework after British rule, there were clear cultural and legal affinities between these European cultures and India. The French territory of Pondicherry was home to an important colony of nationalists in exile, although the French administration assuredly had its own reasons for tolerating their presence, and the nationalists were familiar with the French language and culture.[240] In fact, French culture inspired the nationalists: who among them could have resisted the call of "*liberté, égalité, fraternité*"?[241]

Independent India's initial empowerment of authors and artists took an unexpected twist when the Indian government realized that it could become responsible for moral rights violations affecting cultural works in its own possession. In 1994, it moved to scale back the law of 1957, constraining it within

see Robert Young, *Sir William Jones and the Translation of Law in India* (Nov. 30, 2015), https://lawexplores.com/sir-william-jones-and-the-translation-of-law-in-india/. Young comments that Jones considered the law code of Manu

> ... 'a system so comprehensive and so minutely exact, that it may be considered as the Institutes of Hindu Law' – a remark that transforms the identity of Menu at a stroke into the systematic form of a European legal text.... Even though Jones considers Menu to consist of the 'institutes' of Hindu law, he nevertheless expresses the wish for the law to be systematized further ... it being, he suggests: 'introductory perhaps to a Code, which may supply the many natural defects in the old jurisprudence of this country, and, without any deviation from its principles, accommodate it justly to the improvements of a commercial age.' [Reference omitted]

The 1796 publication is available online at https://archive.org/details/institutesofhind00manu/page/n3/mode/2up. Manu's code has been frequently translated into English since: *see, e.g.*, The Law Code of Manu (Patrick Olivelle, trans., 2009).

[238] A discussion of ancient Indian law is provided by Werner F. Menski, Hindu Law: Beyond Tradition and Modernity (2003). *See generally* Krishnamurti, *supra* note 236.

[239] The influence of civil law systems in India would be an interesting area for further research.

[240] C. Subramania Bharati was among the exiles in Pondicherry; Aurobindo Ghosh was another member of the community and a good friend of the poet. Bharati's case is interesting because his move to Pondicherry was followed by the reestablishment of India, a magazine originally published in British India, which now came under Bharati's de facto editorship. The motto of the magazine was "Liberté; égalité, fraternité." *See* S. Vijaya Bharati, Subramania Bharati (1974); statement by Dr. S. Vijaya Bharati (in personal communication with the author, Apr. 27, 2010).

[241] *See supra* note 245.

more conventional bounds—namely, literal conformity with the text of the Berne Convention.

However, this shift in the official policy towards moral rights was firmly rejected by India's powerful and independent judiciary. Indian judges have evinced a clear sense of responsibility for protecting Indian culture, even safeguarding it, where necessary, from India's political leadership. In the landmark 2005 case of *Amar Nath Sehgal v. Union of India*, the Delhi High Court turned to the international arena for support, invoking international agreements on cultural property to trump the legislative amendments to moral rights in the Indian Copyright Act which it perceived as ill-advised.[242] The decision builds on a tradition of judicial recognition for moral rights in India, initiated in the *Mannu Bandhari* case of 1986,[243] but it moves into new territory by connecting authors' moral rights with the protection of cultural property.

The *Sehgal* case suggests a fascinating new approach to moral rights in the international community. Its pioneering approach to the interpretation of moral rights under section 57 also expands the underlying doctrine. Specifically, the decision points to the relevance of moral rights for the protection of *cultural property*, as distinct from intellectual property. The term used by the Court, "cultural heritage of a nation," also suggests that the principles in this case are applicable to other areas of culture beyond material manifestations such as artworks.

2. Moral Rights and the Protection of Culture: Indian Copyright Law

India adopted its first independent Copyright Act in 1957, and this statute continues to regulate Indian copyright matters today.[244] Since the adoption of the Indian Copyright Act in 1957, it has been amended six times.[245] 1994 and 2012, after the final decision in the *Sehgal* case, were benchmark years for moral rights.

a. The Evolution of Moral Rights in the Indian Copyright Act

i. The 1957 Act: The Birth of Authors' "Special Rights"

Under the rubric of "authors' special rights," section 57 of the 1957 Act included protection for the author's moral rights of attribution and, in broad language reminiscent of France, integrity. It stated:

[242] *Sehgal*, *supra* note 56; Indian Copyright Act, 1957, *supra* note 43.

[243] *Smt. Mannu Bhandari v. Kala Vikas Pictures Pvt. Ltd* (1986) 1987 A.I.R. (Delhi 13) (India). A consideration of this seminal case may be found in Mira T. Sundara Rajan, *Moral Rights in Developing Countries: The Example of India*, 8(5/6) J. Intell. Prop. Rights 357, 449 (2003), http://docs.manupatra.in/newsline/articles/Upload/C5BBF35E-1446-4453-814D-8FFF9885389C.pdf.

[244] Indian Copyright Act, 1957, *supra* note 43. An earlier treatment of these issues may be found in Raghavender, *supra* note 44.

[245] *See* the Copyright Office of the Government of India, http://copyright.gov.in.

Section 57. (1) Independently of the author's copyright, and even after the assignment either wholly or partially of the said copyright, the author of a work shall have the right to claim the authorship of the work as well as the right to restrain, or claim damages in respect of, —

(a) any distortion, mutilation or other modification of the said work; or

(b) any other action in relation to the said work which would be prejudicial to his honour or reputation.

(2) The right conferred upon an author of a work: by sub-section (1), other than the right to claim authorship of the work, may be exercised by the legal representatives of the author.[246]

Notably, the original section 57 imposed no burden of proof upon the author to show damage to honor or reputation. Instead, it allowed an author to make a claim, quite simply, in relation to "*any* distortion, mutilation or other modification of the ... work." The concept of damage to reputation or honor later appeared, instead, as a catch-all to compensate for cases that might have escaped the first provision. [247] Its function was therefore completely different in the Indian Act than in Article *6bis* of Berne. The Indian provision was readily comparable to French law, which traditionally "treat[s] ... [the right of integrity] as an absolute right against alteration."[248] In keeping with French tradition, the Indian legislation implicitly recognized the author as the ultimate judge of how his or her own work was treated. The theory behind the Indian law was what French scholar Henri Desbois characterizes as "individualist" in the French context.[249]

The 1957 version also envisioned the perpetual protection of moral rights.[250] The question of duration was left open by the Act. Accordingly, perpetual protection for moral rights was implied by this omission. There can be little doubt that this approach reflected concerns about the status of Indian culture in the post-colonial period. It was potentially both a symbolic and a practical statement. The perpetual protection of moral rights could help to protect important cultural works in the public domain from harm, and to preserve the integrity of India's historical record.

[246] The original Act of 1957, which included this version of s. 57, is available at https://www.indiacode.nic.in/bitstream/123456789/15356/1/the_copyright_act%2C_1957.pdf (with thanks to Gudibanda Raghavender)

[247] Indian Copyright Act, *supra* note 43, s. 57 (original). It is interesting to note that the structure of s. 57 reflects the traditional importance accorded to the work, independently of its creator, in Indian aesthetic theory. On the relationship between the artist and his or her creation in Indian thought, *see* Sneh Pandit, An Approach to the Indian Theory of Art and Aesthetics 134 (1977).

[248] *See* Staniforth Ricketson, The Law of Intellectual Property para. 15.57 (n.53) (1984). This view is particularly French, as is exemplified, e.g., in the commentary of Henri Desbois, Le Droit d'auteur en France 548–49 (paras. 449–50) (3d ed., 1978).

[249] Id.

[250] No duration of protection was specified, leaving open, by implication, the possibility of perpetual protection. This change was made in response to my scholarship (personal communication from Gudibanda R. Raghavender, January 2013).

If moral rights are to be protected forever, who should exercise them? Should these interests and obligations be entrusted to the author's descendants, his or her legal representatives, cultural organizations, the government, or some combination of these? Indian law resolved this issue very conventionally, by assigning a right of action to the author's heirs.[251]

The original section 57 was a classic post-colonial provision, both more comprehensive and more nuanced than the approach adopted in subsequent versions of the text. As such, it demonstrated the significant influence of national cultural priorities, Indigenous customs, and, possibly, exposure to continental European legal and cultural traditions in India. Taken together, these factors led to an Indian framework for moral rights that considerably exceeded international standards. In the light of subsequent case law, Indian law may even have gone significantly beyond France. In effect, the common law was shown to be little more than a thin veneer obscuring the unique cultural aspirations underlying Indian law.

ii. The 1994 Act: Back to Berne

The original section 57 accomplished two distinct objectives. The first was to preserve the integrity of the work; the second, to protect the author's reputation. This was reflected in the two-pronged statement of the right of integrity in this provision.

In 1994, however, this scheme was revisited and revised by the Indian legislature. The amended section 57 read as follows:

> 57. (1) Independently of the author's copyright, and even after·
> the assignment either wholly or partially of the said copyright, the
> author of a work shall have the right—
> (a) to claim authorship of the work; and
> (b) to restrain or claim damages in respect of any distortion,
> mutilation, modification or other act in relation to the said
> work *which is done before the expiration of the term of copyright*
> *if such distortion, mutilation, modification or other act*
> *would be prejudicial to his honour or reputation:*
> Provided that the author shall not have any right to restrain or
> claim damages in respect of any adaptation of a computer programme
> to which clause (aa) of sub-section (1) of section 52 applies.
> *Explanation.—Failure to display a work or to display it to the*
> *satisfaction of the author shall not be deemed to be an infringement*
> *of the rights conferred by this section.* (italics added)

[251] *See* Indian Copyright Act, *supra* note 238, §57(2).

Two points are noteworthy here. First, the moral right of integrity was modified to remove the original bifurcation of the right into two parts. The second part, which had served as a catch all provision in the 1957 Act and had the flavor of French law, was now eliminated.

The second important amendment imposed a time limit on the moral right of integrity. It would be protected for the same term of protection as copyright overall. The 1994 formula accomplished this adjustment of duration through a backhanded formula, though, which prevented actions being brought for alleged violations of integrity that *occurred after the expiry of copyright,* but did not impose a time limit on when those actions could be initiated in the courts. This seems to reflect an awareness of the general issue of delays in the Indian court system. However, the movement from perpetual protection to a limited term of protection was in any event a profoundly significant change.

An "explanation" also addressed the specific issue of displaying works of art, making the conditions of display exempt from integrity claims. This seems to be a direct response to the situation in the case of Amar Nath Sehgal, which imposed an interim injunction on the Indian government in 1992. The influence of this case upon the 1994 amendment process is discussed in the chronological discussion of Mr. Sehgal's decades-long litigation below.

Overall, the 1994 version of section 57 adheres closely to Article 6*bis* of the Berne Convention. There were still some meaningful differences tending towards greater protection in the Indian provision, including the specific availability of damages under Indian law.[252] Nevertheless, according to the drafter of the new provisions, Mr. Jagdish Sagar, the primary goal of the 1994 amendments was to ensure that Indian law was in line with the Berne Convention.[253]

In general, Berne conformity in the common-law countries has meant a need for *improvements* to the existing moral rights framework. In the Indian context, though, it meant *scaling back* existing provisions to reflect the Berne template. The amendments still departed from the details of Berne in various respects, as noted above. One further such point was the exemption of fair dealings with computer programs from moral rights claims. This showed a precocious sensitivity to the potential collisions between moral rights and exceptions to copyright, at least in the technological context, which continues to be rare, especially in the common-law countries.

But the story of amendments to section 57 did not end here. Further revisions would follow in 2012.

[252] Berne Convention, *supra* note 4, at Art. 6*bis* states: "any distortion, mutilation or *other modification of, or other derogatory action* ["modification or other act" in §57] in relation to, the said work, which would be prejudicial to his honor or reputation."

[253] Jagdish Sagar (in private correspondence with the author, early 2000s).

iii. The Copyright Amendments of 2012: Perpetual Protection Restored

India's copyright amendments of 2012 comprehensively updated Indian copyright law for technology.[254] Against this background, it is especially interesting that only one change was made to the language of the integrity right in section 57.

This involved the term of protection for moral rights. In particular, the proviso that an act infringing the moral right of integrity should be "done before the expiry of the term of copyright" was removed.[255] The current section 57 no longer specifies a precise duration for either the moral right of attribution or the right of integrity. By implication, moral rights are protected, once again, in perpetuity. This is a return in both form and vision, of course, to the 1957 Act. This change was strongly supported by then Indian Copyright Registrar, G.R. Raghavender, and influenced by my own scholarship.[256]

Although no other changes were made, it is important to recognize that the requirement of proof of damage to the author's honor or reputation in section 57 has been significantly weakened by the ruling of the Delhi High Court in the Sehgal case, a complex judgement that is discussed in the following sections. After *Sehgal*, it seems clear that, at least in the case of works that have become part of India's cultural heritage, there is effectively no requirement of proof of damage to the author's honor or reputation, despite the amendments of 1994. It is also possible to predict that the courts, if they continue in the tradition of advocacy established even before *Sehgal* and affirmed in that case, will *not* be especially stringent when examining the question of proof of damage to the author's honor or reputation. In practice, this may lighten or alter the burden of proof upon authors and artists bringing moral rights complaints in India.[257]

[254] Copyright (Amendment) Act, 2012, No. 27 (India), https://www.wipo.int/wipolex/en/text/304385. The Bill was introduced on Apr. 19, 2010.

[255] Id. at s. 36(i).

[256] Raghavender has commented that the move was seen as controversial by some groups in India—hardly surprising given the strong nature of the protection accorded—but that, as demonstrated here, the change was in line with Indian tradition. Raghavender credits my work on moral rights for this change: private conversation with the author, New Delhi, January 2014. Raghavender has subsequently published a paper on moral rights as part of the Symposium Publication based on the Glasgow conference published in April 2019: Raghavender, *supra* note 43.

[257] The issue of proof of damage to reputation is inherently awkward. Should the law act to intervene before the damage is done, or should it be limited to addressing harm after the fact? In other words, is a likelihood of damage sufficient for the court to issue an injunction against potentially harmful future activities? The problem was indirectly addressed in the *Sehgal* case, *supra* note 56, where an interim injunction (1992) enjoined the government from undertaking further actions, such as moving, that might inflict further damage on the mural; however, significant actual damage had already occurred in this case. The problem is a delicate one where damage to artworks is concerned, since original artworks are generally unique works that, by definition, cannot truly be replicated in any way. Once the work is damaged, no real remedy may be possible; artists can only seek compensation, to whatever extent it is meaningful, and both artists and society may also support deterrence for the protection of future works. As discussed in Chapter 7, *infra*, a number of countries accordingly adopt a special approach to

iv. Scope of the Attribution Right

In the original Indian legislation from 1957, the right of *attribution* was, quite simply, the right "to claim authorship of the work." As in French law, there was no explicit attempt to define the scope of attribution in India. Rather, it was left to the courts to decide on nuances such as the extent of protection for the author's right to publish on an anonymous basis or under a pseudonym. [258] The potential application of the right to the problem of forgery—the attachment of one's own name to another person's work—was also left open.[259] This approach remains the same in the current Act.

But Indian law had a peculiarity concerning the attribution right and, in particular, the exercise of the right after an author's death.

This issue is generally a slightly strange aspect of moral rights, and is worth a moment's digression here. In India, subsection 57 (2) of the Indian Copyright Act provides that the author's moral rights can be exercised after the author's death by his or her legal representatives. [260] As such, it is in line with similar provisions elsewhere and is considered to be consistent with the theory that moral rights are inalienable. Notwithstanding the inevitability of death, the relationship between author and work is permanent—and indeed, the work of great authors is often said to be "immortal," or the author is actually called an Immortal.[261] These cultural perspectives may reveal the emotional urge behind perpetual protection: it may be nothing less than a legalistic attempt to negate death, an attempt to affirm human transcendence through creative work.

The legislators behind the Indian Copyright Act of 1957 felt a need to distinguish between the rights of authors and those of their descendants in relation to attribution. [262] The author's legal representatives could assert his or her moral rights

integrity in the artistic context—notably, strengthening the right by allowing integrity claims without a requirement of showing proof of damage to reputation. In any event, where proof of damage to honor or reputation is required, it is advisable to keep in mind that the appropriate standard of proof is, of course, the non-criminal standard of a balance of probabilities.

[258] The French Code de la propriété intellectuelle, *supra* note 60, at art. L121-1 provides only that the author has the right to "respect for his name," but art. L113-6 references anonymous and pseudonymous authorship as protected choices. *See* Chapter 2, *supra* note 104 and accompanying text.

[259] To clarify, the classic attribution problem occurs when a person's own work is not attributed to him or her as its author (i.e., it is attributed to another), so that the author's name is not attached to his or her own work. Forgery effectively means passing off the forger's creation as someone else's. The relevance of the attribution right to forgery remains underexplored in the research on moral rights. See, e.g., the brief discussion in Michel M. Walter, *Dualistic Aspects in Monistic Systems of Moral Rights*, 14(4) JIPLP 318, 325–35 (2019), https://doi.org/10.1093/jiplp/jpz012.

[260] *See generally* S. Ramaiah, *India*, *in* International Copyright Law and Practice (Paul Edward Geller & Melville B. Nimmer eds., 1998); Strömholm, *supra* note 170, vol. 1 (Première Partie: L'Evolution historique et le mouvement international), at 420.

[261] See, e.g., the list of great pianist-composers on the website of Steinway & Sons, *Steinway Artists* (n.d.), https://www.steinway.com/music-and-artists/immortals. The expression is also widely used in Indian culture (e.g., Tamil *amaran, amarar*).

[262] This aspect of Indian moral rights greatly interested Stig Strömholm, *supra* note 275, at 420 (author's translation) who observes, in his seminal 1967 work:

on his or her behalf, but that they could not "claim authorship of the work."[263] This approach appears to have been unique to Indian law and, given the general thoughtfulness with which Indian legislators approached moral rights at that time, it probably reflects deeper features of Indian culture. Was it a reflection of Indian family dynamics in traditional extended families, common in the 1950s? Was it philosophical? A popular Indian theory holds that a great person will be reborn within his or her own family, an idea with emotional resonance for many Indians. There might also have been practical implications related to the broader framework of Indian law, involving, for example, the general limits of personal rights or the extent of family claims, also an interesting feature of historical litigation involving *Scots* law in the case of Robert Burns.[264]

Regardless, as Strömholm notes, there can never have been any doubt that the descendants of Indian authors were entitled to protect the attribution right of their ancestors. [265] It is therefore a welcome relief that the reforms of 2012 finally removed these ambiguous words, of such long standing, from the text of section 57.[266]

> As for the rule which provides that the right to assert paternity of the work may not be exercised by the [author's] descendants, its precise meaning appears to depend on the proper answer to the question of whether the descendants are perceived to be acting in their own capacity against offences to the moral right, or if they are considered to be acting as representatives [of the author]. To resolve this question, it would be necessary to have exact information on the Indian concept of the right of successors mortis causa. If the first possibility is correct, the provision is perfectly logical: the descendants cannot claim for themselves paternity of the work. In this case, it would appear to be possible to allow them, on the other hand, the right to oppose at least some attacks on the right of paternity and, notably, to intervene where the author's name does not appear on copies of a work [first] published during his lifetime under his name.

263 *See* Indian Copyright Act, *supra* note 238, §57(2).

264 This is discussed in detail by Hector L. MacQueen, "Ae Fond Kiss: A Private Matter?" (April 23, 2014) in A Burrows, D Johnston QC and R Zimmermann (eds), Judge and Jurist: Essays in Memory of Lord Rodger of Earlsferry (Oxford, 2013), pp 473-488, Edinburgh School of Law Research Paper No. 2014/14 at Available at SSRN: https://ssrn.com/abstract=2430698 at page 10 and "Robert Burns and Clarinda: A Poet's Passion before the Courts of Law – with Hector MacQueen," Parts 1 and 2, Woman of Culture Podcast, May 25 and June 7, 2024, available at https://podcasts.apple.com/us/podcast/woman-of-culture/id1723723726. See also Chapter 2, *infra,* note 213.

265 Strömholm, *supra* note 170, at 420, also notes that:

> [I]l serait singulièrement arbitraire de refuser aux héritiers le droit de défendre la paternité du de cujus en leur laissant le droit de s'opposer aux modifications, car si celles-ci deviennent souvent désirables après la mort de l'auteur, ... l'usurpation de la paternité ne paraît pas justifiée par le fait que le créateur de l'oeuvre est mort.
>
> [It would be exceptionally arbitrary to deprive the descendants of the right to vindicate the paternity of the deceased author ["de cujus"] while allowing them to retain the right to oppose modifications [of the work].... While modifications often become desirable after the author's death, ... taking over the right of paternity does not seem to be justifiable on the grounds that the creator of the work is dead.]

266 Indian Copyright Act, *supra* note 43, s. 36(ii). At one point, the Indian government made copyright reform proposals available in an online document, organized by section, which was very useful; this document showed the government's intent to remove these words. In December 2009, the government initiated a new round of reform discussions, and the document has since been removed from its website.

b. Performers, Producers, and Bollywood: Moral Rights in Film

A significant point under Indian copyright law is that the author of a film is considered to be its producer. As a result, producers of films acquire moral rights under section 57, since these are simply granted to "authors" without any exceptions. The moral right of the producer is a strange feature that has crept into Indian law and should be revisited.[267] It is unfortunate that film directors and other potential coauthors of a film are neglected under Indian law in favor of the producer. This is an imbalance in India's treatment of film. In an interesting parallel to Hollywood in the United States, this may reflect the power of Bollywood in India.

In 2012, moral rights for performers were introduced into the Act.[268] Increased recognition for performers not only reflected India's membership in the WPPT[269] but also represented a form of legal recognition for Indian musical traditions which emphasize improvisation. This series of amendments also included the creation of an *inalienable* royalty for the use of musical works in films and sound recordings, which could therefore be considered a kind of hybrid right – an economic right with a moral rights dimension. Section 18 was amended in 2012 to provide:

> ... T]he author of the literary or musical work included in a cinematograph film shall not assign or waive the right to receive royalties to be shared on an equal basis with the assignee of copyright for the utilization of such work in any form other than for the communication to the public of the work along with the cinematograph film in a cinema hall, except to the legal heirs of the authors or to a copyright society for collection and distribution and any agreement to contrary shall be void ... [270]

[267] Id. s.2(d)(v), states, "(d) 'author' means,— ... (v) in relation to a cinematograph film or sound recording, the producer."

[268] Id., s. 38B. They are subject to the following, relatively balanced caveat:

> Explanation.—For the purposes of this clause, it is hereby clarified that mere removal of any portion of a performance for the purpose of editing, or to fit the recording within a limited duration, or any other modification required for purely technical reasons shall not be deemed to be prejudicial to the performer's reputation.]

[269] *See* WPPT, *supra* note 226, at Art. 5.

[270] It goes on to state, as well:

> Provided also that the author of the literary or musical work included in the sound recording but not forming part of any cinematograph film shall not assign or waive the right to receive royalties to be shared on an equal basis with the assignee of copyright for any utilization of such work except to the legal heirs of the authors or to a collecting society for collection and distribution and any assignment to the contrary shall be void.

The related §38A(2) provides:

> Once a performer has, by written agreement, consented to the incorporation of his performance in a cinematograph film he shall not, in the absence of any contract to the contrary, object to the enjoyment by the producer of the film of the performer's right in the same film: Provided that, notwithstanding anything contained in this sub-section, the performer shall be entitled for royalties in case of making of the performances for commercial use.

This was a landmark achievement for musicians in the Bollywood film industry, though they have struggled in to realize the benefits in practice. To date, it has proven to be very difficult for musicians to collect the royalty to which they are legally entitled.

In 2012, new provisions on digital rights management were also added, which, though not directly related to moral rights, should be understood as a practical supplement primarily to the attribution right (though also indirectly relevant to integrity). Digital rights management is of particular relevance to music and film in the online context.

c. Authors' and Artists' Resale Right

One further change occurred in 1994: the introduction of a resale right in works of visual art. According to section 53A of the amended Indian Copyright Act, the sale of a work of art for more than 10,000 rupees will attract a royalty of up to 10 percent of the price.[271] This provision resembles a moral right in the sense that it, too, is inalienable.

The resale right lasts for the duration of copyright—the lifetime of the author and sixty years after his or her death. It is worth noting that this limitation of duration presents a contrast to the treatment of true moral rights, which, as noted previously, are protected without limitation in time.[272]

Drawing on Article 14*ter* of the Berne Convention, India extends the resale right to authors' original manuscripts as well, offering this right to the authors of literary works, playwrights, and composers.[273] As in Berne, this is a practical response to the reality that authors' original manuscripts may be valued in much the same way as an original work of art, appreciating considerably in value over time as artworks do.[274]

d. Independence from Economic Rights

In keeping with the Berne Convention, section 57 of the Indian Copyright Act continues to affirm the "independence" of economic and moral rights. An author can assert his or her moral rights even after the assignment of the economic copyright in his work.[275]

[271] Ten thousand rupees is approximately U.S.$215 (as of this printing)—but the sum is more significant in India than its international equivalent.

[272] *See* Indian Copyright Act, *supra* note 43, s. 22. The Copyright Amendment Act 1992 extended the term to prolong copyright in Tagore's works for the benefit of the University founded by him at Shantiniketan. The case of Tagore presents an interesting contrast to Bharati, whose copyright was terminated early for the benefit of society: *see* Mira T. Sundara Rajan, *The Lessons of the Past: C. Subramania and the Nationalisation of Copyright*, 6(2) SCRIPTED (2009), https://script-ed.org/wp-content/uploads/2016/07/6-2-Rajan.pdf.

[273] In contrast, the European resale right, for example, does not apply to original manuscripts.

[274] *See* Indian Copyright Act, *supra* note 238, s. 53A (as amended in 1994).

[275] *See* id., s. 57(1).

At first glance, therefore, moral rights in India are inalienable. But the question of inalienability receives imperfect treatment in the Indian law. The Copyright Act does not address the question of whether moral rights may be waived. Accordingly, in keeping with common-law tradition, Indian lawyers generally accept the possibility of waiver under section 57.[276]

India's judicial landscape makes the implications of waiver different from other common-law countries. In particular, India should be distinguished from the extreme case of Canada, where waivers of moral rights are both usual and comprehensive. In the United Kingdom, the *Frisby* case showed a willingness to read copyright contracts with authors' interests at heart. But no British precedent, to date, can tell us whether a British court would be willing to overrule a waiver of moral rights on similar grounds.[277] Given the proven sympathy of the Indian judiciary for creators, it seems likely that Indian judges would readily overturn attempts to waive moral rights in artists' contracts that they perceive as unbalanced or unfair. This is all the more probable in view of the difficulties and delays faced by Indian authors who attempt to sue, of which judges in that country are well aware. Persistence in a lawsuit means different things in India than elsewhere—the stamina to wait for redress, determination in the pursuit of it, and a level of financial secruity that probably reflects prominence, even eminence, in one's field. In India, where moral rights are concerned, enduring litigation may very nearly justify a presumption of guilt!

e. Remedies

Under Indian law, the specification and choice of remedies available for an infringement of moral rights are both noteworthy. The Indian Act provides that the author has "the right to restrain, or claim damages in respect of" any violation of the integrity interests in his work.[278] The fact that Indian courts have the explicit authority to impose damages, as well as ordering injunctions, is a power that would be associated with moral rights in the civilian tradition. It is hardly typical of the common-law approach.

f. Judicial Chivalry: The Practical Dynamics of India's Moral Rights

To a significant degree, amendments to Indian moral rights represent a reaction to the expansive treatment of moral rights by the Indian judiciary. The tension between legislative and judicial perspectives has exerted a powerful influence on the shape of Indian law. In case after case, on copyright law and beyond, Indian courts

[276] *See* Pravin Anand, *The Concept of Moral Rights under Indian Copyright Law*, 27 COPYRIGHT WORLD 35, 36 (1993) (arguing that "[m]oral rights under Indian law are not transferable, although under an agreement an author may waive his rights under section 57").

[277] *Frisby*, *supra* note 125.

[278] Indian Copyright Act, *supra* note 238, s. 57(1).

invariably choose to define themselves as guardians of civil liberties and individual rights.[279]

This is not to say that the Indian government's concerns about moral rights are unwarranted. On the contrary, they reflect real and important issues. In post-colonial countries, governments often play an especially important role as sponsors of culture. They may commonly be owners of culturally important works. India's government is known for its role in the arts. Not only does the government own artworks, but at least one Indian *state* government has also taken the unusual step of assuming the ownership of copyright in the works of important authors.[280] Extensive provisions on moral rights could lead to liability, affecting the government's ability to support culture. Indeed, the actions of the Tamil Nadu state government in Subramania Bharati's case have led directly to violations of the author's moral rights, and a good case could be made for government liability on both legal and ethical grounds.[281] Where public resources are scarce, the prospect of liability could be overwhelming. Even if a court did not levy financial damages against the government, the intimidating costs of a legal defense might be incurred.

The international consequences of a strong moral rights regime could also be a concern for India. India's membership in the Berne Convention will compel it to extend any moral rights protections which it grants to its own authors to foreign authors as well. Two negative consequences could follow. First, a classic concern: Indian access to foreign materials could be restricted, because Indian users would be obliged to observe additional precautions when using foreign works. Secondly, and on a grander scale, moral rights might make India a less attractive destination for foreign investment in creative enterprises, such as film, by increasing both the costs of "doing business" and the risks of liability for investors. Transformation of existing works into new media, adaptation of foreign works into Indian media,[282] translation, and many other kinds of activities could be affected. Indeed, the same concerns arise in the domestic context, where moral rights could

[279] See the interesting article by S.P. Sathe, *Judicial Activism: The Indian Experience*, 6 J.L. & POL'Y 29 (2001), https://openscholarship.wustl.edu/cgi/viewcontent.cgi?article=1443&context=law_journal_law_policy.

[280] C. Subramania Bharati's case is probably the most famous such example in India, but many others exist. Bharati's copyright was acquired by the state government, but the copyright rests in the hands of the Indian people as a whole. The circumstances are discussed in Sundara Rajan, *Moral Rights in the Public Domain*, *supra* note 177, and an update on purchases of copyright by Tamil Nadu state in 2009 may be found in Sundara Rajan, *The Lessons of the Past*, *supra* note 272. From a legal point of view, the dealings of state governments with copyright are obscure, as copyright is a matter for federal legislation in India. States may therefore purchase it, but it is doubtful whether they then have the authority to give it to the public.

[281] Discussed in detail in Sundara Rajan, *Moral Rights in the Public Domain*, *supra* note 177.

[282] Here, the practice of Bollywood producers who commonly produce Indian remakes of Hollywood films is noteworthy. Citing a 2003 article by Subhash K. Jha, Rachana Desai claims that, "[i]n recent years, nearly eight out of every ten Bollywood scripts have been 'inspired' by one or more Hollywood films": Rachana Desai, *Copyright Infringement in the Indian Film Industry*, 7 VAND. J. ENT. L. & PRAC. 259 (2005).

have a negative impact on investment in industries like film and software. But the international dimension would mean that India's ability to compete for investment with countries where moral rights are less important would, at least in theory, be affected.

But none of these arguments should necessarily lead to the conclusion that lower standards of moral rights protection would be the right choice for India. Should labor standards be reduced in India and China because it makes these countries more competitive for international investment in industries such as clothing manufacture? ... Should the moral rights of individuals be limited in order to promote investment in knowledge industries?

While the Indian government may have had reasonable concerns about moral rights, India's courts did not support the restrictive legislative trend of the 1990s. Indian judges regularly confront the practical side of life in India, especially when it comes to access to justice, and they maintain a degree of aloofness from politics. By upholding moral rights, Indian courts have championed individual rights, supporting the creative and independent efforts of authors and artists. The creative individual walks an arduous and often undervalued path in modern India. Judges have protected authors against the titans of the Bollywood industry[283] and artists against the power and prestige of government.[284] Through moral rights, the courts' focus on the relationship between authors and their works, as under French law, has largely allowed them to avoid the pitfalls of judging artistic *quality* in the courtroom. Instead, as in France, Indian judges have chosen to accept the evidence of artists where the treatment of their own work is concerned. But the legislative context in India, as discussed here, is quite different from that in France.

g. *Amar Nath Sehgal*: Duties of the Government

The case of *Amar Nath Sehgal v. Union of India* unfolded over three decades and established a groundbreaking precedent on the interpretation of the moral right of integrity under Indian law.[285] As Ricketson and Ginsburg note, it is also a helpful

[283] But the courts can also be nationalistic; they have not hesitated to protect Bollywood productions against the claims of individual authors from outside India. The *Bradford* case, involving an Indian television serial based on a novel by U.S. author Barbara Taylor Bradford, is a case in point: *see Bradford v. Sahara Entertainment* (2004) 28 PTC 474 (Cal.). Interestingly, the Indian courts seem more willing to find infringement between India's national film industries producing films in different languages. For a case of Bollywood versus the Bengali film industry, known as Tollywood, see *Shree Venkatesh Film v. Vipul Amritlal Shah*, Civil Suit No. 219/2009, Calcutta High Court, Sept. 1, 2009. The litigation was eventually settled, but the Calcutta court made a number of important points about film copyright at the interim stage of the process. *See* Arpan Banerjee, *Film Copyright Infringement: Bypassing the "Carbon Copy" Handicap*, 5(1) Oxford J. Intell. Prop. L. & Prac. 17 (2010). See also the interesting comments in *Namaste Copyright: Calcutta High Court Reopens the Idea–Expression Debate*, Unwilling Lawyer Blog (Aug. 11, 2009), http://theunwillinglawyer.blogspot.com/2009/08/namaste-copyright-calcutta-high-court.html.

[284] *Sehgal, supra* note 56.

[285] The *Sehgal* case, id., receives a detailed treatment in Sundara Rajan, *Moral Rights and the Protection of Cultural Heritage, supra* note 44.

precedent for the international community clarifying the question of whether the moral right of integrity prohibits the destruction of artworks.[286] The case involved the work of Mr. Amar Nath Sehgal, a celebrated Indian sculptor who died in 2007. In the 1960s, Mr. Sehgal was invited by the government of India to create a mural cast in bronze for the decoration of Delhi's Vigyan Bhavan.[287] The mural was an extraordinary piece of work, massive in scale and scope, and represented several years of Sehgal's creative effort.[288] It eventually came to be considered a national treasure of India.

In 1979, the government of India dismantled the mural and placed it in storage. Carelessness and neglect in the process of moving and storage led it to be damaged. Some parts of the mural were lost, including the piece where the sculptor had placed his name.[289] Sehgal brought a suit against the government, asking for an injunction to prevent further harm to what was left of his work. By the time the Delhi High Court reached its final verdict in the case, in 2005, the harm suffered was severe enough to be considered outright destruction of the work.[290]

i. Interim Ruling: 1992

In a country where it can take decades to receive a final judgment in a case, interim rulings can be powerful indicators of the direction of the law. In Mr. Sehgal's case, the interim ruling itself took thirteen years to emerge, but it clarified two important points about the scope of Indian moral rights. These points were supported and further developed in the Delhi High Court's final judgment of 2005.

(a) Right to Prevent Destruction The *Sehgal* decision established that the moral right of integrity under Indian law can protect an artistic work from outright destruction. This determination goes against the influential international school of thought, which holds that the right of integrity can only protect a work from being mistreated while it remains in existence; it cannot intervene to prevent a work from being destroyed.[291] The rationale for this position may be found in the language of the legal bridge joining the integrity and reputation interests in the Berne Convention. In most jurisdictions, following Article 6*bis* of Berne, the integrity right can only be invoked if the author's reputation has been harmed. Given the fact that the Indian moral rights scheme of 1992 did not require proof of damage

[286] Ricketson & Ginsburg, *supra* note 17, at para. 10.36 (n.106).

[287] The facts are described in detail in Sundara Rajan, *Moral Rights and the Protection of Cultural Heritage*, *supra* note 44. *See also* Anand, *supra* note 264, at 36.

[288] Anand, *supra* note 264, at 36, describes it as being 140 feet long and 40 feet high.

[289] Id. at 36.

[290] *Sehgal*, *supra* note 56.

[291] *See* Ricketson, *supra* note 15, at para. 8.109. Anand, *supra* note 264, at 36 points out that the rationale underlying this view is that, once the work is destroyed, "there would be no subject-matter left to affect the author's reputation."

to the author's reputation, the Court did not need to consider this argument. The comments of the Delhi High Court in 2005, though made in a different legislative context, continued to support this position. It affirmed that, under Indian law, the moral right of integrity can, at the very least, prevent the destruction of works of cultural importance.[292] Moreover, the Court also considered the idea of a "creative corpus"—a body of work. The destruction of any single work could have a powerful impact on the reputation of the artist by reducing his or her creative output, quantitatively or qualitatively, as a whole.[293] This led the Court to consider the destruction of works to be generally included within the ambit of the artist's moral right of integrity.

(b) Duty of Care of the Government The interim judgment also established the important principle of a governmental duty of care towards artworks in its possession. This finding is especially significant in the context of a developing country like India, where the government represents a concentration of power and national resources. Where the powers of government are extensive, there is great potential for both good and evil in government action.[294] In countries like India, the judiciary can play an important role in defining the extent and nature of governmental power, and this responsibility was duly borne by the Court in its interim judgment. Pravin Anand, a leading Indian intellectual property lawyer and counsel for Mr. Sehgal in this litigation, emphasizes this aspect of the case:

> [T]his case raised ... [an] important issue, namely, the right of every citizen to see that works of art which belong to the government, being national wealth, are treated with respect and not destroyed by the government.[295]

(c) Amendments to the Copyright Act The interim ruling in the *Sehgal* case must have given the Indian government food for thought. Although the Indian government claimed that Berne conformity was the primary motivation behind reform of section 57 in 1994, as discussed earlier, the key amendments of 1994 look like a direct response to the interim judgment of 1992 in *Sehgal*.[296]

It is worth drawing the reader's attention to the relationship between those changes and the ruling, which, it should be remembered, delivered an interim

[292] Anand, *supra* note 264, at 36.

[293] The phrase originates in Sundara Rajan, *Moral Rights and the Protection of Cultural Heritage*, *supra* note 44, and was invoked by both Pravin Anand, counsel for Mr. Sehgal, and the Delhi High Court judge.

[294] Frazier points out the power of governments and their ability not only to generate cultural developments but also even to define what is and is not art: Jimmy A. Frazier, *On Moral Rights, Artist-Centered Legislation, and the Role of the State in Art Worlds: Notes on Building a Sociology of Copyright Law*, 70 Tul. L. Rev. 313, 330–54 (1995). Following Frazier's line of argument, it is equally true that governments may influence social attitudes towards art.

[295] Anand, *supra* note 264, at 36.

[296] *Sehgal*, *supra* note 56, where Mr. Sagar comments that conformity with Berne was a concern.

injunction more than a decade after the harm initially occurred. The introduction in 1994 of a requirement to show prejudice to the author's honor or reputation in order to sustain an integrity claim has already been noted. Not only did this change have an impact on how claimants would have to structure their claims in future, but it also had broader implications for the expansion of the integrity right to prevent destruction. In the interim decision on Sehgal's case, the judge was ready to accept that destruction of a work of art was a violation of the author's moral right of integrity, and that the damage to Mr. Sehgal was severe enough to constitute destruction. This argument was arguably bolstered by the separation of the integrity right into two principles under the original section 57: the integrity of the work, on the one hand, and the author's honor or reputation on the other. Under the 1994 version, this structure was changed. The enlargement of the requirement to show prejudice to authorial honor or reputation, making it a basic requirement of the integrity right, created a new connection between the treatment of the work and the effect of that treatment *upon its creator*. This amendment formed a bridge linking the integrity of the work to the author's reputation that did not exist in the earlier version of the Act. It now mirrored Article 6*bis* of Berne.

This is not to say that the link between the status of the work and the author's reputation makes it *impossible* to claim that destruction violates the moral right of integrity. On the contrary, in my 2001 analysis of the case, as noted earlier, I argued that destroying the work reduces the artist's "creative corpus," key language ultimately adopted by the court to resolve Mr. Sehgal's claim.[297]

But the new language implies a philosophical shift. The status of the work is no longer directly in focus. As we will see, the Delhi High Court in its final ruling addressed this issue by proposing that, in certain cases, the status of the work should still take precedence, notwithstanding the new language of the Act.[298]

ii. Final Ruling: 2005

When the moment for a final ruling was at last reached in 2005, the Delhi High Court faced a number of challenges in the interpretation of Indian law. In particular, the Court had to address the issue of a significant legislative amendment that occurred at the midpoint of Mr. Sehgal's case, threatening to invalidate the principles that had been set out in the interim ruling.

This problem of legal interpretation could have been approached in a number of ways. In the absence of transitional provisions in the Indian Copyright Act, the determination of which law to apply was an immediate threshold that had to be crossed. On this point, the judge had at least two clear choices. He could have

[297] Sundara Rajan, *Moral Rights and the Protection of Cultural Heritage*, *supra* note 44.

[298] Moreover, under the new legislation, there would have been no chance of objecting to a failure to display an artwork or to display it in proper conditions. As noted above, this, too, was explicitly eliminated by the 1994 amendments. *See* Explanatory Notes to Indian Copyright Act, *supra* note 43, s. 57(1).

argued that the old provisions of the Indian Copyright Act would apply in Amar Nath Sehgal's case, because they governed the time when the acts of destruction occurred, and also that when the action was initially brought. Alternatively, he could have said that the new provisions should apply because they were in force at the time of the final judgment and expressed the current policy of the Indian government.

In the event, and with the creative flair for which Indian judges are known, he did neither. Rather, he adopted a completely different approach. Where outstanding works of art are concerned, he argued, there is an overriding obligation to protect their integrity. In this sense, it makes little difference whether the old or the new provisions of the Indian Copyright Act are applied. In either case, the letter of Indian law must be read in the light of a higher objective of public policy: the protection of cultural treasures.

How did the judge identify this superior public policy interest? He did so by considering international law. In particular, the policy that he identified was derived, not from intellectual property laws, but from the provisions of international conventions on cultural property. As a signatory to these conventions, India had to respect its obligations under them. Accordingly, its provisions on moral rights should be read in such a way that Indian law remained in harmony with the objectives of the conventions.

Not only does this approach to Indian law address the temporal dimension of Amar Nath Sehgal's case, but it also allows for a clean resolution of the destruction issue. Clearly, it would be incompatible with the objectives of cultural property conventions to allow the destruction of a work of art. And, additionally, the judge was moved by the argument that the overall reputation of an artist is affected by damage to the quantity and quality of his "creative corpus" to accept the prohibition of destruction as part of the artist's integrity right.[299]

The ruling leaves little ambiguity. Even if the new Indian provisions on moral rights mirror the language of the Berne Convention, and even if doubts are raised by international commentators, India's provisions on moral rights do prohibit the destruction of a work. When transplanted into the context of Indian law, the language of the Berne Convention may mean something different. Justice Pradeep Nandrajog concludes,

[299] *Sehgal, supra* note 56, at para. 56, where Justice Pradeep Nandrajog writes:

> There would therefore be urgent need to interpret Section 57 of the Copyright Act, 1957 in its wider amplitude to include destruction of a work of art, being the extreme form of mutilation, since by reducing the volume of the authors creative corpus it affects his reputation prejudicially as being actionable under said section. Further, in relation to the work of an author, subject to the work attaining the status of a modern national treasure, the right would include an action to protect the integrity of the work in relation to the cultural heritage of the nation.

> [T]he various declarations by the international community in the conventions [on cultural property] noted above, lift the moral rights in works of Art if the same acquire the status of cultural heritage of a nation. India is a signatory to the conventions and it would be the obligation of the State to honour its ... declarations.[300]

3. Conclusion

The Indian example illustrates the curious fate of moral rights in the hands of a developing country. Transplanted from Continental law, the doctrine has experienced significant growth and transformation on Indian soil. From a private law doctrine of limited application, it has grown to assume the stature of a public law principle of widespread cultural and moral significance, in the broadest sense of the word. According to the pioneering case of *Amar Nath Sehgal*, moral rights are an instrument for the protection of important cultural works in India. As such, they must be read in conjunction with other national and international instruments that aim at the same target. The case opens up a universe of interesting questions and problems. How should moral rights be treated in works in the public domain? And, to take this question one step further, does India now recognize a moral right in works of cultural property?[301]

Most interesting of all, and in a striking throwback to French tradition, the evolution of moral rights in India is occurring through the intervention of judges. But there is something utterly new and different about the judicial development of moral rights in India. This is the fact that, in India, judicial decision making has been resolute in resisting the currents of change initiated by the Indian government.

This situation is at once inspiring and troubling. In India, the independence of judges functions as a counterweight to political corruption. By an interesting irony, judicial activism helps to build a democratic connection between law and the people that government cannot provide. The problem is not unique to India: in a different context, U.S. judges were asked to decide on the fairness of George W. Bush's claim to the U.S. presidency.[302] At the same time, India can hardly be expected to dispense with government leadership on copyright issues. Given

300 Id. at para. 55. Under the terms of this ruling, it is still possible to argue that a work is not culturally important and would therefore not qualify for protection from destruction. The likelihood of success with this argument seems very slight for two reasons: the Indian judge's emphasis on the concept of "creative corpus," or body of work as a whole; and, as a practical matter, the persistence that would be required of an artist to pursue a claim, financially and otherwise, supporting his or her status as a professional and creative success.

301 *See Bumper, supra* note 215. The case receives an interesting treatment in Richard H. Davis, *Loss and Recovery of Ritual Self*, *in* The Lives of Indian Images 222 (1997).

302 *See Bush v. Gore*, 531 U.S. 98 (2000).

India's position in the vanguard of technological change, government initiatives should be an important part of addressing moral rights in the technological environment, especially with the advent of artificial intelligence. To an impressive degree, both the past and future of Indian culture may benefit from attention to the fundamental principles of disclosure, attribution, and integrity.

The classic copyright dilemma of balancing control and use is poignant in the Indian context. India's is a deeply divided society, and a fundamental challenge faced by Indian law is how to reconcile the interests of a technological superpower with the needs of an impoverished population. The secret may lie in the protection of creative individuals. By helping to generate legal conditions that favor the creative freedom of individuals, the Indian government could promote development and decolonization at a grass-roots level, helping to build confidence and self-esteem among the masses of the Indian people. For India and other post-colonial nations, it is not enough to deal with copyright as a business model; they also need to explore the implications of copyright as a human right.[303]

Whatever copyright may mean to industrialized countries, the principles of copyright law have a special role to play in the developing world. For the sake of development, it is imperative to protect authors' rights. In conditions of general poverty and uncertainty, the position of creators must be stabilized and a base of local knowledge and culture firmly established. India's culture is diverse, and Indians have traditionally held works of the intellect and spirit in great esteem. Indian traditions provide a solid foundation for the protection of individual creativity. The ambition of India's artists and intellectuals is undeniable, and it has always been a potent force underlying the country's drive to modernize. In the words of India's National Poet:

> "What has been shall yet be." Her music will yet be recognized as the most marvellous in the world; her literature, her painting and her sculpture will yet be a revelation of beauty and immortality to the wondering nations; her life and acts will yet be ennobling examples for a grateful humanity.[304]

D. Moral Rights and "Honor" in a Technological Society: Japan

In relation to moral rights, special mention must be made of Japan. Historically remote, Japan's membership in the international copyright system came about as part of its broader engagement with its trading partners at the end of the nineteenth

[303] For a discussion of the relationship between copyright and human rights, see Sundara Rajan, Copyright and Creative Freedom, *supra* note 4, ch. IX ("Copyright and Human Rights"), at 205–33.

[304] *See* C. Subramania Bharati, *Rasa—The Key-Word of Indian Culture*, in Agni and Other Poems and Translations & Essays and Other Prose Fragments 69 (1980).

century. Its opening to international influences was compelled by the United States after more than two centuries of seclusion known as the Edo era, and it was in the subsequent period of the Meiji Restoration that Japan was first exposed to European law.[305] In 1896, the country adopted a civil code derived from German law;[306] the copyright law was adopted in 1899, the same year in which Japan joined the Berne Convention.[307]

Japan's copyright law was initially based on the German model, and a look at the current law shows its continued influence. Japanese law protects three moral rights—disclosure, attribution, and integrity—and the concept of disclosure, as in the German law, is central to the Japanese appreciation of these rights.[308] Attribution includes protection for those writing under a pseudonym, but the right is somewhat restrictive. In particular, it allows the omission of attribution in certain circumstances—when "it is found that there is no risk of damage to the interests of the author in his claim to authorship in the light of the purpose and the manner of exploiting his work and in so far as such omission is compatible with fair practice."[309] In contrast, the integrity right is almost completely open-ended, and the law even goes so far as to specify that any change made "against [the author's] ... will" is a violation of the right.[310] The Japanese law seems to invert international practice in a curious way, making attribution subject to proof of damage to reputation, while integrity is protected without limit. Japanese moral rights are inalienable, although the economic rights in a work may be "transferred in whole or in part."[311]

At first glance, the problem of the duration of moral rights seems basically resolved by protecting moral rights for the term of copyright—under Japanese law, the relatively short duration of fifty years after the death of the author.[312] But the

305 *See* Copyright Research and Information Centre, *History of Copyright System in Japan*, https://www.cric.or.jp/english/csj/csj2.html.

306 Minpō [Minpō] [Civ. C.], no. 89 of 1896 (Japan).

But see the interesting discussion in Charles P. Sherman, *The Debt of Modern Japanese Law to French Law*, 6(3) CAL. L. REV. 198, 200–201 (1918). Sherman shows the interplay of French and German influences that eventually led to the adoption of a Civil Code modeled on German law but still a strong reflection of French legal principles.

307 Chosakukenhou [Copyright Act], Law No. 39 of 1899 (Japan). *See* Sherman, *supra* note 301; Copyright Research and Information Centre, *supra* note 300. Japan originally acceded to the Berne Convention on July 15, 1899.

308 *See* Chosakukenhou [Copyright Act], Law No. 52 of 2021, arts. 18–20 (Japan), https://www.japaneselawtranslation.go.jp/en/laws/view/4207.

309 Id. at art. 19(1)(3):

> It shall be permissible to omit the name of the author where it is found that there is no risk of damage to the interests of the author in his claim to authorship in the light of the purpose and the manner of exploiting his work and in so far as such omission is compatible with fair practice.

310 Id. at art. 20(1); special exceptions to the open-ended integrity principle, including the cases of architectural works and computer programs, are listed in art. 20(2).

311 Id. at art 61.

312 The term is short when compared to the international standard set by the European Union, which is now life plus seventy years. India's term of protection is ten years shorter, at life plus sixty years. Japan's

Japanese formula for accomplishing this is unusual. Japanese copyright law provides for the protection of moral rights, either for this duration or until the author's immediate family members, defined as the "bereaved family," have all died.[313] The "bereaved family" extends from grandparents to grandchildren, and if any of these family members survives the fifty-year period after the author's death, he or she will continue to hold the moral rights until his or her own death.[314] The effective term of protection for moral rights could thereby extend considerably beyond the statutory term of copyright protection, fifty years after the author's death. Interestingly, while the "bereaved family" members are alive, they can make a claim, not only against mistreatment that has occurred but also for the prevention of *potential* damage.[315]

But moral rights do not end with the family. Even after the expiry of the copyright term, it is prohibited to do anything that would be against the author's moral rights. Article 60 of the Japanese copyright law states,

> Even after the death of the author, no person who offers or makes available a work to the public may commit an act which would be prejudicial to the moral rights of the author if he were alive; provided, however, that such act is permitted if it is deemed not to be against the will of the author in the light of the nature and extent of the act as well as a change in social situation and other conditions.[316]

Explicit provision is not made for who is to enforce moral rights after the grandchildren of the author have also passed away. Two implications of this omission should be noted. First, family members in subsequent generations will continue to have a right to assert the author's moral rights, but their rights will not be unlimited. Rather, they will be subject to two tests: ascertaining the "will of the author," a key concept in Japanese moral rights, and determining whether the act complained of is appropriate in the light of a "change[d] ... social situation and other conditions." Secondly, it is obvious that assertion of the moral right is no longer an exclusive prerogative of the authors' descendants. Presumably, any interested person should have the right to assert the author's moral rights on his or her behalf under this provision.[317]

In all of these measures, Japanese law impresses with its pragmatic approach to protection. The Japanese rationale for maintaining moral rights recognizes the

Copyright Act, *supra* note 303, at art. 51 provides for this basic term of protection, with variations for certain types of subject matter.

[313] Id. at art. 116(3).
[314] Id. at art. 116(1).
[315] Id. at art. 112 refers to both "cessation" and "prevention" of infringement. *See also* id. at art. 116(1).
[316] Id. at art. 60.
[317] Id. at art. 62 provides for copyright to revert to the National Treasury if the author has no heirs, but it is not clear that this applies to moral rights.

close connection between authors and their descendants; it is reasonable to think that grandchildren may have known the author, while great-grandchildren most likely would not have had this opportunity. At the same time, one of the frustrations with moral rights law, as apparent in India's *Sehgal* case, is that the remedy comes too late to prevent damage to cultural heritage. By providing that authors may "demand … prevention" of harmful acts, Japanese law makes an attempt to forestall this result.[318]

Two unique features of Japanese moral rights deserve special mention. The first of these has to do with the role of honor and reputation in Japanese law. The concept of "honor" has become nebulous in Western countries and its legal meaning in modern democracies is unclear. In recent amendments to its law, the Republic of Ireland decided to remove it altogether from the legislative formulation of moral rights.[319] Elizabeth Adeney argues that this is a mistake. Although it seems archaic, the use of the word "honor" signifies that the integrity right extends to something more than the protection of reputation alone.[320] In Adeney's view, this "something more" is the recognition of a subjective element in moral rights—the idea that an author's own feelings about the treatment of his or her work should be acknowledged and accepted as legal evidence of infringement.

But there is an element of circularity in this line of reasoning. The question of subjectivity is usually dealt with in the language of the integrity right. If the law requires "proof of damage to honor or reputation," and the author's feelings are said to furnish sufficient proof, then an assertion by the author that his or her reputation has been damaged should meet this requirement. If this is the case, why do we need an additional subjective requirement in the form of "honor"? The same result could be accommodated by an open-ended right of integrity in the French or German style. Adeney argues that the Canadian case of *Snow* provides the example of a common-law court accepting subjective standards. It is true that the court in *Snow* discusses "a certain subjective element or judgment on the part of the author," but only "so long as it is reasonably arrived at." [321] The *Snow* case introduced the evidence of experts on Snow's reputation, thereby satisfying the requirement

318 Id. at art. 112.

319 Copyright and Related Rights Act 2000 (Act No. 28/2000) (Ir.), https://www.irishstatutebook.ie/eli/2000/act/28/enacted/en/html. Section 109(1) of the Act states,

> Subject to the exceptions and qualifications specified in sections 110 and 111, the author of a work shall have the right to object to any distortion, mutilation or other modification of, or other derogatory action in relation to, the work which would prejudice his or her reputation and that right shall also apply in relation to an adaptation of the work.

Despite this apparent modernization in terminology, Ireland also continues to refer to the attribution right as the "paternity right": id. at s. 107(3).

320 *See* Elizabeth Adeney, *The Moral Right of Integrity: The Past and Future of "Honour,"* 2 Intell. Prop. Q. 111 (2005).

321 In *Snow*, *supra* note 77, at para. 7, Judge O'Brien states,

> It is conceded that the sculpture is a 'work' within the meaning of the Copyright Act. I believe the words 'prejudicial to his honour or reputation' in s. 12(7) involve a certain subjective element or judgment on the part of the author so long as it is reasonably arrived at.

that the complaint of damage to the author's reputation should be "reasonable."[322] In legal terms, reasonableness is equivalent to "objectivity."

The answer may lie in the idea that integrity accommodates two distinct types of issues—those involving an author's professional reputation and others involving the author's personal "honor." Adeney draws attention to the statement of the Italian delegate to the Rome revision conference of the Berne Convention in 1928, at which moral rights were first adopted:

> The Italian delegate referred to " ... the [author's] right to prevent his work being altered, deformed, transformed or abridged to the prejudice, not only of his patrimonial interests, but of the even more delicate interests of his scientific, literary or artistic personality, a personality represented by this very work, doing little here to clarify the notion of the intérêts moraux."[323]

The key word in the Italian statement would seem to be "personality," and the idea of damage to the personality, or personal harm, could indeed help to clarify the meaning of "honor." Adeney's instinct that "honor" still matters seems sound.

The Japanese approach to honor accords greater substance to this ancient concept. Notably, Japanese scholarship discusses the suitability of a "public apology" as a remedy for damaged honor or reputation.[324] Indeed, Japan's focus on practical remedies to a violation of moral rights is impressive. The Japanese approach is informed by an awareness that, all too often, it will be impossible to restore the status quo once a violation of moral rights has occurred. *Amar Nath Sehgal* is a case in point: when Mr. Sehgal sued, the best he could do was to ask for an injunction to prevent further damage to his work. Nothing could undo the damage that had already been caused by the mistreatment of his sculpture. In any event, it took him thirteen years to obtain a "preliminary" injunction!

A second point relates to a striking difference between Japanese law and other legal systems of the world: Japan is one of a very small minority of countries to allow companies to hold a moral right.[325] This peculiarity of Japanese law is

Adeney, *supra* note 315, at 128 feels that the case evidences a particular concern with honor rather than reputation.

[322] *Snow*, *supra* note 77.

[323] Adeney, *The Moral Right of Integrity*, *supra* note 315, at 118 (footnote omitted). See the discussion *infra* of "honor" in relation to performers' moral rights; Adeney suggests that the approach to "honor" envisioned by the delegates discussing the WPPT before its conclusion could help to clarify the current meaning of the term in Berne.

[324] For a fascinating discussion of this subject, see Naoya Ichimura, *Restoration-of-Status-Quo Relief to Redress Infringement of Authors' Moral Rights*, Copyright Research and Information Center (n.d.), http://www.cric.or.jp/cric_e/cuj/cuj.html.

[325] As noted, *supra* note 139, Korea also allows corporations to hold moral rights, though in far more limited circumstances than Japan. If a work is attributed to a human author, the corporation's right of attribution will not apply. *See* Korea's 1957 Jeojakgwonbeop [Copyright Act], amended by Act No. 9625, Apr. 22, 2009, art. 9 (S. Kor.), https://www.law.go.kr/engLsSc.do?menuId=1&subMenuId=

accomplished by including corporations within the Japanese definition of authorship.[326] But this provision embodies something more subtle than the legislative separation of moral rights from the personality of a human author. Rather, it seems to reflect Japan's corporate culture, which places unique human responsibilities upon the leaders of companies. Corporate honor has long been a real phenomenon in Japan. Corporate leaders in Japan have even been known to respond to professional disgrace by suicide. Executives cannot live with the damage to their honor.[327] Rather than an example of moral rights supporting corporate power, the Japanese law, when seen in cultural context, is more properly understood as an argument for extending the concept of honor to corporate conduct.[328]

E. Moral Rights and Creative Freedom: Post-Socialist Countries

Post-socialist countries offer a unique window onto moral rights in societies with "an instinctive respect for culture."[329] Their experience highlights the role of artists—and perhaps especially, writers—in establishing the accountability of the state and promoting freedom and democracy. The history of British and European copyright laws already traces a similar historical pattern. Copyright emerged in the United Kingdom out of a struggle against censorship by the monarch, exercised through its organ of control, the Stationers' Company. In France, it was a product of resistance to the Paris printers' monopoly.[330] In Central and Eastern Europe, however, these struggles took place during modern times, and they also happened in countries where the written word enjoyed extraordinary prestige. As Russian

21&tabMenuId=117&query=%EC%A0%80%EC%9E%91%EA%B6%8C%EB%B2%95# (on "Author of Professional Works").

[326] *See* Japan's Copyright Act, *supra* note 303, at arts. 14–16.

[327] *See "Modest" Japanese CEOs Escape Wrath*, Taipei Times 11 (Mar. 23, 2009), http://www.taipeitimes.com/News/biz/archives/2009/03/23/2003439154. Traditional Korean corporate culture (*chaebol*) is similar. For a fascinating overview of Korean moral rights, emphasizing culture as a factor in Korean copyright law, see Ilhyung Lee, *Culturally-Based Copyright Systems? The U.S. and Korea in Conflict*, 79 Wash. U. L.Q. 1103, 1137–40 (2001), https://journals.library.wustl.edu/lawreview/article/2451/galley/19284/view/. Korea's Copyright Act, *supra* note 322, at art. 14 affecting the duration of moral rights, shows the close relationship between Japanese and Korean law; this is also discussed by Lee, *supra*, at 1139, who notes that, notwithstanding these links and resemblances, Korean moral rights are *not* "a matter of mere transplantation."

[328] A similar provision may be found in Korea's Copyright Act, *supra* note 322, at art. 9. The structure of Korean copyright law closely resembles Japanese law and, through it, German law. For a discussion of the colonial history between Japan and Korea, and Korea's distinctive cultural affinity with moral rights, see Lee, *supra* note 326.

[329] Péter Munkácsi, *Moral Rights and the Cultural Aspects of Hungarian Copyright Law: 1945–2000*, in Cambridge Handbook of Intellectual Property in Central and Eastern Europe 51 (Mira T. Sundara Rajan ed., 2019); apparently quoted from the first edition of this book, at 186.

[330] See discussion in Chapter 2, *infra* notes 25-33 and accompanying text.

poet, Osip Mandelstam, commented, "Only in this country is poetry respected—people are killed for it."[331]

Law also had great prestige. In pre-socialist times, many countries in Central and Eastern Europe had laws and constitutions setting out noble aspirations. By the standards of the time, they were often modern, and even advanced. As socialist governments took power, however, a gap between the realities of government and the letter of the law became increasingly wider. Dissidents throughout the region often came to rely upon the language of the law to articulate social grievances, but this appeal to principle had little impact upon irredeemably corrupt and repressive governments.

Copyright itself emerged in these countries as a result of parallel developments to those in the rest of Europe: the establishment of printing technology and the ensuing struggles among church, state, and the intelligentsia for the ear (or eye) of the public. As elsewhere, the evolution of copyright was colored by local culture and, in particular, by the dynamics of the relationships among these groups. For example, Hungarian copyright scholar Péter Mezei writes,

> The development of Hungarian copyright law spans more than two centuries. Over this period, journals teemed with legal disputes similar to those of the Western world, and jurisprudence took a comparable course in unfolding its wings. Classical Hungarian copyright scholars were expected to provide answers to analogous theoretical and practical challenges. But legislative developments lagged behind those of the West. It was only in 1884 that the first Hungarian Copyright Act made up this lag in the progress of copyright legislation. This backlog was further reduced by the Hungarian legislator when the country became a signatory to the Berne Convention in 1922.[332]

Moral rights in the region developed against this background. Consistent with Western European experience, the moral rights idea had established itself in this region by the early nineteenth century. Mezei points out the genesis of moral rights in Hungary in a legal treatise by Ferencz (Schedel) Toldy in 1838, who also emphasized the *meritus publicus*, or public good, of the idea.[333]

But it is also worth mentioning that the situation becomes murkier as we move from Eastern Europe to Western Asia, where many of the countries that were once

[331] Mandelstam's comment to his wife is quoted in Geoffrey Hosking, A History of the Soviet Union 1917–1991 408 (1992).

[332] Péter Mezei, *The Development of Hungarian Copyright Law until the Creation of the First Copyright Act (1793–1884)*, *in* Cambridge Handbook of Intellectual Property in Central and Eastern Europe 37 (footnote omitted) (Mira T. Sundara Rajan ed., 2019).

[333] Although Toldy did not develop this idea further in his 1840 commentary: id. at 40–41. Interestingly, Toldy considered it a type of *property* interest and one with a social benefit: "possession to be respected above all in moral considerations seen as the fruit of offering the noblest of talents to the noblest of ends (*meritus publicus*)": id. at 40.

socialist republics are located. Here, the social context was different, and information about the history of moral rights is more difficult to come by. However, if anything, the prestige of culture as we move from West to East—and of literature, in particular—increases. In a fascinating article about moral rights in Georgia, Georgian lawyer Nino Tsaturova comments,

> The moral rights regime under Georgian legislation serves the needs of Georgian society, on the one hand, by giving authors rights that enable them to have control over their work, while, on the other hand, permitting members of the public to make use of the works in an authentic form. The importance of moral rights for Georgian society deserves further research, but it seems clear that, having a rich and unique culture, Georgians should treat moral rights respectfully, and be able to make use of the wide range of benefits to culture that moral rights can provide.[334]

At the same time, Tsaturova highlights the prestige of culture in Georgia:

> Georgian culture is ancient and unique, stretching back for millennia. Poetry, music, and dance are integral parts of Georgian life. A strong literary tradition arises out of the Georgian language and alphabet. The world-renowned epic poem "The Man in the Panther's Skin" was written by the medieval Georgian poet Shota Rustaveli, and occupies a special place in Georgian culture: quotations are used as proverbs, characters have become role models, and the poem is still one of the most-read books in many Georgian families. Georgian people are also proud of their rich musical culture, which has its roots in ancient times. Throughout the history of Georgia, artists have always played a special role in the development of Georgian society and cultural identity. Despite repeated periods of foreign occupation, the distinctiveness of Georgian culture has been preserved, mainly because of a strong sense of national identity and unity forged by artists.[335]

Tsaturova opens her article with a quote from Rustaveli's work, in which the poet identifies himself as the author of the work, transformed by him, as he writes, from its Persian origins into a "pearl" of Georgian culture. The quote highlights the value of poetic attribution in this tradition. It does so in a manner that is reminiscent of the verses by which Indian poets identify themselves:

[334] Nino Tsaturova, *The Treatment of Authors' Moral Rights in Georgia*, *in* CAMBRIDGE HANDBOOK OF INTELLECTUAL PROPERTY IN CENTRAL AND EASTERN EUROPE 208 (Mira T. Sundara Rajan ed., 2019).
[335] Id.

> This Persian tale, now made into Georgian, has hitherto been like a pearl of great price cast in play from hand to hand; now, I have found it and mounted it in a setting of verse; I have done a praiseworthy deed. The ravisher of my reason, proud and beautiful, willed me to do it.[336]

When Soviet socialism emerged on this scene, it brought a strong ideological influence—a change that may initially have been invigorating for writers and artists but one that quickly became chilling. The idealism of early socialism was inexorably overwhelmed by political ideology. By a bitter irony, the ideological aspect of socialism imbued all human expression with powerful political connotations, and none more so than the socially prestigious and powerful works of authors and artists.

The ideological influence on Soviet and Soviet satellite countries was profound for two reasons. First, Soviet law, like most other aspects of Soviet policy, proceeded on the basis that pre-existing structures would be destroyed and replaced with ideologically infused constructions. In the context of copyright law comment, this meant that socialist copyright ideology replaced the existing copyright laws of these countries, which had been relatively well developed for their times. Accordingly, as Soviet law became increasingly ideological and less connected to external trends, their laws became correspondingly out of date. At the same time, the elimination of underlying concepts that were the norm in other countries, and which were characteristic of modern copyright law from the earliest time of its emergence in Europe, created important disparities in relation to their copyright laws when compared to the rest of the world.

Secondly, under the shared experience of state oppression, the work of authors and artists became increasingly important across all countries of this region—in cultures where it had already been very important before. Literature, music, and the arts came to be deeply associated with the struggle to maintain a sense of cultural identity, as Tsaturova has noted, and, of course, with the right to dissent. In many ways, especially in an environment of restricted access to information that is difficult to understand today, the possibilities of human existence beyond the socialist sphere were kept alive by these efforts.

The repression of free speech and thought are intrinsic features of totalitarian government. To an extent, rights of authorship, like every other aspect of the law, became an instrument of state power against the people. But a study of law and its evolution under totalitarian government can only provide a partial picture of the truth. This is because socialist law was also characterized by another feature, equally pernicious in its own right—a widening chasm between the letter of the law and the government's actions. This is probably one of the key factors

[336] Id. (footnote omitted).

underlying the difficulty of enforcing intellectual property rights in post-socialist countries today. The problem of enforcement points to a fundamental failure of the rule of law, experienced by these societies over an extended period of their history.

Perhaps more than any other system of law, socialist law promoted the enactment of laws with no real intent to enforce them. Indeed, it would be fair to say that socialist governments had no capacity to enforce authors' rights in the usual sense of the term, because the structural features of socialist government imposed practical limits on free expression. In particular, publication in socialist countries was generally controlled by the state. In the Soviet Union, the state was both the publisher of most works and the overseer of private publishing initiatives such as the famed literary journal, *Novy Mir*.[337] It is no accident that anti-state activists in Soviet countries called for practical observance of the law as a first step in lifting repression. "Respect the Constitution!" was the rallying-cry of dissidents in Stalin's time.[338]

The copyright framework that emerges from the post-socialist experience is characterized by a number of unique features distinguishing it from Western norms. These elements intend to atone for the mistreatment of authors under socialist rule by addressing past instances of abuse and establishing a new framework of respect. Accordingly, post-socialist copyright represents an expansion of moral rights into new areas. New moral principles address the mistreatment of dissident authors in Soviet times, attempting to compensate for the practical inability to enjoy the benefits of copyright by providing for a renewed term of protection for many rehabilitated authors.[339] Moral rights not only arise in relation to copyright works but are also recognized in scientific innovation, represented by patents.[340] The protection of works in the public domain through moral rights is a definite priority. And, finally, moral rights are generally considered relevant to new technological creation.

The level of protection for moral rights fluctuates with the general ebb and flow of social reform processes active in these countries. Times of greater sympathy between the government and the people translate directly into improved protection for the moral rights of authors. When the historical wheel comes full circle, and a new cycle of repression rises and subsides, moral rights principles from the past are revisited and, most often, reinstated in reformed laws.

Ironically, the study of Russian law therefore remains an essential part of understanding the legal history of the region—though only one part.[341]

[337] Hosking, *supra* note 325, at 410–11 describes the curious relationship of give-and-take between the editor of *Novy Mir*, Alexander Tvardovsky, and the government.

[338] Id. at 414–26. See also the comprehensive discussion of this issue in Sundara Rajan, Copyright and Creative Freedom, *supra* note 4, ch. V ("Revolution and Reform"), at 107–20.

[339] The circumstances in which this protection is allowed are discussed *infra*.

[340] *See* 2008 Civil Code, *supra* note 38, at arts. 1345 (right of authorship) and 1356.

[341] In view of Russia's current status as an aggressor nation, updates to the discussion of Russian law that follows have deliberately been kept to a minimum. This section has been retained for the sake of

1. Historical Context: Socialism, Russia, and Post-Socialist Countries

Like developing countries, post-socialist countries, too, represent a hybrid legal tradition. The socialist law common to them since the latter half of the twentieth century is known for its extreme emphasis on codification, surpassing even civil law jurisdictions in its affinity for codified laws.[342] This shared political heritage brings a surface veneer of similarity to their laws. So, too, does the behemoth of received Russian law, a product of Soviet expansion into the region and an omnipresent background reality. As I noted in an earlier work,

> It is well-known that Central and East European countries experienced Soviet expansionism in the political arena; what is less obvious is that they were also subject to a form of Russian imperialism in the legal sphere. Any in-depth study of socialist law inevitably turns towards Russian law. Many copyright laws in the "Eastern Bloc" were closely based on Soviet copyright statutes; as for free speech, it was conditioned by the physical or psychological presence of the Soviet Union in Eastern Europe, as well as whatever Indigenous patterns of repression developed.[343]

But if we scratch this polished surface, the extraordinary diversity of post-socialist countries becomes apparent. The socialist era exaggerated similarities by painting over the colors of the region with the uniform grey of the "Iron Curtain." The post-socialist period promotes diversity in all its forms—both positive and negative, from cultural reawakening to social disintegration. The region is affected by a great variety of political affiliations and social trends. Oppression was experienced differently by each country, both at the hands of the Soviet powers and under its own rulers. The re-assessment of the past has also been approached differently by different countries. The diversity of pre-socialist cultural traditions in Central and Eastern Europe, denied by Soviet imperialism, has come to be acknowledged. Factors from European unification to Islamic resurgence affect the area of Eastern Europe and Western Asia roughly known as "post-socialist."[344]

preservation. When Russia rejoins the international community, and if further versions of this work are published, they will be updated at that time.

[342] The characteristics of Soviet legal systems are usefully summarized in GENNADY M. DANILENKO & WILLIAM BURNHAM, LAW AND LEGAL SYSTEM OF THE RUSSIAN FEDERATION 1–10 (1999).

[343] Mira T. Sundara Rajan, *Copyright and Free Speech in Transition: A New International Perspective*, *in* COPYRIGHT AND FREE SPEECH: COMPARATIVE AND INTERNATIONAL ANALYSES 315, para. 13.09 (Jonathan Griffiths & Uma Suthersanen eds., 2005). *See also* Mihály Ficsor, *The Past, Present and Future of Copyright in the European Socialist Countries*, 118 RIDA 33 (1983)—a comprehensive article that includes a discussion of how the European socialist countries traced their copyright laws to Soviet, and through it Russian, law.

[344] The Russia–Europe Agreement marked a thawing point in Russian relations with the European Union, but, of course, it falls far short of Russian membership in the European Union. For a discussion

In this shifting landscape, moral rights have been a surprising historical constant. Virtually all of the countries of Central and Eastern Europe have recognized moral rights in their copyright laws. In some cases, the recognition predates Soviet times—Russia has recognized copyright in the form of an "author's right" since 1828 and protected a very strong moral right of integrity from 1911.[345] This tradition later led to the recognition of a right of "inviolability," first named in the 1961 Soviet legislation, which continues to be mirrored in the post-socialist laws of the region.[346] The Czech Law of April 2000 provides that "[t]he author shall have the right to the inviolability of his work."[347] Hungary and other socialist countries were members of the Berne Convention from pre-socialist times. For Hungary, the adoption of moral rights at the 1928 Berne revision conference led to problems of compatibility between Hungarian copyright law and the Berne Convention; they were resolved through the intervention of Hungary's Supreme Court, the *Kúria*, which recognized moral rights in a series of rulings post-1928.[348] Russia's decision to abstain from membership in Berne was exceptional and reflected a variety of domestic policy issues. There were concerns about "opening Russia to an influx of foreign literature," with "political and cultural as well as economic" implications; even the endorsement of eminent Russian writers was not enough to push Russia into Berne membership.[349] Russia finally joined the Berne Convention in 1995, a mere six years after the United States became a member.

But legislative recognition in socialist countries must be seen in context. The primacy of legislation as a source of law is undeniable; but the practical context in which that legislation functioned must be taken into account. The landmark Soviet law of 1961 is a case in point.[350] The law recognized an author's right to the "inviolability" of his or her work, and at first glance, it appears that earlier and more

of the Agreement on Partnership and Cooperation between the European Union and Russia and its impact on Russian copyright law, see Michiel Elst, *The Interaction of European Community and Russian Copyright Law: A Matter of Partnership and Cooperation*, 22(3) REV. CENT. & E. EUR. L. 267, 276–85 (1996).

[345] Indeed, even the structure of the 1828 legislation lays open the possibility that Russian law implicitly recognized a moral right of disclosure: *see* Sundara Rajan, COPYRIGHT AND CREATIVE FREEDOM, *supra* note 4, at 79–87. Interestingly, the moral right of integrity recognized in the reforms of 1911 sought to protect an author against his or her own publisher—a theme that resurfaced in Soviet legislation and legal theory, which saw the publisher, crudely, as the "capitalist" exploiting the author.

[346] *See* Sundara Rajan, COPYRIGHT AND CREATIVE FREEDOM, *supra* note 4, at 98–99; the language of inviolability dates from 1961.

[347] *See* Tento zákon [Copyright Act], Zákon č. 121/2000 Sb., § 11(3) (Czech), https://wipolex-res.wipo.int/edocs/lexdocs/laws/en/cz/cz029en.pdf.

[348] *See* Péter Mezei, *A Development of Hungarian* Copyright Law *Until the Creation of the First Copyright Act (1793-1884)*, *in* INTELLECTUAL PROPERTY: EASTERN EUROPE & THE CIS 37 (Mira T. Sundara Rajan ed., 2019).

[349] Sundara Rajan, COPYRIGHT AND CREATIVE FREEDOM, *supra* note 4, at 85–87.

[350] Fundamentals of Civil Legislation of the Union of Soviet Socialist Republics and the Union Republics, c. IV, VVS SSSR, 1961, No. 50, Item 525 (1961 Fundamentals). An English translation is available in Newcity, *supra* note 4, at 181–87.

limited language protecting the author's right of integrity has been expanded by the new right of inviolability.[351] Yet, no author could expect to take action against state bodies that controlled the publication of his or her work and, invariably, measured its print-worthiness according to political criteria. By 1961, the reality was that the identity of publisher and government had essentially merged, and the idea of an author being able to act against a publisher was largely meaningless.[352] Perhaps this is why it made sense to remove the terminology of "exclusivity" from Soviet law: under Article 98 of the Russian Civil Code of 1961, the rights of authors were not exclusive in any real sense of the term. The ability of the author to exercise them depended on government cooperation. In other words,

> There can be no doubt that the shape of moral rights in socialist countries, like driftwood caught in the tides, bent under the pressure of political flux. Complex currents were at work. After a brief period of revolutionary *élan*, when nationalization dominated the copyright landscape, copyright rules were swiftly reinforced as part of a state strategy to win the support of authors and artists.[353] At different times in Soviet history, copyright and moral rights were improved—for example, to support reconciliation at the crucial time of reassessment after Stalin's death, known as the "Thaw"—or eviscerated, as in the post-Thaw period when the very idea of "exclusive" rights in one's own work was purged from the legislation, a consideration that was poorly balanced by the introduction of the terminology of "personal" rights for the first time in Russian copyright law.[354]

In summary, socialist copyright law was fundamentally shaped by two influences, clearly illustrated by the Russian example. The first, as noted above, has to do with the peculiarities of the socialist system of government. The Soviet system re-established censorship. In the Soviet Union, publishing was inextricably linked with government approval, and, as a result, the idea of a meaningful relationship between an author and his or her publisher was little more than fiction.

The second influence was also political, but in a much larger sense. The Soviet government always felt a need for the work of authors. Sometimes, as in the early period of the Revolution, the clarion call for support was messianic and full of enthusiasm, and it was heeded by great and rising voices—Mandelstam, Blok, Mayakovsky, among others. At other times, as under Stalin's rule, it was a crude

[351] In fact, in keeping with theories about the "bourgeois" nature of relations between the publisher and the author, the earlier right protected the author explicitly against the unauthorized intervention of the publisher.

[352] Sundara Rajan, COPYRIGHT AND CREATIVE FREEDOM, *supra* note 4, at 85–87, 79–88, 89–97, and 99–100.

[353] For a discussion of the nationalization of copyright in the Bolshevik period, see id. at 89–93. Nationalization has also been tried in India, with various results. *See* Sundara Rajan, *Moral Rights in the Public Domain*, *supra* note 177; Sundara Rajan, *The Lessons of the Past*, *supra* note 272.

[354] *See* Sundara Rajan, COPYRIGHT AND CREATIVE FREEDOM, *supra* note 4, at 98–99.

manipulation of authors for the promotion of state policy, and its victims were just as eminent—Akhmatova, Pasternak, Shostokovich. But, whatever its reasons—(the promotion of ideology in an ideology-based regime, or the demands of development in a "backward" society[355]—), the Soviet state always needed authors and artists.

In keeping with this pattern, Gorbachev's ascent brought new vitality to authors' rights. Gorbachev wanted the support of creative people, and the late 1980s and early 1990s saw reforms that introduced the most pro-author copyright rules in Russian history.[356] In temporary reforms to Russian law, adopted in 1991, moral rights were considerably expanded, and the concept of exclusive rights of authorship was reinstated. Changes to moral rights introduced in Russia's Copyright Act of 1993, valid until 2008, represented new forces that were afoot—the creation of the WTO and its adoption of the TRIPs Agreement, signifying a practical and conceptual shift towards an economic, or commercial, model of copyright law.[357] The amended approach to moral rights in the 1993 legislation was closely, though not perfectly, aligned with the Berne Convention provision on moral rights.

The adoption of new provisions in 2006 represents, once again, a shift in the Russian approach to moral rights. There is a new sense of historicity about the treatment of moral rights in the Civil Code. Characteristically Russian terminology such as "inviolability" is restored from the 1961 Soviet law. The terminology of exclusivity is retained, but it refers only to an author's economic interests in his or her work. Provisions on the copyright of rehabilitated authors are retained in the new law. However, the general trend in the new provisions is actually to scale back Russian protection for moral rights from the levels in the 1993 Copyright Act. In this sense, the Russian legislation is, once again, an enigma—a law that is, in fact, highly Westernized, though it appears in the guise of an orthodox legal framework.

[355] Id. at 100.

[356] For a detailed discussion of the politics behind copyright changes of this period, see id. at 150–69.

[357] *See* Russian Copyright Act 1993, *supra* note 38, at art. 15. Part IV of the Russian Civil Code, *supra* note 38, was said to supersede all previously existing legislation in the field of intellectual property. The speed with which the changes were adopted, their comprehensiveness in repudiating previously existing law, and the relative secrecy in which these provisions were developed were all controversial. A quick overview of the legislation may be found in Sergey Budylin & Yulia Osipova, *Legislative Developments—Total Upgrade: Intellectual Property Law Reform in Russia*, 1(1) COLUM. J. E. EUR. L. 1 (2007). Budylin and Osipova do not draw attention to the novel conceptualization of intellectual property rights in the Code—e.g., the very idea of intellectual "property" is eliminated, and the Code is much closer to a *sui generis* conception of the rights. It is also interesting to note that the new provisions seem to represent some sort of effective compromise between two bureaus of the Russian government that have been charged with intellectual property regulation and have struggled with each other for supremacy: the Private Law Institute of the Russian Federation, reporting directly to the president of Russia; and Rospatent, the Russian patent agency. For a consideration of the Code from a patent law perspective, see Adolf Dietz, *Incorporation of Patent Law into Part Four of the Russian Civil Code: A Structural Analysis*, 6 PATENTS AND TECHNOLOGICAL PROGRESS IN A GLOBALIZED WORLD: LIBER AMICORUM JOSEPH STRAUS 687 (2009).

2. Moral Rights in Transition: The 1991 USSR Fundamentals of Civil Legislation

The first Russian foray into modern copyright law occurred at a true moment of transition: the 1991 Fundamentals came into effect just as the Soviet Union was on the brink of collapse.[358] The Fundamentals, *osnovy* in Russian, were a type of model code used by the member states of the Soviet Union to develop laws; as such, they could be compared to European harmonization directives on copyright among the EU member states.[359] Profound changes were made. The terminology of "exclusive" rights for authors was revived for the first time since 1928.[360] Moral rights included authorship, "the right to his or her name," a right to the integrity of the work, a right of publication, and a right of use with an important "moral" dimension.

a. Publication and Use

The right of use should be read in conjunction with the right of publication, which is identified explicitly. Open recognition of this right is especially meaningful in a country where political obstacles to publication imposed silence on generations of writers.

The author's right of use specifically included the right to produce translations and revised editions of one's own work.[361] It is interesting because it emphasizes authorship over ownership: a publication contract, for example, could not prevent an author from developing a revised edition of his own work.

The right of use presents a contrast to both the long-standing principle of freedom of translation that dominated early Russian copyright law and the idea of government control, which became the accepted norm after Soviet accession to the UCC in 1973. The "right to compensation for the consent to use, and the use of, the work"[362] was part of a comprehensive scheme to remove the possibility of compulsory purchase of an author's work by the state, which was a key feature of the legislation of the 1960s and a focal point of the controversy when the Soviet Union attempted to join the international copyright community by joining, not the Berne Convention but the UCC in 1973.[363] Article 138 of the Fundamentals of 1991

[358] 1961 Fundamentals, *supra* note 344.

[359] But it should be noted, perhaps in contrast to the European situation, that the Russian *osnovy* were often adopted unchanged into the legislation of the Soviet republics. See Dietz, *Incorporation of Patent Law into Part IV*, *supra* note 351, at 691, who feels that this is generally the case in the area of patent law, with greater diversity in the implementation of copyright.

[360] 1961 Fundamentals, *supra* note 268, at art. 138.

[361] Id. at art. 135.2.

[362] Id. at art. 135.2.

[363] *See* Sundara Rajan, Copyright and Creative Freedom, *supra* note 4, ch. V ("Revolution and Reform"), at 100–107.

reiterates that any use of an author's work "can only be done with the consent of the author or his successors, and with payment of compensation." The only exceptions to this rule arise in relation to uses of works by the public that are considered to be exempt from copyright restrictions. The list of fair uses, or fair dealings, in Article 138.2 closely resembles similar provisions in Western copyright laws, and it also provides specifically that "making one copy of a computer program by the owner of the copy" may be lawful.[364]

b. Authorship and Name

In relation to the moral rights of publication and use, the 1991 Fundamentals either introduced new protections or significantly improved upon existing ones. In contrast, the right of authorship and the right to one's name are new rights. They respond to characteristic problems confronted by authors in Soviet times, such as the appropriation of works and the systematic defamation of authors, even extending to the total destruction of their reputations, for political reasons.[365]

c. Integrity as Inviolability

The integrity right is defined in precise and unusually strong terms in the 1991 Fundamentals as the right of the author "to keep his or her work intact." This right evokes the memory of "inviolability," the strong language used to frame the integrity principle in the Soviet law of 1961. If anything, it seems even more powerful: the general idea of inviolability is extended into the absolute clarity of keeping a work "intact." According to this rule, any alteration of the work without the author's consent, even if it is undertaken by a publishing house, is prohibited.

The omission of "prejudice to honour or reputation," an important departure from Article 6*bis* of the Berne Convention, is retained from the Soviet legislation but given new life in the 1991 Fundamentals. This formula for the right of integrity fundamentally responds to the experience of Soviet censorship and, as such, may be even more significant than it is in jurisdictions with traditionally strong moral rights, such as France.

364 *See* art. 136.2(6) of the Fundamentals of Civil Legislation of the USSR and the Republics, ch. IV, Copyright, VSND i VS SSSR, 1991, No. 26, Item 773 (invalidated by Resolution of the Supreme Soviet of the Russian Federation No. 5352-1 of July 9, 1993) (1991 Fundamentals); this was permitted "under the conditions specified by legislation"—meaning, presumably, that specific provisions in legislation on computer programs could inform, and possibly override, this section. Permitted free uses included quotation, news reporting, reproduction for research, and reproduction for blind readers. The subsequent art. 136.3 also allowed use "for exclusively personal purposes."

365 *See, e.g.*, SHEILA FITZPATRICK, THE CULTURAL FRONT: POWER AND CULTURE IN REVOLUTIONARY RUSSIA 183–215 (1992). The case of *Shostakovich* is described by Sheila Fitzpatrick, who offers an analysis of his situation within the broader context of government control, manipulation, and repression of the musical world. Fitzpatrick concludes her discussion by noting that "his disgrace on each occasion proved temporary and his status as an acknowledged 'great Soviet composer' survived these debacles."

d. Inalienability and Inheritance

The Fundamentals of 1991 are generous to the author in their treatment of the inalienability and inheritability of moral rights. Article 135.6 provides that both the author's right to the integrity of the work and his or her right of publication shall be inherited by his or her "successors." In view of the following provision that restricts the rights of the "other successors" to inheriting a right of use only, it is clear that the moral rights, in keeping with their "personal" character, can descend only to the author's heirs, rather than his or her successors in title.[366] Once again, in an environment where it may not have been possible to publish an author's works during his or her lifetime, it seems well advised to make specific provision for the continued exercise of the right of first publication by an author's descendants.

e. Duration

For the first time in Russian or Soviet copyright law, Article 137 of the Fundamentals sets out a specific duration for authors' moral rights. Article 137.3 provides that the rights of authorship, name, and integrity "shall be protected permanently." In this respect, the transitional legislation follows the tradition of protection in strong moral rights jurisdictions, especially France.[367] Presumably, since the moral rights are inherited by the author's heirs, it is their prerogative to enforce them after the author's death. However, in contrast to the current Russian Code, section IV of the Fundamentals does not specifically address the methods of enforcing moral rights after the author's death.[368]

f. Performers

Finally, the Fundamentals took the unusual step of protecting the moral rights of performers, eleven years before an international moral right for performers was established by the WPPT. Article 141.1 provides that performers, actors, stage managers, and conductors all have a right to the protection of their name, as well as a right to the protection of their "performance or rendition" from distortion. The right to be named is protected "without limitation in time."[369] Performers have traditionally been viewed as those who *disseminate* the works of composers rather than creators in their own right. The decision to protect performers' moral rights

[366] The moral right of the author, in contrast to the property rights, is considered to be vested in the author, rather than in the work; it is for this reason that, in the purest application of the doctrine, his personal heirs can inherit the right, but not his successors in title.

[367] *See* Code de la propriété intellectuelle, *supra* note 60, at art. L121-1.

[368] It should be noted that 1991 Fundamentals, *supra* note 358, at art. 135.6 provides for the author's heirs to inherit the moral rights of integrity and publication, but it does not mention the author's right to his name. Given the general framework of protection, it seems consistent with the logic of the legislation to infer that the right to a name is also inherited by the author's heirs and that its protection falls to them after his death.

[369] 1991 Fundamentals, *supra* note 358, at art. 141.5.

carried the Soviet Union forward into the vanguard of a new approach to moral rights.

In addition, an area of ambiguity in the Fundamentals arises in relation to works expressed orally that are not fixed. In keeping with the Russian tradition expressed in the landmark Copyright Act of 1911,[370] works of oral expression are entitled to copyright protection under the Fundamentals. However, the provision seems designed to address specific kinds of public appearances and "performances"—a speech, or music featuring improvisation—as the protection of folklore is specifically excluded.[371] The Fundamentals depart from earlier Russian policy in this respect: although section 1 of the 1911 Act listed only "speeches, lectures, essays, reports, sermons" in the section on oral works, it included other provisions on folklore. For example, section 13 provided for the copyright protection of "combinations of folklore, melodies, details, short stories and similar folk works that exist in aural forms" for fifty years from the date of publication—without, however, precluding others from making their own compilations of the same folk culture. The exclusion of folklore from the Fundamentals may have signified the intention of the Russian government to explore separate legislation on cultural heritage.

3. International Influence: The Russian Copyright Act of 1993

The moral rights provisions in the Russian Copyright Act of 1993[372] reveal a strong Western influence, superimposed upon the post-socialist orientation established by the transitional Fundamentals. Like the measures of 1991, the Act retained a number of features that responded to Soviet-era abuses, although they had a more subtle presence here than in the earlier law.

Both the structure and substance of the 1993 Act reflect the influence of Article 6*bis* of the Berne Convention. The distinctiveness of earlier expressions of moral rights in Russian laws was largely abandoned. A general reduction in their legal stature from 1991 is evident and can probably be attributed to the secondary importance of moral rights, as opposed to economic rights, in the climate for international copyright reform surrounding TRIPs.

However, the Russian Copyright Act of 1993 also retained some unique features to place its moral rights scheme above the minimum level required by Berne. In particular, the Act created a "paying public domain" for the protection of cultural works.[373]

370 *See* Copyright Law of March 20, 1911, POLNOE SOBRANIE ZAKONOV ROSSIISKOI IMPERII (SOB III) [THIRD COMPLETE COLLECTION OF LAWS OF THE RUSSIAN EMPIRE] 1914, Vol. XXXI, Item 34, 935, art. 2 (Russia) (Imperial Copyright Act 1911).

371 1991 Fundamentals, *supra* note 358, at art. 134.5.

372 *See supra* note 38.

373 The schemes are commonly known as *domaine public payant* and refer to the imposition of a royalty on the use of public domain works. The royalty can then be used to support cultural causes. *See*

a. Dualism

For the first time in the history of Russian copyright law, the Act of 1993 introduced a clear separation between the moral and economic rights of authors. The two areas are dealt with in two separate articles. Article 16 on "Economic Rights," like the Fundamentals of 1991, creates an exclusive right. Article 15 on "Moral Rights" provides simply for the "enjoy[ment]" of five moral rights. These include a "right of authorship," which protects the right of the author to be acknowledged as the author of his or her own work; a "right to be named," which allows the author to exploit his or her work, not only in his or her own name but also under a pseudonym or anonymously;[374] a "right of disclosure," which allows the author to determine the circumstances of first publication; as part of disclosure, a distinct right to "disavow or withdraw" the work from circulation; and, finally, a "right to the protection of the author's reputation" that replaces the right of integrity and allows the author to protect his or her work from any distortion or derogatory act that is "liable to prejudice his honour or dignity."[375] The right of use is not carried over from the Fundamentals. It is interesting to note that the right of withdrawal receives extensive treatment: Article 15.2 provides a detailed description of the circumstances in which the right may be exercised, including the author's obligation to compensate the user of the work for any damages resulting from his or her decision to withdraw.

Article 15 also specifies that moral rights are independent of economic rights and may continue to be exercised by the author even after he or she has relinquished the economic rights in a work. The suggestion of inalienability in this provision is not further clarified by provisions on the possibility of waiving moral rights.[376]

The broad and extensive list of rights in the Fundamentals, which is inclusive and not limited to the rights listed in Article 135.2, has been replaced by an apparently "closed" list of moral rights in Article 15 of the Copyright Act. Article 15 provides simply that "[t]he author shall enjoy the following moral rights in relation to his work." The combining of moral and economic rights in one section on the author's rights in the Fundamentals helped to emphasize the overlapping implications of moral and economic interests arising from the creation and use of creative

Adolf Dietz, *Term of Protection in Copyright Law and Paying Public Domain: A New German Initiative*, 22(11) Eur. Intell. Prop. Rev. 506 (2000).

[374] Clearly, the right to exploit the work under a pseudonym, or anonymously, is the crux of the distinction between this right and the preceding right to be acknowledged as the author of the work.

[375] *See* Igor Pozhitkov, *Copyright and Neighbouring Rights Protection in the Russian Federation*, 20(1) Rev. Cent. & E. Eur. L. 53, 62–63 (1994).

[376] For example, the widespread availability of waivers is considered to weaken substantially the moral rights provisions in the UK CDPA, *supra* note 113. *See* William R. Cornish, *Moral Rights under the 1988 Act*, 11(12) Eur. Intell. Prop. Rev. 449, 452 (1989); *see also* Vaver, *supra* note 18, at 274–78 (commenting on both the British and Canadian contexts).

works—for example, in relation to translations. The perspective was lost in the 1993 Act.

b. Duration of Protection: Perpetual Moral Rights and the Question of Inheritance

The Copyright Act of 1993 provides that the right of authorship, and the author's right to his or her name and the protection of his reputation, "shall be protected without limitation in time."[377] While Soviet jurisprudence generally interpreted the duration of moral rights as unlimited,[378] the Copyright Act of 1993 followed the 1991 Fundamentals in providing an explicit answer to the question of duration.

The related question of whether moral rights may be inherited receives a detailed treatment. Article 29, on the "Transfer of Copyright by Succession," refers to "succession," like the Fundamentals, in the specific sense of succession in title. In keeping with their "personal" character, the three principal moral rights of authorship, name, and reputation cannot be transferred by succession; they can only be inherited by the heirs of the author.

The Copyright Act took the laudable step of addressing the potentially problematic issue of who is to enforce an author's moral rights after his or her death. Presumably, this problem was beyond the scope of the transitional copyright provisions in the Fundamentals of 1991. Article 27.2 of the Copyright Act provides that the right to be named as the author of one's own works and the author's right to the protection of his or her reputation can be enforced by an executor appointed for this purpose by the author. In the absence of such an appointment, the author's own heirs or "an agency of the Russian Federation especially empowered to do so" could assert these moral rights after the author's death. It is interesting to note the implied legislative preference for an "executor of moral rights." Practical problems may well arise from entrusting moral rights to the author's heirs. Conflict can arise among the author's descendants, or they may not be sufficiently knowledgeable about the author's work to assert moral rights effectively.[379] However, it may be even more awkward to entrust moral rights to the state. For much of the Soviet period, the state was foremost in failing to respect the moral rights of authors.

In any event, a state agency for administering moral rights after the author's death was never created during the lifetime of the 1993 Copyright Act.[380] Doing so

377 *See* Russian Copyright Act 1993, *supra* note 38, at art. 27.

378 *See* Bella Karakis, *Moral Rights: French, United States and Soviet Compliance with Article* 6bis *of the Berne Convention*, 5 Touro Int'l L. Rev. 105, 133–34 (1994). Karakis's view is in accordance with the interpretation of well-known Soviet legal scholar Serge Levitsky.

379 This issue is discussed in Sundara Rajan, *Moral Rights in the Public Domain*, *supra* note 177, at 177–80.

380 Writing in 1993, Elst mentions the Russian Agency for Intellectual Property, which may have been the natural agency to exercise these rights: Michiel Elst, *New Developments in the Copyright Legislation of the Russian Federation: Part I*, 15(3) Eur. Intell. Prop. Rev. 95, 103 (1993). However, the Agency was abolished by an Edict of October 7, 1993, and a "new" authors' society—what Pozhitkov calls "an independent public organization"—was established: Pozhitkov, *supra* note 368, at 82–83. However, as

would almost certainly have raised issues of credibility in the Russian Federation. After all, Russia does not have a tradition of respecting press freedom, and creative writers have historically paid a very high price for exercising their profession in this restrictive political environment. It now seems incongruous for the post-Soviet state to become responsible for safeguarding authors' moral rights. In the past, the Union of Soviet Writers was charged with the implementation of authors' rights; at the time of Soviet accession to the UCC, the Writers' Union was revamped to deal with the enforcement of Soviet copyright abroad. However, the history of the Union was one of antagonism to the dissident community, and indeed, it often became an instrument of repression against its own members.[381]

c. Moral Rights in the Public Domain: *Domaine public payant*

The Russian Copyright Act of 1993 included a number of provisions geared towards the recognition of the public interest in copyright works. In this, it diverges from the individualistic or corporate character of Western copyright law, particularly as illustrated by the U.S. and common-law models.[382] It might be tempting, at first glance, to assume that the sense of a collective interest in copyright works is a product of the socialist mentality. However, if we think back to the socialist and Soviet approaches to copyright law—for example, in the nationalization decrees and, later, the Soviet Civil Code—we cannot fail to note that the public or collective interest, though identified, was poorly protected. Instead, the state enjoyed the benefits of copyright in more or less the same way that private copyright owners enjoy them in market-driven societies. A major difference, though, was that the rights of the state extended to expropriation. Of course, this is practically unheard-of in modern democratic jurisdictions.[383]

Pozhitkov points out, the society actually reflects the structure and leadership of both that Agency and the earlier Copyright Agency of the USSR (VAAP).

381 See the discussion of the role played by the Union of Soviet Writers (VOUAP) in maintaining ideological conformity between its members and the Communist Party in Hosking, *supra* note 325, at 222–25. The functions of VOUAP are described in Newcity, *supra* note 4, at 25–26, and suggest an outstanding level of state support through the agency for the activities of writers favored by the state. A generally positive view of the agency, in its later incarnation as the VAAP, may be found in an article written shortly after its establishment, from within the Soviet Union: N.S. Roudakov & I.A. Gringolts, *L'agence de l'URSS pour les droits d'auteur (VAAP)*, 81 RIDA 2, 3 (1974). See also the informative article by Elena Muravina, *Copyright Transactions in Russia Part I. The VAAP Era: 1973–1991*, 17 New Matter 4 (1993).

382 The term "corporate" is used here in the sense of relating to an incorporated business and not as referring to a group. In Canada, current amendments to bring Canadian law into conformity with the WIPO Internet treaties have moved it towards fewer allowable public uses. The trend was the subject of a book of critical commentary by Canadian lawyers and professors: *see* Geist, *supra* note 25. The essays are also available for free download under Creative Commons licenses at http://www.irwinlaw.com/store/product/120/in-the-public-interest.

383 In very rare cases, the expropriation of copyright may be used to support public policy. In the United Kingdom, the *Spycatcher* cases saw the House of Lords ordering that copyright royalties from the sale of a book be relinquished to the government—but the reason was extreme. The book, written by a British double agent who had worked in the Soviet Union, represented a flagrant violation of the public trust. The House of Lords was keen to disallow an apparent incentive, in the unusual form of

In specific terms, the Russian Copyright Act of 1993 was quite original in addressing the vulnerability of authors' moral rights in the public domain. The importance of moral rights does not evaporate when copyright in creative works expires and they enter the public domain. On the contrary, moral rights in public domain works assume a broader significance for cultural heritage—a point suggested even in the U.S. context by the decision in the *Shostakovich* case.[384] In a country like the Soviet Union, where the integrity of works as well as authorship, attribution, and reputation were all vulnerable to attack by the state, the continued protection of moral rights in the public domain may have considerable value.

Article 28.2 of the Copyright Act states that the three main moral rights of authorship, name, and reputation must be respected when using works in the public domain. Article 28.3 established a *domaine public payant* scheme for collecting a special royalty from public domain works to be paid into "an authors' professional fund or to an organization for the collective administration of the economic rights of authors." The scheme could contribute to the welfare of the post-Soviet creative community; it also had the symbolic value of representing a benefit flowing from the repression of past writers to future generations of authors. However, practical details of the plan, including who would receive the funds and how they would be spent, were never worked out, and the scheme for a paying public domain was not implemented while the Copyright Act of 1993 was in force.[385]

d. Reputation vs. Integrity

The recasting of the integrity right as a right of reputation in the Copyright Act of 1993 is striking. The right of reputation clearly shows the imprint of Article 6*bis* of the Berne Convention, which prohibits only those acts that would negatively affect an author's "honour or reputation." But the provisions of Article 15 go beyond Article 6*bis*, making reputation the actual focus of the right. Indeed, it is questionable as to whether Article 15 actually met the standard of protection set by the Berne Convention.

Article 6*bis* prohibits "any distortion, mutilation or other modification of, or other derogatory action in relation to, the ... work"; Article 15 prohibited only "any distortion or other derogatory act." The language seems sufficiently precise to imply an intentional restriction on the scope of Article 6*bis*, but much would have depended, here, on the interpretation of the Russian courts. Although Article 15 protected a right of "reputation," it did not explicitly provide for recourse in the

copyright royalties, for this egregious breach of public policy. *See A-G v. Guardian Newspapers Ltd (No. 1)* [1987] All E.R. 316; *A-G v. Guardian Newspapers Ltd (No. 2)* [1988] All E.R. 545 (UKHL).

[384] *Shostakovich*, *supra* note 97.

[385] An interesting discussion of a *domaine public payant* scheme proposed in Germany may be found in Dietz, *Term of Protection*, *supra* note 366, at 508–11. See also the related discussion of *domaine public payant* in Sundara Rajan, *Moral Rights in the Public Domain*, *supra* note 177, at 183–85.

case of damage to an author's reputation; it was only concerned with the possibility of prejudice to his "honour or dignity." However, it did seem to allow a flexible standard of proof, since the derogatory act need only be likely—"liable"—to cause damage. If, indeed, Article 15 did not meet the standard of protection required by Article 6*bis*, the exclusion of moral rights from the TRIPs Agreement meant that the Russian Federation did not face any overwhelming international pressure to improve the protection of the integrity right.

As Pozhitkov, writing in 1994, commented,

> The right to integrity was rescinded and substituted by the right to protection of an author's reputation [in the 1993 Copyright Act] which permits him to object to any distortion of a work or any derogatory action in relation thereto [that is "liable to prejudice his honour or dignity"]. It remains to be seen how broadly the courts will interpret this provision.[386]

When viewed in the context of Russian copyright history, the narrowness of the integrity right in the 1993 Copyright Act is surprising. The right to the "inviolability" of the work is a long tradition in Russian copyright law—it was even paid lip-service in the copyright jurisprudence of Soviet times. The 1991 Fundamentals reflected this tradition and arguably strengthened it, assuring authors that they had the right to keep their work "intact." It is quite probable that the change, once again, was a result of the U.S. influence on Russian law reform. The integrity right is generally acknowledged to be the most powerful moral right of the author, and the U.S. film industry, which has already faced moral rights problems in France, may well have feared the implications of a strong Russian right of integrity for their exports to Russia.[387] In contrast to the integrity right, however, the rights of authorship and name were retained in Article 15 of the Copyright Act, perhaps out of sensitivity to the Soviet-era treatment of authorship.

e. Performers' Moral Rights

Like the earlier Fundamentals, the Copyright Act predated the international community by a number of years with its recognition of moral rights for performers.[388] It recognized the performer's right to be named and to ensure the protection of his or her performance "against any distortion or other derogatory act liable to

[386] Pozhitkov, *supra* note 368, at 63—but he goes on to observe, "Since in the past there was no concept of monetary compensation for moral damage, authors did not usually submit the issues of violations of their moral rights to courts." This analysis of why moral rights claims did not find their way into the Soviet courtrooms is slightly surprising in the Soviet context. What seems more likely is that authors were fearful of bringing cases or thought of legal actions as being pointless.

[387] See *Turner Entertainment*, *supra* note 148, where the colorization of *The Asphalt Jungle* was prohibited by French courts as a violation of the director's right of integrity. It is, of course, clear that moral rights issues may be of concern to other U.S. copyright industries as well.

[388] The WPPT provisions to this effect were drafted in 1996 but came into effect only in 2002.

prejudice his honour or dignity." These protections could be found in Article 27 of the Copyright Act on the "Rights of the Performer." However, these moral rights were applicable only to the performer and, unlike the 1991 Fundamentals, did not offer protection to actors or stage managers. The provisions mirror the concerns of the U.S. film industry about the consequences of allowing actors to claim moral rights. Moreover, Russia, too, may have wanted to protect its historically important film industry from complications arising out of moral rights.

f. *Droit de suite* for the Visual Arts

In addition to extensive provisions on moral rights, the Copyright Act of 1993 made provision for protection of the *droit de suite*, the right of a visual artist to a royalty from the resale of his or her work after he or she initially parts with it to a first buyer. Again, Russian legislation on this issue predated the European initiative, which led to the adoption of a copyright harmonization directive on *droit de suite*, over British objections, in 2004.[389] The right is an accepted method of responding to the tendency of works of visual art to appreciate in value over time, sometimes substantially. Accordingly, where a work is sold at a price that is at least 20 percent greater than that of the previous sale, the seller is required to pay its creator a resale royalty of 5 percent of the resale price. Although the *droit de suite* is not technically a "moral right," it is supported by the rationale of a lasting connection between an author and his or her own work, which is at the heart of moral rights doctrine. Russian law did, indeed, seem to conceive of the *droit de suite* as a kind of moral right: it was protected under Article 17, in conjunction with an additional right of visual artists to continue to have access to their work after it is sold.[390]

g. Disclosure in the Post-Socialist Context

Finally, it is important to note that the issue of disclosure is fundamental to both the economic and moral rights in the Act. Indeed, the Act seems to address the problem of expropriation of authors' works, which was legally and practically tolerated in the Soviet Union, by creating and providing a detailed elaboration of an author's specific right to disclose his or her own work.[391] Disclosure of a work cannot occur without the author's consent, while the author's right to disclose his or her own work is stated in Article 15 on Moral Rights.

[389] The concern was that London would lose its competitiveness as a major art center, particularly vis-à-vis New York. *See* Will Bennett, *Art Sales: New Headache for Dealers*, THE TELEGRAPH (Dec. 20, 2005), http://www.telegraph.co.uk/culture/art/3648899/Art-sales-new-headache-for-dealers.html.

[390] Russian Copyright Act 1993, *supra* note 38, at art. 17.1.

[391] Id. at art. 4.11 ("disclosure of a work").

4. Programmers' Moral Rights: The Law on Computer Programs and Databases and the Recognition of Scientists

Until the adoption of the Civil Code provisions of 2008, the Russian intellectual property system included a number of laws dealing with copyright in addition to the Copyright Act of 1993. The difficulty of locating an authoritative source for the treatment of copyright has been one of the post-socialist problems associated with Russian law. The Civil Code provisions address this problem in two ways. First, the Civil Code consolidates Russian law on copyright into a single source. By doing so, it contributes to the clarity and accuracy of Russian provisions. Secondly, the Civil Code does what previous reforms should have done but did not do: it explicitly cancels other legislation dealing with copyright law.[392]

Prior to the Civil Code, other legislation dealing with copyright issues was adopted to meet the needs of specialized industries, as in the case of computer software, or to address broader social concerns, such as cultural heritage, information, and privacy.[393] A glance at the legislation that formerly dealt with computer programs—the Law on the Legal Protection of Computer Programs and Databases of 1992, last amended in 2002—[394] is helpful. It shows how moral rights in computer programs have been dealt with in the past and gives us a point of comparison on the terms of their inclusion within the new Civil Code.

The Law on Computer Programs supplemented provisions for the copyright protection of software that were already quite extensive in the Russian Copyright Act of 1993. It is therefore not surprising that, in some respects, the provisions of this special law overlapped with the Copyright Act. In others, however, the legislation succeeded in a more laudable objective—the introduction of specific measures directed towards the software industry. In these areas, the coverage of the special law was extraordinarily comprehensive. In effect, the law not only allowed for computer programs to be recognized as a form of literary work like any other but also conferred upon computer programmers a status more or less equivalent to that of authors, more generally, in Russian copyright legislation. Notably, the Law on Computer Programs and Databases created an exclusive right of authorship for programmers, extended to the creators of databases, reserved for "the natural person whose creative effort has brought about the creation of the computer program or database."[395]

[392] Dietz, *Incorporation of Patent Law into Part IV*, *supra* note 351, at 689–90 explains the process by which previous legislation was invalidated, noting that it occurred in several steps, and indeed it cancels all other legislation dealing with intellectual property rights overall.

[393] See, e.g., the comments on privacy law—analogous to intellectual property in many ways—in Mira T. Sundara Rajan, *The Past and Future of Privacy in Russia*, 27(4) Rev. Cent. & E. Eur. L. 625, 627–36 (2001). In particular, the "complexity of Russia's legal framework surrounding information" is cited as a general problem in this area: id. at 628.

[394] Federal Law No. 3523-1 on Computer Programs, Sept. 3, 1992, as amended by Federal Law No. 177-FL, Dec. 24, 2002 (Russ.).

[395] Id. at art. 8.

In fact, the Russian law established a range of moral rights for computer programmers, providing for rights of authorship, name, disclosure, integrity, and even withdrawal, which matched their general availability to authors of other kinds of works under the Copyright Act.[396] A comparison with the French approach is useful. The Russian provisions for programmers' moral rights occurred in the same year that French rules on moral rights in computer programs were elaborated, and they matched the model for protection in France established at that time. Subsequent amendments to the French *Code de la propriété intellectuelle* in 1994 recast the programmers' right of integrity to match the Berne scenario; modifications of the program must cause damage to the programmer's reputation before they can qualify as a violation of his or her right of integrity.[397]

Nevertheless, the right of software corporations in the work of their employees was simultaneously protected by Article 12 of the Russian Computer Law, which specifies that exclusive rights in a program or database created by an author who is an employee "shall [in the absence of contractual provisions] belong to the ... employer." Interestingly, the rights of disclosure and recall were added to the law on computer programs in 2002, along with the rights of employers. The overall logic of the scheme is not entirely clear, as the existence of moral rights independently of the economic—or, in the language of the Russian law, "exclusive"—rights would not have facilitated the dealings of companies with information technology. However, the provisions were consonant with the objectives of protecting free speech and scientific reputations. Oppression of free speech in the Soviet Union affected scientists in much the same way as it affected artists, and the Soviet scientific community can claim its own share of outspoken and courageous dissenters.[398]

5. Return to the Future: The 2008 Civil Code Provisions on Copyright

In 2008, a surprising new set of Russian provisions on intellectual property rights was introduced. The new Part IV of the Russian Civil Code was prepared in an

[396] Id. at art. 9.

[397] *See* French Code de la propriété intellectuelle, *supra* note 60, at art. L121-7, amended in 1994:

> Article L121-7—Modifié par Loi no 94-361 du 10 mai 1994, art. 3 JORF 11 mai 1994:
>
> Sauf stipulation contraire plus favorable à l'auteur d'un logiciel, celui-ci ne peut 1° S'opposer à la modification du logiciel par le cessionnaire des droits mentionnés au 2° de l'article L. 1226, lorsqu'elle n'est préjudiciable ni à son honneur ni à sa réputation; 2° Exercer son droit de repentir ou de retrait.
>
> [In the absence of provisions which are more favorable to the author of a computer program, he may not: (1) object to the modification of the program by the right holder mentioned in Article L122-6 (2), unless it causes prejudice to his honour or reputation; (2) Exercise his right of withdrawal.]

[398] Physicist Andrei Sakharov is probably the best known of these to outsiders.

environment of relative secrecy, with little input from the outside world. However, its pedigree can be traced to a draft version of the Civil Code that had been circulating since 2001, and upon which many of its provisions are closely based.[399]

Russia has not had a Civil Code section on intellectual property law since 1961.[400] By purporting to overrule all pre-existing intellectual property legislation in this field, the Civil Code creates post-socialist Russia's first unified system of intellectual property rights. The new Civil Code deals cleanly with old legislation, explicitly invalidating the Copyright Act of 1993 and related legislation such as the Law on Computer Programs and Databases of 1992.[401]

With respect to copyright law, Part IV signifies a fundamentally new approach. The very theory on which copyright is based is dramatically altered. Copyright is no longer considered a proprietary right. Instead, something akin to the operation of a software license occurs: transactions involving works take place without any real shift of ownership. Property rights subsist in the media in which works are recorded; those "copies" can be owned, but the underlying work remains attached to the author.[402] Dmitry Golovanov points out that, under the new Code,

> the results of intellectual activities as such may not be alienated or transferred. Only economic rights to such results as well as property rights to the material carriers of such results shall circulate on the market. Art 1227 of Part 4 of the Civil Code stipulates that "intellectual rights" shall not be interrelated with ownership rights concerning material carriers. Thus so far the concept of [the] proprietary nature of intellectual property is definitively rejected by the Russian lawmakers.[403]

In keeping with this approach, three different types of interests may arise: moral rights; economic rights, now known as "exclusive rights" in the Civil Code;[404] and what Galavanov calls "other rights blending together both economic and personal elements."[405]

In this last category, the most important right must certainly be the concept of disclosure. Disclosure involves the communication of a work to the public, but it arguably signifies something beyond the concept of publication *stricto sensu*, encompassing also the *intent* or *choice* to make a work public. Publication

[399] The draft Civil Code provisions of 2001 are discussed in detail in Sundara Rajan, COPYRIGHT AND CREATIVE FREEDOM, *supra* note 4, ch. VIII ("The Future of Post-Communist Copyright"), at 188–98.

[400] Before that, Russia included copyright in the Civil Code of 1887: *see* id. at 98–99.

[401] *See* Dietz, *Incorporation of Patent Law into Part IV*, *supra* note 351, at 689–90.

[402] For example, art. 1227 of the 2008 Civil Code, *supra* note 38, supports this view.

[403] Dimitri Golovanov, *Transformation of Authors' Rights and Neighbouring Rights in Russia*, IRIS PLUS (Feb. 2008), https://rm.coe.int/16807833f1.

[404] The terminology of "exclusive rights" was also distinguished from moral rights in the 1993 Copyright Act, *supra* note 38. The use of the term "exclusive" to designate economic rights is clarified in the current provisions of Part IV of the Civil Code.

[405] Golovanov, *supra* note 397, at 5.

specifically means the distribution of a work through professional channels, whereas communication of the work to the public can be accomplished by a variety of methods and technologies. The disclosure concept under the Civil Code extends to both economic and moral rights in a special sense: after the author's death, the current publisher of the work has a right to continue publishing the works unless the author has clearly indicated that this should not be the case.[406]

A second hybrid right is closely related to disclosure: it is the right to withdraw a work from circulation after it is published, which, as in the French model, entails an obligation on the author to compensate the publisher for its loss. The exceptions to the right of withdrawal are interesting ones. The authors of computer programs and of "works integrated into complex works (including audiovisual ones)" are denied the right to withdraw their works from circulation.[407] Once again, in different ways, software and film test the practical limits of moral rights.

Finally, the *domaine public payant* scheme set out in the Copyright Act of 1993 is not carried over into the Civil Code provisions. This decision appears to be based on the practical issue that the paying public domain was never actually implemented under the Copyright Act. If the scheme could not be implemented in the fifteen-year tenure of the Act,[408] it seems clear that the idea was not workable in the Russian context—whether for lack of political will or because of the practical difficulty of collecting royalties in public domain works in a post-socialist state. It is perhaps more significant that, in keeping with the logic of the 1993 Act, moral rights continue to be protected in public domain works.[409] As in the earlier law, any "interested person" can assert moral rights in a work that is in the public domain.[410] This is a potentially important tool for the protection of culture, but it leaves open the practical question of how to determine whether or not, under this broad provision, a given party has standing to sue on behalf of the moral rights in a work.

406 Golovanov, id., says, "After an author's death his or her heirs as well as the publisher (after the work entered the public domain) shall have the right to publish the works unless the author clearly expressed his wish to the contrary (art. 1268, paras. 2, 3)." Presumably, Golovanov is referring to two different scenarios: the persistence of the publisher's right for the duration of copyright protection—the life of the author plus seventy years (*see* 2008 Civil Code, *supra* note 38, at arts. 1281 and 1282)—and the right of the heirs to publish works as they subsequently enter the public domain (id. at art. 1282). Article 1338 concerns the right of the publisher in works that have never been made public. *See also* id. at arts. 1268.2 and 1268.3: the right to publish the works after the author's death is also granted to the heirs of the author. *See* Golovanov, *supra* note 397, at 5 ("Concept of 'Intellectual Rights,' Other Rights").

407 Golovanov, *supra* note 397, at 4–5 ("Concept of 'Intellectual Rights'").

408 Chapter IV of the Civil Code was concluded in 2006, although it did not enter into force until 2008: *see supra* note 398.

409 *See* Golovanov, *supra* note 397, at 4–5 ("Concept of Intellectual Rights").

410 *See* 2008 Civil Code, *supra* note 38, at art. 1267(2). An author may appoint a person to protect his or her moral rights after his or her death. Should he or she have failed to do so, or should the appointed person be unable to act (or be deceased themselves), the heirs, as well as other interested persons, may act.

a. Moral Rights in the Civil Code: General Provisions

The intellectual property section of the Civil Code opens with Chapter 69, which sets out General Provisions relating to intellectual property rights.[411] This choice of structure is somewhat controversial in its own right. Presumably, a general section like this should aid in the interpretation of the specific chapters of the Civil Code dealing with particular kinds of intellectual property rights and help to clarify their content. In fact, there is considerable overlap between the Chapter 69 provisions and the chapters of the Code dealing with specific intellectual property rights. Rather than clarifying their interpretation, the presence of Chapter 69 provisions may actually complicate the interpretation of the Code. From the perspective of transparency, it is not clear why provisions dealing with copyright law should be found in both the general provisions and the chapter on copyright—especially when the copyright provisions in the General section apply to copyright only and not to all areas of intellectual property rights covered by the Code.

The usefulness of a section on general provisions is a question of general interest to civil lawyers, and it is considered by Adolf Dietz in his examination of patents under the new Russian Code. In relation to moral rights, the General Provisions do accomplish the interesting objective of extending moral rights to inventors. Dietz comments,

> [T]he interplay between those "General Provisions" in Chapter 69 and the "special" patent law provisions in Chapter 72 must always be kept in mind. That is particularly true for the general provisions concerning personality rights of "authors" since in Russian terminology an inventor is also called an author (of the invention). The inventor consequently profits from the personality rights granted to authors in general in the introductory Chapter (especially in Article 1228 Point 2).[412]

Chapter 70 deals specifically with copyright and Chapter 71 with "Copyright Neighbouring Rights." Mirroring the General chapter of the Code, both chapters contain provisions on moral rights.

The protection of moral rights in the Russian Civil Code departs substantially from the formula adopted in the 1993 Copyright Act. Indeed, this eventuality was apparent since at least 2001, when a detailed "draft" version of what became Chapter IV was circulating. Interestingly, it is possible to identify a degree

[411] For a complementary analysis of Russian patents under the new Civil Code provisions, see Dietz, *Incorporation of Patent Law into Part IV*, *supra* note 351. For ch. 69, see id. at 688.

[412] Id. at 695 (footnote omitted). But note that 2008 Civil Code, *supra* note 38, at art. 1228.2 also provides that the moral rights of "name and other personal non-property rights" are available "in the cases provided by the present Code"—presumably, as identified in the special sections of the Code. The right of authorship is not subject to this proviso. See also id. at art. 1255.2 in the copyright section of the Code, which provides for moral rights in relation to the author of "products of science, literature and art."

of continuity between the Civil Code provisions, the 2001 Draft, and the 1991 Fundamentals; but there is a definite break with the moral rights provisions of the Copyright Act of 1993.[413]

b. General Principles

Chapter 69 seeks to elaborate the general philosophy of intellectual property rights in the Code, and it establishes principles to guide the interpretation of the specific provisions in subsequent chapters. It specifies the "exclusive" nature of the author's economic rights and the special nature of his or her moral rights.[414]

Moral rights are set out in Article 1228, which defines an author as, "[a] citizen ... whose creative efforts have produced a result of intellectual activity." Article 1228.2 provides for the protection of an author's "personal non-property rights," such as a "right of name."[415] All of the author's personal rights, including the rights of authorship and name, are inalienable and non-transferable, and the Code provides that they cannot be waived by any means. These rights are protected in perpetuity—"without term"—and, in certain circumstances after the death of the author, they may be asserted by "any interested person" on his or her behalf.[416]

Since these provisions appear in the "General" part of the Code, they are presumably applicable to all areas of intellectual property rights in the special sections. Accordingly, moral rights are not unique to copyright works; as appropriate, they will extend into the areas of patents and neighboring rights as well.

The reference to the right of "interested persons" to act is noteworthy. How will the courts interpret it? Would a member of the general public qualify as an "interested person" in relation to moral rights issues?[417] Alternatively, would it be restricted to people who had personal or business dealings with the author, or would it extend to the artistic community in which he or she was involved? In any case, Article 1228.2 represents a substantial commitment to the protection of works in the public domain, their integrity, and their historical accuracy; it achieves this

413 *See* Sundara Rajan, COPYRIGHT AND CREATIVE FREEDOM, *supra* note 4, ch. VIII ("The Future of Post-Communist Copyright"), at 188–98. The discussion of the draft in this book is based on a version of the draft Civil Code, which was translated into English by Oksana M. Kozyr, a drafter of the 1993 Russian Copyright Act, and E.V. Luchits. I am grateful to Professor David Lametti of the Faculty of Law, McGill University, who provided me with a copy of this document. In 2001, Gainan Avilov of the Private Law Research Centre was able to suggest that a revised Civil Code could be adopted at any point over the next decade (personal communication from Gainan Avilov, September 2001). In previous conversations, Dr. Kozyr indicated that a completely new draft was in the making, and the new 2008 Civil Code provisions are presumably the result of those efforts.

414 2008 Civil Code, *supra* note 38, at art. 1228. The "inalienable and nontransferable" quality of these rights is noted. The article specifies that "[w]aiver of these rights is void" and that moral rights are "protected in perpetuity": id. at art. 1228(2).

415 Id. at art. 1228(2). The article states that the author has "the right of name, the right of authorship, and other non-property rights in cases established by this code"; also "*inie lichnie neimushestvennie prava.*"

416 Id. at arts. 1267(2) and 1316(2).

417 Id. at art. 1266(2). In these circumstances, interested persons may request the protection of the author's moral rights. The interested person must be granted standing to sue by the court.

protection by opening the door onto a greatly augmented possibility of moral rights disputes arising out of alterations to the works of deceased authors. The term has a pleasing democratic air—in Russia, any person has the right to act on behalf of culture, which does, after all, become the treasure of the public after the expiry of copyright term. In practice, however, "interested person" may prove to be self-defining. With the possible exception of wealthy art-lovers, only institutions such as museums or universities are likely to have the resources to pursue a moral rights case in Russia.

In the copyright context, an author's right to the protection of his or her name is protected in Article 1265,[418] and his or her right to the inviolability of his or her work is described in Article 1266.

The Civil Code also considers several aspects of the problem of implementing and enforcing moral rights effectively. Article 1251, on the protection of authors' rights and liability for their infringement, deals specifically with moral rights. It provides that a number of specific remedies will be available for the "violation of [the] personal non-property rights of the author." These include the cessation of infringing activities, compensation for "moral harm"—a new concept in post-Soviet civil law, though it is well-known to the civil law of Western Europe—[419] and, in general, an attempt to restore "the situation that existed prior to the violation of the right." Among the remedies available is "publication of a court decision on the committed infringement," a usual remedy against infringement in civilian jurisdictions. Publication of decisions has several implications for moral rights. It allows precedents to develop, which have both legal and practical value, in this civil law system, for the injured parties who may wish to make a claim. Reformers who prepared the Code may also intend to emphasize the importance of shining the light of publicity on infringements of authors' rights. Public information is a sure antidote to the culture of secrecy and persecution historically endured by Russian authors.

In contrast to the old Copyright Act, the Civil Code deals directly with the issue of moral rights infringement. Article 1251 addresses the "violation of personal non-property rights of the author."[420] The remedies provided include, but are not limited to, "recognition of the right, restoration of the situation that existed prior to the violation of the right, stopping effects that are infringing the right or creating the threat of its infringement, compensation for moral harm, [and] publication of a court decision on the committed infringement."

[418] An interesting feature of this article is that it allows the publisher to protect works in cases where publication is anonymous or carried out under a pseudonym: id. at art. 1265(2). The right will expire if the author chooses to declare himself or herself.

[419] See the discussion of indemnification for moral harm in transitional and post-Soviet law in M.I. Braginskii, *The General Part of Civil Codification in Russia*, 99 The Revival of Private Law in Central Eastern Europe: Essays in Honour of F.J.M. Feldbrugge 109 (1996).

[420] 2008 Civil Code, *supra* note 38, at art. 1252 is concerned with "Protection of Exclusive Rights and Liability for Their Infringement."

Finally, it is worth noting that moral rights in "complex objects"—works with multiple components, such as film or databases—are also recognized. Article 1240 provides for the recognition of rights of authorship, name, and inviolability in relation to multifaceted works such as motion pictures and dramatic productions. Article 1240(3) provides that the author of an underlying work that is used in a "complex object," such as a film, enjoys moral rights in his or her contribution, and it clearly specifies that those rights persist through the "process of use" of the contribution.[421] However, in none of the sections where this information should logically fall does the Code specify who should be considered the author of the work. Authorship is not defined in Article 1240 itself, the general provision on authorship; in Article 1228(4), which simply provides for the possibility of recognizing coauthorship; or in Article 1258, the provision on coauthorship in Chapter 70 on copyright, which only provides for equal recognition of authors of a joint work, whether or not the work an be separated into its parts.[422]

The issue receives a partial response in Article 1263, in the Copyright chapter of the Code, on copyright in audiovisual works. This provision states that, in the case of films, the "director, author of scenario, and author of the [original] music [for the film]" will be deemed its coauthors.[423] The problem requires further clarification in relation to "complex" works, which may give rise to competing moral rights claims in the absence of adequate legal measures clarifying their relationships.

c. Copyright

Chapter 70 of the Civil Code, on copyright, reunites the economic and personal rights of the author in a single section. Under the heading, "Authors' Law,"[424] Article 1255 provides for the recognition of rights in "science, literature and art."[425] It goes on to identify five rights of authorship: an "exclusive" right, the term by which economic rights are implied under the new Code; a right of authorship; a right to one's name; the right to the inviolability of one's work; and a right of first publication.[426]

i. Moral Rights Defined

The five moral rights are given a detailed treatment in three separate articles. The right of authorship and the right of name, being especially closely related, are dealt with together in Article 1265. The right to one's name includes the right to work under a pseudonym or anonymously. If the author does not choose to identify him- or herself by name as the author of his or her works, the publisher is charged

[421] Id. at art. 1240(3) states, "In the process of the use of a product of intellectual activity as a part of a complex object, the author of that product has the authorship rights and other personal non-property rights to that product."
[422] Id. at art. 1258(1).
[423] Id. at art. 1263(2).
[424] Like civil law systems, copyright in Russia is known as *droit d'auteur* ("*avtorskoye pravo*").
[425] 2008 Civil Code, *supra* note 38, at art. 1255(1).
[426] Id. at art. 1255.2(5).

with protecting his or her interests as the author's representative until the author chooses to reveal his or her name. In keeping with the general part of the intellectual property provisions, Article 1265 confirms that the rights of authorship and name are inalienable and non-transferable, even if the "exclusive" economic right is transferred to another person.

Article 1266 deals with the right of inviolability of the work, which is restored to all of its formal expansiveness in Soviet copyright law. Indeed, it is a striking feature of the moral rights scheme in the Civil Code that the author's right of "inviolability" is reinstated; it had been drafted down to a "right of reputation" in the 1993 Copyright Act. The principle of inviolability represents a return to the foundations of moral rights in Soviet jurisprudence and exceeds the standard set by Article 6*bis* of the Berne Convention.[427] The right of inviolability offers very strong protection to the integrity of creative works, especially during the lifetime of the author.

In effect, however, this right is actually split into two parts, a powerful right of inviolability for living authors and a strong right of reputation after the author's death. During the lifetime of the author, alterations, abridgments, editions, illustrations, forewords or afterwords, commentaries, and "[any] other explanations whatsoever" are permitted only with the consent of the author. However, after the author's death, previously prohibited changes will be allowed, provided that the person who holds the economic rights during this period consents to them. The alterations will only be allowed if the author has not expressly indicated that changes to the work should not be undertaken after his or her death, and provided that they do not "distort the conception of the author ...[or] derange the integrity of [the audience's] perception of the work." In an interesting overlap with trademark principles, Article 1266(2) also makes it possible for an author to protect the inviolability of his or her work as part of his or her honor, dignity, and "business reputation." The wording of the provision may help to distinguish between "reputation," as it refers to the professional standing of the author, and "honor" and "dignity" as matters of personal reputation.[428]

The right of disclosure is set out in Article 1268. These detailed provisions seem to respond directly to the pressures faced by Soviet writers and dissidents in relation to publication. Article 1268(1) protects the author's right to decide "independently" whether or not his or her work should be disclosed to the public. It is worth

[427] The terminology of "inviolability" dates from the reforms of 1961, which led to the adoption of a new set of Fundamentals in that year. However, the idea of a very strong integrity right, at least against the publisher, goes further back—at least to the early Soviet law of 1928. *See* Sundara Rajan, Copyright and Creative Freedom, *supra* note 4, ch. V ("Revolution and Reform"), at 97–100. *See generally* Serge L. Levitsky, *Continuity and Change in Soviet Copyright Law: A Legal Analysis*, 6 Rev. Socialist L. 425 (1980).

[428] Under this provision, the author is entitled to seek the protection of his "honor" or "dignity" as well. The idea is reminiscent of an interesting moral rights case from India, where the author of a novel sued a filmmaker for distorting her story; in finding for the author, the judge specifically made mention of the damage to the author's reputation that might result from her association with the commercial film industry. *See Mannu Bhandari*, *supra* note 236.

noting that this Article distinguishes between disclosure and publication: it considers publication as only one form of a possible disclosure, including disclosure of the work by electronic means. But Article 1268(3) provides for the publication of posthumous works, which is permissible by the holder of the exploitation rights unless the author has expressly provided otherwise elsewhere in his or her writings—whether published or unpublished, public or private—or in his or her will. This provision addresses the possibility that an author may assign rights to a work but not live to see its publication.[429]

The Code also protects an author's right to withdraw his or her work from publication, but in a limited sense: the author has the right to withdraw a published work from circulation, but he or she must publicly announce his or her decision and also provide financial compensation to the publisher for any potential losses.[430] Despite these safeguards, the right of withdrawal is not granted to the authors of computer programs. The treatment of withdrawal, and its placement in the Code immediately after the Article elaborating the right of first publication, suggests that the drafters of the Code saw it as a limited, but definite, counterpart to disclosure.

ii. Special Features

The duration of copyright is specified as the lifetime of the author and seventy years after his or her death. In contrast, the term of moral rights protection is explicitly provided for in Article 1267(1): the rights of authorship, name, and inviolability are protected "indefinitely," or, in other words, in perpetuity. Moral rights cannot be waived, but they may be asserted after the author's death by his or her heirs.[431]

The treatment of works in the public domain becomes a key issue and is dealt with in Article 1282. As in the 1993 Copyright Act, the use of public domain works must continue to preserve the author's rights of authorship, name, and inviolability. According to Article 1267, the author's moral rights in a work that has fallen into the public domain may be asserted by "other interested persons." Finally, according to Article 1260, it should be noted that translations, compilations, or derivative works must be created while respecting the rights of the original author.

As in the earlier legislation, copyright is extended to oral works, but the provision later specifies that works of folklore shall not be protected by copyright where the authorship of the folkloric creation is indeterminate.[432]

429 It also suggests that contracting for the future publication of the work is acceptable under the Code.

430 2008 Civil Code, *supra* note 38, at art. 1269 provides that, in the case of still unpublished works, the author must compensate "a person who has the exclusive right to the product or who has the right to use the product." If the work has been published, the author is liable for damages resulting from his or her decision to withdraw.

431 Id. at art. 1267(2).

432 Id. at art. 1259(6)(3).

iii. Moral Rights vs. Exclusive Rights

The terminology of "exclusive" rights is worth closer consideration. Russian authors enjoyed "exclusive" rights in their work from the time of the landmark Russian Copyright Act of 1911; when the term was eliminated from the reformed Soviet Civil Code provisions dealing with copyright in 1961, the change of wording dealt a blow to the legal status of authors' rights.[433] "Exclusivity" in the 1993 Copyright Act refers only to the economic rights of authors and owners, but there is no reason to think that an inferior status for moral rights is implied. Rather, given the history of the term in Russian copyright law, the association between exclusivity and economic rights is of long standing. The use of the term in the current Civil Code is perhaps a way of distinguishing between rights that are vested in the author and those that can be controlled by owners. In this sense, the terminology is quite effective. It captures the nature of copyright prerogatives in a way that achieves an effective distinction between the qualities of authorship and the rights of ownership.

iv. Moral Rights and Technology

The Civil Code provisions offer the most detailed treatment of technological issues in any Russian law to date. In fact, the Civil Code consolidates the treatment of technology in the Russian Copyright Act of 1993 and related legislation, such as the 1992 Law on Computer Programs and Databases. The Civil Code includes explicit recognition of computer programs and databases as copyright works, in whatever language they are expressed, and on a par with literary works.[434] The Code implicitly provides for moral rights in computer programs and databases, but certain restrictions apply. Notably, the right of withdrawal, already limited for non-technological works, does not apply to computer programs or databases; to "complex objects," which would include film; or to employment scenarios.[435]

It is worth noting the circumstances in which the free reproduction of computer programs and databases is allowed: this right is extended even to enable the completion of computer programs and cannot therefore be considered a violation of the right of integrity.[436] Alterations made in the interest of improving the program's functioning or correcting errors are permitted, as is copying for the purposes of making an archive or a replacement. The decompilation of programs is also tolerated, but only with a view to making possible, or improving, the functioning of software, and not "for the performance of any ... act prejudicial to copyright." This provision closely resembles India's approach to the same issue.[437]

[433] Sundara Rajan, COPYRIGHT AND CREATIVE FREEDOM, *supra* note 4, ch. V ("Revolution and Reform"), at 98.

[434] 2008 Civil Code, *supra* note 38, at art. 1259 (computer programs and databases protected as literary works).

[435] Id. at art. 1269.

[436] Id. at art. 1280.

[437] See Indian Copyright Act 1957, *supra* note 43, §52(1)(ab), which exempts from infringement "the doing of any act necessary to obtain information essential for operating inter-operability of an

v. Fair Use and Parody

Provisions on fair use, as in the Law on Copyright of 1993, are extensive, and they parallel the approach of Western laws.[438] Special protection is offered to the creators of works of parody, whose works will not constitute violations of the author's moral rights or, indeed, of his or her "exclusive" economic rights.[439] The creator of a parody is under no obligation to compensate the author for his or her "use" of the original work.[440] However, the Civil Code provisions offer a contrast to Western law by providing for the possibility of compulsory licensing.[441] The idea is not unusual by international standards, however, as it reflects similar provisions in developing countries, and it provides for courts, rather than the government, to exercise their judgment about the conditions of the license.

vi. Visual Art

The provisions of the Civil Code include special treatment for works of visual art. Article 1291 distinguishes between the physical possession of an original work and the ownership of its copyright. The purpose of the right may be to allow artists to control the making of reproductions; the following Article provides for artists to enjoy a right of access to their work for the purpose of reproducing it.[442] But the effect of the provision in Article 1291 is to emphasize the effective inalienability of copyright as a whole, drawing attention, once again, to the fact that physical possession of a work is not the same thing as owning its copyright.

In addition to the moral rights identified in the Code, Article 1293 of the Russian law also codifies the visual artist's *droit de suite* (right to a resale royalty). The Russian *droit de suite* shows its kinship to moral rights in the fact of its inalienability. With the exception of a transfer to the author's legal heirs, the artist's resale right cannot be transferred to anyone while copyright in the work subsists. Unlike true moral rights, which are perpetual in Russian law, the artist's resale rights last

independently created computer programme with other programmes by a lawful possessor of a computer programme provided that such information is not otherwise readily available." Note the discussions around the Indian government's introduction of a so-called secret bill proposing copyright amendments in December of 2009, where §52 was reviewed in some detail. The Bill, Bill No. XXIV of 2010, is available at https://iprmentlaw.com/wp-content/uploads/2020/06/CopyrightAmendmentBill2010.pdf; for fascinating insights on the Indian copyright scene, see also RAJYA SABHA [PARLIAMENT OF INDIA] DEPARTMENT RELATED PARLIAMENTARY STANDING COMMITTEE ON HUMAN RESOURCE DEVELOPMENT, REPORT ON THE COPYRIGHT (AMENDMENT) BILL, 2010 (No. 227, Nov. 23, 2010), https://prsindia.org/files/bills_acts/bills_parliament/2010/SCR_Copyright_Bill_2010.pdf. *See also* Shamnad Basheer, *Copyright Amendment Bill*, SPICY IP BLOG (Apr. 20, 2010), http://spicyipindia.blogspot.com/2010/04/copyright-amendment-bill.html.

438 See the list of permitted "free uses" in 2008 Civil Code, *supra* note 38, at arts. 1273–1280.

439 Id. at art. 1274(3).

440 Id. at art. 1274(3).

441 Id. at arts. 1238 and 1239.

442 Id. at art. 1292. This article also allows "demonstration" of a work without the artist's consent, and without the payment of a commission to him or her.

for the duration of the exclusive right—the lifetime of the author plus seventy years.[443]

d. Neighboring Rights

Like corresponding provisions in the 1993 Copyright Act, Chapter 71 of the Civil Code on "copyright neighboring rights" consists of various provisions that create comprehensive rights for performers, the makers of sound recordings, and broadcasting and cable distribution agencies.[444] In addition to providing standard protection for neighboring rights, this chapter also offers recognition for the moral rights of performers.

The Code provides for performers' moral rights of name and integrity on the same terms on which they are enjoyed by authors.[445] Article 1315 protects the performer's right of attribution—his or her name or pseudonym must be associated with the performance—as well as his or her right to protect the performance against "distortion" when it is recorded, reproduced, or broadcast. It is not clear whether the Russian provisions, like the WPPT, exclude protection for performers' moral rights in audiovisual recordings. An important provision is made by Article 1316(2), which specifies that the performer has a right to designate a person who will be responsible for performers' moral rights after his or her death.

e. Patents

Interestingly, the 2008 Civil Code includes an unusual moral right in patents. In Chapter 72, Article 1418 protects the "right of authorship" of plant or animal breeders. Article 1419 allows that the author of the new variety can "determine . . . its denomination," subject to statutory requirements and the approval of the federal agency for the protection of new plant and animal varieties.

6. Improvements to Moral Rights in Russia until the War in Ukraine

While the Copyright Act of 1993 left something to be desired in the protection of authors' personal interests, the moral rights provisions of the Civil Code have set a significantly higher standard of protection. The new law is strongly oriented towards creative authorship and the protection of culture. Its provisions on moral rights reflect concerns about the status of authors and their work in a society that has long suffered the consequences of political oppression. At the same time, it recognizes that moral rights have a contribution to make to the protection and

[443] Id. at art. 1293(3).
[444] Id. at ch. 71.
[445] Id. at arts. 1315 and 1316.

preservation of cultural heritage, and the reach of moral rights is not limited to the protection of individual authors and works. By ensuring that someone will be entrusted with the protection of moral rights in public domain works—an author's legatee; his or her heirs; or, eventually, any "interested person"— Russian reformers have made a laudable attempt to realize their cultural and democratic potential.

Despite the generally positive picture of moral rights that emerges from the Civil Code, a number of questions remained unanswered. For example, Article 1248 of the Civil Code provides that "a court" shall deal with copyright claims, including the assertion of moral rights. However, Russia's court system is complex, and it is not immediately apparent which forum will be most appropriate for dealing with authors' moral rights. Copyright matters are usually dealt with in the *arbitrazh* courts, the branch of the Russian judicial system concerned with copyright matters. It is true that moral rights have important commercial implications; nevertheless, their main purpose is personal and non-commercial, and commercial courts may therefore not be the best forum for adjudication. If not, who should make decisions on moral rights? Would a specialist tribunal dealing with intellectual property rights—such as the Supreme Patent Chamber, for example—be the ideal forum? Or would the Constitutional Court, which should be building expertise on the protection of individual rights, ultimately be more suited to dealing with authors' personal interests?

The role of government in copyright matters is also far from clear. Both the Copyright Act of 1993 and the Civil Code make provision for the active involvement of government agencies in protecting authors' moral rights. But how will it be possible to entrust the Russian government with the protection of authors' rights when it has been the main instrument of their oppression in the past? A similar question arises in relation to the role of writers' or artists' unions in Russia's new copyright system. How can the collective administration of rights be made into a viable proposition in a country where the writers' union was essentially a tool of government oppression, rather than an authentic mouthpiece for writers' needs?[446]

Another area of concern is the question of how moral rights relate to technology. The Civil Code, like the Copyright Act before it, allows moral rights in computer programs and databases. When is the right of integrity in a computer program infringed? When can the author claim a right of attribution? For example, if an author produces a computer program, and this work is used by insurance companies to collect personal data about health-related matters, can the author object that the use is against his or her principles and therefore violates his or her honor and right to the integrity of the work? Previous Russian tradition recognized a moral right

[446] An interesting perspective on this issue arose in the *Russian Kurier* case, *supra* note 144. The Russian journalists' union was unable—or perhaps unwilling—to provide the New York appeals court with a list of its members, making it impossible for the court to grant it standing to sue on their behalf.

related to the use of a work, but this concept now seems to have been purged from Russian law.

The application of moral rights raises serious concerns about the ability of information technology to develop and to be used to its full potential. For this reason, India, with its dynamic information technology industry, imposes certain limits on the availability of moral rights for computer programs.[447] What are Russia's interests in relation to information technology, and how does its approach to moral rights support them?

A number of questions concerning moral rights also arise in relation to works of art whose creation has been made possible by technology. For example, in a computer-generated artwork, where the only creative activity of the author is to write the computer program, should the complete range of moral rights be available? What happens in the case of a multimedia work that is composed of images, sound, and text from a variety of sources which have now been compiled and reworked in an innovative way through digital technology? To what extent should attribution and integrity in relation to the original works be preserved? For artists and creative people, the question of how digital technology will affect their creative potential is the key to their future in the Digital Age. Yet, questions like these are not addressed in the Russian Civil Code provisions on moral rights.

7. A New Moral Right in Russian Law: The Renewal of Copyright Terms for Rehabilitated Authors

In Russia, the importance of moral rights is immediately apparent in two features of the copyright law. The first is the prominent place of moral rights in the copyright legislation. Russian moral rights in the 1991 Fundamentals of Civil Legislation[448] gave explicit protection to a great variety of interests, including new rights not featured in previous Russian law or in the Berne Convention and framed in expansive language. The rights were scaled back in the Copyright Act of 1993, introduced after the collapse of the Soviet Union in 1991; but the Copyright Act simultaneously continued to recognize certain rights which may not be traditionally classified as moral rights in themselves but support moral rights in a broader sense. This broad preoccupation with the ethics of copyright continues to characterize the latest provisions in Part IV of Russia's Civil Code.[449] In this context, a

[447] Pravin Anand suggests that the idea was developed in *Statart Software Pvt Ltd v. Karan Khanna*, cited in Anand, *supra* note 264, at 35–36, and later became the subject of a legislative amendment. *See* the Copyright (Second Amendment) Bill, 1994, Bill No. 105C of 1992, http://parliamentofindia.nic.in/ls/bills/1994/1994-31.htm.

[448] 1991 Fundamentals, *supra* note 358.

[449] 2008 Civil Code, *supra* note 38.

second feature of Russian copyright law should be noted: the attempts of Russian copyright law in the post-socialist era to redress the injustices of the past.

It is well known that the Soviet government had a policy of bringing calumny on authors and artists who fell afoul of its policies. To offer but one well-known example, the life of the composer, Shostakovich, was a microcosm of the general situation in one individual case: over his lifetime, he endured unimaginable ups and downs in his official reputation due to the direct intervention of Stalin.[450] Accordingly, post-Soviet law, from the transitional Fundamentals of 1991 to the present Civil Code, has always included provisions for the "rehabilitation" of authors.[451]

Rehabilitation not only involved official apologies and recognition; there was also a copyright dimension. In the case of authors who had been victimized by the state and were posthumously rehabilitated, the term of copyright protection in their works would run anew from the time of rehabilitation.[452] This amounts to an extension of copyright term for humanitarian reasons: it effectively allows the term of copyright protection after an author's death to be reinstated for rehabilitated authors.

There is still a slight issue of prejudice in distinguishing between those who were rehabilitated posthumously and those who were rehabilitated during their lifetimes. The point is illustrated by the case of Andrei Siniavsky and Yuli Daniel, two writers who were prosecuted for their writings by the Soviet Union in a notorious "show trial" of the 1960s.[453] Siniavsky lived to see their rehabilitation in 1991, but Daniel died in 1988. Siniavsky himself died in 1997, six years after his official rehabilitation. Accordingly, the Russian provision on the extension of copyright for rehabilitated authors would apply to Daniel but not to Siniavksy. In effect, Siniavsky's copyright would endure for fifty years after his death in 1997, but Daniel's would endure for the slightly longer period *post mortem auctoris* of

[450] Fitzpatrick, *supra* note 359, at 183–215. Fitzpatrick offers an analysis of his situation within the broader context of government control, manipulation, and repression of the musical world; she concludes her discussion by noting that "his disgrace on each occasion proved temporary and his status as an acknowledged 'great Soviet composer' survived these debacles."

[451] 2008 Civil Code, *supra* note 38, at art. 1281(4).

[452] *See* Russian Copyright Act 1993, *supra* note 38, at art. 27(5):

> Copyright in a posthumous work shall have effect for 50 years following the publication of the work.
>
> If the author has been rehabilitated posthumously after having been the subject of repressive measures, the period of protection of rights under this Article shall begin on January 1 of the year following that of the said rehabilitation.

The 2008 Civil Code, *supra* note 38, at art. 1281(4), increases this term of protection to seventy years ("If the author of a work has been subjected to repression and posthumously rehabilitated, the effective term of the exclusive right shall be deemed extended, and 70 years shall be counted from January 1 of the year following the year of rehabilitation of the author of the work"). A further four years is also granted to war veterans of the "Great Patriotic War" (roughly World War II), which was also the case in the 1993 Copyright Act.

[453] *See* Sundara Rajan, COPYRIGHT AND CREATIVE FREEDOM, *supra* note 4, at 133 and ch. VI ("Creative Freedom on Trial"), at 123–49.

fifty-three years after his death in 1988. Is this extra duration a form of compensation for the especially egregious wrong of allowing an author to die before the restoration of his or her name? If so, the families of these authors received a small though perhaps largely symbolic benefit through prolonged copyright protection in honor of their ancestors.

The fact that the provision is limited to cases of "posthumous" rehabilitation may be a simple recognition of the tragedy that most authors and artists did not live to see it occur: the persecution of writers in the Stalinist period occurred decades before the end of the Soviet regime was in sight. But, in the interest of fairness, the Russian government probably should have framed the provision to include both posthumous rehabilitation and the rehabilitation of living authors. Otherwise, the provision reads faintly like a penalty: if you enjoyed any of your copyright without persecution during your lifetime, you would forfeit any possible extension of copyright term.

The extension of copyright term in the case of posthumous rehabilitation, though not a moral right itself, certainly has the flavor of a moral right. At least three interpretations seem possible. Is it a new aspect of the right of integrity that an author is entitled to enjoy copyright protection provided by law without inhumane interference? Indeed, as noted below, the Russian Copyright Act of 1993 recognized a right of reputation even in preference to the usual formula represented by the Berne Convention, where reputation and integrity are linked. In the Russian Act, the reputation right was simply an author's right to protect oneself from damage to one's reputation.[454] Alternatively, is it a new dimension of disclosure? The idea that an author should not be forced to disclose his or her works in an environment of abuse seems apt, since publication in such a context would be damaging, rather than beneficial, to the author's career. Finally, it could also represent a response to an implicit right against excessive or unreasonable criticism. In this case, because the criticism is propagated by the state and the state is also responsible for copyright protection, the remedy seems most appropriate.

8. Conclusion

The evolution of moral rights in Russian legislation shows increasing reliance on Russian legal tradition, which is generally preferred to international law in the Civil Code provisions on moral rights. The influence of the Berne Convention in Russia has actually translated into a scaling back of Russian protection for moral rights, reflected in the Copyright Act of 1993. It meant fundamental readjustments to the Russian concept of moral rights, particularly in relation to the right of integrity.

[454] *See* Russian Copyright Act 1993, *supra* note 38, at art. 15(1).

Known as the right of "inviolability" since 1961, the right of integrity was finally implemented into the 1993 Act in a modified form that converted it into a simple right of reputation. The 2008 Civil Code has now reinstated the Russian right and the associated terminology of "inviolability".

The history behind this situation reflects an interesting experience of translating international norms into domestic laws. Golovanov suggests that this interpretation of the integrity right reflected "an incorrect translation of Art. 6bis of the Berne Convention." He points out that Professor Gavrilov, a senior expert on Russian copyright, has argued for the right of adaptation as the true legal mechanism for the protection of the integrity of a work in Russia. Golovanov points out that the right of adaptation has been amended in Article 1266 of the new Code to prevent any modifications to a work that would violate the author's wishes or ideas. However, it is difficult to agree with Golovanov's hope that the adaptation right could compensate for a shift from integrity to reputation. The problem is not only that adaptation is fundamentally an economic right, now defined with moral dimensions in the new Civil Code; any change to a work would also have to meet the definition of adaptation to qualify as a violation of moral rights. The rule is reminiscent of the U.S. approach, which, in the Monty Python case, converted an edited version of the work into an unauthorized adaptation in order to establish that the edited version violated the authors' copyright.[455] This was not a finding that the moral right of integrity had been violated, but it offered a solution to the moral rights problem in U.S. law.[456]

In the Russian Civil Code, key elements of a post-socialist approach remain intact. The Russian law recognizes both traditional moral rights and new rights with moral dimensions, such as the special rights of rehabilitated authors. It gives precedence to the protection of moral rights over economic rights in the sense that it requires the protection of moral rights in almost every circumstance of individual authorship and even extends these requirements into the public domain, where economic rights have completely expired. Russian law is also in the vanguard of technological change, recognizing moral rights in software and scientific inventions. Its very emphasis on the concept of disclosure has powerful technological resonance—disclosure, whether moral or economic, is a key concept for the copyright law of the Digital Age. In practical terms, disclosure may be the one act that remains unequivocally within an author's control in the technological environment.

[455] *Gilliam*, *supra* note 132.

[456] The Canadian case of *Théberge*, *supra* note 30, presents the reverse scenario: a moral rights concern claimed as a violation of economic rights failed because of the additional standard of proof required for moral rights, which, the majority of the Canadian Supreme Court said, Théberge should not have evaded.

F. Conclusion: The Modern Doctrine

In both space and time, moral rights have traveled a great distance from their origins in continental Europe. The rights have spread around the globe to diverse countries, representing an immense variety of cultures and legal traditions. In this process of global migration, moral rights have themselves been transformed.

Moral rights were originally an individual right of the author. In French law, they were a form of recognition for the author's creative powers, while German jurisprudence emphasized respect for the personality of the author. In both of these traditions, moral rights were independent of all other rights, including economic rights in a work. They were inalienable and generally could not be waived. The duration of moral rights was at least equivalent to the duration of economic rights in a work, as in the German system, but the rights could also last forever, as in France.

The spread of moral rights to new jurisdictions has led to a startling variety of new interpretations of the doctrine. The basic principles of independence and inalienability have been universally maintained. However, moral rights in the common-law countries show relaxation of the theory in various ways. Waivers of moral rights are possible in some circumstances.[457] Different approaches to duration have been explored. An extreme insistence on the separation of economic and moral rights in Canada seems to imply that the same set of facts probably cannot lead to litigation on both grounds: one set of rights must be preferred.[458] The possibility of protecting moral rights through tort law is one that U.S. lawyers, in particular, are interested in exploring. Among other things, this approach implies that protection for moral rights will be limited to the lifetime of the author. Common-law countries have also considered the applicability of practical formalities to the enjoyment of moral rights, including the controversial UK and New Zealand requirement that the moral right of attribution must be asserted. The proposed Australian bill on an "Indigenous communal moral right" would have established moral rights in works of Indigenous culture, but it also imposed certain formalities on the enjoyment of this special right.

The recognition of moral rights in developing and post-socialist jurisdictions has raised interesting possibilities for their expansion. Moral rights are said to exist in cultural heritage; they can also help to address the problems of political repression, to protect an author's reputation from destruction, and to compensate an author for the abuse of his or her reputation. These countries follow more traditional moral rights in jurisdictions like France, by recognizing moral rights in works of new technology such as computer programs and film—although questions

[457] But note that waivers are also permitted, under limited circumstances in German law. See the discussion in Chapter 2, *infra* notes 148–59 and accompanying text.
[458] *Théberge*, *supra* note 30.

surround the management of the complex relationships between the different personalities involved in the making of a film. The general trend is to exclude at least some aspects of moral rights where employment situations arise, as is often the case in relation to computer programs. The special case of Japan seems to have generated new principles in its own right: a moral right for companies, restoration of the status quo as a principle guiding compensation, and moral rights that may be time-limited in name but perpetual in practice.

The near-universal recognition of moral rights is convincing proof of their relevance to diverse countries and cultures. They are not limited by the contours of European culture or, indeed, Romanticism. The willingness to explore and extend the doctrine of moral rights in "new" jurisdictions is convincing evidence of its flexibility and malleability—its potential for growth. This feature of moral rights is a key element underlying their relevance in the technological context.

A distinction should be drawn between the suppleness of moral rights doctrine and the rigidity of other copyright norms. Moral rights have successfully served many policy interests—the protection of individual rights, the preservation of cultural heritage, the recognition of oppressed cultures, the accommodation of technological creativity, and the validation of human rights—and the doctrine has proven to be an effective instrument for the practical achievement of social goals.

This analysis of moral rights in a number of the world's major jurisdictions shows beyond doubt that the doctrine of moral rights continues to be vital and deeply relevant in the technological context. In all their permutations and combinations, global and historical, moral rights remain personal and cultural rights. Their purpose is to recognize and protect authorship and, through it, cultural heritage. Whether that heritage offers itself in the form of paintings or poems, ancient bronzes or computer programs is of little importance. If it is worth protecting, as shown by the experience of moral rights around the globe, moral rights can probably adapt to embrace this new need.

Above all, moral rights continue to affirm the value of authorship, and the broad commitment to these rights around the world can be taken as an encouraging sign of a deeper collective commitment to creativity and culture. The rights are arguably more important than ever before as human creativity faces new headwinds with the rise of artificial intelligence technologies.[459] The moral right of the author is nothing less than the human face of copyright law. Like the author, moral rights, too, are here to stay.

[459] The subject of Chapter 5, *infra*.

5

The Machine as Author

Moral Rights and Artificial Intelligence

We risk losing touch with the facts of history.

—Margaret Mitchell, founder of Google's Ethical Artificial Intelligence research team and now ethics chief at Hugging Face[1]

[A]rtificial intelligence poses an existential threat to [the] creative professions.

—Screen Actors' Guild[2]

Nobody remembers that I won the first match.

—Garry Kasparov, chess grandmaster, on his historic games with IBM's Deep Blue computer[3]

A. **Authenticity: The Keyword of Our Era** 334
B. **Authorship: The Human Heart of Copyright Law** 336
C. **Are Machines Authors? Approaches and Prospects under Copyright Law** 340
1. Copyright in "Computer-Generated" Works: The UK Model 341
2. The Authors of Authors? Moral Rights for AI Creators 343
3. Copyright Registration: An Initial Test of Machine Authorship? 347
D. **The Machine as Infringer** 348
1. AI Artists: In-Stability 349
2. AI Writers: Settlements and Lawsuits 354
a. The Hollywood Writers' Strike 354
b. *NYT v. OpenAI* and Its Sister Lawsuits 356
3. The Machine as Performer: "Performance Cloning" and the Hollywood Actors' Strike 358
E. **The Machine as Enforcer: Moral Rights** 366
F. **Are Machines Creative? Existentialism Redux** 368
G. **Attribution and Integrity: Keys to Our Future** 369

[1] Quoted in Will Knight, Kari Johnson & Morgan Meaker, *Meet the Humans Trying to Keep Us Safe from AI*, Wired (June 27, 2023), https://www.wired.com/story/meet-the-humans-trying-to-keep-us-safe-from-ai. All websites cited in this chapter were last visited on July 15, 2023.

[2] Quoted in Shiona McCallum, *The Black Mirror Plot about AI That Worries Actors*, BBC News (July 14, 2023), https://www.bbc.com/news/technology-66200334.

[3] Daryl Chen, *"Machines Have Objectivity, Humans Have Passion": Garry Kasparov Speaks at TED2017*, Ted Blog (Apr. 25, 2017), http://blog.ted.com/humans-must-face-our-fears-garry-kasparov-speaks-at-ted2017 (reproduced here under the terms of the CC BY-NC-ND 4.0 license). Also quoted in Jane Wakefield, *Ted 2017: I Won First Match with Deep Blue, Says Kasparov* (Apr. 25, 2017), https://www.bbc.com/news/technology-39701222.

1. Authors' Moral Rights of Attribution and Integrity 370
2. Beyond Authorship: Attribution and Integrity as Stand-Alone Principles 372
H. The EU AI Act: The Role of Moral Rights in a Risk-Based Approach 375
I. Recommendations 378
J. Conclusion: Being Human in the Age of AI 380

A. Authenticity: The Keyword of Our Era

The stunning rise of artificial intelligence (AI) means that it is no longer possible, as Annemarie Bridy wrote in 2012, to hope for "a reprieve from the reactive, crisis-driven model of policymaking that has dominated copyright law in the digital era."[4] On the contrary, the need for guidance in this area is arguably more urgent than anything that has been previously known in the history of copyright law. Though harnessing artificial intelligence will ultimately require a multidisciplinary approach, it seems clear that copyright law and policy should be in the forefront of these efforts.

In the digital era, copyright law has come to play a unique role in mediating the relationship between technology and society. This has occurred in spite of the limitations of the copyright framework: it is not ideally equipped for this role and has arguably failed in key areas such as fostering creativity and innovation across all areas of useful social endeavor, effectively balancing the needs of authors, right holders, and the public, and supporting core social values such as human rights and social justice. Indeed, copyright has potential in these areas that has not been realized. But it remains a fact that, more than any other area of law, or of intellectual property regulation in particular, copyright has become synonymous with innovation in the digital context. AI is therefore a natural and unavoidable next step for copyright law and policy.

Copyright is said to "incentivize" creativity by protecting exclusive rights in works. While the concept of "incentivizing" creativity can be problematic, it is clear that in relation to AI, at least, protecting the economic value in AI creations can serve both to encourage creativity in this field and to determine who will be its primary economic beneficiaries. These stakes were identified by the Indian government in a 2021 Report:

> As regards the economic impact of AI, ... an Accenture research report ... estimated that the benefits from AI related innovations, if drawn in an

[4] Annemarie Bridy, *Coding Creativity: Copyright and the Artificially Intelligent Author*, 5 Stanford Tech. L. Rev. 2, 2 (2012), http://stlr.stanford.edu/pdf/bridy-coding-creativity.pdf.

optimal manner, would add USD 957 billion by 2035 to the Indian economy. However, in order to extract benefits from AI, revisiting of IPR legislations and implementing a strong IPR framework is desirable.[5]

However, addressing artificial intelligence through copyright law has proven to be fraught with difficulty. Policymakers around the world have so far been unable to rise to this challenge. Indeed, AI technology poses fundamental challenges to copyright law and exposes the inadequacy of the existing copyright framework in the face of social needs. Two decades of highly politicized evolution in the digital environment have limited copyright's development and redirected it into ever narrower channels. It is arguably more difficult now than ever to achieve what is needed from copyright law in relation to AI—clear policy objectives, sound understanding and application of the concepts underlying the modern copyright framework, and a suitably nuanced approach to regulation.

And yet, copyright law may also hold the secret to meeting the broader social challenges posed by AI. This hidden potential of copyright may be found in the relatively neglected area of moral rights.

In the discussions of AI regulation to date, there has been very little consideration of the role of moral rights. This is in keeping with the general trend in modern copyright law, going back at least to the 1980s, which has greatly emphasized the economic aspects of copyright over moral rights. In the technological context, though, and as suggested in the previous edition of this book,[6] this has proven to be a serious oversight. Moral rights are highly relevant in this environment—perhaps even more so, in certain respects, than economic rights—and they should have played an important role in policy development throughout this period. Instead, they have been largely neglected, and many of the problems caused by technology and the inadequate regulation of innovation have grown unchecked. But moral rights continue to offer solutions to many technological challenges. Fundamentally, they can help to address the large-scale and increasingly serious deterioration of the environment for information, knowledge, and culture in the technological context by assuring authenticity.

Accordingly, when it comes to AI, moral rights are arguably more important than ever before. Moral rights can help to re-establish authenticity in this new environment. They can also accomplish something essential by providing a means to reaffirm the value of human creativity at its most vulnerable.

[5] Rajya Sabha [Parliament of India] Department Related Parliamentary Standing Committee on Commerce, Review of the Intellectual Property Rights Regime in India (Report No. 161, July 23, 2021), https://files.lbr.cloud/public/2021-07/161_2021_7_15.pdf?VersionId=S01fCQEC5DzDqKNymsGgxal6YXmJbUwM.

[6] Mira T. Sundara Rajan, Moral Rights: Principles, Practice, and New Technology (2011).

B. Authorship: The Human Heart of Copyright Law

Authorship is the basic principle out of which modern copyright law as a whole has emerged. It is the core of copyright. Modern copyright law was established when authors were granted rights in their own works for the first time, in the British Statute of Anne of 1710. As has been discussed previously, that right was a right in literary property arising out of the creative labor of the author.[7] Although British copyright law quickly came to be extended to other forms of creativity beyond the production of literature, the Statute of Anne, and copyright in this first iteration, was fundamentally concerned with books. The Statute of Anne specifies its own purpose as follows:

> Whereas printers, booksellers, and other persons have of late frequently taken the liberty of printing, reprinting, and publishing, or causing to be printed, reprinted, and published, books and other writings, without the consent of the authors or proprietors of such books and writings, to their very great detriment, and too often to the ruin of them and their families: for preventing therefore such practices for the future, and *for the encouragement of learned men to compose and write useful books*. . . .[8]

The right of the author was established by the Statute as a direct counterweight to the previous exercise of censorship by the British Crown. The sovereign exercised censorship by controlling what was printed in the realm, restricting the right to print to those who received printing "privileges" directly from the sovereign, the powerful printing monopoly known as the Stationers' Company.[9]

At this early date, the idea of individual rights was generally underdeveloped in British society, and authors' rights in the Statute of Anne were accordingly limited. Nevertheless, copyright under the Statute was an individual right of authorship. It arose directly out of the author's creative labor, and it was established for a fixed period of time so that authors could, in the words of the statute, "earn a livelihood." This last point is important, because it shows that copyright, from its earliest manifestation in the modern world, was linked to the protection of an individual human author. The purpose of the right of literary property established by copyright law was to allow the author some possibility of subsistence through the creative act of writing. This support was provided both for the author's benefit and for the sake of the greater good in learning—expressed, in those days, as "encouraging learned men to write books." The Statute was also a response to developments in

[7] See discussion of copyright history in Chapter 2 *infra*.

[8] Statute of Anne, 8 Anne. c. 19 (1710), §I (emphasis added) (Eng.), https://avalon.law.yale.edu/18th_century/anne_1710.asp.

[9] See discussion in Chapter 2 *infra*. This history has been discussed extensively in the work of Lyman Ray Patterson and others.

technology—at that time, new printing technology that promised to transform society by making the written word more accessible to all.

In the light of these considerations, it is important to notice how far modern copyright law has moved from the author-centered approach in the Statute of Anne without, however, replacing or significantly updating the copyright paradigm represented by the statute. A simple example arises in relation to the duration of copyright protection. The duration of copyright protection has steadily been increasing since the Statute of Anne, and in 1908, the Berne Convention introduced the benchmark principle that copyright should last for at least the lifetime of the author and fifty years after the author's death.[10] The extension of term had to do with the growing social prominence of authors and the perception that authors should be able to acquire the means of supporting their families.[11] The rationale by which this happened is, in a sense, an intellectual "property" rationale, but only to a limited extent. Unlike material property, this intellectual property could only be held by the author and the author's heirs for a limited time. Interestingly, in the technological era, policymakers are now beginning to consider the question of whether, in principle, holding large amounts of property such as that acquired by tech billionaires should also be limited in time.[12]

In modern copyright law, corporations are allowed to hold copyright, usually acquiring it through the operation of the work-for-hire or employment rule, which grants employers the copyright in the underlying work of their employees. This is a standard feature of copyright laws in common-law countries.[13] Corporations

10 The term of life plus fifty years was introduced at the Berlin revision conference in 1908, but it was made mandatory only at the Brussels revision conference in 1948: International Convention for the Protection of Literary and Artistic Works, adopted at Berne on Sept. 9, 1886, completed at Paris on May 4, 1896, revised at Berlin on Nov. 13, 1908 (Berlin Act, 1908); International Convention for the Protection of Literary and Artistic Works, adopted at Berne on Sept. 9, 1886, completed at Paris on May 4, 1896, revised at Berlin on Nov. 13, 1908, completed at Berne on Mar. 20, 1914, revised at Rome on June 2, 1928, at Brussels on June 26, 1948 (Brussels Act, 1948). *See* Sam Ricketson & Jane Ginsburg, *Chapter 9: Duration of Protection (Articles 7 and 7bis; TRIPS Agreement, Article 12; WCT, Article 9)*, *in* International Copyright and Neighbouring Rights: The Berne Convention and Beyond 527 (3d ed., 2022), https://doi.org/10.1093/oso/9780198801986.003.0009. (The information is noted in the abstract.) *See also* International *Convention for the Protection of Literary and Artistic Works*, adopted at Berne on Sept. 9, 1886, completed at Paris on May 4, 1896, revised at Berlin on Nov. 13, 1908, completed at Berne on Mar. 20, 1914, revised at Rome on June 2, 1928, at Brussels on June 26, 1948, at Stockholm on July 14, 1967, and at Paris on July 24, 1971, and amended on Sept. 28, 1979, S. Treaty Doc. No. 99-27 (1986), https://www.wipo.int/treaties/en/ip/berne. Interestingly, John Locke is said to have suggested a similar duration for copyright as early as 1695: "[F]or those who purchase copies from authors that now live and write, it may be reasonable to limit their property to a certain number of years after the death of the author, or the first printing of the book, as, suppose, fifty or seventy years." *See* History of Copyright, *Early Writings & the Beginning of Book Printing* (n.d.), https://historyofcopyright.org/pb/wp_27fa9cd0/wp_27fa9cd0.html, citing Lord Peter King, The Life of John Locke 208 (1829).

11 *See, e.g.*, Mark Twain, discussed in Chapter 1, *supra* note 91 and accompanying text.

12 It should be noted that the taxation of inheritances has never been a major impediment to the accumulation of wealth in Western countries either.

13 *See, e.g.*, Copyright Act, 17 U.S.C. § 101 (U.S.) (Definitions section), https://www.copyright.gov/title17/92chap1.html#101; Copyright, Designs and Patents Act 1988, c. 48 (CDPA), § 11(2) (UK),

acquire copyright based on the underlying contributions of a human author—their employees—and the duration of protection for corporate copyright, though no longer measured against the lifetime of the author, is still calibrated against that standard. Accordingly, corporations acquire extended durations of copyright protection in the works that they own.[14] Not surprisingly, the duration of copyright protection has become an intensely controversial issue,[15] but in the process, the initial purpose of extending copyright term—to allow individual *human* authors to provide for themselves and their children, as suggested by Mark Twain[16]—has been all but forgotten.

These transformations of copyright law through time—of which, the extension of duration is only one example—have led to a blurring of lines when it comes to the purpose and scope of modern copyright protection. Copyright's underlying rationale ostensibly remains the protection of authors, but the extent to which modern copyright law actually achieves this is questionable. Instead, in many countries, corporations now appear to be the primary beneficiaries of copyright through the operation of work for hire. However, the concept of an author's right continues to lie at the heart of modern copyright regulation, and in the increasingly specialized situation where individual authors are not working as employees, they remain the first holders of copyright in their own works.

But artificial intelligence shakes our understanding of authorship to the core. With its ability to mimic human creation, including the acts of writing and creating images, AI has, first and foremost, generated a profound sense of insecurity. In a landscape where AI is becoming a significant presence and may have the potential to replace human beings in many spheres, the value of human creativity itself has been brought into question. And it is worth remembering that creativity plays a role in human activities at many levels, with the creation of creative, artistic, or intellectual works being only one type of activity that lies at the apex of human culture. AI creation may therefore threaten the viability of a great range of human activities and livelihoods.[17]

https://www.legislation.gov.uk/ukpga/1988/48/section/11; Copyright Act, R.S.C. 1985, c. C-42, s. 13(3) (Can.), https://laws-lois.justice.gc.ca/eng/acts/C-42/section-13.html.

[14] *See, e.g.*, U.S. Copyright Act, *supra* note 13, at ch. 3 (esp. § 302(c) on duration of copyright in works for hire created after Jan. 1, 1978), https://www.copyright.gov/title17/92chap3.html.

[15] Most recently, a further extension to life of the author plus seventy years was acrimoniously debated in the United States—the term originally adopted by the European Union in 1993 under Council Directive 93/98/EEC of 29 October 1993 harmonizing the term of protection of copyright and certain related rights, 1993 O.J. (L 290) 9, https://eur-lex.europa.eu/legal-content/EN/ALL/?uri=CELEX%3A31993L0098, since repealed and replaced by Directive 2006/116/EC of the European Parliament and of the Council of 12 December 2006 on the term of protection of copyright and certain related rights, 2006 O.J. (L 372) 12, https://eur-lex.europa.eu/LexUriServ/LexUriServ.do?uri=OJ:L:2006:372:0012:0018:EN:PDF, with which U.S. legislators wished to harmonize U.S. copyright law. *See, e.g.*, *Eldred v. Ashcroft* 537 U.S. 186 (2003); *see also* Chapter 3, *infra* note 142 and accompanying text.

[16] From Chapter 1, *supra* note 91 and accompanying text.

[17] *See, e.g.*, Kate Morgan, *The Jobs AI Won't Take Yet*, BBC News (May 8, 2023), https://www.bbc.com/worklife/article/20230507-the-jobs-ai-wont-take-yet. A more optimistic view is offered in *Your*

The problem goes even deeper then this: AI awakens basic insecurities about the value of being human at all. After all, technology may have the potential to do much of what we do better than we can. AI is rapidly becoming more "productive" and more "efficient" than humans can ever be in areas from writing journalism to the practice of law. But there is also a murmur of dissatisfaction—not a ray of hope, but a warning. AI as it currently exists is prone to mistakes and even falsifies information systematically—problems which, if they escape human detection, as they are likely to do if they occur on a large scale, could lead to dramatic, even apocalyptic, consequences for society. It is no wonder that many experts are warning that the unchecked development of AI could end in humanity's destruction.[18] They are urgently calling for regulation.

In the field of copyright, we therefore face two challenges. The first, more familiar issue, is to deal effectively with AI as a new area of human innovation. AI has the potential to develop in chaotic and possibly detrimental ways if we do not arrive at clear policy goals and effective means of implementing them. In particular, if we cannot find a way to harness the power and promise of AI technology, the potential benefit to society could be lost. In this sense, copyright regulation is part of a typical process of regulating a new technology, AI in this case, in a responsible and beneficial way.

But the second challenge is vast: to ensure that our approach to regulating AI through copyright law and policy is in step with the larger purpose of reaffirming human values in the AI environment. In some ways, copyright is uniquely positioned to lead in this area. Copyright is fundamentally preoccupied with human creativity. Its historical emergence was a response to threats that were, within their contexts, existential threats to human well-being as AI may be today—notably, censorship. Copyright's focus on authorship is important in the AI landscape. Even more importantly, authorship rights—the inalienable moral rights of authors—may actually hold some of the keys to effective regulation in this area. Moral rights also offer another, potentially exciting prospect: they may be able to guide us on AI regulation, not only within copyright law, but also beyond the traditional bounds of the copyright framework itself.

Job Is (Probably) Safe from Artificial Intelligence, THE ECONOMIST (May 7, 2023), https://www.economist.com/finance-and-economics/2023/05/07/your-job-is-probably-safe-from-artificial-intelligence (with subscription).

[18] Countless media articles have appeared on this theme, and AI experts themselves are divided on it. *See, e.g.*, Chris Vallance, *Artificial Intelligence Could Lead to Extinction, Experts Warn*, BBC NEWS (May 30, 2023), https://www.bbc.com/news/uk-65746524; Steve Rose, *Five Ways AI Might Destroy the World: "Everyone on Earth Could Fall Over Dead in the Same Second,"* THE GUARDIAN (July 7, 2023), https://www.theguardian.com/technology/2023/jul/07/five-ways-ai-might-destroy-the-world-everyone-on-earth-could-fall-over-dead-in-the-same-second.

C. Are Machines Authors? Approaches and Prospects under Copyright Law

In view of this history of copyright, it would be deeply problematic to recognize artificial intelligence as an "author" under copyright law. Copyright, by definition, emerges out of the act of human authorship. Its aim is to recognize and protect the author as a human individual.

Indeed, it is possible to go a step further and say that copyright protects the author specifically as a *biological* entity, seeking to ensure the author's subsistence, as well as his or her ability to provide for dependents. As Mark Twain commented to the Committee on Patents of the Senate and the House in 1906, a time when the extension of copyright term was being considered,

> I like that extension of copyright life to the author's life and fifty years afterward. I think that would satisfy any reasonable author, because it would take care of his children. Let the grand-children take care of themselves. That would take care of my daughters, and after that I am not particular. I shall then have long been out of this struggle, independent of it, indifferent to it.[19]

Copyright also supports the protection of human rights in another sense. The copyright concept originally emerged as a means of limiting the exclusive control of publishing by the state, transferring control over the written word to those who wrote: authors. It thereby affirmed the basic human rights of individuals. It also conferred a profound social benefit by laying the foundation for democracy. Authors and the public had a shared interest in the freedom to write, publish, and, of course, read. It is this inherent independence of the word, this symbolic integrity of speech and thought, that was embodied in the copyright. While copyright has evolved in various directions since its genesis in eighteenth-century Britain, this basic core of the copyright idea should never be forgotten.

Given the importance of AI technology, from both economic and social perspectives, a strong case can be made that some form of regulation should be found for it. Notwithstanding the centrality of human authorship to copyright law, there is at least some possibility that copyright—on its own or, as seems more likely, in conjunction with other legal mechanisms[20]—could be an appropriate form of protection for AI creations. However, a basic question must first be answered. If a copyright were to subsist in computer-generated works, who would be entitled to

[19] Quoted in the marvelous post, Steve Courtney, *Mark Twain's Copyright Fight*, MARK TWAIN HOUSE AND MUSEUM (Fall 2017), https://www.uspto.gov/learning-and-resources/newsletter/inventors-eye/mark-twains-copyright-fight.

[20] Privacy protections come to mind, and privacy is represented in the EU AI Act: *see, e.g.*, Elizabeth Gibney, *What the EU's Tough AI Law Means for Research and ChatGPT*, NATURE (Feb. 16, 2024), https://www.nature.com/articles/d41586-024-00497-8.

hold that copyright, and why? In theory, at least three initial possibilities present themselves: the creator of the AI, the owner of the AI, or the AI itself.

1. Copyright in "Computer-Generated" Works: The UK Model

The UK Copyright, Designs and Patents Act 1988 (CDPA) is one of the few examples of direct legislative treatment of AI works, and it seems to be inspired by the general approach discussed here—although its language is oblique.[21]

The CDPA allows copyright protection in computer-generated works. The protection is granted to the creator of the underlying program. Section 9(3) states that, "In the case of a literary, dramatic, musical or artistic work which is computer-generated, the author shall be taken to be the person by whom the arrangements necessary for the creation of the work are undertaken."[22] As Bridy notes, a similar approach is taken in a number of common-law countries, including New Zealand and India.[23]

There has been only one case on this issue: *Nova v. Productions v. Mazooma Games*, from 2007. The case affirms the authorship of the person creating the "arrangements" for computer-generated creation. As Charlotte Ebutt summarizes,

> [In] *Nova Productions Ltd v. Mazooma Games Ltd [2007] EWCA Civ 219*, ... the Court of Appeal held that a person playing a computer game was not the author of screenshots taken while playing the game and had not undertaken any of the arrangements necessary for the creation of the images. Instead, the court held that the persons who made the arrangements necessary for the creation of the screenshots were the game's developers.[24]

[21] CDPA, *supra* note 13.

[22] Id.

[23] Bridy, *supra* note 4, at paras. 67–68. Bently provides a chart of countries that have adopted the UK approach as slide 25 in Lionel Bently, *The UK's Provisions on Computer-Generated Works: A Solution for AI Creations?* (June 2018), https://europeancopyrightsociety.org.files.wordpress.com/2018/06/lionel-the-uk-provisions-on-computer-generated-works.pdf. At slides 21–22, Bently cites the examination of this issue in the Whitford Committee Report on Copyright and Designs Law (Cmnd 6732, 1977), and the White Paper, Department of Trade and Industry, Intellectual Property and Innovation (Cmnd 9712, 1986), to arrive at the overall position that "no special treatment" and "no special provisions" were needed (slides 21-22). For a helpful overview of the treatment of computer-generated works under UK law, see Jyh-An Lee, *Computer-Generated Works under the CDPA 1988, in* Artificial Intelligence and Intellectual Property 177 (Jyh-An Lee, Reto Hilty & Kung-Chung Liu eds., 2021).

[24] Charlotte Ebbutt, *Creative Genius by Artificial Intelligence—But Who Owns the Copyright?*, Rwk Goodman (Dec. 17, 2019), https://www.rwkgoodman.com/info-hub/creative-genius-by-artificial-intelligence-but-who-owns-the-copyright.

Importantly, this ruling effectively established the rights of developers against all other claimants—including those who might make use of the computer to develop further computer-generated creations, such as consumers of the technology who were playing an interactive video game, as well as the computer creator "itself."

Is this link sufficient to allow moral rights to be extended, as well, to "the person by whom the arrangements necessary for the creation of the work are undertaken"? This problem, too, must be solved in the United Kingdom and in other countries where the moral rights of authors are recognized. There are at least three possible approaches: excluding moral rights in AI works, granting them, or granting some moral rights but not others.

Let us turn, once again, to the CDPA, which is one of the few examples of direct legislative treatment of this issue.[25] The UK approach is to create exceptions to the moral rights of attribution and integrity in computer-generated works, excluding moral rights from arising in these works.[26] Moral rights are therefore generally not allowed in AI creations under UK law.

Strangely, though, protection from false attribution, a distinct moral right under the UK scheme, is not addressed in relation to AI works. As a result, the moral right against false attribution may still subsist, uniquely among UK moral rights, in relation to computer-generated works. As Simon Stokes points out, this omission could, in theory, lead to a valid claim under UK law for false attribution of a computer-generated work by the author of the original software.[27] Why is this one attribution-related claim allowed?

As noted in the detailed discussion in Chapter 2 *supra*, the UK scheme for moral rights is exceptionally complex and fragmented. A plausible explanation for this inconsistency is that the UK drafters kept the right against false attribution of a computer-generated work because it is effectively a right against passing off, which is well accepted under UK law to protect business and corporate interests. This tradition of tort protection also helps to explain the presence of the right against false attribution in the CDPA.

The UK law has created a new copyright framework for the recognition of technologically generated works—one where the economic dimension of copyright is preserved, thereby continuing to function as a system of incentives and reward for those who develop AI, but not for the works that are directly generated by the computer. The moral rights dimension is generally eliminated. It should be emphasized that this approach does not completely sever the link between copyright and authorship under UK law in relation to computer-generated works. A human author still benefits from the copyright in the computer-generated work: that

[25] CDPA, *supra* note 13.

[26] *See* id., § 9(3). See the exceptions to attribution in § 79(2)(c) and the exceptions to the right to object to derogatory treatment in § 81(2).

[27] *See* Simon Stokes, *Implications of Moral Rights for the Digital Environment*, *in* Art and Copyright 95 (2003).

author is the programmer who created the technology. The technology, in its turn, generates the "artificial" work. In other words, the link between human author and computer-generated work is clearly considered sufficient for copyright as a whole to arise, but it is *not* strong enough to lead to moral rights in the computer-generated work.

In addition, if the computer-generated work is created in an employment context, the initial copyright holder will be the employer, and not the human creator of the technology.[28] The standard rule applicable in an employment context applies to copyright in computer-generated works, as well.

2. The Authors of Authors? Moral Rights for AI Creators

Could "the person who makes the necessary arrangements" for the creation of the AI work be granted moral rights in that work? [29] While this does not happen under UK law, let us consider the example of India, where it may.

At first glance, India takes a similar approach to the United Kingdom in dealing with AI. Like the United Kingdom, India grants the initial copyright in computer-generated works to the maker of the AI. Section 2(d)(vi) of the Indian Copyright Act, 1957 states,

> (d) "author" means...
>
> (vi) in relation to any literary, dramatic, musical or artistic work which is computer-generated, the person who causes the work to be created;

The Indian Copyright Act provides that the "author" of "any literary, dramatic, musical or artistic work which is computer-generated" is "the person who causes the work to be created." Like the UK Act, the Indian Act identifies the programmer as the creator of the work. However, it is also subtly different. Under the Indian Act, creation of the work is "cause[d] by" the author; the programmer is a "creator". Under the UK Act, this person is not a "creat[or]" but only a person who

[28] CDPA, *supra* note 13, section 11(2) contains the "employment rule," providing that the employer is the first owner of copyright in a "literary, dramatic, musical, or artistic work, or a film" created in the course of employment ("subject to any agreement to the contrary," as is usual in employment or work-for-hire relationships). This provision must be read with section 9(3), which provides for the copyright protection of "a literary, dramatic, musical or artistic work which is computer-generated." In other words, the condition that a work be literary, dramatic musical or artistic (known as the LDMA categories) is an explicit prerequisite for copyright protection under the UK Act.

[29] Interestingly, the point was noted as a concern in the African context, more than a decade ago: see Caroline B. Ncube, *Copyright Protection of Computer Programs, Computer-Generated Works and Databases in Zimbabwe*, 2 J. INFO. L & TECH (2002), http://www2.warwick.ac.uk/fac/soc/law/elj/jilt/2002_2/ncube. See section 2.1.2 on "*Computer-Generated Works*," where Ncube observes, "Zimbabwean legislation is thus deficient as it fails to comprehensively cater for computer generated works, which are actually being produced on a significant scale."

"undertakes" the "arrangements necessary for the creation of the work." This wording suggests that the Indian Act conceives of the person behind the computer as an author in the traditional sense of the word. The UK Act does not.

Section 57 of the Indian Copyright Act grants moral rights to "authors," and it does so without any exception or exclusion related to the computer-generated works identified as works of authorship earlier in the Act. Moreover, amendments to the Act in 2012, which led to both substantive change and some drafting improvements to section 57, did not introduce an exception to moral rights protection for the authors of computer-generated works. In the Indian context, at least for now, the question "Can machines be creative?" is not yet relevant. Instead, the Act implicitly asks whether the *creator of a technology with the capacity to generate works* can be creative, and its answer to this question is a clear "Yes." Accordingly, that creator enjoys moral rights, just as other authors do under the Indian Copyright Act.

But one caveat remains. The Indian Copyright Act does not define "person." Ankit Sahni, the owner of the art-generating AI tool Raghav, has argued that "person" under Indian law should be interpreted as including both natural and legal persons.[30] His position is based on a provision in another Indian law, the General Clauses Act,[31] whose purpose is to "shorten" the language used in Indian laws.

However, a closer look at the General Clauses Act (GCA) undercuts Sahni's reading of the definition of person in the GCA. Section 30 of the Act states,

> Person.—"Person" shall include any company or association or body of individuals, whether incorporated or not;

While this does extend the definition of "person" to include companies, it likens that entity to a "body of individuals," suggesting that the basis for recognizing a company as a person under this provision is that it represents a coalition of human individuals. Looking at this section, it would seem that extending the definition of person to include artificial persons could only be accomplished if that artificial person could somehow be linked to a collective of human individuals, as is done here in relation to the other legal entities involved. That would not be strictly impossible in relation to AI—for example, there is a connection between the functionality ("life" or "activity") of the artificial intelligenceAI and the human input on which it was trained. But this link, though factual, would seem to be a tenuous basis for establishing the legal personhood of AI. At the very least, the unresolved conflicts between the providers of the works used in training and the creators of AI

[30] Sahni's attempts to register Raghav as an author in its own right in various copyright offices are discussed *infra*: *see, e.g.*, note 31.

[31] As noted by Sukanya Sarkar, *Exclusive: Indian Copyright Office Issues Withdrawal Notice to AI Co-author*, MANAGING IP (Dec. 13, 2021), https://www.managingip.com/article/2a5d0jj2zjo7fajsjwwlc/exclusive-indian-copyright-office-issues-withdrawal-notice-to-ai-co-author.

technology mandate against such a recognition. In these circumstances, accepting Sahni's argument would be a supremely ironic, if not cynical, approach to the question of AI personhood.

In the case of a computer-generated work, it seems clear that the closest we can come to locating a relevant human "author" is the programmer: the person who creates the computer program whose purpose it is to generate a further work, whether that subsequent work might be another computer program; an artwork involving visual art, musical works, text, or some combination of these; or some other kind of work altogether. This is what UK law means by "the person by whom the arrangements necessary for the creation of the work are undertaken."

Although the work is ultimately generated by a machine—a computer— there is an identifiable human intelligence behind the machine itself. But how meaningful is the link between that human intelligence and the *products* of the computer program? Is it strong enough to imply a connection between author and work such that the author may be harmed by damage to his or her creation?

If the link is initially strong, at what point, if any, does it break? Does the breaking of the connection between the author of a generative technology and its output depend on the nature of the creation? If, unlike most traditional works of art, a program were to generate its creations over an extended period of time, with ever more intricate variations, how strong must the connection of the human author with these works remain over time for us to continue to consider that person their author? A program might be explicitly designed to generate a chaotic and unforeseeable series of events, which then coalesce into a work. Is it now correct to call the programmer the author, even though he or she cannot predict the form of the final "work"?

The impact of uncertainty is particularly difficult to assess. At this point, computer-generated creation seems eerily reminiscent of human creativity. To what extent does any author or artist truly predict the form of his or her final creation? The answer might depend on the artist's individual personality, the nature of the work, and many other ephemeral factors. Is the uncertainty inherent in a computer-generated work greater than that involved in purely human creation? Is it qualitatively different? While the general answer may be "Yes," the purpose of this discussion is only to determine whether uncertainty about the product should deprive the creator of the generative technology of his or her own rights.

The difficulty of identifying the author of unpredictable works is also matched by uncertainty about the nature of the computer-generated work. What exactly is the "work"? Is it the computer program that generates the end product, the end product itself, or both? If the work is executed through time, at what stage of its existence does it become a final product rather than a work-in-progress, thereby becoming capable of protection by copyright?

Again, this last question is not unique to computer programs. It can arise in many contexts, traditional ones as well as those where technology is involved in the creative process. For example, deciding on the final version of a film can be challenging.[32] Even in the case of traditional copyright works, such as literature, authors may continue to make changes to their work even after a so-called "final" version is published. Thomas Hardy revised the chapters of certain of his novels that had appeared in serialized versions for magazine publication in order to establish a "definitive" version of the text.[33] F. Scott Fitzgerald was known for making further revisions of his works even at the proof stage.[34] In all of these cases, however, a human author, or a group of them, ultimately decides on a "final" version of the work, at least for the purpose of publication as such. Authorial intent is implicit in the protections granted by copyright law.[35]

Moral rights for programmers who create AI could be justified. Given the uncertainty involved, however, are there any overwhelming arguments either in favor of or against such a grant? Arguably, there is a powerful argument in favor of moral rights for AI creators: the value of attribution and integrity for maintaining knowledge about the source of the AI works, helping to distinguish those works from direct human creation, and impeding the use of those works for nefarious purposes that might represent threats to the integrity right of the AI creator (and others).[36] Whether or not these justifications truly fit within the theory of a special relationship between author and creative work, on which moral rights are traditionally based, is unclear. It may depend on the specifics of each AI scenario. However, it is clear that there is a wider benefit to be gained from recognizing these rights. The question of how to treat attribution and integrity interests as distinct from the moral rights of authors is a much larger issue, and it is given its own treatment in section G below.

[32] This is recognized in the French Intellectual Property Code, where it is a central issue in the regime for film copyright. *See* Loi 92-597 du 1 juillet 1992 relative au Code de la propriété intellectuelle (partie législative) [Law 92-597 of July 1, 1992, relating to the Intellectual Property Code (Legislative part)], Journal officiel de la République française [J.O.] [Official Gazette of France], Feb. 8, 1994 (Code de la propriété intellectuelle), arts. L121-5 and L113-7 (Fr.), https://www.legifrance.gouv.fr/codes/texte_lc/LEGITEXT000006069414.

[33] *See, e.g.*, Mary Ellen Chase, Thomas Hardy from Serial to Novel (1927) (summarizing Hardy's own notes to this effect).

[34] *See, e.g.*, Kenneth Eble, *The Craft of Evision:* The Great Gatsby, 36(3) American Literature 315 (1964), https://doi.org/10.2307/2923547. *See also* Don Skemer, *Digitization of The Great Gatsby Autograph Manuscript and Galleys*, PUL Manuscripts News (May 24, 2013), https://blogs.princeton.edu/manuscripts/2013/05/24/538.

[35] Indeed, it is worth noting that copyright protects both an economic right of first publication and a moral right of disclosure, recognizing the author's intent to publish as the core of the rights involved in copyright: *see* Chapter 1 *infra*.

[36] For example, in *Confetti Records v. Warner Music UK Ltd* [2003] EWHC (Ch) 1274, the first UK judgment on moral rights under the CDPA, *supra* note 13, the plaintiff argued that the association between his musical compositions and drug culture offended his moral right of integrity. The case was ultimately unsuccessful, but for the amusing reason that the judges felt that they could not be sure of the meaning of the words used in the offending musical performance .

3. Copyright Registration: An Initial Test of Machine Authorship?

Nevertheless, by recognizing computer-generated creation as works under copyright law, the UK law goes much further than other laws, which prefer to ban copyright in computer-generated works altogether. Notably, the United States Copyright Office specifies that non-human authors cannot be protected by copyright.[37] In other countries, where there is no such specification in law or policy documents, the issue remains murky. It has been tested indirectly in both Canada and India, with slightly different outcomes in each country. The copyright offices in these two countries have both considered the possibility of registering an AI tool called Raghav—used to create an image based on Vincent Van Gogh's painting "Starry Night"—as the author of a copyright work. In Canada, as a possible first step on a different path, registration of Raghav as a "coauthor" was permitted. But this approach is tantalizing without really establishing any legal principles. Copyright Office registrations have little evidentiary value in Canada—they are far less significant than in the United States, with a long history of registration-based copyright protection that is not shared by Canada— and the influence of the Canadian Copyright Office is more limited.[38]

Interestingly, India originally refused the request to register Raghav as the author of the image, but it subsequently granted the possibility of Raghav's "authorship" if the human inventor of Raghav were to be named as a coauthor of the work. However, this grant of coauthorship was subsequently withdrawn, a decision that has been disputed by Mr. Sahni, the owner of the technology—and an intellectual property lawyer himself.

One further question arises: should the author or owner be named as a coauthor in the application? Indian law allows both authors and owners to register copyright.[39] However, accurate information about those named in the registration must presumably be preserved. This example, in itself, serves to highlight

[37] U.S. Copyright Office, Compendium of U.S. Copyright Office Practices s. 313.2 (3d ed., Jan. 28, 2021), https://www.copyright.gov/comp3 (in a chapter on "Copyrightable Authorship: What Can Be Registered," the section states, unequivocally, "To qualify as a work of 'authorship' a work must be created by a human being").

[38] Though it should also be noted that, under Canada's Copyright Act, *supra* note 13, the significance of registration is largely symbolic. The Canadian Copyright Office states,

> Benefits of registration—The Copyright Act states that a certificate of registration of copyright is evidence that copyright exists and that the person registered is the owner of the copyright. However, the Copyright Office is not responsible for policing or checking on registered works and how people use them. It also cannot guarantee that the legitimacy of ownership or the originality of a work will never be questioned.

See Canadian Intellectual Property Office, *A Guide to Copyright* (n.d.) https://ised-isde.canada.ca/site/canadian-intellectual-property-office/en/guide-copyright#benefitsRegistration.

[39] *See* Copyright Act 1957, ch. X (esp. ss. 44 and 45) (India), http://copyright.gov.in/Documents/CopyrightRules1957.pdf.

the relevance of moral rights in the AI environment. The accurate preservation of knowledge is one of the goals of the copyright registration process, just as it is behind the requirement of identifying inventors under patent law. This requires us to name those involved in the technology in their proper roles; an owner presumably cannot register as an "author" of the work. This information then becomes available to the public, and its credibility is established.

D. The Machine as Infringer

The role of copyright-protected works—artworks and text—in training generative AI raises a fundamental question. Is this an infringement of copyright in the underlying works? If not, on what legal basis are they being used?

The predictable response on the part of AI companies (reflected so far in OpenAI's public comments[40]) is that such use is "fair" because AI technology ultimately has the potential to be highly useful to society. But is that usefulness, whatever it may be, such as to justify the cost to the creators of the works that are being used? The cost is one that should be measured in years of biological life and perhaps many other human investments—emotion and hope—as well as money invested (or lost) and opportunities foregone. And what about the great economic inequality between the creators of copyright works and leading technology companies? Is this "fair"?

It should also be added that inequality of bargaining power in the making of agreements is another dimension of this problem. Blanket licenses covering all potential future developments in technology have never seemed so unfair. These clauses are arguably unethical[41] to begin with; if they are now to be used to justify the free and non-consensual use of such works for the potentially lucrative purpose of AI development, this would be an indictment of modern contract practice.

Added to this, AI derived from existing human creations is not only lucrative but also has the potential to supplant the original works. The AI-created works emulate the human originals without being actual "copies."[42] This is a thorny issue for copyright law and for moral rights as well. It serves to highlight the potential shortcomings of accepted copyright concepts and norms when faced with the reality of AI.

[40] *See, e.g.*, Hayden Field, *OpenAI Responds to New York Times Lawsuit, Says "Regurgitation" of Content Is a "Rare Bug,"* CNBC (Jan. 8, 2024), https://www.cnbc.com/2024/01/08/openai-responds-to-new-york-times-lawsuit.html.

[41] "Unconscionable," in the terminology of contract law—as discussed in all the standard textbooks. *See, e.g.*, Ewan McKendrick, Contract Law: Text, Cases and Materials 20 (10th ed., 2022).

[42] The wording of the trial court in *Designers Guild v. Russell Williams* [2001] FSR 113 (UKHL) comes to mind: "altered copying."

1. AI Artists: In-Stability

Copyright has long held closely to the proposition that the copying of style is not restricted by copyright. An example that often serves to illustrate this proposition is that of pointillism, the technique created by impressionist painter Georges Seurat—while Seurat's particular paintings would have qualified for copyright protection, any other painter would be free to adopt the pointillistic style in making his or her own work. This approach to copyright is often framed in terms of the "idea expression dichotomy,"[43] which provides for the expression of ideas in works to be protected, while leaving the ideas themselves "free as the air"[44] in order to encourage the spread of learning.

But this approach may not be well adapted to the age of artificial intelligence—and to image generators in particular. At least two things happen that should be of concern. First, images that imitate the style of a living artist may end up being confused with works originally made by that artist. This would affect the artist in at least two ways, potentially undercutting the market for that artist's works by offering a cheaper substitute, and also leading to potential damage to the artist's reputation by creating confusion in the mind of the public between original works and AI copies. This was the kind of problem that previously arose in the *Théberge* case in relation to the then new technique of creating canvas backed reproductions from a postcard image made of Théberge's paintings.[45] Secondly, these effects would follow from prompts input by the user of the system into the AI algorithm—prompts that would probably involve the use of the artist's name or intentionally invoke the artist's identity through some other choice of words. The artist's moral rights of attribution and integrity are both affected by these processes.

For the artists whose works were initially popular on DALL-E, described by its maker as "an AI system that can create realistic images and art from a description in natural language," this situation raised the specter of artistic identity theft – a new and powerful affront to their lives and livelihoods.[46] Artist Greg Rutkowski states, "People are pretending to be me. I'm very concerned about it; it seems unethical."[47] Rutkowski says that his work "has been used in AI more than Picasso."[48] He argues, as this chapter suggests below, that "A.I. should exclude living artists

[43] *See* U.S. Copyright Act, *supra* note 13, § 102 ("ideas shall not be protectable").

[44] A phrase famously used by Justice Brandeis in his dissent in *International News Service v. Associated Press* 248 U.S. 215 (1918) 248 (U.S.S.C.), https://supreme.justia.com/cases/federal/us/248/215.

[45] *Théberge v. Galerie d'Art du Petit Champlain Inc.* [2002] 2 S.C.R. 336, 2002 SCC 34 (Can.), https://scc-csc.lexum.com/scc-csc/scc-csc/en/item/1973/index.do.

[46] *See* https://openai.com/index/dall-e-2/.

[47] Beatrice Nolan, *Artists Say AI Image Generators Are Copying Their Style to Make Thousands of New Images—And It's Completely out of Their Control*, Tech (Oct. 17, 2022), https://www.businessinsider.com/ai-image-generators-artists-copying-style-thousands-images-2022-10?amp.

[48] Quoted in Clare Hutchinson & Phil John, *AI: Digital Artist's Work Copied More Times Than Picasso*, BBC News (July 20, 2023), https://www.bbc.com/news/uk-wales-66099850.

from its database."[49] Artists have also spoke about the "aggression" that is sometimes apparent in these new uses of technology. Simon Stålenhag, a Swedish artist and designer, comments,

> People are selling prints made by AI that have my name in the title ... Something like—"Rusty Robot in a field in the style of Simon Stålenhag"—which is a super aggressive way of using this technology ... People have tagged me and said that [they'll] ... make me lose my job ... they're really harsh and aggressive.[50]

Not surprisingly, both DALL-E and ChatGPT are currently being sued for copyright infringement. A class action lawsuit filed by a number of artists against Midjourney, DeviantArt, Runway, and Stability AI in the summer of 2023 was initially dismissed by U.S. District Court Judge William H. Orrick of the Northern District of California on the grounds that "many of the artworks cited as being infringed by the AI companies had not actually been registered for copyright by the artists with the U.S. Copyright Office."[51] However, this formality was open to correction, and an amended and expanded complaint was subsequently filed, including more artists—among them, Greg Rutkowski.[52]

In principle, violations of the artists' moral rights are clearly apparent. The use of prompts containing the names of artists arguably should be considered a new form of violation of the artist's attribution right.[53] It can be considered either a presumptive association of the artist's name with the AI creation or, simply, an abusive use of the artist's name with the intent to create a substitute for the artist's work. The production of works that look like the artist's work without being actual

[49] Quoted in Vittoria Benzine, *"A.I. Should Exclude Living Artists from Its Database," Says One Painter Whose Works Were Used to Fuel Image Generators*, ARTNET NEWS (Sept. 20, 2022), https://news.artnet.com/art-world/a-i-should-exclude-living-artists-from-its-database-says-one-painter-whose-works-were-used-to-fuel-image-generators-2178352.

[50] Quoted id.

[51] For a discussion of the original claim, see, e.g., Zachary Small, *Sarah Silverman Sues OpenAI and Meta Over Copyright Infringement*, NEW YORK TIMES (July 10, 2023), https://www.nytimes.com/2023/07/10/arts/sarah-silverman-lawsuit-openai-meta.html.

[52] *See* Carl Franzen, *The Copyright Case against AI Art Generators Just Got Stronger with More Artists and Evidence*, VENTUREBEAT (Dec. 1, 2023), https://venturebeat.com/ai/the-copyright-case-against-ai-art-generators-just-got-stronger-with-more-artists-and-evidence. In the United States, registration is required prior to bringing a lawsuit; there are no timing requirements to register a work, but timely registration can preserve the valuable entitlement to statutory damages under the Copyright Act, or secure certain other advantages to the author. For a full discussion, see "Myth #3: Registration Isn't Necessary," in Janet Fries & Jennifer T. Criss, *Debunking Copyright Myths*, 11(6) LANDSLIDE (2019), https://www.americanbar.org/groups/intellectual_property_law/publications/landslide/2018-19/july-august/debunking-copyright-myths. See also the case summary of the latest U.S. Supreme Court precedent on this issue in *Copyright Registration Is a Prerequisite to Suing for Infringement*, WILEY (Mar. 4, 2019), https://www.wiley.law/alert-Copyright-Registration-Is-A-Prerequisite-to-Suing-for-Infringement.

[53] Some commentators argue that prompts are a new form of authorship, but Daniel Gervais makes a persuasive case against this: Daniel Gervais, *Humans as Prompt Engineers*, KLUWER COPYRIGHT BLOG (June 14, 2023), https://copyrightblog.kluweriplaw.com/2023/06/14/humans-as-prompt-engineers.

reproductions of it may not infringe copyright, but it could infringe the artist's moral right of integrity by causing damage to his or her reputation—as discussed in the *Théberge* case both by the artist and by the court, though ironically to the artist's detriment in that case.[54]

If reputational damage occurred through the proliferation of new images, this would amount to a violation of the artist's moral right of integrity. It would also be a new type of affront to that right, through the particular features of this new technology. The violation of the artist's right of integrity would be caused by the actual and potential volume of images generated, their capacity to overwhelm the original creations of the author, and the difficulty of verifying their provenance in the absence of rules on the attribution of AI content—or, of course, simply in the absence of accurate attribution of the artists whose works are behind the production of these images, and, as noted above, in the use of their names to "prompt" the creation of these images. Attribution and integrity are clearly closely linked in this technological context.

None of these claims can actually be made under U.S. copyright law including the Visual Artists Rights Act of 1990 (VARA), which only deals with the direct alteration of original works and not the treatment of images. In Canada, the *Théberge* case was decided under a similar rationale.[55] In this sense, VARA is a failure. It has failed to protect artists from exploitation by new technologies. VARA's focus on "originals" should be fundamentally reconsidered in the digital environment, since many effects on artist's reputations may be felt through the digital manipulation of images, even as the "original" work remains "intact." In some cases, though, these manipulations may also affect the integrity of the original works by destroying context or other essential features of the works.[56]

Although the moral right of attribution cannot be claimed under U.S. copyright law, the revised claim is littered with references to the issue of missing "credit" to the artists whose works have been used. Indeed, the importance of attribution in

[54] This idea is similar to the problem of passing off under trademark law—and, indeed, the resemblances between moral rights and trademark law are well known, especially in the United States, where the Lanham Act has historically allowed trademark designation of origin to step in for the moral right of attribution. *See, e.g.*, the Monty Python case, *Gilliam v. ABC*, 538 F.2d 14 (1976) (U.S.), https://casetext.com/case/gilliam-v-american-broadcasting-companies-inc.

[55] Otherwise, in the case of direct treatment of an artwork, there would have been no need to show proof of damage to the author's honor or reputation under Canadian copyright law, as illustrated by *Théberge*, *supra* note 45. *See* Mira T. Sundara Rajan, *Moral Rights and Economic Rights: Overlapping Protection of Authors under Copyright Law*, *in* OVERLAPPING INTELLECTUAL PROPERTY RIGHTS 303 (Neil Wilkof, Shamnad Basheer & Irene Calboli eds., 2d ed., 2023).

[56] It should also be noted that this situation is fundamentally different from the use of technology to produce images of works by well-known artists, where attribution and reputation are also well established. The issues are discussed in Chapter 8 *infra*. The importance of context is emphasized by Jean-Louis Andral, curator of the Picasso Museum in Antibes, in a letter released to the public: *see* Save Oslo's Y-block with mural by Picasso, FACEBOOK (May 31, 2020), https://m.facebook.com/243059203235939/photos/a.601125957429260/610685876473268/?type=3&hx0026;source=57&hx0026;__tn__=EH-R (also in private conversation, June 2020).

the claim can hardly be overstated, because the issue of credit appears alongside that of consent throughout this document. This only serves to highlight the importance of the moral right of attribution, despite its absence from U.S. law, and the artists involved here should bear in mind that, outside the United States, legal recourse of some kind will be available for violations of their attribution right.

The availability of fair use in the context of artworks may also be different from the situation of literary works. *Google v. Oracle* expanded fair use in the software context in 2020,[57] but *Warhol v. Goldsmith* pulled it back in the artistic context—correctly—in 2023.[58] It therefore seems unlikely that the uses of works made by DALL-E and other technologies based on "scraping" can be easily justified as fair uses under U.S. copyright law.

More generally, it is important to note that this situation is detrimental to the public by encouraging false information to proliferate, making it difficult to establish who is the true creator of these images and how they were created. Moral rights can play a crucial contribution to the preservation of historical truth—a reality that is laid bare in the environment of artificial intelligence. What happens in circumstances like those confronting artists through generative AI today, if moral rights are not affirmed? The social harms will be felt far beyond the artistic community.

For example, let us consider Shakespeare. As scholars throughout the past few centuries have noted,[59] it is difficult to confirm the poet's identity as the author of the plays because of the failure to preserve proper attribution of these works. This has happened in spite of the importance of the works: they are fundamental to English cultural identity, and they are widely recognized as among the greatest treasures of human cultural heritage. Indeed, in Shakespeare's turbulent times, political and religious currents created a situation that was dangerous for writers and where, if anything, the author's identity may have been consciously concealed for reasons of safety.[60] We continue to feel the effects of this censorious regime today—and they will probably be felt forever. Will we ever know for certain who Shakespeare was, or who wrote the works attributed to him?

Of course, a further question could be asked—"Does it matter?" After all, Shakespeare's plays are available, and they appear to be reasonably well preserved. Perhaps we know all that we need to know about Shakespeare from the texts

[57] *Google v. Oracle*, 141 S. Ct 1163 (2021) (U.S.S.C), https://www.supremecourt.gov/opinions/20pdf/18-956_d18f.pdf.

[58] *Warhol v. Goldsmith*, No. 21-869 (May 18, 2023) (U.S.S.C.), https://www.supremecourt.gov/opinions/22pdf/21-869_87ad.pdf.

[59] *See, e.g.*, Elizabeth Winkler, *Doubting Shakespeare's Identity Isn't a Conspiracy Theory*, Literary Hub (Mar. 15, 2023), https://lithub.com/doubting-shakespeares-identity-isnt-a-conspiracy-theory. This is also a theme of Michael Wood's work, discussed *infra* note 60.

[60] Discussed in detail in Michael Wood's documentary on Shakespeare: *see In Search of Shakespeare*, BBC (2004), https://www.imdb.com/title/tt0398492/. Wood refers to the Tudor regime as a "police state."

themselves. And yet, in the technological context, this answer seems unsatisfying. Technology feeds on rapid change, and information quickly becomes obsolete—often within hours or even faster—triggering a cycle driven by technology's insatiable hunger for more, newer information.[61] The quality of information is inevitably eroded. This process ends up being different in both tempo and style from the natural processes of human memory and understanding, artificially hastening and distorting them.

In addition, false information has proven to proliferate in the technological environment, a tendency that is exaggerated by AI. ChatGPT, an AI tool that generates text in response to prompts, has a demonstrated tendency to generate false information—potentially leading to profound human embarrassment, as in the "cringe-inducing" case of a lawyer whose reliance on it generated a "legal brief for a case in Federal District Court that was filled with fake judicial opinions and legal citations."[62] Much of what happens in the modern world seems to depend upon the manipulation of speech, ideas, and images, often with a view to manipulating people and politics in a way that might be familiar to Renaissance Italians who had read Machiavelli's *The Prince*.[63] Through technology, the spread of false information has become a threat to such fundamentals as democracy, environmental safety, and human rights. In this environment, preserving the historical truth of identity and authorship are arguably even more important than they have been at any time in the past. Moral rights clearly have a role, narrow but valuable, to play in this broader struggle.

Is this all pessimism? After all, humans have always developed tools and worked with them to promote its progress. Is there any reason why AI should be fundamentally different? As chess grandmaster Gary Kasparov argues, "Machine's triumph is [hu]man's triumph."[64] In the hands of artists, could AI be a creative and interesting tool? In theory, the answer would seem to be the same as in relation to any other tool: "Yes." But crucially, as artist Stålenhag notes, AI-image generators are "not in the hands of artists right now. It's in the hands of early adopters of tech."[65] The incentives operating in these two communities are clearly not aligned.

[61] An issue noted in my much earlier work, MIRA T. SUNDARA RAJAN, *Introduction*, *in* COPYRIGHT AND CREATIVE FREEDOM: A STUDY OF POST-SOCIALIST LAW REFORM (2006).

[62] See, e.g., the early case of a lawyer who wrote a brief using ChatGPT that ended up filled with false information, as described in numerous sources including Benjamin Weiser & Nate Schweber, *The ChatGPT Lawyer Explains Himself*, NEW YORK TIMES (June 8, 2023), https://www.nytimes.com/2023/06/08/nyregion/lawyer-chatgpt-sanctions.html. It is disturbing that Mr. Schwartz claimed, "I did not comprehend that ChatGPT could fabricate cases."

[63] *See Niccolò Machiavelli*, BRITANNICA (n.d.), https://www.britannica.com/biography/Niccolo-Machiavelli.

[64] From a TED talk by Kasparov in 2017, quoted in Wakefield, *supra* note 3.

[65] Id.

2. AI Writers: Settlements and Lawsuits

a. The Hollywood Writers' Strike

In the summer of 2023, Hollywood screenwriters went on strike to protest the use of AI in films. It was soon followed by a strike of performers in response to concerns about AI that struck at the heart of their profession.

The writers were on strike for 148 days—nearly 5 months—and the settlement that ended their strike revealed some interesting solutions to their concerns, while also defining, just as interestingly, crucial terrain for potential disagreements and lawsuits in the future.

The important benchmark established by the settlement took the form of restrictions on the use of AI-generated content to replace screenwriters. Under the terms of the agreement, writers cannot be compelled to use AI, and any production company that wants to use it must acquire the consent of its screenwriters to do so. The use of AI in the creation of a script, in any capacity, must be indicated, whether that use is partial or more comprehensive. At the same time, AI cannot be credited as an author in its own right. This is in keeping with copyright policy which, so far, has refused to allow non-human authors to gain authorial status under copyright laws. The correctness of this policy must be emphasized; it has its roots in the birth of modern copyright law, and copyright offices should not deviate from it in the AI environment.

These provisions all suggest a certain attitude towards AI: it is a tool to be used by human writers and not a replacement for human authorship. Not only is the use of AI to replace the activity of human writers prohibited, but the potentially unique creative input of human writers, in the form of literary work, is also acknowledged.

But the insistence on labeling work created by AI is more broadly interesting. Artists and authors are not usually required to disclose the tools that they use in the creation of their work.[66] A requirement that the use of AI should be indicated suggests that AI is somehow qualitatively different from other tools—including those available through modern technology—that are used in the creation of works. What is that qualitative difference? Being able to identify it could be important for AI policy. Much of what happened during the Hollywood writers' strike was clearly a response to the writers' fear of being replaced by AI. It should be explicitly pointed out that such a fear could only arise in two sets of circumstances: where the AI-generated content is qualitatively "better" than that produced by human writers, or where human input, whatever its distinctive characteristics might be, is not highly valued. Given the difficulty of identifying what makes a "better" product in relation to a potentially artistic work like a screenplay, we can turn our attention immediately to the second area of concern as more relevant for our analysis. Once

[66] A point noted by Ela Orleans in an interview, Jan. 22nd, 2024; forthcoming podcast episode from Woman of Culture Podcast (Nov. 2024), http://womanofculturepodcast.com.

we divest ourselves of concerns about artistic quality, the advantages offered by AI are obvious. AI can produce vast, probably infinite quantities of output, and it does so at vastly reduced costs. Doing business with humans is costly in terms of time, resources, and the basic requirements of human relationships, all of which can be dispensed with through the use of AI.

Labeling AI writing as such, in Hollywood, supports a "human-friendly" environment for the production of films. A flood of AI-generated material could be forestalled through accurate labeling, and human work would not be at risk of being overwhelmed by a stream of AI-generated products, vanishing into an infinitely fractured landscape for films.

In this case, the interest of screenwriters also supports the public interest in knowing the provenance of information. Interestingly, it is not universally accepted that the labeling of information generated by AI is necessary. However, the dangers of misinformation seem to support labeling as a prerogative, bringing it perhaps greater emphasis to this aspect of preserving knowledge than has ever been the case in the past. Although it may be difficult to articulate the reasons behind the need to label information originating with AI, in particular, the broader imperative to preserve attribution in relation to any and all knowledge that is circulating today, is very clear.

As a result of these terms, although the United States does not recognize moral rights for writers in any context, including screenwriters, this agreement effectively upholds the moral right of attribution of Hollywood screenwriters. Once again, through the back door, and to a correspondingly limited extent, writers have succeeded in vindicating their moral right of attribution in a contractual context. What about the right of integrity? Is it a concern for screenwriters in the AI environment, and is it reflected in this agreement?

Indeed, the most subtle point in the agreement may be a provision that AI cannot be used to rewrite "literary" material.[67] This provision bears a clear relationship to the moral right of integrity, which prevents the distortion, mutilation, or other objectionable modification of an author's work—either upon the simple objection of the author, as in France, or as part of protecting the author's reputation, as under the Berne Convention. If we consider the provision in the screenwriters' contract as a manifestation of the moral right of integrity, some interesting points emerge. Banning AI from the modification of literary work implies that, *a priori*, AI manipulation is considered a violation of the author's moral right of integrity. There is also a consensus that writers can achieve a higher level of creation, which the agreement calls literary, and that when they do so, interference with that work through AI is fundamentally unacceptable. From a legal point

[67] The settlement is helpfully summarized in Jake Coyle, *In Hollywood's Battle against AI, Human Win (for Now)*, Associated Press (Sept. 27, 2023), https://apnews.com/article/hollywood-ai-strike-wga-artificial-intelligence-39ab72582c3a15f77510c9c30a45ffc8.

of view, this provision presents all kinds of problems, because it may prove to be difficult in practice to distinguish between literary and non-literary work created by screenwriters. Indeed, this has been the basic difficulty confronting copyright law throughout its history: what constitutes an original work of authorship that should benefit from copyright regulation, with all the provision for incentives and rewards inherent in the copyright framework. This question continues to be fundamentally relevant in the technological context.

How will this difficulty be resolved in Hollywood? If the answer to this question is that it will be settled by those most able to sue, then the practical effect of the provision will be minimal, though not non-existent. And this highlights the difficulty of relying on private ordering: it is ultimately driven by inequality of bargaining power, open to manipulation by the most powerful actors, and largely unfit for protecting the public interest. Issues such as fairness and equity for those working in Hollywood should be recognized as broader public policy issues, since most Americans, like most people worldwide, would probably like to live in a fairer, and therefore safer and healthier, society.

b. *NYT v. OpenAI* and Its Sister Lawsuits

But the Hollywood writers' settlement allowed studios to continue to train AI on human-authored scripts. This issue is of broad concern to writers and publishers across all genres, since the advent of ChatGPT has clearly shown that AI has the capacity to generate vast amounts of text. In fact-based writing, such as news, the products of AI may be able to compete directly with the work of human writers; more generally, generative AI has the potential to lead to overwhelming disinformation and to profound degradation of the environment for the written word.

These points of general concern are included in the New York Times complaint against OpenAI, the maker of ChatGPT. Predictably, OpenAI argues that its use of vast amounts of written material, including articles from the New York Times, amounts to fair use under U.S. copyright law because it is "transformative" in nature. In doing so, OpenAI is relying upon the the precedent established by the Google Books litigation a decade ago.[68] However, in the case of generative AI, there is no guarantee that this legal strategy will succeed as it did in relation to Google Books. Indeed, as has been discussed elsewhere,[69] the differences between Google Books and OpenAI are fundamental, technologically and otherwise. Perhaps most importantly, the products of OpenAI are in direct competition with the creations of human authors, with the obvious potential to undercut the marketplace for their works by flooding the market with artificially generated material. In

[68] The relevance of Google Books is discussed in Mira T. Sundara Rajan, *Is Generative AI Fair Use of Copyright Works?* NYT v. OpenAI, Kluwer Copyright Blog (Feb. 29, 2024), https://copyrightblog.kluweriplaw.com/2024/02/29/is-generative-ai-fair-use-of-copyright-works-nyt-v-openai/.

[69] Id.

this environment, the free use of literary works as training data seems downright odious, since it appropriates the work of the authors of the published articles, offering neither recognition for the agency of authors nor payment for the use of their works in return. Showing fair use requires finding a balance among the different factors involved in the four-factor test under U.S. copyright law,[70] and transformative use is not meant to circumvent this process.[71] Rather, if transformative use can be shown, it must be weighed against all of the considerations identified in the four-factor test. It is difficult to see how the economic impact on authors could be sufficiently counterbalanced by the benefit to society from generative AI to justify the use of their works as "fair."

Since the moral rights of writers are not protected under U.S. copyright law, uniquely in the world, one would not expect the New York Times complaint to raise moral rights. Yet, the claim does reference moral rights—indirectly.[72]

It does so in relation to attribution. The complaint points to two attribution-related problems: first, that "these [AI] tools ... wrongly attribute false information to The Times" and, secondly, that, "[b]y design, the training process does not preserve any copyright-management information, and the outputs of Defendants' GPT models removed any copyright notices, titles, and identifying information" from the articles.

The problem of imputing false information to articles deserves a moment's reflection. Without involving the direct mistreatment of the articles per se, it is still a fundamental attack on the integrity of journalistic works. The suggestion that these articles contain false information could destroy the reputations of the articles, their authors, and the publication itself. Not only is the moral right of integrity held by the authors of the articles affected, but the integrity of the publication as a whole is also at issue. While the status of the publication is not a problem that is reached by the traditional doctrine of moral rights, as corporate moral rights are not traditionally recognized, it still presents a fascinating scenario where something akin to a corporate moral right, at the level of the publishing house, seems intuitive, and possibly warranted.[73]

Rights management information is a feature of U.S. law, and its presence in the claim becomes more interesting, for our purposes, when we consider its place in the broader context of the U.S. Copyright Act. While the law does not grant moral rights to writers, U.S. copyright law does prohibit the removal of digital rights management information from literary (and other) works.[74] The provision on rights

[70] *See* U.S. Copyright Act, *supra* note 13, § 107.

[71] Pierre Leval, *Toward a Fair Use Standard*, 103 Harv. L. Rev. 1105 (1990).

[72] The sole exception being moral rights under the U.S. Visual Artists Rights Act of 1990 (VARA), 17 U.S.C. § 106A (1990), https://www.copyright.gov/title17/92chap1.html#106a.

[73] As noted previously, corporate moral rights are recognized in Japan and Korea, and the rationale for doing so perhaps reflects cultural norms surrounding relations between corporations and society, and the conduct of corporations. *See* Chapter 4, *supra* notes 322–25 and accompanying text.

[74] *See* U.S. Copyright Act, *supra* note 13, § 1202 ("Integrity of Copyright Management Information").

management has also been put forward as a practical stand-in for the moral right of attribution under U.S. copyright law, in an environment dominated by technology, as noted by the U.S. Copyright Office in a 2017 report on moral rights protection in the United States.[75]

Along with a number of other points of principle raised in the complaint, this element draws attention to a broader picture: the potentially uncontrollable spread of false information in the AI environment. AI can generate vast amounts of information and falsify it in new ways. At this stage, AI chatbots are even known to "hallucinate" information—creating problems for users of the technology by generating everything from false narratives to made-up citations for legal cases, with potentially dramatic consequences.[76] It is in this environment that works of NEW YORK TIMES journalism, like other works of human authorship, will have to compete—not only for money but also for attention, legitimacy, authority, and human connection.

This leaves us with the intriguing possibility that, if the TIMES complaint were being considered under copyright laws in other countries, it might include many more elements having to do with the violation of the moral rights of attribution and integrity of the authors of the articles published in the NEW YORK TIMES—and even, in certain jurisdictions, the possible violation of the attribution and integrity of the NEW YORK TIMES organization itself. This point is of more than theoretical interest because the products generated by ChatGPT, as well as the generative technology itself, are functioning beyond U.S. borders. Quite apart from fair use, what is ultimately deemed permissible in the United States may be considered a violation, not of copyright law, but of the moral rights that are recognized elsewhere. This would significantly restrict the scope, relevance, and growth prospects of the technology worldwide, unless it could be adapted to the reality of moral rights in other jurisdictions.

3. The Machine as Performer: "Performance Cloning" and the Hollywood Actors' Strike

One of the most startling manifestations of AI technology is when it is used to mimic humans directly.[77] Digital replicas of actors have been able to appear in films for a long time; with AI technology, these digital impersonations could convincingly stand in for human beings.[78] Artificial intelligence can be used to imitate

[75] Referencing, as a source for this idea, the previous edition of this book. *See* U.S. COPYRIGHT OFFICE, AUTHORS, ATTRIBUTION, AND INTEGRITY: EXAMINING MORAL RIGHTS IN THE UNITED STATES (Apr. 23, 2019), https://www.copyright.gov/policy/moralrights/full-report.pdf.

[76] *See, e.g.*, Weiser & Schweber, *supra* note 61.

[77] The expression "performance cloning" was cited in the article by Shiona McCallum, *supra* note 2.

[78] Of course, human actors have also impersonated previous actors: a notable example occurs in Woody Allen's 1972 film, *Play It Again Sam*, in which another actor impersonates Humphrey Bogart: *see*

voices, impersonating human beings in the audio sphere. It can be used to create "deepfakes," videos that substitute one person's image for another in a video, creating the illusion that someone is saying or doing something entirely false.[79] Liam Budd, speaking for Equity, the UK actors' union, comments, "We're seeing this technology used in a range of things like automated audiobooks, synthesised voiceover work, digital avatars for corporate videos, or also the role of deepfakes that are being used in films."[80]

It is clear that dealing effectively with these issues will need to be a cross-disciplinary endeavor within the law, because so many types of issues are potentially involved, from the protection of privacy to identity theft and defamation. In the performance context, though, the moral rights of performers could have an important role to play by establishing legal benchmarks in this area. Indeed, it is hardly surprising that a huge contingent of Hollywood actors went on strike in mid-2023, asking for "guarantees that artificial intelligence (AI) and computer-generated faces and voices will not be used to replace actors."[81] The key to unlocking the power of moral rights in this context may lie in the idea of reputation: copying an actor's face or voice to use in another context where the actor does not actually appear could arguably be a major source of potential damage to the actor's reputation. Moral rights implicitly understand the importance of potential rather than actual damage to reputation, since the fundamental goal of the rights is to *prevent* the harm from occurring, rather than attempting to compensate for it once it has occurred. This is why injunctive relief is so important in the moral rights arena. But the fact that actors lose control of their performances once computer-generated images are substituted for them is qualitatively different and more serious even from the problem of potential damage. Rather, it could be called an inherent form of damage to reputation, which occurs in the act of robbing the performer of his or her agency.

To the extent that such use of a performance might rely on excerpting the previous performance of the actor, the creation and use of such an excerpt should be considered a violation of the performer's moral right of integrity. This, again, reflects an updated view of the integrity right. Even if the performance can be found intact in an original version, the replication of the performance for use in a new

https://www.imdb.com/title/tt0069097/. Humans copy, too—but the consequences of their copying are different. AI operates on a different scale, both qualitatively and quantitatively, and commentators who argue that AI is simply doing what humans do already are mistaken.

[79] *See, e.g.*, John Healey, *Real-Time Deepfakes Are a Dangerous New Threat. How to Protect Yourself*, Los Angeles Times (May 11, 2023), https://www.latimes.com/business/technology/story/2023-05-11/realtime-ai-deepfakes-how-to-protect-yourself.

[80] McCallum, *supra* note 2.

[81] Bernd Debusmann, Jr. & Samantha Granville, *SAG Strike:* Avatar *and* Gladiator *Sequels Look Set to Be Hit as Actors Walk Out*, BBC News (July 14, 2023), https://www.bbc.com/news/entertainment-arts-66196357.

form threatens its integrity through the multiplication of the actor's appearances, and the potential effects of that multiplication upon the actor's reputation.

Similar considerations apply in relation to the moral rights of musical performers. However, actors are greatly disadvantaged in comparison to musicians by the severe limitations on the protection of their moral rights under the Beijing Treaty—limits that are not present in the World Intellectual Property Organization (WIPO) Performances and Phonograms Treaty, which applies to audio performers only.[82] When it comes to actors, the Beijing Treaty is presumably expected to fulfill a role much like Article 6*bis* of the Berne Convention in relation to authors, providing a template for protecting the moral rights of actors that all member countries of Beijing are expected to implement in their national legislation. However, protection of the moral rights of actors under Beijing is so severely limited by the footnote to irrelevant provision, Article 5, that it is questionable whether moral rights for actors are protected in anything more than name under Beijing.

The celebratory tone taken by WIPO in this regard has been very disappointing for observers, who had been hoping for a sincere and significant effort to recognize the moral rights of actors in the international community. Beijing may be an "act of justice," in the words of actor Javier Bardem, but it is an extremely limited kind of justice.[83] Through the Beijing Treaty, WIPO managed to deliver symbolic recognition, but little else. With the growing presence of AI technologies, however, and the real risks to performers, particularly in the audiovisual context, Beijing already seems terribly out of date.

In Hollywood, all of this is, unfortunately, of limited relevance. Given that the United States has no moral rights protection under its copyright law outside the visual arts, it is difficult to see how the Beijing Treaty could ever be ratified—unless it was on the familiar but also tired basis that existing U.S. law is somehow sufficient to satisfy the requirements of moral rights for actors under Beijing. The extent of the exceptions and qualifications in the footnote to Article 5 just might make such

[82] *See* World Intellectual Property Organization (WIPO) Performances and Phonograms Treaty, adopted Dec. 20, 1996, S. Treaty Doc. No. 105-17, 36 I.L.M. 76 (1997) (WPPT) entered into force May 20, 2002), Art. 5, https://www.wipo.int/wipolex/en/treaties/textdetails/12743 (general information available at https://www.wipo.int/treaties/en/ip/wppt); WIPO Beijing Treaty on Audiovisual Performances, June 24, 2012 (Beijing Treaty), https://www.wipo.int/edocs/pubdocs/en/wipo_pub_228.pdf (general information available at https://www.wipo.int/treaties/en/ip/beijing). See discussion of the WPPT and the Beijing Treaty in Chapter 3, *supra* notes 66–67 and accompanying text.

[83] *See, e.g., Javier Bardem at WIPO on Actors, Film and Digital Technologies*, WIPO (July 19, 2011), https://www.wipo.int/copyright/en/activities/copyright_dialogue (includes links to video interviews with Bardem and other actors). See also *Javier Bardem Hails New Treaty for Actors' Rights*, France24 (Jan. 28, 2020), https://www.france24.com/en/20200128-javier-bardem-hails-new-treaty-for-actors-rights, on the coming into force of the Beijing Treaty (on Apr. 28, 2020), noting that there are thirty signatory countries, including the United States. The United States has not yet ratified the Treaty. India, another major film producer, is not yet a signatory; Nigeria, Africa's film powerhouse, has both signed and ratified the Treaty. *See* WIPO, *WIPO-Administered Treaties* (n.d.), https://www.wipo.int/wipolex/en/treaties/ShowResults?start_year=ANY&end_year=ANY&search_what=C&code=ALL&treaty_id=841.

an argument credible. But this would effectively amount to saying that Beijing itself provides no real recognition for the moral rights of actors. Compliance with the Treaty should therefore not be considered a true measure of success; rather, the Treaty itself may be a failure where the moral rights of performers are concerned.

But the United States could also argue that such matters are taken care of through private ordering—in this case, Hollywood Guild contracts for the protection of actors.[84] It is true that provisions on moral rights have been negotiated into these contracts (notably, in relation to credit, or in other words, attribution), but it should be remembered that these contracts depend on private negotiations between actors and production companies. They do not reflect the public good in the way that the legislative process is supposed to do. It is therefore questionable whether contracts that result from Hollywood negotiation processes should truly be considered equivalent to the protection of moral rights under federal copyright law.

In the current climate, however, fighting for contractual provisions that will protect them from incursions by AI technology may be the only hope for Hollywood actors to gain recognition of their moral rights—at least in the United States. For now, their efforts have been a success. After 118 days on strike—close to 6 months on the picket lines, with Hollywood writers simultaneously striking for much of that period[85]—actors were able to secure new contractual provisions.[86] Though concerns about AI triggered the strike action, it is worth noting that the actors also raised the need for increased payments and benefits in the streaming environment during the negotiation process, and settling these was also essential to finding a resolution.

In relation to AI, the settlement focuses on securing actors' consent to the use of the technology for creating "synthetic performers" based on real human actors. As journalist Ramishah Maruf notes, writing for CNN,

> Studios will have to provide informed consent for the creation of any kind of digital replica of a performer or background actor, with a specific description of the intended use, the union officials said. Compensation for the replica will vary.[87]

In many ways, "digital replicas" intersect with copyright works and can be seen as analogous to them. In fact, they are a curious hybrid creation: their existence

[84] *See* U.S. Copyright Office, *supra* note 74, at "Conclusion."
[85] Coyle, *supra* note 66.
[86] Angela Watercutter & Will Bedingfield, *Hollywood Actors Strike Ends with a Deal That Will Impact AI and Streaming for Decades*, Wired (Nov. 8, 2023), https://www.wired.com/story/hollywood-actors-strike-ends-ai-streaming.
[87] Ramishah Maruf, *Artificial Intelligence and Synthetic Performers*, CNN Business (Nov. 10, 2023), https://www.cnn.com/sag-aftra-deal-terms/index.html.

depends both on the *work* of the actor, as embodied in that actor's previous performances on film, and on the actor's human attributes and personality, including his or her appearance, voice, and mannerisms. The latter is inseparable from the former. The consent requirement can be seen as the primacy of a disclosure principle for the creation or use of "digital replicas." The settlement effectively amounts to a form of contractual recognition for the principle of disclosure underlying *both* moral rights and copyright law as a whole, and extending to other areas of law as well, such as privacy and general personality rights. Indeed, personality rights, as noted by Desbois, are at the origin of moral rights.

The fact that the disclosure principle intersects with a variety of legal domains is to be expected, because moral rights embody the creative interests of performers as a whole. Given the underlying relationship between artists and their work, in which artists are implicated in multiple professional and personal ways, it is clear that moral rights do not represent a "watertight" category in the law; moral rights and other categories of legal rights will necessarily overlap. The uses of actors' performances made possible by AI impinge upon the privacy as well as the agency of actors. Similarly, the fact that AI can replace actors outright was the primary concern of the union, but, looking into the future, a further underlying concern is also the potential impact of such replicas on the reputations of real actors. Without some assurance of reputational security, especially in the current political climate, a human actor's work life would be precarious. The ubiquity of the replica, its words and actions, and its potential influence on perceptions of the underlying human actor should all be matters of concern.

But are the provisions put in place by the deal—the so-called "guardrails" implemented for AI—sufficient? The deal remains controversial, and at least two important limitations should be noted. First, the agreement contains a number of loopholes, including provision for doing what is otherwise not allowed—creating and using digital likenesses without the consent of the people on whom they are based—in some situations. Notably, such a loophole "allows employers to use digital doubles without a performer's consent when the project is 'comment, criticism, scholarship, satire or parody, a docudrama, or historical or biographical work.'" As noted by actress Justine Bateman, adviser to the Screen Actors' Guild–American Federation of Television (SAG-AFTRA) negotiating committee and leadership on AI,[88] who is quoted here by Conor Murray at Forbes, "Actors may find themselves in a 'project you never consented to, doing things you never were informed of, for no compensation at all.'"

The language of the loophole suggests that production companies are implicitly relying on a "fair use" rationale to allow the use of performances in these contexts in spite of the consent requirements of the settlement. Fact-based works, and most

[88] *See* @JustineBateman, Twitter (Nov. 6, 2023) https://twitter.com/JustineBateman/status/1721738381636616501.

of the specific categories of works referenced here, such as parody[89] and biographical work[90] – with satire being a notable exception[91] – have all been found to be fair uses of copyright works in the past and are therefore exempt from the usual requirement that right holders must consent to the use of the work. This suggests that the studios do indeed see digital replicas as some form of intellectual creation, probably copyright works (in the absence of other credible options); it also represents a troubling generalization of fair use concepts beyond the copyright framework and provides a further argument why the disclosure principle should be recognized as such in this context.

The approach of the studios highlights the extent to which fair use in the United States has increasingly become a tool enabling the use of copyright-protected works by technology corporations without consent and, presumably, the payment of licensing fees.[92] It is also peculiar for other reasons. The issues of fairness and ethics involved in the use of AI-generated performers are implicitly resolved as copyright issues, but it is doubtful whether copyright law—particularly in the United States, and particularly in its current iteration—is equipped to handle the

[89] On parody as fair use, see *Campbell v. Acuff-Rose Music*, 510 U.S. 569 (1994), https://www.law.cornell.edu/supct/html/92-1292.ZS.html. Writing for the majority, Justice Souter comments, id. at 581 (reference omitted):

> The fact that parody can claim legitimacy for some appropriation does not, of course, tell either parodist or judge much about where to draw the line. Like a book review quoting the copyrighted material criticized, parody may or may not be fair use, and petitioner's suggestion that any parodic use is presumptively fair has no more justification in law or fact than the equally hopeful claim that any use for news reporting should be presumed fair... The Act has no hint of an evidentiary preference for parodists over their victims, and no workable presumption for parody could take account of the fact that parody often shades into satire when society is lampooned through its creative artifacts, or that a work may contain both parodic and non parodic elements. Accordingly, parody, like any other use, has to work its way through the relevant factors, and be judged case by case, in light of the ends of the copyright law.

[90] Fact-based works are generally exempt from copyright protection in the United States and internationally: *see, e.g.*, Berne Convention, *supra* note 10, at Art. 2(8) (on the protection of "news of the day or ... miscellaneous facts having the character of mere items of press information"). A useful (though minimally organized) summary of a number of cases on fair use is provided by Stanford Libraries, https://fairuse.stanford.edu/overview/fair-use/cases/, which notes, "The content for the Copyright and Fair Use Overview section is from NOLO, with much of it taken from the book *Getting Permission* (October 2019) by Richard Stim. Thanks!"

[91] This is due to the general nature of the "criticism," or social commentary, offered by satire: unlike parody, copying of the original work may not be required for the making of a successful satirical work. The distinction is explained by the U.S. Supreme Court in *Campbell*, *supra* note 89: "Parody needs to mimic an original to make its point, and so has some claim to use the creation of its victim's (or collective victims') imagination, whereas satire can stand on its own two feet and so requires justification for the very act of borrowing" (notes omitted). *See, e.g.*, Copyright Alliance, *Why Is Parody Considered Fair Use but Satire Isn't?* (n.d.), https://copyrightalliance.org/faqs/parody-considered-fair-use-satire-isnt/; Joe Vesper, *Parody, Satire, and "Fair Use,"* Daniel Ross Law Firm (June 9, 2021), https://www.danielrosslawfirm.com/2021/06/09/parody-satire-and-fair-use/.

[92] In a more traditional context, *Warhol v. Goldsmith*, *supra* note 58, took a more restrictive approach to fair use. The policy is not necessarily bad—but a duel between large companies over software, such as *Google LLC v. Oracle Am., Inc.* 141 S. Ct. 1163 (2021) (U.S.), https://www.supremecourt.gov/opinions/20pdf/18-956_d18f.pdf (summarized at https://www.copyright.gov/fair-use/summaries/google-llc-oracle-am-inc-2021.pdf), and the requirements of actors and artists are likely to be quite different.

problems involved. As William F. Patry has noted, copyright is called upon to respond to a staggering range of social issues, many of which considerably exceed its traditional bounds.[93] If we bring moral rights into these discussions, it is also apparent that what is allowed under the copyright system of the United States, which does not include moral rights, may not be acceptable under the copyright laws of other jurisdictions where moral rights *are* protected, including Europe, Asia, and the rest of the world. But now, at a purely *legal* level, we are venturing into a domain where there are many questions and few answers. What is the relationship between moral rights and parody, or between moral rights and exceptions and limitations of copyright more generally—whether those restraints on copyright take the form of fair use, fair dealing, or free use as these exceptions are known, with subtle variations of the basic principles involved, in different places?

At least two opportunities to provide answers to these questions have arisen, one in the United Kingdom and one in Europe. In the United Kingdom, a parody exception was adopted in the UK copyright law in 2014, providing for parody to be recognized as a permissible exception to copyright law as a whole. This means, of course, that the parody can be made without the consent of the author of the original work. At the time, moral rights were well established in the UK Act, dating from 1988, but the language of the parody exception was silent on whether the use of a work in a parody could violate the moral rights of the author. In view of this silence, it must be presumed that parodies are not exempt from moral rights requirements under the UK Act, but this assertion remains to be proven in case law.

In Europe, the *Deckmyn* case sought the opinion of the European Court of Justice on whether a parody that created a racist version of an original cartoon was a permissible use of the work as an exception or limitation to copyright law. As discussed earlier,[94] the Court said that it was not, justifying its decision on the basis of the incompatibility of such a parody with European human rights legislation. However, had the Court been willing to invoke the artist's moral right of integrity, the case could also have been decided on the basis that the parody would have had a negative (or simply undesired) [95] effect on the reputation of the cartoon's creator.

As a result, the question of moral rights in relation to these proposed uses of AI remains unsettled. While this issue is not a concern under U.S. copyright law at the present time, given the absence of moral rights from the U.S. legal framework,

[93] *See, e.g.*, Bill Patry's interview at Google (Feb. 21, 2012), https://www.youtube.com/watch?v=tGkvjVl3uSg, esp. at 3:19–4:12.

[94] *See* Chapter 1, *supra* notes 115–20 and accompanying text.

[95] Under Belgian copyright law, the author has a broad integrity right, as in France: *Code de droits économique* [Code of Economic Rights] (Belg.), art. XI.165, https://www.sofam.be/dbfiles/mfile/1500/1535/Code_de_droits_economique_.pdf. However, the general right to prohibit modification of the work can be waived; modifications that are damaging to the author's honor or reputation cannot be waived. *See also* the basic explanation provided by Bart Van Besien, *Main Principles of Copyright Protection under Belgian Law*, Finnian Columba (n.d.), https://finniancolumba.be/en/copyright-2/frequent-questions-belgian-copyright/.

it is of interest everywhere else in the world. There is a real possibility that such uses of performances may be deemed unacceptable outside the United States, severely restricting the lawful distribution of works using AI performances beyond U.S. borders. In other words, the potential for a revival of the *Huston* scenario, but on a much grander scale given the nature of the technology and the worldwide expansion of moral rights since 1988, is possible.

The negotiated settlement also highlights another, troubling reality. In the environment of AI, inequality of bargaining power between authors and artists and those using their works, always a problem, has arguably reached undreamt-of heights. The ability of individual performers to negotiate contractual provisions is more limited than ever before, and the union played an absolutely essential role in compelling the settlement that has been reached between actors and production companies. In the absence of appropriate legislation, actors are increasingly, perhaps entirely, reliant upon their union to secure any meaningful level of fairness or professional protection in the movie marketplace. Much turns upon the effectiveness of the union, which is not, by any means, assured.

Of course, when Hollywood movies are shown abroad, the actors fully enjoy the protections offered by foreign copyright laws.[96] Those who work in Hollywood today remain stuck where John Huston found himself in 1990—in his case, reliant upon the mercy of the French courts to protect his U.S. film.[97] *Plus ça change, plus c'est la même chose.*

Commenting on national treatment under Berne, Professor Jane Ginsburg, a consummate authority on the matter, observes,

[96] This is the result of Berne Convention, *supra* note 10, at Art. 5, which stipulates national treatment for all claimants from member states. Article 5(2) specifies that "the extent of protection, as well as the means of redress afforded to the author to protect his rights, shall be governed exclusively by the laws of the country where protection is claimed," and Art. 5(3) states that, "when the author is not a national of the country of origin of the work for which he is protected under this Convention, he shall enjoy in that country the same rights as national authors." The French courts have interpreted this provision as signifying that French law is applicable to all copyright claims brought in France, which effectively means that all foreign claimants will benefit from French provisions on moral rights in France: *see* Cour de cassation [Cass.] [supreme court for judicial matters] 1e civ., Apr. 10, 2013, ECLI:FR:CCASS:2013:C100347, http://www.legifrance.gouv.fr/affichJuriJudi.do?oldAction=rechJuriJudi&idTexte=JURITEXT000027303750&fastReqId=204836325&fastPos=1. The case is discussed by Brad Spitz, *French Supreme Court on 5(2) BC: National Law Determines Who Is the Copyright Owner*, Kluwer Copyright Blog (May 28, 2013), https://copyrightblog.kluweriplaw.com/2013/05/28/french-supreme-court-on-52-bc-national-law-determines-who-is-the-copyright-owner. However, the U.S. interpretation of the Berne Convention, *supra* note 10, at Art. 5(2) is quite different, with the 1998 *Russian Kurier* case providing that domestic law applies to questions of substantive law and infringement, but not to the *ownership* of copyright: *ITAR-TASS Russian News Agency v. Russian Kurier*, 153 F.3d. 82, 26 Media L. Rep. 2217 (2d Cir. 1998) (U.S.). The 2018 *Fahmy* case specifically provides that foreign claimants cannot rely on either their home legislation or the Berne Convention to claim moral rights in the United States: *Fahmy v. Jay-Z*, No. 16-55213 (9th Cir. 2018) (U.S.).

[97] *See Huston v. La Cinq*, Cour de cassation [Cass.] [supreme court for judicial matters] 1e civ., May 28, 1991, Bull. civ. I, No. 172 (Fr.), https://www.legifrance.gouv.fr/juri/id/JURITEXT000007026649.

> National treatment is a rule of non-discrimination: A member state may not accord foreign authors less protection than it grants its own. But a second principle buttresses the first: Whatever level of protection national law provides, a treaty member state must grant foreign authors protection commensurate with the treaties' substantive standards. Most often that obligation means that member states whose domestic laws fall below the treaty minima must accord more protection to foreign authors than they do to their own. Berne's drafters anticipated that *the political precariousness of such an outcome would result in a general raising of the level of domestic protection as well.*[98]

How unfortunate that this has not happened.

Not only are improved provisions for the moral rights of actors needed, but those provisions must also update the interpretation of moral rights doctrine to address the increasingly complicated relationship between humans and machines. Daniel Gervais notes that machines, unlike authors, do not need to be paid royalties.[99] Nor do machines need any of the rights, recognition, cooperation, humoring, or possibly pampering that human actors may need, want, and deserve—making them much more inconvenient and complicated to deal with than machines, perhaps, but commanding the love and attention of human audiences in a deeply human way.[100] If all the world's a stage, what role should machines play? Will the ensuing production be farce, tragedy, or something in between?

E. The Machine as Enforcer: Moral Rights

But there is a paradox to consider. AI technologies create new possibilities for appropriating, misrepresenting, and coopting human knowledge—and in particular, works created by human authors—. At the same time, they also generate new possibilities for identifying and verifying knowledge. This affirms in a new form "the general maxim," as noted by Edward Stone in 1763, "that many natural maladies carry their cures along with them or that their remedies lie not far from their causes."[101]

[98] Jane C. Ginsburg, *Minimum and Maximum Protection under International Copyright Treaties*, 44 Colum. J. L. & Arts 1, 2 (emphasis added) (2020), https://journals.library.columbia.edu/index.php/lawandarts/article/view/7308/3883.

[99] Gervais, *supra* note 53.

[100] Neuroscience research also shows that humans prefer human performances to those by machines: *see, e.g.*, Darren Bridger, *Perception of AI Voices* (July 4, 2023), https://cloud.army/resources/blog/perception-of-ai-voices?.

[101] He was writing of the bark of the willow tree, from which aspirin (ASA) was ultimately derived. *See* Edward Stone, *An Account of the Success of the Bark of the Willow in the Cure of Agues*, *in* Philosophical Transactions XXXII (1763), https://royalsocietypublishing.org/doi/10.1098/rstl.1763.0033; Niall Boyce & Gareth Evans, *Nothing But Flowers*, The Lancet (Oct. 4, 2011), https://www.thelancet.com/journals/lancet/article/PIIS0140-6736(11)61543-2/fulltext.

In contrast to copyright more generally, which stands in direct conflict with new technologies that can reproduce and disseminate works, technology and moral rights are strangely and powerfully complementary. This situation is illustrated by the example of DALL-E; in fact, the very problem created by DALL-E is, in a sense, a reflection of this reality, since it is the resemblance between the works that it generates and the creations of living authors that is problematic. In this sense, attribution of authorship is, ironically, built into DALL-E. This becomes problematic because the images resembling the works of artists are not what they seem to be: they are a form of false attribution, or, in other words, forgeries.[102] Once again, the moral right of attribution should be invoked against the creation of these "altered copies," to repurpose the language of the English court in the *Russell Williams* case—which was subsequently affirmed by the House of Lords, and which may now have found a new application.[103] In this sense, the enforcement of moral rights in the AI environment—as in the technological environment overall—is both more natural and more straightforward than the enforcement of copyright, because the need for moral rights is an integral part of many technological systems, including AI. Databases are an unequalled tool for enforcing attribution across all kinds of creativity. This is illustrated by the case of Joyce Hatto, the classical pianist whose recordings were fabricated out of other pianists' work—a fraud that was ultimately unmasked by Apple's iTunes.[104]

The same may be said of the integrity right. While the integrity of works can be more easily affected by manipulation through technology, technology, particularly in the commercial context, also favors the careful preservation of works. When creative works or cultural products are disseminated through technology, such as downloading or streaming music, it is in the user's interest to receive authentic files that are not only properly attributed to their creators but also provided to the public at the highest possible levels of technical and artistic integrity. Compromising on these issues would make the entire enterprise of online music unattractive.

In addition, in view of the speed and reach made possible by technology, it is also worth noting that the right of disclosure, in both its economic and moral dimensions, may also be more important than ever before. Once a work has been made available online, the personal intervention of the artist or right-holder to ensure its status is more difficult in the technological environment, where the sheer volume of material presents a daunting obstacle to human intervention. Although the marketplace and the public may have a strong underlying preference for authentic works, the marketplace can be flooded, and the public can be deceived. For this

[102] Historically made by humans, of course—van Meegeren being the most famous. *See, e.g.*, Peter Schjeldal, *Dutch Master: The Art Forger Who Became a National Hero*, THE NEW YORKER (Oct. 20, 2008), https://www.newyorker.com/magazine/2008/10/27/dutch-master.

[103] *Designers Guild v. Russell Williams*, *supra* note 42.

[104] See, e.g., a fascinating article by Mark Singer, *Fantasia for Piano*, THE NEW YORKER (Sept. 17, 2007), http://www.newyorker.com/magazine/2007/09/17/fantasia-for-piano.

reason, the author's right to decide to disclose or withhold works from the public is especially important, since a decision to release works may have far-reaching consequences, both for the author's livelihood and for his or her reputation.[105]

F. Are Machines Creative? Existentialism Redux

Artificial intelligence is often put forward as an existential challenge to human creativity, but the question asked here is a slightly different one. Why should the value of human creativity be questioned? Instead, the considerations reviewed here so far lead inevitably to questions about the meaning and purpose, not of human creativity, but of AI as a cultural force.

Let us first question the raison d'être of the machine as creator. While the exciting potential of AI in fields like medicine, energy, and transportation are apparent,[106] what role is AI called upon to play in the cultural sphere? While AI may have the potential to enhance creativity and culture, the initial intrusions of the technology seem to suggest just the opposite—that it leads to the devaluation of human creativity by offering potential replacements for human creators that are "cheaper" and "easier." How does this "improve" culture or creative works—and how does it benefit the public? As things currently stand, the technology benefits *its* creators and the corporations who own them. It does so at the expense of human creators, and of the public, which is ultimately forced to accept a lower standard of cultural production whose only purpose is to satisfy the greed of corporations. An alternate universe might be possible: machine creativity could also prove to be inspiring and uplifting, pushing human beings to new and more creative frontiers, and enriching society and culture. But that eventuality could only arise in a dramatically different cultural context. In such a scenario, rather than being driven by greed, AI would develop and thrive in an environment where technology truly empowered the public at large and affirmed the inherent value of human creativity rather than devaluing it. This would be a very different universe from the one that we inhabit. It would be characterized by an utterly new mindset with respect to technology. It implies nothing less than leaving behind forever the values, priorities, and goals of the Digital Age to pursue something new.

For now, this remains nothing more than a utopian vision. As Justine Bateman, a filmmaker and director, comments,

[105] A recent case involving the release of recordings made by singer Jessye Norman, but not approved by her for release during her lifetime, raises a number of interesting questions in this regard. *See, e.g.*, Zachary Woolfe, *Jessye Norman Rejected These Recordings. Should They Be Released?*, New York Times (Feb. 23, 2023), https://www.nytimes.com/2023/02/23/arts/music/jessye-norman-unreleased-recordings.html. Norman, who passed away in 2019, is considered one of the greatest singers of our era.

[106] Areas identified by the European Parliament: *see, e.g.*, European Parliament, *EU AI Act: First Regulation on Artificial Intelligence* (June 14, 2023), https://www.europarl.europa.eu/news/en/headlines/society/20230601STO93804/eu-ai-act-first-regulation-on-artificial-intelligence.

> Tech should solve a problem and there's no problem that those using AI solves. We don't have a lack of writers, we don't have a lack of actors, we don't have a lack of film-makers—so we don't need AI...
>
> The problem it solves is for the corporations that feel they don't have wide enough profit margins—because if you can eliminate the overhead of having to pay everyone you can appease Wall Street and have greater earnings reports.[107]

G. Attribution and Integrity: Keys to Our Future

Even at this early stage of development, it already seems clear that AI stands to play a major role in the further erosion of our cultural environment. Artificial intelligence enormously encourages the creation and spread of false and abusive information, and this problem is growing rapidly.

"Cultural environment" is a term that is deliberately chosen here. The problem of misinformation, in all its diverse forms, is most accurately characterized as a cultural problem. What other word is truly sufficient to describe the breadth and importance of the difficulties that the world is facing, all of which are created or exacerbated by "misinformation"? Lack of access to education; lack of integrity in public life; the widespread acceptance of online abuse, harassment, and discrimination; the disempowerment of individuals; corrupt and exploitative politics—all of this is initiated, promoted, and fed by the corruption of information, knowledge, and culture surrounding us. Cultural degradation is as serious a form of "pollution" as environmental degradation—perhaps more so, since, unlike environmental harm, it directly prevents us from making any concerted effort to try to address social problems. In the meantime, AI is likely to become ubiquitous, touching and transforming everything from exam papers and legal briefs to encyclopedia entries, employment contracts, social media posts, and, of course, political advertising.

Moral rights have a key role to play in addressing these challenges. It is all the more important to emphasize that potential here because moral rights are often neglected or ignored by policymakers who are preoccupied with the economics of copyright and the money-making potential of technology. The suggestion here is not to ignore the economic potential of technology but, on the contrary, to establish an environment where technology can develop in a way that is conducive to human well-being. Moral rights can contribute to its creation in two ways. First, moral rights protect human authorship. Secondly, the doctrine of moral rights serves as a kind of generative technology in its own right—in this case, a human generative technology that generates the core principles of attribution and

[107] McCallum, *supra* note 2.

integrity, invaluable tools in the struggle to re-establish truth and authenticity in our cultural environment.

1. Authors' Moral Rights of Attribution and Integrity

In a sense, we live in an unprecedented age of authorship. The technologies that have become ubiquitous, from the Internet to social media, rely on text. Even AI technologies for generating images, like DALL-E, rely on the input of text in the form of prompts to generate results—in the case of DALL-E, quasi-artistic images derived from pre-existing artistic works.

Given copyright's historically low requirements in relation to the originality that is required of copyright works, much of this text crosses the minimum boundary to be considered a literary work under copyright law. Most of it is well above that threshold: posts on social media often require considerable personal or creative input, and actual articles posted on sites such as LinkedIn are simply traditional copyright literary works in a new setting. The overextension of the status of "author" under copyright law in this environment is a separate issue worthy of its own discussion. For now, Daniel Gervais's discussion of whether AI "prompts" should be considered literary works under copyright law is to the point:

> The question of copyright in the prompts themselves inevitably surfaces. After all, engineers like to protect their outputs. Can a prompt be protected as a work of authorship? It should, if it is (a) created by one or more humans; (b) not de minimis; and (c) embodies creative choices. The hard question is whether those creative choices—the originality, if any—of the prompt is "transferable" into the product or output of the AI machine. Owning a prompt could then mean owning all outputs generated by the machine (which can generate dozens and dozens of outputs based on the same prompt, in various "genres," styles", etc.). This gets dangerously close to owning the underlying idea, and thus goes against a fundamental principle of international copyright law.[108]

[108] Gervais, *supra* note 53. "Tweets" might have been deemed uncopyrightable because they are so short—not satisfying the "de minimis" requirement, rather like titles, which are usually (though not always) unprotectable under copyright law: *see, e.g., Exxon Corp. v. Exxon Insurance Consultants International Ltd* [1982] Ch. 119 (UK). The issue is discussed from a practical perspective in James Williams, *Does Embedding a Tweet Count as Copyright Infringement?*, TINGEN (Oct. 20, 2020), https://tingen.law/2020/does-embedding-a-tweet-count-as-copyright-infringement/45352. If tweets are now generally considered copyrightable, then at least two justifications can be offered for this: first, they are short because of the requirements of the medium, and this should not exclude an entire category of work; and second, the precision of a tweet may actually require greater "creativity" or "originality" than a longer piece of expression. Polonius's words are doubly ironic in the universe of Twitter.

To the extent that works attract copyright protection, they also attract moral rights. Accordingly, the moral rights of authors can serve two important functions that will help to preserve the integrity of information in the technological environment. First, when applied to traditional creative and intellectual works—such as the artworks and books fed into DALL-E or ChatGPT- the rights of attribution and integrity can help to maintain accurate information about the source of information and support its preservation in an uncorrupted form. Again, these are the traditional functions of moral rights of authorship applied in relation to traditional works of authorship or works that are highly analogous to them in form and substance.

Due to the relatively low standard of originality required by modern copyright laws,much of the text that is used in socially ubiquitous technologies also attracts copyright, and the authors of these kinds of works will also acquire moral rights. This means that people who post information in the form of text—or, indeed, as images, music, or other forms that attract copyright protection—will also be eligible for the protection of their moral rights. This means that the attribution of information to its source, in relation to these kinds of publications, should also be maintained. Similarly, reposting or referencing this information in such a way that its integrity is compromised would violate an author's moral right of integrity.

Does protection of moral rights make sense in relation to this second category of works? If there is a problem here, it lies not in moral rights but in copyright law, which would almost certainly consider such works sufficiently original to qualify for copyright. Copyright deems them works of authorship. This would be the case everywhere in the world, including in the continental European countries, which have traditionally had somewhat more rigorous standards for the recognition of copyright; even the old "creativity" standard may not have been sufficient to exclude the protection of work such as articles or posts on social media.[109]

But the basic premise underlying the moral rights of authors is that of a special relationship between author and work. Does that relationship exist in the environment of social media? It may not be possible to arrive at a general answer to this question. Why is a tweet potentially less deserving of protection than a tiny haiku poem? This question goes to the underlying artistry and significance of a particular piece of writing, an area from which judges usually abstain. Copyright law does not currently offer the means of making this kind of assessment. This is why the law errs, if at all, on the side of inclusiveness.[110]

[109] On the "creativity" standard, see, e.g., Gerhard Schricker, *Farewell to the "Level of Creativity" (Schöpfungshöhe) in German Copyright Law?*, 26(1) Int'l Rev. Indus. Prop. & Copyright L. 41 (1995).

[110] See Justice Holmes's famous commentary on this point in *Bleistein v. Donaldson Lithographing Co.*, 188 U.S. 239 (1903), e.g., at 188:

> The copy is the personal reaction of an individual upon nature. Personality always contains something unique. It expresses its singularity even in handwriting, and a very modest grade of

2. Beyond Authorship: Attribution and Integrity as Stand-Alone Principles

But it is possible to go a step further and examine attribution and integrity, not as artefacts of a special relationship between authors and their work, but as abstract principles governing the preservation of knowledge. For it is clear that the principles of attribution and integrity are immensely powerful ideas in their own right.

Attribution of authorship through the moral right of the author can be seen as part of a much broader concept of identifying sources. As such, it is a concept that enjoys broad cultural recognition, and it is recognized in an amazing diversity of ways. Attribution of authorship itself transcends copyright law: from the *mudras* used by ancient Indian poets to identify themselves in their verses to Alfred Hitchcock's cameos in his films or Elena Ferrante's pseudonym, there are few real limits to the forms in which authors can choose to identify themselves. In the current era, blockchain technologies are effectively forms of attribution;[111] so, too, are digital rights management technologies and the establishment of databases like the U.S. music rights database established in 2018, the Mechanical Licensing Collective.[112] Non-fungible tokens (NFTs) are based on attribution; as Kevin Roose of the NEW YORK TIMES notes:

> [Y]ou can think of NFTs as like the certificate of authenticity you might get if you bought an expensive sculpture. The sculpture could be copied or forged—or someone could break into your house and steal it—but because you have the certificate of authenticity, you can prove that you are the owner of the original.[113]

More generally, attribution itself can mean many different things, from attribution of authorship to attributing place, company, manufacturer, cultural group, tradition, or ownership. Again, attribution can be implicit as well as explicit, as in the form of a parody, which must be based on a recognizable original work to function as a parody; homage can also implicitly involve attribution. But an explicit right of attribution is needed in environments that are vulnerable to alteration and manipulation, and it can play an extremely valuable role in ensuring the authenticity of the knowledge sphere.

> art has in it something irreducible which is one man's alone. That something he may copyright unless there is a restriction in the words of the act.

[111] *See, e.g.*, Chris Baraniuk, *Blockchain: The Revolution That Hasn't Quite Happened*, BBC NEWS (Feb. 11, 2020), https://www.bbc.com/news/business-51281233.

[112] *See* Orrin G. Hatch–Bob Goodlatte Music Modernization Act, or Music Modernization Act (MMA), H.R. 1551, 115th Cong. (2018), https://www.congress.gov/115/plaws/publ264/PLAW-115publ264.pdf.

[113] Kevin Roose, *The Latecomer's Guide to Crypto: What Are NFTs?*, NEW YORK TIMES (Mar. 18, 2002), https://www.nytimes.com/interactive/2022/03/18/technology/nft-guide.html.

Given the breadth of attribution as a concept, what is its value in the context of artificial intelligence, and how should it be implemented? First and foremost, attribution is clearly a way to distinguish between the creations of human beings and those made by AI. This distinction should be a core principle of regulation in the age of AI. It immediately allows us to distinguish between information that has fundamentally different qualities—that is distinct in terms of reliability, purpose, and function—separating out potentially false, abusive, misleading, or dangerous information over which human beings, and human systems of accountability, may not have a significant degree of control. Again, as noted above, this is not to say that humans are incapable of generating false information, but its occurrence through AI suggests scale, scope, and, potentially, a new kind of ruthlessness in the generation and propagation of what is false.

At the same time, labeling information as emanating from human beings could be something akin to labeling fine wines from a famous vintner or any type of goods emanating from a trusted producer. This aspect of the "human-made" designation would make particular sense in the arts and culture, where it might help to ensure the authenticity of artworks, so that purchasers know that they are supporting individual artists, or of literary works, so that readers can be assured of the authenticity of the text. Let us use Shakespeare as an example: reading a play by an AI technology that can write in iambic pentameter is not the same experience, and the work should be labeled as what it is. This is also important from the point of view of historical preservation, because, 500 years from now, if AI technologies like these had proliferated and created large bodies of work, doubts could arise about what is authentically Shakespeare—or Renaissance poetry, or drama, more generally—as opposed to machine creations. If AI creations became common, how would human beings sustain their commitment to creative literature, their belief in their creative capacity, or, indeed, the profession of literature? As Gervais notes, "many media companies would try to reduce and possibly eliminate human authors because machines are 'not owed royalties.'"[114] Recognizing an attribution right distinguishing human and artificial creations, as well as providing information about the source of the creations, is essential in this environment. Beyond this foundational principle, the norms of attribution could potentially be broad, including not only the moral right of authors but also attribution requirements for the broader context of information, knowledge, or culture surrounding the work. Similar rights already exist in the areas of trademark and geographical indications law: the concept is already known in law, even if it has not so far been applied in the context of copyright.

The importance of integrity in the technological environment can hardly be overstated. Like attribution, it is the core of social needs, and it is only likely to

[114] Gervais, *supra* note 53.

grow in importance with the surge in AI technologies. Maintaining the integrity of the informational environment could be facilitated by recognizing a general right of integrity in published information. An author's moral right of integrity allows that individual to object to alteration of the work, particularly if the treatment of the work might cause damage to the author's reputation. Interestingly, the Federal Trade Commission has initially chosen to question ChatGPT's penchant for generating false information as an issue of *reputation*. As the BBC notes,

> The Federal Trade Commission (FTC) sent a letter to the Microsoft-backed business requesting information on how it addresses risks to people's reputations.[115]

But a right to the integrity of information and knowledge would be a much broader right attached to the information itself. It could potentially be asserted by any one of a number of interested parties—including members of the general public, where appropriate, as well. Such a right would be clearly linked to the principle of attribution, since part of maintaining the integrity of information is to maintain information about its source, which allows those who come into contact with it to understand it in context. But the integrity of right could also mean that the public should know, not only where the information came from, but also whether it has been altered since it was originally published, and how. Simple means of maintaining informational integrity might involve a mention of when, and how, a published article has been altered; this already occurs, in a basic form, in many news publications, where corrections or updates are made.[116]

These principles are sufficiently important that policymakers should create broad frameworks like charters of rights in other contexts to guide the development and use of AI technologies. Attribution and integrity, both as moral rights of authorship and as general principles governing the treatment of information, knowledge, and culture, provide the means of maintaining authenticity in the information sphere. Most importantly of all, they are principles that are simple, elegant, and intelligible to all. The regulation of AI need not require highly technical and specialized rules that the general public, and non-computer scientists in particular, might find inaccessible. The basic principles involved are simple, and regulation should be driven by the overwhelming social need for authenticity that is already apparent. It is only likely to intensify as AI develops further. It is not often that a scholar can argue that the future of humanity depends upon any one particular idea, but if there ever were such a situation, a strong case could be made for the twin legal principles of attribution and integrity in the age of artificial intelligence.

[115] *See ChatGPT Owner in Probe over Risks around False Answers*, BBC NEWS (July 14, 2023), https://www.bbc.com/news/business-66196223.

[116] But it should be noted that, unfortunately, this is not always the case.

H. The EU AI Act: The Role of Moral Rights in a Risk-Based Approach

The European Union (EU) has frequently been in the forefront of regulating new technologies, and AI is no exception.[117] The EU Artificial Intelligence Act, under development since 2020[118] and finalized in January 2024,[119] is the first comprehensive international regulation on AI. While a full analysis of the Act is beyond the scope of this chapter, some important observations should be made in relation to moral rights.

The Act approaches AI regulation from the perspective of risk. It prohibits "high-risk" uses of AI and introduces a system of graduated responses to the use of AI according to the level of risk that the proposed use presents.

Moral rights are not referenced directly in the Act. However, the concept of attribution is fundamental to the EU AI Act, as is the role of human oversight. The European Parliament notes,

> Parliament's priority is to make sure that AI systems used in the EU are safe, transparent, traceable, non-discriminatory and environmentally friendly. AI systems should be overseen by people, rather than by automation, to prevent harmful outcomes.[120]

When it comes to generative AI, the Act provides that "compl[iance] with transparency requirements" means

> Disclosing that the content was generated by AI
> Designing the model to prevent it from generating illegal content
> Publishing summaries of copyrighted data used for training[121]

All three of these requirements clearly involve interests resembling moral rights, and the third is directly connected to moral rights. Labeling content as being

[117] For the final draft of and updates on the European Parliament Legislative Resolution of 13 March 2024 on the proposal for a regulation of the European Parliament and of the Council on laying down harmonised rules on Artificial Intelligence (Artificial Intelligence Act) and amending certain Union Legislative Acts (Jan. 21, 2024), COM(2021)0206 – C9-0146/2021 – 2021/0106(COD)), https://www.europarl.europa.eu/doceo/document/TA-9-2024-0138_EN.pdf, *see* Future of Life Institute, *The EU Artificial Intelligence Act: Up-to-date developments and analyses of the EU AI Act* (2024), https://artificialintelligenceact.eu/.

[118] A timeline of the Act's development is available at European Council, *Timeline—Artificial Intelligence* (n.d., complete to Aug. 1, 2024 when the AI Act entered into force), https://www.consilium.europa.eu/en/policies/artificial-intelligence/timeline-artificial-intelligence/.

[119] *See* the Act Texts, available at https://artificialintelligenceact.eu/the-act.

[120] European Parliament, *EU AI Act: First Regulation on Artificial Intelligence* (Dec. 19, 2023) (First Regulation), https://www.europarl.europa.eu/topics/en/article/20230601STO93804/eu-ai-act-first-regulation-on-artificial-intelligence.

[121] Id.

AI-generated, as has been noted elsewhere in this chapter, is a new and unprecedented form of attribution. It is not a moral right of the author, but the distinction that is drawn between human and machine authorship recognizes some special quality in works of human authorship. It may also be taken to imply the recognition of a significant relationship between human beings and their creations. This recognition takes the negative form of identifying AI-created works; it is a negative machine counterpart to the positive right of human authors to be named through the moral right of attribution. It should be remembered that attribution of authorship is a requirement of all copyright laws in the world excepting only that of the United States (and involving a controversial assertion requirement in the United Kingdom[122]). Attribution is even required by the Creative Commons licensing system, which seeks to provide an alternative to copyright for authors who wish to make their works freely available to the public.[123]

Ensuring that generative AI is designed to avoid illegal outputs implies both a need for transparency, or attribution, in terms of how the models are designed and trained, and integrity, meaning the integrity of the AI systems themselves; integrity in the use of inputs, including works protected by copyright that are used for training; and the integrity of the final outputs. This final point means, at a minimum, that AI outputs should not be unlawful, which presumably extends to the requirement that they should not violate copyright or the moral rights of authors. In other words, works that are "substantially similar" to pre-existing works (as in the *NYT v. OpenAI* case[124]) may be unlawful; so, too, may outputs that could be mistaken for the work of human authors protected by moral rights, leading to misattribution or reputational harm.

Finally, requiring the publication of summaries of copyright-protected data used in training AI systems is a clear and important manifestation of the attribution right. In this context, it is worth noting that the moral principle of attribution[125] also works with copyright protection to protect against copyright infringement. The tendency of modern copyright policy to view economic and moral rights as separate, often treating them as self-contained and independent protections, is not reflected at a practical level. Instead, the interdependent and

[122] *See* CDPA, *supra* note 13, § 78.

[123] See Chapter 9, *infra*, for a detailed exploration of attribution and other moral rights implicated in Creative Commons. *See also* Mira T. Sundara Rajan, *Creative Commons: America's Moral Rights?*, 21 FORDHAM INTELL. PROP. MEDIA & ENT. L.J. 905 (2011), https://ir.lawnet.fordham.edu/iplj/vol21/iss4/3.

[124] For the ongoing complaint, *see* https://nytco-assets.nytimes.com/2023/12/NYT_Complaint_Dec2023.pdf.

[125] Since copyright-protected data is involved, referencing the "authors' moral right of attribution" here would also have been appropriate. "Principle" has been preferred to capture the broader and more comprehensive attribution that might be required for transparency. Regardless, at a minimum, maintaining authors' attribution where copyright works are involved will clearly be one layer of necessary and useful attribution in this context.

mutually reinforcing character of economic and moral rights is evident in the technological context.[126]

But the Act also misses an important opportunity to build on moral rights in their traditional form. It requires that the providers of AI systems comply with the copyright requirements of the EU Copyright Directive[127]—in which, however, moral rights have not been harmonized. If the Directive had harmonized moral rights,[128] this provision would have ensured that AI systems, in both their training phase and their outputs, maintained the attribution of authorship and the integrity of works of authorship, including the reputations of their creators in the AI environment across the EU. This could have been an incredibly efficient, effective, and elegant way of reinforcing the AI Act's rules on transparency and lawfulness—allowing regulators to create a regulatory framework layering the rights of the authors and owners of copyright protected works, as well as protections for culturally important works,[129] with the new, specific rules on AI. The result would be a robust system of interwoven and mutually reinforcing norms, uniquely drawing upon the sophisticated heritage of European law in this area.

As noted above, AI development in the EU would still appear to be bound by the moral rights requirements in the copyright laws of the member states. But it is to be hoped that further development of the AI Act might take moral rights explicitly into account and begin to explore the idea that these rights could bring support to the regulatory priorities that the Act seeks to advance.

Importantly for the EU, moral rights are an area in which European countries have a considerable competitive advantage in terms of regulatory expertise—perhaps an unusual way of characterizing moral rights norms but arguably accurate, all the same. Rather than reject or neglect this area of law because it has remained underexplored in international copyright regulation—or because of preconceptions about the tension between culture and economics or technology—a more reasonable approach would be to consider moral rights as a potentially useful regulatory tool in this important area.

It is equally important to note the potential of moral rights to respond to the many concerns about inequities that AI has already generated. Moral rights can help to bring greater balance to the relationship between human authors, technology, and society in this environment. They can help to affirm the humanistic and democratic values that are most threatened by the abuses that AI will bring,

[126] This point has been noted in my previous work, including the first edition of this book. *See* Chapter 6 *infra* on moral rights and the music industry.

[127] Directive (EU) 2019/790 of the European Parliament and of the Council of 17 April 2019 on copyright and related rights in the Digital Single Market and amending Directives 96/9/EC and 2001/29/EC, 2019 O.J. (L 130) 92 (DSM Directive), https://eur-lex.europa.eu/eli/dir/2019/790/oj.

[128] Or, of course, if they had been harmonized in EU law by some other means, such as a directive specifically on moral rights.

[129] A distinction made in view of perpetual protection for moral rights in some EU countries, including France and Italy.

especially in the absence of visionary policymaking. Why should this valuable instrument of copyright law and information policy, of social justice and the public interest, an area of rich European legal heritage, continue to be neglected at a time when *all* our human ingenuity is needed?

I. Recommendations

Moral rights are uniquely adapted to the problems posed by AI. They should be a centerpiece of regulation in this area. In the process, our understanding of moral rights, themselves, should also be refined and updated to reflect the technological challenges of the Age of AI. This approach involves three broad recommendations.

First, the moral rights of authors should be recognized and enforced across all areas of human creativity where they are currently recognized. In particular, the moral rights of attribution and integrity, as set out in Article 6*bis* of the Berne Convention, are highly relevant to the challenges of AI. The moral right of disclosure, implicit in the Berne Convention, can also play an important role, supporting privacy and control in the technological environment.

Secondly, updating our interpretation of the moral rights of attribution and integrity requires us to develop an understanding of what is happening to human creativity in the Age of AI. The use of prompts for generative AI that include the names of living artists—and, more broadly, of artists whose works are still within the term of copyright protection—should qualify as a clear violation of the author's moral right of attribution.

Of course, it should also be noted that generating AI creations in this way involves both economic and moral effects: in addition to the potential for damage to the artist's reputation, these works can also undercut the market for the artist's original work. Once again, separating artists' economic and moral interests in this context is an artificial exercise: this distinction is necessitated by law, but it does not reflect the lived experience of artists. The intention of those using AI systems should also be taken into account. Why should the users of these systems who intend to cause harm to artists, as noted by Simon Stålenhag in his comments on DALL-E,[130] be protected from the consequences of their actions? If the use of prompts that *intend* to destroy an artist's reputation, or the market for his or her work, cannot be prevented by the moral rights of authors, then the doctrine has failed. It would not have accomplished its original purpose under the 1928 revisions to the Berne Convention. In this regard, it is also worth noting that "intention" to harm an artwork is already instrumental in the implementation of moral rights for artists in the United States.[131] Our understanding of moral rights should

[130] Nolan, *supra* note 46.

[131] Though under VARA, *supra* note 71, it is the harming of an artwork, rather than the artist, through "intention" or "gross negligence." The essence of moral rights doctrine is that harm to the

be refined for the technological environment, just as copyright law as a whole must be adapted to new technologies. Existing concepts under copyright law, including moral rights, must be used effectively to confront technological insults.

It is also clear that insults to individual artists can have a much broader negative impact on our cultural environment. For example, a recent seminar in honor of the Canadian pianist, Glenn Gould, discussed the use of AI to create a system that can generate performances, in Gould's style, of musical works *that the pianist had never played in his lifetime.*[132] The seminar concluded with the question, "Are creative artists an endangered species?"[133]

What would happen if a large number of these artificially generated performances were to be made publicly available? If proper attribution were not maintained, in order to distinguish these new creations from Glenn Gould's own recordings, how would the public know what the pianist actually played? These technologies are designed to copy Gould as closely as possible. But Gould had strong, definite ideas about the music that he chose to interpret and record. He preferred the works of certain composers, including Bach—and will be linked forever with certain works, including Bach's *Goldberg Variations*, which he recorded twice.[134]

The example of Gould is especially poignant because the pianist was also deeply passionate about technology. He embraced technology to an extraordinary degree, and he remains the only classical musician in history to forego live performance for a career based exclusively on recording. But, ironically, it seems clear that developments in AI could have a powerful impact on Gould's legacy—including his reputation among future listeners.[135] Gould loved technology, but he was also fanatically

artwork causes harm to the artist, and the treatment of intention in VARA is therefore directly relevant to the discussion.

[132] *See, e.g.*, *The Canadian Premiere of "Dear Glenn," an AI System That Plays Like Gould*, ALLEVENTS (Sept. 24, 2022), https://allevents.in/mobile/amp-event.php?event_id=10000412366397997:

> The Canadian premiere of Dear Glenn, developed by Yamaha Japan in consultation with The Glenn Gould Foundation. This deep-learning technology has analyzed the elements of Gould's performing style and can produce a performance of any repertoire in the style of Glenn Gould (including music never performed by Gould in his lifetime).

[133] The system is called "Dear Glenn" and is also the subject of a podcast episode: *see* Mira T. Sundara Rajan, *Is Artificial Intelligence Creative? Glenn Gould, Pianist and Technological Visionary, and "Dear Glenn," the AI Inspired by Him—with Dr. Akira Maezawa of Yamaha*, WOMAN OF CULTURE PODCAST (Jan. 14, 2024), https://womanofculturepodcast.com/is-artificial-intelligence-creative-glenn-gould-pianist-and-technological-visionary-and-dear-glenn-the-ai-inspired-by-him-with-dr-akira-maezawa-of-yamaha.

[134] The two versions were recorded in 1952 and 1980: *see, e.g.*, Frances Wilson, *Returning to the Studio*, INTERLUDE (July 15, 2018), https://interlude.hk/returning-studio/.

[135] It is worth noting that a disregard for moral rights, or inadequate care for them, can point the way to similar outcomes even without the added impact of AI: see, e.g., the case of Jessye Norman, *supra* note 105.

perfectionist about his recordings.[136] And Glenn Gould is only one artist. His is but one example of the possible impact of AI on an artist's legacy.

Moral rights doctrine has something even more to offer than the direct protection of authors and artists. While the moral rights of authors give us language and concepts to support human creativity, they also provide us with the powerful framework of attribution and integrity interests. Attribution and integrity are principles that can be applied directly, in their own right, to information, knowledge, and culture. Maintaining the attribution of these intangibles protects historical truth—"the facts of history"—and the integrity of the cultural sphere surrounding us.[137] Like the biosphere that is our physical environment, the cultural sphere is the intangible environment that surrounds human beings and influences our actions. Like the biosphere, it is endangered, and the proliferation of generative AI will dramatically increase its fragility. But the principles of attribution and integrity, when attached to the creation and dissemination of these intangibles, can play a valuable role in ensuring the integrity of the cultural sphere—and, through it, the viability of crucial social infrastructure, including education, democracy, and(of course) culture.

J. Conclusion: Being Human in the Age of AI

Our reaction to AI developments so far reveals much about what it means to be human. There is fear and fascination; something existential animates the words of commentators on this subject. The question that seems to draw the most publicity and attention—as much or more then the practical question of whether AI will replace jobs—has to do with something else: creativity.

Google's Magenta project has embarked upon a truly unsettling enterprise. In the words of its designers, Magenta "directly addresses the question, 'Can machines be creative?' "[138] Skeptics might ask how interesting this question really is—or whether it merely reflects, as some might argue, the limitless hubris of software engineers (or ambition of Google). It still leads us on a path towards ever more profound questions. Some philosophers of AI argue that the entire universe is a computer simulation, leading to the conclusion that "God," as we know It, is a supreme form of AI.[139] But this may only serve to demonstrate that every era seeks

[136] This can be seen in action in many films of Gould at work, including, e.g., Roman Kroiter & Wolf Koenig, ON THE RECORD (1959), https://www.nfb.ca/film/glenn_gould_on_record.

[137] Margaret Mitchell, quoted in Knight et al., *supra* note 1.

[138] Google Magenta, *Make Music and Art Using Machine Learning* (n.d.), https://magenta.tensorflow.org.

[139] *See, e.g.*, Stephen Kelly, *The Matrix: Are We Living in a Simulation?*, BBC SCIENCE FORUM (Jan. 16, 2022), https://www.sciencefocus.com/future-technology/the-matrix-simulation (citing Nick Bostrom's work).

to remake God in the image of what it values most.[140] In the nineteenth century, the Creator of the universe was an artist, an author, as Voltaire wrote (*auteur*);[141] in the twenty-first, the supreme Being may manifest Itself (usually Himself) as a programmer and, ultimately, a machine. As Philip Ball of the BBC puts it, these explorations amount to "spinning webs from a thread of ignorance,"[142] but they are endlessly fascinating.

These paradoxes and limitations are neatly sidestepped in a visionary speech delivered by Garry Kasparov, the chess grandmaster who played against Deep Blue, the chess-playing AI machine and, as he points out, both won and lost to it.[143] He proclaims,

> Machine's triumph is man's triumph ... Deep Blue was victorious, but was it intelligent? Chess could be crunched by brute force once algorithms got smart enough, but it didn't offer the dreamt-of insights into the mysteries of human intelligence.... We should not worry about what machines can do today, we should worry about what they cannot do.[144]

The issues raised by Deep Blue have since been revisited in the context of Go, a Chinese game of strategy that is said to be more complex than chess, in a series of games played by Lee Sedol, a leading Go player, against AlphaGo, an AI system of amazing sophistication designed by DeepMind, a London lab now owned by Google.[145] Like Kasparov, Lee Sedol responded with awe, wonder, and enthusiasm to the experience of playing the machine—a reaction shared by many observers, and beautifully reflected in Cade Metz's comments for WIRED magazine:

> In Game Two, the Google machine made a move that no human ever would. And it was beautiful. As the world looked on, the move so perfectly demonstrated the enormously powerful and rather mysterious talents of modern artificial intelligence.

[140] This is perhaps taking Voltaire's famous words a step further—"Si Dieu n'existait pas, il faudrait l'inventer": VOLTAIRE, EPÎTRE À L'AUTEUR DU LIVRE DES TROIS IMPOSTEURS (OEUVRES COMPLÈTES DE VOLTAIRE, VOL. 10 402–405 (Louis Moland ed., 1877–85) (1768), reproduced in its entirety on the website of the Voltaire Society of America, https://www.whitman.edu/VSA/trois.imposteurs.html.

[141] Id.

[142] Philip Ball, *Several Physicists Have Suggested That Our Universe Is Not Real and Is Instead a Giant Simulation. Should We Care?*, BBC NEWS (Sept. 5, 2016), http://www.bbc.co.uk/earth/story/20160901-we-might-live-in-a-computer-program-but-it-may-not-matter.

[143] The term "visionary" is desperately overused in Silicon Valley, but Kasparov's speech seems to deserve it.

[144] Quoted in Wakefield, *supra* note 3.

[145] "AlphaGo, an artificially intelligent system designed by a team of researchers at DeepMind, a London AI lab now owned by Google": Cade Metz, *In Two Moves, Alphago and Lee Sedol Redefined the Future*, WIRED BUSINESS (Mar. 16, 2016), https://www.wired.com/2016/03/two-moves-alphago-lee-sedol-redefined-future.

> But in Game Four, the human made a move that no machine would ever expect. And it was beautiful too. Indeed, it was just as beautiful as the move from the Google machine—no less and no more. It showed that although machines are now capable of moments of genius, humans have hardly lost the ability to generate their own transcendent moments. And it seems that in the years to come, as we humans work with these machines, our genius will only grow in tandem with our creations.[146]

When machines are already capable of such superlative sophistication, there can be no doubt that they have an important capacity to produce "works" resembling the creative works traditionally created by humans. Moreover, with the Magenta project and beyond, those interested in AI have explicitly set themselves and their creations the challenge of discovering whether they have creative abilities "like" those of humans.

Ironically, these efforts may ultimately say more about human thought processes than anything else. Creativity is paramount; the ability to emulate creativity and to overcome it with "superior" displays of creativity, whether in the context of chess, Go, or the composition of music, appears to be a kind of ultimate test of success for AI. This is not to say that AI developers do not value tools that function in all kinds of ways, but there is still something especially tantalizing and important about creativity—even for them. This is true even for those who may claim that their ultimate goal is to prove that human creativity can be emulated and even transcended by machines.

And yet, as Kasparov illustrates so clearly, the very terms of such a discourse are meaningless. Modern society may see creativity as a luxury, but the larger history of humanity is one where creative and, indeed, artistic activities have always been prioritized. Indian poet C. Subramania Bharati writes, "Where woman comes, comes Art," but this could be neatly paraphrased: "Where humans come, comes Art."[147] Art, in one form or another, has always been with humanity.[148] We could even call art one of the first and most sophisticated of human "technologies"—in this case, a technology to achieve nothing less than transcendence of our physical and personal limitations, both as individuals and as a species. It is impossible to talk meaningfully about creativity or art without reaching for mystical language, and this is as it should be. Whether or not machines are creative is a question that the developers of AI are exploring, and we will someday arrive at an answer. The answer may ultimately be that such a question is meaningless. But there can be no question about whether humans are creative.

[146] Id.

[147] C. Subramania Bharati, *The Place of Woman, in The Coming Age: Collected English Writings* 69, 70 (Mira T. Sundara Rajan ed., 2021).

[148] This is the thesis of Ellen Dissanayake's beautifully argued book, Ellen Dissanayake, Homo Aestheticus: Where Art Comes From and Why (1992).

The real danger that we face today is life in a society that places so little value on human creativity.[149] At best, human creativity in artistic fields is considered secondary, non-essential; at worst, it is seen as fragile and vulnerable to exploitation. Indeed, the treatment of artists and authors by AI technologies amounts to exploitation of the most crude and direct kind. It is the exploitation of those whose mistreatment is, at a certain level, widely ignored, if not accepted, by society.

And yet, the public knows the difference between artificially generated products and the work of human creativity. AI technology demands a response, and the time has perhaps come at last for us to reject a future where those who control technology are allowed, and even encouraged, to exploit human creativity in favor of one that acknowledges that we are fundamentally creative beings. Artificial intelligence should be treated, first and foremost, as an instrument of human creativity and ingenuity. It is our tool. What kind of world will we make with it?

[149] Except, of course, in technical fields; the focus, here, is on artistic and intellectual creativity.

6

More Than Musicians

Music Copyright, Moral Rights, and Music in the Technological Environment

Born in the heart of the poet, [aesthetic experience] flowers as it were in the actor ... and bears fruit in the spectator. All three in the serene contemplation of the work, form in reality a single knowing subject fused together.

—*Bharata, Natya Shastra*[1]

Accurate metadata is essential to the healthy digital future of music creators, it is also critical to the healthy digital future of each and every Citizen Creator. The potential to report 100% accurate usage is the greatest promise cyberspace makes to Creators. Yet, in your Moral Rights submission, the RIAA seems to approach attribution and the accuracy that metadata provides as if it were a threat.

—*Global Music Rights Organizations*[2]

A. Introduction 386

B. State of the Art: Music Streaming, the Culmination of a Revolution in Sharing Music 387

C. Beginnings: The Creative Potential of Digital Music Discovered by Classical Musicians 390

D. *Blurred Lines* and *Stairway to Heaven*: The Limits of Music Copyright vs. Moral Rights 396

E. The Impact of New Musical Technologies: Moral Rights in Creation, Production, and Dissemination 402

1. Creation or Production? Technologies for the Creation of Musical Works 402
   a. Sampling 402
   b. Mixing 408
   c. Production 413
2. Communication 418
   a. File-Sharing: Moral Rights and Illegality 419
   b. Downloading: Moral Rights as Corporate Obligation 421
   c. Streaming: The Future of Moral Rights? 425

[1] Translated in Sneh Pandit, An Approach to the Indian Theory of Art and Aesthetics 134 (1977).

[2] Letter to the Recording Industry Association of America (RIAA) from global music rights organizations (August 2017) (in response to the RIAA position on proposed U.S. moral rights reform): Richard Smirke, *Songwriters Write Open Letter to RIAA Criticizing "Moral Rights" Stamce. Call It "Irresponsible"*

F. **Musical Transformations: From Mobile Ringtones to the Streaming Era** 432
1. Moral Rights and Excerpts 433
a. Integrity of a Ringtone: Germany Leads the Way 433
i. Excerpts 433
ii. Modifications 434
2. Licensing: An Implicit Waiver of Moral Rights? 435
G. **Musical Performers: The New Authors** 438
1. Authors and Artists: Two Solitudes 438
a. Attribution of Performances 440
b. Protecting the Performer's "Honor" as an Element of the Integrity Right 442
c. Performance in a New Context 443
2. Performers and Their Public: Future Symbiosis? 444
3. Layers of Rights: The Performer Finds a Place 446
4. Recognizing the Performer: An Issue of Equity 447
5. Recording and Broadcasting 451
H. **Recommendations** 453
I. **Conclusion: The Public Interest in Music** 455

A. Introduction

Music may be the oldest form of creative expression known to humanity.[3] As such, it is ironic that music has now become emblematic of the challenges facing creative expression in the technological environment. Music is a complete reflection in microcosm of the digital revolution, an embodiment of the themes of unfettered creation and, above all, communication; new relationships; new hierarchies among artists, their producers, and their public; and the near-death experience and consequent transformation of an industry.

and a "Betrayal," Music News (Aug. 17, 2017), https://www.billboard.com/pro/songwriters-coalition-open-letter-riaa-moral-rights-copyright-law. For the full text of the letter, see Chris Castle, *Global Songwriter and Composer Organizations Send an Open Letter to RIAA Proposing Solution to Massive Failures to Accord Credit and Respect International Laws of Moral Rights*, Music Technology Policy Blog (Aug. 16, 2017), https://musictechpolicy.com/2017/08/16/global-songwriter-and-composer-organizations-send-open-letter-to-riaa-proposing-solution-to-massive-failures-to-accord-credit-and-respect-international-laws-of-moral-rights. All websites cited in this chapter were last visited on June 17, 2024.

[3] In this regard, India's ancient Vedic poems, which are usually chanted, provide an extraordinary example: that of a *wordless* Veda whose patterns of sound more closely resemble birdsong than any known language. Sanskrit philosophy discusses the relationship of sound, word, and meaning extensively, and interested readers can investigate the terms *sabda* (word) and *sruti* (sound, also the Vedas). Although Encyclopedia Britannica's coverage of India leaves something to be desired, the entries on Indian philosophy are a useful starting place: *see, e.g.*, https://www.britannica.com/topic/shabda and, more generally, https://www.britannica.com/topic/Indian-philosophy. For *sruti*, there are separate entries, but the same word has multiple senses (and may be transliterated differently into English): https://www.britannica.com/topic/Shruti and https://www.britannica.com/art/sruti. The wordless Veda is discussed in Michael Wood, *Beginnings*, The Story of India ep.1 (2007), https://www.youtube.com/watch?v=i1yqkOanQwg; further details about this series , including a Q&A with Michael Wood, are available at Public Broadcasting Service, *The Story of India* (n.d.), https://www.pbs.org/thestoryofindia/about/episode_summaries. For further information on Wood's work, *see Michael Wood Biography* (2008), https://www.pbs.org/thestoryofindia/about/episode_summaries.

The digital transformation of the music industry has profound implications for the moral rights of musicians—affecting musical "authors," such as composers and songwriters, as well as performers. Indeed, copyright, as a whole, is in the midst of a fundamental transformation in relation to the art of music. This chapter will show how moral rights raise questions but also provide answers to many of the complex challenges before us, suggesting a new, and perhaps more equitable, shape for the music industry of the future.

This chapter draws attention to three exciting contributions of moral rights to the music industry: their role in the continuing fight against music piracy led by music industry stakeholders, including, of course, musicians; the seamless fit between moral rights and the imperatives of new musical technologies themselves, in apparent contrast to copyright law as a whole; and, finally, the essential role of moral rights in securing and maintaining the musical reputations of artists. This last point is among the most subtle and important considerations involving moral rights in the online universe of music. The vast amount of musical material available online suggests that, without moral rights, there is every chance that music will ultimately become decoupled from its creators, leading to a situation where all but the most famous of musical artists cannot expect to build reputations or audiences through the dissemination of their recordings. All indicators suggest that reputation, rather than any single product or creation, will be among the most valuable of both economic and artistic assets for musicians in the digital environment.

In the light of these considerations, this chapter examines the acceptance of moral rights by major players in the online environment for music, which, overall, continues to lag behind the desires and needs of artists. It offers some recommendations on how, and to what extent, those rights should be recognized, and argues for the broader exploration of creative means of using new technologies to support the moral rights of musicians.

The discussion of musical genres in this chapter is free and quite wide-ranging. Examples are drawn from classical music, jazz, and Indian classical music, among other genres, as well as hip-hop and pop music, where many of the major controversies confronting music in the online environment, such as pop singer Taylor Swift's dispute with Spotify, have played out. No genre of music has been left behind by technology; the challenges and opportunities for musicians in different genres are sometimes similar, but often different as well. Analyzing the prospects of each genre is beyond the scope of this chapter, but the discussion here may help to generate some interesting reflections for musicians and all those who work with them, in every genre, in the online context.

B. State of the Art: Music Streaming, the Culmination of a Revolution in Sharing Music

When the digital revolution first made it possible to copy and disseminate high-quality sound files, the advent of this inexpensive and relatively uncomplicated technology signaled the end of an era in the music industry. That era was the age of music recordings. It began roughly at the start of the twentieth century, with the capacity to record live musical performances, and ultimately burgeoned into a music industry based on the growing market for recordings that were disseminated in the fixed, physical form of records (LPs) and, later, compact discs (CDs). In the early twenty-first century, the reliance on physical products melted away. Quite simply, the music industry moved from a context where the distribution of music was controlled to one with profound limitations on the ability to control either the reproduction or the movement of musical works—the movement from physical products to the digital embodiment of those products, limitlessly reproducible, infinitely susceptible to dissemination. The digital era of music has often threatened to lurch into an age of no control, but, interestingly, it has always been able to pull back from that brink.

Not surprisingly, the process of transformation from an analog to a digital industry has involved major casualties. The trigger for these changes was the development of file-sharing technology in the late 1990s, with Napster being the dominant force in this market. Napster, and other services like it, allowed music files to be shared online so that users of the system could acquire music without being obliged to purchase music recordings from labels. This was the onset of an age of copyright piracy, and all of the large music companies ultimately had to adapt to this new technological reality, with downsizing and streamlining being the order of the day.

The breakdown of an old order, by definition, opens the door for something new. These technological developments, while they were greatly feared by the major players in the industry, opened the door for innovation—most strikingly, in relation to the distribution of music, but, no less radically, in terms of the creation and production of music, as well. What came to be known as "illegal" file-sharing would create an incentive to explore the possibilities of a legal counterpart, with Apple stepping in as the first major player in this new marketplace, to be followed, in short order, by Amazon and other file-sharing services. File-sharing, itself, would eventually be superseded by a newer and more exciting technology: music streaming. New entities have stepped in to develop and exploit this new technological realm, with platforms like Spotify and YouTube, which disseminates both music and video, now among the most dynamic entities in the music industry. In contrast to file-sharing, music streaming has offered a new universe of possible products, arising not only from the making available of works, but also from the organization and curation of what has effectively become a vast quantity of musical works and performances available online. These services often interface with technology in countless way. It is possible to identify music by cross-referencing information available through databases—through iTunes, for example—and, through technology, music also interacts with countless applications that offer users support with meditation, therapy, fitness, and education, to name only a few possibilities.

But the labels have not been the only stakeholders affected by this wave of change. Far from it: the primordial losses have been those felt by artists. The obsolescence of the analog world and the further movement from digital reproduction technologies to streaming has paradoxically left musicians fighting for their earnings in a marketplace where all indicators suggest that there is an extremely strong and growing demand for their work—for music.

As the streaming era has taken flight, musicians have struggled to realize earnings from this new form of dissemination. A lack of transparency combined with outsize music industry influence among streaming providers has left even well-known popular musicians earning pennies for their music. Their struggle was brought unforgettably before the public eye when one of the best-known musicians in the world, Taylor Swift, withdrew her entire catalogue from Spotify. In an opinion piece published in the WALL STREET JOURNAL, she argued,

> Music is art, and art is important and rare. Important, rare things are valuable. Valuable things should be paid for. It's my opinion that music should not be free, and my prediction is that individual artists and their labels will someday decide what an album's price point is. I hope they don't underestimate themselves or undervalue their art.[4]

Three years later, after a concerted series of steps aimed at securing her position that show how shrewd a businesswoman she truly is, Swift renewed her relationship with Spotify and posted her new album with the service.[5]

Swift's return to Spotify did not reflect major improvements in the service's payments to musicians. Her public calling-out of the company focused attention on the problem, which had been simmering just below the surface of the streaming industry for years, and created hope among other musicians with less industry clout than Swift about the potential for positive change and improved payments to musicians featured on streaming sites. However, Swift's return was as much an acknowledgment of the changing shape of the music industry and the impossibility of turning back technology once it has become familiar to the public as any declaration of victory—or concession of defeat—against Spotify.

The reality is that the use of streaming services like Spotify has become a "normal" expectation in the industry—normal for industry players; for musicians;

[4] Taylor Swift, *For Taylor Swift, the Future of Music Is a Love Story: The Singer-Songwriter Says Artists and Fans Will Still Form Deep Bonds, But They Will Do It in New Ways*, WALL STREET JOURNAL (July 7, 2014), https://www.wsj.com/articles/for-taylor-swift-the-future-of-music-is-a-love-story-1404763219.

[5] Tim Ingham, *Taylor Swift Is Getting Friendly with Spotify Ahead of Her New Album, Lover. Times Have Changed*, MUSIC BUSINESS WORLDWIDE (Aug. 20, 2019), https://www.musicbusinessworldwide.com/taylor-swift-is-getting-friendly-with-spotify-ahead-of-her-new-album-lover-times-have-changed.

and, above all, for the public. Yet, the true culprits behind the absurdly low royalties payed by streaming services are, in a sense, not the services themselves. Rather, widespread piracy in the music industry—the "free" availability of music files on file-sharing services during the late 1990s—effectively reduced the real "price" of music to near zero. However, obtaining music by file-sharing involved risk—the risk of doing something illegal and potentially getting caught and penalized. The brilliance of Spotify was to recognize that the public would be willing to pay something for the protection of using music legally; but that it would only be willing to do so when the cost of that legal service could be compared to the free availability of the same goods by means of piracy and found to be valuable. The price of legal music was real, but it was also low. Indeed, Apple's iTunes was an earlier reflection of the same philosophy; but Apple launched its legal download service in an environment where music was still less widely available than it has become with the advent of streaming services.

To complete this broad analysis of the music landscape in the era of streaming, it seems clear that the public must accept its share of responsibility for the low earning potential of music on streaming sites. But the attitude of the public seems natural: why pay for what is (or has been) available for free?

Streaming services signal a new inflection point in the development of the music industry: a world where copyright royalties have little value, not because of illegal activity, but because the digital dissemination of music has opened the Pandora's box of "free" access to music. While the public apparently remains sympathetic to creators, the lure of cheap music seems to be irresistible. Yet, musicians are left with the need to put food on the table. How will they do so? If not through copyright, then perhaps through the wealth generated indirectly by the protection of moral rights: reputation.

A secondary and perhaps less obvious answer to this question is that they must do so with the help of the public. As yet, no industry model has found the answer to the question of *how* the public can help creators without foregoing free music as a matter of principle. Would the public be willing to make a sacrifice like this to support those who create music? And what form would that sacrifice take—taxes and subsidies to musicians, a general artist's fund with mandatory or voluntary contributions, or public shaming around the use of pirated or low-cost music? And who would the public be willing to support—which artists, which genres? Celebrities or unknown artists, both or neither?

C. Beginnings: The Creative Potential of Digital Music Discovered by Classical Musicians

It is worth remembering that the first musicians to recognize the potential of technology were classical musicians. In many ways, classical music continues to be on the cutting edge of technology, exploring, for example, innovative and potentially controversial uses of artificial intelligence in music-making, such as the recreation of the performance styles of renowned artists from the past.[6]

The classical art is perhaps uniquely preoccupied with the idea of "perfection." Johannes Brahms once said that he was not primarily concerned with whether his compositions were beautiful but with the question of whether they were perfect.[7] Pianist Artur Schnabel famously commented that he was "attracted only to music which I consider to be better than it can be performed"—the suggestion of an ideal, though Schnabel hated recording.[8] On the other hand, Canadian pianist Glenn Gould—for whom, Schnabel was "a God"—suggested that the environment of the recording studio is a more likely place for the attainment of an ideal than the concert hall.[9]

But, for interested classical artists, technology promised something more than this: the democratization of an art that was deeply mired in convention, not all of it serving the higher purpose of artistic excellence. Technology could break down the barriers between artist and audience; it could transform the passive experience of the listener into active engagement with the music. The Canadian pianist Glenn Gould was, in some sense, the living embodiment of this dream.

Gould was the first prominent musician to become excited about the creative possibilities brought to classical music by technology, and he courageously reshaped his own career to reflect his vision. In 1964, he retired permanently from concert-giving. He was thirty-two years old. He preferred, instead, to focus on what he saw as the musical art of the future: recording. His manager, Walter Homburger, warned him that public tastes were fickle. Gould might be unable to maintain his livelihood as a classical artist through recordings.[10] But Gould's experiment

[6] But note the groundbreaking work of classical sound engineers, such as Steve Epstein: *see, e.g.*, ArgerichHD, *Glenn Gould plays Bach - The Goldberg Variations, BMV 998 (Zenph re-performance)*, YouTube (May 25, 2013), https://www.youtube.com/watch?v=Ah392lnFHxM&t=959s.

[7] Jan Swafford, Johannes Brahms: A Biography 120 (1997).

[8] But note, nevertheless, that Schnabel disliked recording, not only because of the circumstances in which he recorded but also on principle. In an extraordinary letter to his wife, written on March 26, 1932, he refers to it as ""destruction through preservation" ("What cannot die has never lived"), commenting that the experience of recording Beethoven's Sonatas was "sheer torture": *see* Allan Evans, *A First Hearing of Artur Schnabel*, Arbiter Records (2019), https://arbiterrecords.org/a-first-hearing-of-artur-schnabel (reproducing the letter in full from a text provided by the Schnabel Music Foundation, available at https://schnabelmusicfoundation.com). *See also* Brian C. Thompson, *Liner Notes to Great Pianists: Artur Schnabel: BEETHOVEN: Piano Works Vol. 6Piano Sonata No. 17 "Tempest" • Piano Sonata No. 18 • Piano Sonata No. 21 "Waldstein,"* Naxos (n.d.), https://www.naxos.com/MainSite/BlurbsReviews/?itemcode=8.110760&catnum=8110760&filetype=AboutThisRecording&language=English. Glenn Gould, who greatly admired Schnabel, commented that Schnabel was "a person who didn't really care very much about the piano as an instrument. The piano was a means to an end, for him, and the end was to approach Beethoven": quoted in Geoffrey Payzant, Glenn Gould: Music and Mind 6 (1984) (1978).

[9] *See* Glenn Gould, *Glenn Gould and Humphrey Burton on Beethoven—Part 1 (Official)*, YouTube (Dec. 15, 2017), https://www.youtube.com/watch?v=PiRySfETBdg.

[10] See the comments in Peter F. Ostwald, Glenn Gould: The Ecstasy and Tragedy of Genius 210 (1997)(Foreword by Oliver Sacks).

proved to be a brilliant success. Not only did he craft some of the iconic recordings of the twentieth century—his early and late versions of the Goldberg Variations are two examples from his peerless discography[11]—but he also wrote and lectured extensively on the theme of recording. He thought it the ultimate musical art form. Writing in 1966, Gould commented,

> In an unguarded moment some months ago, I predicted that the public concert as we know it today would no longer exist a century hence, that its functions would have been entirely taken over by electronic media. It had not occurred to me that this statement represented a particularly radical pronouncement. Indeed, I regarded it almost as self-evident truth and, in any case, as defining only one of the peripheral effects occasioned by developments in the electronic age.[12]

Gould's passion for technology was not limited to the joys of the recording studio, whose privacy, concentration, and opportunities for multiple takes provided the perfect setting in which to examine a work comprehensively, to approach it in a mode of consistent creative exploration.[13] Gould was also interested in digital music in its own right. He commented, controversially and with typical self-deprecation, that the Moog synthesizer produced the most perfect interpretation imaginable of Bach.[14]

Gould may have been the first person to see the "democratizing" potential of technology for the hierarchical and elite art of classical music. In Gould's view, technology offered new opportunities for the listener to intervene in a creative work—to change the sound of a recording, to alter the balance among multiple

[11] Glenn Gould, *Goldberg Variations* (1955; 1981). Both versions were recorded by Columbia Masterworks.

[12] Glenn Gould, *The Prospects of Recording*, 16(4) High Fidelity 46 (1996), http://www.collectionscanada.gc.ca/glenngould/028010-4020.01-f.html. The online version appears with comments by a number of leading musical figures. See also the extremely interesting comments on Gould's attitude to recording in the Canadian Encyclopedia online, *Gould, Glenn*, The Encyclopedia of Music in Canada (Aug. 17, 2008), https://www.thecanadianencyclopedia.ca/en/article/glenn-gould ("For Gould, recording had fundamentally altered the traditional relationship of composer, performer, and listener").

[13] Gould's creative process in studio is the subject of a book by his long-time—and apparently long-suffering—producer, Andrew Kazdin: Andrew Kazdin, Glenn Gould at Work: Creative Lying (1989). Kazdin's reflections are sometimes bitter, but his expert and insider view of his work with Gould make the book required reading for anyone interested in Gould's work or in the art of recording more generally.

[14] The personality of the performer could not "interfere" with the integrity of the composition if the performance, as in the case of the Moog synthesizer, was mediated by a machine. A Canadian Broadcasting Corporation (CBC) broadcast features Gould's comments on the Moog synthesizer, as well as two interesting interviews related to "automation" and music: *Hear Glenn Gould Celebrate the Moog Synthesizer & Wendy Carlos' Pioneering Album* Switched-On Bach *(1968)*, Open Culture (Aug. 12, 2019), http://www.openculture.com/2019/08/glenn-gould-sings-the-praises-of-the-moog-synthesizer-and-wendy-carlos-switched-on-bach.html. An interview with Wendy Carlos from BBC program *Horizon*, originally shown in 1989, can be seen at *Watch Composer Wendy Carlos Demo an Original Moog Synthesizer (1989)*, Open Culture (Sept. 30, 2019), http://www.openculture.com/2019/09/watch-composer-wendy-carlos-demo-an-original-moog-synthesizer-1989.html.

"voices" or performers, to adjust the speed of the music. The possibilities for intervention in a work of recorded music are much greater now than they were even in Gould's time.

The legendary jazz pianist Bill Evans, coincidentally a friend of Gould's, was also interested in technology.[15] He used it to accomplish something slightly different—a pathbreaking record called *Conversations with Myself*, in which he used the then novel technique of "overdubbing" his own playing, superimposing one recorded performance of a piece upon another, to achieve a new level in his exploration of musical ideas.[16] Recorded in 1963, the album won the young pianist a Grammy Award. Jason R. Laipply describes the work as an "instant classic." He comments,

> Overdubbing was sneered at by most jazz people, looked at as "gimmicky" and "synthetic." But Evans, one of the most lyrical musicians of the jazz world, was intrigued with taking the "conversational" approach his trio had been practicing to a new level. If three musicians could practice and play together long enough to be able to carry on musical conversations during a song, then wouldn't the musical ideas expressed and explored in multiple tracks by the same musician create a new and unique kind of musical dialogue?[17]

These early experiments were in the avant-garde of a phenomenon that is now commonplace: the manipulation of music through technology. Gould and Evans felt that technology allowed them to approach, more closely than ever before, the realization of an artistic vision. Curiously, experiments with technology in the world of classical music seem to have largely stalled since then, with the classical music world of today seeming to turn inward in a way that was not the case during the 1960s. Today's musicians largely seem to wish to recreate the illusion of being present in a concert hall—an idealized concert hall, minus the coughs and whispers—whereas Gould spoke of wanting to create a novel and more intimate experience of listening. Adopting Gould's perspective, the sense is one of underutilized technology, of opportunities for profound change that have remained largely unexplored.

But unprecedented events have generated new uses for technology: it has been marshalled to serve classical music in a new way in the era of the novel coronavirus pandemic of 2020–2021. With concert halls closed, and the public throughout the world in enforced isolation, artists performed upon stages in empty rooms,

[15] In his biography of Bill Evans, Peter Pettinger notes their friendship: PETER PETTINGER, BILL EVANS: HOW MY HEART SINGS 221 (1998). It is difficult to find much more on their relationship, but some interesting and apparently reliable information is available at http://www.glenngould.org/f_minor/msg07197.html.

[16] Apparently, Evans used Gould's Steinway piano, CD 318, for the recording of the album *Conversations with Myself*: Pettinger, *supra* note 15. *See also* KEVIN BAZZANA, WONDROUS STRANGE: THE LIFE AND ART OF GLENN GOULD 88 (2004).

[17] Jason R. Laipply, *Conversations with Myself: Bill Evans* [Review], ALL ABOUT JAZZ (Oct. 1, 1997).

recording and sharing those performances online. Orchestras, who could not perform together for fear of spreading the virus through their breath, broadcast recordings made before the pandemic in "virtual concert hall" settings. This was an effort to create community in a new form—virtual "community" online. In a broadcast of the Seattle Symphony, 90,000 listeners tuned in—a fascinating contrast to the 4,835 tickets that were actually sold for a 3-day run of the performance in September of 2018.[18] This was a deep repudiation of the claimed "irrelevance" of classic music during humanity's greatest hour of need.[19]

In contrast, the impact of technology on popular music has been simply explosive. Entire new genres, notably hip-hop, are based on technological intervention, which includes the use of samples and mixing techniques that alter sounds or songs, voices or riffs, presenting them in a new context or manufacturing new ones outright. The DJ is now well established as a musical creator in his or her own right.[20]

The democratizing effect of technology that was so interesting to Gould has had a more ambiguous trajectory. On the one hand, the availability of platforms for showcasing works theoretically involves greater autonomy for artists, who can bypass labels to release their own work online. For example, YouTube, which allows users to post their own videos online, has become one major vehicle for publicizing new talent. Singer Susan Boyle became an overnight sensation when her performance on the television program, *Britain's Got Talent*, posted on YouTube, made an unlikely star of the modest forty-seven-year-old Scotswoman, defying a media environment hungry for youth and glamour.[21] To date, Boyle's YouTube video has apparently received a staggering 300 million hits, and subsequent sales of her debut album set new records.[22] She is only one example of a performer whose fame has been bolstered by YouTube, and the impact of the platform is not limited to music. Far from it—YouTube has given birth to a bewildering new array of performance

[18] *See* Brooke Jarvis, *Livestreaming the Seattle Symphony Became a Source of Connection in Dark Times*, NEW YORK TIMES MAGAZINE (Mar. 24, 2020), https://www.nytimes.com/2020/03/24/magazine/coronavirus-music-live-stream-concert.html.

[19] On this theme, see a fascinating article by Anna Goldsworthy, *The Lost Art of Listening: Has Classical Music Become Irrelevant?*, THE MONTHLY (Oct. 2015), https://www.themonthly.com.au/issue/2015/october/1443621600/anna-goldsworthy/lost-art-listening#mtr.

[20] A program on this theme has been produced by the CBC: Chris Brookes, Paolo Pietropaolo & Jowi Taylor, *The Wire: The Digital Democracy of Sound*, CBC NEWS (Aug. 14, 2017), https://www.cbc.ca/radio/ideas/the-wire-the-digital-democracy-of-sound-1.4234253.

[21] *See* Scott Collins & Janet Stobart, *Talent Trumps All for YouTube Sensation Susan Boyle: An Appearance on "Britain's Got Talent" Propels the 47-Year-Old Singer onto the World Stage—with Nary a Speck of Glitz or Glamour*, LOS ANGELES TIMES (Apr. 17, 2009), http://www.latimes.com/entertainment/la-et-susan-boyle17-2009apr17,0,2767635.story.

[22] *See* Sarah Lyall, *Unlikely Singer Is YouTube Sensation*, NEW YORK TIMES (Apr. 18, 2009), http://www.nytimes.com/2009/04/18/arts/television/18boyle.html. Boyle's celebrity has also translated into outstanding album sales. *See Susan Boyle Sets US Chart Record*, BBC NEWS (Dec. 2, 2009), http://news.bbc.co.uk/2/hi/8391777.stm. The problems of attributing posted videos to their creators and of maintaining the integrity of videos are briefly noted by Damien O'Brien & Brian Fitzgerald, *Digital Copyright Law in a YouTube World*, 9(6/7) INTERNET L. BULL. 71 (2006).

content, including "vloggers," "esports players," and make up artists, as well as offering a platform to musicians of every genre from around the world.

And, of course, musicians, particularly well-known ones, have the option of bypassing platforms altogether and releasing music on their own websites. This option was famously chosen by the rock band *Radiohead*, which made its album *In Rainbows* available on its website in 2008, with the zen-like stipulation upon downloading that "You pay what you want."[23] This approach raised the hackles of other performers. For example, Robert Smith of the Cure commented,

> You can't allow other people to put a price on what you do, otherwise you don't consider what you do to have any value at all.[24]

Once again, the issues transcend genre: classical pianist Vikingur Ólafsson released three albums of music on his own label. His music ultimately drew the notice of the most prestigious classical music label in the world, Deutsche Gramophon, which has since signed him as one of its own artists.[25]

In spite of these changes, labels continue to exist, and, indeed, as noted above, the volume of music available online is creating a new need for services—this time, services such as curation, search, and organization—which is being filled by new music services based on streaming. Musicians have not so much escaped from labels as watched their relationship with labels metamorphose into something new. Moreover, which of these services will prove to have longevity, and whether longevity is indeed a test of success in the online environment, has yet to be determined.

In the process, however, one great unanswered question remains—and it is not the question of how industry will survive these changes. Decades into the digital revolution, it seems clear that there are opportunities for almost everyone in the new environment, and that most organizations involved in the music industry, including large corporations, can adapt their services to survive in the new environment. Industry will not only survive but also thrive, somehow, for the simplest of reasons—because the demand for music exists, and it shows no sign of abating.

Instead, in the contest over music rights, the fate of artists is uncertain. One universal truth in the music industry, as noted, is that the price of music has fallen.

[23] *See* Josh Tyrangiel, *You Pay What You Want*, Time (Oct. 1, 2007). See also the interesting follow-up by Greg Sandoval, *Radiohead Won't Repeat "In Rainbows" Giveaway* (Apr. 30, 2008), https://www.cnet.com/culture/radiohead-wont-repeat-in-rainbows-giveaway/?search=toaþp.

[24] *See* Michael Leonard, *Robert Smith Blasts "Idiot" Radiohead: Pay What You Want? Not for The Cure* (Feb. 24, 2009), https://www.musicradar.com/news/guitars/robert-smith-blasts-idiot-radiohead-197836 ("The Cure's frontman Robert Smith says he 'disagreed violently' with Radiohead allowing their fans to pay what they wanted for the band's last album, *In Rainbows*.").

[25] See the interview with the pianist, *Meet the Artist—Vikingar Ólafsson, Pianist*, The Cross-Eyed Pianist (May 25, 2017), https://crosseyedpianist.com/2017/05/25/meet-the-artist-vikingur-olafsson-pianist. Ólaffson makes numerous works available online on his own website and a number of albums on Spotify: *see* https://www.vikingurolafsson.com/#music.

Once again, the reality underlying this change is so fundamental that it is difficult to imagine how it can ever be undone. The movement from analog to digital music has meant, in a nutshell, that music became easily available—in the era of piracy, for free, and in the period of the resurgence of the music industry following that nadir, at a cost that remained below its previous high point and continued to reflect the plentiful availability of music in the digital environment. The discussion of possible solutions has focused on economic rights—though, given the structural factors at work, there has been little concrete progress on finding mechanisms to pay artists better. Moral rights have been almost entirely neglected.

In a landscape dominated by corporations, this is, perhaps, hardly surprising. But musicians, themselves, have begun to raise the issue of the moral rights in their music. It is remarkable that a group of people who are said to be naïve about their rights, who are traditionally disadvantaged in the process of forming contracts with those responsible for commercializing their music—managers, agents, labels— and who are often in immediate need of financial returns from their work, have still thought it worthwhile to draw attention to their moral rights.

D. *Blurred Lines* and *Stairway to Heaven*: The Limits of Music Copyright vs. Moral Rights

In this regard, the U.S. copyright case involving the song *Blurred Lines* is a fascinating example. One of the best-known cases on music copyright of the decade of the 2010s, the case focused on a song by pop singer, Robin Thicke, called *Blurred Lines* and arose when the descendants of Marvin Gaye, one of the best-known singers of a previous era and an icon of musical style, alleged that Thicke and his co-writers had copied from one of Gaye's songs, *Got to Give It Up*.[26]

The case was an unusual one in the sense that it did not hinge on the copying of particular elements from one song into the new song. Instead, the issue was the similarity of the "feel" between the two songs, with a jury finding that, indeed, this was a situation of copyright infringement. The court awarded damages of more than 5 million dollars in the case.[27] For many observers in the United States, and for a dissenting appeals judge in the case, the verdict raised concerns that music copyright had ventured into territory that was once forbidden by allowing

[26] In fact, Gaye's children wanted responsibility for the copying to be assigned to all of those involved in writing the new song and distributing it. The court ultimately found liability, but only on the part of Robin Thicke and one of his co-writers, Pharell Williams. *See* Ben Sisario, *Both Sides in "Blurred Lines" Copyright Suit Signal a Continuing Battle*, New York Times (Mar. 18, 2015), https://www.nytimes.com/2015/03/19/business/media/both-sides-in-blurred-lines-copyright-suit-signal-a-continuing-battle.html?_r=0.

[27] The trial court awarded US$7.4 million, but of this "only" $5.3 million was upheld on appeal. *See* id.; Ben Sisario, *"Blurred Lines" Verdict Upheld by Appeals Court*, New York Times (Mar. 21, 2018), https://www.nytimes.com/2018/03/21/business/media/blurred-lines-marvin-gaye-copyright.html.

restrictions on musical "style"—which, they argued, was, and always had been, beyond the scope of copyright protection.[28] The problem is a classic illustration of what is known in copyright law as the "idea–expression" dichotomy, which provides that ideas per se can never be protected by copyright; it is only the concrete *expression* of those ideas in a work, such as a song,[29] that can be protected. The purpose of this distinction, artificial as it may seem, is to protect the public domain, where ideas circulate freely, providing a general incentive to create further works.

In the *Blurred Lines* case, the apparent similarity in the two songs, while striking, is difficult to explain in terms other than style. In this sense, the case resembled the UK case of *Russell Williams v. Designers' Guild*, which dealt with the entirely different area of copyright in fabric designs, but found, similarly, that copyright in the original design had been infringed in spite of the fact that no actual elements from the first design were reproduced in the second. In a brilliant and subtle ruling, Lord Hoffman dealt with the idea–expression dichotomy by effectively dismantling it, pointing out that every element of a work is an embodiment of the idea underlying it, and that separating idea and expression can be, in practice, an artificial exercise. From a U.S. perspective, this effectively opens the door—even if it is ever so slightly—to the copyright protection of ideas. And yet, in *Blurred Lines*, we are left with what may have been, in effect, the copying of a song, without any other way of recognizing that possibility within the toolbox of copyright law. For example, Robin Thicke has explicitly stated that he knew, and was inspired by, Gaye's song.[30] Does that mean, as the dissenting judge argued, that Thicke's process should be tolerated by copyright law for the sake of maintaining freedom of expression in the musical realm?

A practical answer may be found in the statements of the Gaye family, made in an extraordinary letter to the public, which they drafted in the wake of the suit.[31] For them, the primary matter of concern was that Thicke and his co-writers crafted their song with the explicit intention of writing a song "with the same groove,"[32] yet neither Gaye nor his song received any credit for their role in the composition of the new song.

[28] As summarized by Sisario, *"Blurred Lines" Verdict, supra* note 27: "In a dissent, Judge Jacqueline H. Nguyen harshly criticized the decision as one that 'allows the Gayes to accomplish what no one has before: copyright a musical style.' She further warned that the decision 'establishes a dangerous precedent that strikes a devastating blow to future musicians and composers everywhere.'"

[29] But it should be noted that a song almost always consists of multiple parts: music and lyrics, which generate their own copyrights; the recording of the music and lyrics, which generates its own rights; and vocal and musical performances, which generate performance rights.

[30] *See* Stelios Phili, *Robin Thicke on That Banned Video, Collaborating with 2 Chainz and Kendrick Lamar, and His New Film*, GQ (May 6, 2013), https://www.gq.com/story/robin-thicke-interview-blurred-lines-music-video-collaborating-with-2-chainz-and-kendrick-lamar-mercy.

[31] The letter, "An Open Letter from the Children of Marvin Gaye 3/18/15," is reproduced in full in Britanny Spanos, *Marvin Gaye's Children: What Our Father Would Say about Lawsuit*, ROLLING STONE (Mar. 18, 2015), https://www.rollingstone.com/music/music-news/marvin-gayes-children-what-our-father-would-say-about-lawsuit-172597.

[32] Id.

Licensing could have been a solution to this problem. Gaye's children write:

> Like most artists, they could have licensed and secured the song for appropriate usage; a simple procedure usually arranged in advance of the song's release. This did not happen. We would have welcomed a conversation with them before the release of their work. This also did not happen. [33]

Interestingly, though, the Gaye family's interest in licensing was not only an issue of money. They outline the problem clearly, as follows:

> Great artists like our dad intentionally build their music to last, but we as the caretakers of such treasures, have an obligation to be vigilant about preserving the integrity of the music so that future generations understand its origins and feel its effect as the artist intended, and to assure that it retains its value.[34]

For anyone familiar with moral rights, the language that they chose is striking. They speak of the "origins" and "integrity of the music"—their wish that the audience can experience the music "as the artist intended." They do affirm, as well, that music should "retain … its value," which implies the retention of economic value; but this is only one of the elements that they emphasize. It is also important to note that the retention of economic value for "future generations" involves inherent limits, since even the current long duration of copyright protection in the United States—seventy years after the lifetime of the artist or author, following the European model[35]—means that copyright lasts one or, at maximum, two generations after the artist's death. At most, it is to the grandchildren's benefit; but the non-economic considerations of "origin" and "integrity" are qualitatively different.

Overall, this paragraph, penned by Gaye's family, reads like a classic statement of moral rights. It does so in one of the doctrine's most traditional forms—as illustrated, notably, by the finding of the French court in the famous *Huston* case on colorizing black-and-white movies[36]—by emphasizing that the intention of the author should be a determinative factor in how his or her work is treated. Of course, this is only one possible interpretation of moral rights doctrine, but it has traditionally characterized the French approach. Gaye's children go on to conclude

[33] Id.

[34] Id.

[35] Originally under Council Directive 93/98/EEC of 29 October 1993 harmonizing the term of protection of copyright and certain related rights, 1993 O.J. (L 290) 9, https://eur-lex.europa.eu/legal-content/EN/ALL/?uri=CELEX%3A31993L0098; since repealed and replaced by Directive 2006/116/EC of the European Parliament and of the Council of 12 December 2006 on the term of protection of copyright and certain related rights, 2006 O.J. (L 372) 12, https://eur-lex.europa.eu/LexUriServ/LexUriServ.do?uri=OJ:L:2006:372:0012:0018:EN:PDF.

[36] *Huston v. La Cinq*, Cour de cassation [Cass.] [supreme court for judicial matters] 1e civ., May 28, 1991, Bull. civ. I, No. 172 (Fr.), https://www.legifrance.gouv.fr/juri/id/JURITEXT000007026649. See discussion in Chapters 1, 3, and 5, *supra*, and Chapter 7, *infra*.

that if Gaye were alive now, "he would be vigilant about safeguarding the artist's rights; a sacred devotion to not only the artist, but key in encouraging and supporting innovation. He also gave credit where credit is due."[37]

In the United States, of course, there are no moral rights for musicians. It is worth noting that this remains the case in spite of the fact that the United States is now a member of the Berne Convention and, further, that it has also ratified the World Intellectual Property Organization (WIPO) Performances and Phonograms Treaty, which provides for moral rights for performers in its Article 5.[38] A review of moral rights in the United States conducted in 2016 and 2017 led the Recording Industry Association of America (RIAA) to make its opposition to moral rights known in a submission to the U.S. Copyright Office, leading to a rebuke for this "betrayal" by a large coalition of groups representing songwriters from many countries. They state,

> The RIAA's argument prioritizes the inconvenience of dealing with accurate metadata over the principle of the protection of the rights of the people upon whose work the music business is built. In our view, and the view of many in the creator community, this is not only irresponsible, it represents a betrayal of the "greater common purpose" to which so many of us are committed—a purpose with which the RIAA claims to agree.
>
> ... [T]he RIAA comments have inspired very active opposition, including that from UK and European music creators whose work is consumed widely across the USA but whose moral rights are not recognized, in part, due to your position. The Berne Convention, revised in 1928 to include moral rights, has 172 countries around the world signed up to it; it is only the U.S. that refuses to assert them.
>
> ... [E]nforceable rights of attribution (in the form of statutorily protected metadata) can be useful, if not indispensable, tools in achieving the kind of accountability from the internet that, in other submissions, the RIAA seeks to establish.[39]

Accordingly, there was no opportunity under U.S. law for the Gaye family to consider bringing a unique or additional claim of moral rights violations against Thicke and his co-writers for *Blurred Lines*. From their letter, however, it appears that they were primarily concerned about moral rights—the attribution and integrity of their father's works. This leads to a number of interesting questions.

[37] Spanos, *supra* note 31, at concluding paragraph of the Gaye letter.

[38] The United States ratified the Treaty on September 14, 1999; the Treaty ultimately entered into force when it acquired the required minimum number of ratifications in 2002. *See* WPPT Notification No. 8 (Sept. 14, 1999), https://www.wipo.int/treaties/en/notifications/wppt/treaty_wppt_8.html. See also discussion in Chapter 3, *infra* notes 67, 84–85, and 119 and accompanying text.

[39] In the final paragraph, the group points to a paper by Maria Schneider, a "composer and conductor," submitted to the U.S. Copyright Office as part of this review process (on file with the author).

The subsequent case involving Led Zeppelin's song, *Stairway to Heaven* also deserves mention as an example of copyright litigation where moral rights may have offered an elegant solution.[40] This case was brought by Mr. Skidmore, a friend and collaborator of Randy Wolfe, who composed the original song, *Taurus*, who argued that *Taurus* had actually been copied by Led Zeppelin in their famous song, *Stairway to Heaven*. The suit was quite a poignant one, as Skidmore asked for "equitable relief for a claim that he titled 'Right of Attribution—Equitable Relief—Falsification of Rock n' Roll History.'" The case pitted competing experts on music against one another, and the claim ultimately failed. Seen from a moral rights perspective, however, the case probably never should have been brought as a claim of copyright infringement. The underlying issue seems to have been concerned about unfairness to Randy Wolfe, the composer of *Taurus*. But under U.S. copyright law, there is no way to recognize such a claim. As we know well, musicians do not have a moral right of attribution under the U.S. Copyright Act. This suggests, once again, wasteful and perhaps pointless litigation that is poorly adapted to the desires and objectives of the litigants.

First, if moral rights were available in a case like this, could copyright litigation be avoided? The advantage of doing so would be to avoid the development of convoluted rules on copyright law—to avoid the situation where a court needs to adjudicate the question of whether a work inspired by another has, in fact, "copied it" when the particular elements of copying are difficult to pinpoint, leading to concerns about the (improper) copyright protection of ideas. Instead, the court could determine whether a credit should have been given to an earlier original work that "inspired" the new creation. The standards applied to the two findings would be different, since the idea of "substantial copying," which is the foundation of copyright infringement, is not the issue in moral rights; rather, the "identifiability" of the work and, further, of its author, is what matters in a case where attribution (credit) is sought. This would allow us to avoid a finding of copying and copyright infringement in favor of a finding of failure to attribute the author of a work that was used in the creation of a new one.

Secondly, could litigation have been completely avoided? Had a discussion been opened between Thicke and the Gaye family, could they have requested a credit to Gaye, and would this have been enough for them to forego litigation altogether? Based on the public statements of Gaye's children, as quoted above, this was a real possibility.

[40] *Skidmore v. Zeppelin*, No. 16-56057 (9th Cir. 2020) (U.S.), https://law.justia.com/cases/federal/appellate-courts/ca9/16-56057/16-56057-2020-03-09.html. Leave to appeal to the Supreme Court was refused: *Michael Skidmore v. Led Zeppelin et al.*, Case No. 20-142 (S. Ct 2020) (U.S.). For an analysis, see, e.g., Eriq Gardner, *Supreme Court Won't Hear "Stairway to Heaven" Copyright Fight*, The Hollywood Reporter (Oct. 5, 2020), https://www.hollywoodreporter.com/business/business-news/supreme-court-wont-hear-stairway-to-heaven-copyright-fight-4071344.

Thirdly, would it have been possible to fashion more appropriate remedies for this complaint than a damages award? Notably, the Gaye family wanted to limit circulation of the new song until an agreement could be reached between the parties upon the terms of circulation.[41] This is reminiscent of a remedy that is more typical of moral rights than copyright infringement: injunction. In the Gaye case, any injunctive remedy imposed would have had to accommodate the necessary steps to ensure that copies of the work in circulation included the necessary attribution.[42]

All of this suggests that the absence of moral rights, even in the United States, is ultimately a strain on the copyright system.[43] Not only this, but the failure to recognize moral rights also fails the creative community in key respects by suppressing recognition of their contributions where it is clearly needed. The community itself has identified moral rights as valuable and even thinks of them as essential. There is strong evidence that at least one of the stakeholder communities in the music world—musicians—believes that moral rights need legal protection. As the *Blurred Lines* case shows, the inherently ephemeral nature of a musical work can make it difficult to arrive at the clear-cut solutions for disputes that copyright law requires. At the same time, the subtle interests involved—which may not be any less important, from the musician's point of view, because they are subtle—are captured by moral rights, which can help to clarify and reinforce the rights and interests of musicians in a new way. This argument holds especially true in the digital environment, where, without the protection of intangible interests like attribution

[41] Kory Grow, *Marvin Gaye's Family Seeks to Halt Sales of "Blurred Lines,"* ROLLING STONE (Mar. 15, 2015), https://www.rollingstone.com/music/music-news/marvin-gayes-family-seeks-to-halt-sales-of-blurred-lines-86000.

[42] It is helpful to think of the facts in the Monty Python case, *Gilliam v. ABC*, 538 F.2d 14 (2d Cir. 1976) (U.S.), where the desired remedy was the broadcast of the works in their unedited form and/or the withdrawal of the edited versions from circulation.

[43] Indeed, subsequent rulings in two cases, the *Stairway to Heaven* and *Dark Horse* musical copyright infringement complaints, suggest that U.S. courts are being careful about extending the type of findings in the *Blurred Lines* case too broadly. However, the *Stairway to Heaven* case is controversial for another reason: it relies on the principle that music copyright in older songs (pre-1976) will be protected only in the form of the musical score. In the United States, registration of copyright in a work continues to be required before a lawsuit can be filed, and this approach reflects the fact that, in the earlier era, the musical score was submitted to the Copyright Office for registration purposes (and it should be noted that, in this era, copyright protection in the United States was not automatic but, in contrast to the Berne approach, required registration). This is a regressive view of music copyright, which fails to recognize that music is not the same thing as a musical score. The true musical "work," though this is unfortunate from a copyright perspective, is the ephemeral music itself; it is not the written approximation of what is ephemeral, which is akin to the "instructions," or "recipe," for recreating the music that is provided in the score. The rejection of the "inverse ratio rule," which effectively allows for a lower standard of proof regarding infringement if the original music is popular and widely available, is also a questionable approach. Both cases receive useful and interesting treatment in Chris Cooke, *Ninth Circuit Upholds Led Zeppelin's Win in* Stairway To Heaven *Copyright Case*, CMU (Mar. 10, 2020), https://completemusicupdate.com/article/ninth-circuit-upholds-led-zeppelins-win-in-stairway-to-heaven-copyright-case, and *Judge Overturns* Dark Horse *Song-Theft Judgement*, CMU (Mar. 18, 2020), https://completemusicupdate.com/article/judge-overturns-dark-horse-song-theft-judgement. *See also* Chris Cooke, *U.S. Court Dismisses* You Raise Me Up *Song-Theft Case, Criticises Musicologist Report*, CMU (Apr. 7, 2020), https://completemusicupdate.com/article/us-court-dismisses-you-raise-me-up-song-theft-case-criticises-musicologist-report.

and integrity, it cannot be taken for granted that "our musical treasures will always be valued."[44]

E. The Impact of New Musical Technologies: Moral Rights in Creation, Production, and Dissemination

The current challenges facing music reflect the impact of technology on every aspect of the making and dissemination of recorded music. Each step in this technological evolution has moral rights implications, just as it has had implications for economic rights. This chapter systematically examines the moral rights aspect of new musical technologies by tracing the development of new techniques in the creation, production, and, of course, dissemination of musical works alongside the discussion of moral rights.

1. Creation or Production? Technologies for the Creation of Musical Works

a. Sampling

Paradoxically, new technologies transform our relationship with the past. One of the joys of musical creation through technology is the opportunity to explore pre-existing musical performances. Recorded music has allowed access to the music of the past throughout the twentieth century, but the digital scenario is different. Recorded works can now be used in the creation of new works—not through inspiration or idea alone, but directly, through the actual use of previously recorded music in the creation of new works.[45]

The champion of this new creative act is the DJ, or "disc jockey." When it was coined in the early twentieth century, the term initially meant a person who organized a radio program that featured recorded music and commentary. David Michael points out that the key is "playing recorded music to an audience," as opposed to broadcasting live music.[46] John Peel, a British DJ famous for his pioneering

[44] Spano, *supra* note 31.

[45] The ability to sample, or reuse, old recordings in new works has widespread implications. For example, in the context of a movie soundtrack, Kim Novak observed that the director of 2012 film *The Artist* had used the actual soundtrack from Hitchcock's 1958 film *Vertigo*, in which she starred. The music was one of the scores composed by the famous film composer and musical partner in many of Alfred Hitchcock's films, Bernard Herrmann. *See Artist Director Responds to Kim Novak Vertigo Claim*, BBC NEWS (Jan. 10, 2012), https://www.bbc.com/news/entertainment-arts-16482624 (where both Novak's claim and the response by the director of *The Artist* are discussed).

[46] David Michael, *DJing: A (Very) Brief Lesson in Early History*, PASSIONATE DJ.COM (Mar. 15, 2013), https://passionatedj.com/djing-a-very-brief-lesson-in-early-history. Another term is "turntablism"—the subject of an episode of a Public Broadcasting Service (PBS) program, *The Art of Turntablism*, HISTORY DETECTIVES: SPECIAL INVESTIGATIONS (n.d.), https://www.pbs.org/opb/historydetectives/feature/the-art-of-turntablism.

work at the BBC, championed new popular music and helped to create careers for little-known bands that he found interesting.[47] Over the past half-century, the art of the DJ has expanded considerably, and it now includes "performance" and "composition" based on the use of segments from recorded music and synthesized sound. The use of these "samples" can lead to a distinctive new style, and many DJs have become celebrity musicians through their work. Sampling gave birth to a new genre of music, hip-hop, which is extensively derived from the practice.[48]

A number of interesting cases have arisen in both the United States and Europe on the use of music samples. They are all cases about economic rights, in Europe as well the United States, examining the question of whether sampling infringes copyright.[49] Arguments that it would not infringe copyright have been based on the size of the sample and the possibility that using a sample might amount to a fair use or, the corresponding principle under German law, "free use."

The answer in both jurisdictions was restrictive. Two principles emerged. The first was that the small size of a sample will not offer protection from a finding of infringement. In the United States, this principle was established in the *Bridgeport* case, which saw the U.S. Court of Appeals for the Sixth Circuit deciding that a mere three notes was enough to constitute the taking of a substantial part of a musical work, leading to a finding of copyright infringement.[50] However, it has subsequently been rejected by the U.S. Ninth Circuit in *Salsoul*.[51] In Europe, it was settled in the twenty-two-year litigation over *Kraftwerk*.[52] According to the

[47] *Legendary Radio DJ John Peel Dies*, BBC NEWS (Oct. 26, 2004), http://news.bbc.co.uk/2/hi/entertainment/3955289.stm.

[48] For a fascinating quick summary of some key points in hip-hop's development, see *The Art of Tunrtablism*, *supra* note 46. This phenomenon is multicultural. Ian Condry explores the world of Japanese hip-hop, considering, among other things, the fascinating question of how a U.S. cultural export like hip-hop can adapt to a new cultural environment: IAN CONDRY, HIP-HOP JAPAN: RAP AND THE PATHS OF CULTURAL GLOBALIZATION (2006). He remarks, "For some, the presence of hip-hop implies a 'loss of Japanese culture.' But what if hip-hop is used to express one's Japaneseness?" No discussion of sampling could be complete without a reference to Herbie Hancock's *Rockit*— a hip-hop tour de force made by one of the most celebrated jazz musicians in history. *See* Nate Chinen, *Two Turntables and a Keytar: The Night Herbie Hancock Rocked the Grammys*, NEW YORK TIMES (Feb. 8, 2016), https://www.nytimes.com/2016/02/09/arts/music/grammys-herbie-hancock-rockit.html.

[49] *MG Salsoul v. Ciccone* 824 F.3d 871 (9th Cir. 2016) (U.S.) ("we find Bridgeport's reasoning unpersuasive"). See the interesting discussion of the two decisions in Daniel Esannason, *Note, Get a License or Don't Sample: Using Examples from Popular Music to Raise New Questions About the* Bridgeport v. Dimension Films Holding, 29 HARV. J.L. & TECH. 551, 557–58 (2016). Although moral rights are protected in the member states of the European Union, they are not harmonized at the EU level, which has probably been a factor in music copyright lawsuits.

[50] *See Bridgeport*, *supra* note 51. It depends which three notes: for example, Rachmaninoff's famous first prelude for piano (*Opus 3, No. 2*, in C-sharp minor) is instantly recognizable by its first three notes. See also *Frisby v. BBC* [1967] Ch. 932 (UK), in which the deletion of a single line from a radio play was considered an effective violation of the dramatist's copyright and significant enough that the change required express contractual permission. As in the U.S. example, the UK court had to have recourse to copyright infringement doctrines in the absence of statutory protections for moral rights. If the case were to be considered today, it could be approached as a question of the violation of the author's moral right of integrity.

[51] *Bridgeport Music, Inc. v. Dimension Films*, 410 F.3d 792 (6th Cir. 2005) (U.S.).

[52] The *Kraftwerk* "saga" is helpfully summarized in an excellent note by Susan Bischoff, *The Next Chapter in the "Metall auf Metall" Saga: Pastiche to be Clarified by the CJEU*, KLUWER COPYRIGHT BLOG

European ruling, even a minimal use of a work for sampling purposes will trigger an infringement of copyright law.

While this finding has been criticized as imposing "chilling effects" on freedom of creativity, it also seems reasonable to conclude that a small part of a work might still be significant. For example, in the British case of *Frisby v. BBC*,[53] the removal of a single line from the broadcast of a radio play was considered to violate the author's right to prevent "structural" changes to his work—though the matter was decided under the contractual provision to this effect, since the United Kingdom did not yet recognize an author's moral right of integrity in its copyright law.[54]

This principle may also be partly explained by the second principle: the use of a sample may potentially be justified as a fair use. Though restrictive in its own way, this is a more nuanced idea that can help to explain the logic by which the first, more controversial conclusion is reached. In *Kraftwerk*, the Court of Justice of the European Union (CJEU) relied on the concept of "freedom of the arts" in order to determine when a sample could be used. If a sample is taken from a pre-existing work and refashioned into a form where it is no longer recognizable, then the use of that sample is justified, notwithstanding copyright law, on the grounds of "freedom of the arts," which is interpreted by the Court as the freedom to create something new from a pre-existing work. The sample must be "embodied" in the new recording "in a modified form unrecognisable to the ear;" as such, it would not constitute a reproduction of the original work within the meaning of copyright law and would therefore not infringe copyright.[55]

"Freedom of the arts" is a concept enshrined in the Charter of Fundamental Rights of the European Union.[56] In *Kraftwerk*, it plays a crucial role by allowing the CJEU to balance the copyright of the record producer against the right of a new musician to create works based on the existing work; the "public interest" is

(Sept. 21, 2023), https://copyrightblog.kluweriplaw.com/2023/09/21/the-next-chapter-in-the-metall-auf-metall-saga-pastiche-to-be-clarified-by-the-cjeu/. *See also Kraftwerk Wins 20-Year Sampling Case over Metal on Metal,* BBC News (July 30, 2019), https://www.bbc.com/news/entertainment-arts-49162546; Court of Justice of the European Union (CJEU), *Sampling without Authorisation Can Infringe a Phonogram Producer's Rights* (Press Release No. 98/19, July 29, 2019), https://curia.europa.eu/jcms/upload/docs/application/pdf/2019-07/cp190098en.pdf. The original judgment is Case C-476/17, *Pelham GmbH and Others v. Ralf Hütter and Florian Schneider-Esleben*, ECLI:EU:C:2019:624 (July 29, 2019), https://curia.europa.eu/juris/document/document.jsf?text=&docid=216552&pageIndex=0&doclang=en&mode=req&dir=&occ=first&part=1&cid=683291.

[53] *Frisby, supra* note 51.

[54] The case is typically said to stand for the protection of the moral right of integrity under UK law through contractual (i.e., alternative) means: id.

[55] CJEU, *supra* note 50. For the judgment, see, e.g., id. at para. 31, discussion at paras. 31–37, and—with a shift to restating the producer's rights in these terms—paras. 38–39.

[56] Article 13 of the Charter of Fundamental Rights of the European Union, 2012 O.J. (C 326) 391, https://eur-lex.europa.eu/legal-content/EN/TXT/PDF/?uri=CELEX:12012P/TXT, is entitled "Freedom of the arts and sciences," and states, "The arts and scientific research shall be free of constraint. Academic freedom shall be respected."

also invoked.[57] But the Court takes the very conventional approach of treating "freedom of the arts" or "creative freedom" primarily as a *digital creator's* right. The term is almost never discussed in relation to the freedom of artists to create their work in the first place, although there is a need to continue to recognize this aspect of creative freedom, as well, in the technological environment. It is one of the ways in which, for example, the creativity of artists can be affirmed against oppressive governments or unwanted commercialization.[58] It is also a way of recognizing the dangers to artists who may, because of unusual or revolutionary ideas, be maligned by some parts of the public, even to the extent that they might eventually be deterred from producing work at all.[59] In circumstances like these, artist and public are both affected: the overall effect is to dampen creativity.

In *Kraftwerk*, ironically, "freedom of the arts" is a broad term that is ultimately used by the Court in a narrow and restrictive sense to *limit* the creative freedom of a digital creator. Because the sample involved in the case is so small, it is questionable whether this discussion helps to bring greater clarity to the concept of artistic freedom as embodied in the *original* work. Instead, the digital creator's "freedom of art" is affirmed but still limited when weighed against Kraftwerk's rights in a two-second sample.[60]

In the United States, there is no constitutional provision on copyright beyond the famous clause empowering Congress to legislate on intellectual property.[61] The balancing approach is therefore accommodated exclusively through the idea of copyright fair use—notably, in this case, the specific idea of "transformative use," where an existing work is used to make an original new work, exempting that use from a finding of copyright infringement.[62]

[57] CJEU, *supra* note 50, at paras. 5 and 32; the public interest aspect is derived from Recital 3 of the Directive 2001/29/EC of the European Parliament and of the Council of 22 May 2001 on the harmonization of certain aspects of copyright and related rights in the information society, 2001 O.J. (L 167) 10 (InfoSoc Directive).

[58] The example of anti-Soviet artists and the development of the idea of "freedom of creativity" in this context are discussed in my earlier work, MIRA T. SUNDARA RAJAN, COPYRIGHT AND CREATIVE FREEDOM: A STUDY OF POST-SOCIALIST LAW REFORM (2006).

[59] This was the case of South Indian writer Perumal Murugan, whose first novel about a controversial Indian social practice caused such an outcry that he was compelled to declare, "Perumal Murugan the writer is dead. Leave him alone." *See* Parul Sehgal, *One of India's Most Original and Controversial Novelists Returns with a Powerful Parable*, NEW YORK TIMES (Dec. 11, 2019), https://www.nytimes.com/2019/12/11/books/review-story-of-goat-perumal-murugan.html.

[60] See the helpful discussion in *German Federal Supreme Court Decides in Spectacular Music Sampling Case – for the Fourth (and Last?) Time*, Bird & Bird (May 1, 2020), https://mediawrites.twobirds.com/post/102j3jn/german-federal-supreme-court-decides-in-spectacular-music-sampling-case-for-the.

[61] *See* U.S. Const. art. 1, § 8, cl. 8, https://www.law.cornell.edu/constitution/articlei#section8. See also the helpful overview in Cornell Law School, *Intellectual Property Clause* (n.d.), https://www.law.cornell.edu/wex/intellectual_property_clause.

[62] The idea of "transformative use" was instrumental in the finding that Google Books was "fair use." Google's creation of an online library out of the scanned books in its collection was considered "transformative" because it created a valuable new resource for the public. *See* Pierre N. Leval, *Toward a Fair Use Standard*, 103(5) HARV. LAW REV. 1105 (1990), https://doi.org/10.2307/1341457.

It should be noted that sampling involves a degree of schizophrenia for the U.S. music lobby. While the RIAA has generally been unrelenting in its quest for higher levels of copyright protection, sampling presents a quandary. Excessive restrictions could limit the expansion of a lucrative genre, and the RIAA has accordingly resisted the temptation to condemn sampling outright. Among other issues with sampling is the fact that restrictions may favor established musicians who can afford to pay for the use of samples over newcomers. In this sense, could the excessive restriction of sampling ultimately make it an art of the establishment—a rich sampler's art that, over time, might lose its voice of creative rebellion?

Sampling raises a number of moral rights issues alongside these concerns. As yet, there is little case law on moral rights in music sampling. As Elizabeth Adeney points out, the relatively later adoption of moral rights in many jurisdictions is one reason why case law remains limited[63]—others being the unfamiliarity of moral rights claims and, more generally, questions about the availability of financial remedies for moral rights violations.[64] But moral rights are important for two reasons. First, they provide an additional layer of rights by which musical artists may secure what they see as more appropriate and satisfactory remedies for their concerns. Secondly, they provide new options for litigation—for framing complaints and for fashioning remedies that may, once again, lead to greater fairness in the outcomes. Moral rights may promote sustainability in emerging creative genres. They may also lead to a quieting of controversy. As Adeney points out, much of the organized opposition to copyright does not oppose moral rights principles and, indeed, often endorses them in practice.[65] The restoration of a degree of reasonableness to discussions about copyright would be a contribution in its own right to an overly polarized environment that is detrimental to good law and policy.

Sampling from pre-existing recordings involves both the moral rights of attribution and integrity of the creators of the works that are sampled. Attribution would serve musicians in this field, because it would effectively support the reputation of the original artist and allow his or her work to continue to live by circulating it to the public in a new form. This is something that intuitively seems like a very good thing for most artists. Their music, rather than being available only in the "museum" of music recordings, would also be currently available. Without attribution, though, this positive development of a musical tradition through sampling

[63] Adeney points out that Australia adopted its provisions only in 2000, making moral rights "an emerging area of jurisprudence": Elizabeth Adeney, *The Sampling and Remix Dilemma: What Is the Role of Moral Rights in the Encouragement and Regulation of Derivative Creativity?*, 17(2) Deakin L. Rev. 338 (2012).

[64] Discussed in Chapter 1, *supra* note 16 and accompanying text, and at notes 167–71 and accompanying text.

[65] Adeney, *supra* note 61, at 341–46. This point is also discussed in depth, and specifically in reference to the Creative Commons and Open Source movements, in Chapter 10, *infra*. *See also* Mira T. Sundara Rajan, *Creative Commons: America's Moral Rights?*, 21 Fordham Intell. Prop. Media & Ent. L.J. 905 (2011), https://ir.lawnet.fordham.edu/iplj/vol21/iss4/3.

would not occur in the same way. Without proper attribution, music from the past would be appropriated by current composers. The unfairness of this seems clear. The problem is not just a moral one: it also has economic dimensions. An artist whose work is sampled could stand to make earnings as well as further reputation. In this sense, the moral right of attribution could potentially work with economic rights to lay the foundation for fairness, in terms of both recognition and payment.

Attribution could also pre-empt actions for copyright infringement rights claim. This last point might represent an innovation in the traditional treatment of moral rights, where injunctive remedies have been preferred to damages, but this seems like a desirable innovation: recognition can be given to the situation of unjust enrichment out of another person's creation. Importantly, if financial compensation is allowed as part of an attribution claim, the additional need to prove copyright infringement can be avoided, and with it the development of awkward rules on copying in the digital environment.

How should works be credited in the online environment? Doing so in the body of the new song may not be possible, but the attribution could be provided on liner notes. This raises a separate issue—the fact that many songs are now heard by online streaming or purchased with online music services such as Apple's iTunes or Amazon.com. In this case, they may be broadcast or sold without announcements or liner notes, and attribution cannot occur in the moment. This problem could be addressed through the provision of links with full attribution, information that would be circulated and could become easily known online.

Another issue in this environment has proven to be the problem of incomplete attribution. For example, a jazz recording available on Apple's iTunes service might credit the featured artist but not the supporting players in a trio; a classical recording might identify the orchestra but not the soloist. Amplifying this limited attribution is important—not only to recognize the performers of the past, but also to give due credit to new or obscure groups whose music could become popular through sampling. Sampling could bring publicity to music that might not have a chance to become popular unless the work is championed by a famous name. The long-term benefits could be celebrity and success in terms of both reputation and money. In spite of the relatively "new" nature of these musical genres, they remain traditional in their reliance on reputation; the emphasis on reputation has, if anything, increased in the digital environment as it becomes necessary to find new and often indirect means of translating reputation into earnings. It is the bedrock of modern musical stardom.

Finally, sampling could involve the moral right of integrity as well. Is the use of a sample from an original work an inherent violation of the right of integrity because it shows only a portion of the work that may not be representative? An unexpected example of sampling like this might be the use of musical extracts in advertising a work. For example, a music website might offer previews of each work recorded as small excerpts from each recording. The excerpts may or may not make sense in terms of showcasing the ability of the artist or, indeed, give an overall sense of the qualities of the recording—all the more so if the excerpts are automatically selected by an algorithm.[66] If the work were large—an orchestral work or a suite of related pieces by a classical composer, for example—the possibility of misrepresenting it by presenting brief extracts might be even greater.

Could sampling violate the artist's right of integrity by presenting the extract in a new musical context? Or would it simply amount to a new perspective on the work—a new window through which to view it? In a sense, the latter is the most basic definition of creative listening.

The answer to both questions must be "It depends": it will depend on the specific context of the sampling. As is usual in copyright law, the making of a difficult artistic determination will be left in the hands of the courts or, at the very least, to those who the courts decide are the "experts."

b. Mixing

Remixing the sample changes it. It seems clear that changes to the work could affect the original artist's right of integrity and may cause damage to the artist's reputation.

Would the recognition of an integrity right in relation to remixing be feasible in this musical genre? It would certainly impose a duty of care when using samples—care for the work of the original author. The real difficulty lies in the subjectivity of the integrity principle in these circumstances. If, as in the French tradition, the objections of the author were sufficient to find that integrity had been violated, this would undoubtedly "chill" the activity: any remixing could only be done with the blessing and effective collaboration of the original author, and the person making the remixed version would be accordingly constrained. But would this be a serious or unfair obstacle to musical creativity? Even in France, the idea of "balance" has found its way into the integrity principle—what the CJEU in *Kraftwerk* calls balancing the "freedom of the arts" of a digital creator against the prerogatives of an author. With this in mind, a more "objective" standard of integrity could be applied to remixing, requiring proof of damage to reputation before an integrity violation could be found. A "balanced" approach is arguably better than either excluding integrity or giving absolute priority to the author of the original work: sampling could be encouraged, and digital creativity given fair play, while the reputation of the original author and his or her work would be protected from harm. In relation to sampling, the Berne standard makes sense.

A cross-cultural dimension to the problem also exists, and here, remixing can become controversial. A DJ takes a vocal sample from Indigenous artists and

[66] On the other hand, in theory, if an algorithm were programmed to be so sophisticated that it could identify sections of the recording that were well suited to a preview, it might select extracts more effectively than a human listener.

creates an electronic music composition out of it. If the composition eventually becomes popular, or lucrative, what is the situation of the Indigenous group?[67] The implications raise questions about moral rights, as well as economic interests, in the form of questions about fair remuneration.[68] In terms of moral rights, all of the classical moral rights of disclosure, attribution, integrity, and withdrawal are implicated in this scenario.

As noted by the Australia Council for the Arts,

> While works by individual artists ... are protected by copyright, there are often no legal rights around the broader reproduction and use of Indigenous cultural heritage material. Australia does not yet have a law that prevents alteration, distortion or misuse of traditional symbols, songs, dances, performances or rituals that may be part of the heritage of particular Indigenous language groups.[69]

Given the popularity of remixing, respect for the context in which a musical work, or an extract from it, is placed may be an important new moral interest in the Digital Age. At least one traditional jurisdiction, Germany, provides that a change of context may amount to a violation of the moral right of the author; as Stefan Michel comments, "Scholarly literature and the judiciary agree that even an unaltered performance may constitute a derogatory treatment if it occurs in a prejudicial context that is capable of jeopardizing the honor and reputation of the artist."[70]

[67] For a fascinating example from a context that is much less discussed, see the discussion of the collaboration between Indigenous music and Western *classical* music in Eileen Cunniffe, *In Harmony: Lakota Music Project Models Cross-Cultural Collaboration* (Sept. 12, 2019), https://nonprofitquarterly.org/in-harmony-lakota-music-project-models-cross-cultural-collaboration.

[68] *See* AUSTRALIA COUNCIL FOR THE ARTS, PROTOCOLS FOR PRODUCING INDIGENOUS MUSIC (2d ed., 2007), https://creative.gov.au/wp-content/uploads/2021/07/music.pdf. The document discusses moral rights extensively, considering how these can be used to protect Indigenous music, but it also notes that, "The potential for moral rights to increase copyright protection for Indigenous musicians has not been fully explored." In the Council's view, the tradition of moral rights as individual rights is an obstacle to their use for Indigenous communities (id. at 27), and it considers the proposed Australian "Indigenous communal moral rights" provisions of 2003 as offering potential solutions. The 2003 proposals are discussed in Chapter 4, *supra* notes 197, 200–201. While they were exciting in the sense that they represented a new way of approaching moral rights that could help Indigenous peoples, they remained problematic in terms of their fit with Indigenous culture and modern Indigenous realities. Future proposals are sure to be more nuanced.

[69] Australia Council for the Arts, *supra* note 66.

[70] *See* Stefan Michel, *You Can't Always Get What You Want? A Comparative Analysis of the Legal Means to Oppose the Use of Campaign Music*, 18 J. MARSHALL REV. INTELL. PROP. L. 169, 190 (2018). Michel draws a contrast between the German position and the more restrictive position in, notably, UK law, which, he suggests, does not allow integrity claims based on context because of its reliance on the idea of derogatory "treatment"—a contrast to Art. 6*bis* of the Berne Convention, which also seeks to restrain "other derogatory action in relation to the work, which would be prejudicial to his honor or reputation": id. at 186. For the full text of Article 6*bis* of the Berne Convention, see International Convention for the Protection of Literary and Artistic Works, adopted at Berne on Sept. 9, 1886, completed at Paris on May 4, 1896, revised at Berlin on Nov. 13, 1908, completed at Berne on Mar. 20, 1914, revised at Rome on June 2, 1928, at Brussels on June 26, 1948, at Stockholm on July 14, 1967, and at Paris on July 24, 1971, and amended on Sept. 28, 1979, S. Treaty Doc. No. 99-27 (1986), https://www.wipo.int/treaties/en/ip/berne.

The issue of changing musical context can be compared to the requirement for the visual artists, that an artistic work should be displayed in appropriate conditions. This right is recognized as part of the moral right of integrity in France and Australia, but it is explicitly rejected in other jurisdictions, such as Canada and India.[71]

In the United States, the use of music in political campaigns is an interesting example of a situation where a musician might wish to assert a moral right of integrity, not because of direct mistreatment of the music, but because of the context in which that music is heard.[72] The problem is essentially one of false endorsement. While moral rights in music are not protected in the United States, the issue has become controversial enough that the primary U.S. music rights society, the American Society of Composers, Authors and Publishers (ASCAP), has created

[71] *See* Copyright Act, R.S.C. 1985, c. C-42, s. 28.2(3)(a) (Can.), https://laws-lois.justice.gc.ca/eng/acts/c-42 ("a change in the location of a work, the physical means by which a work is exposed or the physical structure containing a work" will not violate the artist's right of integrity); Copyright Act, No. 14 of 1957, "Explanation" to s. 57(1)(b) (India), http://copyright.gov.in/Documents/CopyrightRules1957.pdf ("Failure to display a work or to display it to the satisfaction of the author shall not be deemed to be an infringement of the rights conferred by this section"); and *Copyright Act 1968* (Cth) s. 195AK(b) (Austl.) (which provides that the integrity right can be invoked in the case of "an exhibition in public of the work that is prejudicial to the author's honour or reputation because of the manner or place in which the exhibition occurs"). In France, the issue is not addressed explicitly in the Loi 92-597 du 1 juillet 1992 relative au Code de la propriété intellectuelle (partie législative) [Law 92-597 of July 1, 1992, relating to the Intellectual Property Code (Legislative part)], Journal officiel de la République française [J.O.] [Official Gazette of France], Feb. 8, 1994 (Code de la propriété intellectuelle) (Fr.), https://www.legifrance.gouv.fr/codes/texte_lc/LEGITEXT000006069414. However, the case of the refrigerator panels painted by Bernard Buffet, later separated and sold without the artist's knowledge, confirmed that the "dismantling" of an artwork into its component parts would violate the right of integrity: *see*)Code de la propriété intellectuelle commenté 101 (para. 43) (Pierre Sirinelli, Sylviane Durrande, Antoine Latreille & Jeanne Daleau eds., 2009). *See also* John Henry Merryman, *The Refrigerator of Bernard Buffet*, 27 Hastings L.J. 1023 (1976).

[72] A similar issue, in a deeply disturbing context, is the use of music during U.S. government torture operations. For a thought- and outrage-provoking overview, see Anna J. Mitran, *Facing the Music: Moral Intellectual Property Rights as a Solution to Artist Outrage about Music Torture*, 101 Cornell L. Rev. 505, http://scholarship.law.cornell.edu/clr/vol101/iss2/5. Mitran notes, "Although artists may be outraged, there is unfortunately very little that they can do to prevent Guantánamo Bay from using their music under the United States' current intellectual property system": id. at 511 (footnotes omitted). In particular, Mitran is doubtful about the ability to opt out of such uses under the blanket licenses that are typically issued by collecting societies:

> [M]ost copyright-owning musical artists in the United States have blanket licensing agreements with the American Society of Composers, Authors and Publishers (ASCAP); Broadcast Music, Inc. (BMI); or the Society of European Stage Authors and Composers (SESAC). Artists transfer their copyright or public performance right to these blanket-licensing organizations, and the organizations provide consumers access to their vast catalogues of music in exchange for a fee, out of which the organizations compensate the artists. These organizations must license public performance rights for their members' work to anyone willing to pay the rates. As such, artists that take advantage of these organizations' services could not choose to deny public performance rights for use in Guantanamo Bay if the United States were willing to pay the licensing fee. Of course, artists could choose not to register their works with ASCAP, BMI, or SESAC, but these organizations are nearly ubiquitous in the music industry, and failure to register would vastly, perhaps prohibitively, increase artists' transaction costs.

Mitran also notes the similarities between this and the issue of music use in political campaigning: id. at 529.

guidelines advising politicians that the unauthorized use of music may violate copyright law.[73] They make the interesting point that, even if the campaign has an ASCAP license, which would ordinarily allow the licensee to use any of the works in the catalogue, "ASCAP members may ask ASCAP to exclude specific songs from a particular political campaign's license. In that event, ASCAP will notify the campaign of the excluded works."[74] ASCAP also goes on to point out that "other" rights may be violated, including the artist's right of publicity, the Lanham Act, or the right against false endorsement—all traditional stand-ins for moral rights under U.S. law, though, in the wake of recent case law, their continued relevance is not certain.[75]

Interestingly, Germany has a long tradition of cases finding that the use of music in a political context can violate the performer's moral right of integrity.[76] As Stefan Michel points out,

> Scholarly literature and the judiciary agree that even an unaltered performance may constitute a derogatory treatment if it occurs in a prejudicial context that is capable of jeopardizing the honor and reputation of the artist.... Because the decontextualization of an otherwise unaltered work constitutes a derogatory treatment, German law enables artists to assert an integrity right claim [footnotes omitted].[77]

Cross-cultural issues in music mixing are not limited to Indigenous music. For example, classical Indian music is often used in Western popular music remixes. From the perspective of Indian culture, this could be considered an inclusive step (remembering Ravi Shankar and the Beatles) or a complete misrepresentation of an art form that is thousands of years of old and steeped in a devotional tradition that has no real parallels in the West. For Indian *rasikas*, as classical music aficionados are called,[78] the association between the Indian saint-composers and the

[73] ASCAP, *Using Music in Political Campaigns: What You Should Know* (n.d.), https://www.ascap.com/~/media/files/pdf/advocacy-legislation/political_campaign.pdf. For a quick and useful overview of U.S. music rights societies, including their histories, see Julie Pajuheshfar, *An In-Depth Look at Performing Rights Organizations in the US*, TUNE REGISTRY (Nov. 9, 2018), https://www.tuneregistry.com/blog/an-in-depth-look-at-performing-rights-organizations-in-the-us.

[74] ASCAP, *supra* note 74. As Mitran, *supra* note 71, at 528 (footnotes omitted) concludes: "Whether an artist uses the attribution, integrity, or withdrawal right to frame her claim, though, she is likely to succeed because the unauthorized use of one's music for torture purposes is an affront to the personality theories upon which the moral rights system is built." This conclusion may partly result from the incomplete discussion of the *Shostakovich* litigation in the article: it does not mention the reasoning behind a French court's decision to grant relief to the composers although the Soviet government asserted moral rights on their behalf.

[75] *See* ASCAP, *supra* note 74. It should be noted, though, that the *Dastar* case has brought into question the continued usefulness of the Lanham Act as a proxy for moral rights: *see* the discussion in Chapter 4, *infra* notes 121–46 and accompanying text.

[76] For an excellent overview of German case law on this issue, see Michel, *supra* note 68, at 187–93.

[77] Id. at 190, 193.

[78] The term *rasikas* is used by Indians to denote the audience; it specifically means those who enjoy the music. It is derived from the word *rasa*, identified by India's national poet as the "key-word of Indian

music is so powerful that even when songs are heard in purely instrumental performances, the devotional mood of the underlying poem, known by the Sanskrit word *bhakti*, is invoked. Is it justified to mingle the composition of an Indian saint-composer such as Tyagaraja with modern pop culture? If not, would it be possible, or even desirable, to invoke moral rights to protect music that is hundreds of years old?

An issue that presents some interesting parallels actually arose in Italy—not in relation to the ephemeral art of music, but in relation to a sculpture that is several centuries old and considered to be a treasure of Italian cultural heritage. The question involved an ad for a gun by a U.S. company. In the advertising image, the gun was placed in the arms of Michelangelo's David, a work of art that dates from the early 1500s.[79] Since Italian copyright law allows for the protection of moral rights in perpetuity, a valid legal claim could in theory have been made.[80] Italian law allows for the Ministry of Culture to take action on behalf of the public interest, avoiding the difficult problem of who should assert moral rights in old works on behalf of their authors.[81] In the digital environment, images of artworks have also taken on a new significance, sometimes even supplanting the original work in terms of reach and power. Altering an image of the work, in this context, arguably amounts to an alteration of the work itself. The case could also have been made that the image represented an objectionable change of context in which the work was

culture": THE COMING AGE: C. SUBRAMANIA BHARATI'S COLLECTED ENGLISH WRITINGS 87 (Mira T. Sundara Rajan ed., 2021). The history of this aesthetic and philosophical concept receives a beautiful treatment in Pandit, *supra* note 1.

[79] An image of the ad is available at Alberto Bellan, *Exclusive Rights in Classical Art Works: The "Armed David" Case*, THE IPKAT (Mar. 11, 2014), http://ipkitten.blogspot.com/2014/03/exclusive-rights-in-classical-art-works.html.

[80] Bellan, id., provides much interesting detail on the background to the case—and an update on its resolution: the image was ultimately withdrawn by the company, with apologies. However, Bellan concludes that moral rights could not be claimed in a case such as this without explaining why not. His argument seems to hinge on proving a violation of the public interest ("Does the public interest so require?"), but the issue is not discussed in the blog. The interesting treatment in another blog, ART AND ARTIFICE, emphasizes the issue of "ownership" of the statue, which is actually irrelevant to moral rights: *ArmaLite in Italy's Sights over Gun-Toting David Ad*, ART AND ARTIFICE BLOG (Mar. 11, 2014), http://aandalawblog.blogspot.com/2014/03/armalite-in-italys-sights-over-gun.html. A further case involving the David and the Italian government's attempt to restrict the use of the image receives thought-provoking commentary from Roberto Caso in a third blog: Roberto Caso, *Michelangelo's David and Cultural Heritage Images. The Italian Pseudo-Intellectual Property and the End of Public Domain*, KLUWER COPYRIGHT BLOG (June 15, 2023), https://copyrightblog.kluweriplaw.com/2023/06/15/michelangelos-david-and-cultural-heritage-images-the-italian-pseudo-intellectual-property-and-the-end-of-public-domain.

[81] *See* art. 23 of the Italian Copyright Law, Legge 22 aprile 1941, n. 633, G.U. July 16, 1941, n.166 (It.), http://www.interlex.it/testi/l41_633.htm, which states, "If the public interest should so require, such action may also be taken by the President of the Council of the Ministers after hearing the competent professional association." An unofficial English translation of the Law is available on the WIPO website, https://www.wipo.int/edocs/lexdocs/laws/en/it/it211en.pdf. See the related discussion in Caso, *supra* note 78.

viewed—a relatively novel argument from a moral rights perspective, but one that has gained acceptance in some jurisdictions.[82]

Issues such as these stretch the imagination of the intellectual property community. Yet, the question should be asked: why do copyright laws contain provisions for the protection of moral rights "in perpetuity" if countries do not intend to recognize these rights?

In relation to the example of Indian music, as noted above, it was actually Ravi Shankar, a Hindustani classical artist, who pioneered the popularization of Indian classical music in the West by his work with the Beatles. It is an interesting epilogue to Shankar's career that his two daughters have become leading musicians: Anoushka Shankar, a sitar player, and Norah Jones, a popular singer-songwriter.

c. Production

As these examples show,[83] sound recording is an activity of fundamental importance in the digital era. With digital technology, the role of the sound engineer has expanded dramatically. Sound engineers have always played an essential role in the quality of a recording, but the means and methods behind sound recording have grown. If art can be defined as the creative exercise of choice, artistry in sound engineering may now be possible as never before.

The transformation of the recorded music industry supports the emergence of an artist-engineer in a curious way. In the heyday of recording, teams of engineers worked as employees of a recording label, and the label would have its own "sound"—Decca or Deutsche Gramophon in the world of classical music, for example. As the recorded music industry has contracted, it is now common for sound engineers to work as individuals freelancers. The characteristic sound of a given label may have vanished; but the sound of the individual engineer has a place in this new landscape.[84]

Paul Greene's definition seems apt: sound engineering is "the technological empowerment to engineer music, culture, soundscapes, and lifeways."[85] The work of

[82] See the discussion of this issue in Chapter 8, *infra.*

[83] This section makes use of the terms "production," "sound engineering," "audio engineering," and "making a recording" interchangeably. In relation to recording, the English language is somewhat lacking in precision; in contrast, consider the German term *Tonmeister*, as opposed to *Tontechniker* and *Toninegenieur*, which specifically distinguishes the creative side of sound engineering from its hardware aspects. *See, e.g.,* Martha de Francisco, *Meeting the Challenge of Producing Classical Music for Global Audiences in the Digital Era*, 14(4) JIPLP Symposium on Moral Rights 327 (2019), https://doi.org/10.1093/jiplp/jpz009. *See also* Industry Canada, Intellectual Property Policy—Assessing the Economic Impacts of Copyright Reform on Performers and Producers of Sound Recordings in Canada (2003), https://publications.gc.ca/collections/collection_2021/isde-ised/C23-117-2003-eng.pdf.

[84] I am indebted to sound engineers Martha de Francisco and Steve Epstein for illuminating the world of sound engineering for me and sharing their vast knowledge of the recorded music industry.

[85] *See* Paul D. Greene, *Engineering Spaces in Nepal's Digital Stereo Remix Culture*, Paper delivered at the panel, "Sound Engineering as Cultural Production," Society for Ethnomusicology meeting (Austin, TX) (Nov. 19, 1999). Greene's website, dedicated to panel research on Sound Engineering as Cultural

a sound engineer involves myriad creative features, from the choice of equipment and the placement of microphones to the mixing of sound to create a suitable environment for the music being recorded.[86]

The emerging concept of "virtual recording" is interesting in a classical music culture obsessed with "authenticity." In classical music, history plays an important part in establishing authenticity, and this preoccupation probably explains the modern interest in rebuilding instruments from historical periods to be used for performing the works of the composers of the times. Virtual recording seems to turn this ideal on its head by focusing on the re-creation of a sound that theoretically exists (or existed) somewhere in space and time. It is reminiscent of Glenn Gould's idea of "creative cheating" in his quest for musical perfection.[87]

If the awareness of sound recording as an art form lags behind, at least the skill involved in recording has been recognized for some time in copyright law. The special right in a sound recording exists independently of the matter recorded; it is an additional layer of rights beyond the rights of the composer and performer of the music.[88] In most jurisdictions, the sound recording right is available for a period of fifty to seventy years after the making of the recording.[89] The right can be classified as a "neighboring" right, and it effectively recognizes a contribution made in creating a work that is derived from the original work of a higher-level creator—the composer or the performer, or both.

Sound production often happens in a corporate environment. Accordingly, companies acquire copyright in sound recordings through the operation of the work-for-hire rule, which makes an employer the first owner of copyright in a work

Production, is an extremely useful resource that includes a helpful bibliography up to 2011: *see* http://pmssem.wikidot.com/sound-engineering-as-cultural-production.

[86] For example, a project undertaken by *tonmeister* Martha de Francisco, a leading classical sound engineer, with her colleagues at McGill University involves the creation of "virtual concert halls" based on the sound environments of well-known concert venues, which are effectively re-created using special speaker and microphone techniques. The project features performances by Tom Beghin and engineering by Wieslaw Wozczyk at McGill's Center for Music, Media and Technology, and a description can be found in *The Virtual Haydn*, http://www.music.mcgill.ca/thevirtualhaydn. The recordings are produced by Naxos, and the set of Blu-ray discs includes a three-hour documentary film on the project, http://www.naxos.com/catalogue/item.asp?item_code=NBD0001-04. The project receives an interesting review by Paul Wells, *You've Never Heard Haydn Like This*, MACLEAN'S (Oct. 1, 2009), https://macleans.ca/culture/youve-never-heard-haydn-like-this.

[87] The expression "creative cheating" is used in Payzant, *supra* note 8, at 119. Note also the echo of the term in Andrew Kazdin's title, *supra* note 13.

[88] For helpful clarification of this point, see U.S. Copyright Office, *Copyright Registration for Sound Recordings* (Circular No. 56, Mar. 2021), https://www.copyright.gov/circs/circ56.pdf; U.S. Copyright Office, *Copyright Registration of Musical Compositions and Sound Recordings* (Circular No. 56A, Mar. 2021), https://www.copyright.gov/circs/circ56a.pdf.

[89] *See* HECTOR L. MACQUEEN, CHARLOTTE WAELDE & GRAEME T. LAURIE, CONTEMPORARY INTELLECTUAL PROPERTY: LAW AND POLICY 223 (para 7.5) (2008). A helpful comparison of the U.S., UK, and EU positions on sound recording rights is provided by Susanna Monseau, *"Fit for a Purpose": Why the European Union Should Not Extend the Term of Related Rights Protection in Europe*, 19(3) FORDHAM INTELL. PROP., MEDIA & ENT. L.J. 629 (2009).

that has been created in the course of employment, or a contract for the producer's services.[90] However, copyright law does not have a general mechanism to recognize the creative contribution of the sound engineer. Notably, rights of attribution and integrity for sound engineers are not protected.

This framework does not provide for the recognition of a creative or intellectual contribution by sound engineers to the quality of a musical recording. The situation seems all the more anomalous in consideration of two factors: first, that copyright law has increasingly been used to recognize creation in a technical context, with computer programming being a case in point; and, secondly, that the level of creativity or intellectual contribution typically required for copyright protection remains relatively low. This is the case even in view of refinements to the notion of originality in the common-law countries, beginning with the U.S. case of *Feist*,[91] which initiated the movement from the notion of labor being inherently worthy of copyright protection—colorfully known as the "sweat of the brow" doctrine—to the idea that "a modicum of creativity" must be present before copyright can arise.[92]

In doing so, the common-law standard moved towards the traditionally higher, European standard of "creativity" for copyright protection, implicitly promoting international harmonization.[93] At the same time, the technological background to *Feist* and Justice O'Connor's decision should be emphasized: *Feist* arose in the emerging digital context, and it firmly established that simply amassing data should no longer be enough to generate a powerful right of ownership.[94]

This issue leads to another interesting point: moral rights have traditionally been important in civil law countries, but, historically, those countries have also

[90] *See, e.g.*, 17 U.S.C. § 201(b). The corresponding Canadian provision provides for transfer of ownership in the case of a "work made in the course of employment": Canadian Copyright Act, *supra* note 69, at s. 13(3). *See* Stephen Fraser, *Who Owns the Copyright in a Canadian Film? Answer: It Depends (And That's the Problem)*, PLAYBACK (Jan. 3, 2005), https://playbackonline.ca/2005/01/03/legal-20050103 (noting the important distinction between the two). The Canadian provision leads to some ambiguity about the circumstances in which the "employer's" copyright prevails.

[91] *Feist Publications Inc. v. Rural Telephone Service Co.*, 499 U.S. 340 (1991), https://supreme.justia.com/cases/federal/us/499/340.

[92] *Feist*, id., was followed by the 2008 *Eastern Book Company* case in the Indian Supreme Court, which looked towards, and explicitly emulated, the Canadian case of *CCH Canadian Ltd v. Law Society of Upper Canada* [2004] 1 S.C.R. 339, 2004 SCC 13, https://decisions.scc-csc.ca/scc-csc/scc-csc/en/item/2125/index.do. Both cases established that some standard of originality beyond mere labor will now be required in these jurisdictions, although the *CCH* standard is still considered to be lower than that in *Feist*.

[93] *See, e.g.*, Gerhard Schricker, *Farewell to the "Level of Creativity" (Schöpfungshöhe) in German Copyright Law*, 26(1) INT'L REV. INDUS. PROP. & COPYRIGHT L. 41 (1995). Schricker discusses the evolution of the creativity standard in the German context.

[94] The issue is one of breadth: do the standards apply to all copyright works, or only to fact-based works, such as databases and telephone directories? *Feist*, *supra* note 89, moved all the way to a "creativity" standard, but *CCH*, *supra* note 90, establishes only that the standard falls somewhere on the spectrum between labor and creativity. Precisely where the Canadian standard crystallizes is unclear, and the emphasis on "skill and judgement" at the Supreme Court of Canada is not entirely helpful. *See* Nicholas Stuart Wood, *Protecting Creativity: Why Moral Rights Should Be Extended to Sound Recordings under New Zealand Copyright Law*, 32(1) VICTORIA UNIV. WELLINGTON L. REV. 8 (2001).

had a higher threshold of originality for copyright works. But, a consideration of the work of sound engineers suggests that it would be comfortably grounded even in a higher standard of originality as in Europe, or as developed by *Feist*.[95] The work of sound engineers clearly reflects the additional feature of human imagination that would lead to the recognition of a creative copyright, as well as a moral right in the European context. Crucially, the creative nature of their work suggests that sound engineers themselves will ultimately want a moral right and see it as relevant to their work.

If a sound engineer's moral rights were to be recognized, the attribution right would not present any special difficulties: a sound engineer's involvement in a recording project can be indicated on liner notes just as other album information is provided.[96] Where integrity is concerned, however, the scope of the sound engineer's prerogative is unclear. As in the case of copyright, more generally, moral rights in a sound recording confront layers of coexisting and potentially competing rights. How would a sound engineer's moral rights be evaluated against those of a composer or performer of the musical works in a recording?

In particular, sound recordings highlight the importance of the fundamental relationship underlying the art of recording—that between musical performer and engineer. The sound engineer, of course, has no work without the performer. But the performer depends on the sound engineer too, albeit in a different sense. Performers rely on sound engineers to present their performances to the public in the desired light. "Desired" will mean different things to different artists. For Glenn Gould, it meant intimacy, detail, and clarity of sound; for another pianist, it may mean creating the illusion of listening in the concert hall; for a historical performer, it might mean recreating a sound as we imagine it to have been 300 years ago.[97] For the creator of a film score, sound aesthetics might involve something different yet again—a slightly out of tune piano to evoke nostalgia,[98] or an orchestral score presented in spectral clarity to suggest the vast stillness of outer space.[99]

In the late 1960s, the first Bill Evans Trio made a legendary series of recordings, including the classic album, *Live at the Village Vanguard*. Decades later, reflecting on that recording, drummer Paul Motian comments,

[95] *See Feist*, *supra* note 89; CCH, *supra* note 90.

[96] But, once again, sale without liner notes will create a problem. This issue is discussed, in the context of downloaded music, *infra* notes 160–61 and accompanying text.

[97] See the fascinating analysis in Gould, *The Prospects of Recording*, *supra* note 12, at "Change of Acoustic".

[98] Such as the sound of the piano in the film *Hannah & Her Sisters*, written and directed by Woody Allen: *see, e.g.*, Roger Ebert, *Hannah and Her Sisters* (Feb. 7, 1986), https://www.rogerebert.com/reviews/hannah-and-her-sisters-1986.

[99] As was done by Stanley Kubrick, who used classical music in the film *2001 Space Odyssey* (with which Richard Strauss's *Also Sprach Zarathustra* now seems indelibly associated. *See e.g.* https://www.youtube.com/watch?v=vI6MUYJIAtM).

> You know what I like best on that record? … The sounds of all those people, glasses and chatter—I mean, I know you're supposed to be very offended and all, but I like it. They're just there and all.[100]

For Adam Gopnik, the record offers "[n]ot a timeless experience of a general emotion but a permanent experience of a particular moment."[101] Editing could "clean up" this recording, but it would go against the sensibility of the one surviving member of the trio. And, in the process, something irreplaceable would, perhaps, be lost.

Accordingly, the exercise of the moral right of integrity by performer and sound engineer should be protected in such a way as to be *mutually reinforcing*. The possibility of a disagreement between performer and sound engineer about a recording exists, but the nature of the art form lends itself to collaboration. Even differences in temperament seem to be superseded by the practical need for collaborative work.[102] The two moral rights coexist to protect the integrity of the recording.

At some level, this discussion raises the issue of disclosure. What happens if there is a dispute between engineer about the release of a recording in a particular form? In that scenario, the right of disclosure of the engineer could conflict with that of the performer.

In situations of conflict, the performer's right of disclosure should probably predominate because it is his or her recorded performance; but this proposition does leave a lingering sense of unease, since it is entirely possible that the performer will not be the best judge of the quality of a recording, and the decision about the recording is probably best taken in consultation with the engineer.[103] In situations where the recording of works is controversial—for example, recordings of music from non-mainstream cultural groups in some of the contexts discussed above—granting a right of disclosure to the maker of the recording could reinforce existing biases against the rights and interests of the artists themselves. Moreover, there is a natural hierarchy in operation: without the performer (and/or the composer), the sound engineer has no material on which to work his or her magic. Only with the performer's participation can the sound engineer's work be brought before the public at all. In this sense, there is something integral about the hierarchy between performer and engineer that should probably be preserved for the good of the music. Added to this is one final consideration: if the engineer objects to the quality of the recording that the *performer* chooses to disclose, he or she can always

[100] The quote appears in a remarkable article by Adam Gopnik, *That Sunday*, New Yorker (Aug. 13, 2001), https://www.newyorker.com/magazine/2001/08/13/that-sunday-2.

[101] Id.

[102] The working relationship between Glenn Gould and his sound engineer Andrew Kazdin seems to have been a case in point. Their collaboration yielded a number of outstanding recordings over a period of fifteen years. *See* Kazdin, *supra* note 13.

[103] For example, this situation has been experienced by Martha de Francisco (in private conversation with the author, March 2020).

rely on the moral rights of attribution or integrity to control his or her association with the final product, or to require improvements to that product, particularly for the protection of the producer's reputation. It is worth noting that this is a different solution to the problem of managing moral rights between collaborators than that which might be offered for another type of collaborative work: film. Under French law, the joint authors of a film must agree on the final version of the film before it can be released; thereafter, no joint author will have an action in moral rights against any of the other co-creators. This solution seems undesirable for recording rights due to the special nature of the relationship between musician and producer, and its embodiment in the musical recording.

A final point: producers should be protected from moral rights complaints based on good-faith attempts at restoration of sound quality, whether they are made by the engineer who made the original recording or a new one. This provision is required by the reality of constant technical improvements that make restoration a growing industry, and by the subtlety of restoration, which may transmute it to the level of an art. Once again, the surprising parallel between a work of visual art and a sound recording makes sense, and the exemption from moral rights for conservation efforts in the visual arts that is provided in many jurisdictions can help to mark the limitations of the performer's moral right.[104]

2. Communication

If the first prong of our piracy era, as the present time could reasonably be called, is the digital reproduction of music, the second is the online dissemination of those files. To date, the discussion about rights in the online dissemination of music has been dominated by economic rights. However, the music streaming era has led to a growing awareness of moral rights—spearheaded, not by performers, but by music composers, who are concerned about their attribution for music that they have *written* when it is listened to via streaming services.[105]

It is to be hoped that this new awareness of moral rights will help those in the music industry to become more generally aware of how widespread moral rights issues are for musicians and of the importance of moral rights recognition for the future of musical creativity in the industry context. In this, as in so much else, the music industry also represents a test case. As such, the development of positive

[104] *See, e.g.*, Canadian Copyright Act, *supra* note 69, at s. 28.2(3)(b). *See also* Visual Artist Rights Act, 17 U.S.C. §§ 106A and 106A(c)(2) (1990) (U.S.), https://www.copyright.gov/title17/92chap1.html#106a (VARA)—although this section provides that cases of "gross negligence" in conservation efforts will constitute a violation of the right of integrity.

[105] *See, e.g.*, Smirke, *supra* note 2. The text of the letter is available in full at Bruce Houghton, *Coalition of Songwriter Groups Protest RIAA "Moral Rights" Stance in Strongly Worded Letter*, Hypebot (Aug. 16, 2017), https://www.hypebot.com/hypebot/2017/08/coalition-of-songwriter-groups-protest-riaa-moral-rights-stance-in-strongly-worded-letter.html.

industry practices relating to moral rights in the music industry would be well placed to generate greater respect for moral rights in the online environment, overall.

This section considers moral rights within all the models of online music dissemination that have arisen so far in the industry: moral rights as they relate to illegal file-sharing,[106] as they arise in legal download environments, and as they face new challenges in the streaming context.

a. File-Sharing: Moral Rights and Illegality

When Napster established itself in 1999 as the first platform for sharing music files online, the recorded music industry faced the first major challenge in the century of its existence. Once copyright-protected music was digitized, nothing could restrain its dissemination online. Music copyright had become almost impossible to enforce, and music companies saw file-sharing as a fight to the death. The industry's response was to launch into battle against the technology.

In practice, this meant that music companies would try to extend the rules of the game, and copyright protection as they knew it, into the new environment of online music-sharing. This translated into frenetic lobbying coupled with dramatic copyright lawsuits against those engaging in file-sharing—even against private individuals, seeking to impose draconian penalties on ordinary citizens in the hope of generating a powerful deterrent effect against future piracy.[107] But the effects were mixed. These strategies greatly soured music industry relations with the public. They have arguably led to a general deterioration in the public view of copyright law, making it, in this sense, more difficult to enforce than ever.[108]

[106] After the rulings in *MGM Studios, Inc. v. Grokster, Ltd*, 545 U.S. 913 (2005) and *Sony BMG Music Entertainment v. Tenenbaum*, No. 03-CV-11661 (D. Mass. July 31, 2009), file-sharing is clearly illegal in the United States. However, the issue is not as clear-cut in other jurisdictions, such as Canada, where the distinction between private and public activities may still be sufficient to define file-sharing as a private activity outside the scope of copyright law. See, e.g., the ambiguous statements of the Federal Court, at both the trial and appeal level in *BMG Canada Inc. v. John Doe (F.C.)*, 2004 FC 488 (CanLII), [2004] 3 FCR 241 (Can.), http://www.canlii.org/en/ca/fct/doc/2004/2004fc488/2004fc488.html. *See also BMG Canada Inc. v. John Doe*, 2005 FCA 193, [2005] 4 R.C.F. 81 (Can.). The criteria for copyright infringement are discussed in James J.S. Holmes & Afigo I. Okpewho, *Transformative in the Eye of the Beholder*, 22(5) Intell. Prop. & Tech. L.J. 12, 15 (2010). Of the four criteria that can meet the U.S. standard for a finding of infringement, the issue of the economic harm caused by music downloading is clearly satisfied.

[107] Tenenbaum, *supra* note 4. *See, e.g., US Music File-Sharer Must Pay Damages*, BBC News (Aug. 24, 2012), https://www.bbc.com/news/technology-19370862.

[108] There are a number of industry examples where the fear of copying has encouraged restrictions on technology that have little to do with copyright law per se. In relation to copyright, region codes for DVDs—a ubiquitous feature of the market for DVDs—are worth mentioning. Region codes essentially require a purchaser to buy the same product more than once because he or she wants to use it in different parts of the world. In theory, the technology may help to inhibit piracy by making it difficult for anyone to buy a DVD in a country or region known for piracy and take it to their home country for viewing. Nevertheless, there are several problems with this argument. Region coding seems to operate on the premise that all items purchased in a country with piracy problems are somehow "contaminated": legal purchasers of the work are in no better position than those who bought pirated copies. Indeed, the region coding system may even create an incentive to acquire pirated goods, since a person

What was the situation of moral rights in this new context for the dissemination of musical works? At least two useful observations can be made. First, as in the case of copyright protection more generally, file-sharing presented a threat to moral rights. It made it more difficult to enforce interests such as the correct attribution of works and the maintenance of their integrity, in the sense that it became more difficult to know what was happening to works as they were clandestinely shared.

However, this brings us to the second, and perhaps more salient, observation. While moral rights *theoretically* became more difficult to enforce—as a matter of law—the *practice* of file-sharing revealed an unexpected symbiosis with moral rights: the interests underlying moral rights became important in a new way when sharing files. It turned out that the activity of sharing itself would benefit from respect for moral rights, at least in some form. In particular, the universal desire for quality music files could encourage the recognition of moral rights. This might happen in at least three ways.

First, attribution of the musicians: those uploading files would want other users of the system to know which songs were being uploaded. Without that information, the uploads would be useless. Moreover, from the musician's point of view, if a popular piece were to be misattributed, that misattribution would be at risk of perpetuation through the file-sharing network. This could have a negative impact on musical reputations and, therefore, careers—especially if the music was written or performed by a lesser-known artist who was at the stage of attempting to build a reputation.

Secondly, attribution of the file-sharer: the community of file-sharers would benefit from knowing the source of musical files. If files uploaded by a particular user were typically of good quality, or if files from a particular source identified by the user were of good quality, both features would make those uploads more valuable on a file-sharing system. Here, attribution of the source of the work is as important, in its own way, as the attribution of the creators of the work. But it is a different attribution interest, not the author's right of attribution. It might overlap with the author's attribution right, but only if, for example, the file was sourced

who travels frequently is not rewarded for buying legitimate merchandise in a zone where piracy is common. It could be simpler and cheaper to buy and use pirate copies while traveling, then discard them upon departure. Similarly, the logic by which the codes are imposed seems senseless: a DVD purchased in the United Kingdom, where it may be at its highest world price, cannot be viewed in the United States or Canada without code-breaking technology. An analogous situation arises in the case of "format-shifting"—i.e., making copies of a work that a user has purchased so that he or she can transfer it to another device. This activity was initially considered illegal under copyright law, even though members of the public often believed that it was permitted. Attempts to create an exception to this rule and make format-shifting legal have been opposed by right-holder organizations, and the results have been mixed. *See, e.g.*, Isabel Teare, *Do You Copy? UK's New Format-Shifting Exception Found Illegal*, MILLS & REEVE: TECHNOLOGY LAW UPDATE (June 26, 2015), https://www.mills-reeve.com/insights/blogs/technology/june-2015/do-you-copy-uk-s-new-format-shifting-exception-fou; in the Australian context, see the advice to the public offered by Anthony Caruana, *When Is It OK To "Copy" Content?*, LIFEHACKER (July 17, 2018), https://www.lifehacker.com.au/2018/07/when-is-it-ok-to-copy-content.

from the author's own website or another source where identification of the author was an integral aspect of that source.

Thirdly, the musician's integrity right: the quality of the file made available on the file-sharing network was, once again, of primary importance to users. A musical file that was damaged, distorted, or maligned in some way—if parts of the music were missing or inaudible, for example—would be of reduced interest, and perhaps even of little value, to the users of a file-sharing system. On the contrary, to an important extent, the viability of the system depended on the quality of the music files that it made available. While there might be trade-offs where listeners were willing to compromise on some level of quality in order to obtain the files for free, there would still be an evident interest among users of the system in having access to files of high quality.

This self-policing aspect of both attribution and integrity reflects the basic premise that the circulation of corrupted music files is likely to be of little interest to the file-sharing community.

There is also another layer to these considerations: there may be an intrinsic drive towards the enforcement of moral rights generated by the technical architecture of file-sharing systems. When music is transformed into data, the authenticity and integrity of the information comprising the file become paramount considerations. Indeed, the protection of the integrity of the data, itself supported by the maintenance of some level of attribution of its source, may be essential for protecting the integrity of the network as a whole. The concepts of attribution and integrity are therefore familiar to the peer-to-peer community not only in what might be called a social or cultural sense—preserving the relative musical integrity of the music that is shared so that it can be enjoyed as fully as possible—but also in the technical sense of preserving the integrity of the file-sharing system itself. While rights of attribution and integrity in data are far removed from the idea of authorial moral rights that seek to protect the personality of the author as expressed in his or her work, a closer look shows how the protection of information—data—plays a vital role in supporting authors' and artists' moral rights in their music. They are overlapping interests, uniting the creative and the technical in a single objective: the preservation and communication of musical quality.

b. Downloading: Moral Rights as Corporate Obligation

Music downloading arose as a legal alternative to file-sharing. It was an ingenious solution to the problem, allowing users to have the convenience of file-sharing without the inconvenience of illegality—for a price. What would that price be—what would the public be willing to pay for music once it had had the taste of enjoying it without paying anything? It is no exaggeration to say that file-sharing was like a wildfire that had already ravaged the system of music copyright to the point where re-establishing the previous status quo was not possible. The value added by legal downloading was, effectively, to legalize an illegal activity. Music downloading was first offered by Apple's iTunes service before its historic transformation to reflect the overarching importance of music streaming as a way of delivering music.[109]

But recognition of moral rights in the downloading environment remains uncertain. A general issue arises out of the international spread of technologies like iTunes, where music is available in environments with different rules about moral rights or, in the case of the United States, no moral rights requirement for musicians at all. Since Apple's iTunes, like most other large technology companies, originated in the United States, it can safely be assumed that the point of departure for the service is towards less recognition of moral rights, since these remain outside the requirements of U.S. copyright law.

Nevertheless, as noted in the discussion on illegal downloads, some level of both attribution and integrity are necessary for music downloads to be valuable to users of the system. Attribution of music tracks and albums makes it possible for customers to locate the works that interest them, while maintaining the integrity of music allows the user to gain access to the file in a valuable state. With respect to the right of attribution on download services, two fundamental questions needed to be answered and have still not received a fully satisfactory response in the musical context.

First, who should be held responsible for maintaining the attribution of musical works? There are at least two possibilities here: the music companies who license music to iTunes or iTunes itself. It is generally accepted that record labels bear the burden of providing information on musical works—an obligation that they acquire through their contractual relationships with artists. Attribution of music on iTunes is often unsatisfactory, including partial and incomplete credits for composers and performers. Labels often fail to provide full information on attribution for use in the iTunes system, but it is also true that Apple has not insisted on having it for the benefit of their users.

Should Apple be made responsible for providing users with attribution information on the music files that it makes available for download through iTunes? The ubiquity of digital music files potentially makes this an important issue, as incomplete or imperfect attribution effectively erases players from the stage of musical history.[110]

[109] *See* Andrew Flanagan & Jasmine Garsd, *iTunes' Death Is All About How We Listen to Music Today*, NPR (June 3, 2019), https://www.npr.org/2019/06/03/729290123/itunes-death-is-all-about-how-we-listen-to-music-today. Other early players were Sony, Microsoft, and Amazon; the entire industry has now been transformed by streaming. For a UK perspective on legal download providers, in 2009, when streaming was not yet widespread, see, e.g., Jessica Brown, *Prick Up Your Ears—You Can Download Music Online and Keep It Legal*, The Guardian (Apr. 24, 2009), https://www.theguardian.com/money/2009/apr/25/download-music-online-legally#maincontent.

[110] For a detailed discussion of this issue, see "Mira T. Sundara Rajan, *Is Apple Deleting the History of Music? Moral Rights on iTunes*, 1709 Blog (May 29, 2012), http://the1709blog.blogspot.com/2012/05/is-apple-deleting-history-of-music.html, including comment by Paul Edward Geller.

But there is another reason, also compelling yet quite different, why Apple should participate as fully as possible in recognizing attribution rights. Apple's iTunes represents a tremendous opportunity for the validation of musical attribution through technical means. It was the first technology to offer the possibility of identifying musical works that are introduced to the system by automatically matching them with tracks that are already in its database. This was dramatically illustrated in 2007, by the case of Joyce Hatto, a reclusive pianist who became famous late in life for a series of celebrated recordings.[111] Six months after her death, it was revealed that the recordings issued as hers were, in fact, constructed from the performances of other pianists. These original recordings had been used by Hatto's husband, a sound engineer by profession, to create the new recordings that were attributed to Hatto. They were "mash-ups."

The fraud was discovered when a listener placed Hatto's CD into his iTunes music player only to have Gracenote, the database used by iTunes, identify the performances as originating in the recordings of other pianists.[112] The debacle not only revealed the power of iTunes as a force for correct musical attribution; it also generated a quiet cultural storm as the classical music community had to confront a number of difficult questions about the Hatto story. Why had Hatto's recordings received such an enthusiastic reception when many of the pianists whose works were put forward as hers were denied similar recognition? Was musical quality alone insufficient to build a reputation in a crowded field with an abundance of exciting talent but a reputation for elitism?[113]

Questions surrounding the nature and meaning of attribution in the digital context also merit consideration. Apple's iTunes has come to offer multiple answers to the question of how to attribute music in the context of downloading—although, taken together, the solutions seem to amount to more of a patchwork than a systematic approach to attribution. Album information is potentially attached to music; there is also a "Song Info" feature in iTunes that provides more detailed information on the music, including various levels of attribution.[114] Again, however, these features are not standardized.

In this regard, it is also interesting to consider Apple's history of ambivalence towards the preservation of digital rights management (DRM) information from music companies. In itself, DRM has proven to be a dual-edged sword: while the

[111] This case is also discussed in Chapter 1, *supra* note 154.

[112] *See, e.g.*, Mark Singer, *Fantasia for Piano*, The New Yorker (Sept. 17, 2007), http://www.newyorker.com/magazine/2007/09/17/fantasia-for-piano.

[113] This fascinating topic is discussed widely. *See e.g.* Chris Lloyd, *Is Classical Music "Elitist"? No, But You Might Be!*, Interlude (July 21, 2019), https://interlude.hk/classical-music-elitist-might; Candace Allen, *Class, Race and Classical Music*, The Guardian (Apr. 4, 2014), https://www.theguardian.com/music/musicblog/2014/apr/04/class-race-and-classical-music-candace-allen.

[114] Sandy Writtenhouse, *How to Get Details about Any Song on Apple Music in the Music App or iTunes*, iDB (Aug. 17, 2023), https://www.idownloadblog.com/2019/04/10/details-song-info-itunes-apple-music.

information can make it inconvenient or impossible to use a musical file across many devices, it has historically been an important way of preserving attribution information in the digital context. The unpopularity of DRM is unfortunate, but it is primarily a reflection of what is arguably overreach on the part of music companies, which, at one point, sought to control activities involving files for which customers had already paid.[115] DRM undoubtedly remains a useful technological tool for attribution in the online environment, but this goal should be kept in view and properly served by it.

The situation of integrity rights in the downloading context presents several new considerations. One of them involves the shift from albums to individual songs: the iTunes model is built on the sale of single tracks rather than collections, a structure that mirrors peer-to-peer file-sharing.[116] The iTunes approach has some potential advantages for the listener, who might be interested in a song or two rather than an entire album. Songs might be of uneven quality; the listener might like one track but not be interested in owning an entire album or hearing more performances by the same musicians.

Nevertheless, some musicians also see an album as a whole as an integral artistic work. This is readily apparent in classical music, where splitting an album into its component parts can separate the movements of a multi-part work such as a symphony, concerto, chamber music piece, or individual work with many parts. This is mildly ironic, because, at least in relation to some kinds of works, nineteenth-century conventions would favor the independent performance of separate movements, whereas the twentieth century has preferred that works be presented to audiences in their entirety.[117] In relation to multi-movement instrumental works, though, the results can be truly disconcerting. For example, individual variations from Bach's Goldberg variations, as performed by Glenn Gould, could be made available for sale, completely destroying what the performer thought of as thematic unity throughout the piece and which he affirmed to be among the fundamental goals of his recording project.[118]

[115] *See, e.g.*, Roberto Baldwin, *Kill the DRM in Your Old iTunes Music Purchases*, WIRED (Mar. 18, 2014), https://www.wired.com/2014/03/kill-itunes-drm.

[116] Ironically, the file-sharing model also invokes the early era of rock music, when the release of singles was an important step. The single as cultural icon is explored by Andrew O'Hagan, *The Sad Death of a Pop Single*, THE TELEGRAPH (Jan. 29, 2005), http://www.telegraph.co.uk/culture/music/3635867/The-sad-death-of-the-pop-single.html. But his pessimism is not universally shared: *see Pop Single Still Hits Right Note*, SYDNEY MORNING HERALD (Aug. 24, 2004), http://www.smh.com.au/articles/2004/08/25/1093246622880.html. The idea of combining singles with ringtones in a CD format available for purchase was first explored by Sony-BMG in 2007. The package, called a "ringle," is discussed by Martyn Wolf, *Howlin' Wolf*, BRAVE NEW WORLD (Sept. 11, 2007), https://bookseller-association.blogspot.com/2007/09/howlin-wolf.html.

[117] See, e.g., the discussion in KENNETH HAMILTON, AFTER THE GOLDEN AGE: ROMANTIC PIANISM AND MODERN PERFORMANCE (2007).

[118] One of the reasons given by Gould for re-recording a work that had already received a classic treatment at his hands was the discovery of a unifying "pulse" throughout the variations that, he felt, had not been adequately reflected in his first version: *see* Peter A. Martens, *Glenn Gould's "Constant Rhythmic Reference Point": Communicating Pulse in Bach's Goldberg Variations, 1955 and 1981*, 13(4)

The first case on the issue of song versus album seems to have emerged when Pink Floyd sued EMI records for splitting up an album and offering individual tracks for download. The group argued that this treatment of their work violated their right to "preserve the artistic integrity of the albums"[119]—their moral right of integrity, claimed, in this case, under a contractual clause.

Another issue of more general importance involves the overlap between technical quality and the musician's moral right of integrity. When download services were first offered, the technical quality of music files represented a step down from CD quality. Is there a point at which this deterioration in quality becomes a violation of the artist's moral right of integrity? And, if so, by what standard should the integrity violation be determined: the artist's "subjective" assertion; "objective" information about audience preferences, as reflected, for example, in declining sales or poor reviews; or more truly "objective" evidence, such as neuroscience studies showing that audiences may perceive and enjoy music differently at different levels of technical quality?[120]

The tendency towards increasingly compressed formats continues with music streaming, which makes music available on a continuous basis online and has led to a further decline in the technical quality of music. This aspect of musical integrity is therefore becoming a more serious concern in an industry evolving towards an ever-greater dependence on music streaming.

c. Streaming: The Future of Moral Rights?

As noted earlier, music streaming has overtaken downloading to become the primary means of disseminating musical works in the current environment. The change involves ease and convenience for consumers—they can avoid the need to find digital storage space for music files while having instantaneous access to music of interest wherever an Internet connection is available.

But streaming has also brought about significant and deeply troubling changes in the way that music is created and heard. Notably, the development of streaming has allowed the music industry to generate exciting new levels of revenue, but musicians, as a group, have not benefited widely from that growth. Rather, the current models by which musicians are paid for streaming result in extremely limited payments to musicians and generally benefit well-known musicians far more than

Music Theory Online (2007), https://www.mtosmt.org/classic/mto.07.13.4/mto.07.13.4.martens.html. It was very unusual for Gould to re-record a work.

[119] *See, e.g.*, *Pink Floyd Win EMI Court Ruling over Online Sales*, BBC News (Mar. 11, 2010), http://news.bbc.co.uk/2/hi/entertainment/8561963.stm; Reuters, *Pink Floyd Wins Court Battle with EMI over Downloads*, New York Times (Mar. 12, 2010), http://www.nytimes.com/2010/03/12/business/media/12pink.html.

[120] *See, e.g.*, Darren Bridger, *Perception of AI Voices* (July 4, 2023), https://cloud.army/resources/blog/perception-of-ai-voices?.

newcomers.[121] Worse yet, the systems by which payments to musicians are made are frustratingly opaque. Spotify, the pioneering streaming service for music, is a prominent offender on both counts.[122]

Streaming services seem inherently susceptible to problems with attribution. This essentially comes down to the fact that, even in comparison to music downloading, the visual element of the streaming experience is truly minimal.[123] Within this framework, some level of attribution is still possible, probably involving creative ways of managing information through links, suggestions of further music arising out of the deeper levels of attribution on a song—songs by the same songwriter, for example, or other means of attribution. Once again, attribution means reputation—the currency of the online environment. The issue has arguably taken on a new importance in the light of musicians' frustrations over their limited revenues through streaming. If the models of artist payment in streaming deprive musicians, particularly songwriters, of a livelihood, the failure to attribute them properly deprives them of any *prospect* of a livelihood. Without attribution, they cannot build any reputation in the music industry—or, at least, they cannot expect to do so through the streaming of their songs.

Here, as in other situations, the interplay of economic and moral rights should not be underestimated. Attributing music is important for a fundamental *economic* reason: only correct attribution can enable the payment of royalties due, especially where payment depends on the number of streams associated with a particular piece. As Paula Mejía notes, "Crossed wires and bad metadata have contributed to a 'royalty black box' of unpaid money, thought to be somewhere at least in the millions."[124] In a report for *The Verge*, Dani Deahl observes,

[121] For a superb treatment of this situation, see the clear and succinct analysis in Paula Mejía, *The Success of Streaming Has Been Great for Some, But Is There a Better Way?*, NPR (July 22, 2019), https://www.npr.org/2019/07/22/743775196/the-success-of-streaming-has-been-great-for-some-but-is-there-a-better-way. As Mejía notes, "while streaming continues to evolve at a breakneck pace, the system through which artists are paid for the music being listened to hasn't evolved in tandem—meaning that, as dissenters note, many artists are still paid little, after services and labels take their respective cuts." *See also* John Seabrook, *Will Streaming Music Kill Songwriting?*, The New Yorker (Feb. 8, 2016), https://www.newyorker.com/business/currency/will-streaming-music-kill-songwriting.

[122] See, e.g., discussion of Taylor Swift *supra* notes 4–5 and accompanying text.

[123] With reference to songwriters, in particular composers, Becca E. Davis notes,

> For songwriters, CDs are the ideal vehicle for musical consumption because they list every single contributing writer on the packaging…
>
> Unfortunately for songwriters, listeners streaming music will likely not encounter songwriting credits unless they go out of their way to search for them. While listening to a song on iTunes, for example, the consumer sees the names of the performing artist and the label, the technical attributes of the song, and typically a list of the other songs the performing artist has available on iTunes. There is no mention of the songwriter.

See Becca E. Davis, *Moral Rights for Musical Compositions in the United States: It's Not Just Fair, It's an Obligation*, 40 Hastings Comm. & Ent. L.J. 67, 87–88 (footnotes omitted) (2018), https://repository.uchastings.edu/hastings_comm_ent_law_journal/vol40/iss1/3.

[124] Mejía, *supra* note 120.

> It's critical that metadata is distributed and entered accurately, not just for a song or album's discoverability, but because metadata helps direct money to all the folks who made that music when a song is played, purchased, or licensed. Documenting everyone's work is also important because, "That attribution could be how someone gets their next gig," says Joshua Jackson, who leads business development for Jaxsta, an Australian company that authenticates music information.[125]

A more creative approach is clearly needed overall to make those attributions more comprehensive and, accordingly, more meaningful to both listeners and musicians.[126]

The Music Modernization Act of 2018 offers a potential solution to this problem. It creates a Mechanical Licensing Collective (MLC),[127] which administers the payment of royalties based on a single, public database specifying ownership details of every piece of music available for streaming as of January 1, 2021. In effect, the Act succeeds in creating exactly what recognition of the moral right of attribution requires: a reliable source for proper attribution information about musical works. However, it does so without making any reference to musicians' moral rights at all. This is especially curious in light of the review of moral rights in the United States

[125] *See* Dani Deahl, *Metadata Is the Biggest Little Problem Plaguing the Music Industry*, The Verge (May 29, 2019), https://www.theverge.com/2019/5/29/18531476/music-industry-song-royalties-metadata-credit-problems. Deahl also points out,

> Entering the correct information about a song sounds like it should be easy enough, but metadata problems have plagued the music industry for decades. Not only are there no standards for how music metadata is collected or displayed, there's no need to verify the accuracy of a song's metadata before it gets released, and there's no one place where music metadata is stored. Instead, fractions of that data is [*sic.*] kept in hundreds of different places across the world.

[126] For some more detailed thoughts on this issue, see Sammy Andrews, *Streaming Music Discovery Is More Than Just Showing Album Credits*, Music:)ally (July 22, 2015), https://musically.com/2015/07/22/streaming-music-discovery-sammy-andrews-cooking-vinyl. Andrews notes,

> [T]he new age of discovery goes so far beyond display. The true beauty and value in discovery via streaming stems from recommendation, curation and data—mountains of lovely data exploration leading to rich paths of sonic enlightenment. These are the paths that truly add value to the entire industry.... If musicians and creators want to be found, heard and appreciated for their work the answer lies not in showing listeners album credits they will see briefly, but likely won't remember or follow up. The answer is allowing them to search for and interact with the data that they are shown.

[127] *See* The MLC, *About Us* (n.d.), https://www.themlc.com/our-story. The MLC is sometimes referred to in songwriters' information—incorrectly, but understandably—as the Music Licensing Collective: *see, e.g.*, Bobby Oswinski, *What Every Songwriter Needs to Know about the Music Licensing Collective*, Hypebot (July 30, 2019), https://www.hypebot.com/hypebot/2019/07/what-every-songwriter-ought-to-know-about-the-music-licensing-collective.html; Monica Corton, *The Music Licensing Collective (MLC)/Unclaimed Royalties Study: What's the Deal?*, Synchtank (Feb. 12, 2020), https://www.synchtank.com/blog/the-music-licensing-collective-mlc-unclaimed-royalties-study-whats-the-deal. The term "mechanical royalties" refers to payment for the use of musical compositions to the owner of the song—usually a music publisher: *see, e.g.*, Kevin Zimmerman, *Understanding Mechanical Royalties*, Songwriter 101 (Mar. 28, 2005), https://www.bmi.com/news/entry/Understanding_Mechanical_Royalties. *See also* Royalty Exchange, *Mechanical Royalties Guide* (Feb. 2, 2021), https://www.royaltyexchange.com/blog/mechanical-royalties#sthash.vI1uQjD9.dpbs ("mechanical royalties are payments to the writer of a song whenever that song is reproduced in some form").

undertaken by the U.S. Copyright Office in 2016 and 2017.[128] The time would have been as opportune as any to propose some recognition of the moral right of attribution, at least for musicians, under U.S. copyright law.

But, in a stunning twist to all but the most jaded industry players, the RIAA lobbied against the recognition of a musician's moral right of attribution at the U.S. Copyright Office. This led to an outraged response by a group of musicians' rights organizations, who drafted an open letter to the RIAA, complaining of a "betrayal" by their own industry body. They write,

> It was with great disappointment that we read the recent RIAA comments to the Copyright Office in connection with moral rights; in particular, with regard to the right of attribution. The RIAA's argument prioritizes the inconvenience of dealing with accurate metadata over the principle of the protection of the rights of the people upon whose work the music business is built. In our view, and the view of many in the creator community, this is not only irresponsible, it represents a betrayal of the "greater common purpose" to which so many of us are committed—a purpose with which the RIAA claims to agree.[129]

In a striking turn, the letter goes on to comment,

> Even anti-copyright groups like Creative Commons understand the importance of attribution. If the RIAA is seen as *less* artist-friendly than Creative Commons, the copyleft and all who seek to undervalue our work will benefit. What's more, this could make the job of aligning creators with the RIAA around our combined interests infinitely more difficult.[130]

The RIAA responded that "we fully support attribution for songwriters, and all the others who contribute to a musical recording."[131] It went on to make two arguments: first, that the focus of its submissions to the Copyright Office was not the provision of metadata but, instead, "publicly visible identification," and, secondly, that private measures, like contractual provisions, would better serve the goal of protecting the moral right of attribution than legislation. It commented,

[128] *See* U.S. Copyright Office, Authors, Attribution, and Integrity: Examining Moral Rights in the United States (Apr. 23, 2019), https://www.copyright.gov/policy/moralrights/full-report.pdf. The public comments—including those by Maria Schneider referenced in the dispute between the songwriters and the RIAA, https://www.regulations.gov/document?D=COLC-2017-0003-0012—are available at https://www.copyright.gov/policy/moralrights.

[129] For the text of the letter, see Castle, *supra* note 2.

[130] *See* Chapter 10, *infra*, on Creative Commons and moral rights; an earlier version of this work was published as Sundara Rajan, *Creative Commons*, *supra* note 64.

[131] The letter can be seen at *RIAA Rebuts Songwriter Moral Rights Critics: "We Love Metadata Too!,"* Hypebot (Aug. 23, 2017), https://www.hypebot.com/hypebot/2017/08/riaa-responds-to-songwriter-groups-re-moral-rights-credit-solutions.html.

> It is this form of attribution that was the focus of our filing with the Copyright Office—publicly visible identification, and not—as your letter suggests—metadata that may be included with a file but that is not publicly displayed to those listening to a music file or watching a music video. Even if all possible information were included in the metadata, that wouldn't solve the attribution problem unless that information was also rendered on-screen in a form visible to the human eye. In other words, while metadata might be a means to an end, it is not an end in itself if the end is public-facing attribution.
>
> Since it appears that you were focused more on metadata than public attribution, let us be clear: we do not oppose, indeed we support, including in metadata information about all creators of a musical recording, and we encourage the use of available mechanisms to give credit to creators. We simply believe that these measures should not be legislated, but rather should be voluntary, or based on freely negotiated contractual obligations, as they always have been in the United States.[132]

The latter position expresses the classic position of U.S. law on this issue—or, rather, the arguments that are typically made in the United States by those who would like to avoid legislative implementation of an attribution right.[133] The question remains: if moral rights are already adequately protected in typical copyright contracts, what is being lost by including recognition for them in the Copyright Act? The answer would no doubt be "choice"—but contract law theory has long since rejected the presumption of free choice in the majority of contracts. Power imbalances drive the choices of the parties. The imbalance of power between authors and publishers, creators and owners, can be, and often is, significant.[134]

As a disturbing footnote to this dispute, songwriters have also expressed concern about the ways in which streaming is reshaping the market for music and, through it, the art form itself. As Paula Mejía points out,

[132] Id. For some interesting commentary on the dispute, see Chris Cooke, *Songwriter Groups Hit Out at the Major Labels' Position on Moral Rights*, CMU (Aug. 17, 2017), https://completemusicupdate.com/article/songwriter-groups-hit-out-at-the-major-labels-position-on-moral-rights.

[133] In contrast, see Jane Ginsburg's arguments in favor of one, made at the U.S. Copyright Office Symposium on Moral Rights: a video recording of her presentation (and of the other symposium presentations) is available at https://cip2.gmu.edu/conferences-events/authors-attribution-and-integrity-examining-moral-rights-in-the-united-states/.

[134] See, e.g., *Macaulay v. Schroeder Music Publishing Co. Ltd* [1974] 1 WLR 1308 (UK), a finding against a musician's contract for payment of future royalties on the basis of the inequality of bargaining power between the young musician and the publisher. See also the discussion in Sundara Rajan, COPYRIGHT AND CREATIVE FREEDOM, *supra* note 59, about the early socialist perspective on power relations in the creative sector. If this position must be labeled "socialist," then so be it! It is still a reflection of a reality with ample evidence to support it. The EU Digital Single Market (DSM) Directive is explicitly concerned with authors' inequality of bargaining power and seeks to address it in various ways: Directive (EU) 2019/790 of the European Parliament and of the Council of 17 April 2019 on copyright and related rights in the Digital Single Market and amending Directives 96/9/EC and 2001/29/EC, 2019 O.J. (L 130) 92 (DSM Directive), https://eur-lex.europa.eu/eli/dir/2019/790/oj.

> Money (for artists) aside, naysayers also point to the shift towards mood and purpose-driven playlisting instead of full-length albums or EPs ... "Their product is more valuable if people just listen more," says Liz Pelly, a contributing editor for *The Baffler* and journalist who covers streaming. "If people just don't stop streaming. So in some ways, it seems to me that a result has been this situation where music that is being surfaced by the platform is music people won't turn off: This background experience, where music isn't really as intentional of a thing, and it's more music that people could just stream for hours and really not think about." As a consequence, streaming isn't just changing consumption habits but how people write music altogether...[135]

Streaming services also offer help, advice, and recommendations on what to stream, often determined by proprietary algorithms, adding to convenience—if that is what the listener wants. Moral rights cannot offer solutions to all of these problems, but they are clearly relevant to many of them. For example, the issue of anodyne playlists represents a changing context for music, and parallels can be drawn with the separation of Pink Floyd's album into individual songs as a violation of the integrity of the group's music.[136]

As noted in the context of downloading, the digital dissemination of music raises the interesting question of how technical standards will relate to the musician's integrity right. Notably, any significant deterioration in the quality of communication would offer a clear basis on which to find a violation of the moral right of integrity: the direct experience of the music would be distorted for the listener, and the reputation of the artist could suffer.

For Neil Young, the famous Canadian singer and songwriter, the point where technology affects integrity has long since been passed by the digital dissemination of music. Profiling the musician for the New York Times, David Samuels writes,

> If you want to envision how Young feels about the possibility of having to listen to not only his music but also American jazz, rock 'n' roll and popular song via our dominant streaming formats, imagine walking into the Metropolitan Museum of Art or the Musée d'Orsay one morning and finding that all of the great canvases in those museums were gone and the only way to experience the work of Gustave Courbet or Vincent van Gogh was to click on pixelated thumbnails.[137]

[135] Mejía, *supra* note 120.

[136] *Pink Floyd Music and anor v. EMI Records Ltd* [2010] EWCA Civ 1429 (UK). See also the case summary, City Legal Research, *What Is a Record?* Pink Floyd v. EMI (Jan. 25, 2011), https://citylegalresearch.wordpress.com/2011/01/25/what-is-a-record-pink-floyd-v-emi/. It was widely discussed in the media; *see, e.g.*, Reuters, *Pink Floyd Wins Court Battle with EMI over Downloads*, New York Times (Mar. 11, 2010), https://www.nytimes.com/2010/03/12/business/media/12pink.html.

[137] *Neil Young's Lonely Quest to Save Music: He Says Low-Quality Streaming Is Hurting Our Songs and Our Brains. Is He Right?*, New York Times (Aug. 20, 2019), https://www.nytimes.com/2019/08/20/magazine/neil-young-streaming-music.html.

As Samuels explains,

> At ground level, which is to say not the level where technologists live but the level where artists write and record songs for people who care about the human experience of listening to music, the internet was as if a meteor had wiped out the existing planet of sound. The compressed, hollow sound of free streaming music was a big step down from the CD. "Huge step down from vinyl," Young said. Each step eliminated levels of sonic detail and shading by squeezing down the amount of information contained in the package in which music was delivered. Or, as Young told me, you are left with "5 percent of the original music for your listening enjoyment."
>
> Producers and engineers often responded to the smaller size and lower quality of these packages by using cheap engineering tricks, like making the softest parts of the song as loud as the loudest parts. This flattened out the sound of recordings and fooled listeners' brains into ignoring the stuff that wasn't there anymore, i.e., the resonant combinations of specific human beings producing different notes and sounds in specific spaces at sometimes ultraweird angles that the era of magnetic tape and vinyl had so successfully captured.[138]

Young's concerns are especially interesting because, at this point, they remain largely the subjective concerns of an individual artist—indeed, of an individual listener. Again, given the current state of knowledge, what would be the standards to apply to a complaint by a musician about technical quality? Courts, particularly in the common-law countries, will be in search of "objective" measures to evaluate the impact of lower-quality audio on music. This is a niche to be filled, perhaps, by neuroscientists as much as by musicians, or experts who evaluate the impact, real or potential, of file quality on sales of a given musical work.

It is also important to note that the market for music is dynamic and that listeners, notwithstanding the overwhelming market forces that often seem to be working against their best interests, are surprisingly persistent in searching for ways to improve the quality of their experience. In parallel to the growth of streaming, the music industry has witnessed a surprising trend: the resurgence of interest in buying vinyl records. Timothy J. Seppala calls them "not competitors, but complementary formats that deliver different benefits to fans."[139] Seppala draws an interesting contrast between discovering new music and enjoying music to which listeners are more deeply committed. He argues that streaming helps listeners to discover the new, while the quality of vinyl allows them to have a better

[138] Id.

[139] Timothy J. Seppala, *Music Streaming Is Fueling Vinyl's Resurgence*, ENGADGET (Dec. 4, 2018), https://www.engadget.com/2018-12-04-music-streaming-is-fueling-vinyls-resurgence.html. Seppala notes that, "[i]n the past three years, vinyl sales in the U.S. have steadily risen about $2 million annually."

experience of the beloved. Citing industry professionals that he has interviewed, he writes,

> Streaming is a good method for discovery while vinyl is for investing in the artists and albums you love. The unfortunate side effect is that streaming has commoditized music. Every music app more or less looks the same, and you pick tunes much like you would scan your inbox, by dragging your finger through a list of data. But it fills a vacuum in an era when terrestrial radio is no longer a reliable way to discover new music.[140]

F. Musical Transformations: From Mobile Ringtones to the Streaming Era

The use of music in mobile ringtones is now largely obsolete—at least for the moment[141]— but a look back at this once vibrant market offers a rare and interesting case study for moral rights in the digital environment.

At one time, using a piece of music as a mobile ringtone to alert the user of a call was an exciting new use of music made possible by technology. As Breeanna Hare of CNN comments,

> In the early- to mid-2000s, the ability to play a customized sound for incoming calls—usually a blaring few seconds of a favorite song called a "mastertone"—was a fun novelty for people buying their first cellphones. Ringtones became an aural fashion accessory, as people scrambled to personalize their phones with the newest or coolest tunes.
>
> Mastertones mimicked the clarity of what one could hear on the radio, making the ringtone an easy and addictive way to hear snippets of one's favorite music. People also could assign different ringtones to different callers -- say, "Take This Job and Shove It" when your boss calls, ha ha -- as a sonic form of Caller ID.
>
> At the same time, much was made of the millions of dollars ringtone sales brought to a grateful music industry that was struggling to adapt to the digital age.
>
> At the same time, much was made of the millions of dollars ringtone sales brought to a grateful music industry that was struggling to adapt to the Digital Age.[142]

[140] Id.

[141] Looking at the status of ringtones today, Stuart Sweet notes, "Ironically, choosing to put the phone away or intentionally leaving it in the other room may finally cause some people to take their phones 'off vibrate' and that may actually cause a ringtone renaissance. Hey, stranger things have happened. I mean, vinyl records are back so why not ringtones?" *See* Stuart Sweet, *Will Ringtones Go Silent in 2019?*, Solid Signal Blog (Jan. 27, 2019), https://blog.solidsignal.com/news/editorials/will-ringtones-go-silent-in-2019.

[142] Breeanna Hare, *Whatever Happened to the Ringtone?*, CNN (May 16, 2013), https://www.cnn.com/2013/05/09/tech/mobile/ringtones-phones-decline/index.html. For a perspective on the

By definition, this use of the song involved the creation of an excerpt, possibly remixing the song into a new version, alterations in the technical quality of the recording, and, of course, unpredictability—as the length of the excerpt, or the number of times it is heard, were determined by how quickly the call was answered. In two ways, musical ringtones represented an interesting and valuable test of moral rights in the digital environment: first, as an example of how musical works can be subject to technological manipulation in the light of new market demands and, secondly, as an exploration of where the limits may lie when it comes to collective licensing of works for common uses in the digital environment. Both of these issues are of growing relevance to the digital marketplace in music.

1. Moral Rights and Excerpts

The issue of moral rights in mobile ringtones presents a microcosm of the challenges that can arise in relation to digital uses of sound. The interest mainly lies in the area of integrity rights; attribution can be addressed without difficulty by ensuring that proper information is attached to the digital excerpt when it is made available for purchase or use. Crucially, though, making available a work in a new technical format like a ringtone will depend on a presumption that the new use does not violate moral rights per se: a technological transformation should not be objectionable in its own right. However, the quality of the transformation should arguably remain open to the creator's judgement.

a. Integrity of a Ringtone: Germany Leads the Way

In 2006, Germany's Supreme Court the *Bundesgerichtshof* (BGH), delivered an authoritative ruling on moral rights in mobile ringtones.[143] In doing so, it discussed two specific issues: whether the technological manipulation of music might violate moral rights and, if so, when; and how moral rights should be dealt with in an environment dominated by the collective licensing of works.

i. Excerpts

Without allowing the making of an excerpt, it would be impossible to use a work as a ringtone. For the German court, the key issue in assessing the moral right of integrity was, therefore, that of consent. The author's consent to the use of the work as a ringtone should be obtained by the producer of the ringtone. Once it is

ringtones market in its heyday, see Edna Gunderson, *Ringtone Sales Ring Up Music Profits*, USA Today (Nov. 29, 2006), https://www.crb.gov/proceedings/2006-3/riaa-ex-l-102-dp.pdf. Other terms include "realtones."

143 *Klingeltöne* [*Ringtones*] case, Bundesgerichtshof [BGH] [Federal Court of Justice] Dec. 18, 2008, I ZR 23/06 (Ger.), https://openjur.de/u/73874.html.

obtained, however, an author should no longer be able to object to the use of the work as a ringtone per se; the author cannot argue that the use of an excerpt in itself constitutes a violation of the moral right of integrity. This was the eminently sensible finding of the BGH.[144]

ii. Modifications

But, once the musical work has been transformed, it can be subject to further modification. Is it possible that the moral right of integrity might be infringed in this process? On this question, the German court's position was more ambiguous. The judges state that the use of excerpts is presumed for the conversion of music into ringtones; but they also go on to comment that "digital ... process[ing]" of a work is to be presumed.[145] This second point is troublesome. Is there scope for considering technical quality in a digital transformation of a work? Is the issue relevant to musicians?

In the heyday of ringtones, the answer to this question would probably have been, "Yes." In the mid-2000s, there was a movement towards the use of ever more reliable reproductions of music that attempt to preserve the quality and characteristics of the original recording.[146] The technical quality of a ringtone was prized by musicians, some of whom would even release music as a ringtone. A high-quality ringtone could encourage subsequent sales of a song and boost the artist's reputation.[147]

[144] Id. The decisions of the BGH can be reviewed only on constitutional grounds, by the Federal Constitutional Court. However, not all commentators agree with this perspective. For example, Arnold Vahrenwald, writing in 2005, argued strongly that transforming a song into a ringtone might amount to a violation of integrity in its own right:

> The reduction of the work to a product with a duration of a few seconds is likely to violate the author's right of integrity. There seems to be little doubt that the treatment to which the producer of a ring tone subjects the work of music might be derogatory, or a mutilation, or other prejudicial treatment. In the case of digital sound sampling where only parts of a work of music are taken, the fragmentation may be considered as an infringement of the substance of the work. Even if the producer has obtained the right to adapt the work for the production and distribution of a ring tone. his conduct may nevertheless infringe the author's moral rights.

Arnold Vahrenwald, *Reflecting the Sound of Ring Tones and Copyright*, 16(4) Ent. L. Rev. 68 (footnotes omitted) (2005). He notes, "Based on the moral rights of its authors, the EMI company required the companies which offered ring tones to stop such conduct which allegedly infringed the authors' moral rights, even when the companies had acquired the 'ring-tone rights' from the relevant collecting societies": id. (footnote omitted).

[145] Quoted in Lutz Riede, *Mobile Ringtones: German Supreme Court Rules on the Licensing of Music as a Ringtone for Mobile Phones* (April 2009) (unpublished article) (on file with author).

[146] *See* Paul R. La Monica, *Ringtones: The Sound of Money*, CNN Money (Apr. 12, 2006), https://money.cnn.com/2006/04/12/commentary/mediabiz/: "Ringtones, particularly master tones, which play actual sections from the studio version of a song, often cost between $2.50 and $3.50 to download."

[147] Id. He quotes from Tom Ryan, then senior vice-president of digital and mobile strategy and development at EMI, to highlight the aesthetics of this marketplace:

> He even jokes that even though most users are now more interested in downloading master ringtones because of the better quality, it wouldn't surprise if there were a pick up in sales of polyphonic ringtones—basically versions of songs that sound like they are being played on a cheesy Casio keyboard.

The BGH identified "technological necessity" as one of the criteria for determining whether or not the integrity of a work has been violated—an entirely appropriate standard to moral rights. If something is technologically "necessary," then, if the artist has consented to the use, that aspect of the transformation should be exempt from liability for violating the artist's right of integrity. Similar ideas can be found in other areas of copyright regulation: for example, the tests for infringement of copyright in a computer program establish that "functional" features of a program cannot be protected by copyright, and copying these features cannot lead to infringement.[148] The issue is essentially one of where to draw the line between necessity and choice when deciding on questions of integrity in the mobile context.

Has the German ruling gone too far? Neither of the two criteria introduced by the court—the presumption of excerpting and the permissibility of digital modifications—entirely precludes success on an integrity claim. However, technological necessity sets a high threshold of proof for any claim that a ringtone violates the author's integrity. Still, as Lutz Riede argues, the decision does not completely pre-empt moral rights in mobile ringtones; the right of integrity can still be invoked in cases of egregious mistreatment—what he calls "extraordinary" circumstances:

> [T]he decision is certainly not expected to prejudice the rights of composers to object to mutilations of [their] ... work in extraordinary cases, e.g. when the ringtone significantly varies from the original or puts ... [the music] into a context detrimental to the composer's reputation.[149]

2. Licensing: An Implicit Waiver of Moral Rights?

The ringtones issue arose in the context of a wider dispute about the powers of GEMA, the body responsible for the collective licensing of German music rights.[150] In particular, did the general license between GEMA and its members, German musicians, give GEMA the right to permit the use of musical works in ringtones?

To this question—an important one, as collective rights management, already significant in the music industry, has become crucial to supporting authors in the streaming era—the BGH provided a mixed answer. The issue of whether a general license is applicable to a new technological use that was not envisioned at the time the license was entered into has affected the use of works in many contexts;

"There could be a retro comeback because of the kitsch factor," said Ryan.

See Brandon Caldwell, *Remember When Ringtone Rap Ruled the World?*, HOUSTEN PRESS (Sept. 11, 2015), https://www.houstonpress.com/music/remember-when-ringtone-rap-ruled-the-world-7751438 on hip-hop and ringtones.

[148] *See., e.g., Delrina v. Triolet Systems Inc.* (2000), 58 O.R. (3d), 17 C.P.R. (4th) 289 (Ont. C.A.).

[149] Riede, *supra* note 142.

[150] Gesellschaft für musikalische Aufführungs- und mechanische Vervielfältigungsrechte [Society for Musical Performing and Mechanical Reproduction Rights], https://www.gema.de/en (available in both German and English).

for example, in the United States and Canada, major rulings have had to examine the use of news articles in online archives when the possibility of such archives did not exist at the time the articles were acquired, and license agreements could not have provided for them.[151] In the case of a dispute about whether or not an existing license can be extended to a new technological use, a court might well find that the necessary meeting of minds between author and publisher on how the work would be disseminated never took place. Moreover, in the pre-digital era, relations between author and publisher were often informal, and this led to more extreme situations, such as the Canadian case of *Robertson*, where no written contract at all existed between the freelancer and the newspaper.[152] It was left to the Canadian Supreme Court to clarify the nature of the relationship between the two and, in particular, the extent of the rights acquired by the publisher. With no written contractual basis for the use of the work, this case embodied the ultimate nightmare of copyright lawyers everywhere.

In its deliberations, the German BGH reviewed different versions of the licensing agreements with members that had been used by GEMA in recent years. It concluded that composers who had made arrangements with GEMA for music rights *in 1996 or before*—in effect, prior to the advent of the digital era—had not consented to the use of their work as ringtones under the general terms of the license. However, in the updated versions of the license from 2002 and 2005, the Court found that GEMA had effectively acquired permission from its members to allow their work to be used in ringtones.

Accordingly, for works licensed through GEMA after 2002, *no additional permission was required* to use the work as a mobile ringtone. If the work was licensed prior to 2002, however, *additional permission had to be sought* before it could be used as a ringtone.

Importantly, the ruling delivered a new perspective on moral rights in the German music licensing system. Prior to this ruling, the German music industry operated on the basis of what was known as a "two-step" licensing scheme for ringtones which was being practiced by some music publishers.[153] This arrangement reflected the presence of moral rights in German copyright law. A company wanting to use music for ringtones needed to seek permission from two

[151] *See Robertson v. Thomson Corp.* [2006] 2 S.C.R. 363, 2006 SCC 43 (Can.), https://scc-csc.lexum.com/scc-csc/scc-csc/en/item/2317/index.do?q=Canada+Evidence+Act; *New York Times Co. v. Tasini*, 533 U.S. 483 (2001). One of the interesting points in the *Pink Floyd* ruling, *supra* note 134, is that the UK court considered the terms of a pre-digital license to be applicable in the digital context. But the license that continued to be honored was one that restricted certain treatments of the work; it was not, as in the *Robertson* case, the possibility of extending a contractual omission—in that case, the absence of a contract—into the digital environment.

[152] *See Robertson*, *supra* note 148.

[153] *See* Riede, *supra* note 42.

sources: GEMA, for economic rights, but also, the creator of the music, who would have to authorize the use as being consistent with his or her moral rights.[154]

The BGH eliminated the need for this practice, establishing two principles. First, the use of music in ringtones was permitted under current GEMA licenses. Secondly, the GEMA license effectively covered moral rights as well. If an author agreed to the use of the work in a mobile ringtone, he or she had implicitly agreed to the *necessary modifications* that would be made to transform the work into this new format.

But this aspect of the ruling is controversial for two reasons. The first, as noted earlier, is the question of how much technological modification is truly "necessary" for the use of music in a ringtone. But, secondly, a troubling administrative issue arises. The fundamental quality of a moral right is its personal nature: it cannot be claimed by anyone but the author. This situation changes only at the point of death, when the heirs or executors of the author may exercise it, not in the author's stead, but on his or her behalf. On maintaining the personal connection between an author and his or her moral rights, German law is quite strict. General waivers of moral rights through contracts are not allowed in German law, though specific waivers may be permitted.[155]

Did the BGH decision on ringtones effectively allow the German collective agency, GEMA, to exercise moral rights on behalf of its members? There are two limiting factors to consider. First, GEMA would not be dealing directly with moral rights, because the inclusion of moral rights in the GEMA licenses was read in by the court and was, therefore, implicit rather than overt. Secondly, as noted above, if modifications to the music exceeded the requirements of technological "necessity," the moral right of integrity could then be invoked by the author. If any waiver of moral rights had occurred by authors in favor of GEMA, it was partial, covering only the circumstances of "technological necessity." Still, the standard of damage that the author would need to show for a moral rights violation in this technological context would clearly be high. The position is summarized by Stefan Michel, as follows:

> The court [in the mobile ringtones case] concluded that the general licensing agreement implies the consent to commonplace and predictable uses by licensees. This conclusion is however troublesome, as it contradicts the personal and inalienable notion of moral rights; the economical licensing agreement with the

[154] *But see German Publishers Retain Veto over Ringtones*, CMU Editorial (Mar. 19, 2010), https://completemusicupdate.com/article/german-publishers-retain-veto-over-ringtones (expressing this idea slightly differently as a "veto right" of music publishers).

[155] *See* Michel, *supra* note 68, at 188, 195 (including n.243), and 198. See also the in-depth discussion by Michel M. Walter, *Dualistic Aspects in Monistic Systems of Moral Rights*, 14(4) JIPLP 318 (2019), https://doi.org/10.1093/jiplp/jpz012.

collecting societies preempts the exercise of moral rights by the individual (*footnotes omitted*).[156]

A final consideration: given the importance of moral rights in German law, could reading them into the general provisions of the GEMA license invalidate the license as a whole? The BGH did not address this issue, but it established a clear precedent on moral rights: where technological manipulation of works is involved, only cases of egregious distortion will allow a composer, or performer, to assert that his or her moral right of integrity has been infringed.

G. Musical Performers: The New Authors

Western culture, in particular, has long emphasized the leading role of the composer as the creator of a musical work. If musical relationships could be depicted as a pyramid, the composer would find himself—possibly herself, but female composers were traditionally rare[157]—at its apex, with the devoted audience constituting its base. The performer's place is between the two. He or she is a vehicle to transmit the greatness of the composer's larger genius to the world.

The international recognition of moral rights for musical performers in the WIPO Performances and Phonograms Treaty (WPPT) of 2002 reflected a dramatically new perspective on performance at the international level.[158] As noted earlier, performers have effectively been raised to a new level in a musical hierarchy traditionally defined by the supremacy of authors. At the same time, this transformation is not complete, as the WPPT implements new limitations on the enactment of moral rights in the performance context.

What do the new rights signify for performers? How do performers and their art stand to benefit? How do the limitations affect the ability of performers to benefit from this new recognition by the international copyright community?

1. Authors and Artists: Two Solitudes

With moral rights, the performer is recognized as an original creator in his or her own right, but it must still be acknowledged that the nature of a performance is

[156] Michel, *supra* note 68, at 192–93.

[157] For example, Clara Schumann substantially neglected her efforts at composing—though they were supported by her husband, Robert Schumann—in favor of her performance career and, as Robert Schumann wrote, her duties as a mother. *See* NANCY B. REICH, CLARA SCHUMANN: THE ARTIST AND THE WOMAN 211–15 (rev'd. ed., 2001).

[158] *See* WPPT, *supra* note 38, at Art. 5. These provisions are discussed in more detail in Chapter 3, *supra* notes 11–17 and accompanying text, and notes 208–26 and accompanying text.

perhaps intrinsically different from a musical composition. In particular, when a composer records his or her work in writing, the work comes to exist as an objective entity, distinct from the person of the composer (who is also, presumably, the work's first performer). In contrast, the secret of the *performer's* art lies in the ethereal details of musical execution—style, touch, gesture, and breath (the most ephemeral of all)—as well as, of course, interpretation.

It is also worth pointing out that the art of composing and the art of performing are different enough that, perhaps paradoxically, a composer may not always be the "best" interpreter of his or her own work. Classical music provides some fascinating illustrations. For example, Russian twentieth-century composer and pianist Sergei Rachmaninoff said that the legendary pianist Vladimir Horowitz played his work better than he played it himself.[159] However, Horowitz also took the liberty of modifying some of Rachmaninoff's works in his performances. In the case of Rachmaninoff's second piano sonata, originally published in 1913 but revised by him in 1931, these changes were quasi-compositional, as Horowitz created a new, hybrid version of the work.[160] As a *performer*, there could have been no real need to do so—Rachmaninoff's original versions still exist— but it seems clear that, at least to some extent, Horowitz also saw himself as a *composer*.[161] Rachmaninoff was, perhaps, sympathetic to Horowitz because, as a brilliant virtuoso in his own right, he had exercised his own prerogative as *performer* when dealing with other composers' works—for example, altering the speed, and thereby, the mood, of the Prelude, Opus 11 No.8, a short composition by his friend, the great pianist and mystic Alexander Scriabin.[162] Scriabin felt that Rachmaninoff had misinterpreted it. However, Rachmaninoff's devotion to his friend's music was so sincere that, when Scriabin died suddenly of an infection, Rachmaninoff, the great composer, went on tour as a *pianist,* playing only Scriabin's music in his concerts.[163] He must have believed in his own view of Scriabin's piece; it was no mere parody.

[159] Rachmaninoff is widely said to have made this remark in relation to his third piano concerto. *See, e.g.*, David Michael Wolf, *Zen and the Art of Piano*, THE CAROLINA PHILHARMONIC (Dec. 8, 2015), https://www.carolinaphil.org/zen-and-the-art-of-piano/tag/horowitz+meets+rachmaninoff. Horowitz also made revisions to Rachmaninoff's second piano sonata, which Rachmaninoff himself also revised: *see, e.g.*, Gerhardus Petrus Maritz, Rachmaninoff, Horowitz, and the Discursive Arena between (Re)Composition and Performance: The Case of Rachmaninoff's Piano Sonata, Opus 36 (January 2014) (M.Mus. thesis, Nelson Mandela Metropolitan University), https://core.ac.uk/download/pdf/145053122.pdf.

[160] See the interesting review of this situation, which perhaps downplays Horowitz's involvement (or interprets it as more improvisational than compositional), in Dominik Rahmer, *Preface, in* PIANO SONATA NO. 2, B FLAT MINOR OP. 36, VERSIONS 1913 AND 1931 (Dominik Rahmer, ed., & Marc-André Hamelin, fingering, n.d.), https://www.henle.de/media/5a/a4/19/1697725924/1256-1697725924-sync.pdf.

[161] Private conversation with pianist Jeffrey LaDeur (Spring 2020).

[162] Prelude Op. 11, No. 8, in F-sharp minor. *See*Max Lima, *Rachmaninoff plays Scriabin: Prelude in F sharp minor, Op. 11, No. 8*, YOUTUBE (June 8, 2012), https://youtu.be/y2RgiIWcZZk?si=NO7YdLJWlCXZJf8l.

[163] *See, e.g.*, FAUBION BOWERS, SCRIABIN: A BIOGRAPHY 281 (rev'd. ed., 1996). This book, at times damaging to the composer's reputation in many respects, is still Scriabin's only modern biography in

In the past, performance was valued; but preserving the essence of a performer's art, or recognizing it in any form apart from the living person of the performer, was practically impossible. Recording changed this. Without the aid of recording technology, the greatness of a performer would pass away as gently as a cloud, and all that he or she had worked for would become dependent on memory and word of mouth. Great performers became legends, and their art was described in a kind of folklore—in stories about the performer that were passed down as oral tradition from teacher to student or written down in books about him or her, or about music in general. Through the grace of recording, and only through this, performance can now be preserved.

In this sense, performance is perhaps the art that most closely mirrors life: its essential quality is impermanence. The fragility of improvisatory music, like jazz, seems especially poignant: the art of improvisers unfolds in live performance and *only there*. The impact of the recording medium on improvisatory music is therefore tremendous, bearing witness not only to performance but to something more—the awesome genius of composition in action. As Bill Evans wrote, "Direct deed is the most meaningful reflection."[164] Once again, technology makes a record of that reflection possible.

When it comes to moral rights for performers, the uniqueness of performance, and an awareness of the different roles that performers may fulfil in different kinds of musical genres, requires a sensitive adaptation of accepted principles of moral rights to this context. Keeping in mind that the WPPT now serves both as a model for countries ready to implement moral rights for performers, and as a legal requirement setting out minimum standards for performers to be implemented in signatory countries, how well has it succeeded in this regard?

a. Attribution of Performances

The attribution interest, in relation to both live music and recorded music, would require that all musicians in a performance be properly credited, but attribution could also be omitted if that were "dictated by the manner of the use of the

English, and is therefore cited here (comments based on private correspondence with Simon Nicholls, September 2023).

[164] See Bill Evans' classic liner notes to the pioneering jazz album, *Kind of Blue*: *Bill Evans' Kind of Blue Liner Notes*, SFJazz (Mar. 2, 2018), https://www.sfjazz.org/onthecorner/bill-evans-kind-blue-liner-notes/. Evans elaborates:

> There is a Japanese visual art in which the artist is forced to be spontaneous. He must paint on a thin stretched parchment with a special brush and black water paint in such a way that an unnatural or interrupted stroke will destroy the line or break through the parchment. Erasures or changes are impossible. These artists must practice a particular discipline, that of allowing the idea to express itself in communication with their hands in such a direct way that deliberation cannot interfere. The resulting pictures lack the complex composition and textures of ordinary painting, but it is said that those who see well find something captured that escapes explanation.

performance."[165] This limitation, ostensibly to factor technological constraints into the equation, is further strengthened by the identification of the attribution right as a right "to claim to be identified" as the performer rather than to be identified per se.

This amounts to a watered-down version of the strong moral right of attribution for authors in Berne. It is ironic that the hesitation about performers' attribution appears to be driven by fears about the potential difficulties of recognizing moral rights in a technological context—although the impact of technology on performances was a primary factor behind the adoption of moral rights in the WPPT, as pointed out by Adeney, and as is apparent in the record of discussions surrounding the development of the WPPT in the first place.[166]

Moreover, there is no real reason to think that it will be more difficult to provide attribution in the digital environment then it was in the pre-digital era. On the contrary, technology offers a new range of options for attributing performances and works alike, including the provision of complete metadata and DRM information for performances. For example, Richard Arnold identifies a number of possible means of recognizing a performer in the digital environment:

> In the case of a performance that is broadcast, the right is to be identified in a manner likely to bring the performer's identity to the notice of a person seeing or hearing the broadcast. A credit at the end of the broadcast is the conventional way of doing this, but other methods are not excluded. In an appropriate case, for example, it may be sufficient to refer the audience to list of performers displayed on the website. In the case of a sound recording ... [t]his may include, for example, including the performer's name in a digital file in such a way that it is displayed when the file is played. In any of these cases, it is sufficient to identify the performer in whatever manner may be agreed between the performer and the person who produces, broadcasts, etc. the performance. By contrast with authors' paternity right, there is no requirement that the identification be clear and reasonably prominent.[167]

Like any obligation, there is a level of care required to fulfill these requirements of attribution; but the presence of rights in international agreements requiring

[165] WPPT, *supra* note 38, at Art. 5(1):

> Independently of a performer's economic rights, and even after the transfer of those rights, the performer shall, as regards his live aural performances or performances fixed in phonograms, have the right to claim to be identified as the performer of his performances, except where omission is dictated by the manner of the use of the performance, and to object to any distortion, mutilation or other modification of his performances that would be prejudicial to his reputation.

[166] See discussion in Chapter 4, *supra*.

[167] RICHARD ARNOLD, PERFORMERS' RIGHTS para. 7.06 (5th ed., 2015). He goes on to discuss the use of "some particular form of identification (like a pseudonym)": id. at para. 7.07.

the attribution of performances should represent a real commitment rather than a symbolic promise. It can be disconcerting that the language of final provisions does not always reflect the level of commitment of its members, as evinced, for example, in preparatory discussions; but, in a sense, this is also of secondary importance from a legal point of view, since the provisions as formulated in international copyright agreements only represent minimum standards of protection. It is up to the member countries to choose how they will implement these provisions, and it is the interpretative treatment of courts in the member jurisdictions that will bring clarity to their practical application.

A further consideration is that, in most situations, performers' right to attribution is already widely recognized, and there are well-established means of realizing attribution in practice. Where individual artists or small groups are concerned, each musician can be credited without difficulty by means of concert programs or, indeed, in announcements made during the event. Credit can also be given by means of websites. The situation could theoretically become more complicated in relation to large groups, such as orchestras, but here, too, industry norms are already in operation; for example, concert programs typically list the names of all of the orchestra members.

b. Protecting the Performer's "Honor" as an Element of the Integrity Right

As set out in the WPPT, an alteration of the performance is objectionable if it is likely to have a negative effect on the reputation of the performer.[168] As noted earlier, this right is narrower than its counterpart in Article 6*bis* of the Berne Convention, because it removes the word "honor" from the formulation. In other words, an alteration of the work may violate the performer's moral right integrity if, and only if, it may cause prejudice to the performer's *reputation.*

Of necessity, the mere omission of a term from a legal provision, however indeterminate that term may be, must be seen, *a priori*, as a significant change. Given the lack of legal precedent to guide us in this area, however, it is difficult to say how significant this omission is. As discussed earlier, based on her examination of the drafting history of Berne, and conference discussions around the adoption of "honor" when Article 6*bis* was adopted in 1928, Elizabeth Adeney suggests that the word "honor" has some personal connotations beyond the idea of (professional) reputation.[169] If we accept both propositions, they lead us to two conclusions: first, at the international level, protection for the performer's moral right of integrity is weaker than it is for that of the author; and, secondly, it is specifically weakened with respect to the performer's personal interest in his or her performance.

[168] But it should be noted that there is some lack of clarity about the test: is it "likelihood of damage to the author's reputation," actual damage, or potential damage—or any of the above?

[169] *See* Chapter 3, *supra* note 113.

But the latter consequence is unfortunate: as noted in the discussion above, a performer has the distinction of being more closely and more personally associated with his or her work, and the performance, then any author—simply by virtue of the fact that it is he or she who embodies the performance by voice, physical presence, movements, and other *personal* characteristics. Accordingly, the performer is more at risk of being harmed personally—that is to say, in relation to his or her "honor"—than a composer. In the case of performers, it is also possible to distinguish quite clearly between personal "honour"—for example, embarrassment or personal distress—and professional "reputation" in the case of a performance—as evidenced by loss of sales or a poor review, perhaps more so, once again, than in relation to a composer. Moreover, performers are especially vulnerable on this account in an environment where they are depending on online circulation of their performances, both live and recorded, to build professional reputations; but the online environment is increasingly rife with false information and campaigns that target particular individuals for a variety of reasons, many of which may be personal in nature. Some consolation may be found in noting that the removal of the term "honor" from Article 5 of the WPPT allows, and perhaps encourages, the countries implementing the Treaty to remove it; but, of course, it does not require them to do so.

c. Performance in a New Context

Finally, the removal of the prohibition on "other derogatory action" in relation to performances limits the applicability of the WPPT to performances taken out of context—as in the examples of songs used in a political campaign or in the context of abuse, as discussed above.[170] This actually departs from the practice of a number of member countries concerning the moral rights of both composers and performers in a performance, including, notably, Germany.[171] Like the other modifications to the Berne framework for authors discussed earlier, this change seems poorly adapted to the digital environment, where one of the most basic forms of "creative expression" in relation to music has rapidly become the "mash-up—in essence, the presentation of an existing work, transformed or otherwise, in a new musical context.

[170] Richard Arnold notes the significance of this position, giving the example of music associated with Nazism, and citing the work of Adeney and Ricketson on international copyright law: *see* Arnold, *supra* note 63, at para. 7.28 (n.52).

[171] *See* Elizabeth Adeney, The Moral Rights of Authors and Performers, An International and Comparative Analysis paras. 9.146–147 (2006). Writing in 2006, Adeney comments on art. 74, which creates a moral right of attribution for performers, as a "recent addition" modeled on the provisions on authorial attribution in art. 13 of the Act: id. *See* Urheberrechtsgesetz (UrhG) vom 9 Sept. 1965 [Act on Copyright and Related Rights of Sept. 9, 1965], berücksichtigt die Änderung(en) des Gesetzes durch Artikel 25 des Gesetzes vom 23. Juni 2021 (BGBl. I S. 1858) [as amended by article 25 of the Act of June 23, 2021 (Federal Law Gazette I, p. 1858)], art. 14 (Ger.), https://www.gesetze-im-internet.de/englisch_urhg/englisch_urhg.html (translation provided by Ute Reusch).

Moreover, when the placing of musical works into a new context generates an affront to musical integrity or artistic reputations, it would be most efficient to allow performers and songwriters (or composers) to make claims together for the violation of their moral rights. Otherwise, a potentially artificial situation arises where a performer, as the public face of the musical work, finds that his or her reputation is threatened; but only the songwriter or composer can sue. Providing a right of action for both would also help to strengthen the integrity of the musical work, which is protected from damaging associations on two levels, those of composition and performance. In the online environment, stronger, more coordinated, and more systematic measures like these may be needed to make real inroads against misrepresentation, misinformation, and abuse, which have become endemic to online communication, as well as more conventional problems like music piracy.

2. Performers and Their Public: Future Symbiosis?

One of the most serious issues affecting performers in the digital environment is their vulnerability to unauthorized recordings by members of the public. The problem is a broader one, with musicians and their audiences across every genre of music affected by the distractions of cell phone use during their performances.

Is an audience causing distractions by using their devices causing harm to a performer's moral right of attribution? If the performer feels that his or her performance is affected by the distraction, a strong subjective case can be made that it is; and there is undoubtedly much objective evidence about the deterioration of environments like this and their impact on performers, which such cases could draw upon to show a likelihood of damage to performers' reputations. If obvious problems occur, such as a performer forgetting the words or the notes to a song in the midst of a performance, these shortcomings, whether seen in the theatre or preserved in recordings, are obvious ways in which performers' reputations may be harmed.

The case of unauthorized recordings is especially egregious because of the potential breadth of dissemination, and the consideration that those who see the recording may be unaware of the problems that the performer encountered while on stage. While this situation is pronounced enough in Western countries, a sense of concert etiquette has sometimes helped to discourage filming during concerts. In a country like India, where cellphone use is ubiquitous and concert etiquette quite different from Western norms,[172] the

[172] During Chennai's famed "December Music Season," the prompt departure of listeners for dinner at 8:00 "sharp," often mid-percussion solo, is a standing joke. But the Season organizers may be partly "to blame" for providing delicious food in the celebrated music "canteens" located on site, which draw

unauthorized filming of classical musicians is a serious problem noted by musicians' advocates.[173]

It is helpful that concerns about an environment of distractions may be shared by the audience. In their discussion of two examples where performers interrupted their performances to deal with an audience member who was filming them, Michael Paulson and Michael Cooper, writing for the NEW YORK TIMES, note the supportive reaction of the audience:

> Both artists were cheered—first in person, later on social media—for taking a stand against the growing ranks of smartphone addicts who cannot resist snapping pictures and making recordings that are often prohibited by rule or by law, that are distracting to performers and patrons, and that can constitute a form of intellectual property theft.[174]

At the same time, as these writers note, audiences do not always side with performers, arguing, instead, that prohibiting phones is "elitist" or "snobbish" at a time when, for example, classical music is in need of expanding its audience.[175] Another powerful argument is that phones may serve multiple purposes, even allowing audience members to "take notes" or engage with the performance in special ways by following along with online features, as has been experimented with by some U.S. orchestras. There is also the issue of safety and needing to maintain connectivity in a society that expects to be able to reach people at all times for emergencies. In all of these cases, though, access to phones may be handled creatively to maintain an environment of appropriate concentration for performers while treating audiences with respect and recognizing their needs. Paulson and Cooper identify a number of such possibilities in their article; the solution may be as simple as applying a seal on the phone camera that can be removed after the performance or letting audience members know when an appropriate opportunity for photographs arises. For example,

> When Bruce Springsteen was on Broadway in 2017 and last year, the production put an insert in the Playbill, urging fans accustomed to rock concerts not

customers in their own right during the music festival: *see, e.g.*, unpublished article by the author, available upon request.

[173] *See, e.g.*, *Artists and Musicians Told to Come Together to Safeguard Their Work*, THE HINDU (Feb. 2, 2011), https://www.thehindu.com/news/cities/chennai/Artists-and-musicians-told-to-come-together-to-safeguard-their-work/article15123964.ece.

[174] *See* Michael Paulson & Michael Cooper, *Filming the Show: Pardon the Intrusion? Or Punish It? A Seized Phone. A Stopped Concert. A Text from Rihanna. All Are New Fuel for a Heated Debate about Theater Etiquette in the Digital Age*, NEW YORK TIMES (Oct. 19, 2019), https://www.nytimes.com/2019/10/06/theater/theater-etiquette-cellphone-anne-sophie-mutter.html.

[175] Id.

> to use their phones during the show, but promising that Mr. Springsteen would stay onstage during the curtain call long enough for people to take pictures. The Metropolitan Opera offers similar advice on its website: "Tip: Snap a pic of the cast during curtain call!"[176]
>
> They go on to point out,
>
> The issue is complicated because so many audience members have become habituated to photographing and videotaping sporting events, pop concerts, even dinner. And the truth is that live performers, who have long battled piracy and bootlegging, also rely on fan-fueled social media to bolster ticket sales.

The relationship between artist and audience has always been symbiotic. In the digital environment, this symbiosis has taken on a new intimacy and urgency. It is up to both artists and their public to rise to the challenge of working together to create a better environment—one of greater confidence, safety, and opportunity—for performers.

3. Layers of Rights: The Performer Finds a Place

Performers' moral rights become more complicated in the context of a recording, which is a complex work involving many layers of rights. These now include the moral rights of both composers and performers, which they continue to hold personally even after the copyright may be transferred or licensed, and which subsist alongside the rights of producers as well as those who own the recordings by virtue of employment or contractual arrangements.

Moral rights of performers in a musical recording therefore involve two kinds of negotiations. First, the moral right of the performer must be balanced against those of the composer. What happens in situations where a composer is dissatisfied with a performer's interpretation (or cover) of his or her work? In no sense can moral rights legislation derived from (or inspired by) the WPPT expect to limit the performer's moral rights to situations where the composer is satisfied with the performance—this would have the ultimate effect of depriving performers' moral rights of their meaning.

The provision that integrity violations depend on showing damage to reputation or, where the author is concerned, honour, can help to clarify the circumstances where performers and composers might bring each others' integrity into question. The standard of proof in such a situation would obviously be quite demanding,

[176] Id.

since evidence would have to be adduced to satisfy this requirement of proof of damage to reputation or, potentially, honour.

Another approach might be to make provision for the moral right of integrity in the licensing arrangements between composer and performer. Contractual provisions could be adopted, to the effect that the composer agrees to recognize the performer's creative freedom, or that the performer agrees to secure the composer's agreement to his or her version of the song; in some jurisdictions, notably in common-law countries, the composer and performer might agree to waive their moral rights, but only with respect to each other. Since all of these arrangements will reflect the personal relationships between, notably, songwriters and performers, fashioning solutions through contractual provisions reflecting their meeting of minds makes sense. At the same time, those provisions should arguably be shaped by the background of legislative protection for moral rights—a different culture for entering into contracts than an environment, as in the United States, without moral rights for music.

To the extent that the author–performer relationship is characterized by inequality of bargaining power, legislative rules on the management of moral rights could be helpful. Interestingly, the power imbalance may not be what we think it is, as it is *performers* who might be likely to have power over *songwriters* in many genres of music. In the case of legislation seeking to mitigate any imbalances, the model of European countries regulating film moral rights may help. In particular, the French approach, which requires coauthors to agree on the final version of a film before its release, thereby pre-empting—and ultimately eliminating—conflicts about moral rights among the coauthors by the time the film is released, may be helpful.

4. Recognizing the Performer: An Issue of Equity

By its very nature, music leaves ample room for confusion about the roles of composer and performer. In modern pop music, this is confusion about the roles of singers versus songwriters; sometimes, they are one and the same person, but they are often different individuals (or groups).

But the problem already existed in earlier historical periods. Western classical music illustrates how the creative roles of composer and performer were already starting to shift in the nineteenth century, when the art of performance gained enormously in public prestige and visibility with the rise, notably, of virtuoso pianists.[177] Here, too, composer and performer were sometimes one and the same

[177] *See* Hamilton, *supra* note 115.

person, but not always; and the enlargement of the performer's role set the scene for later contests between the two.[178]

There was an interesting gender dimension to this split. Composers were generally male, and the few women who tried their hand at composition faltered under early discouragement. Notable examples were Felix Mendelssohn's sister, Fanny, and Robert Schumann's wife, Clara. A selection of Fanny's works was eventually published under her brother's name.[179] In Clara's case, family life left her with little time for composition. But the situation was actually deeply concerning to her husband, who wrote,

> Clara has composed a series of small pieces, which show a musical and tender ingenuity such as she has never attained before. But to have children, and a husband who is always living in the realm of imagination, does not go together with composing. She cannot work at it regularly, and I am often disturbed to think how many profound ideas are lost because she cannot work them out.[180]

But Clara, herself, seems to have been more constrained by gender conventions than her conscientious husband. She comments,

> I once believed that I possessed creative talent, but I have given up this idea; a woman must not desire to compose—there has never yet been one able to do it. Should I expect to be the one?[181]

At the same time, the audience for classical music appears to have been even predominantly female. Playing the piano was a desirable accomplishment for women of the eighteenth century, and by the nineteenth, a significant number of amateur

[178] Id. Notably, examples of composer-pianists include Johannes Brahms, who gave up his performance career to compose, and Robert Schumann, whose early brilliance as a performer was terminated by a hand injury, self-inflicted in his effort to improve his technique. Clara Schumann, Robert Schumann's wife and one of the most famous virtuoso pianists of her day, became the ideal performer of works by both composers. Her influence extended deep into the compositional efforts of both. Notably, Clara Schumann was responsible for helping to popularize Schumann's compositions, while remaining restrained in her public presentation of others—important artistic judgements that shaped the development of his legacy. *See* Reich, *supra* note 154, at 257–66. Franz Liszt was a composer who believed that his composing career had been ruined by his excessive financial dependence on performance. One of the last in this line was twentieth-century composer-pianist Sergei Rachmaninoff, whose concerts in the United States led to such a busy career that he had little time left for composing. No doubt, the sadness of exile also colored his attitude to composition in the United States, where he lived after 1918. His friend Alexander Scriabin was a remarkable composer-pianist who remained focused on composition. The tradition of the pianist-composer may yet be revived in the twenty-first century by the uniquely talented Canadian pianist and composer, Marc-André Hamelin: *see* https://www.marcandrehamelin.com/.

[179] *See* R. Larry Todd, Mendelssohn: A Life in Music (2003).

[180] Joint diary of Robert and Clara, quoted in Reich, *supra* note 154, at 215.

[181] Quoted id. from Clara Schumann's diary, 1839. *See also* Nancy B. Reich, *Clara Schumann*, in Women Making Music: The Western Art Tradition 1150–1950 249, 267 (Jane Bowers & Judith Tuck eds., 1987). Clare was only twenty years old at the time.

musicians—including students of the great composers—were female. This is an interesting aspect of the slow recognition of performers as creators in Western culture.

The insistence of Western copyright laws on written forms for music reflects a cultural bias—one that places oral traditions at a disadvantage. In this sense, the recognition of performers may address another equity concern by granting copyright to systems of world music that are not based primarily on written forms. For example, in India, classical compositions are often composed orally, memorized, and taught to students by an outstanding composer and his or her disciples.[182] In 1994, to accommodate this tradition, the Indian Copyright Act was modified to include protection for music that is not written down.[183] Given the millennial emphasis on oral tradition in Indian music, the late adoption of this approach to the protection of musical works in India is incongruous. Still, it was not unusual by world standards. Canada enacted a similar amendment in 1993,[184] following a case in which the transmission of music by wire was found not to infringe copyright because the musical score had not actually been copied. In the case of Canada, this change could be especially helpful to Indigenous groups, and traditional music of all kinds could benefit. In the United States, however, reliance on a written score, at least for works composed and registered for copyright before 1976, was affirmed as late as 2020.[185] With performers' moral rights, it should generally become easier to accord status to oral and improvised music, though it remains to be seen how different countries will implement these rights.

The establishment of moral rights for performers has interesting implications for live performance. In the past, the supremacy of the composer's interest in the presentation of the work was obvious, and it was he or she who was the final authority on how the work should be performed. A performance that did not accord with the composer's view of his or her own music could amount to a violation of the composer's right of integrity. Now that the performer also enjoys a moral right

[182] Statement by Dr. S. Vijaya Bharati (in personal communication with the author, Apr. 27, 2010). Ravi Shankar notes,

> The tradition of Indian classical music is an oral one. It is taught directly by the guru to the disciple, rather than by the notation method used in the West. The very heart of Indian music is the raga: the melodic form upon which the musician improvises. This framework is established by tradition and inspired by the creative spirits of master musicians.

See Ravi Shankar, *On Appreciation of Indian Classical Music*, The Ravi Shankar Foundation (n.d.), https://www.ravishankar.org/music.html.

[183] The amending Bill is available on the Parliament of India website at https://copyright.gov.in/Documents/Public_Notice_inviting_reviews_and_comments_of_stakeholders_on_draft_guidelines/Musical_Work.pdf. *See* amendment of s. 2(p): "(p) 'musical work' means a work consisting of music and includes any graphical notation of such work but does not include any words or any action intended to be sung, spoken or performed with the music."

[184] *See Composers, Authors and Publishers Assoc. of Canada Ltd v. CTV Television Network Ltd* [1968] S.C.R. 676 (Can.), https://www.canlii.org/en/ca/scc/doc/1968/1968canlii89/1968canlii89.html. The amendment was enacted in 1993: *see* Government of Canada, *History of Copyright in Canada* (n.d.), https://www.canada.ca/en/canadian-heritage/services/history-copyright-canada.html.

[185] *Skidmore v. Zeppelin*, *supra* note 40.

to the integrity of the performance, the balance of power in this relationship has shifted. The performer's art is recognized as creative and original; he or she is also entitled to present his or her view of the composition. The hierarchy inherent in the relationship between composer and performer has not been entirely removed, but it is more ambiguous than in the past. This reflects new technologies for music, and also, social change. At what point is the performer's creativity limited by the composer's rights? Should a performer be allowed to present the work of a composer in some way that circumvents his or her artistic intent? And how is this to be judged—by the accuracy with which performers follow indications in the score or by some other criterion? For example, the legendary Russian pianist Vladimir Sofronitsky was considered almost to "incarnate" the music of Alexander Scriabin in his performances; and yet, there are instances in his recordings where he does not conform to the composer's directions.[186] At the very least, the threshold at which this determination is made should be set at a higher point now than in the past. The composer should not be able to intervene in questions of style and expression that represent the performer's art. The performer will also be entitled to make choices in order to preserve the integrity of his or her own performance.

Such an issue arose in the Netherlands in a rather different context. A Dutch theater company, De Haarlemse Toneelschuur, decided to mount a production of Samuel Beckett's play, *Waiting for Godot*, with an all-female cast. This iconic play focuses on four male characters, but there are many reasons, both practical and idealistic, why a female production might be attempted. Theater scholar, David Bradby, sees it as a simple issue of gender equality:

> With the increasing empowerment of women in theater, many attempts have been made to perform Godot with an all-female cast. One such was in 1988, in Holland, a society where women's liberation was accepted earlier than elsewhere.[187]

This Dutch production aroused the ire of Beckett, who felt that women actors could not convey what he intended in his play. His explanation that "women do not have prostates" may offend at first glance, but the main character, Vladimir, actually suffers from an enlarged prostate. This becomes known to the audience through his frequent visits offstage to relieve himself. Bradby comments,

> [H]is remark about prostates, although typically economical and rather puckish, deserves to be taken seriously because of its emphasis on the body. As Krejča

[186] See, e.g., his extraordinary performance of Scriabin's second sonata, where he departs from some dynamics in the score: truecrypt, *Vladimir Sofronitsky plays Scriabin Sonata no. 2, Op 19*, YouTube (Jan. 16, 2008),
0:45–0:48, https://www.youtube.com/watch?v=gT4IFD5ue0k.

[187] David Bradby, Beckett: Waiting for Godot 155–56 (2001).

pointed out, the play came to life when the actors were able to use their own flesh, avoiding "impersonating" in favor of "being."[188]

Beckett brought an action against the Dutch theater company through the French *Société des auteurs et compositeurs dramatiques* (SACD), the collective agency responsible for dramatic rights. But the theater company received a sympathetic hearing from the Dutch judge, who commented that "the play was about the human condition in general" and therefore "transcended the sexual identity of men and women." He also noted that the interpretation of the play by the female actors and director showed great fidelity to Beckett's text. For this reason, it was impossible to establish that the integrity of the work had been violated.[189]

Bradby feels that the judge should have been more sympathetic towards Beckett's artistic vision for the play. Beckett rejected traditional conventions of location and, it could be added, traditional notions of plot. The innovative nature of the play lies in its ability to create a tremendous sense of indeterminacy. The extension of this underlying aesthetic to the issue of gender might be a valuable creative insight. Yet Beckett objected.

The case reveals the interesting possibility of a schism within the artistic personality itself. Creative innovation and social conservatism may coexist in one mind. The resulting inner tension can lead the author to invoke moral rights to the possible *detriment* of his or her own artistic work. This may have been what happened in this case.

On the French theory of moral rights in its purest form, the artistic quality of the alteration is irrelevant: the fact that the author does not want it is reason enough to ban it. But the Dutch court took a broader perspective on moral rights, acknowledging the author's right to control his own creation, but balancing it a a broader social interest in culture. The issue could also be framed as one of competing moral rights—dramatic author, theater director, and performers—and how to manage their coexistence. Bradby comments that the discussion surrounding the case in Holland did touch on the issue of "the director's creative freedom."[190]

Beckett's response to the court case was to ban all productions of his plays in Holland.

5. Recording and Broadcasting

The extension of moral rights to performers brings a new layer of complexity to recordings. Performers' moral rights coexist alongside an existing framework of both

[188] Id. at 157.
[189] Id.
[190] Id.

economic and moral rights. From the artists' perspective, the territorial borders of composition and performance must now be redrawn. From the perspective of the public, when it comes to use of the work, there is an additional layer of rights to recognize and negotiate—permissions to seek, payments to make.

The complex relationship between composer and performer means that, in most cases, the successful release of a recording will involve a degree of cooperation between the two. The purchase of music rights by the performer from the composer may not be enough to clarify matters. Notwithstanding the potential role of collective agencies, the moral rights will still be held personally by the composer and must be dealt with as a distinct issue. At the same time, a composer's objections to the interpretation of his or her work should not be allowed to stray into areas of the art that are properly the domain of performers. As the area of performers' rights develops, courts are likely to find themselves in the awkward position of trying to determine and delimit the creative spaces inhabited by each. Prominent members of the musical community need to address this issue in their own writing, speaking, and collaborative work. It should not be left primarily in the hands of outsiders.

The potential for conflict between composers and performers is likely to affect the largest and most powerful musical communities, represented by popular music in all its genres. They are built upon the work of living composers and recent composers. Classical music is also affected, to a lesser extent, when work by current composers is performed. Where perpetual protection for moral rights exists, as in France, moral rights issues could theoretically arise in the performance of classic works, although this has never happened. On the other hand, the need to attribute modern editors of classic works has been recognized in the UK case of *Sawkins v. Hyperion Records*.[191]

A largely untapped market for Western classical music exists in other parts of the world. The controversial music critic Norman Lebrecht,[192] writing for Bloomberg News, comments,

[191] *See Sawkins v. Hyperion Records* [2005] E.M.L.R. 29 (CA), an interesting UK case on moral rights that involved a record company's failure to attribute authorship to the editor of works by a French baroque composer, Richard de Lalande. The editor, Dr. Sawkins, was a musicologist and authority on the works of Lalande, and his work on each of the four editions used extended over some 300 hours. Hyperion had thanked Dr. Sawkins "for his preparation of performance materials for this recording." The English Court of Appeal noted that there was no fixed formula for attribution in circumstances such as these. Nevertheless, Mummery LJ, like the judge at first instance, felt that this was insufficient: "Although the CD sleeve named Dr Sawkins, it did not identify his authorship" (id. at para. 69). Interestingly, Mummery LJ commented that Hyperion's acknowledgment was in line with usual practice, but this did not excuse the failure to attribute authorship.

[192] *See, e.g., Grigory Sokolov Refuses Award Because It Has Previously Been Won by Norman Lebrecht*, Gramophone (Sept. 28, 2015), https://www.gramophone.co.uk/classical-music-news/article/grigory-sokolov-refuses-award-because-it-has-previously-been-won-by-norman-lebrecht. For an interesting comment on this incident, see *Churnalism Is Destroying Classical Music*, On an Overgrown Path (Sept. 29, 2015), https://www.overgrownpath.com/2015/09/churnalism-is-destroying-classical-music.html.

> Taking a different measure, classical recording is bucking the industry slump in key areas, according to the International Federation of the Phonographic Industry [IFPI]. Sales are on the rise in France and Poland, where they constitute 9 percent of the market, in Austria and Hungary at 11 percent, and in Germany and Australia at 6 percent.
>
> The biggest surge is in China w[h]ere one in six recordings that are legally traded is of Western classical music, show figures just released by the IFPI. In South Korea, the share is 18 percent. In the U.S., the classical share of record sales is just under 1 percent.
>
> It's in the young tiger markets, more than at the mature American concert halls, that classical music is finding its future.[193]

Though Lebrecht's focus on China is understandable, Western classical music has long been well established in India and has a very distinguished history there.[194]

H. Recommendations

Moral rights in music should be recognized and protected in the digital context. The recognition of moral rights should be subject to certain adaptations which are appropriate to this environment. The form in which digital music rights develop will almost certainly help to frame policies around digital moral rights in other areas of interest, such as film.

The moral right of attribution should be respected, but it should be exercised with technological necessity in mind. Notably, in the context of specialized uses of music such as mobile ringtones, attribution in the sound of the ringtone would be unpredictable because of the nature of the ringtone. Different methods of attribution, such as video attribution or attribution in an attached file, should be explored. But the importance of attribution in the digital environment should be recognized. In the future, music is likely to be distributed primarily through online channels—pay-per-download services like iTunes, global licensing schemes, or new models that develop as a result of new experiences in the coming years. If the attribution of works is not maintained, we will experience a gradual loss of musical history. As the names of musicians disappear, so, too, do their stories. Much of our knowledge about music is derived from our knowledge of the lives, careers, and compositions of great musicians of the past. In this light, there can be no doubt

193 He concludes, "The signs are that recession is once again accelerating the need for the spiritual consolation that only a symphony can deliver." *See* Norman Lebrecht, *Recession Blues Spurs Classical Music*, BLOOMBERG (June 8, 2009).

194 *See, e.g.*, Ananya Barua, *Lost Tales: How Mysore's Maharaja Created History in Western Classical Music*, THE BETTER INDIA (Aug. 20, 2019), https://www.thebetterindia.com/192140/mysore-maharaja-wadiyar-western-classical-music-history-india.

that the principle of attribution needs to include, not only composers, but also performers. The WPPT has set an important benchmark in this regard, although its recognition of performers excludes the world of film and is, therefore, incomplete.

The right of integrity remains an essential right in the environment of new music. It plays an important role in preserving musical culture, and it lends invaluable support to the establishment of artistic reputations, on which musical careers continue to be built. In most digital scenarios, the integrity right should be restricted to situations of damage to reputation. Given the extent to which music is "handled" in the downloading context, an open-ended right of integrity might prove counterproductive, and lead to an unwillingness to disseminate music via digital means.

In the digital context, it is particularly important to recognize a third, and fundamental, moral right: the right of disclosure. The principle of disclosure assumes a new significance in the digital world—indeed, it may be the only right that can be unequivocally protected in practice *and* justified in theory, where digital technology is concerned. When it comes to moral rights in the Digital Age, the right of disclosure should no longer be taken for granted, implied into the existing legal framework for moral rights.[195] It should be stated openly, alongside the author's economic right to release his or her work to the public. In the monist tradition, disclosure should be recognized as both an economic and moral prerogative of authorship.

Extending moral rights to technical musicians, such as sound engineers, makes sense in an environment where art and technology are ever more closely connected. The nature of the special relationship between performer and engineer must be considered, as the work of the engineer is dependent upon the performer for its raw material. This factor will affect the framing of moral rights for sound engineers. The rights that they enjoy may need to remain subordinate to the performer's rights; at the same time, sound engineers are entitled to attribution for their labor, creativity, and individuality in the creation of a sound environment appropriate for the performer's work. In a sense, the sound engineer is like the jeweler who places an exquisite gem in its setting—without the setting, the gem shows little splendor.

In order to acquire practical significance, moral rights must be recognized across a wide variety of jurisdictions. In this process, the countries of the European Union have a special role to play. Moral rights should be harmonized across European member states as part of a pan-European licensing scheme for music downloads. European countries are well placed, as a bloc, to demand compliance with moral

[195] For example, it is arguably implicit in Art. *6bis* of the *Berne* Convention, *supra* note 70. *See* Mira T. Sundara Rajan, *Moral Rights and Copyright Harmonisation: Prospects for an "International Moral Right"*? nn.42–65 and accompanying text, Paper presented to the Seventeenth BILETA Annual Conference (Apr. 5–6, 2002), https://www.bileta.org.uk/wp-content/uploads/Moral-Rights-and-Copyright-Harmonisation-Prospects-for-an-International-Moral-Right.pdf.

rights from music companies. If European countries are determined to command respect for moral rights across the EU region, a level of corporate acquiescence is likely to be achieved. Given the size and importance of this pan-European market, it seems unlikely that respect for moral rights will dampen the European music market vis-à-vis the United States. On the contrary, if companies are required to respect moral rights in Europe, it seems likely that they will choose to circulate moral rights information in other jurisdictions as well, rather than removing it for the U.S. market.

The European experience of both collective licensing and moral rights is extensive, placing European Union countries in a good position to develop rules on specific moral rights issues, such as the separation of individual tracks on an album. It should also be noted that respect for moral rights is in harmony with the legal systems of a number of powerful countries—India, Japan, Russia, and even China—and may actually help to open up further markets for the U.S. music industry overseas.

I. Conclusion: The Public Interest in Music

As the first area of the arts to become intimately engaged with technology, music represents an important test case for the protection of moral rights in the digital context. From the DJ phenomenon to the composition of electronic music, technology brings new challenges to the principles of attribution and integrity. The practices that evolve through music are likely to serve as invaluable guideposts for recognizing moral rights in other contexts.

The importance of access to music is often invoked by advocates of the public interest. But why is the discussion of the public interest so narrowly circumscribed? The broader interest in the integrity of cultural heritage, which is ultimately the treasured possession of the public, also deserves attention. The integrity of cultural heritage is a vast area, encompassing the protection of both material cultural property and the preservation of the general environment for culture. Only by encouraging interest in culture, education, and the creative ability of individuals who are alive today can cultural heritage as a concept continue to exist.

Protecting the moral rights of composers and performers upholds their human rights and helps to preserve an important part of our cultural heritage: musical history. Through technology, this ancient art form can extend its reach across time and space, and reach individuals who are alive today. In this sense, technology mirrors the magic of music itself, which can transport us instantly into the intimate state of mind of the composer. Contact with music means contact with its creator, and moral rights can help to maintain the integrity and vitality of this relationship. Without a connection to the musicians of our world—past, present, and future—the digital cosmos could prove to be a lonely place.

7

Authors and *Auteurs*

Copyright and Moral Rights in Film

I believe the people who are coloring movies have contempt for the audience by claiming, in effect, that viewers are too stupid and too insensitive to appreciate black and white photography—that they must be given, like infants or monkeys, bright colors to keep them amused.

—Woody Allen[1]

- A. **Introduction** 457
- B. **Commerce Meets Creation: Authorship of a Film** 460
- C. **The Film as a Derivative Work: An Argument against Moral Rights?** 474
- D. **Practical Challenges: Film Litigation in India and France** 477
  - 1. India: Moral Rights in a Culture of Adaptation 482
    - a. Producer vs. Author: *Mannu Bhandari* 482
      - i. Moral Rights and Film Contracts 486
      - ii. "Certain Modifications" 487
      - iii. Remedies 489
      - iv. Cultural Heritage 489
    - b. Digital Re-creation: *Anand Patwardhan* 492
  - 2. Colorization: Producers vs. Directors in France 494
- E. **Film as a Technological Work** 499
  - 1. Editing, Creative Allusion, and Reuse: From Fan Films to Family Movies 500
  - 2. The Communication of Films Online 508
  - 3. Fame beyond the Grave: Reviving Deceased Actors through Artificial Intelligence 510
- F. **Recommendations** 511
- G. **Conclusion** 514

A. Introduction

Film has been called the one truly original art form of the twentieth century.[2] Countless artistic elements merge in the creation of a film—images, drama, words,

[1] Woody Allen, *The Colorization of Films Insults Artists and Society*, New York Times (June 28, 1987).

[2] James H. Billington, Librarian of Congress, has commented, "The moving picture is not so much the art form as the language of the twentieth century.... Future generations will wonder why so little

music, and, of course, the technology that binds all of these together and creates the look of the finished work. However spectacular in themselves, the whole is still somehow greater than the sum of these parts. The complex nature of this art form presents a fundamental challenge to the image of the artist as individual, whose work reflects a unified artistic concept, embodied in the nineteenth-century doctrine of moral rights. But moral rights have also proven their capacity to accommodate film. With the notable exception of the United States, moral rights in this medium are recognized in most countries of the world.[3]

Their practical relevance to film is beyond doubt.[4] A number of leading international cases on moral rights have arisen out of the treatment of films. In this process, something peculiar has happened: films originating in the United States, now the world's third largest producer of movies, have found themselves at the heart of international conflicts involving moral rights.[5] The colorization of black-and-white films has become the single most widely litigated conflict in film moral rights. The issue, essentially a dispute between the competing Hollywood interests of filmmakers and production companies, received a seminal legal treatment from the French courts in the case of *Turner Entertainment v. Huston*.[6] Moral rights issues have arisen in the creative products of a country that does not recognize moral

of such a marvelously accessible and appealing record was ever preserved or seriously studied by the strangely transparent and otherwise exuberant society that produced it all." *See* Library of Congress, *National Film Preservation Board* (n.d.), https://www.loc.gov/programs/national-film-preservation-board/preservation-research/film-preservation-study/overview. All websites cited in this chapter were last visited on Oct. 28, 2024.

[3] Most Western European countries, including France, Germany, Italy, Austria, Spain, and Belgium, have special provisions on moral rights in film. For useful comparative analyses of the different regimes of film copyright in European countries, see Irini Stamatoudi, *Moral Rights of Authors in England: The Missing Emphasis on the Role of Creators*, 8(4) INTELL. PROP. Q. 478, 500–503 (1997); for a more detailed treatment, see PASCAL KAMINA, FILM COPYRIGHT IN THE EUROPEAN UNION 284–337 (2002).

[4] This chapter uses the terminology of film, audiovisual works, and cinematographic works interchangeably; all of these appear in international laws dealing with copyright and moral rights in motion pictures. For a helpful analysis of their different uses and connotations, see IRINI A. STAMATOUDI, *Audiovisual Works, in* COPYRIGHT AND MULTIMEDIA PRODUCTS: A COMPARATIVE ANALYSIS 104, para 6.1 (2002). She notes, "There is no definite way of distinguishing between audiovisual works, films and cinematographic works, and most national copyright laws use one of the terms to include the others or use all or some of the terms interchangeably": id. at 110 (footnotes omitted).

[5] There is some variability about which is considered the largest film industry in the world, but the largest producer of films appears to be India, which combines the Hindi-language popular film industry, known as "Bollywood"—because it is based in Mumbai, formerly known as Bombay—with cinema in a variety of other national languages of India. Nigeria is also highly productive and possibly in second place; its film industry is now known as "Nollywood." *See, e.g.*, *Nigeria Surpasses Hollywood as World's Second Largest Film Producer—UN*, UN NEWS (May 5, 2009), https://news.un.org/en/story/2009/05/299102-nigeria-surpasses-hollywood-worlds-second-largest-film-producer-un (noting that "Key to Nollywood's explosive success is Nigerian filmmakers' reliance on video instead of film, reducing production costs, and, as the survey points out, the West African country has virtually no formal cinemas, with about 99 per cent of screenings in informal settings, such as home theatres.").

[6] *Turner Entertainment v. Huston Heirs*, Cour d'appel [CA] [regional court of appeal] Versailles, chs Réunies, Dec. 19, 1994, 164 RIDA 389 (1995), *on remand from* Cour de cassation [Cass.] [supreme court for judicial matters] 1e civ., May 28, 1991, 149 RIDA 197 (1991) (Fr.).

rights in film and, perhaps more importantly, where moral rights protection is vigorously opposed by the powerful Motion Picture Academy Association (MPAA), Hollywood's lobbying wing.[7] As a result, the contribution of U.S. filmmakers to the art has been vindicated outside U.S. borders, while little scope to recognize it exists under U.S. law.

At the same time, U.S. courts have built a certain familiarity with artistic and cultural issues in film. The well-known case of *Shostakovich*, from 1948, involved the use of music by four celebrated Soviet composers in an anti-Soviet film. In a lawsuit brought in the New York Supreme Court, the composers argued that their right of integrity had been violated by the association of their works with the incompatible political views expressed in the film.[8] Despite the silence of U.S. copyright legislation on moral rights, the U.S. judge gave an impressive assessment of the issues. His reasoning undertook the difficult task of determining whether moral rights could exist at U.S. law even though the U.S. copyright statute did not provide explicitly for them. The reasons for Justice Koch's eventual finding against a moral right were practical ones—he felt that the absence of legislative guidance on this issue would create intolerable uncertainty about the nature of the rights and the practical implications of protecting them. However, in the judge's view, there was no underlying reason of law or culture why moral rights could not be accepted on the U.S. scene.[9] Indeed, the judge found that, in certain circumstances, a moral right could be invoked to protect works in the public domain. In this respect, the ruling still represents a novel way of thinking about the public domain in the United States, where it is usually considered an area of near-absolute freedom.[10]

The twenty-first century transformation of film has brought many new possibilities to this art form. Digital images of personalities from film history can be used to recreate actors and characters from the past. Movies can be communicated to viewers by Internet, with access on an individual and near-instantaneous basis. Films can be copied and broken down into their component parts with relative ease and potentially reused in the making of new videos or films.

[7] For an analysis of how the MPAA's role developed in the context of U.S. bilateral and international trade negotiations, see Stephen Fraser, *Berne, CFTA, NAFTA and GATT: The Implications of Copyright Droit Moral and Cultural Exemptions in International Trade Law*, 18 Hastings Comm. & Ent. L.J. 287 (1996), at 308–11 on film and the Canada–U.S. Free Trade Agreement, and at 316–18 on film and U.S.–France discussions during the Uruguay Round of General Agreement on Tariffs and Trade (GATT) negotiations leading to the establishment of the World Trade Organization (WTO).

[8] *Shostakovich v. Twentieth Century-Fox Film Corp.*, 80 N.Y.S.2d 575 (N.Y. Sup. Ct 1948), *aff'd*, 87 N.Y.S.2d 430 (N.Y. App. Div. 1949) (U.S.). Given the copyright-related practices in the Soviet Union of the time and Shostakovich's own precarious position, it seems clear that the Soviet government took it upon itself to act for the composers. William Strauss notes that the plaintiff was acting as "assignee" of the composers: William Strauss, *The Moral Right of the Author*, 4 Am. J. Comp. L. 506, 534–35 (1955). The case is discussed in Chapter 4, *supra* notes 121–31 and accompanying text. See also the discussion of this aspect of the case in Mira T. Sundara Rajan, Copyright and Creative Freedom: A Study of Post-Socialist Law Reform 104–105 (2006).

[9] Id. (a detailed discussion of the case can be found at ch. 4, *supra*).

[10] See the comments on the U.S. public domain in Sundara Rajan id.

A newly global film community has also come into being. India now surpasses the United States as the world's largest maker of films, and India's insatiable appetite for stories has translated into numerous "Bollywood" remakes of Hollywood films. In contrast to the United States, India has embraced moral rights in films. Indeed, its pioneering jurisprudence on film has paved the way for moral rights in other aspects of culture to be recognized by the Indian courts.[11] It is also interesting to note that Indian moral rights have kept alive a cultural discussion around film, although it is a poor counter to the deterioration of India's art-film tradition, which parallels Bollywood's rise.

All of these new activities, and the many more that are certain to arise in the digital environment, involve questions about moral rights. In this context, will Hollywood continue to oppose moral rights in film? And if so, what will be the potential losses to U.S. and international filmmakers?

B. Commerce Meets Creation: Authorship of a Film

The complexity of moral rights issues in film is unmatched by any other form of creative expression. The nature of the work itself is at fault. Film combines technological and creative elements in a way that no other form of intellectual creation attempts.

Film is the prototype of a technological work. It is a composite work that is largely compiled from the original work of a number of contributors. Those who contribute to a film include the writer of the screenplay or dialogue, the composer of film music and the arranger of the film score, the performers who act in the film, and the technicians responsible for physically creating and shaping the final product. Indeed, countless individuals are involved in the technical and cosmetic aspects of production that give a particular film its characteristic look, from costumes and set design to cinematography.[12] The director requires special mention. He does not contribute a separate work, but his labor, vision, and editorial control are instrumental in realizing the final character of the work. The contribution of

[11] For an overview of the development of moral rights jurisprudence in India, including of the seminal 1986 case *Smt Mannu Bhandari v. Kala Vikas Pictures Pvt Ltd* 1987 AIR (Delhi 13) (India), https://indiankanoon.org/doc/331111, which deals with moral rights in a film adaptation of a novel, see Mira T. Sundara Rajan, *Moral Rights in Developing Countries: The Example of India*, 8(5/6) J. INTELL. PROP. RIGHTS 357, 449 (2003). The *Mannu Bhandari* case is also discussed by U.S. lawyer, Jeffrey Dine: Jeffrey M. Dine, *Authors' Moral Rights in Non-European Nations: International Agreements, Economics,* Mannu Bhandari, *and the Dead Sea Scrolls*, 16 MICH. J. INT'L L. 545 (1995).

[12] The use of costumes is a striking creative issue. Among major directors, Alfred Hitchcock is well known for his attention to this detail; in just one example from his 1960 film *Psycho*, the viewer watches the metamorphosis of a female character from white to black clothing to signify her moral corruption. For an unusual discussion of this and other aspects of the film, see J. Poole, *Psycho: Queering Hitchcock's Classic*, *in* BRIGHT LIGHTS 61 (G. Morris ed., 2008), https://libres.uncg.edu/ir/uncg/f/J_Poole_Psycho_2008.pdf.

the producer is essential, but it is different from all others—financial in nature, but potentially creative, as well.

From a copyright perspective, it is not necessarily important to identify the author of the film. Copyright law, whatever its apparent protests to the contrary, is oriented towards the protection of owners of copyright, rather than authors per se. In relation to film, this focus is clearly apparent. The primary objective of copyright, particularly in the common-law countries, is to protect the investment of economic resources into the making of a film, a rationale that fits well with the labor theory of copyright that traditionally holds sway in these countries.[13] But this approach is more than a common-law tradition; it is pragmatic. A large investment of resources is required to make a film and, as a result of these financial stakes, the industry has acquired certain special characteristics. The focus on production makes sense. At its origins, film was a corporate product; but it has evolved progressively towards a higher identity, becoming an increasingly creative and individual art form.[14]

Where moral rights are concerned, the first question that needs to be addressed is that of authorship. The moral right is vested in the human author of a work, and its existence depends on the expression of creative personality in the work. The fact that a film is a composite work does not necessarily make moral rights inappropriate—indeed, moral rights may be relevant to many group phenomena, from folklore and traditional knowledge in India to the corporate culture of Japan.[15] The rationales for recognizing moral rights in these kinds of works are diverse. Protection of the author is only one perspective on moral rights, and a

[13] The principle that copyright is available in practically any work involving the investment of labor into its creation is a classic proposition of English law. See the seminal English cases *Kenrick v. Lawrence* [1890] 25 Q.B.D. 99 and *University of London Press v. University Tutorial Press* [1916] 2 Ch. 601. In recent years, this standard has slowly evolved upward, towards the creativity standard required for copyright protection in civil law countries. This trend was initiated by the U.S. Supreme Court in *Feist Publications Inc. v. Rural Telephone Service Co.*, 499 U.S. 340, 362–63 (1991), which identified a "modicum of creativity" as a requirement for copyright and led to a reconsideration of standards of originality in other jurisdictions such as Canada, *CCH Canadian Ltd v. Law Society of Upper Canada* [2004] 1 S.C.R. 339, 2004 SCC 13 (Can.), and India, *Eastern Book Co. and ors v. DP Modak and anor*, 2008 (36) PTC 1, 2008 (1) SCC 1 (India). Interestingly, the *Eastern Book Company* case relied explicitly on the Canadian ruling in *CCH* for its resolution of closely similar facts: *see* Supreme Court of India judgments, https://indiankanoon.org/doc/1062099.

[14] In the French context, the progress of film from corporate creation to individual art form is famously described in François Truffaut's landmark essay: François Truffaut, *Une Certaine Tendance du cinéma français* [*A Certain Tendency in French Cinema*], *in* THE FRENCH NEW WAVE: CRITICAL LANDMARKS 17 (Ginette Vincendeau & Peter Graham trans., 2009). The original article appeared as François Truffaut, *Une Certaine Tendance du cinéma français* [*A Certain Tendency in French Cinema*], CAHIERS DU CINÉMA 31 (January 1954).

[15] Japan includes moral rights for corporations in its copyright law: *see* Copyright Law, art. 15(1) and (2) (Japan), on the attribution of authorship to a legal person. The Copyright Law of Japan (February 2020 edition), Copyright Research and Information Center, https://www.cric.or.jp/english/clj/index.html. *See also* Chapter 4, *supra* notes 325–28 and accompanying text.

consideration of moral rights in non-Western jurisdictions shows that the preservation of culture in its less individualistic forms can also be supported by the doctrine.

Is it possible to identify an author whose creative personality is expressed in a film? From a moral rights perspective, it is essential to be able to answer this question. Without an author, there would be no clear rationale for recognizing moral rights in films. In the absence of an author, who would benefit from these rights—and how, and why?

The legal response to this question is astonishingly vague. Major jurisdictions, including the United States, do not clarify the basic question of who can claim authorship in a film.[16] The initial approach in the United Kingdom was to make the producer the owner of copyright, but the director was entitled to moral rights even though he or she was not considered an author. Writing at the time of the adoption of these provisions, William Cornish noted,

> The moral rights are in some cases given to film directors, who are not authors at all and so never acquire initial copyright. In consequence, qualification for moral rights does not necessarily depend, so far as the matter is one of status, upon the position of the person enjoying the right. Dualism on this scale opened the way, during the Parliamentary process, to a highly pragmatic outcome, in which the pressures of interest have played a noteworthy part.[17]

Since then, the UK approach has been modified in a series of 1996 revisions that define the producer and director as "authors" of the film. Unless these are one and the same person, a film is specifically to be considered "a work of joint authorship".[18]

British law also offers the possibility that a film may be physically copied without infringing copyright. The case of *Norowzian v. Arks*[19] found that the essence of a film is to be found in its narrative aspect. If the narrative element is not copied, even the use of similar techniques to create a film that looks very much like the original will not lead to an infringement of copyright.[20] The implications for moral rights are interesting. Under British law, the physical treatment of a film may not be the only factor that can lead to a violation of the moral right of integrity. Acts

[16] See the comments in F. Jay Dougherty, *Not a Spike Lee Joint? Issues in the Authorship of Motion Pictures under U.S. Copyright Law*, 49 UCLA L. Rev. 225, 269–70 (2001).

[17] William R. Cornish, *Moral Rights under the 1988 Act*, 11(12) Eur. Intell. Prop. Rev. 449, 449 (1989). Cornish's use of the term "dualism" in this context is interesting.

[18] Section 10(1A) of the Copyright, Designs and Patents Act (CDPA), 1988 c. 48 (UK), https://www.legislation.gov.uk/ukpga/1988/48/. *See*§§ 9(2)(ab) (authorship of a film), 77(1), (6), and (8) (right to be identified as author or director), 80(1) and (6) (right to object to derogatory treatment of work).

[19] *Norowzian v. Arks Ltd (No. 1)* [1998] EWHC (Ch) 315; *Norowzian v. Arks Ltd (No. 2)* [2000] EMLR 67, [2000] FSR 363 (UKCA).

[20] *See Norowzian (Nos 1 and 2)*, *supra* note 19, especially the comments of Buxton LJ in *Norowzian (No. 2)*, *supra* note 19, at 77–78.

that compromise the integrity of the film as a work of narrative art may also be a relevant concern. The use of images or excerpts in contexts that misrepresent the original narrative could constitute a violation of the right of integrity.

The French approach is to classify the film as a "collaborative" work of "coauthor[ship]."[21] "Coauthors" are defined in the Intellectual Property Code as the scriptwriter, the author of any adaptation, the writer of the dialogue, the composer of music that is especially created for the film, and the director.[22] Coauthorship is the approach of choice in most civil law jurisdictions, including the post-socialist civilian systems of Central and Eastern Europe.[23]

French law has the most comprehensive approach to the problem of film authorship in any major jurisdiction. While production is underway, the relationship of the coauthors plays an instrumental role in shaping the film. Finalizing the film depends upon their mutual agreement and consent. After the final product is complete, the focus turns outward, to the relationship of the creators with the outside world. In this scenario, the producer is not an "author" or "coauthor" of the film, but his or her agreement is necessary in order to settle upon the final version of the film.[24] Under French law, this version is considered the "*version définitive*," which will stand as the copyright work and in which moral rights subsist.[25]

The life of a film therefore unfolds in two phases. The first phase is the creative period, in which the work develops out of the collaborative efforts of the various contributors to the film. This phase concludes with the establishment of the "final version" of the work. This version is a product of agreement between the producer and the coauthors, and once it is decided upon, it becomes illegal to destroy the matrix of this version of the film.[26] It is certainly possible that moral rights issues could arise at this stage of the film's existence out of conflicts between the coauthors about the artistic development of the work. French law does not seem to address the question of how to finalize a work when the coauthors have differences of opinion, except for the indirect assertion that the agreement of all is required before the final version of the film can be established.

[21] *See* Loi 92-597 du 1 juillet 1992 relative au Code de la propriété intellectuelle (partie législative) [Law 92-597 of July 1, 1992, relating to the Intellectual Property Code (Legislative part)], JOURNAL OFFICIEL DE LA RÉPUBLIQUE FRANÇAISE [J.O.] [OFFICIAL GAZETTE OF FRANCE], Feb. 8, 1994 (Code de la propriété intellectuelle), arts. L113-7 and L121-5 (Fr.), https://www.legifrance.gouv.fr/codes/texte_lc/LEGITEXT000006069414.

[22] Id. at art. L113-7.

[23] See, e.g., the provisions of the 2008 Russian Civil Code on intellectual property. Article 1263.2 of the Grazhdanski Kodeks Rossiiskoi Federatsi, Chast' Chetvërtaya [Civil Code of the Russian Federation, Part IV], Federal Law No. 230-FZ of December 18, 2006, *Rossijskaja Gazeta* No. 289 (4255) of December 22, 2006 = *Sobranie zakonodatel'stva RF* (SZ RF) No. 52 (Part I) of December 25, 2006, Item 5496, at 14803 (2008 Russian Civil Code).

[24] *See* French Code de la propriété intellectuelle, *supra* note 21, at art. L121-5.

[25] CODE DE LA PROPRIÉTÉ INTELLECTUELLE COMMENTÉ 120 (para II.A.3) (Pierre Sirinelli, Sylviane Durrande, Antoine Latreille & Jeanne Daleau eds., 2009).

[26] The wording of the statute is that it is *interdit* ("forbidden" or "prohibited") to destroy this version: French Code de la propriété intellectuelle, *supra* note 21, at art. L121-5.

In a sense, what this provision really specifies is a kind of *composite* right to disclose the film. If even one of the coauthors disagrees on the final version proposed by the other authors, that version cannot be established as the "*version définitive*" of the film.[27] In their commentary on the French Intellectual Property Code, Pierre Sirinelli and his colleagues point out that this "slight bending of the traditional rules" on moral rights can be understood in conjunction with the following provision, which sets out the procedures for the completion of a project in the case where one author drops out part-way.[28] It is also interesting to note that, in this phase, the treatment of the moral rights of the coauthors is egalitarian. The director's moral rights do not now have any precedence over the moral rights of the other authors. In the end, French law seems to visualize a practical solution to the problem of artistic conflicts: if the parties concerned cannot agree, the film cannot be released. From the producer's point of view, however, this result could present a highly undesirable outcome, and alternatives may not always be available to complete a work when one of the original authors objects to its realization. No provision is made for the indemnification of the producer in the case of truly irreconcilable artistic differences.

In the second phase of a film's life, the film as a work has been finalized. Moral rights issues may arise, no longer in the course of production, but in the course of exploitation, the commercial distribution of the film. Not only the users of the film but also the producer must respect the moral rights of the coauthors. It is clear that moral rights subsist in the final version of the film only. In this sense, although film is considered a work of coauthorship, the director is given a certain pride of place in the French system. This transition occurs as part of the movement from creative process to product in the life of the film.

But the interpretation of this rule is a subtle point. A moral right may continue to exist in the underlying work that has been incorporated into a film, such as the script or the musical score, and this right would be held by the author of that work. In fact, each author would be the author of two works—his or her own component part and the film as a whole. He or she could therefore object to both the misuse of his or her own portion and to problematic uses made of the film as a whole.

In the final analysis, French law does not provide formal clarification about what is to happen in the case of disputes among the coauthors involving their respective moral rights. A practical solution seems implicit in this separation of a film into its pre- and post-production life: authors should have reconciled their

[27] Sirinelli et al., *supra* note 25, at 119, call it "veto power," and they observe:

Il y aurait donc bien deux phases distinctes dans l'opposabilite du droit moral et l'articulation de l'ensemble fait que l'essentiel des debats ou risques de contentieux se manifesteront au moment d'etablir la version definitive puisque chacun des coauteurs aura alors un pouvoir de veto.

[Accordingly, there would be two distinct phases in the opposability of moral rights and the articulation of the whole such that points of debate or the risk of litigation will occur at the moment when the final version is established because each of the coauthors will have veto power.]

[28] Id. (in the original French, "léger infléchissement aux règles traditionnelles").

artistic differences before the film is finalized. After that point, any one of the authors has a right to object to abuse of the film as a whole, or of any part that he or she created. However, the right to restrict the use of one's individual contribution cannot apply against one's own coauthors or, indeed, be invoked by the authors against the producer: it is only a right against the outside world. The case of the film as a whole is different. For example, the conversion of a black-and-white film into a colorized version, though authorized by its own producer, might amount to a violation of the director's moral right of integrity—this is what happened in the *Huston* case, where Ted Turner was responsible for the colorization of films that he owned, including Huston's classic *The Asphalt Jungle*.[29] The company that bought the rights to broadcast the film in its colorized version was also responsible for violating the integrity of the film.[30] In this scenario, any of the coauthors should have standing to sue for the moral right of integrity.

The German approach can be said to defuse the potential tensions of producer–director relations through two features of the law. First, German law does something important: it restricts the general rules on moral rights in order to accommodate the special nature of film. It does so through a number of specialized provisions. The law includes a separate section on film rights,[31] and in this part, the possibility of distortion of a film is weighed against the requirements of commercial exploitation. In particular, where the "production and exploitation" of the film is concerned, the German provision will only allow "gross distortions" to be prevented. Importantly, "[e]ach author or right holder shall take the others and the film producer into due account when exercising the right."[32] As an additional point, the producer of the film is also granted a kind of quasi-moral right against distortion, which allows him or her "to prohibit any distortion or abridgment of the video recording or video and audio recording which may jeopardize his legitimate interests."[33] Of course, the producer's right against distortion is not a moral right in the usual sense—it is a right arising from economic considerations, and it may be transferred.[34] But the objective is clearly to achieve fair recognition of the producer's contribution to the production of a film. As a final point, it should be

[29] *Turner Entertainment*, *supra* note 6. A number of well-known directors objected to colorization: *see, e.g.*, Woody Allen, *supra* note 1.

[30] The case concerned the broadcast of the film by France's La Cinq network. It is interesting that overdubbing of foreign films in French does not seem to attract the sanction of moral rights, and this remains a common practice in France.

[31] *See* Urheberrechtsgesetz (UrhG) vom 9 Sept. 1965 [Act on Copyright and Related Rights of Sept. 9, 1965], berücksichtigt die Änderung(en) des Gesetzes durch Artikel 25 des Gesetzes vom 23. Juni 2021 (BGBl. I S. 1858) [as amended by article 25 of the Act of June 23, 2021 (Federal Law Gazette I, p. 1858)], Pt. III ("Special provisions on films") (Ger.), https://www.gesetze-im-internet.de/englisch_urhg/englisch_urhg.html (translation provided by Ute Reusch). *See* especially id. at art. 93 ("Protection against distortion; claim to identification").

[32] Id. at art. 93.

[33] Id. at art. 93.

[34] Id. at art. 94.

noted that the moral right of an author to withdraw his or her work from circulation, whether for a change of opinion or for concern about the inadequate exploitation of the work, is not available to those involved in the making of a film.[35]

Secondly, German law provides a useful criterion for evaluating the claims of potential coauthors of a film: "separability." The test to be applied is whether a contribution can be commercially exploited on its own as a "separate" work; if not, then the creators of those inseparable elements will be considered joint authors of the work.[36] The application of this criterion considerably reduces the claims of coauthorship, excluding, in particular, the possibility of scriptwriters and composers of musical scores being treated as joint authors of the film.[37] The device is a clever way of isolating the creative contribution of the makers of a film. If the creative contribution truly applies to the film as a whole, and not merely to a component part, then the person making that contribution is entitled to claim authorship. As Pascal Kamina observes, "[U]nder such a rule, only the director, the director of photography and possibly the editor could claim co-authorship in the film."[38]

The contrast with the U.S. approach could not be stronger. In so far as rules on coauthorship apply to a film, as F. Jay Dougherty points out, "an independently copyrightable contribution is required."[39] If the logic of the German scheme is to isolate the original contribution of the filmmaker, U.S. law looks, instead, at the substantiality—no doubt, in quality as well as quantity—of a given contribution to a work. If the contribution is sufficient to qualify for copyright on its own, the contributor may merit the title of "author."

U.S. law is firmly anchored in an economic understanding of film. The producer can be identified as the owner of the film, and the issue of who is its author is therefore of nominal importance. The question is left open—U.S. law does not identify any individuals as the author, or joint authors, of a film.[40] The solution to authorship problems in the U.S. context is generally thought to lie in the work-for-hire doctrine, with the practical realization that most of the contributors to a film work as employees of the producer. Contractual arrangements for the making of a film can also clarify matters; although contracts imply flexibility, the general practice is to assign all rights to the producer.[41]

These traditions have their roots in the studio system, which saw directors and other creative contributors to a film working as employees of the studio.[42]

[35] Id. at art. 90 ("Limitation of Rights").
[36] Id. at art. 8.1.
[37] Kamina, *supra* note 3, at 157.
[38] Id. at 157.
[39] Dougherty, *supra* note 16, at 276–77. This rule has been upheld by the Ninth Circuit, in particular.
[40] Id. at 269.
[41] Id. at 269–71.
[42] *See* U.S. Copyright Office, *Technological Alterations to Motion Pictures and Other Audiovisual Works: Implications for Creators, Copyright Owners, and Consumers (A Report of the Register of Copyrights, Washington, DC 1989)*, 10 Loyola Ent. L.J. 1, 22–25 (1990).

Conflicts between studio and artist are, of course, an integral part of Hollywood history; and, in a notorious chapter of U.S. life, the McCarthy era blacklist tore apart these relationships as some studios condemned creative people suspected of Communist sympathies.[43] The blacklist episode was not only a clash between studio and artist; like all repressive movements, it also led to a general contamination of the environment, with artists turning against one another under conditions of extraordinary pressure.[44] The potential for conflict is inherent in human relationships, but overwhelming evidence supports the power of environment to shape relationships. Legal norms can influence individual and collective behavior in extraordinary ways beyond the courtroom, and litigation is only one of the many measures of the "success" of a law.[45] A moral rights framework could alter the entire chemistry of film industry relationships, even with little or no increase at all in the number of lawsuits.

In the case of *Aalmuhammed v. Lee*,[46] the Ninth Circuit Court of Appeals showed extreme reluctance to grant the status of a coauthor to Mr. Aalmuhammed, a consultant who made an important contribution to Spike Lee's 1992 film on the controversial African-American Muslim activist, Malcolm X. Aalmuhammed was credited on the film as "Islamic Technical Consultant," but he felt that this designation did not provide fair recognition of his work. The situation was complicated by the fact that, unusually, there was no written contract between Aalmuhammed and either Spike Lee or the film's producers.[47] Dougherty describes Aalmuhammed's involvement in the film:

> There was evidence he suggested script revisions that were included in the film, directed [star Denzel] Washington and other actors in several scenes, created at least two entire scenes with new characters, translated material from Arabic for subtitles, provided voice-overs in his own voice, and edited parts of the film.[48]

Dougherty argues that Hollywood convention should have allowed Aalmuhammed to cross the threshold into coauthorship. Instead, in the absence

[43] A fascinating collection of notes and interviews from the people targeted on the blacklist can be found in PATRICK MCGILLIGAN & PAUL BUHLE, TENDER COMRADES: A BACKSTORY OF THE HOLLYWOOD BLACKLIST (1999); PAUL BUHLE & DAVID WAGNER, BLACKLISTED: THE FILM LOVER'S GUIDE TO THE HOLLYWOOD BLACKLIST (2003).

[44] *See* McGilligan & Buhle, *supra* note 43.

[45] It should be duly noted that lack of litigation can also indicate the success of a regulatory framework.

[46] *Aalmuhammed v. Lee* 202 F.3d 1227 (9th Cir. 2000) (U.S.).

[47] *See* Dougherty, *supra* note 16, at 276 (n.277). Dougherty's informative comments about contract practices in the movie industry conclude with the remark that, "Perhaps Aalmuhammed's arrangement was not formally documented because he did not fall into one of those categories at the inception of his relationship with the production company."

[48] Id. at 277 (footnotes omitted).

of explicit contractual arrangements to that effect, it now appears that it will be exceptionally difficult to qualify as a joint author of an U.S. film.

In the *Spike Lee* case, the court's consideration of film authorship in U.S. law could have provided an interesting clarification of this point. But the court's comments generated further confusion on an already peculiar issue. Questions of authorship primarily arise in U.S. law when the work-for-hire doctrine does not apply, or in the absence of specific contractual arrangements between the parties. Ownership of the work is what counts. Unless and until the authorship of a film implies concrete rights and obligations, the designation of author may have little importance. From a moral rights perspective, a clarification of these issues under U.S. law is imperative, because the exercise of moral rights depends on establishing authorship. At the same time, it seems unlikely that the producer's contribution to a film will be sufficient for him or her to qualify as the holder of the moral right, leading, once again, to the classic potential for conflict between producer and director, owner of the copyright and author of the work.[49]

The court found that there was enough evidence of an authorial contribution to Spike Lee's film to justify its examination of the possibility of coauthorship, but it proceeded to find that the contribution of a coauthor must be more than simply a contribution that is "creative" in nature. According to Dougherty, the required contribution amounts to "an extreme expression of the romantic authorship concept."[50] The test established by the judge in this case was to assess two factors: the degree of "control" over the work exercised by the person claiming joint authorship, and the extent to which that person's contribution is ultimately responsible for the work's "public appeal." Dougherty is rightly skeptical about these tests:

> Judge Kleinfeld's laudable goal was to encourage authors' consultation with others during the creative process and to limit the risk of claims by overreaching contributors. His approach may encourage authors to consult, but it will arguably discourage other people from consulting with them. It does not solve the problem of overreaching contributors, because it may be considered entrenchment for the author to use any minimally creative expressive material a contributor provides. Also, it may not really benefit production companies because the tests of control and of audience appeal are inherently unpredictable and uncertain.[51]

Of course, the emphasis on contractual arrangements for film is not, by any means, unique to the United States, or to common-law countries. Contractual arrangements also enjoy pride of place in regulating the relationships among different

[49] Dougherty describes the transformation of the roles of producer and director through the history of film and concludes that, "today, studio production executives focus more on business matters and the director's importance has correspondingly increased" (footnote omitted): id. at 312.

[50] Id. at 277.

[51] Id. at 281.

contributors to a film in the continental systems. From one perspective, the role of contracts makes sense: contracts provide a measure of flexibility to deal with the complexities of individual relationships and circumstances involved in the making of a film. On the other hand, the issues that arise are likely to have many points in common from one film production scenario to the next, and some basic level of regulation to establish rules that reflect these commonalities would make sense. The failure to do so is little more than a form of tacit cooperation on the part of governments with the power of production houses, which are likely to enjoy the advantages of disproportionate bargaining power when film contracts are concluded.

Money is important, but without creative input, how can a viable film be developed for either critical or mass-market tastes? In fact, both financial resources and creative skill are needed for any film venture to succeed. The problem of unequal bargaining power is recognized in both common law and European countries, but the specific issue of bargaining inequality in artistic relationships seems to receive greater attention in the European context. In particular, moral rights play a role in alleviating this inequality. In Europe, restrictions on the scope of artistic contracts, and on the allowability of waivers of moral rights, leads to a situation where film relationships function in an environment of greater legal rigidity, but in which, fairness for artists may become an achievable goal.[52]

Appropriately enough, the regulation of author–producer relationships receives interesting consideration in Italian law. Italy, a country with a brilliant tradition of intellectual cinema, has some of the most elegant provisions on film moral rights among the European Union countries. Italian law clearly identifies the "author of the subject-matter, the author of the scenario, the composer of the music and the artistic director" as joint authors of the film; rights of exploitation are, however, held by producers.[53] The Italian law provides that a producer has the right to make "necessary" modifications to the contributions for the purpose

[52] An example of how this occurs in the Russian context is discussed by Elena Muravina & Karina Ayrapetova, *Making the Twain Meet: Cross-Border Entertainment Transactions between Russia and the United States*, *in* Intellectual Property: Eastern Europe and the CIS (Mira T. Sundara Rajan ed., 2010).

[53] *See* arts. 44 and 45 of the Italian Copyright Act, respectively: Legge 22 aprile 1941, n. 633, G.U. July 16, 1941, n.166 (It.), http://www.interlex.it/testi/l41_633.htm. An earlier version of the law is available in English translation through the World Intellectual Property Organization (WIPO) Collection of Laws for Electronic Access: *see* WIPO, *Law No. 633 of April 22, 1941, for the Protection of Copyright and Other Rights Connected with the Exercise Thereof (as amended up to April 9, 2003)* (n.d.), https://www.wipo.int/wipolex/en/text/477668. The Library of Congress has information on further updates to the Italian Copyright Law: *see* Library of Congress, *Italy: Copyright Law Updated for Digital Era* (Dec. 27, 2021), https://www.loc.gov/item/global-legal-monitor/2021-12-27/italy-copyright-law-updated-for-digital-era. The Library of Congress information is current to Nov. 8, 2021, and it includes details of Italian implementation of Directive (EU) 2019/790 of the European Parliament and of the Council of 17 April 2019 on copyright and related rights in the Digital Single Market and amending Directives 96/9/EC and 2001/29/EC, 2019 O.J. (L 130) 92 (DSM Directive), https://eur-lex.europa.eu/eli/dir/2019/790/oj. *See also* Eleonora Rosati, *Italy Has Transposed the DSM Directive*, The IPKat (Nov. 7, 2021), https://ipkitten.blogspot.com/2021/11/italy-has-transposed-dsm-directive.html.

of "cinematographic adaptation," presumably with commercial viability in mind.[54] Importantly, any disagreement between an author and a producer about modifications to the film are subject to adjudication by a government panel.[55]

This provision adds a nice touch of objectivity to the thorny question of disputes over cinematographic transformation.[56] The Italian terminology is evocative, because it draws attention to a curious fact: in a sense, a film is always an adaptation of the underlying work of the contributors. When a screenplay becomes a film, for example, the director is involved in retelling the story originally expressed in the medium of the screenplay through a completely different form of narration—the composite work, blending images and sound with words, that is the film. What works well in the screenplay may or may not be effective in the context of the film.

Film moral rights become even more interesting in the case of a film that is an adaptation of a pre-existing work, such as a book. Not only are the moral rights of film coauthors involved, but the rights of the original author of the underlying work must also be considered. Selling the rights to film a novel, for example, will not take away the novelist's moral rights.[57] The problem of maintaining the integrity of a literary work in the case of a film adaptation can be exceptionally difficult. The demands of the new medium may be very different from the conventions of the original form. What is perfection in one genre may be dysfunctional in another.

In an interview, director Alfred Hitchcock claimed that he would not film a great work of literature such as Dostoevsky's *Crime and Punishment*, because "in Dostoyevsky's novel there are many, many words and all of them have a function .... [T]o really convey that in cinematic terms, substituting the language of the camera for the written word, one would have to make a six- to ten-hour film." His interlocutor, François Truffaut adds, "Theoretically, a masterpiece is something that has already found ... its definitive form."[58]

Italian law also provides explicitly that the authors shall enjoy a right of attribution that includes their names and details of their roles in the production. In contrast to German law, it also provides that a producer's failure either to finish production or, indeed, to show the work within a period of three years will release

[54] Italian Copyright Act, *supra* note 53, at art. 47. The first part states, "The producer shall have the right to make such modifications in works utilized in a cinematographic work as are necessary for their cinematographic adaption."

[55] Id. at art. 47 states,

In the absence of agreement between the producer and one or more of the authors referred to in Article 44 of this Law, the question whether modifications effected or to be effected in a cinematographic work are necessary shall be decided by the Chairman of the Council of Ministers in accordance with the rules contained in the Regulations. The findings of the College shall be final.

[56] Of course, it must be assumed that the government body charged with this determination makes an objective assessment and is not unduly influenced by the power of the producer or vulnerable to corruption.

[57] For an interesting Indian case on this issue, see *Mannu Bhandari, supra* note 11. The case involved the Bollywood adaptation of a literary Hindi novel and was a seminal moral rights precedent.

[58] François Truffaut, with the collaboration of Helen G. Scott, Hitchcock 72 (rev'd. ed., 1984).

all participants from their contractual obligations and render them free to do whatever they choose with their respective contributions.[59]

Russia is a post-Communist country with an important tradition of filmmaking. Its new Civil Code provisions, valid from January 1, 2008, include moral rights in film.[60] As in the civil law countries of Western Europe, Russian law considers the film to be an expression of coauthorship, and the authors of the film are the director-producer,[61] the author of the screenplay,[62] and the composer of original musical works, with or without words, used in the film. In Russian law, however, it is clear that two works exist at all times: moral rights subsist in the screenplay for the film, for example, and also, in the film as a finished product. As Elena Muravina and Karina Ayrapetova point out, Russian industry practice is to transfer rights in both the screenplay and the film from the screenwriter to the person exploiting the film, notably, the producer.[63] However, these kinds of licensing arrangements can only clarify the exploitation of economic rights: moral rights remain with the authors and cannot be transferred or waived under Russian law. Again, Muravina and Ayrapetova illustrate how Russian agreements work within the moral rights framework by providing that the transfer of rights to a producer occurs "to the full extent now or hereafter permitted by applicable law."[64] Crucially, the moral rights available to the authors of the film are limited to rights of name and the inviolability of the work;[65] they do not benefit from a right of withdrawal either in relation to the underlying work or with respect to the film itself.[66] But Russian law, too, is unsatisfactory in failing to clarify the relationships among coauthors. In particular, the role of the director in finalizing the use of screenplay and music is not recognized; in the absence of clarification, it would appear that the moral rights of all three coauthors are treated on an equal basis. This model of filmmaking is apparently collaborative in nature; but how practical is it? Without any provision for the special, or supervisory, role of the director, the moral rights of the screenwriter or the film composer could interfere with the process of finalizing the film. Unlike French law, no reference is made in Russian law to the need for collaborative agreement among the authors in order establish the final version of the film.

On the question of film authorship, the example of India offers some insight. It is typical for India to represent, and somehow reconcile, apparent contradictions. This rule of Indian culture applies perfectly to film. India is a developing country

[59] Italian Copyright Act, *supra* note 53, at art. 50.

[60] The subject had been closely addressed in the draft Civil Code provisions of 2001, which were largely, though not entirely, followed in the 2008 Civil Code, *supra* note 23. *See* Sundara Rajan, Copyright and Creative Freedom, *supra* note 8, at 188–98. See also the remarks on updates to Russian law in this book, in Chapter 4, *supra* notes * and accompanying text.

[61] The Russian term is *regissër-postanovshchik*. *See* 2008 Civil Code, *supra* note 23, at art. 1263.2(1).

[62] *Avtor stsenariya*. *See* id. at art. 1263.2(2).

[63] *See* Muravina & Ayrapetova, *supra* note 52.

[64] Id.

[65] *See* 2008 Russian Civil Code, *supra* note 23, at art. 1228(2).

[66] Id. at art. 1269.

that is also the world's largest producer of films. The garishness of its commercial film industry may be unparalleled; the delicacy of its art cinema is as exquisite as the petals of a rose.[67]

The divide between economic ownership and creative integrity plays itself out in the Indian film industry with unique intensity. As in Indian copyright law as a whole, the Indian treatment of film reveals an inner tension between a common-law tradition and a post-colonial perspective. Under the Indian Copyright Act, there is no ambiguity about the authorship of a film: the legislation states that the author of a film is the producer.[68] However, the extensive treatment of moral rights in the Indian Copyright Act makes no special provision for film. Instead, section 57 of the Indian Copyright Act simply identifies the "author" of a work as the beneficiary of moral rights of attribution and integrity.[69] Since moral rights are not excluded from "cinematographic works," two logical results follow. First, moral rights of attribution and integrity arise in Indian films. Secondly, these rights are enjoyed by the producer.

This position is clearly anomalous. Producers, who are the economic forces behind the work, enjoy moral rights. But moral rights are normally held by the individuals who represent the creative forces engaged in a work. In addition, section 2(l)(uu) of the Indian Copyright Act specifies only that the producer must be "a person who takes the initiative and responsibility for making the work." Nothing in the Indian Copyright Act specifies that a human person, alone, is entitled to moral rights.[70] By defining the producer as the "author" of a film, Indian law creates an unusual situation, where a corporation could hold moral rights in a film.[71] The relative lack of clarity about personhood under the Act also leaves open the issue of whether works created by artificial intelligence would be protectable as copyright works under the act.[72]

Indeed, the situation of economic rights in film is also far from clear-cut in Indian law. Problems arise because the layering of rights in a film is acknowledged,

[67] Internationally, the most famous of Indian art-film directors is certainly Satyajit Ray (1921–1992), whose Bengali films have acquired a passionate following. A wide selection of his works, including creative writing, is published by Penguin India: *see* https://penguin.co.in/book_author/ray-satyajit.

[68] *See* Copyright Act, 1957, No. 14, s. 2(d)(v) (India), http://copyright.gov.in/Documents/CopyrightRules1957.pdf. A look at the amendment Bill shows that this provision was to remain the same: see the Bill and commentary on the legislation when it was still under discussion, available at https://prsindia.org/billtrack/the-copyright-amendment-bill-2010.

[69] Act 27 of 2012, s. 36 (w.e.f. 21-6-2012) amended the Act to remove a time limit on the moral right of integrity, which, between 1994 and 2012, was limited by the words "which is done before the expiration of the term of copyright".

[70] Accordingly, nothing in the Indian Copyright Act, *supra* note 68, excludes the possibility of moral rights for corporations. See discussion in Chapter 5, *supra* notes 30–31 and accompanying text.

[71] The same result occurs in Japanese law, where the "author" holds moral rights, but "author" is not defined to exclude corporations; on the contrary, the Japanese law explicitly provides that a "legal person" may hold more moral rights. *See* Copyright Law of Japan, *supra* note 15, at art. 15(1) and (2).

[72] *See* Chapter 5 *supra*. The issue is also discussed briefly by Rommel Khan, *India: AI Works—The Future Of Intellectual Property Law*, Mondaq (Feb. 20, 2023), https://www.mondaq.com/india/copyright/1284668/ai-works--the-future-of-intellectual-property-law.

but the relationships that it leads to are not clarified. Soundtracks are a case in point. *Filmi* music is a gigantic industry in India. Regarding the soundtrack to a film, the Indian Copyright Act suggests that there is a separate copyright for a musical work used in the film and that this copyright may itself be split into the rights of music composer and lyricist.[73] And yet, as pointed out by a paper produced for the Indian Ministry of Human Resource Development, the producer has a right to authorize the sale of a film soundtrack. The study states,

> Music is an integral part of any cinematographic work. In India, film soundtracks account for almost 80% of the total music market. Even if [the] film producer has the copyright in the film, the music included in the film is the outcome of efforts undertaken by a separate group of creative people such as the composer, lyricists etc.—each of which is a rightholder of its own right. Generally the producer sells this right to a music company who makes cassettes/CDs of such songs for sale in the market. The incidence of a large number of rights in a single work and the involvement of a variety of right holders make the copyright issue very complicated in cinematographic works.[74]

The internal contradictions in this statement are difficult to reconcile. In particular, if the copyright in the musical works used in the film rests with the composers of those works, the producer can only sell musical rights in so far as is permitted by the contractual arrangements between the producer and the artists. But in this case, it is not clear why the definition of "cinematographic work" in the Copyright Act includes the musical soundtrack.[75] This framework then raises the problem of competing moral rights among the different participants in the creation of a film. Will the film composer and the director see eye to eye on the use of the music in the film? And, if they do not, what right does an Indian director have to promote his or her own view? By a supreme irony, the copyright law of the country of Satyajit Ray never so much as mentions the word "director" as the author of a film.[76]

[73] The Indian Copyright Act, *supra* note 68, §2(p), defines a "musical work" as "a work consisting of music and [that] includes any graphical notation of such work *but does not include any words or any action intended to be sung, spoken or performed with the music*" (emphasis added). The Act clearly attempts to separate musical, literary, and dramatic works, as nearly as possible, into watertight compartments—to the extent that a song that includes both music and words is essentially seen by the Act as a composite product containing two works: one musical; one literary.

[74] *See* N.K. Nair, A.K. Barman & Utpal Chattopadhyay, Study on Copyright Piracy in India (1999), http://copyright.gov.in/Documents/STUDY%20ON%20COPYRIGHT%20PIRACY%20IN%20INDIA.pdf.

[75] But there is little doubt that it does. *See* Indian Copyright Act, *supra* note 68, §2(f) (emphasis added; footnote omitted):

(f) "cinematograph film" means any work of visual recording on any medium produced through a process from which a moving image may be produced by any means *and includes a sound recording accompanying such visual recording* and "cinematograph" shall be construed as including any work produced by any process analogous to cinematography including video films.

[76] Id. The word "director" appears three times in §69 and is used in the Indian sense of head, or "director," of a company or firm.

C. The Film as a Derivative Work: An Argument against Moral Rights?

As these examples show, the composite nature of film has an important legal consequence: it implies an awkward situation of coexisting rights, belonging to different persons, in the same work. When considering moral rights in film, it is essential to resolve the issue of potentially competing rights. An approach that arises in the U.S. context is to consider a film as a "derivative work"—notably, a work derived from the screenplay.

Assessing the meaning of derivative work in U.S. law is an important exercise, especially from a moral rights perspective. This is because the doctrine of unauthorized derivative works operates as one of the most powerful substitutes for formalized moral rights protection in the United States. The argument is a practical one, and it goes as follows. If the editing of a work is sufficiently interventionist, it can create a new work, deemed "derivative" by U.S. courts. Copyright rules require, of course, that the making of any derivative work be authorized by the creator of the original work. Unauthorized editing can therefore lead to a finding of copyright infringement. When plaintiffs object to unauthorized editing because it distorts the original work, the argument becomes a practical substitute for the moral right of integrity. This argument led the Monty Python troupe of comedians to victory in their well-known lawsuit against the ABC network, *Gilliam v. ABC*.[77] ABC broadcast edited versions of skits by the comedy troupe, apparently in order to protect viewers from material that they could find offensive. But the comedians felt that removing off-color references from their work deprived their humor of its original quality.[78]

As illustrated by *Gilliam*, U.S. law shows a broad appreciation of what constitutes a derivative work. Yet, even in the U.S. context, it does not seem entirely correct to adopt the terminology of "derivative" work for a film. There is some truth in the idea that a film is derived from an underlying screenplay and other component parts, such as music. However, a connotation of inferiority seems implicit in the term "derivative." It conveys the idea that there is something "secondary" about the work—that, like a performance in relation to a composition, a film depends fundamentally on another work for its existence. There is a definite hierarchy involved; the original work takes precedence over the "derivative" work.[79]

[77] *Gilliam v. American Broadcasting Companies*, 538 F.2d 14 (2d Cir. 1976) (U.S.).

[78] Id. The British case of *Frisby v. BBC* [1967] Ch. 932 (Ch) is similar, involving the removal of single "obscene" word from a radio play for broadcast by the BBC. These cases are interesting because they remind us of the rebellious and nonconformist aspects of creative expression, which can easily place artists at odds with social norms in the normal exercise of their professions.

[79] But see Kamina, *supra* note 3, at 291–92 ("Basic problems of moral rights protection in relation to films"), who suggests that this may be appropriate and comments that,

> ... audiovisual works are almost always derivative works, the production of which involves the use or adaptation of numerous pre-existing or underlying works (literary works, scripts, music, etc.). As a consequence, moral rights problems arise not only between film contributors and producers or

To modern eyes, it seems unsatisfactory to characterize a film in this way. When we do so, the hierarchy that is established places the director below the screenwriter. This view may have made sense at an earlier point in film history, when this form of creative expression was itself less developed. Pascal Kamina's observations about the initial approach to film copyright are interesting, although he seems to draw inadequate attention to the practical reasons why the director gradually grew into authorship. Kamina points out the role of aesthetic theories of filmmaking:

> Following the success of sound movies, in the 1930s and the 1940s, the director as creator became secondary to the writer. This conception of the director as a mere technician was clearly adopted in Europe in pre-war case law and legal literature. In this respect, it is interesting to observe that, under the list of co-authors set by the Italian Act of 1941 and the French Act of 1957, the director comes last, the first author mentioned being the scriptwriter. Then came the so-called *auteur* theory, initiated by French film critics.[80]

A consideration of the relationship between a film and its component parts may help to clarify this issue. For example, it is true that a film depends on performances, but there are several reasons why it would be inaccurate to characterize a film as a work "derived" from those performances. Notably, a performance can be provided by more than one actor. Countless examples of actor substitutions exist in Hollywood history. Even a film destined to become as famous as Alfred Hitchcock's *Vertigo* saw the director settling for his second choice of female lead, actress Kim Novak—who went on to deliver a classic performance.[81]

Indeed, it is difficult to say that the underlying performance truly qualifies as an *independent* copyright work at all, since the purpose of the performance is to be used in conjunction with the other elements of the film. A screenplay could be published as such, or rewritten as a play; the musical score could be produced independently of the film. But this would certainly take these works out of the context in which their realization was first imagined; it might also require some

users, but also between film authors and authors of adapted or included works. This creates potential conflicts of interests (too often, film directors are ready to claim, as creators, rights they refuse to authors of adapted works). Of course, when the law acknowledges the collaborative nature of audiovisual works, such conflicts can also exist between the co-authors of the film. In practice, producers and users are faced with an unprecedented number of potential moral rights claims, and with the difficulty of identifying their origins.

It seems unnecessarily problematic to place collaborators and the director into the same relationship as author of adapted work and director.

80 Id. at 155–56 (footnotes omitted).

81 *See* Truffaut, *supra* note 58. The influential critics' poll by Sight & Sound magazine is conducted every ten years; the 2012 edition saw *Vertigo* emerge as the second-best film of all time (after Orson Welles's *Citizen Kane*); in the subsequent poll of 2022, it fell to second place after Chantal Akerman's Jeanne Dielman, 23 Quai du Commerce, 1080 Bruxelles: see British Film Institute, The Greatest Films of All Time, https://www.bfi.org.uk/sight-and-sound/greatest-films-all-time.

adaptation of the works in question. It is not too fine a point of legal analysis to call these versions of a film's component parts new works—no more than saying that an edited version of Monty Python's television skits is a new, "derivative" work in its own right[82]—but the interdependence of the works makes the question difficult. Moreover, the interdependence between a film and its component parts reflects a new kind of hierarchy. The final version of the film is at the summit of this pyramid; it represents a higher-level work than any one component considered on its own terms.

This is not to attempt to devalue the importance of contributions to a film by the artists whose work makes it possible. Rather, the objective is to try to understand the creative process of filmmaking more accurately. As this discussion suggests, the process is clearly collaborative; but there is an undeniable element of hierarchy involved. Someone must be responsible for coordinating the countless elements that combine to make a film. And in that process, it is at least possible that the creative vision of that person, or persons, is engaged.

The principle of creative authorship in films has been recognized at least since the 1960s. The pioneering article, *A Certain Tendency in French Cinema*, by French film critic and, later, director, François Truffaut, is considered a manifesto of the "authorship" theory of filmmaking. With a nod to Truffaut and the directors of the French "New Wave,"[83] directors whose creative contribution is recognized are known as "*auteurs.*" France has pioneered the recognition of a director's moral rights in its copyright law. The director's role in the creation of a film is one of practical leadership. To varying degrees, and according to the type of film, it may also be creative in its own right.

It is worth emphasizing this last point. Film is not just a technological creation; it is also a pure, classic example of creative expression. In contrast to computer programs or databases— other examples of works where the author confronts the dual task of assembling pre-existing components and developing a higher-level, possibly creative approach to those parts—there is no need here for discussions about the nature of the contribution made by the filmmaker. The form may be new, but the essence is traditional. The end result is clearly an original creative work in the sense in which creativity has been recognized at least since the Romantic era. We do not need to ask whether the investment of labor should be sufficient to recognize moral rights. Moral rights, which seek to protect the creative expression of the author, are in natural sympathy with film.

Perhaps the director can be properly compared to the conductor of a symphony. The conductor plays no musical instrument directly, but he or she coordinates

[82] *Gilliam, supra* note 76. Colin Tapper suggests that a useful test to determine whether a new "original" work has been created is to consider whether the derivative creation requires—or justifies—a new title (in private communication with the author, June 16, 2010).

[83] In the French, *Nouvelle Vague.*

and guides the playing of the musicians in the orchestra. Indeed, without the conductor's overarching comprehension of the musical score and vision about how the different parts are meant to work together, it is questionable whether an orchestra of even the most renowned individual players could realize a symphony as it is meant to be heard. In this sense, the conductor's instrument is the orchestra as a whole. The conductor is in a position to see the larger picture; so, too, is the director of a film.

If we accept the *auteur* theory of filmmaking, even to a limited extent, it becomes difficult to justify the exclusion of moral rights from film. As a matter of principle, they should be protected. In practice, however, the striking complexity of the human relations embedded in a film may lead to intractable legal problems. Legal responses to these concerns must be extraordinarily well conceived before they can hope to succeed.

D. Practical Challenges: Film Litigation in India and France

Given the complexity of this form of creative expression, it should come as no surprise that the protection of moral rights in film has proven to be a controversial issue for the international community. Two kinds of problems arise. The first involves the practical impact of moral rights on an expensive industry. Michael Handler characterizes film as "the product of an interdependent relationship between collaborative artistic creation and economic investment,"[84] and Schuyler M. Moore offers striking statistics to show that "[m]ost films lose money."[85]

The second is the potential for competing interests among those involved in the making of a film. Conflicts can arise in three ways: between the author of a film and the performers featured in it;[86] among the different "authors" of a film, themselves, such as conflicts between the director, screenwriter, or composer of original film music;[87] and, specifically, in the competing claims and interests dividing the director and the producer of a film.

[84] Michael Handler, *Continuing Problems with Film Copyright* (UNSW Law Research Paper No. 2008-51, 2008), https://papers.ssrn.com/sol3/papers.cfm?abstract_id=1399195, originally published as Michael Handler, *Continuing Problems with Film Copyright*, *in* New Directions in Copyright Law ch. 7 (Fiona Macmillan ed., 2007).

[85] Schuyler M. Moore, *Financing Drama: The Challenges of Film Financing Can Produce as Much Drama as Takes Place on the Screen*, 24 Los Angeles Law 2 (2008). *See also* Independent Film & Television Association (IFTA), *Film Financing in a VOD World with Schuyler Moore* (June 17, 2022) https://www.youtube.com/watch?v=c9xRdIz-b_0.

[86] Of course, conflict can also arise with other contributors to a film who do not enjoy authorship status—notably, those responsible for the technical aspects of its creation.

[87] See French Code de la propriété intellectuelle, *supra* note 21, at art. L113-7 on the authorship of a film, which not only identifies these three persons as co-authors of the film but also includes the possibility of an author of a spoken text, or the author of an adaptation, in this group.

This last relationship is perhaps the most difficult of all. In the common-law countries, authorship of a film has traditionally been accorded to the producer. This continues to be the case, implicitly in the United States, and explicitly in India.[88] However, better recognition for cinema as a creative art has led to an improved status for directors in the common-law world. In the United Kingdom, current law reflects the need to harmonize the British tradition of recognizing producers with the continental preference for directors. The result, however, creates some awkwardness: the producer is still considered the "author" of a film, but the British moral rights in the film are enjoyed by the director. Canada has no provisions clarifying who is to be the author of a "cinematographic work," leading to a situation of persistent ambiguity about moral rights in film.[89]

The resistance of the U.S. film lobby to moral rights is well known, and it is easy enough to understand the industry's fears about moral rights.[90] With so many creative elements coming together in the making of a film, moral rights could translate into legal chaos, depriving films of their chance to reach the public. The economic consequences could be disastrous. Filmmaking requires a heavy financial commitment, and if moral rights led to the suppression of a film, the losses could make the industry unsustainable. Indeed, even the delay of a release date could translate into lost marketing opportunities.[91] For a medium based in the year-round paradise of Southern California's climate, Hollywood remains a seasonally driven industry.[92]

But there is nothing new about these concerns. In fact, many of the same issues could arise in relation to economic rights as well. Competing economic rights and conflicts over the uses of works could present a serious challenge to the successful release of a film. Screenwriters and composers can certainly lay claim to copyright in their own work. Why do these same concerns militate against moral rights?

The answer to this question is partly practical, partly psychological. From a practical point of view, mechanisms exist to address the "layering" of economic rights in a film but these are not available for moral rights. In particular, two possibilities should be noted. First, within copyright law itself, the "work-for-hire" doctrine allows the copyright in a work to be acquired by the purchaser. The doctrine is usual in the common-law countries, but, in keeping with the tradition of protecting authors' rights, it does not operate in many civil law countries. Secondly, copyright contracts can address the ambiguities of film collaboration, clarifying the extent of rights and limitations when an underlying work becomes an integral component of the film.

[88] *See* Indian Copyright Act, *supra* note 68, §2(d)(v).

[89] *See* Stephen Fraser, *Who Owns the Copyright in a Canadian Film? Answer: It Depends (And That's the Problem)*, PLAYBACK (Jan. 3, 2005), https://playbackonline.ca/2005/01/03/legal-20050103.

[90] For an analysis of Hollywood's position, see Fraser, *Berne, CFTA, NAFTA and GATT*, *supra* note 7.

[91] *See* Dustin Putman, *Hollywood's Theories on Movie Release Dates* (Oct. 20, 2000), http://www.themovieboy.com/essays_releasedates.htm.

[92] Id.

The example of a screenplay provides a helpful illustration of how film contracts can work. Copyright in the screenplay may be transferred to the producer or director of the film; alternatively, the right to use the screenplay in the film may be licensed. No contract can be perfect, and copyright contracts are no exception. There is often room for dispute over the terms of a contractual relationship.[93] But a contract can hope to be reasonably comprehensive in defining the mutual obligations of the parties. Its success is ultimately measured by whether it is able to provide an effective working environment for the relationship. Beyond the terms of the contract, artists still have recourse against one another under tort law and can sue, for example, for defamation. They may also find themselves in a position where the terms of the contract are considered unfair and are corrected by judges who imply new terms into the contractual relationship.[94] Doctrines such as unconscionability, duress, and the outright claim of unequal bargaining power are at their disposal.[95]

The introduction of moral rights into a creative relationship would alter this situation in some ways, but how significant those changes would be is unclear. Two difficulties can occur. First, in an important contrast with economic rights, moral rights are not automatically conveyed to the buyer when economic rights are transferred. For example, the sale of a screenplay does not necessarily mean that its author will forego his or her moral rights. On the contrary, unless explicit provision is made for the moral rights, they will continue to rest with the author. If, as in the French scenario, the law provides that moral rights *cannot* be waived, this leads to what a common-law lawyer might see as chronic imperfection in the assignment of copyright.[96] A contract cannot be used to waive moral rights. In theory, at the very least, the uncertainty generated by a continuing right of the author becomes a permanent part of the relationship. The screenwriter could revoke his or her permission to use the screenplay at any stage of the creative process, and the production would then be affected.

When attempting to assess the seriousness of these consequences, a consideration of the French example may be instructive. The French experience suggests how moral rights litigation works in practice—the practical solutions to disputes over film. The results seem reassuring. France's recognition of moral rights is extensive, and in relation to film, France recognizes at least three potential "authors"

93 Examples include *Shostakovich*, *supra* note 8, and *Turner Entertainment*, *supra* note 6.

94 *See, e.g., Schroeder Music Publishing Co. v. MaCaulay (Instone)* [1974] 1 W.L.R. 1308 (UK).

95 The doctrine of unconscionability, in particular, is directly relevant to copyright contracts as it specifically embodies the problem of unequal bargaining power. As John D. McCamus points out, an allegation of unconscionability places the stronger party in the position of having to prove that the agreement is not unfair, unjust, or unreasonable: John D. McCamus, The Law of Contracts 405 (2005). The doctrine is clearly explained in Ewan McKendrick, *Unconscionability and Inequality of Bargaining Power*, *in* Contract Law: Text, Cases and Materials 667 (3d ed., 2008).

96 French Code de la propriété intellectuelle, *supra* note 21, at art. L121-1 provides that moral rights are "*inaliénable et imprescriptible* [inalienable and non-transferable]." These important issues are examined in the notes to art. L121-1 in Sirinelli et al., *supra* note 25.

of the work: the director, the author of the screenplay, and the composer of the original musical works used in the film.[97] There have been a number of cases on film which involve conflicts between creative authors.[98] But the outcome of those cases has not been the suppression of a film. Rather, corrections are required before the film can be released. The goal is still to circulate the film to the public and to let it achieve its audience potential. A moral rights claim is not likely to lead to the suppression of a film. Although French law provides for the moral right of withdrawal, it is difficult to see how the right could be exercised successfully by a single participant without the agreement of the others involved in the making of the film.[99]

There is no doubt that the world of French cinema is a different place from Hollywood. It is a smaller industry, perhaps with limited commercial potential in an English-dominated world. France may also represent a less litigious society than the United States, although it is not clear that French artists are especially hesitant to sue for their moral rights. But France also has relatively substantial experience with moral rights in film, and French patterns of litigation can certainly help to inform policies on film in other countries.

The power of the inalienability principle could also be mitigated by making it possible to waive moral rights in at least some circumstances. The special nature of film could justify a system of permitted waivers. In fact, the French provision that considers the moral right in a film to be limited to action against outsiders could be understood as a temporary suspension of disclosure and integrity rights, if not outright waiver of those rights, in favor of one's coauthors.

However, a system such as Canada's approach to moral rights, which allows moral rights to be waived comprehensively, does not seem ideal for film. It might encourage the standardized use of waivers in film contracts, which is what tends to occur more generally in Canadian publishing,[100] and could invalidate the entire moral rights scheme in practice.[101]

[97] As noted above, the French Code de la propriété intellectuelle, *supra* note 21, also makes provision for the adaptation of a film from another work. Article L113-7 includes, as the authors of a film: the author of the screenplay; the author of the adaptation; the author of the spoken text; the author of the musical compositions, with or without words, specially composed for the film; and the director.

[98] *See* Sirinelli et al., *supra* note 25, at 119–21, for a selection of principles from cases.

[99] Note the French Code de la propriété intellectuelle, *supra* note 21, at art. L121-6, which allows for the completion of a film in circumstances where one of the coauthors withdraws prematurely from the project.

[100] The Screen Composers Guild of Canada (SCGC), in its model contract, suggests that composers agree to a waiver of integrity but requires attribution to be maintained: *see, e.g.*, *SCGC Model Contract v. 2.4* (March 2020), https://screencomposers.ca/membership/model-contract. However, it should be noted that these model contracts are very poorly drafted, in the sense that they include contradictory provisions on moral rights in the text. It is also worth noting that the Writers' Union of Canada once advised authors to "beware," or "stay away from," contractual clauses that require them to give up their moral rights, but it no longer appears to provide advice on moral rights to writers: *see, e.g.*, ch. 7, n.99, in the first edition of this book. It would be interesting to learn how often Canadian authors who want to retain their moral rights are actually able to do so, because they are often in a position of greatly unequal bargaining power vis-à-vis publishers.

[101] *See* Copyright Act, R.S.C. 1985, c. C-42, s. 14(2)–(4) (Can.), https://laws.justice.gc.ca/eng/acts/c-42/index.html; id. at s. 14(3) provides a mitigating consideration—that an assignment of copyright does not, by itself, imply waiver of moral rights.

It is also worth noting that the general availability of waivers may or may not protect a filmmaker from a lawsuit. It depends on the judges. In theory, judges might support a waiver of moral rights as evidence of industry practice, but they might also strike it down as evidence of unequal bargaining power between the parties involved.[102] In Canada, existing case law on moral rights, including the *Théberge* case,[103] suggests that the courts will favor a restrictive interpretation of moral rights. This is unfortunate in view of the paradox apparent in Canadian law: copyright legislation includes general recognition for moral rights while standard-form contracts demand that moral rights be waived. In a practical sense, Canada's current legislative framework for moral rights flirts with hypocrisy. No challenge to standard-form waivers of moral rights has ever been brought before the Canadian courts.

This situation is complicated by the fact that, as noted earlier, Canadian legislation does not identify who is considered the author of a film.[104] It is therefore not clear who would be entitled to hold the first copyright in a film. Additionally, Canada's employment rule, in the film context, offers only a rough analogy to the U.S. work-for-hire doctrine. As Stephen Fraser aptly notes, before copyright can be transferred from an author to an owner under Canadian law, an employment relationship must exist between the two.[105] Is the relationship between the producer of the film and its director such a relationship? Between the producer and the other creative collaborators on the film? It is conceivable that these relationships would be more akin to those between an employer and a consultant—a person hired to work in special circumstances on a given project. If this were the case, the individual would retain copyright in his or her work, even though it might be a component part in a film. From the perspective of moral rights, the failure to identify an author is, of course, profoundly troublesome, because it leads to a situation of potential conflict involving the moral rights of a number of people. The environment provided by the Canadian Copyright Act for filmmaking is clearly an uncertain universe.

102 The question of how judges see balance-of-power issues in copyright contracts deserves to be investigated in its own right.

103 *Théberge v. Galerie d'Art du Petit Champlain Inc.* [2002] 2 S.C.R. 336, 2002 SCC 34 (Can.), https://scc-csc.lexum.com/scc-csc/scc-csc/en/item/1973/index.do.

104 This point is also discussed, albeit circuitously, by David Vaver:

The Federal Court of Canada has, however, in at least three decisions said that s. 34.1(1)(b) presumes that the film's "maker" is the copyright owner of the "work" unless the contrary is proved: see *Interbox Promotion Corp v 9012- 4314 Québec Inc* 2003 FC 1254 at [24]–[26]; *CBC v Conservative Party of Canada* 2021 FC 425 at [32]; *Bell Canada v L3D Distributing Inc* 2021 FC 832 at [47].

See David Vaver, *Copyright Ownership of Movies and Films in Canada: Who's On First?*, Osgoode Digital Commons (2022), https://digitalcommons.osgoode.yorku.ca/cgi/viewcontent.cgi?article=1222&context=public_writing.

105 Fraser, *Canadian Film*, *supra* note 88.

India presents a fascinating comparison with both France and the United States. India's "Bollywood" is the Hindi-speaking cinema of North India; it caters to 300 million Hindi speakers in India and to a large international market that includes parts of Africa.[106] What is less well known is that India has an extraordinary tradition of intellectual cinema, though it is now largely eclipsed by Bollywood and its national counterparts, such as "Kollywood," the film industry of South India.[107] The idea of film as art—director as author—is certainly one that India has historically shared with France. At the same time, the reality of Indian film as mass-market powerhouse is closely aligned with the U.S. experience.

1. India: Moral Rights in a Culture of Adaptation

In India, development in the entire field of moral rights litigation was initiated by film. The seminal case arose in 1986, not as a dispute among different film authors but as a conflict over the adaptation of a novel into a film.[108]

a. Producer vs. Author: *Mannu Bhandari*

Mannu Bhandari is a well-known Indian novelist writing in Hindi. Rights to her novel, *Aap ka Bunty*, were purchased by Kala Vikas Pictures, a film production company interested in adapting her book into a film. In the agreement between Ms Bhandari and the production company, the novelist agreed to allow the director and screenwriter of the film to make changes, in consultation with her, as "necessary" for the production of a "successful" film.[109] Ms Bhandari would be credited as the author of the original novel.

As the project developed, Ms Bhandari grew dissatisfied. The film's title was changed by the producers to *The Flow of Time*. It was no longer offered as the story of "Bunty," the main character, as in the original title of the novel. The portrayal of the characters, the dialogue, and changes to the ending of the film were all objectionable in her view.[110] Ms Bhandari finally brought a complaint against the production house, alleging that these modifications amounted to a violation of her moral right of integrity under section 57 of the Indian Copyright Act.

[106] *See, e.g.*, Brian Larkin, *Nigerian Films and Indian Lovers: Media and the Creation of Parallel Modernities*, 67(3) AFRICA (1997), https://www.wcas.northwestern.edu/projects/globalization/secure/articles/larkin2.pdf.

[107] The Bengali film industry is known as "Tollywood"; as noted earlier, Nigeria's large, video-based industry is known as "Nollywood."

[108] *Mannu Bhandari*, *supra* note 11.

[109] *See* Dine, *supra* note 11, at 561: he quotes the clause in the contract as allowing "certain modifications in [her] novel for the film version, in discussion with [her,] to make it suitable for a successful film."

[110] These grounds for the author's dissatisfaction with a film are identified by Dine, *supra* note 11, at 144, who also provides a detailed description of what these changes involved.

At trial, the judge considered the extent to which the recognition of moral rights is likely to interfere with the successful production and release of a film. The decision turned on an analysis of the contract between writer and producer. The fact that Ms Bhandari had authorized changes that might be "necessary" to a film adaptation was subject to interpretation. In the court's view, the changes made by the producers fell within these terms.[111] Ms Bhandari had effectively forfeited her right to object to modifications by the terms of her contract.

But the court then went on to make an apparent error of legal interpretation. At that time, India's moral rights provisions clearly stipulated that "any distortion, mutilation or modification" of a work would violate an author's right of integrity. A second clause provided that "any other action in relation to the said work which would be prejudicial to his honour or reputation" would also violate integrity. However, actions that were *prima facie* "modification[s]" objected to by the author did not require a demonstration that the author's honor or reputation would be affected by the mistreatment of the work. Section 57 has since been amended; but the language of the old provisions is unequivocal.[112] Any modification of the work could violate the right of integrity.

Not only did the court apply the standard of damage to honor or reputation to Ms Bhandari's complaint, but it also did so in an eccentric manner. Jeffrey Dine calls it "an odd holding." As quoted by the Delhi High Court, the district court judge stated,

> In my view *prima facie* the plaintiff has not been able to establish on record that the defendants have changed the theme[,] distorted or mutilated the novel[,] or damaged the underlying idea thereof. The Plaintiff had *prima facie* authorized the defendants to make necessary changes in order to make a successful film based on the novel.... [T]the film is not at all going to harm the reputation of the plaintiff in any manner. The plaintiff's reputation can be harmed in the eyes of those only who have read her novel and seen the film also. Those who have read her novel and seen the film may change their views about the producer, [or] director of the film but not about the plaintiff.[113]

[111] *See Mannu Bhandari*, *supra* note 11, at para. 6 (quoting from para. 12 of the trial judgment). *See also* id. at para. 12, disposing of the issue.

[112] For the pre-1994 §57 provisions of the Indian Copyright Act, *supra* note 68, see the website of the Commonwealth Legal Information Institute, https://copyright.gov.in/documents/copyrightrules1957.pdf. The old §57(1) provides that

> the author of a work shall have the right to claim the authorship of the work as well as the right to restrain, or claim damages in respect of—(a) any distortion, mutilation or other modification of the said work; or (b) any other action in relation to the said work which would be prejudicial to his honour or reputation.

[113] *Mannu Bhandari*, *supra* note 11, at para. 6. *See* Dine, *supra* note 11, at 561.

The lower court seemed to feel that the poor quality of the adaptation would make the producers, rather than the author, look deficient in the eyes of the public. But, as Jeffrey Dine suggests, there can be little doubt that the film effectively represents the work of the author to all those who see it.[114] If the film is successful, it may draw a readership to the author. But the issue is a delicate one. A poor adaptation may bring readers to an author who are in search of something that she cannot provide—a happy ending, a sexually explicit story, or, as in the present case, "vulgar dialogue"—or, for the same reasons, it could drive potential readers away. A faithful adaptation may succeed in conveying the vision of the author but lead to the commercial (or critical) failure of the film. This situation could reduce the author's readership or, if people sense that the original work is good despite the flaws of the film version, increase it. But it is difficult to imagine a situation where the adaptation of the work would leave the author of the original work completely untainted. The court's apparent skepticism about Bollywood movies might not be shared by other Indians. Its assessment of reputation seems bizarre.[115]

Ms Bhandari did not allow the issue to rest here: she pursued an appeal to the High Court of Delhi. The parties then settled their dispute, with Kala Vikas Pictures agreeing to remove all references to Ms Bhandari and her work from the film and Ms Bhandari relinquishing her right to claim "any right or interest" in the film, or to object in any way to its release or distribution. But the parties, nevertheless, asked the High Court of Delhi to deliver its legal opinion in order to establish a much-needed precedent on the making of film adaptations. Ms Bhandari "insisted that, as a committed author, she would like the Court to authoritatively resolve the question of the right of the authors as the problem is repeatedly faced by... authors and there is no judicial decision."[116] The concerns of the defendants seem typical of the concerns of filmmakers in common-law countries around moral rights:

> "The defendants' grievance, on the other hand, was that they had made a huge investment and ... entered into contracts with the distributors. According to the defendants, the plaintiff... filed the suit with the ulterior motive of extracting more money than that paid under the contract."[117]

The request for a decision was a valuable one. Despite the best efforts of Indian judges, it can take decades for a case to progress through the Indian legal system. Few, indeed, are the litigants who can see a complaint through to its ultimate end. For this very reason, judgments may fail to accomplish the purpose

[114] Dine, *supra* note 11.

[115] The court also felt that Ms. Bhandari waited too long to bring her claim and made a finding of laches on her part. In particular, it felt that she should not have waited until the film was completed to make her complaints known, as appears to have happened in this case.

[116] *Mannu Bhandari, supra* note 11, at para. 16.

[117] Id. at para. 3.

of deterrence—however strongly the Indian courts protect the moral rights of authors, it seems unlikely that an author or his or her heirs would have the stamina to wait out a lawsuit. Justice, alas, is primarily accessiblee to the wealthy. In India, artistic excellence may not lead to wealth for the artist or the artist's descendants. Indian cultural traditions are partly to blame, as material wealth and intellectual contributions are often seen as incompatible. Colonialism, which discouraged and even outlawed the activities of many Indian authors, is also a major factor.[118]

Given the extraordinary resources of time and money required to succeed in litigation, Indian legal practice has developed some interesting evolutionary modifications. Notably, an interim judgment in India can be surprisingly influential as a precedent. An interesting example of such a case arose in the moral rights litigation of *Amar Nath Sehgal v. Union of India*. A 1992 interim decision by the Delhi High Court led the Indian government to amend the provisions on moral rights in India's Copyright Act.[119]

In Ms Bhandari's case, the writer found strong support in the High Court of Delhi.[120] By upholding her claim, the High Court established a pattern that it was to follow unerringly in future cases: the Court acted as an advocate for the individual artist against what it perceived as powerful and corrupt forces that threatened to demean her. For Mannu Bhandari, those forces were represented by the might of Bollywood; in the subsequent litigation of *Amar Nath Sehgal*, the Indian government, itself, was to blame.

[118] *See* Mira T. Sundara Rajan, *Moral Rights in the Public Domain: Copyright Matters in the Works of Indian National Poet C. Subramania Bharati*, SINGAPORE J. LEGAL STUD. 161 (July 2001).

[119] *Amar Nath Sehgal v. Union of India* 2005 (30) PTC 253 (Delhi High Court); the previous hearing was held in 1992, Suit No. 2074 (Delhi HC), (1994) 19 IPLR 160 (India). As noted previously, when queried on this issue, Mr. Jagdish Sagar, who was responsible for drafting the amendments to India's moral rights scheme enacted in 1994, commented only that India was then concerned about implementing the provisions of the Berne Convention on moral rights successfully (Jagdish Sagar, in personal communication with the author, February 2009). And, indeed, the 1994 language mirrors the language of Art. 6*bis* of the Berne Convention: International Convention for the Protection of Literary and Artistic Works, adopted at Berne on Sept. 9, 1886, completed at Paris on May 4, 1896, revised at Berlin on Nov. 13, 1908, completed at Berne on Mar. 20, 1914, revised at Rome on June 2, 1928, at Brussels on June 26, 1948, at Stockholm on July 14, 1967, and at Paris on July 24, 1971, and amended on Sept. 28, 1979, S. Treaty Doc. No. 99-27 (1986), https://www.wipo.int/treaties/en/ip/berne. However, changes to the provisions would also make it difficult for an author to succeed on a claim for destruction of an artwork and impossible to be able to proceed with a claim without showing damage to reputation. They respond directly to the circumstances of *Sehgal*.

[120] *See* Dine, *supra* note 11. In fact, Ms. Bhandari was unsuccessful at trial, where the judge found that "a bad film reflects poorly only on the filmmakers" and not on the original author of the work. Interestingly, the holding of the trial court in Ms. Bhandari's case was explicitly rejected by the High Court, which found that distortions in a work of adaptation can also offend the original author's moral rights: *Mannu Bhandari*, *supra* note 11, at paras. 4–12. Clearly, the High Court viewed the nature of the relationship between an original work and an adaptation somewhat differently from the trial court, and it saw the adaptation as being, in essence, a reproduction of the original work rather than a new creative work in its own right. This perception was probably due to the Court's general interest in considering the case from the position of Ms. Bhandari and others like her, who might find themselves in relationships of unequal bargaining power.

The High Court of Delhi made three points that sought to clarify the terms on which film production and moral rights would coexist in the Indian context. First, it considered the role of moral rights in the interpretation of artists' contracts, with special attention to the question of whether, and to what extent, authors' moral rights may be waived under Indian law. Secondly, it examined the meaning of the term "modifications" under section 57 of the Indian Copyright Act and considered its application to the film context. Finally, the Court discussed the social context, which brings a special importance to authors' moral rights in India.

i. Moral Rights and Film Contracts

In the contract between producer and author for the making of the film, Mannu Bhandari had agreed to allow "certain modifications" to her novel, to be made upon "discussion with [the writer]," in the interest of creating a "successful" film adaptation.[121] In contrast to the trial judge, the High Court found that Ms Bhandari's contractual consent to some modification of her work did not deprive her of the moral rights in section 57. "Certain modifications" were allowed; but others could still amount to violations of the integrity right.

Key to the Court's ruling was the notion that the terms of the contract for the assignment of copyright had to be read in conjunction with the provisions of section 57. Accordingly, modifications that were different from those agreed upon in the contract could violate the right of integrity; but so, too, could changes that were egregious in the eyes of the court. Interpretation of the contract on its own terms is not the central issue. Rather, the contract itself must fundamentally respect the terms of section 57. As a result, an author's moral rights in Indian law may override the provisions of the contract in much the same way that other kinds of public policy concerns predominate over contractual terms.[122] Justice Wad states,

> Reading the contract with Section 57 it is obvious that modifications which are permissible are such modifications which do not convert the film into an entirely new version from the original novel. The said "certain modifications" should also not distort or mutilate the original novel .... As a show business or as a box office collection, a film may be a success, but, it may do no credit to the reputation or the honour of the author. That is why Section 57 insists on the special protection to honour and reputation of the author.[123]

[121] Clause (b) of the contract between the parties. The contract is reproduced by the Delhi High Court: *see Mannu Bhandari, supra* note 11, at para. 8.

[122] An interesting British analogy is the *Spycatcher* case: *A-G v. Guardian Newspapers Ltd (No. 1)* [1987] All E.R. 316; *A-G v. Guardian Newspapers Ltd (No. 2)* [1988] All E.R. 545 (UK). The publication of memoirs by a secret service agent who worked as a double agent during the Cold War led to the effective expropriation of the author's copyright by the British government. In its ruling, the House of Lords felt that it must offer a strong public policy decision to discourage such nefarious activities.

[123] *Mannu Bhandari, supra* note 11, at para. 11.

The judge's position was, he felt, supported by the contract itself, which required that the author should be provided "proper publicity" for her contribution to the film. He comments,

> The contract requires that "proper" publicity should be given. The word "proper" has to be interpreted in contradistinction to "notoriety" or "bad name," causing harm to the honour and reputation of the author.[124]

This was an additional point; clearly, section 57 could have been invoked whether or not this terminology was incorporated into the contract itself.

The effect of the Court's position was to support the view that moral rights are generally inalienable under Indian law and, in definite contrast to the approach in other common-law countries, cannot be waived in their entirety in a film contract.[125] As summarized by S. Ramaiah,

> [T]he author's special rights as provided in Section 57 of the *Copyright Act* may override the terms of [a] contract of assignment of copyright. To put it differently, the contract of assignment of copyright has to be read subject to the provisions of Section 57, and the terms of [the] contract cannot negate the special rights and remedies granted by Section 57.[126]

ii. "Certain Modifications"

But balance is at the heart of the High Court's approach. Within the terms of this contract, the author clearly did not have a right to object to any changes, but only to changes that went beyond "certain modifications" made to her work. The Court had a sympathetic understanding of the needs of adaptation and commented,

> Filming a novel is quite different from literary re-production. There is a change in the medium. The theme of the novel is conveyed through audio-visual effects.[127]

In fact, the Court felt that it would be ideal to have the benefit of expert evidence on the adaptation of a literary work into film. Justice Wad apparently made this suggestion to the parties, only to be refused:

[124] Id.

[125] Moral rights legislation in both Canada and the United Kingdom supports the availability of waiver as part of their moral rights schemes. *See* Canadian Copyright Act, *supra* note 100, at s. 14(2)–(4). The UK provisions are discussed in David Vaver, *Moral Rights Yesterday, Today and Tomorrow*, 7(3) Int'l J. Tech. & L. 270, 274, 277–78 (1999).

[126] S. Ramaiah, *India*, *in* International Copyright Law and Practice (Paul Edward Geller & Melville B. Nimmer eds., 1998).

[127] *Mannu Bhandari*, *supra* note 11, at para. 4.

> It is better to have [the] assistance of informal assessors ... such as storywriter, directors and producers. I made this suggestion. But one party was not agreeable to have the assistance of [his] ... peers.[128]

In attempting to define the scope of the "certain modifications" permissible under the contract, the High Court explored the meaning of the term "modifications" as it appeared in the Indian copyright legislation.[129] Could the legislative definition of this term help to set general limits on changes to a literary work during the process of adaptation, thereby establishing a fair and feasible equilibrium between the interests of author and producer?

The Court observed that the term, "modifications" should be read "*ejusdem generis* with the words 'distortion' and 'mutilation,'" which appear alongside it in section 57 of the Copyright Act.[130] Extrapolating from this contract, the Court establishes a useful rule for adaptations. The criterion is that the modifications should be "necessary for converting the novel into a film version."[131] In the process, however, they should not distort or mutilate the original work.[132]

But a "modification" need not be obviously or unquestionably "negative" to infringe the author's moral right. Rather, "necessary" modifications to an original work would be allowed under section 57.[133] As distinguished intellectual property lawyer, Pravin Anand, points out,

> Thus, in this case, even though the author had permitted the film producer under a written agreement to make modifications, the court held that there was a breach of section 57 as the extent of the modifications was more than necessary for converting the novel into a film version or for making the film a successful venture.[134]

It is well worth noting that "necessity" is open to interpretation.[135] The question of what is actually "necessary" arises repeatedly in the technological context, and

[128] Id.

[129] Indian Copyright Act, *supra* note 68, §57(1)(a).

[130] *Mannu Bhandari, supra* note 11, at para. 11; *Anand Patwardhan v. Director General, Directorate General of Doordarshan and others*, Suit No. 2259 of 2004, 36.

[131] *Mannu Bhandari, supra* note 11, at para. 12. This contract had other implications, as well, discussed *infra*.

[132] Id.

[133] For a quick overview of the Indian scheme, see P. NARAYANAN, LAW OF COPYRIGHT AND INDUSTRIAL DESIGNS paras. 7.06–7.10 (esp. para. 7.07) (3d ed., 2002). Narayanan gives much weight to the common law tradition surrounding quasi-moral rights actions in India and the United Kingdom, including the British case *Frisby, supra* note 77. That court interpreted §57(1)(a) to mean that an intellectual work is "inviolable."

[134] *Anand Patwardhan, supra* note 129, at 37. *See also* Dine, *supra* note 11, at 564: "The court appears to have made moral rights inalienable, while placing outside the prohibition on modifications such changes as are necessary to make the transition to a different medium."

[135] As Shakespeare's King Lear comments, "O, reason not the need! Our basest beggars/Are in the poorest thing superfluous;/Allow not nature more than nature needs,/Man's life is cheap as beast's": WILLIAM SHAKESPEARE, KING LEAR act 2, sc. 4, ll. 304–307.

it is rarely confined to purely technical manipulation.[136] In the case of a film adaptation of a novel, for example, it will be the rare example where dialogue can be lifted directly from the novel to the film.[137] Indeed, it is often the case that dialogue cannot be effectively transposed even from drama to film.

Finally, the Court's approach to the question of balancing the author's rights against the producer is important. It comments that "The basic question is how to balance [the] freedom (of expression) of the author with that of the director in th[is] ... field of art."[138] For the High Court of Delhi, the author's right to fidelity in the transformation of her artistic vision from page to screen is fundamental—it is a feature of her own freedom of expression. Far from seeing the moral right as a part of the ownership interest bound up with intellectual property, the Court links moral rights with human rights. It does so while arriving at an eminently pragmatic test for the authenticity of adaptations.

iii. Remedies

In its search for an appropriate remedy, the Court considers the substance of the complaint and assesses each point raised by the plaintiff to decide whether or not the objections of the writer should lead to changes in the film. If the case had been decided by the Court, it would have been possible, with these changes, to release the film. The changes were relatively minor ones which could probably have been accommodated in a minimum of editing sessions. Once again, the Court's approach is utterly practical. The producer would have secured the release of the film, and the writer would have achieved her reputation-saving measures. But there is something incongruous about a judge being called upon to decide what qualifies as a valid change for the purpose of literary adaptation in a film. To Justice Wad's credit, he engaged in this exercise against his own will; and his comments on the issue suggest that expert evidence should be preferred in cases on moral rights in adaptations.

iv. Cultural Heritage

The opportunity presented by this litigation was an important one for India's judiciary. It was the first major case, not only on moral rights in film adaptations, but also on the general concept of the moral right in Indian law. The Court understood that this was an opportunity on the grand scale and commented,

> The hallmark of any culture is [the] excellence of [its] arts and literature .... Art needs [a] healthy environment and adequate protection. The protection

136 See, e.g., the discussion in Chapter 6, *supra* notes * and accompanying text, of "necessity" in the context of technological modifications to music that is used in ringtones.

137 Colin Tapper (in personal communication with the author, June 10, 2010).

138 *Mannu Bhandari*, *supra* note 11, at para. 5.

> which law offers is thus not the protection of the artist or author alone. [The] [e]nrichment of culture is of vital interest to ... society. Law protects this social interest. Section 57 of the Copyright Act is one such example of legal protection. Section 57 lifts authors' status beyond the material gains of copyright and gives it a special status.[139]

The case of *Mannu Bhandari* has a special resonance in the Indian context. In a sense, the Indian cultural scene is built on the art of adaptation. Adaptation is the foundation of everything. The example of India's ancient Sanskrit epics is illustrative. It is believed that the twin epics of the Ramayana and Mahabharata—both gripping stories of heroism, love, and war—began life as history and folk stories, until the traditional "warehouse" of cultural treasures, in the Renaissance sense of the term, was crystallized in their verses.

These works are *living* legends. Each one is many times the size of Leo Tolstoy's modern Russian "epic," *War and Peace.* In India, these poems gradually spread across the entire subcontinent, and touched the entire array of its cultures and languages. The Ramayana was translated into local languages in different parts of India—but what translations! It hardly seems fair to call them by this modest name. Local poets adapted the existing stories to the local environment, essentially creating new works that were completely innovative in language and imagery, yet bore the hallmark of spiritual fidelity to the original. Adaptations, like the Tamil version composed by twelfth-century poet Kamban, have become classics in their own right. Memorized by village *pandits*, the works were widely disseminated throughout India's social classes, and there is probably no individual alive in the Indian subcontinent today who does not know the personalities within them as well as members of his or her own family. In this way, cultural adaptation has been the foundation of Indian unity from very ancient times until the present. As a quintessentially Indian art, it reflects the shimmering interplay of authorial invention, scholarship, and poetic genius to create something authentically Indian.

For better or worse, film, too, has epic consequences in India. How else is it possible to explain the mass suicides that followed the death of M. G. Ramachandran, a Tamil film star of the 1930s?[140] Film has clearly inherited the capacity of the ancient epics to transcend social barriers, including the continuing obstacle of

[139] Id. at para. 8. These words are echoed in the interim ruling in *Amar Nath Sehgal, supra* note 118. For an analysis that shaped the final ruling, see Mira T. Sundara Rajan, *Moral Rights and the Protection of Cultural Heritage*: Amar Nath Sehgal v. Union of India, 10(1) Int'l J. Cultural Prop. 79 (2001).

[140] *See e.g., From MGR to Karunanidhi, a Leader's Death Triggers Wave of Suicides*, The Newsmen (Sept. 17, 2022), https://thenewsmen.co.in/politics/from-mgr-to-karunanidhi-a-leaders-death-triggers-wave-of-suicides/83870. *See also* Amrit Dhillon, *Mass Suicide Fears after Death of Revered Lady in Green, Jayaram Jayalalithaa*, Sydney Morning Herald (Dec. 6, 2016), https://www.smh.com.au/world/mass-suicide-fears-after-worshipped-indian-female-politician-jayaram-jayalalithaa-dies-20161206-gt4pm7.html.

illiteracy. Against this background, it hardly seems surprising that Indian courts consider the moral rights of the author in a film adaptation to be an important cultural issue.[141]

By establishing a high threshold that must be met in the making of adaptations, the Court tries to support authors in a context where, as a group, they are relatively weak, both economically and socially. The Court recognized that there is an important connection between the integrity of an author's work and the maintenance of his or her reputation. In the case of popular film adaptations of creative works, there may be, *prima facie*, an implication that modifications to a work are likely to damage the author's reputation. The Court's approach suggests that, even where modifications are qualified by the requirement of prejudice, as in the case of the current section 57, Indian authors may have extensive moral rights protection in relation to film adaptations. Dine refers to these considerations as "the unique conditions of the Indian film business bearing upon ... [the issue of] damage to the author's reputation."[142] The Court says,

> It is widely believed that there are investments and collections of crores of rupees in a successful Hindi movie and the heroes and heroines are paid fabulous amounts for their services. If the complaint of the author (of mutilation and distortion of the novel) is correct[,] the lay public and her admirers are likely to conclude that she has fallen prey to big money in the film world and has consented to such mutilation and distortions. The apprehension of the author cannot be dismissed as imaginary. It is reasonable. Her admirers are likely to doubt her sincerity and commitment and she is likely to be placed in the category of cheap screenplay writers of the common run [of] Bombay Hindi films.[143]

[141] Interestingly, the tradition of cultural adaptation may also mean that Indian courts will be slow to recognize copyright infringement in the adaptation of stories. A lawsuit brought by Barbara Taylor Bradford for the apparent copying of her novel, *A Woman of Substance*, in an Indian television serial was unsuccessful. Despite close similarities between the themes, Bradford was offered the rebuke that she did not have a monopoly on the story of a woman's rise from rags to riches. In another case, Warner's suit against a Bollywood production making a film entitled *Hari Puttar* was thrown out on the grounds that there was no likelihood of confusion among the relevant population between "Hari Puttar" and Harry Potter. *See* Nyay Bhushan, *Warner Bros. Warns Bollywood: Don't Touch "Button,"* REUTERS (Apr. 7, 2009), https://www.reuters.com/article/us-india/warner-bros-warns-bollywood-dont-touch-button-idUSTRE5370LZ20090408. For an interesting perspective, see also Hariqbal Basi, *Indianizing Hollywood: The Debate over Bollywood's Copyright Infringement*, 18 UCLA ENT. LAW REV. 33 (2011), https://escholarship.org/content/qt0zg193zk/qt0zg193zk.pdf. He refers to "Indianization" as a valid defense against charges of copyright infringement in the Bollywood context.

[142] Dine, *supra* note 11, at 565. Not only is the Indian popular film industry the largest in the world, but it also relies on much formulaic film-making for its success, with elements including popular music, the exploitation of current fasion trends, conventional values, and blatant appeal to viewers' sentiments. Critics, including the present author, will not hesitate to point out that Indian popular films and Indian art films come from different worlds..

[143] *Mannu Bhandari*, *supra* note 11, at para. 17, quoted in Dine, *supra* note 11, at 565.

b. Digital Re-creation: *Anand Patwardhan*

India's first moral rights case dealt with film; a more recent case involves movies and the role that they play in spreading political and philosophical messages to the public.[144] In a 2009 ruling, the Bombay High Court addressed the question of moral rights in the re-use of images from an existing film to make a new documentary. The film in question dealt with a sensitive national issue—the Bihar Movement, a student uprising that led to India's Declaration of Emergency in 1975.

The original film aired in 1977, but the new documentary, broadcast in 2003, presented the events in a completely new light. The new film is said to have "contained substantial footage from the suit film made in 1974–75," although the footage was apparently used with a different soundtrack. The perspective "differs radically and fundamentally" from the opinions offered by the original film. The director of the original film, who "follows a secular democratic ideology," alleged that the new film reflected political biases. It promoted the "Hindutva" ideology, a form of religious extremism based on controversial interpretations of Hinduism. For these reasons, could the new film be said to violate the copyright in the original work?

The makers of the new documentary claimed that they owned the copyright in the first film. They immediately confronted problems here, because they could not demonstrate ownership in the form of a written agreement. In construing the contract between the two parties, the judge found that only telecast rights had been assigned to the defendants. Accordingly, any use made of the images in the film was, to begin with, an infringement of copyright.

But the Court proceeded to a more interesting question: had the creator's right of integrity under Indian law been violated? The argument was made on two specific grounds—the association of the images in the film with new music, rather similar to the issue of associating music with an incompatible political ideology that arose in the U.S. case of *Shostakovich*,[145] and the use of the images to present political and religious view that were "completely contrary [to] and different" from the perspective of the original work.[146]

The Court found that it had. It draws a parallel with the *Amar Nath Sehgal* litigation, where damage and partial destruction of a work of sculpture were considered to violate the artist's moral right of integrity. "This case," says the Court,

[144] *Anand Patwardhan*, *supra* note 129.

[145] *Shostakovich*, *supra* note 8.

[146] A similar point arose in the UK case of *Confetti Records v. Warner Music UK Ltd* [2003] EWHC (Ch) 1274, which saw an allegation that the association of a song with gangsterism violated the composer's moral rights because of his ideological objections. The facts of the case led to a tongue-in-cheek treatment of the argument by the court: the original performance of the song had been carried out by a group filmed in gangster outfits.

> is much the same. The Plaintiff has by his own labour, skill, art and knowledge produced the suit film .... [T]he use of the part of the suit film, being contrary to the written agreement between the parties, would be tantamount to distortion and mutilation.[147]

The argument is tantalizing. Why is this case "the same" as the *Sehgal* litigation? In Sehgal's case, there was no question of a wrongful association on political or religious grounds, no issue of distortion by use in a derivative work. Is the essence of the ruling that cutting and pasting images from the original film, notwithstanding the fact that the original film continued to be available in an unaltered form, amounted to a violation of the integrity of the original work, and could be compared to damaging a work of art? Or is it that the repurposing of the material cut from the original film for new political ends in itself violated the director's moral rights?

The Court does not offer an explicit consideration of whether the complaint meets the criteria for damage to the author's reputation, as is now required by the revised section 57 of the Indian Copyright Act. However, it does examine the question of whether the new film "defamed the Plaintiff" by "lower[ing] ... his image [as] ... a secular democratic person in the eyes of his relatives, friends and acquaintances." As an aside, the plaintiff apparently came to know of the existence of the new film when a cousin called him about it during the broadcast.[148] Interestingly, the Court defines the test for defamation as being able to show actual damage to reputation and finds that the plaintiff has not succeeded in establishing it.[149] Under the moral rights provisions of the Indian Copyright Act as well, the plaintiff would have had to establish damage to reputation; but whether the damage needs to be actual or constructive, concrete or reasonably anticipated, is not stated.

In the final Order, damages for defamation are refused. Damages are awarded for copyright infringement, in the amount of 1 million rupees—approximately 25,000 dollars at current rates—and provision is also made that the "Defendants shall not screen or re-screen the impugned film ... showing any stills/shots/images from the suit film." Has the Court effectively found a violation of the moral right of integrity without showing the required damage to reputation? The final ruling in the *Amar Nath Sehgal* case bypassed this requirement by relying on the status of Mr. Sehgal's work as an important part of India's cultural heritage and invoking Indian membership in international cultural property conventions as a kind of higher-level norm that must inform the interpretation of moral rights under India's Copyright Act. In this case, too, the Court concludes with its assessment of the

[147] *Anand Patwardhan*, *supra* note 129, at para. 109.
[148] Id. at para. 77.
[149] Id. at paras. 120–21.

plaintiff as "a talented artist" and "a film maker of repute," and states that the film is unique:

> The production, editing, [and] photography of the suit film[,] aside from being a work of art[,] is seen to be the only such work of art on a historical topic which is both informative and educative[,] and reflecting character and constitutional ideology worth emulating in the Plaintiff's name rather than plagiarising...

The Indian Court makes it clear that a film can be both a work of art and an important part of a nation's heritage. Moral rights apply, and they should be interpreted with broad principles of public policy in mind.

2. Colorization: Producers vs. Directors in France

The debate surrounding the colorization of black-and-white films presents a sobering case study of moral rights in film. Colorization led to the first major discussion of moral rights in film at the national level in the United States. The experience laid bare the wound of a raw internal conflict within the United States' own film industry, and this is where its continued significance lies. The conflict between directors and producers was at least provisionally resolved on the producers' side—in favor of colorization. But the issue was specifically resolved, not through the recognition of film directors' moral rights, but by the National Film Preservation Act of 1988, which prohibits the "material alteration"[150] of films that are "culturally, historically, or aesthetically significant."[151] The term, "material alteration," is defined to include colorization.[152] At the same time, international attention brought to the issue by the *Huston* case, generated strong support for the plight of U.S. directors in Europe, especially France.[153] This led to an embarrassing situation, where U.S. directors found greater sympathy for their opinions, and better protection for their rights, outside the borders of their own country. This continues to be the case. As Woody Allen comments, "American films are a landmark heritage that do our nation proud all over the world, and should be seen as they were intended to be."[154] Perhaps in France, but not in the United States.

[150] *See* National Film Preservation Act, Pub. L. No. 100-446, § 11(a)(5), 102 Stat. 1774 (1988) (NFPA), http://www.gpo.gov/fdsys/pkg/STATUTE-102/pdf/STATUTE-102-Pg1774.pdf.

[151] Id. § 2.

[152] *See* id. § 5: colorization is mentioned first, followed by "other fundamental post-production changes," made for "marketing purposes." The section "does not include changes made in accordance with customary practices and standards and reasonable requirements of preparing a work for distribution or broadcast." Section 13 provides, among other things, an exception for the "personal use" of films.

[153] Represented by the *Turner Entertainment* case, *supra* note 6.

[154] Allen, *supra* note 1.

The question of where artists can expect to enjoy their moral rights is worth a closer look. Since the United States joined the Berne Convention in 1989, the possibility of differential protection for the moral rights of Americans and non-Americans on U.S. soil has been raised as a possible solution to the problem of reconciling U.S. law with the Berne Convention.[155] As discussed in Chapter 3 *supra*, this is a truly troubling prospect.[156] The logic of national treatment is that the regime of rights one grants to one's own citizens should also be available to foreign nationals. The goal is egalitarian—to avoid discrimination against foreigners. The protection of the law should be extended to everyone within the borders of one's own country. To offer protection to foreign nationals without granting it to one's own citizens would turn the very idea of national treatment on its head.

In copyright matters, the prospect of favoring foreigners is not a new idea. Once upon a time, the idea was considered by the Soviet Union in its first official foray into international copyright law—its application for membership in the Universal Copyright Convention (UCC), which it eventually joined in 1973. The Soviet move to join the UCC raised an outcry in both the international and Soviet literary communities. The fear was precisely this—that the protections of the UCC would be granted to non-Soviet authors within Soviet territory, while the rights of Soviet authors would continue to be "regulated," or eviscerated, by internal Soviet rules.[157]

In particular, Soviet copyright law of the time allowed the government to acquire works from writers on a "compulsory" basis. Once it did so, the decision to publish or not to publish them fell into the hands of the government.[158] Just as the Soviet government suppressed the publication of works by dissidents within the Soviet Union, its formal ownership of copyright in those works could empower it, through the UCC, to prevent their publication outside the country. Other member countries of the UCC would be obliged to recognize Soviet copyright rules. This new development would have deprived repressed Soviet authors of one of their traditional outlets: publication abroad. In a statement whose authors are identified by THE TIMES only as "a group of internationally-known Soviet dissident writers," the writers mourned,

155 But see the discussion in Chapter 4, *supra* at notes 154–58 and accompanying text. See also the interesting article by Graeme Austin on the theme of U.S. compliance with the Berne Convention after *Dastar*: Graeme W. Austin, *The Berne Convention as a Canon of Construction: Moral Rights after* Dastar, 61 N.Y.U. ANN. SURV. AM. L. 111 (2005).

156 *See* Chapter 3, *supra* note *.

157 As Mihály Ficsor points out, "There is the possibility of having also *provisions* which are not compatible with the conventions, but those can prevail only for *internal situations* (for the relations between national authors and users, where no international obligation is involved)": Mihály Ficsor, *The Past, Present and Future of Copyright in the European Socialist Countries*, 118 RIDA 33 (1983). See the quotation and related discussion in Sundara Rajan, COPYRIGHT AND CREATIVE FREEDOM, *supra* note 8, at 51–53.

158 In other words, by compulsory purchase of a writer's work, the Soviet government effectively acquired control of the author's moral right of disclosure.

> Our books will be stifled not only during the lives of their authors, but forever, until the end of publishing on earth. This situation did not exist even in Stalin's time for the books then ended by coming to the surface, at least posthumously.[159]

Even a commentator as knowledgeable as Michael Newcity wondered how seriously these claims should be taken, although his "depressing" conclusion that the Soviet Union had plentiful tools for the repression of writers without recourse to copyright law is hardly reassuring.[160] In fact, the subsequent comments of the Soviet government left little doubt about the intentions of the Soviet government. THE TIMES of December 28, 1973, reported,

> In an interview, Mr. Boris Pankin [head of the new Russian copyright agency] denied accusations made last spring by six Soviet intellectuals, including Dr Andrei Sakharov, the nuclear physicist, that this was a prime reason behind the Soviet decision to join the Universal Copyright Convention on May 27.

However, he left no doubt that his agency from now on would prosecute foreign publishers of dissident works and Soviet citizens who supplied them:

> Mr. Pankin said his agency, set up in September, is now the sole legal Soviet body authorized to deal with foreign publishers on questions of copyright.[161]

Clearly, this is not the sort of memory that the United States wants to evoke in its own approach to membership in the Berne Union. It is true that U.S. authors, unlike their Soviet counterparts, do not face routine state persecution; but the United States is a passionately democratic country, and it should jealously guard the ideals of free speech. It is difficult to see how treating one's own nationals poorly can set a positive example—or indeed, how this approach can support the United States' international leadership on copyright issues. It seems profoundly unjust.

The conflict over colorization arose in the early 1990s. It presented the spectacle of the first large-scale technological issue to affect the moral interests of filmmakers. The colorization experience was important for three reasons. First, colorization was widely protested by a number of prominent U.S. filmmakers,

[159] The letter is signed, "The Stifled *Samizdat*": *see Soviet Dissidents Accuse UNESCO*, THE TIMES 8 (Mar. 27, 1973). The quote also appears in Sundara Rajan, COPYRIGHT AND CREATIVE FREEDOM, *supra* note 8, at 106 (within discussion at 100–107), and in MICHAEL NEWCITY, COPYRIGHT LAW IN THE SOVIET UNION 152 (n.12) (1978).

[160] See the discussion in Sundara Rajan, COPYRIGHT AND CREATIVE FREEDOM, *supra* note 8, at 100–107.

[161] *Bar on Publication Abroad of Solzhenitsyn Works*, THE TIMES 6 (Dec. 28, 1973). The issue of Soviet membership in the Universal Copyright Convention (UCC) received wide coverage in THE TIMES of 1973–74. The period after 1973 was one of cultural stagnation in the Soviet Union, and it is difficult to assess the role of the UCC in it. Certainly, membership in the UCC did not help to open Soviet society to the West.

from Martin Scorsese to Woody Allen. John Huston was deeply offended by the colorization of films that he had shot in black and white, including *The Maltese Falcon* and *The Asphalt Jungle*. His films became the subject of a seminal case on the issue in France, as previously discussed.[162]

The debate over colorization pitted these directors against their own producers, who authorized the colorization of their works.[163] In this process, the identity of U.S. filmmakers as independent artists and genuine creators hardened into a new mold. Fine fissures appeared in the image of a U.S. cinema controlled by production values. The shift is captured by Woody Allen's commentary:

> Yet another question: "Why were directors not up in arms about cutting films for television or breaking them up for commercials, insulting them with any number of technical alterations to accommodate the television format?" The answer is that directors always hated these assaults on their work but were powerless to stop them …
>
> Still, when the assaults come too often, there is a revolution. The outrage of seeing one's work transformed into color is so dramatically appalling … that … all the directors, writers and actors chose to fight.[164]

The debate was also an alarm bell that alerted the U.S. film community to the possibilities of digital technology. Modifying film was going to be possible in a way that had never before been imagined. Through the miracle of digital intervention, the integrity of film was vulnerable, not only to alteration, but also to what Woody Allen aptly called "assault." If a right of integrity for films was not necessary in the past, it might now make eminent sense to recognize one. The integrity right would be a fitting response to the rise of new technological possibilities for manipulating film.

Finally, the colorization debate brought the issue of moral rights to the forefront of the U.S. legal and cultural consciousness. This may or may not have been a good thing. Why should moral rights be examined on the testing-ground of the most treacherous copyright terrain that exists, the world of the audiovisual work? While the colorization debate brought the issue of film integrity before the U.S. public, the principles that emerged from the controversy did not necessarily promote the cause of moral rights. The conflict ultimately reinforced Hollywood's resistance to the idea and, more generally, U.S. caution about the Berne Convention.

[162] *Turner Entertainment*, *supra* note 6.

[163] For example, Turner Entertainment had colorized *The Asphalt Jungle*; Turner had become part of Metro-Goldwyn-Mayer, the original producers of the film, by merger. *See Turner Entertainment*, *supra* note 6. The decision has been translated into English in ENT. L. REP. 3 (March 1995). A version is available on the website of Professor Andrew Chin of the University of North Carolina Law School, http://www.unclaw.com/chin/teaching/iip/turner.pdf.

[164] Allen, *supra* note 1.

In John Huston's case, protest against the colorization of his films came to a head when France's Channel 5 network, *La Cinq*, reached an agreement with Turner Entertainment to broadcast a colorized version of the film. The broadcast was scheduled for the evening of June 20, 1988, at eight thirty. Huston was by then deceased; but a suit was filed by his heirs, including his daughter, the actress Angelica Huston, and Ben Maddow, the screenwriter of *The Asphalt Jungle*. The plaintiffs argued that showing the film on television would amount to an affront on the director's moral rights. The judge at first instance agreed; he stated that the broadcast "could cause intolerable and irreparable damage to those who, defending the integrity of the work 'The Asphalt Jungle,' invoke respect for the will of John Huston."[165] The conclusion of the appeals tribunal was even stronger. It quoted Huston's own words about the film—"I filmed it in black and white, as a sculptor chooses to shape clay, to mold his work in bronze, to sculpt in marble."[166] The court then goes on to comment,

> It is not debated that his aesthetic sense, which was widely celebrated, rests on the play of black and white that allowed him to create an atmosphere in the context of which he directed the actors and chose the decor; that, in acting in a certain and direct manner on the sensibility of the viewer, colorization is likely to modify these impressions; thus, that the colorization of the film at issue, even in only some formats, against the will of the plaintiffs, amounts to an attack on their moral right; that, accordingly, they are entitled to demand that Channel 5 be prohibited from proceeding to the television broadcast of the film Asphalt Jungle in its colorized version.[167]

The *Huston* case established a number of important points of law concerning moral rights in the international community. First, as the case initially occurred before the United States had become a signatory to the Berne Convention, the French court affirmed that the enjoyment of moral rights did not depend on the nationality of the author.[168] Rather, under French law, moral rights would be generally

[165] *Turner Entertainment, supra* note 6: "pouvait entraîner un dommage intolérable et irréparable pour ceux qui, défendant l'intégrité de l'œuvre Asphalt Jungle, invoquent le respect et la volonté de John Huston."

[166] Id.: "Je l'ai tourné en noir et blanc, comme un sculpteur choisit de façonner l'argile, de couleur [*sic*] son travail dans le bronze, de sculpter dans le marbre."

[167] Id.:

> Qu'il n'est pas contesté que son esthétisme, qui lui a valu une grande notoriété, repose sur le jeu noir et blanc qui permettait de créer une atmosphère en fonction de laquelle il dirigeait l'acteur[s] et choisissait les décors; qu'en agissant de façon certaine et directe sur la sensibilité du téléspectateur, la colorisation est susceptible d'en modifi er les impressions; qu'ainsi, la colorisation du fi lm en cause, même sur certains supports seulement, contre le gré des demandeurs, constitue une atteinte à leur droit moral; qu'ils sont dès lors fondés à demander qu'il soit fait interdiction à La Cinq de procéder à la télédiffusion du film Asphalt Jungle dans sa version colorisée.

[168] The Berne Convention entered into force in the United States on March 1, 1989: Berne Notification No. 121 (Nov. 21, 1988), https://www.wipo.int/treaties/en/notifications/berne/treaty_berne_121.html.

available to creators belonging to any country. Secondly, the fact that moral rights were unavailable in the country of origin of the work, the United States, was irrelevant to the claim. Instead, what mattered was the fact that both France and the United States were members of the UCC, which would allow Americans to enjoy the privilege of national treatment under French copyright law.[169] While the UCC did not make any mention of moral rights, the court ruled that it also did not impose any restrictions on the ability of member states to recognize moral rights. Thirdly, the aesthetic vision of the director was gleaned from the direct evidence of his work and his words. Through them, the director himself could lay claim to the status of individual artist, fully entitled to the protection of his moral rights.

As an epilogue to *Huston*, it should finally be noted that the practice of colorization itself has virtually died out. By the mid-1990s, Turner Broadcasting, which colorized 200-odd films from the "cream of the crop" of its film collection, had completely ceased to colorize films. Ironically, Turner Classic Movies now offers classic films, including silent movies, in their original formats.[170] There is no longer any fear that black and white has become obsolete. As James Danziger pointed out in a 1998 interview with the New York Times, "Young people won't watch black and white? ... That's certainly been disproved by MTV. Many of the most interesting and avant-garde videos have been done in black and white." But this trend was foreseen at the height of the colorization debate by Woody Allen, who commented,

> Probably false ... is the claim that young people won't watch black and white. I would think they would, judging from the amount of stylish music videos and MTV ads that are done in black and white, undoubtedly after market research.[171]

E. Film as a Technological Work

Where moral rights are concerned, the situation of film is already difficult to handle. The addition of a technological element into the process of filmmaking leads to scenarios that reach a new level of complexity. The future of filmmaking, like most other fields of human creativity, will increasingly feel the influence of digital technology. In particular, the blending of technological and human elements is likely

[169] The French Cour de cassation states,

In admitting the claim, this judgment referred in substance to the Universal Copyright Convention signed in GENEVA on 6th September 1952, ratified by the UNITED STATES, to deduce that this convention provides citizens of member States in FRANCE with the benefit of the Law of 11th March 1957, notably Section 6, which provides that the moral right is attached to the person and is perpetual, inalienable and imprescribable.

As translated by Professor Chin, *supra* note 162.

[170] *See* Rick Lyman, *Black and White Is Back: Color "Em Wrong,"* New York Times (Jan. 11, 1998), http://www.nytimes.com/1998/01/11/weekinreview/ideas-trends-black-and-white-is-back-color-em-wrong.html?pagewanted=1.

[171] Allen, *supra* note 1.

to add a new layer of complexity to what is already the multilayered wedding cake of moral rights. The potential for digital intervention allows the editing of a film, reusing its parts in a new film or multimedia work, communicating the film via the Internet, and introducing radical new elements into the creation of a film, such as the "re-animation" of deceased actors through technology, allowing the appearance of their images, voices, and performances in current films. What are the implications of these filmmaking techniques for moral rights?

1. Editing, Creative Allusion, and Reuse: From Fan Films to Family Movies

In the digital environment, it seems, nothing need be forever.[172] Even a version of a film that has been agreed upon and finalized by all those involved in its creation—producer, director, writer, composer, actors, and technicians—can subsequently be altered by a viewer, or "user." This scenario is illustrated by the 2006 case of *Clean Flicks*.[173]

In the *Clean Flicks* case, films were edited with a specific purpose in mind—removing parts that could be considered "sensitive," making the film fit for viewing by families with children. In continental and developing countries, this kind of editing would clearly violate the author's moral right of integrity. Even in a country like India, which has faced many controversies over film censorship because of the objections—often violent—of militant social groups, a court has never found social objectionability to be a valid reason to curtail the author's moral right of integrity.[174] Indeed, the trial court in the *Bhandari* case actually commented that it is not the court's mandate to decide on the social acceptability of particular content when assessing the right of integrity.[175]

A different kind of problem arises in relation to fan films, a new genre of video creativity. In a fan film, an admirer of an existing film, television program, or video game will make a video based on the world of the original film—its characters and

[172] In another sense, the online environment is "forever" in many ways, leading to arguments in favor of a "right to be forgotten": *see, e.g.*, Ben Wolford, *Everything You Need to Know about the "Right to Be Forgotten,"* GDPR.EU (n.d.), https://gdpr.eu/right-to-be-forgotten. On the issues involved for young people, see, e.g., Kate Eichhorn, *Why an Internet That Never Forgets Is Especially Bad for Young People*, MIT TECH. REV. (Dec. 27, 2019), https://www.technologyreview.com/2019/12/27/131123/internet-that-never-forgets-bad-for-young-people-online-permanence. Eichhorn notes, powerfully,

> Identities and political perspectives will be hardened in place, not because people are resistant to change but because they won't be allowed to shed their past. In a world where partisan politics and extremism continue to gain ground, this may be the most dangerous consequence of coming of age in an era when one has nothing left to hide.

[173] *Clean Flicks of Colorado, LLC v. Soderbergh*, 433 F. Supp. 2d, 1236 (D. Colo. 2006) (U.S.).

[174] On film censorship in India, see the interesting comment by Shammi Nanda, *Censorship and Indian Cinema: The Case of* War and Peace, 38 BRIGHT LIGHTS FILM J. (2002), http://www.brightlightsfilm.com/38/indiacensor.php.

[175] *Mannu Bhandari*, *supra* note 11, at para. 22.

locales and, possibly, its storylines. As the name suggests, it is a form of homage to the original production. Fan films can be highly original in their own right, and some of them are made with the investment of substantial resources and talent.

Depending on its actual content, it is possible that a fan film could infringe copyright. A fan film could be considered a derivative work based on the original film, for which the permission of the original author would be required. In contrast, however, moral rights are not obviously implicated in fan films. Where attribution is concerned, the idea of crediting the creators of the original work seems implicit in the very definition of a fan film. As for integrity, the fan film would usually not involve the use of footage from the original work, eliminating the likelihood of a violation of the right on the grounds that the work has suffered direct mistreatment.[176]

But one possible violation of the right of integrity should be considered: the use of characters from the original film in the new work. This situation resembles the *Hugo* case, in which a descendant of the writer attempted to prevent the publication of a "sequel" to Hugo's monumental *Les Misérables* that pursued the further adventures of its characters—including the resurrection of the deceased Inspector Javert.[177] In its ruling, the French *Cour de cassation* found that a decision in favor of the plaintiffs would amount to an excessive limitation on the new writer's right to free speech.[178] The judgment can be criticized on the grounds that the author and publisher clearly hoped to exploit Hugo's reputation for their own commercial benefit—the main reason leading Hugo's great-great-grandson to pursue legal action in the first place.[179] The fan film case seems much more sympathetic, as the films are traditionally not made for profit.

The film industry is increasingly supportive of fan films. In this sense, the industry seems to have learned something from the public relations mishaps that have dogged the music industry. However, situations do arise where fan films clash with copyright policy. A recent example is the case of the German fan film *Damnatus*, inspired by a British videogame called *Warhammer*.

Damnatus was directed and produced by Huan Vu over a period of four years. When it was completed, the release of the film was blocked by Games Workshop, the makers of the *Warhammer* game, because of concerns about the copyright implications of Huan Vu's work under German law. In particular, Games Workshop noted that German copyright law grants rights to authors that cannot be waived. The company had hoped to acquire all rights in *Damnatus* from Mr. Wu, but the

176 *See, e.g., Shostakovich, supra* note 8.

177 *Pierre Hugo v. Editions Plon*, Cour d'appel [CA] [regional court of appeal] Paris, 1e ch., Mar. 31, 2004, 202 RIDA (Oct. 2004), *reversed* Cour de cassation [Cass.] [supreme court for judicial matters] 1e civ., Jan. 30, 2007, Bull. civ. I, No. 125 (Fr.), https://www.legifrance.gouv.fr/juri/id/JURITEXT000017627153.

178 For an interesting overview in English, see Kim Willsher, *Heir of Victor Hugo Fails to Stop Les Mis II*, THE GUARDIAN (Jan. 31, 2007), http://www.guardian.co.uk/world/2007/jan/31/books.france.

179 *Pierre Hugo, supra* note 176.

structure of German law would prevent it from doing so. Games Workshop felt that Mr. Wu's copyright in *Damnatus* would imply that he also had rights of ownership over *Warhammer*. As reported by the BBC, a Games Workshop spokesman claimed that allowing Mr. Wu to release his film would mean that, "Games Workshop would essentially be giving up the title to the Warhammer 40,000 intellectual property."[180] Accordingly, in the words of Andy Jones, the head of Games Workshop's legal department,

> To lose control of Warhammer or Warhammer 40,000 is simply unthinkable. So we must be vigilant, and perhaps sometimes seemingly heartless in our decisions to safeguard the IP for the future success of the business and the hobby.[181]

The outcome of this dispute was devastating for Vu, who commented to the BBC, "It's really horrible for an artist not being able to show off their own work."

The ultimate irony of the situation is that Games Workshop's analysis of the legal differences between German and British copyright law is questionable. There appear to have been two main concerns. First, the fact that German law would confer ownership of *Damnatus* on Mr. Vu, the "author" of the film, rather than Games Workshop as the "owner" of the copyright in the original work, seems to have presented a problem. German law does not allow the outright transfer of copyright.[182] But it is difficult to see why Games Workshop could not simply license the use of *Damnatus* in connection with its video game, rather than seeking to acquire the copyright in *Damnatus*.

Secondly, the comment regarding concerns about rights that cannot be waived could also be a reference to Germany's protection of the moral rights of authors, far more extensive than their counterpart in British law.[183] As Fan Cinema Today comments,

> Under German copyright law, the filmmakers are given rights to their work that they can't give away, even if they want to—art is considered to be an extension of the creator him- or herself.[184]

[180] Mark Ward, *Copyright Law Scuppers Fan Film*, BBC News (Nov. 6, 2007), http://news.bbc.co.uk/2/hi/technology/7010484.stm.

[181] Quoted id.

[182] *See* UrhG, *supra* note 31, at art. 29 ("Transfer of Copyright"): "Copyright may be transferred in execution of a testamentary disposition or to coheirs as part of the partition of an estate. Copyright shall not otherwise be transferable."

[183] *See* id. at art. 39 ("Alteration of [a] Work"): "(1) The holder of an exploitation right may not alter the work, its title or the designation of author (Article 10(1)), unless otherwise agreed. (2) Alterations to the work and its title which the author cannot reasonably refuse shall be permissible."

[184] *See* Clive Young, *Legendary Banned Warhammer 40,000 Fan Film Damnatus Leaked Online*, Fan Cinema Today (Jan. 30, 2009), http://fancinematoday.com/2009/01/30/legendary-banned-warhammer-40000-fan-film-damnatus-leaked-online.

But this interpretation of the law is puzzling. Once again, it seems that Games Workshop had little to fear. Huan Vu could not claim attribution or integrity rights in the products of Games Workshop; he could only enjoy those rights if, for example, the company created new products that were directly derived from his film. It is difficult to see how Games Workshop developed the notion that their own rights in their video game would be compromised by allowing Vu to retain his rights in an obviously derivative work. Wu would not own *Warhammer*; he would only own *Damnatus*.

If anything, an argument could be made that Vu's moral rights as an author were violated by Games Workshop. It initially authorized the making of his fan film but then refused to allow him to disclose it on what were, essentially, unreasonable grounds. In the end, Vu effectively secured the release of his film by "leaking" it to the online community via the Pirate Bay. Ironically, the leaked version makes little mention of the origin of the film—no doubt, because of Mr. Vu's experience with Games Workshop. Fan Cinema Today says that the film appeared "with little indication of its relation to" the original game, jeopardizing the very interest that Games Workshop had wanted to protect: its association with its own work.

In the United States, which recognizes no right of integrity in films, the approach to editing movies is a difficult copyright problem. In this sense, editing presents a strong contrast to the question of reusing film images in a new context, as happened in the Indian case of *Anand Patwardhan*,[185] which is actually quite easy to resolve under the conventions of U.S. law. Unless it can be shown to be fair use, reusing substantial parts of a film without the owner's consent is a clear infringement of the owner's copyright. It amounts to the making of a derivative work without the owner's permission. As in the *Gilliam* case, the doctrine of derivative works can capture this moral rights problem in the United States.[186]

Film editing is a different issue. In *Clean Flicks*, the process by which family-friendly versions of films were distributed—sanitized or sterilized, according to one's perspective—infringed copyright. The process of "cleansing" films occurred as follows. First, a DVD of the original film was purchased, either by the consumer or by Clean Flicks itself. The company would then copy the film onto a computer hard drive and run the movie in a program that would allow the user to modify the areas of concern. Deletions and additions were both possible. The editing might be seamless, or the final version could include visible changes obscuring the unwanted scenes.[187] The edited version was then copied onto a DVD for sale to the consumer, or to a retailer of movies.

[185] *Anand Patwardhan*, *supra* note 129.

[186] *Gilliam*, *supra* note 76.

[187] The editing process is described in detail by Suresh Pillai, *Mr. Soderbergh Goes to Washington: How Congress and the Clean Flicks Court Created Moral Rights for Filmmakers*, 17 DePaul-LCA J. Art & Ent. L. 339, 341–42 (2007).

These facts beautifully illustrate the copyright paradox of ownership versus authorship. From the perspective of copyright ownership, there is little in these activities to trigger the response of U.S. copyright law.[188] Indeed, the activities of Clean Flicks almost certainly generated benefits to the copyright-owners, since many of the people who bought these films might not have purchased them otherwise. At no point were the owners of the films deprived of their royalties: Clean Flicks always carried out its work on a version of the film that was lawfully purchased, either by the company or by the consumer. Its money was made out of its services and not from the film.

For the filmmakers, money may not be the essence of the matter. Rather, it is the misrepresentation of their work that generates discomfort. Interference with artistic control, possible damage to reputation, and confusion about the authenticity of the final work are all implicated in the "cleansing" process.

In fact, the United States has passed a federal law dealing with the issue of objectionable content in films—the Family Home Movie Act of 2005.[189] The Act was passed as part of a larger piece of legislation, the Family Entertainment and Copyright Act, which is actually a piece of anti-piracy legislation targeting two activities: unauthorized recording of a movie while it is being shown in a theater and the disclosure of a movie to the public prior to its official release date.[190] The rules on objectionable content are offered as an exception to copyright infringement under 17 U.S.C. §110(11).[191] "Skipping audio and video content," or the act of "making [material] imperceptible" through technology, in the words of the statute, is allowed for the purpose of rendering the film fit for "private home viewing."[192] The caveat comes in the concluding words: only if "no fixed copy of the altered version of the motion picture is created by such computer program or other technology" can the exemption to copyright infringement be claimed.[193]

Here, and only here, could the Clean Flicks defense fail: by copying the modified movies onto DVDs, it had made fixed copies of the works. On this ground, the

[188] *But see Gilliam, supra* note 76: filmmakers could argue that the edited versions were new derivative works, made without their consent.

[189] The Family Home Movie Act (FHMA) is part of the Family Entertainment & Copyright Act, Pub. L. 109–9, 119 Stat. 218 (2005).

[190] Id. § 102, also applies to computer software and music (id., § 103).

[191] *See* 17 U.S.C. § 202, amending the FHMA, *supra* note 188, § 110 ("Exemption from Infringement for Skipping Audio and Video Content in Motion Pictures"), which prohibits

... the making imperceptible of limited portions of audio or video content of a motion picture, during a performance in or transmitted to that household for private home viewing, from an authorized copy of the motion picture, or the creation or provision of a computer program or other technology that enables such making imperceptible and that is designed and marketed to be used, at the direction of a member of a private household, for such making imperceptible, if no fixed copy of the altered version of the motion picture is created by such computer program or other technology.

[192] *See* FHMA, *supra* note 188, § 110(11).

[193] In effect, this seems like a statutory exemption to the scenario in *Gilliam, supra* note 76: FHMA, *supra* note 188, § 110(11).

Colorado court found that the filmmakers' copyright had been violated by Clean Flicks.

In effect, the wording of the statute was flawed. It was drafted with a certain kind of technology in mind. Since the case, new methods of "cleansing" films have continued to be available, such as DVD software that allows objectionable scenes to be blacked out while the film is playing. Some commentators have argued that the court's ruling effectively creates a moral right of integrity, and indeed, it has outlawed the creation of permanent records of the sanitized versions of films.[194] But this right is incomplete: public broadcast of the altered versions and the development of software that allows the films to be viewed or broadcast after purging are still entirely permissible. The court has given a push to the development of "cleansing" technology in alternate directions.

Is the court's emphasis on fixation justified? From a moral rights perspective, it makes perfect sense. Fixation is a powerful method of establishing the authenticity of a given version of a creative work. In a digital environment, the concept of fixation is increasingly difficult to define. The court in *Clean Flicks* decided that fixation should remain the prerogative of the filmmaker, while post-film editing should not be granted an equivalent status by allowing the edited version to be fixed.

But in terms of policy, the court's decision is incomplete. The idea seems to be that no permanent damage to a work will occur if the modified versions of films are not fixed. They are ephemeral, perhaps the passing fad or fancy of a day, but the fixed version remains and is authentic. The court's position supports authenticity; but it does not address the possibility of damage to reputation, which can still occur if it is possible to view a modified version of the film. Under the ruling, it would be acceptable to broadcast edited versions of films provided that no fixation occurred. When an edited film is viewed, could it not have a negative impact on the reputation of the filmmaker? The character of a motion picture could be changed fundamentally by obscuring or deleting scenes to make them "imperceptible," in the language of the Act.

This was the scenario in the *Huston* case: what mattered was the fact that the public would have been exposed to colorized versions of the director's films when they were broadcast on television. It was irrelevant to ask whether the colorized version was fixed. Rather, the issue was the "performance" of the film, which reached the viewer in an altered—corrupted—form. In *Huston*, the court was concerned with the director's artistic reputation—not with the issue of preserving the integrity of the film. Until the question of reputation is clarified, the provisions of the Family Movie Act can be considered helpful for preserving authenticity, but they do not amount to a full-fledged moral right of integrity. Integrity, as it

194 See, e.g., the perceptive remarks made by Pillai, *supra* note 186, at 363–68.

is currently understood, would need to include both authenticity and reputation interests within its scope.

In this sense, the *Clean Flicks* decision fits well with the general approach to film in the United States. A growing awareness of the importance of maintaining authenticity in films found expression in the National Film Preservation Act of 1988.[195] The Act makes provision for establishing a registry of films that are "culturally, historically, or aesthetically significant;" it is also an offense to distribute or exhibit to the public any film from the registry that has been "materially altered" or colorized. The Act has some limitations: the number of films that can be selected for inclusion on the registry is limited to twenty-five per year, and the film itself must be at least ten years old.[196]

In these respects, the right conferred by the Act falls far short of what could be accomplished through a moral right of integrity, but it still represents an important achievement. Once a film is considered "significant," its status changes. It is no longer a mere commercial product; it is recognized as a culturally important work. The idea echoes the Indian approach to moral rights, as articulated in the *Amar Nath Sehgal* case, which affirms prerogatives for cultural treasures that transcend the usual limits of copyright law.[197]

For the proponents of economic rights in films, limiting the scope of integrity may be a good thing. As Suresh Pillai argues, imposing limits on moral rights would avoid the problem of a "chilling pall on the rights enjoyed by purchasers of protected material" that could flow from their recognition.[198] But Pillai goes on to suggest that a restrictive approach to moral rights should be promoted, not only for practical reasons, but also because restricting moral rights would keep copyright law within the legal limits defined by the copyright clause in the U.S. Constitution.[199]

[195] NFPA, *supra* note 149. The Act has subsequently been renewed a number of times, and its provisions have expanded to include new administrative procedures. The current iteration is now in force until 2026. *See* Library of Congress, *National Film Preservation Board: Mission* (n.d.), https://www.loc.gov/programs/national-film-preservation-board/about-this-program/mission; Library of Congress, *National Film Preservation Board: Legislation Impacting Film Preservation* (n.d.), https://www.loc.gov/programs/national-film-preservation-board/resources/legislation-impacting-film-preservation.

[196] Details of the Act can be found on the National Film Preservation Board website, *supra* note 194. The creation of the Registry is part of a larger project to preserve films that are of historical importance. In a fascinating paragraph, the National Film Preservation Board summarizes its mandate:

> The Foundation's primary mission is to save orphan films, films without owners able to pay for their preservation. The films most at-risk are newsreels, silent films, experimental works, films out of copyright protection, significant amateur footage, documentaries, and features made outside the commercial mainstream. Orphan films are the living record of the twentieth century. Hundreds of American museums, archives, libraries, universities, and historical societies care for "orphaned" original film materials of cultural value. The Foundation will work with these film preservation organizations to preserve orphan films and make them accessible to "present and future generations of Americans."

[197] See discussion of the *Amar Nath Sehgal* case in Chapter 4, *supra* notes * and accompanying text.

[198] Pillai, *supra* note 186, at 368.

[199] Id. at 344–70.

This point is conventional among U.S. copyright lawyers, but it deserves a closer look. It touches on a much larger issue: the relationship between copyright and freedom of speech in the United States.[200] The potential for conflict between moral rights and the U.S. Constitution is a debatable point and an issue on which copyright scholars may be too quick to pronounce judgment. Moral rights certainly challenge free speech, but so, too, do the economic rights enjoyed by copyright holders. In fact, proponents of moral rights could argue that they are less offensive to free speech than economic rights, because they are essentially a form of recognition for the human rights of creators without direct economic consequences.[201] Indeed, a right to protect the work from intrusive editing could be seen as one aspect of the director's own right to free expression. The moral right is also a right to free creative speech.

As for the "chilling pall" that moral rights would impose on the rights of purchasers, the connotations of the expression are strongly negative, but the effect described is the very objective of the moral right. There is no escaping this conclusion. It was Ted Turner's nightmare—in response to the colorization controversy, Turner is said to have remarked, "Last time I checked, I owned those films."[202] Moral rights mean that one cannot do absolutely anything with a work that one owns; certain kinds of treatment are disallowed. Almost every case that has dealt with the right of integrity, whether in India, France, or Canada, is about setting limits on the right to use a work, *even if* one owns it. Film is a form of creative expression in which both authors and owners are engaged in the exploitation of the work, and it can be difficult to define the limits of ownership. As the colorization conflict shows, film can become a battleground that pits authors against owners, unless and until the terms of a lasting peace can be achieved.

[200] This relationship is the theme of a multinational book of essays, COPYRIGHT AND FREE SPEECH: COMPARATIVE AND INTERNATIONAL ANALYSES (Jonathan Griffiths & Uma Suthersanen eds., 2005).

[201] For a detailed discussion of the connections between moral rights and human rights, see Sundara Rajan, COPYRIGHT AND CREATIVE FREEDOM, *supra* note 8, at ch. IX ("Copyright and Human Rights"). Other literature on this increasingly popular issue includes the seminal work of Peter Drahos, *Intellectual Property and Human Rights*, 3 INTELL. PROP. Q. 349 (1999). Of course, the economic rights of creators could also be seen as human rights, and they are noted as such in both the United Nations Declaration of Human Rights (UNDHR) and the International Covenant on Civil and Political Rights (ICCPR): G.A. Res. 217 (III) A, Universal Declaration of Human Rights (Dec. 10, 1948), http://www.un.org/en/documents/udhr; G.A. Res. 2200 (XXI) A, International Covenant on Civil and Political Rights (Dec. 16, 1966), https://www.ohchr.org/en/instruments-mechanisms/instruments/international-covenant-civil-and-political-rights. Article 27(2) of the UNDHR states, "Everyone has the right to the protection of the moral and material interests resulting from any scientific, literary or artistic production of which he is the author"; Art. 15(c) of the ICCPR mirrors this language, saying "To benefit from the protection of the moral and material interests resulting from any scientific, literary or artistic production of which he is the author." But the special connection between moral rights and human rights should probably be noted; commercial gain is not involved.

[202] Russell Baker, *We Trashed Those Films Long Ago*, ST PETERSBURG TIMES 25A (Nov. 28, 1986).

2. The Communication of Films Online

Like music, films are increasingly available online. Moral rights are clearly implicated in this form of communication. However, film has enjoyed some distinct advantages over music. The communication of video is slower than sound, and this has meant that the communication of films online has not kept pace with file-sharing in the music industry. The problems faced by the music industry have not developed as quickly in the film scenario, and, as a result, the film industry is, at least theoretically, in a position to benefit from the music experience.

In particular, the emergence of a legal framework for downloading films, such as Apple's iTunes, presents a likely solution to the vulnerability of film copyright. The extra-legal film counterpart to the iTunes model is YouTube, and here, as in the case of peer-to-peer music file-sharing, problems of copyright protection have arisen. When the YouTube service was first launched, its purpose was ostensibly to allow users to post their original videos; but much of the material posted to YouTube was copied from television broadcasts of programs protected by copyright that viewers uploaded to the service. In 2007, entertainment giant Viacom filed a billion-dollar lawsuit for copyright infringement against YouTube, but the case has become mired in procedural tangles and shows little sign of moving towards a hearing.[203]

YouTube has responded by vaunting a newfound hair-trigger sensitivity to potential copyright infringement. Absurd claims of copyright infringement have prompted calls for affected users of YouTube to sue it and its parent company, Google, for the removal of their videos.[204] YouTube has also adopted the more strategic approach of limiting the length of videos that can be posted on its site in an effort to control the uploading of illegally copied videos.[205]

[203] *Viacom Int'l Inc. v. Youtube, Inc.*, 940 F. Supp. 2d 110 (2013) (U.S.), https://casetext.com/case/viacom-intl-inc-v-youtube-inc-2. For an overview of the litigation, see Jonathon Stempel, *Google, Viacom Settle Landmark YouTube Lawsuit*, REUTERS (Mar. 18, 2014), https://www.reuters.com/article/us-google-viacom-lawsuit/google-viacom-settle-landmark-youtube-lawsuit-idUSBREA2H11220140318.

[204] An interesting example was the case of Stephanie Lenz's video of her baby son dancing to the Prince song, *Let's Go Crazy*; when the video was removed from YouTube, Ms. Lenz sued Universal Music and obtained a judgment in her favor. Copyright-owners are now required to make a good faith assessment of whether the video is a fair use of copyright-protected material before sending a takedown notice (under the Digital Millennium Copyright Act). *See* Robert Plummer, *Lawyers Go Crazy at Baby Prince Fan*, BBC NEWS (Sept. 8, 2008), http://news.bbc.co.uk/2/hi/business/7599921.stm. On a similar story, see Marshall Kirkpatrick, *YouTube Copyright System Gone Mad, EFF Prepares to Sue*, READWRITEWEB (Feb. 3, 2009), https://readwrite.com/youtube_copyright_system_eff_action.

[205] YouTube's copyright compliance strategy, as described by Glenn Brown, product counsel for Google, is summarized by Daniel B. Wood, *Lawsuit over YouTube video: It's What Everyone's Watching*, CHRISTIAN SCIENCE MONITOR (Mar. 23, 2007), http://www.csmonitor.com/2007/0323/p02s02-usju.html?page=1. Wood comments,

> Those additional measures include an automated takedown tool that can provide a quick search for copyrighted content, which YouTube offers to anyone who asks, he says. YouTube also has a 10-minute limit on videos, which limits abuse; a three-strikes provision that cancels the account of any three-time rule breaker; and a digital "hashing" feature that records when a file has been taken down to help prevent re-uploading of the same or similar material.

The film industry has a chance to learn what the music industry took too long to discover—that viable alternatives to free Internet material should be offered in order to satisfy the "unmet demand" for access to entertainment via the Internet. At the same time, measures for dealing with potential copyright infringement should not be draconian. An overly strict approach leads to bad public relations, on the one hand, and to bad legal practice, on the other. Viacom's decision to sue YouTube instead of attempting to target individual users of the site reflects a lesson well learned from the music experience.

It seems unlikely that any legal developments will inhibit the growth of video file-sharing. As video technologies improve, the incentives to share videos will only increase. If the Viacom suit is successful, it may help to change the legal framework for video file-sharing in much the same way that the model of music file-sharing has been transformed over the past decade. As in the case of music, collective licensing or pay-per-use models are likely to be the way of the future for video downloads.

As in the case of music, downloading exposes the vulnerability of moral rights. The attribution and integrity of films can both be compromised by users in a YouTube scenario; in an iTunes-style model, moral rights are also likely to suffer neglect at the hands of the companies controlling downloads. Many of the same concerns affect music and film—maintaining the integrity and attribution of films is both a social issue surrounding the integrity of knowledge and an issue of fairness affecting authors and artists. As in the case of music, the international legal dimension creates additional difficulties, because moral rights are not recognized in the United States, one of the world's largest producers—and consumers—of films.[206]

Issues of moral rights can also arise in user-made videos. For example, the posting of a private video that becomes a hit, as has happened a number of times on YouTube, can generate extensive reuse of the video, leading to a corresponding loss of control for its creator. In addition, the making of fan films can lead to concerns about the moral rights of the authors of the original work. Should a special exception along the lines of a parody exemption—primarily based on the intentions of the author—be created for these kinds of works?

206 It is well worth noting that, under French law, the insertion of advertisements into a film without the authors' consent is a violation of moral rights: *see* Sirinelli et al., *supra* note 25, at 121, 3 ("*Modalités de la diffusion* [Conditions of Broadcast]") and 11 ("*Coupures publicitaires* [Interruptions for advertising]").

3. Fame beyond the Grave: Reviving Deceased Actors through Artificial Intelligence

In Woody Allen's 1972 film, *Play It Again Sam*, the main character is fixated on Humphrey Bogart—his ideal of a man with a perfect understanding of women. In the film, Bogart coaches Allen's character towards a decision to do the right thing, in the process, recreating the famous final scene of the 1942 classic *Casablanca*, starring Bogart and Ingrid Bergman, in an entirely new context.

In Allen's film, Bogart is played by actor Jerry Lacy. But artificial intelligence now offers another possibility. Bogart's own image could potentially be taken from his old films and re-used—made to speak and act, to say new things that the character did not say and might never have said otherwise. Jerry Lacy is no longer needed. He would now be unemployed or in search of new roles that did not exploit his ability to impersonate Bogart.

Allen's comedy offers an especially interesting context in which to explore this problem because it involves a situation where there *was* an impersonation—not by means of artificial intelligence, but by another human actor. In some situations, this act of copying by a human impersonator could itself violate moral rights, defamation or, in the United States, the right of publicity.[207]

But there are arguably important qualitative differences between the two kinds of copying. As noted above, the use of another actor created a new human opportunity. It gave that impersonating actor a vehicle to develop his or her own creativity, albeit in a specialized direction. His or her ability to make films would also be constrained by biological realities: he or she could not generate large numbers of such performances, and those that he or she did deliver would differ subtly from one another, whether by intention as he or she honed his or her craft, or an unintentionally, as he or she became fatigued. Using artificial intelligence also generates opportunities, but they would primarily be opportunities for programmers—not actors. But programmers have little difficulty finding employment for their skills and time; actors do. In other words, the availability of artificial intelligence that can recreate actors' personas does not necessarily mean that it should be used in this context. There is a strong need for decision making in the public interest in situations such as these.

[207] In the United States, despite the terminology, the "right of publicity" actually protects celebrities' privacy rights. Publicity rights are discussed widely, but see, e.g., Kristin Bria Hopkins, *Put My Money in the Grave: Creating a Federally Protected Post-Mortem Right of Privacy*, ENT. & SPORTS LAWYER (Apr. 28, 2023), https://www.americanbar.org/groups/entertainment_sports/publications/entertainment-sports-lawyer/esl-39-01-spring-23/when-i-die-put-my-money-the-grave-creating-federally-protected-postmortem-right-publicity/, which specifically explores an issue that seems reminiscent of moral rights: protection after the death of the person involved. In common-law countries, personal torts can be invoked only during a person's lifetime; afterwards—except in those cases in which special legislation might address the protection of a personality after his or her death—there is no obvious legal solution.

Moral rights are well equipped to deal with this situation, for two reasons. First, they are fundamentally concerned with protecting artists' reputations. As such, they target precisely the kinds of issues that are raised by the reuse of actors' images, whether living or deceased, in films. This highlights the second advantage of moral rights: they persist after an artist's death and may even be recognized in perpetuity. In contrast to torts, they offer a method of protecting the integrity of a personality after the death of the individual concerned.

A further point is worth noting: the international copyright arena has expanded the definition of moral rights to reflect the possibility of moral rights for performers in the WIPO Performances and Phonograms Treaty and, specifically for actors, in the Beijing Treaty. Unfortunately, though, as discussed in Chapter 3, the extent of moral rights protection in both contexts is limited. In the Beijing Treaty, it is extraordinarily restricted by the terms of the footnote to article 5. This leads to the ironic situation that actors, who may need moral rights in the age of artificial intelligence more than almost anyone else, also have more limited access to them. It comes as no surprise, then, that Hollywood actors have been up in arms about the encroachments of artificial intelligence (AI). This situation must be remedied, and it remains to be seen whether the power of actors' unions is able to compel what Hollywood's creative workers have had to settle for in the past: contractual recognition of rights that the U.S. Copyright Act, influenced by Hollywood's perennially influential copyright lobby, refuses to give them. In this case, the guarantees offered by some kind of quasi moral rights protection in the guise of contractual clauses preventing the assumption of actors' identities by AI tools will be beyond compromise. They are, indeed, "bargaining for our very existence."[208] As noted by Hamilton Nolan, writing for The Guardian, the creators of movies must "win—for all of us, not just writers and actors."[209]

F. Recommendations

The art of film has developed throughout the twentieth century into an increasingly sophisticated medium of expression. It has proven its potential to convey the artistic vision of its creators. The history of film has been one of steady movement towards greater recognition for filmmakers as creative artists. It therefore seems natural that a parallel legal development would see moral rights as appropriate for film. Moral rights should play an integral role in valuing the creativity of

208 *See* Lois Beckett & Kari Paul, *"Bargaining for Our Very Existence": Why the Battle over AI Is Being Fought in Hollywood*, The Guardian (July 22, 2023), https://www.theguardian.com/technology/2023/jul/22/sag-aftra-wga-strike-artificial-intelligence.

209 Hamilton Nolan, *The Hollywood Strike Can and Must Win—For All of Us, Not Just Writers and Actors* (July 19, 2023), https://www.theguardian.com/commentisfree/2023/jul/19/the-hollywood-strike-can-and-must-win-for-all-of-us-not-just-writers-and-actors.

filmmakers. The challenge of recognizing moral rights in film is tremendous, but it is well worth the application of legal and creative ingenuity.

The traditional moral rights of disclosure, attribution, and integrity are all appropriate for film. However, each right should be tailored to the practical requirements of the medium. Disclosure cannot be the prerogative of all those involved in the creation of the film; but the concept of film disclosure can serve to represent, as in the French example, the agreement of the filmmakers on the final product.[210] Attribution is already accommodated in films, in the form of film credits, and should be maintained by companies engaged in the distribution of movies via the Internet. Individuals should also be educated about the need to attribute videos properly when posting content to the Internet, a requirement that could also support copyright more broadly on Internet video sites.

The moral right of integrity should be recognized in both its dimensions, as a right of authenticity that preserves the integrity of the director's vision in a film and a right of reputation that protects all the creative contributors to a film. These would include the director, writers of the screenplay and dialogue, composers of the soundtrack, and, in accordance with the principles in the Beijing Treaty,[211] actors' performances in films. As moral rights come to be recognized in more technical work, such as that of sound engineers and cinematographers, provision for the protection of their reputations could also make sense.

Moral rights provisions should offer clarity in defining the relationships among the different parties involved in the making of a film. Once again, the French approach, which requires agreement on the final version among producers and coauthors, is a solid one. At the same time, it may make sense to craft specific provisions that allow the director's moral right to override the rights of other creative contributors after the final version of a film is established. This would avoid a situation where, for example, a bad review of an actor's performance triggered a moral rights suit against the director, based on the integrity principle.

Evidence from the countries where film moral rights are recognized supports this approach. All the countries of continental Europe, and countries with major traditions of filmmaking such as India and Russia, recognize the moral rights of the authors of a film. In the common-law world, the example of India, which includes film comprehensively in its moral rights regime, is striking; but film moral rights are also recognized in the legislation of the United Kingdom, Canada, Australia, and New Zealand. The presence of moral rights does not appear to have "chilled" the film industry in any of these countries.[212] Indeed, India has both the largest and most flagrantly commercial film industry in the world.

[210] French Code de la propriété intellectuelle, *supra* note 21, at art. L121-5.

[211] World Intellectual Property Organization (WIPO) Performances and Phonograms Treaty, adopted Dec. 20, 1996, S. Treaty Doc. No. 105-17, 36 I.L.M. 76 (1997) (WPPT), https://www.wipo.int/wipolex/en/treaties/textdetails/12743.

[212] Of the four countries, Canada is the only long-term example of a country with moral rights (from 1931); since it allows comprehensive waiver of moral rights, it is difficult to say what impact they have

Once again, the position of the United States is quite anomalous. Based on the experience of other countries with film moral rights, the fears of Hollywood appear difficult to justify; and Hollywood's neglect of moral rights translates into U.S. disregard for its own filmmakers. When other countries demonstrate their willingness to recognize the work of Americans, as has often happened in the history of film moral rights, the situation can generate national embarrassment.

In the era of AI, the United States, in particular, must rethink its strategy. In doing so, the global experience with film moral rights should help. Hollywood may have something concrete to gain from moral rights. In particular, popular U.S. films are increasingly noticed by India's Bollywood film industry. Many Bollywood films are simply remakes of Hollywood features—although it should be noted that Hollywood, too, is famous for its remakes of world cinema and television.[213] In cases such as Barbara Taylor Bradford's, *A Woman of Substance*, remade as the television program, *Karishma—The Miracles of Destiny*, or the Hindi film, *Hari Puttar*, playing on the popularity of *Harry Potter* films, Indian courts, usually pro-author, have been completely unwilling to support Hollywood interests against Indian producers.[214] From an Indian perspective, Bollywood may be continuing an age-old tradition of exuberant adaptation. But how are Hollywood films, themselves, faring in India? Is India a potential marketplace for them? Do the new, "derivative" adaptations of U.S. stories produced by Bollywood support Hollywood interests by creating a taste with local viewers for the original; do they harm Hollywood by supplanting the U.S. films; or, though it seems increasingly unlikely, are the film markets in the two countries insulated from one another? Moral rights, already well supported by the Indian courts, could help to persuade Indian judges that certain limits should be imposed on Bollywood's gain, even when the films in question represent popular cultural "adaptations" in India.[215]

had on Canada's film industry. Moreover, it is probably fair to say that Canada's focus has generally been on the production of art and specialty films. For an interesting overview of the Canadian film landscape, see Fraser, *Canadian Film, supra* note 88. His earlier article, Berne, CFTA, NAFTA and GATT, *supra* note 7, at 304–11, offers a more detailed treatment of Canadian film and cultural issues from an international trade perspective.

213 Of course, Hollywood, too, has had its share of remakes for cinema and television. To cite a couple of examples, 1980s comedy program *Three's Company* was based on British sitcom *Man About the House*, and 1987 Hollywood comedy *Three Men and a Baby* was based on French film *Trois Hommes et un couffin*.

214 For an overview of the *Bradford* case and other Indian cases involving Hollywood films, see Rachana Desai, *Copyright Infringement in the Indian Film Industry*, 7 Vand. J. Ent. L & Prac. 259 (2005); Ayan Roy Choudhury, *The Future of Copyright in India*, 3(2) J. Intell. Prop. L. & Prac. 102, 109–13 (2008).

215 The pursuit of such an argument by an American filmmaker in India would be interesting but complicated. In particular, where film is concerned, Indian courts firmly adhere to the notion that there can be no copyright in ideas—the ground on which the *Bradford* case failed. *But see* T.S. Krishnamurti, *Copyright—Another View*, 15(3) Bull. Copyright Soc'y USA 217 (1968) (suggesting that the ancient Indian practice was to recognize "copyright in ideas"). It seems likely that the recognition of ideas had more to do with preserving the attribution interest than assuring any kind of financial benefit for the author.

G. Conclusion

As the original art form of the twentieth century grows into maturity, the technological landscape of the twenty-first presents new and unprecedented threats to film. These cultural shifts require a new and more sympathetic orientation towards those involved in the creation of films. The development of AI alternatives to human creativity, in particular, are of immense concern in this sector. And, importantly, the public interest is almost certainly on the creators' side: human beings continue to be interested in human performance, and, perhaps even more to the point, they *deserve* authentic human performance.

A thoughtful approach to moral rights could help to recognize the contributions of filmmakers to modern culture and lend support to the preservation of film as a vital cultural artefact. The ideas of authenticity and integrity have captured the imagination of those involved with cinema throughout the world. Many countries have adopted useful and interesting provisions on film moral rights, and future decades should see the refinement of these provisions to reflect the sophistication of new technologies and their potential impact on film.

The United States, a world leader in movies and in copyright matters, should not be left behind. The United States has produced some of the world's great film artists. Production no longer occurs within a strict studio system, and legal support for greater equality of bargaining power between the producers and the authors of a film would reflect this practical reality. U.S. directors, in particular, deserve to be recognized in their own country as they are already appreciated abroad. The introduction of moral rights would herald a cultural shift, but international experience suggests that there is little need for the U.S. film industry to be fearful. On the contrary, moral rights can help to affirm pride of achievement in an industry whose excellence depends on human creativity. They can help to preserve authentic human expression from unfair exploitation by means of AI.

When stories fail, films fail. Neither money nor machines can rescue them then. Films are products of the human imagination, and ultimately, narrative vehicles for the art of human performance. What does the United States have to lose?

8
The Master Hand
Moral Rights in the Visual Arts

Music resembles poetry, in each
Are nameless graces which no methods teach,
And which a master hand alone can reach.

—*Alexander Pope*[1]

A. Special Rights and Privileges: Moral Rights for Artists 516
B. *Sanctum Sanctorum*: Originality and the Special Status of Art 516
C. Moral Rights for Visual Artists Alone: The Approach in the Visual Artists Rights Act 1990 (VARA) 518
1. The Dis-United States: The Genesis of VARA in State Legislation for the Protection of Art 520
2. The Workplace: Employees Are Not Artists 520
3. Attribution: Remedying Integrity Violations 521
4. The Integrity Right: Intentional Harm 523
5. The Prohibition of Destruction: Cultural Heritage Bows before Property 525
6. *5Pointz*: Threading the Eye of the Needle 527
7. The VARA Time Machine 529
8. Waiving Moral Rights 531
D. Integrity without Reputation: Canada's Approach to Art 532
E. Context and Conservation: Alteration of the Work? 533
F. Context and Meaning: "Framed by the Sky" 534
G. Author's Right Meets the Public Interest: "General Cultural Interests," "National Treasure," and "Recognized Stature" 539
H. Creative Destruction: Should Artists Be Allowed to Destroy Their Own Work? 543
I. Perpetual Moral Rights: A Bridge between Intellectual and Cultural Property 544
1. Artworks: Property or Heritage? 547
2. Moral Rights and the Life-Cycle of an Artwork 549
a. Phase 1: Intellectual Property 549
b. Phase 2: *Post Mortem Auctoris* 549
c. Phase 3: Cultural Property and Moral Rights 552
d. The Public Domain: Shiva Nataraja's Rights of "Attribution" and "Integrity" 556
i. Legal Issues Assessed by the Courts 560
ii. A Moral Rights Perspective 563

[1] ALEXANDER POPE, *An Essay on Criticism, Part I*, *in* POETRY FOUNDATION (1711), https://www.poetryfoundation.org/articles/69379/an-essay-on-criticism. All websites cited in this chapter were last visited on October 29, 2024.

J. Architectural Works: Balancing Public Needs with Artistic Prerogative 565
K. Moral Rights and Virtual Galleries 569
1. Digital Images: New Technology to Reach Old Masters 569
2. Building Virtual Galleries 572
3. Artistic Innovation: From Collages to Parodies 573
L. Copy or Original? 3D Printed Artworks 575
M. A Critique of Originality: Bill Reid and Haida Art 579
N. A Further Critique: Yumbulul and the Legal Paradox of Living Traditions 582
O. Recommendations and Conclusion 584

A. Special Rights and Privileges: Moral Rights for Artists

The visual arts are different.[2] Where moral rights in artistic works are concerned, in contrast to every other sphere of creative expression, legislators stand ready to intervene. Artists receive greater protection for moral rights than any other group of authors. This chapter examines two questions. First, why are artists working in the fine arts treated differently? Secondly, are there broader lessons to be learned from the treatment of the visual arts, including the relatively in-depth jurisprudence on moral rights in this area, for other creators?

B. *Sanctum Sanctorum*: Originality and the Special Status of Art

Regarding the issue of special treatment, we may ask what differentiates artistic works from other types of creative works. Two primary distinctions can be drawn. First, an artistic object is usually unique: the archetype of an artwork is an "original" work[3] that cannot be "copied" in any meaningful sense.[4] This presents a strong contrast to text, music, and even film, where digital copies can be made without any significant degradation of the original work.[5]

[2] It should be noted that *droit de suite*, as a form of "hybrid" right, is not discussed in this chapter, but it is treated in Chapter 3 (on the Berne Convention), *supra* notes 62-66 and accompanying text.

[3] "Original" is used here in the sense of a work that did not exist previously.

[4] Technologies such as 3D printing, but also the application of artificial intelligence (AI) techniques, create the first ever potential for ambiguity in this regard and are discussed *infra*.

[5] 3D printing has the potential to change this in relation to artworks, as discussed *infra*. The perfection of the 3D copy will also depend on the quality of the scanning. The technology holds promise as a boon for conservation and a potential way out of intractable disputes over art and cultural property (by allowing "sharing" through the making of a 3D replica, as could be done, for example, in the case of the Elgin Marbles). As a tool for dramatic improvement in the quality of forgeries, it also presents a threat.

For this reason, damage to a work of art has uniquely serious consequences. Once the work has been harmed, it may be impossible to set it right, and the artwork may never be truly restored to its original state. If it is destroyed, there is no hope of recovery. For this reason, it makes immediate sense to have strong rights in place to protect works of art—above all, for their *deterrent* effect, since the ultimate goal is to prevent damage to artworks. In relation to art, the goal of prevention should always be prioritized. This fragile reality may explain why moral rights in artworks are accorded a higher standard of protection in most places than that provided to other works. It may also be the reason why moral rights for artists meet with greater receptivity in the United States, an otherwise skeptical jurisdiction when it comes to moral rights.

The work is not only unique but also—to be more precise—"original." Originality is a concept of unrivaled significance in the art world, where this notion acquires a spectacular, even fanatical importance. Works of art are even referred to as "originals," and the meaning involved here is something very specific: the idea that a work physically originates from the "master hand" of the artist.[6] Pope specifically speaks of the subtle greatness of the "master hand" of the musician or poet, but the notion has been most enthusiastically embraced in relation to the visual arts. In the art world, originality amounts to authenticity, and it signifies provenance. These connotations are wholeheartedly imported into the art world, where they create extraordinary complexity and confusion.[7]

"Original" works by recognized artists become immensely, perhaps insanely, valuable because of their provenance directly from the artist's "master hand."[8] Even a small sketch by a celebrated artist—a Gauguin or a Van Gogh—might be worth millions, to say nothing of a painting, sculpture, or other substantial work. But this definition of originality can only be comfortably applied to a relatively small subset of artistic works—those that are of known and uncontested authorship, and made without any need for technological intervention. For example, Rodin's large works in bronze depended on casting at the Rudier Foundry, which realized all of his important artistic works of monumental scale such as the Gates of Hell. By creating models for these works, Rodin did not physically create the works themselves—he could not—but he established what were, in a sense, detailed artistic blueprints for their creation. The originality of these works has been preserved by limiting the number that can be cast and vesting the authority to cast them in the Rodin Museum, an institution established by the artist before his death to oversee his legacy. French copyright law protects the originality that is established by these

[6] Pope, *supra* note 1.

[7] This situation is wonderfully illustrated in a documentary portrait of the art world, Nathaniel Kahn, *The Price of Everything* (2018), https://kinolorberedu.com/film/the-price-of-everything-dvd-1

[8] Nathaniel Kahn's film, id., brilliantly examines the seemingly insane valuations of artworks in the modern art market.

means, and making further copies would amount to piracy.[9] It is worth noting that, by doing so, the law upholds the market value of the works; but it also serves another purpose, which is to maintain a degree of authenticity in Rodin's creations that would be unsustainable if unauthorized copies were to become widespread. It is not difficult to see how copying could lead to the degradation of quality, with the details of the artist's vision becoming eroded over time.

C. Moral Rights for Visual Artists Alone: The Approach in the Visual Artists Rights Act 1990 (VARA)

Moral rights in works of art receive at least two kinds of special treatment. First, as is most striking in the case of the United States, they are recognized even where moral rights are *not* generally recognized within a given legislative framework. Secondly, as is apparent in countries with general recognition for moral rights, visual artists routinely enjoy stronger moral rights than those granted to other kinds of creators.

The United States is uniquely illustrative of the first case, offering moral rights protection *only* to visual artists.[10] More than two decades after joining the Berne Convention, the United States has made little progress towards the general implementation of moral rights in its copyright law.[11] But moral rights in visual works were established soon after Berne membership, with the introduction of special legislation known as the Visual Artists Rights Act of 1990 (VARA).[12]

[9] This is explained in Rodin Museum, *Respecting Rodin's Moral Right: A Warning to Collectors about the Notion of Authenticity* (n.d.), https://www.musee-rodin.fr/en/professionnals/respecting-Rodins-moral-right (also providing references to relevant provisions of French law). A long-awaited successful judgment on an infringement issue was obtained by the Musée Rodin against two U.S. dealers in 2019: *see, e.g.*, Vincent Noce, *Two Art Dealers Sentenced over "Fake-Genuine" Rodin Sculptures after 18 Year Legal Battle*, The Art Newspaper (Apr. 24, 2019), https://www.theartnewspaper.com/2019/04/24/two-art-dealers-sentenced-over-fake-genuine-rodin-sculptures-after-18-year-legal-battle.

[10] But moral rights, though not explicitly designated as such, are implicit in at least one other area of U.S. copyright law: *see* National Film Preservation Act, Pub. L. No. 100-446, 102 Stat. 1774 (1988) (NFPA), http://www.gpo.gov/fdsys/pkg/STATUTE-102/pdf/STATUTE-102-Pg1774.pdf. The Act has been renewed a number of times, and its provisions have expanded to include new administrative procedures. The current version is in force until 2026. *See* Library of Congress, *National Film Preservation Board: Mission* (n.d.), https://www.loc.gov/programs/national-film-preservation-board/about-this-program/mission; Library of Congress, *National Film Preservation Board: Legislation Impacting Film Preservation* (n.d.), https://www.loc.gov/programs/national-film-preservation-board/resources/legislation-impacting-film-preservation. The Act is discussed in more detail in Chapter 4, *supra* note 176 and accompanying text, and Chapter 7, *supra* notes 149–51, 194 and accompanying text.

[11] See the detailed discussion of the approach to moral rights in the United States in Chapter 4, *supra* notes 100-85 and accompanying text.

[12] *See* Visual Artist Rights Act, 17 U.S.C. § 106A (1990), https://www.copyright.gov/title17/92chap1.html#106a (VARA). The original Bill and accompanying information are available at https://www.congress.gov/bill/101st-congress/house-bill/2690. William Patry provides a useful analysis of case law

How did VARA come to be adopted? Review of the congressional debates at the time of Berne accession,[13] as well as the study of VARA itself, show that VARA did not emerge out of a legal vacuum. On the contrary, there were very strong antecedents in U.S. law for the protection of moral rights in works of visual art: pre-existing state-level statutes for the protection of artworks, particularly California legislation. VARA is clearly a product of these precedents, and, in some cases, it represents a re-examination of established state-level practices before their adoption in the new, federal context.

The bill was introduced by Representative Kastenmeier from Wisconsin. His comments are worth quoting at some length here:

> The second goal was to protect the works of art themselves. Society is the ultimate loser when these works are modified or destroyed. They should be preserved in the way the artist intended, and as the *important part of our cultural heritage* that they are. *Eleven States have already recognized this fact. These laws have not disrupted the market for the sale of works of art, and they have given artists the ability to protect their reputations and their works of art. H.R. 2690 [which ultimately became VARA] builds on the experiences of these States by protecting works of visual art from modification and destruction.*
>
> The third goal of H.R. 2690 was *to provide a nationwide standard for these protections.* H.R. 2690 will preempt State laws in certain circumstances. While the States are free to continue to explore their own solutions in areas not covered by this bill, a *Federal law will provide the uniformity and certainty that individual States cannot.*[14]

related to VARA: William Patry, *No VARA Trophy* (June 18, 2006), http://williampatry.blogspot.com/2006/06/no-vara-trophy.html. In a second post, he provides an interesting look at the interpretation of VARA in relation to "site-specific art" and whether its removal can violate an artist's rights under the legislation: William Patry, *The First Circuit Misses the Boat Again* (Aug. 22, 2006), http://williampatry.blogspot.com/2006/08/first-circuit-misses-boat-again.html.

[13] 136 Cong. Rec. 9 (1990), 101st Cong., 2d Sess., https://www.congress.gov/bound-congressional-record/1990/06/05/136/house-section/article/12591-12683?q=%7B%22search%22%3A%5B%22visual+artists+rights+act%22%5D%7D&s=6&r=5&overview=open#content.

[14] Id. at 12607–608 (emphasis added). The astonishing comments that precede this (id. at 12607) suggest that VARA should be considered primarily as a response to U.S. public policy concerns rather than a means of Berne implementation:

> We began this examination with the Berne convention implementing legislation. The convention requires its members to provide artists with a certain level of protection. The Congress, in passing the implementation act, decided that United States law was already sufficient to comply with the convention and we therefore joined Berne, effective March 1989. This did not, however, end debate over the issue. While our laws may be sufficient to comply with Berne, this does not necessarily mean that they are sufficient for all purposes.

1. The Dis-United States: The Genesis of VARA in State Legislation for the Protection of Art

The interaction of state and federal law in the United States is a largely unique phenomenon in the international community. The highly federalist U.S. system encourages pro-active law-making at the state level, and the area of art preservation is a case in point. When federal legislation in a given field is adopted, of course, it preempts state legislation—but there is an important caveat to this rule. Where state legislation deals with areas that are not dealt with in the federal statute, or where it provides more extensive protection than the federal law, it remains in force. This is the case with certain state-level laws involving art. A number of states, including New York, Louisiana, Connecticut, Pennsylvania, New Mexico, Maine, New Jersey, Rhode Island, Nevada, and Massachusetts,[15] as well as California, have enacted statutes in this area. Of these, special status must be accorded to California's landmark art preservation statute, the California Art Preservation Act (CAPA) of 1979, which was expanded in a subsequent piece of legislation, the Cultural and Artistic Creations Preservation Act (CACPA) of 1982.[16] California law, which also served as the inspiration for New York's subsequent Artists' Authorship Rights Act (1984). Interestingly, certain provisions of CACPA were reassessed and scaled down in the corresponding New York legislation.

2. The Workplace: Employees Are Not Artists

As noted previously, employees do not have moral rights under VARA. The definition of "a work of visual art" in section 101 of the U.S. Copyright Act specifically provides that a "work of visual art does not include ... any work made for hire."[17] This accompanies the general work-for-hire rule under U.S. law, which provides that the copyright in employee-created work that is made "in the course of employment" is owned by the employer.[18] This issue has twice come up in case law—*Carter v. Helmsley-Spear*,[19] the first major precedent on VARA, and *Community*

[15] For details, see Edward J. Damich, *State Moral Rights Statutes: An Analysis and Critique*, 13 COLUM.-VLA J.L. & ARTS 291 (1988), discussing statutes in New York, Connecticut, Massachusetts, Rhode Island, Louisiana, and other states. *See also* Christopher J. Robinson, *The "Recognized Stature" Standard in the Visual Artists Rights Act*, 68 FORDHAM L. REV. 1937, 1944 (2000).

[16] Cal. Civ. Code § 989 (West Supp. 2000) (U.S.), https://codes.findlaw.com/ca/civil-code/civ-sect-989. Massachusetts followed suit with a similar provision: *see* Mass. Ann. Laws ch. 231, § 85S (Law. Co-op. 1986 & Supp. 1999), https://malegislature.gov/Laws/GeneralLaws/PartIII/TitleII/Chapter231/Section85S.

[17] *See* Copyright Act, 17 U.S.C. § 101 (definitions), https://www.copyright.gov/title17/92chap1.html. Correspondingly, moral rights under VARA, *supra* note 12, § 106A can be held only by "the author of a work of visual art."

[18] *See* U.S. Copyright Act, *supra* note 17, § 101.

[19] This case is discussed in detail in Chapter 4, *supra* note 161: in spite of the work-for-hire doctrine, the court created a new and controversial "two-tiered" test relating to "recognized stature" under

for Creative Nonviolence v. Reid, a seminal 1989 ruling on work for hire.[20] This is not coincidental, as much artistic creation is commissioned for various purposes, and the exclusion of moral rights from the work for hire setting is a major limitation on the moral rights of artists in the United States.

The *Carter* case is a particularly bitter illustration of this exclusion. The artist plaintiffs had successfully brought suit through two levels of court. Their complaint was finally overturned by the Supreme Court, which ruled that their work had been carried out as employees and not as independent contractors. In other words, moral rights violations had occurred, but they were not actionable because moral rights cannot arise in a work-for-hire context. The ruling only serves to highlight the importance of the exclusion, and its potential unfairness.

3. Attribution: Remedying Integrity Violations

VARA recognizes the basic moral rights of attribution and integrity, as per Berne requirements; but it does so through sometimes unusual formulae. Attribution under VARA explicitly includes two aspects of attribution—the right to claim authorship,[21] and the opportunity for the author to reject the false attribution of another person's work to him or her.[22] In the context of the visual arts, the right against false attribution could help to address the problem of forgery.[23] In contrast, commenting on the Berne Convention, Silke von Lewinski argues that "moral rights only protect the relation of the author to her own work," leading to the general situation that "cases of false attribution are not covered by the right to claim authorship."[24] In this sense, VARA may surpass international standards, and moral rights as defined by VARA may offer an additional weapon in the fight against art forgery.

VARA. *See Carter v. Helmsley-Spear, Inc.*, 861 F. Supp. 303, 325 (S.D.N.Y. 1994) (U.S.), https://law.justia.com/cases/federal/district-courts/FSupp/861/303/2261919:

> Thus, for a work of visual art to be protected under this Section, a plaintiff must make a two-tiered showing: (1) that the visual art in question has "stature," *i.e.* is viewed as meritorious, and (2) that this stature is "recognized" by art experts, other members of the artistic community, or by some cross-section of society. In making this showing, plaintiffs generally, but not inevitably, will need to call expert witnesses to testify before the trier of fact. [Note omitted.]

The appeal is *Carter v. Helmsley-Spear, Inc.*, 71 F.3d 77 (1995) (U.S.), https://casetext.com/case/carter-v-helmsley-spear-inc.

20 *Community for Creative Non-Violence v. Reid*, 490 U.S. 730 (1989) (U.S.), https://supreme.justia.com/cases/federal/us/490/730.

21 *See* VARA, *supra* note 12, § 106A(a)(1)(A).

22 *See* id., § 106A(a)(1)(B).

23 *See* id., § 106A(a)(1)(B), providing that the artist has the right "to prevent the use of his or her name as the author of any work of visual art which he or she did not create." In relation to literary works, a similar right could serve to provide effective protection against plagiarism.

24 Silke von Lewinski, International Copyright Law and Policy para. 5.99 (2008).

However, there is another side to attribution under VARA: it is also presented as a remedy to violations of the right of integrity. The statute states that the "author ... shall have the right to prevent the use of his or her name as the author of the work of visual art in the event of a distortion, mutilation, or other modification of the work which would be prejudicial to his or her honor or reputation."[25] In other words, in the case of any detrimental treatment of a work that would damage the author's reputation, VARA takes the view that reputational damage can be forestalled or corrected by removing the artist's name from the work—thereby, severing his or her association with it. The author will no longer be known as its original creator.

In this sense, the attribution right under VARA is technically broader than Berne requirements, yet, when it comes to the intersection of the artist's attribution right with the integrity right, it is also double-edged. When moral rights claim their own efficacy in the removal of an artist's name from the work, the right of attribution seems to be functioning at cross-purposes with itself.[26] In looking at the VARA provisions, it is helpful to remember that the moral right of integrity in the Berne Convention effectively protects two distinct interests—the integrity of the work and the reputation of the author—which are formally linked through the language of Article 6*bis*. The provision in VARA can be considered an extreme version of the integrity right that seeks to protect *only* the author's reputational interest. But, importantly, this negative aspect of the "attribution" right in VARA should not have the effect of precluding the artist from separately asserting the moral right of integrity. And, indeed, under this provision, it does appear that artists can separately exercise a distinct moral right of integrity.

[25] *See* VARA, *supra* note 12, § 106A(a)(2): the author "shall have the right to prevent the use of his or her name as the author of the work of visual art in the event of a distortion, mutilation, or other modification of the work which would be prejudicial to his or her honor or reputation."

[26] See the interesting moral rights litigation under VARA initiated by David Ascalon, a well-known sculptor, in July 2010. Ascalon's sculpture for a Holocaust memorial in Harrisburg, Pennsylvania, was subject to restoration work that defaced the sculpture and effectively destroyed the artistic concept behind it. Among other forms of damage, the sculptor's name was ground off the work. Monika Bruss provides an interesting post on the case: Monika Bruss, *Moral Rights and Unhappy Bedfellows*, 1709 Blog (Aug. 16, 2010), http://the1709blog.blogspot.com/2010/08/it-is-fact-universally-acknowledged-at.html. Bruss comments that "by grinding off Mr. Ascalon's name the Defendants successfully avoided violation of § 106A(a)(2)." But this interpretation seems mistaken; rather, Ascalon's statement of claim identifies the removal of his name as part of the severe harm done to the work by the defendants, the Harrisburg Department of Parks and Recreation, and David Grindle, hired by the Department to restore the work. Ascalon's counsel writes: "The Federation's direction to Grindle, or alternatively its acceptance of Grindle's decision, to remove Ascalon's name from the Memorial amounts to grossly negligent and intentional destruction of the Memorial and prejudice to Ascalon's honor and reputation in violation of Ascalon's rights under 17 D.S.C.§106A(a)(3)(B)." It would seem that the right to remove the artist's name from his or her work, granted by VARA, is a choice that is supposed to remain with the artist. It may be a practical means of dealing with damage to a work that cannot be sufficiently corrected to restore the artist's reputation—or, at least, to forestall further damage to it. The Statement of Claim in the Ascalon litigation is available at http://websites.uwlax.edu/kincman/474%20Legal/Ascalon%20Complaint.pdf.

4. The Integrity Right: Intentional Harm

The integrity right under VARA is framed in broadly familiar terms, incorporating much of the language of Article 6*bis* of the Berne Convention. However, it also introduces a new concept: that of "intention." VARA states that the author will have the right "to prevent any intentional distortion, mutilation, or other modification of that work which would be prejudicial to his or her honor or reputation and any intentional distortion, mutilation, or modification of that work is a violation of that right."[27] The introduction of intention narrows the right as compared to Berne. It effectively excludes violations of the integrity right through accidents or good-faith actions, such as conservation, that go awry.

But the formula is also curiously circular. What does it mean that "any intentional distortion, mutilation, or modification of that work is a violation of that right"? A straightforward reading of this provision suggests that, if intentional harm to a work can be established, there is *no additional requirement* to show damage to the author's honor or reputation for an integrity violation under VARA. In a sense, this right is a Berne-plus formulation, because it eliminates that secondary requirement. However, VARA also introduces a new requirement, in lieu of showing proof of damage to the artist's honor or reputation, that of "intentional" harm.[28]

What exactly qualifies as intentional? Is this concept broad enough to encompass negligence? In fact, the VARA provisions introduce at least three instances of legal terminology that call for clarification: intention, "gross negligence," and the meaning of "recognized stature."

In relation to the first term, "intention," the objective of the statute is clearly to introduce a high standard of proof that will be met with difficulty. Accidents or mishaps will not be covered by this provision unless the accident occurs as a result of truly substantial irresponsibility. Negligence, already a high standard of disregard, will probably not be sufficient under this provision, for the simple reason that intention is distinguished from *gross* negligence, the following possibility. Unless the relatively high standard of "gross negligence" under U.S. law is met, destruction of a work will not amount to a violation of VARA.[29]

The third term, "recognized stature" has received some judicial commentary, though it is questionable how helpful that commentary proves to be. In the case of *Carter v. Helmsley Spear*, the first case decided under VARA, the court of first instance sought to define a work of "recognized stature" by introducing

[27] *See* VARA, *supra* note 12, § 106A(a)(3)(A).

[28] Private communications with representatives of the U.S. Copyright Office (Spring 2021).

[29] The gross negligence standard has not been tested specifically in relation to VARA, but for a discussion of its general meaning in U.S. law, see, e.g., the definition and explanation at Cornell Law School Legal Information Institute, *Gross Negligence* (n.d.), https://www.law.cornell.edu/wex/gross_negligence.

a two-pronged requirement of proof, which it calls a "two-tiered showing," that would need to be satisfied.[30] The test reads as follows:

> Thus, for a work of visual art to be protected under this Section, a plaintiff must make a two-tiered showing: (1) that the visual art in question has "stature," i.e. is viewed as meritorious, and (2) that this stature is "recognized" by art experts, other members of the artistic community, or by some cross-section of society. In making this showing, plaintiffs generally, but not inevitably, will need to call expert witnesses to testify before the trier of fact. Finally, in order to be entitled to injunctive relief, a plaintiff must show that the defendant has commenced destruction of, or intends to destroy, the subject work.[31]

In this paragraph, reliance on the opinion of experts, the old, familiar recourse of common-law courts dealing with the moral rights of artists, makes its expected—though, as the court says, "not inevitabl[e]"[32]—appearance.[33] U.S. courts have confronted some interesting factual permutations, such as the 1996 case of two California artists whose home was destroyed by "a city garbage truck that ... rolled down a hill."[34] The city's actions were found not to be "intentional or grossly negligent," but the court's consideration of "recognized stature," though not determinative of the outcome, is noteworthy. It allowed recognized stature to be inferred. This inference was based upon the reputations of the artists, and it was made in spite of the fact that many of the works had actually not been seen by the public.[35] As Christopher J. Robinson notes, "The court looked to evidence, excluded at trial on motions *in limine*, of the Lubners' active forty-year careers as painters and art instructors."[36] But Robinson adds an important cautionary remark:

> The court's finding of recognized stature by inference is a creative solution. It is doubtful, however, that inferred recognized stature would have been so easily accepted by this or any other court had the outcome of the case depended on it.[37]

How helpful is the *Carter* test? Perhaps the Court in *Carter*, while trying to walk a tightrope between judicial interpretation of the VARA provisions and the effective creation of new rules, lost its balance. With the introduction of the term

[30] *See Carter, supra* note 19.
[31] Id. at 325 (footnotes omitted).
[32] Id. *See also* Robinson, *supra* note 15, at 1950.
[33] U.S. courts have indicated that certain other types of evidence may satisfy the *Carter* test, e.g., "certain newspaper and magazine articles, including a letter from an art gallery director and a letter to the editor of *The Indianapolis News*, all in support of the sculpture": *Martin v. City of Indianapolis*, 192 F.3d 608 (7th Cir. 1999) (U.S.), cited in *5Pointz, infra* note 39.
[34] Robinson, *supra* note 15, at 1952.
[35] Id.
[36] Id.
[37] Id.

"recognized stature," *Carter* seems to introduce a new standard beyond what Congress intended. In the early years of VARA, at least, courts were willing to work with it.[38] But *Carter* fell short of providing greater clarity. The Court may also have unnecessarily complicated the interpretation of VARA: the "new standard" is not self-explanatory and therefore requires further interpretation in its own right.

With time, the approach to "recognized stature" in *Carter* has come to be treated as non-binding. The most significant case on this issue is that of the 5Pointz mural complex in the borough of Queens, New York City, which offers a thought-provoking picture of the post-*Carter* landscape and is discussed below.[39]

5. The Prohibition of Destruction: Cultural Heritage Bows before Property

VARA includes remarkable language that explicitly prohibits the destruction of artworks, but the provision can only be invoked in extraordinarily limited circumstances. Still, this language is a rare instance among world copyright laws, and it is also remarkable that such an esoteric provision has led to the largest punitive award of damages against a property owner for destroying artworks on his property.[40]

VARA explicitly prohibits the "*intentional* or *grossly negligent destruction* of a work of *recognized stature*."[41] Preventing the destruction of artworks, in any circumstances,[42] is more than the Berne Convention requires.[43] In India, the destruction of artworks has also been prohibited, provided, though, that those works "have attained the status of national treasures."[44] The Indian result has been accomplished through judicial interpretation of the law—moral rights in section 57 of the Indian Copyright Act,[45] as well as instruments of

[38] *See, e.g.*, id. at 1956 (discussing *Martin v. City of Indianapolis*, *supra* note 33, at 1955–58).

[39] *Castillo v. G&M Realty L.P.*, Nos 18-498-cv (L), 18-538-cv (CON), 2020 U.S. App. LEXIS 5228 (2d Cir. Feb. 20, 2020), https://www.mintz.com/sites/default/files/media/documents/2020-03-25/18-498_amd_opn.pdf.

[40] Id.

[41] Emphasis added.

[42] But it should be noted that the discussion of the treatment of artworks during wartime is excluded from this chapter, and the relevant provisions in the Hague Convention are not discussed. The reader who is specifically interested in this issue should bear those in mind: United Nations Convention for the Protection of Cultural Property in the Event of Armed Conflict, May 14, 1954, 249 U.N.T.S. 215, https://en.unesco.org/protecting-heritage/convention-and-protocols/1954-convention [Hague Convention].

[43] For an assessment of where destruction of an artwork stands in international copyright law, see Sam Ricketson, The Berne Convention for the Protection of Literary and Artistic Works: 1886–1986 para. 8.109 (1987). See also the comments in von Lewinski, *supra* note 24, at para. 5.103. For a discussion of the debate surrounding the issue of whether or not destruction of a work is encompassed by the right of integrity, see Chapter 1, *supra* notes 79–86 and accompanying text.

[44] *Amar Nath Sehgal v. Union of India*, 2005 (30) PTC 253 (Delhi High Court) (India), https://indiankanoon.org/doc/1990275.

[45] Copyright Act, 1957, No. 14 (India), http://copyright.gov.in/Documents/CopyrightRules1957.pdf.

international cultural property law to which India is a signatory—not in statutory language.[46]

All of VARA's provisions on the integrity right are further limited when it comes to artworks that are incorporated into buildings. Section 113(d) of the Copyright Act deals specifically with potential conflicts surrounding the removal of such works from their sites. Under its terms, if a work can be removed without destroying or damaging it, then "a diligent, good faith attempt" to advise the artist of the plan to remove the work must be made.[47] The Act also explains what such an attempt would be: "notice by registered mail to the author at the most recent address of the author that was recorded with the Register of Copyrights."[48] The latter point may represent a possible administrative hurdle to the artist's rights, since the following provision provides for a register of artist information to be maintained, but it does not require artists to participate: they "may" do so.[49] Any artist who has created a public artwork on or in a building that he or she cares about would be well advised to register an address in accordance with this provision and to keep it updated, notwithstanding its apparently elective character.

When it comes to artworks that are integrated into buildings, there are also two specific caveats under VARA. First, the property owner is obliged to involve the artist only if there is a *possibility* that the work can be removed without damage.[50] Otherwise, if the work *cannot* be removed without damage, by implication, the property owner can simply remove the work.

Secondly, VARA imposes the obligation to remove the work *upon the artist* or, alternatively, to pay for the costs of removing it.[51] An artist must be able to manage these costs. If he or she cannot do so, that is the artist's problem—not the property owner's, who has performed his or her statutory duty by informing the artist of the need to move the work under these provisions.

[46] Previously discussed in Chapter 4, *supra* note 295 and accompanying text.

[47] *See* U.S. Copyright Act, *supra* note 17, § 113(d)(2)(A) and (B) (regarding costs), https://www.copyright.gov/title17/92chap1.html#113.

[48] Id.:

> For purposes of subparagraph (A), an owner shall be presumed to have made a diligent, good faith attempt to send notice if the owner sent such notice by registered mail to the author at the most recent address of the author that was recorded with the Register of Copyrights pursuant to paragraph (3). If the work is removed at the expense of the author, title to that copy of the work shall be deemed to be in the author.

[49] See id., §113(d)(3), which states:

(3) The Register of Copyrights shall establish a system of records whereby any author of a work of visual art that has been incorporated in or made part of a building, may record his or her identity and address with the Copyright Office. The Register shall also establish procedures under which any such author may update the information so recorded, and procedures under which owners of buildings may record with the Copyright Office evidence of their efforts to comply with this subsection.

[50] *See* id., §106(d)(2): "If the owner of a building wishes to remove a work of visual art which is a part of such building and which *can* be removed from the building without the destruction, distortion, mutilation, or other modification of the work as described in section 106A(3)." (*See* VARA, *supra* note 12, § 106A.)

[51] This is clear upon reading Copyright Act, *supra* note 47, § 113(d)(2)(A) and (B) together.

The right of integrity will also not be applicable to works installed in buildings before 1990, when VARA came into effect, or in the case where there is a signed agreement between the artist and the property owner specifying that the work may be "subject … to destruction, distortion, mutilation, or other modification, by reason of its removal."[52]

Crucially, works of "recognized stature" are *not exempt* from these provisions. They, too can be removed at the discretion of the property owner, provided that the conditions regarding notice and prior agreement set out in section 113(d) are met.

Only if the work was created after VARA, and there is *no signed agreement* between the parties on the possibility of removal, is the treatment of works installed in buildings subject to the artist's moral right of integrity under VARA. In the case of works of recognized stature, they cannot then be destroyed. *5Pointz* fell into this narrow category of works.

By now, it should be apparent that this entire scheme takes great care to clarify what is expected of property owners in order to minimize any potential liability for them that could arise from ambiguity. There is an indisputable need to balance the interests of property owners and artists in these situations, but VARA is heavily weighted towards property owners. Once the property owner has complied with these notice provisions, the artist no longer has a moral right of integrity.[53] Moreover, if the work cannot be saved, removal takes the priority, and the artist is literally left with "a handful of dust."

6. *5Pointz*: Threading the Eye of the Needle

In view of these limitations, it is remarkable that a valid legal action arose in the *5Pointz* case, and even more remarkable that the artists won. As noted above, *5Pointz* fell into an extremely narrow category of works: the paintings were created after VARA, and there was no agreement between the parties on the possibility that the works might ultimately be damaged upon their removal from the site.

[52] *See* id., § 113(d)(2)(B):

> the author consented to the installation of the work in the building either before the effective date set forth in section 610(a) of the Visual Artists Rights Act of 1990, or in a written instrument executed on or after such effective date that is signed by the owner of the building and the author and that specifies that installation of the work may subject the work to destruction, distortion, mutilation, or other modification, by reason of its removal, then the rights conferred by paragraphs (2) and (3) of section 106A(a) shall not apply.

[53] *See* id., § 113(d)(2):

> (2) If the owner of a building wishes to remove a work of visual art which is a part of such building and which can be removed from the building without the destruction, distortion, mutilation, or other modification of the work as described in section 106A(3), the author's rights under paragraphs (2) and (3) of section 106A(a) shall apply *unless*[italics added].

5Pointz was a popular complex of graffiti art, well known across the country and internationally. The graffiti was painted on walls of a number of buildings and was threatened with destruction when the owner of the site decided to tear the walls down to redevelop the property. The artists sued. They obtained a brief stay while awaiting a longer hearing on the issue of whether a preliminary injunction against the destruction of their works was warranted.

However, on November 12, 2013, the court denied the plaintiffs' request for a preliminary injunction. The court analyzed the potential for "irreparable harm" to the plaintiffs, the applicable standard under U.S. law for the grant of a preliminary injunction, and considered the "balance of hardships" between plaintiff and defendant. The judge concluded that the destruction of the works could be adequately compensated by monetary damages, thereby making this a case where there was no danger of "irreparable harm" in the absence of a preliminary injunction. In arriving at this conclusion, the judge compared the situation to the sale of an artwork, which seems like an odd comparison: apparently, in the eyes of the court, there was no essential difference between selling a painting for money and losing ownership of it as a result of its destruction. At the same time, the judge also noted that "plaintiffs' works can live on in other media"–namely, photographs of the works–an approach that completely disregarded the importance of the "original" work in all assessments of works of art, including valuations.

Finally, Judge Block concluded his analysis with an examination of the public interest. In perhaps the strangest turn of all, he suggested that the public interest could be adequately served both by the new residential complex and by the possibility that, within it, new spaces might be created, once again, for art. He observed,

> As for the public, its general interests will be served by the new apartments, including the 75 affordable housing units, and while the present walls will no longer exist, the public's aesthetic interests were addressed by the City Planning Commission by requiring 3,300 square feet of the exterior of the new buildings to be made available for art. Defendants can do even more. They can make much more space available, and give written permission to Cohen to continue to be the curator so that he may establish a large, permanent home for quality work by him and his acclaimed aerosol artists. For sure, the Court would look kindly on such largesse when it might be required to consider the issue of monetary damages; and 5Pointz, as reincarnated, would live.[54]

But how could the possibility of making new works be compared to the value of pre-existing works? The works would be different: what guarantee is there that

[54] *See Cohen v. G&M Realty L.P.*, 988 F. Supp. 2d 212, 225–27 (E.D.N.Y. 2013) (U.S.), https://casetext.com/case/cohen-v-gm-realty-lp.

Leonardo could have painted his Mona Lisa twice? There is also the fact of human mortality: what if an artist died before he or she could paint a new work?

However, the judge also concluded with a warning to Wolkoff, the developer:

> Since ... VARA protects even temporary works from destruction, defendants are exposed to potentially significant monetary damages if it is ultimately determined after trial that the plaintiffs' works were of "recognized stature."[55]

This warning proved to be prescient. Astoundingly, just a few days later, Wolkoff went ahead and had the walls whitewashed.[56] The workers came during the night and worked in haste. The coverage of the painted walls was messy and haphazard, adding injury to insult—as the artists later recounted in court. And this was ultimately the poignancy of the case. Although the artists carried it forward, and ended up with a resounding victory, the works were gone. Nothing could be done to recover them.

In its final ruling, the court in *5Pointz* established a number of valuable points of law, all of which should be generalizable beyond the narrow exception under which this particular case succeeded. First, the Court determined that "ephemeral" works like graffiti could still qualify as artworks under the U.S. Copyright Act, partly relying upon expert evidence to support this proposition. Secondly, it established an important precedent by awarding an extremely large award of damages to the artists, and by doing so as a punitive measure. In particular, its censure of the behavior of the property owner in the case, Mr. Wolokoff, was powerful. Notwithstanding the narrowness of the underlying legal action, this should certainly give property owners pause before they choose to destroy artworks on their property. Finally, the case reaffirmed that the two-pronged test in the *Carter* case need not be applied to the judicial determination of "recognized stature" and, instead, maintained a practical focus on the evidence at hand, including expert opinions.[57]

7. The VARA Time Machine

As noted above, the VARA rules on destruction are also conditioned by VARA's temporal parameters. VARA entered into force in June of 1991,[58] and the moral

55 Id. at 227.

56 *See, e.g.*, Bruce Wallace, *Remembering 5Pointz: A Five-Story Building That Told Plenty More*, NPR (Nov. 21, 2013), https://www.npr.org/2013/11/21/246549375/remembering-5pointz-a-five-story-building-that-told-plenty-more.

57 *See Moral Rights around the World: Two Case Studies*, The Art Law Podcast (Mar. 29, 2021), http://artlawpodcast.com/2021/03/29/moral-rights-around-the-world-two-case-studies.

58 Section 9(a) of the Bill provided that VARA would enter into force six months after the date of enactment, which was June 1, 1990; Patry notes an effective date of June 1, 1991 (*The First Circuit Misses the Boat Again*, *supra* note 12). *See* Bill to Amend Title 17, United States Code, to Provide Certain

rights that it creates are applicable to works created on or after the date of entry into force of the statute. In general, the provision is not crafted to respond to threats against Picassos or Renoirs; VARA relates to works made in the current era and the recent past.

Nevertheless, artworks that were created before VARA still exist, and may be subject to destruction. If they are of "recognized stature," can VARA protect them?

The answer to this question is an extremely cautious and qualified "Yes." This issue turns on the passage of title in the original work. VARA does not exclude pre-existing artworks from the ambit of protection; but it tells us that, for artworks created before 1991, eligibility for protection will depend on whether or not the "title" in the work continues to rest with the original artist. Section 106A(d)(2) of VARA provides that, for "works created before the effective date set forth in subsection (a) but title to which has not, as of such effective date, been transferred from the author," the rights "shall be coextensive with, and shall expire at the same time as, the rights conferred by section 106"—the copyright provisions, which, in the United States, now endure for the lifetime of the author and seventy years after his or her death.[59]

Is there a potential ambiguity here, as ownership of an artwork and copyright in that work, if it has been sold, will still be distinct from one another? In this context, what, exactly, does "title" mean? According to William F. Patry, the transfer of "title" under VARA should be taken at face value: it simply means transfer of ownership. In other words, if the artwork has been sold by the artist prior to 1991, VARA cannot be invoked. Patry addresses this issue, noting that, at the time when VARA was adopted –

> The House agreed to limit VARA to copies (including the original) of "works of visual art" created before the effective date (June 1, 1991), the title to which had not, as of that date, been transferred by the author. The term "title" refers to title to the physical copy of the work of visual art at issue, and not to title to any intellectual property rights.[60]

Rights of Attribution and Integrity to Authors of Works of Visual Art, H.R. 2690, 101st Cong., 2d Sess., s. 9 ("Effective Date") (1990), https://www.congress.gov/bill/101st-congress/house-bill/2690/text. *See generally* Jane C. Ginsburg, *Copyright in the 101st Congress: Commentary on the Visual Artists Rights Act and the Architectural Works Copyright Protection Act of 1990*, 14 Colum.-VLA J. L. & Arts 477 (1990), https://scholarship.law.columbia.edu/faculty_scholarship/3735.

[59] Detail of the complex rule on copyright term in the United States, particularly in view of the transitional period surrounding Berne and following adoption of the 1976 U.S. Copyright Act, is set out in the extremely useful chart available at https://guides.library.cornell.edu/copyright/publicdomain.

[60] Quoted in Mira T. Sundara Rajan, *Saving Picasso's Le Tricorne and Other Pre-1991 Artworks: Can VARA Help?*, 1709 Blog (June 12, 2014), http://the1709blog.blogspot.com/2014/06/saving-picassos-le-tricorne-and-other.html. But it is interesting to note that this perspective is not universally shared: see Nicholas O'Donnell, discussing a pending lawsuit on behalf of Los Angeles artist Victor Henderson in Sullivan & Worcester LLP, *VARA Likely to Apply Retroactively to Victor Henderson "Brooks Avenue Painting Claim,"* Lexology (n.d.), https://www.lexology.com/library/detail.aspx?g=e6f39e9c-1fe2-4d79-916e-e8ad5a87c01f, who comments,

8. Waiving Moral Rights

Finally, and significantly, U.S. law, like the laws of other common-law countries, allows moral rights to be waived, although the U.S. provisions are more specific than the blanket waivers available under Canadian law.[61] According to section 106E, any waivers must be agreed to in "a written instrument signed by the author," and that "instrument shall specifically identify the work, and uses of that work, to which the waiver applies."[62] This section also considers works of joint authorship, providing that, in relation to "a joint work prepared by two or more authors, a waiver of rights under this paragraph made by one such author waives such rights for all such authors." This provision is useful in recognizing the situation of joint authors and addressing some of the complexity that can arise in relation to moral rights when more than one author of a work is concerned. However, the solution itself is doubtful. While convenient, it violates a fundamental principle of joint authorship, that each of the joint authors is considered a full author of the work in his or her own right. Beyond the practical aspect, it is difficult to see why one author's desire to waive moral rights should prevail over another's desire to retain them. Equally practical solutions might be arrived at without disrupting the theory of joint authorship, and indeed, of moral rights—and such solutions should arguably be pursued by policymakers, so that the law is not only enforceable but also makes sense. For example, waiving moral rights in works of joint authorship could be made to depend upon a written agreement between the authors, or a waiver of one author's moral rights might be allowed while those of the other author continued to subsist.

An early study by the U.S. Copyright Office of the provisions on waiving moral rights included extensive information-gathering on this issue. Predictably enough, survey responses and sample contracts seemed to suggest that artists in the United States must function in a position of great bargaining inequality that has not been

The effective date of VARA is June 1, 1991. This paragraph thus first means that as long as the original author (Henderson) still holds the copyright, his VARA rights will exist as long as his copyright does, and expire at the same time. Assuming that Henderson had never transferred the copyright in the 1969 mural, those rights would not have expired, and his VARA rights would still be enforceable for a previously-created work.

[61] *See* VARA, *supra* note 12, § 106A(e)(1). Canadian law even provides that waivers can be extended to a third party who acquires rights from the person exploiting the copyright: *see* Copyright Act, R.S.C. 1985, c. C-42, s. 14.1(4) (Can.), https://laws-lois.justice.gc.ca/eng/acts/c-42. Canadian copyright reform to bring the Copyright Act into conformity with the World Intellectual Property Organization (WIPO) Performances and Phonograms Treaty (WPPT) extended the same regime, mutatis mutandis, to performers' moral rights: *see Copyright Modnernization Act,* Bill C-32, 40th Parl., 3d Sess., 59 Eliz. II, 2010, ss 17.1 and 17.2. The WPPT provides for performers' moral rights in Art. 5: *see* World Intellectual Property Organization (WIPO) Performances and Phonograms Treaty, adopted Dec. 20, 1996, S. Treaty Doc. No. 105-17, 36 I.L.M. 76 (1997), https://www.wipo.int/wipolex/en/text/295578.

[62] *See* VARA, *supra* note 12, § 106A(e)(1); *see also* the further provisions id., § 106A(e)(2).

substantially improved by VARA, and that the waiver provisions may play a role.[63] Strikingly, the Copyright Office noted,

> However, most art contracts continue to be oral and therefore cannot contain valid waiver clauses under the terms of VARA. Many artists decried the complexity of art contracts and stated that legal requirements were too burdensome and legal advice too costly.[64]

D. Integrity without Reputation: Canada's Approach to Art

The second case of special treatment for moral rights in works of visual art provides stronger protection than usual by adjusting the scope of the right of integrity. It is illustrated by the Canadian Copyright Act.[65] In Canada, the moral right of integrity in a visual work is an unconditional right that can be invoked upon any unwanted change to an artist's work. The artist is under no obligation to prove damage to the artist's reputation or honor.[66] This treatment amounts to a complete departure from the usual approach to integrity in Canadian law, which depends upon proof of damage to the author's reputation or honor.[67]

However, the apparent liberality of this provision towards artists is constrained by the fact that, to date, the provision has not been considered applicable to *copies* of an artistic work. Accordingly, in the case of *Théberge*, where the Canadian Supreme Court discussed the moral right of the artist in relation to copies of the work that were both unauthorized and qualitatively doubtful, this standard was not applied. On the contrary, the decision of the majority of the Supreme Court turned upon the need to prove damage to the plaintiff's reputation, not only for a claim of an integrity violation to succeed, but also, to *exclude* the possibility of relief for regular copyright infringement where integrity may (also) have been violated.

This precedent is both controversial and out of date, but the basic principle that copies of a work are not covered by the special provision on the artist's moral right of integrity under Canadian law has not been revisited. This issue could be corrected by broadening the language of the provisions. For example, Australian law, while maintaining the principle that damage to an artist's or author's moral right

[63] U.S. Copyright Office, *Executive Summary*, *in* Waiver of Moral Rights in Visual Artworks (Oct. 24, 1996), https://www.copyright.gov/reports/exsum.html.

[64] Id.

[65] Id.

[66] VARA, *supra* note 12, § 28.2(2) ("Where prejudice deemed").

[67] For the standard rule on integrity under Canadian law, see Canadian Copyright Act, *supra* note 61, at s. 28.2(1); *Théberge v. Galerie d'Art du Petit Champlain Inc.* [2002] 2 S.C.R. 336, 2002 SCC 34 (Can.), https://scc-csc.lexum.com/scc-csc/scc-csc/en/item/1973/index.do. Among the many intricacies of *Théberge* was damage to the reputation of a visual artist cause by "copies" of his paintings made on a canvas backing that could, the artist felt, lead to a degree of confusion between these copies and his originals.

of integrity requires a showing of reputational harm, also provides that damage to an author's or artist's honor or reputation may occur through "anything else in relation to the work."[68] This should be sufficient to extend consideration to the treatment of copies of artworks, although the point remains untested in court. The artist's right against false attribution is explicitly relevant to copies as well as to original artworks.[69] As compared to Canadian law, the Australian provision is better adapted to the needs of the technological environment.

E. Context and Conservation: Alteration of the Work?

But the broader scope of the integrity right may also be qualified by certain specific limitations that apply to the visual arts. Initially, Canadian law provides a useful illustration of this approach. The Canadian Copyright Act explicitly states that attempts made in good faith to restore a work of art will not lead to a violation of the artist's integrity right.[70] This provision offers a potentially useful safety net for conservators of artworks, ensuring that conservation activities are not unduly inhibited by fears of liability. In this regard, it mirrors a similar provision in VARA—and, indeed, it may have been one of the models for the provision in VARA—but VARA also provides that conservation efforts that are "gross[ly] neglig[ent]" will, nevertheless, amount to violations of the artists moral right of integrity.[71] The Canadian law includes no such limitation. The Canadian provision also amounts to an indirect introduction of the idea of intention into the Canadian formulation of the integrity right, used here as a defensive measure against potential violations of integrity: the intention to conserve a work exempts the conservator from liability. In contrast, the U.S. stance is that intentional damage is *required* before the moral right of integrity can be claimed.

The Canadian Copyright Act also provides for a more controversial exception involving the display of a work. Under Canadian law, the conditions in which a work of art is displayed generally cannot lead to a violation of the integrity right. In particular, "a change in the location of a work, the physical means by which a work is exposed or the physical structure containing a work" will not be actionable.[72] In the United States, VARA also provides that "modification of a work of

68 *See Copyright Act 1968* (Cth) s 195AK(c) (Austl.), https://www.legislation.gov.au/Details/C2019C00042; this also applies to other types of works.

69 Id. at s 195AE.

70 *See* Canadian Copyright Act, *supra* note 61, at s. 28.2(3)(b).

71 *See* VARA, *supra* note 12, § 106A(c) on "exceptions"; § 106A(c)(2) specifically provides: "(2) The modification of a work of visual art which is the result of conservation, or of the public presentation, including lighting and placement, of the work is not a destruction, distortion, mutilation, or other modification described in subsection (a)(3) unless the modification is caused by gross negligence."

72 Canadian Copyright Act, *supra* note 61, at s. 28.2(3)(a) exempts "a change in the location of a work, the physical means by which a work is exposed or the physical structure containing a work" from the moral right of integrity in works of visual art.

visual art which is the result ... of the public presentation, including lighting and placement, of the work is not a destruction, distortion, mutilation, or other modification ... unless the modification is caused by gross negligence."[73] Once again, though, publicly presenting the work in a way that is grossly negligent, even if only "lighting and placement, of the work" are involved, is actionable under VARA.

In comparison, the Indian Copyright Act goes further than either Canada or the United States in protecting those who display works, with a detailed stipulation in an "explanation" to section 57 of the Act that integrity will simply *not* be violated by conditions of display.[74] This position is too extreme. In particular, it seems problematic in the technological environment, where the conditions in which an artwork are seen can lead to drastic alterations of appearance or meaning, and potentially have dramatic implications for the reputations of artists.

Australia has a noteworthy provision in this regard. Section 195AK(b) of the Australian Copyright Act provides that "an exhibition in public of the work that is prejudicial to the author's honour or reputation because of the manner or place in which the exhibition occurs" will amount to a derogatory treatment of the artist's work, which is prohibited by the Act. Like UK law, the prohibition of derogatory treatment is how the Australian act defines a violation of the author's moral right of integrity. The provisions on display of an artwork have not yet been examined in court—and, in fact, the only cases involving the moral rights of visual artists in Australia, so far, deal with photographs.[75]

F. Context and Meaning: "Framed by the Sky"[76]

How important is the context in which a work of art is displayed? Considering these examples, there is evidently considerable variation in how this issue is treated in different countries. The Canadian, U.S., Indian, and Australian provisions on the moral rights of artists each arrive at a different balance between the interest of an artist and that of the person engaged in displaying the work.

[73] *See* VARA, *supra* note 12, § 106A(c)(2).

[74] *See* Indian Copyright Act, *supra* note 45, Explanation to §57: "Explanation.—Failure to display a work or to display it to the satisfaction of the author shall not be deemed to be an infringement of the rights conferred by this section."

[75] See, e.g., for an extremely useful summary of Australian moral rights cases so far, including some potential litigation that has been settled, Bennett, *An Australian Overview of the Moral Rights Regime*, LEXOLOGY (July 29, 2019), https://www.lexology.com/library/detail.aspx?g=e28d8b9b-6eac-4dc0-9fab-a6303772dc2c. The facts point to a very curious collection of cases, of which the most prominent so far appears to be successful litigation by Pitbull to prevent an altered version of one of his songs being circulated prior to a cancelled concert tour of Australia: *Fernandez v. Perez* [2012] NSWSC 1242 (Austl.).

[76] The words of Gro Nesjar, quoted in Gareth Harris, *Saga of Picasso Murals Ripped from Oslo Building Continues as Heirs Head to Court*, THE ART NEWSPAPER (Jan. 14, 2021), https://www.theartnewspaper.com/2021/01/14/saga-of-picasso-murals-ripped-from-oslo-building-continues-as-heirs-head-to-court.

But in relation to certain types of work, the conditions of display may be an integral part of the work. In this case, the approach taken by Canadian and Indian law, which effectively eliminate liability for violating the artist's moral right of integrity by the manner in which the work is displayed, is inappropriate. These issues are illustrated by a contentious case in Norway involving prestigious works of public art: murals created by Norwegian artist Carl Nesjar, a close collaborator of Pablo Picasso, who "translated" Picasso's drawings into monumental, three-dimensional works of art using a special method of sculpting with concrete developed by him, known as "Betograve." Nesjar claims to have been the only person ever to correct a drawing by Picasso.[77] The two collaborated over many years and created twenty-four works of art, scattered around the world.

Two of these works formed part of Oslo's government buildings: *The Fishermen*, a mural on the exterior wall of the Y-Block, and *The Seagull*, a smaller mural installed in the lobby of a neighboring building, the H-Block.[78] In 2011, these works were damaged in a terrorist attack. The Oslo government decided to remove the murals and redevelop the area, but this prospect generated a wave of protest in Norway, and internationally. Many Norwegians felt that removing the murals from the highly public settings in which they were located effectively completed the destruction first initiated by the terrorist—a "cruel irony," as noted by expert Mari Hvattum. As affirmed by Janne Wilberg, Oslo's director of cultural heritage, "We don't want the ministry to tear down the building when the terrorist didn't manage to do that."[79]

These issues came to a head in 2020, when Gro Nesjar, the daughter of Carl Nesjar, and the grandchildren of Erling Viksjø, the architect who originally designed the building, decided to pursue an action against the Oslo government to stay the removal of the murals until further study of the issue could be undertaken, and a solution that was widely acceptable to the public could be achieved. In particular, Ms Nesjar had become interested in moral rights as a potential course of action.[80] In an extended interview given to Stephen Stapleton at the ART NEWSPAPER and published on July 8, 2020, she noted,

[77] He is quoted in a wonderful obituary by Margalit Fox, *Carl Nesjar, Sculptor Who Added Dimension to Picasso, Dies at 94*, NEW YORK TIMES (June 20, 2015), https://www.nytimes.com/2015/06/21/arts/design/carl-nesjar-sculptor-who-added-dimension-to-picasso-dies-at-94.html.

[78] *Picasso Mural Removed from Oslo's Y-Block Despite International Protest*, ARTFORUM (July 30, 2020), https://www.artforum.com/news/picasso-mural-removed-from-oslo-s-y-block-despite-international-protest-83638.

[79] Quoted in Mira T. Sundara Rajan, *The Moral Rights of the Artists in Oslo's Y-Block: Can a Case against the Demolition Be Made under Copyright Law?*, 15(10) JLPIP 838, 838–39 (2020), https://doi.org/10.1093/jiplp/jpaa129.

[80] Moral rights came to their attention through Mira T. Sundara Rajan, *"The Art Is on the Wall": Picasso, Nesjar, and the Moral Rights of the Artists in Oslo's Y-Block*, THE IPKAT (June 4, 2020), https://ipkitten.blogspot.com/2020/06/guest-post-art-is-wall-picasso-nesjar.html. I am very grateful to my former LL.M. students Martine Valland and Beatrice Ignacius, both from Oslo, who made me aware of the controversy and generously provided their research assistance for this blog post.

> Well, we now have an attorney and have found the right legal grounds to contest the government's decision. It turns out that because under Norwegian law the Y Block mural is considered a co-authored art work by Picasso and my father and the architect, we do have what are called "moral rights", as long as we can prove that the murals are a collaboration—that my father was not just a fabricator for Picasso but part of the artistic process. And Erling Viksjø also has the rights, because the industrial and artistic techniques that made these murals possible, and which made my dad and then Picasso interested in doing this project in the first place, is something he developed with his engineer, Sverre Jystad.[81]

Since the murals were integrated into the walls of the buildings where they were situated, removing them involved real risks that they would be physically destroyed in the process. However, this was not the only concern that preoccupied Nesjar. The works had been situated in locations where they were easily accessible to the public, and, according to Nesjar, it had been the intention of the artists to make them works of public art that would be widely accessible to everyone in Oslo. Moving them would change their character. And, indeed, Gro Nesjar and Espen Viksjø, Erling Viksjø's grandson, particularly objected to the proposed new placement of the works, which would place them out of sight in a new and inaccessible location. According to Ms Nesjar, *The Fishermen* should have been "placed in the park, where the Y-block was, and framed by the sky as it was intended to be."[82]

Under Norwegian copyright law, the author's moral right of integrity, described in Section 5 and further elucidated in Section 108 of the Norwegian Copyright Act, receives extensive protection. Norwegian law clearly exceeds the minimum requirements of Article 6*bis* of the Berne Convention.

Section 108 states:

> Even if the term of protection of copyright has expired, an artistic work may not be made available to the public in a manner or context that is prejudicial to the

[81] Stephen Stapleton, *With Demolition of Oslo's Picasso–Nesjar Murals Imminent, Norwegian Sculptor's Daughter Speaks Out*, The Art Newspaper (July 8, 2020), https://www.theartnewspaper.com/2020/07/08/with-demolition-of-oslos-picasso-nesjar-murals-imminent-norwegian-sculptors-daughter-speaks-out.

[82] Harris, *supra* note 76:

> But Gro Nesjar, Carl Nesjar's daughter, and Espen Viksjø, Erling Viksjø's grandson, say they have a claim to copyright on the murals and are subsequently entitled to approve the new location. "*The Fishermen* will not be as accessible in the new location [A-block]. We want it to be placed in the park, where the Y-block was, and framed by the sky as it was intended to be," Gro Nesjar says. "*The Seagull* has to be inside and there are a couple of good options [under consideration]," she adds."

> reputation or individuality of the artist or the work, or that may otherwise be considered harmful to general cultural interests.[83]

Several points are noteworthy here. First, the duration of protection for moral rights is indeterminate, and it must therefore be presumed, as in the case of Indian law, that they do not expire. Secondly, the idea of prejudice to the reputation of the author is maintained, but the concept of prejudice to the "individuality of the artist or the work" is added to the more familiar phrase. Not only does this expression capture something beyond artistic reputation, in the form of the artist's "individuality," but it also addresses prejudice to the individuality of the *work*. Although it is framed in terms that resemble those of Article 6*bis* of the Berne Convention, this distinct reference to the work reflects a pure integrity right: it does not depend on the effects of the treatment upon its creator. As I noted in my previous commentary on the case,

> Under section 5 of the Norwegian law, which operates according to a so-called "objective" standard of proof for moral rights violations, if the artist can show the possibility of damage to his or her reputation, or to the status of the work—its "reputation" or "individuality," in the language of the Act—the person responsible for the alterations should be held liable for these acts.[84]

Thirdly, this provision makes reference to a concept of "general cultural interests." This is a highly innovative approach to moral rights that links the recognition of the moral right of integrity to the cultural interest of the public. However, as is often the case when such provisions are adopted, a number of questions remain about how it is to be implemented in practice. Who can assert these claims on behalf of the "general cultural interests," and how can they be upheld in practice? Sadly, in this particular instance, reliance upon the government remained the only legal

[83] *See* Lov om opphavsrett til åndsverk mv. (åndsverkloven) [Act on copyright to intellectual property etc. (Intellectual Property Act)], § 108 (Nor.), https://lovdata.no/dokument/NL/lov/2018-06-15-40/KAPITTEL_8#KAPITTEL_8. *See also* id., § 5.

[84] See id., § 5, which states, on the integrity right:

> A work must not be changed or made available to the public in a way or in a context that is offensive to the reputation or uniqueness of the author or the work.

The author cannot waive the right under the first and second paragraphs, unless it concerns a use of the work that is limited by nature and scope.

If a work is made available in such an infringing manner or in a context as mentioned in the second paragraph, the author, even if consent to the use has been given, has the right to demand that it not take place under the author's name or that it is stated in a satisfactory manner that the changes are not written by the originator. The holder cannot waive this right.

See Sundara Rajan, *The Moral Rights of the Artists in Oslo's Y-Block*, *supra* note 79, at 841 (discussing the Norwegian legal framework for moral rights and their interpretation under the various provisions in detail).

recourse, and impeded the very realization of this legislative objective. As I previously commented,

> A wealth of evidence attests to the cultural importance of the Y-Block sculptures. However, the protection of "general cultural interests" relies upon the government to assert the right. We have come full circle: under these innovative provisions, the government is effectively assigned the role of custodian of the public interest in the integrity of artistic works. What remedy can the Norwegian public now hope to rely upon when the government, itself, is moving inexorably forward with plans that carry a very real risk of damage to unique and irreplaceable works of art?[85]

The claims finally foundered on what is an extremely familiar scenario to those dealing with the moral rights of artists: the difficulties of obtaining a preliminary injunction to prevent further action until matters can be clarified. Under Norwegian law, if a preliminary injunction had been granted, but the case was ultimately dismissed, the cost to the government in the meantime would have had to have been borne by the plaintiffs. The government could have elected to forego this right to damages, but they chose not to do so. As I concluded,

> This story has a bitter moral: cost remains a significant obstacle to the ability of many, if not most, artists to vindicate their moral rights in court. This situation is only reinforced by the difficulty of obtaining a preliminary injunction, a powerful legal remedy whose availability depends on the satisfaction of rigorous tests. Yet, in moral rights cases involving works of art, a preliminary injunction may be a necessary step on the path towards a truly just resolution of the conflict.[86]

This was the case in spite of the seriousness of the issues raised. This case involved historically important works of art by leading artists of the twentieth century, including a celebrity artist of the stature of Picasso. It also generated passionate public involvement of a kind that any democratically elected government would seem to be under a moral obligation to recognize. The seriousness of the consequences faced by the artworks must also be noted. They might have been significantly damaged or even physically destroyed in the process of relocating them. But a more refined understanding of these issues suggests something far more troubling: even if the artworks remained physically intact, the act of removing them from their established location may still have brought about their effective destruction. By destroying their setting, not only would the physical environment for viewing the artworks be altered, but the spiritual environment for experiencing

[85] *See* id. at 846.
[86] Id. at 846.

them would also have been irrevocably harmed. For site-specific artworks such as these, moving them might destroy them *as works of art,* even while their physical form was preserved.[87]

This point is eloquently made by Jean-Louis Andral, the curator of the original Picasso museum, in Antibes, who courageously objected to the removal of the works even though the Picasso foundation had agreed to it.[88] In a letter to government authorities in Oslo, he wrote:

> I truly hope that your government will reconsider the demolition decision, to preserve this modernist heritage by the great Norwegian architect, Erling Viksjø, rare example of the "synthesis of the arts" in which the integration between art and construction is essential, for your country, for your people, and for the entire world.[89]

At the time of writing, the murals are in storage, and the government plans to relocate them to the new site once it is complete. But is the time of their flourishing already behind them?

G. Author's Right Meets the Public Interest: "General Cultural Interests," "National Treasure," and "Recognized Stature"

In the light of this discussion, it is important to revisit a question that has already come up on several occasions: whether the artist's moral right of integrity prevents the destruction of a work of art. As noted previously, traditional commentary on Article 6*bis* of the Berne Convention has taken the view that it does not prevent the destruction of artworks. This is because the integrity right ultimately depends upon a showing of damage to the artist's "honor or reputation." According to this view, once the work has been destroyed, mistreatment can no longer affect the artist's reputation negatively because the work no longer exists.

This position was disapproved by the Delhi High Court in *Amar Nath Sehgal v. Union of India.* It accepted my own commentary pointing out that the absence of a work from an artist's catalogue can, in itself, cause harm to the artist's reputation. The Court also considered the fundamental purpose of the integrity right.

[87] But this is certainly *not* the position in the United States: *see* Patry, *The First Circuit Misses the Boat Again, supra* note 12 (citing U.S. authority to note that, "The purpose of VARA is 'not … to preserve a work of visual art where it is, but rather to preserve the work as it is'" [note omitted]).

[88] Also in private conversation, where this point was explained, in June 2020.

[89] *See* Save Oslo's Y block with mural by Picasso, Facebook (May 31, 2020), https://m.facebook.com/243059203235939/photos/a.601125957429260/610685876473268/?type=3&hx0026;source=57&hx0026;__tn__=EH-R (also in private conversation, June 2020).

Allowing works to be destroyed could potentially fall within a technical, legalistic reading of Article 6*bis*, but destruction clearly violates at least one of the underlying purposes of this provision: to protect the integrity of valuable artistic works.

Examples from India, the United States, and Norway, have now been considered in relation to the destruction of artworks. Two observations should be made.

First, notwithstanding the various limitations that are typically imposed upon the artist's moral right of integrity, it is clear that both legislators and courts remain uneasy about the prospect of artworks being destroyed. Rather than accepting the possibility of destruction as a natural limitation flowing from the framing of the moral right of integrity in Article 6*bis* of Berne, moral rights regimes, across disparate jurisdictions, have developed special rules preventing the destruction of artworks. Unfortunately, these rules are not especially broad in their application, but they do, at least, seek to prevent important works of art from being destroyed.

Accordingly, the Delhi High Court has developed the language of "national treasure," while U.S. and Norwegian legislators have arrived, respectively, at works of "recognized stature" and "general cultural interests" to accommodate this idea. The language remains indeterminate, and decisions about whether or not a work is of the requisite quality to trigger these protections most ultimately be made on a factual basis. Evidence of various kinds will be relevant to this determination, including credible expert evidence, publicity surrounding the work online, and, potentially, other factors. This limitation on the right to prevent destruction is unfortunate because it will not always be possible to capture valuable works within established legal definitions and precedents. Unless there is some kind of general recognition that the destruction of artworks is more broadly problematic, works of value to future generations, perhaps including the most innovative new works, are likely to remain vulnerable to destruction. For example, in the *5Pointz* case, it was a challenge for the court to assess works of street art according to the criterion of "recognized stature," and this is largely why the case is considered a legal landmark: it was able to incorporate a new type of artistic creation within this category, vindicating the artists who sued.

Elizabeth Adeney has suggested that artists would be better off not to be linked with notions of national cultural heritage. She argues:

> As one leading barrister put it in 1978: "I think that artists need to be wary of tying themselves to the 'integrity of national cultural heritage' or to perpetual protection bodies. One only needs to have average paranoia to imagine how such notions could be used against artists." The speaker here raises issues of the misuse of moral rights under ultra-nationalist regimes and the vilification of artists who do not conform to distorted concepts of "national culture."[90]

[90] Elizabeth Adeney, *Australia's Experience of Moral Rights*, 14(4) JIPLP SYMPOSIUM ON MORAL RIGHTS 312, 313 (note omitted) (2019), https://doi.org/10.1093/jiplp/jpz001.

But this analysis is worlds away from the contexts in which such terminology is currently used. Adeney links it to the treatment of artists under repressive regimes, including Nazism. However, as the examples discussed here have shown, this language has not been adopted in order to promote repression. On the contrary, the purpose of the language is to prevent the destruction of works that might otherwise be vulnerable to destruction. In the Indian case, the idea of a "national treasure" was explicitly anti-government: it was meant to accord status to an artist who was facing the violation of his rights by the national government. If anything, the language adopted by the Delhi High Court, including the terminology of "national treasure," served to empower the artist against official ideology, affirming his status against the power of the state. Indeed, this is the function that the Indian courts have taken upon themselves: acting as a democratic counterweight to politically expedient policies on the part of the government. This is the exact opposite of the scenario outlined by Adeney.

Secondly, these legal measures involve serious difficulties of interpretation. We must decide, not only whether a work is important, but also, at times, whether the work has actually been destroyed. As the examples discussed show, neither determination is especially straightforward. If the case of *5Pointz* was a victory for an innovative new artistic genre, the Oslo murals were, in contrast, a rather depressing illustration of how even works that are obviously important may not be adequately protected as cultural heritage. Once again, in Norway, the government was the offender. When the government is also the sole body empowered to intercede on behalf of threatened cultural works, what recourse is actually available under the law in a case such as this?

The example of the Oslo murals raises the further question of how to assess destruction itself. Physical destruction was a risk—Gro Nesjar described the works as being so integrated with the underlying structure of the buildings that "the art is the wall"[91]— but the government decided to take it. What is now happening to the works in storage? Are they physically preserved? Will they be taken out safely when the time comes to install them in their new location?

This was precisely the situation that occurred in Amar Nath Segal's case: works that had been dismounted by the government in order to renovate the building ended up being severely damaged while in storage. Ironically, the Indian government argued that, because the damage was so bad, the works had effectively been destroyed, and Mr. Sehgal would have no legal recourse under section 57 of the Indian copyright law, which protected the artist's moral right of integrity. The court resoundingly, even angrily, rejected this reasoning, explicitly proclaiming its own status as a forum for advocacy on behalf of artists. The status of Mr. Sehgal's work was well established through factual evidence, but the crux of the decision was the

[91] Sundara Rajan, "*The Art Is on the Wall*," *supra* note 80.

Court's determination to connect the artist's moral right of integrity in section 57 with a much broader issue: the protection of cultural heritage. This rationale was essentially based on the idea of a public interest in culture.

To support its position, the court linked the moral rights in section 57 of the Indian Copyright Act to India's broader commitments to international cultural property conventions, of which the country was a member. Given that my own 2001 work provided the scaffolding for these arguments, it will come as no surprise to the reader that I support this view again here. The additional point can be made that the court effectively built a new bridge—just as Article 6*bis* of the Berne Convention had built a bridge between the artist's reputation and the integrity of the work—in this case, between the rights of individual artists and the public interest in maintaining the integrity of cultural heritage. This remains an extremely strong argument in favor of including destruction among the acts prohibited by the artist's moral right of integrity.

Sehgal's case raises at least one more interesting issue that should not be neglected here. Is the principle elucidated by the court—that culturally important works considered "national treasures" should be protected from destruction by the author's moral right of integrity under section 57 of the Indian Copyright Act—applicable *beyond* the category of artworks? Arguably, it is. While the court did base its arguments on India's membership of international cultural property conventions, its reasoning transcended the context of material culture. The Court relied on the broad principle of cultural protection, and described its own role as that of advocate, both for artists and for the public interest in culture. It is therefore an intriguing possibility that literary, musical, or other forms of heritage may ultimately seek the protection of the courts as, in Indian terms, "national treasures."[92]

This brings us back to the example of the Norwegian murals. For, in that case, those who are most knowledgeable about these matters—Gro Nesjar, Jean-Louis Andral, and other experts—were in profound agreement with the broader public, which feared that removing the works from their established location would effectively destroy them. The passion of the public was expressed in highly symbolic terms: these works had ultimately come to symbolize the resilience and freedom of Norwegian culture against attacks like the terrorist incident the damaged these buildings. The destruction of material heritage was not the primary framework within which this discussion occurred. As in Sehgal's case, there was even more

[92] Indeed, those familiar with C. Subramania Bharati's case have suggested that the government should be sued for its acquisition of his copyright, which has led to significant—and perhaps irreparable—damage to the integrity of the poet's works, and to his reputation. For a discussion of this history, see Mira T. Sundara Rajan, *Moral Rights in the Public Domain: Copyright Matters in the Works of Indian National Poet C. Subramania Bharati*, SINGAPORE J. LEGAL STUD. 161 (2001). A recent book on Bharati's copyright is an affront to Bharati and is emblematic of the kinds of problems involved; it is not cited here to avoid further publicity to the work and its author. *See* Mira T. Sundara Rajan, *Reclaiming the Legacy of Tamil Poet Subramania Bharati*, FRONTLINE (Sept. 8, 2020), https://frontline.thehindu.com/profile/author/Mira--T--Sundara-Rajan-17550.

at stake than the material existence of the objects. Ironically, Mr. Sehgal, whose work was physically destroyed, was victorious at a much higher level in the wake of this tragic incident. In Oslo, the works were physically preserved, but the voice of the Norwegian people, sounding in unison with those of the artists' heirs, was silenced.

H. Creative Destruction: Should Artists Be Allowed to Destroy Their Own Work?

The limited U.S. prohibition against destruction of an artwork of recognized stature is still a striking step—a bold expansion of the integrity right to cover a circumstance that is still ambiguous in international law. The language framing the U.S. provision resembles the approach adopted by the Delhi High Court in the *Amar Nath Sehgal* case. Destruction that is intentional or "grossly negligent," and that affects a work "of recognized stature," is prohibited by U.S. law; in parallel, the Indian Court stated that, when a work of art becomes a "national treasure," its status raises the artist's moral rights to a new level of protection.[93] When it comes to artworks that are an important part of national cultural heritage, U.S. and Indian law are closely aligned with one another. But a similar legal result is achieved in the two jurisdictions by different means—legislative reform in the United States, and judicial precedent in India.

Prohibiting destruction leaves an intriguing question open: what happens when an artist wants to destroy his or her own work? The point is neatly illustrated by Adolf Dietz, who offers the example of Munich's Olympic Stadium. Even the architect who designed the stadium was apparently willing to redesign it for new needs, but the decision to do so was opposed by the German authority for the protection of monuments, which also happened to represent public opinion in this case.[94]

The potential conflict between the public interest in protecting heritage and the artist's moral rights of integrity and withdrawal presents a harrowing choice. There may be many reasons why an artist wants a work of art destroyed. It is difficult to argue that the artist's desire to see his or her own work removed from a catalogue of works should be disregarded. At the same time, an artist is not always the best judge of the quality or importance of his or her own work.

When it comes to traditional knowledge, this question acquires new connotations. Moral rights, in contrast to other intellectual property rights, may be a more compatible form of intellectual property recognition. However, some works of traditional culture are meant to be destroyed—Tibetan sand mandalas, for

[93] *Sehgal*, *supra* note 44.

[94] *See* Adolf Dietz, *The Importance of Moral Rights for Cultural Heritage and Diversity*, Paper presented at the 2008 ALAI Congress 51 (on file with the author).

example.[95] Is an outright prohibition on destruction the best way to deal with the potential conflict between private desires and public needs? Rather, moral rights in traditional culture must be appropriately translated into the new context, reflecting the needs and desires of the people that they serve.

I. Perpetual Moral Rights: A Bridge between Intellectual and Cultural Property

These examples lead to a further question: what is the nature of the relationship between the works of individual artists and the cultural heritage of a nation? The cultural heritage of every nation is composed of the work of artists, whether living or dead, known or unknown, or working as individuals or collectives. Fundamentally, what distinguishes the works of individual artists from cultural heritage is the passage of time.

From a legal point of view, this leads to a regulatory schism. On one side, where the works of living or recently deceased individuals are concerned, intellectual property laws apply. This is private law, governed by the standard principles of standing, territoriality, and enforceability that surround the dealings of private parties. On the other side, works of cultural heritage are protected by an elaborate system of public law, primarily public international law agreements on the protection of culture to which states parties may adhere, adapting their national legal frameworks for compatibility with these instruments. When the Indian court in the *Amar Nath Sehgal* case made reference to India's membership in international conventions on cultural property, it was invoking this public law framework in the context of the case brought by Mr. Sehgal. Given the usual separation of intellectual and cultural property matters under the law, this was a radical approach.

The two frameworks also interact formally, but in an awkward and limited way. As noted earlier, certain general provisions on intellectual property appear in instruments of public international law like the Universal Declaration of Human Rights[96] and the International Covenant on Economic, Social, and Cultural Rights.[97] The appearance of these provisions protecting artists and authors in international public law conventions amounts to a declaration of principle. There is no recognized legal means of linking these two frameworks with one another.[98]

[95] See, e.g., the interesting discussion of these creations by Alexander Nguyen, *Sacred Tibetan Sand Mandala a Reminder of Universe's Impermanence*, KPBS (Nov. 30, 2023), https://www.kpbs.org/news/faith-spirituality/2023/11/30/sacred-tibetan-sand-mandala-a-reminder-of-universes-impermanence.

[96] G.A. Res. 217 (III) A, Universal Declaration of Human Rights (Dec. 10, 1948), Art. 27, http://www.un.org/en/documents/udhr.

[97] G.A. Res. 2200 (XXI) A, International Covenant on Civil and Political Rights (Dec. 16, 1966), Art. 15, https://www.ohchr.org/en/instruments-mechanisms/instruments/international-covenant-civil-and-political-rights.

[98] The distinction in terminology between cultural property and cultural heritage should be duly noted and has been greatly emphasized in the seminal scholarship of Prott and O'Keefe: LYNDEL PROTT & PATRICK J. O'KEEFE, LAW AND THE CULTURAL HERITAGE, VOL. 3 (1990). For an interesting

But a possible bridge exists: perpetual moral rights. Their function in linking the intellectual property of today with the cultural property of hereafter is not widely recognized. Instead, discussions of perpetual moral rights focus on concerns about the freedom of speech of the general public. At a certain level, without downplaying their importance altogether, these discussions may still amount to a kind of "MacGuffin."[99] They have a place in debates of intellectual property policy. But they should not trump broader discussions of cultural policy.

The purpose of perpetual moral rights is to maintain the attribution of works to their authors and to preserve the integrity of those works after the usual period of protection for artistic creations expires. They're implicitly based on a belief about the value of maintaining the work and knowledge of its authorship for generations to come. They are concerned with the preservation of culture, and with historical truth.

An interesting thought experiment can be developed in relation to one of the greatest examples of human heritage, although it is in the literary rather than the artistic field: the works of Shakespeare. As has been documented in fascinating research by Elizabeth Winkler, substantial uncertainty surrounds the identity of the Bard. In itself, there is perhaps nothing especially surprising about this: Shakespeare lived at a time when writers could be punished for what they wrote by a powerful and cruel state. Their families and friends could suffer terrible consequences. Historian Michael Wood refers to the England of Shakespeare's time as the "Elizabethan police state."[100] Were details of Shakespeare's identity deliberately concealed? Or did they simply slip away into the mists of time?

There was no copyright law in the British realm at the time of Shakespeare. Copyright only came into existence in 1709, with the adaption of the Statute of Anne, and it was the product of decades of lobbying by writers and others who were concerned about the absence of freedom of speech in Great Britain. In Shakespeare's time, the sovereign controlled printing by granting exclusive printing privileges to the Stationers' Company. Not only is there uncertainty about Shakespeare's identity today, but also, as highlighted by Winkler,[101] attempts to investigate the truth of

review and overview of the work, see Charles Sparrow, *Review (Untitled)*, 40(1) Int'l & Comp. L.Q. 248 (1991). Invoking the power of property while attempting to recognize the special nature of heritage, the discussion in this chapter makes use of both expressions.

[99] *See, e.g.*, Joseph Temple, *Dial P for Pinot Noir: Hitchcock and the Origins of the Most Famous Wine Bottle in Movie History*, The International Wine & Food Society (Apr. 18, 2014), https://blog.iwfs.org/2014/04/dial-p-for-pinot-noir-hitchcock-the-origins-of-the-most-famous-wine-bottle-in-movie-history.

[100] Michael Wood, *In Search of Shakespeare* (2003), https://www.mayavisionint.com/project/in-search-of-shakespeare.

[101] *See, e.g.*, Elizabeth Winkler, *Doubting Shakespeare's Identity Isn't a Conspiracy Theory*, Literary Hub (May 15, 2023), https://lithub.com/doubting-shakespeares-identity-isnt-a-conspiracy-theory. This is also discussed in my podcast interview with Winkler, Mira T. Sundara Rajan, "*Was Shakespeare a Woman—and Does It Matter? An Interview with Elizabeth Winkler, Journalist, Book Critic, and Author of* Shakespeare Was A Woman and Other Heresies, Woman of Culture Podcast (Jan. 27, 2024), https://womanofculturepodcast.com/was-shakespeare-a-woman-and-does-it-matter-an-interview-with-elizabeth-winkler-journalist-book-critic-and-author-of-shakespeare-was-a-woman-and-other-heres

Shakespeare's identity have been met with hostility, mockery, and derision—even by scholars, whose profession it is to investigate the truth, no matter how unlikely it may seem. The inquiry has been called "immoral."[102] Winkler explores why she thinks Shakespeare's identity is such a fraught issue, arguing convincingly that the construction of the Bard has been a historical, cultural, and even colonial enterprise, rather than primarily a search for truth.

From the perspective of moral rights, two observations can be made. First, if a moral right of attribution had been recognized in Shakespeare's time, much could have been done to preserve the true identity of the Bard. Secondly, however, the preservation of authorial attribution may or may not have been a desirable goal, from the writer's point of view, in the political environment of Elizabethan England. Ultimately, the moral rights of authors are fragile; they have little meaning except in a context where freedom of expression is generally respected. They can help to preserve historical truth, but only in a society where truth is valued. Faced with power, the meaning of moral rights crumbles. In the absence of basic human freedoms, moral rights, an instrument meant to protect authors and artists, quickly devolve into a parody of themselves—a means of oppression instead.

If we recognize perpetual moral rights, a most important question remains to be answered: who will assert them? The *Hugo* case saw a descendant of Victor Hugo bring a claim on the author's behalf; it failed, and the awkwardness of allowing an individual who was, in this case, so removed from Hugo's context to bring a claim was apparent in this case. However, the example of the Oslo murals, which involved artworks by living artists that had already become part of Norwegian cultural heritage, shows the dangers of entrusting government with the enforcement of moral rights protection of cultural heritage. In Amar Nath Sehgal's case, as well, the Indian government was at fault in the destruction of the work, and its response to its own potential liability seems to have been, coincidentally or otherwise, to change the law. It is clear that those responsible for taking care of cultural heritage must be simultaneously passionate and disinterested, and arguably connected with that heritage in some meaningful way.

For example, Picasso's granddaughter, Diana Widmaier Picasso, is now an art historian and an expert on her grandfather's works.[103] In the Indian context, C. Subramania Bharati's granddaughter, S. Vijaya Bharati, became the leading scholar of her grandfather's works. The latter example highlights some of the special difficulties faced by developing countries in the preservation of culture. Much of the information about Bharati was difficult to preserve after his death in 1921: as

ies. On copyright in Shakespeare's time, see the fascinating article from the archives of *The Atlantic* magazine, Horace Davis, *Shakespeare and Copyright*, The Atlantic (Feb. 1893), https://www.theatlantic.com/magazine/archive/1893/02/shakespeare-and-copyright/634523/.

[102] *See* Sundara Rajan, "*Was Shakespeare a Woman?*," *supra* note 101.

[103] *See, e.g.*, Kelly Crow, *Picasso's Determined Granddaughter Catalogs His Sculptures*, Wall Street Journal (July 19, 2013), https://www.wsj.com/articles/SB10001424127887323297504578579824284030506.

a pro-freedom writer, he had struggled to publish his writing at the time of British colonial domination in India. It was only through the heroic efforts of his wife that many details were ultimately preserved.[104] However, the treatment of women and widows in India during that era was oppressive, and Bharati's wife had to struggle against Indian society. These circumstances created serious obstacles to the preservation of this heritage.

1. Artworks: Property or Heritage?

In modern legal terminology, a work of art is classified as one of two things: intellectual property or cultural property. Intellectual property is almost entirely governed by national laws on copyright, and these, in their turn, are shaped by the requirements of international copyright agreements. Copyright law is an area of "private" law, having to do with the rights of private individuals and corporations, who either create works or purchase the right to exploit them.[105] In the case of intellectual property disputes, anyone can be a plaintiff—individuals, groups, or, as occasionally happens, governments of countries.[106] Intellectual property rights are modeled on rights in tangible property, among the most fundamental rights protected in modern democracies.[107] In order to claim intellectual property rights in a work, certain criteria must be met: the work must be artistic or intellectual in nature, original, and "fixed" in a tangible medium.[108] It must also have an identifiable author.[109]

[104] Discussed by S. Vijaya Bharati, who was raised by Chellamma, in S. Vijaya Bharati, *Chellamma, The Heroine of Bharati's Poetry—Part I* (Feb. 23, 2013), https://subramaniabharati.com/2013/02/23/chellamma-the-heroine-of-bharatis-poetry-part-i.

[105] Although international copyright agreements represent both private and public frameworks, the "public" ones, regulated by WIPO, function on a largely "private" basis and depend on domestic laws for their enforcement.

[106] *Bumper Development Corporation Ltd v. Commissioner of Police for the Metropolis and others* [1991] 1 WLR 1362 (C.A.). The case is summarized in two useful notes: Sandy Ghandhi & Jennifer James, *The God That Won*, 1 Int'l J. Cult. Prop. 369 (1992) and, focusing on its Canadian angle, Robert K. Paterson, *The "Curse of the London Nataraja,"* 5(2) Int'l J. Cult. Prop. 330 (1996).

[107] *See also* Organization of African Unity [OAU] African Charter on Human and Peoples' Rights, at Art. 14 (1981) (Banjul Charter), http://www.claiminghumanrights.org/au_charter.html, which protects property as a human right.

[108] But, traditionally, it has been extraordinarily easy to satisfy this requirement in common-law countries, which have applied a labor standard to originality and defined it as virtually anything not copied: *see* the seminal British case of *Kenrick v. Lawrence* (1890) L.R. 25, Q.B.D. 99 (Eng.). This approach has now changed, with common-law countries apparently moving to higher standards of originality that are closer to the position that was previously associated with civil law jurisdictions. The movement started with the U.S. case of *Feist Publications, Inc. v. Rural Telephone Service Co.*, 499 U.S. 340 (1991), which dealt with databases and demonstrates the increasing influence of civil law concepts of copyright in the digital environment. Higher standards of originality have also been supported in Canada, in the case of *CCH Canadian Ltd v. Law Society of Upper Canada* [2004] 1 S.C.R. 339, https://decisions.scc-csc.ca/scc-csc/scc-csc/en/item/2125/index.do; *CCH*, in turn, was followed in the Indian case of *Eastern Book Co. and ors v. DP Modak and anor*, 2008 (36) PTC 1, 2008 (1) SCC 1.

[109] It is worth noting that joint authors are often explicitly included in this scheme: *see, e.g.*, Canadian Copyright Act, *supra* note 61, at s. 9(1). The case of works created under a pseudonym or anonymously is also addressed by many copyright laws, including that of Canada.

In contrast, international conventions on cultural property reflect the framework of public international law at its most traditional: they formally empower states to act in favor of cultural heritage at the international level. Even this course of action is subject to some important limitations. Cultural property conventions set out rights of ownership associated, not with individuals, but with a country of origin. No specific "author," either individual or group, is implicated. The conventions affect relations between countries and, potentially, they will allow legal action to be brought to restore an object to its country of origin.

A suit for the return of cultural property must be brought by the government of a country. Typically, legal action will be brought in the country where the object has been seized, and the government bringing suit faces the disadvantages associated with a foreign legal claim. Since cultural property that is illegally exported from its country of origin is very often from developing countries, the cost of an attempted recovery can be prohibitive.[110] Indeed, even a successful suit can involve surprising costs: a third party who has purchased the object in the reasonable belief that it was legally available for sale may be entitled to compensation.[111] Whatever their potential at the international level, it is clear that cultural property laws can do little to influence the treatment of cultural heritage on the domestic stage. At most, it may be hoped that countries will craft domestic laws on cultural heritage that are influenced by the international conventions.

Clearly, these two different legal frameworks represent fundamentally different ways of thinking about cultural heritage. From a legal point of view, the two categories do not overlap. Intellectual property law and cultural property law are not connected with each other in any meaningful way. But perpetual moral rights offer another way of looking at these two legal regimes, offering the promise of substantially refining and enhancing the law's potential to protect cultural heritage.

[110] Interestingly, greater prominence has been brought to this issue in recent years as museums and galleries face requests for the return of artworks confiscated from private owners by the Nazis. *See, e.g., Return Nazi-Looted Art: Austrian Panel*, CBC NEWS (July 12, 2010), https://www.cbc.ca/news/entertainment/return-nazi-looted-art-austrian-panel-1.935438. See also the note on British policy, which cites and reproduces Jasper Copping, *National Galleries to Hand Back Nazi Art*, THE TELEGRAPH (Oct. 18, 2008), *reproduced in* http://www.elginism.com/20081020/1446. The Council for British Archeology (CBA) noted in 2009 that the Heritage Protection Bill had since been dropped: *see* Dan Hull, *Heritage Bill Dropped Again!*, CBA INFORMATION (July 1, 2009). *See also* Secretary of State for Culture, Media and Sport, *Draft Heritage Protection Bill* (April 2008), https://publications.parliament.uk/pa/cm200708/cmselect/cmcumeds/821/821.pdf.

[111] *See* Art. 7(b)(ii) of the United Nations Educational, Scientific and Cultural Organization (UNESCO) Convention on the Means of Prohibiting and Preventing the Illicit Import, Export and Transfer of Ownership of Cultural Property, Nov. 14, 1970, 823 U.N.T.S. 231 (UNESCO Convention), http://portal.unesco.org/en/ev.php-URL_ID=13039&URL_DO=DO_TOPIC&URL_SECTION=201.html.

2. Moral Rights and the Life-Cycle of an Artwork

The distinction between intellectual and cultural property could be understood as one of authorship status.[112] If we think of it in these terms, it becomes apparent that the natural life-cycle of most works of art involves a *legal* transformation—a movement from the category of intellectual property to classification as cultural heritage. In fact, from a legal point of view, it is possible to identify three distinct stages in the life of an artwork: early life as intellectual property, mid-life under copyright protection after the author's death, and a final phase as cultural property.

a. Phase 1: Intellectual Property

The artwork begins life as the creation of an author. Authorship of the work may take many forms. The work may be created by an individual or by joint authors; the author might be named or unnamed. But copyright law is capable of capturing most of these situations—even anonymous authorship—and it seems fair to say that the initial status of a work of art is that of a work of authorship protected by copyright law.

b. Phase 2: *Post Mortem Auctoris*

The death of the author initiates a period of transition. For a time, the work continues to be classified as intellectual property. The precise duration of that status is defined by national legislation, which, in its turn, operates according to certain minimum terms of copyright protection defined by international agreements.[113] The history of duration in copyright law has been one of progressive increase, and at present, most copyright works are protected for a period of seventy years after the author's death.[114]

Would an increased term of protection *post mortem auctoris* contribute to the protection of cultural heritage? In India, the issue arose, once again, in relation

[112] Note, once again, the distinction between "property" and "heritage." The term "objects" used in this chapter is meant in both the material and metaphorical senses.

[113] *See* Art. 7 of the International Convention for the Protection of Literary and Artistic Works, adopted at Berne on Sept. 9, 1886, completed at Paris on May 4, 1896, revised at Berlin on Nov. 13, 1908, completed at Berne on Mar. 20, 1914, revised at Rome on June 2, 1928, at Brussels on June 26, 1948, at Stockholm on July 14, 1967, and at Paris on July 24, 1971, and amended on Sept. 28, 1979, S. Treaty Doc. No. 99-27 (1986) (Berne Convention), https://www.wipo.int/wipolex/en/text/283698.

[114] This term of protection currently applies in the EU member states, and other countries have attempted to harmonize their laws to this level. The extension of copyright term has always been contentious. In the United States, the extension of the term of protection to life of the author plus seventy years from the previous international standard of life plus fifty years led to a legal challenge on the grounds that the increase in the term of copyright protection was unconstitutional. The case was put forward by Creative Commons founder Lawrence Lessig. Extension of term for performers has been a more recent controversy in the United Kingdom and Europe. *See* Chapter 6 *supra*.

to literature. In 1992, India's Parliament voted to prolong the duration of copyright protection from fifty to sixty years after the author's death.[115] The explicit rationale behind this move was to extend protection for the works of India's Nobel Laureate in literature, Bengali poet Rabindranath Tagore (1861–1941), whose copyright would otherwise have expired at that time. Tagore's copyright was administered by Viswa Bharati University in Shantiniketan, founded by the poet. It was thought that the extension of copyright term would help to protect his important literary legacy by prolonging the rights of Viswa Bharati—which, of course, would presumably benefit financially from this arrangement, as well. The Indian Government stated,

> Gurudev Rabindranath Tagore died in the year 1941 and copyright in his published works, which stood vested in Visva Bharati was to expire on 31st December 1991. There had been numerous demands for according extended protection to his works in view of their national importance. While it was not considered feasible and appropriate to extend the term of copyright in respect of one author alone, the Government reviewed the whole question of what should be the appropriate term of copyright and decided to extend the term of copyright generally in all works protected by the Copyright Act.[116]

But an earlier series of similar discussions around the contributions of C. Subramania Bharati, the leading modern Tamil writer who occupies a similar position to Tagore in his own cultural context, led to the opposite conclusion. Bharati's copyright was nationalized in 1949. Soon afterwards, it was given to the people of India as a "gift." A copyright that would otherwise have expired in 1971, according to Indian copyright law of the time, was terminated in 1949.[117] This, too, was said to be for the good of culture.

The Indian case is not unique. Pre-Revolutionary Russia also amended its copyright term out of respect for a single author's work. A petition from Madame Pushkin saw the extension of copyright term for the sake of Pushkin's copyright. In the Russian case, the objective appears to have been practical rather than

[115] *See* Copyright (Amendment) Bill, 1992, Bill C-35 (Mar. 17, 1992) (India), https://www.wipo.int/wipolex/en/legislation/details/17860.

[116] *See* the Statement of Objects and Reasons to the Amendment Act 13 of 1992, reprinted in Professional, The Copyright Act, 1957: Bare Act with Short Comments 4 (2006).

[117] See the detailed discussion of these transactions in Sundara Rajan, *Moral Rights in the Public Domain*, *supra* note 92. The government of Tamil Nadu state continues to favor nationalization as an approach to literary heritage: Mira T. Sundara Rajan, *The Lessons of the Past: C. Subramania Bharati and the Nationalization of Copyright*, 6(2) SCRIPTed 201 (2009), https://script-ed.org/wp-content/uploads/2016/07/6-2-Rajan.pdf.

cultural—to ensure that Pushkin's wife continued to have means of subsistence from her husband's work.[118]

During the period of copyright's validity after an author's death, there is one obvious and crucial change in the status of the work: there is no living author to take care of it. Usually, copyright is inherited by the heirs of the author. Depending on the circumstances of the author's family, the work may or may not be well cared for by the author's descendants. It might be widely publicized or greatly restricted. Of course, it is also possible for the author to bequeath the copyright deliberately to anyone of his or her choice.[119] The inheritor of the copyright then becomes its administrator. This approach, too, can have its positives and negatives in practice.

Once the term of copyright protection expires, the work falls into the public domain. Its connection with its creator has become relatively remote; on the other hand, its connection with country or community may be stronger than ever. At this point, a distinction arises between material works of art and intangible ones. Two points should be noted. First, the expiry of copyright in a work of visual art is less significant than it is in relation to other kinds of works. Copyright is generally of secondary importance where artworks are concerned, because material possession of the work is normal and supersedes any questions of copyright.

Illustrating this principle, the 1741 case of *Pope v. Curll* considered the separation of literary copyright from ownership of the work in relation to letters written by the author. It was found that material ownership of the letters did not translate into a right to publish them, which remained vested in the author.[120] In the context of artworks, a vestige of copyright control can perhaps be said to remain with the author in the form of the artist's *droit de suite*, or resale right, which allows an artist to claim a percentage of proceeds from future sales of his works. In a fascinating twist, *droit de suite* is also recognized in the literary context. The Berne Convention provides that it is a legitimate right in relation to the sales of original manuscripts. India is among the few countries that recognize this right explicitly in their copyright lcgislation.[121]

The expiry of copyright in an artwork therefore signifies something different from the end of copyright term in other kinds of works. Most probably, this will not be the mechanism by which the work moves out of its owner's control. However, when copyright expires, the owner can no longer control derivative uses of his or

[118] Mira T. Sundara Rajan, Copyright and Creative Freedom: A Study of Post-Socialist Law Reform (2006).

[119] Chellamma Bharati intended to bequeath the copyright in her husband's work to the public of India after death; since circumstances compelled her to part with it much earlier, she did not have the chance to do so. See the epigraph in Sundara Rajan, *Moral Rights in the Public Domain*, *supra* note 92.

[120] *Pope v. Curll* (1741) 2 Atk. 342, 26 Eng. Rep. 608 (Eng.).

[121] *See* Indian Copyright Act, *supra* note 45, §53A ("Resale Share Right in Original Copies"); the provision was adopted in the 1994 amendments to Indian copyright law. The principle is explicitly excluded by Recital 19 of Directive 2001/84/EC of the European Parliament and of the Council of 27 September 2001 on the resale right for the benefit of the author of an original work of art, 2001 O.J. (L 272) 32, https://eur-lex.europa.eu/legal-content/FR/TXT/?uri=celex%3A32001L0084.

her works. This would include, for example, the making of pictures, photographs, and other reproductions of them.

c. Phase 3: Cultural Property and Moral Rights

Once copyright has expired, material works of art fall into the public domain. At that time, they may become "cultural property" in the legal sense of the term. The treatment of the work is no longer restricted by copyright laws; instead, the work may be freely used by the public. The use of the work must not contravene cultural property conventions; but, in practice, all this means is that works of cultural property must not be stolen, leave their countries of origin illegally, or be imported illegally.[122] The conventions on cultural property have little to say about how works should be treated by their lawful owners within borders, how disputes over their treatment should be resolved, or what practices the public should observe when dealing with art. On the other hand, intangible works are freely available for use once copyright in those works has expired.

But this explanation leaves one issue unresolved: moral rights. In those countries where moral rights expire with the expiry of copyright,[123] the question of moral rights in the public domain is irrelevant. Even here, there is an unexpected twist, as the possibility of moral rights in public domain works may receive a *more* sympathetic consideration in case law than the moral rights of living or recent artists. The United States provides a surprising illustration of this point. To date, both the first and last U.S. cases on moral rights—*Shostakovich* in 1949 and *Dastar* in 2003—have assessed the possibility of moral rights in public domain works. The earlier judgment in *Shostakovich* sympathetically explored moral rights for public domain works under U.S. law, but the attempt to recognize them failed because of the principle was deeemed too ambiguous in the absence of legislative guidance. The *Dastar* case rejected moral rights in public domain works on the grounds that restricting the public domain would be contrary to U.S. traditions of free use where the public domain is concerned.[124]

[122] The two most significant international conventions are the UNESCO Convention, *supra* note 111, and the International Institute for the Unification of Private Law (UNIDROIT) Convention on Stolen or Illegally Exported Cultural Objects, June 24, 1995, 34 I.L.M. 1322, https://www.unidroit.org/instruments/cultural-property/1995-convention. A number of major art-market countries have joined the UNESCO Convention since the turn of the millennium, including the United Kingdom (2002) and Switzerland (2003); the United States has been a member since 1983, and Canada joined in 1978. For a list of states parties and the dates of their ratification or accession, as well as dates of entry into force in the member states, *see* https://www.unesco.org/en/legal-affairs/convention-means-prohibiting-and-preventing-illicit-import-export-and-transfer-ownership-cultural?hub=416#item-2 and https://www.unidroit.org/instruments/cultural-property/1995-convention/status/.

[123] Or before—though this goes against the Berne Convention, *supra* note 113. See, e.g., the UK right against false attribution: Copyright, Designs and Patents Act 1988 (CDPA), c. 48, §§84 and 86(2) (UK). This right is arguably not a true moral right: see discussion in Chapter 2, *supra* notes 262-63 and accompanying text.

[124] *See* Chapter 4, *supra* notes 109-47 and 184, and accompanying text.

In countries where moral rights continue to exist even after the expiry of copyright, they provide a clear link between the worlds of intellectual property and cultural property. With no legal basis for excluding them, principles of attribution and integrity continue to apply to works that are classified as cultural property. Moral rights could be an extraordinarily powerful tool for protecting the status of these works, thereby helping to maintain the integrity of cultural heritage.

As noted above, a fundamental practical question is that of *who should be empowered to act* on behalf of this cultural property. In the absence of specific legislative provisions governing moral rights in the public domain, and identifying those who will have the capacity to assert them, the rights would be largely meaningless.[125] In relation to sensitive works, such as cultural property based on traditional knowledge, or works that document past historical eras, government may be particularly ill suited to undertake the protection of moral rights.[126] In the Norwegian and Indian examples, government has shown itself to be a poor trustee for moral rights and, at least in these instances, for cultural heritage overall.

Where duration of moral rights is concerned, it is worth briefly reviewing India's history. Indian moral rights were initially protected without the specification of a precise duration of protection, and it was reasonable to assume that the rights could be protected in perpetuity. This implied significant potential for the use of moral rights to protect cultural heritage that was no longer protected by other aspects of copyright law.[127]

In 1994, however, a new phrase on timing was introduced.[128] The integrity of the work would be protected against "any distortion, mutilation, modification or other act in relation to the said work which is done before the expiration of the term of copyright if such distortion, mutilation, modification or other act would be prejudicial to ... [the author's] honour or reputation."[129] With this specification,

[125] The same problem is generally confronted in relation to the protection of folklore: see, on authorities, UNESCO Model Provisions for National Laws on the Protection of Expressions of Folklore against Illicit Exploitation and Other Prejudicial Actions (May 6, 1985), s. 9, https://unesdoc.unesco.org/ark:/48223/pf0000063799. A major weakness of the scheme may be the idea that "borrowing expressions of folklore for creating an original work of an author or authors" requires no authorization—perhaps reflecting the fact that the model provisions pre-date the digital environment, where information is readily available and intellectual property strongly valued.

[126] *See* Mira T. Sundara Rajan, *Moral Rights in Developing Countries: The Example of India, Part I*, 8(5) J. INTELL. PROP. RIGHTS 357 (2003), https://nopr.niscpr.res.in/bitstream/123456789/4907/1/JIPR%208%285%29%20357-374.pdf (printed with some errors).

[127] Mira T. Sundara Rajan, *Moral Rights and the Protection of Cultural Heritage:* Amar Nath Sehgal v. Union of India, 10(1) INT'L J. CULTURAL PROP. 79 (2001).

[128] Copyright (Amendment) Act, No. 38 of 1994 (India). *See* Sundara Rajan, *Moral Rights in Developing Countries*, *supra* note 126, at 368–71; Sudhir Ahuja, *Latest Amendments to the Indian Copyright Act*, 44 COPYRIGHT WORLD 38 (1994).

[129] *See* Indian Copyright Act, *supra* note 45, s. 57(1)(b) (emphasis added). The subsection goes on to state that "the author shall not have any right to restrain or claim damages in respect of any adaptation of a computer programme to which clause (aa) of sub-section (1) of section 52 applies." Section 52(1)(aa) provides for exceptions to copyright infringement of computer programs for fair dealing and for the purposes of regular use or making back-up copies.

the amended section does not quite say that moral rights will expire with the end of economic rights; but, in practice, it will lead to that result. The Indian integrity right provides that legal action for moral rights can only flow from acts that occur while the work is still within the term of copyright protection. However, there is no limitation period on suing for those violations. In theory, at least, damage that occurred in 1978, as in Amar Nath Sehgal's case,[130] could be brought before the courts for the first time in 2010—provided only that Sehgal's copyright was still in force in 1978.[131] But damage to the work after the expiry of Sehgal's copyright—calculated at sixty years from the author's death in December of 2007, Sehgal's copyright would expire in 2067—could not be subject to a moral rights suit.

But the *Amar Nath Sehgal* case led to another, altogether extraordinary, possibility. In Indian law, where "cultural heritage of a nation" is concerned, the precise language of the statute may not matter. Instead, the doctrine of moral rights found in the Indian Copyright Act could be substantially enlarged by interpreting it in the light of international cultural property conventions signed by India. In particular, destruction of works of art was effectively prohibited in certain circumstances.

On this crucial point, the Court found that international conventions on cultural property take priority over national law. The Court considered Sehgal's work to be a part of India's cultural heritage—a "national treasure." In this situation, the moral rights provisions should be read in the larger context of Indian membership in international conventions for the protection of cultural property. In order to honor these obligations at international law, India would have to intervene to protect damage and destruction affecting important cultural works.

The reasoning of the Indian judge established two important principles where artworks are concerned. First, there can be no doubt that destroying a work of art affects the reputation of the artist. It does so by damaging his or her overall "creative corpus."[132] After this precedent, it seems clear that, whatever the international position, the destruction of artworks is prohibited in India by section 57 of India's Copyright Act.[133] Secondly, where an outstanding work of art is involved, there is an overriding obligation to protect its integrity.

The interpretation of Indian moral rights is, to this extent, dependent on the nature of the work. In the *Amar Nath Sehgal* case, the work had not yet entered the public domain. Nevertheless, the status of the sculpture and its creator were such that the work could be classified as a "national treasure"—already an important contribution to Indian cultural patrimony while the artist was still alive.

[130] *Sehgal, supra* note 44. The case is discussed in detail in Chapter 4, *supra* notes 285-300 and accompanying text.

[131] See the detailed discussion of the evolution of India's moral rights in Chapter 4, *supra* notes 246-66 and accompanying text.

[132] Sundara Rajan, *Amar Nath Sehgal, supra* note 127, at 83; *Sehgal, supra* note 44, at para. 31.

[133] This does not, however, resolve the issue of what happens if an artist wants to destroy his or her own work.

It is worth pointing out that the judge did not need to enter into an assessment of the quality of the work: the sculptor and the work were so well known in India that any threshold would easily have been crossed. This might not always be the case. Similar issues could be much more difficult to deal with if the artist were younger and less established—although he or she might have grown old in the course of this litigation, which spread across nearly three decades from 1978 to 2005. If the artwork had been controversial, the Court might have found itself in difficulty. However, Indian judges have consistently adopted a deferential attitude towards artists who pursue legal complaints. In theory, any significant work of visual art might meet the court's definition of valuable cultural heritage. Given the extraordinary delays and difficulties of litigation in India, the court's approach can easily be justified on practical grounds.[134]

When does a work of art becomes a "national treasure"? In the case of Sehgal's sculpture, the work had already attained iconic status upon its completion because of its history—it was personally appreciated by then Indian Prime Minister Nehru—and location.[135] Mr. Sehgal had many years left to live. As a contrast, when Vincent van Gogh was alive, it seems doubtful that the Dutch government would have dreamed of calling any of his paintings "national treasures." The problem of belated recognition is inevitably an undercurrent running through all discussions of art. Nevertheless, moral rights that persist after an author's death, whether for the limited duration of the author's copyright or beyond, can clearly enrich the protection of cultural heritage. They can do so by harnessing the power of an intellectual property concept in the service of cultural property. As a legal instrument, the moral right can protect cultural heritage from harm in a way that goes beyond what can be accomplished by international cultural property agreements.

It should be noted that visual art moves more easily into the category of national treasure than other kinds of works, and the treatment of these treasures is more straightforward. Avoiding damage to a work of art may be inherently simpler than assessing damage to music or poetry.

Nevertheless, if we separate moral rights from the legal idea of cultural heritage—which is largely, though not entirely, focused on property[136]—it is apparent that moral rights can also protect cultural heritage in its intangible forms, such as literature, music, and folk culture. In this regard, poet Bharati's case is

[134] On the challenges facing the Indian legal system, especially its judges, see Soutik Biswas, *Supreme Court: Why India's Powerful Top Court Is in a "Crisis,"* BBC NEWS (July 31, 2023), https://www.bbc.com/news/world-asia-india-66292895. This issue receives in-depth and high-quality reporting by Vidhi Doshi, *India's Long Wait for Justice: 27m Court Cases Trapped in Legal Logjam*, THE GUARDIAN (May 5, 2016), https://www.theguardian.com/world/2016/may/05/indias-long-wait-for-justice-27-million-court-cases-trapped-in-a-legal-logjam.

[135] It is also worth noting that his work was well placed to do so by its association with Nehru and the Vigyan Bhavan: *see* Sundara Rajan, *Amar Nath Sehgal*, *supra* note 127.

[136] *See, e.g.*, UNESCO, *Safeguarding without Freezing* (n.d.), https://ich.unesco.org/en/safeguarding-00012. These resources suggest that there is increasing recognition for intangible heritage in the international community.

illustrative: his writings are considered "national literature," and the copyright was acquired by the government, and then made public, for this reason.

What would have happened if the continued existence of moral rights in the poet's work had been publicly acknowledged by the government when it gave this gift?[137] Indeed, the first independent Indian Copyright Act was adopted only in 1957, but it created moral rights; would Bharati's works be entitled to these? As a practical matter, there can be no doubt that much of what has occurred in the treatment of Bharati's works since 1949 would amount to violations of his moral rights of attribution and integrity.[138] The Indian government, itself, claimed to recognize the value of copyright for protecting intangible cultural heritage when it prolonged Tagore's rights in 1992.

At least where works of visual art are concerned, and possibly beyond, Indian moral rights may be much greater than they seem. They are not just what is stated by the rather conventional language of section 57. Through their relationship with cultural property conventions, they may take flight beyond the normal bounds of moral rights protection.

d. The Public Domain: Shiva Nataraja's Rights of "Attribution" and "Integrity"

What happens to perpetual moral rights when the work has otherwise entered the public domain? There are at least two possible answers to this question. The first is that, where moral rights are concerned, the work never fully enters the public domain—at least, not in the U.S. sense of the public domain as an area where all rights have expired and there are *no restrictions* on the use of the work. This is not the case: moral rights continue to exist. This leads to situations like the French *Hugo* case, where the great-great-grandson of writer Victor Hugo brought a suit for the protection of *Les Misérables* in 2008—148 years after it was first published in 1862.

But let us say that we travel into the future by another 200 years. By this time, the descendants of Hugo may or may not know of their ancestry or be able to prove their connection to the great author. They will probably have merged with the general population. If the work is still in publication, who will have the right to assert moral rights?

A further step forward takes us into the world of folklore and traditional knowledge. Works of folklore may be culturally valuable and important, but their creators are, or have become, unknown. Moral rights may still have a role to play in protecting the integrity of these kinds of works. They can also support attribution, if not to an individual author, then to the group or country to which the work

[137] In this discussion, I adopt the position of India's first Copyright Act of 1957, which included moral rights, even though Bharati died in 1921.

[138] *See* Sundara Rajan, *Moral Rights in the Public Domain*, *supra* note 92.

belongs. Indeed, the emphasis of cultural property laws on the "country of origin" seems tantamount to recognition of the attribution principle in a new guise. But who shall assert the rights? And on what legal basis can they do so?

In an interesting example, which occurred while the Russian Copyright Act of 1993 was still in force, the Tretyakov Gallery in Moscow sued for the right to assert moral rights in artworks that it owns in order to prevent the use of pictures of them in literary books produced by a Moscow publishing house.[139] The museum had to bring its claim under old legislation that assigned the right to act to an "agency empowered by the state." No such agency had been created by the Russian government. The Gallery therefore made a creative, yet convincing, argument. In the absence of an identifiable state body, the Gallery itself should be considered legally equivalent to a state agency empowered to act by the legislation.

In the common-law countries, as noted in the Indian example of Amar Nath Sehgal's case, solutions may also be found in case law. As illustrated by *Sehgal*, those solutions may be highly innovative. The *Sehgal* judgment emerged out of legislative provisions on moral rights; its conclusions are still defined by its connection to the Indian Copyright Act. But it is also possible for entirely novel doctrines to develop out of case law, bringing extraordinary and unforeseen elements to bear on the issue of moral rights in cultural heritage.

The British judgment in *Bumper Development Corporation v. Commissioner of Police for the Metropolis* is such a case.[140] Decided in 1991, this precedent remains valid, and no attempt has been made to discredit it in subsequent case law. Some U.S. commentary has called the decision "bizarre" and "exotic," though it probably would not seem either of those things to Indians.[141] It is a unique decision. The judgment is as much idea-driven as it is derived from legalities; yet its sophistication where cultural differences are concerned makes it a compelling legal precedent.[142]

The *Bumper* case centers on a bronze statue of the Indian deity Nataraja, traditionally portrayed as a dancer in ecstatic motion and known as the Lord of the Cosmic Dance. The image of the divine dancer is laden with symbolism and

[139] *See* Sundara Rajan, Copyright and Creative Freedom, *supra* note 118, at 202–203.

[140] *Bumper*, *supra* note 106.

[141] *See* John Henry Merryman, *Book Review*: The Ethics of Collecting Cultural Property: Whose Culture? Whose Property?, 85 Am. J. Int'l L. 737, 739 (1991). Merryman not only assesses the *Bumper* decision as "bizarre" but also goes on to refer to the Shiva lingam as, "a phallus-shaped stone emblem"—a bald description that makes no sense when expressed out of context, as here. Merryman fails to express any understanding of the lingam as part of Shaivite Hindu ritual, where this "object" would occupy a space analogous to the sanctum sanctorum of a church. Meanwhile, Paul Bator considers the naming of the deity as a claimant in the *Bumper* case and in the *Norton Simon* case to be "an exotic feature," and goes on to refer to the deity incorrectly as a "goddess": Paul M. Bator, *An Essay on the International Trade in Art*, 34 Stan. L. Rev. 275, n.13 (1982). The terminology "goddess" is also used with reference to the *Bumper* case by John E. Bersin, *The Protection of Cultural Property and the Promotion of International Trade in Art*, 13 N.Y.L. Sch. J. Int'l & Comp. L. 125, 151 (n.67) (1992).

[142] *See Bumper*, *supra* note 106.

represents one of the great mystical traditions of India. The story of the Nataraja bronze in this case is quite typical of conflicts over cultural property that have arisen at various times and places, always across borders; but its legal resolution is unique.

The incident at the heart of this case occurred in 1976. A bronze figure of Nataraja was unearthed in the South Indian state of Tamil Nadu by Ramamoorthi, a laborer. Sacred images made in bronze have been the pride of Tamil craftsmanship for more than a millennium. Famous examples have been prized by art collectors all over the world. These bronze statues were made, not to adorn museums, but for active worship. Nevertheless, their antiquity and excellence has called for special preservation measures even in South India, where a display gallery of unparalleled beauty has been built for them at the Madras Museum.[143]

The bronze, known as the Pathur Nataraja for the town where it was discovered, was found by a poor laborer named Ramamoorthi.[144] Ramamoorthi lived in a hut that was adjacent to the site of a ruined temple. He was digging foundations to build a cow shed when he struck a metal object. The object which he discovered, buried alongside a number of other bronze figures, was the Nataraja statue.

Immediately aware that he had uncovered something of value, Ramamoorthi reburied the objects. He contacted a friend, who put him in touch with a dealer in stolen art objects. The dealer purchased the Nataraja from Ramamoorthi and sold it to another dealer. The Nataraja eventually resurfaced in London, where a dealer named Sherrier sold the object to Bumper Corporation on the basis of a false certificate of origin. The irony of the transaction is that the buyer, Bumper Corporation's chairman Robert Borden, bought the bronze with good intentions: he wanted to add it to a collection of art for display in Canadian museums. Borden apparently held "deep concern for the understanding of cultures," and, as Richard H. Davis observes in his detailed study of the incident, a "conviction that exhibiting works of art can aid this understanding by demonstrating the quality and depth of other civilizations past and present."[145]

But the bronze had been concealed underground for centuries, and it was in a state of great deterioration. The Corporation decided against transporting it immediately to Canada.[146] Instead, it was taken to the staff of the British Museum for an appraisal and conservation work prior to travel. While the bronze was at the

[143] For a description, see the website of the museum, http://www.chennaimuseum.org/draft/gallery/01/arch.htm. Mr. and Mrs. John D. Rockefeller III, well-known for their passion for Asian Art, owned at least one of these statutes in their collection. See the information on an exhibition of Chola bronzes from their collection: Asia Society, *Asian Society Presents Rare Assemblage of Some of the Finest Examples of Indian Bronze Sculptures* (Oct. 6, 2009–Feb. 7, 2010), http://asiasociety.org/files/Chola%20Bronzes%20press%20release.pdf.

[144] Richard H. Davis, *Loss and Recovery of Ritual Self, in* Lives of Indian Images 222 (1997).

[145] Id. at 238 (quoting Borden from trial testimony, and then citing it for his information).

[146] The bronze was believed to have been buried to protect it from destruction at the hands of Muslim invaders. *See* Ghandhi & James, *supra* note 106, at 370.

British Museum, it came to the attention of the Metropolitan Police, who seized it with a view to returning it to its rightful owner.

Bumper Corporation brought an action against the police, seeking the return of the statue with damages. The Corporation argued that it had purchased the bronze in good faith, based on the certificate of provenance that had been provided by the dealer. Its claim was opposed by the Indian government, which hoped to secure the return of the bronze to India.

The dispute eventually led to the English Court of Appeal, which found itself confronting a difficult legal problem. The Indian government had brought the suit, but it had never "owned" the object. Fundamentally, this litigation was about a right to possess, and, in keeping with the norms of British property rules, the Indian government would have to be able to show a title that was superior to Bumper's. In the hope of meeting this test, a number of plaintiffs were added to the suit. They included some highly unusual characters—for example, the ruined temple where the bronze had been discovered, which was represented by its custodian, Sadagopan. Ultimately, the God Shiva, Himself, was included. He was represented by a stone carving that had been discovered with the bronze, known as a Shivalingam.[147] The Shivalingam was also put forward as a claimant on the grounds that it represented the "pious intention" of the thirteenth-century notable who had endowed the temple.[148]

At trial, Justice Kennedy found in favor of the Indian claimants and awarded possession of the statue and compensation for the costs of the proceedings to India.[149] His decision was later upheld by the English Court of Appeal. The Corporation was said to have bought the image in good faith. Its role in the transactions seems extraordinarily naïve—how could Robert Borden not have known that the image was probably, almost certainly, removed illegally from India? In an earlier case involving a bronze Nataraja from Sivapuram acquired by the Norton Simon Foundation, Mr. Simon commented, "Hell, yes, it was smuggled .... I spent between $15 million and $16 million over the last year on Asian art, and most of it was smuggled."[150] Davis notes that Borden "consciously disregarded all questions

[147] *See* Davis, *supra* note 144, at 249. A Shivalingam is a stone sculpture that is a symbol of cosmic unity and, as such, represents the god, Shiva. In traditional Shaivite temples, the lingam is the main focus of worship, and this is perhaps one of two reasons why the case focused on the claim of the Shivalingam rather than the Nataraja itself; a second reason might be the need to avoid the awkwardness of an object asserting "ownership" over itself! Since the case focused on "ownership," it perhaps makes sense to identify another object as the "owner" of the disputed one. At trial, Justice Kennedy studied Hindu law to reach the conclusion that, as Davis explains, "the pious aim of the founder continues to reside in the physical idol as representing and symbolizing that aim." Sadagopan, who claimed as the representative of the temple, also sued as a third claimant on his own behalf.

[148] *See Bumper*, *supra* note 106, at 1367; *see also* Ghandhi & James, *supra* note 106, at 369–70.

[149] The English Court of Appeal substantially followed the judgment of the trial court, delivered by Justice Ian Kennedy.

[150] Quoted by Davis, *supra* note 144, at 241.

of provenance when purchasing the Nataraja."[151] This sounds like negligence, and Justice Kennedy, while not questioning Borden's intentions, nevertheless issued an order for the complete reimbursement of the legal costs of the Indian plaintiffs, which exceeded £300,000.[152]

i. Legal Issues Assessed by the Courts

The *Bumper* rulings are innovative in two respects. First, the case was unusual for its time in ordering the unconditional restoration of the disputed object to the Indian claimants. Secondly, the line of reasoning that led to this result was unique.[153]

In particular, the courts made a valiant attempt to take into account the cultural perspective of the Indian claimants, which probably could not be more removed from a modern British context. For South Indians, Nataraja is an ecstatic figure, the visible embodiment of myth and magic on a cosmic scale, and the originator of an entire tradition of mysticism. He is celebrated with unparalleled splendor in the temple of Chidambaram that is dedicated to him.[154] In assessing the Indians' plea for the return of this bronze, British judges made a remarkable effort to bridge the gap in values between the concerns of the Indian claimants, whose arguments were based on the ancient traditions of a developing country, and the Bumper Corporation, whose dealings with the bronze were standard market activities in a leading art-market country. The trial judge, Justice Kennedy, was able to achieve something almost impossible: translating an awareness of different cultural values into a viable legal framework within the traditions of the common law.[155]

Both at trial and in the subsequent consideration given to the case by a highly sympathetic Court of Appeal, it is apparent that the courts are driven by more than strictly legal considerations. Indeed, the appellate court asks bluntly, "What does justice demand in a case such as this?"[156] The discussion is framed in legal terms, but the approach to the dispute demonstrates the high priority given to the non-legal rationales underlying the positions of the parties.

[151] Id. at 240. Davis quotes Borden as commenting, at trial, "I have bought enough objects to know that one simply doesn't ask those questions."

[152] Davis, *supra* note 144, at 251. Paterson, *supra* note 106, at 333–35, argues that the approach of the courts has important implications for the legal regime regulating the international movement of cultural property.

[153] Paterson, *supra* note 106, at 330.

[154] See the interesting analysis of Siva's dance on the Temple's website, http://www.chidambaramnataraja.org/about_temple.html ("tillai," for the "milky mangrove" tree, common to the region, seems to have been the original name of the place).

[155] The English Court of Appeal's findings were subsequently approved in Canada by the Alberta Court of Queen's Bench: *see India (Union) v. Bumper Development Corp.* [1995] A.J. No. 380 (Q.B.) (Alberta judgment) (Can.).

[156] *Bumper*, *supra* note 106, at 1373.

(a) Title The first and most important legal issue involved title to the object, which would then confer the right to sue on its owner. At trial, Justice Kennedy followed three routes leading to title for the Indian claimants. First, he determined that the ruined Hindu temple, suing through its rightful representative, had a title to the Nataraja that was superior to Bumper's. Secondly, Justice Kennedy found that the intentions of the notable who endowed the temple were represented in the Shivalingam which had been discovered with the statue, and that the title of the Shivalingam was therefore superior to that of Bumper. Finally, the trial judge noted that the Indian state of Tamil Nadu, where the bronze was discovered, would have title to the Nataraja under Tamil Nadu cultural property statutes. In keeping with principles of international comity, a British court was bound to respect this right.[157]

In appealing the issue of title, Bumper specifically questioned the trial judge's attribution of legal personality to the temple, whether directly or through its representative, and to the Shivalingam. Bumper argued that none of the claimants had succeeded in showing that it had a title to the bronze which could be recognized in an English court.

(b) Legal Capacity under Local Law In order to determine whether the temple could be recognized in English law as a legal person, the trial judge first considered the issue of legal capacity under local law—the law of Tamil Nadu, where the bronze originated. In British law, determining the substance of foreign law is a matter of fact, which must be established by expert evidence. However, Justice Kennedy not only relied upon the testimony of the experts presented to the court by the disputing parties, but he also undertook research of his own into the nature of legal personality under Indian law. While the Court of Appeal acknowledged certain restrictions on the ability of the trial judge to investigate factual matters beyond the testimony of the experts, it upheld the bases of his finding that the ruined temple would have legal personality under Indian law.[158]

(c) "Juristic Entity" in English Law Having determined that the temple could sue in an Indian court, the English Court of Appeal went on to consider the issue of whether the capacity of the temple to sue would be recognized under English law. The court adopted the phrase "juristic entity" to signify a "person, body of persons or object" that would be capable of holding title to an object and exercising the rights associated with its ownership in England.[159] In particular, could a foreign

[157] Details of these statutes are noted by Ghandhi & James, *supra* note 106, at 372.

[158] The Court of Appeal pointed out that the trial judge must restrict his research to texts which have been referred to by the expert witnesses, since they have been introduced into evidence by the experts: *see Bumper*, *supra* note 106, at 1367–71. *See also* Ghandhi & James, *supra* note 106, at 375–76.

[159] *Bumper*, *supra* note 106, at 1366.

legal person who was not recognized as a legal person under English law sue in an English court?[160] In order to decide this issue, the court relied on three principles.

First, the Court of Appeal considered the extension of legal personality to entities other than individuals under English law. It pointed out that the assignment of legal personality in English law is usually restricted to corporations or other, similar "groups or series of individuals."[161] Under English law, legal personality has its basis in the "animate content" that the legal person represents.[162]

However, the Court of Appeal recognized that there is no reason of logic or policy to limit the recognition of legal persons in this way. It observed that restricting legal personality to groups of persons is a matter of "tradition and practice" in English law, and is not compelled by analytical or practical necessity.[163] As a result, the recognition of the ruined temple as a juristic entity could be considered comparable to the attribution of legal personality to corporations.

Secondly, the Court of Appeal went on to consider the recognition of legal personality in institutions by assessing the hypothetical case of a Catholic cathedral which was assigned personality by the legislation of its country. The Court argued that the principle of "comity of nations" encouraged British courts to recognize the legal personality of the cathedral in order to show respect for the laws and customs of its country of origin.[164] In the modern context, it felt that a non-Christian institution would be equally entitled to claim legal personality in Britain.[165]

Finally, the Court of Appeal argued that the recognition of legal personality in a foreign institution under English law would promote English objectives of public policy. As noted above, the Court quoted from English precedent to ask what it saw as the fundamental question at issue: "'What does justice demand in such a case as this?'"[166] The Court of Appeal pointed out that artificial procedural considerations should not prevent the recognition and enforcement of a legitimate legal right. With these arguments, it upheld the trial judge's finding that the Indian temple had a title to the Nataraja which was superior under English law to the title acquired by Bumper Corporation. In view of this finding, the Court felt that it did not need to go on to consider whether the Shivalingam would also be entitled to assert ownership of the statue in an English court.

[160] Id. at 1367.

[161] Id.

[162] Id.

[163] Id. at 1372.

[164] This aspect of the Court's reasoning is reminiscent of the U.S. case of *Autocephalous Greek Orthodox Church of Cyprus v. Goldberg*, 917 F.2d 278 (7th Cir. 1990). In *Autocephalous*, a Cypriot church sought to recover a series of elaborately decorated mosaics that had become an important symbol of the history of Greek Cypriot culture. A group of these mosaics was removed from the church in the 1970s and brought to the United States by an art dealer. In deciding to return the mosaics to the church, the court developed the idea of a due diligence requirement for purchasers. The court also considered the church to have ownership of the mosaics through the Archbishopric of the Church of Cyprus. *See Autocephalous*, *supra*, at 289–90; *see also* Bersin, *supra* note 141, at 125–27.

[165] *Bumper*, *supra* note 106, at 1372–73.

[166] Id., quoting Viscount Simonds in *National Bank of Greece & Athens S.A. v. Metliss* [1958] A.C. 509, 525 (UK).

ii. A Moral Rights Perspective

Do moral rights offer a useful perspective on this dispute? For moral rights to be invoked, two criteria would have to be met. First, perpetual moral rights must be found to exist under the relevant legislation. Would English or Indian law apply? England did not recognize moral rights by any statutory means. The common law generally leaves open a degree of flexibility in English law, but the ancient rejection of a common-law copyright in *Donaldson v. Beckett* has meant that English courts are constrained in their ability to develop a jurisprudential doctrine of moral rights. However, following the reasoning of the Court of Appeal in the *Bumper* case, and considering the later U.S. decision on the subsistence of copyright in the Russian *Kurier* case, it would clearly be more appropriate to apply the Indian Copyright Act to what is essentially a question about the subsistence of rights.[167] Until 1994, the Indian Act arguably did grant perpetual protection to moral rights.

Secondly, some provision must be made to clarify who is entitled to assert moral rights when the work is of great antiquity, placing it beyond the reach of authors and their heirs or appointed trustees. In India, at the time of this dispute, moral rights existed and were not limited in time, but no provision was made for their exercise once heirs could no longer be traced.

The concept of attribution is important for cultural property, touching upon so many aspects of its existence. Attribution represents provenance; attribution of "authorship," and, possibly, ownership, may both be appropriate to a situation like the Nataraja's. A focus on attribution could help to establish the legal status of cultural property, and make it more difficult to offer works of improper or unknown attribution for sale. At the same time, it would become more difficult for a buyer to claim ignorance of an object's status. In the most extreme cases, attribution could also provide a powerful rationale for the repatriation of an object—especially if, as in the case of the Nataraja bronze, the object has been removed from its country of origin in contravention of export regulations.[168]

The integrity principle is also of fundamental importance to cultural property. One of the major reasons why the illicit trade in art is so distressing is because it places cultural property in grave danger of damage, destruction, or loss. In the case of the Nataraja, the bronze was deliberately broken by the "dealers" who acquired it from Ramamurti; they wanted to see whether the statue was actually made of gold, in which case, as Davis observes, "presumably they would have reduced the image to its raw material."[169] But, once again, the principle of integrity does not necessarily offer an easy resolution to the question of repatriation. It has been argued in the past that cultural objects from developing countries will be better preserved

[167] *Itar-Tass Russian News Agency v. Russian Kurier, Inc.* 153 F.3d 82 (2d Cir. 1998) (U.S.).

[168] *See* UNESCO Convention, *supra* note 111, at Art. 6. Essentially, every member country of the Convention undertakes to prohibit the export of valuable cultural property without appropriate documentation.

[169] Davis, *supra* note 144, at 235.

in developed countries, and that this justifies their presence in the Western world as part of the heritage of "humanity"—an approach put forward by the work of John Henry Merryman.[170] It is really our understanding of "integrity" that must be brought to bear upon this issue. If we take it at face value, as a question of physical preservation, then the argument might make sense. However, a cultural "object," no matter how splendid and alluring it might be as a work of art, represents much more than its physical presence. The Nataraja bronze illustrates this point perfectly. Its *raison d'être* is to provide a focus for active worship in a temple—surrounded by clouds of incense and smoke from oil lamps, bathed regularly in ablutions of milk and ghee, adorned by profusions of roses and jasmine. It was not meant to sit in splendid isolation in a dust-free museum.

Nevertheless, even within India, it may not be practical to "use" these ancient objects in the traditional way, and attempts have been made to create suitable modern spaces for them such as the Government Museum in Egmore.[171] There is something important about leaving these choices in the hands of the people whose ancestors produced the works. If anyone is qualified to define what is really meant by the integrity of these works, it is probably them.

Against this example stands the situation of works such as the Buddha of Bamiyan, destroyed by the modern warlords of the Taliban in the name of their religion. The Taliban have now returned to power in Afghanistan, and the Afghan people have begun to discuss the idea of restoring the Buddhas. Writing for the International Herald Tribune, Carlotta Gall notes,

> [S]imply preserving what remains is daunting. Once the niches, grottos and caves were covered with murals, but 80 percent were obliterated by the Taliban, [Japanese historian Kasaku] Maeda said. Art thieves also did damage, using ropes to climb into caves 30 meters up on the cliff face and hacking away priceless medallions depicting seated Buddhas. One of these made its way to Tokyo, where an art dealer, suspecting its illicit provenance, showed it to Maeda, who has managed to retrieve more than 40 stolen artefacts.
>
> "One day I hope we will return them to Afghanistan," he said.[172]

[170] Merryman disturbingly co-opts the language of a shared humanity when he argues that cultural property is perhaps best seen as "components of a common human culture": *see, e.g.*, John Henry Merryman, *Two Ways of Thinking about Cultural Property*, 80(4) AM. J. INT'L L. 831 (1986).The growing trend towards repatriation of cultural objects lays bare the underlying hypocrisies of Merryman's work on these issues.

[171] But Davis describes a sadder product of modern-age India: an Icon Centre built at Tiruvarur in Tamil Nadu state to protect statues in danger of theft but housing them in utterly unsuitable conditions. *See* Davis, *supra* note 144, at 257–59.

[172] See the interesting comment by Carlotta Gall, *Afghans Consider Rebuilding Bamiyan Buddhas—Asia-Pacific-International Herald Tribune*, NEW YORK TIMES (Nov. 5, 2006), http://www.nytimes.com/2006/12/05/world/asia/05iht-buddhas.3793036.html. The Taliban's weird follow-up to this destruction is described in Gabe Joselow & Rachel Elbaum, *The Taliban Destroyed Afghanistan's Ancient Buddha Statues. Now They're Welcoming Tourists*, NBC NEWS (Nov. 24, 2021), https://www.nbcnews.com/news/world/taliban-destroyed-afghanistans-ancient-buddhas-now-welcoming-tourists-rcna6307.

J. Architectural Works: Balancing Public Needs with Artistic Prerogative

Works of art that are situated in public locales pose a unique challenge to moral rights doctrine, especially in view of its generous treatment of visual artists. The specter of conflict between artistic intent and the practical requirements of the public looms over moral rights in public art. The law is confusing. The United Kingdom explicitly provides that anyone can make a photograph or image of public art.[173] In the United States, this issue is not addressed explicitly by copyright law, but, depending on the nature of the use, photography of public art may be restricted.[174] As far as moral rights are concerned, neither the UK Copyright, Designs and Patents Act of 1988 nor the U.S. Visual Artists Rights Act clarifies the status of moral rights in public artworks.

In Canada, the Copyright Act states that photographing a work of public art will not be an infringement of copyright. However, the provision is not quite as straightforward as it might seem at first glance. In fact, the advice on interpretation provided by the Act itself leaves open the possibility that this section may be intended to allow photography only for private and noncommercial purposes.[175] At least one Canadian municipality—the city of Duncan, situated on Vancouver Island and famous for its totem poles—has enacted a policy stating that any commercial use of photographs of these poles must first be approved by the City. The purpose of the policy is essentially to support the protection of Indigenous cultural heritage in the city's public spaces by controlling the public spread of images. Where appropriate, the City hopes to secure some economic benefit for the creators of the poles and, in cases where it has acquired rights from the artists, for the City, itself.[176] The policy is also intended to support the artists' moral rights of attribution and integrity.[177]

[173] *See* CDPA, *supra* note 123, §62.

[174] Public art is not explicitly addressed in U.S. copyright legislation, but fair use provisions in the U.S. Code identify "the purpose and character of the use" with a focus on whether or not it is commercial, and the "nature of the copyrighted work" as relevant factors in making this determination: 17 U.S.C. § 107, http://www.copyright.gov/title17/92chap1.html#107.

[175] *See* Canadian Copyright Act, *supra* note 61, at ss. 32.2(1)(b)(ii) and 32.2 (on interpretation).

[176] *See* Shannon Moneo, *Do You Have a Permit to Take That Photo?*, THE GLOBE & MAIL (Oct. 4, 2007), https://www.theglobeandmail.com/news/national/do-you-have-a-permit-for-that-photo/article18146486/. See the interesting article inspired by the issue, David Spratley, *Copyright Law Offers Poor Protection for Aboriginal Cultural Property*, LAWYERS WEEKLY (Nov. 23, 2007). The municipality of Duncan followed up on the issue by developing a policy to clarify the issue: *see* Mira T. Sundara Rajan, Opinion on Duncan Totem Policy prepared for the City of Duncan (January 2008) (on file with author) . The focus of the totem policy was on implementing measures to provide for respectful treatment of these works of art: "The development of a policy should encourage photographers to treat the works with deference, and in particular, to think carefully about the suitability of proposed uses".

[177] Id. *See also* City of Duncan, *About the Totems* (n.d.), https://duncan.ca/visitors/totems-tour/about-the-totems.

In Spain, a similar issue arose, not in relation to public artworks per se, but in relation to works of architecture. The case involved a bridge designed by celebrated architect, Santiago Calatrava, who is known for the flamboyance and elegance of his bridge designs. For the convenience of pedestrians, the city of Bilbao decided to add a footbridge to Calatrava's structure. Calatrava sued for the violation of his moral right of integrity. At first instance, the trial court disagreed with his claim and came to the practical conclusion that the public interest in pedestrian access to the bridge outweighed the artist's prerogative. The addition of the footbridge could not qualify as a violation of the architect's right of integrity.[178]

The decision is entirely understandable from a practical point of view, yet it leaves a slightly bitter aftertaste. A bridge is a difficult thing to classify. It serves a practical purpose, but the greatest bridges often become iconic representations of the cities where they are built—Paris's Pont-Neuf, London's Tower Bridge, New York's Queensboro, San Francisco's Golden Gate, Vancouver's Lion's Gate—and how many more? As William Patry notes,

> To me the works of these designers and others were not only art, but great art. Calatrava's bridge at Bilbao is art by anyone's definition. In New York City, he designed the new Path transportation Station at the World Trade Center, and has designed a wild apartment building at 80 South Street consisting of stacked cubes. Despite his training as an engineer, Mr. Calatrava asserts that function follows form, and there can be no doubt that his works are sculptural.[179]

Alterations to a bridge may become necessary, and it is possible to see the fairness of limiting the availability of moral rights for works that have an essential practical function. The practical shortcomings of Calatrava's bridge are apparently significant. Elizabeth Nash, writing for the INDEPENDENT newspaper, notes,

> Initially ridiculed for "leading from nowhere to nowhere," Calatrava's footbridge is beautiful, but not exactly user-friendly. Its limpid glass floor tiles, designed to reflect the grey-green waters of the river Nervion that flow beneath,

[178] THE IPKAT blog comments:

The IPKat is glad that common sense has prevailed here. It would make life extremely difficult if architects could object to alterations to buildings which others have commissioned from them, and would enable them to control other people's "real property." More fundamentally, the IPKat questions the wisdom of granting a right of integrity over works of architecture in the first place. This wouldn't be such a problem in the UK since an architect's right of integrity only gives him the right to have his name removed from buildings which have been altered in a way which is derogatory to his reputation.

Anon., *Right of Integrity over Bridge Fails*, THE IPKAT (Dec. 4, 2007), http://ipkitten.blogspot.com/2007/12/right-of-integrity-over-bridge-fails.html.

[179] William Patry, *Calatrava, Bridges, and Moral Rights*, THE PATRY COPYRIGHT BLOG (links omitted) (Oct. 29, 2007), http://williampatry.blogspot.com/2007/10/calatrava-bridges-and-moral-rights.html.

> are notoriously slippery when wet. For 10 years residents and visitors have complained of skidding and tumbling.[180]

But functional works that can lay claim to a certain aesthetic stature should also be treated with care. There can be little doubt that works of architecture constitute an important part of a nation's cultural heritage—Greece's Parthenon and India's Taj Mahal are but two examples. In this regard, moral rights can help to supplement laws for the protection of monuments by opening up the important requirement of including the artist-architect in discussions about modification of the work. In Calatrava's case, for example, a simple solution may have been to ask the architect himself to assist with the alteration plans, rather than making the unfriendly gesture of engaging a rival architect to undertake the work.[181] An architect may or may not agree to be involved in the alteration of his or her own work; and the law could limit the architect's rights by giving him or her a first right of refusal in cases such as these.

In his interesting analysis of the case, Spanish copyright lawyer Juan José Marín López notes,

> The judge criticized the actions of the city council, stating that it had been wrong not to have put Mr. Calatrava himself in charge of the extension to his bridge. But no penalty was imposed.[182]

The dilemma between art and function is neatly expressed by the court. The Court comments (in López's translation),

> In addition to constituting a singular artistic creation suitable for protection, the work is [a] public one, offering a service to the citizens, and thus satisfies a public interest. If we weigh these interests, the public must prevail over the private.[183]

In fact, the court expressed sympathy for the idea that Calatrava should have been asked to modify his own work. For José J. Izquierdo Peris, the judgment of the court provides useful guidance on upholding the architect's right to make any

180 Elizabeth Nash, *Calatrava Sues for "Violation of Copyright" over Bridge Changes*, The Independent (Oct. 26, 2007), http://www.independent.co.uk/news/world/europe/calatrava-sues-for-violation-of-copyright-over-bridge-changes-397965.html.

181 In the recently filed *Ascalon* case, the sculptor offered to undertake restoration work on his sculpture himself. Monika Bruss, *supra* note 26, observes, "Mr. Ascalon offered to carry out any necessary restoration work, but was eventually not taken up on that offer." Instead, the work was carried out by another person.

182 Juan José Marín López, *In the Courts: Bridging Moral Rights and Public Utility*, WIPO Magazine (Feb. 2008), http://www.wipo.int/wipo_magazine/en/2008/01/article_0004.html.

183 Id.

alterations to his own work that become necessary. However, the court's statement on this issue is not entirely authoritative, and Peris advises:

> Ultimately, one sees how difficult it is for an architect, who is commissioned to complete a functional work, to retain any possibility ... [of] stop[ping] modifications done by [the] public authorities ... On the positive side, in one way or another, the owner of the work is expected to contract changes to the author, not to a third party. But this expectation is far from being other than an obiter dictum. For ... [this] reason, when receiving a contract from a public authority, designers and architects should perhaps negotiate an explicit provision, to help the author retain at least some contractual rights in case alteration is done under circumstances like those in this suit.[184]

On appeal, the perspective of the provincial court hearing Mr. Calatrava's complaint was entirely different. In contrast to the practical resolution of the case offered by the court at first instance, the higher court felt that Mr. Calatrava had already provided a public service by constructing the bridge. Further convenience for the public was not reason enough to overrule the architect's moral right of integrity. In particular, the decision to construct a footbridge was a matter of choice, and the authorities could have chosen other means of facilitating public access to the bridge without ruining Calatrava's design. The higher court's perspective is summarized by López:

> Mr. Calatrava's bridge, on its own, already served the public interest by providing a means to cross the river at a place where it was not previously possible. After crossing the bridge, pedestrians had to go down one flight of stairs and up another to reach the residential area. The footbridge added to Mr. Calatrava's bridge fulfilled a function of simple comfort, as it allowed a direct connection with the residential area, without the need to go up or down stairs. The Court considers that, in these circumstances, the footbridge does not represent a public interest that prevails over and above the author's moral right. Simple comfort is not then, at least in this case, a public interest prevailing over the moral right.[185]

Crucially, the higher court noted that Calatrava's stature as an architect was relevant to its determination. The city should not have expected to hire an architect of his reputation and style, and then alter his work without his consent. As López notes,

[184] José J. Izquierdo Peris, *A Bridge Too Far: Calatrava's Bridge Is Copyright-Protected, But Not Enough*, 3(4) J. Intell. Prop. L. & Prac. 218 (2008).

[185] Juan José Marín López, *Copyright in the Courts: Moral Right in Architecture (Part II)*, WIPO Magazine (June 2009), http://www.wipo.int/wipo_magazine/en/2009/03/article_0012.html.

The Town Hall recruited a prestigious architect, such as Mr. Calatrava, not in order to plan the complete work provided for in the urban plan, but only to design and construct a bridge over the river. Some time later, once the bridge was complete, it decided to add the footbridge in order to connect the bridge to the residential area. According to the Court, the Town Hall could have made good on the provision made in the urban plan, by facilitating direct access to the residential area, in a manner that did not harm Mr. Calatrava's moral right. However, as it did not do so, it infringed the copyright.[186]

K. Moral Rights and Virtual Galleries

Technology complicates the lives of art and artefacts. Two crucial developments have occurred: the ability to reproduce images of artworks on a scale that was previously unknown and the possibility of communicating those images with extraordinary ease via the Internet. Apart from the potential for copyright infringement, the moral rights implications of digital imagery are striking.

1. Digital Images: New Technology to Reach Old Masters

The circulation of an image such as a photograph of an artwork leads to new and interesting questions. An initial concern is whether moral rights are infringed when the photograph is circulated without attributing the artist who created the work, or in a manner that is likely to be derogatory. In the case of artworks created by living artists, or whose creators are still known, the problem is obvious. Provided that moral rights have not expired, failure to attribute and derogatory treatment will both constitute violations of the artist's moral rights.

When we explore the idea of a moral right in public domain works or cultural property, the question becomes more difficult to answer. The photograph is a picture of an artefact or cultural object; it does not portray an artwork created by an identifiable artist. Once again, attribution could be interpreted in a number of ways to support the idea that, in such cases, the provenance of a work should be indicated. How far back in the pedigree of a work should such attribution extend? For example, in the case of the Nataraja bronze owned by the Rockefeller Foundation, should it be displayed with an indication that it belongs to the Rockefeller collection? That it is from India? Tamil Nadu? The town of origin? Concerns about the status of cultural property suggest that attribution should generally be as complete as possible.

186 Id.

Integrity is a subtler issue. Where the reproduction of an artwork is concerned, at least two distinct problems can arise. The first is the quality of the reproduction: does a poor-quality digital reproduction constitute a violation of the artist's right of integrity? The argument that it does has been made in relation to the reproduction of music for use as mobile ringtones in Germany. In that scenario, the German *Bundesgerichtshof* found that the conversion of music into files suitable for a ringtone implied a certain degree of alteration due to "digital ... process[ing]."[187] In its assessment, the Court may have been a bit behind the times—fidelity and quality came to be prized in ringtones[188]—but its analysis is directly applicable to reproductions of visual art. Is a degree of deterioration to be expected in a digital reproduction and, accordingly, to be tolerated? On the other hand, does it make more sense to argue that art galleries and museums are under an obligation to represent their collections in the most favorable light possible, and that deterioration in the quality of images is a serious affront to the right of integrity? The solution here involves striking the right balance between the standard of care expected of museums, which should be high, and a degree of reasonableness in applying it.

In relation to three-dimensional works, such as sculptures, reproducing them in two-dimensional photographs involves a fundamental change. A poor-quality photograph of a sculpture may misrepresent the work, and this could, indeed, be considered a violation of the sculptor's right of integrity. At the same time, the threshold for making such a determination should be quite high, as a change in quality is definitely implied by photography of a three-dimensional object. If the artist has given permission, it should be harder to establish that the act of photography has violated his or her moral rights.

Secondly, where painting is concerned, the question of authenticity is potentially disturbing. This is because of a degree of overlap between the nature of the original work and the form of the reproduction. For example, it is possible that a photographic image could be used to generate new "hard copies" of the original work. To make matters more complicated, it may not be the fault of the author-photographer or owner-gallery that new hard copies surface. Unless the image files are somehow devised to make printing impossible, anyone who has access to them could print them.

The problem of potential confusion between an original artwork and unauthorized copies arose in the Canadian case of *Théberge*. In this case, the facts showed an interesting twist: the reproductions were not photographs. Instead, they were made by a process of lifting ink from postcards—which were, themselves, authorized reproductions of Théberge's original paintings—and superimposing the ink

[187] *See* Chapter 6, *supra* notes 144-60 and accompanying text.
[188] Id.

onto canvas.[189] The artist felt that these canvas-backed reproductions could create confusion in the mind of the public, which might mistake them for his original works. At the same time, Théberge was also concerned that these reproductions could ultimately degrade the saleability of his original work.[190]

The artist's moral rights of attribution and integrity were clearly implicated in this case. Nevertheless, the suit failed. But the failure was an extremely interesting one: it raised the fundamental question of how to decide on the characterization of a claim as moral or economic under the terms of Canadian copyright law. In fact, Théberge had not framed his claim as a moral rights complaint. His cautious counsel probably wanted to avoid making a legal claim based on moral rights because it is generally difficult to obtain a positive judgment in this area from Canadian courts. In particular, it has proven to be difficult to offer the courts persuasive evidence of damage to reputation. In Théberge's case, the decision to avoid moral rights was probably a strategic error, but his situation presents something of a "catch-22." Justice Binnie, writing for the majority of the Canadian Supreme Court, emphasized the different and higher standard of proof required to show a violation of moral rights, reflected in the requirement that an author must be able to prove damage to his or her reputation.[191] Théberge had made no attempt to satisfy it; if he had, it is hard to say whether he would have been successful.

To add to these ambiguities, the creation of a photograph can lead to new moral rights in the image itself—the moral rights of the photographer. If a museum plans to use photographs, it needs to be aware of these overlapping rights. Appropriate steps should be taken to protect both the moral rights of the photographer, as the creator of the image, and the moral rights of the underlying artist or cultural group.

Finally, it is worth noting that displaying an image of an artwork changes the environment in which the artwork is perceived. In a sense, this is one of the most exciting aspects of the artistic experience. Linking apparently disparate works and artists through novel combinations of images can illuminate connections that we never knew were there—juxtaposing Picasso's paintings with traditional African art, or showing van Gogh's and Gauguin's paintings side by side.[192] When individuals can create their own collections of images, finding connections that might

[189] *Théberge*, *supra* note 67.

[190] Id. at para. 20. The artist commented, "Being a party to the distribution of these things means that they [clients and friends] assume that I hatched a plot in which I am a participant. I'm getting money, royalties or ... that I make money off of it—otherwise, it's just not possible. How can you allow such a thing, Mr. Théberge?"

[191] But note that Canadian Copyright Act, *supra* note 61, at s. 28.2 (2) infers damage to reputation if distortion of a painting is found to have occurred.

[192] See, e.g., the Van Gogh Museum's exhibition, *Van Gogh and Gauguin: The Studio of the South*: Art Institute Chicago, *Van Gogh and Gauguin: The Studio of the South* (2001), https://www.artic.edu/print-publications/65/van-gogh-and-gauguin-the-studio-of-the-south. Britain's National Gallery featured an exhibition entitled *Picasso: Challenging the Past*, in which paintings by Picasso were

be quite original, the experience of viewing art is unexpectedly democratized.[193] Discovering the unity of apparently unrelated things is an essential part of creative expression. But could this approach to images lead to violations of the artist's moral right of integrity?

2. Building Virtual Galleries

The specific question of how museums and galleries use images of their own collections is worth a closer look. Museums are increasingly creative in their use of images, and many of them have undertaken to build true "virtual galleries." A virtual gallery is no mere collection of reproduced artworks or artefacts. More than replicating the real-world structure of the museum, a virtual gallery creates original pathways and experiences through the medium of the Internet. Its purpose is to show viewers how to appreciate a collection by guiding them through the experience of viewing.

Museum websites may also allow viewers to generate their own virtual galleries.[194] Interactive websites allow viewers to assemble their own collections of images from the museum's collection. This is a creative attempt at outreach by museums to their public and encourages individuals to engage with art in an interesting way through technology. The potential for public education seems endless. All of these opportunities offer the extraordinary and useful opportunity to "visit" a museum in "virtual" form without having to travel to its physical location.

In these situations, more than ever, questions might surface about the context in which a work is "virtually" displayed. Most likely, when an image of an artwork appears online, it is presented in a new way that may differ from the conditions in which the work of art is viewed on site or even alter them fundamentally. These technological developments strongly suggest that principles surrounding the display of artworks should be revisited. If anything, the context of online display is becoming ever more important in the post-COVID-19 era, when people may be less willing or able to travel as public health risks increase.

This issue is of particular concern in relation to contested artworks or artefacts from vulnerable cultures. Juvenal Nsengimana, legal officer at the Rwandan

displayed alongside earlier classic works of the same types of subject matter: The National Gallery, *Picasso: Challenging the Past* (Feb. 25–June 7, 2009), https://www.nationalgallery.org.uk/exhibitions/past/picasso-challenging-the-past.

[193] Although, as Russell Smith of the GLOBE & MAIL notes, expert curators may be skeptical about the value of interactive tools for cultivating artistic taste: *see* Russell Smith, *The Cloud Sees a Milk Jug, Curators See Vermeer*, GLOBE & MAIL (June 30, 2010), https://www.theglobeandmail.com/arts/the-cloud-sees-a-milk-jug-curators-see-vermeer/article1374298.

[194] *See, e.g.*, the Virtual Collections of the Pitt Rivers Museum, Oxford, https://www.prm.ox.ac.uk/collections-online#/search.

museums, speaks of the misunderstandings that can arise from the presentation of African artworks in European museums, highlighting that this is an educational issue. Problems like this could multiply online, especially in light of the rising tide of misinformation, and reduced opportunities to travel to sites in person might increase their influence. In many circumstances online, what the Indian government calls a "failure to display a work properly" may, indeed, violate the moral rights of creators.

This problem is one that calls for a sensitive approach. The viewing experience offered by a virtual gallery can be a precious gift. It can allow viewer to experience art in a new way, with privacy and intimacy. This kind of experience has previously been reserved to music, perhaps—or to the private owners of valuable artworks. Sam Hamill speaks of the "beautiful aloneness" prized by the masters of Haiku.[195] Moreover, the value of images of artworks should not be underplayed. The popular art historian, Sister Wendy Beckett, speaks of the photographs that stirred her passion for art when her ability to travel to see the original works was limited.[196] Similar experiences may now be in the hands of the public, not only online, but also in physical form, through 3D printing.

Where virtual "private collections" remain private, there is no need to talk about moral rights. But in the case of images or collections which are publicly accessible, whether they belong to museums or to private collectors, accountability will be important. Maintaining accurate attribution of works is a must, and, in the online context, the notion of attribution should probably be enlarged to include details such as the place where the physical work is displayed and information on the provenance of the work or object.[197] The rising prevalence of artificial intelligence, which had its first major public impact through the generation of artistic images,[198] not only means that attribution should be scrupulously maintained, but also that it should identify the human origin of artistic works. Works should be appropriately labeled when they feature artificial intelligence or other significant technological elements—whether in creation, conservation, or commentary on the works.

3. Artistic Innovation: From Collages to Parodies

There is nothing new about the collision between modern art and copyright law. The example of Andy Warhol, his Campbell's soup cans, and his reproductions

[195] *See* Sam Hamill, *Introduction*, *in* THE SOUND OF WATER: HAIKU BY BASHO, BUSON, ISSA, AND OTHER POETS xv (Sam Hamill trans., 2000).

[196] *Sister Wendy Beckett, TV Art Historian, Dies at 88*, BBC NEWS (Dec. 26, 2018), https://www.bbc.com/news/uk-46687275.

[197] See the general discussion in Chapter 5, *supra* regarding the attribution right in the context of artificial intelligence.

[198] See discussion of DALL-E in Chapter 5, *supra* notes 46, 51, and accompanying text.

of Marilyn Monroe's photographs, suffices to illustrate the point.[199] It is ironic, though perhaps in the natural order of things, that the Warhol Foundation is now vigilant against violations of Warhol's copyright in his own works.[200]

The availability of digital images greatly enriches the potential for creative innovation in new artistic forms—from collages to parodies, from virtual galleries to commercial web pages. The artist who wants to use images for the creation of new works faces formidable legal and ethical challenges involving questions of copyright ownership as well as moral rights. The artist must respect the moral rights of attribution and integrity of all those who came before him or her, although the practicalities of doing so are not easy to contemplate. Similarly, galleries that wish to show the work of modern artists engaged in experimental work may find themselves facing difficulties because of the need to respect moral rights.

At first glance, any form of art that makes use of pre-existing images will face the problem of moral rights. In these situations, two questions arise. First, it is not clear that every use of a pre-existing image will lead to a moral rights violation. Rather, in keeping with the theory behind moral rights, the component of the work that is used must retain a real connection with the original author. An appropriate test is needed.

The general test for copyright infringement is one of substantiality: if the copied image represents a substantial part of the original work, it will constitute an infringement of copyright.[201] What is substantial depends on a number of factors, and both quantity and quality are relevant to this determination. In the case of moral rights, similar principles can be used to assess the strength of the link between a particular image and its creator. For example, merely copying a color may not be sufficient to establish a link with the author of the work. On the other hand, if the color is highly distinctive, or if it invokes the artist in the context in which it is used—Mark Rothko's or Matisse's Red, for example—it may be a violation of moral rights to copy it. This is not to suggest that any artist could, or should, restrict the use of a color. Rather, the idea is to prevent something unfair: the exploitation of the work of the original artist without identifying him or her. A useful connection can be made here between moral rights and trademark principles. Trademark law will only protect an image that invokes its brand when its use raises this association

[199] An image of Warhol's soup cans can be viewed on the website of the Museum of Modern Art (MoMA), https://www.moma.org/collection/works/79809; see also the commentary on his "Gold Marilyn," https://www.moma.org/collection/works/79737.

[200] See, e.g., the discussion of licensing rights on the website of the Andy Warhol Foundation for the Visual Arts, https://warholfoundation.org/warhol/licensing/. In the latest case involving the Warhol Foundation, the U.S. Supreme Court held the Foundation liable for Warhol's unlicensed use of a photograph by Linda Goldsmith: *see Warhol Foundation v. Goldsmith* (Oct. 12, 2022), https://www.supremecourt.gov/opinions/22pdf/21-869_87ad.pdf.

[201] *Ladbroke v. William Hill* [1964] 1 WLR 263 (UK); *University of London v. University Tutorial Press* [1916] 2 Ch. 601 (Ch.D.) (UK).

in the mind of the viewer. Nothing is protected, or restricted, in the abstract. This principle of association seems to be well suited to the context of digital art.

The second question has to do with the practical issue of how moral rights should be recognized. What constitutes adequate attribution? If a work is extremely well known, is it fair to argue that the use of the work implies attribution to its original creator? This appears to be the principle behind parody, which can only operate as a defense to copyright infringement if the work and its author are well known. Without this expectation of recognition from the public, the use of a little-known work, without giving credit to the author, cannot be justified as a parody.

The format of an artwork may not lend itself to easy attribution. Web pages can be broken up into component parts, and the presence of attribution in any part of the page may be sufficient. But what happens when the image can be printed or physically reproduced in some other way, and separated from the attribution information? What about the case of original works such as collages, which may be signed by the artist but are not likely to include attribution to the artists whose earlier works are integrated into the collage? It is also worth noting that the increasingly popular U.S. doctrine of transformative works—which provides that an original work made out of pre-existing works will not infringe copyright if it "transforms" those works sufficiently[202]—does not help to resolve the questions of attribution and integrity raised by the use of pre-existing works.[203]

L. Copy or Original? 3D Printed Artworks

The prospect of 3D printing raises new questions about the meaning of originality. 3D printing is based on detailed scanning of an original object. Scanning captures key information that can then be used by a 3D printer to create a replica of the object that is identical to the original, or identical in scale, based on the details that have been scanned. Something analogous happens in the case of musical technologies like Zenph and others, which recreate "original" performances by musicians who are no longer alive by using various forms of information gathering and artificial intelligence-based technologies. The performances of jazz great Oscar

[202] Pierre Leval, *Toward a Fair Use Standard*, 103 Harv. L. Rev. 1105 (1990).

[203] For a helpful early examination of the interplay between derivative works, transformative uses, and fair use under U.S. copyright law, see Mary W.S. Wong, *"Transformative" User-Generated Content in Copyright Law: Infringing Derivative Works or Fair Use?*, 11(4) Vand. J. Ent. L. & Tech. 1075, 1104–37 (footnote omitted) (2009), https://scholarship.law.vanderbilt.edu/jetlaw/vol11/iss4/11:

> The fundamental idea seems to be that if the use will advance knowledge and enable progress (in the constitutionally mandated manner), it may be fair and thus permissible, subject to the other factors in the case; more specifically, such a use could be transformative in that it does more than "supersede the objects" of the original work—it also generates new and socially desirable "knowledge."

Peterson[204] and classical great Glenn Gould[205] have both been made available on this basis.

What is created through methods like these amounts to a new form of copying. And yet, this seems inadequate to capture the level of accuracy and precision that can be attained through 3D printing. What is the value of an original when a 3D-printed copy exists?

This is the essential problem that confronts the Rodin museum in Paris. The museum has made 3D scans of the works in its collection, both for research and for commercial purposes. This scans are sought after by a U.S. public domain advocate, Cosmo Wenman, who has turned to French administrative law to obtain an opinion that the scans qualify as administrative documents under French law and should therefore be made freely available to all members of the public, including himself.[206] Wenman's goal is to make 3D-printed copies of the artist's work from these scans and to sell them, presumably for profit. He comments,

> I would freely redistribute [the scans] ... as I did in 2019 with the 3D scan of the bust of Nefertiti in Berlin's Egyptian Museum. I would love to show off my commercial digital-to-bronze capabilities by using the Musée Rodin's scans to produce my own bronze replicas at far higher quality than the museum's own gift shop offerings.[207]

As of the time of writing, the museum has not made the scans available to him on the grounds that the report of CADA (the *Commission d'accès aux documents administratifs*)[208] does not constitute a binding authority on the museum. Then director, Catherine Chevillot, has expressed concerns that allowing Wenman's reproductions—and, potentially, others like them—would undercut the market for the museum's own reproductions of Rodin's works, which are a major source of revenue for the museum. In fact, the museum is the only self-financing cultural institution of its kind in France. In this light, her concerns seem entirely understandable. Ironically, though, Wenman himself claims that these fears are overblown:

[204] *See, e.g., Oscar Peterson—Unmistakable Album EPK from Zenph & Sony Masterworks* (2011), https://www.youtube.com/watch?v=i5Ls24d7Dog.

[205] Yamaha claims that its invention "reproduces the masterful touch of Glenn Gould to provide an inspiring and interactive experience of co-creation between an AI pianist and human musicians": Yamaha, *Dear Glenn: An A.I. System Crafted by Love* (n.d., concert and event on Sept. 7, 2019), https://www.yamaha.com/en/stories/new-values/dear-glenn/.

[206] See, for a fascinating discussion of the case, Anna Sansom, *Musée Rodin Could Be Forced to Release 3D Scans of Bronze Sculptures—Including The Thinker—to the Public*, The Art Newspaper (Mar. 5, 2021), https://www.theartnewspaper.com/2021/03/05/musee-rodin-could-be-forced-to-release-3d-scans-of-bronze-sculpturesincluding-the-thinkerto-the-public.

[207] Id.

[208] CADA, Conseil 20190026 (Feb. 7, 2019), https://www.cada.fr/20190026.

> Rodin replicas are already ubiquitous [and the Museum] ... knows full well that the high-end art market prizes authenticity above all else and accepts no substitutes; authenticity cannot be reproduced via a scan.

The essence of Wenman's claim is that the reproductions made by the museum are "authentic" in a way that his own reproductions cannot be. According to him, there is a different market for both types of reproductions. Market demand for authentic reproductions will therefore not be negatively affected by the demand for his own, non-authentic and presumably cheaper, copies.

But at what point does the quantity of reproductions on the market shift to this equation? If, as Wenman says, the market is already "flooded" with Rodin reproductions, why exactly is he interested in making more? His comments suggest that he is driven to prove a point, and he claims that he is doing so in the public interest, but none of this should be taken at face value. The Rodin Museum was founded by the artist himself, and its mandate is to preserve the artist's legacy in line with *his own* vision. It is in this context, as well, that the museum is responsible for exercising the artist's moral rights, which exist in perpetuity under French law. It is also worth bearing in mind that Rodin struggled to establish the museum, which was his way of providing for his works after his death and assuring the continuation of his artistic legacy—ultimately, his gift to the French people and to the world. The French government was not cooperative in this process, and the fact that Rodin's efforts were ultimately successful is a testament to the persistence and determination of the artist.

The French administrative body's decision that the scans made by the museum should be publicly available for any purpose seems to flow from the fact that the works are in the public domain. The report mentions moral rights, but it does so only to state that access to the scans cannot be refused on this account:

> Finally, the Commission emphasizes that the [Museum's] status [as] the artist's right holder, responsible for ensuring that the moral rights of the sculptor are respected, is an equally unsuitable basis for a refusal to communicate [the scans], and it is the responsibility of the museum to ensure respect for the integrity of the works in the course of the reuse of the solicited documents.[209]

This statement is interesting, because it seems to leave open the possibility that the use of the scans as Wenman proposes might violate the moral rights of the artist.

[209] *See* id.:

> La commission souligne, enfin, que la qualité d'ayant droit de Rodin, chargé de faire respecter le droit moral du sculpteur est également insusceptible de fonder un refus de communication, à charge pour le musée, comme il le fait aujourd'hui, de veiller au respect de l'œuvre lors de la réutilisation des documents sollicités.

It would cost the Museum resources to pursue this idea, but the effort might be worth it.

Given that Wenman is American, the significance of this legal barrier may not be fully apparent to him. However, at least two possible bases for moral rights claims come to mind. First, given that the scans are the museum's own, and that the 3D replications made by Wenman might be functionally indistinguishable from them, this implies the possibility that members of the public might be confused between these scans and those made by the museum. This could be a *prima facie* violation of Rodin's moral right of attribution as exercised by the museum on the artist's behalf. At the very least, Wenman's scans should be labeled in such a way that they clearly indicate that they are not authorized by the museum. To state, further, that the scans were originally made by the museum might even amount to a violation of the moral right of attribution in itself. Such a statement could create a false impression in the marketplace that the reproductions are somehow made with the cooperation of the museum, or even authorized by it. The issue of proper labeling would thus need to be handled with great care by Wenman to avoid implicating the museum in any way.

These copies could also violate the museum's *own* right of attribution, but only if the creation of the scans can be attributed to individual "authors" at the museum. This is, admittedly, a speculative argument, as it is questionable whether the scans themselves would qualify as works under French copyright law. Like extremely accurate photographs of artworks, they may lack the requisite element of originality—bringing us full circle.

Could the plentiful availability of the scans also tarnish the marketplace for Rodin reproductions or damage the artist's reputation in the eyes of the public? This would presumably not be caused by the quality of the reproductions but by their ubiquity. Again, Wenman claims that unauthorized reproductions are already ubiquitous, but this raises the question of why he wants to produce more.

Such an interpretation of the artist's moral right of integrity resembles the trademark concept of dilution. The marketplace for reproductions of Rodin's works, and the artist's reputation in that marketplace, would both be negatively affected by the availability of the scans.

Of course, this situation demonstrates the intertwining of artistic and commercial prerogatives involved in moral rights. This is, perhaps, a more realistic appreciation of the practical realities underpinning moral rights than the doctrine usually affords, made possible in the context of a concrete example. Arguably, the practical implications of moral rights should be more emphasized by those interested in the future of the arts, since neither individual artists nor culture as a whole benefit when the doctrine is treated as primarily theoretical and impractical. Statements of principle seem woefully inadequate to meet the challenges facing culture in the technological environment. In many ways, with so much to gain financially, it is a predatory environment. But moral rights were born in the courts, at a moment in time that was also highly innovative, and they emerged in response to authors' practical needs. In our current era of rapid technological innovation, they are arguably needed once again.

In the case of the Rodin reproductions, we are no longer dealing with the artist's "master hand," but with the intentions that guided it, and with the artist's vision of the future lives of his works. Can moral rights help to keep his gift to the public—his museum, his legacy—intact in the technological era?

M. A Critique of Originality: Bill Reid and Haida Art

But the emphasis on originality can corrupt the creative environment in which living artists work —all the more so if the artists represent non-mainstream traditions. This should in no way be interpreted as a negative comment on the value of artistic attribution. Rather, the discussion here aims to criticize the concept of artist as brand—"authenticity" as it is prized by the art market, in Cosmo Wenman's words—and the role played by the concept of originality in perpetuating it. The appearance of authenticity is different from authenticity itself—a lesson that must be borne in mind in our era.

A sobering lesson can be found in the legacy of Bill Reid, a path-breaking Canadian artist who belonged to the Haida people of North America's West Coast and was considered a master sculptor. By the time of his death in 1998, at age seventy-eight, Reid had reinvigorated the Haida tradition of sculpture. Perhaps he belonged to that rare class of artists who are Renaissance-makers. The Italian philosopher, Mazzini, writes about the conditions in which artistic genius may flourish, arguing that both times of great prosperity and great despair may produce great people. Based on his theory, Indian nationalist writer C. Subramania Bharati speculates that, at times of extreme oppression, "sages may be born to redeem [a] nation."[210] Bill Reid may well be admired by his people as one of these.

But in the year following his death, Reid was the subject of a controversial article in Canada's MACLEAN'S MAGAZINE.[211] The article drew attention to the role of the artists working for Reid, exceptional craftsmen who were largely responsible for realizing the concrete details of Reid's artistic vision through their skill. The fact that Reid was suffering from Parkinson's disease throughout the 1990s shows how important, both practically and spiritually, their involvement must have been.

The article cited interviews with a number of the artists involved and found mixed feelings—humiliation and disappointment for some but, for others, a sense

[210] Quoted in S. VIJAYA BHARATI, SUBRAMANIA BHARATI: PERSONALITY AND POETRY (1975).
[211] Jane O'Hara, *Reid Controversy*, MACLEAN'S MAGAZINE (Dec. 16, 2013), https://www.thecanadianencyclopedia.ca/en/article/reid-controversy.

of honor and privilege. None of these artists had been forced to work by Reid. On the other hand, all of them lived by their art and needed the work.

This problem clearly involves moral rights.[212] It appears that the contribution of these artists was never recognized publicly by Reid. According to the MACLEAN'S piece, every formal context in which Reid was honored was one in which he, and he alone, received the credit for the work.

Looking at this situation through the lens of artists' moral rights, what can we conclude? There can be no doubt that it was both wrong and illegal under existing Canadian law to deny attribution to these artists.[213] How should they have been attributed? As joint authors alongside Reid? As his assistants? Or as unique creators of the works, or portions of the works, which were made with their own hands? It is now openly acknowledged that *Raven and the First Men*, perhaps Reid's most famous work, was not physically carved by Reid. And yet, as the Maclean's article notes, the sculpture was "[b]ased on an original eight-centimetre boxwood carving done by Reid in 1970." The artist was then at the height of his creative powers, physically as well as mentally. It seems that the concept behind the work was clearly, undeniably, Reid's.

Modern copyright law, as we know it, frowns upon such an assessment. From a copyright perspective, the origin of the concept behind the work is of limited importance. Even on the most liberal interpretation, copyright law cannot protect ideas in the absence of a thinker's eventual involvement in the physical creation of the work.[214] And yet, without the concept, no work can exist. And it is rare, indeed, that artists are recognized primarily for their craftsmanship—although Bill Reid at first saw himself, first and foremost, as the maker of the "well-made object."[215] An artist is undoubtedly known for his or her artistic vision: the greater the vision,

[212] But this is not to say that financial considerations were not important. The article points out that many of the artists involved felt that they were poorly paid for their work and that Bill Reid's actions were partly driven by his own need for financial success: id.

[213] *See* Canadian Copyright Act, *supra* note 61, at s. 14.1(1), defining the right of attribution. It is a peculiarity of Canadian law that attribution must be "reasonable in the circumstances."

[214] The House of Lords case of *Designer Guild Ltd v. Russell Williams (Textiles)* [2001] 1 All E.R. 700 (UKHL), https://publications.parliament.uk/pa/ld199900/ldjudgmt/jd001123/design-1.htm, has come closer than any other common-law ruling to claiming that ideas may be protected by copyright law. Lord Hoffman made the eminently sensible argument that idea and expression are united in any creative work; rather than viewing them as opposites, his discussion suggests a spectrum along which copyright protection moves from idea to expression. As the idea becomes increasingly detailed, copyright protection crystallizes. Alluding to Isaiah Berlin, Lord Hoffman points out that, "Copyright law protects foxes other than hedgehogs." This position would appear to be supported by recent reassessments of the fixation (and originality) criteria in UK copyright law, including *Sawkins v. Hyperion Records* [2005] EWCA Civ 565 —which, to the chagrin of many law professors, affirms the controversial pre-1911 case (when originality was first introduced into the UK copyright statute) of *Walter v. Lane* [1900] AC 539 (UKHL). The traditional artistic law of India is, apparently, an exception to the traditional rule, requiring the protection of ideas as well as expression: T.S. Krishnamurti, *Copyright—Another View*, 15(3) BULL. COPYRIGHT SOC'Y USA 217, 217-18 (1968).

[215] Reid, quoted in O'Hara, *supra* note 211.

the greater the artist. Vision is arguably what separates a true artist from the merely successful author of poem or painting.

Reid's case unfolded against a background of Western norms in which Haida culture operates—the models of authorship and creativity to which Indigenous art is subject, and the Western art market's insistence on developing the brand names of artists as the basis of artistic valuation. Western society idolizes the artist made in a certain mold: the individual, original, independent, and often male genius[216] who creates valuable works. To every work its artist. The Western model is based on the presence of individual and readily identifiable contributions to a work of art. As soon as the nature of the creative work becomes more complex, this model founders.

Work such as Reid's acquires its extraordinary power from the culture behind it. The work is a product of tradition; it seeks to give new life to that tradition. It embodies the relationship of artist, community, and creation in an incredibly sophisticated way. The very fact that Reid's work was made as it was—through the collaborative efforts of several outstanding artists—suggests that there may not have been any other way to make it. Perhaps it was too massive, physically and spiritually, for any one person to control.

Of course, to the extent that the MACLEAN's reportage is based on facts, there can be no defense of Reid's behavior towards his fellow artists. And Allan Antliffe is absolutely right to point out that Reid missed an important opportunity to fight the inequities and stereotypes of the art world.[217]

But it is also apparent that Reid was himself the victim of a system—a system that demands that artists should look a certain way, talk a certain way, and, of course, work in a certain way. As a society, we seem to have lost any sense of diffidence when confronted with true genius. If we acknowledge its existence at all, we often think of it as something predictable and well defined, but a little observation would reveal the errors involved in this kind of complacency. If the emergence of genius were predictable, artists and authors could never rise up from disadvantaged backgrounds. In many ways, Bill Reid resisted social stereotypes. But, in this particular regard, Reid played along, intentionally or not, with society's expectations.

The modern stereotypes of artistic creation are also of questionable use to Western artists. If an artist is able to survive long enough, he or she may be able to use the system for his or her benefit, but the decision could come at a spiritual cost. Should an artist be obliged to conform to socially accepted notions of what it means to be an artist? This is bound to limit creativity.

[216] This theme is explored in depth in a fascinating and disturbing podcast episode, Julie Beauzac, *Picasso, séparer l'homme de l'artiste, Venus s'épilait-elle la chatte?*, VÉNUS: LE PODCAST (May 18, 2021), https://www.venuslepodcast.com/episodes/picasso%2C-s%C3%A9parer-l'homme-de-l'artiste.

[217] Lucianna Ciccocioppo, *On Determining Authenticity and Authorship in Art*, FOLIO (Oct. 29, 1999)..

For artists who are not so clever, or so lucky, the situation becomes more troublesome. An artist may be a visionary who is, as the expression goes, ahead of his or her time. In other words, it will take some time for society to be able to recognize the artist's worth. It often happens that an artist does not actually live long enough to enjoy the benefits of that recognition. Vincent van Gogh is the classic illustration of this paradox. The impoverished painter who sold but one painting in his entire lifetime is now the most expensive and elite name on the international art market. The delayed recognition of an artist's value reflects the inherent difficulty of perceiving the outstanding nature of the artists who live among us. The real explanation behind society's unwillingness to allow artists to break free of stereotypes may be simple ignorance. Whatever the reason, there can be little doubt that the stereotype of impoverished genius works against the artist. Sadly, it accomplishes little other than serving to justify the misery and poverty of many artists' lives in the eyes of society—thereby inhibiting any pangs of conscience that might motivate the public to try to improve their circumstances.

N. A Further Critique: Yumbulul and the Legal Paradox of Living Traditions

More broadly, where traditional cultures are concerned, their intrinsic patterns of cultural development may collide directly with modern notions of original authorship. This happened in the Australian case of *Yumbulul v. Reserve Bank of Australia*.[218] Decided in 1991, neither Australia nor any other jurisdiction has yet been able to address in its copyright law the concerns about the treatment of traditional artworks that this litigation raised.[219]

Yumbulul was an Aboriginal artist, initiated by his clan into the knowledge needed to make a ceremonial "morning star pole"—a mystical object which embodies Aboriginal knowledge of astronomy and reflects the spiritual worldview of the people who imagined it. Yumbulul was approached by the Australian government about the possibility of designing an image of a morning star pole to appear on a banknote. He agreed, but later attempted to withdraw his agreement. In fact, he was faced with the difficult prospect of displeasing his own community by allowing the Pole and the knowledge that it embodied—held as restricted and privileged by them—to be disseminated in this form. When the dispute between Yumbulul and the Australian government eventually went to court, the judge openly acknowledged the limits of copyright law, pointing out that "the question

[218] *Yumbulul v. Reserve Bank of Australia* (1991) 21 I.P.R. 481 (Austl.).

[219] Australia toyed with the idea of an "Indigenous communal moral right" in a 2001 Bill, but the law was never passed. Had it succeeded, it would have left much to be desired in clarifying Aboriginal cultural rights. *See* Chapter 4, *supra* notes 186-218 and accompanying text.

of statutory recognition of Aboriginal communal interests in the reproduction of sacred objects is a matter for consideration by law reformers and legislators."[220]

Once again, the models of creativity that support the Western copyright system fail to adapt to a different reality. Copyright law considers Yumbulul, the individual creator of this specific Pole, to be its author. The Aboriginal community has no right to intervene in an author's decision to disclose his or her own work. The community has no role in "creating" the work.

From an Aboriginal point of view, however, this insistence on individual authorship is unhelpful. The creator of the work has certain rights and privileges; so, too, does the community of which he or she is part. Cultural rules define the parameters of this relationship, and those rules may not have much in common with the rules governing copyright transactions.

In fact, the attempt to apply copyright concepts to this kind of problem is of questionable value. Copyright cannot help to clarify the nature of the rights and obligations involved, nor does copyright language really help to translate Aboriginal cultural reality into Western concepts—a process that would ultimately benefit both. Rather, copyright superimposes Western relationships and concepts onto the underlying reality of Aboriginal thought. The results are often highly incongruous. In the Yumbulul scenario, neither Yumbulul nor his Aboriginal community can have been happy with the result. The trust in the relationship was broken. In every such instance, a process of healing and rehabilitation will surely be required.

But the question of moral rights is different. The attribution and integrity interests protected by moral rights are clearly important to Aboriginal cultures in some form. Not only can they help to empower communities, if they can be adapted to reflect the symbiotic relationship between Aboriginal artists and their communities, but they can also play a role in defending Aboriginal cultures from misappropriation. This is a non-traditional use of intellectual property rights, and it also reflects an adaptation of these rights to a new cultural environment.

For Aboriginal groups, the intellectual property concept may represent, first and foremost, a threat. It can empower outsiders to lay claim to Aboriginal cultural symbols, stories, and knowledge. The danger lies in the ease with which copyright can be acquired by outsiders. Even in a post-*Feist* context, a work with a minimal level of creativity will satisfy the originality requirements for copyright protection. At the same time, Aboriginal cultural knowledge is not associated with a single identifiable author or with a group of joint authors in the copyright sense of the term. Moral rights in Aboriginal culture remain abstract until they can coalesce around an identifiable and unified entity, whether it is an individual or a group.

A possible solution to the dangers of cultural appropriation would be to recognize an Aboriginal moral right that would be vested in the community concerned.

[220] *Yumbulul, supra* note 218, at para. 20.

While the cultural work, knowledge, or tradition is in use within the community, the moral right would remain latent. In the situation where an appropriation of the work is attempted without the consent of the community, the moral right could be invoked in an action for infringement.[221]

But there are always at least two layers of transactions in these kinds of dealings. The first layer, in which Aboriginal right and newcomer's attempt confront one another, is relatively easy to address through legal measures. The second layer, however, may be completely impenetrable by Western law. It is the problem of relationships within each Aboriginal community—between different groups associated with the same cultural tradition, among the different members of a group hailing from a particular cultural tradition, and between the givers and receivers of ceremonial knowledge.

The practical difficulties of applying an Aboriginal moral right led to controversy over the provisions of the Australian government's bill on the "Indigenous communal moral right" proposed in 2002.[222] If the principle of cultural self-determination is to be upheld, Western law cannot serve to regulate relationships within Indigenous communities. And yet, there is a danger that Indigenous cultures, like every other human environment, can also become spheres of injustice where unfair claims are made, and individuals may be subject to mistreatment or exploitation. Tradition can be a two-edged sword. The fact that something has been done in a certain way "since time immemorial" does not necessarily justify the practice. To some extent, each generation reinvents tradition, and it can even be difficult to know with certainty what exactly is "traditional." Ideally, these conflicts would be resolved according to principles of fundamental justice. But who is entitled to decide what constitutes justice in cases such as these? Would it be appropriate to subject them to rulings by councils of elders or judges in Indigenous communities? And would these councils be recognized as lawmakers by Western courts? This is one of many possible compromise solutions. If moral rights are ultimately seen as a valuable framework for cultural rights, compromise, in some form or another, will be unavoidable.

O. Recommendations and Conclusion

The moral rights of artists have always been given preferential treatment in the copyright laws of Common law countries, and they are more important than ever

[221] Interestingly, this is reminiscent of how Creative Commons licenses operate: *see* Chapter 9, *infra*.

[222] Copyright Amendment (Indigenous Communal Moral Rights) Bill 2003 (Cth) (Austl.). Notably, the Indigenous moral right could be invoked only in cases where the Aboriginal artist and his or her community had entered into an agreement about the work. This clumsy attempt to forestall conflicts within communities seems utterly impractical. See the discussion in Chapter 4, *supra* notes 186-218 and accompanying text.

before in the technological environment. The rise of artificial intelligence only serves to emphasize the threats to authenticity confronting artists. While creations in all genres are affected, and human creativity overall is under threat, artists are, in many ways, in the vanguard. Generative artificial intelligence has dramatically highlighted the dangers faced by artists, and the perhaps unprecedented importance of maintaining artistic attribution and integrity in this environment. Not only are the moral rights of artists more important than ever before, but the recognition and interpretation of artists' moral rights must also be adapted to the particular challenges, concerns, and infringements made possible through technology. By doing so, a template of protection for human creativity and knowledge can be developed. Policymakers should not miss this opportunity.

The objective of protecting cultural heritage must remain in focus, alongside the human rights of artists. No lesser concerns than these can justify the imposition of restrictions on the creative use of artistic images. Technology such as artificial intelligence and 3D printing clearly translates into new dangers of misappropriation, misrepresentation, and abuse. These injustices require an adequate response from the law. Moreover, by supporting authenticity and historical truth in a fluid technological environment, moral rights also support the educational and aesthetic goals of new creative projects.

Attribution should be treated in a nuanced manner to accommodate the specific needs created by interactions with technology. Integrity rights in works of art should be carefully framed. The traditional requirements stipulated by the Berne Convention, that alterations of a work must be shown to damage an author's honor or reputation, may not be appropriate. In contrast to other kinds of creative expression, damage to a visual work may be beyond correction or redemption. As such, the extra care that can be achieved by making any modification a *prima facie* violation of the integrity right—as attempted, to varying degrees, by Canadian, U.S., Australian, Norwegian, and even Indian law (in this last case, by judges rather than legislators) —makes eminent sense. The moral right of integrity should address specific issues, including the use of artificial intelligence, the reasonable protection of good-faith conservation efforts, the evaluation of the context in which an artwork is displayed, and prohibition of the outright destruction of a work of art.

Consideration should be given to the potentially important idea that moral rights should be available to protect works of art in the public domain. As India's *Sehgal* case suggests, moral rights can make an important contribution to the protection of cultural heritage, supplementing relatively weak international agreements such as the UNESCO and UNIDROIT conventions on cultural property with a powerful legal alternative. The laws of many countries already recognize this principle by granting perpetual moral rights to artists, and to authors as well.

9

Friends or Enemies?

Moral Rights and Open Access

The writer as a writer has but one heir—the public domain.

—Victor Hugo[1]

A. **Open Access: An Alternative to Copyright** 588
B. **The Cult of Copyleft** 589
C. **Creative Commons: A Licensing System Based on Moral Rights** 592
  1. Copyright Infringement and Creative Commons: License or Contract? 593
  2. The Basic License: Attribution Affirmed 595
  3. Integrity in the Basic License 596
  4. Derivative Works: Integrity or Attribution? 596
  5. Reputation: The Heart of Open Access 598
  6. The Dark Side of Open Access: Art as a Profession in Decline 599
D. **Open Access: A Practical Need for Moral Rights** 602
E. **Collective Creation: Wikipedia** 609
F. **Freedom to Create: The Price and Promise of Copyleft Movements** 615
G. **Recommendations** 617
H. **Conclusion** 619

[1] The quote has been widely attributed to Hugo in the context of the recent French case, *Hugo v. Editions Plon*, about the right of an author to write a sequel to *Les Misérables. See, e.g.*, Kim Willsher, *Heir of Victor Hugo Fails to Stop Les Mis II: France's Highest Appeal Court Allows Modern Sequel to 1860s Masterpiece*, The Guardian (Jan. 31, 2007), http://www.guardian.co.uk/world/2007/jan/31/books.france. *See Pierre Hugo v. Editions Plon*, Cour d'appel [CA] [regional court of appeal] Paris, 1e ch., Mar. 31, 2004, 202 RIDA (Oct. 2004), *reversed* Cour de cassation [Cass.] [supreme court for judicial matters] 1e civ., Jan. 30, 2007, Bull. civ. I, No. 125 (Fr.), https://www.legifrance.gouv.fr/juri/id/JURITEXT000017627153. In his speech at the International Literary Congress held in Paris in 1878, Hugo affirmed, ("Le livre, comme livre, appartient à l'auteur, mais comme pensée, il appartient—le mot n'est pas trop vaste—au genre humain" ["The book, as a book, belongs to the author, but the thought belongs—the term is not too vast—to the human race"]. All websites cited in this chapter were last visited on August 25, 2023.

A. Open Access: An Alternative to Copyright

Throughout the digital era, copyright has become an increasingly contentious issue. As technology has made it exponentially easier to copy and share creative works, the copyright industries have resorted to increasingly desperate measures to try to preserve the economic value of what they own. Based on the current understanding of copyright law, which has not shifted fundamentally during this period, the economics of the creative industries can only be maintained by preserving exclusivity of access to creative works. However, technology presents profound, even existential challenges to this model of copyright law—and to the status quo in the creative industries. This technological upheaval has resulted in the fundamental transformation of the music industry. Film has not been far behind.

Not surprisingly, attempts by the copyright industries to control access to works in this environment have led to a powerful backlash by those who believe that access to works in this environment should be "free"—as free as free-flowing technology could potentially allow them to be in the absence of other restrictions. Open access, and the Creative Commons movement in particular, is an expression of this position.

In two respects, Creative Commons has been truly revolutionary. First, it has created a relatively simple system whereby anyone who wishes to make their work available to others can do so by means of a general license to the public. Creative Commons provides template licenses on its website, and anyone can make use of one of these model licenses to release their work to the public. When people choose to release their work under a Creative Commons license, this means that anyone can make use of it without having to ask the permission of the right holder or anticipating the need to pay any royalties. This effectively sidesteps the major usual requirements for anyone normally wishing to use a work that is still within the term of copyright protection.

Secondly, the Creative Commons licensing system has made an important contribution to the evolution of copyright in the technological context—with both positive and negative implications for authors and artists. Creative Commons licenses are built on attribution. The basic license that anyone wanting to release their work through Creative Commons can use is a license that allows anyone to use the work, without permission or payment, provided that the person attributes the work to its author. In other words, at its core, Creative Commons means a license based on the moral right of attribution. It is worth remembering that Creative Commons emerged in the United States, a country that has no general moral right of attribution for authors in its copyright law. Creative Commons licensing therefore offers something that U.S. copyright law does not—a guarantee of attribution for authors—while also dispensing with something that U.S. copyright law insists upon: payment for the use of an author's work.

Creative Commons is arguably the only true alternative to the copyright system that has emerged during the digital era. But it is sobering that Creative Commons licensing essentially forces authors to choose, at least in the United States, between earnings from their work and the right to be attributed as its author. Outside the United States, notwithstanding the hype surrounding Creative Commons—especially in its heyday earlier in the millennium—the licenses offer a convenient way for authors to give their work to the public, but they do not add anything more. The only scenario that could be considered an exception to this rule arises in a small number of countries like the United Kingdom and New Zealand, where authors must assert their moral right of attribution under the Copyright Act. In these countries, a Creative Commons license may amount to a form of assertion of the author's moral rights. Everywhere else, however, authors automatically have moral rights of attribution under their national copyright laws. They do not need a Creative Commons license to provide them with the equivalent of a moral right of attribution.

B. The Cult of Copyleft

Creative Commons is also known by the coinage Copyleft, which captures its antipathy to copyright. It was born out of the admiration of Larry Lessig, a Stanford law professor, for Richard Stallman, a pioneer of the concept of "open access" software. The key ideology underlying Copyleft can be summed up in the movement's use of the word "free."

"Free" means different things to different people. In the context of music downloads, to most members of the public, "free" means available without payment. But advocates of "free" software and "free" culture claim something more. Richard Stallman, the founder of the Free Software Foundation, defines free software as

> a matter of liberty, not price. To understand the concept, you should think of "free" as in "free speech," not as in "free beer."[2]

Larry Lessig, the founder of Creative Commons, acknowledges a profound debt to Richard Stallman in his own work, FREE CULTURE, and describes the idea in similar terms:[3]

[2] *See* GNU Operating System, *The Definition of Free Software* (n.d.), https://www.gnu.org/philosophy/free-sw.en.html.

[3] LAWRENCE LESSIG, FREE CULTURE: HOW BIG MEDIA USES TECHNOLOGY AND THE LAW TO LOCK DOWN CULTURE AND CONTROL CREATIVITY (2008). Ironically enough, the book is no longer available for free download, but it can be purchased via Amazon buttons on Lessig's website, "Amazon:supporting the Creative Commons project" or "Amazon:supporting Public Knowledge" (a third button also allows purchasers to "Support your local bookseller"): Lawrence Lessig, *Free Culture* (n.d.), https://lessig.org/product/free-culture.

> [W]e come from a tradition of "free culture"—not "free" as in "free beer" (to borrow a phrase from the founder of the free-software movement), but "free" as in "free speech," "free markets," "free trade," "free enterprise," "free will," and "free elections." A free culture supports and protects creators and innovators. It does this directly by granting intellectual property rights. But it does so indirectly by limiting the reach of those rights, to guarantee that follow-on creators and innovators remain as free as possible from the control of the past. A free culture is not a culture without property, just as a free market is not a market in which everything is free. The opposite of a free culture is a "permission culture"—a culture in which creators get to create only with the permission of the powerful, or of creators from the past.[4]

The activists behind the Creative Commons movement are, in a sense, an unlikely group—law professors—while those behind open source, or free software, are programmers. The person who remains mostly off-stage is the author. There is no real reason why the sympathies of the open access movement should tend against authors. In fact, the anger of open access movements is more properly directed at the corporate owners of copyright works, who overwhelmingly enjoy the financial rewards of copyright control. Current practice in Western copyright industries gives short shrift to the author, who is typically entitled to royalties on sales of his or her work in the range of 1–15 percent of net receipts.[5] The situation in non-Western countries is perhaps even worse. In a country like India, the featured country at the London Book Fair of 2009, authors often pay to have their work published. The fact that Indian books are increasingly of international interest has done little to alter Indian publishing practices, solidly rooted in a cultural tradition that artists do not, and should not, care about money.

Ironically enough, it is socialist countries who have most boldly acknowledged the potential for conflict between authors and publishers. A 1938 commentary on the Russian copyright law noted,

[4] Lessig, Free Culture, *supra* note 3, at xiv.

[5] The calculation of royalties is a contentious matter. There is significant variation in royalty rates depending on the type of book involved: a scholarly book might attract a royalty of 2.5 percent, while the rate for a trade book might be as high as 15 percent. Calculating the actual amount of the royalty may depend not on the list price of the book but on the amount for which it was actually sold. It is common for publishers to sell books at "deep discounts" to various buyers, including bookstores and libraries, book clubs, and other types of bulk order and special sales. On the general state of the writing profession in the twenty-first century, see Authors Guild, *Authors Guild Issues Report Exploring the Factors Leading to the Decline of the Writing Profession* (Feb. 19, 2020), https://authorsguild.org/news/authors-guild-issues-report-exploring-the-factors-leading-to-the-decline-of-the-writing-profession. A presentation by Siobhan O'Connor, Associate Director of the Writers' Union of Canada, addresses the equally (or more) troubling situation of writers in that country: Siobhan O'Connor, *The State of Writing in Canada: A Cautionary Tale* (Sept. 2022), https://authorsguild.org/app/uploads/2022/09/The-Writers-Union-of-Canada_Siobhan-OConnor.pdf.

> [It] is characteristic that, except for a small group of bourgeois authors, the author's right is the property, in bourgeois society, not of the author, but of the publisher, of a big capitalist, an industrialist .... [T]he author's right in capitalist countries is made into a tool of the interests of the monopolist-publisher, a means of exploiting the author and retarding the cultural growth of the masses of the people ....[6]

The structure of modern publishing puts the author in an awkward position. In order to enjoy any economic reward from his or her work, the author depends on sales. However, the vast majority of the money made from sales accrues to the publisher; only a small—often tiny—proportion of those receipts finds its way into the hands of the author, in the form of royalties. Without those royalties, however, the author has nothing at all. The position of authors can make them simultaneously dependent on their publishers and antipathetic to them—at once for and against free access. Not surprisingly, authors are often sympathetic to the goals of open access movements, but the problem of economic survival—to say nothing of the desire for financial success—may align them with publishers.

This point takes us back to the question of "freedom" and what it means in the Digital Age. Lessig's definition of "free" is an appealing one, as is his call for a balanced approach to copyright law. The easing of copyright restrictions makes eminent sense. But the difficult question becomes where, exactly, should the line be drawn? Open access movements offer active alternative to corporate control, and as such, their contribution to copyright discourse is important. However, the apparent absence of the author from "Copyleft" discussions is a serious deficiency. In fact, the strong stand of open access movements against the corporate ownership of knowledge is, in its own way, equally extreme. Corporations want to be overpaid for copyright works; open access wants copyright works for nothing.

The entire debate is defined, not by authorship, but by ownership.[7] Corporate interests claim to own knowledge; for the copyleft advocate, the public owns it. This is an important point. Whether or not proponents of Copyleft use the terminology of ownership, the effect of Copyleft is to confer ownership of works on the public. This is because the point of Copyleft is public access: to say that "no one" owns knowledge may not be quite enough to convey the practical thrust of

[6] *See A Text Writer's Opinion, I Grazhdanskoe Pravo (Civil Law) 254 (1938), in* MATERIALS ON SOVIET LAW 35 (John N. Hazard trans., 1947). See MIRA T. SUNDARA RAJAN, COPYRIGHT AND CREATIVE FREEDOM: A STUDY OF POST-SOCIALIST LAW REFORM 93–97 (2006) for a detailed discussion of this perspective.

[7] I am indebted to Colin Tapper for pointing out that the concept of ownership is, itself, potentially misleading when used in relation to knowledge (personal communication with the author, July 14, 2010). Nevertheless, the concept of "intellectual property" is definitely built upon the analogy between intangible knowledge and tangible property, however imperfect it may be. The purpose of the discussion here is to emphasize the contrast between the idea of "ownership" that informs intellectual property law and the concept of "authorship" as it is refers to the creators of artistic and intellectual work.

Copyleft. If no one owns knowledge, there may still be other reasons for restricting it—for example, in the case of sacred knowledge protected by cultural traditions.[8] But Copyleft is fundamentally against restricting access to knowledge. For both sides, pro and anti, the terms of the argument are accordingly defined by the practical concept of ownership.

When Copyleft writers talk about the "public interest," they are actually referring to something quite specific: the public interest in access to works. However, there is little reference to other aspects of the "public interest." Preserving the integrity of culture is surely a public interest issue; so, too, is the authenticity of knowledge. There is a public interest in encouraging artists, as Lessig notes, but in his view, that appears to be adequately recognized by providing some copyright protection.[9]

Yet—perhaps paradoxically—moral rights have quietly crept into open access movements. This chapter will examine the recognition of authors' moral rights in open access movements, with a view to answering three questions.

First, how significant is the presence of authors' moral interests in model agreements for open access licensing? Is it truly a form of recognition for moral rights? Second, what is the rationale behind the presence of moral rights in open access licenses? In particular, what are the philosophical reasons, as well as the legal explanations, for their presence? Third, does the recognition of moral rights compensate for the reduction or elimination of economic rewards to the author in the open access model? Four case studies will be considered: Creative Commons; open source software; projects for the collective creation of works, such as WIKIPEDIA; and the creation of Internet libraries, including the Google Books project.

C. Creative Commons: A Licensing System Based on Moral Rights

Acquiring the right to use a copyright-protected work usually involves two steps. First, the user must obtain permission to use the work; and secondly, the user is generally obliged to pay a fee for that use. Both factors can inhibit the creative re-use of a work, notably in scenarios involving remixing. While certain attempts to re-use a work may fall within the definition of "fair use" or "fair dealing," there is no bright line conveniently separating allowable uses from an infringement of copyright.[10] Copyright infringement is classically about the "quality" of copying

[8] *Yumbulul v. Reserve Bank of Australia* (1991) 21 IPR 481 (Austl.).

[9] Lessig, FREE CULTURE, *supra* note 3, at xiv.

[10] This can also be considered the line between fair use in the making of a derivative work or adaptation of the original work, which is generally resolved to the original author: *see, e.g., U.S. Supreme Court Agrees with Authors Guild in Fair Use Case*, THE AUTHORS' GUILD (June 6, 2023), https://authorsguild.org/news/us-supreme-court-agrees-with-authors-guild-in-fair-use-case (discussing *Warhol v. Goldsmith*, Docket No. 21-869, May 18, 2023, https://www.supremecourt.gov/opinions/22pdf/21-869_87ad.pdf, from an authors' rights point of view).

as much as the quantity.[11] In the case of works whose copyright owners are impossible to locate, often known as "orphan" works, the use of the work will not be legally possible unless there are rules allowing access to orphan works in the jurisdiction in question.

The objective of Creative Commons is to circumvent this system entirely. Creative Commons aims to promote the dissemination of works without the restrictions of copyright law. It provides an alternative to copyright protection by proposing that authors release their works under the terms of a license to the general public. The exact terms of the license vary according to a number of possible models provided by Creative Commons, and examples may be seen on the Creative Commons website.[12]

All Creative Commons licenses aim at the common goal of allowing any person to use a work without permission or payment. However, the Creative Commons use of a work is not entirely free of conditions. A closer examination of the Creative Commons licenses reveals the presence of the author in a new and interesting form.

1. Copyright Infringement and Creative Commons: License or Contract?

The general license to the public generated by Creative Commons operates very much like a contract between private parties, which can override the terms of copyright law. For example, a copyright statute might provide that the initial copyright in a work is owned by an individual's employer, known in the United States as "work-for-hire," or the employment rule in other common-law countries.[13] But an individual's contract of employment may provide that the employee retains copyright in his or her own work. This contractual arrangement would prevail.[14] In the case of the Creative Commons licenses, should the new user of the work fail to respect the conditions of use specified in the license to the general public, he or she will become liable for infringing the copyright in the original work.

Copyright infringement is a means of enforcing the Creative Commons license. While the terms of the license are respected, it is an action held in reserve. Once an

[11] See, e.g., the judgment in *Ladbroke (Football) Ltd v. William Hill (Football) Ltd* [1964] 1 WLR 273 (UK).

[12] *See* Creative Commons, *Licenses List* (n.d.), https://creativecommons.org/licenses.

[13] See Copyright Act, R.S.C. 1985, c. C-42, s. 13.3 (Can.), https://laws-lois.justice.gc.ca/eng/acts/c-42, which states, in part,

> Where the author of a work was in the employment of some other person under a contract of service or apprenticeship and the work was made in the course of his employment by that person, the person by whom the author was employed shall, *in the absence of any agreement to the contrary*, be the first owner of the copyright. [Emphasis added]

[14] And, as noted id., the formulation of work for hire and of the employment rule is framed accordingly.

improper use of the work is made—a use that is not allowed under the terms of the license—the license is invalidated, and copyright infringement can be invoked by the author of the original work.

The relationship between Creative Commons licenses and contracts is considered in the 2008 case of *Jacobsen v. Katzer.*[15] The court interprets the terms of the license as equivalent to the "conditions" of a contract, which are therefore binding upon those who make use of the work. Judge Jeffrey S. White comments,

> Thus, if the terms of the Artistic License allegedly violated are both covenants and conditions, they may serve to limit the scope of the license and are governed by copyright law. If they are merely covenants, by contrast, they are governed by contract law.[16]

The court goes on to offer a detailed analysis of the Creative Commons framework for software, explaining how the economic and moral elements of the license work together to accomplish important practical goals:

> The clear language of the Artistic License creates conditions to protect the economic rights at issue in the granting of a public license. These conditions govern the rights to modify and distribute the computer programs and files included in the downloadable software package. The attribution and modification transparency requirements directly serve to drive traffic to the open source incubation page and to inform downstream users of the project, which is a significant economic goal of the copyright holder that the law will enforce. Through this controlled spread of information, the copyright holder gains creative collaborators to the open source project; by requiring that changes made by downstream users be visible to the copyright holder and others, the copyright holder learns about

[15] *Jacobsen v. Katzer*, 535 F.3d 1373 (Fed. Cir. 2008), *remanded*, 609 F. Supp. 2d 925, 89 U.S.P.Q.2d 1441 (N.D. Cal. 2009), settled Feb. 16, 2010 (U.S.).

[16] Id. at 1380. The case was settled on February 19, 2010, and drew the comment: "Th[e] … Terms [of the settlement] can include an affirmative obligation of a commercial developer to 'give back' its own changes to the code for the benefit of others. They invariably also include an obligation to acknowledge the authorship of those that had created the earlier code." *See* Andy Updegrove, *A Big Victory for F/OSS:* Jacobsen v. Katzer *Is Settled*, ConsortiumInfo (Feb. 19, 2010), https://www.consortiuminfo.org/intellectual-propery/intellectual-property-rights/a-big-victory-for-f-oss-jacobsen-v-katzer-is-settled/. See also the comment by Ashley West, *Little Victories: Promoting Artistic Progress through the Enforcement of Creative Commons Attribution and Share-Alike Licenses*, 36(4) Fla. St. Univ. L. Rev. 903, 913 (footnotes omitted) (2009), who notes that,

> After the Federal Circuit released the Jacobsen opinion, the technology blogosphere praised the decision, announcing that the judicial system had finally given a definitive answer that public licensing regimes are enforceable as a matter of law. Part of this enthusiasm likely stemmed from the simple fact that Jacobsen was the first case to specifically discuss the Creative Commons movement in a significant way.

the uses for his software and gains others' knowledge that can be used to advance future software releases.[17]

2. The Basic License: Attribution Affirmed

According to the terms of a Creative Commons license, someone who wants to use a work released under the license must meet one fundamental condition: the new user must credit the creator of the original work.[18] The Creative Commons attribution license cannot cancel the copyright in the original work. The statutory copyright remains as an underlying right of the author. Instead, the license suspends the operation of copyright.

Under the attribution license, if someone were to use the work without attributing it to the original creator, the user could be sued for copyright infringement. Copyright becomes a fall-back position—it implicitly serves to enforce the terms of the Creative Commons license.

A closer look at the attribution license reveals something else interesting: the license represents a total rejection of copyright restrictions. Any use can be made of a work released under this license, including commercial uses. So, for example, a photograph released under the attribution license could be used in a commercially released documentary or feature film. But the profit from the film would go exclusively to its producers; the person making the photograph would have no claim on any earnings from the project. This would be the case regardless of how significant the image was—even if it were central to the successful marketing of the film, for example, appearing on publicity posters. But the condition of attribution remains, and attribution must be made according to the terms set out by the original author.[19]

Attribution is the foundation of moral rights, and as such, the attribution license could be called a "moral rights" license for the use of the work. It is a license that protects the author's right of attribution without imposing any financial obligations on the user, or providing economic rewards to the author. Creative Commons also states that "No warranties are given. The license may not give you all of the permissions necessary for your intended use. For example, other rights such as publicity, privacy, or moral rights may limit how you use the material."[20]

In other words, and with particular reference to countries where the author enjoys moral rights under the copyright statute, the attribution license explicitly operates in addition to the existing legal framework for the protection of authors'

[17] *Jacobsen*, *supra* note 15, at 1382.

[18] *See* Creative Commons, *supra* note 12.

[19] See the explanation at the Creative Commons website: Creative Commons, *CC by 4.0 Deed: Attribution 4.0 International* (n.d.), https://creativecommons.org/licenses/by/4.0.

[20] Id.

moral rights. If the copyright law of a country offers extensive protection for moral rights, the attribution license is merely reinforcing the law. But, in the case of a country where moral rights are not well protected, the Creative Commons license may offer moral rights protection that is not otherwise available in this form—for example, in the United States.

This situation presents a contrast to the author's economic entitlement under copyright law, which the author effectively "contracts out of" by the attribution license.

3. Integrity in the Basic License

But Version 4.0 of the basic license, in contrast to earlier iterations, also has implications for integrity. It states,

> You must give appropriate credit, provide a link to the license, and indicate if changes were made. You may do so in any reasonable manner, but not in any way that suggests the licensor endorses you or your use.[21]

This right is a kind of "attribution of integrity," and it allows the authenticity of the work to be preserved by keeping a record of changes. This, again, looks very similar to the practices of programmers.

Prohibiting the making of changes would be equivalent to a pure moral right of integrity, unlike the moral right of integrity in Article 6*bis* of the Berne Convention: it would protect the work from alteration without reference to the creator's reputation. This Creative Commons license does not prohibit alterations, but it does impose a standard of "reasonable[ness]" on what the user may do with the work. It is not clear what exactly this might mean from a legal standpoint, but it is possible to speculate that changes like those in the *Deckmyn* case[22]—creating discriminatory associations by re-purposing the work, a violation of basic human rights in Europe—could be caught by this provision as an "unreasonable" use.

4. Derivative Works: Integrity or Attribution?

Creative Commons licenses build upon each another in consecutive steps, each group more restrictive than the last. Based on the attribution concept, the second

[21] Id.

[22] Case C-201/13, *Deckmyn v. Vandersteen*, ECLI:EU:C:2014:2132 (Sept. 3, 2014), https://eur-lex.europa.eu/legal-content/EN/TXT/?uri=CELEX%3A62013CJ0201, discussed in Chapter 1, *supra* notes 117–28 and accompanying text.

level of license provides, first, for a "share- alike" principle. Should an author create a new work out of the creative re-use of an existing work, the new work will need to be released under the same type of Creative Commons license as the original work.[23] At the same level, a second, "attribution noncommercial" license prevents anyone re-using the work from doing so for commercial purposes.[24] This license is noteworthy because of its considerable restrictiveness: any subsequent use of the work which leads to commercial gain, whether intentionally or accidentally, would invalidate the license, placing the user of the work in a situation of potential copyright infringement.

In terms of the moral right of integrity, the third license in this group adds a "no-derivatives" principle to the attribution license. Under this license, no person should *make public* a derivative work based on the original work, although private uses of the work remain, of course, at the user's discretion. The Creative Commons group explains:

> If you remix, transform, or build upon the material, you may not distribute the modified material.[25]

At the next level, two types of licenses can be found. The first combines attribution with the principles of noncommercial use and the need to "share alike"—to allow the use of the new work only on the same terms as the original work.[26] Secondly, a more restrictive version of the "no-derivatives" license includes this rule alongside noncommercial use.[27] This license is said to provide "free advertising" for the creator of the original work, as it allows the work to circulate freely in noncommercial contexts, provided that attribution of the author is maintained and the work itself is not altered.

The principle of restricting the creation of derivative works includes within it the integrity right, which would prohibit alterations to the original work in certain circumstances. But the no-derivatives principle is both larger and more general than the integrity right. It completely prohibits the making of derivative works for public circulation, even where the derivative creation might not violate the integrity of the original work. At the same time, it cannot protect a work from minimal interventions that will not result in the outright creation of a new, ostensibly "derivative," work. Only in cases where the alteration of the work is so extensive as,

[23] Creative Commons, *CC by-SA 4.0 Deed: Attribution-ShareAlike 4.0 International* (n.d.), https://creativecommons.org/licenses/by-sa/4.0.

[24] Creative Commons, *CC by-NC 4.0 Deed: Attribution-NonCommercial 4.0 International* (n.d.), https://creativecommons.org/licenses/by-nc/4.0.

[25] Creative Commons, *CC by-ND 4.0 Deed: Attribution-No Derivatives 4.0 International* (n.d.), https://creativecommons.org/licenses/by-nd/4.0.

[26] Creative Commons, *CC by-NC-SA 4.0 Deed: Attribution-NonCommercial-ShareAlike 4.0 International* (n.d.), https://creativecommons.org/licenses/by-nc-sa/4.0.

[27] Id.

in effect, to create a new work, *and that new version is seen by the original author as unfavorably modified*—the Monty Python scenario[28]—will the integrity right and the no-derivatives principle be truly equivalent. This additional factor for the moral right, that modifications to the work must be seen as negative by the author—or, depending on the jurisdiction, that they must be "objectively" harmful to the author's reputation or "honor"—is what differentiates the moral right of integrity from the no-derivatives principle. There is a qualitative element in the moral rights determination that may not be applicable in the no-derivatives context.

As in the case of the attribution right, any statutory moral rights will continue to exist alongside the no-derivatives principle. Once again, given the international use of Creative Commons licenses, the persistence of statutory moral rights is important. Even if the user of the work did something less dramatic than the creation of a derivative work, but altered the original work—for example, sharing a piece of music with one of the stanzas of a song removed—this could potentially qualify as a violation of the moral right of integrity. The integrity of the work would be violated even though a derivative work would not necessarily have been created by removing the single stanza from the song.

The close relationship between derivative works and the integrity principle is important in U.S. law, and there is every reason to interpret Creative Commons licenses with this legal culture in mind. However, as this discussion seeks to show, the "no-derivatives" idea is a distorted reflection of the moral right of integrity. In fact, the real significance of the restriction on making derivative works lies in the consideration that derivative works must traditionally be authorized by the copyright-holder. In Creative Commons, the "no-derivatives" idea is not just a species of integrity right; it is also related to economic copyright.[29] Its purpose is to allow the author to control what is done with the work, an economic right under U.S. copyright law.

5. Reputation: The Heart of Open Access

The presence of attribution and "no-derivatives" requirements in the Creative Commons model amounts to a form of recognition for moral rights. The attribution principle occupies a central role in Creative Commons licenses. As for the principle of "no derivatives," it could be considered an extremely specialized form of the integrity right, but it should also be recognized as a manifestation of the attribution principle. In addition, Creative Commons licenses specifically allow moral rights, as defined by copyright laws, to coexist with the licenses. In contrast,

[28] *Gilliam v. American Broadcasting Companies*, 538 F.2d 14 (2d Cir. 1976) (U.S.), https://casetext.com/case/gilliam-v-american-broadcasting-companies-inc.

[29] *See, e.g., Jacobsen, supra* note 15.

under a Creative Commons license, the author chooses to "opt out" of his or her economic rights at copyright law.

Why does Creative Commons build its licensing system around moral rights principles, rather than simply providing for works to be available without an attribution requirement? At some level, and in spite of its populist rhetoric, Creative Commons is paradoxically preoccupied with authorial control. An overall consideration of the components of Creative Commons licenses suggests that, seen in context, the requirement of attribution, like the "share-alike" and "no-derivatives" principles, aims to promote the individuals behind the creation of works. In particular, all three principles accomplish the same goal: they affirm the author's right to control his or her own work.

The formulation of the attribution right in the Creative Commons attribution license offers an interesting illustration of this principle. Not only is the author's attribution protected, but the author also chooses the method by which he or she wants to be attributed. While moral rights statutes do provide for authors to choose to be anonymous, or to use pseudonyms, Creative Commons goes even further than this.

But the type of author imagined by Creative Commons is a specific kind of individual. Entrepreneurial and tech-savvy, the Creative Commons author is, above all, an amateur. Notwithstanding Lessig's idealistic definition of "free," embracing the goal of "Free Culture" in practice means forfeiting the opportunity to be paid for one's work. None of the Creative Commons licenses provide for payment for the uses of a work. Name—in other words, reputation—is everything; money is nothing. Creative Commons therefore cannot be a comprehensive solution to the problems of excessive copyright protection. It is a solution for those who do not need or want to earn money from their work.

What happens to authors and artists in a world where they have to choose between corporate control over their works through the copyright system, and the "free" distribution of their works, with credit and some measure of guaranteed control, through Creative Commons? The answer is obvious: academia. It is the ideal Creative Commons career. Academics earn a salary independent of earnings from publications or other public manifestations of their work and thereby enjoy the luxury of being able to afford to distribute their work to the public free of charge. At least, law professors do.

6. The Dark Side of Open Access: Art as a Profession in Decline

What happens when intellectuals and artists can no longer expect to be paid for their work? Two consequences follow. First, artists will cease to be "professionals." Being unable to earn a living from creative work means that the artist must earn his or her living by some other means. The lucky ones might come from independently wealthy families. For others, the ubiquitous "day job" can guarantee a double life to look forward to—the tension of a lifetime spent in struggle to find the time to do what the artist wants to do and, perhaps, what he or she does best.

But making intellectual creation "free" does something even larger: it negates society's principal method of recognizing value. Money is the means by which society acknowledges value, whether that value arises in things, labor, or information. No doubt, it is a flawed system for assigning value. How flawed is it?

The classic example of how money valuation is misdirected in the cultural arena is to point out that a work of mass culture will generate more money than a work of art. But in fact, it is probably more accurate to say that the life cycles of these two kinds of works are different. A popular work generates its returns in the initial period of its publication, but a work of art generates its revenues over the long term. As Ernest Hemingway commented, "Good books always make money eventually."[30] Van Gogh's paintings were worthless during his lifetime, but he is now the highest grossing artist of all time.[31] F. Scott Fitzgerald's novel, The Great Gatsby, did not sell out its original print run; it is now considered one of the greatest works in English of the twentieth century and is currently in print in new editions. The fact remains: money is the principal method by which society recognizes value. It is not the only one, and, when it comes to culture, there are other ways of showing appreciation—for example, creating a new work, in homage or in parody, or helping to publicize work that deserves an audience. But it is not clear that any alternative can provide a totally adequate substitute for money. To remove money valuation altogether from creative works is to create an instant bias against the recognition of their value by society.

And why should the person who is capable of intellectual creation be deprived of money because he or she happens to have the misfortune of an intellectual gift in lieu of business capital? George Bernard Shaw claimed that a true artist could never be happy doing anything for a living but art.[32] However, throughout most of human history, this is exactly what artists have had to do. Turning the clock backwards, and finding ourselves in any European capital some 200 years ago, we could have witnessed this story playing itself out in the lives of artists who have since become famous—musicians like Mozart and Beethoven, writers like Jane Austen or Voltaire. Franz Schubert was famously torn between his living as a schoolteacher

[30] Ernest Hemingway, Green Hills of Africa 23 (1935).

[31] *See, e.g.*, Kelly Grovier, *Klimt's Lady with a Fan: The Painting That Sold for £85.3m*, BBC News (June 27, 2023), https://www.bbc.com/culture/article/20230621-klimts-lady-with-a-fan-the-painting-thats-valued-at-65m; *The Art Gems That Broke the Bank*, BBC News (June 19, 2006), http://news.bbc.co.uk/2/hi/entertainment/4883296.stm. The issue is discussed in Chapter 1, *supra* note 18 and accompanying text. The art market is explored in the brilliant film, *The Price of Everything* (Nathaniel Kahn dir., 2018).

[32] "The true artist will let his wife starve, his children go barefoot, his mother drudge for a living at seventy, sooner than work at anything but his art": George Bernard Shaw, Man and Superman: A Comedy and a Philosophy (1903), http://www.gutenberg.org/files/3328/3328-h/3328-h.html.

and his work as a composer. There is a psychological theory that inner conflict such as this produces great art. But the reality can be painful, even cruel.

Indeed, prior to the Romantic era, the means of sustenance for artists were few. Those who were successful sometimes came from aristocratic families; more often, their talents won favor for them from a wealthy patron, a king or a duke who was willing to support them, if only for a time. Independence was a luxury that few artists could afford.

Patronage provided a poor infrastructure for intellectual life. With the expansion of mass culture in the nineteenth century, many intellectuals were understandably eager to entrust themselves to the public for their livelihood.[33] Experiences could be bitter—Friedrich Schiller's faith in the public led to disappointment and bankruptcy[34]—but the alternatives were equally unsatisfactory in their own ways.

Looking further afield, in both space and time, we can consider the history of India. The birthplace of a number of the world's great intellectual and artistic traditions, Indian culture developed a highly formal relationship between intellectual and material wealth. Intellectuals and artists earned a livelihood from their work, but they did so largely by indirect means. Tradition compelled the wealthy and worldly castes to provide financially for their educators and learned men.

By separating intellectual work from money, Creative Commons is therefore not proposing anything truly new. Without providing an alternate system for the support of creative individuals, however, the movement leaves a fundamental question unanswered. How does society intend to support the creation of culture? If the marketplace will not support artists, who will? Is it time for a new system of patronage, perhaps in the form of state support? After all, if society can go so far as to claim "co-authorship" of creative works, as at least one commentator has suggested, does society not have a corresponding obligation to provide financial support?[35] And if so, should the support not be generous, to free an artist for intellectual life, in every sense, from all extraneous demands? In the absence of market opportunities to sell his or her work, what would be the use of a pension that allows an artist less than what he or she needs to survive, and, in this new scenario where works would be available free of charge, would deprive him or her of any chance at financial stability?

The question of artistic livelihood leads to another, troubling consideration: how can an artist or intellectual build material stability if society prevents it? In contrast

[33] In India, the experience was felt into the twentieth century: Tamil Renaissance poet C. Surbramania Bharati satirized his experiences at the court of the Ettayapuram Maharaja (and the Majaraja himself) in the delightful short novel, CHINNA SHANKARAN KATHAI [THE STORY OF LITTLE SHANKARAN].

[34] *See* CALVIN THOMAS, THE LIFE AND WORKS OF FRIEDRICH SCHILLER 71 (2004) (1901) (describing the experience as Schiller's attempt to live as a "literary free-lance who served no prince, but only the public").

[35] *See* Roberta Rosenthal Kwall, *The Author as Steward "For Limited Times,"* 88 B.U.L. REV. 685 (2008)—a review of LIOR ZEMER, THE IDEA OF AUTHORSHIP IN COPYRIGHT (2007).

to a person who is able to amass material property, the profit from an artist's creation is taken away by society, apparently for the general benefit. No one takes away the property of a landowner or the assets of a businessperson. In the worst case, it is taxed. But the bulk of it remains, supporting the entrepreneur throughout his or her life and, for some period afterwards, his or her descendants. This is not considered to be detrimental to society. Rather, the accumulation of capital is seen as a positive achievement in most modern democracies—one that benefits society by "creating wealth" and "creating jobs."

On the other hand, the value that could be generated out of an artist's work does not evoke a comparable response. Art, it is said, belongs to society; sooner or later, it enters the public domain. Yet, the effect of rendering artists' works into the public domain means that they are deprived of their own livelihood—their own "assets." And, certainly, they have no chance of leaving anything for their families in the form of an inheritance. An artist's family is condemned to eternal poverty—unless at least some of his or her descendants learn how to do other things.[36] Each generation has to begin over again and cannot build on the achievements of its ancestor—they are deemed to be public property. But the heirs of businessman are generally considered to be "entitled" to their wealth and the social advantages that it secures.

It is easy to forget that a person with purely intellectual or creative capabilities may have nothing else of equal value to contribute to society. Yet, society considers itself the rightful owner, and the rightful beneficiary, of what he or she creates. What is the fundamental difference between property and creative work? The capacity to exclude—society can take away the product of an artist's mind, so it does. It cannot do the same to an entrepreneur, a businessman who makes money. It is difficult to remove property, to confiscate money without the owner's consent. And if conflicts escalate, the owner has the resources to compel the law to his or her side—to launch suits, to propagate his or her point of view through the use of his material resources, to advertise and generate publicity on his or her side. An artist, who lacks material resources, cannot command the same things from society. This is the dark side of "open access"—the dispossession of human beings.

D. Open Access: A Practical Need for Moral Rights

The history of copyright law is a curiously poetic one. Poetry lies in the means, if not in the end: copyright is built on the development of analogies.[37] Each form of copyright protection is accepted because it is somehow akin to previously known

[36] Pierre Hugo, a great-great-grandson of Victor Hugo, who brought suit against Francois Cérésa for his sequels to *Les Miserables*, is apparently a goldsmith by trade. *See* Willsher, *supra* note 1.

[37] Poets played an important role in the impetus behind the Statute of Anne, and leadership on international copyright law was famously provided by Victor Hugo, who was instrumental in the adoption of the Berne Convention: *see* Chapter 2, *supra* notes 89–91, 109–21 and accompanying text.

forms—film grows out of photographs; music, like literature, is also a form of written expression.[38] The protection of computer software, widely debated in its early history, was no exception to this rule. Software eventually became subsumed under one of copyright's metaphors—after all, computer programs are written forms of intellectual expression, "like" literary works.

But there is nothing inevitable about copyright protection for software. Through the early 1990s, a number of alternative approaches to software were debated.[39] Software might be patentable as a scientific invention, or it might be entitled to a new form of protection, a system of *sui generis* rights, reflecting its own novelty.[40] An important possibility remained the option of no "protection" at all—free and unrestricted access to software. When copyright won out, it represented a victory for major players in this burgeoning industry, such as the Microsoft Corporation, who would enjoy the benefits of automatic and extended protection for their works. Established software designers stood to benefit; for new companies and would-be innovators, copyright protection introduced new restrictiveness to what had previously been an open playing field.

When copyright protection for software was accepted, it seems natural that alternative regimes for rights in software should have died a natural death. In fact, this did not happen. The persistence of other approaches probably reflects the dissatisfaction generated by a premature attempt to resolve the software conundrum. Alternative approaches to the recognition of software as a new form of intellectual creation remain. If anything, they have gained strength with the passage of time. They coexist alongside copyright protection, raising interesting questions about the nature and extent of intellectual rights in software, and the consequences of restricting growth in this crucially important field.

Alternatives to copyright protection share the common intuition of a poor fit between software as a new form of intellectual creation and the conventional principles of copyright law. Patents in software respond to this concern by introducing protection that is both more specialized and more limited than copyright. They can protect the specific aspects of software associated with the functions of programs, without crippling further development.[41] In contrast, copyright could impose

38 Canadian history on this issue is instructive. A 1968 case found that a musical broadcast did not infringe copyright because the true copyright work was not the music but the written score of the music. Canada's copyright law was subsequently amended to include a definition of music that accepted both the written score and the music itself as subject to copyright protection. *See Capac v. CTV Television Network* [1968] S.C.R. 676, 68 D.L.R. (2d) 98 (Can.).

39 In fact, Colin Tapper points out, "the argument about whether copyright or patent was most appropriate for software was at its height in the 1960s" (personal communication with the author, July 14, 2010). He observes that "the debate was closer then because it pre-dated the personal computer, and the software in issue was system software (normally in machine code)."

40 *But see* Jane C. Ginsburg, *Four Reasons and a Paradox: The Manifest Superiority of Copyright over* Sui Generis *Protection of Computer Software*, 94 Colum. L. Rev. 2559 (1994). Ginsburg is skeptical about the possibility.

41 In addition, Colin Tapper notes (in personal communication with the author, July 14, 2010) that

> ... the main advantage of patent as a means of protecting software is that it allows the idea (or aim) of the software to be protected given that software is so versatile that the same effects can

large-scale protection on computer programs, restricting features that should be generally available for the development of the technology. In the landmark ruling of State Street Bank, a U.S. court found that software could be patented as a "business model" under U.S. law, unleashing a spate of new precedents granting patents in software.[42] At the same time, patent protection is subject to the rigors of registration and review before it can be granted, and the duration of protection never exceeds twenty years, as compared to copyright's seventy.[43]

However, the possibility of patent protection for software has met with a perhaps insurmountable obstacle—the formalization of copyright protection for software in international regulation.[44] In particular, the Agreement on Trade-Related Aspects of Intellectual Property Rights (TRIPs Agreement) provides that computer programs must be recognized as copyright works by the member countries of the World Trade Organization (WTO). In an important phrase, TRIPs specifies that they should be protected "as literary works."[45] No distinction is made between computer programs and other types of literary works. The implication is that any and all rights enjoyed in literary works will be available for computer programs as well. In most of the member countries of the WTO, with the notable exception of the United States, this classification implies that the moral rights of authors must be recognized in computer programs, as in all other literary works.

In terms of patent rights, TRIPs involves serious limitations. If computer programs must be protected as literary works under copyright law, how can software patents be recognized? Will they exist as an additional form of protection for a program alongside copyright in the work? There is no prohibition in intellectual property law or theory against the coexistence of different types of intellectual property rights in a single work; but this option always raises the possibility of excessive protection for a given type of intellectual creation.[46] Indeed, concerns

be created by any number of different sequences of instructions in any number of different software systems.

[42] *State Street Bank & Trust Co. v. Signature Financial Group, Inc.*, 149 F.3d 1368 (Fed. Cir. 1998) (U.S.).

[43] Copyright term for software in the United States is currently seventy years from the date of making. The term of copyright protection was extended in 2002, and a constitutional challenge, arguing that the extended term contravened the limits on copyright in the U.S. Constitution, failed in 2003: *Eldred v. Ashcroft*, 239 F.3d 372 (3d Cir. 2001), *aff'd*, 537 U.S. 186 (2003) (U.S.), http://www.law.cornell.edu/supct/html/01-618.ZS.html. of the U.S. Const. art. I, § 8, cl. 8 states, "The Congress shall have power … to promote the progress of science and useful arts, by securing for limited times to authors and inventors the exclusive right to their respective writings and discoveries."

[44] *See* Ginsburg, *supra* note 40, at 2–3.

[45] *See* Art. 10.1 of the TRIPS Agreement: Agreement on Trade-Related Aspects of Intellectual Property Rights, opened for signature Apr. 15, 1994, entered into force Jan. 1, 1995, Annex 1C to Marrakesh Agreement Establishing the World Trade Organization, 1869 U.N.T.S. 299, 33 I.L.M. 1197 (1994), https://www.wto.org/english/docs_e/legal_e/27-trips_01_e.html.

[46] For example, the Canadian Supreme Court addressed the question of overlapping trademark and copyright protection in what is widely known as the case of the chocolate bar wrappers: *Euro-Excellence Inc. v. Kraft Canada Inc.* [2007] 3 S.C.R. 20, 2007 SCC 37 (Can.).

about excessive restrictions on software led to the rejection, in 2005, of a proposal for the recognition of software patents in the European Union.[47]

Open access stands in direct opposition to intellectual property rights in software. But open access movements also share something interesting with copyright: a moral dimension to their views. In the case of open access, the moral argument can mean two things. The first is a moral perspective in the largest sense of the term: many proponents of open access believe that it is morally wrong to restrict access to a technology of such importance to society. Richard Stallman, the founder of the Free Software Foundation, is the leading advocate for the moral imperative of access to software.[48] His comments on the different connotations of copyright for books and software are instructive:

> The copyright system was created expressly for the purpose of encouraging authorship. In the domain for which it was invented—books, which could be copied economically only on a printing press—it did little harm, and did not obstruct most of the individuals who read the books....
>
> The case of programs today is very different from that of books a hundred years ago. The fact that the easiest way to copy a program is from one neighbor to another, the fact that a program has both source code and object code which are distinct, and the fact that a program is used rather than read and enjoyed, combine to create a situation in which a person who enforces a copyright is harming society as a whole both materially and spiritually; in which a person should not do so regardless of whether the law enables him to.[49]

But, secondly, open access also recognizes certain interests that resemble, at least superficially, the moral rights of authors in the literary and artistic context. The interests of attribution and integrity are present in the terms of open access software, both in the Free Software Foundation's GNU license and beyond. No doubt, this assertion would be rather unpopular with Stallman himself, who includes a rebuttal of the natural rights basis of "ownership" in his essay, *Why Software Should Not Have Owners*:

> Authors often claim a special connection with programs they have written, and go on to assert that, as a result, their desires and interests concerning the program simply outweigh those of anyone else—or even those of the whole rest of the

[47] For a summary of the positions surrounding the proposed European Software Patents Directive, see *Software Patents Bill Thrown Out*, BBC News (July 6, 2005), http://news.bbc.co.uk/1/hi/technology/4655955.stm. An analysis of the problems from an open source perspective is provided by Heather J. Meeker, *The Fuzzy Software Patent Debate Rages On*, Linux Insider (Feb. 23, 2005), https://www.linuxinsider.com/story/the-fuzzy-software-patent-debate-rages-on-40676.html.

[48] *See* http://www.fsf.org.

[49] Richard Stallman, *The GNU Manifesto*, GNU Operating System (n.d.), http://www.gnu.org/gnu/manifesto.html.

> world. (Typically companies, not authors, hold the copyrights on software, but we are expected to ignore this discrepancy.)[50]

But Stallman's critique of natural rights theories of authorship approaches the issue with a blunt tool rather than a finely tuned instrument. His analysis of natural rights raises three major issues. First, the analogy between a work and material objects is, indeed, overstretched, as natural rights theory would argue that the damage resulting from the mistreatment of one's work is fundamentally different from material harm. The concept of moral harm is not well developed in common-law countries, but it is a foundation of civil law systems.[51] Secondly, the point that authors are not the main beneficiaries of the copyright ownership is noted by him, but the role of authors' natural rights as a counterweight to the interests of the copyright-owner is not discussed. Finally, his analysis is quite United States-centric. What about the role of natural rights theories in other copyright systems of the world, which are author-focused in a way that U.S. law is not? Do natural rights of authorship lead to unethical situations, in Stallman's terms, in those cultural contexts?

[50] Stallman goes on to comment,

> To those who propose this as an ethical axiom—the author is more important than you—I can only say that I, a notable software author myself, call it bunk.
>
> But people in general are only likely to feel any sympathy with the natural rights claims for two reasons.
>
> One reason is an overstretched analogy with material objects. When I cook spaghetti, I do object if someone else eats it, because then I cannot eat it. His action hurts me exactly as much as it benefits him; only one of us can eat the spaghetti, so the question is, which one? The smallest distinction between us is enough to tip the ethical balance.
>
> But whether you run or change a program I wrote affects you directly and me only indirectly. Whether you give a copy to your friend affects you and your friend much more than it affects me. I shouldn't have the power to tell you not to do these things. No one should.
>
> The second reason is that people have been told that natural rights for authors is the accepted and unquestioned tradition of our society.
>
> As a matter of history, the opposite is true. The idea of natural rights of authors was proposed and decisively rejected when the U.S. Constitution was drawn up. That's why the Constitution only permits a system of copyright and does not require one; that's why it says that copyright must be temporary. It also states that the purpose of copyright is to promote progress—not to reward authors. Copyright does reward authors somewhat, and publishers more, but that is intended as a means of modifying their behavior. The real established tradition of our society is that copyright cuts into the natural rights of the public—and that this can only be justified for the public's sake.

See Richard Stallman, *Why Software Should Not Have Owners*, GNU OPERATING SYSTEM (n.d.), http://www.gnu.org/philosophy/why-free.html.

[51] *See* P.R. Handford, *Moral Damages in Germany*, 27(4) INT'L COMP. L.Q. 849, 851 (1978) (remarking that, "The civil law offers a refreshing contrast to the common law, not only because of its wholehearted acceptance of claims for injury to feelings and other non-pecuniary loss, but also because of its orderly appearance in comparison to the patchwork quilt of the common law."). This was also the initial problem in the *5Pointz* case, leading to the denial of a preliminary injunction: the court felt that material damages could ultimately compensate the artists for the destruction of their work. *See Castillo v. G&M Realty L.P.*, Nos. 18-498-cv (L), 18-538-cv (CON), 2020 U.S. App. LEXIS 5228 (2d Cir. Feb. 20, 2020), https://www.mintz.com/sites/default/files/media/documents/2020-03-25/18-498_amd_opn.pdf (the *5Pointz* case), discussed in Chapter 8, *supra* notes 53–57 and accompanying text.

In fact, the Free Software movement recognizes attribution, integrity, and disclosure; but it recognizes them in precise and narrow forms. Attribution of the author of software may help to protect the integrity of source code. Knowing who has made given modifications can help to identify and correct problems. Stallman confirms:

> It is also acceptable for the license to require that, if you have distributed a modified version and a previous developer asks for a copy of it, you must send one, or that you identify yourself on your modifications.[52]

This right of attribution is not focused on the author per se. Rather, its objective is to protect the "work"—in this case, software—for the good of the community that uses and enjoys it, works with it, and, very possibly, attempts to improve it.[53] It is akin to a right to protect the integrity of a work of art for the sake of cultural heritage—the rationale of the Indian court in the *Amar Nath Sehgal* case.[54]

The person working with software also has the right to choose whether or not he or she will release those changes publicly—a classic statement of the right of disclosure.[55] There is an interesting contrast here between the apparent rejection of authorship as it confers any special privileges on the individual programmer, and the right to maintain control over your own modifications. "Freedom" apparently does not include the right to have access to other people's modifications of software. Stallman also makes another concession to authorship in his comments on the "motivations" behind free software: professional reputation and the admiration of one's fellows are recognized motives behind the making of free software.[56] These are exactly the same human drives underlying the moral rights of attribution and integrity.

In relation to software, Stallman's concept of "free" essentially has to do with the fact that the software is nonproprietary in nature. In describing the fundamental differences between free software and open source, Stallman comments,

> For the free software movement, free software is an ethical imperative, because only free software respects the users' freedom. By contrast, the philosophy of

[52] Richard Stallman, *What Is Free Software?*, GNU Operating System (n.d.), http://www.gnu.org/philosophy/free-sw.html.

[53] Although, in keeping with the principle of "freedom," any modification is allowed, even if it may not amount to an "improvement" in the next person's opinion: id.

[54] *Amar Nath Sehgal v. Union of India*, 2005 (30) PTC 253 (Del H.C.) (India).

[55] *See* Stallman, *supra* note 52: "You should also have the freedom to make modifications and use them privately in your own work or play, without even mentioning that they exist. If you do publish your changes, you should not be required to notify anyone in particular, or in any particular way."

[56] "To be admired. If you write a successful, useful free program, the users will admire you. That feels very good. Professional reputation. If you write a successful, useful free program, that will suffice to show you are a good programmer": Richard Stallman, *Motives for Writing Free Software*, GNU Operating System (n.d.), http://www.gnu.org/philosophy/fs-motives.html.

> open source considers issues in terms of how to make software "better"—in a practical sense only. It says that nonfree software is an inferior solution to the practical problem at hand. For the free software movement, however, nonfree software is a social problem, and the solution is to stop using it and move to free software.[57]

On the other hand, commercial uses of free software are accepted, and even encouraged, as long as the software that is sold continues to be "free"—amenable to modification and distribution at the will of the user. Many models of open access or open source software exist, and one approach is to restrict the right of a user to use the software for commercial purposes.

From a "free software" perspective, this issue is not important, as it is the right to use software freely that is really at the heart of this movement. Indeed, the preference for publishing software through "Copyleft" models of licensing over simply releasing software into the public domain is due to the desire to prevent software from becoming anyone's property. In the "Copyleft" scenario, anyone who attempts to convert the software into intellectual property will be legally liable for two things: breaking the terms of the software license, which he or she accepted when he or she acquired the software, and, potentially, violating the "author's" copyright in the software. As Stallman comments,

> Copyleft says that anyone who redistributes the software, with or without changes, must pass along the freedom to further copy and change it. Copyleft guarantees that every user has freedom.
>
> Copyleft also provides an incentive for other programmers to add to free software. Important free programs such as the GNU C++ compiler exist only because of this.[58]

This reliance on the Copyleft model again makes the attribution and integrity interests important. Attribution is needed because of copyright's dependence on an author to sue; integrity is needed in order to examine what kind of unauthorized use has occurred and whether it would qualify as an infringement of copyright in the work. In particular, it would be important to show unauthorized appropriation, use, or the creation of an "unauthorized" derivative work. The threshold will be low; practically any evidence of modification will do, but some evidence must be offered.

The appearance of moral rights in alternative models of software regulation comes as a surprise. However, the practical relevance of moral rights to the needs

57 *See* Richard Stallman, *Why Open Source Misses the Point of Free Software*, GNU Operating System (n.d.), http://www.gnu.org/philosophy/open-source-misses-the-point.html.

58 Id.

of software is immediately apparent. A right of attribution can preserve accountability and access to help when problems arise; it can also protect useful knowledge and build community by drawing attention to the accomplishments of highly skilled and creative programmers. The integrity principle also has something to contribute to software. Preserving the integrity of code helps to develop knowledge while protecting subsequent users from problems such as flaws, errors, or sabotage.

Moral rights also reflect certain philosophical parallels with the free software and open software movements. The integrity principle can offer practical support to the goals of these movements. In the case of free software, it could prevent proprietary treatments of code; and, in effect, Stallman's concept that the conversion of free software into property would violate its moral integrity, in the larger sense of the term, finds ready sympathy in the moral right of integrity recognized in much of the world. Once again, this approach to integrity finds parallels in a right for the protection of cultural heritage. It is not so much an author-focused right as a work-focused principle.

Nevertheless, the author, too, makes an appearance in free software and open software movements. Reputation matters. The needs of programmers may be different from those of artists, but that does not make the claims of artists unreasonable. Rather, as Stallman himself notes, the nature of their work is different. In the creation of software, attribution can support the needs of authorship; but the nature of the medium demands a willingness to change and be changed. Without the ability to change what comes before, to build upon it in freedom and without fear of limitation, a meaningful software community might cease to exist. The drive towards further development is a reality of all forms of human knowledge, but the degree of flexibility required, and the intensity of the intervention, will vary according to the nature of the work. If the need to intervene creatively in a work of classic literature could be colored a soft pearl grey, the software environment presents the case of a brilliant fuchsia. Where software is concerned, intervention is the key to innovation.

E. Collective Creation: Wikipedia

Collective creation is a fascinating new opportunity made possible through technology. The Internet facilitates an unprecedented level of human cooperation, uniting people across vast distances who may never have been able to work together in the absence of technology. The work might be undertaken anonymously or in an explicit partnership—by a small group of collaborators or a large community worldwide.

WIKIPEDIA illustrates the latter case. The ubiquitous online encyclopedia was built almost entirely on the contributions of the general public, who initiated the coverage of new topics or modified existing entries in order to correct and improve their content.[59] The founders of WIKIPEDIA also hoped that this phenomenon would ultimately expand into languages other than English, an ambition that has been realized on a vast scale.[60]

Online collaboration can take many forms. Music offers a number of interesting examples. South Indian classical music is now taught in the United States by teachers in India who may never have travelled by plane.[61] Musicians from Western and non-Western traditions build artistic collaborations online, holding workshops and performances, exploring and developing new forms of musical expression.[62] These developments were intensified by the challenges of the Covid era. The creative possibilities are broad. They hint at a world of new potential for the development of culture through technology.

To return to the example of WIKIPEDIA, what is the legal status of contributors? Under the terms of copyright law, they are authors. They write the texts that form the basis of WIKIPEDIA entries, and, according to universally recognized principles of copyright law, the low level of originality required of a text writer would almost certainly be met by contributions to WIKIPEDIA.[63] Small modifications to

[59] *But see* Alex Krotoski, *Liberty, Wikipedia and a Voice for All*, BBC BLOG (July 21, 2009), http://www.bbc.co.uk/blogs/digitalrevolution/2009/07/liberty-wikipedia-and-a-voice.shtml. For an update on Wikipedia's shifting approach to its content, see, e.g., Joe Pinsker, *The Covert World of People Trying to Edit Wikipedia—For Pay*, THE ATLANTIC (Aug. 11, 2015), https://www.theatlantic.com/business/archive/2015/08/wikipedia-editors-for-pay/393926.

[60] For a list of non-English Wikipedias, *see* https://en.wikipedia.org/wiki/List_of_Wikipedias#:~:text=Non%2DEnglish%20editions%20were%20soon,currently%20active%20and%2013%20closed. The diversity of entries in these alternative versions is an interesting question. *See e.g.* https://en.wikipedia.org/wiki/Tamil_Wikipedia (on the growth of the Tamil language Wikipedia). The history behind these goals is discussed by Emma Barnett, *Jimmy Wales Interview: Wikipedia Is Focusing on Accuracy*, THE TELEGRAPH (Nov. 17, 2009), http://www.telegraph.co.uk/technology/wikipedia/6589487/Jimmy-Wales-interview-Wikipedia-is-focusing-on-accuracy.html. WIKIPEDIA is generally considered reliable but also biased (even by its own assessment): *see, e.g.*, Liam Mannix, *Evidence Suggests Wikipedia Is Accurate and Reliable. When Are We Going to Start Taking It Seriously?*, SYDNEY MORNING HERALD (Sept. 13, 2022), https://www.smh.com.au/national/evidence-suggests-wikipedia-is-accurate-and-reliable-when-are-we-going-to-start-taking-it-seriously-20220913-p5bhl3.html; Wikipedia, *Reliability of Wikipedia* (n.d.), https://en.wikipedia.org/wiki/Reliability_of_Wikipedia.

[61] The South Indian school of classical music is called Carnatic music, while the North Indian branch is known as Hindustani. Both schools represent a common system of music with different styles, scales, and instruments. Teaching of Carnatic music in the United States is done via Skype—the free online software that allows Internet users to call each other from their computers by audio only or by video and audio transmission. The U.S. connections made by Carnatic artists are widely publicized in India.

[62] See, e.g., the interesting discussion of cross-cultural musical conversations in Gary Giddins, *A Passage to India: Rudresh Mahanthappa Chooses a Heritage*, THE NEW YORKER (Mar. 2, 2009), https://www.newyorker.com/magazine/2009/03/02/a-passage-to-india. The article is among the first publications outside India to draw attention to the remarkable talent of South Indian saxophonist Kadri Gopalnath (now deceased) and his brilliant group, including leading violinist, A. Kanyakumari. On Kadri's career (from a Western perspective), see Giovanni Russonnello, *Kadri Gopalnath, 69, Dies; Brought the Saxophone to Indian Music*, NEW YORK TIMES (Nov. 4, 2019), https://www.nytimes.com/2019/10/31/arts/music/kadri-gopalnath-dead.html.

[63] It seems likely that this would be the case whether the jurisdiction in question recognized the "sweat of the brow," labor-oriented standard of creativity in classic cases such as *University of London Press v. University Tutorial Press* (1916) 2 Ch. 601 (Eng.) and *Ladbroke (Football) v. William Hill (Football)* 1964 1 All E.R. 465 (UKHL); the higher requirement of "skill and judgement," in *CCH Canadian Ltd v. Law Society of Upper Canada* [2004] 1 S.C.R. 339 (Can.) and *Eastern Book Co. and ors*

existing text might not qualify for copyright protection but larger changes and, of course, new contributions, would. However, these contributions are made in the foreknowledge that they will be subject to change. The integrity of the original contribution cannot be maintained—that was never intended to be the case. The very purpose of the contribution is to make something available to others for modification.

These circumstances could place WIKIPEDIA in an ambiguous situation in countries where moral rights of attribution and integrity are recognized—something that is especially relevant to WIKIPEDIA's global expansion. If there are restrictions on an author's ability to waive moral rights, as in France and Germany, the potential problem of an author who want to assert rights of attribution and integrity could threaten the viability of this resource.

The persistence of moral rights in a technological context whose very objective is to transcend the limits of individual authorship seems like a strange anomaly. If policymakers in countries with strong moral rights wish to encourage technology-based collaborations on the WIKIPEDIA model, they should consider modifying the legal limits on waivers. For example (as is often done), a three-step test could be established. The criteria could be anonymity, the expectation of unlimited modification, and the goal of general public access. In these circumstances, an author might be said to have agreed to suspend his or her moral rights in relation to a given project.[64]

The terminology of "suspension" seems to be a more accurate reflection of what should happen in the WIKIPEDIA context than a "waiver" of rights. Waiver suggests that rights exist but are set aside. In the WIKIPEDIA context, however, it seems that authorial involvement falls entirely outside the scope of moral rights. To put it another way, you, as the contributor of text to WIKIPEDIA, are not, in any meaningful sense, the *author* of that text. Instead, the *author* is a collective entity, made up of the efforts of individual contributors, who is effectively a being which is greater than the sum of its parts. Analogies could be drawn with the recognition of Indigenous cultural creation or cultural heritage discussed in Chapter 8. On this surprising terrain, the old and the new meet.

Notwithstanding these arguments, it is also clear that the concepts of attribution and integrity may also be relevant to WIKIPEDIA. Attribution of contributors could help to establish that a particular piece of knowledge is authoritative—for example, a person with specialist or insider knowledge of a given subject may be in a position to make a valuable contribution to a WIKIPEDIA entry. At the same

v. DP Modak and anor, 2008 (36) PTC 1, 2008 (1) SCC 1 (India); or the "modicum of creativity" in *Feist Publications, Inc. v. Rural Telephone Service Co.*, 499 U.S. 340 (1991) (U.S.).

[64] WIKIPEDIA editors can still be those who contribute anonymously or regular editors who are identified through the system. For a discussion of the editing process and ongoing changes to it, see Barnett, *supra* note 60.

time, attribution for special contributors would probably go against the ethos of WIKIPEDIA, which is democratic in the purest sense of the term. WIKIPEDIA relies upon the contributions of the general public, and its audience is the general public, which seeks out information or knowledge on a particular subject.

One approach to the attribution problem might be to adopt a simple, cosmetic solution. Individual authors could be attributed by WIKIPEDIA—for example, in a list of contributors to a particular page, to which any person modifying the page could add his or her name—while the possibility of removing or modifying another person's name could be excluded.

This leads to a second point—the importance of maintaining the integrity of an information resource like WIKIPEDIA. Here, too, the problem presents a fundamental challenge to the philosophy underlying this public encyclopedia. Inaccurate information online is a serious problem, and the reach of WIKIPEDIA means that this resource, without proper oversight, could become a significant source of public misinformation.

A third point should also be noted. Moral rights are not not only held by the contributors to WIKIPEDIA; they are also enjoyed by many of the people who become the subjects of WIKIPEDIA entries. Notably, moral rights are important where individuals are engaged in creative or other work that attracts copyright. Inaccurate information could damage an individual's reputation—or "honor." Inappropriate comments about a person's work or personal life could amount to violations of the subject's moral rights of integrity or reputation.[65]

From a moral rights perspective, collective creation along the lines of WIKIPEDIA presents a fundamental challenge. Collective works are a dramatic demonstration of work whose essential purpose is to receive and modify texts provided by others. WIKIPEDIA offers a more open model of knowledge than even free software. In the case of software, the nature of the medium demands the freedom to modify preexisting works, and all models of nonproprietary software—free or open, commercial or nonprofit, pure or hybrid—rely on open access to at least some part of the

[65] This is a fine legal point. As noted by the court in the U.S. case *Shostakovich v. Twentieth Century-Fox Film Corp.*, 80 N.Y.S.2d 575 (N.Y. Sup. Ct. 1948), *aff'd*, 87 N.Y.S.2d 430 (N.Y. App. Div. 1949), modification of the work is usually a precondition to a finding that integrity has been violated. False information or reviews of a work could arguably qualify as a form of direct "modification"; perhaps for this reason, the French law recognizes a specific right against excessive criticism, although it is now a part of French personal law rather than the Intellectual Property Code. *See* GEORGES MICHAÉLIDÈS-NOUAROS, LE DROIT MORAL DE L'AUTEUR: ÉTUDE DE DROIT FRANÇAIS, DE DROIT COMPARÉ ET DE DROIT INTERNATIONAL paras. 168–70 (1935); LAW AND THE GORBACHEV ERA: ESSAYS IN HONOR OF DIETRICH ANDRÉ LOEBER 287–89 (Donald D. Barry ed., 1988). Comments about one's personal life do not violate the integrity of the work, but they may affect one's personal reputation; a moral right of reputation would be violated, but not the moral right of integrity. In relation to WIKIPEDIA misinformation, a notorious incident in 2005 involved the falsification of journalist John Siegenthaler's biography, discovered by him four months after it was first posted: see the comment by Charles Cooper, *Perspective: Wikipedia and the Nature of Truth*, CNET NEWS (Dec. 2, 2005), https://www.cnet.com/culture/wikipedia-and-the-nature-of-truth. Since then, false information online has become a much more serious and pervasive problem.

code embedded in the software.[66] But in the case of WIKIPEDIA, the text cannot exist without the freedom to modify it. The underlying philosophy is that collective efforts will gather enough knowledge, expertise, and commitment to arrive at largely correct information: the phenomenon of "crowdsourcing."[67] The principle of preserving the integrity of knowledge would then become self-executing through the law of averages.

This is an idealistic vision. In the technological context, it is a hope that must be treated with skepticism. The myth of modern media as nondiscriminatory is dead. On the contrary, in the age of artificial intelligence, media are rife with bias, and the incentives to spread misinformation (for some) are strong. In the AI context, bias is imported from the works used in training AI systems. It is also recognized that bias may inevitably arise in the minds of editors and contributors to entries, and from the self-selection or self-reinforcement of those who participate in "collective" endeavours online. The idea of the Internet as a space with truly democratic potential is long gone. It has been replaced by a predatory, commercial, and outright dangerous reality. Writing in 2010, Jaron Lanier was already arguing that Internet collectivism suppresses individuality and encourages the development of a mob-rule mentality.[68] Reviewing his book for the NEW YORK TIMES, Michiko Kakutani writes,

> Lanier sensibly notes that the "wisdom of crowds" is a tool that should be used selectively, not glorified for its own sake. Of Wikipedia he writes that "it's great that we now enjoy a cooperative pop culture concordance" but argues that the site's ethos ratifies the notion that the individual voice—even the voice of an expert—is eminently dispensable, and "the idea that the collective is closer to the truth." He complains that Wikipedia suppresses the sound of individual voices, and similarly contends that the rigid format of Facebook turns individuals into "multiple-choice identities."

Lanier's is not an isolated voice. An earlier and controversial book by Andrew Keen complained of the Internet's creation of a "cult of the amateur," where the quality of knowledge and skill are no longer valued. The book touched a nerve in the open access community; among other reactions, it received a bitter response from Larry

[66] Colin Tapper notes (in personal communication with the author, July 14, 2010) that "modification can be accomplished either by access to source code or object code (the route from the former to the latter is no more than the application of another program, a compiler)," and he observes that "the more skilled the programmer the more he will choose to modify object code so as to achieve precisely the result that is sought."

[67] Julia Angwin & Geoffrey J. Fowler, *Volunteers Logoff as Wikipedia Ages*, WALL STREET JOURNAL (Nov. 27, 2009), https://www.wsj.com/articles/SB125893981183759969. WIKIPEDIA gives its own current—and more optimistic—assessment, summarizing shifting opinions over the years: Wikipedia, *Predictions of the End of Wikipedia* (n.d.), https://en.wikipedia.org/wiki/Predictions_of_the_end_of_Wikipedia.

[68] *See* JARON LANIER, YOU ARE NOT A GADGET: A MANIFESTO (2010).

Lessig.[69] For all its flaws—among other things, Keen is not as clear as he should be on what he means by "amateur"—the book raises some valuable questions about the future of culture. If anything, the strident reaction to it seems to lend support to his theory. Keen might be wrong; but why not consider the points that he raises? If the wisdom of the crowd is truly better, why not let it prove itself in action?

It is a truism that few technologies in the world are inherently good or evil. Rather, the use that is made of technology will give it its moral character.[70] New technology offers tremendous hope for improving the conditions of life in many parts of the world—the excitement of bringing information and education to remote places like those in rural India, for example, helping to empower the lives of poor people. However, technology also serves increasingly destructive ends, exploiting the vulnerabilities of individuals and destabilizing social institutions, threatening democracy and the rule of law. What will we decide to use it for?

It is rumored that WIKIPEDIA is moving towards a more hierarchical structure, with increased editorial supervision of its pages. If so, then one of the reasons for this shift is clearly concern for the integrity of WIKIPEDIA's entries.[71] The popularity of WIKIPEDIA may also be declining among users, who complain of overzealous editing.[72] The general vulnerability of WIKIPEDIA to virtual "vandals" who deliberately post misinformation or advertising is also a concern.[73] As early as 2009, Julia Angwin and Geoffrey J. Fowler had already noted that the culture of WIKIPEDIA was in transition:

> Wikipedia contributors have been debating widely what is behind the decline in volunteers. One factor is that many topics already have been written about. Another is the plethora of rules Wikipedia has adopted to bring order to its unruly universe—particularly to reduce infighting among contributors about write-ups of controversial subjects and polarizing figures.[74]

Developments in an increasingly challenging environment for information will determine whether the WIKIPEDIA ethos ultimately succeeds or fails. At the least, it is clear that its pure-democracy vision, a naïve remnant of an earlier technological era, has been significantly watered down over time. Every modern idealist should save one sigh for WIKIPEDIA.

[69] *See* Lawrence Lessig, *Why I Want to Run*, LESSIG BLOG ARCHIVES, https://archives.lessig.org/indexb827.html?p=3388.

[70] Something that needs to be remembered as AI technology develops: see the extensive discussion in Chapter 5 *supra*.

[71] A premature declaration of U.S. Senator Ted Kennedy's death is one example: *see* Angwin & Fowler, *supra* note 67.

[72] These editors are known as "deletionists," and the rate at which new contributions were deleted in 2010 was one out of four, as compared to one out of ten in 2005: *see* id. *See also* Wikipedia, *Deletionism and Inclusionism in Wikipedia* (n.d.), https://en.wikipedia.org/wiki/Deletionism_and_inclusionism_in_Wikipedia.

[73] *See* Angwin & Fowler, *supra* note 67.

[74] Id.

F. Freedom to Create: The Price and Promise of Copyleft Movements

Copyleft movements have been quick to grasp two fundamentals of the technological era. First, it is not practical to restrict every act of copying with a view to monetizing each transformation of a work.[75] The example of the music industry proves how difficult, polarizing, and ultimately unsuccessful such a strategy would be.

Secondly, it is not right to restrict access to works. Access to knowledge has been a painful battleground throughout much of human history, and restricting knowledge has been a universal tactic of oppression. The digital era signifies nothing less than an opportunity to break fundamentally with our past. Ignorance may be the single root cause of human conflict. But the power of technology can spread knowledge to disadvantaged groups in every society and to virtually every corner of the world. In a sense, realizing the truth of human interdependence is no longer an esoteric dream of *yogis* seeking spiritual enlightenment; it is now obvious. The importance of improving education through technology can hardly be overstated. It may be the key to our survival as a species.

But the goal of technology should be to connect human beings—not to replace human relationships with the relationship between man and machine. This would only deepen our growing alienation from our physical and spiritual environment, a process that was prophetically explored by E.M. Forster in an early short story, *The Machine Stops*.[76] Information can be spread through technology; but education depends on the ability of human beings to communicate with each other about the significance of that information and its place in our lives. Behind every piece of knowledge, culture, or entertainment is at least one human being. The emphasis on "free" culture in the open access movements seems to negate the existence of that person.

In fact, culture can almost never be "free" in the sense of "free of cost." Culture represents the efforts of human beings. Notwithstanding the role of social or historical forces, the human person remains essential to the act of creation. Medieval thought considered the author a "vessel" for inspiration, and modern criticism seems to see

[75] As noted by Hector L. MacQueen, *The Google Book Settlement*, 40(3) Int'l Rev. Intell. Prop. Competition L. 247, 249 (2009).

[76] First published in 1909, the story has now become ubiquitous: E.M. Forster, *The Machine Stops* (1909), https://www.cs.ucdavis.edu/~koehl/Teaching/ECS188/PDF_files/Machine_stops.pdf. As noted elsewhere in this book, the parallels between the degradation of the environment and the global degradation of culture are well worth exploring. The loss of biodiversity is strikingly matched by a worldwide loss of linguistic diversity. In the words of researcher Anthony Aristar, "When a language dies, it's just the same as when a species dies. You lose a part of the network of life, and you lose everything it could impart." On the loss of Indigenous languages, see United Nations Department of Economic and Social Affairs, *Protecting Languages, Preserving Cultures* (n.d.), https://www.un.org/en/desa/protecting-languages-preserving-cultures-0. The issue receives an interesting analysis in Anthony Löwstedt, *Loss of Language, Loss of Soul*, Vienna Review (Mar. 1, 2009).

the author as a "channel" of social forces. But the author is still present, and it is the author's life that must be invested in order to create awork. Without the author, there is nothing.

The humanity of the author must be recognized. When the image of the author rises before our eyes, it is not appropriate to talk only of state policies and economic priorities. We must turn to language that can express human priorities. The survival of the author—full-time or part-time, professional or amateur, but above all, as a creative being—is a human right.

From a legal perspective, there is nothing particularly radical about the idea of an author's human right. It falls within the classical definition of human rights: individual rights arising from human characteristics that are universally shared, including, in this case, the potential for intellectual and creative activity. In the digital era, human beings are subject to new kinds of treatment. Through the mediation of technology, our position in the world is different. Human identities are affected by the collection and communication of personal data and information; human personalities are implicated in the development of digital media; human creative expression is influenced by new instruments for the creation and communication of our work. The digital world created by human beings is an ever-widening spider's web of amazing complexity. The spider at the center remains, spinning its web, but it is becoming increasingly difficult to see.

In the world of new technology, the fragility of the human personality makes it urgent to protect human rights. The digitization of an author's work initiates a vast pool of ripple effects involving the transformation and re-transformation of the work for new media contexts, including artificial intelligence. Without the work, technology has nothing to work upon; once a work enters into the technological circuit, however, the link between the work and its human creator becomes increasingly remote. The author becomes a mere "content provider," and the value of an author's work is increasingly defined by what technological re-mixing can achieve with it. The intrinsic value of the work is of secondary interest: its "value" is determined by what technology can make of it and whether society will buy it. The utter degradation of the human creator in this scenario is something that should be universally rejected, in part, with the help of the law.

Our technological era is already generating new human rights. The possibility that Internet access should be recognized as a human right has been widely explored, and, since the COVID-19 pandemic, the idea has come to be generally accepted .[77] The rise of artificial intelligence should generate a new understanding of human rights, including the need to distinguish between human-created and artificially-generated information, texts, images, sound, and performances.[78]

[77] *See, e.g.*, Article 19, *UN: Human Rights Council Adopts Resolution on Human Rights on the Internet* (July 15, 2021), https://www.article19.org/resources/un-human-rights-council-adopts-resolution-on-human-rights-on-the-internet.

[78] See the discussion in Chapter 5, *supra*.

The human right of the author is a perfect example of "respect [for] the fundamental rights and freedoms of natural persons" in this new environment. A creator's human right could help to balance technological developments and social needs with the prerogatives of individuals. A creator's human right could be framed as a right to create work with the intention of forming and maintaining a human connection to the world. By this formula, works that are primarily generated by technology can be readily distinguished from work that includes a significant component of human creativity. The moral rights of the author are an established form of legal recognition for the relationship between an author and his or her own work. As such, rights of attribution, integrity, and, as appropriate to the digital environment, disclosure could provide the basis for defining a digital human right of creativity.[79] The purpose of the right would be to protect the integrity of the human personality behind every work—a new need in the technological context—for the benefit of both creators and the public.

A human rights approach could help to elevate the problems of authorship in the technological environment to a new level of seriousness. However, the conceptual appeal of human rights also has some profound practical disadvantages. International human rights law suffers from vagueness and subjectivity. It can be notoriously difficult to agree upon human rights norms. They can be difficult to enforce. Attempting to define moral rights at a higher degree of abstraction, as required by human rights instruments, could ultimately harm, rather than help, the interests involved. But it may still be useful to employ human rights language to talk about moral rights within the copyright framework. Invoking the terminology of human rights could help to clarify that the problems of creative authorship involve issues of human integrity and infuse discussion about them with humanitarian ideals.

G. Recommendations

Open access movements generally recognize the importance of moral interests. These movements are ideologically diverse, but in all of them, moral rights seem to emerge out of practical concerns about maintaining the integrity of the open source environment. The language of natural rights of authorship is explicitly—perhaps disingenuously—rejected by the free software community, but the Copyleft community makes use of it.

Indeed, moral rights are fundamental to Copyleft. The examination of Copyleft models in this chapter leads to a striking conclusion. Not only should moral rights

[79] The right is analogous to the "right to create," or *droit de créer*, which has occasionally been recognized as a part of the moral rights package. Strömholm is skeptical, but a case for the right as a way of recognizing an author's right to free speech is made by Sundara Rajan, *supra* note 6, at 218–24, 228–31.

be recognized in the digital environment, but their recognition should also be expanded in two important ways. First, as access to knowledge comes to be recognized as a human right, a corresponding human right of creators should be established. Moral rights can provide the foundational principles of such a right—disclosure, attribution, and integrity. Moral rights can also provide the proper practical framework: the doctrine behind moral rights firmly excludes the possibility of corporate ownership or possession. They are personal rights of an author, dependent on the presence of a human being to invest them with meaning, and to exercise them. The recognition of a human creative right is important, not only to protect authors and their works, but also to shield society as a whole from the consequences of losing contact with its own humanity. Intellectual life is an intrinsic part of human existence. Technology cannot replace culture; a machine cannot replace a human being.

The second area of growth for moral rights may, surprisingly, carry them into the area of economic rights. Much of the attitude of open access movements is based on the idea of "free" access. While the free software movement and Creative Commons both emphasize the importance of freedom in an ideological sense, in practice, the Creative Commons licensing system also implies freedom from payment.[80] In this sense, the model of "free" use has its appeal and purposes. But it does not respond to the problem of how to maintain artistic professions or, in a more fundamental sense, how to establish social value for intellectual creation in the absence of an economic valuation.

Historically, intellectuals have often been an impoverished group. Given this reality, the denial of economic benefits to authors seems like nothing other than a new form of oppression. It is cultural oppression, and it perpetuates stereotypes—the impoverished artist at work in his or her attic studio, caring little for the pleasures of the world—that can implicitly justify the oppression.[81]

In a more just society, some economic value would be guaranteed to an author who made a work of quality. It would last for his or her lifetime and, in order to provide capital for future generations, beyond it—perhaps, as Mark Twain argued, for at least the lifetime of the author's children. At this point, it might make sense to release the work to the public for free use. But in an ideal society, both intangible wealth and material capital should probably be released into the public domain for the benefit of society. Needless to say, such a change, however worthy, would be much more difficult to bring about than a few adjustments to the law of copyright!

[80] Or the connection is presumed. The distinction between the two meanings of "free" is easily noted in French, through the use of two separate words to signify these separate ideas: "*gratuity*," for free of charge; and "*libre*," for the larger idea of freedom. The distinction is appreciated by Stallman, who offers a list of translations of the expression "free software" into an amazing array of languages and makes use of these terms on his website: Richard Stallman, *Translations of the Term "Free Software,"* GNU Operating System (n.d.), http://www.gnu.org/philosophy/fs-translations.html.

[81] No doubt there are artists who fit this model. The argument here is that it should not be imposed on all artists.

Both the substance and the language of copyright should evolve to meet these concerns. Copyright law should be meticulous in distinguishing between the author of a work and the owner of rights in it—once again, a clarification favored by the moral rights tradition. It should also distinguish between human and machine creation.

In the technological context, it is clear that the right of disclosure, in both its moral and economic dimensions, has acquired a new importance. The one right that can be definitely controlled by the author is the initial publication of the work. This initial release in digital form should perhaps generate the bulk of the author's earnings from the work. The problem of works appreciating in value over time could then be dealt with as in the artist's resale right (*droit de suite*), by levying an author's royalty as a small percentage of the sale price on subsequent transactions. An author's royalty could also be processed more easily through collective licensing schemes .

H. Conclusion

At least superficially, open access movements and moral rights have important points in common. Both represent fundamentally anti-corporate approaches to creativity. Each focuses on human rights in its own way—for open access movements, the (immediate) rights of the public; for moral rights, the right of the author. To an extent, the two frameoworks also share a preoccupation with culture—though any false equivalence between the two perspectives should be carefully avoided. Moral rights protect culture by maintaining the connection between the human personality and creative work. Copyleft seeks to promote its own vision of culture by encouraging people to use and re-use works to create new works.

Both models have value, but the culture that emerges from each will be different. Even Copyleft recognizes that there are limits to "creative destruction:" with no sense of preservation at all, even the "free" culture of Copyleft cannot exist. This probably explains the migration of moral rights ideas into Copyleft, which recognizes attribution and integrity as important, even foundational principles.

In the technological environment, the relationship between author and public has been transformed. Unlike the hierarchies of the past, communication and exchange occur with a potential for equality and direct access made possible by technology. At different times, individuals may find themselves at different points in the cycle of creativity, sometimes using, sometimes shaping, and sometimes creating work. Technology has invited many people to discover the author within themselves. It has promised a new world of creativity.

How far has this promise been realized? The prospect of "free culture" heralded by Creative Commons—inspired by software and eagerly transplanted to the soil of the creative arts—has been accompanied by a hollowing out of the creative professions. Since the onset of the digital era, Creative Commons licensing has presided over a steady decline in the livelihoods of most authors and artists. The rise of artificial intelligence now threatens to expand and accelerate this process to a degree that was previously unimaginable. Will our experience of "remix culture" enable us to approach this new environment with greater agency, skepticism, and determination than we had in the early days of the technological revolution? Have we learned the lessons of the past?

10
Conclusion
Moral Rights in the Age of Artificial Intelligence

This exploration of moral rights in the world's legal systems reveals a robust and flexible doctrine. Moral rights are universally accepted around the world. They have come to be included in the laws of countries representing diverse cultures and legal traditions, from common law to civil law, and developing to post-socialist jurisdictions. The presence of moral rights has also encouraged the blurring of these distinctions between legal systems—a generally beneficial trend that has enriched the modern understanding of copyright law and policy.

The international acceptance of moral rights has ultimately been accelerated by the curious marriage of the Berne Convention for the Protection of Literary and Artistic Works and the Agreement on Trade-Related Aspects of Intellectual Property Rights (TRIPs Agreement). Article 6*bis* of the Berne Convention serves as a moral rights template for many countries; TRIPs requires Berne membership, and adherence to the terms of the Berne Convention by WTO member states, but it also excludes moral rights from the dispute-settlement mechanisms at the World Trade Organization (WTO).

In spite of this ambiguity in the international copyright system, moral rights have now spread their wings across a wider swathe of the world's countries and cultures than ever before. It is ironic that this has occurred in spite of the exclusion of moral rights from WTO dispute settlement. In fact, moral rights have achieved their greatest expansion ever in the post-TRIPs era. This is true, not only because more countries recognize moral rights than ever before, but also because common-law countries, which have historically been reluctant to adopt moral rights, have all chosen to include them in their copyright laws.

Indeed, the twenty-first century expansion of moral rights in the common-law countries is a striking development. The common-law countries deal with moral rights in many different ways. As ever, the United States is the most restrictive jurisdiction, recognizing moral rights only for artists and *not* authors, and its courts have pared back common-law doctrines that once stood in for moral rights in the U.S. legal system of the past. However, technological analogues to moral rights, such as digital rights management, which primarily focuses on identifying copyright ownership, have flourished in the United States. The Music Modernization Act, whose aim is to create a comprehensive database of rights information for musical works, brings fresh support, albeit indirectly, to the foundational moral rights concept of attribution. The award of large damages to artists suing for their moral rights in the United States has also brought greater prominence to moral rights, and respect for them—though the irony of respecting moral rights for their economic consequences should be noted. Although the United States remains the country where the recognition of moral rights is most limited, that recognition, when it is effective, can lead to exceptionally strong practical consequences.

In contrast, comprehensive protection for authors and artists in Australia has been achieved, but that protection remains subject to "reasonableness" requirements that are widely present in Australian law.[1] Australia's ambition to develop a new kind of moral right adapted to Aboriginal culture remains, for now, beyond reach. The continued evolution of Australian moral rights in this regard seems both desirable and increasingly possible in the light of a more receptive cultural and political climate for Indigenous rights. Uniquely among prominent jurisdictions, Ireland has rejected the nebulous concept of "honor," perhaps making its provision on the moral right of integrity more transparent, efficient, and up to date than elsewhere. However, this interpretaion of the integrity right may also make Ireland's law the narrowest provision of this kind in the world. By eliminating honor, Irish law may fail to touch the heart of what moral rights represent.

Canada, the only common-law country with a significant French tradition, seems confused and somewhat skeptical about moral rights. But India, another common-law country with a mixed heritage—including contact with French and even Portuguese law—has made use of its palimpsest of laws to emphasize moral rights. Its position arguably reflects the underlying vibrancy of Indian cultural heritage, and the great emphasis placed by Indian judges on the compassionate, remedial, and sometimes highly active role of the courts in law-making. The practical difficulty of access to justice for Indian authors and artists is tempered by a balance of rules and judicial interpretations that may shift the balance in their favor once their complaints actually reach the ears of judges.

Around the world, the trajectory of moral rights has been one of spectacular growth. Countries that are technologically advanced have extended moral rights to new technologies, from computer programs to collaborative works such as databases and film. Those that are rich in traditional culture have explored the extension of moral rights to Indigenous cultural traditions, folklore, and even inanimate features of the natural landscape that are culturally significant, such as rivers and mountains. Moral rights have been treated as an aspect of freedom of speech and thought in countries emerging from political oppression. As noted previously, not all of these experiments have led to successful law reform; but there can be little

[1] *See Copyright Act 1968* (Cth) (Austl.), https://www.legislation.gov.au/C1968A00063/2019-01-01/text, at ss 195AA and 195AB, 195ABE and 195ABE, 195AR and 195AS, 195AXD and 195AXE (and the nature of identification in s 195 is itself the right to "be identified by any reasonable form of identification").

doubt that the worldwide trend is towards greater acceptance of moral rights, and greater flexibility and nuance in the understanding of the moral rights doctrine than ever before.

Britain's separation from the European Union (EU) also raises a fascinating possibility, though it remains entirely theoretical at this stage—that the EU may attempt to harmonize moral rights in the future. Should it do so, this will certainly become one of the most significant developments in the history of copyright law since the adoption of the Berne Convention. In the light of technological developments, including the special challenges to authorship posed by artificial intelligence (AI), the EU should arguably brave this experiment. Harmonizing moral rights could add relevance and power to Europe's treatment of AI. The EU AI Act has been adopted in advance of AI regulation in any other jurisdiction in the world. This nascent regulatory regime is built on the foundational principles of human safety and dignity. Moral rights could connect it with the deeper cultural and humanistic priorities represented by the doctrine. The EU is ideally placed to test the theory that moral rights, an idea born in the heart of continental Europe, may be uniquely equipped to shape our relationship with technology, and with each other, in the age of AI.

The expansion of moral rights has invariably been accompanied by introspection, and the doctrine has often resurfaced in new forms. While the general principles of attribution, integrity, and disclosure seem to apply universally to creative expression, the precise legal forms in which they are recognized vary according to context. The moral right of a computer programmer differs from the moral right of an artist. The rights of a performer will be different from those of a composer, and also, from those of a *Tonmeister*.[2]

The development of moral rights has taken place during a dramatic and continually unfolding technological revolution. Information, once a scarce and therefore treasured resource, is now readily available. Indeed, the world is awash in information. The challenge now lies in ensuring that information is reliable and trustworthy—distinguishing truth from lies. This is an elemental concern. In the absence of authenticity, the flood of information in the technological environment has shown itself to be a profound threat. Misinformation endangers social values and institutions: human rights, justice, democracy, and the rule of law, itself, are all at stake. Fundamentally, these problems are not purely technological problems: they are also cultural problems and should be recognized as such. It is for this reason that moral rights could play a valuable role in the construction of our future.

The recognition of moral rights has often been tempered by a cautious legal community that is preoccupied with finding balance. However, in our commercially

[2] An issue discussed by Martha de Francisco, *Meeting the Challenge of Producing Classical Music for Global Audiences in the Digital Era*, 14(4) JIPLP 327 (2019), https://doi.org/10.1093/jiplp/jpz009.

driven world, the imbalanced lives and livelihoods of authors and artists are often ignored. Lawyers today may struggle to talk about humanistic or spiritual values, and it has been difficult for the legal profession to prioritize a non-commercial doctrine like moral rights. In the world of copyright, money rules. When it comes to art and artists, cynicism or disillusionment may prevail.

The tragedy of the COVID-19 pandemic has at least raised some questions about the status quo—although much of the world has had a tendency to fall back into the old ways of doing things. Still, hints of awareness, autonomy, and a broader search for meaning are apparent, offering whispers of hope to a world in crisis. There is both a need and a unique opportunity to explore new and different ideas.

For those interested in copyright law, a greater awareness of the legitimacy and importance of moral rights may be possible precisely *because* they do not fit with the economic logic of modern copyright law. This book has sought to show the value of such an approach. Its goal is to advocate for authors and artists, for culture, and also, for the legal profession—for its right to grow, to refine itself, and to change.

The doctrine of moral rights is also a crucible in which the prototypical concepts of attribution and integrity have been forged. In an environment where AI is rapidly becoming ubiquitous, attribution and integrity can act as foundational principles that help us to distinguish between human and artificial intelligence, information and misinformation, and truth and lies, in a way that is simple, elegant, and accessible. By doing so, moral rights can help to preserve and promote authenticity in the AI environment.

In a book about the rights of authors and artists, the final words must be reserved for culture. In our era, culture is often thought of as a luxury or a superfluity. But culture, in all its forms, emerged in the earliest times of our existence as a species, and it has accompanied us throughout our journey of 200,000 years on Earth. It is among the most basic of all human artefacts.

As a reminder of the essential place of culture in human life and history, the cover of this book features the image of a handprint from the Lascaux Caves in France. These caves house some of the oldest works of art still in existence, which are estimated to have been made around 17,000 years ago. These ancient artists not only painted images of the world around them, but they also made prints of their own hands, integrating them into their artistic creations as in this cover image.

We see the hand of the artist. Though it was made at a remove of 17,000 years from us, this handprint looks no different from our own.[3]

[3] But the Lascaux caves do not contain the world's oldest existing artworks. In Southeast Asia, for example, cave art dating from 45,500 to 65,000 years ago has been discovered, and expert Professor Paul Pettitt cautions that, even here, "minimum ages are just that—minimums—and cannot definitively be used to claim discovery of 'the world's oldest figurative art'": quoted by Rachel Nuwer, *The World's Oldest Animal Paintings Are on This Cave Wall: Depictions of Pigs Found in Indonesia Date Back at Least 45,500 Years*, SCIENTIFIC AMERICAN (Jan. 14, 2021), https://www.scientificamerican.com/article/the-worlds-oldest-animal-paintings-are-on-this-cave-wall.

Handprints offer ancient echoes of *attribution*—an assertion by the artist of presence, achievement, desire, and communication. They symbolize the artist's claim to immortality. This connection between creator and work, which clearly dates from time immemorial, is at the heart of the modern idea of moral rights.

Wherever humans are, wherever they go, they create culture. At the conclusion of *The Farthest*, a film about the Voyager spacecraft— which became, in 2012, the first human-made object to enter interstellar space[4]—the visionary scientists behind Voyager discuss the famous "Golden Record." This record, which was created to travel on the spacecraft, features music from around the world, and it was made to last for at least a billion years.[5] The Golden Record will almost certainly outlive humanity itself.

In such a literal sense, culture may ultimately be all that remains of us. It deserves to be honored as humanity's unique contribution to the universe.[6]

[4] There were two Voyager spacecraft: Voyager 1 was the first to cross out of the solar system (beyond our sun's sphere of influence, the heliopause) and into interstellar space, which it did on Aug. 25, 2012. *See* NASA, *Interstellar Mission* (n.d.), https://voyager.jpl.nasa.gov/mission/interstellar-mission.

[5] There were actually two parts to the record—the first including languages, natural sounds, and images—and one copy traveled on each of the two Voyager spacecraft. *See, e.g.*, Ashley Strickland, *One of the Most Iconic Pieces of Space Exploration History Goes up for Auction*, CNN (July 26, 2023), https://www.cnn.com/2023/07/26/world/sagan-voyager-golden-record-auction-scn/index.html.

[6] *See, e.g.*, Leslie Felperin, *The Farthest Review—Nasa Documentary Voyages to the Outer Limits*, The Guardian (Sept. 1, 2017), https://www.theguardian.com/film/2017/sep/01/the-farthest-review-nasa-documentary-voyager-i-ii (writing about the Golden Record, the cultural mission envisioned by Carl Sagan):

> Although the main purpose of the trip was data collection, the thing most people remember about the Voyagers is that each of them contain a golden LP encoded with images, aural greetings in many Earth languages and, on the B-side, a playlist of top tunes (Beethoven, Bach, Pygmy tribespeople, Chuck Berry) to tickle the eardrums of any alien life form they might meet.

Sagan's son speaks extensively about the Golden Record in the film.

Index

For the benefit of digital users, indexed terms that span two pages (e.g., 52–53) may, on occasion, appear on only one of those pages.

Aalmuhammed v. Lee, 467, 467n.46
Abhinavagupta, 63–64
Aboriginal culture(s), 211–12, 212n.6, 257–59, 260, 260n.209, 260n.210
Actors
  artificial intelligence threats to, 148, 338, 359–60, 514
  strike (Hollywood), 333, 358–66
  substitutions between (Hollywood), 475
Adeney, Elizabeth, 22n.66, 27n.79, 63n.5, 80n.87, 126n.262, 406n.63, 443n.171, 540, 540n.90
Aesthetics, role in filmmaking, 475, 476–77
Agreement on Trade-Related Aspects of Intellectual Property Rights (TRIPs Agreement), 16–17n.49, 37n.105, 89n.126, 124, 166n.53, 169–72, 211–12n.4, 214–15, 604n.45, 621
  computer programs as literary works, 312, 604
  copyright protection for software, 603, 604
  exclusion of moral rights from, xix, 44, 171, 186–87, 309–10, 477, 520–21, 621
  harmonization in, 124, 188, 189
  moral rights in, 46–49, 91–92, 126–33, 149–208
  moral rights in computer programs, 89n.124, 312, 313, 322, 325–26
  most-favored nation treatment, 196–97
  protection of moral rights in, 35, 106, 113, 140, 309, 316–17, 324–25, 329, 412–13, 455, 477, 519
Akhmatova, Anna [Anna Andreyevna], 300–1
Allen, Woody, 200n.180, 358–59n.78, 416n.98, 457n.1, 465n.29, 494, 497–99, 502n.181
Amar Nath Sehgal v. Union of India, Indian case, 24n.72, 28n.82, 40, 96n.148, 151–52n.5, 205, 219–20n.44, 271, 282–83, 485n.119, 490n.139, 525n.44
Anand, Pravin, 280n.276, 283–84, 284n.293, 326n.447, 488
Anderson, Jane, 258–59, 258n.202, 259n.206, 260, 261n.212
Andral, Jean-Louis, 25n.73, 224, 351n.56, 539–15, 542–43. *See also* Picasso-Nesjar murals
Angwin, Julia, 613n.67, 614
Anti-circumvention measures, 53, 177–78. *See also* Technological protection measures
Apple's iTunes, 367, 407, 421–22, 423, 508
Appropriation art, 47–48, 94
Arnold, Richard, 19n.59, 127n.269, 441, 441n.167, 443n.170
Art, as biological necessity, 146, 148
Art, as essential human activity, 148, 624–25
Art, as profession, 599–602, 618
Artefacts
  moral rights and, 569–75
  ownership and repatriation of, 7, 564, 572–73
  3D printing of, 175n.94
  and virtual galleries, 572–73
Artificial intelligence (generative), ch. 5 and passim, 334, 335, 338, 340, 359, 368
Artistic works
  copyright protection of, 79n.84, 107n.193, *See also* Work(s)
  differentiated from computer program, 47, 289n.310
  Artist's resale right, 32, 106n.189, 108–9n.201, 168, 168n.63, 279, 323–24, 551, 619. *See also droit de suite*
Artists
  threats from artificial intelligence, 148, 333, 584–85
  work used in training of artificial intelligence systems, 344–45, 376–77
Artworks
  attribution of, 371, 373, 521–22
  authenticity of, 373
  destruction of, 24n.71, 29–30, 59, 250, 282–83, 525–27, 539, 540, 554
  integrity of, 21
  intentional or grossly negligent destruction of, 250
  modern, 573–75
  preferential treatment, 59, 516–18
    in Canada, 223–26
    in United States, *see* treatment in Visual Artists Rights Act
  treatment in Visual Artists Rights Act 1990 (VARA), 518–30
  valuation of, 517n.8
Attribution, general principle as opposed to moral right, 623

Attribution, moral right of, 17–18, 84, 101–2, 125, 165–66, 242, 245, 253, 275, 330, 351–52, 351n.54, 355, 357–58, 367, 375–76, 378, 400, 406–7, 427–28, 441, 443n.171, 444, 453–54, 546, 578, 588–89
  definition 17–20
  in Australian Copyright Act, 23, 88n.121, 256, 534
  Berne Convention, 24, 25, 27–28, 30–31, 32, 37n.106, 39n.112, 50, 50n.147, 58, 66n.16, 71n.39, 80, 96, 97, 106–7, 107n.193, 123n.248, 124n.252, 128–29, 128n.275, 140, 150–52, 153–68, 159n.29, 162n.42, 175, 179, 180, 182, 198–99, 198n.174, 202n.186, 203, 205, 207n.202, 245, 246, 247n.153, 274n.252, 309, 320, 337, 378, 516n.2
  in Canadian Copyright Act, 165, 220n.48, 547n.109
  in Creative Commons license, 308n.382, 588–89, 593n.12, 595–97
  in cultural property, 271, 287n.301, 542, 549, 552–56
  in free software movement, 590, 607, 618
  in German Copyright Act, 101n.168, 102
  and Google Book Settlement, 111n.209, 208n.204, 615n.75
  in Japanese Copyright Law, 289–90
  and modern art, 573–75
  in Visual Artists Rights Act of 1990, 92n.132, 171–72, 178n.106, 216, 224, 238–39, 351, 357n.72, 518–30, 520n.16
  and Wikipedia, 609–12
Audience,
  as author, 49, 224
  and author, relationship between, 5–6, 105
  as participant in creative experience, 48–49
Audiovisual works, xvii–xviii, 89–90, 89n.125 *See also* Cinematographic works, Work(s), Films
  as derivative work, 474n.77
  French moral rights in, 79–80, 95, 105n.185
  performers' moral rights, 117n.231, 177–79, 181, 182, 184, 206, 215n.24, 215–16n.26, 227–29, 235, 268n.233, 292n.323, 304–5, 310–11, 324, 446, 449, 451–52, 531n.61
  WIPO Performance and Phonograms Treaty, 89n.125, 169n.67, 222, 268n.233, 360, 360n.82, 399, 512n.211, 531n.61
Australia,
  computer programs, moral rights in, 89n.124, 312, 322
  Copyright Amendment Indigenous Communal Moral Rights Bill (2003), 256–62, 409n.68, 584
  Copyright Amendment (Moral Rights) Act 2000, 172n.78, 215n.25, 228n.78, 256n.186, 256–57nn.189–94
  duration of moral rights in, 256–57
Australian Copyright Act, 23, 256, 534
  right of attribution, 101–2, 330
  right of integrity, 23, 108, 256, 410n.71
Austrian Copyright Law, 99, 103–4, 108n.197, 109n.203
  comparison with German Copyright Law, 106
  "Designation of Author," 108, 108n.198
  "Obligations of Owners of Works," 108–9, 109n.202
  "Protection of Authorship," 108, 108n.197
  "Protection of Works," 108
  right of attribution, 101–2
  right of disclosure, 107–8, 607
Auteurs of film, 476–77
Author(s). *See also* Authorship
  audience as, 48–49
  designation of, 108, 108n.198, 468, 502n.183
  individual rights of, 75, 115
  moral rights after death, 551n.119
  performer as, 182
  preventing moral harm to, 22
  programmer as, 343–44
  relationship between audience and, 5, 48–49, 441
  right against abusive criticism, 78
  right of disclosure, 37, 78, 175n.95, 195, 346n.35, 495n.158
  right of integrity, 20–21, 28, 43, 90–91, 125, 223, 299–300, 373–74, 403n.50, 483
  right of reputation, 320
  right of withdrawal, 79, 103
  right to destroy own work, 5, 7, 16, 17, 29, 115, 126, 302, 306, 307, 521, 599
  rights as individual rights, 75, 115
  sui generis right, 36, 162n.44, 603
Authorship, *See also* Author(s)
  American law, 141
  British law, 140
  Canadian law, 165, 223, 226–27, 228
  creative, 108, 330, 336–37
  economic rights of, 3, 23, 76, 98, 143, 306, 309, 322
  French law, 77, 82, 509n.206
  German law, 101n.165, 103
  Indian law, 273, 280n.276, 486
  individual rights of, 75, 115

individual rights of, in Statute of Anne, 112–13, 115, 116n.228, 117
Italian law, 336–39, 412–13, 469–71
problems of, 617
right to claim, in Visual Artists Rights Act of 1990, 2n.5, 92n.132, 152n.6, 171–72, 216, 224, 236, 238–39, 239n.119, 351, 357n.72, 518, 527n.52
Russian law, 22n.65, 201–2n.185, 202, 218n.39, 246, 246n.149, 297–98, 297–98n.341, 299n.345, 301, 305, 310, 311, 312, 313, 322, 323–24, 325–28, 329, 471, 471n.60
shared human and machine, 375–76, 615
use of pre-existing material, xx, 44, 143–44, 147
Autocephalous Greek Orthodox Church of Cyprus v. Goldberg, 562n.164
Ayrapetova, Karina, 469n.52, 471, 471n.63

Bach, Johann Sebastian, 50–51, 50n.151, 114n.219, 379, 391n.6, 392, 392n.14, 424, 424–25n.118, 625n.6
Basho, 573n.195
Bargaining inequality, in artistic relationships, 33, 469, 531–32
Beckett, Samuel, 42–43, 450
Beckett, Sister Wendy, 573, 573n.196
Bently, Lionel, 70n.38, 71–72n.43, 97n.151, 161n.38, 341n.23
Bergman, Ingrid, 510
Berne Convention for the Protection of Literary and Artistic Works, 2–3, 4n.11, 9, 63n.5, 113n.216, 141n.315, 150–51, 155n.18, 160n.32, 189, 213–14, 214n.15, 237–38, 246, 525n.43
age of authorship, 153–58, 370
Article 6*bis*, development and evolution of, 540
bilateral agreements and, 217n.33
Brussels Act (1948), evolution of moral rights in, 158–59, 158–59n.28
Canadian membership in, 214–15
on choice of law, 202–3
and codification of tort in Article 6*bis*, 150–51
commercial age, moral rights in, 158–59, 269–70n.237
and the common law, 156
computer programs, as literary works, 90–91
computer programs, moral rights in, 313, 322, 325–26
enforceability of, 544
moral rights, evolution of, 328–29
India's membership in, 205, 281–82, 542, 544
Japan's membership in, 288–89
minimum standards of, 165, 197–98, 199, 246, 247, 440, 441–42
most-favored nation treatment, 204
national treatment under, 246, 365, 498–99
practical implications of, 578–79
protection of moral rights in, 111, 199–200, 204, 215–16
resale right (*droit de suite*) in, 32, 168
right of attribution, 126, 164, 165–66, 180n.110
right of integrity, 20–21, 50, 90–92, 96, 176–77n.99, 184, 199–200
right of reputation in, 309, 320, 328, 612n.65
Rome Act (1928), original text of moral rights, 63n.5
Russian membership in, 298–99n.344
Stockholm Act (1967), amendment of moral rights in, 159–61
technological creation, 163–64, 188–89, 207
United States membership in, 152, 237–38, 240
Bharata, 48–49, 288n.304, 411–12n.78, *See also Rasa* theory
Bharati, C. Subramania, 6–7, 6–7n.17, 10n.28, 49n.143, 73n.49, 145n.324, 175n.95, 252n.177, 270n.240, 279n.272, 281n.280, 288n.304, 382, 382n.147, 411–12n.78, 485n.118, 542n.92, 546–47, 547n.104, 550, 550n.117, 579, 579n.210
Bharati, S. Vijaya, 175n.95, 270n.240, 449n.182, 546–47, 547n.104
Bihar Movement, 492
Bilateral agreements, 204
Billington, James H., 457–58n.2
Blacklist (Hollywood), and studio-artist tensions, 467n.43
BMG v. John Doe, Canadian case, 173–74
Bogart, Humphrey, 358–59n.78, 510
Bollywood, 278–79, 281n.282, 282, 282n.283, 458n.5, 460, 470n.57, 482, 484, 485, 491n.141, 513
Bradby, David, 450, 450n.187, 451
Bradford, Barbara Taylor, Indian case, 282n.283, 491n.141, 513nn.214–15
Brahms, Johannes, 29, 391, 391n.7, 448n.178
Bridgeport Music v. Dimension Films, 403n.49, 403nn.50–51
Brown, Glenn, 508n.205
Brown, Gregory S., 10n.28, 72, 72n.46
Bruguière, Jean-Michel, 77n.68, 84
Brunet, Claude, 220–21, 221nn.49–50, 221n.53
Buffet, Bernard, the refrigerator of, 5n.12, 410n.71
Bundesgerichtshof (BGH), 183n.122, 433n.143, 570

Burden of proof, 24–25, 81, 157, 224, 272, 275
Bush, George W., 287–88

Calatrava, Santiago, 132n.285, 566–69, 566n.179, 567n.180, 568n.184
Canada, 216–35
 authorship in, 157, 165
 film moral rights and, 447, 458–59, 512
 history of moral rights in, 217–19
 inalienability of moral rights, 83–84, 135–37, 226–27, 304
 membership in Berne Convention, 237–38
 monism and dualism, 99
 moral rights in computer programs, 313, 322, 325–26
 rarity of moral rights cases, 22
 right of attribution, 580n.213
 right of integrity, 219, 223, 227, 257n.193
 Visual Artists Rights Act of 1990, 2n.5, 92n.132, 152n.6, 171–72, 216, 224, 236, 238–39, 239n.119, 351, 357n.72, 518, 527n.52
 Waiver, 34, 157, 178–79, 221n.52, 226, 280, 480, 531
  general availability, 313, 481
  of moral rights, 481, 512–13n.212
 Writers' Union of Canada, 55n.165, 221n.52, 480n.100, 590n.5
Canadian Copyright Act, 37–38, 84n.104, 92n.131
 moral rights of authors in, 605
 moral rights of performers in, 177–78
 photographing a work of public art, 565
 right of integrity in visual work, 518
 waiver of moral rights, 83, 481, 512–13n.212
Carlos, Wendy/William, 392n.14
Casablanca, 510
Cave art, 624n.3
CCH Canadian Ltd. v. Law Society of Upper Canada, Canadian case, 415n.92
Certain Tendency in French Cinema, A, 461n.14, 476
Chapelier, Le, 71–72, 71–72n.43, 73
"Charming Betsy" principle, 242n.133
Choice of law, 200–3
Cinematographic works. *See also* Work(s)
 authorship of, 202n.186, 473, 478
 colorization of, 179n.108
 deceased actors, reviving, 499–500, 510–11
 as derivative work, 243, 321, 474–77, 596–98
 digital technology and, 3–4, 7–8, 48n.142, 49, 51, 105, 187–88, 326
 internet and communication of, 459, 499–500
 litigation in India and France, 477–99
 ownership of copyright in (under the Berne Convention), 202n.186
Clean Flicks of Colorado v. Soderbergh, 500–7
Code de la propriété intellectuelle (CPI), France, 5n.13, 67n.20, 76n.66, 96, 167n.58, 224n.60, 239, 313, 346n.32, 410n.71, 463n.21, 463n.25
Collective creation, 592, 609–14
Collective licensing, 192, 192n.160, 193, 193n.162, 433, 435, 455, 509, 619
Colombet, Claude, 30–31, 31n.88, 71n.40, 175, 176, 176n.97, 233n.93
Colorization of films, 182–83, 200n.180, 457n.1, 464–65
Comity of nations, 151–52n.5, 562
Commissioner of Police of the Metropolis v. Bumper Corporation, 262n.215, 557–64
Common law copyright, 61, 90, 118–19, 122–24, 122n.244, 142–43, 563
 birth of, 140–42
 moral rights and, 174n.89, 361–62, 454n.195
Communication to the public, right of in WIPO Copyright Treaty, 133, 174, 174–75n.90, 175, 189, 206, 278
Computer-generated work, 47, 134, 340–41, 341n.23, 342–43, 343n.29, 344, 345
Computer software/programs, 96, 162, 162n.41, 265n.219, 504n.190, 602–3, 603n.40, *See also* Open Source
 Australian approach to moral rights, 261
 as business methods, 288, 603–4
 Canadian approach to moral rights, 222, 480
 copyright protection of, 162, 162n.41, 305, 312, 343n.28, 343n.29, 397, 400
 differentiated from artistic creativity, 13
 European approaches to moral rights in, 214–15
 France, approach to moral rights in, 20–21, 26, 27n.78, 38–39, 91, 94–95, 96, 98, 100–1, 134, 239, 313, 398–99, 438–39, 463
 India approach to moral rights in, 506
 infringement of moral rights in, 23n.67, 37–38, 137n.307, 230–31
 as copyright works, 603
 Japanese approach to moral rights in, 292
 as literary work, 604–5
 moral rights in, 313, 322, 325–26
 New Zealand approach to moral rights in, 341
 patentability, 603–5
 practical impact of moral rights in, 32, 477
 programmers, 90–91, 312
 relationship between programmers and, 312–13
 sui generis right in, 36, 162n.41, 162n.44, 265n.219, 603, 603n.40
 waiver of moral rights, 435–38

Confetti Records v. Warner Music Ltd., UK case, 125n.257, 191n.157, 220n.46, 346n.36, 492n.146
Conservation, 533–34
Continued access right, 16
Contracts, for films, 361, 468–69, 478, 479, 486–87
Copyleft licensing model, of free software, 589–92
  price and promise of, 615–17
Copyright Act of 1842 (UK), 217n.33
Copyright Act of 1921 (Canada) 217n.33
Copyright Act of 1993 (Russia), 305–11, 314, 315, 322, 324–25, 328, 557
  authors' moral rights in the public domain, 309
  domaine public payant scheme, 309, 309n.385, 315
  droit de suite (artist's resale right) for visual arts, 168, 311
  dualism, 306–7
  duration of protection, 19, 100–1, 162, 182, 198n.174, 239, 272n.250, 307–8, 337–38, 337n.10, 537, 553, 603–4
  performers' moral rights, 117n.231
  right of disclosure, 306, 320–21
  right of integrity, 310, 328–29
  right of reputation, 154, 154n.14, 320, 328–29, 612n.65
Copyright Amendment (Moral Rights) Act 2000 (Australia), 172n.78, 228n.78, 256n.186, 256–57nn.189–90
Copyright (Amendment) Act, 2012 (India), 275
Copyright infringement. *See* Infringement
Copyright law
  future of, 298n.343, 495n.157, 513n.214
Copyright protection
  of artistic works, 341, 343–44, 536–37
  of audiovisual works, 89–90, 319, 466n.42, 497
  circumventing, 53, 53n.155, 593
  of literary works, 16–17n.49, 46, 370, 604–5
  of musical works, 278, 427–28, 621–22
Cornish, William, 124, 124n.256, 125, 125n.260, 129n.277, 136, 136n.304, 137, 137n.307, 138, 138n.309, 140, 306n.376, 462, 462n.17
Coudert, Fanny, 173–74, 174n.88
Creative authorship, in films, 3–4, 324–25, 476, 617
Creative cheating, 414, 414n.87
Creative Commons and, 45–46n.135, 593–95
Creative Commons license, 308n.382
  copyright infringement and, 593–95
  derivative works, creation of, 597–98
  right of attribution in, 375–76
  right of integrity in, creation of, 597–98. *See also* Derivative works
Creative freedom, moral rights and, 293–329
Criticism, right against, 78, 612n.65
Cultural heritage, xix, 7, 21, 28, 139, 158, 193n.164, 251–54, 544–47, 549–50
  and films, 255–56, 489–91
  France, 74
  India ("cultural heritage of a nation"), 271, 275, 287, 554–56
  Indigenous, 262
  Italian, 36
  United States, 59, 241
Cultural property, 544–47
  assessed by courts, 560–62
  moral rights of, 557
  in public domain, 552–56
  works in copyright, 552
Czech Copyright Act of 2000, 299

Danziger, James, 499
Dastar v. Twentieth-Century Fox Film Corp., 141n.316, 240–45, 240n.121, 240n.122
Davies, Gillian, 84n.104
Davis, Miles, 114n.219
Deazley, Ronan, 118, 118n.235
Declaration of the Rights of Man, 75, 75n.58
Defamation test in India, 241, 493
Democratization, of art, 105, 105n.183, 147n.331, 391
Derivative works, creation of, 596–98. *See also* Work(s)
Desbois, Henri, 4n.10, 25, 25–26n.74, 26, 26n.75, 27, 27n.78, 86n.114, 111n.211, 142n.318, 154n.15, 272, 272n.248, 361–62
Dickens, Charles, 155–56, 156n.19, 160–61
Dietz, Adolf, 1, 1n.1, 28n.80, 37, 37n.107, 45n.132, 98, 99, 99n.157, 106, 106nn.187–88, 143n.320, 144, 301n.357, 302n.359, 305–6n.373, 309n.385, 312n.392, 314n.401, 316, 316n.411, 543, 543n.94
Digital Age, moral rights in, 172–85
Digital images, in modern art, 459
Digital media, 616. *See also* Media
Digital Millennium Copyright Act, 53n.156, 105n.182, 236, 508n.204
Digital re-creation, 492–94
Digital Single Market Directive (DSM), 41n.123, 155, 155n.16, 377n.127, 429n.134, 469n.53
Digital technology and films, 413, 454
Dine, Jeffrey, 460n.11, 482n.109, 482n.110, 483, 483n.113, 484, 484n.114, 485n.120, 488n.134, 491, 491n.142, 491n.143

Directives, EU Copyright. *See* European Union Copyright Directives
Disclosure right, 75, 311, 464
  in employment, 91–92, 134
  in free software movement, 590, 607–8
  in French law, 70–73, 346n.32, 464
  in German Copyright Law, 106, 502
  in Japanese Copyright Act, 289–90
  in Russian Copyright Act of 1993, 301n.357, 305–11, 557
"Distortion of the Work," right against, 106–7, 107n.192, 130
Divulgation right, 78
  WIPO Copyright Treaty, 169, 169n.67, 173, 189–90
DJ (disc jockey), 394, 402–3, 402–3nn.46–47, 408–9, 455
Domaine public payant, 305–6n.373, 308–9, 309n.385, 315
Donaldson v. Beckett, xix–xx, 62n.3, 74n.55, 111–12, 116–17, 116n.229, 122–23, 142–43, 563
Dostoyevsky, F. [Fyodor Mikhailovich], 470
Dougherty, F. Jay, 462n.16, 466n.39, 467–68, 467n.47, 468n.49
Droit d'accèss, 16n.44
Droit de destination, 2n.4, 210, 233n.93
Droit de suite, 108–9n.201, 168, 195n.168
  for visual arts, 311, 323–24, 551. *See also* Artist's resale right
Droits innés, 98n.152
Droit moral, 5n.12, 19n.58, 64n.11, 67, 252n.175
Droits patrimoniaux, 76n.65
Dualism (*le dualisme*), 82–89, 306–7
  inalienability of moral rights, France, 83–84
  perpetual protection of moral rights, France, 106
  Russian Copyright Act of 1993, 305–11, 312, 322, 328, 557
  vs. monism, 230–34
DVDs, region codes for, 419–20n.108, 504–5

Eastern Book Company & Ors. v. DP. Modak & Anr., Indian case, 415n.92, 461n.13, 547n.108
Economic consequences, of moral rights, 14–15, 221n.50, 242, 478, 507, 621–22
Economic rights, 32–33, 36–38, 40n.116
  distinguished from moral rights, 314n.404
  independence of, 32–33, 35, 340
Eden v. Whistler, 79–80
Electronic music, 408–9, 455
Elgin Marbles, 175n.94
Eliot, T.S., 57n.171
EMI, 190n.152, 425, 425n.119, 430n.136, 434n.144, 434–35n.147
Employment, right of disclosure in, 91–92, 593n.13
Enforcement of moral rights, 52–54, 102, 170, 367, 421, 546
European Union Copyright Directives, 10–11n.29, 168, 185–86n.134, 236
  Computer Programs Directive (1991), 188–89
    computer programs as literary works, 16–17n.49, 322n.434, 602–3, 604
    moral rights in computer programs, 313, 322, 325–26
  Database Directive (1996)
    sui generis right in, 162n.44
  Directive on Copyright in the Information Society (2001), 94–95, 189
  Green Paper (1995), 187, 187n.138
  Harmonization of moral rights, lack of, 207, 623
  role of adjudication, 190
Evans, Bill, 181–82n.117, 393, 393nn.15–16, 393n.17, 416, 440, 440n.164
Exclusive rights vs. moral rights, Russian law, 322

Fair dealing, 93n.137, 93n.138, 135n.297, 363–64, 553n.129, 592–93
Fair use, 323, 352, 356–57, 356n.68, 357n.71, 358, 362–64, 363nn.89–91, 363n.92, 403, 404, 405, 405n.62, 503, 508n.204, 565n.174, 575nn.202–3, 592–93, 592n.10
  Russian Civil Code Provisions on Copyright (2008), 326
Fame, 14, 50–52, 50n.148, 51n.152, 391–92, 510–11
Family Entertainment and Copyright Act, (2005), 504
Family Movie Act, (2005), 505–6
Fan films, 500–7, 509
Farran, Sue, 269, 269n.236
Feist Publications Inc. v. Rural Telephone Service Co., 415n.91, 461n.13
Ficsor, Mihály, 180, 180n.112, 298n.343, 495n.157
File-sharing of music files, 388–90, 419–22, 419n.106, 424, 424n.116, 508, 509
Films, 500–7 (*See also* audiovisual works, cinematographic works)
  authorship of, 460–73, 477n.87, 478
  colorization of, 182–83, 200n.180, 457n.1, 464–65
  deceased actors, reviving, 499–500, 510–11
  as derivative work, 474–77, 493, 501, 503, 592n.10, 597, 598, 608
  digital technology and, 7–8
  employees, directors and actors as, 466–67
  internet and communication of, 459, 499–500
  litigation in France and India, 477–82

First publication, right of, 31, 37, 70, 100, 176, 190, 304, 319, 321, 346n.35
Fitzgerald, F. Scott, 345–46, 600
Fitzpatrick, Sheila, 303n.365, 327n.450
5Pointz, 137–38, 249–51, 527–29
damages (settlement), 56, 59
experts, use of in lawsuits, 81n.88
new artistic genre recognized (graffiti), 541
preliminary injunction, 606n.51
recognized stature, 525, 540
Fixation (under copyright law), 107n.196, 207, 233–34, 268, 505, 580n.214
Floyd, Pink, 425, 425n.119, 430, 430n.136, 436n.151
Format shifting, 419–20n.108
Fowler, Geoffrey J., 613n.67, 614, 614n.71, 614n.73
France, 66–96
defenses to a moral rights claim, 93–95
dualism (*dualisme*), 35, 82–89
dualism vs. monism, 230–34
file-sharing, 419–21
film litigation in, 477–99
film moral rights in, 447, 469–70, 512, 513
ghostwriting in, 84, 95, 136n.301
influence on Russian Civil Code (2008), 26n.75, 313–14, 463n.23
moral rights (*droits moraux*), 11, 77–82, 78n.71
moral rights in audiovisual works, 185
moral rights in computer programs, 313, 322, 325–26
moral rights and revolutionary ideals, 67–75
moral rights reforms, 385n.1
pre-eminence of moral rights, 76–77
Fraser, Stephen, 5n.14, 15n.41, 89n.125, 415n.90, 459n.7, 478n.89, 478n.90, 481, 481n.105, 512–13n.212
Free, the term, 44–45, 389–90, 588, 589–90, 591, 599, 600, 607, 608, 615–16, 618, 618n.80
Freedom of "function," 435
Freedom of the press, 115, 122
Free software, 589, 589n.2, 590, 607–8, 607n.56, 609, 612–13, 617, 618n.80
right of attribution, 607
right of integrity, 607
right of disclosure, 607
distinguished from open source, 607–8
copyleft licensing model, 608
Free Software Foundation, 605
GNU license, 605
Free speech, 44–46, 122–23
protecting, 122–23, 313
French law
and authorship, 26, 31
moral rights in computer programs, 89

Gall, Carlotta, 564, 564n.172
Games Workshop, 501–2, 503
Gatsby, The Great, 346n.34, 600
GEMA, 190, 435, 436, 437, 438
General cultural interests (Norway), 536–38, 539–43
German Basic Law, 109n.205
German Copyright Act, 101n.168, 102
comparison with Austrian Copyright Act, 102, 107–8
comparison with Russian Copyright Act (1993), 104
computer programs as literary works, 604
German law and film moral rights, 66, 105n.186, 465–66, 502
Germany, 97–111, 433–35
integrity of ringtones, 433–35
monism, 100–6
Nazi oppression, 548n.110
right of attribution, 106–7, 470–71
right of disclosure, 106–7
right of integrity, 154
Gervais, Daniel, 350n.53, 366, 370, 373
Gilliam v. American Broadcasting Companies, 38n.108, 199n.177, 242n.136, 329n.455, 351n.54, 401n.42, 474, 474n.77, 476n.82, 598n.28
Ginsburg, Jane, 7n.21, 17n.52, 37n.106, 71–72, 71n.39, 72n.44, 110n.208, 113n.216, 128n.275, 151n.3, 156n.20, 162n.41, 166n.52, 167n.57, 199n.178, 203n.189, 214n.17, 253, 265n.219, 337n.10, 365, 366n.98, 429n.133
Global licensing, 453–54
Gogh, Vincent van, 50–51, 50n.150, 163, 347, 430, 517–18, 555, 571–72, 571–72n.192, 582, 600
Goldstein, Paul, xxiii
Google,
Book Rights Registry, 506n.196
Book Settlement, 111n.209, 208n.204, 615n.75
quality of archives, 435–36, 506n.196
Google v. Oracle, 352, 352n.57
Gopnik, Adam, 181–82n.117, 417, 417n.100
Gould, Glenn, 47n.138, 48, 379–80, 379nn.132–33, 391, 391n.6, 391nn.8–9, 391–92nn.10–11, 392n.12, 392nn.13–14, 393n.16, 414, 416, 417n.102, 424–25n.118, 576n.205
and artificial intelligence ("Dear Glenn"), 379nn.132–33

Government of India, 175n.95, 271n.245, 282–83
amendments to the Copyright Act, 284–85
duty of care towards artworks, 284. *See also* Amar Nath Sehgal
Greene, Paul, 413–14, 413–14n.85

Haiku, 371, 573, 573n.195
Handler, Michael, 477, 477n.84
Hari Puttar, 491n.141
Harmonization, as analogy drawn from music, 114, 114–67nn.218–20
Harmonization of moral rights, 207, 623
European Union Copyright Directive, 164–65, 187, 236, 377
Hart, Michael, 189, 189n.148
Hatto, Joyce, 52, 367, 423
Hemingway, Ernest, 15n.40, 29nn.83–84, 600, 600n.30
Herrmann, Bernard,
Hesse, Carla, 7–8, 8n.22, 40n.120, 62n.4, 67–68, 73–74, 73n.48, 74n.52, 110n.208
Hindutva, 492
Hitchcock, Alfred, 6n.15, 18, 372, 402n.45, 460n.12, 470, 470n.58, 475, 545n.99
Hoffman, Lord, 397, 580n.214
Hollywood, 5n.14
actors' strike, 358–66
writers' strike, 354–56
Homburger, Walter, 342
Honor, 20–21, 22–24, 96n.147
Horowitz, Vladimir [Vladimir Samoylovich], 99–100nn.160–61, 117
Hugo, Victor, 35, 35n.101, 35n.102, 81–82, 85, 85–86n.112, 87n.116, 150–51, 155–56, 156n.21, 501n.178, 546, 556, 587n.1, 602n.36, 602n.37
Hungarian copyright law, 63n.6, 188n.142, 293n.329, 294, 294n.332, 299, 299n.348
Huston, Angelica, 498
Huston, John, 27, 183n.121, 199–200, 202–3n.188, 365, 496–97, 498, 498n.165

Inalienability of moral rights, 83–84, 135–37. *See also* Waiver
in Canada, 226–27
in France, 83
in Germany, 34, 100–1, 330
in India, 280, 487
in Japan, 289
in Russia, 323–24
in United Kingdom, 330
India, 269–71, 280–82
colonialism, 484–85
Cultural heritage in, *see* Cultural heritage.
defamation test in, 23, 493–94
digital re-creation in, 492–94
duties of the government. *See* Government of India
exposure to European civil law, 270
film moral rights in, 470
literature, 50n.149, 69–70, 197–98, 288, 549–50, 555–56
membership in Berne Convention, 142, 152, 156n.20, 160–61, 205, 281–82
moral rights in computer programs, 506
music and film soundtracks in, 279
producer vs. author in, 482–91
protection of moral rights in, 272
support from judiciary, 271, 280–81, 489
Indian Copyright Act, 24n.71, 88n.121
author of computer-generated work in, 343–44
author's personal rights in, 6
computer programs, moral rights in, 313, 322, 325–26
cultural heritage, relationship with, 556
independence from economic rights, 279–80
perpetual protection of moral rights, 272, 275
remedies for infringement of moral rights, 137n.307
right of integrity in visual work, 518
Section 57, 271, 279, 284–85, 344, 472, 482, 483, 486, 487, 488, 489–90, 491, 493, 525–26, 541–42, 554, 556
"Special Rights of the Author," 516
term of protection for moral rights, 228, 289–90
Indigenous communal moral right (Australia), 257–58, 257n.199, 258n.202, 258n.203, 262, 315, 409n.68, 584n.222
Infringement of copyright distinguished from subsistence of copyright, 202
Infringement of moral rights, 137n.307, 230–31
of moral rights in software, 329
remedies for, 137n.307
Inheritance of moral rights, in India, 307–8
Innate rights (*droits innés*), 98n.152
Integrity right, 442–43, 523–25. *See also* Berne Convention for the Protection of Literary and Artistic Works, Australian Copyright Act, Japanese Copyright Act
author's reputation, protection of, 239
in Berne Convention, 217
in Canadian Copyright Act, 37–38, 165, 217, 227
in Russian Copyright Act of 1993, 305–11, 328
in Russian Civil Code of 2008, 313–14, 463n.23
cultural heritage, preservation of, 158
in cultural property, 455

in free software movement, 609
in Indian Copyright Act, 482
as inviolability, 303
modern art, 573–74
works of architecture, overlap with, 566n.178
vs. right of reputation (pure integrity right), 537
in Visual Artists Rights Act of 1990, 2n.5, 92n.132, 152n.6, 171–72, 216, 224, 236, 238–39, 239n.119, 351, 357n.72, 518, 527n.52
Wikipedia, in relation to, 612n.65
Intellectual Property Code (France), 5n.13, 67n.20, 167n.58, 224n.60, 346n.32, 410n.71, 463, 463n.21
Interested persons, right of
Japan, 317–18
Russian Civil Code Provisions on Copyright (2008), 326
International copyright regime, moral rights in, 149–208
Berne Convention, 153–64
bilateral agreements, 204
choice of law, 200–3
European Union Copyright Directive, 187
minimum standards of, 197–98, 199, 246, 247, 440, 441–42
most-favored nation treatment, 204
practical implications, 199–200, 276–77, 578–79
Russian Kurier case, 248, 325n.446, 365n.96, 563
TRIPs Agreement. *See* Agreement on Trade-Related Aspects of Intellectual Property Rights (TRIPs Agreement)
WIPO Copyright Treaty, 169, 169n.67, 173, 189–90
WIPO Performances and Phonograms Treaty, 173, 189, 222, 268n.233, 438, 511
International Covenant on Economic, Social and Cultural Rights, 204–5, 205n.193, 544
Internet, 2
and privacy, 173–74
Interpretation of moral rights, 18n.55, 149, 157n.25, 217, 271, 366, 398–99, 481, 493–94
Inviolability principle, 320
integrity as, 303
Irish Copyright and Related Rights Act of 2000, 3n.9, 24
Italian law, 412–13, 469–71

Jacobsen v. Katzer, 594
Japan
membership in Berne Convention, 288–89
membership in international copyright system, 213–14
rationale for maintaining moral rights in, 290–91
Japanese Copyright Act, 289–90
corporate (company) moral rights, 292–93
duration of moral rights in, 289–90
honor in, 291, 292–93
prevention of harm, 290–91
protection after the author's death, 290
right of attribution, 289
right of disclosure, 289
right of integrity, 289, 291–92
term of protection for, 289–90
Jones, Andy, 501–2
Juristic entity in English law, 515, 562

Kakutani, Michiko, 613
Kamban (also Kambar), 490
Kamina, Pascal, 161–62n.39, 233n.93, 466, 466n.37, 474–75n.79, 475
Keen, Andrew, 613–14
Keyes, A.A., 220–21, 221nn.49–50, 221n.53
Knowledge
digital transformation of, 387
dissemination of, 259
Kollywood, 482

La Cinq, 27n.76, 158n.27, 203n.190, 365n.97, 398n.36, 465n.30, 498, 498n.167
Lacy, Jerry, 510
Laipply, Jason R., 393, 393n.17
Lanham Act, 39–40, 141, 141n.316, 228, 237n.107, 240, 242, 244, 245–46, 351n.54, 410–11, 411n.75
Lascaux caves, 624, 624n.3
Law
distinguished from doctrine of moral rights, 314n.404
Law on the Legal Protection of Computer Programs and Databases of 1992 (Russia), 312
Lenz, Stephanie, 508n.204
Lessig, Lawrence, 116n.227, 549n.114, 589, 589n.3, 590n.4, 591, 592, 592n.9, 599, 614n.69
Literary property, 10n.28, 46–47, 68, 69, 71–72, 72n.46, 143, 144
Literary theft, 14n.37
Literary works. *See also* Work(s)
analogy with, in copyright law, 37n.105, 47, 161, 163–64
computer software as, 162, 504n.190
copyright protection of, 343n.28

Live performance, 51–52, 179, 268n.233, 379–80, 440, 449–50
Locke, John, 11n.31, 40n.118, 69, 115, 115–16n.226, 117–18, 337n.10
López, Juan José Marín, 567, 567n.182, 568n.185
Lucas, André, 54–55, 54n.159

MacQueen, Hector, xxiii, 109n.204, 110, 111n.209, 112n.213, 116n.229, 414n.89
Maddow, Ben, 498
Maggs, Peter B., 201, 246n.149
Mahabharata, 70n.36, 145, 490
Making available, right of, 173–74
Mandelstam, Osip, 293–94, 294n.331, 300–1
Mannu Bhandari v. Kala Vikas Pictures Pvt. Ltd., 271n.243, 320n.428, 460n.11, 470n.57, 482–91, 482n.108, 483n.111, 483n.113, 484n.116, 485n.120, 486n.121, 486n.123, 487n.127, 488nn.130–31, 489n.138, 491n.143, 500n.175
Mansfield, Lord, xix–xx, 117–20, 121, 122, 122n.244, 123, 142–43
Maugham, W. Somerset, 61, 61n.1
McCarthy era blacklist (Hollywood), 466–67
McCamus, John D., 33n.95, 479n.95
MGM Studios v. Grokster, 419n.106
Media, digital, 616
Merryman, John Henry, 5n.12, 410n.71
  Bumper Corporation case, 557n.141
  opposition to repatriation of artworks, 563–64
Michaélidès-Nouaros, Georges, 62–63, 63n.5, 79–80, 79n.81
Millar v. Taylor, UK case, 3n.9, 62n.3, 74n.55, 111–12, 116–22, 142–43, 213, 213n.11
Milton, John, 40n.118, 115, 115n.224, 115–16n.226, 117–18, 119
Mixing, in music, 394, 408–14, 616
Mobile technology, and music,
  media neutrality, 92n.134, 232
  mobile ringtones, 183, 432–38, 434n.145, 434n.146, 453–54, 570
Modern art. *See also* Artwork
  digital images in, 459, 574
  virtual galleries, building, 569–75
Monism, 36, 66
  birth of, 98–99
  distinguished from French dualism, 98
  vs. dualism, 230–34
  duration of moral rights protection, 106n.187
  inalienability of moral rights in: *see* Waiver
  in WIPO Internet Treaties, 169
Moog synthesizer, 392, 392n.14
Moore, Schuyler M., 477, 477n.85
Moral interests, protection of, 39–40
Moral rights, 4–8
  aesthetic reality of, 13–15
  characteristics of, 27n.78
  defences to a moral rights claim, 93–95
  defined, 77–82
  distinguished from economic rights, 314n.404
  doctrine of, xix, 4–8
  doctrine, distinguished from law, 9–12
  droits moraux, les, 77–82
    integrity vs. reputation rights, 80–82
    right against abusive criticism, 403
    right of disclosure, 78
    right of withdrawal, 79–80. *See also* Withdrawal, right of
  enforcement of, 52–54
  vs. exclusive rights, 322
  harmonization of, 207, 623
  implicit recognition of, 120
  in Russian Civil Code Provisions on Copyright (2008), 324
  in developing countries, 265–88
  in software. *See* Computer software
  inalienability of, 83–84
  legal implications, 32–36
  origins of doctrine, 12–13, 62–66
  perpetual protection of, 34–36, 275
  as personal rights, 2–3, 43, 98, 141, 317
  practical implications, 199–200
  pre-eminence of, in French law, 76–77
  similarities between trademark and, 94n.140
Moral rights in films, 460–73
  alleviating bargaining inequality, 469
  artistic development of work and, 463
  authorship and, 303
  British law and, 115
  Canadian law and, 217
  commercial circulation of film and, 464
  complexity of, 239, 460, 477
  fan films and, 500–7
  films and argument against, 474–77
  French law and, 89–90
  German law and, 465–66
  Indian law and, 472
  integrity and, 509
  Japanese law and, 293n.328
  of directors, 476
  practical challenges, 477–99
  pre-existing work and, 87
  Russian law and, 326–28
Moral rights in public domain works, 324–25, 552
Moral rights protection
  duration of, 307–8
  perpetual protection, 34–36

Morillot, André, 97, 97n.151, 98nn.154–55
Most-favored nation treatment, 204
Motian, Paul, 416
Motion Picture Academy Association (MPAA), 458–59
Muravina, Elena, 62–63, 63n.8
Murugan, Perumal, 405n.59
Music
  downloading, 421–25
  electronic music, 408–9, 455
  file-sharing of music files, 419–21
  and film soundtracks, in India, 181–82n.117
  global licensing, 453–54
  mixing, 408–13
  mobile technology, 183, 432–38, 434n.145, 434n.146, 453–54, 570
  performers, 438–53
  policy recommendations, 59
  sampling technique, 402–8
  sound recording, 222, 278n.270, 413, 414, 414n.89
Music Modernization Act 2018, 253–54, 372n.112, 427–28, 621–22
Musical score, 401n.43, 449–50, 466n.38, *See also* Musical works
Musical works. *See also* Work(s)
  analogy with literary copyright, 551
  versus musical score, 401n.43

Name, right of
  in Russian Civil Code Provisions on Copyright (2008), 463n.23
  in USSR Fundamentals of Civil Legislation, 302–5
Nash, Elizabeth, 566, 567n.180
Nataraja. *See* Shiva Nataraja
National Film Preservation Act (1988), 253, 253n.178, 457–58n.2, 494, 494n.150, 506, 506nn.195–96, 518n.10
National Film Preservation Board, 253n.178, 457–58n.2, 506nn.195–96, 518n.10
National treasure (of India), 282–83, 286n.299, 539–43, 554–55
Natural law, 11–12, 123
Neighboring right, 151n.3, 154n.14, 324
  Russian Civil Code Provisions on Copyright (2008), 326
Nesjar, Carl, 535n.77, *See also* Picasso-Nesjar murals
Nesjar, Gro, 55n.163, 224, 535–36, 541, 542–43. *See also* Picasso-Nesjar murals
Newcity, Michael, 201, 201–2n.185, 211–12n.4, 246n.149, 299n.350, 308n.381, 496, 496n.159
New Zealand, 211–12, 215–16, 262–64, 330, 341, 512
Nigeria, 7nn.19–20, 360n.83, 458n.5, 482n.107
Nimmer, David, 124n.254, 161n.34, 276n.260, 487n.126
Nollywood, 458n.5, 482n.107
Norowzian v. Arks, 131n.282, 462–63, 462nn.19–20
Novak, Kim, 6n.15, 402n.45, 475

Open access
  and contract, 588–89, 598–609
  and license, 592
  and moral rights, 619
Open source, 14, 59–60, 406n.65, 590, 592, 594–95, 617
Originality of visual art, 516–18
Orphan
  films, 506n.196
  works, 71, 592–93
Overdubbing, 393, 465n.30
Ownership,
  vs. authorship, 504
  of copyright, 99
  of open source, 592–602

Painting, moral rights in, 79–80, 163, 331, 349, 571–72
Pandit, Sneh, 14n.37, 48–49, 63–64n.9, 64n.12, 272n.247, 385n.1
Pankin, Boris, 496
Paris, Thomas, 65, 65n.15
Parochialism, 113
Parody 21, 93–95, 111, 135, 323
  amendments in UK CDPA, 21n.64, 125, 135
  Deckmyn v. Vandersteen (unified concept of parody under EU law), 41–42
  defense in French copyright law, 93
  in French law, 78, 82n.93. *See also* Pastiche
  Russian Civil Code Provisions on Copyright (2008), 313–24
Pasternak, Boris [Boris Leonidovich], 51n.152, 68–69, 300–1
Pastiche 78, 93–95, 135n.297
  defense in French copyright law, 93
Patents 21n.64, 117n.231, 125, 126–33, 165–66, 166n.50, 239n.117, 324, 337–38n.13, 341, 462n.18, 552n.123, 565, 603–4
  in Russian Civil Code Provisions on Copyright (2008), 313–24
Paternity, right of, versus attribution 16, 16n.45, 17, 219n.43, 276–77n.262, 277n.265, 291n.319

Patry, William F., 10n.28, 120, 120n.239, 363–64, 518, 530, 566, 566n.179
Patterson, Lyman Ray, 40, 115n.223, 115–16n.226, 116–17n.230, 117n.232, 119
Patwardhan, Anand, 488n.130, 488n.134, 492–94, 492n.144, 493n.147, 503, 503n.185
Peel, John, 402–3, 403n.47
Performers, 227–29, 278–79, 304–5, 310–11, 438–53
  as author, 98, 138, 181, 192, 192n.159, 227, 256, 333–83, 462n.18, 482
  in Canadian Copyright Act, 37–38, 84n.104, 92n.131, 165, 217, 217n.33, 220n.48, 221n.51, 222–23n.56, 223, 223n.58, 223n.59, 224n.62, 225–26, 225n.68, 227, 227n.70, 227n.72, 228, 230–31, 230n.81, 231n.85, 232n.86, 232n.92, 257n.193, 415n.90, 418n.104, 481, 487n.125, 532, 532n.67, 533–34, 533n.70, 533n.72, 547n.109, 565n.175, 571n.191, 580n.213
  in Russian Copyright Act of 1993, 305–11, 312, 322, 328, 557
  in USSR Fundamentals of Civil Legislation, 302–5
  moral rights, in WIPO Performances and Phonograms Treaty, xvii–xviii, xix, 89n.125, 169n.67, 173, 189, 222, 268n.233, 360, 360n.82, 399, 438, 511, 512n.211, 531n.61
Performers, music, 178–79, 181, 206
  audiovisual works, xvii–xviii, 89–90, 89n.125, 179n.109, 185, 194, 268n.233, 319, 458n.4, 466n.42, 474–75n.79
  live performance, 51–52, 179, 268n.233, 379–80, 440, 449–50
  recording and broadcasting, 451–53
Peris, José J. Izquierdo, 567–68, 568n.184
Perpetual protection, of moral rights, 5, 34–36, 275
Photographer, moral rights of, 133, 202–3, 571
Photography, copyright protection of, 161, 457, 466, 494, 565, 570
Picasso, Diana Widmaier, 546–47
Picasso, Pablo, 50n.150, 571–72n.192
  Le Tricorne, 54–57, 530–31n.60
  treatment of women, 581n.216
Picasso-Nesjar Murals, xxiv, 25n.73, 55n.163, 224
  change of context, 33n.93, 534–39
Pillai, Suresh, 503n.187, 505n.194, 506, 506n.198
Pirate Bay, 503
Post mortem auctoris protection, for moral rights, 160n.33
Pound, Ezra, 159, 159n.29
Pozhitkov, I., 306n.375, 307–8n.380, 310, 310n.386
Press publication (*titre de presse*), 92–93
Private international law, 204
Producers 278–79, 431, 494–99
  vs. directors, 494–99
  moral rights of, in India, 278, 472, 473
Programmers, 312–13
  as author, 98, 138, 181, 227, 256, 333–83, 462n.18, 474–75n.79
  moral rights of, 90–91, 185, 312–13
  relationship with work, 35
Publication right 92–93, 118
  in French copyright law, 71, 93, 94, 94n.139, 110n.208, 154–55, 202–3, 498–99, 517–18, 578
  in German copyright law, 105n.186, 106, 106n.190, 109, 371n.109, 415n.93, 436–37, 501–2
  in USSR Fundamentals of Civil Legislation, 302–5
Public interest, 7n.20, 18–19, 21, 29–30, 36n.104, 43, 46, 47n.138, 73–74, 89, 93–94, 110, 158, 196–97, 204, 215–16n.26, 252, 255–56, 308, 355, 356, 404–5, 412n.80, 412n.81, 455, 510, 514, 528, 538, 539–43, 567, 568, 577
  against the prerogatives of authors, balancing, 73–74
  in music, 48, 51–52, 403n.49, 406, 410–12, 433, 453, 455
  in protecting heritage and artist's moral rights of integrity and withdrawal, conflict between, 543
Python, Monty, 199n.177, 242, 329, 351n.54, 401n.42, 474, 475–76, 597–98

Rachmaninoff, Sergei [Sergei Vasilyevich], 403n.50, 448n.178
  and Horowitz, 439
  and Scriabin, 439
Ramachandran, M.G., 490–91
Ramaiah, S., 276n.260, 487, 487n.126
Ramayana, 490
Rasa theory of aesthetics/art, 48–49, 49n.143, 63–64n.9, 288n.304, 411–12n.78
Recht, Pierre, 33n.93, 77, 77n.67, 83, 154n.15
Recording and broadcasting, 451–53
  audiovisual works, 89–90, 89n.125, 179n.109, 185, 194, 268n.233, 319, 458n.4, 466n.42, 474–75n.79
Recording Industry Association of America (RIAA), 385–86n.2, 399
Recognized stature, 249–51, 523–26, 527, 529, 530, 539–43
Region coding system, DVDs, 419–20n.108

Reid, Bill, 184n.126, 249, 249n.163, 520–21, 521n.20, 579–82, 579n.211, 580n.212
Remedies 280, 489
 and the Berne Convention, 237–48, 299
 in Canada, 37–38, 55n.165, 66n.16, 81n.89, 83, 136n.299, 157, 157n.25, 161n.37, 165, 211–12, 212n.5, 215–16, 216n.29, 217, 217n.33, 219n.42, 220n.48, 221n.49, 221n.50, 221n.52, 228–29, 230, 231–33, 234n.97, 235, 240, 308n.382, 330, 347, 351, 392n.12, 413n.83, 449, 449n.184, 481, 481n.104, 532, 547n.108, 560n.155, 565, 579, 590n.5
 and the common law, 34n.96, 67n.18, 112–13, 123n.249, 211–12, 213–64
 in India, xix, 14n.37, 66n.16, 69–70, 70n.36, 129n.277, 131–32n.283, 151–52n.5, 175n.95, 185, 205, 219–20n.44, 225n.66, 258n.201, 269–70n.237, 270n.239, 271, 272n.247, 273, 275, 275n.256, 276, 276n.261, 278, 279n.271, 280, 281n.280, 282, 286, 287–88, 290–91, 300, 335n.5, 344, 449, 453, 460n.11, 461–62, 472–73, 473n.74, 477–99, 487n.125, 488n.133, 500n.174, 507, 513, 513n.214, 525–26, 542, 543, 549–50, 554, 555, 563, 564, 601n.33, 610, 610n.61
 for infringement of moral rights, 137n.307
 in Japan, 8, 289n.305, 292–93, 357n.73
 and music, 48n.140, 49n.144, 147, 385–455, 392n.14, 471, 504n.190
 in Russia, 10–11n.29, 22n.65, 62–63, 63n.8, 154n.14, 156n.20, 201, 298–99n.344, 300, 301, 301n.357, 302, 304, 305, 308n.381, 310, 312, 312n.393, 314n.403, 316, 317–18, 318n.419, 319n.424, 322, 323–29, 471
 in the UK, 83n.102, 93n.136, 112–13, 131–33, 133n.289, 166n.51, 219–20n.44, 306n.376, 364, 452, 492n.146, 566n.178
 in the United States, 2n.5, 7n.20, 10–11n.29, 11n.31, 12, 16n.45, 17–18, 30n.86, 35, 37–38, 48n.139, 59, 63n.5, 71n.40
Remixing, 408–9, 433, 592–93
Repatriation of artworks/cultural property, 563–64
Representation, in WIPO Copyright Treaty, 169, 169n.67, 173, 189, 190
Reputation, 20–30, 80–82, 88–89, 309–10, 532–33, 598–99. *See also* Fame
Reputation right
 in Creative Commons license, 598–99
 in German Copyright Act, 101n.168, 102
 vs. right of integrity/disclosure, 154n.14, 218–19, 220–21, 309–10, 328, 612n.65
 in Russian Copyright Law, 201, 298–99n.344, 300, 302–3, 306, 310, 322, 326–27, 590
Resale right (*droit de suite*), of visual artists, 32, 168, 279, 323–24, 551, 619
Ricketson, Sam, 4n.11, 37n.106, 71n.39, 113n.216, 124n.252, 151n.3, 155n.18, 175, 214n.15, 214n.17, 266, 337n.10, 525n.43
Riede, Lutz, 434n.145, 435
Right of paternity, 16n.45, 17, 276–77n.262, 277n.265, *See also* Attribution right
Right of recall, 79. *See also* Withdrawal, right of
Ringtones, mobile, 183, 432–38, 434n.145, 453–54, 570
 attribution, 17–20, 126–27
 excerpts, 433–38
 licensing, 435–38, 592–602
 modifications, 434–35, 487–89
Robertson v. Thompson, Canadian case, 92n.134, 232, 232n.88, 436n.151
Rodin, Auguste, 175n.94, 518n.9, 576–79
Romanticism, 10n.28, 144, 145–47, 211, 331
Rose, Mark, 118, 118n.233
Royalties, 51–52, 108–9n.201, 131–32n.283, 192, 254, 278, 279, 308–9n.383, 315, 366, 373, 389–90, 426, 427–28, 427n.127, 429n.134, 504, 571n.190, 588, 590, 590n.5, 591
Russia, 10–11n.29, 22n.65, 62–63, 63n.8, 154n.14, 156n.20, 201, 298–99n.344, 300, 301, 301n.357, 302, 304, 305, 308n.381, 310, 312, 312n.393, 314n.403, 316, 317–18, 318n.419, 319n.424, 322, 323–29, 471
 Civil Code Provisions on Copyright (2008), 313–24. *See also* Russian Civil Code Provisions on Copyright (2008)
 continuing improvements to moral rights in, 324–26
 Copyright Act of 1911, 305, 322
 Copyright Act of 1993, 301, 305–11, 312, 314, 315, 316–17, 324–25, 326–27, 328–29, 557. *See also* Copyright Act of 1993 (Russia)
 copyright terms for rehabilitated authors, renewal of, 326–28
 film moral rights in, 89, 96, 126, 127, 131n.282, 138, 140, 171, 179, 183n.121, 185, 185n.132, 202–3n.188, 206, 222, 241, 247n.152, 251, 253, 255–56, 278–79, 310, 315, 319, 330–31, 372, 453, 457–514
 joint authorship, 261, 462, 468, 531
 Law on the Legal Protection of Computer Programs and Databases of 1992, 312
 membership in Berne Convention, 152, 237–38, 299

Russia (*cont.*)
place in post-socialist world, xix, 39, 39n.113, 58–59, 63n.7, 105n.184, 154n.14, 188, 208n.203, 211–12n.4, 293–329
rehabilitation of authors, 327
right of inviolability, 299–300, 320
Russian Civil Code Provisions on Copyright (2008), 313–24
duration of copyright, 31n.90, 71n.42, 168n.64, 197–98, 223n.57, 230n.84, 279, 315n.406, 321, 337–38, 338n.14, 398, 549–50
fair use, 14, 93n.137, 93n.138, 115n.223, 192n.161, 194, 302–3, 323, 352, 356–57, 356n.68, 357n.71, 358, 362–64, 363n.89, 363n.90, 363n.91, 363n.92, 403, 404, 405, 405n.62, 503, 508n.204, 565n.174, 575n.202, 575n.203, 592–93, 592n.10
general provisions, 316–17, 438, 544
moral rights, defined, 98
moral rights vs. exclusive rights, 322
moral rights and technology, 52, 54, 322
neighboring rights, 22n.65, 107n.194, 151n.3, 154n.14, 175n.93, 181, 188n.144, 218n.39, 267n.227, 317, 324
parody, 21, 21n.64, 41–42, 78, 82, 82n.93, 93–95, 93n.136, 93n.137, 93n.138, 94n.139, 111, 125, 135, 135n.297, 167, 167n.58, 167n.59, 167n.60, 194–95, 206–7, 323
patents, 21n.64, 92n.131, 125, 126–33, 165–66, 167, 220, 239n.117, 297, 316, 316n.411, 317, 324, 337–38n.13, 341, 462n.18, 552n.123, 565, 603–5, 605n.47
right of "interested persons," 317–18
treatment of works in public domain, 321
Russian Copyright Act of 1993, 305–11, 312, 322, 328, 557

Sag-AFTRA, 361n.87, 362, 511n.208
Sakharov, Andrei, 313n.398, 496
Sampling technique, in music, 402–3, 407, 434n.144
Samuelson, Pamela, 162n.44
Schiller, Friedrich, 601, 601n.34
Schnabel, Artur, 391, 391n.8
Schovsbo, Jens, 34n.97, 104, 104n.180, 105
Schumann, Clara, 438n.157, 448, 448n.178, 448n.181
Schumann, Robert, 438n.157, 448, 448n.178
Scorsese, Martin, 496–97
Screenplay and film contracts, 89–90, 460–61, 470, 471, 474, 475–76, 479–80, 480n.97, 491, 512
Scriabin, Alexander [Alexander Nikolayevich], 439, 449–50
Sculpture, moral rights in, 28, 28n.82, 40, 205, 230, 292, 412–13, 518n.9, 522n.26, 580. *See also* Modern art; Visual art
Separability test, of film coauthorship, 319, 463, 464, 466, 468, 471
Seville, Catherine, 190, 190n.152, 191n.155
Shakespeare, William, 50–51, 50n.150, 115n.222, 352–53, 352n.59, 352n.60, 373, 488n.135, 545–46, 545n.100, 545–46n.101
Shankar, Anoushka, 413
Shankar, Ravi, 411–12, 413, 449n.182
Shaw, George Bernard, 600–1, 600n.32
Shiva Nataraja (Shivalingam), 557n.141, 561, 562
Shostakovich, Dmitri Dmitriyevich, 10n.26, 88n.120, 165n.49
Shostakovich v. Twentieth-Century Fox Film Corp., 10n.26, 88n.120, 165n.49
integrity of the public domain, 240–42
Singh, Jaspal, 88n.121, 286
Sirinelli, Pierre, 11, 76n.66, 77, 410n.71, 463n.25, 464n.27
Smith, Robert, 395, 395n.24
Sofronitsky, Vladimir Vladimirovich, 449–50, 450n.186
Solzhenitsyn, Alexander, 68–69
Sound recording, 177–79
Soviet Union, 10–11n.29, 302–3, 326–28. *See also* Russia
Stallman, Richard, 589, 605, 605n.49, 606n.50, 607n.52, 607n.56, 608n.57, 618n.80
Stamatoudi, Irini, 28n.80, 123n.249, 126n.264, 133n.291, 140n.314, 190n.153, 458n.3, 458n.4
Standard-form contracts, 34, 481
Statute of Anne (1710), 2n.3, 65, 72n.47, 73, 115–23, 336, 336n.8
and right of disclosure, 30–31, 32, 37, 37n.106, 71, 78, 79, 100, 106–8, 110, 111n.209, 120–21, 133, 173–76, 175n.95, 175n.96, 190, 195, 218–19, 233n.93, 239, 299n.345, 306, 320–21, 346n.35, 367–68, 378, 417–18, 454, 495n.158
right of printing, 117
Sterling, J.A.L., 54, 54n.158
Stromholm, Stig, 4n.11, 10n.27, 13, 13n.36, 16n.44, 31n.89, 33n.94, 54, 62, 62n.2, 63n.5, 64, 64n.11, 65, 65n.14, 66n.17, 97, 97n.150, 97n.151, 98, 98n.152, 98n.153, 98n.155, 98n.156, 100, 100n.161, 100n.163, 145–46, 217n.31, 252, 252n.175, 276n.260, 276–77n.262, 277, 277n.265, 617n.79

Sui generis right, 36, 162n.44, 603
computer software, 96, 162, 162n.41, 265n.219, 312, 504n.190, 603n.40

Tagore, Rabindranath, 185–86n.134, 197–98, 197n.172, 230n.84, 549–50
Tapper, Colin, xxiv, 114n.220, 156n.22, 162, 476n.82, 489n.137, 591n.7, 603n.39, 603–4n.41, 613n.66
Technological protection measures (TPMs), 53
Tenenbaum, 419n.106, 419n.107
Term of protection, for moral rights, 85
Théberge, 2n.4, 35n.100, 38n.109, 81n.89, 106n.188, 157n.24, 157n.25, 157n.26, 175n.91, 217, 217n.30, 226, 231, 232, 232n.87, 232n.89, 233, 234, 234n.95, 234n.97, 234n.98, 235, 329n.456, 330n.458, 349, 349n.45, 350–51, 351n.55, 481, 481n.103, 532, 532n.67, 570–71, 571n.189
Thomson, James, 116–17
3D printing, 65, 175n.94, 516nn.4,5, 573, 575–79, 585
"Three strikes" laws, 508n.205
Tolstoy, Leo [Lev Nikolayevich], 490
Totem Policy, for City of Duncan, 565n.176
Trademark and moral rights, similarities between, 94n.140
"Relation to Berne Convention," 170–71
Truffaut, François, 461n.14, 470, 470n.58, 476
Tunisia, 211, 266–67, 267n.228, 268n.231
Copyright Act of 1966, 267n.228
Turner, Ted, 464–65, 507
Turner Broadcasting, 499
Turner Classic Movies, 499
Turner Entertainment v. Huston Heirs, 171n.75, 200n.179, 247n.152, 310n.387, 458–59, 458n.6, 465n.29, 479n.93, 494n.153, 497n.162, 497n.163, 498, 498n.165
"Two-step" licensing scheme, Germany, 436–37

UK Copyright, Designs and Patents Act 1988, 131–32, 341, 565
author of computer-generated work in, 47, 134, 340–43, 341n.23, 343n.29, 344, 345, 347
moral rights in, 9, 13, 56, 91–92, 113, 126–33, 136, 140n.314
moral rights in computer programs, 89n.124, 312, 313, 322, 325–26
UK Fine Arts Copyright Act of 1862, 161n.38

Unconscionability, doctrine of, 76n.66, 136–37, 479, 479n.95
United International Bureaux for the Protection of Intellectual Property (BIRPI), 172–73n.83
United Kingdom, 111–42, 111n.210, 113n.216, 117n.231, 256n.187
assertion of attribution right, xix, 32
conceptual confusion about moral rights, 137–38
Copyright, Designs and Patents Act 1988, 21n.64, 117n.231, 126–33, 165–66, 166n.50, 239n.117, 337–38n.13, 341, 462n.18, 552n.123, 565
cultural sensibilities and moral rights, 113
early rejection of moral tights, 61–65
formalities for exercise of moral rights, 330
practical difficulties in implementation of moral rights, 584
Statute of Anne (1710), 2n.3, 65, 72n.47, 73, 115–23, 336, 336n.8
waiver of moral rights, availability, 83, 100–1, 280, 435–38, 480n.101, 481, 512–13n.212, 532n.63
United States, 236–56, 255n.184, 266n.222, 520
constitutional framework supporting copyright law, 236–37
cultural scene, and "remix" culture, 237
integrity of public domain, 240–42
Lanham Act, 39–40, 141, 141n.316, 237, 237n.107, 240, 242, 242n.134, 244, 245, 246, 351n.54, 410–11, 411n.75
U.S. law and coauthorship, 466–68
limits on legal mechanisms for moral rights, 40, 141, 242–45
membership in Berne Convention, 16–17n.49, 128–29, 129n.277, 161
national treatment, 198–204, 204n.191, 211–12n.4, 246–48, 366
prohibition against destruction of an artwork, 543
protection of moral rights in, 35, 106, 113, 140, 309, 316–17, 324–25, 329, 412–13, 455, 477, 519
Visual Artists Rights Act of 1990 (VARA), 2n.5, 92n.132, 152n.6, 171–72, 216, 224, 236, 238–39, 239n.119, 351, 357n.72, 518, 527n.52, *See also* Visual Artists Rights Act of 1990
Universal Copyright Convention (UCC), 237–38, 495, 496n.161
Universal Declaration of Human Rights, 40, 40n.121, 204n.192, 219n.41, 507n.201, 544, 544n.96

UPOV (International Union for the Protection of New Varieties of Plants) Convention of 1961, 177
sui generis right in, 36, 162n.44, 603
USSR Copyright Law (1928)
inviolability, right of, 154n.14, 299–300, 303, 310, 318, 319, 320, 328–29
USSR Fundamentals of Civil Legislation (1961), 299n.350
USSR Fundamentals of Civil Legislation (1991), 302–5, 303n.364, 326–27
authorship and name, 303, 310, 317, 319–20
duration for authors' moral rights, 304
inalienability of moral rights, 100–1, 330
inheritance of moral rights, 223, 307–8
integrity as inviolability, 303
moral right for performers, 173, 177, 206, 304–5
right of publication, 31n.89, 115–16n.226, 302, 304
right of use, 302–3, 304, 306

Vaver, David, 48n.140, 83n.101, 94n.140, 107n.196, 136n.299, 156–57, 157n.23, 157n.24, 172n.80, 214n.18, 217n.32, 218n.34, 219, 219n.42, 219n.43, 219–20n.44, 220n.48, 230n.81, 242n.135, 306n.376, 481n.104, 487n.125
Version definitive, 463, 464–65
Vertigo (1958 film) 402n.45
Viacom, 508, 508n.203, 509
Virtual concert halls, 414n.86
Virtual galleries, building, 569–75
Virtual recording, 414
Visual and applied arts in German Basic Law, 109n.205
Visual Artists Rights Act of 1990 (VARA), 2n.5, 92n.132, 351, 357n.72, 518
problem of false attribution of another person's work to the author, 521
right of attribution, 16n.45, 249, 522
right of integrity, 223, 224, 250, 256–57
right to claim authorship, 101n.167, 101n.168, 154, 272, 521
waiver of moral rights, 83, 100–1, 280, 435–38, 480n.101, 481, 512–13n.212, 532n.63
Visual artists 251–52, 518–30
droit de suite for, 311
Visual arts. 223–26, 311, 515–85, *See also* Artwork
Aboriginal communal moral right in (Australia), 260, 260n.209, 582n.219
in Civil Code Provisions on Copyright (2008), 312, 313–24, 317n.413, 471
copyright protection of, 162, 162n.41, 305, 312, 343n.28, 343n.29, 397, 400
as cultural property, 549, 553
hybrid moral rights for, 32, 108–9, 168, 195n.168, 315, 516n.2
intentional or grossly negligent destruction of, 525–26
as intellectual property, 6–7, 549
moral rights for, 151–52n.5, 182, 185, 213–14, 224, 229, 378–79, 516, 517, 621–22
originality of, 517–18
post mortem *Auctoris*, 72n.47, 160n.33, 185–86n.134, 223n.57, 327–28, 549–52
property or heritage, 547–48
recommendations for, 378–80, 387, 453–55, 511–13, 584–85, 617–19
right of attribution, 17–18
right of integrity, 283–84, 351, 408, 410, 410n.71, 435, 533, 539, 540, 542
true moral rights for, 323–24
Vivant, Michel, 84n.105
Voyager (spacecraft), 625
Vu, Huan, 501–2, 503

Wad, Justice, 486, 487, 489
Waiver of moral rights, 33–34, 83, 101, 101n.167, 226, 280, 416n.99, 435–38, 480–81, 512–13n.212
implicit (through collecting societies), 435–38
in Australia, 256–57
in Austria and Germany, 100–3, 108n.197
in Canada, 36n.104, 157, 165, 177–78, 217n.33, 220–21, 226–27, 236n.102, 532n.67, 533n.70
in films, 480 (Canada), 487 (India)
in France, 83–84
in India, 280
in United Kingdom, 135–37, 138n.310
in the United States, 531–32
and Wikipedia, 611
Warhammer, 501–2, 502n.184, 503
Warhol, Andy, 574n.200, *See also Warhol v. Goldsmith*
Warhol v. Goldsmith, 44, 352n.58, 363n.92, 574n.200, 592n.10
Web 2.0, 609–14
Werkers, Evi, 174n.88
White, Jeffrey S. Judge, 594
Wieck, Clara. *See* Clara Schumann
Wikipedia, 592, 609–14
legal status of contributors to, 610–11
moral rights in, 611–12
WIPO Copyright Treaty (WCT), 169n.68
language of, 182n.119

moral rights in, 152n.7, 153, 154–55, 157, 160, 163–64, 165–66, 172–85, 206, 222, 268n.233, 324, 399, 405n.60
preamble of, 174
right of communication, 174–75n.90, 175, 176, 190
right of disclosure (*divulgation*), 37
right of *représentation*, 175, 189
WIPO Internet Treaties, 162n.40, 172–85, 222n.54, 228–29, 308n.382
moral rights in, 179–81, 206, 222, 268n.233, 324, 399, 405n.60
WIPO Performances and Phonograms Treaty (WPPT), xvii–xviii, xix, 89, 169n.67, 173, 222, 360, 399
audiovisual works in, 268n.233
limitations on moral rights in, 139
as modelled on the Berne Convention, Article 6*bis*, 16–17, 19, 20–21, 24, 25, 58, 91–92, 96, 124, 126, 128n.275, 140, 149–208, 213–14, 215–16, 219, 222, 225–26, 227, 229, 249, 250, 252, 272, 274, 283–85, 303, 307n.378, 309, 320, 360, 378, 442, 522, 523, 536, 537, 539, 542, 596, 621
Canadian implementation, 531n.61
moral rights in, 179–81, 206, 222, 268n.233, 324, 399, 405n.60
moral rights of performers, 177–79, 256, 304–5, 446
practical implications, 66, 199–200, 276–77, 459, 578–79
right of attribution, 227, 441
right of integrity, 7, 21n.64, 26, 27–28
Withdrawal, right of, 5, 30–31, 119
in architecture, 132
interpretation in Canada, 221n.50
in French law, 78, 79–80, 313n.397
in software/computer programs, 91–92
in German law 103, 106
in Russian law (computer programmers), 228n.75, 306, 313, 315, 321, 471, 479–80
Woman of Culture podcast, 55n.163, 112n.213, 224n.65, 379n.133, 545–46n.101
Work(s), copyright,
audiovisual, (France) 89–90, 179n.109, 185, 194, 268n.233, 319, 458n.4, 497
cinematographic, 458n.4, 472, 473, 473n.74, 478
damage to, 20–21, 22, 37–38, 167n.59, 292, 505, 522n.26, 553–54, 555
derivative, 37–38, 243, 321, 474–77, 474–75n.79, 493, 501, 503, 504n.188, 596–98, 608
disintegration of, 298
literary, 2n.5, 16–17n.49, 21, 37, 46, 68, 150n.2, 151n.4, 174, 174–75n.90, 214n.14, 237–38, 278n.270, 279, 312, 322n.434, 352, 354, 355–58, 370, 373, 463n.23, 474–75n.79, 487, 602–3, 604n.45, 605n.49
as "spiritual child" of the author, 4n.11
World Intellectual Property Organization (WIPO), 177n.102, 268n.233, 360n.82, 404n.53
World Trade Organization (WTO), 16–17, 74n.53, 169n.70, 212n.7, 604–5, 604n.45, 621
dispute-settlement system, 169–70, 190, 215n.20, 215n.22, 621
Writers' Union of Canada, 55n.165, 221n.52, 480n.100, 590n.5
Work for hire doctrine, or employment rule, 202–3, 337–38, 343n.28, 462n.19, 466, 468, 593n.14

YouTube, 51, 51n.153, 388–89, 394–95, 508–9
Yumbulul v. Reserve Bank of Australia, 259–60, 266n.221, 582–84, 592n.8